HOLT McDOUGAL

Literature

Grade 6

Janet Allen

Arthur N. Applebee

Jim Burke

Douglas Carnine

Yvette Jackson

Carol Jago

Robert T. Jiménez

Judith A. Langer

Robert J. Marzano

Mary Lou McCloskey

Donna M. Ogle

Carol Booth Olson

Lydia Stack

Carol Ann Tomlinson

Special Contributor: Kylene Beers

HOLT McDOUGAL

HOUGHTON MIFFLIN HARCOURT

SENIOR PROGRAM CONSULTANTS

JANET ALLEN Reading and Literacy Specialist; creator of the popular "It's Never Too Late"/"Reading for Life" Institutes. Dr. Allen is an internationally known consultant who specializes in literacy work with at-risk students. Her publications include *Tools for Content Literacy; It's Never Too Late: Leading Adolescents to Lifelong Learning; Yellow Brick Roads: Shared and Guided Paths to Independent Reading; Words, Words, Words: Teaching Vocabulary in Grades 4–12;* and *Testing 1, 2, 3 . . . Bridging Best Practice and High-Stakes Assessments.* Dr. Allen was a high school reading and English teacher for more than 20 years.

ARTHUR N. APPLEBEE Leading Professor, School of Education at the University at Albany, State University of New York; Director of the Center on English Learning and Achievement. During his varied career, Dr. Applebee has been both a researcher and a teacher, working in institutional settings with children with severe learning problems, in public schools, as a staff member of the National Council of Teachers of English, and in professional education. He was elected to the International Reading Hall of Fame and has received, among other honors, the David H. Russell Award for Distinguished Research in the Teaching of English.

JIM BURKE Lecturer and Author; Teacher of English at Burlingame High School, Burlingame, California. Mr. Burke is a popular presenter at educational conferences across the country and is the author of numerous books for teachers, including *School Smarts: The Four Cs of Academic Success; The English Teacher's Companion; Reading Reminders; Writing Reminders;* and *ACCESSing School: Teaching Struggling Readers to Achieve Academic and Personal Success.* He is the recipient of NCTE's Exemplary English Leadership Award and was inducted into the California Reading Association's Hall of Fame.

DOUGLAS CARNINE Professor of Education at the University of Oregon; Director of the Western Region Reading First Technical Assistance Center. Dr. Carnine is nationally known for his focus on research-based practices in education, especially curriculum designs that prepare instructors of K–12 students. He has received the Lifetime Achievement Award from the Council for Exceptional Children and the Ersted Award for outstanding teaching at the University of Oregon. Dr. Carnine frequently consults on educational policy with government groups, businesses, communities, and teacher unions.

YVETTE JACKSON Executive Director of the National Urban Alliance for Effective Education. Nationally recognized for her work in assessing the learning potential of underachieving urban students, Dr. Jackson is also a presenter for the Harvard Principal Center and is a member of the Differentiation Faculty of the Association for Supervision and Curriculum Development. Dr. Jackson's research focuses on literacy, gifted education, and cognitive mediation theory. She designed the Comprehensive Education Plan for the New York City Public Schools and has served as their Director of Gifted Programs.

CAROL JAGO Teacher of English with thirty-two years of experience at Santa Monica High School in California; Author and nationally known Lecturer; and President of the National Council of Teachers of English. With varied experience in standards assessment and secondary education, Ms. Jago is the author of numerous books on education and is active with the California Association of Teachers of English, editing its scholarly journal *California English* since 1996. Ms. Jago also served on the planning committee for the 2009 NAEP Framework and the 2011 NAEP Writing Framework.

ROBERT T. JIMÉNEZ Professor of Language, Literacy, and Culture at Vanderbilt University. Dr. Jiménez's research focuses on the language and literacy practices of Latino students. A former bilingual education teacher, he is now conducting research on how written language is thought about and used in contemporary Mexico. Dr. Jiménez has received several research and teaching honors, including two Fulbright awards from the Council for the International Exchange of Scholars and the Albert J. Harris Award from the International Reading Association.

JUDITH A. LANGER Distinguished Professor at the University at Albany, State University of New York; Director of the Center on English Learning and Achievement; Director of the Albany Institute for Research in Education. An internationally known scholar in English language arts education, Dr. Langer specializes in developing teaching approaches that can enrich and improve what gets done on a daily basis in classrooms. Her publications include *Getting to Excellent: How to Create Better Schools* and *Effective Literacy Instruction: Building Successful Reading and Writing Programs.*

ROBERT J. MARZANO Senior Scholar at Mid-Continent Research for Education and Learning (McREL); Associate Professor at Cardinal Stritch University in Milwaukee, Wisconsin; President of Marzano & Associates. An internationally known researcher, trainer, and speaker, Dr. Marzano has developed programs that translate research and theory into practical tools for K–12 teachers and administrators. He has written extensively on such topics as reading and writing instruction, thinking skills, school effectiveness, assessment, and standards implementation.

DONNA M. OGLE Professor of Reading and Language at National-Louis University in Chicago, Illinois; Past President of the International Reading Association. Creator of the well-known KWL strategy, Dr. Ogle has directed many staff development projects translating theory and research into school practice in middle and secondary schools throughout the United States and has served as a consultant on literacy projects worldwide. Her extensive international experience includes coordinating the Reading and Writing for Critical Thinking Project in Eastern Europe, developing integrated curriculum for a USAID Afghan Education Project, and speaking and consulting on projects in several Latin American countries and in Asia.

CAROL BOOTH OLSON Senior Lecturer in the Department of Education at the University of California, Irvine; Director of the UCI site of the National Writing Project. Dr. Olson writes and lectures extensively on the reading/writing connection, critical thinking through writing, interactive strategies for teaching writing, and the use of multicultural literature with students of culturally diverse backgrounds. She has received many awards, including the California Association of Teachers of English Award of Merit, the Outstanding California Education Research Award, and the UC Irvine Excellence in Teaching Award.

CAROL ANN TOMLINSON Professor of Educational Research, Foundations, and Policy at the University of Virginia; Co-Director of the University's Institutes on Academic Diversity. An internationally known expert on differentiated instruction, Dr. Tomlinson helps teachers and administrators develop effective methods of teaching academically diverse learners. She was a teacher of middle and high school English for 22 years prior to teaching at the University of Virginia. Her books on differentiated instruction have been translated into eight languages.

SPECIAL CONTRIBUTOR:
KYLENE BEERS Special Consultant; Former Middle School Teacher; nationally known Lecturer and Author on reading and literacy; and former President of the National Council of Teachers of English. Dr. Beers is the nationally known author of *When Kids Can't Read: What Teachers Can Do* and co-editor of *Adolescent Literacy: Turning Promise into Practice,* as well as articles in the *Journal of Adolescent and Adult Literacy.* Former editor of *Voices from the Middle,* she is the 2001 recipient of NCTE's Richard W. Halley Award, given for outstanding contributions to middle-school literacy.

ENGLISH LEARNER SPECIALISTS

MARY LOU McCLOSKEY Past President of Teachers of English to Speakers of Other Languages (TESOL); Director of Teacher Development and Curriculum Design for Educo in Atlanta, Georgia. Dr. McCloskey is a former teacher in multilingual and multicultural classrooms. She has worked with teachers, teacher educators, and departments of education around the world on teaching English as a second and foreign language. She is author of *On Our Way to English, Voices in Literature, Integrating English,* and *Visions: Language, Literature, Content.* Her awards include the Le Moyne College Ignatian Award for Professional Achievement and the TESOL D. Scott Enright Service Award.

LYDIA STACK International ESL consultant. Her areas of expertise are English language teaching strategies, ESL standards for students and teachers, and curriculum writing. Her teaching experience includes 25 years as an elementary and high school ESL teacher. She is a past president of TESOL. Her awards include the James E. Alatis Award for Service to TESOL (2003) and the San Francisco STAR Teacher Award (1989). Her publications include *On Our Way to English; Wordways: Games for Language Learning;* and *Visions: Language, Literature, Content.*

CURRICULUM SPECIALIST

WILLIAM L. McBRIDE Curriculum Specialist. Dr. McBride is a nationally known speaker, educator, and author who now trains teachers in instructional methodologies. A former reading specialist, English teacher, and social studies teacher, he holds a Masters in Reading and a Ph.D. in Curriculum and Instruction from the University of North Carolina at Chapel Hill. Dr. McBride has contributed to the development of textbook series in language arts, social studies, science, and vocabulary. He is also known for his novel *Entertaining an Elephant,* which tells the story of a burned-out teacher who becomes re-inspired with both his profession and his life.

MEDIA SPECIALISTS

DAVID M. CONSIDINE Professor of Instructional Technology and Media Studies at Appalachian State University in North Carolina. Dr. Considine has served as a media literacy consultant to the U.S. government and to the media industry, including Discovery Communications and Cable in the Classroom. He has also conducted media literacy workshops and training for county and state health departments across the United States. Among his many publications are *Visual Messages: Integrating Imagery into Instruction,* and *Imagine That: Developing Critical Viewing and Thinking Through Children's Literature.*

LARKIN PAULUZZI Teacher and Media Specialist; trainer for the New Jersey Writing Project. Ms. Pauluzzi puts her extensive classroom experience to use in developing teacher-friendly curriculum materials and workshops in many different areas, including media literacy. She has led media literacy training workshops in several districts throughout Texas, guiding teachers in the meaningful and practical uses of media in the classroom. Ms. Pauluzzi has taught students at all levels, from Title I Reading to AP English IV. She also spearheads a technology club at her school, working with students to produce media and technology to serve both the school and the community.

LISA K. SCHEFFLER Teacher and Media Specialist. Ms. Scheffler has designed and taught media literacy and video production curriculum, in addition to teaching language arts and speech. Using her knowledge of mass communication theory, coupled with real classroom experience, she has developed ready-to-use materials that help teachers incorporate media literacy into their curricula. She has taught film and television studies at the University of North Texas and has served as a contributing writer for the Texas Education Agency's statewide viewing and representing curriculum.

TEACHER ADVISORS

These are some of the many educators from across the country who played a crucial role in the development of the tables of contents, the lesson design, and other key components of this program:

Virginia L. Alford, MacArthur High School, San Antonio, Texas

Yvonne L. Allen, Shaker Heights High School, Shaker Heights, Ohio

Dave T. Anderson, Hinsdale South High School, Darien, Illinois

Kacy Colleen Anglim, Portland Public Schools District, Portland, Oregon

Jordana Benone, North High School, Torrance, California

Patricia Blood, Howell High School, Farmingdale, New Jersey

Marjorie Bloom, Eau Gallie High School, Melbourne, Florida

Edward J. Blotzer, Wilkinsburg Junior/Senior High School, Wilkinsburg, Pennsylvania

Stephen D. Bournes, Evanston Township High School, Evanston, Illinois

Barbara M. Bowling, Mt. Tabor High School, Winston-Salem, North Carolina

Kiala Boykin-Givehand, Duval County Public Schools, Jacksonville, Florida

Laura L. Brown, Adlai Stevenson High School, Lincolnshire, Illinois

Cynthia Burke, Yavneh Academy, Dallas, Texas

Hoppy Chandler, San Diego City Schools, San Diego, California

Gary Chmielewski, St. Benedict High School, Chicago, Illinois

Delorse Cole-Stewart, Milwaukee Public Schools, Milwaukee, Wisconsin

Kathy Dahlgren, Skokie, Illinois

Diana Dilger, Rosa Parks Middle School, Dixmoor, Illinois

L. Calvin Dillon, Gaither High School, Tampa, Florida

Dori Dolata, Rufus King High School, Milwaukee, Wisconsin

Jon Epstein, Marietta High School, Marietta, Georgia

Helen Ervin, Fort Bend Independent School District, Sugar Land, Texas

Sue Friedman, Buffalo Grove High School, Buffalo Grove, Illinois

Chris Gee, Bel Air High School, El Paso, Texas

Paula Grasel, The Horizon Center, Gainesville, Georgia

Rochelle L. Greene-Brady, Kenwood Academy, Chicago, Illinois

Christopher Guarraia, Centreville High School, Clifton, Virginia

Michele M. Hettinger, Niles West High School, Skokie, Illinois

Elizabeth Holcomb, Forest Hill High School, Jackson, Mississippi

Jim Horan, Hinsdale Central High School, Hinsdale, Illinois

James Paul Hunter, Oak Park-River Forest High School, Oak Park, Illinois

Susan P. Kelly, Director of Curriculum, Island Trees School District, Levittown, New York

Beverley A. Lanier, Varina High School, Richmond, Virginia

Pat Laws, Charlotte-Mecklenburg Schools, Charlotte, North Carolina

Diana R. Martinez, Treviño School of Communications & Fine Arts, Laredo, Texas

Natalie Martinez, Stephen F. Austin High School, Houston, Texas

Elizabeth Matarazzo, Ysleta High School, El Paso, Texas

Carol M. McDonald, J. Frank Dobie High School, Houston, Texas

Amy Millikan, Consultant, Chicago, Illinois

Eileen Murphy, Walter Payton Preparatory High School, Chicago, Illinois

Lisa Omark, New Haven Public Schools, New Haven, Connecticut

Kaine Osburn, Wheeling High School, Wheeling, Illinois

Andrea J. Phillips, Terry Sanford High School, Fayetteville, North Carolina

Cathy Reilly, Sayreville Public Schools, Sayreville, New Jersey

Mark D. Simon, Neuqua Valley High School, Naperville, Illinois

Scott Snow, Seguin High School, Arlington, Texas

Jane W. Speidel, Brevard County Schools, Viera, Florida

Cheryl E. Sullivan, Lisle Community School District, Lisle, Illinois

Anita Usmiani, Hamilton Township Public Schools, Hamilton Square, New Jersey

Linda Valdez, Oxnard Union High School District, Oxnard, California

Nancy Walker, Longview High School, Longview, Texas

Kurt Weiler, New Trier High School, Winnetka, Illinois

Elizabeth Whittaker, Larkin High School, Elgin, Illinois

Linda S. Williams, Woodlawn High School, Baltimore, Maryland

John R. Williamson, Fort Thomas Independent Schools, Fort Thomas, Kentucky

Anna N. Winters, Simeon High School, Chicago, Illinois

Tonora D. Wyckoff, North Shore Senior High School, Houston, Texas

Karen Zajac, Glenbard South High School, Glen Ellyn, Illinois

Cynthia Zimmerman, Mose Vines Preparatory High School, Chicago, Illinois

Lynda Zimmerman, El Camino High School, South San Francisco, California

Ruth E. Zurich, Brown Deer High School, Brown Deer, Wisconsin

COMMON
CORE

OVERVIEW
Student Edition

LESSONS WITH EMBEDDED COMMON CORE INSTRUCTION

COMMON CORE   Look for the COMMON CORE symbol throughout the book. It highlights targeted objectives to help you succeed in mastering the knowledge and skills you will need for college or for a career.

COMMON CORE CONTENTS

© Getty Images

COMMON CORE

CONTENTS IN BRIEF

Online at

Log in to learn more at **thinkcentral.com**, *where you can access most program resources in one convenient location.*

LITERATURE AND READING CENTER
- Author Biographies
- *PowerNotes* Presentations with Video Trailers
- Professional Audio Recordings of Selections
- Graphic Organizers
- Analysis Frames
- NovelWise

WRITING AND GRAMMAR CENTER
- Interactive Student Models*
- Interactive Graphic Organizers*
- Interactive Revision Lessons*
- *GrammarNotes* Presentations and Practice

also available on WriteSmart CD-ROM

VOCABULARY CENTER
- *WordSharp* Interactive Vocabulary Tutor
- Vocabulary Practice Copy Masters

MEDIA AND TECHNOLOGY CENTER
- MediaScope: Media Literacy Instruction
- Digital Storytelling
- Speaking and Listening Support

RESEARCH CENTER
- Writing and Research in a Digital Age
- Citation Guide

Assessment Center
- Program Assessments
- Level Up Online Tutorials
- Online Essay Scoring

MORE TECHNOLOGY

Student One Stop
Access an electronic version of your textbook, complete with selection audio and worksheets.

Media⬤Smart DVD-ROM
Sharpen your critical viewing and analysis skills with these in-depth interactive media studies.

What's Happening?
PLOT, CONFLICT, AND SETTING

• FICTION • INFORMATIONAL TEXT • POETRY • DRAMA • MEDIA

COMMON CORE UNIT 1

Vocabulary Strategies

Denotations and connotations, *p. 44*
Suffixes, *p. 64*
Synonyms, *p. 76*

Literal and figurative meanings, *p. 102*
Prefixes and Latin roots: *ject, p. 124*
Reading a dictionary entry, *p. 136*

Person to Person
ANALYZING CHARACTER AND POINT OF VIEW
• FICTION • INFORMATIONAL TEXT • POETRY • MEDIA

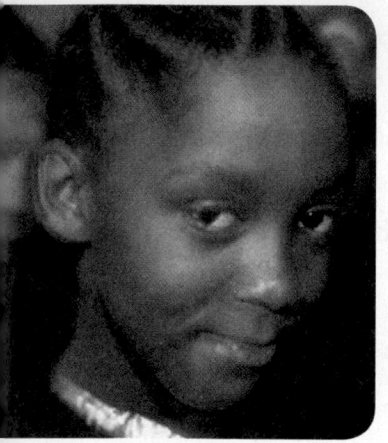

Vocabulary Strategies

Spanish words used in English, *p. 205*
Syllabication and pronunciation, *p. 218*
Compound words, *p. 232*

Context clues, *p. 258*
Latin roots: *press, p. 273*
Prefixes that mean "not," *p. 286*

The Big Idea
UNDERSTANDING THEME

COMMON CORE

UNIT 3

• FICTION • POETRY

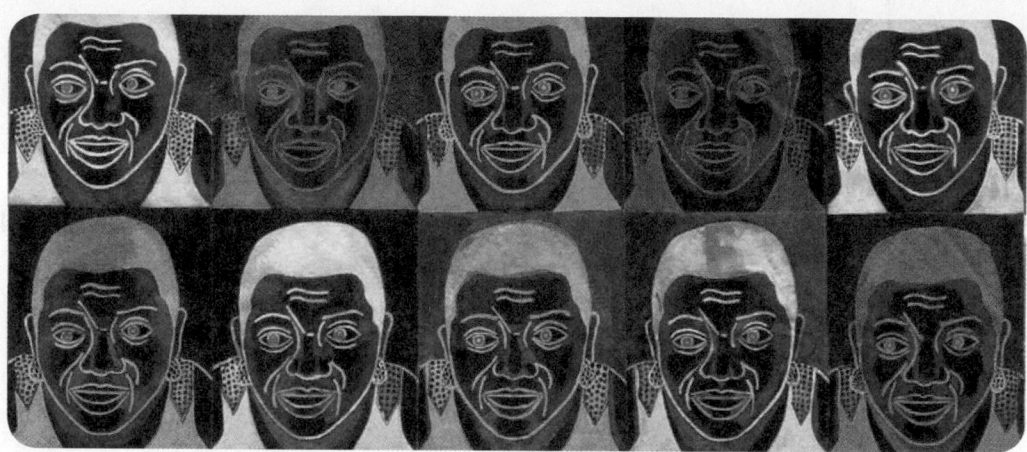

COMPARING FABLES

POETRY

Vocabulary Strategies

Latin roots: *rupt, p. 338*   Part-to-whole analogies, *p. 376*
Noun-forming suffixes, *p. 358*   Multiple-meaning words, *p. 392*

Writer's Craft
SENSORY LANGUAGE, IMAGERY, AND STYLE

• FICTION • INFORMATIONAL TEXT • POETRY • DRAMA • MEDIA

INFORMATIONAL TEXT: LITERARY NONFICTION

Vocabulary Strategies

Similes as context clues, *p. 455*
Figurative language in context, *p. 484*

Latin roots: *pro, p. 506*
Use a dictionary to determine part of speech, *p. 517*

Word Pictures
THE LANGUAGE OF POETRY

STANDARDS FOCUS
Structure, Sound Devices, Refrain, Meter, Figurative Language, Imagery

Video link at
HISTORY thinkcentral.com
Structure of a Poem, Reading Poetry Aloud

Video link at
HISTORY thinkcentral.com
Rhyme, Recognize Meter

Imagery, Understand Refrain

Imagery and Metaphor, Paraphrase

Vocabulary Strategies

Greek roots, *p.599*   Latin roots: *lect, p. 635*

COMMON CORE
UNIT 6

Timeless Tales
MYTHS, LEGENDS, AND TALES

Vocabulary Strategies

Words derived from Latin and Greek, *p. 690* Analogies, *p. 745*
Greek and Latin affixes, *p. 704* General context clues, *p. 758*
Use reference aids, *p. 723* Recognizing base words, *p. 778*

Life Stories
BIOGRAPHY AND AUTOBIOGRAPHY
• INFORMATIONAL TEXT • POETRY • MEDIA

Vocabulary Strategies

Idioms, *p. 820*   Foreign words in English, *p. 858*
Analogies, *p. 839*

Know the Facts
INFORMATION, ARGUMENT, AND PERSUASION

● INFORMATIONAL TEXT ● MEDIA

INFORMATIONAL TEXT: LITERARY NONFICTION

Investigation and Discovery
THE POWER OF RESEARCH

Student Resource Bank

Selections by Genre

Features

WriteSmart CD-ROM

Media⬥Smart DVD-ROM

STUDENT GUIDE TO ACADEMIC SUCCESS

STUDENT GUIDE

© Jupiterimages/Getty Images

The Common Core for Uncommon Achievement

Carol Jago

*"If you don't know where you are going,
any road will get you there."* – Lewis Carroll

The Common Core State Standards make clear where students are going. They describe what today's children need to know and be able to do to thrive in post-secondary education and the workplace. By focusing on results — the destination — rather than on the how — the means of transportation — the Common Core allows for a variety of teaching methods and many different classroom approaches. The challenge for teachers is to turn the daily journey towards this destination into an intellectual adventure.

One way to think about the Common Core is as a kind of GPS device to situate curriculum. While some students may choose the road less traveled, the objective is fixed. When students become lost through a wrong turn, teachers recalculate the route, providing a calm and confident voice that guides all students to academic achievement and deep literacy.

Shared Responsibility for Students' Literacy Development

The Common Core State Standards insist that the responsibility for helping students achieve literacy is not the sole responsibility of the English teacher. The introduction states clearly that, "instruction in reading, writing, speaking, listening, and language (should) be a shared responsibility within the school" (4). Citing NAEP Reading assessment test specification guidelines, the Common Core recommends that 55% of what students read in grade 8 and 70% in grade 12 should be informational text. These percentages are not meant to reflect the balance of reading materials in English class alone but rather the totality of what students should be reading across the curriculum in history/social studies, science, and technical subjects as well as in English. Given the type of reading that will be required of students in college and of graduates in the workplace, this distribution is both relevant and practical.

Understanding of Other Perspectives and Cultures

The Common Core also makes clear the importance of literature in the education of America's children. "Through reading great classic and contemporary works of literature representative of a variety of periods, cultures, and worldviews, students can vicariously inhabit worlds and have experiences much different from their own" (7). Reading literature demands that readers look inward, examine their beliefs in light of new information, consider the world through different eyes, take time for reflection. Such reading is a key to student learning.

The Purpose of Exemplar Texts

To describe the quality and complexity of the works students should read at each grade level, the Common Core offers lists of "exemplar texts." While some may choose to treat the texts on these lists as required reading, such usage would represent a misunderstanding of their purpose. "The choices should serve as useful guideposts in helping educators select texts of similar complexity, quality, and range for their own classrooms. They expressly do not represent a partial or complete reading list" (Appendix B, 2). The poems, stories, novels, and nonfiction that appear on the Common Core lists are intended as models for guiding — not dictating — text selection.

The Difference Between Persuasion and Argument

The Common Core writing standards describe the types and purposes for writing that students need to master. You will find extended definitions of argument, informative/ explanatory writing, and narrative writing in Appendix A. Of particular note is the distinction the Common Core draws between persuasion and argument. "When writing to persuade, writers employ a variety of persuasive strategies. One common strategy is an appeal to the credibility, character, or authority of the writer (or speaker). A logical argument, on the other hand, convinces the audience because of the perceived merit and reasonableness of the claims and proofs offered rather than either the emotions the writing evokes in the audience or the character or credentials of the writer" (24). Because of its importance for college and workplace readiness, argument holds a special place in the Common Core writing standards.

> *One way to think about the Common Core is as a kind of GPS device …*

Complex Literary and Informational Texts

Throughout the Common Core document you will notice the anchor standard, "Read and comprehend complex literary and informational texts independently and proficiently." It isn't enough for students to read with a teacher by their side. They need to be able, often with a little help from their friends or from the habits of mind they learned from their teachers, to read for themselves. They need to be able, like Huck Finn, to head out for the territory on their own. Such a journey requires confidence in one's ability to navigate uncharted waters and to overcome challenges their teachers can't foresee or even imagine. As we guide students on the academic adventure that is middle and high school, let us never forget that the path we tread is the path to intellectual freedom.

WORKS CITED

Common Core State Standards for English Language Arts and History/Social Studies, Science, & Technical Subjects. 2010.

Appendix B. Common Core State Standards for English Language Arts and History/Social Studies, Science, & Technical Subjects. 2010.

Carol Jago has taught middle and high school for over 30 years and was a member of the Common Core Initiative feedback team. She serves as president of the National Council of Teachers of English.

Understanding the Common Core State Standards

What are the English Language Arts Common Core State Standards?

The Common Core State Standards for English Language Arts indicate what you should know and be able to do by the end of your grade level. These understandings and skills will help you be better prepared for future classes, college courses, and a career. For this reason, the standards for each strand in English Language Arts (such as reading informational text or writing) directly relate to the College and Career Readiness Anchor Standards for each strand. The Anchor Standards broadly outline the understandings and skills you should learn by the end of middle school so that you are well-prepared for high school, for college, or for a career.

How do I learn the English Language Arts Common Core State Standards?

Your textbook is closely aligned to the English Language Arts Common Core State Standards. Every time you learn a concept or practice a skill, you are working on mastery of one of the standards. Each unit, each selection, and each workshop in your textbook connects to one or more of the standards for English Language Arts listed on the following pages.

The English Language Arts Common Core State Standards are divided into five strands: Reading Literature, Reading Informational Text, Writing, Speaking and Listening, and Language.

Reading Literature (RL)

This strand concerns the literary texts you will read at this grade level: stories, drama, and poetry. The Common Core State Standards stress that you should read a range of texts of increasing complexity as you progress through middle school.

Reading Informational Text (RI)

Informational text includes a broad range of literary nonfiction, including exposition, argument, and functional text, such as personal essays, speeches, opinion pieces, memoirs, and historical and technical accounts. The Common Core State Standards stress that you will also read a range of informational texts of increasing complexity as you progress from grade to grade.

Writing (W)

The Writing strand focuses on your generating three types of texts: arguments, informative or explanatory texts, and narratives, as well as using the writing process and technology to develop and share your writing. The Common Core State Standards also emphasize research and specify that you should write routinely for both short and extended time frames.

Speaking and Listening (SL)

The Common Core State Standards focus on comprehending information presented in a variety of media and formats, on participating in collaborative discussions, and on presenting knowledge and ideas clearly.

Language (L)

The standards in the Language strand address the conventions of Standard English grammar, usage, and mechanics; knowledge of language; and vocabulary acquisition and use.

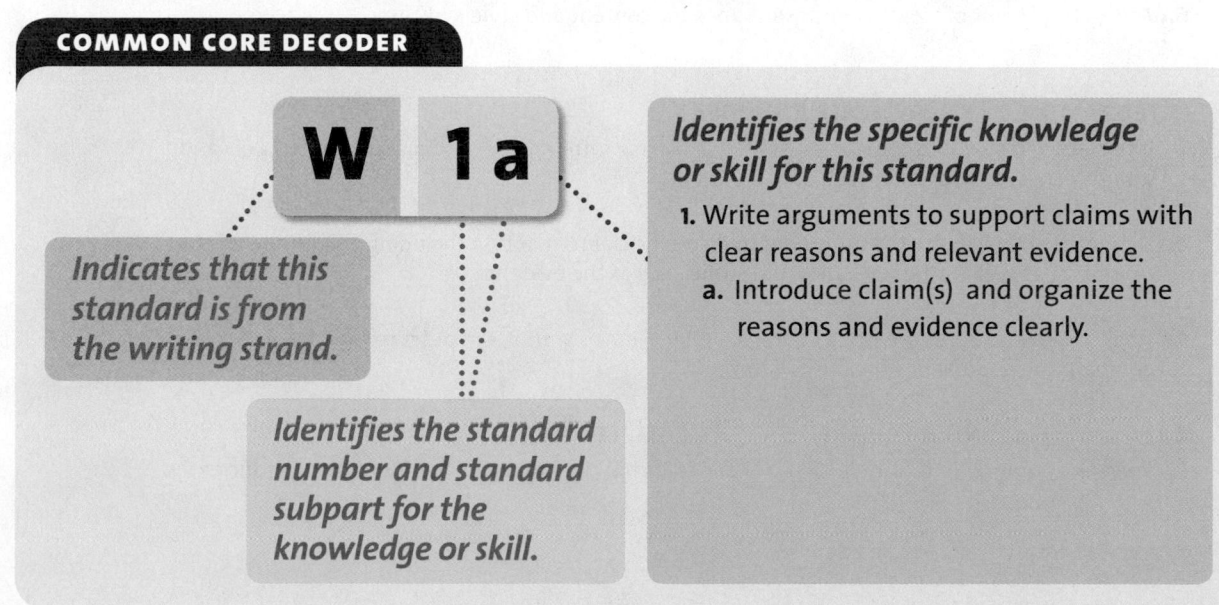

COMMON CORE DECODER

W **1 a**

Indicates that this standard is from the writing strand.

Identifies the standard number and standard subpart for the knowledge or skill.

Identifies the specific knowledge or skill for this standard.

1. Write arguments to support claims with clear reasons and relevant evidence.
  a. Introduce claim(s) and organize the reasons and evidence clearly.

COMMON CORE

English Language Arts
Common Core State Standards

Listed below are the English Language Arts Common Core State Standards that you are required to master by the end of grade 6. To help you understand what is required of you, we have provided a summary of the concepts you will learn on your way to mastering each standard.

College and Career Readiness Anchor Standards for Reading

COMMON CORE STATE STANDARDS

KEY IDEAS AND DETAILS

1. Read closely to determine what the text says explicitly and to make logical inferences from it; cite specific textual evidence when writing or speaking to support conclusions drawn from the text.

2. Determine central ideas or themes of a text and analyze their development; summarize the key supporting details and ideas.

3. Analyze how and why individuals, events, and ideas develop and interact over the course of a text.

CRAFT AND STRUCTURE

4. Interpret words and phrases as they are used in a text, including determining technical, connotative, and figurative meanings, and analyze how specific word choices shape meaning or tone.

5. Analyze the structure of texts, including how specific sentences, paragraphs, and larger portions of the text (e.g., a section, chapter, scene, or stanza) relate to each other and the whole.

6. Assess how point of view or purpose shapes the content and style of a text.

INTEGRATION OF KNOWLEDGE AND IDEAS

7. Integrate and evaluate content presented in diverse formats and media, including visually and quantitatively, as well as in words.

8. Delineate and evaluate the argument and specific claims in a text, including the validity of the reasoning as well as the relevance and sufficiency of the evidence.

9. Analyze how two or more texts address similar themes or topics in order to build knowledge or to compare the approaches the authors take.

RANGE OF READING AND LEVEL OF TEXT COMPLEXITY

10. Read and comprehend complex literary and informational texts independently and proficiently.

Reading Standards for Literature, Grade 6 Students

COMMON CORE STATE STANDARD	WHAT IT MEANS TO YOU
KEY IDEAS AND DETAILS	
1. Cite textual evidence to support analysis of what the text says explicitly as well as inferences drawn from the text.	You will use information from the text to support its main ideas—both those that are stated directly and those that are suggested.
2. Determine a theme or central idea of a text and how it is conveyed through particular details; provide a summary of the text distinct from personal opinions or judgments.	You will analyze a text's main idea or theme by showing how they unfold throughout the text. You will also summarize the main idea of the text as a whole without adding your own ideas or opinions.
3. Describe how a particular story's or drama's plot unfolds in a series of episodes as well as how the characters respond or change as the plot moves toward a resolution.	You will describe the events that make up a story or drama's plot and how those events affect the characters.
CRAFT AND STRUCTURE	
4. Determine the meaning of words and phrases as they are used in a text, including figurative and connotative meanings; analyze the impact of a specific word choice on meaning and tone.	You will analyze specific words, phrases, and patterns of sound in the text to determine what they mean and how they contribute to the text's larger meaning.
5. Analyze how a particular sentence, chapter, scene, or stanza fits into the overall structure of a text and contributes to the development of the theme, setting, or plot.	You will analyze how a specific section of a text contributes to its larger meaning.
6. Explain how an author develops the point of view of the narrator or speaker in a text.	You will analyze how an author shapes the narrator's point of view in a text.
INTEGRATION OF KNOWLEDGE AND IDEAS	
7. Compare and contrast the experience of reading a story, drama, or poem to listening to or viewing an audio, video, or live version of the text, including contrasting what they "see" and "hear" when reading the text to what they perceive when they listen or watch.	You will compare and contrast how events and information are presented in visual and non-visual texts.
8. (Not applicable to literature)	
9. Compare and contrast texts in different forms or genres (e.g., stories and poems; historical novels and fantasy stories) in terms of their approaches to similar themes and topics.	You will analyze how different forms of texts treat the same themes and topics.
RANGE OF READING AND LEVEL OF TEXT COMPLEXITY	
10. By the end of the year, read and comprehend literature, including stories, dramas, and poems, in the grades 6–8 text complexity band proficiently, with scaffolding as needed at the high end of the range.	You will read and understand grade-level appropriate literary texts by the end of grade 6.

Spotlight on Common Core

COMMON CORE

RL 9 Compare and contrast texts in different forms or genres (e.g., stories and poems; historical novels and fantasy stories) in terms of their approaches to similar themes and topics.

Literature: Comparing and Contrasting Texts

The Common Core State Standards require you to look at two similar texts to find how they are alike and how they are different. You will look at texts from different genres, or kinds of literature, and compare the authors' approach to their topics and their themes.

The **topic** of a piece of literature is the subject of the text, what the text is about. The **theme** is the writer's message about the topic. It expresses the lesson the writer wants to share with the reader. Here is an example of each.

Topic (writer's subject): facing fears
Theme (writer's message): Facing your fears makes you stronger.

Throughout this book, you will find works of literature with similar topics and themes. Study the following example:

Read the following poem and story excerpt. Then respond to the question that follows.

"On Turning Ten"
by Billy Collins

The whole idea of it makes me feel
like I'm coming down with something,
something worse than any stomach ache
or the headaches I get from reading in bad light—
a kind of measles of the spirit,
a mumps of the psyche,
a disfiguring chicken pox of the soul.

You tell me it is too early to be looking back,
but that is because you have forgotten
the perfect simplicity of being one
and the beautiful complexity introduced by two.
But I can lie on my bed and remember every digit.
At four I was an Arabian wizard.
I could make myself invisible
by drinking a glass of milk a certain way.
At seven I was a soldier, at nine a prince.

But now I am mostly at the window
watching the late afternoon light.
Back then it never fell so solemnly
against the side of my tree house,
and my bicycle never leaned against the garage
as it does today,
all the dark blue speed drained out of it.

continued

This is the beginning of sadness, I say to myself,
as I walk through the universe in my sneakers.
It is time to say good-bye to my imaginary friends,
time to turn the first big number.

It seems only yesterday I used to believe
there was nothing under my skin but light.
If you cut me I would shine.
But now when I fall upon the sidewalks of life,
I skin my knees, I bleed.

from "Eleven"
by Sandra Cisneros

*In this story, the narrator is embarrassed on her eleventh birthday when her
teacher insists that an ugly old sweater that has been in the coatroom for a
month belongs to her and makes her put it on.*

This is when I wish I wasn't eleven, because all the years inside of me—
ten, nine, eight, seven, six, five, four, three, two, and one—are pushing
at the back of my eyes when I put one arm through the sleeve of the
sweater that smells like cottage cheese, and then the other arm through
the other and stand there with my arms apart like if the sweater hurts me
and it does, all itchy and full of germs that aren't even mine.

   That's when everything I've been holding in since this morning, since
when Mrs. Price put the sweater on my desk, finally lets go, and all of a
sudden I'm crying in front of everybody. I wish I was invisible but I'm
not. I'm eleven and I'm crying like I'm three in front of everybody. I put
my head down on the desk and bury my face in my stupid clown-sweater
arms. My face all hot and spit coming out of my mouth because I can't
stop the little animal noises coming out of me, until there aren't any more
tears left in my eyes, and it's just my body shaking like when you have the
hiccups, and my whole head hurts like when you drink milk too fast.

   But the worst part is right before the bell rings for lunch. That
stupid Phyllis Lopez, who is even dumber than Sylvia Saldívar, says she
remembers the red sweater is hers! I take it off right away and give it to
her, only Mrs. Price pretends like everything's okay.

   Today I'm eleven. There's a cake Mama's making for tonight, and
when Papa comes home from work we'll eat it. There'll be candles and
presents and everybody will sing Happy birthday, happy birthday to you,
Rachel, only it's too late.

continued

I'm eleven today. I'm eleven, ten, nine, eight, seven, six, five, four, three, two, and one, but I wish I was one hundred and two. I wish I was anything but eleven, because I want today to be far away already, far away like a runaway balloon, like a tiny *o* in the sky, so tiny-tiny you have to close your eyes to see it.

1. Compare and contrast the topic and the theme of the poem by Collins and the story excerpt by Cisneros.

LEARN HOW Comparing and Contrasting Texts When you compare and contrast two texts, follow these steps.

Step One: Identify the texts' topics and themes.
Read the first text. Ask yourself what it is about. This is the text's **topic**. Read the text a second time. Then ask yourself what message about life or human nature the writer wants to get across. This is the text's **theme**. Now look for the topic and theme of the second text. Here are one student's notes.

	"On Turning Ten"	**"Eleven"**
Topic	*getting older*	*getting older*
Theme	*Getting older is sad.*	*Being older is better than being young.*

When you have identified both texts' topics and themes, compare them. What do the texts have in common? In this case, the texts share the topic of getting older.

Step Two: Compare and contrast what each text has to say about the common topic or theme.
One thing the texts have in common is their topic. Next, find out what each text has to say about this topic. Re-read the texts, and write down words that show the writer's thoughts and feelings. This will help you discover the message, or theme, that the writer wants to express. Here are one student's notes.

"On Turning Ten"	**"Eleven"**
The thought of turning ten makes him feel sick.	*She wishes she wasn't eleven. When you are eleven, you sometimes still act like a younger child.*
He remembers being younger as a happy time.	*She cries like she was three.*
"This is the beginning of sadness."	*"There'll be candles and presents and everybody will sing Happy birthday, happy birthday to you, Rachel, only it's too late."*
"But now when I fall upon the sidewalks of life/ I skin my knees, I bleed."	*She wishes she were older than eleven. Then the embarrassment of the day would be far away.*

Next, go over your notes to see what is the same and different.

Step Three: Write about what you have found.
Finally, write a few sentences about what is the same and different about the texts. Start by stating their common topic or theme. Then tell about similarities and differences in the authors' messages. What thoughts and feelings do they express? Here is one student's response to the prompt.

1. Compare and contrast the topic and theme of the poem by Collins and the story excerpt by Cisneros.

> In "On Turning Ten" and "Eleven," Collins and Cisneros both write about getting older. However, their thoughts and feelings about this topic are very different. The speaker of "On Turning Ten" remembers childhood as a magical time. He regrets getting older and leaving innocence behind. The narrator of "Eleven" finds childhood painful. She is powerless to speak up for herself, and she can't control her own emotions. She can't wait to grow up.

Reading Standards for Informational Text, Grade 6 Students

COMMON CORE STATE STANDARD	WHAT IT MEANS TO YOU
KEY IDEAS AND DETAILS	
1. Cite textual evidence to support analysis of what the text says explicitly as well as inferences drawn from the text.	You will cite information from the text to support its main ideas—both those that are stated directly and those that are suggested.
2. Determine a central idea of a text and how it is conveyed through particular details; provide a summary of the text distinct from personal opinions or judgments.	You will analyze the development of a text's main idea. You will also summarize the text without adding your own ideas or opinions.
3. Analyze in detail how a key individual, event, or idea is introduced, illustrated, and elaborated in a text (e.g., through examples or anecdotes).	You will analyze how an author treats a key person, event, or idea throughout a text.
CRAFT AND STRUCTURE	
4. Determine the meaning of words and phrases as they are used in a text, including figurative, connotative, and technical meanings.	You will discover the meaning of specific words and phrases in the text.
5. Analyze how a particular sentence, paragraph, chapter, or section fits into the overall structure of a text and contributes to the development of the ideas.	You will examine the major sections of a text and analyze how each one adds to the whole.
6. Determine an author's point of view or purpose in a text and explain how it is conveyed in the text.	You will understand the author's point of view and explain how the author gets his or her point of view across.

Reading Standards for Informational Text, Grade 6 Students, continued

COMMON CORE STATE STANDARD	WHAT IT MEANS TO YOU
INTEGRATION OF KNOWLEDGE AND IDEAS	
7. Integrate information presented in different media or formats (e.g., visually, quantitatively) as well as in words to develop a coherent understanding of a topic or issue.	▶ You will use information from visual and non-visual sources to understand a topic or issue.
8. Trace and evaluate the argument and specific claims in a text, distinguishing claims that are supported by reasons and evidence from claims that are not.	▶ You will evaluate the author's claims and reasoning and identify any weaknesses in them.
9. Compare and contrast one author's presentation of events with that of another (e.g., a memoir written by and a biography on the same person).	▶ You will compare and contrast two different authors' treatments of the same subject.
RANGE OF READING AND LEVEL OF TEXT COMPLEXITY	
10. By the end of the year, read and comprehend literary nonfiction in the grades 6–8 text complexity band proficiently, with scaffolding as needed at the high end of the range.	▶ You will demonstrate the ability to read and understand grade-level appropriate literary nonfiction texts by the end of grade 6.

Spotlight on Common Core

 **COMMON CORE** **RI 5** Analyze how a particular sentence, paragraph, chapter, or section fits into the overall structure of a text and contributes to the development of the ideas.

Informational Text: Analyzing Text Structure and Development of Ideas

The Common Core State Standards require you to analyze a text to understand how the parts fit together to create the whole. Those parts might be sentences, paragraphs, or chapters that make up an essay, an article, or a textbook. If the parts fit together well, the ideas in the text will be expressed clearly and coherently. If you understand the structure of the texts that you read, you can apply that same skill to become a better writer.

There are a few text structures, or patterns of organization, that writers of informational texts often use:

- chronological order
- compare-and-contrast organization
- cause-and-effect organization
- problem-solution order
- proposition-support organization

Each of these text structures has a characteristic pattern—sentences, paragraphs, and sections are organized in a predictable way. For instance, a problem-solution essay often begins by introducing the problem and then moves on to describing one or more solutions. A compare-and-contrast essay might be subject-by-subject or point-by-point. In a subject-by-subject organization, all the information about the first subject is given before moving to the second subject. In a point-by-point organization, both subjects are compared on one point before moving to the second point.

Throughout this book and your school career, you will be asked to analyze informational texts. If you can identify their structures and understand how their parts fit together, you will be better able to understand their overall meaning. Study the following example.

Read the following excerpt from an article about the surprising intelligence of some birds. Then answer the questions that follow.

from "Bird Brains"
by Gareth Huw Davies

PLAYING GAMES WITH HUMANS

Some birds seem to indulge in "intelligent" play. The kea, a New Zealand parrot, has been filmed ripping (inedible) windshield wipers off cars. Young keas, in a neat variation on ringing the doorbell and running away, are known to drop rocks on roofs to make people run outside.

Jack the jackdaw was raised by wildlife film producer John Downer. As soon as Jack was mature, he was released into the wild. However, he couldn't stay away. "One thing he is totally fascinated by is telephones," said Downer. "He knows how to hit the loudspeaker button and preset dial button. Once we came into the office to find him squawking into the telephone to the local travel agent."

Jack also likes to fly down onto the mirror of the production car when he sees somebody going out. "He turns into the wind, gets his head down and surfs on the air current until we reach about 30mph when he gives up. . . ."

ADJUSTING TO OTHERS

Scientists believe it is not physical need that drives creatures to become smarter, but social necessity. The complexities of living together require a higher level of intelligence. . . .

1. Which sentence tells you the main idea of the first section of the excerpt?

2. What kind of information do the other sentences in the first section give you? How do they relate to the main idea?

3. What do you predict the second section, "Adjusting to Others," will be about? Why do you think so?

4. How do these two sections relate to the main idea of the article —that some birds are surprisingly intelligent?

LEARN HOW Analyzing Structure The questions that follow the excerpt ask you to **analyze** it—that is, to figure out how each part fits together with the other parts to create the whole. To do this, you have to decide what each sentence means and what its purpose is. How does each sentence relate to the other sentences? How does it relate to the section? How does the section relate to the whole article? Let's take a closer look at the questions and how one student answered them.

1. Which sentence tells you the main idea of the first section of the excerpt?

> *1. The first sentence of the section states the main idea: "Some birds seem to indulge in 'intelligent' play."*

2. What kind of information do the other sentences in the first section give you? How do they relate to the main idea?

> *2. The other sentences in the section give examples of birds being playful. They support the main idea.*

3. What do you predict the second section, "Adjusting to Others," will be about? Why do you think so?

> *3. I predict the second section will be about birds being smart because they have to cooperate with others. I think so because of the heading and because the first sentence of the section probably states the main idea.*

4. How do these two sections relate to the main idea of the article —that some birds are surprisingly intelligent?

> *4. These two sections support the main idea of the article.*

> The sentences, paragraphs, and sections of this excerpt fit together to create a proposition-support text structure. This structure develops the writer's idea that birds are surprisingly intelligent.

As you analyze the structure of informational texts throughout the book, think about how the individual parts of a text contribute to the ideas that the writer wants to express.

Sometimes, as in this excerpt, writers state main ideas directly. Other times, you might have to infer, or guess, the main idea. In some informational texts, you can also use the headings of sections to help you figure out their main ideas. For instance, the heading of this section, "Playing Games with Humans," suggests that the section will be about playfulness.

Once a pattern has been established in a text, it becomes easier to predict what kind of information will come next. For instance, in this excerpt, the writer establishes a pattern in the first section. He states the main idea and then gives examples to support it. The reader can predict that the next section will follow the same pattern.

College and Career Readiness Anchor Standards for Writing

COMMON CORE STATE STANDARDS

TEXT TYPES AND PURPOSES

1. Write arguments to support claims in an analysis of substantive topics or texts, using valid reasoning and relevant and sufficient evidence.

2. Write informative/explanatory texts to examine and convey complex ideas and information clearly and accurately through the effective selection, organization, and analysis of content.

3. Write narratives to develop real or imagined experiences or events using effective technique, well-chosen details, and well-structured event sequences.

PRODUCTION AND DISTRIBUTION OF WRITING

4. Produce clear and coherent writing in which the development, organization, and style are appropriate to task, purpose, and audience.

5. Develop and strengthen writing as needed by planning, revising, editing, rewriting, or trying a new approach.

6. Use technology, including the Internet, to produce and publish writing and to interact and collaborate with others.

RESEARCH TO BUILD AND PRESENT KNOWLEDGE

7. Conduct short as well as more sustained research projects based on focused questions, demonstrating understanding of the subject under investigation.

8. Gather relevant information from multiple print and digital sources, assess the credibility and accuracy of each source, and integrate the information while avoiding plagiarism.

9. Draw evidence from literary or informational texts to support analysis, reflection, and research.

RANGE OF WRITING

10. Write routinely over extended time frames (time for research, reflection, and revision) and shorter time frames (a single sitting or a day or two) for a range of tasks, purposes, and audiences.

Writing Standards, Grade 6 Students

COMMON CORE STATE STANDARD	WHAT IT MEANS TO YOU
TEXT TYPES AND PURPOSES	
1. Write arguments to support claims with clear reasons and relevant evidence.	You will write and develop arguments with clear reasons and strong evidence that include
a. Introduce claim(s) and organize the reasons and evidence clearly.	**a.** a clear introduction and organization of claims
b. Support claim(s) with clear reasons and relevant evidence, using credible sources and demonstrating an understanding of the topic or text.	**b.** clear, accurate support for claims
c. Use words, phrases, and clauses to clarify the relationships among claim(s) and reasons.	**c.** use of clear words, phrases, and clauses to link information
d. Establish and maintain a formal style.	**d.** a formal style
e. Provide a concluding statement or section that follows from the argument presented.	**e.** a strong concluding statement that connects to the argument
2. Write informative/explanatory texts to examine a topic and convey ideas, concepts, and information through the selection, organization, and analysis of relevant content.	You will write clear, well-organized, and thoughtful informative and explanatory texts with
a. Introduce a topic; organize ideas, concepts, and information, using strategies such as definition, classification, comparison/contrast, and cause/effect; include formatting (e.g., headings), graphics (e.g., charts, tables), and multimedia when useful to aiding comprehension.	**a.** a clear introduction and organization, including headings and visuals (when appropriate)
b. Develop the topic with relevant facts, definitions, concrete details, quotations, or other information and examples.	**b.** strong supporting details and background information
c. Use appropriate transitions to create cohesion and clarify the relationships among ideas and concepts.	**c.** clear transitions to link ideas
d. Use precise language and domain-specific vocabulary to inform about or explain the topic.	**d.** precise language and vocabulary
e. Establish and maintain a formal style.	**e.** a formal style
f. Provide a concluding statement or section that follows from the information or explanation presented.	**f.** a strong conclusion that connects to the topic.

Writing Standards, Grade 6 Students, continued

COMMON CORE STATE STANDARD	WHAT IT MEANS TO YOU
3. Write narratives to develop real or imagined experiences or events using effective technique, relevant descriptive details, and well-structured event sequences.	You will write clear, well-structured, detailed narrative texts that
a. Engage and orient the reader by establishing a context and introducing a narrator and/or characters; organize an event sequence that unfolds naturally and logically.	**a.** draw your readers in with a clear topic that unfolds logically
b. Use narrative techniques, such as dialogue, pacing, and description, to develop experiences, events, and/or characters.	**b.** use narrative techniques to develop and expand on events and/or characters
c. Use a variety of transition words, phrases, and clauses to convey sequence and signal shifts from one time frame or setting to another.	**c.** use a variety of transition words to clearly signal shifts between time frames or settings
d. Use precise words and phrases, relevant descriptive details, and sensory language to convey experiences and events.	**d.** use precise words and sensory details that keep readers interested
e. Provide a conclusion that follows from the narrated experiences or events.	**e.** have a strong conclusion that connects to the topic

PRODUCTION AND DISTRIBUTION OF WRITING

4. Produce clear and coherent writing in which the development, organization, and style are appropriate to task, purpose, and audience. (Grade-specific expectations for writing types are defined in standards 1–3 above.)	You will produce writing that is appropriate to the task, purpose, and audience for whom you are writing.
5. With some guidance and support from peers and adults, develop and strengthen writing as needed by planning, revising, editing, rewriting, or trying a new approach.	With help from peers and adults, you will revise and refine your writing to address what is most important for your purpose and audience.
6. Use technology, including the Internet, to produce and publish writing as well as to interact and collaborate with others; demonstrate sufficient command of keyboarding skills to type a minimum of three pages in a single setting.	You will use technology to share your writing and to provide more information on your topic. You will also develop keyboarding skills to type at least three pages in a single setting.

RESEARCH TO BUILD AND PRESENT KNOWLEDGE

7. Conduct short research projects to answer a question, drawing on several sources and refocusing the inquiry when appropriate.	You will conduct short research projects to answer a question using multiple sources and altering your topic when needed.

Writing Standards, Grade 6 Students, continued

COMMON CORE STATE STANDARD	WHAT IT MEANS TO YOU
8. Gather relevant information from multiple print and digital sources; assess the credibility of each source; and quote or paraphrase the data and conclusions of others while avoiding plagiarism and providing basic bibliographic information for sources.	You will gather, quote, or restate information from different sources, and assess the strength of each source. You will also provide information for a bibliography.
9. Draw evidence from literary or informational texts to support analysis, reflection, and research. • Apply *grade 6 Reading standards* to literature (e.g., "Compare and contrast texts in different forms or genres [e.g., stories and poems; historical novels and fantasy stories] in terms of their approaches to similar themes and topics") • Apply *grade 6 Reading standards* to literary nonfiction (e.g., "Trace and evaluate the argument and specific claims in a text, distinguishing claims that are supported by reasons and evidence from claims that are not").	You will paraphrase, summarize, quote, and cite primary and secondary sources to support your analysis, reflection, and research.
RANGE OF WRITING 10. Write routinely over extended time frames (time for research, reflection, and revision) and shorter time frames (a single sitting or a day or two) for a range of discipline-specific tasks, purposes, and audiences.	You will write for many different purposes and audiences both over short and longer periods of time.

Spotlight on Common Core

COMMON CORE

W 10 Write routinely over extended time frames (time for research, reflection, and revision) and shorter time frames (a single day or two) for a range of tasks, purposes, and audiences.
W 4 Produce clear and coherent writing in which the development, organization, and style are appropriate to task, purpose, and audience.

Writing: Maintaining Clarity and Coherence

The Common Core State Standards require you to write in a variety of forms and situations. For instance, you might spend as long as several weeks writing a research report and only twenty minutes writing a descriptive paragraph. No matter what your writing task, purpose, or audience, your writing will be better if you start with a plan. Here are some questions you can ask yourself to make a plan for any writing task.

- **What is my purpose, or reason, for writing?**
  Do I want to explain how to do something, express a feeling, or persuade people to take an action?

- **What is my task, or final product?**
  What am I being asked to write? A poem? A how-to explanation? A letter?

- **Who is my audience?**
  Am I writing a spooky story to read to my cousins or a research report to enter in a school-wide contest? What will my audience expect from my writing? What information does my audience need to understand my topic? What am I comfortable sharing with my audience?

- **How much time do I have to write?**
  Do I have to finish my writing by the end of class, or do I have two weeks to finish it?

- **What is my topic?**
  Did my teacher assign a topic or a range of topics from which to choose? What do I want to write about? Do I have enough time to write about the topic I have chosen, or do I need to narrow my topic?

Once you have a plan for your writing, it will be easier to develop your ideas clearly and coherently in a way that fits your task, purpose, and audience. **Clear writing** is writing that your readers can understand—it makes sense. **Coherent writing** is writing that your readers can follow—the ideas are in a logical order and they all fit together.

The Writing Workshops in this book give many strategies to help students become successful writers. Here are some examples of the types of strategies you'll find:

DEVELOPMENT	WHAT DOES IT LOOK LIKE?
• **Engage** your audience with an interesting introduction and memorable conclusion. • **Focus** your ideas with a thesis statement or controlling idea. • **Develop your ideas** with relevant support (logical reasoning and relevant evidence, including facts, definitions, concrete details, quotations, and examples).	What did sailors once mistake for a mermaid but is actually closer in size to a car? If you guessed "manatee," you are right. These unique marine mammals grow to be around 1,000 pounds and 10 feet long. Despite their large size, however, they are not dangerous. Manatees are herbivorous, which means that they eat only plants, and spend much of their time placidly grazing, a habit which may have given them their nickname: sea cow.

ORGANIZATION	WHAT DOES IT LOOK LIKE?
• **Organize ideas logically** using patterns (such as definition, classification, compare/contrast, cause/effect, and chronological order) to help readers follow your ideas. • **Use transitions** to clarify the relationships among ideas and create coherence. • **Include formatting, graphics, and multimedia** to help your audience understand your ideas.	*Habitat* Manatees live in the coastal waters and rivers of the Caribbean and the Gulf of Mexico, the Amazon Basin, and West Africa. They prefer to live in warm, shallow water and often swim through estuaries, where rivers open into the sea, to reach freshwater springs where the water temperature stays more constant. In fact, manatees are so fond of warmth that they like to gather in the water heated by power plants.

LANGUAGE/STYLE	WHAT DOES IT LOOK LIKE?
• **Use an appropriate style and tone** (formal for academic tasks). • **Use precise words** and relevant descriptive details to bring the writing to life. • Write with correct grammar, usage, capitalization, and punctuation.	Unfortunately, the manatees' habitats are threatened by human activity. Development of coastal areas has led to a loss of habitat for manatees. In addition, many manatees are injured and even killed by violent crashes with fast motor boats and their propellers. The slow-moving, graceful manatees are curious and cannot move out of the way in time. In order to avoid hurting these gentle giants, the ships NASA uses when passing through manatee habitats are powered by water jets, rather than propellers.

College and Career Readiness Anchor Standards for Speaking and Listening

COMPREHENSION AND COLLABORATION

1. Prepare for and participate effectively in a range of conversations and collaborations with diverse partners, building on others' ideas and expressing their own clearly and persuasively.

2. Integrate and evaluate information presented in diverse media and formats, including visually, quantitatively, and orally.

3. Evaluate a speaker's point of view, reasoning, and use of evidence and rhetoric.

PRESENTATION OF KNOWLEDGE AND IDEAS

4. Present information, findings, and supporting evidence such that listeners can follow the line of reasoning and the organization, development, and style are appropriate to task, purpose, and audience.

5. Make strategic use of digital media and visual displays of data to express information and enhance understanding of presentations.

6. Adapt speech to a variety of contexts and communicative tasks, demonstrating command of formal English when indicated or appropriate.

Speaking and Listening Standards, Grade 6 Students

COMMON CORE STATE STANDARD	WHAT IT MEANS TO YOU
COMPREHENSION AND COLLABORATION	
1. Engage effectively in a range of collaborative discussions (one-on-one, in groups, and teacher-led) with diverse partners on grade 6 topics, texts, and issues, building on others' ideas and expressing their own clearly.	You will actively participate in a variety of discussions in which you
a. Come to discussions prepared, having read or studied required material; explicitly draw on that preparation by referring to evidence on the topic, text, or issue to probe and reflect on ideas under discussion.	a. have read any required material beforehand and have come to the discussion prepared
b. Follow rules for collegial discussions, set specific goals and deadlines, and define individual roles as needed.	b. work with others to set goals and processes within the group
c. Pose and respond to specific questions with elaboration and detail by making comments that contribute to the topic, text, or issue under discussion.	c. ask and respond to questions that relate to the topic
d. Review the key ideas expressed and demonstrate understanding of multiple perspectives through reflection and paraphrasing.	d. review and restate different points of view

Speaking and Listening Standards, Grade 6 Students, continued

COMMON CORE STATE STANDARD	WHAT IT MEANS TO YOU
2. Interpret information presented in diverse media and formats (e.g., visually, quantitatively, orally) and explain how it contributes to a topic, text, or issue under study.	You will analyze main ideas and details of various media and relate them to a topic under study.
3. Delineate a speaker's argument and specific claims, distinguishing claims that are supported by reasons and evidence from claims that are not.	You will evaluate a speaker's argument and identify any false reasoning or evidence.

PRESENTATION OF KNOWLEDGE AND IDEAS

4. Present claims and findings, sequencing ideas logically and using pertinent descriptions, facts, and details to accentuate main ideas or themes; use appropriate eye contact, adequate volume, and clear pronunciation.	You will organize and present information to your listeners in a logical sequence and style that is appropriate to your task and audience.
5. Include multimedia components (e.g., graphics, images, music, sound) and visual displays in presentations to clarify information.	You will use audio and/or visual materials to clarify and add to presentations.
6. Adapt speech to a variety of contexts and tasks, demonstrating command of formal English when indicated or appropriate.	You will adapt the formality of your speech appropriately.

Spotlight on Common Core

COMMON CORE SL 5 Include multimedia components (e.g., graphics, images, music, sound) and visual displays in presentations to clarify information.

Speaking and Listening: Including Multimedia Components and Visual Displays in Presentations

The Common Core State Standards ask that you include a variety of media in presentations. Media can consist of pictures, photographs, music, sounds, and graphics. Including multimedia can help your audience understand the information and ideas you are presenting. Use of multimedia components can also make your presentations more interesting and entertaining!

In this book, you will learn how to give several kinds of presentations—an oral response to literature, a persuasive speech, and an informational power presentation. In the workshops for these presentations you will learn how to incorporate graphics and other multimedia components. Here are some additional tips for including multimedia and visual displays to clarify information.

Visuals

What?	Why?	Examples
Pictures, photographs, and diagrams	To show what someone or something unfamiliar looks like; to show how something works; to show the parts of something; to help an audience understand or relate to the subject of a presentation	Sandra Cisneros
Charts	To show relationships among ideas and data. A **flowchart** can be used to show a sequence of events, while a **pie chart** can be used to show how the parts of something relate to the whole	**Recycled Materials** Aluminum cans 25%, Glass 15%, Paper 40%, Plastic 20%
Graphs	To show numeric data; to show how things change over time and in relationship to one another	Size of Ancient Empires (Area in Square Miles): Akkadia, Assyria, Babylonia, Sumer. Source: *Institute for Research on World Systems*
Tables	To show detailed information in a clear and accessible way; to compare and contrast	See table below
Timelines	To show events that have happened during a given period of time; to clarify when an event happened in relation to other events	See timeline below

Greek and Roman Gods

Description	Greek	Roman
Supreme god	Zeus	Jupiter
Supreme goddess	Hera (wife of Zeus)	Juno (wife of Jupiter)
God of the sea	Poseidon	Neptune
God of music and poetry	Apollo	Apollo

November 1860—Abraham Lincoln is elected president of the United States.

December 1860—South Carolina secedes from the Union; other states follow.

1860 A.D.   **1861 A.D.**

February 1861— Southern states form the Confederacy.

April 1861—Confederate soldiers attack Fort Sumter.

Other Multimedia Components

What?	Why?	Examples
Music	To "illustrate" a presentation about music; to create a mood for your presentation; to create context for a presentation on a historical time period.	You are doing a presentation on the birth of hip hop. You want your audience to hear what hip hop music sounded like at various stages in its history.
Sounds	To help audiences to understand what something sounds like; to get the audience's attention.	You are doing a presentation on the novel *To Kill a Mockingbird*. You want your audience to hear what a mockingbird sounds like.
Video Clips	To clarify how something works, particularly in a how-to presentation; to help your audience understand the topic of your presentation.	You are doing a presentation on how to do a skateboard trick. You show a brief video clip of yourself doing the trick. Or, you are doing a presentation on the book *The Lightning Thief*. You show a brief clip from the movie based on that book.

Read the following excerpt from the text of one student's research paper about cats in ancient Egypt. Then answer the questions that follow about how to incorporate multimedia components into a presentation of the paper.

Before about 4000 B.C. in Egypt, cats were wild. They were also bigger than the pet cats we know today. When Egyptians began to farm, they had to store their grain, but mice got into the grain and ate it. Cats attacked the mice and rats. People realized that cats could help keep the grain safe. For that reason, cats became valuable to people.

continued

Big, wild cats also killed poisonous snakes. People must have noticed this and then figured out that it would be good to keep cats around their homes. People began to feed the cats to make sure that they stayed around. At some point, they probably began to pet and enjoy the cats, too. Bisno says that the cats "found a good source of food living around people's homes" and that cats and people started to have a friendly relationship. By 2000 B.C., many cats were pets instead of wild animals.

Cats and people interacted for a few thousand years before people began thinking of cats as sacred. That happened beginning about 1000 B.C. At that time people began to believe that cats were the special favorite of a goddess named Bastet. In fact, in some works of art, Bastet has a female body and the head of a cat.

1. What picture might you use to help your audience understand the main idea in the first paragraph of this research paper?

2. In addition to the dates given in the excerpt above, several more dates important to the domestication of cats appear in the paper. What type of visual aid might you use in a presentation to clarify the dates and order of events for your audience?

3. What image would help an audience understand the possibly unfamiliar ideas in the last paragraph of the excerpt?

LEARN HOW Including Multimedia Components and Visual Displays in Presentations

1. The first question asks you to identify the main idea of the first paragraph. Identifying the main idea will help you choose a visual to illustrate that main idea. In this case, the main idea is that cats were useful as mousers. You might want to include a picture of a cat pouncing on a mouse or a rat.

2. The second question asks you which type of visual is best for the data you want to present. Analyzing your information will help you choose the right type of visual to represent it. A timeline is the best choice to clarify dates and the order of events for your audience.

3. The third question asks you to consider your audience. Identifying information that they might be unfamiliar with will help you choose an image. The concept that seems the most unfamiliar is the image of Bastet, who has the body of a woman and the head of a cat. To illustrate this part of the presentation, you would want to find a slide or other representation of artworks of Bastet.

Regardless of the subject of your presentation, try to include media from a wide range of sources, including films, videos, newspapers, magazines, Web sites, and CDs. Remember, though, that a few well chosen images are all you need. Choose visuals and multimedia components to clarify and enhance your presentation, not to clutter it.

College and Career Readiness Anchor Standards for Language

COMMON CORE STATE STANDARDS

CONVENTIONS OF STANDARD ENGLISH

1. Demonstrate command of the conventions of standard English grammar and usage when writing or speaking.

2. Demonstrate command of the conventions of standard English capitalization, punctuation, and spelling when writing.

KNOWLEDGE OF LANGUAGE

3. Apply knowledge of language to understand how language functions in different contexts, to make effective choices for meaning or style, and to comprehend more fully when reading or listening.

VOCABULARY ACQUISITION AND USE

4. Determine or clarify the meaning of unknown and multiple-meaning words and phrases by using context clues, analyzing meaningful word parts, and consulting general and specialized reference materials, as appropriate.

5. Demonstrate understanding of word relationships and nuances in word meanings.

6. Acquire and use accurately a range of general academic and domain-specific words and phrases sufficient for reading, writing, speaking, and listening at the college and career readiness level; demonstrate independence in gathering vocabulary knowledge when considering a word or phrase important to comprehension or expression.

Language Standards, Grade 6 Students

COMMON CORE STATE STANDARD	WHAT IT MEANS TO YOU

CONVENTIONS OF STANDARD ENGLISH
1. Demonstrate command of the conventions of standard English grammar and usage when writing or speaking.
  a. Ensure that pronouns are in the proper case (subjective, objective, possessive).
  b. Use intensive pronouns (e.g., *myself, ourselves*).
  c. Recognize and correct inappropriate shifts in pronoun number and person.*
  d. Recognize and correct vague pronouns (i.e., ones with unclear or ambiguous antecedents).*
  e. Recognize variations from standard English in their own and others' writing and speaking, and identify and use strategies to improve expression in conventional language.*
	You will correctly understand and use the conventions of English grammar and usage, including
	
	  a. making sure pronouns are in the proper case
	
	  b. using intensive pronouns
	
	  c. correcting shifts in pronoun number and person
	
	  d. correcting unclear connections between pronouns and antecedents
	
	  e. identifying your own and others' errors in speaking and writing and using strategies to improve expression.

Language Standards, Grade 6 Students, continued

COMMON CORE STATE STANDARD	WHAT IT MEANS TO YOU
2. Demonstrate command of the conventions of standard English capitalization, punctuation, and spelling when writing.	You will correctly use the conventions of English capitalization, punctuation, and spelling, including
a. Use punctuation (commas, parentheses, dashes) to set off nonrestrictive/parenthetical elements.*	**a.** punctuation to set off information that is not essential to the meaning of the sentence
b. Spell correctly.	**b.** spelling

KNOWLEDGE OF LANGUAGE

3. Use knowledge of language and its conventions when writing, speaking, reading, or listening.	You will apply your knowledge of language in different contexts by
a. Vary sentence patterns for meaning, reader/listener interest, and style.*	**a.** using various sentence patterns
b. Maintain consistency in style and tone.*	**b.** keeping a consistent style and tone

VOCABULARY ACQUISITION AND USE

4. Determine or clarify the meaning of unknown and multiple-meaning words and phrases based on grade 6 reading and content, choosing flexibly from a range of strategies.	You will understand the meaning of grade-level appropriate words and phrases by
a. Use context (e.g., the overall meaning of a sentence or paragraph; a word's position or function in a sentence) as a clue to the meaning of a word or phrase.	**a.** using context clues
b. Use common, grade-appropriate Greek or Latin affixes and roots as clues to the meaning of a word (e.g., *audience, auditory, audible*).	**b.** using Greek or Latin roots
c. Consult reference materials (e.g., dictionaries, glossaries, thesauruses), both print and digital, to find the pronunciation of a word or determine or clarify its precise meaning or its part of speech.	**c.** using reference materials
d. Verify the preliminary determination of the meaning of a word or phrase (e.g., by checking the inferred meaning in context or in a dictionary).	**d.** inferring and verifying the meanings of words in context
5. Demonstrate understanding of figurative language, word relationships, and nuances in word meanings.	You will understand figurative language, word relationships, and slight differences in word meanings by
a. Interpret figures of speech (e.g., personification) in context.	**a.** interpreting figures of speech in context
b. Use the relationship between particular words (e.g., cause/effect, part/whole, item/category) to better understand each of the words.	**b.** analyzing relationships between words
c. Distinguish among the connotations (associations) of words with similar denotations (definitions) (e.g., *stingy, scrimping, economical, unwasteful, thrifty*)	**c.** distinguishing among words with similar definitions
6. Acquire and use accurately grade-appropriate general academic and domain-specific words and phrases; gather vocabulary knowledge when considering a word or phrase important to comprehension or expression.	You will learn and use grade-appropriate vocabulary.

Spotlight on Common Core

 COMMON CORE

L 1e Recognize variations from standard English in their own and others' writing and speaking, and identify and use strategies to improve expression in conventional language.

Language: Standard English

The Common Core State Standards require you to be able to recognize variations from standard English and to improve your ability to use conventional language. What is standard English? It is English that follows the rules and conventions of grammar and usage. Here is an example of a sentence written incorrectly and correctly.

INCORRECT: We don't have no homework tonight.

CORRECT: We don't have any homework tonight.

Which version should you use when speaking to the principal of your school? Which version might you use when speaking to a friend?

Nobody uses standard English all the time when speaking to friends and family. We all use variations, regionalisms, and slang. However, the ability to recognize and use standard English is important because it is the most widely accepted form of English. It is used in formal situations, such as in speeches and writing for school, and in informal situations, such as in conversation and everyday writing. Knowing when and how to use standard English is a skill that you will need throughout your school and work careers.

Here are some common variations on standard English that you may recognize in your writing and speaking. Note the strategies for turning the variations into standard English.

TURNING VARIATIONS INTO STANDARD ENGLISH		
INCORRECT	**STRATEGY**	**CORRECT**
Our team hasn't never lost a game.	Make sure that you use only one of these negative words in a sentence: *aren't, can't, haven't, hasn't, isn't, hardly, never, nobody, none, not, nothing.*	*Our team has never lost a game.* *Our team hasn't ever lost a game.*
Youse are welcome to come with us! *Y'all are welcome to come with us!*	Remember that if you want to emphasize that you are using the plural form of you, add the word *all. Youse* and *y'all* are not standard English.	*You all are welcome to come with us!* *You are all welcome to come with us!*
I read where the play was supposed to start at 5 p.m.	Don't use "where" to mean "that."	*I read that the play was supposed to start at 5 p.m.*
Bring them books to class tomorrow.	Remember that *them* is a pronoun. Do not use *them* as an adjective. Use *those* instead.	*Bring those books to class tomorrow.*

Read this passage from a personal narrative and see if you can identify and fix the instances of incorrect usage.

> I noticed where the tryouts for the band would be on Saturday. I had been playing the drums ever since I could get the pots and pans out of the kitchen cabinets and bang on them with a wooden spoon, but I hadn't never been in a band. As Saturday got closer, I got more and more nervous. I practiced every day and went to bed early on Friday night. I couldn't hardly sleep a wink, though, I was so excited.
>
> Saturday morning, my mom drove me to the tryouts. It was in one of them music studios downtown. As we pulled up, I could hear the music throbbing from the building. A line of about ten guys stood outside.
>
> "Youse can wait in here," shouted someone from inside the building.

Here is a corrected version.

> I noticed **that** the tryouts for the band would be on Saturday. I had been playing the drums ever since I could get the pots and pans out of the kitchen cabinets and bang on them with a wooden spoon, but I hadn't **ever** been in a band. As Saturday got closer, I got more and more nervous. I practiced every day and went to bed early on Friday night. I **could** hardly sleep a wink, though, I was so excited.
>
> Saturday morning, my mom drove me to the tryouts. It was in one of **those** music studios downtown. As we pulled up, I could hear the music pulsing from the building. A line of about ten guys stood outside.
>
> "Youse can wait in here," shouted someone from inside the building.

Note: Discuss with your teacher why the corrected version still includes the nonstandard word *youse*.

When you receive feedback from teachers and others that you have used English inappropriately in your speaking and writing, make a note of the incorrect usage and try to correct it in the future.

The Power of Ideas

INTRODUCING
THE ESSENTIALS

- Genres Workshop
- Reading Strategies Workshop
- Academic Vocabulary Workshop
- Writing Process Workshop

What Are Life's Big Questions?

The challenges we face in life can raise many questions, including the ones shown here. Such universal questions get us thinking about ideas—such as friendship, freedom, and fitting in—that affect our lives. Through our attempts to find answers, we come closer to understanding our choices, actions, and mistakes. Sometimes, reading a powerful piece of literature can help us make sense of how we got where we are and where we want to go now.

What is a FRIEND?

There's nothing better than spending time with a true friend—whether that friend is someone your own age, an older person with wisdom to share, or even a family pet. How do you know for certain that you have a friend you can count on in good and bad times? Many of the stories, poems, and plays you'll read in this book will help you think about what it takes to be a friend.

Who's really IN CHARGE?

Some people want to tell you how to live your life, giving opinions about everything from what you should wear to what you should be when you grow up. It's good to listen to advice, but how can you be sure you're charting your own course? In this book, you'll meet all kinds of characters and real people who have to decide who's *really* in charge.

When is STRENGTH more than muscle?

Strength isn't always physical. Emotional strength and courage can be just as powerful. This book is filled with characters who find an inner source of strength when standing up to bullies, confronting deadly creatures, or experiencing impossible problems.

When is CHANGE good?

Change is all around you. Leaves turn from green to red, birds migrate from north to south, day turns to night. You deal with change at the start of each school year when you're faced with new classes, new friends, and new problems. Why is change both exciting and scary? You'll consider this question as you read about people who confront changes big and small.

Reading Text Types

You've been reading for most of your life, from childhood fairy tales to the novels, plays, and Web sites you encounter today. What more can you learn about reading? In this book, you'll take reading to a new level. Get started by discovering how literary and nonfiction texts can help you explore ideas that matter.

The Genres

COMMON CORE

Included in this workshop:
RL 1, RL 2, RL 4, RL 5, RI 1, RI 2, RI 7

Think about the ideas that are important to you. For example, are you curious about what it means to be respected or trusted? Writers often explore these same ideas, choosing a **genre,** or category of literature and nonfiction, in which to express their thoughts. A genre is characterized by its unique style, form, or content.

Within each genre, writers use different forms to share their ideas with readers. Writers of stories may create novels or folk tales, for instance.

GENRES AT A GLANCE

STORIES
Stories are made-up narratives about characters and events.
• short stories   • novels   • novellas   • folk tales

POETRY
Poetry is a type of literature in which words are chosen and arranged in a precise way to create specific effects.
• odes   • limericks   • narrative poems

DRAMA
Dramas are stories that are meant to be performed.
• comedies   • historical dramas   • radio plays

NONFICTION
Nonfiction tells about real people, places, and events.
• autobiographies   • essays   • news articles
• biographies   • speeches   • technical articles

TYPES OF MEDIA

The word *media* refers to communication that reaches many people.
• TV shows   • advertising   • Web sites

READING STORIES

Short stories, novels, and novellas are different forms of narratives.

- A **short story** usually centers on one idea and can be read in one sitting.
- A **novel** is a longer work in which the characters and story line are thoroughly developed.
- A **novella** is longer than a short story but shorter than a novel.

Whatever you read, there's nothing like being swept away by a good story. These strategies can help make the most of your journey.

- **Make connections.** Ask: Have I experienced situations similar to those of these characters?
- **Picture the scene.** Note descriptions of characters and settings. Use these descriptions to help you visualize lifelike pictures in your mind.
- **Predict what will happen.** At each twist and turn, ask: What's going to happen next? Then read on to find out if you guessed correctly.
- **Track the events.** Every story follows a **plot,** or a series of events that traces a problem. Keep track of the events in your **Reader/Writer Notebook.**

Read the Model Annemarie is a young girl living in Denmark in 1943. German soldiers who occupy her city intend to imprison all Jewish people, including Annemarie's friend Ellen. In this excerpt, Annemarie is racing with Ellen. Use the strategies to explore the idea of fear.

LITERARY TERMS FOR STORIES

- plot
- conflict
- character
- setting
- theme
- point of view

from

Number the Stars

Novel by **Lois Lowry**

Annemarie outdistanced her friend quickly, even though one of her shoes came untied as she sped along the street called Østerbrogade, past the small shops and cafés of her neighborhood here in northeast Copenhagen. Laughing, she skirted an elderly lady in black who carried
5   a shopping bag made of string. A young woman pushing a baby in a carriage moved aside to make way. The corner was just ahead.

Annemarie looked up, panting, just as she reached the corner. Her laughter stopped. Her heart seemed to skip a beat.

"*Halte!*" the soldier ordered in a stern voice.
10   The German word was as familiar as it was frightening. Annemarie had heard it often enough before, but it had never been directed at her until now.

Close Read

1. What do you think the soldier will say to Annemarie? Make a prediction, based on what you've read so far.

2. **Exploring a Big Question** If you were in a scary situation like Annemarie's, would you be able to hide your fear? Would most people be able to? Explain.

READING POETRY

A red wheelbarrow, windshield wipers, war—a poet can create poems about anything. Yet poets express their ideas differently than fiction writers do. Poets arrange their thoughts in **lines,** rather than sentences. Lines are often grouped into **stanzas,** instead of paragraphs. Use these strategies to fully appreciate any poem you read.

- **Examine the form.** First, notice how the poem looks on the page. Are the lines long or short? Are they grouped into stanzas?

- **Notice the punctuation.** In a poem, a single sentence can continue over many lines. Use the punctuation to help you figure out when to pause while reading.

- **Read the poem aloud.** Listen for the poem's musical rhymes or rhythms.

- **Form a mental picture.** Look for words and phrases that can help you imagine what's being described.

Read the Model As you read this poem, notice how the writer uses the description of an old quilt to explore the idea of family.

LITERARY TERMS FOR POETRY
- form
- line
- stanza
- rhythm
- rhyme

Quilt

Poem by
Janet S. Wong

Our family
is a quilt

of odd remnants[1]
patched together

5 in a strange
pattern,

threads fraying,
fabric wearing thin—

but made to keep
10 its warmth

even in bitter
cold.

---

1. **remnants:** leftovers; remainders.

Close Read

1. Read the poem aloud, pausing only where there is punctuation. How many sentences are in this poem? How many lines and stanzas are there?

2. **Exploring a Big Question** This poem compares a family to a quilt. How does this comparison help you understand the positive qualities of family?

READING DRAMA

A drama is meant to be acted out for an audience. To read drama, you have to visualize in your mind the action that would take place in the theater. These strategies can help.

- **Read the play silently, then aloud with others.** Sometimes, hearing the dialogue can help you better understand what's happening.

- **Read the stage directions.** Often printed in *italic type,* **stage directions** are the writer's specific instructions about everything from the setting and props to the characters' feelings and movements. Use these notes to help you picture the setting, action, and characters.

- **Get to know the characters.** Characters' words and actions tell you what they are like. Pay attention to their **dialogue,** or what they say, as well as the stage directions.

Read the Model Sara is treated like a princess at school because of her family's wealth. After her family fortune is lost, however, she must become a servant. In this excerpt, Becky, the school maid, comforts Sara. The two girls have always been friends, despite their different circumstances. What is the author suggesting about the idea of differences?

LITERARY
TERMS FOR
DRAMA

- plot
- character
- act
- scene
- dialogue
- stage directions

from

The Little Princess

Novel by **Frances Hodgson Burnett**
Dramatized by **Adele Thane**

Becky. I just wanted to ask you, miss—you've been such a rich young lady and been waited on hand and foot. What'll you do now, miss, without any maid? Please, would you let me wait on you after I'm done with my pots and kettles?

5 **Sara** (*with a sob*). Oh, Becky! Do you remember when I told you that we were just the same? Not a rich girl and a poor girl, but just two girls.

Becky. Yes, miss. You said it was an accident that I was not you and you were not me.

Sara. Well, you see how true it is, Becky. There's no difference now. I'm

10 not a princess any more. (BECKY *presses* SARA's *hand to her cheek.*)

Becky. Yes, miss, you are! Whatever happens to you, you'll be a princess just the same—and nothing could make it any different.

Close Read

1. How does Becky feel about Sara? How does Sara feel about Becky? How can you tell?

2. **Exploring a Big Question** Becky and Sara are friends, even though they come from different backgrounds. What other differences can people overcome in the name of friendship?

READING NONFICTION

From articles on the Web to front-page news, informational texts are all around you. Informational text includes not only encyclopedia entries and news articles, but also autobiographies, personal narratives, memoirs, essays, and speeches. By reading all these different types of nonfiction, you can learn about real people, places, events, and issues that matter.

TERMS FOR NONFICTION

- purpose
- organization
- main idea
- text features

TYPES OF INFORMATIONAL TEXTS

AUTOBIOGRAPHY/ BIOGRAPHY
The true story of a person's life, told by that person (autobiography) or by someone else (biography)

NEWS ARTICLE
Factual writing that reports on recent events

Homeless Dolphins to Get Back Together in Bahamas

JACKSON, Miss. (AP) — Several dolphins that were swept out to sea by Hurricane Katrina will soon be reunited at a resort in the Bahamas.

A resort on Paradise Island in the Bahamas will take on 17 dolphins from the Marine Life Oceanarium—eight of which were rescued from open water in September.

"The dolphins, I think, are a symbol of everything that's happened on the Gulf Coast and to find a new home for them—that's something that we hope will happen for everybody on the coast," said Howard Karawan, president and managing director of the company that owns the resort.

PERSONAL NARRATIVE/ AUTOBIOGRAPHICAL ESSAY
A short piece of writing about a single subject

What Video Games Taught Me

REFERENCE ARTICLE
Informative writing that provides facts and background on a specific subject

COYOTES
Wildlife Sense and Safety

SPEECH
An oral presentation of a speaker's ideas or beliefs

CONSUMER DOCUMENT
Printed material that usually comes with a product or a service

HOW TO USE YOUR *DIGITAL* **MP3 PLAYER**
A STEP-BY-STEP GUIDE

Strategies For Reading

- **Consider the purpose.** Is the writer trying to persuade, inspire, or inform? Understanding the author's purpose can help you know what to look for in the text.

- **Note the main ideas.** As you read, look for the **main ideas,** or the most important points about a topic. Record these ideas in a notebook to help you remember them.

- **Preview the text.** Some types of nonfiction have **text features,** like subheadings or captions. Before you read, look at the features to get a sense of what the text is about.

- **Examine the graphic aids.** Photographs and illustrations also convey information. Tables, charts, and diagrams may also provide additional information about a topic.

MODEL 1: READING A BIOGRAPHY

This excerpt is from a biography about Steven Spielberg, a famous movie director. How does it help you understand the idea of inspiration?

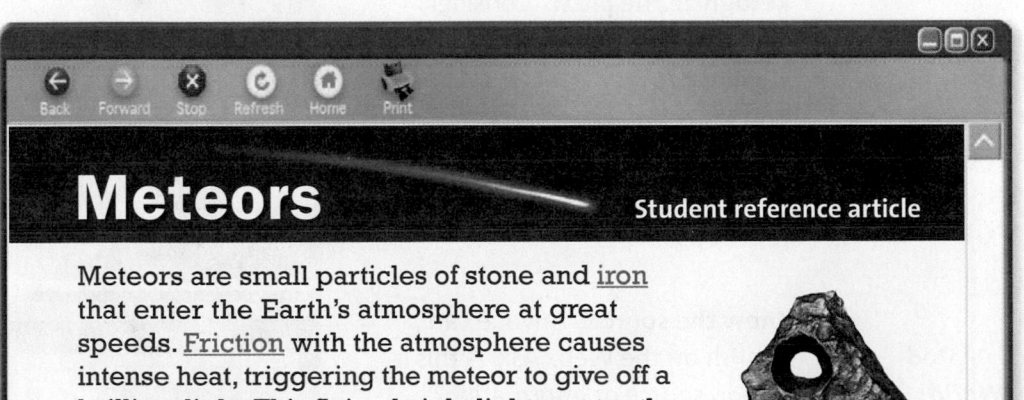

from
Steven Spielberg:
Crazy *for* Movies

Biography by
Susan Goldman Rubin

When Steven Spielberg was ten, his father woke him up and took him out to the desert near where they lived in Phoenix, Arizona. They spread out a blanket and lay on their backs looking up at the sky. Steven's father, Arnold Spielberg, liked astronomy and hoped to see a comet
5 that was supposed to appear. Instead, they saw a meteor shower. "The stars were just tremendous," recalled Arnold. "They were so intense it was frightening." He gave Steven a scientific explanation of what was happening.
   "But I didn't want to hear that," said Steven. "I wanted to think of
10 them as falling stars." That memory of falling stars stayed with him and inspired his first full-length movie, *Firelight*.

Close Read

1. What do you learn about Steven Spielberg from this excerpt?

2. **Exploring a Big Question**
   The memory of a meteor shower led Spielberg to create science fiction films. What other experiences might inspire people to pursue certain careers?

MODEL 2: READING A REFERENCE ARTICLE

Turning a moment of inspiration into a life-long career takes more than just wishing on a falling star. Hard work and a curious mind are essential. As you read this Web article, think about the idea of curiosity.

Meteors
Student reference article

Meteors are small particles of stone and <u>iron</u> that enter the Earth's atmosphere at great speeds. <u>Friction</u> with the atmosphere causes intense heat, triggering the meteor to give off a brilliant light. This flying bright light creates the appearance of a shooting or falling star.

Meteorites

Most meteors burn up before they reach the Earth's surface. Occasionally, though, very large meteors—called meteorites—make impact with the Earth's surface.

This meteorite was found at the edge of the Kalahari Desert.

Close Read

1. What do you learn about this article simply by previewing the title, the subheading, and the photograph?

2. **Exploring a Big Question**
   People have always been fascinated by mysteries of science and nature. What scientific mysteries have sparked your curiosity?

READING MEDIA

Has an ad ever persuaded you to buy something you didn't need? Do you ever find yourself glued to the television or unable to tear yourself away from the Web? Media messages influence your life in all kinds of ways. That's why it's important to become **media literate**—that is, learn how to "read," analyze, and evaluate what you see and hear. You can begin by identifying the structural features of each medium and using those features to help you find the information you want.

TERMS FOR MEDIA

- medium
- message
- target audience

TYPE OF MEDIA	STRATEGIES FOR VIEWING	
FILMS AND TV SHOWS Motion pictures, shown in movie theaters or broadcast on television, that tell stories	• **Know what's happening.** Ask a friend or an adult if you're confused about the plot. • **Spot the techniques.** Ask yourself: How does the director use sound and visuals to make the story more interesting?	
NEWS MEDIA Reports of recent events in newspapers and magazines and on TV, the radio, and the Web	• **Get the facts.** Make sure the report answers the questions *who, what, when, where, why,* and *how?* • **Evaluate the information.** Ask yourself: Can I trust what I'm seeing and hearing?	
ADVERTISING The promotion of products, services, and ideas using print and broadcast media	• **Recognize the pitch.** Consider what the sponsor wants the audience to buy, believe, or do. • **Don't be duped by dazzle.** Visuals and sounds can be persuasive. Don't let flashy techniques influence your decisions.	
WEB SITES Collections of related pages on the World Wide Web; include hyperlinks and menus	• **Know the source.** Anyone can publish on the Web. Ask: Is this a good source of information? • **Don't get lost!** Always remember your purpose for visiting a site so you don't veer too far off course.	

Literature and Nonfiction Strategies

Write your reactions and observations in your **Reader/Writer Notebook.**

❶ Ask Yourself the Right Questions

Sometimes, reading texts can be a challenge. The following features will help you find answers to the questions you may have while you read.

Where to Look	What You'll Find
Text Analysis Workshops (at the beginning of every unit)	▶ Interactive practice models and Close Read questions
Side notes, discussion questions, and instructional notes	▶ Questions that focus on the analysis of literary and nonfiction elements
Analysis Frames THINK central Go to **thinkcentral.com.** KEYWORD: HML6-11	▶ Guided questions for analyzing different genres

❷ Make Connections

A text is more meaningful when you connect to it personally. Use these strategies to "get into" a text.

- **Connect to Your Life** Is fear paralyzing? What makes a family? Think about how your own experiences can help you understand big ideas in literature and nonfiction.

- **Connect to Other Subjects** The effects of fear, meteor showers, careers—the subjects you read about can help you learn more about the world. If a subject interests you, investigate it on the Web.

❸ Record Your Reactions

Jot down your questions, thoughts, and impressions about what you are reading. Record discussions about the stories you have read. Try a variety of formats.

JOURNAL
Write your reactions as you read.

The Little Princess

Becky treats Sara like a princess, even though Sara is no longer rich. It's interesting that Becky still views Sara the same way.

GRAPHIC ORGANIZER
After reading, create a graphic organizer to deepen your understanding of events and characters.

Becky's Traits	Evidence
polite	calls Sara "miss"
comforting	presses Sara's hand to her cheek
loyal	tells Sara she is still a princess no matter what

Becoming an Active Reader

To really appreciate stories, poems, plays, and articles, you have to be able to understand what you're reading. The following strategies can help you unlock the meaning of all kinds of texts, including novels, newspapers, blogs, and even movie scripts. Which strategies do you recognize? Which are new to you?

SKILLS AND STRATEGIES FOR ACTIVE READING

Preview
Look at the title, the pictures, and the first paragraph. What do they tell you about what you're about to read?

Set a Purpose
Know *why* you are reading—for information, for enjoyment, or to understand a process?

Connect
Think about whether the characters or situations remind you of people or experiences in your own life.

Use Prior Knowledge
Jot down what you already know about a topic. Use these notes to help you make sense of what you read.

Predict
Guess what will happen next. Look for details in the selection that serve as clues.

Visualize
Picture the scene in your mind, using the writer's descriptions of settings, characters, and events.

Monitor
Check your understanding as you read.

- **Question** what is happening and why.
- **Clarify** what is unclear by rereading or asking for help.

Make Inferences
Make logical guesses about characters and events by considering details in the text and your own experiences.

Details in "The Circuit"	What I Know	My Inference
"Ito, the strawberry sharecropper, did not smile" when the season was ending.	People in charge get worried or unhappy when business slows down.	Ito is probably unhappy that the strawberry-picking season is over because that's how he makes a living.

MODEL: SHORT STORY

Panchito is a young Mexican American boy whose family frequently
moves in search of farm work. The time has come for Panchito's family to
move—again. How will he react? As you read an excerpt from this story,
use the Close Read questions to practice the strategies you just learned.

COMMON CORE

Included in this workshop:
RL 1

from

The Circuit

Short story by **Francisco Jiménez**

t was that time of year again. Ito, the strawberry sharecropper, did not
smile. It was natural. The peak of the strawberry season was over and
the last few days the workers, most of them *braceros*,[1] were not picking as
many boxes as they had during the months of June and July.

5   As the last days of August disappeared, so did the number of *braceros*.
Sunday, only one—the best picker—came to work. I liked him.
Sometimes we talked during our half-hour lunch break. That is how I
found out he was from Jalisco, the same state in Mexico my family was
from. That Sunday was the last time I saw him.

10   When the sun had tired and sunk behind the mountains, Ito signaled
us that it was time to go home. *"Ya esora,"*[2] he yelled in his broken
Spanish. Those were the words I waited for twelve hours a day, every
day, seven days a week, week after week. And the thought of not hearing
them again saddened me.

15   As we drove home, Papa did not say a word. With both hands on the
wheel, he stared at the dirt road. My older brother, Roberto, was also
silent. He leaned his head back and closed his eyes. Once in a while he
cleared from his throat the dust that blew in from outside.

    Yes, it was that time of year. When I opened the front door to the
20 shack, I stopped. Everything we owned was neatly packed in cardboard
boxes. Suddenly I felt even more the weight of hours, days, weeks, and
months of work. I sat down on a box. The thought of having to move
to Fresno and knowing what was in store for me there brought tears
to my eyes.

---

1. *braceros* (brä-sĕ'rôs) *Spanish:* Hispanic farm workers.
2. *Ya esora:* a made-up spelling for the sharecropper's pronunciation of the Spanish expression
    Ya es hora (yä' ĕs ô'rä), which means "It is time."

Close Read

1. **Monitor** Reread the
    boxed text. Why is
    Panchito sad to hear
    the words *Ya esora* this
    time?

2. **Connect** If you suddenly
    found out that you were
    moving, would you
    react as Panchito does?
    Think about whether
    you would get used to
    moving or dread it every
    time.

That night I could not sleep. I lay in bed thinking about how much I
hated this move.

A little before five o'clock in the morning, Papa woke everyone up.
A few minutes later, the yelling and screaming of my little brothers and
sisters, for whom the move was a great adventure, broke the silence of
dawn. Shortly, the barking of the dogs accompanied them.

While we packed the breakfast dishes, Papa went outside to start
the "Carcanchita." That was the name Papa gave his old '38 black
Plymouth. He bought it in a used-car lot in Santa Rosa in the winter of
1949. Papa was very proud of his car. *"Mi Carcanchita,"* my little jalopy,[3]
he called it. He had a right to be proud of it. He spent a lot of time
looking at other cars before buying this one. When he finally chose the
"Carcanchita," he checked it thoroughly before driving it out of the car
lot. He examined every inch of the car. He listened to the motor, tilting
his head from side to side like a parrot, trying to detect any noises that
spelled car trouble. After being satisfied with the looks and sounds of
the car, Papa then insisted on knowing who the original owner was. He
never did find out from the car salesman. But he bought the car anyway.
Papa figured the original owner must have been an important man,
because behind the rear seat of the car he found a blue necktie.

Papa parked the car out in front and left the motor running. *"Listo,"*[4]
he yelled. Without saying a word, Roberto and I began to carry the
boxes out to the car. Roberto carried the two big boxes and I carried the
smaller ones. Papa then threw the mattress on top of the car roof and
tied it with ropes to the front and rear bumpers.

Everything was packed except Mama's pot. It was an old large
galvanized pot she had picked up at an army surplus store in Santa
Maria the year I was born. The pot was full of dents and nicks, and the
more dents and nicks it had, the more Mama liked it. *"Mi olla,"*[5] she
used to say proudly.

I held the front door open as Mama carefully carried out her pot by
both handles, making sure not to spill the cooked beans. When she got
to the car, Papa reached out to help her with it. Roberto opened the rear
car door, and Papa gently placed it on the floor behind the front seat.
All of us then climbed in. Papa sighed, wiped the sweat off his forehead
with his sleeve, and said wearily, *"Es todo."*[6]

As we drove away, I felt a lump in my throat. I turned around and
looked at our little shack for the last time. . . .

---

3. **jalopy:** a shabby, old car.

4. **listo** (lē'stô) *Spanish:* ready.

5. **mi olla** (mē ô' yä) *Spanish:* my pot.

6. **Es todo** (ĕs tō'dô) *Spanish:* That's everything.

Close Read

3. **Make Inferences**
Reread lines 25–30.
Why would younger
kids view moving more
as an adventure than
someone Panchito's age
would?

4. **Visualize** What details
in lines 31–44 help you
picture the family car
and the father's initial
inspection of it?

5. **Predict** Do you think
Panchito will eventually
adjust to life in Fresno?
Try to guess what will
happen once he arrives.

Strategies That Work: Reading

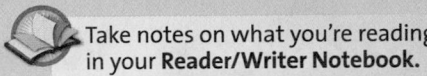 Take notes on what you're reading in your **Reader/Writer Notebook**.

❶ Read Independently

The best way to improve your reading skills is to read as much as you can, whenever you can. Follow your interests to find new and exciting things to read.

What Should I Read?	Where Should I Look?
Novels 	 **Get Novel Wise** **THINK** central Go to **thinkcentral.com**. KEYWORD: HML6-15
Magazines **Newspapers** **Web sites** 	Every time you pick up a newspaper or magazine, you are reading. Ask your friends for suggestions on what to read and where to look for information that interests you.

❷ Take Notes

Writing down your impressions as you read can deepen your understanding of a selection. In your notebook, create a two-column chart. In one column, write details or quotations from the selection. In the other, record your thoughts.

"The Circuit"	My Thoughts
Panchito worked "twelve hours a day, every day, seven days a week, week after week." (lines 12–13).	That seems like an impossible amount of work. I hope Panchito won't have to work so hard when his family moves to Fresno.

❸ Build Your Vocabulary

When you encounter words that are unfamiliar to you, look them up. Create a list of these words and their meanings, and add new words as you come across them.

- **Choose your words.** Consider writing down the vocabulary words for each selection, as well as any other words you find challenging.
- **Know more than the definition.** Knowing synonyms (same meaning), antonyms (opposite meaning), and context (use in a sentence) adds to your total understanding of a word's meaning. Use a thesaurus or dictionary to find out more about each new word you encounter.

Word	Meaning
surplus (n.) "The Circuit," line 51	**Definition:** extra materials or supplies **Synonym:** excess **Antonym:** shortage **Sentence:** The owners donated the restaurant's surplus of canned goods to a local hospital.

What Is Academic Vocabulary?

Your vocabulary is made up of words you use in everyday speaking and writing. Increasing the number of words you know helps you better communicate with friends, teachers, and classmates. **Academic vocabulary** refers to the language you use to talk and write about school subjects, such as language arts, math, science, and social studies. Building your academic vocabulary will help you improve your reading and comprehension skills in *all* subjects, not only in your English class.

You will often encounter academic-vocabulary terms in lessons in this book, on homework assignments, and on test questions. Knowing the meaning of academic vocabulary words will help you become more successful in school and on assessments. The web diagram below shows examples of academic vocabulary words from different subject areas.

COMMON CORE

Included in this workshop:
L 4a–d, L 6

SOCIAL STUDIES
Explain how citizens can **influence** the political process.

LANGUAGE ARTS
In what ways does the setting **affect** the plot in "All Summer in a Day"?

WORLD HISTORY
Describe common **characteristics** of developing nations.

ACADEMIC VOCABULARY
The language you use to talk and write about different school subjects.

SCIENCE
Evaluate the **impact** of scientific research on the environment.

MATHEMATICS
Illustrate the relationships between angles in a triangle.

HEALTH
Demonstrate an understanding of basic first-aid procedures.

Use the following chart to preview some of the academic vocabulary words you will use in this textbook. As you read, look for the activities on After Reading pages labeled "Academic Vocabulary in Writing" and "Academic Vocabulary in Speaking." These activities provide opportunities to use academic vocabulary in your writing and discussions.

Word	Definition	Example
achieve	to bring about an intended result; accomplish	How did Eli Whitney **achieve** his claim to fame?
affect	to produce a response or reaction	How did Hurricane Katrina **affect** the residents of New Orleans?
associations	connections between thoughts, ideas, or images	What **associations** can you make between your life and the life of the narrator in "The School Play"?
characteristics	features or qualities that help identify, describe, or recognize something	Describe the **characteristics** of a story told in the first-person point of view.
conclude	to form an opinion about something based on evidence, experience, or reasoning	What can you **conclude** about the author's purpose for writing this article?
convey	to communicate something and make it known	Make sure you **convey** your personal opinions in your essay.
formulate	to develop a plan, system, or method	**Formulate** a plan for gathering resources before you begin your research.
impact	to have a direct effect on	What **impact** will this decision have on the environment?
implicit	not stated directly	The main idea of the article is **implicit** rather than directly stated.
interpret	to explain the meaning of something	How did you **interpret** the results of the experiment?
obvious	easy to see or understand	What is one **obvious** sign of Lyme disease?
relevant	having a logical connection with something else	Which Web sites will you consult for information **relevant** to your research topic?
reliable	able to be trusted or accurate	How can you tell which sources are **reliable?**

Academic Vocabulary in Action

The terms below are academic vocabulary terms found in your state standards. Knowing the meanings of these terms is essential for completing the activities and lessons in this book as well as mastering test items.

formulate *(verb)*

Defining the Word

One meaning of the word *formulate* is "develop a plan, system, or method." A governor might formulate a new state policy, your coach might formulate a strategy, and a lawyer might formulate an argument for court.

Using the Word

Once you understand the meaning of a word root, you will be able to understand the meanings of other words built from the same root. The word *formulate* comes from the Latin root *form*, meaning "shape."

- In a chart like this one, make a list of other words you know formed from the root *form*.
- Look up each word in a dictionary and write down its meaning.
- Write a sentence using each word.

Word	Definition	Sentence
transform	to change in form, appearance, or structure	A caterpillar <u>transforms</u> into a butterfly in the pupal stage.

structure *(noun)*

Defining the Word

The word *structure* can be used as either a verb or a noun. As a noun, a *structure* is something that is built or the *way* that something is built. A poem might follow a certain structure, for example, or pattern of organization. In biology, a structure might refer to the way atoms or other particles are organized.

Using the Word

Now that you know the definitions of the word *structure*, practice using them in various contexts.

- Use a chart like the one shown to identify different *structures* you've learned about in different subject areas. You might scan this book as well as textbooks in other subject areas for ideas.
- Write a brief definition of each meaning of *structure*.

Subject Area	Structure	Definition
social studies	pyramid (as found in ancient Egypt)	a massive monument found in ancient Egypt having a rectangular base and four triangular sides joining at an apex at the top

Strategies That Work: Vocabulary

 Record new vocabulary words in your **Reader/Writer Notebook.**

❶ Use Context Clues

The most important step in building your vocabulary is learning to identify unfamiliar words as you read. When you encounter an unfamiliar word, look at the **context,** the words, phrases, or sentences that surround that word. Often, the context can give you important clues to an unfamiliar word's meaning. See the following example from "The Dog of Pompeii" (page 333):"

> The water—hot water—splashing in his face <u>revived</u> him. He got to his feet, Bimbo steadying him, helping him on again.

If you do not know the meaning of *revived* in the first sentence, look at the context. The next sentence, "He got to his feet," helps you figure out that *revived* means "brought back to life."

❷ Clarify Word Definitions

If a word's context does not help you understand its meaning, it's time to use a dictionary. Most dictionary entries provide a word's meaning, as well as its pronunciation, part of speech, origin, and alternative meanings. When using a textbook like this one, you will find definitions for unfamiliar words in a glossary at the back of the book.

dazzling (dăz′lĭng) *adj.* beautiful; amazing.

❸ Keep a Word List

List new academic vocabulary words in your **Reader/Writer Notebook.** Add to your list each time you take on a new reading assignment. In addition to listing the word and its definition, also note examples to remind you of the word's meaning. Challenge yourself to use words from the list in your writing and discussions. The more frequently you use the words, the easier they will be to remember.

Interactive Vocabulary **THINK**central

Go to <u>thinkcentral.com.</u>
KEYWORD: HML6-19

For a complete list of terms in this book, see the **Glossary of Academic Vocabulary in English & Spanish** *on pages R115–R116.*

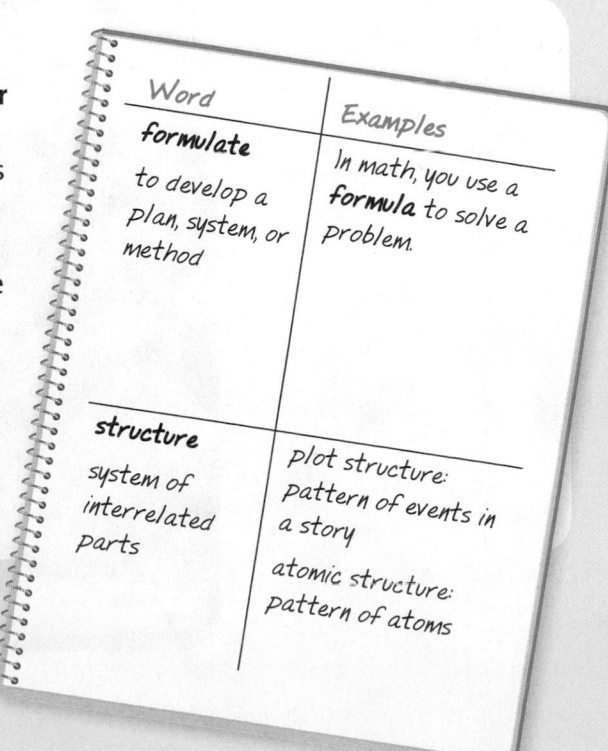

Word	Examples
formulate to develop a plan, system, or method	In math, you use a **formula** to solve a problem.
structure system of interrelated parts	Plot structure: pattern of events in a story atomic structure: pattern of atoms

Expressing Ideas in Writing

Writing is a way of discovering what you think and feel, and also a way to share ideas with others. You may write with a practical need—e-mailing a friend with a homework question, for example. Or, you may have a grander purpose, such as persuading a politician to see your viewpoint. Either way, writing can help you find your voice and share it with the world.

COMMON CORE

Included in this workshop:
W 4, W 5

Consider Your Options

Are you writing a speech for your school assembly, a thank-you letter to a relative, or a message-board posting about last night's episode? Before you write your ideas on paper, make sure you know your **purpose, audience,** and **format.**

PURPOSE	AUDIENCE	FORMAT
Why am I writing? • to entertain • to inform or explain • to argue or persuade • to describe • to express thoughts and feelings	**Who are my readers?** • classmates • teachers • friends • myself • community members • Web users • customer service at a company	**Which format will best suit my purpose and audience?** • essay • report • poem • short story • script • speech • journal entry • personal letter • narrative • letter to the editor • Web site • review

Continue the Process

Every writer eventually discovers the process that best suits his or her working style. The **Writing Workshops** in this book are designed to help you find the path to your best writing. The process described here can serve as your starting point.

THE WRITING PROCESS

PLANNING/PREWRITING

Consider your **audience** and **purpose** as you decide on a topic. Explore your ideas in a graphic organizer or by freewriting. Then decide what you want to write about.

▶

WHAT DOES IT LOOK LIKE?

It must be scary living in a town where soldiers patrol the streets. But some kids in the world deal with that in their daily lives. Maybe I will write about what it takes to be brave in scary situations.

DRAFTING

Turn your ideas into a first draft. If you're writing a formal essay, you may want to **draft from an outline.** If you're doing more informal writing, consider **drafting to discover,** letting your ideas take shape as you go.

▶

WHAT DOES IT LOOK LIKE?

1. Being brave in the face of fear takes determination and a calm attitude.

A. Annemarie doesn't let the soldiers' presence stop her from racing her friend.

B. She remains calm when the soldier addresses her.

REVISING

Review what you've written. Now is the time to look for ways to improve development, organization, and style. Make sure your writing is clear and **coherent,** or easy to follow.

- Check your work against a **rubric** (page 22).
- Ask a **peer** to give you feedback.
- Consider trying a new approach if something simply is not working.

▶

ASK A PEER READER

- Is the main idea of the essay clearly stated?
- Does the essay start with an engaging sentence?
- Are there enough details to support the main idea?

EDITING AND PUBLISHING

- Edit your draft to correct any distracting errors.
- Use the **Proofreader's Checklist** to help you catch common mistakes.
- Where you publish depends on your **purpose, audience,** and **format.**

▶

PROOFREADER'S CHECKLIST

√ Revise sentence fragments and run-on sentences.

√ Fix mistakes in subject-verb agreement and pronoun agreement.

√ Capitalize and use punctuation marks correctly.

√ Revise fragments.

Scoring Rubric

Score	COMMON CORE TRAITS
6	• **Development** Includes a meaningful, memorable introduction; develops ideas with varied, relevant evidence; ends powerfully • **Organization** Is effectively and logically organized; uses varied transitions to create cohesion (flow) and link ideas • **Language** Uses precise language in original ways; effectively maintains an appropriate style; shows a strong command of grammar, mechanics, and spelling
5	• **Development** Has an effective introduction; develops ideas with relevant evidence; has a strong concluding section • **Organization** Is logically organized; uses transitions to create cohesion and link ideas • **Language** Uses precise language; maintains an appropriate style; has a few errors in grammar, mechanics, and spelling
4	• **Development** Has an introduction, but it could be more interesting; lacks support for one or two ideas; has an adequate concluding section • **Organization** Is logically organized, with one or two exceptions; could use a few more transitions • **Language** Generally uses precise language; has one or two lapses in style; includes a few distracting errors in grammar, mechanics, and spelling
3	• **Development** Has a superficial introduction that lacks interest; includes some unsupported ideas or irrelevant evidence; has a weak ending • **Organization** Has some flaws in organization; needs more transitions • **Language** Uses words correctly, though language is unoriginal; has frequent lapses in style; has some critical errors in grammar, mechanics, and spelling
2	• **Development** Has a weak, uninteresting introduction; does not support most ideas; ends abruptly • **Organization** Has a weak organization; lacks transitions throughout • **Language** Uses vague language and misuses some words; has an inappropriate style in many places; contains many distracting errors in grammar, mechanics, and spelling
1	• **Development** Lacks an introduction, support for ideas, and a concluding section • **Organization** Has no organization or transitions; is confusing and disconnected • **Language** Uses many words incorrectly; has an inappropriate style; has major problems with grammar, mechanics, and spelling

Strategies That Work: Writing

Jot down your writing plans, ideas, and notes in your **Reader/Writer Notebook**.

❶ Use Prewriting Strategies

Try different strategies to get your ideas flowing. Find one that works best for you and for the assignment.

- **Freewrite.** For ten minutes, jot down whatever crosses your mind.
- **Get graphic.** Generate ideas in a web or a chart.
- **Look and listen.** Carry a notebook around with you each day. Record interesting sights and conversations.
- **Ask: What if?** What if kids were in charge of the town for a day? You can find an intriguing topic by answering a "what if" question.

❷ Get Friendly Feedback

Consider exchanging work with other writers. Feedback can help at any stage of the process, but remember these guidelines as you work.

When You're the Writer	When You're the Reader
• Ask for specific feedback. Do you want readers to comment on ideas, or simply check grammar and spelling? • Be open, patient, and polite when listening to others' suggestions. • Consider all feedback, and be willing to think about your writing in new ways.	• Tell the writer what you like, as well as what you think needs improvement. • Support your opinions with specific examples. • Ask questions to learn more about the writer's goals and ideas. • Don't rewrite the work yourself.

❸ Pay Attention to Details

Even minor mistakes, such as errors in grammar, punctuation, and spelling, can distract readers and keep them from taking your ideas seriously.

Use these spelling tips to make sure your writing is polished and correct.

- Review spelling rules on pages R72–R74.
- Avoid misusing commonly confused words, such as *affect* and *effect*. (See page R75 for more examples.)
- Use the spell-check feature in your word-processing program or a dictionary.
- Read your draft backwards to catch mistakes your eye might miss while scanning over sentences you are very familiar with.

> Do you know how to become the most unpopular kid in school? Write an essay ~~recommending~~ recommending that people give up watching television one night a week. You'll be surprised at the ~~effect~~ affect this suggestion will have.

Writing Online

THINK central

Go to **thinkcentral.com**.
KEYWORD: HML6N-23

UNIT 1

What's Happening?

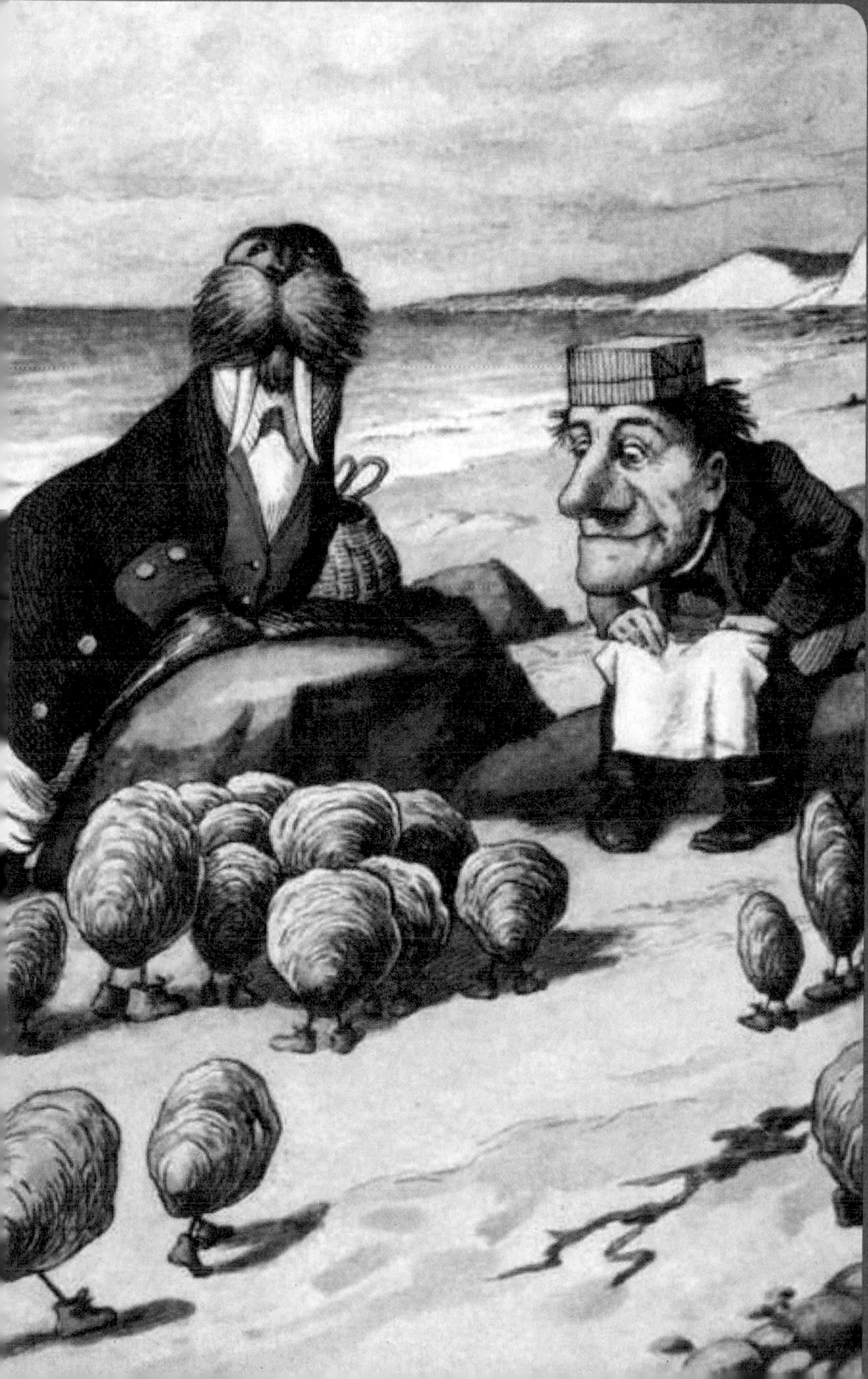

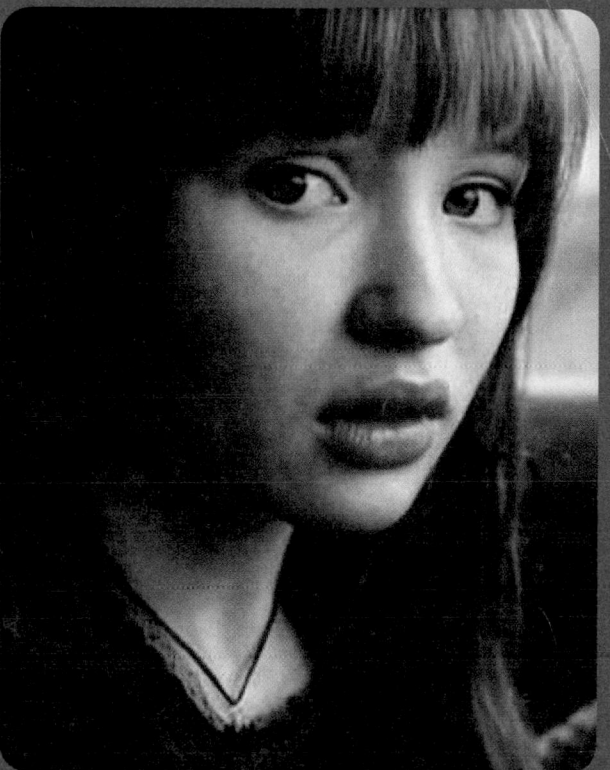

PLOT, CONFLICT, AND SETTING

- In Fiction
- In Nonfiction
- In Poetry
- In Drama
- In Media

How do you build a STORY?

A story can take many different shapes, but all stories share some basic elements. Like a bricklayer building a wall, a writer builds a story layer by layer. The writer might start with an interesting character and add an important event. Or, he or she might start by describing a place far away and see where that leads. If the writer is successful, the finished story will capture the reader's attention and never let go.

ACTIVITY Think of one of your favorite stories—it might be based on fact, such as a book about an ancient mystery, or pure fantasy, such as the classic story *Alice's Adventures in Wonderland*. Ask yourself these questions:

• What made the story interesting?

• What did the story make you feel?

• What part of the story do you remember most clearly?

In a small group, discuss your answers to the questions and consider what makes a story powerful.

Find It Online!

Go to **thinkcentral.com** for the interactive version of this unit.

Preview Unit Goals

TEXT ANALYSIS
- Describe how a story's or drama's plot unfolds
- Describe how characters respond as the plot moves toward a resolution
- Analyze how a sentence, scene, or stanza contributes to the development of the setting or plot
- Compare authors' purposes and draw conclusions about texts

READING
- Cite textual evidence to support inferences drawn from the text.
- Integrate ideas across texts

WRITING AND LANGUAGE
- Support an opinion
- Use intensive pronouns correctly
- Maintain pronoun-antecedent agreement
- Identify and correct sentence fragments and run-on sentences
- Use commas in compound sentences correctly

SPEAKING AND LISTENING
- Participate in a discussion

VOCABULARY
- Use roots and affixes as clues to the meaning of a word
- Use a dictionary or thesaurus to determine or clarify the precise meaning of a word

ACADEMIC VOCABULARY
- affect
- analyze
- evidence
- impact
- provide

MEDIA AND VIEWING
- Interpret information presented in media

Media Smart DVD-ROM

Setting and Conflict in Movies

View the scenes from *Lemony Snicket's A Series of Unfortunate Events* to see how conflict and suspense are created. Page 110

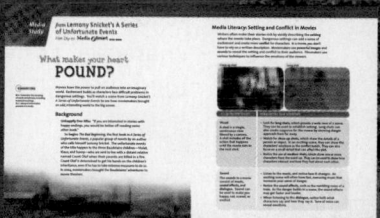

Text Analysis Workshop

What Makes a Good Story?

Can the hero save the city from danger? Will the lost hikers reach home? Good stories capture our attention and make us curious about what will happen next. Although stories are different in many ways, all good stories share certain parts.

Part 1: Parts of a Story

COMMON CORE

Included in this workshop:
RL 3 Describe how a story's plot unfolds as well as how the characters respond as the plot moves toward a resolution.
RL 5 Analyze how a particular sentence fits into the structure of a text and contributes to the development of the setting or plot.

Consider two very different stories. One is about a city detective struggling to solve a case. The other is about space aliens invading Earth. Even these stories have parts in common—the setting, characters, and conflicts—which are described in the chart below.

BASIC PARTS	EXAMPLES
SETTING Setting is the time and place of the action. The **time** can be the past, present, or future. It can also be a season or a time of day. The **place** can be a room, a country, or any place you imagine. Often, the setting affects the story's problem and how it is solved.	• a rainy day on the planet Venus • a tropical island in the present day • a city park in the year 2086 • a palace in England in 1547
CHARACTERS Characters are the people, animals, or creatures who take part in the story's action. The most important characters are **main characters.** Less important ones are **minor characters.** The characters' qualities, such as courage, affect the story's events and conflict.	• a 12-year-old girl • a wizard with mysterious powers • a baseball coach • a family's pet dog
CONFLICT A conflict is the problem or struggle that a character faces in a story. The struggle can be between characters or between a character and the setting or a force of nature, such as a storm. A conflict can also be within a character, as he or she struggles with difficult problems.	• A girl is made fun of by her friends. (girl vs. friends) • A family seeks shelter from a storm. (family vs. storm) • A boy must decide between telling the truth and lying to protect his friend's feelings. (telling the truth vs. lying)

MODEL 1: SETTING AND CHARACTERS

In this excerpt, a woman panics when her grandson Dewey disappears. Notice the details that describe the time and place of the action.

from *Trouble River*

Novel by **Betsy Byars**

She rose and moved to the open doorway where she looked out over the golden prairie.

"Dewey!" she called, her voice breaking with anxiety. "D*eweeeeeee.*"

When there was no answer, she went back to her rocking chair.

5 "Dewey Martin," she called from her chair. "Oh, *Deweee.*"

After a moment she went to stand in the doorway again. For as far as she could see there was only the prairie, the long waving line of grass on the horizon with not one single cabin or chimney in sight.

The sun was dropping behind the horizon, and she knew how quickly

10 darkness would cover the land, how quickly the colorful prairie would become desolate and cold.

Close Read

1. In what way does the setting add to the woman's anxiety? Find two details that describe her surroundings. One detail has been boxed.

2. What do you learn about the woman from the way she reacts to her grandson's absence? Support your answer.

MODEL 2: CONFLICT

A boy named Aaron has just left his village to sell his family's goat. What unexpected conflict will he face on his journey?

from Zlateh the Goat

Short story by **Isaac Bashevis Singer**

The sun was shining when Aaron left the village. Suddenly the weather changed. A large black cloud with a bluish center appeared in the east and spread itself rapidly over the sky. A cold wind blew in with it. The crows flew low, croaking. At first it looked as if it would rain,

5 but instead it began to hail as in summer. It was early in the day, but it became dark as dusk. After a while the hail turned to snow.

In his twelve years Aaron had seen all kinds of weather, but he had never experienced a snow like this one. It was so dense it shut out the light of the day. In a short time their path was completely covered. The

10 wind became as cold as ice. The road to town was narrow and winding. Aaron no longer knew where he was.

Close Read

1. Find three details that convey the dangers of the weather. One detail has been boxed.

2. In your own words, describe the conflict that Aaron is facing. Whom or what is the conflict with?

Part 2: What Happens in a Story?

The power of a story comes from the action—what happens as the story develops. While the action varies from story to story, most stories follow a pattern called a plot. A **plot** is the series of events in a story. A typical plot begins by introducing a character who has a conflict. Suspense builds as the character tries to resolve, or work out, the conflict. Shortly after the conflict is resolved, the story comes to a close. Some plots will seem like real-life events to you, while others will seem contrived, or completely invented. A contrived plot is more fantastic than it is realistic. It can even be unbelievable.

Most plots have five stages. Learning about these stages can help you keep track of a story's events and answer the question "What happened?" when someone asks you about a story. Thinking about what happened and why will also help you judge if a plot is realistic or contrived.

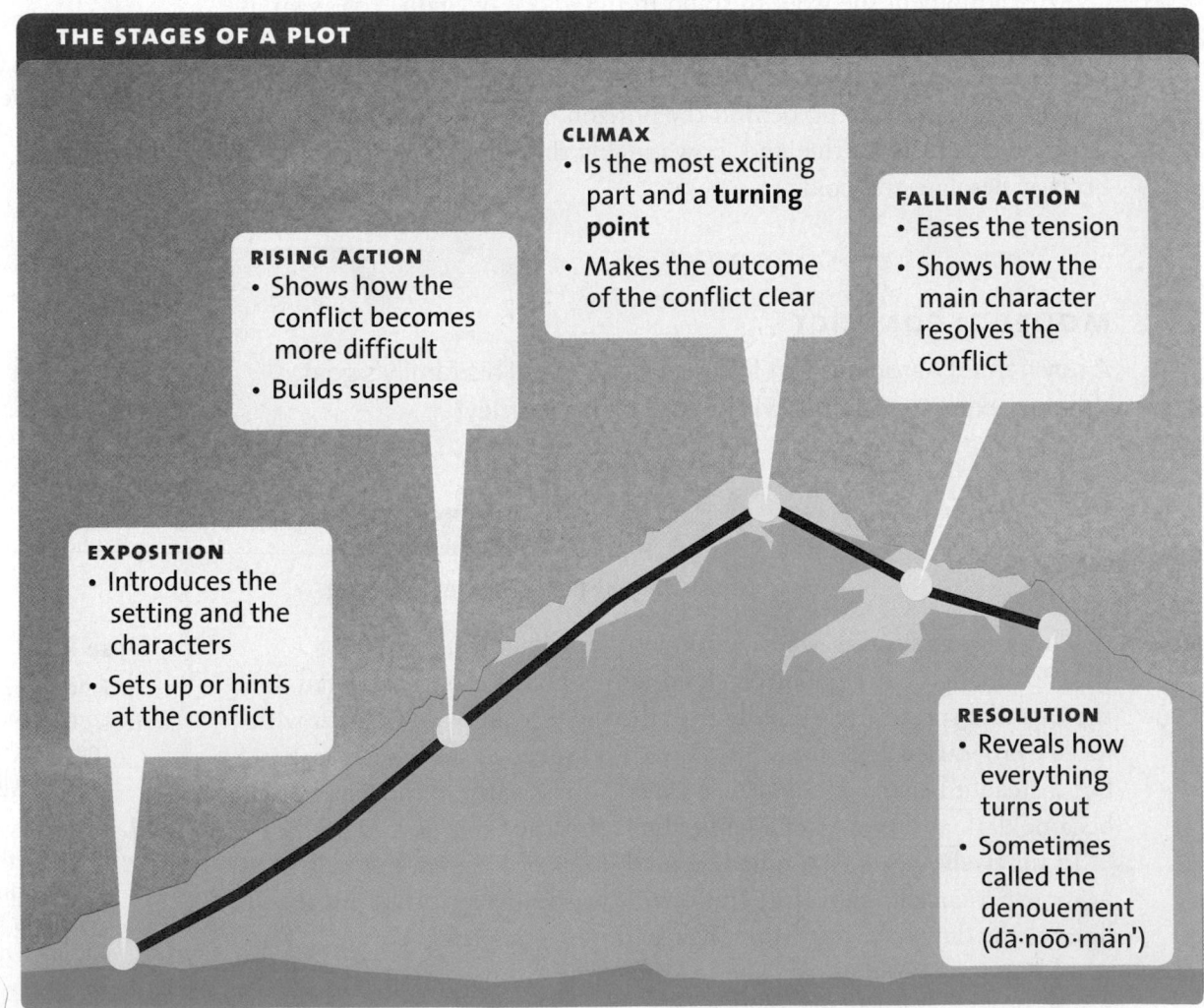

THE STAGES OF A PLOT

CLIMAX
- Is the most exciting part and a **turning point**
- Makes the outcome of the conflict clear

RISING ACTION
- Shows how the conflict becomes more difficult
- Builds suspense

FALLING ACTION
- Eases the tension
- Shows how the main character resolves the conflict

EXPOSITION
- Introduces the setting and the characters
- Sets up or hints at the conflict

RESOLUTION
- Reveals how everything turns out
- Sometimes called the denouement (dā·nōō·män')

MODEL 1: EXPOSITION

This story is about a young Japanese-American girl. What do you learn about the setting and the conflict in the exposition of the story?

from THE BRACELET

Short story by **Yoshiko Uchida**

It was April 21, 1942. The United States and Japan were at war, and every Japanese person on the West Coast was being evacuated by the government to a concentration camp. Mama, my sister Keiko, and I were being sent from our home, and out of Berkeley, and eventually out
5 of California.

The doorbell rang, and I ran to answer it before my sister could. I thought maybe by some miracle, a messenger from the government might be standing there, tall and proper and buttoned into a uniform, come to tell us it was all a terrible mistake; that we wouldn't have to
10 leave after all.

Close Read

1. Where and when does this story take place?

2. Reread the boxed details. Explain the conflict that the girl's family has. How does the setting influence their situation?

MODEL 2: RISING ACTION

Billy is overjoyed when his mother buys him a bike for his birthday. What happens when Billy rides his prized possession to school? Find out by reading this excerpt from the rising action of the story.

from You're Not a **WINNER**
Unless Your Picture's in the Paper

Short story by **Avi**

The racks were not sufficient for all the bikes, so lots of them were just dumped on the ground. Billy wouldn't do that to his bike. He leaned it carefully against a tree. The tree being in leaf, it shaded the bike from a too-hot sun.
5 On Wednesday, right after three o'clock dismissal, when Billy came to collect his bike, it was gone.

At first Billy thought he had just forgotten where he had left it, and went searching. But as more and more kids claimed their bikes and took off, it became obvious that his bike wasn't just gone, it had been *stolen*.

Close Read

1. Describe what you learn about Billy's conflict in the boxed lines. What is Billy's initial reaction?

2. In lines 8–9, Billy concludes that his problem is worse than he first realized. How does the conflict become more complicated?

Part 3: Analyze the Text

Jenny has heard stories about a ferocious boar—a wild pig—that roams the woods near her home. Will she be the first person to come face-to-face with the dreaded creature? Use what you've learned in this workshop to analyze the elements of plot development in this suspenseful story.

BOAR OUT THERE

Short story by **Cynthia Rylant**

Everyone in Glen Morgan knew there was a wild boar in the woods over by the Miller farm. The boar was out beyond the splintery rail fence and past the old black Dodge that somehow had ended up in the woods and was missing most of its parts.

5　Jenny would hook her chin over the top rail of the fence, twirl a long green blade of grass in her teeth and whisper, "Boar out there."

And there were times she was sure she heard him. She imagined him running heavily through the trees, ignoring the sharp thorns and briars that raked his back and sprang away trembling.

10　She thought he might have a golden horn on his terrible head. The boar would run deep into the woods, then rise up on his rear hooves, throw his head toward the stars and cry a long, clear, sure note into the air. The note would glide through the night and spear the heart of the moon. The boar had no fear of the moon, Jenny knew, as she lay in bed,
15　listening.

One hot summer day she went to find the boar. No one in Glen Morgan had ever gone past the old black Dodge and beyond, as far as she knew. But the boar was there somewhere, between those awful trees, and his dark green eyes waited for someone.
20　Jenny felt it was she.

Close Read
Exposition (lines 1–15)

1. Where and when does this story take place? Find three details in lines 1–16 that help you to visualize the setting. One detail has been boxed.

Close Read
Rising Action (lines 16–46)

2. Explain what Jenny decides to do in lines 16–20. What conflict do you think might result from her plan of action?

Moving slowly over damp brown leaves, Jenny could sense her ears tingle and fan out as she listened for thick breathing from the trees. She stopped to pick a teaberry leaf to chew, stood a minute, then went on.

Deep in the woods she kept her eyes to the sky. She needed to be
25 reminded that there was a world above and apart from the trees—a world of space and air, air that didn't linger all about her, didn't press deep into her skin, as forest air did.

Finally, leaning against a tree to rest, she heard him for the first time. She forgot to breathe, standing there listening to the stamping of
30 hooves, and she choked and coughed.

Coughed!

And now the pounding was horrible, too loud and confusing for Jenny. Horrible. She stood stiff with wet eyes and knew she could always pray, but for some reason didn't.

35 He came through the trees so fast that she had no time to scream or run. And he was there before her.

His large gray-black body shivered as he waited just beyond the shadow of the tree she held for support. His nostrils glistened, and his eyes; but astonishingly, he was silent. He shivered and glistened and was
40 absolutely silent.

Jenny matched his silence, and her body was rigid, but not her eyes. They traveled along his scarred, bristling back to his thick hind legs. Tears spilling and flooding her face, Jenny stared at the boar's ragged ears, caked with blood. Her tears dropped to the leaves, and the only
45 sound between them was his slow breathing.

Then the boar snorted and jerked. But Jenny did not move.

High in the trees a bluejay yelled, and, suddenly, it was over. Jenny stood like a rock as the boar wildly flung his head and in terror bolted past her.

50 *Past* her. . . .

And now, since that summer, Jenny still hooks her chin over the old rail fence, and she still whispers, "Boar out there." But when she leans on the fence, looking into the trees, her eyes are full and she leaves wet patches on the splintery wood. She is sorry for the torn ears of the
55 boar and sorry that he has no golden horn.

But mostly she is sorry that he lives in fear of bluejays and little girls, when everyone in Glen Morgan lives in fear of him.

3. Reread lines 21–34. What details help to build suspense about what might happen next?

4. The conflict becomes clear in line 36. How do Jenny and the boar react to each other when they finally meet?

5. Would the story be different if Jenny met the boar in a different setting? Explain how the setting in the woods influences the story.

Close Read
Climax (lines 47–50)

6. What is surprising about what happens at the climax, or the turning point in the story?

Close Read
Falling Action and Resolution, or Denouement (lines 51–57)

7. The tension eases after Jenny's encounter with the boar. How has her impression of the boar changed?

The School Play

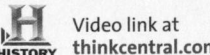 Video link at thinkcentral.com

Short Story by Gary Soto

VIDEO TRAILER THINK central KEYWORD: HML6-34

What do you FEAR most?

⋯ **COMMON CORE**

RL 1 Cite evidence to support analysis of the text. **RL 3** Describe how a plot unfolds as well as how the characters respond as the plot moves toward a resolution. **RL 5** Analyze how a particular sentence fits into the structure of a text and contributes to the development of the setting or plot.

Have you ever jumped at the sight of a harmless bug? Or, maybe you have waited a long time to ride a roller coaster only to change your mind when it was your turn? Things that frighten people range from big to small, from living to nonliving, from the seen to the unseen. In "The School Play," a student struggles to overcome a fear many people face.

SURVEY What are you most afraid of? Some of the most common fears people have are listed in the survey below. Rank the fears from one to ten, with one being the thing you are most afraid of. Then survey the class to find out what is the most common fear in your classroom.

SURVEY

FACE YOUR FEARS!

Rank the following fears to see what scares you the most:

___ **Heights**

___ **Spiders and Insects**

___ **Being in the Dark**

___ **Dentists**

___ **Thunder and Lightning**

___ **Failing a Test**

___ **Being Bullied**

___ **Airplane Rides**

___ **Public Speaking**

___ **Being in a Crowd**

TEXT ANALYSIS: PLOT ELEMENTS

Everything in a story happens for a reason. The series of events is the story's **plot.** The plot usually follows a pattern.

- **Exposition** introduces the characters and setting. It may also hint at what the **conflict,** or problem, will be.
- **Rising action** shows how the conflict develops.
- The most exciting part is the **climax,** a turning point in which you discover how the conflict is settled.
- Tension eases during the **falling action,** and events unfold as a result of the climax.
- The **resolution,** or **denouement,** is the final part of the plot, in which the reader learns how the problem is solved.

As you read "The School Play," notice the events that occur in each stage of the story's plot.

READING STRATEGY: MONITOR

Have you ever forgotten what you just read? To avoid this problem, **monitor** your reading by pausing occasionally to check your understanding. One way to monitor is to ask yourself questions about what you are reading. Sometimes you'll need to reread to find the answer. Other times you'll find the answer later on in the story.

As you read "The School Play," record questions about what is happening in a chart like the one shown.

My Questions	Answers
What is inside the cardboard box?	

VOCABULARY IN CONTEXT

Soto uses the boldfaced words below to help relate a student's experience in a school play. To see which words you know, replace each boldfaced word with a different word or phrase.

1. Robert's friend delivers the **narrative** about the background of the play.
2. The audience's **relentless** talking distracts the actors.
3. The main **prop** in the play is a map of the West.
4. Belinda wanted to **smirk** when the actor forgot his lines.

 Complete the activities in your **Reader/Writer Notebook.**

Meet the Author

Gary Soto
born 1952

True to Life
Gary Soto draws upon his childhood memories of growing up in Fresno, California, as an inspiration for his writing. He is often asked what his family thinks about his writing. He jokes that they don't read much of his work, "so they're not fully aware of how they've been brought to the page."

A Star Is Born
At age ten, Soto was cast in his school play. He only had to remember one line: "I have the glasses," but he was so fascinated with the fake beard he was wearing that he forgot what to say.

BACKGROUND TO THE STORY
The Donner Party
In the spring of 1846, a group of men, women, and children from Illinois and nearby states set out for California. George and Jacob Donner led the group.

While trying to cross the Sierra Nevada Mountains in eastern California, the Donner Party was trapped in a snowstorm. The travelers ran out of food, and members of the group began dying of starvation. In desperation, some of them ate the bodies of the dead. Only half the people made it through that grim winter.

Author Online
THINK central
Go to **thinkcentral.com.**
KEYWORD: HML6-35

THE SCHOOL PLAY

Gary Soto

In the school play at the end of his sixth-grade year, all Robert Suarez had to remember to say was, "Nothing's wrong. I can see," to a pioneer woman, who was really Belinda Lopez. Instead of a pioneer woman, Belinda was one of the toughest girls since the beginning of the world. She was known to slap boys and grind their faces into the grass so that they bit into chunks of wormy earth. More than once Robert had witnessed Belinda staring down the janitor's pit bull, who licked his frothing chops but didn't dare mess with her. **Ⓐ**

The class rehearsed for three weeks, at first without costumes. Early 10 one morning Mrs. Bunnin wobbled into the classroom lugging a large cardboard box. She wiped her brow and said, "Thanks for the help, Robert."

Robert was at his desk scribbling a ballpoint tattoo that spelled DUDE on the tops of his knuckles. He looked up and stared, blinking at his teacher. "Oh, did you need some help?" he asked.

Analyze Visuals ▶

Examine the art on page 37. In what way do the exaggerated **details** create a humorous effect?

Ⓐ PLOT: EXPOSITION
What background information have you learned about Robert?

She rolled her eyes at him and told him to stop writing on his skin. "You'll look like a criminal," she scolded.

Robert stuffed his hands into his pockets as he rose from his seat. "What's in the box?" he asked.

20 She muttered under her breath. She popped open the taped top and brought out skirts, hats, snowshoes, scarves, and vests. She tossed Robert a red beard, which he held up to his face, thinking it made him look handsome.

"I like it," Robert said. He sneezed and ran his hand across his moist nose.

His classmates were coming into the classroom and looked at Robert in awe. "That's bad," Ruben said. "What do I get?"

Mrs. Bunnin threw him a wrinkled shirt. Ruben raised it to his chest and said, "My dad could wear this. Can I give it to him after the play is done?"

30 Mrs. Bunnin turned away in silence.

Most of the actors didn't have speaking parts. They just got cutout crepe-paper snowflakes to pin to their shirts or crepe-paper leaves to wear.

During the blizzard in which Robert delivered his line, Belinda asked, "Is there something wrong with your eyes?" Robert looked at the audience, which at the moment was a classroom of empty chairs, a dented world globe that had been dropped by almost everyone, one limp flag, one wastebasket, and a picture of George Washington, whose eyes followed you around the room when you got up to sharpen your pencil. Robert answered, "Nothing's wrong. I can see."

40 Mrs. Bunnin, biting on the end of her pencil, said, "Louder, both of you."

Belinda stepped up, nostrils flaring so that the shadows on her nose quivered, and said louder, "Sucka, is there something wrong with your eye-balls?"

"Nothing's wrong. I can see."

"Louder! Make sure the audience can hear you," Mrs. Bunnin directed. She tapped her pencil hard against the desk. She scolded, "Robert, I'm not going to tell you again to quit fooling with the beard."

"It's itchy."

50 "We can't do anything about that. Actors need **props.** You're an actor. Now try again."

Robert and Belinda stood center stage as they waited for Mrs. Bunnin to call "Action!" When she did, Belinda approached Robert slowly. "Sucka face, is there anything wrong with your mug?" Belinda asked. Her eyes were squinted in anger. For a moment Robert saw his head grinding into the playground grass. **B**

"Nothing's wrong. I can see."

Language Coach

Oral Fluency   Reread line 27 aloud. When the letter *w* is followed by the letter *r*, the *w* is usually silent, as in *wrinkled*. Think of two other words that have a silent *w* before an *r*.

prop (prŏp) *n.* an object an actor uses in a play

B PLOT: RISING ACTION
Reread lines 42–56. What **conflict**, or struggle, is developing?

Robert giggled behind his red beard. Belinda popped her gum and **smirked.** She stood with her hands on her hips.

60 "What? What did you say?" Mrs. Bunnin asked, pulling off her glasses. "Are you chewing gum, Belinda?"

"No, Mrs. Bunnin," Belinda lied. "I just forgot my lines." **C**

Belinda turned to face the snowflake boys clumped together in the back. She rolled out her tongue, on which rested a ball of gray gum, depleted of sweetness under her **relentless** chomp. She whispered "sucka" and giggled so that her nose quivered dark shadows.

The play, *The Last Stand,* was about the Donner party just before they got hungry and started eating each other. Everyone who scored at least twelve out of fifteen on their spelling tests got to say at least one line.
70 Everyone else had to stand and be trees or snowflakes.

Mrs. Bunnin wanted the play to be a success. She couldn't risk having kids with bad memories on stage. The nonspeaking trees and snowflakes stood humming snow flurries, blistering wind, and hail, which they produced by clacking their teeth.

Robert's mother was proud of him because he was living up to the legend of Robert De Niro, for whom he was named. Over dinner he said, "Nothing's wrong. I can see," when his brother asked him to pass the dishtowel, their communal napkin. His sister said, "It's your turn to do dishes," and he said, "Nothing's wrong. I can see." His dog, Queenie,
80 begged him for more than water and a dog biscuit. He touched his dog's own hairy beard and said, "Nothing's wrong. I can see."

One warm spring night, Robert lay on his back in the backyard, counting shooting stars. He was up to three when David, a friend who was really his brother's friend, hopped the fence and asked, "What's the matter with you?"

"Nothing's wrong. I can see," Robert answered. He sat up, feeling good because the line came naturally, without much thought. He leaned back on his elbow and asked David what he wanted to be when he grew up. **D**

"I don't know yet," David said, plucking at the grass. "Maybe a fighter
90 pilot. What do you want to be?"

"I want to guard the president. I could wrestle the assassins and be on television. But I'd pin those dudes, and people would say, 'That's him, our hero.'" David plucked at a stalk of grass and thought deeply.

Robert thought of telling David that he really wanted to be someone with a supergreat memory, who could recall facts that most people thought were unimportant. He didn't know if there was such a job, but he thought it would be great to sit at home by the telephone waiting for scientists to call him and ask hard questions.

smirk (smûrk) *v.* to smile in an insulting way

C MONITOR
What is the actual line Belinda is supposed to say?

relentless (rĭ-lĕnt'lĭs) *adj.* refusing to stop or give up

Language Coach

Word Forms Some nouns have related adjective forms. To create an adjective from a noun, add to or change the ending of the noun. In line 81, for example, "hair" (*n.*) + y = "hairy" (*adj.*). Think of another example of a noun that can change into an adjective.

D MONITOR
Reread lines 75–88. Why does Robert respond with his line when someone speaks to him at home?

The three weeks passed quickly. The day before the play, Robert felt
happy as he walked home from school with no homework. As he
turned onto his street, he found a dollar floating over the currents of wind.

"A buck," he screamed to himself. He snapped it up and looked for
others. But he didn't find any more. It was his lucky day, though. At
recess he had hit a home run on a fluke bunt—a fluke because the catcher
had kicked the ball, another player had thrown it into center field, and
the pitcher wasn't looking when Robert slowed down at third, then burst
home with dust flying behind him.

That night, it was his sister's turn to do the dishes. They had eaten
enchiladas with the works, so she slaved with suds up to her elbows.
Robert bathed in bubble bath, the suds peaked high like the Donner Pass.
He thought about how full he was and how those poor people had had
nothing to eat but snow. I can live on nothing, he thought and whistled
like wind through a mountain pass, raking flat the suds with his palm. **E**

The next day, after lunch, he was ready for the play, red beard in hand
and his one line trembling on his lips. Classes herded into the auditorium.
As the actors dressed and argued about stepping on each other's feet,
Robert stood near a cardboard barrel full of toys, whispering over and
over to himself, "Nothing's wrong. I can see." He was hot, itchy, and
confused when he tied on the beard. He sneezed when a strand of the
beard entered his nostril. He said louder, "Nothing's wrong. I can see,"
but the words seemed to get caught in the beard. "Nothing, no, no. I can
see great," he said louder, then under his breath because the words seemed
wrong. "Nothing's wrong, can't you see? Nothing's wrong. I can see you."
Worried, he approached Belinda and asked if she remembered his line.
Balling her hand into a fist, Belinda warned, "Sucka, I'm gonna bury your
ugly face in the ground if you mess up." **F**

"I won't," Robert said as he walked away. He bit a nail and looked into
the barrel of toys. A clown's mask stared back at him. He prayed that his
line would come back to him. He would hate to disappoint his teacher
and didn't like the thought of his face being rubbed into spiky grass.

The curtain parted slightly, and the principal came out smiling onto
the stage. She said some words about pioneer history and then, stern
faced, warned the audience not to scrape the chairs on the just-waxed
floor. The principal then introduced Mrs. Bunnin, who told the audience
about how they had rehearsed for weeks.

Meanwhile, the class stood quietly in place with lunchtime spaghetti
on their breath. They were ready. Belinda had swallowed her gum because
she knew this was for real. The snowflakes clumped together and began
howling. ◆

E MONITOR
Think about how Robert
feels the day before the
play. How might this
affect his performance?

F PLOT: RISING
ACTION
How has the tension
increased now that it is
the day of the play?

◆ GRAMMAR IN
CONTEXT
Look at the sentences
in lines 136–139. The
sentences in this
paragraph are complete
sentences, not sentence
fragments. Every
sentence contains a
subject (*class, they,
Belinda, snowflakes*) and
a predicate that says
something about the
subject.

140　　Robert retied his beard. Belinda, smoothing her skirt, looked at him
and said, "If you know what's good for you, you'd better do it right."
Robert grew nervous when the curtain parted and his classmates who
were assigned to do snow, wind, and hail broke into song.

　　Alfonso stepped forward with his **narrative** about a blot on American
history that would live with us forever. He looked at the audience, lost for
a minute. He continued by saying that if the Donner party could come
back, hungry from not eating for over a hundred years, they would be
sorry for what they had done.

　　The play began with some boys in snowshoes shuffling around the
150　stage, muttering that the blizzard would cut them off from civilization.
They looked up, held out their hands, and said in unison,[1] "Snow." One
stepped center stage and said, "I wish I had never left the prairie." Another
one said, "California is just over there." He pointed, and some of the first
graders looked in the direction of the piano.

　　"What are we going to do?" one kid asked, brushing pretend snow off
his vest.

　　"I'm getting pretty hungry," another said, rubbing her stomach.

**Analyze
Visuals ▲**

What do the facial
expressions of the
audience members
suggest about the
actor's performance?

narrative (năr′ə-tĭv)
n. a story

---

1. **in unison** (yōo′nĭ-sən): at the same time.

The audience seemed to be following the play. A ribbon of sweat ran down Robert's face. When his scene came up, he staggered to center stage and dropped to the floor, just as Mrs. Bunnin had said, just as he had seen Robert De Niro do in that movie about a boxer. Belinda, bending over with an "Oh, my," yanked him up so hard that something clicked in his elbow. She boomed, "Is there anything wrong with your eyes?"

Robert rubbed his elbow, then his eyes, and said, "I can see nothing wrong. Wrong is nothing, I can see." **G**

"How are we going to get through?" she boomed, wringing her hands together at the audience, some of whom had their mouths taped shut because they were known talkers. "My husband needs a doctor." The drama advanced through snow, wind, and hail that sounded like chattering teeth.

Belinda turned to Robert and muttered, "You mess-up. You're gonna hate life."

But Robert thought he'd done okay. At least, he reasoned to himself, I got the words right. Just not in the right order.

With his part of the play done, he joined the snowflakes and trees, chattering his teeth the loudest. He howled wind like a baying hound and snapped his fingers furiously in a snow flurry. He trembled from the cold.

The play ended with Alfonso saying that if they came back to life, the Donner party would be sorry for eating each other. "It's just not right," he argued. "You gotta suck it up in bad times." **H**

Robert figured that Alfonso was right. He remembered how one day his sister had locked him in the closet and he didn't eat or drink for five hours. When he got out, he hit his sister, but not so hard as to leave a bruise. He then ate three sandwiches and felt a whole lot better.

The cast then paraded up the aisle into the audience. Belinda pinched Robert hard, but only once because she was thinking that it could have been worse. As he passed a smiling and relieved Mrs. Bunnin, she patted Robert's shoulder and said, "Almost perfect."

Robert was happy. He'd made it through without passing out from fear. Now the first and second graders were looking at him and clapping. He was sure everyone wondered who the actor was behind that smooth voice and red, red beard. ∾ **I**

G PLOT: TURNING POINT/CLIMAX
The **climax** is the story's most exciting moment, when you find out how the problem or conflict will be resolved. How is the delivery of Robert's line a turning point in the story?

H PLOT: FALLING ACTION
What effect does Robert's delivery of his lines have on the end of the play?

I PLOT: RESOLUTION/ DENOUEMENT
How do Robert, Belinda, and Mrs. Bunnin feel about Robert's performance?

Comprehension

1. **Clarify** Does repeating his line again and again help Robert remember it?

2. **Clarify** Reread lines 86–98. What does Robert want to be when he grows up?

3. **Summarize** What happens on the day of the performance?

Text Analysis

4. **Monitor** Review the chart you filled in as you read. Which questions and answers were most helpful for understanding the story? Explain.

5. **Compare and Contrast** Do you think Belinda is nervous about performing in front of the student audience? Compare and contrast her actions with Robert's on the day of the play.

6. **Make Inferences** How does the audience react to the play? Support your answer with specific details from the story.

7. **Examine Plot Elements** The plot of "The School Play" centers on Robert's fear of forgetting his line. Go back through the story and make a list of important events. Place the events on a diagram like the one shown to identify what happens at each stage of the plot. Do you think the plot of this story is realistic? Why or why not?

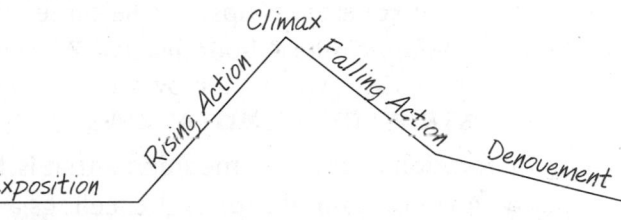

8. **Analyze Character's Effect on Plot** In addition to fear, Robert shows other personal qualities as the plot develops. Identify two of these qualities and explain how they help Robert resolve the conflicts he meets.

Extension and Challenge

9. **Creative Project: Drama** With a partner, choose a part of the story to act out. Rely on the details provided by Soto to accurately portray the characters. Present your performance to the class.

10. **Inquiry and Research** The United States expanded in the 1800s as people followed trails from eastern states to western territories. Research to find the trail used by the Donner Party. Using a map you can write on, sketch the trail and label the Donner Pass, which Robert describes in line 110.

> ### What do you FEAR the most?
> Are some fears more real than others? Explain.

COMMON CORE

RL 1 Cite textual evidence to support analysis of what the text says explicitly as well as inferences drawn from the text. **RL 3** Describe how a plot unfolds as well as how the characters respond as the plot moves toward a resolution. **RL 5** Analyze how a particular sentence fits into the structure of a text and contributes to the development of the setting or plot.

Vocabulary in Context

▲ VOCABULARY PRACTICE

Choose the letter of the word or phrase that has the same, or nearly the same, meaning as the boldfaced word.

1. a thrilling **narrative:** (a) argument, (b) story, (c) debate, (d) notice
2. **prop** for the play: (a) script, (b) costume, (c) object, (d) director
3. **relentless** noise: (a) constant, (b) deafening, (c) frightening, (d) occasional
4. to **smirk** at someone: (a) stare rudely, (b) laugh quietly, (c) yell loudly, (d) smile defiantly

ACADEMIC VOCABULARY IN SPEAKING

> • affect   • analyze   • evidence   • impact   • provide

With a partner, **analyze** the resolution of "The School Play." How would the story be **affected** if Robert was upset as he came offstage? Use at least two Academic Vocabulary words in your discussion.

VOCABULARY STRATEGY: DENOTATIONS AND CONNOTATIONS

A word's **denotation** is its literal meaning—that is, the definition you find in a dictionary. A word's **connotation** is the feelings and ideas associated with a word. You might find words that have similar denotations but different connotations in a **thesaurus,** or book of synonyms. For example, if you looked up *smile* in a thesaurus, you would likely find the Vocabulary word *smirk* listed as a synonym. The words have similar denotations but different connotations. *Smile* suggests happiness while *smirk* suggests smugness. You can also use a thesaurus to vary your word choice when writing, as well as to build up the new words in your vocabulary.

PRACTICE Use a thesaurus (either a printed version or an online version) to find a word with the same denotation as the boldfaced word, but with a negative connotation. Then use it in a sentence to show the negative meaning.

1. a **serious** speech
2. her **funny** hat
3. **eager** to get started
4. **enthusiastic** about the project
5. a **youthful** outlook

.·˙ **COMMON CORE**

L 4c Consult thesauruses, both print and digital, to clarify meaning. **L 5c** Distinguish among the connotations (associations) of words with similar denotations (definitions).

Interactive **THINK** central
Vocabulary

Go to **thinkcentral.com.**
KEYWORD: HML6-44

Language

COMMON CORE

L1 Demonstrate command of the conventions of grammar. **W2** Write informative/explanatory texts to convey ideas.

◆ **GRAMMAR IN CONTEXT:** Avoid Sentence Fragments

A **sentence fragment** is exactly what it says it is—a piece of a sentence. A fragment lacks a **subject** (whom or what the sentence is about), a **predicate** (what the subject is or does), or both. Don't let the punctuation at the end of a fragment fool you. What might look like a sentence is still a fragment if a complete thought is not expressed. A fragment can usually be combined with the sentence before it to make a complete sentence.

> *Original:* Robert was cast in a play. About the Donner Party.
>
> *Revised:* Robert was cast in a play about the Donner Party.

PRACTICE Rewrite this paragraph, correcting the four sentence fragments.

> The story would end very differently. If Robert had forgotten his line completely. He might run off the stage. Leaving Belinda to go on without him. Belinda would be angry. At Robert. However, Mrs. Bunnin would have another chance next year. To direct a perfect school play.

*For more help with fragments, see page R64 in the **Grammar Handbook**.*

READING-WRITING CONNECTION

YOUR TURN

Broaden your understanding of "The School Play" by responding to this prompt. Then use the **revising tip** to improve your writing.

WRITING PROMPT	REVISING TIP
Short Constructed Response: Review Drama critics write reviews of plays to give their opinion of a performance. In **one paragraph,** write a review of Robert's play for his school newspaper. Use your imagination to fill in the details.	Review your response. Have you avoided using sentence fragments? If not, revise your writing.

Interactive Revision **THINK** central

Go to **thinkcentral.com**.
KEYWORD: HML6-45

The Good Deed
Short Story by Marion Dane Bauer

Can first
IMPRESSIONS
be trusted?

COMMON CORE

RL 3 Describe how the characters respond as the plot moves toward a resolution. **L 6** Gather vocabulary knowledge when considering a word important to comprehension or expression.

Whenever you meet someone, you form an impression, or idea of what that person is like. You base your opinion on how the person looks, talks, and acts. Sometimes, after you get to know the person, you realize that your first impression was wrong. In "The Good Deed," a young girl finds out whether her first impression of someone was accurate.

LIST IT Think of someone you have known for a year or two. Make a list of words that describe your first impression of that person. When you are finished, decide if your impression has changed. Make a second list of words describing how you currently feel about that person.

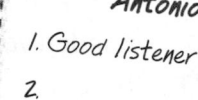

Antonio
1. Good listener
2.

● TEXT ANALYSIS: CONFLICT AND CLIMAX

Most characters face a problem or struggle. It is this struggle, or **conflict,** that makes a story interesting. There are two main types of conflict.

- An **external conflict** is a struggle with a force outside the character, such as another character.
- An **internal conflict,** such as overcoming a fear, takes place inside the character and is expressed through the character's thoughts and actions.

A strong plot pulls you in and moves the story towards a **climax,** the turning point in the story when you find out how the conflict will be resolved, or worked out.

● READING STRATEGY: CONNECT

Stories introduce us to new people and sometimes to new places and times. As you read a story, you may find that you can **connect,** or identify with, the feelings of the characters or the events and situations in the story.

As you read, use a chart like the one shown to record the connections you make.

What Is Happening?	My Connection
Heather is scared to talk to Miss Benson.	I was nervous to meet my pen pal at the Senior Center for the first time.

▲ VOCABULARY IN CONTEXT

The author uses these words to show how powerful first impressions can be. See which ones you already know. Place each word in the correct column of a chart like the one shown.

WORD LIST			
accusation	impaired	pert	
generic	incredibly	trite	

Know Well	Think I Know	Don't Know

 Complete the activities in your **Reader/Writer Notebook.**

Meet the Author

Marion Dane Bauer
born 1938

A Life Spent Writing
Marion Dane Bauer spent much of her childhood making up stories. Her first written work was a poem dedicated to her teddy bear. For Bauer, writing is a habit. She says, "It's what I get up in the morning to do." In 1987 her efforts were rewarded when she received the Newbery Honor for her novel *On My Honor.*

Inspiration
Many events in Bauer's life have inspired her writing, but she draws her stories less from real life than from her need to connect with someone else's feelings. "It may start with ... a newspaper article, from something overheard in the grocery store, or told to me by a friend," she says. Then Bauer thinks about how to turn the information into a story. She explains, "It must first pass through my own thoughts and feelings. ... And when it does, the story is true. Not because it 'really happened,' but because, for me, it is real."

Author Online

THINK central

Go to thinkcentral.com.
KEYWORD: HML6-47

47

The Good Deed

Marion Dane Bauer

Analyze Visuals ▶

What do the lines and colors in this painting lead you to focus on?

Miss Benson was my good deed for the summer. Every girl in our scout troop was assigned someone. My friend Melody had Mr. Stengle. He's the oldest resident of the Riverview Nursing Home. He must be at least one hundred and two. He used to be a farmer, and all he ever talks about is the weather. Anne Marie got Mrs. Mechlenburg. Mrs. Mechlenburg has four children, all under five, and kind of bewildered, cocker spaniel eyes. Like maybe she doesn't know how they all got there. But I was assigned Miss Benson.

Miss Benson is old. Not old like Mr. Stengle, but old enough. And she's
10 blind. "Sight **impaired**, Heather," our scout leader said. But whether you say "sight impaired" or "blind," the truth is, Miss Benson can't see a thing.

impaired (ĭm-pârd′) *adj.* being in a less than perfect condition

"What do I do?" I asked. "What do I say?" **Ⓐ**

"Start with 'hello,'" our scout leader said, like that was some kind of help. Then she added, "She's a retired teacher. I'll bet she'd just love it if you'd read to her." And she was off talking to Anne Marie about diapers.

The problem was I'd never been alone with a blind person before. Come to think of it, I don't suppose I'd ever even met one. And the thought of trying to talk to Miss Benson kind of scared me. Melody and
20 Anne Marie and I all had the same number of badges though, the most of anyone in the troop, and I wasn't about to let either of them get ahead of me. So the next day I called Miss Benson—she sounded normal enough on the phone—then I set out to meet her. **Ⓑ**

Her place wasn't hard to find. She lived in the apartment building right next to the Piggly Wiggly, only a few blocks from my house. Which meant I got there really fast. Too fast. Then I kind of stood in front of her door, waiting, though I couldn't have said what I was waiting for. To figure out what I was going to say, I guess. After "hello," I mean. But before I even got around to knocking, the door across the hall from
30 Miss Benson's apartment popped open and this girl I'd never seen before stuck her head out.

"What do you want?" she said, like it was her door I was standing in front of.

"I'm visiting Miss Benson," I told her, which was perfectly obvious.

The girl had long brown hair. Kind of a reddish brown. But it was a tangled mess. I'll swear she'd pulled it into a ponytail that morning without ever passing it by a brush. "Why are you visiting her?" she wanted to know.

It would have sounded really dumb to say, "Because I'm a Girl Scout,
40 and she's my good deed for the summer." So I said instead, "I've come to read to her." And then I added, just in case this girl didn't know anything at all, "She's sight impaired, you know."

"No, she's not," the girl answered, with a toss of that tangled hair. "I've seen her. She's blind as a bat."

Behind the girl, from inside her apartment, a whole lot of noise was going on. It sounded like the beginnings of World War III. Or like a herd of runaway horses maybe. Just then two little kids came hurtling up to the doorway and stopped to peer out from each side of the girl. I couldn't tell whether they were boys or girls or one of each. They looked kind of
50 **generic.** Is that the word? Their hair wasn't combed either, and their noses were snotty. . . . I decided maybe reading to a blind woman wasn't so bad after all and turned to knock on the door.

Ⓐ CONNECT
Reread lines 1–12. Think of a time when you felt nervous about meeting someone. What is adding to Heather's nervousness?

Ⓑ CONFLICT
Reread lines 17–23. What conflict is Heather facing?

generic (jə-nĕr′ĭk) *adj.* having no particularly distinctive or noteworthy quality

"Wait," the girl said. "I'll come with you."

Just like that she said it, as though she'd been invited.

And the truth was, I didn't know whether to be annoyed at her for being so pushy or relieved that I didn't have to go in there alone. What if a good deed didn't count if you had help? But though there wasn't a reason in the world for me to do what that girl said, I found myself standing there with my hand in the air, waiting.

60 "Tell Mama I've gone across the hall," the girl told the two snotty-nosed kids. And she stepped out and closed the door behind herself.

"Mama," I heard the kids yodel as they stampeded back into the apartment. And then there was nothing left to do but to knock on Miss Benson's door.

The rest wasn't nearly as hard as I'd expected. After a moment a tall woman with curly, salt-and-pepper hair opened the door and said, "You must be Heather. Come in." I could tell she couldn't see me, because she looked right over my head like there was something interesting on the wall across the way, but her voice didn't *sound* blind.

70 I don't know what I mean by that exactly, except that she didn't sound like she was missing anything at all. And I guess she wasn't, because when the girl said, "Hi!" and followed me into the apartment Miss Benson asked right away, "Who's your friend?"

Of course, I didn't have a clue who my "friend" was, but she answered, just as **pert** as you please, "Risa. My mom and me and my little brothers"—so they *were* boys—"just moved in across the hall."

"Welcome, Risa," Miss Benson replied. Her voice sort of had a smile in it. "I'm glad to see you."

Just like that she said it. *I'm glad to see you!* Like she could.

80 Miss Benson led the way, one hand trailing lightly across the furniture she passed or sometimes just grazing the wall. "I hope you don't mind if we go to the kitchen," she called back. "It's the cheeriest place."

The kitchen was a cheery place. The sun was all spread out across a table made out of some kind of golden wood. And in the middle of the table, sweating coolness, sat a pitcher of lemonade and a big blue plate heaped with oatmeal-raisin cookies. There were glasses, too. Just two of them though.

"Mmmm, cookies," Risa said.

"Help yourselves, girls," Miss Benson told us. "I made them for you."

90 And it was a good thing she extended the invitation, because Risa already had one in her hand.

Miss Benson went to the cupboard and got out another glass and began to pour lemonade for everyone. She stopped pouring before she overflowed the glasses too, though I couldn't figure how she did it.

COMMON CORE L 6

Language Coach

Homonyms Words that have the same pronunciation but different meanings are called **homonyms.** What homonyms for *there* in line 57 do you know?

pert (pûrt) *adj.*
offensively bold; saucy

I expected Risa to gobble her cookie, just the way she had grabbed it off the plate without being invited, but she didn't. She just took a couple of nibbles, then tucked the rest into the pocket of her cutoffs. Can you imagine that? An oatmeal cookie in your pocket? **C**

"Tell me about yourselves, girls," Miss Benson said, sitting across from us at the table, and before I could even open my mouth, Risa was off and running.

She told about her three little brothers—there was a baby I hadn't seen; he probably had a snotty nose too—and about how her mom had moved to Minnesota for a better job, only Risa didn't like her mom's new job because the boss wouldn't even let her take telephone calls from her children when she was at work.

C CONNECT
What do Heather's internal thoughts and feelings tell you about her impression of Rita? Have you ever felt the same way about someone you just met?

▼ **Analyze Visuals**
Does the dining table in this painting seem as cheery as Miss Benson's kitchen? Explain.

Detail of *Breakfast Room II,* Marty Walsh. Oil on panel, 24″ × 24″. © Marty Walsh.

I told Miss Benson how many badges I'd earned and how my parents and I had gone to Disney World over spring break. I could tell, just by the way Risa looked at me, that she'd never been near any place like Disney World and that she hated me for saying I'd been there. But what was I supposed to do? It was the truth.

When Miss Benson pushed the cookies toward us and said "Help yourself" again, quick as a flash, Risa took another cookie and put that one into her pocket too. I figured she must be stashing them for the snotty-nosed brothers at home, and I was almost impressed. It was kind of nice of her, really, to think of her brothers that way. It made me wish I had a little brother or sister to take cookies home for, but if I had one, I'd teach mine how to use a tissue. ◆

And then I offered to read, so Miss Benson sent me to her bedroom to check out her bookshelf. I found a tall blue book—it looked kind of tattered, so I figured it had been around awhile and was, maybe, a favorite—called *Stories That Never Grow Old.* There was a picture on the cover of a woman wearing a long dress reading a book to some children.

When I came back with the book, Risa looked at it and said low, under her breath, "Dummy. That one's for little kids."

I shrugged, like I didn't care, but still my cheeks went hot when I opened it and saw she was right. It was a lot of old-timey stories like "The Little Engine That Could" and "Hansel and Gretel" and "Why the Bear Has a Stumpy Tail," things like that. Probably not what a grown-up, even one who used to be a teacher, would want to hear.

But then Miss Benson asked, "What book did you get?" and when I told her, she clapped her hands and said, "Perfect!" So I shot Risa a look and started to read. "'Bruin, the young brown bear, was feeling very hungry.'" **D**

Risa leaned across the corner of the table so she could see the page too. She even started silently shaping the words with her mouth as I read, like she was tasting each one. I figured she must not be a very good reader though, because I'd given up reading with my lips when I was in the first grade.

As soon as I'd finished the story I knew I was right about her not being a good reader, because Miss Benson said, "Okay, Risa. Why don't you read the next one?"

While I was reading, she couldn't get close enough to the book, but suddenly she couldn't get away from it fast enough. "Oh no!" she said, pushing away from the table so hard that her chair screeched against the floor. "Anyway, you don't want to hear any more from that old thing. I'll do something else for you instead." **E**

◆ **GRAMMAR IN CONTEXT**
A **run-on sentence** is created when two sentences are written as if they were one sentence. Read lines 116–118. The writer avoids using a run-on sentence by inserting a comma and the coordinating conjunction *but* between two thoughts.

D CONFLICT
Reread lines 124–134. What evidence is there that the tension between Heather and Risa has increased?

E CONFLICT
Why doesn't Risa want to read aloud?

Miss Benson's face was round and soft. "What do you want to do instead?" she asked, and she folded her hands in her lap, waiting.

150 For a moment Risa looked around, whipping that tangled ponytail back and forth like she was expecting to find an idea for something she could do hanging on the wall. Then it must have come to her, because her face lit up and she settled back in her chair. "How about," she said, "if I give you an eye bouquet."

"An eye bouquet?" The way Miss Benson leaned forward you could tell she was expecting something grand.

An eye bouquet? I thought. *How dumb!*

But Risa explained. "I'll make a picture for you with words."

"What a wonderful idea!" Miss Benson said.

160 And it was a wonderful idea. I wished I'd thought of something half as wonderful. Though Miss Benson seemed to like the story I'd read well enough.

Risa thought for a few seconds, then she began. "The lilac bushes are blooming in front of the apartments."

Miss Benson nodded. "It's been years since I've seen those old lilac bushes, but they're still there, are they?"

"Yes," Risa said. "And they're that shimmery color, halfway between silver and purple. You know what I mean?"

"Shimmery. Halfway between silver and purple." Miss Benson nodded
170 again. "That's it. That's it exactly. I can see them now."

I couldn't stand being bested by a girl who still read a little kiddy book with her lips, so I jumped in. I hadn't especially noticed the bushes she was talking about, but I'd seen lilac bushes all my life. "The leaves are shaped like little hearts," I said. "And they're green." I could see Miss Benson was waiting for something more, so I added, kind of feebly, "Green like grass." **F**

But that wasn't any good, and I knew it. What could be more ordinary than "green like grass"? It's what my English teacher would call **trite**.

"The green of horses munching," Risa said, offering the words up like
180 a gift, and Miss Benson tipped her head back and laughed out loud.

"Well," I said, getting up so fast I had to catch my chair to keep it from tipping over. "I guess I'd better be going. My father"—I leaned heavily on the word since it was obvious Risa didn't have one of those—"told me he'd take me and my friends to the beach this weekend." **G**

It wasn't a lie. Daddy was taking me and Melody and Anne Marie to the beach, but not until Sunday afternoon. This was Saturday.

Miss Benson stood up too. "Thank you, Heather," she said, "for the nice visit. I enjoyed it. I enjoyed it very much."

COMMON CORE RL 3

F CONFLICT
Conflict is the struggle that makes a story interesting and keeps you reading to see what happens next. There are two main types of conflict. In an **external conflict** a character struggles against an outside force. A character who confronts a school bully or is trapped in a terrifying storm is facing an external conflict. An **internal conflict** takes place within a character's mind. A character who is tempted to cheat at a game faces an internal conflict. You can learn about the development of conflicts by paying attention to the thoughts and feelings of a character as the plot moves toward a resolution. Reread lines 171–176. What kind of conflict do these lines reveal?

trite (trīt) *adj.* boring because overused; not fresh or original

G CONNECT
Have you ever tried to make someone jealous? Why is Heather trying to make Risa jealous?

54 UNIT 1: PLOT, CONFLICT, AND SETTING

"I'll be back," I promised. "I'll come and read again on Monday."
190 *By myself,* I wanted to add, but I said instead, "I'll put your book away before I go." And I carried it back to the bedroom.

When I got to the bookshelf I stood looking at the empty space where the book had stood. *Risa lives right across the hall,* I was thinking. *What if she decides to come back on her own? Maybe she'll even decide to read to Miss Benson, and this is the book she'll want, one that doesn't have too many big words.*

And then there I was, looking around for some place to put the book where she wouldn't find it. After all, Miss Benson herself certainly wasn't going to be wanting to look at it again while I was gone.

200 The wastebasket next to the bookshelf, rectangular and deep and perfectly empty, was just the right size. I slipped the book inside. It would be safe there, waiting for me. **H**

H CONFLICT
Reread lines 192–202. Why does Heather decide to hide the book?

When I got to the door, Risa was there, standing beside Miss Benson. She had to go home too, she said, though I knew she didn't have plans for going anywhere special like the beach. But I said all the polite things you're supposed to say to someone you've just met, to her and to Miss Benson too, and I left. My good deed was done for the day.

On my way out of the apartment building, I couldn't help but notice. The blooms on the lilac bushes were a crisp brown, the color of tea. So the
210 girl was a liar, too, besides being a poor reader.

A couple of days later when I came to visit Miss Benson again, I stopped in front of her door, half expecting Risa to pop out of the apartment across the hall. All seemed quiet over there this time except for cartoons blaring from a TV. I breathed a sigh of relief and knocked on Miss Benson's door.

This time the blue plate on the table held sugar cookies, creamy white, just beginning to be brown at the edges, and sparkling with sugar.

"I'll get a book," I said, after we had each eaten a cookie and sipped some cocoa, chatting about this and that. And I hurried off to Miss
220 Benson's bedroom to get *Stories That Never Grow Old*.

Only the book wasn't there.

I looked in the wastebasket, of course. I even picked it up and turned it upside down and shook it, as though something as big as a book could disappear. But the wastebasket was empty. Just the way it had been the first time I'd come into the room. I wondered, in fact, why Miss Benson had a wastebasket at all since she didn't seem to put anything into it. **I**

Then I hurried to the shelf. Maybe Miss Benson had reached a hand into the basket and found it there and put it away herself. Or maybe someone who came and cleaned for her had discovered it. Now that I
230 thought about it, a wastebasket was about the dumbest place in the world to hide a book.

The space left behind when I took *Stories That Never Grow Old* out, right between two fatter books—*A Literary History of England* and *The Oxford Companion to English Literature*—was still there, empty, accusing. *You did it!* the space said. *You've lost Miss Benson's book! Probably her favorite book in all the world.*

Did she empty her own wastebaskets? She wouldn't have been able to see what was in there. Or maybe somebody else emptied them for her and thought, seeing it there, that she meant to throw it away. My heart beat
240 faster just thinking about the possibilities. **J**

There was nothing else to do, so I picked out another book, a collection of poems by Robert Frost, and brought that out instead.

I CONNECT
Based on your own experiences, what emotions do you think Heather feels when she realizes the book is missing?

J CONFLICT
Reread lines 227–240. How has Heather's conflict become more complicated?

"I have some poems," I told Miss Benson, and before she had a chance to say whether she was disappointed that I hadn't brought the blue book, I opened the collection and began to read.

"I'm going out to clean the pasture spring."[1]

She settled back to listen, a small smile tipping the corners of her mouth, but though she looked perfectly happy, I couldn't get past feeling that maybe she'd rather have heard *Stories That Never Grow Old*.

250 I read several poems—I especially liked the one about the boy who died after cutting himself with a chainsaw; it was so sad—but I kept feeling this weight in the pit of my stomach. The blue book was gone. Miss Benson had probably had it since she was a little kid.

I guess I quit reading without even noticing I'd stopped, because the next thing I knew Miss Benson was saying, "How about an eye bouquet now? What can you make me see?"

Her asking took me by surprise, because I'd already proven on Saturday that "eye bouquets" weren't really my thing. When I didn't answer right away though, she said, "I'll give you one first."

260 "All right," I said, though I couldn't help wondering what kind of eye bouquet a blind woman could come up with.

"Freckles," she said, "and hair the color of pulled taffy.[2] Green eyes, a misty green like the sea."

For a moment I just sat there, feeling dumb, until gradually what Miss Benson had said began to dawn. *I* had freckles, though I didn't like to think they were the first thing a person saw. And my hair . . . well, it's the color people like to call "dirty blond," though I always hated that description. I keep my hair as clean as anybody's. But if you were being real nice, you could say it's the color of pulled taffy. And my eyes? Were 270 they green like the sea? (I guess that would be better than green like horses munching.)

And then slowly, gradually, the truth dawned. Miss Benson had gotten her eye bouquet from . . .

"Risa's been here," I said. It came out sounding like an **accusation**.

"Yes. She came Sunday afternoon. She's a very nice girl. I'm sure the two of you are going to be great friends."

I ignored that, about Risa's being a nice girl and about the two of us being friends, because an idea was rising in me like dinner on a rocking boat. Risa had been in Miss Benson's apartment since the last time I'd 280 been there. The blue book was gone from the place where I'd hidden it. Risa had taken it. I already knew she was a liar. Now I knew she was a thief, too! **K**

---

1. **I'm going . . . pasture spring:** the first line of Robert Frost's poem "The Pasture." (See page 62.)
2. **pulled taffy:** a boiled candy usually of molasses or brown sugar that is stretched until light-colored.

accusation
(ăk′yōō-zā′shən) *n.* the act of charging someone with wrongdoing

K CONFLICT
Reread lines 272–282. How does Miss Benson's eye bouquet increase Heather's conflict with Risa?

◀ **Analyze Visuals**

Does the girl in this painting look more like Heather or Risa? Explain.

"Okay," I said, "I can give you an eye bouquet. Hair . . ." I was going to say *Hair that's never seen a brush,* but something stopped me. Instead I said, "Hair the color of chestnuts." I paused. That was pretty good. And Risa's hair was a nice reddish brown. "And eyes . . . eyes like little bits of sky." I didn't even know I'd noticed those things about Risa—what a rich color her hair was, tangled or not, and the brilliant blue of her eyes—until I'd named them, but even as I did, I was standing up.

290   "Sor . . . sorry," I said, stumbling over my feet and my tongue at the same time. "I'm afraid I've got to go. I mean, there's something I've got to do. But I'll be back. Tomorrow. I promise."

Miss Benson stood too. "Is your daddy taking you to the beach again?" she asked.

"No . . . no." I was backing toward the door. "Not today. He's working today. But"—I'd reached the front door—"he'll probably take us again next weekend."

"That's nice." Miss Benson had followed. "Come back anytime, dear. I like having you here."

300 *Come back anytime!* She wouldn't say that when she found out her book was missing. Then she would think I was the thief. Because I was the one who'd had the book last, wasn't I? She'd never think of suspecting Risa of stealing a book, Risa who'd refused to read, Risa with her pretty eye bouquets.

As soon as Miss Benson closed the door behind me, I stalked across the hall and knocked on Risa's door . . . hard. I could hear the television still, Road Runner[3] cartoons, but no one answered. The girl was hiding from me!

I knocked again, harder, and when still no one came, I turned the
310 handle. Surprised to find the door unlocked—some people are **incredibly** careless!—I opened it slowly and peeked in. Two pairs of sky-blue eyes stared back at me from the couch. Without taking his thumb out of his mouth, one of the little boys mumbled, "Who're you?"

"I'm a friend of Risa's," I lied. "Is she here?"

They stared at one another and then, without answering, turned back to the TV.

"Where's Risa?" I said more loudly.

The one who had talked before pulled his thumb out of his mouth this time. "She took Andrew and went," he said. "She told us to sit right here."
320 He gave me a warning look. "She told us not to let anybody in, and we're not supposed to talk to strangers."

I stepped closer. Who was Andrew? The baby, probably. And where was their mother? Was she going to come marching in, demanding to know what I was doing in her apartment bullying her little kids? Not likely. This was Monday. She must be working. And Risa was supposed to be here taking care of the little boys. Well, so much for counting on her for anything. "When will she be back?" I demanded to know, stepping closer. "She's got something of mine."

No answer, so I moved between the couch and the coyote zooming
330 across the screen, facing down the two small, dirty-faced boys. And that's when I saw it. The tattered blue book lay on the couch between them, open to a picture of a cheerful train puffing up a steep hill.

I snatched up the book. "Where did you get this?"

incredibly
(ĭn-krĕd′ə-blē) *adv.*
unbelievably

COMMON CORE L 6

Language Coach

Onomatopoeia The word *zooming* in line 329 is an example of onomatopoeia (on′ä-mät′a-pē′a) because its sound imitates its meaning, like *buzz*. Can you think of other examples of onomatopoeia?

---

3. **Road Runner:** a bird cartoon character who is constantly chased but never caught by Wile E. Coyote.

"Risa give it to us," the talker replied. The other one just leaned over until he had almost toppled onto his side, trying to peer around me to see the TV. Maybe he didn't know how to talk.

"I'll bet she did," I said. I could have burst. That buttinski girl who thought she was so great was a thief. Just as I'd thought.

The voice came from the doorway behind me. "Miss Benson gave it to 340 me, and I gave it to them." I whirled around to see Risa, standing there holding an armful of baby. He was asleep with a fat cheek pressed against her shoulder. Risa looked small under his weight.

"Miss Benson gave it to me," she said again, as though she knew I didn't believe her, "when I went over there on Sunday."

"Where did you find it?" I demanded to know.

"Why did you hide it?" she countered.

The question hung in the air. The instant she asked, I realized I couldn't answer. Why had I hidden the book anyway? Something about not wanting Risa to horn in[4] on my good deed. Was that it? **L**

350 I tried another attack. "How come you went off and left your little brothers? Something terrible could have—"

She interrupted. "Andrew was sick. His temperature got really high. I couldn't get hold of my mom, so I went looking for a doctor." As she said it, she kind of staggered, like she couldn't hold up that lump of a baby for another minute.

Suddenly I could see how scared she'd been, scared for the baby, scared to go off and leave her brothers, probably scared to walk into a strange doctor's office alone too. "Here," I said, moving toward her. "Let me take him. Is he going to be all right?"

360 When I lifted the baby away from her, I could feel how hot he was. And how heavy, too. **M**

"Yeah." She rubbed her nose with the back of her hand. Had she been crying? "The doctor gave him a shot. And he called my mom too. Her boss didn't have any choice. He had to let the doctor talk to her. She's coming home real soon."

I walked over to the couch and laid the sleeping baby down beside the other two boys. His cheeks were bright red. I took a tissue out of my pocket and wiped his nose.

"I'll bet Miss Benson would have come over to watch the boys while 370 you went looking for the doctor," I said. And for a moment we both stood there, considering the word *watch*.

Risa nodded. "I didn't think of that," she said softly. But then she lifted her chin and added, like it was what we were talking about still, "I found her book in the wastebasket."

L CLIMAX
Reread lines 346–349. How does Risa's question affect Heather?

M CLIMAX
What causes Heather to suddenly change her attitude towards Risa? Why is this a turning point?

---

4. **horn in:** to push one's way in without invitation.

"Did you tell her?"

Risa tossed her head. Her pretty chestnut hair had been brushed that morning, and it flowed with the movement like a horse's tail. "Of course not. What do you take me for?"

Something deep inside my chest loosened a bit. **N**

380 "Miss Benson said if I read out loud to my brothers it will help me get better. Better at reading, I mean." As Risa said it, a slow blush touched her cheeks, made her ears flame, even reached the roots of her hair. And that's why I knew she was telling the truth. Never in a thousand years would she have admitted that she needed help with reading except as a way of letting me know she hadn't stolen the book. "I'm going to read to her sometimes too," she added.

"That's . . . that's really great," I stammered. And I knew it was. Really. "You'll be helping her, and she'll be helping you. A kind of a good deed both ways."

390 "A good deed?" Risa laughed. "Is that what you call it?"

"Risa," one of the boys interrupted, the one I'd thought couldn't talk, "would you read to us some more?"

She looked sideways at me, and I knew that it was me—snotty me—who'd kept her from reading out loud before. "Why don't we take turns reading to them?" I said. "That would be fun."

Risa considered my offer long and carefully. "Okay," she said at last. "Just so it doesn't count as a good deed."

"It doesn't," I said. "I promise." **∿ O**

N CONNECT

Think of a time when you realized your first impression of someone was wrong. How does that experience help you to understand how Heather is feeling?

O CONFLICT

What is the **resolution**, or end, of the conflict between Heather and Risa?

Heber Valley Pastures (2005), Douglas Aagard. Oil, 11″ × 14″. © 2005 Meyer-Milagros Gallery. All rights reserved.

The *Pasture*

Robert Frost

I'm going out to clean the pasture spring;
I'll only stop to rake the leaves away
(And wait to watch the water clear, I may):
I shan't be gone long.—You come too.

5 I'm going out to fetch the little calf
That's standing by the mother. It's so young
It totters when she licks it with her tongue.
I shan't be gone long.—You come too.

Comprehension

1. **Recall** How does Heather meet Risa?

2. **Clarify** Reread lines 260–274. Why is Miss Benson able to describe Heather?

3. **Represent** Sketch one of the eye bouquets described in "The Good Deed." Which of the author's words helped you form a mental picture of the image?

COMMON CORE

RL 3 Describe how the characters respond as the plot moves toward a resolution. RL 9 Compare and contrast texts in different genres in terms of their approaches to similar topics.

Text Analysis

4. **Connect** Pick one of the connections you listed on the chart you kept while reading. Explain how the connection helped you to understand the character's actions.

5. **Identify Conflicts** An **external conflict** is a character's struggle against an outside force. An **internal conflict** takes place inside a character's mind. Create a "portrait" of Heather like the one shown. Go back through the story and record examples of the internal and external conflicts she faces.

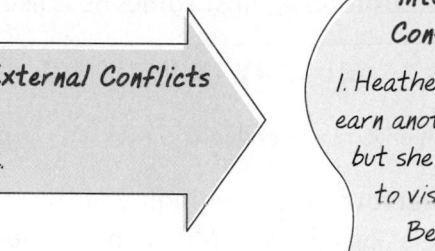

External Conflicts
1.
2.

Internal Conflicts

1. Heather wants to earn another badge, but she is scared to visit Miss Benson.
2.

6. **Identify Climax** What event leads to the resolution between Heather and Risa?

7. **Evaluate** Do you think Heather accomplishes her "good deed" by the end of the story? Use examples to support your answer.

8. **Connect Literary Works** In line 246, Heather begins to read Robert Frost's poem "The Pasture" to Miss Benson. Reread the entire poem on page 62. Do you think the **speaker,** or the voice in the poem that talks to the reader, would treat Risa the way Heather did, or the way Miss Benson did? Support your opinion with examples from the poem and "The Good Deed."

Extension and Challenge

9. **Inquiry and Research** What challenges does a blind person face on a daily basis? Research the strategies, tools, and resources available to help them actively participate in every aspect of life, just as Miss Benson does.

Can first IMPRESSIONS be trusted?

What did Heather's experiences teach you about the wisdom of trusting first impressions?

Vocabulary in Context

▲ VOCABULARY PRACTICE

Show that you understand the vocabulary words by deciding if each statement is true or false.

1. A **generic** shirt is hard to find.
2. If you give a **pert** answer, other people will think you are quiet and shy.
3. A room that is **incredibly** noisy is very loud.
4. A **trite** statement usually suggests a new way of looking at something.
5. If my ability to hear is **impaired,** I can hear very well.
6. A false **accusation** against someone is likely to make that person angry.

accusation
generic
impaired
incredibly
pert
trite

ACADEMIC VOCABULARY IN WRITING

> • affect • analyze • evidence • impact • provide

Heather is nervous at the beginning of the story. How did her nervousness **affect** her relationship with Miss Benson? Support your answer with examples from the text. Use at least two Academic Vocabulary words in your response.

VOCABULARY STRATEGY: SUFFIXES

A **suffix** is a word part that appears at the end of a root or base word to form a new word. Suffixes can change a word's part of speech. For example, the suffix in *accusation* changes the verb *accuse* to a noun. If you can recognize the base word, you can usually figure out the meaning of the new word. See the chart for common suffixes and their meaning.

PRACTICE For each boldfaced word, identify the base word and its meaning. Then use your knowledge of the word and the information in the chart to define the boldfaced word.

1. The sudden noise broke his **concentration.**
2. Our swimming **instructor** was a teenager.
3. She received a weekly **allowance** for buying lunch.
4. I have always had a **fascination** with frogs and toads.

⋯ **COMMON CORE**

L 4b Use common affixes as clues to the meaning of a word.

Suffixes	Meanings
-er, -or	person or thing that
-ance, -ence, -ion, -tion, -ation	act or condition of

Interactive Vocabulary **THINK** central

Go to **thinkcentral.com**.
KEYWORD: HML6-64

Language

◆ **GRAMMAR IN CONTEXT:** Avoid Run-On Sentences

A run-on sentence is two or more sentences written as one sentence. To correct the error, use a **period** to make two separate sentences, or use a **comma** and **coordinating conjunction** (*and, but, or*) to divide the parts of the run-on.

> *Original:* Heather politely says goodbye to Miss Benson, she barges into Risa's home uninvited.
>
> *Revised:* Heather politely says goodbye to Miss Benson, but she barges into Risa's home uninvited.

PRACTICE Rewrite the following sentences, making changes in punctuation and, if necessary, capitalization to correct the run-on sentences. Add coordinating conjunctions where needed.

1. Risa walked in the door, she asked me to give her the book.
2. I accused Risa of stealing the book, she blushed and looked down.
3. Risa told me she planned to return the book after she read it to her brothers, she asked me not to tell Miss Benson.
4. I wasn't sure what to do, I really liked Miss Benson.

*For more help with run-on sentences, see page R64 in the **Grammar Handbook**.*

READING-WRITING CONNECTION

Broaden your understanding of "The Good Deed" by responding to this prompt. Then use the **revising tip** to improve your writing.

WRITING PROMPT	REVISING TIP
Short Constructed Response: Comparison Outwardly, Heather treats Miss Benson differently than she treats Risa. Write **one paragraph** comparing Heather's behavior toward Miss Benson with her behavior toward Risa.	Review your response. Have you avoided using run-on sentences in your writing? If not, revise your writing.

◯ **COMMON CORE**

L1 Demonstrate command of the conventions of grammar.
W2 Write informative/explanatory texts to convey ideas.

Interactive Revision **THINK** central

Go to **thinkcentral.com**.
KEYWORD: HML6-65

All Summer in a Day

Short Story by Ray Bradbury

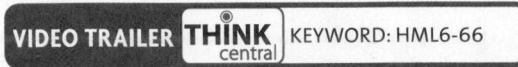

VIDEO TRAILER THINK central KEYWORD: HML6-66

What if your whole WORLD changed?

COMMON CORE

RL 1 Cite textual evidence to support inferences drawn from the text. **RL 3** Describe how the characters respond as the plot moves toward a resolution. **RL 5** Analyze how a particular sentence fits into the structure of a text and contributes to the development of the setting or plot.

People often become comfortable in the familiar world of their family, friends, and daily routines. However, people move and traditions change. When your world changes, whether by a little or a lot, it can have an impact on your life. In "All Summer in a Day," a young girl feels lost in a new place.

SKETCH IT Think about the people, places, events, and ideas that are most precious to you. Create a sketch of your world, showing some of the things that make it a special place. How would you feel if any of these things disappeared?

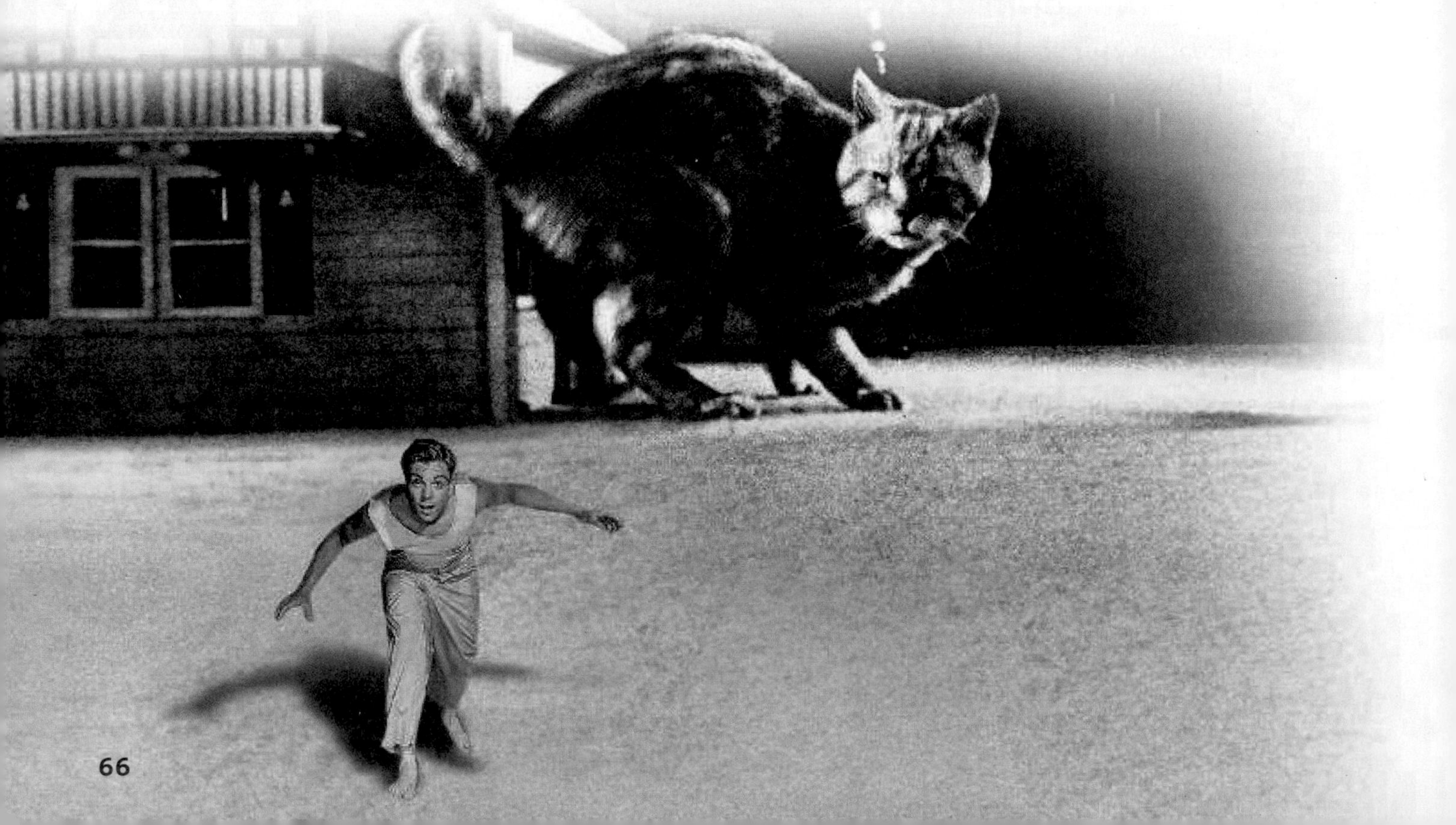

● TEXT ANALYSIS: PLOT AND SETTING

The **plot** is the series of events that make up a story, including the conflict and its resolution. **Setting** is *where* and *when* a story takes place. In science fiction stories, the setting is often the distant future. This setting usually causes the events of the plot to unfold in an unexpected way. As you read "All Summer in a Day," look for clues that tell you when and where the story takes place. Then think about the setting's influence on the story's conflict and resolution, or denouement.

Review: **Conflict**

● READING SKILL: MAKE INFERENCES

As a reader you are a detective. Details, events, and dialogue in a story are your clues. You put the clues together with your own knowledge to **make inferences,** or guesses.

As you read "All Summer in a Day," use an equation like the one shown to record the inferences you make about the characters' feelings and their actions.

Clues from the Story	+	My Knowledge	=	Inference
Margot is not part of the group.	+	Not being part of a group can make you feel sad.	=	Margot feels sad.

Review: **Identify Cause and Effect**

▲ VOCABULARY IN CONTEXT

Ray Bradbury uses the words below to create a world that is very different from our own. Complete each sentence with an appropriate word from the list.

WORD	apparatus	resilient	slacken
LIST	immense	savor	tumultuously

1. The leaves shook _____, and we were scared.
2. The _____ planet offered many areas to explore.
3. The sturdy shelters are built to be _____.
4. After the storm, the wind began to _____.
5. The _____ used to open the hatch was broken.
6. She sat quietly to _____ everything around her.

 Complete the activities in your **Reader/Writer Notebook.**

Meet the Author

Ray Bradbury
born 1920

Vivid Imagination
As a boy in Illinois, Ray Bradbury had a passion for adventure stories, secret code rings, and comic strips. He started writing fiction to create his own imaginary worlds.

Creative Genius
While some of Bradbury's most famous stories are science fiction, he doesn't think of himself as a science fiction writer. Instead, he thinks of himself as someone who simply writes what he sees, just "through a different lens." Though he writes about future technology and space travel, Bradbury is a bit old-fashioned. He has never learned to drive a car, preferring to get around by riding a bicycle.

BACKGROUND TO THE STORY
Beyond Summer
When Bradbury wrote "All Summer in a Day" in 1954, very little was known about Venus. The mysterious planet lay hidden beneath a very heavy layer of clouds. Scientists learned a few years later that this dense cloud cover did not result in constant rain, as occurs in Bradbury's story. Instead, the clouds appear to trap heat. The temperature at the surface of the planet is about 860°F, which is much too hot for rainfall.

Author Online
THINK central

Go to **thinkcentral.com.**
KEYWORD: HML6-67

67

All Summer in a Day

Ray Bradbury

"Ready?"

"Ready."

"Now?"

"Soon."

"Do the scientists really know? Will it happen today, will it?"

"Look, look; see for yourself!"

The children pressed to each other like so many roses, so many weeds, intermixed, peering out for a look at the hidden sun.

It rained.

10 It had been raining for seven years; thousands upon thousands of days compounded and filled from one end to the other with rain, with the drum and gush of water, with the sweet crystal fall of showers and the concussion[1] of storms so heavy they were tidal waves come over the islands. A thousand forests had been crushed under the rain and grown up a thousand times to be crushed again. And this was the way life was forever on the planet Venus, and this was the school room of the children of the rocket men and women who had come to a raining world to set up civilization and live out their lives. **Ⓐ**

Analyze Visuals ▶

What words would you use to describe this photograph?

Language Coach

Dialogue Reread lines 1–8. Notice that Bradbury does not not identify who is speaking. Who is speaking?

Ⓐ SETTING
Reread lines 7–18. What do the **details** in each sentence tell you about where and when the story takes place?

---

1. **concussion** (kən-kŭsh′ən): pounding.

"It's stopping, it's stopping!"

20   "Yes, yes!"

Margot stood apart from them, from these children who could never remember a time when there wasn't rain and rain and rain. They were all nine years old, and if there had been a day, seven years ago, when the sun came out for an hour and showed its face to the stunned world, they could not recall. Sometimes, at night, she heard them stir, in remembrance, and she knew they were dreaming and remembering gold or a yellow crayon or a coin large enough to buy the world with. She knew that they thought they remembered a warmness, like a blushing in the face, in the body, in the arms and legs and trembling hands. But then they

30 always awoke to the tatting drum,[2] the endless shaking down of clear bead necklaces upon the roof, the walk, the gardens, the forest, and their dreams were gone.

All day yesterday they had read in class, about the sun. About how like a lemon it was, and how hot. And they had written small stories or essays or poems about it:

> "I think the sun is a flower,
> That blooms for just one hour."

That was Margot's poem, read in a quiet voice in the still classroom while the rain was falling outside.

40   "Aw, you didn't write that!" protested one of the boys.

"I did," said Margot. "I *did.*"

"William!" said the teacher.

But that was yesterday. Now, the rain was **slackening,** and the children were crushed to the great thick windows.

"Where's teacher?"

"She'll be back."

"She'd better hurry, we'll miss it!"

They turned on themselves, like a feverish wheel, all tumbling spokes.

Margot stood alone. She was a very frail girl who looked as if she had

50 been lost in the rain for years and the rain had washed out the blue from her eyes and the red from her mouth and the yellow from her hair. She was an old photograph dusted from an album, whitened away, and if she spoke at all her voice would be a ghost. Now she stood, separate, staring at the rain and the loud wet world beyond the huge glass.

"What're *you* looking at?" said William.

Margot said nothing.

---

2. **tatting drum:** a continuous, soft, beating sound.

SCIENCE CONNECTION

Exploration of Venus began with a "flyby" spacecraft from the Soviet Union in 1961 and another from the United States in 1962. Since then, orbiting spacecraft and robotic equipment have provided pictures and information about conditions on Venus.

Language Coach

Dialogue Reread lines 40–42. How can you tell who is speaking in line 40?

slacken (slăk′ən) *v.* to slow down or lessen

"Speak when you're spoken to." He gave her a shove. But she did not move; rather, she let herself be moved only by him and nothing else.

They edged away from her, they would not look at her. She felt them
60 go away. And this was because she would play no games with them in the echoing tunnels of the underground city. If they tagged her and ran, she stood blinking after them and did not follow. When the class sang songs about happiness and life and games, her lips barely moved. Only when they sang about the sun and the summer did her lips move, as she watched the drenched windows.

And then, of course, the biggest crime of all was that she had come here only five years ago from Earth, and she remembered the sun and the way the sun was and the sky was, when she was four, in Ohio. And they, they had been on Venus all their lives, and they had been only two years old
70 when last the sun came out, and had long since forgotten the color and heat of it and the way that it really was. But Margot remembered. **B**

"It's like a penny," she said once, eyes closed.

"No it's not!" the children cried.

"It's like a fire," she said, "in the stove."

"You're lying; you don't remember!" cried the children.

But she remembered and stood quietly apart from all of them and watched the patterning windows. And once, a month ago, she had refused to shower in the school shower-rooms, had clutched her hands to her ears and over her head, screaming the water mustn't touch her head. So after
80 that, dimly, dimly, she sensed it, she was different and they knew her difference and kept away. **C**

There was talk that her father and mother were taking her back to Earth next year; it seemed vital to her that they do so, though it would mean the loss of thousands of dollars to her family. And so, the children hated her for all these reasons, of big and little consequence. They hated her pale, snow face, her waiting silence, her thinness and her possible future.

"Get away!" The boy gave her another push. "What're you waiting for?"

Then, for the first time, she turned and looked at him. And what she
90 was waiting for was in her eyes.

"Well, don't wait around here!" cried the boy, savagely. "You won't see nothing!"

Her lips moved.

"Nothing!" he cried. "It was all a joke, wasn't it?" He turned to the other children. "Nothing's happening today. *Is* it?"

They all blinked at him and then, understanding, laughed and shook their heads. "Nothing, nothing!" **D**

B CONFLICT
What is the conflict between Margot and her classmates?

C MAKE INFERENCES
Why does Margot refuse to take a shower?

D SETTING
Reread lines 88–97. If Venus had a climate like Earth's, do you think Margot would have a problem with the boy? Explain how a change in setting would affect the conflict.

"Oh, but," Margot whispered, her eyes helpless. "But, this is the day, the scientists predict, they say, they *know*, the sun . . ."

100 "All a joke!" said the boy, and seized her roughly. "Hey, everyone, let's put her in a closet before teacher comes!"

"No," said Margot, falling back.

They surged about her, caught her up, and bore her, protesting, and then pleading, and then crying, back into a tunnel, a room, a closet, where they slammed and locked the door. They stood looking at the door and saw it tremble from her beating and throwing herself against it. They heard her muffled cries. Then, smiling, they turned and went out and back down the tunnel, just as the teacher arrived. **E**

"Ready, children?" She glanced at her watch.

110 "Yes!" said everyone.

"Are we all here?"

"Yes!"

The rain slackened still more.

They crowded to the huge door.

The rain stopped.

It was as if, in the midst of a film concerning an avalanche, a tornado, a hurricane, a volcanic eruption, something had, first, gone wrong with the sound **apparatus,** thus muffling and finally cutting off all noise, all of the blasts and repercussions and thunders, and then, secondly, ripped

120 the film from the projector and inserted in its place a peaceful tropical slide which did not move or tremor. The world ground to a standstill. The silence was so **immense** and unbelievable that you felt that your ears had been stuffed or you had lost your hearing altogether. The children put their hands to their ears. They stood apart. The door slid back and the smell of the silent, waiting world came in to them.

The sun came out. **F**

It was the color of flaming bronze and it was very large. And the sky around it was a blazing blue tile color. And the jungle burned with sunlight as the children, released from their spell, rushed out, yelling, into the

130 summer-time.

"Now, don't go too far," called the teacher after them. "You've only one hour, you know. You wouldn't want to get caught out!"

But they were running and turning their faces up to the sky and feeling the sun on their cheeks like a warm iron; they were taking off their jackets and letting the sun burn their arms.

"Oh, it's better than the sun-lamps, isn't it?"

E CAUSE AND EFFECT
A **cause** is an event that makes something happen. An **effect** is what happens as a result of a cause. What causes the other children to dislike Margot? What do they do to her as a result?

apparatus (ăp′ə-răt′əs) *n.* a device or set of equipment used for a specific purpose

immense (ĭ-mĕns′) *adj.* extremely big; huge

F PLOT
Reread lines 115–126. What changes do the children notice when the sun comes out? What impact does the setting have on the plot in line 126?

"Much, much better!"

They stopped running and stood in the great jungle that covered Venus, that grew and never stopped growing, **tumultuously,** even as you watched it. It was a nest of octopuses, clustering up great arms of flesh-like weed, wavering, flowering in this brief spring. It was the color of rubber and ash, this jungle, from the many years without sun. It was the color of stones and white cheeses and ink. **G**

The children lay out, laughing, on the jungle mattress, and heard it sigh and squeak under them, **resilient** and alive. They ran among the trees, they slipped and fell, they pushed each other, they played hide-and-seek and tag, but most of all they squinted at the sun until tears ran down their faces, they put their hands up at that yellowness and that amazing blueness, and they breathed of the fresh fresh air and listened and listened to the silence which suspended them in a blessed sea of no sound and no motion. They looked at everything and **savored** everything. Then, wildly, like animals escaped from their caves, they ran and ran in shouting circles. They ran for an hour and did not stop running. **H**

And then—

In the midst of their running, one of the girls wailed.

Everyone stopped.

The girl, standing in the open, held out her hand.

"Oh, look, look," she said, trembling.

They came slowly to look at her opened palm.

tumultuously
(tŏŏ-mŭl′chōō-əs′lē)
adv. in a wild or disorderly way

G SETTING
What is unusual about the plants on Venus?

resilient (rĭ-zĭl′yənt) *adj.*
flexible and springy

savor (sā′vər) *v.* to take great pleasure in

H CAUSE AND EFFECT
Reread lines 144–153. How do the children react to the change in the weather?

160 In the center of it, cupped and huge, was a single raindrop.

She began to cry, looking at it.

They glanced quickly at the sky.

"Oh. Oh."

A few cold drops fell on their noses and their cheeks and their mouths. The sun faded behind a stir of mist. A wind blew cool around them. They turned and started to walk back toward the underground house, their hands at their sides, their smiles vanishing away.

A boom of thunder startled them and like leaves before a new hurricane, they tumbled upon each other and ran. Lightning struck ten miles away, 170 five miles away, a mile, a half-mile. The sky darkened into midnight in a flash.

They stood in the doorway of the underground for a moment until it was raining hard. Then they closed the door and heard the gigantic sound of the rain falling in tons and avalanches everywhere and forever.

"Will it be seven more years?"

"Yes. Seven."

Then one of them gave a little cry.

"Margot!"

"What?"

180 "She's still in the closet where we locked her."

"Margot."

They stood as if someone had driven them, like so many stakes, into the floor. They looked at each other and then looked away. They glanced out at the world that was raining now and raining and raining steadily. They could not meet each other's glances. Their faces were solemn and pale. They looked at their hands and feet, their faces down.

"Margot."

One of the girls said, "Well . . . ?"

No one moved.

190 "Go on," whispered the girl. ◆

They walked slowly down the hall in the sound of cold rain. They turned through the doorway to the room, in the sound of the storm and thunder, lightning on their faces, blue and terrible. They walked over to the closet door slowly and stood by it.

Behind the closet door was only silence.

They unlocked the door, even more slowly, and let Margot out. ❧ ❶

◆ **GRAMMAR IN CONTEXT**
A **speaker tag,** such as the phrase *whispered the girl* in line 190, identifies who is speaking. Since the quotation comes before the speaker tag, Bradbury correctly places a comma at the end of the quotation before the quotation mark and a period at the end of the speaker tag.

❶ **MAKE INFERENCES**
How might the children feel toward Margot now that they, too, have seen the sun?

Comprehension

1. **Recall** How often does the sun shine on Venus?

2. **Clarify** Why is Margot the only child who remembers the sun?

3. **Summarize** What is the conflict and resolution of this story?

Text Analysis

⬤ 4. **Make Inferences** Review the inferences that you recorded as you read the story. Were any of your ideas wrong or incomplete based on what you learned later on in the story? Adjust your equations as needed.

⬤ 5. **Identify Cause and Effect** A cause-and-effect relationship occurs when one event causes another event to happen. What events in the story and prior to the story lead to Margot's unhappiness?

⬤ 6. **Analyze Setting** Think about what happens on a sunny day on Earth. How is that day different from the sunny day in the story? Use a Y chart to **compare and contrast** which details might stay the same and which might be different.

Sunny Day on Earth

Sunny Day on Venus
The children prepare by doing activities about the sun.

Similarities
Children enjoy time in the sun.

⬤ 7. **Examine Conflict** An **external conflict** is a struggle between a character and an outside force. An **internal conflict** occurs when a character is struggling with his or her own feelings. Reread lines 182–196. Are the children facing an external or internal conflict as they walk to the closet and unlock the door for Margot? Explain.

⬤ 8. **Analyze Plot and Setting** How does the **setting** of this story influence the **plot,** including the conflict and resolution? Would there still be a story if Bradbury's Venus had less extreme weather? Explain.

Extension and Challenge

9. 🔬 **SCIENCE CONNECTION** Venus and Earth have often been referred to as "twin planets." Research Venus and Earth to learn more about their similarities and differences.

What if your whole WORLD changed?

Describe what you sketched for your vision of your world. What elements of your world would you most hate to see disappear, and why?

COMMON CORE

RL1 Cite textual evidence to support inferences drawn from the text. **RL3** Describe how characters respond as the plot moves toward a resolution. **RL5** Analyze how a particular sentence fits into the structure of a text and contributes to the development of the setting or plot.

Venus   Earth

Vocabulary in Context

▲ VOCABULARY PRACTICE

For each numbered item below, choose the word that differs most in meaning from the other words.

1. (a) prepare, (b) appreciate, (c) enjoy, (d) savor
2. (a) appliance, (b) device, (c) apparatus, (d) operator
3. (a) slacken, (b) lessen, (c) decrease, (d) enlarge
4. (a) enormous, (b) immense, (c) gigantic, (d) distant
5. (a) tumultuously, (b) carefully, (c) thoughtfully, (d) cautiously
6. (a) elastic, (b) nervous, (c) flexible, (d) resilient

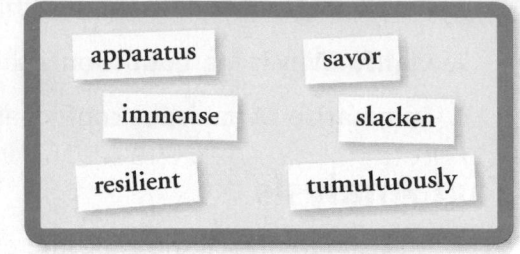

apparatus   savor

immense   slacken

resilient   tumultuously

ACADEMIC VOCABULARY IN SPEAKING

• affect   • analyze   • evidence   • impact   • provide

With a partner, discuss the possible **impact** on Margot of being shut in the closet. **Provide evidence** from the text to support your response. Use at least two Academic Vocabulary words in your discussion.

VOCABULARY STRATEGY: FIND THE BEST SYNONYM

A **synonym** is a word that has the same or similar meaning as another word. A book of synonyms is called a **thesaurus.** You can use a thesaurus, which is available in print and online versions, to find words that express a specific meaning. When you look up a common word like *big* in a thesaurus, you will find many alternate word choices: *immense, enormous, huge,* and so on. In this story, the writer uses *immense* to describe the silence that occurs after the rain stops. This word gives the reader a clearer sense of the silence than a word like *enormous* or *huge* would.

PRACTICE Choose the synonym from the box that best fits the meaning of each sentence. Use a thesaurus if you need help.

1. The _____ poster did not fit into the small frame.
2. The _____ theater easily held the 600 students.
3. Fields of wheat stretched for miles across the _____ plains.
4. The _____ package was hard to lift.

COMMON CORE

L 4c Consult thesauruses, both print and digital, to clarify meaning.

Synonyms for *big*
hefty
oversized
spacious
vast

Interactive Vocabulary THINK central

Go to **thinkcentral.com**.
KEYWORD: HML6-76

Language

◆ **GRAMMAR IN CONTEXT:** Punctuate Dialogue Correctly

Keep the following rules in mind when you write **dialogue:**

- Put quotation marks before and after a speaker's exact words.
- Place punctuation marks such as commas and periods inside the quotation marks.
- If a speaker tag, such as *he said,* comes before the quotation, set a comma after the speaker tag.
- If a speaker tag follows the dialogue, set a comma after the quotation (before the closing quotation mark) and a period after the speaker tag.

> *Original:* Margot said I have seen the sun.
>
> *Revised:* Margot said, "I have seen the sun."

PRACTICE Rewrite the following sentences. Correct the misplaced punctuation marks and insert any missing marks.

1. "It's been raining for years" the girl said.
2. "Let's go outside the teacher said."
3. The boy said "What are you waiting for?"
4. The sun looks like a penny Margot said

*For more help with punctuating dialogue, see page R50 in the **Grammar Handbook.***

READING-WRITING CONNECTION

YOUR TURN Broaden your understanding of "All Summer in a Day" by responding to this prompt. Then use the **revising tip** to improve your writing.

WRITING PROMPT	REVISING TIP
Extended Constructed Response: Dialogue What would Margot say to her classmates and teacher now that she has been freed? How would they respond to her? Write a **brief dialogue** that begins at the moment Margot walks out of the closet.	Review your response. Have you used correct punctuation in your dialogue? If not, revise your writing.

COMMON CORE

L 2 Demonstrate command of the conventions of punctuation. **W 3** Write narratives to develop imagined events.

Interactive Revision

THINK central

Go to **thinkcentral.com**.
KEYWORD: HML6-77

Settling in Space

 Video link at **thinkcentral.com**

- Magazine Article, page 79
- Online Article, page 80
- Illustrations, page 84

Use with "All Summer in a Day," page 68.

What's the Connection?

In "All Summer in a Day," you read about people living in a colony on Venus. What is Venus *really* like? What would it be like to live in a space colony? Study the articles and images on the next few pages to get the science facts about Bradbury's science fiction setting.

Standards Focus: Synthesize Ideas Across Texts

When you read several texts on the same topic, you naturally connect the ideas you find in each piece. You can then synthesize , or integrate, this information by putting it all together. Follow these steps to synthesize the ideas in the selections that follow:

1. **Find the Main Idea** The **main idea** is the most important point the writer makes about a topic. When you have to find the main idea of a piece of nonfiction, ask yourself, "What's the subject?" Sometimes the title tells you what the subject is. Now ask yourself, "What about it?" Your answer to that question is the main idea. Remember that a text may contain more than one main idea.

2. **Make Connections** Think about the relationships among the main ideas of all of the texts. In what ways are they connected? How are they different? How does one idea relate to or expand on another?

3. **Synthesize Ideas** To **synthesize** information means to take individual pieces of information and combine them in order to gain a better understanding of a topic.

Organize your ideas about each of the three selections in a chart like the one below.

Selection	Main Ideas	Supporting Details
"Weather That's Out of This World"	• Venus's weather is much worse than Earth's weather.	• The temperature on Venus can melt lead. • Acid rain constantly falls on Venus.
"Space Settlements"		

COMMON CORE

RI 1 Cite textual evidence to support what the text says explicitly.
RI 2 Determine a central idea of a text and how it is conveyed through details. **RI 7** Integrate information presented in different media or formats to develop a coherent understanding of a topic.

Weather That's Out of This World! Alan Dyer

**If you think Earth's weather is wild,
just wait until you see what it's like elsewhere in the solar system.**

Hot, Sizzling Venus

"This is VTN—the Venus Television Network—with the latest forecast for the second planet from the Sun: hot today, hot tomorrow, and hot the following day. It will also be cloudy, with no sign of any sunshine. Take your glass umbrella—we're in for more acid rain."

If there were meteorologists on Venus, that's the kind of forecast they would have to give. Venus is a nasty place to live. Think of the hottest day you can remember. Then imagine what it would be like if it were 10 times hotter—that's what it's like on Venus.

10 Venus is the hottest planet in the solar system. The temperature at its surface is a searing 860 degrees Fahrenheit, day and night. The superhigh temperature surprised many astronomers, who once thought Mercury would be hotter, since it is closer to the Sun. But Venus has something very important that Mercury lacks—an <u>atmosphere</u>. Unlike Earth's atmosphere, which is made of oxygen and nitrogen, the air on Venus is mostly carbon dioxide gas, one of the so-called greenhouse gases. Like the glass in a greenhouse, carbon dioxide in the air traps heat coming from the Sun. With no place to go, the heat builds up. In the case of Venus, its thick carbon dioxide blanket has made the planet so hot that
20 some metals, such as lead, would melt on its surface.

Adding to Venus's unpleasant weather is a constant drizzle from the thick clouds that surround the planet. But it's not water that falls from the sky there. Instead, the rain is made of droplets of sulfuric acid, a corrosive liquid that burns anything it touches. Between the blistering heat and the sizzling acid rain, Venus's weather is much worse than anything we could find on Earth. **A**

FOCUS ON FORM
A **science article** is a short piece of nonfiction about a scientific subject. The author's purpose for writing a science article is usually to inform or explain. Science articles often use **text features,** like illustrations and bulleted lists, to help present information more clearly.

For more information about text features, see page R3 in the **Reading Handbook.**

A FIND THE MAIN IDEA
State the **main idea** of this article. What details support the main idea? Add this information to your chart.

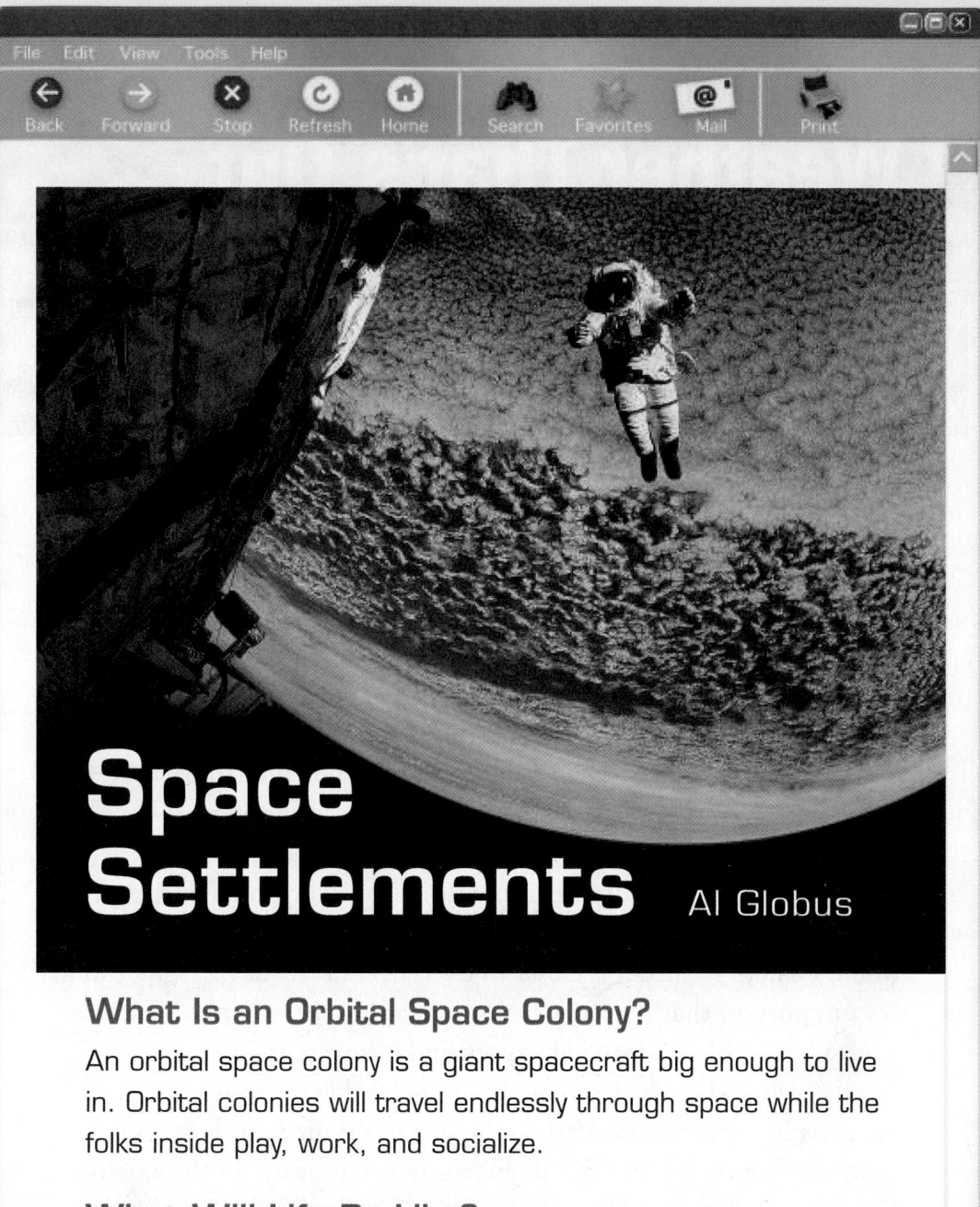

What Is an Orbital Space Colony?

An orbital space colony is a giant spacecraft big enough to live in. Orbital colonies will travel endlessly through space while the folks inside play, work, and socialize.

What Will Life Be Like?

Living inside a space colony will, in many ways, be like living on Earth. People will have houses or apartments. They will go to work and to school. There will be shops, sports teams, concerts, and movies. People will go to parties with their friends, just like
10 on Earth. However, there will also be many differences. **B**

B SYNTHESIZE IDEAS ACROSS TEXTS
What is the topic of this online article? How might space colonies enable people to study Venus?

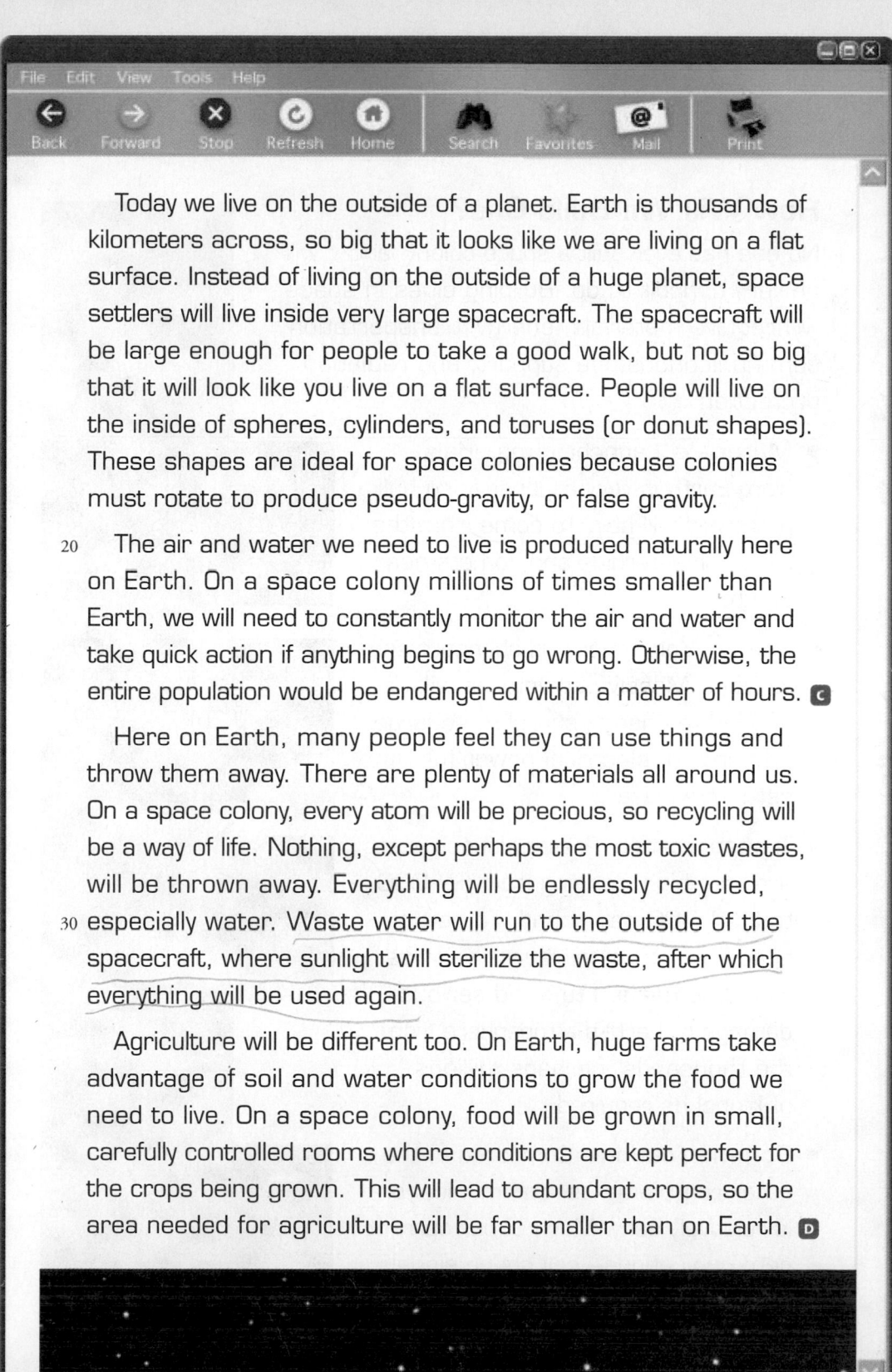

File   Edit   View   Tools   Help

Back   Forward   Stop   Refresh   Home   Search   Favorites   Mail   Print

Today we live on the outside of a planet. Earth is thousands of kilometers across, so big that it looks like we are living on a flat surface. Instead of living on the outside of a huge planet, space settlers will live inside very large spacecraft. The spacecraft will be large enough for people to take a good walk, but not so big that it will look like you live on a flat surface. People will live on the inside of spheres, cylinders, and toruses (or donut shapes). These shapes are ideal for space colonies because colonies must rotate to produce pseudo-gravity, or false gravity.

20   The air and water we need to live is produced naturally here on Earth. On a space colony millions of times smaller than Earth, we will need to constantly monitor the air and water and take quick action if anything begins to go wrong. Otherwise, the entire population would be endangered within a matter of hours. **C**

Here on Earth, many people feel they can use things and throw them away. There are plenty of materials all around us. On a space colony, every atom will be precious, so recycling will be a way of life. Nothing, except perhaps the most toxic wastes, will be thrown away. Everything will be endlessly recycled,

30 especially water. Waste water will run to the outside of the spacecraft, where sunlight will sterilize the waste, after which everything will be used again.

Agriculture will be different too. On Earth, huge farms take advantage of soil and water conditions to grow the food we need to live. On a space colony, food will be grown in small, carefully controlled rooms where conditions are kept perfect for the crops being grown. This will lead to abundant crops, so the area needed for agriculture will be far smaller than on Earth. **D**

Internet

C SYNTHESIZE IDEAS ACROSS TEXTS
What information about air and water quality on a space colony is provided in this paragraph? How does the quality of life in a space colony compare to the quality of life on Venus as described in the previous article? Add this information to your chart.

D SYNTHESIZE IDEAS ACROSS TEXTS
How will conditions for growing food enable people to survive in space?

E FIND THE MAIN IDEA
Reread lines 40–44. Then skim the bulleted items that follow. How does each support the main idea?

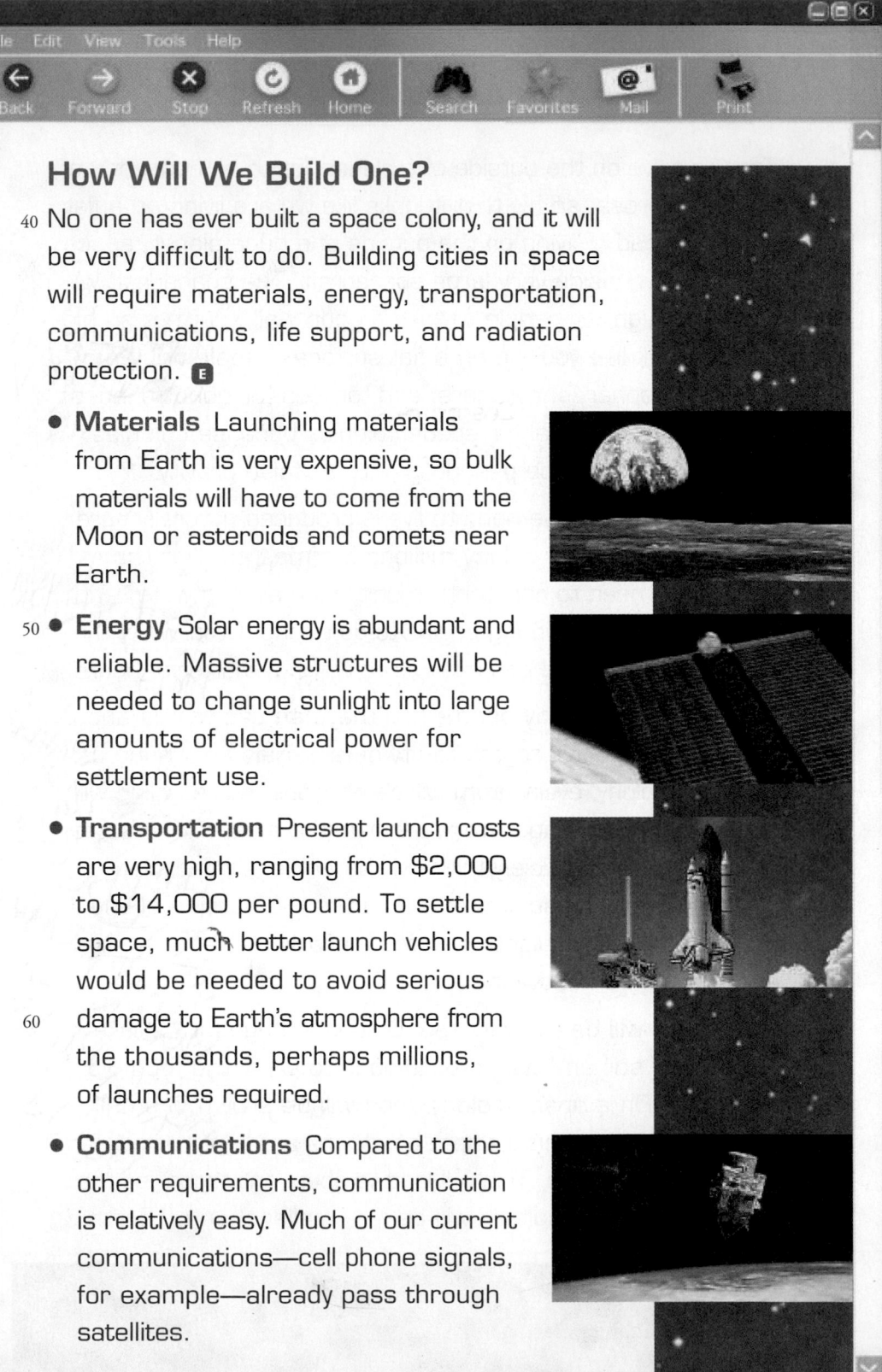

How Will We Build One?

40 No one has ever built a space colony, and it will be very difficult to do. Building cities in space will require materials, energy, transportation, communications, life support, and radiation protection. **E**

- **Materials** Launching materials from Earth is very expensive, so bulk materials will have to come from the Moon or asteroids and comets near Earth.

50 - **Energy** Solar energy is abundant and reliable. Massive structures will be needed to change sunlight into large amounts of electrical power for settlement use.

- **Transportation** Present launch costs are very high, ranging from $2,000 to $14,000 per pound. To settle space, much better launch vehicles would be needed to avoid serious

60 damage to Earth's atmosphere from the thousands, perhaps millions, of launches required.

- **Communications** Compared to the other requirements, communication is relatively easy. Much of our current communications—cell phone signals, for example—already pass through satellites.

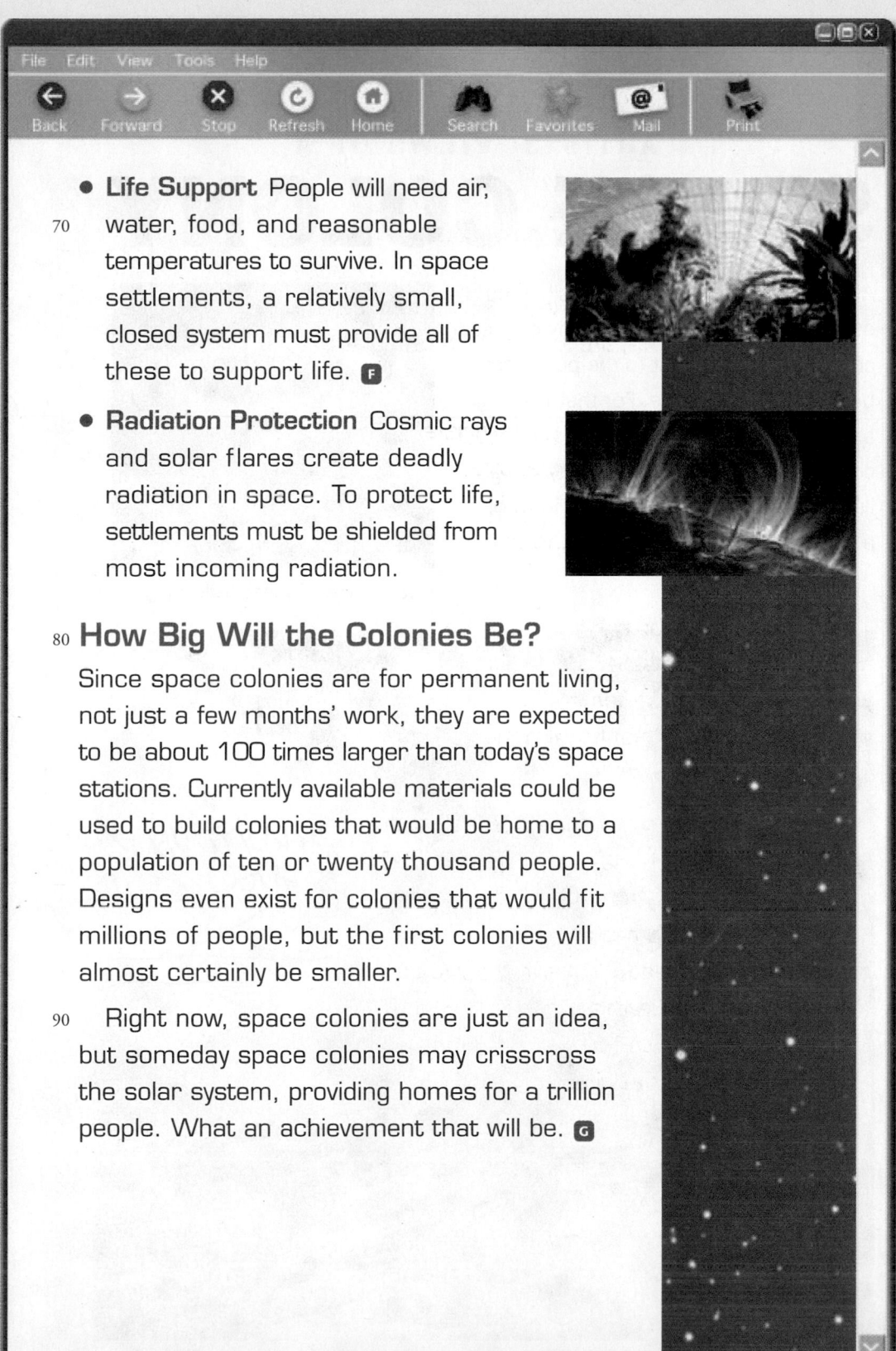

- **Life Support** People will need air,
70 water, food, and reasonable
temperatures to survive. In space
settlements, a relatively small,
closed system must provide all of
these to support life. **F**

- **Radiation Protection** Cosmic rays
and solar flares create deadly
radiation in space. To protect life,
settlements must be shielded from
most incoming radiation.

80 How Big Will the Colonies Be?

Since space colonies are for permanent living,
not just a few months' work, they are expected
to be about 100 times larger than today's space
stations. Currently available materials could be
used to build colonies that would be home to a
population of ten or twenty thousand people.
Designs even exist for colonies that would fit
millions of people, but the first colonies will
almost certainly be smaller.

90   Right now, space colonies are just an idea,
but someday space colonies may crisscross
the solar system, providing homes for a trillion
people. What an achievement that will be. **G**

COMMON CORE RI 1

F **SYNTHESIZE IDEAS ACROSS TEXTS**
To fully understand a topic like space exploration, you need to **synthesize**, or combine facts, details, and ideas from different sources. When you integrate this information, you will be able to form new ideas about the topic. Recall what you learned about Venus's weather in "Weather That's Out of This World" (page 79). How does that information add to your understanding of the necessity of the life support described in lines 69–74?

G **SYNTHESIZE IDEAS ACROSS TEXTS**
How did the information from this online article improve your understanding of living in space? Why is it more likely that people would live in space colonies rather than try to settle on the surface of planets like Venus?

ARTISTS' VIEWS OF A
SPACE COLONY

As scientists explore the possibilities of how to colonize space, many of the concepts they present to the public can be difficult to visualize. For that reason, artists often work with scientists to help convey their ideas. Here, artists have illustrated inside and outside views of a possible space colony.

Exterior view of a space colony **H**

H **SCIENCE ARTICLE**
In an informational text, the visual elements on the page are deliberately instructive. In scientific articles, an artist's illustrations provide supporting and clarifying information. How do these illustrations add to your understanding of living in a space colony?

Interior view of a space colony

Comprehension

1. **Recall** What do you learn about Venus from the Venus Television Network "broadcast"?

2. **Summarize** Briefly describe the main features of the orbital space colony shown in the two illustrations on page 84.

Text Analysis

3. **Find the Main Idea** Name three ways that life on a space colony would differ from life on Earth, according to "Space Settlements."

4. **Analyze Characteristics of Form** What are three characteristics of "Space Settlements" that make it a **science article?** Explain.

5. **Synthesize Ideas Across Texts** Consider what you know of neighborhoods on Earth and what you learned about orbital space colonies in the articles you read. Do you think the illustrations of an orbital space colony are realistic? Why or why not?

COMMON CORE

RI 1 Cite textual evidence to support what the text says explicitly. **RI 2** Determine the a central idea of a text and how it is conveyed through details. **RI 7** Integrate information presented in different media or formats to develop a coherent understanding of a topic. **W 2** Write informative/ explanatory texts to examine a topic.

Read for Information: Synthesize Ideas Across Texts

WRITING PROMPT

The three texts you just read provide different ideas about living in space. In a paragraph, explain what you learned about living in space. Consider the facts in "Weather That's Out of This World!" and the facts in "Space Settlements." Think about how the illustrations in "Artists' Views of a Space Colony" added to your understanding. Finally, use the chart you created as you read to **integrate,** or combine, what you learned into a paragraph.

To answer this prompt, follow these steps:

1. Review the chart you created as you read each selection.

2. Make sure the information in the chart represents the main ideas in each selection and includes details that support each selection's main idea.

3. Make connections between the texts by drawing lines on your chart to link ideas that appear in more than one text.

4. Write a paragraph in which you sum up what you've learned about living in space.

Lob's Girl
Short Story by Joan Aiken

How powerful is LOYALTY?

COMMON CORE

RL 1 Cite textual evidence to support what the text says explicitly. RL 5 Analyze how a particular sentence fits into the structure of a text and contributes to the development of the plot. L 4b Use common affixes as clues to the meaning of a word.

Has there ever been a time when a friend stood by you in a time of need? If so, then you know how important loyalty, or devotion, can be. A reliable friend or family member can help you overcome the toughest problems. In "Lob's Girl," a girl and her family discover just how powerful loyalty can be.

WEB IT Create a web of the people and pets to which you are loyal. Then explain how you show your loyalty to each.

● TEXT ANALYSIS: FORESHADOWING

Sometimes writers build excitement and curiosity by providing a hint about something that will happen later in the story. This hint is known as **foreshadowing.** Foreshadowing may appear in

- what the characters say (*"I wish we could play with him every day."*)
- what the characters do (*Don came home very late and grim-faced.*)
- descriptions of setting (*narrow, steep, twisting hillroad*)

As you read "Lob's Girl," look for examples of foreshadowing.

● READING SKILL: IDENTIFY SEQUENCE

A story's events are presented in a specific order, or **sequence.** Certain words and phrases can help you identify the sequence of events, such as

- the next day
- at ten o'clock
- at the same time
- by this morning
- then
- a few minutes later

As you read, record the story's sequence of events on a timeline like the one shown. Above each event, record the clue words or phrases that signal it.

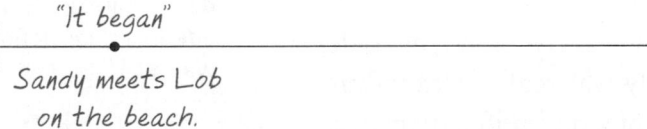

"It began"

Sandy meets Lob
on the beach.

▲ VOCABULARY IN CONTEXT

The boldfaced words below help Joan Aiken tell the story of a very determined dog. To show how many you already know, provide a definition for each boldfaced word.

1. The **agitated** owner searches for his lost pet.
2. When they see the dog, the children **erupt** with joy.
3. The dog is **reluctant** to leave his new friends.
4. As he turns to leave, the dog looks **melancholy.**
5. The dog licks his owner as if to **atone** for running away.
6. He runs **decisively** toward his beloved new owner.

Complete the activities in your **Reader/Writer Notebook.**

Lob's Girl

Joan Aiken

S ome people choose their dogs, and some dogs choose their people. The Pengelly family had no say in the choosing of Lob; he came to them in the second way, and very **decisively.**

It began on the beach, the summer when Sandy was five, Don, her older brother, twelve, and the twins were three. Sandy was really Alexandra, because her grandmother had a beautiful picture of a queen in a diamond tiara and high collar of pearls. It hung by Granny Pearce's kitchen sink and was as familiar as the doormat. When Sandy was born everyone agreed that she was the living spit[1] of the picture, and so she was called Alexandra and
10 Sandy for short. **A**

On this summer day she was lying peacefully reading a comic and not keeping an eye on the twins, who didn't need it because they were occupied in seeing which of them could wrap the most seaweed around the other one's legs. Father—Bert Pengelly—and Don were up on the Hard[2] painting the bottom boards of the boat in which Father went fishing for pilchards.[3] And Mother—Jean Pengelly—was getting ahead with making the Christmas puddings because she never felt easy in her mind if they

decisively (dĭ-sī′sĭv′lē) *adv.* in a clear, definite way

A SEQUENCE
What words signal the first important event?

Analyze Visuals ▸

What can you **infer** about the dog based on the details in the image?

---

1. **the living spit:** an exact likeness, often worded as "the spitting image."
2. **Hard:** a landing place for boats.
3. **pilchards** (pĭl′chərdz): small fish similar to sardines.

German Shepherd. ©Keiler Sensenbrenner.

weren't made and safely put away by the end of August. As usual, each member of the family was happily getting on with his or her own affairs.

20 Little did they guess how soon this state of things would be changed by the large new member who was going to **erupt** into their midst.

Sandy rolled onto her back to make sure that the twins were not climbing on slippery rocks or getting cut off by the tide. At the same moment a large body struck her forcibly in the midriff, and she was covered by flying sand. Instinctively she shut her eyes and felt the sand being wiped off her face by something that seemed like a warm, rough, damp flannel. She opened her eyes and looked. It was a tongue. Its owner was a large and bouncy young Alsatian, or German shepherd, with topaz eyes, black-tipped prick ears, a thick, soft coat, and a bushy, black-tipped tail.

30 "*Lob!*" shouted a man farther up the beach. "Lob, come here!"

But Lob, as if trying to **atone** for the surprise he had given her, went on licking the sand off Sandy's face, wagging his tail so hard while he kept on knocking up more clouds of sand. His owner, a gray-haired man with a limp, walked over as quickly as he could and seized him by the collar.

"I hope he didn't give you a fright?" the man said to Sandy. "He meant it in play—he's only young."

erupt (ĭ-rŭpt') *v.* to release one's anger or enthusiasm in a sudden, noisy way

atone (ə-tōn') *v.* to seek pardon; to make up for

Analyze Visuals ▾

What **details** do you notice in this illustration?

"Oh, no, I think he's *beautiful*," said Sandy truly. She picked up a bit of driftwood and threw it. Lob, whisking easily out of his master's grip, was after it like a sand-colored bullet. He came back with the stick, beaming, and gave it to Sandy. At the same time he gave himself, though no one else was aware of this at the time. But with Sandy, too, it was love at first sight, and when, after a lot more stick-throwing, she and the twins joined Father and Don to go home for tea, they cast many a backward glance at Lob being led firmly away by his master.

"I wish we could play with him every day," Tess sighed.

"Why can't we?" said Tim.

Sandy explained. "Because Mr. Dodsworth, who owns him, is from Liverpool, and he is only staying at the Fisherman's Arms till Saturday."

"Is Liverpool a long way off?"

"Right at the other end of England from Cornwall, I'm afraid."

It was a Cornish[4] fishing village where the Pengelly family lived, with rocks and cliffs and a strip of beach and a little round harbor, and palm trees growing in the gardens of the little whitewashed stone houses. The village was approached by a narrow, steep, twisting hillroad and guarded by a notice that said LOW GEAR FOR 1½ MILES, DANGEROUS TO CYCLISTS. **B**

The Pengelly children went home to scones with Cornish cream and jam, thinking they had seen the last of Lob. But they were much mistaken. The whole family was playing cards by the fire in the front room after supper when there was a loud thump and a crash of china in the kitchen.

"My Christmas puddings!" exclaimed Jean, and ran out.

"Did you put TNT in them, then?" her husband said.

But it was Lob, who, finding the front door shut, had gone around to the back and bounced in through the open kitchen window, where the puddings were cooling on the sill. Luckily only the smallest was knocked down and broken.

Lob stood on his hind legs and plastered Sandy's face with licks. Then he did the same for the twins, who shrieked with joy.

"Where does this friend of yours come from?" inquired Mr. Pengelly.

"He's staying at the Fisherman's Arms—I mean his owner is."

"Then he must go back there. Find a bit of string, Sandy, to tie to his collar." **C**

4. **Cornish:** in or from the English county Cornwall.

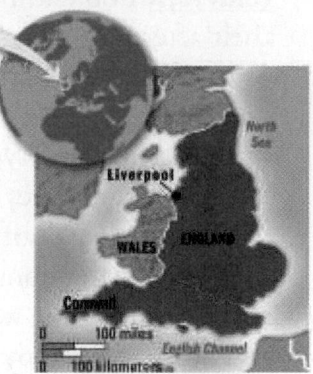

SOCIAL STUDIES CONNECTION

Cornwall is a county in southwestern England. Liverpool is a large city in northern England.

B FORESHADOWING
Reread the sentence In lines 54–56. How might this be an example of foreshadowing?

C SEQUENCE
What happens after Lob's owner takes him back to Fisherman's Arms? As you read, record the events on your timeline.

"I wonder how he found his way here," Mrs. Pengelly said, when the **reluctant** Lob had been led whining away and Sandy had explained about their afternoon's game on the beach. "Fisherman's Arms is right round the other side of the harbor."

Lob's owner scolded him and thanked Mr. Pengelly for bringing him back. Jean Pengelly warned the children that they had better not encourage Lob any more if they met him on the beach, or it would only lead to more trouble. So they dutifully took no notice of him the next day until he spoiled their good resolutions by dashing up to them with joyful barks, wagging his tail so hard that he winded Tess and knocked Tim's legs from under him.

They had a happy day, playing on the sand.

The next day was Saturday. Sandy had found out that Mr. Dodsworth was to catch the half-past-nine train. She went out secretly, down to the station, nodded to Mr. Hoskins, the stationmaster, who wouldn't dream of charging any local for a platform ticket, and climbed up on the footbridge that led over the tracks. She didn't want to be seen, but she did want to see. She saw Mr. Dodsworth get on the train, accompanied by an unhappy-looking Lob with drooping ears and tail. Then she saw the train slide away out of sight around the next headland, with a **melancholy** wail that sounded like Lob's last good-bye.

Sandy wished she hadn't had the idea of coming to the station. She walked home miserably, with her shoulders hunched and her hands in her pockets. For the rest of the day, she was so cross and unlike herself that Tess and Tim were quite surprised, and her mother gave her a dose of senna.[5]

A week passed. Then, one evening, Mrs. Pengelly and the younger children were in the front room playing snakes and ladders.[6] Mr. Pengelly and Don had gone fishing on the evening tide. If your father is a fisherman, he will never be home at the same time from one week to the next.

Suddenly, history repeating itself, there was a crash from the kitchen. Jean Pengelly leaped up, crying, "My blackberry jelly!" She and the children had spent the morning picking and the afternoon boiling fruit.

But Sandy was ahead of her mother. With flushed cheeks and eyes like stars she had darted into the kitchen, where she and Lob were hugging one another in a frenzy of joy. About a yard of his tongue was out, and he was licking every part of her that he could reach.

"Good heavens!" exclaimed Jean. "How in the world did *he* get here?"

"He must have walked," said Sandy. "Look at his feet."

reluctant (rĭ-lŭk′tənt) *adj.* unwilling

melancholy (mĕl′ən-kŏl′ē) *adj.* sad; gloomy

---

5. **senna** (sĕn′ə): medicine made from the leaves of senna, a tree or shrub that grows in warm regions.

6. **snakes and ladders:** a board game in which game pieces climb ladders and slide down.

They were worn, dusty, and tarry. One had a cut on the pad.

"They ought to be bathed," said Jean Pengelly. "Sandy, run a bowl of warm water while I get the disinfectant."

"What'll we do about him, Mother?" said Sandy anxiously.

Mrs. Pengelly looked at her daughter's pleading eyes and sighed.

"He must go back to his owner, of course," she said, making her voice firm. "Your dad can get the address from the Fisherman's tomorrow, and phone him or send a telegram. In the meantime he'd better have a long drink and a good meal."

120 Lob was very grateful for the drink and the meal, and made no objection to having his feet washed. Then he flopped down on the hearth rug and slept in front of the fire they had lit because it was a cold, wet evening, with his head on Sandy's feet. He was a very tired dog. He had walked all the way from Liverpool to Cornwall, which is more than four hundred miles. ◆

The next day Mr. Pengelly phoned Lob's owner, and the following morning Mr. Dodsworth arrived off the night train, decidedly put out,[7] to take his pet home. That parting was worse than the first. Lob whined, Don walked out of the house, the twins burst out crying, and Sandy crept
130 up to her bedroom afterward and lay with her face pressed into the quilt, feeling as if she were bruised all over.

Jean Pengelly took them all into Plymouth to see the circus on the next day and the twins cheered up a little, but even the hour's ride in the train each way and the Liberty horses[8] and performing seals could not cure Sandy's sore heart.

She need not have bothered, though. In ten days' time Lob was back—limping this time, with a torn ear and a patch missing out of his furry coat, as if he had met and tangled with an enemy or two in the course of his four-hundred-mile walk.
140 Bert Pengelly rang up Liverpool again. Mr. Dodsworth, when he answered, sounded weary. He said, "That dog has already cost me two days that I can't spare away from my work—plus endless time in police stations and drafting newspaper advertisements. I'm too old for these ups and downs. I think we'd better face the fact, Mr. Pengelly, that it's your family he wants to stay with—that is, if you want to have him."

Bert Pengelly gulped. He was not a rich man, and Lob was a pedigreed dog.[9] He said cautiously, "How much would you be asking for him?"

---

7. **put out:** annoyed.

8. **Liberty horses:** groups of trained horses, often all white or all black, that perform simultaneously on vocal or visual command.

9. **pedigreed** (pĕd′ĭ-grēd′) **dog:** dog whose ancestry is known and recorded, making the dog more valuable.

COMMON CORE L 4b

Language Coach

Prefixes *Dis-* is a prefix that means "lack of" or "opposing." You may be familiar with this prefix in words such as *dishonest,* which means "lacking honesty." You can use prefixes to help you determine the meaning of words. How does the prefix *dis-* affect the meaning of *disinfectant* in line 113? How will using disinfectant help Lob's cut?

◆ **GRAMMAR IN CONTEXT**
Notice the sentence that begins "Then he flopped . . ." in line 121. The author has used an apostrophe followed by an *s* to show whose feet Lob rests his head on. The word *Sandy's* is an example of a singular possessive pronoun.

"Good heavens, man, I'm not suggesting I'd *sell* him to you. You must have him as a gift. Think of the train fares I'll be saving. You'll be doing me a good turn." **D**

"Is he a big eater?" Bert asked doubtfully.

By this time the children, breathless in the background listening to one side of this conversation, had realized what was in the wind and were dancing up and down with their hands clasped beseechingly.

"Oh, not for his size," Lob's owner assured Bert. "Two or three pounds of meat a day and some vegetables and gravy and biscuits—he does very well on that."

Alexandra's father looked over the telephone at his daughter's swimming eyes and trembling lips. He reached a decision. "Well, then, Mr. Dodsworth," he said briskly, "we'll accept your offer and thank you very much. The children will be overjoyed and you can be sure Lob has come to a good home. They'll look after him and see he gets enough exercise. But I can tell you," he ended firmly, "if he wants to settle in with us, he'll have to learn to eat a lot of fish."

So that was how Lob came to live with the Pengelly family. Everybody loved him and he loved them all. But there was never any question who came first with him. He was Sandy's dog. He slept by her bed and followed her everywhere he was allowed.

Nine years went by, and each summer Mr. Dodsworth came back to stay at the Fisherman's Arms and call on his erstwhile dog. Lob always met him with recognition and dignified pleasure, accompanied him for a walk or two—but showed no signs of wishing to return to Liverpool. His place, he intimated, was definitely with the Pengellys.

In the course of nine years Lob changed less than Sandy. As she went into her teens he became a little slower, a little stiffer, there was a touch of gray on his nose, but he was still a handsome dog. He and Sandy still loved one another devotedly. **E**

One evening in October all the summer visitors had left, and the little fishing town looked empty and secretive. It was a wet, windy dusk. When the children came home from school—even the twins were at high school[10] now, and Don was a full-fledged fisherman—Jean Pengelly said, "Sandy, your Aunt Rebecca says she's lonesome because Uncle Will Hoskins has gone out trawling,[11] and she wants one of you to go and spend the evening with her. You go, dear; you can take your homework with you."

Sandy looked far from enthusiastic.

D SEQUENCE
What event finally leads Lob's owner to give him to the Pengelly family?

E SEQUENCE
Note on your timeline the nine-year break in the story after Lob comes to live with the Pengellys. What might have happened during that time?

---

10. **high school:** In Great Britain, students go to high school when they are about 11 years old.

11. **trawling** (trô´lĭng): fishing with a net pulled behind a boat along the sea bottom.

"Can I take Lob with me?"

"You know Aunt Becky doesn't really like dogs—Oh, very well." Mrs. Pengelly sighed. "I suppose she'll have to put up with him as well as you."

190 Reluctantly Sandy tidied herself, took her schoolbag, put on the damp raincoat she had just taken off, fastened Lob's lead to his collar, and set off to walk through the dusk to Aunt Becky's cottage, which was five minutes' climb up the steep hill. **F**

The wind was howling through the shrouds[12] of boats drawn up on the Hard.

"Put some cheerful music on, do," said Jean Pengelly to the nearest twin. "Anything to drown that wretched sound while I make your dad's supper." So Don, who had just come in, put on some rock music, loud. Which was why the Pengellys did not hear the truck hurtle down the hill and crash against the post office wall a few minutes later. **G**

200 Dr. Travers was driving through Cornwall with his wife, taking a late holiday before patients began coming down with winter colds and flu. He saw the sign that said STEEP HILL. LOW GEAR FOR 1½ MILES. Dutifully he changed into second gear.

"We must be nearly there," said his wife, looking out of her window. "I noticed a sign on the coast road that said the Fisherman's Arms was

---

12. **shrouds** (shroudz): ropes or cables on a boat's mast, the vertical pole that supports the sails.

F **FORESHADOWING**
Reread the sentence in lines 189–192. Why might the narrator be drawing attention to the steep hill again?

G **FORESHADOWING**
Reread lines 195–199. What might the description of the crash suggest?

◄ **Analyze Visuals**
What **details** in the illustration suggest that the hill is steep?

two miles. What a narrow, dangerous hill! But the cottages are very pretty—Oh, Frank, stop, *stop!* There's a child, I'm sure it's a child—by the wall over there!"

210 Dr. Travers jammed on his brakes and brought the car to a stop. A little stream ran down by the road in a shallow stone culvert,[13] and half in the water lay something that looked, in the dusk, like a pile of clothes—or was it the body of a child? Mrs. Travers was out of the car in a flash, but her husband was quicker.

"Don't touch her, Emily!" he said sharply. "She's been hit. Can't be more than a few minutes. Remember that truck that overtook us half a mile back, speeding like the devil? Here, quick, go into that cottage and phone for an ambulance. The girl's in a bad way. I'll stay here and do what I can to stop the bleeding. Don't waste a minute."

Doctors are expert at stopping dangerous bleeding, for they know the
220 right places to press. This Dr. Travers was able to do, but he didn't dare do more; the girl was lying in a queerly crumpled heap, and he guessed she had a number of bones broken and that it would be highly dangerous to move her. He watched her with great concentration, wondering where the truck had got to and what other damage it had done.

Mrs. Travers was very quick. She had seen plenty of accident cases and knew the importance of speed. The first cottage she tried had a phone; in four minutes she was back, and in six an ambulance was wailing down the hill.

Its attendants lifted the child onto a stretcher as carefully as if she were
230 made of fine thistledown.[14] The ambulance sped off to Plymouth—for the local cottage hospital did not take serious accident cases—and Dr. Travers went down to the police station to report what he had done.

He found that the police already knew about the speeding truck—which had suffered from loss of brakes and ended up with its radiator halfway through the post-office wall. The driver was concussed[15] and shocked, but the police thought he was the only person injured—until Dr. Travers told his tale.

At half-past nine that night Aunt Rebecca Hoskins was sitting by her fire thinking aggrieved thoughts about the inconsiderateness[16]
240 of nieces who were asked to supper and never turned up, when she was startled by a neighbor, who burst in, exclaiming, "Have you heard about Sandy Pengelly, then, Mrs. Hoskins? Terrible thing, poor little soul, and

---

13. **culvert** (kŭl'vərt): a gutter or tunnel that runs along or under a road.

14. **thistledown** (thĭs'əl-doun'): the soft, fluffy part of a thistle, a plant with a prickly stem and purple flowers.

15. **concussed** (kən-kŭsd'): suffering from a concussion, an injury that results from being struck in the head.

16. **aggrieved thoughts about the inconsiderateness:** offended feelings over the thoughtlessness.

they don't know if she's likely to live. Police have got the truck driver that hit her—ah, it didn't ought to be allowed, speeding through the place like that at umpty miles an hour, they ought to jail him for life—not that that'd be any comfort to poor Bert and Jean." **H**

Horrified, Aunt Rebecca put on a coat and went down to her brother's house. She found the family with white shocked faces; Bert and Jean were about to drive off to the hospital where Sandy had been taken, and the twins were crying bitterly. Lob was nowhere to be seen. But Aunt Rebecca was not interested in dogs; she did not inquire about him. **I**

"Thank the Lord you've come, Beck," said her brother. "Will you stay the night with Don and the twins? Don's out looking for Lob and heaven knows when we'll be back; we may get a bed with Jean's mother in Plymouth." **J**

"Oh, if only I'd never invited the poor child," wailed Mrs. Hoskins. But Bert and Jean hardly heard her.

That night seemed to last forever. The twins cried themselves to sleep. Don came home very late and grim-faced. Bert and Jean sat in a waiting room of the Western Counties Hospital, but Sandy was unconscious, they were told, and she remained so. All that could be done for her was done. She was given transfusions to replace all the blood she had lost. The broken bones were set and put in slings and cradles.

"Is she a healthy girl? Has she a good constitution?"[17] the emergency doctor asked.

"Aye, Doctor, she is that," Bert said hoarsely. The lump in Jean's throat prevented her from answering; she merely nodded.

"Then she ought to have a chance. But I won't conceal from you that her condition is very serious, unless she shows signs of coming out from this coma."[18]

But as hour succeeded hour, Sandy showed no signs of recovering consciousness. Her parents sat in the waiting room with haggard faces; sometimes one of them would go to telephone the family at home, or to try to get a little sleep at the home of Granny Pearce, not far away.

At noon next day Dr. and Mrs. Travers went to the Pengelly cottage to inquire how Sandy was doing, but the report was gloomy: "Still in a very serious condition." The twins were miserably unhappy. They forgot that they had sometimes called their elder sister bossy and only remembered how often she had shared her pocket money with them, how she read to them and took them for picnics and helped with their homework. Now there was no Sandy, no Mother and Dad, Don went around with a gray, shuttered face, and worse still, there was no Lob. **K**

---

17. **constitution:** physical makeup.
18. **coma:** a sleeplike state in which a person cannot sense or respond to light, sound, or touch.

H SEQUENCE
What sequence of events caused the accident?

I FORESHADOWING
Where might Lob be?

J SEQUENCE
Who is out looking for Lob? Record this event on your timeline.

K SEQUENCE
How long has Lob been missing?

The Western Counties Hospital is a large one, with dozens of different departments and five or six connected buildings, each with three or four entrances. By that afternoon it became noticeable that a dog seemed to have taken up position outside the hospital, with the fixed intention of getting in. Patiently he would try first one entrance and then another, all the way around, and then begin again. Sometimes he would get a little way inside, following a visitor, but animals were, of course, forbidden, and he was always kindly but firmly turned out again. Sometimes the guard at the main entrance gave him a pat or offered him a bit of sandwich—he looked so wet and beseeching and desperate. But he never ate the sandwich. No one seemed to own him or to know where he came from; Plymouth is a large city and he might have belonged to anybody.

At tea time Granny Pearce came through the pouring rain to bring a flask of hot tea to her daughter and son-in-law. Just as she reached the main entrance the guard was gently but forcibly shoving out a large, **agitated,** soaking-wet Alsatian dog.

"No, old fellow, you can *not* come in. Hospitals are for people, not for dogs."

"Why, bless me," exclaimed old Mrs. Pearce. "That's Lob! Here, Lob, Lobby boy!"

Lob ran to her, whining. Mrs. Pearce walked up to the desk.

"I'm sorry, madam, you can't bring that dog in here," the guard said.

Mrs. Pearce was a very determined old lady. She looked the porter in the eye.

"Now, see here, young man. That dog has walked twenty miles from St. Killan to get to my granddaughter. Heaven knows how he knew she was here, but it's plain he knows. And he ought to have his rights! He ought to get to see her! Do you know," she went on, bristling, "that dog has walked the length of England—*twice*—to be with that girl? And you think you can keep him out with your fiddling rules and regulations?"

"I'll have to ask the medical officer," the guard said weakly.

"You do that, young man." Granny Pearce sat down in a determined manner, shutting her umbrella, and Lob sat patiently dripping at her feet. Every now and then he shook his head, as if to dislodge something heavy that was tied around his neck.

Presently a tired, thin, intelligent-looking man in a white coat came downstairs, with an impressive, silver-haired man in a dark suit, and there was a low-voiced discussion. Granny Pearce eyed them, biding her time.

"Frankly . . . not much to lose," said the older man. The man in the white coat approached Granny Pearce.

"It's strictly against every rule, but as it's such a serious case we are making an exception," he said to her quietly. "But only *outside* her bedroom door—and only for a moment or two."

agitated (ăj′ĭ-tāt′əd)
adj. disturbed; upset
agitate *v.*

Without a word, Granny Pearce rose and stumped upstairs. Lob followed close to her skirts, as if he knew his hope lay with her.

They waited in the green-floored corridor outside Sandy's room. The door was half-shut. Bert and Jean were inside. Everything was terribly quiet. A nurse came out. The white-coated man asked her something and she
330 shook her head. She had left the door ajar and through it could now be seen a high, narrow bed with a lot of gadgets around it. Sandy lay there, very flat under the covers, very still. Her head was turned away. All Lob's attention was riveted on the bed. He strained toward it, but Granny Pearce clasped his collar firmly.

"I've done a lot for you, my boy, now you behave yourself," she whispered grimly. Lob let out a faint whine, anxious and pleading.

At the sound of that whine, Sandy stirred just a little. She sighed and moved her head the least fraction. Lob whined again. And then Sandy turned her head right over. Her eyes opened, looking at the door.
340 "Lob?" she murmured—no more than a breath of sound. "Lobby, boy?"

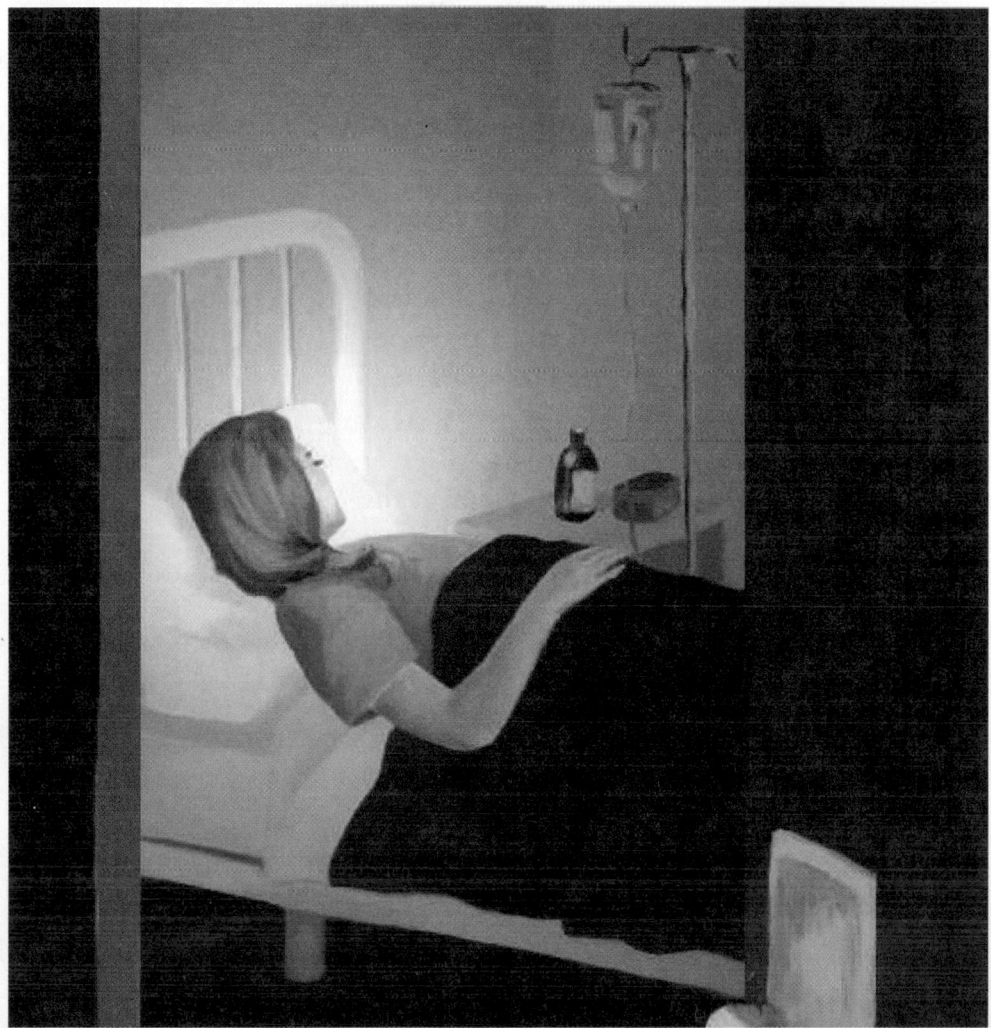

◀ **Analyze Visuals**
What **mood,** or feeling, does this illustration create?

The doctor by Granny Pearce drew a quick, sharp breath. Sandy moved her left arm—the one that was not broken—from below the covers and let her hand dangle down, feeling, as she always did in the mornings, for Lob's furry head. The doctor nodded slowly.

"All right," he whispered. "Let him go to the bedside. But keep a hold of him."

Granny Pearce and Lob moved to the bedside. Now she could see Bert and Jean, white-faced and shocked, on the far side of the bed. But she didn't look at them. She looked at the smile on her granddaughter's face as
350 the groping fingers found Lob's wet ears and gently pulled them. "Good boy," whispered Sandy, and fell asleep again.

Granny Pearce led Lob out into the passage again. There she let go of him, and he ran off swiftly down the stairs. She would have followed him, but Bert and Jean had come out into the passage, and she spoke to Bert fiercely.

"*I* don't know why you were so foolish as not to bring the dog before! Leaving him to find the way here himself—"

"But, Mother!" said Jean Pengelly. "That can't have been Lob. What a chance to take! Suppose Sandy hadn't—" She stopped, with her
360 handkerchief pressed to her mouth.

"Not Lob? I've known that dog nine years! I suppose I ought to know my own granddaughter's dog?"

"Listen, Mother," said Bert. "Lob was killed by the same truck that hit Sandy. Don found him—when he went to look for Sandy's schoolbag. He was—he was dead. Ribs all smashed. No question of that. Don told me on the phone—he and Will Hoskins rowed a half mile out to sea and sank the dog with a lump of concrete tied to his collar. Poor old boy. Still—he was getting on. Couldn't have lasted forever."

"*Sank him at sea?* Then what—?"
370 Slowly old Mrs. Pearce, and then the other two, turned to look at the trail of dripping-wet footprints that led down the hospital stairs.

In the Pengellys' garden they have a stone, under the palm tree. It says: "Lob. Sandy's dog. Buried at sea." ❧

Comprehension

1. **Recall** What causes the accident that injures Sandy?

2. **Clarify** Where does Mr. Dodsworth live?

3. **Summarize** How does Lob show his loyalty toward Sandy?

Text Analysis

4. **Make Inferences** Reread lines 84–96. Why do you think Sandy wishes she had not gone to the train station to see Lob leave?

5. **Identify Sequence** Review your timeline to find the point in the story when you learned what happened to Lob. When did Sandy's brother Don most likely find Lob? Support your answer with evidence from the story.

6. **Analyze Foreshadowing** Find details that foreshadow what happened to Lob in the story. Record the hints and what happened to him in a diagram like the one shown. Did these hints prepare you for the story's ending? Explain.

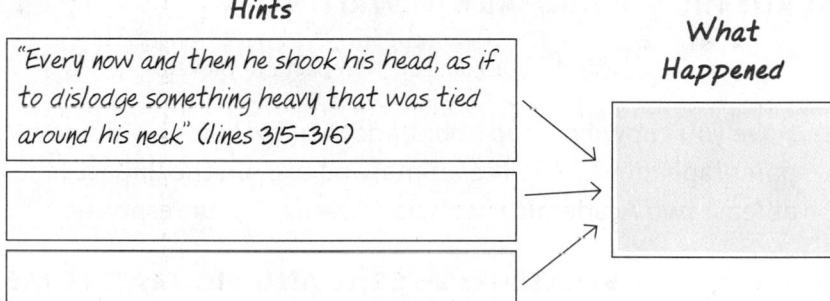

Hints

"Every now and then he shook his head, as if to dislodge something heavy that was tied around his neck." (lines 315–316)

What Happened

7. **Analyze Setting** The setting has a strong influence on the events in the story. Compare and contrast the details of the setting on the day Sandy meets Lob and on the evening of the accident. How do the settings influence the plot of the story?

8. **Evaluate Plot** How realistic or contrived is the plot of "Lob's Girl"? Think about the elements of the plot that make it a good story. Explain your answer with details from the story.

Extension and Challenge

9. **Readers' Circle** What if Mrs. Pengelly hadn't let Sandy take Lob with her to Aunt Rebecca's house? In a small group, discuss how this would affect the rest of the story. Support your responses with evidence from the story.

10. **SOCIAL STUDIES CONNECTION** Mr. Dodsworth has to travel from Liverpool to Cornwall every time Lob runs away to the Pengellys. Review the map on page 91. Research to find the names of other cities Mr. Dodsworth might travel through on his way to pick up Lob.

How powerful is LOYALTY?

What are the qualities of a devoted friend or pet?

COMMON CORE

RL 1 Cite textual evidence to support what the text says explicitly. **RL 5** Analyze how a particular sentence fits into the structure of a text and contributes to the development of the plot.

Vocabulary in Context

▲ VOCABULARY PRACTICE

Answer each question below to show your understanding of the vocabulary words.

1. If a person is about to **erupt,** is that person angry or calm?
2. If I am **reluctant** to see a movie, have I heard good or bad things about it?
3. Does a baseball team **decisively** win a game by one run or six runs?
4. Do people show they are **agitated** by taking a nap or by yelling?
5. Would someone who is **melancholy** sit alone in a corner or dance?
6. Would you **atone** for an action that is praiseworthy or unlawful?

agitated

atone

decisively

erupt

melancholy

reluctant

ACADEMIC VOCABULARY IN WRITING

• analyze • affect • evidence • impact • provide

Have you known or read about another loyal pet or animal? Write a paragraph identifying the animal and explain the **impact** of its actions. Use at least two Academic Vocabulary words in your response.

VOCABULARY STRATEGY: LITERAL AND FIGURATIVE MEANINGS

The **literal** meaning of a word is its most common and basic definition. Over time, though, some words take on **figurative** meanings that expand the basic definition. For example, the literal meaning of *erupt* is "to explode from a volcano with fire and noise." Sometimes the word *erupt* is used figuratively to refer to a person or animal "exploding" with emotion. When you encounter words that have both a literal and figurative meaning, use context clues to help you recognize which meaning the writer intends.

COMMON CORE

L 5 Demonstrate understanding of figurative language in word meanings. **L 6** Acquire and use accurately academic words.

PRACTICE Explain the figurative meaning of each boldfaced word. Then explain how this meaning relates to the word's literal meaning.

1. After the candidate's support increased, he won by a **landslide.**
2. The family created a warm **cocoon** of affection in which their children thrived.
3. Everyone relied on Mrs. Casey to be the **pillar** of the volunteer group.
4. Calling home daily was the **crutch** that helped Maria get through her loneliness.

Interactive Vocabulary **THINK** central

Go to **thinkcentral.com.**
KEYWORD: HML6-102

Language

◆ **GRAMMAR IN CONTEXT:** Punctuate Possessives Correctly

⋯COMMON CORE

L 2 Demonstrate command of the conventions of punctuation.
W 2 Write informative/explanatory texts to convey ideas.

The possessive form of a noun shows ownership or relationship. When forming a possessive noun, be sure to put the **apostrophe** in the correct place. A misplaced apostrophe can be confusing. Follow these guidelines for punctuating possessive nouns correctly:

- **Singular nouns:** Add an apostrophe and *s*, even if the word ends in *s* (*Sandy's dog, octopus's body*).
- **Plural nouns ending in *s*:** Add an apostrophe (*patients' beds*).
- **Plural nouns not ending in *s*:** Add an apostrophe and *s* (*fishermen's boat*).

  Original: Sandy was walking to her aunts' cottage.
             (*only one aunt*)

  Revised: Sandy was walking to her aunt's cottage.

PRACTICE Correct the possessive nouns in the following sentences.

1. Dr. Travers' wife called for an ambulance.
2. The familys' dog is missing.
3. Both nurses shifts at the hospital are ending.
4. The police said that the steep hill is a danger to peoples safety.

*For more help with possessives, see page R50 in the **Grammar Handbook.***

READING-WRITING CONNECTION

Broaden your understanding of "Lob's Girl" by responding to this prompt. Then use the **revising tip** to improve your writing.

WRITING PROMPT	REVISING TIP
Short Constructed Response: Evaluation Much of the story focuses on how Lob showed his loyalty toward Sandy. Do you think Sandy is equally loyal to Lob? In **one paragraph,** give your evaluation.	Review your response. Have you punctuated possessives correctly in your evaluation? If not, revise your writing?

Interactive Revision   THINK central

Go to thinkcentral.com.
KEYWORD: HML6-103

Bud, Not Buddy

COMMON CORE

RL 10 Read and comprehend literature.

Historical Novel by Christopher Paul Curtis

Meet Christopher Paul Curtis

Christopher Paul Curtis knew from an early age that he wanted to be a writer. "I must have been 10 or 11 years old," he remembers. "I said to my brothers and sisters, 'One day, I'm going to write a book.'" They just laughed at him. For a long time, it looked like Curtis's siblings were right. He worked full-time at an auto factory for 13 years and had little time to write.

Finally, Curtis's wife convinced him to quit his job. With time to focus on his life's dream, Curtis turned his attention to writing *The Watsons Go to Birmingham—1963*. The novel was named a Newberry Honor Book. *Bud, Not Buddy* received both the Newbery Medal and the Coretta Scott King Award.

Other Books by Christopher Paul Curtis

- *The Watsons Go to Birmingham—1963*
- *Mr. Chickee's Funny Money*

Try a Historical Novel

Great **historical novels** make the past come alive by mixing references to real events, people, and places with fictional plots and characters. *Bud, Not Buddy* takes place in Curtis's hometown of Flint, Michigan, during the Great Depression of the 1930s. It was a time when jobs were hard to find and many Americans were without food, warm clothing, and shelter.

Reading Fluency refers to how easily and well you read. Fluent readers read with expression. To increase your fluency, practice reading aloud the first twenty-three lines of *Bud, Not Buddy* (page 105) with a partner. When reading aloud, think about your purpose for reading a text. Be sure to group words into meaningful phrases that sound like natural speech.

Read a Great Book

Times are hard when ten-year-old Bud, an orphan, runs away from a horrible foster home. With only a music flyer to guide him, he is determined to find the man he's convinced is his father. First, though, he has to get some much-needed food.

from

BUD, NOT BUDDY

CHRISTOPHER PAUL CURTIS

Uh-oh. My eyes opened and I could see the sun behind the branch of a Christmas tree.

I jumped up, folded my blanket inside my suitcase, hid it and started running the six or seven blocks down to the mission.

I turned the corner and said, "Whew!" There were still people lined up waiting. I started walking along the line. The end was a lot farther away than I thought. The line turned all the way around two corners, then crossed over one street before I saw the last person. Shucks. I walked up to get behind him.

10 He said, "Line's closed. These here folks are the last ones." He pointed at a man standing next to a woman who was carrying a baby.

I said, "But sir . . ."

He said, "But nothing. Line's closed. These here folks are the last ones."

It was time to start lying. If I didn't get any food now I'd have to steal something out of someone's garbage or I wouldn't be able to eat until the mission opened for supper.

I said, "Sir, I—"

The man raised his hand and said, "Look, kid, everybody's got
20 a story and everybody knows the rules. The line closes at seven o'clock. How's it fair to these people who been here since five o'clock that you can sleep until"—he looked at his wristwatch—"until seven-fifteen, then come busting down here expecting to eat?

You think you got some kind of special privilege just 'cause you're skinny and raggedy? Look in the line, there's lots of folks look just like you, you ain't the worst.

"Supper starts at six P.M., but you see how things is, if you plan on getting fed you better be in line by four. Now get out of here before I get rough with you."

30 Shucks, being hungry for a whole day is about as bad as it can get. I said, "But . . ."

He reached into his pocket and pulled something out that looked like a heavy black strap and slapped it across his hand. Uh-oh, here we go again.

He said, "That's it, no more talk, you opened your mouth one time too many. You rotten kids today don't listen to no one, but I'ma show you something that'll improve your hearing." He slapped the strap on his hand and started walking toward me.

I was wrong when I said being hungry for a day is about as bad as 40 it can get, being hungry plus having a big knot on your head from a black leather strap would be even worse.

I backed away but only got two steps before I felt a giant warm hand wrap around my neck from behind. I looked up to see whose doggone hand was so doggone big and why they'd put it around my neck.

A very tall, square-shaped man in old blue overalls looked down at me and said, "Clarence, what took you so long?"

I got ready to say, "My name's not Clarence and please don't choke me, sir, I'll leave," but as soon as I opened my mouth he gave 50 my head a shake and said, "I told you to hurry back, now where you been?" He gave me a shove and said, "Get back in line with your momma."

I looked up and down the line to see who was supposed to be my momma when a woman pointed her finger at her feet and said, "Clarence, you get over here right now." There were two little kids hanging on to her skirt.

I walked over to where she was and she gave me a good hard smack on the head. Shucks, for someone who was just pretending to be my momma she sure did slap me a good one.

60 I said, "Ow!"

The big square man who'd grabbed my neck looked at the man with the strap and said, ". . . Like you said, these kids today don't listen to nobody."

The strap man looked at the size of the man who called me Clarence and walked back to the end of the line.

When the overall man got back in line I said, 'Thank you, sir, I really tried to get—" But *he* popped me in the back of the head, hard, and said, "Next time don't be gone so long."

70 The two little kids busted out laughing and said, "Nyah-nyah-nyah-nyah-nyah, Clarence got a lickin', Clarence got a lickin'."

I told them, "Shut up, and don't call me—" Then *both* my pretend poppa and my pretend momma smacked my head.

She looked at the people direct behind us and said, "Mercy, when they get to be this age . . ."

The people weren't too happy about me taking cuts in the line, but when they looked at how big my pretend daddy was and they saw how hard him and my pretend momma were going upside my head they decided they wouldn't say anything.

80 I was grateful to these people, but I wished they'd quit popping me in the head, and it seems like with all the names in the world they could've come up with a better one for me than Clarence.

I stood in line with my pretend family for a long, long time. Everybody was very quiet about standing in line, even my pretend brother and sister and all the other kids. When we finally got around the last corner and could see the door and folks going in it seemed like a bubble busted and people started laughing and talking. The main thing people were talking about was the great big sign that was hanging over the building.

90 It showed a gigantic picture of a family of four rich white people sitting in a car driving somewhere. You could tell it was a family 'cause they all looked exactly alike. The only difference amongst them was that the daddy had a big head and a hat and the momma had the same head with a woman's hat and the girl had two big yellow pigtails coming out from above her ears. They all had big shiny teeth and big shiny eyes and big shiny cheeks and big shiny smiles. Shucks, you'd need to squint your eyes if that shiny family drove anywhere near you.

You could tell they were rich 'cause the car looked like it had room for eight or nine more people in it and 'cause they had movie star clothes on. The woman was wearing a coat with a hunk of fur around the neck and the man was wearing a suit and a tie and the kids looked like they were wearing ten-dollar-apiece jackets.

Writ about their car in fancy letters it said, THERE'S NO PLACE LIKE AMERICA TODAY!

My pretend daddy read it and said, "Uh-uh-uh, well, you got to give them credit, you wouldn't expect that they'd have the nerve to come down here and tell the truth."

When we finally got into the building it was worth the wait. The first thing you noticed when you got inside was how big the place was, and how many people were in it and how quiet it was. The only sound you could hear was when someone scraped a spoon across the bottom of their bowl or pulled a chair in or put one back or when the people in front of you dragged their feet on the floor moving up to where they were spooning out the food.

After we'd picked up our spoons and bowls a lady dug a big mess of oatmeal out of a giant pot and swopped it down into our bowls. She smiled and said, "I hope you enjoy."

Me and my pretend family all said, "Thank you, ma'am." Then a man put two pieces of bread and a apple and a big glass of milk on your tray and said, "Please read the signs to your children. Thank you."

We all said, "Thank you, Sir." Then we walked past some signs someone'd stuck up on the wall.

One said, PLEASE DO NOT SMOKE, another said, PLEASE EAT AS QUICKLY AND QUIETLY AS POSSIBLE, another one said, PLEASE BE CONSIDERATE AND PATIENT—CLEAN UP AFTER YOURSELF—YOUR NEIGHBORS WILL BE EATING AFTER YOU, and the last one said, WE ARE TERRIBLY SORRY BUT WE HAVE NO WORK AVAILABLE.

My pretend daddy read the signs to my pretend brother and sister and we all sat at a long table with strangers on both sides of us.

The oatmeal was delicious! I poured some of my milk into it so it wouldn't be so lumpy and mixed it all together.

My pretend mother opened her pocketbook and took out a little brown envelope. She reached inside of it and sprinkled something on my pretend brother's and sister's oatmeal, then said to them, "I know that's not as much as you normally get, but I wanted to ask you if you minded sharing some with Clarence."

They pouted and gave me a couple of dirty looks. My pretend mother said, "Good," and emptied the rest of the envelope over my oatmeal. Brown sugar!

Shucks, I didn't even mind them calling me Clarence anymore. I said "Thank you, Momma, ma'am."

She and my pretend daddy laughed and he said, "It took you long enough to catch on, Clarence." He acted like he was going to smack me again but he didn't.

After we'd finished all our food we put our bowls up and I thanked my pretend family again, I asked them, "Are you going to be coming back for supper?"

My pretend momma said, "No, dear, we only come here mornings. But you make sure you get here plenty early, you hear?"

I said, "Yes, Momma, I mean, ma'am."

I watched them walking away. My pretend brother looked back at me and stuck out his tongue, then reached up and took my pretend mother's hand. I couldn't really blame him, I don't think I'd be real happy about sharing my brown sugar and my folks with any strange kids either. ∾

Keep Reading

Poor Bud—on his own, struggling to find food and a place to sleep. Think about what you have learned about Bud from his experience in the mission. Will he succeed in finding his father? Read the rest of *Bud, Not Buddy* to find out. As Bud continues on his journey, he will have to overcome hunger, fear, and prejudice. Will his struggle be worth it in the end?

from Lemony Snicket's A Series of Unfortunate Events

Film Clip on **Media Smart** DVD-ROM

What makes your heart
POUND?

COMMON CORE

RI 4 Determine the meaning of words and phrases, including technical meanings.
SL 2 Interpret information presented in media.

Movies have the power to pull an audience into an imaginary world. Excitement builds as characters face difficult problems in dangerous settings. You'll watch a scene from *Lemony Snicket's A Series of Unfortunate Events* to see how moviemakers brought an odd, interesting world to the big screen.

Background

Unhappily Ever After "If you are interested in stories with happy endings, you would be better off reading some other book."

So begins *The Bad Beginning,* the first book in *A Series of Unfortunate Events,* a popular group of novels by an author who calls himself Lemony Snicket. The unfortunate events of the title happen to the three Baudelaire children—Violet, Klaus, and Sunny—who are sent to live with a distant relative named Count Olaf when their parents are killed in a fire. Count Olaf is determined to get his hands on the children's inheritance, even if he has to take extreme measures to do so. In 2004, moviemakers brought the Baudelaires' adventures to movie theaters.

Media Literacy: Setting and Conflict in Movies

Writers often make their stories rich by vividly describing the **setting** where the events take place. Dangerous settings can add a sense of excitement and create more **conflict** for characters. In a movie, you don't have to rely on a written description. Moviemakers use **powerful images** and **sounds** to reveal the setting and conflict to their audience. Filmmakers use various techniques to influence the emotions of the viewers.

Close-up shot

Long shot

FILM TECHNIQUES	STRATEGIES FOR VIEWING
Visual A **shot** is a single, continuous view filmed by a camera. A shot includes all the action that happens until the movie cuts to the next shot.	• Look for **long shots,** which provide a wide view of a scene. They can be used to establish setting. Long shots can also create suspense for the viewer by showing danger approach from far away. • Watch for **close-up shots,** which show the details of a person or object. In an exciting scene, they can show the characters' emotions as the conflict builds. They can also focus on a small detail that can affect the plot. • Notice the use of **medium shots,** which show one or more characters from the waist up. They can be used to show how characters interact and how they feel about each other.
Sound The **sounds** in a movie consist of **music, sound effects,** and **dialogue.** Sound can be used to make you happy, sad, scared, or excited.	• Listen to the **music,** and notice how it changes. An exciting scene will often have fast, menacing music that increases your sense of danger. • Notice the **sound effects,** such as the rumbling noise of a train. As the danger builds in a scene, the sound effects may get faster and louder. • When listening to the **dialogue,** notice both what characters say and how they say it. Tone of voice can reveal emotions.

Viewing Guide for

Lemony Snicket's A Series of Unfortunate Events

In this scene, the dastardly Count Olaf uses a remote control to lock the Baudelaire children in his car after parking it on train tracks. The children must use their wits and special talents to foil Olaf's plans. Violet is an inventor, Klaus has read many books on many subjects, and the baby, Sunny, has her own surprising skills.

Pay attention to the rising excitement as you watch the scene. You can watch the clip more than once, then use these questions to help you analyze it.

NOW VIEW

FIRST VIEWING: Comprehension

1. **Recall** Why doesn't Mr. Poe understand the danger the children are in when he talks to Violet on the car phone?

2. **Clarify** How do the children pull the track-switching lever so that the train misses the car?

CLOSE VIEWING: Media Literacy

3. **Identify Conflict** What is the conflict in the scene, and how do the children first become aware of the danger they are in?

4. **Analyze Shots** Think about the moment in the scene after Violet gets off the phone with Mr. Poe. The train is bearing down on the children and they can't get out of the car. Why do you think the director chose this moment to show a **close-up** of Violet?

5. **Evaluate Sound** Listen carefully to the **music** and **sound effects** in the scene. What part of the scene is the most exciting? What sound elements make it exciting?

6. **Analyze Setting** Throughout the movie, Violet, Klaus, and Sunny find themselves in dangerous places and situations. Which details in this scene's **setting** make it exciting to you?

Write or Discuss

Evaluate Suspense Think about the racing train scene you viewed. Do you think the moviemakers do a good job of building suspense? Are the film techniques you learned about used effectively? Write a brief evaluation of the scene. Is it as exciting as other movies you've enjoyed? Think about the following parts of the scene:

- the types of shots and the length of shots
- the use of music and sound effects
- the dangers in the setting that threaten the children

Produce Your Own Media

Create a Storyboard Imagine you're a director and you've been asked to make a movie based on one of the stories in this unit. Work with a partner to create a storyboard for the most exciting scene from a story you read. A **storyboard** is a device used to plan the shooting of a movie. It is made up of drawings and brief descriptions of what happens in each shot in a scene.

HERE'S HOW Here are a few suggestions for making your storyboard:

- Imagine the scene happening in your head before you begin. Describe what you see to your partner.
- Think about the characters' emotions and the setting. Use what you learned about **camera shots** to decide what types of shots will work best.
- Draw the shots that show what happens in four to six individual frames.
- Write a brief description of what is happening under each drawing. Include any **dialogue** or **sound effects** you'd hear.

STUDENT MODEL

Klaus says, "Violet, I don't mean to rush you . . ."

The elf's head swings around the track switcher.

Close-up of Violet's smiling face.

Medium shot of Violet and Klaus pulling the strap.

Long shot of the approaching train. The music is fast and exciting.

The train rumbles by loudly. Medium shot of Klaus and Violet.

COMMON CORE

SL1 Engage effectively in collaborative discussions (one-on-one, in groups).

Media Tools
THINK central

Go to **thinkcentral.com**.
KEYWORD: HML6-113

Tech Tip

Try using a computer drawing program to make the frames for the storyboard.

from **Woodsong**
Memoir by Gary Paulsen

Does nature demand
RESPECT?

COMMON CORE

RI 4 Determine the meaning of words and phrases as they are used in the text.
RI 6 Determine an author's purpose and explain how it is conveyed in the text.
RI 10 Read and comprehend literary nonfiction.

Nature can be a powerful force. It might be a thunderstorm rumbling in the night, a wave crashing onto the beach, or a lion's mighty roar. In *Woodsong*, Gary Paulsen shares a lesson he learned about respect for nature.

QUICKWRITE Think about your most memorable or intense encounter with nature. Describe this experience in a journal entry. What did you learn from the experience?

● TEXT ANALYSIS: NARRATIVE NONFICTION

Woodsong is a type of narrative nonfiction called a **memoir,** in which the writer tells true life stories. Writers of narrative nonfiction use many of the same literary elements that are found in fiction, such as

- a **conflict,** or struggle between opposing forces
- **suspense,** or the anxious curiosity you feel about what happens next
- **imagery,** or words and phrases that appeal to your senses

As you read, notice how the writer explains the conflict, builds suspense, and creates vivid scenes with imagery.

● READING SKILL: IDENTIFY AUTHOR'S PURPOSE

A writer's main reason for writing is called the **author's purpose.** For example, a writer might write to

- explain or provide information about a topic or event
- share thoughts or feelings about an issue or event
- persuade people to think or act in a certain way
- entertain the reader with a moving story

As you read, use a chart to record clues about Paulsen's main purpose for writing this memoir.

Author's Purpose

Explain/Inform   Share Thoughts   Persuade   Entertain

▲ VOCABULARY IN CONTEXT

For each numbered word or phrase, choose the word from the list that is closest in meaning.

WORD	coherent	hibernation	scavenge
LIST	eject	novelty	truce

1. throw out
2. agreement
3. find leftovers
4. new thing
5. sensible
6. sleep

Complete the activities in your **Reader/Writer Notebook.**

Woodsong

Gary Paulsen

We have bear trouble. Because we feed processed meat to the dogs, there is always the smell of meat over the kennel. In the summer it can be a bit high[1] because the dogs like to "save" their food sometimes for a day or two or four—burying it to dig up later. We live on the edge of wilderness, and consequently the meat smell brings any number of visitors from the woods.

Skunks abound, and foxes and coyotes and wolves and weasels—all predators. We once had an eagle live over the kennel for more than a week, **scavenging** from the dogs, and a crazy group of ravens has pretty
10 much taken over the puppy pen. Ravens are protected by the state, and they seem to know it. When I walk toward the puppy pen with the buckets of meat, it's a toss-up to see who gets it—the pups or the birds. They have actually pecked the puppies away from the food pans until they have gone through and taken what they want. **Ⓐ**

Analyze Visuals ▶

Examine the painting closely. What do you see?

scavenge (skăv′ənj) v. to search for discarded scraps

Ⓐ NARRATIVE NONFICTION
Reread lines 1–14. What imagery does Paulsen use to depict life at the edge of the wilderness?

---

1. **it can be a bit high:** the smell can be rather strong.

Ursus, Susan Brearey. Oil and wax on wood with beech leaf and birch bark, 11⅛″ × 11″ × 1⅜″. © Susan Brearey represented by Gerald Peters Gallery, Santa Fe, New Mexico.

Analyze Visuals

What **details** in the painting suggest that the house is in the wilderness?

Golden Autumn (1901), Stanislav Joukovski. Oil on canvas, 87.5 cm × 107.5 cm. Museum of Art, Serpukhov, Russia. © Bridgeman Art Library.

Spring, when the bears come, is the worst. They have been in **hibernation** through the winter, and they are hungry beyond caution. The meat smell draws them like flies, and we frequently have two or three around the kennel at the same time. Typically they do not bother us much—although my wife had a bear chase her from the garden to the house one morning—but they
20 do bother the dogs.

They are so big and strong that the dogs fear them, and the bears trade on this fear to get their food. It's common to see them scare a dog into his house and take his food. Twice we have had dogs killed by rough bear swats that broke their necks—and the bears took their food.

We have evolved an uneasy peace with them, but there is the problem of familiarity. The first time you see a bear in the kennel it is a **novelty**, but when the same ones are there day after day, you wind up naming some of them (old Notch-Ear, Billy-Jo, etc.). There gets to be a too-relaxed attitude. We started to treat them like pets.

30 A major mistake. **B**

There was a large male around the kennel for a week or so. He had a white streak across his head, which I guessed was a wound scar from some hunter—bear hunting is allowed here. He wasn't all that bad, so we didn't mind him. He would frighten the dogs and take their hidden stashes now and then, but he didn't harm them, and we became accustomed to him hanging around. We called him Scarhead, and now and again we would joke about him as if he were one of the yard animals.

hibernation (hī'bər-nā'shən) *n.* the state of being inactive through the winter

novelty (nŏv'əl-tē) *n.* something new and unusual

B NARRATIVE NONFICTION
Reread lines 15–30. At what point are you excited or anxious about what happens next? Note the details that create suspense.

At this time we had three cats, forty-two dogs, fifteen or twenty chickens, eight ducks, nineteen large white geese, a few banty hens . . .
40 ten fryers which we'd raised from chicks and couldn't (as my wife put it) "snuff and eat," and six woods-wise goats.

The bears, strangely, didn't bother any of the yard animals. There must have been a rule, or some order to the way they lived, because they would hit the kennel and steal from the dogs but leave the chickens and goats and other yard stock completely alone—although you would have had a hard time convincing the goats of this fact. The goats spent a great deal of time with their back hair up, whuffing and blowing snot at the bears— and at the dogs, who would *gladly* have eaten them. The goats never really believed in the **truce.** ● C

50 There is not a dump or landfill to take our trash to, and so we separate it—organic, inorganic[2]—and deal with it ourselves. We burn the paper in a screened enclosure, and it is fairly efficient; but it's impossible to get all the food particles off wrapping paper, so when it's burned, the food particles burn with it.

And give off a burnt food smell.

And nothing draws bears like burning food. It must be that they have learned to understand human dumps—where they spend a great deal of time foraging. And they learn amazingly fast. In Alaska, for instance, the bears already know that the sound of a moose hunter's gun means there
60 will be a fresh gut pile when the hunter cleans the moose. They come at a run when they hear the shot. It's often a close race to see if the hunter will get to the moose before the bears take it away. . . . ● D

Because we're on the south edge of the wilderness area, we try to wait until there is a northerly breeze before we burn, so the food smell will carry south, but it doesn't always help. Sometimes bears, wolves, and other predators are already south, working the sheep farms down where it is more settled—they take a terrible toll[3] of sheep—and we catch them on the way back through.

That's what happened one July morning. ● E
70 Scarhead had been gone for two or three days, and the breeze was right, so I went to burn the trash. I fired it off and went back into the house for a moment—not more than two minutes. When I came back out, Scarhead was in the burn area. His tracks (directly through the tomatoes in the garden) showed he'd come from the south.

---

truce (trōōs) *n.* an agreement to end an argument or fight

● C **NARRATIVE NONFICTION**
Reread lines 42–49. What conflicts exist between the animals?

● D **AUTHOR'S PURPOSE**
Reread lines 56–62. Why do you think Paulsen wants you to know these facts about bears?

● E **NARRATIVE NONFICTION**
Look back at lines 30, 55, and 69. How does Paulsen build suspense by using single sentence paragraphs? Why is this an effective technique?

---

2. **organic, inorganic:** *Organic* refers to plant or animal material that breaks down naturally. *Inorganic* refers to man-made material that will not break down naturally.

3. **take a terrible toll:** destroy a large number.

He was having a grand time. The fire didn't bother him. He was trying to reach a paw in around the edges of flame to get at whatever smelled so good. He had torn things apart quite a bit—ripped one side off the burn enclosure—and I was having a bad day, and it made me mad.

80 I was standing across the burning fire from him, and without thinking—because I was so used to him—I picked up a stick, threw it at him, and yelled, "Get out of here." ◆

I have made many mistakes in my life, and will probably make many more, but I hope never to throw a stick at a bear again.

In one rolling motion—the muscles seemed to move within the skin so fast that I couldn't take half a breath—he turned and came for me.

⋯ COMMON CORE L5

Language Coach

Multiple-Meaning Words *Bit* is an example of a multiple-meaning word, or a word with more than one meaning. In line 77, *bit* means "a small amount." The word *bit* is also the past tense of the word *bite* and can mean "cut off with teeth." Reread lines 75–78 and identify at least two more multiple-meaning words.

◆ **GRAMMAR IN CONTEXT**

Read the sentence beginning "I was standing . . ." on line 79. Notice the writer uses correct pronoun-antecedent agreement. The singular pronoun *it* agrees with the noun *stick*.

◀ **Analyze Visuals**

What words would you use to describe the bear in this work of art?

Close. I could smell his breath and see the red around the sides of his eyes. Close on me he stopped and raised on his back legs and hung over me, his forelegs and paws hanging down, weaving back and forth gently as he took his time and decided whether or not to tear my head off. **F**

90   I could not move, would not have time to react. I knew I had nothing to say about it. One blow would break my neck. Whether I lived or died depended on him, on his thinking, on his ideas about me—whether I was worth the bother or not.

I did not think then.

Looking back on it, I don't remember having one **coherent** thought when it was happening. All I knew was terrible menace. His eyes looked very small as he studied me. He looked down on me for what seemed hours. I did not move, did not breathe, did not think or do anything.

And he lowered.

100   Perhaps I was not worth the trouble. He lowered slowly and turned back to the trash, and I walked backward halfway to the house and then ran—anger growing now—and took the rifle from the gun rack by the door and came back out.

He was still there, rummaging through the trash. I worked the bolt and fed a cartridge in and aimed at the place where you kill bears and began to squeeze. In raw anger, I began to take up the four pounds of pull necessary to send death into him.

And stopped.

Kill him for what?

110   That thought crept in.

Kill him for what?

For not killing me? For letting me know it is wrong to throw sticks at four-hundred-pound bears? For not hurting me, for not killing me, I should kill him? I lowered the rifle and **ejected** the shell and put the gun away. I hope Scarhead is still alive. For what he taught me, I hope he lives long and is very happy, because I learned then—looking up at him while he made up his mind whether or not to end me—that when it is all boiled down, I am nothing more and nothing less than any other animal in the woods. ✏ **G**

F NARRATIVE NONFICTION
Reread lines 84–89. What imagery helps you understand what it's like to be in Paulsen's shoes?

coherent (kō-hîr′ənt) *adj.* clear; logical

eject (ĭ-jĕkt′) *v.* to throw out from inside

G AUTHOR'S PURPOSE
What does Paulsen now think about his place in nature? Identify the line that tells you this.

NEWSPAPER ARTICLE Gary Paulsen's love of nature is not limited to the wilderness. In this article, based on an interview with Caroline Scott, Paulsen describes a typical day on his sailboat, on which he lives alone most of the year.

Section 4   C4

A Life in the Day of
Gary Paulsen

At 5:30 A.M. I have a bowl of oatmeal, then I go to work. First up, I stow all the gear away. Then I take the covers off the sails and fire the engine up to get out of the harbor. I hate the motor—once it's off, there's silence. I have a steering vane so I can go below and cook or sit and write. Sailing is an inherently beautiful thing. To me it's like dancing with the wind and the water; it's like running with wolves—a perfect meeting of man and nature. . . .

On the boat there is nothing, and I know I work better that way. I think that the writer in the city, with the traffic and the parties and the theater, is at a disadvantage, because the distractions are so enormous. I work in the city when I have to, but I find it really hard. I don't need much. The way I live is nobody's idea of luxury, but that's the way I like it. I use a battery to charge my laptop and I just head out to sea. Sometimes I go 150 miles out and 150 miles back; sometimes I head out and keep right on going. . . .

I write all morning, then I have a two-hour break to answer mail. I get around 400 letters a day from children and I have a secretary in New York who helps me answer them all. I owe a great deal to dogs and a great deal to children, and I try to help both of those species. A lot of what I write is fiction based on my life. . . . I spent my whole childhood running away. A lot of kids know this through my books, so I look for mail from kids in the same situation. It helps them to know you care. I'll try and get in touch with their school to let them know this child is in trouble. I'm aware I might be the only person they've told. I got a letter once from a girl who said, "My only friends in the world are your books.". . .

I don't get lonely. There was a time when I [wished I had] somebody who I could turn to and say, "Look at that!" I'd be leaning over the bow strip to touch the dolphins swimming alongside the boat. One time, three of them somersaulted in the air and crashed into the water, which was golden with the sinking sun. It was the most beautiful thing, and I felt so happy I just wanted to tell someone. But I realized that I'm telling it through my writing the whole time. . . .

I used to think I should be fulfilled by awards or by earning a million dollars, but with age has come some kind of self-knowledge. My rewards are less tangible: they're the killer whales who reared up out of the water to look at me. Or a 15-knot wind across my beam. Those are my moments of pure joy.

Comprehension

1. **Recall** What smell draws the bears to Paulsen's cabin?

2. **Clarify** Why does Scarhead show up the day Paulsen burns the trash even though the wind is blowing away from the wilderness?

3. **Summarize** What happens when Paulsen confronts Scarhead?

Text Analysis

4. **Make Inferences** Reread lines 42–49. Why don't the bears bother the yard animals?

5. **Analyze Author's Purpose** Review the clues you recorded in your chart as you read *Woodsong*. What is Paulsen's main purpose for sharing his experience? Support your answer with examples from the memoir.

6. **Examine Narrative Nonfiction** Although *Woodsong* is a memoir, you probably noticed literary language and devices that you commonly find in short stories. Record examples of imagery from *Woodsong* and note the senses to which these images appeal. What is memorable about Paulsen's use of imagery? Support your answer with details from the chart.

Imagery	Senses
"…there is always the smell of meat over the kennel."	smell, sight

7. **Synthesize Ideas Across Texts** Consider Paulsen's descriptions of nature in *Woodsong* and in the newspaper article on page 122. Based on the details in these texts, how would you define Paulsen's attitude toward nature? Support your response with specific examples from both selections.

Extension and Challenge

8. **Creative Project: Art** Sketch the area where Paulsen lives, using details found in the memoir.

9. **Inquiry and Research** Paulsen explains that bears are very hungry in the spring after hibernating through the winter. Research to find out more about the hibernation process. In two or three paragraphs, explain why a bear hibernates, how it prepares for hibernation, and what happens to its body.

Does Nature Demand RESPECT?

Review your journal entry on your encounter with nature. Did you gain respect for nature after your experience? Explain.

COMMON CORE

RI 4 Determine the meaning of words and phrases as they are used in the text. RI 6 Determine an author's purpose and explain how it is conveyed in the text. RI 10 Read and comprehend literary nonfiction.

Vocabulary in Context

▲ VOCABULARY PRACTICE

Choose the letter of the word or phrase that best completes each sentence below.

1. A **coherent** message (a) is very long, (b) makes sense, (c) is a surprise.
2. A bear might **scavenge** in (a) garbage, (b) streams, (c) caves.
3. **Hibernation** involves (a) growling, (b) eating, (c) resting.
4. Enemies who call a **truce** (a) go to war, (b) stop fighting, (c) sink a ship.
5. After I **eject** the CD-ROM, I (a) put it away, (b) play it, (c) buy it.
6. A bear would be a **novelty** in (a) a zoo, (b) the wilderness, (c) a house.

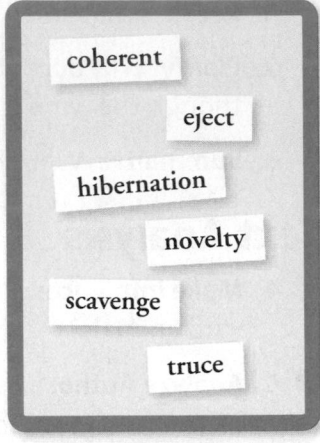

coherent

eject

hibernation

novelty

scavenge

truce

ACADEMIC VOCABULARY IN WRITING

• analyze • affect • evidence • impact • provide

With a partner, **analyze** the imagery Paulsen uses to describe the animals in *Woodsong*. How do his descriptions **affect** the way you imagine the animals? Which animals seem more lifelike or dangerous because of Paulsen's descriptions? Use at least two Academic Vocabulary words in your response.

VOCABULARY STRATEGY: PREFIXES AND THE LATIN ROOT *ject*

A **prefix** is a word part that appears at the beginning of a base word to form a new word. For example, consider the word *uneasy* (un + easy) in line 25 of *Woodsong*. *Un-* is a prefix that means "not," so *uneasy* means "not easy."

Prefixes may also be added to **roots,** which are word parts that can't stand alone. The vocabulary word *eject* contains the Latin root *ject,* which means "to throw." This root is combined with various prefixes to form English words. To understand the meaning of words containing *ject,* use your knowledge of the root's meaning and the meanings of the prefixes used with it.

PRACTICE Use the information in the chart and the meaning of the root *ject* to write a definition for each boldfaced word.

1. The emperor **subjected** his people to a harsh government.
2. Dad keeps his antique movie **projector** in the basement.
3. This **injection** will protect you from the illness.
4. The actor **rejected** the role offered to him.

COMMON CORE

L 4b Use Latin affixes and roots as clues to the meaning of a word.

Prefix	Meaning
e-, ex-	from; out of
in-	in; into
pro-	forward; in front of
re-	back; again
sub-	under; down

Interactive Vocabulary

THINK central

Go to **thinkcentral.com**.
KEYWORD: HML6-124

Language

◆ **GRAMMAR IN CONTEXT:** Maintain Pronoun-Antecedent Agreement

A **pronoun** is a word that is used in place of a noun or another pronoun. The word that the pronoun refers to is its **antecedent.** For example, notice how the pronoun *his* refers to the antecedent *Gary* in the following sentence: *Gary walked out of his house.*

Pronouns should always **agree in number** with their antecedents. Be careful when using antecedents that are indefinite pronouns, such as *anyone, nobody, no one,* and *somebody.* These indefinite pronouns should always be paired with singular pronouns. In the revised sentence, notice how the singular pronoun (in yellow) and the singular antecedent (in green) agree in number.

> *Original:* Somebody threw a stick, and they yelled, "Get out of here."
>
> *Revised:* Somebody threw a stick, and he yelled, "Get out of here."

PRACTICE Correct the following pronoun-antecedent errors.

1. Anyone in this situation would have turned to face their enemy.
2. For what seemed like an hour, nobody moved from their spot.
3. Someone had to be reasonable. They would need to walk away.
4. No one wanted their life cut short that day.

*For more help with pronouns, see page R52 in the **Grammar Handbook**.*

READING-WRITING CONNECTION

YOUR TURN
Broaden your understanding of *Woodsong* by responding to this prompt. Then use the **revising tip** to improve your writing.

WRITING PROMPT	REVISING TIP
Short Constructed Response: Author's Purpose Paulsen says that the bear gave him more respect for nature and taught him that he is just another animal in the woods. In **one paragraph,** explain how this lesson might change the way Paulsen will interact with nature in the future.	Review your response. Do all pronouns agree with their antecedents in your paragraph? If not, revise your writing.

COMMON CORE

L 1c Recognize and correct inappropriate shifts in pronoun number and person. **W 2** Write informative/explanatory texts to convey ideas.

Interactive Revision **THINK** central

Try it at thinkcentral.com.
KEYWORD: HML6-125

The Horse Snake
From the Memoir *The Land I Lost*
by Huynh Quang Nhuong

When is there strength in NUMBERS?

COMMON CORE

RI 3 Analyze in detail how a key event is introduced, illustrated, and elaborated in a text. **RI 5** Analyze how a particular sentence, paragraph, or section fits into the structure and contributes to the development of ideas. **L 5** Demonstrate understanding of nuances in word meanings.

No matter who you are, life will present you with challenges. Perhaps you'll face danger from a natural disaster. Perhaps you'll find you have more work than you can do. Maybe you'll be asked to carry emotional burdens that seem impossibly heavy. Will you be strong enough to take on every challenge alone? In "The Horse Snake," a community depends on teamwork to face a threat that is too big for just one person.

LIST IT With a group of classmates, make a list of goals and challenges that would be easier to meet if you worked with a team rather than by yourself. Discuss why teamwork would help bring success in each situation.

TEXT ANALYSIS: SETTING IN NONFICTION

Like all authors of **memoirs,** Huynh writes about actual events in his life. Since these events actually happened to him, Huynh provides real details about the setting. These details help you visualize the small village where he grew up. As you read, look for images and details that help you experience life in the Vietnamese countryside. Then think about how the setting affects the villagers and their conflict with the snake.

Notice that this piece of literary nonfiction shares many of the features you have studied in this unit, including plot, characters, and setting.

READING SKILL: TRACE CHRONOLOGICAL ORDER

Often, writers of narrative nonfiction present events in the same order in which they happened in real life. This is called **chronological order,** or time order. Look for words and phrases that reveal time order, such as *at nightfall,* or *the next day.*

As you read, use a timeline to track the order of events and the time of day each event occurred.

Friend bangs on door

Night

▲ VOCABULARY IN CONTEXT

The author uses the words in the list below to show the fear caused by a dangerous snake. Complete each phrase with the correct word from the list.

WORD LIST	assume	nocturnal	stealthily
	gait	petrify	succumb

1. One look at the deadly snake could _____ anyone.
2. It was a _____ animal, so it was seldom seen in daylight.
3. We must _____ responsibility for killing the snake.
4. To be safe, make sure you approach the snake _____.
5. So you don't scare it, walk with a quiet, careful _____.
6. After a hard fight, you might get the animal to _____.

 Complete the activities in your **Reader/Writer Notebook.**

Meet the Author

Huynh Quang Nhuong
1946–2001

Village Life
Growing up in a small village in Vietnam, Huynh Quang Nhuong was tending rice fields by the time he was six years old. He also watched over his family's water buffaloes, including his favorite, Tank. There were no stores, cars, or televisions in the village. For entertainment, Huynh, his family, and his neighbors listened to one another tell stories. When he was older, Huynh received a scholarship to Saigon University, and he left home. He planned to return to his village as a teacher.

Distant Memories
Instead, Huynh was drafted into the army of South Vietnam in the 1960s. After being paralyzed by a bullet, he traveled to the United States for treatment. Huynh never returned to Vietnam. However, his memoirs, poems, and plays brought his memories of Vietnam and the stories he heard there to audiences in the United States.

BACKGROUND TO THE MEMOIR
"The Horse Snake" is a chapter in Huynh's memoir *The Land I Lost.* The memoir is set in Huynh's childhood village, which was surrounded by jungle on one side and mountains on the other. Huynh describes the realities of living close to fascinating and dangerous animals.

Author Online
THINK central
Go to thinkcentral.com.
KEYWORD: HML6-127

The Horse Snake

Huynh Quang Nhoung

Analyze Visuals ▶

What does this photo suggest about the importance of the horse snake in relation to the village?

Despite all his courage there was one creature in the jungle that Tank always tried to avoid—the snake. And there was one kind of snake that was more dangerous than other snakes—the horse snake. In some areas people called it the bamboo snake because it was as long as a full-grown bamboo tree.[1] In other regions, the people called it the thunder or lightning snake, because it attacked so fast and with such power that its victim had neither time to escape nor strength to fight it. In our area, we called it the horse snake because it could move as fast as a thoroughbred.

---

1. **a full-grown bamboo tree:** a bamboo tree can grow as tall as 120 feet.

10   One night a frightened friend of our family's banged on our door and asked us to let him in. When crossing the rice field in front of our house on his way home from a wedding, he had heard the unmistakable hiss of a horse snake. We became very worried; not only for us and our friend, but also for the cattle and other animals we raised. **Ⓐ**

    It was too far into the night to rouse all our neighbors and go to search for the snake. But my father told my cousin to blow three times on his buffalo horn,[2] the signal that a dangerous wild beast was loose in the hamlet. A few seconds later we heard three long quivering sounds of a horn at the far end of the hamlet[3] answering our warning. We presumed
20 that the whole hamlet was now on guard. **Ⓑ**

    I stayed up that night, listening to all the sounds outside, while my father and my cousin sharpened their hunting knives. Shortly after midnight we were startled by the frightened neighing of a horse in the rice field. Then the night was still, except for a few sad calls of **nocturnal** birds and the occasional roaring of tigers in the jungle.

T he next day early in the morning all the able-bodied men of the hamlet gathered in front of our house and divided into groups of four to go and look for the snake. My father and my cousin grabbed their lunch and joined a searching party. **Ⓒ**

30   They found the old horse that had neighed the night before in the rice field. The snake had squeezed it to death. Its chest was smashed, and all its ribs broken. But the snake had disappeared.

    Everybody agreed that it was the work of one of the giant horse snakes which had terrorized our area as far back as anyone could remember. The horse snake usually eats small game, such as turkeys, monkeys, chickens, and ducks, but for unknown reasons sometimes it will attack people and cattle. A fully grown horse snake can reach the size of a king python.[4] But, unlike pythons, horse snakes have an extremely poisonous bite. Because of their bone-breaking squeeze and fatal bite they are one of the
40 most dangerous creatures of the uplands.

    The men searched all day, but at nightfall they gave up and went home. My father and my cousin looked very tired when they returned. My grandmother told them to go right to bed after their dinner and that she would wake them up if she or my mother heard any unusual sounds.

Ⓐ CHRONOLOGICAL ORDER
Reread lines 10–14. What is the first event in this selection? Record the event and the time of day on your timeline.

Ⓑ SETTING
Reread lines 15–20. What do the night sounds reveal about this setting?

nocturnal (nŏk-tûr′nəl) *adj.* active at night

Ⓒ CHRONOLOGICAL ORDER
What words or phrases in this paragraph help you understand the order of events?

COMMON CORE L5
Language Coach
Multiple-Meaning Words *Game* usually means "contest." What is the meaning of *game* as it is used in line 35? What words in the sentence give you a clue to its meaning?

---

2. **buffalo horn:** The horns of water buffalo are sometimes used to produce music or other sounds.

3. **hamlet:** a small village.

4. **king python:** large, heavy snake that can grow to a length of 20 feet and kills its prey by squeezing it to death.

The men went to bed and the women prepared to stay up all night. My mother sewed torn clothing and my grandmother read a novel she had just borrowed from a friend. And for the second night in a row, they allowed my little sister and me to stay awake and listen with them for 50 as long as we could. But hours later, seeing the worry on our faces, my grandmother put aside her novel and told us a story:

Once upon a time a happy family lived in a small village on the shore of the South China Sea. They respected the laws of the land and loved their neighbors very much. The father and his oldest son were woodcutters. The father was quite old, but he still could carry home a heavy load of wood.

One day on his way home from the jungle he was happier than usual. He and his son had discovered a wild chicken nest containing twelve eggs. Now he would have something 60 special to give to his grandchildren when they pulled his shirtsleeves and danced around him to greet him when he came home.

The father looked at the broad shoulders of his son and his steady **gait** under a very heavy load of wood. He smiled. His son was a good son, and he had no doubt that when he became even older still his son would take good care of him and his wife.

As he was thinking this he saw his son suddenly throw the load of wood at a charging horse snake that had come out of 70 nowhere. The heavy load of wood crashed into the snake's head and stunned it. That gave them enough time to draw their sharp woodcutting knives. But instead of attacking the horse snake from the front, the elder shouted to his son to run behind the big bush of elephant grass nearby while he, who was a little too old to run fast, jumped into the front end of the bush. Each time the snake passed by him the old man managed to hit it with his knife. He struck the snake many times. Finally it became weak and slowed down; so he came out of his hiding place and attacked the snake's tail, while his 80 son attacked the snake's head. The snake fought back furiously, but finally it **succumbed** to the well-coordinated attack of father and son.

When the snake was dead, they grabbed its tail and proudly dragged it to the edge of their village. Everyone rushed out to

SOCIAL STUDIES CONNECTION

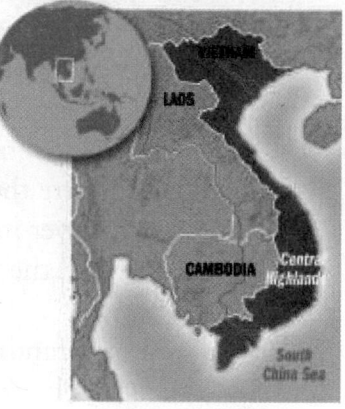

The uplands, or the central highlands, of Vietnam are a mountainous area bordering Laos and Cambodia.

gait (gāt) *n.* manner of walking or moving on foot

Language Coach

Homophones
Words that sound the same but are spelled differently and mean different things are called **homophones**. For example, the word *weak* (line 78), sounds the same as the word *week*. Which word means "the time between Sunday and Saturday"? Which word means "not strong"?

succumb (sə-kŭm') *v.* to give in; die

see their prize. They all argued over who would have the honor of carrying the snake to their house for them.

90   The old woodcutter and his son had to tell the story of how they had killed the snake at least ten times, but the people never tired of hearing it, again and again. They all agreed that the old woodcutter and his son were not only brave but clever as well. Then and there the villagers decided that when their chief, also a brave and clever man, died, the old woodcutter was the only one who deserved the honor of replacing him. **D**

When my grandmother finished the story, my little sister and I became a bit more cheerful. People could defeat this dangerous snake after all. The silent darkness outside became less threatening. Nevertheless, we were still too scared to sleep in our room, so my mother made a makeshift bed in the sitting room, close to her and our grandmother. **E**

D CHRONOLOGICAL ORDER
Would you include the events in grandmother's story in your timeline? Explain.

E SETTING
What two details in lines 94–99 help you picture the setting?

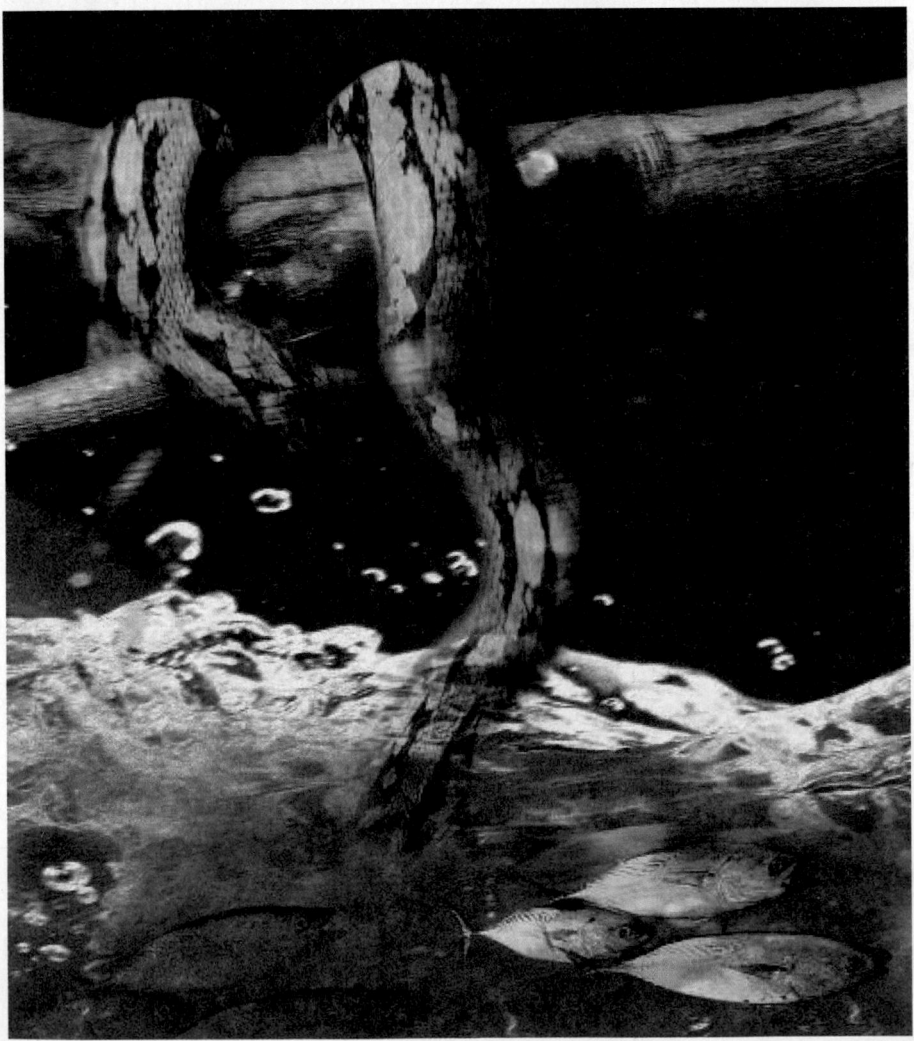

◀ **Analyze Visuals**
What **mood,** or feeling, does this work of art create?

100 When we woke up the next morning, life in the hamlet had almost returned to normal. The snake had not struck again that night, and the farmers, in groups of three or four, slowly filtered back to their fields. Then, late in the afternoon, hysterical cries for help were heard in the direction of the western part of the hamlet. My cousin and my father grabbed their knives and rushed off to help. **F**

It was Minh, a farmer, who was crying for help. Minh, like most farmers in the area, stored the fish he had caught in the rice field at the end of the rainy season in a small pond. That day Minh's wife had wanted a good fish for dinner. When Minh approached his fish pond he heard
110 what sounded like someone trying to steal his fish by using a bucket to empty water from the pond. Minh was very angry and rushed over to catch the thief, but when he reached the pond, what he saw so **petrified** him that he fell over backward, speechless. When he regained control he crawled away as fast as he could and yelled loudly for help.

The thief he saw was not a person but a huge horse snake, perhaps the same one that had squeezed the old horse to death two nights before. The snake had hooked its head to the branch of one tree and its tail to another and was splashing the water out of the pond by swinging its body back and forth, like a hammock. Thus, when the shallow pond became dry, it
120 planned to swallow all the fish.

All the villagers rushed to the scene to help Minh, and our village chief quickly organized an attack. He ordered all the men to surround the pond. Then two strong young men approached the snake, one at its tail and the other at its head. As they crept closer and closer, the snake **assumed** a striking position, its head about one meter above the pond, and its tail swaying from side to side. It was ready to strike in either direction. As the two young men moved in closer, the snake watched them. Each man tried to draw the attention of the snake, while a third man crept **stealthily** to its side. Suddenly he struck the snake with his
130 long knife. The surprised snake shot out of the pond like an arrow and knocked the young man unconscious as it rushed by. It broke through the circle of men and went into an open rice field. But it received two more wounds on its way out. **G**

The village chief ordered all the women and children to form a long line between the open rice field and the jungle and to yell as loudly as they could, hoping to scare the snake so that it would not flee into the jungle. It would be far easier for the men to fight the wounded snake in an open field than to follow it there.

But now there was a new difficulty. The snake started heading toward
140 the river. Normally a horse snake could beat any man in a race, but since this one was badly wounded, our chief was able to cut off its escape by

F CHRONOLOGICAL ORDER
Reread lines 100–105. When are the cries for help heard? Mark the time and the event on your timeline.

petrify (pĕt′rə-fī′)
v. to paralyze with astonishment or fear

VISUAL VOCABULARY

hammock n. canvas or heavy netting hung between two supports and used as a swinging bed

assume (ə-soom′) v. to take on

stealthily (stĕl′thə-lē) adv. secretly; sneakily

G SETTING
Reread lines 121–133. How does the setting affect the way the villagers attack the snake?

sending half his men running to the river. Blocked off from the river and jungle, the snake decided to stay and fight.

The hunting party surrounded the snake again, and this time four of the best men attacked the snake from four different directions. The snake fought bravely, but it perished. During the struggle one of the men received a dislocated shoulder, two had bruised ribs, and three were momentarily blinded by dirt thrown by the snake. Luckily all of them succeeded in avoiding the fatal bite of the snake. ◆

150   We rejoiced that the danger was over. But we knew it would only be a matter of time until we would once again have to face our most dangerous natural enemy—the horse snake. ◠

◆ **GRAMMAR IN CONTEXT**
A sentence made up of two or more independent clauses is called a **compound sentence.** Reread lines 145–146. Notice that the writer uses a comma and a conjunction ("but") to join one clause ("The snake fought bravely") to another ("it perished") to create a compound sentence.

Comprehension

1. **Recall** Why is the horse snake more dangerous than other snakes?

2. **Clarify** Why does the grandmother tell the story about the father and son who face a horse snake?

3. **Summarize** Reread lines 106–120. What happens to Minh when he goes to his pond.

Text Analysis

● 4. **Understand Chronological Order** Use the timeline to determine over what period of time the events in this selection take place. Then note when the most important events occur.

5. **Make Inferences** Huynh does not directly state his actions during the battle with the horse snake. Reread lines 121–149. What do you think his role was in the battle? Support your inference with evidence from the text.

6. **Analyze Imagery** In lines 10–25, Huynh brings the setting alive with imagery. Which of the five senses does he appeal to in these lines? Support your answer with examples from the text.

● 7. **Examine Setting** Review "The Horse Snake" and find details that describe the setting. Write the details on a chart like the one below. How does the setting affect the conflict between the villagers and the horse snake? Support your answer with details from your chart.

Details About Setting		
Location	Time of Day	Surroundings

8. **Draw Conclusions** How is this memoir similar or different in structure to other stories you have read in this unit? Explain. What other features does it have? What makes it different?

Extension and Challenge

9. **Creative Project: Art** Sketch Huynh's village, using imagery and details from the text.

When is there strength in NUMBERS?

What role did teamwork play in defeating the snake? How is teamwork important in your life?

COMMON CORE

RI 3 Analyze in detail how a key event is introduced, illustrated, and elaborated in a text. **RI 5** Analyze how a particular sentence, paragraph, or section fits into the structure and contributes to the development of ideas.

Vocabulary in Context

▲ VOCABULARY PRACTICE

In each numbered item below, choose the letter of the word or phrase that is not related in meaning to the other words.

1. (a) pace, (b) step, (c) gait, (d) feet
2. (a) stealthily, (b) secretly, (c) slyly, (d) swiftly
3. (a) frighten, (b) petrify, (c) confuse, (d) horrify
4. (a) sunny, (b) nocturnal, (c) moonlit, (d) dark
5. (a) take on, (b) move on, (c) undertake, (d) assume
6. (a) succumb, (b) reject, (c) refuse, (d) throw away

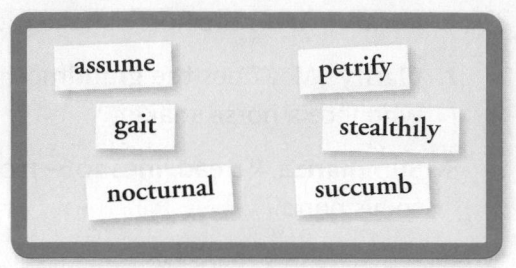

assume   petrify
gait   stealthily
nocturnal   succumb

ACADEMIC VOCABULARY IN WRITING

• affect   • analyze   • evidence   • impact   • provide

Analyze the **impact** of the horse snake on the village. What **evidence** can you cite to show that the villagers have been fighting snakes like these for years? Use at least two Academic Vocabulary words in your discussion.

VOCABULARY STRATEGY: READING A DICTIONARY ENTRY

A dictionary entry contains more than just a definition. You can use a dictionary to determine the pronunciation and parts of speech of unfamiliar words. Dictionary entries may also provide information about a word's origin in an **etymology**. Etymologies help you understand the meaning of an unfamilar word by telling you its history.

> **ballot** (băl′ət) *intr. v.* to cast a vote. [From Italian *ballotta*, small ball or pebble. Italian citizens once voted by casting a small ball or pebble into one of several boxes.]

The pronunciation of the word *ballot* is indicated immediately after the entry word. The sounds represented by the symbols in the pronunciation guide are explained in a key in the dictionary. After the pronunciation, you find the word's part of speech. *Ballot* is an intransitive verb, or a verb that does not take an object. The definition appears after the part of speech. After the definition of the word, you find the word's etymology. This etymology tells you that the word comes from the Italian word for *ball*, which citizens once used to vote.

PRACTICE Look up each word in a dictionary. First, identify the pronunciation and part of speech of each word. Then write down the origin of each word and explain how the history will help you remember the meaning.

1. algorithm   2. hippopotamus   3. radar   4. safari

COMMON CORE

L 4c Consult dictionaries to find the pronunciation of a word or determine its precise meaning or part of speech.

Interactive Vocabulary **THINK** central

Go to **thinkcentral.com**.
KEYWORD: HML6-136

Language

◆ **GRAMMAR IN CONTEXT:** Create Compound Sentences

A run-on sentence is two or more sentences written as one. You can change a run-on sentence to a **compound sentence** by using a comma and a coordinating conjunction (such as *and, but, or, for,* or *so*) to separate the two sentences.

> *Original:* The villagers tried to trap the snake, the snake escaped.
>
> *Revised:* The villagers tried to trap the snake, but the snake escaped.

PRACTICE Rewrite the following sentences. Use a comma and a coordinating conjunction to create a compound sentence.

1. Grandma wanted me to calm down, she read me a story.
2. The villagers searched for the snake, they could not capture him.
3. We heard the cries for help, we raced into the forest.
4. One man had bruised ribs, another injured his arm.

READING-WRITING CONNECTION

Broaden your understanding of "The Horse Snake" by responding to the prompt. Then use the **revising tip** to improve your writing.

WRITING PROMPT	REVISING TIP
Short Constructed Response: Analysis In this section of his memoir, Nhuong describes the way his community overcomes a treacherous foe. In **one paragraph,** describe the qualities that allow Nhuong's village to defeat the horse snake	Review your paragraph. Have you used a comma and coordinating conjunction to create compound sentences? If not, revise your writing.

COMMON CORE

L1 Demonstrate command of the conventions of grammar.
W2 Write informative/explanatory texts to examine a topic.

Interactive Revision **THINK** central

Go to thinkcentral.com.
KEYWORD: HML6-137

Le Mat Village Holds On to Snake Catching Tradition

Radio Transcript

Use with "The Horse Snake," page 128.

COMMON CORE

RI 3 Analyze in detail how a key idea is introduced, illustrated, and elaborated in a text.
RI 6 Determine an author's purpose and explain how it is conveyed in the text.

What's the Connection?

In "The Horse Snake," set in Vietnam in the 1950s, villagers fight off a large snake that threatens their community. In the following radio transcript, you'll read about a modern Vietnamese village that prides itself on its tradition of catching snakes.

Standards Focus: Analyzing an Author's Purpose

There are many different reasons, or **purposes,** an author might have for writing. Here are common examples of an **author's purpose:**

- to inform
- to express feelings
- to persuade
- to entertain

Most authors will not come right out and state their reason for writing. Their purpose will be **implied,** or suggested through the information they present. You will have to read between the lines to determine the author's purpose yourself. To determine an author's purpose, ask yourself:

- For what reason is the author telling me *this?*
- Why is the author telling me this *in this way?*
- What *point* do the author's ideas make?

Use a chart like the one below to discover the author's purpose in the following radio transcript. As you read, list the important details the author shares about snake hunting. Then, study the details and state the main idea of the text. (Hint: the main idea may often be found in the title or in the final paragraph of an informational text.) Finally, decide what purpose the author wanted to achieve in writing.

"Le Mat Village Holds On to Snake Catching Tradition"
Detail 1: All Le Mat villagers, regardless of age or gender, know how to catch snakes.
Detail 2: (Add as many details as you need)
Main Idea:
Author's Purpose:

Le Mat Village Holds On to Snake Catching Tradition

FOCUS ON FORM
This **radio transcript** is a written version of a radio broadcast. Radio broadcasts may include music and sound effects to engage the listener. Radio broadcasts can be created for any number of purposes, including to inform, to persuade, or to entertain.

Le Mat on the outskirts of Hanoi has long been famous for its tradition of catching snakes. Le Mat villagers, regardless of their age and gender, all know how to catch snakes. Although the trade is fading and many villagers now make a living from other jobs, local people's skills and love for catching snakes remain strong. Many can talk with visitors for hours about their village's unique tradition.

Legend has it that snake catching in the village dates back to the 11th century. King Ly Thai Tong's daughter was carried
10 away by a giant snake when she was on a boat on the Duong River. The King announced that anyone who found his daughter's body would be rewarded. **A**

A **AUTHOR'S PURPOSE**
What is the most important detail in lines 8–12? How might this detail hint at the author's purpose?

COMMON CORE RI 3

B CULTURE AND
HISTORY
"The Horse Snake"
and this transcript
both present an
aspect of Vietnamese
culture in the legends
they relate. Legends
are stories about
extraordinary people
and extraordinary
events. Most legends
are based on long-ago
historical facts, to which
storytellers have added
over the ages. In "The
Horse Snake," Nhuong's
grandmother tells the
frightened children
a story about a brave
woodcutter who kills
a ferocious snake. The
woodcutter is honored
by being named chief
of the village. Reread
lines 13–23. What honor
is bestowed on Trung?
What conclusion can
you draw from the
rewards offered in these
two legends? What do
these rewards tell you
about the value of snake
catchers in Vietnamese
culture?

A villager from Le Mat, Hoang Duc Trung, went to the part of the river where the princess was taken away. Trung killed the snake and brought back the princess's body. The King kept his promise and rewarded Trung, but he refused the reward and just asked the King to allow Le Mat's poor villagers to reclaim and settle in the area west of Thang Long Citadel. Under the leadership of the young man, villagers were able to turn a swampy area full of wild 20 grass and poisonous snakes into a fertile and prosperous land. This is now the area of Ngoc Khanh, Lieu Giai, Cong Vi, and Kim Ma in Hanoi. Hoang Duc Trung taught the villagers how to catch snakes and was recognized as the Genie of Le Mat. . . . **B**

Le Mat villagers know well the difference between poisonous and harmless snakes. They also know the characteristics of each snake species, and they all agree that snakes that do not react quickly are maybe the most dangerous. Despite the passage of time and changes in their lives, Le Mat people still love their special tradition and continue to catch any snake they see.

Comprehension

1. **Recall** What have villagers learned about snakes from practicing snake catching? Name at least three examples.

2. **Clarify** How does the snake catching tradition benefit the Le Mat village?

Text Analysis

3. **Draw Conclusions** Reread the legend in lines 8–23. What is the author's purpose for including the legend in the transcript?

4. **Analyze Author's Purpose** What is the main purpose of the transcript? Support your response with the information you recorded in your chart.

COMMON CORE

RI 6 Determine an author's purpose and explain how it is conveyed in a text. **W 2** Write informative/explanatory texts to examine a topic.

Read for Information: Compare Authors' Purposes

WRITING PROMPT

Huynh Quang Nhuong's memoir "The Horse Snake" and the radio transcript you just read discuss life in a Vietnamese village. Though the topic of each work is similar, the author's purpose for each work is very different. In three paragraphs, compare and contrast the author's purpose for writing each work.

To answer this prompt, follow these steps.

1. For each selection, complete a chart like the one shown. Record important details, identify the main idea, and determine the writer's purpose.

"The Horse Snake"
Detail 1: The villagers search for a snake that has squeezed a horse to death.
Detail 2: (Add as many details as you need.)
Main Idea:
Author's Purpose:

2. Write one paragraph analyzing the author's purpose for writing "The Horse Snake." Then write a second paragraph analyzing the author's purpose for writing the radio transcript. Finally, write a paragraph in which you compare and contrast each author's purpose for writing about snake catching. Be sure to provide details from your charts to support your response.

The Walrus and the Carpenter
Narrative Poem by Lewis Carroll

Have you ever been FOOLED?

COMMON CORE

RL 5 Analyze how a particular stanza fits into the structure of a text and contributes to the development of the setting or plot.

It can be fun to trick people—to watch their faces as you convince them to believe that something wacky is actually true. It can even be fun to be tricked. Has anyone ever told you that you were going somewhere boring when in fact you were headed to a surprise party? But not all tricks are fun or funny. In "The Walrus and the Carpenter," we see how easy it is to be fooled into doing something unwise.

CHART IT With a group of classmates, discuss what types of tricks are harmless and fun and what types of tricks can be harmful and cruel. Use a chart like the one shown to note your ideas.

Harmless	Harmful

● TEXT ANALYSIS: NARRATIVE POETRY

"The Walrus and the Carpenter" is a **narrative poem,** a poem that tells a story. Narrative poems contain all the elements of poetry—such as rhythm, rhyme, and sound effects—but they also include the same narrative elements that any work of fiction does, such as

- plot
- setting
- characters

Identifying these elements will help you understand the ideas in a narrative poem.

As you read "The Walrus and the Carpenter," note details about the plot events, setting, and characters in a story map like the one shown.

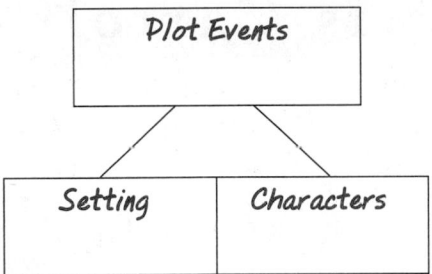

● READING STRATEGY: VISUALIZE

You're about to read a poem with a vivid setting and some very unusual, fantastical characters. You'll probably enjoy the poem more and understand it better if you can **visualize,** or picture in your mind, the setting and characters. To visualize, follow these steps:

- Pay attention to the descriptions on the page.
- Take time to form sensory images based on the words in the descriptions.
- Use your imagination to fill in the blanks.

As you read Lewis Carroll's poem, pay attention to details that will help you visualize the story the poem is telling.

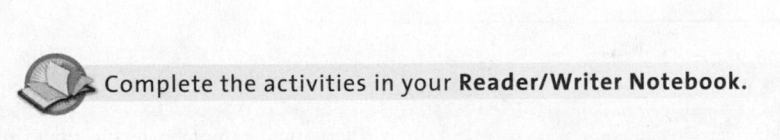
Complete the activities in your **Reader/Writer Notebook.**

Meet the Author

Lewis Carroll
1832–1898

A New Name

In 1865 a British man named Charles Lutwidge Dodgson published his first book for children, *Alice's Adventures in Wonderland.* Instead of using his name, however, Dodgson chose a "pen name," a made-up name. The book was a huge success, and the pen name, Lewis Carroll, became very famous.

Children's Entertainer

Dodgson enjoyed entertaining children throughout his life. As the eldest son in a family of 11, he made up games for his brothers and sisters. As an adult, he told stories and drew pictures for the children he befriended—including a real-life Alice. By training, Dodgson was a mathematician, and even in this field he often focused on young people. He used his math skills to make up puzzles and brainteasers.

BACKGROUND TO THE POEM

Poetic Lessons

In the 1800s in Great Britain, children were often required to memorize long, boring poems that taught lessons about how young people should behave. In "The Walrus and the Carpenter," Carroll makes fun of this approach to education. But he might have slipped in a good lesson for children at the same time.

Author Online
THiNK central
Go to **thinkcentral.com**.
KEYWORD: HML6-143

The *Walrus and the Carpenter*

Lewis Carroll

Analyze Visuals ▶

How would you describe the **setting** in this illustration?

The sun was shining on the sea,
    Shining with all his might:
He did his very best to make
    The billows[1] smooth and bright—
5 And this was odd, because it was
    The middle of the night. **A**

The moon was shining sulkily,[2]
    Because she thought the sun
Had got no business to be there
10   After the day was done—
"It's very rude of him," she said,
    "To come and spoil the fun!"

The sea was wet as wet could be,
    The sands were dry as dry.
15 You could not see a cloud because
    No cloud was in the sky:
No birds were flying overhead—
    There were no birds to fly. **B**

A **VISUALIZE**
Reread the first stanza. What words help you to visualize the setting?

B **NARRATIVE POETRY**
What have you learned so far about the time, place, and weather conditions of the setting? Record details in your graphic organizer.

---

1. **billows:** large waves.
2. **sulkily:** in a gloomy, pouting way.

Illustrations by Sir John Tenniel from
Through the Looking-Glass by Lewis Carroll.

The Walrus and the Carpenter
20   Were walking close at hand:
They wept like anything to see
      Such quantities of sand:
"If this were only cleared away,"
      They said, "it *would* be grand!" **C**

25 "If seven maids with seven mops
      Swept it for half a year,
Do you suppose," the Walrus said,
      "That they could get it clear?"
"I doubt it," said the Carpenter,
30   And shed a bitter tear.

"O Oysters, come and walk with us!"
      The Walrus did beseech.[3]
"A pleasant walk, a pleasant talk,
      Along the briny[4] beach:
35 We cannot do with more than four,
      To give a hand to each."

The eldest Oyster looked at him,
      But never a word he said:
The eldest Oyster winked his eye,
40   And shook his heavy head—
Meaning to say he did not choose
      To leave the oyster-bed.

But four young Oysters hurried up,
      All eager for the treat:
45 Their coats were brushed, their faces washed,
      Their shoes were clean and neat—
And this was odd, because, you know,
      They hadn't any feet.

C NARRATIVE POETRY
What **characters** have you met? Note them in your graphic organizer. Add new characters as they are introduced in the poem.

---

3. **beseech:** to beg anxiously.
4. **briny:** containing a fair amount of salt.

Four other Oysters followed them,
50   And yet another four;
And thick and fast they came at last,
        And more, and more, and more—
All hopping through the frothy waves,
        And scrambling to the shore.

55 The Walrus and the Carpenter
        Walked on a mile or so,
And then they rested on a rock
        Conveniently low:
And all the little Oysters stood
60   And waited in a row. **D**

"The time has come," the Walrus said,
        "To talk of many things:
Of shoes—and ships—and sealing-wax—
        Of cabbages—and kings—
65 And why the sea is boiling hot—
        And whether pigs have wings."

"But wait a bit," the Oysters cried,
        "Before we have our chat;
For some of us are out of breath,
70   And all of us are fat!"
"No hurry!" said the Carpenter.
        They thanked him much for that.

"A loaf of bread," the Walrus said,
        "Is what we chiefly need:
75 Pepper and vinegar besides
        Are very good indeed—
Now, if you're ready, Oysters dear,
        We can begin to feed." **E**

D VISUALIZE
Reread lines 55–60.
What do you see in your
mind? Why might it be
important that the rock
is "conveniently low"?

E NARRATIVE POETRY
What's happening at
this point in the poem?
Note the **plot events** in
your graphic organizer.

"But not on us!" the Oysters cried,
80   Turning a little blue.
"After such kindness, that would be
      A dismal⁵ thing to do!"
"The night is fine," the Walrus said.
      "Do you admire the view?" **F**

85 "It was so kind of you to come!
      And you are very nice!"
The Carpenter said nothing but
      "Cut us another slice.
I wish you were not quite so deaf—
90   I've had to ask you twice!"

"It seems a shame," the Walrus said,
      "To play them such a trick.
After we've brought them out so far,
      And made them trot so quick!"
95 The Carpenter said nothing but
      "The butter's spread too thick!"

"I weep for you," the Walrus said:
      "I deeply sympathize."
With sobs and tears he sorted out
100   Those of the largest size,
Holding his pocket-handkerchief
      Before his streaming eyes. **G**

"O Oysters," said the Carpenter,
      "You've had a pleasant run!
105 Shall we be trotting home again?"
      But answer came there none—
And this was scarcely odd, because
      They'd eaten every one.

F NARRATIVE POETRY
The **climax** of a plot is
the turning point. What
do the Oysters finally
realize in this stanza?

G VISUALIZE
Picture in your mind
the Walrus crying while
sorting the Oysters.
What details in the
poem help you to do so?

---

5. **dismal:** particularly bad; dreadful.

Comprehension

1. **Recall** What do the Walrus and the Carpenter invite the Oysters to do?

2. **Clarify** What trick do the Walrus and the Carpenter play on the Oysters?

Text Analysis

● 3. **Make Inferences** Reread lines 37–42. Why might the eldest Oyster have lived longer than any of the other oysters in the oyster bed?

● 4. **Visualize** A **stanza** is a group of lines within a poem. Choose a stanza on page 146 and describe the mental picture you form when you read it. Then use a diagram like the one shown to note what helped you visualize.

5. **Identify Rhyme** The repetition of a sound at the ends of different words—as in *knows* and *rose*—is called **rhyme.** The words at the ends of lines 2, 4, and 6 rhyme. Which words in lines 7–12 rhyme? Which words rhyme in lines 13–18? Look through the rest of the poem and describe any pattern you notice.

● 6. **Evaluate Narrative Poetry** Using the story map that you created as you read, summarize "The Walrus and the Carpenter." Tell what happened, where it happened, and who took part. Do you find the events in the poem funny or disturbing? Explain your reaction.

7. **Draw Conclusions** On the basis of this poem, what do you think Carroll might advise young people to do to avoid being tricked? Use evidence from the poem to support your answer.

COMMON CORE

RL 5 Analyze how a particular stanza fits into the structure of a text and contributes to the development of the setting and plot. **SL 1c** Pose and respond to specific questions with elaboration and detail.

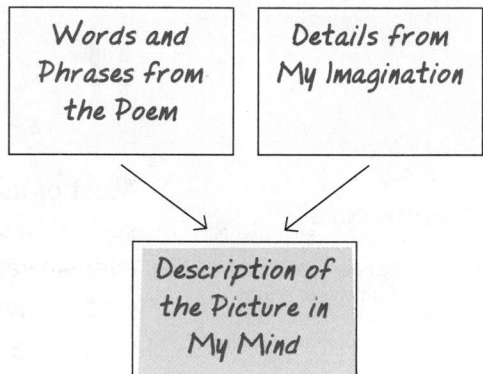

Extension and Challenge

8. **Readers' Circle** With a partner, look over the fiction and nonfiction you have read in this unit. Decide which selection might serve as a good basis for a narrative poem and why. Then discuss how the selection would change if told in poem form. Would it be funnier, or more serious?

9. **Creative Project: Drama** Poems often lend themselves to being read aloud. Put together a cast of classmates to read "The Walrus and the Carpenter." Assign one person to be the narrator and others to perform the speaking parts. Then do a dramatic reading of the poem.

Have you ever been FOOLED?

Consider the oysters. Is it ever acceptable to fool someone? Explain why or why not.

The Prince and the Pauper

Novel by Mark Twain
Dramatized by Joellen Bland

HISTORY. Video link at thinkcentral.com

Who would you BE if you could?

COMMON CORE

RL 3 Describe how a particular drama's plot unfolds as well as how the characters respond or change as the plot moves toward a resolution.

Most of us can name at least one person who has a life we sometimes envy. This person may be an actor, an athlete, a singer, or even a friend. However, you might not envy him or her if you knew what his or her life was really like. In *The Prince and the Pauper,* two characters learn unexpected lessons about themselves and each other when they trade places.

ROLE-PLAY With a classmate, choose two famous people whose lives you admire. Make a list of questions you would want to ask them and think of the answers the people would give. Be sure to include things in their lives that might not be perfect. Then take turns being the interviewer and present your interviews of the famous people to the class.

● TEXT ANALYSIS: CONFLICT IN DRAMA

In drama, as in short stories, the **plot** revolves around a central **conflict.** Since drama is meant to be performed by actors, a drama's conflict usually unfolds through action and dialogue (conversation between characters).

Unlike a book, which has chapters, a play is divided into acts and scenes. This play takes place in eight scenes that revolve around two boys who switch identities. As you read, notice how their behavior affects the plot and how the boys change as the plot moves toward a resolution.

● READING STRATEGY: READING A PLAY

In a drama, **stage directions** provide key information that readers would normally see or hear in a performance, such as

- the setting, scenery, and props (*Westminster Palace, England,* Scene 1, line 2)

- the music, sound effects, and lighting (*Fanfare of trumpets is heard,* Scene 3, line 282)

- the characters' movements, behavior, or ways of speaking (*surprised, standing up quickly,* Scene 4, line 345)

As you read the play, record examples of stage directions and tell what they help you to understand.

Stage Direction	Type of Direction	What It Tells Me
Fanfare of trumpets is heard (Scene 3, line 282)	Sound effects	Someone is entering.

▲ VOCABULARY IN CONTEXT

Replace each boldfaced word below with a different word or words that have the same meaning.

1. The king expected his son to be his **successor.**
2. Tom looked like a prince, but he was a **pauper.**
3. An **affliction** seemed to make the prince forgetful.
4. The king began to doubt that his son was **sane.**
5. The boy had no **recollection** of where he put the seal.
6. Was he the real prince or an **impostor?**

 Complete the activities in your **Reader/Writer Notebook.**

Meet the Author

Mark Twain
1835–1910

Boyhood Adventures
Two of Mark Twain's best-known works focus on the adventures, or misadventures, of two young boys— Huckleberry Finn and Tom Sawyer. In developing these stories, Twain drew upon his own experiences and those of his childhood friends. Many of his tales take place along the Mississippi River, where Twain spent much of his time as a child and young adult.

Have Pen, Will Travel
Twain loved to travel. His frequent trips throughout the United States and to Europe resulted in a series of funny and clever stories. Twain set some of his novels, including *The Prince and the Pauper,* in England, where he was greatly admired. Though he wrote *The Prince and the Pauper* as a novel, Joellen Bland later adapted the story as a play.

BACKGROUND TO THE PLAY
True Royalty
The prince in Twain's story is based on Edward, son of King Henry VIII of England. After Henry's death in 1547, the nine-year-old Edward took the throne, becoming King Edward VI.

Author Online
THINK central
Go to **thinkcentral.com.**
KEYWORD: HML6-151

The Prince and the Pauper

Mark Twain
Dramatized by Joellen Bland

CHARACTERS

Edward, Prince of Wales

Tom Canty, the Pauper

Lord Hertford

Lord St. John

King Henry VIII

Herald

Miles Hendon

John Canty, Tom's father

Hugo, a young thief

Two Women

Justice

Constable

Jailer

Sir Hugh Hendon

Two Prisoners

Two Guards

Three Pages

Lords and Ladies

Villagers

SCENE ONE

Time: *1547.*

Setting: *Westminster Palace, England. Gates leading to courtyard are at right. Slightly to the left, off courtyard and inside gates, interior of palace anteroom[1] is visible. There is a couch with a rich robe draped on it, screen at rear, bellcord, mirror, chairs, and a table with bowl of nuts, and a large golden seal on it. Piece of armor hangs on one wall. Exits are rear and downstage.*

---

1. **anteroom** (ăn′tē-rōōm′): an outer room that leads to another room and is often used as a waiting room.

Photographs by Crown Media
Distribution, LLC.

At Curtain Rise: Two Guards—*one at right, one at left—stand in front of gates, and several*
10 Villagers *hover nearby, straining to see into courtyard where* Prince *may be seen through fence, playing.* Two Women *enter right.*

1st Woman. I have walked all morning just to have a glimpse of Westminster Palace.

2nd Woman. Maybe if we can get near enough to the gates, we can have a glimpse of the young Prince. (Tom Canty, *dirty and ragged, comes out of crowd and steps close to gates.*)

Tom. I have always dreamed of seeing a real
20 Prince! (*Excited, he presses his nose against gates.*)

1st Guard. Mind your manners, you young beggar! (*Seizes* Tom *by collar and sends him sprawling into crowd.* Villagers *laugh, as* Tom *slowly gets to his feet.*)

Prince (*rushing to gates*). How dare you treat a poor subject of the King in such a manner! Open the gates and let him in! (*As* Villagers *see* Prince, *they take off their hats and bow low.*)

Villagers (*shouting together*). Long live the
30 Prince of Wales! (Guards *open gates and* Tom *slowly passes through, as if in a dream.*)

Prince (*to* Tom). You look tired, and you have been treated cruelly. I am Edward, Prince of Wales. What is your name?

Tom (*looking around in awe*). Tom Canty, Your Highness.

Prince. Come into the palace with me, Tom. (Prince *leads* Tom *into anteroom.* Villagers *pantomime conversation, and all but a few exit.*)
40 Where do you live, Tom?

Tom. In the city, Your Highness, in Offal Court.

Prince. Offal Court? That is an odd name. Do you have parents?

Tom. Yes, Your Highness.

Prince. How does your father treat you?

Tom. If it please you, Your Highness, when I am not able to beg a penny for our supper, he treats me to beatings.

Prince (*shocked*). What! Beatings? My father
50 is not a calm man, but he does not beat me. (*looks at* Tom *thoughtfully*) You speak well and have an easy grace. Have you been schooled?

Tom. Very little, Your Highness. A good priest who shares our house in Offal Court has taught me from his books.

Prince. Do you have a pleasant life in Offal Court?

Tom. Pleasant enough, Your Highness, save when I am hungry. We have Punch and Judy
60 shows, and sometimes we lads have fights in the street.

Prince (*eagerly*). I should like that. Tell me more.

Tom. In summer, we run races and swim in the river, and we love to wallow in the mud.

Prince (*sighing, wistfully*). If I could wear your clothes and play in the mud just once, with no one to forbid me, I think I could give up the crown!

Tom (*shaking his head*). And if I could wear
70 your fine clothes just once, Your Highness . . .

Prince. Would you like that? Come, then. We shall change places. You can take off your rags and put on my clothes—and I will put on yours. (*He leads* Tom *behind screen, and they return shortly, each wearing the other's clothes.*) Let's look at ourselves in this mirror. (*leads* Tom *to mirror*)

Tom. Oh, Your Highness, it is not proper for me to wear such clothes.

80 **Prince** (*excitedly, as he looks in mirror*). Heavens, do you not see it? We look like brothers! We have the same features and bearing.[2] If we went about together, dressed alike, there is no one

---

2. **features and bearing:** parts of the face and ways of standing or walking.

who could say which is the Prince of Wales and which is Tom Canty!

Tom (*drawing back and rubbing his hand*). Your Highness, I am frightened. . . .

Prince. Do not worry. (*seeing* Tom *rub his hand*) Is that a bruise on your hand?

90 **Tom.** Yes, but it is a slight thing, Your Highness.

Prince (*angrily*). It was shameful and cruel of that guard to strike you. Do not stir a step until I come back. I command you! (*He picks up golden Seal of England[3] and carefully puts it into piece of armor. He then dashes out to gates.*) Open! Unbar the gates at once! (*2nd Guard opens gates, and as* Prince *runs out, in rags,* 1st Guard *seizes him, boxes him on the ear, and knocks him to the ground.*)

100 **1st Guard.** Take that, you little beggar, for the trouble you have made for me with the Prince. (Villagers *roar with laughter.*)

Prince (*picking himself up, turning on* Guard *furiously*). I am Prince of Wales! You shall hang for laying your hand on me!

1st Guard (*presenting arms; mockingly*). I salute Your Gracious Highness! (*Then, angrily,* 1st Guard *shoves* Prince *roughly aside.*) Be off, you mad bag of rags! (Prince *is surrounded* 110 *by* Villagers, *who hustle him off.*)

Villagers (*ad lib,[4] as they exit, shouting*). Make way for His Royal Highness! Make way for the Prince of Wales! Hail to the Prince! (*etc.*)

Tom (*admiring himself in mirror*). If only the boys in Offal Court could see me! They will

---

3. **Seal of England:** a device used to stamp a special design, usually a picture of the ruler, onto a document, thus indicating that it has royal approval.

4. **ad lib:** talk together about what is going on, but without an actual script.

not believe me when I tell them about this. (*looks around anxiously*) But where is the Prince? (*Looks cautiously into courtyard. Two Guards immediately snap to attention and salute. He quickly ducks back into anteroom as* Lords Hertford *and* St. John *enter at rear.*)

Hertford (*going toward* Tom, *then stopping and bowing low*). My Lord, you look distressed. What is wrong?

Tom (*trembling*). Oh, I beg of you, be merciful. I am no Prince, but poor Tom Canty of Offal Court. Please let me see the Prince, and he will give my rags back to me and let me go unhurt. (*kneeling*) Please, be merciful and spare me!

Hertford (*puzzled and disturbed*). Your Highness, on your knees? To me? (*bows quickly, then, aside to* St. John) The Prince has gone mad! We must inform the King. (*to* Tom) A moment, your Highness. (Hertford *and* St. John *exit rear.*)

Tom. Oh, there is no hope for me now. They will hang me for certain! (Hertford *and* St. John *re-enter, supporting* King. Tom *watches in awe as they help him to couch, where he sinks down wearily.*)

King (*beckoning* Tom *close to him*). Now, my son, Edward, my prince. What is this? Do you mean to deceive me, the King, your father, who loves you and treats you so kindly?

Tom (*dropping to his knees*). You are the King? Then I have no hope!

King (*stunned*). My child, you are not well. Do not break your father's old heart. Say you know me.

Tom. Yes, you are my lord the King, whom God preserve.

King. True, that is right. Now, you will not deny that you are Prince of Wales, as they say you did just a while ago?

Tom. I beg you, Your Grace, believe me. I am the lowest of your subjects, being born a **pauper,** and it is by a great mistake that I am here. I am too young to die. Oh, please, spare me, sire!

King (*amazed*). Die? Do not talk so, my child.
160 You shall not die.

Tom (*gratefully*). God save you, my king! And now, may I go?

King. Go? Where would you go?

Tom. Back to the alley where I was born and bred to misery.

King. My poor child, rest your head here. (*He holds* Tom's *head and pats his shoulder, then turns to* Hertford *and* St. John.) Alas, I am old and ill, and my son is mad. But this shall pass. Mad
170 or **sane,** he is my heir and shall rule England. Tomorrow he shall be installed and confirmed in his princely dignity! Bring the Great Seal!

Hertford (*bowing low*). Please, Your Majesty, you took the Great Seal from the Chancellor two days ago to give to His Highness the Prince.

King. So I did. (*to* Tom) My child, tell me, where is the Great Seal?

Tom (*trembling*). Indeed, my lord, I do not know.

180 **King.** Ah, your **affliction** hangs heavily upon you. 'Tis no matter. You will remember later. Listen, carefully! (*gently, but firmly*) I command you to hide your affliction in all ways that be within your power. You shall deny to no one that you are the true prince, and if your memory should fail you upon any occasion of state, you shall be advised by your uncle, the Lord Hertford.

Tom (*resigned*). The King has spoken. The
190 King shall be obeyed.

King. And now, my child, I go to rest. (*He stands weakly, and* Hertford *leads him off, rear.*)

Tom (*wearily, to* St. John). May it please your lordship to let me rest now?

St. John. So it please Your Highness, it is for you to command and us to obey. But it is wise that you rest, for this evening you must attend the Lord Mayor's banquet in your honor. (*He pulls bellcord, and* Three Pages *enter and kneel*
200 *before* Tom.)

Tom. Banquet? (*Terrified, he sits on couch and reaches for cup of water, but* 1st Page *instantly seizes cup, drops on one knee, and serves it to him.* Tom *starts to take off his boots, but* 2nd Page *stops him and does it for him. He tries to remove his cape and gloves, and* 3rd Page *does it for him.*) I wonder that you do not try to breathe for me also! (*Lies down cautiously.* Pages *cover him with robe, then back away and exit.*)

210 **St. John** (*to* Hertford, *as he enters*). Plainly, what do you think?

Hertford. Plainly, this. The King is near death, my nephew the Prince of Wales is clearly mad and will mount the throne mad. God protect England, for she will need it!

St. John. Does it not seem strange that madness could so change his manner from what it used to be? It troubles me, his saying he is not the Prince.

220 **Hertford.** Peace, my lord! If he were an **impostor** and called himself Prince, that would be natural. But was there ever an impostor, who being called Prince by the King and court, denied it? Never! This is the true Prince gone mad. And tonight all London shall honor him. (Hertford *and* St. John *exit.* Tom *sits up, looks around helplessly, then gets up.*)

Tom. I should have thought to order something to eat. (*sees bowl of nuts on table*) Ah! Here are
230 some nuts! (*looks around, sees Great Seal in armor, takes it out, looks at it curiously*) This will make a good nutcracker. (*He takes bowl of nuts, sits on couch and begins to crack nuts with Great Seal and eat them, as curtain falls.*)

SCENE TWO

Time: *Later that night.*

Setting: *A street in London, near Offal Court. Played before the curtain.*

At Curtain Rise: Prince *limps in, dirty and tousled. He looks around wearily. Several* Villagers *pass by, pushing against him.*

Prince. I have never seen this poor section of London. I must be near Offal Court. If I can only find it before I drop! (John Canty *steps out of crowd, seizes* Prince *roughly.*)

Canty. Out at this time of night, and I warrant you haven't brought a farthing[5] home! If that is the case and I do not break all the bones in your miserable body, then I am not John Canty!

Prince (*eagerly*). Oh, are you his father?

Canty. *His* father? I am *your* father, and—

Prince. Take me to the palace at once, and your son will be returned to you. The King, my father, will make you rich beyond your wildest dreams. Oh, save me, for I am indeed the Prince of Wales.

Canty (*staring in amazement*). Gone stark mad! But mad or not, I'll soon find where the soft places lie in your bones. Come home! (*starts to drag* Prince *off*)

Prince (*struggling*). Let me go! I am the Prince of Wales, and the King shall have your life for this!

Canty (*angrily*). I'll take no more of your madness! (*raises stick to strike, but* Prince *struggles free and runs off, and* Canty *runs after him*)

SCENE THREE

Setting: *Same as Scene 1, with addition of dining table, set with dishes and goblets, on raised platform. Throne-like chair is at head of table.*

At Curtain Rise: *A banquet is in progress. Tom, in royal robes, sits at head of table, with* Hertford *at his right and* St. John *at his left. Lords and Ladies sit around table eating and talking softly.*

Tom (*to* Hertford). What is this, my Lord? (*holds up a plate*)

Hertford. Lettuce and turnips, Your Highness.

Tom. Lettuce and turnips? I have never seen them before. Am I to eat them?

Hertford (*discreetly*). Yes, Your Highness, if you so desire. (Tom *begins to eat food with his fingers. Fanfare of trumpets[6] is heard, and* Herald *enters, carrying scroll. All turn to look.*)

---

5. **farthing:** a former British coin worth one-fourth of a British penny.

6. **fanfare of trumpets:** a short tune or call, usually indicating that something important is about to occur.

Herald (*reading from scroll*). His Majesty, King Henry VIII, is dead! The King is dead! (*All rise and turn to* Tom, *who sits, stunned.*)

All (*together*). The King is dead. Long live the King! Long live Edward, King of England! (*All bow to* Tom. Herald *bows and exits.*)

290 **Hertford** (*to* Tom). Your Majesty, we must call the council. Come, St. John. (Hertford *and* St. John *lead* Tom *off at rear.* Lords *and* Ladies *follow, talking among themselves. At gates, down right,* Villagers *enter and mill about.* Prince *enters right, pounds on gates and shouts.*)

Prince. Open the gates! I am the Prince of Wales! Open, I say! And though I am friendless with no one to help me, I will not be driven from my ground.

300 **Miles Hendon** (*entering through crowd*). Though you be Prince or not, you are indeed a gallant lad and not friendless. Here I stand to prove it, and you might have a worse friend than Miles Hendon.

1st Villager. 'Tis another prince in disguise. Take the lad and dunk him in the pond! (*He seizes* Prince, *but* Miles *strikes him with flat of his sword. Crowd, now angry, presses forward threateningly, when fanfare of trumpets is heard offstage.* Herald, 310 *carrying scroll, enters up left at gates.*)

Herald. Make way for the King's messenger! (*reading from scroll*) His Majesty, King Henry VIII, is dead! The King is dead! (*He exits right, repeating message, and* Villagers *stand in stunned silence.*)

Prince (*stunned*). The King is dead!

1st Villager (*shouting*). Long live Edward, King of England!

Villagers (*together*). Long live the King! 320 (*shouting, ad lib*) Long live King Edward! Heaven protect Edward, King of England! (*etc.*)

Miles (*taking* Prince *by the arm*). Come, lad, before the crowd remembers us. I have a room at the inn, and you can stay there. (*He hurries off with stunned* Prince. Tom, *led by* Hertford, *enters courtyard up rear.* Villagers *see them.*)

Villagers (*together*). Long live the King! (*They fall to their knees as curtains close.*)

SCENE FOUR

Setting: *Miles' room at the inn. At right is table* 330 *set with dishes and bowls of food, a chair at each side. At left is bed, with table and chair next to it, and a window. Candle is on table.*

At Curtain Rise: Miles *and* Prince *approach table.*

Miles. I have had a hot supper prepared. I'll bet you're hungry, lad.

Prince. Yes, I am. It's kind of you to let me stay with you, Miles. I am truly Edward, King of England, and you shall not go unrewarded. (*sits at table*)

340 **Miles** (*to himself*). First he called himself Prince, and now he is King. Well, I will humor him. (*starts to sit*)

Prince (*angrily*). Stop! Would you sit in the presence of the King?

Miles (*surprised, standing up quickly*). I beg your pardon, Your Majesty. I was not thinking. (*Stares uncertainly at* Prince, *who sits at table, expectantly.* Miles *starts to uncover dishes of food, serves* Prince *and fills glasses.*)

350 **Prince.** Miles, you have a gallant way about you. Are you nobly born?

Miles. My father is a baronet,[7] Your Majesty.

Prince. Then you must also be a baronet.

Miles (*shaking his head*). My father banished me from home seven years ago, so I fought in

---

7. **baronet:** a rank of honor in Britain, below a baron and above a knight.

the wars. I was taken prisoner, and I have spent the past seven years in prison. Now I am free, and I am returning home.

Prince. You have been shamefully wronged!
360 But I will make things right for you. You have saved me from injury and possible death. Name your reward and if it be within the compass of my royal power, it is yours.

Miles (*pausing briefly, then dropping to his knee*). Since Your Majesty is pleased to hold my simple duty worthy of reward, I ask that I and my <u>successors</u> may hold the privilege of sitting in the presence of the King.

Prince (*taking* Miles' *sword, tapping him lightly*
370 *on each shoulder*). Rise and seat yourself. (*returns sword to* Miles, *then rises and goes over to bed*)

Miles (*rising*). He should have been born a king. He plays the part to a marvel! If I had not thought of this favor, I might have had to stand for weeks. (*sits down and begins to eat*)

Prince. Sir Miles, you will stand guard while I sleep? (*lies down and instantly falls asleep*)

Miles. Yes, Your Majesty. (*With a rueful look*
380 *at his uneaten supper, he stands up.*) Poor little chap. I suppose his mind has been disordered with ill usage. (*covers* Prince *with his cape*) Well, I will be his friend and watch over him. (*Blows out candle, then yawns, sits on chair next to bed, and falls asleep.* John Canty *and* Hugo *appear at window, peer around room, then enter cautiously through window. They lift the sleeping* Prince, *staring nervously at* Miles.)

Canty (*in loud whisper*). I swore the day he was
390 born he would be a thief and a beggar, and I won't lose him now. Lead the way to the camp Hugo! (Canty *and* Hugo *carry* Prince *off right, as* Miles *sleeps on and curtain falls.*)

SCENE FIVE

Time: *Two weeks later.*

Setting: *Country village street.*

Before Curtain Rise: Villagers *walk about.* Canty, Hugo, *and* Prince *enter.*

Canty. I will go in this direction. Hugo, keep my mad son with you, and see that he doesn't
400 escape again! (*exits*)

Hugo (*seizing* Prince *by the arm*). He won't escape! I'll see that he earns his bread today, or else!

Prince (*pulling away*). I will not beg with you, and I will not steal! I have suffered enough in this miserable company of thieves!

Hugo. You shall suffer more if you do not do as I tell you! (*raises clenched fist at* Prince) Refuse if you dare! (Woman *enters, carrying wrapped*
410 *bundle in a basket on her arm.*) Wait here until I come back. (Hugo *sneaks along after* Woman, *then snatches her bundle, runs back to* Prince, *and thrusts it into his arms.*) Run after me and call, "Stop, thief!" But be sure you lead her astray! (*Runs off.* Prince *throws down bundle in disgust.*)

Woman. Help! Thief! Stop, thief! (*rushes at* Prince *and seizes him, just as several* Villagers *enter*) You little thief! What do you mean by robbing a poor woman? Somebody bring the
420 constable! (Miles *enters and watches.*)

1st Villager (*grabbing* Prince). I'll teach him a lesson, the little villain!

Prince (*struggling*). Take your hands off me! I did not rob this woman!

Miles (*stepping out of crowd and pushing man back with the flat of his sword*). Let us proceed gently, my friends. This is a matter for the law.

Prince (*springing to* Miles' *side*). You have come just in time, Sir Miles. Carve this rabble to rags!

430 **Miles.** Speak softly. Trust in me and all shall go well.

Constable (*entering and reaching for* Prince). Come along, young rascal!

Miles. Gently, good friend. He shall go peaceably to the Justice.

Prince. I will not go before a Justice! I did not do this thing!

Miles (*taking him aside*). Sire, will you reject the laws of the realm, yet demand that your subjects respect them?

Prince (*calmer*). You are right, Sir Miles. Whatever the King requires a subject to suffer under the law, he will suffer himself while he holds the station of a subject. (Constable *leads them off right. Villagers follow. Curtain.*)

SCENE SIX

Setting: *Office of the Justice. A high bench is at center.*

At Curtain Rise: Justice *sits behind bench.* Constable *enters with* Miles *and* Prince, *followed by* Villagers. Woman *carries wrapped bundle.*

Constable (*to* Justice). A young thief, your worship, is accused of stealing a dressed pig from this poor woman.

Justice (*looking down at* Prince, *then* Woman). My good woman, are you absolutely certain this lad stole your pig?

Woman. It was none other than he, your worship.

Justice. Are there no witnesses to the contrary? (*All shake their heads.*) Then the lad stands convicted. (*to* Woman) What do you hold this property to be worth?

Woman. Three shillings and eight pence, your worship.

Justice (*leaning down to* Woman). Good woman, do you know that when one steals a thing above the value of thirteen pence, the law says he shall hang for it?

Woman (*upset*). Oh, what have I done? I would not hang the poor boy for the whole world! Save me from this, your worship. What can I do?

Justice (*gravely*). You may revise the value, since it is not yet written in the record.

Woman. Then call the pig eight pence, your worship.

Justice. So be it. You may take your property and go. (Woman *starts off, and is followed by* Constable. Miles *follows them cautiously down right.*)

Constable (*stopping* Woman). Good woman, I will buy your pig from you. (*takes coins from pocket*) Here is eight pence.

Woman. Eight pence! It cost me three shillings and eight pence!

Constable. Indeed! Then come back before his worship and answer for this. The lad must hang!

Woman. No! No! Say no more. Give me the eight pence and hold your peace. (Constable *hands her coins and takes pig.* Woman *exits, angrily.* Miles *returns to bench.*)

Justice. The boy is sentenced to a fortnight[8] in the common jail. Take him away, Constable! (Justice *exits.* Prince *gives* Miles *a nervous glance.*)

Miles (*following* Constable). Good sir, turn your back a moment and let the poor lad escape. He is innocent.

Constable (*outraged*). What? You say this to me? Sir, I arrest you in—

Miles. Do not be so hasty! (*slyly*) The pig you have purchased for eight pence may cost you your neck, man.

---

8. **fortnight:** 14 days.

Constable (*laughing nervously*). Ah, but I was merely jesting with the woman, sir.

Miles. Would the Justice think it a jest?

Constable. Good sir! The Justice has no more sympathy with a jest than a dead corpse! (*perplexed*) Very well, I will turn my back and see nothing! But go quickly! (*exits*)

510 **Miles** (*to* Prince). Come, my liege.[9] We are free to go. And that band of thieves shall not set hands on you again, I swear it!

Prince (*wearily*). Can you believe, Sir Miles, that in the last fortnight, I, the King of England, have escaped from thieves and begged for food on the road? I have slept in a barn with a calf! I have washed dishes in a peasant's kitchen, and narrowly escaped death. And not once in all my wanderings did I see a courier[10] searching for 520 me! Is it no matter for commotion and distress that the head of state is gone?

Miles (*sadly, aside*). Still busy with his pathetic dream. (*to* Prince) It is strange indeed, my liege. But come, I will take you to my father's home in Kent. We are not far away. There you may rest in a house with seventy rooms! Come, I am all impatience to be home again! (*They exit,* Miles *in cheerful spirits,* Prince *looking puzzled, as curtains close.*)

SCENE SEVEN

530 **Setting:** *Village jail. Bare stage, with barred window on one wall.*

At Curtain Rise: Two Prisoners, *in chains, are onstage.* Jailer *shoves* Miles *and* Prince, *in chains, onstage. They struggle and protest.*

Miles. But I tell you, I am Miles Hendon! My brother, Sir Hugh, has stolen my bride and my estate!

Jailer. Be silent! Impostor! Sir Hugh will see that you pay well for claiming to be his dead 540 brother and for assaulting him in his own house! (*exits*)

Miles (*sitting, with head in hands*). Oh, my dear Edith . . . now wife to my brother Hugh, against her will, and my poor father . . . dead!

1st Prisoner. At least you have your life, sir. I am sentenced to be hanged for killing a deer in the King's park.

2nd Prisoner. And I must hang for stealing a yard of cloth to dress my children.

550 **Prince** (*moved; to* Prisoners). When I mount my throne, you shall all be free. And the laws that have dishonored you shall be swept from the books. (*turning away*) Kings should go to school to learn their own laws and be merciful.

1st Prisoner. What does the lad mean? I have heard that the King is mad, but merciful.

2nd Prisoner. He is to be crowned at Westminster tomorrow.

Prince (*violently*). King? What King, good sir?

560 **1st Prisoner.** Why, we have only one, his most sacred majesty, King Edward the Sixth.

2nd Prisoner. And whether he be mad or not, his praises are on all men's lips. He has saved many innocent lives, and now he means to destroy the cruelest laws that oppress the people.

Prince (*turning away, shaking his head*). How can this be? Surely it is not that little beggar boy! (Sir Hugh *enters with* Jailer.)

Sir Hugh. Seize the impostor!

570 **Miles** (*as* Jailer *pulls him to his feet*). Hugh, this has gone far enough!

Sir Hugh. You will sit in the public stocks for two hours, and the boy would join you if he were not so young. See to it, jailer, and after

---

9. **my liege** (lēj): my lord.

10. **courier** (kŏŏr′ē-ər): messenger.

two hours, you may release them. Meanwhile, I ride to London for the coronation![11] (Sir Hugh *exits and* Miles *is hustled out by* Jailer.)

Prince. Coronation! What does he mean? There can be no coronation without me! (*curtain falls.*)

SCENE EIGHT

580 **Time:** *Coronation Day.*

Setting: *Outside gates of Westminster Abbey, played before curtain. Painted screen or flat at rear represents Abbey. Throne is in center. Bench is near it.*

At Curtain Rise: Lords *and* Ladies *crowd Abbey. Outside gates,* Guards *drive back cheering* Villagers, *among them* Miles.

Miles (*distraught*). I've lost him! Poor little chap! He has been swallowed up in the crowd!

590 (*Fanfare of trumpets is heard, then silence.* Hertford, St. John, Lords *and* Ladies *enter slowly, in a procession, followed by* Pages, *one of whom carries crown on a small cushion.* Tom *follows procession, looking about nervously. Suddenly,* Prince, *in rags, steps out from crowd, his hand raised.*)

Prince. I forbid you to set the crown of England upon that head. I am the King!

Hertford. Seize the little vagabond!

600 **Tom.** I forbid it! He is the King! (*kneels before* Prince) Oh, my lord the King, let poor Tom Canty be the first to say, "Put on your crown and enter into your own right again." (Hertford *and several* Lords *look closely at both boys.*)

Hertford. This is strange indeed. (*to* Tom) By your favor, sir, I wish to ask certain questions of this lad.

---

11. **coronation:** the act of crowning someone king or queen. In England coronations usually take place at a large church in London called Westminster Abbey.

Prince. I will answer truly whatever you may ask, my lord.

610 **Hertford.** But if you have been well trained, you may answer my questions as well as our lord the King. I need a definite proof. (*thinks a moment*) Ah! Where lies the Great Seal of England? It has been missing for weeks, and only the true Prince of Wales can say where it lies.

Tom. Wait! Was the seal round and thick, with letters engraved on it? (Hertford *nods*.) I know where it is, but it was not I who put it there. The rightful King shall tell you. (*to* Prince)

620 Think, my King, it was the very last thing you did that day before you rushed out of the palace wearing my rags.

Prince (*pausing*). I recall how we exchanged clothes, but have no **recollection** of hiding the Great Seal.

Tom (*eagerly*). Remember when you saw the bruise on my hand, you ran to the door, but first you hid this thing you call the Seal.

Prince (*suddenly*). Ah! I remember! (*to* St. John)

630 Go, my good St. John, and you shall find the Great Seal in the armor that hangs on the wall in my chamber. (St. John *hesitates, but at a nod from* Tom, *hurries off.*)

Tom (*pleased*). Right, my King! Now the scepter[12] of England is yours again. (St. John *returns in a moment with Great Seal.*)

All (*shouting*). Long live Edward, King of England! (Tom *takes off his cape and throws it over* Prince's *rags. Trumpet fanfare is heard.* St.

640 John *takes crown and places it on* Prince. *All kneel.*)

Hertford. Let the small impostor be flung into the Tower!

Prince (*firmly*). I will not have it so. But for him, I would not have my crown. (*to* Tom) My poor boy, how was it that you could remember where I hid the Seal, when I could not?

Tom (*embarrassed*). I did not know what it was, my King, and I used it to . . . to crack nuts. (*All*

650 *laugh, and* Tom *steps back.* Miles *steps forward, staring in amazement.*)

Miles. Is he really the King? Is he indeed the sovereign of England, and not the poor and friendless Tom o' Bedlam[13] I thought he was? (*He sinks down on bench.*) I wish I had a bag to hide my head in!

1st Guard (*rushing up to him*). Stand up, you mannerless clown! How dare you sit in the presence of the King!

660 **Prince.** Do not touch him! He is my trusty servant, Miles Hendon, who saved me from shame and possible death. For his service, he owns the right to sit in my presence.

Miles (*bowing, then kneeling*). Your Majesty!

Prince. Rise, Sir Miles. I command that Sir Hugh Hendon, who sits within this hall, be seized and put under lock and key until I have need of him. (*beckons to* Tom) From what I have heard, Tom Canty, you have governed

670 the realm with royal gentleness and mercy in my absence. Henceforth, you shall hold the honorable title of King's Ward! (Tom *kneels and kisses* Prince's *hand.*) And because I have suffered with the poorest of my subjects and felt the cruel force of unjust laws, I pledge myself to a reign of mercy for all! (*All bow low, then rise.*)

All (*shouting*). Long live the King! Long live Edward, King of England! (*curtain*)

---

12. **scepter** (sĕp'tər): a baton or other emblem of royal authority.

13. **Tom o' Bedlam:** an insane person, such as someone hospitalized at St. Mary of Bethlehem Hospital, or Bedlam Hospital, in London.

Comprehension

1. **Recall** How do most of the adults explain the boys' claims that they are not who they appear to be?

2. **Clarify** Explain how the constable tricks the woman into selling the pig. How does Miles use the trick to get Edward released?

3. **Summarize** How has Edward's experience as a pauper influenced him?

Text Analysis

4. **Make Inferences** Scan the play to find examples of how Miles treats the prince and how the members of the royal court treat Tom. What motivates their behavior toward the boys?

● 5. **Evaluate Stage Directions** Look over the stage directions you listed in your chart. Which ones seemed most useful for understanding the play?

● 6. **Analyze Conflict in Drama** Use a chart like the one shown to summarize the main events of each scene. This will help you see how the conflict develops and the boys change over the course of the play. In which scene is the conflict resolved?

Scene 1: The guards mistake the Prince for Tom, and the King thinks that Tom is the Prince.
Scene 2:

7. **Analyze Character** Tom's behavior at court leads people to believe the "prince" is mad. Why does Tom behave this way? How does the boys' behavior affect the plot?

8. **Evaluate Resolution** What lessons did the boys learn about themselves and each other by trading places?

Extension and Challenge

9. **Inquiry and Research** During the time of Henry VIII and Edward VI, the British king was very powerful. Since then, the power of the royal family has decreased. Research Henry VIII's reign and compare it with that of Queen Elizabeth II. Focus on how royal powers and responsibilities have changed over time. Present your findings to the class.

> ## Who would you BE if you could?
>
> What does *The Prince and the Pauper* teach readers about wanting to be someone else?

COMMON CORE

RL 3 Describe how a particular drama's plot unfolds as well as how the characters respond or change as the plot moves toward a resolution. **W 7** Conduct short research projects to answer a question, drawing on several sources.

King Henry VIII

Twain's Tale Transplanted to Today
Film Review

What's the Connection?

The play version of Twain's *The Prince and the Pauper* keeps the same basic setting, characters, and plot as the novel. A recent movie version of *The Prince and the Pauper* updates the story to modern times. Read the following film review to understand the differences between the play and the film.

Use with *The Prince and the Pauper*, page 152.

COMMON CORE

RL 1 Cite textual evidence to support analysis of what the text says explicitly. **RL 7** Compare and contrast a drama to a video version of the text.

Standards Focus: Compare and Contrast Versions of a Story

Some stories are so popular and timeless that they exist in different forms, or versions. (Think about different versions of well-known fairy tales that you have heard or seen, such as "Snow White" or "Cinderella.") Some versions of a story are even told through a different genre, or type, of literature. For example, a novel might become a Broadway play, which is then made into a movie, which in turn becomes a musical that gets turned into another movie! Although different versions of a story might have slightly different characters or take place in different settings—or even different time periods—the basic plot, or story line, usually remains similar.

In this lesson, use the information in the movie review to find similarities and differences between the drama version and the film version of *The Prince and the Pauper*. First, in the center column, record what you know about the play. Then, as you read, record in the right-hand column what you learn about the setting, characters, and plot of the film. You will use the chart to assess similarities and differences between the play and the film.

The Prince and the Pauper		
	Play	Film
Setting	sixteenth-century England	
Characters	Tom Canty, a pauper	
Plot		

Twain's Tale
TRANSPLANTED TO TODAY

Does the world really need another version of Mark Twain's classic story *The Prince and the Pauper*? The creators of the 2007 film *The Prince and the Pauper: A Modern Twain Story* thought so—probably because they were counting on large numbers of young viewers jumping at the chance to see "twin sensations" Cole and
10 Dylan Sprouse in a story seemingly tailor-made for these twin brothers.

Sprouse twins on the red carpet

The Prince and the Pauper: A Modern Twain Story transplants the often-told tale to today's world. In fact, certain details in this update are more faithful to Twain's original story than one might expect. For example, Dylan Sprouse's character is named Tom Canty, the same as the pauper character in Twain's story, and Cole Sprouse plays Eddie Tudor, a clever updating of the name of Edward, the Tudor prince. There's also a helpful adult friend named Miles. The basic outline of the plot remains essentially the same: two boys from "opposite sides of
20 the track" meet accidentally. One is rich and famous and the other is not, but they are the spitting image of each other. Each boy is unhappy with his own life and thinks the other boy's life has certain advantages. The boys suddenly decide to switch identities in order to see whether the grass really is greener on the other side. When the boys are unexpectedly separated after trading places, each boy gets trapped in a life that's not his own. As in Twain's story, each boy is surrounded by adults who fear he is going insane—or worse. The boys have to overcome various obstacles in order to return to their rightful places, and no one believes that the boys are who they say they are until a final
30 reunion reveals the truth to all. **A**

FOCUS ON FORM
A **film review** is a short essay about a movie the writer has seen. The author's purpose for writing a film review is to express an opinion. A film review also includes details that describe major events in the film.

A COMPARE AND CONTRAST VERSIONS
Reread lines 12–30. What similarities and differences in the characters and plot does the reviewer note? Add them to your chart.

The updates to Twain's story are cleverly handled. Instead of sixteenth-century England, the setting is Palm Beach and Miami Beach in the present day. Instead of events revolving around a royal court, they revolve around the world of movies and acting. The "prince" is what might be considered royalty today—a teen actor with millions of fans. The "pauper" is a kid from a difficult background who has to work for his grandfather's landscaping business. In this version of the story, however, the two boys are united by more than physical appearance: they both feel lonely, and they both feel misunderstood by the adults in their lives. Acting is what they have in common, though in different ways: Tom, who idolizes Eddie, wants more than anything to be an actor. Eddie, who is an actor, resents the time his career takes up and would rather be playing with other kids. **B**

As in Twain's story, when the boys change places, each gets the opportunity to learn something important about life. Eddie Tudor, the "prince" in this film, is not the thoughtful observer of life that the prince in Twain's novel is, and he has a long way to go in becoming a wiser person. Tom Canty is, from the beginning, a better person than his idol Eddie in every way—even, as it turns out, as an actor. Like his pauper namesake in the Twain novel, Tom makes a great substitute for the real "prince." **C**

When Eddie finally makes it back to the movie set, he just wants to beat the stuffing out of Tom for impersonating him. Only after a slapstick chase scene and a final winding-down of events does Eddie show signs that he has become a better person from living Tom's life: he hugs his mother (his film producer) and tells her he understands that she is hard on him because she loves him.

Tom benefits the most directly from the switch, for he learns that his dreams of being an actor are not idle fantasies. He really *can* act. Eddie's transformation is less direct and comes through a plot twist involving Tom's adult friend Miles, a washed-up actor who had attempted to teach Eddie (thinking he was Tom) the importance of treating other people with kindness and respect.

In a nice touch, the film ends with Tom and Eddie acting together in a traditional film version of *The Prince and the Pauper,* reminding us of the timelessness of this story. Although this direct-to-video film is unlikely to win any awards or become a classic, it is a pleasant family film with plenty of humor and a few gentle messages that kids should hear and adults shouldn't forget. **D**

B COMPARE AND CONTRAST VERSIONS
Reread lines 31–43. What differences in character and setting does the reviewer mention? Add them to your chart.

C COMPARE AND CONTRAST VERSIONS
Reread lines 44–51. How is the prince in the play different from the "prince" in the movie? Note the details in your chart.

D FILM REVIEW
Reread lines 64–69. What opinion does the author express about the film version of *The Prince and the Pauper?*

Comprehension

1. **Recall** What is the setting of the updated version of *The Prince and the Pauper*?

2. **Recall** What things do the two boys in the film have in common? How is this different from what the two boys in the play have in common?

3. **Summarize** According to the reviewer, what are the main differences between the film and Twain's original version of the story?

Text Analysis

4. **Analyze Setting and Characters** How might the setting and characters of the film especially appeal to audiences today? What other settings and characters would work well for an updated version of this story?

5. **Compare and Contrast Versions of a Story** How are the "prince" character and the "pauper" character in the film similar to and different from the prince and the pauper of the play? Which character in the film version seems closer to his counterpart in the play version? Explain.

6. **Compare and Contrast Versions of a Story** Based on your reading of the play and of this review, how faithful do you think this updated film version of *The Prince and the Pauper* is to the plot of Twain's original story? Would you say that the film keeps the same basic story line as the play, or is the story line different? Explain.

COMMON CORE

RL 1 Cite textual evidence to support analysis of what the text says explicitly. **RL 7** Compare and contrast a drama to a video version of the text. **W 2** Write informative/explanatory texts to examine a topic.

Read for Information: Compare and Contrast Versions of a Story

WRITING PROMPT

Compare and contrast the drama version of *The Prince and the Pauper* with the film version. How are the setting, characters, and plot similar and different in the two versions?

To answer this prompt, follow these steps:

1. Review the chart you filled out about the play and the film.

2. In one paragraph, explain the similarities between the setting, characters, and plot in the two versions.

3. In a second paragraph, explain the differences between the setting, characters, and plot in the two versions.

Writing Workshop
ARGUMENT

Supporting an Opinion

Think about the stories or novels you've read recently. Which one stands out in your mind? Why? Perhaps the story has a page-turning plot, a conflict you can relate to, or an unusual setting. In this workshop, you will write an argument in which you tell other readers why the story is so memorable. You will strengthen your argument by supporting your opinion with reasons and evidence.

 Complete the workshop activities in your **Reader/Writer Notebook.**

WRITE WITH A PURPOSE

WRITING TASK

Pick a story that's memorable to you. Which element—for example, a suspenseful plot, a realistic setting, or a humorous conflict—is most responsible for making the story unforgettable? Write an **argument** that persuades readers to agree with your viewpoint, or claim.

Idea Starters
- the conflict between Heather and Risa in "The Good Deed"
- the surprise ending of "Lob's Girl"
- the dangerous setting in *Hatchet*
- an important lesson in *Esperanza Rising*

THE ESSENTIALS

Here are some common purposes, audiences, and formats for writing an argument.

PURPOSES	AUDIENCES	FORMATS
• to convince others to agree with your claim • to explore how a literary element, such as plot, affects readers	• classmates and teacher • friends and family members • book club • newspaper readers • Web users	• essay for class • book review in school or local newspaper • online book review • blog posting

COMMON CORE TRAITS

1. DEVELOPMENT OF IDEAS
- includes an engaging **introduction** with a **claim,** or position
- provides **clear reasons** and **relevant evidence** to support the claim
- offers a **concluding section** that follows from the argument presented

2. ORGANIZATION OF IDEAS
- **organizes** reasons and evidence in a **logical way**
- uses **transitions**—words, phrases, and clauses—to show the relationships among claims and reasons

3. LANGUAGE FACILITY AND CONVENTIONS
- maintains a **formal style** and **tone**
- uses **intensive pronouns** to add emphasis
- employs correct **grammar, mechanics,** and **spelling**

Writing Online
Go to **thinkcentral.com.**
KEYWORD: HML6N-170

Planning/Prewriting

COMMON CORE

W 1a–e Write arguments to support claims with clear reasons and relevant evidence. **W 5** Strengthen writing by planning. **W 9a (RL 5)** Draw evidence from literary texts; analyze how a scene contributes to development of theme, setting, or plot.

Getting Started

CHOOSE A STORY AND ELEMENT

Use the Idea Starters on page 170, brainstorm with a friend, or browse through the unit to help you identify stories or novels that you enjoyed reading. List your favorites. Then choose the work that had the strongest impact on you. Consider which element—plot, setting, or conflict, for example—makes the work so memorable. Ask yourself why this particular element is so powerful. Jot down as many reasons as you can think of to support your **opinion.** Strong **reasons** tell why you believe what you do.

▶ WHAT DOES IT LOOK LIKE?

Title: *Hatchet*
Most Powerful Element: *Setting*
Reasons:

   1. *creates exciting action*

   2. *forces a brave character to battle intense conflicts*

   3. *teaches the main character an important lesson*

THINK ABOUT AUDIENCE AND PURPOSE

Keep in mind the **purpose** of your argument—to convince your readers to agree with your opinion. To do this, you need to think about what background information your **audience** must have in order to follow your ideas.

▶ ASK YOURSELF:

- Who will read my argument?
- How much do my readers already know about my chosen story or novel?
- What are the most important details about the story or novel that my readers need to know?

STATE YOUR CLAIM

Begin your argument with a strong **claim,** or a formal statement that expresses your opinion. Your claim should identify the element you've chosen. Write your claim, improving the language until it says exactly what you hope to prove in your argument. Make sure your claim is a statement that you can support with reasons and evidence. If you discover that your claim can't be supported easily, then you should rework it.

▶ WHAT DOES IT LOOK LIKE?

Original Claim	Rewritten Claim
The setting in Hatchet makes the novel memorable.	*An exciting plot, a brave character, and a meaningful lesson all result from the setting, making Hatchet a truly memorable novel.*

Planning/Prewriting *continued*

Getting Started

GATHER EVIDENCE TO SUPPORT YOUR CLAIM

An effective argument includes two or three strong reasons. Each of your reasons should be supported by **relevant**, or related, **evidence.** Evidence includes direct quotations, examples, and descriptive details from the story or novel. Skim the story or novel, jotting down evidence that is directly related to each of your reasons.

- **direct quotation**—"slamming him back and down into the water"
- **example**—He rushes out to signal the plane only to see it disappear.
- **descriptive detail**—He is so desperate that he eats choke cherries and even raw turtle eggs.

▶ WHAT DOES IT LOOK LIKE?

Reasons	Evidence
setting creates exciting plot	• almost dies after a moose charges him • "slamming him back and down into the water"
setting shows a brave character battling intense conflicts	• tornado demolishes almost everything he has made or acquired • he says "I might be hit but I'm not done"
setting teaches the main character an important lesson	• "what doesn't kill you makes you stronger"

PLAN YOUR CONCLUDING SECTION

Your argument should end with a strong, persuasive **concluding section.** In this section, you will restate your claim and provide a brief summary of your reasons. You might also end with a thought-provoking quotation from the story or novel, or a question or insight to keep your audience thinking about the ideas in your argument. At this stage, jot down ideas that you might want to include, such as a thought-provoking quotation or a brief summary of your claim and reasons.

▶ TIPS

- Avoid simply repeating your claim and reasons Instead, try to expand on them, since your audience has a greater familiarity with your subject after reading most of your argument. For example, rather than just restating "setting affects the character of Brian," you might offer a related insight: "As a result of Brian's ordeal in the wilderness, he changes from a boy into a man."
- Avoid introducing any new ideas in your concluding section. Quotations, questions, or insights should relate to the points that you have made throughout your argument.

PEER REVIEW Share with a peer your claim and supporting reasons. Then list the evidence that you have gathered. Ask: Do I have enough relevant evidence? Does each piece of evidence strongly support a reason? If the evidence isn't as strong or relevant as you might like, ask: What new approach could I take to strengthen my claim?

YOUR TURN In your *Reader/Writer Notebook*, write your claim. Then complete a chart similar to the one on this page identifying your reasons and your evidence from the text. Add quotations, questions, or related insights you might want to include in the concluding section.

Drafting

 **COMMON CORE** **W 4** Produce clear and coherent writing appropriate to task, purpose, and audience. **W 6** Demonstrate sufficient command of keyboarding skills.

The following chart shows how to organize your draft to create a clear and **coherent**, or easy to follow, argument.

Organizing an Argument

INTRODUCTION

- Grab the audience's attention with a **question** or **comment.**
- Provide the necessary **background information** about your work of literature, including the title, the author, and a brief plot summary, if appropriate.
- State your opinion in a strong **claim.**

▼

BODY

- Present your reasons in a **logical order**, such as order of importance.
- Support each reason with **direct quotations, examples, descriptive details,** and **other types of evidence** from the story or novel.
- Use **transitions**—words, phrases, and clauses, such as *furthermore* and *in addition*—to show the relationships between your claims and reasons.
- Maintain a **formal style** by using a serious tone (or attitude), a confident voice, and thoughtful words.

▼

CONCLUDING SECTION

- Restate your **claim** and your reasons.
- End with a **quotation, question**, or **insight** that relates to your claim.

GRAMMAR IN CONTEXT: PRACTICE KEYBOARDING SKILLS

Good keyboarding skills help you express your ideas quickly and easily. To strengthen your keyboarding skills, keep these tips in mind:

- Place your keyboard directly in front of you. Set it low enough so that you can keep your arms bent and relaxed as you type.

- Clear your work space of items you don't need.

- Sit up straight and keep both feet on the floor.

- Look up at the screen rather than down at your fingers.

- Familiarize yourself with the home row keys. The letters *J* and *F* upon which you rest your forefingers have raised ridges to help you position your fingers correctly.

- Use your right little finger to hit the *enter* (return) key.

- Increase your speed and accuracy by doing online drills or keyboarding games.

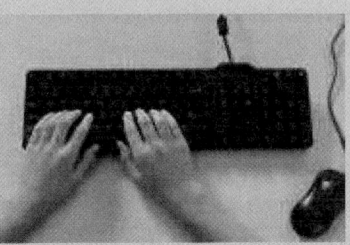

Revising

The first draft of an essay always needs improvement. The revising stage gives you a chance to improve your ideas, wording, organization, and style. Use the chart shown to help you revise and rewrite where necessary. Check that you achieve your purpose, which is to convince your audience to agree with your opinion.

ARGUMENT

Ask Yourself	Tips	Revision Strategies
1. Does the introduction grab the audience's attention?	▶ **Draw a star** next to the attention-grabbing text.	▶ **Add** a question or comment to interest the audience.
2. Do I provide the background information that my audience needs?	▶ **Underline** the details of the background information, such as title, author, and brief plot summary.	▶ **Add** details to answer general questions such as: "Who is the main character?" "Where does this story take place?" "What happens?" **Delete** unnecessary details.
3. Does the introduction have a strong claim?	▶ **Bracket** the claim. Ask a peer to read it and explain your viewpoint.	▶ **Reword** and strengthen your claim, being sure to identify the work and the element you have chosen.
4. Are there at least two clear reasons that support the claim? Does at least one piece of relevant evidence support each reason?	▶ **Highlight** the reasons that support the claim. **Draw an arrow** from the evidence to the reason.	▶ If necessary, **add** clear reasons that support the claim. **Add** relevant evidence to support each reason.
5. Does my argument include transitions that show the relationships among my claim and reasons?	▶ **Circle** the words, phrases, and clauses that connect your claim and reasons.	▶ **Add** one or two transitions, such as *furthermore, one reason,* or *in addition,* to show the relationships among your claims and reasons.
6. Does the concluding section follow logically from the argument and restate my claim and reasons?	▶ **Draw a wavy line** under your claim and restatement of your reasons.	▶ **Add** a restatement of your claim and a summary of your reasons if either is missing.

YOUR TURN **PEER REVIEW** Working with a peer, review your drafts together. Answer each question in the chart to identify which parts of your drafts need reworking or a new approach.

ANALYZE A STUDENT DRAFT

COMMON CORE **W 1c** Use words, phrases, and clauses to clarify the relationships among claim(s) and reasons. **W 1d** Maintain a formal style. **W 5** Strengthen writing by revising, editing, rewriting, and trying a new approach.

Read this student's draft and the comments about it as a model for revising your own argument.

Setting—The Key Element in *Hatchet*
by Malachi Brown, Addison Central School

① How would you survive if you found yourself alone in the Canadian wilderness, surrounded by forests and a lake, miles from help? That is the question facing Brian Robeson, the 13-year old main character in the novel *Hatchet* by Gary Paulsen. After Brian's plane crashes, he must find a way to meet the challenges of the dangerous environment with only a hatchet and the clothes on his back. A suspenseful plot, a remarkable character, and an important lesson all result from the setting, making *Hatchet* a truly memorable novel.

② Brian's struggles to survive in the wilderness setting and the dangers he confronts create an exciting plot. He must find food, build a shelter, and figure out how to start a fire if he is to live more than a few days. Several times, he is injured or almost killed by wild animals. For example, he is attacked by an angry moose that charges him, "using her head and front hooves . . . , slamming him back and down into the water." He barely escapes with his life from this encounter.

③ The setting brings out Brian's bravery. At first, he feels hopeless and sorry for himself. Then he realizes that these emotions won't accomplish anything. His growing inner strength is shown most clearly when a tornado destroys his shelter and food supply. The tornado also slams him like a rag doll against his cave wall. Afterwards, instead of giving up, Brian thinks to himself, "I might be hit but I'm not done." He figures that what he made once with his hatchet, he can make again. If not for the setting, Brian may not have shown such bravery and strength.

> Malachi provides the audience with necessary **background information**.

> Malachi introduces his **claim** in the last sentence of the first paragraph. This sentence sets up the support that he provides in the next paragraphs.

> Malachi includes an example from the text and a direct quotation as **evidence**.

> Malachi needs to add a **transition** to show the relationship between his reasons.

LEARN HOW Use Transitions In the first sentence of Malachi's third paragraph, he states his second reason. The sentence does not show how the reason connects to the previous paragraph. To help the audience better understand the relationship between the reasons, he rewrote the sentence, adding a transition.

MALACHI'S REVISION TO PARAGRAPH ③

~~The setting brings out Brian's bravery.~~ At first, he feels hopeless and sorry for himself. *In addition to the exciting plot details, the setting reveals Brian's bravery.*

4   Another reason the setting is the most memorable story element is that it teaches Brian an important lesson. He discovers that he can triumph over difficulties with patience and determination. For example, it takes him dozens of attempts to start a fire. Each time the flame flickers out, he improves the nest of materials he has arranged to catch the sparks until finally the fire takes. Hey, "what doesn't kill you makes you stronger." Kind of an important lesson for all of us, isn't it! It is important never to give up, but to look within yourself to find ways to solve tough problems.

5   The setting is the key to this novel, affecting every part of it. The conflicts between Brian and nature keep readers guessing, uncertain if he will be able to overcome them. His ordeal changes him from a boy into a man and teaches him valuable lessons about never giving up in any situation. Brian will never forget the 54 days he spends in the wilderness. Neither will readers, who remain haunted by the question, "Could I have survived?"

> Malachi needs to use a more **formal style and tone** to strengthen this part of the essay.

> Malachi's **concluding section** restates his claim and reasons, provides an insight, and leaves the audience with a question for thought.

LEARN HOW **Maintain a Formal Style and Tone** Some of the sentences in Malachi's fourth paragraph use an informal style. The conversational tone and the incomplete sentence weaken his important points. In his revision, he rewrote those ideas using a more serious tone, a confident voice, and thoughtful words.

MALACHI'S REVISION TO PARAGRAPH 4

      Each time the flame flickers out, he improves the nest of materials he has arranged to catch the sparks until finally the fire takes. *His actions and attitude prove the saying that* ~~Hey,~~ "what doesn't kill you makes you stronger." ~~Kind of an important lesson for all of us, isn't it!~~ It is important never to give up but to look within yourself to find ways to solve tough problems.

YOUR TURN   Use feedback from your peers and your teacher as well as the two "Learn How" lessons to revise your argument. Evaluate how well you show a clear connection among your ideas, use a formal style throughout your essay, and convince your audience to agree with your claim.

Editing and Publishing

COMMON CORE

W 5 Strengthen writing as needed by revising and editing. **L 1b** Use intensive pronouns. **L 2** Demonstrate command of the conventions of standard English capitalization, punctuation, and spelling. **L 3b** Maintain consistency in style and tone.

In the editing stage, it's important to proofread your essay for grammar, spelling, and punctuation errors. You don't want mistakes to distract your audience from the important points you are making in your argument.

GRAMMAR IN CONTEXT: PUNCTUATING DIALOGUE

Intensive pronouns are used to emphasize the noun or pronoun they follow. Notice the difference that the insertion of an intensive pronoun makes in the sentences below.

Type of Intensive Pronoun	Example
Singular intensive pronouns—*myself, yourself, himself, herself, itself*	The mayor gave a commendation to Brian for his courage.
	The mayor himself gave a commendation to Brian for his courage. (emphasizes the importance of the occasion by drawing attention to who gave the commendation)
Plural intensive pronouns—*ourselves, yourselves, themselves*	In a rare move, the class members asked to continue their discussion of Hatchet.
	In a rare move, the class members themselves asked to continue their discussion of Hatchet. (emphasizes how unusual such a request is)

When Malachi edited his essay, he inserted intensive pronouns to draw attention to specific ideas.

> Neither will readers themselves, who remain haunted by the question, "Could I have survived?"

PUBLISH YOUR WRITING

Share your essay with an audience.
- Make copies of your essay and distribute them to your classmates.
- Submit your essay to a newspaper as part of its book review section.
- Use your essay as a springboard for an informal class discussion.
- Post your essay on a blog. Ask others for their opinions on your claim.

YOUR TURN Proofread your essay, looking for places where you can add emphasis with an intensive pronoun. Then choose the publishing option that will best reach your intended audience.

Scoring Rubric

Use the rubric below to evaluate your argument from the Writing Workshop or your response to the on-demand task on the next page.

ARGUMENT

SCORE	COMMON CORE TRAITS
6	• **Development** Effectively presents a strong claim; supports the claim with clear reasons and relevant evidence; has a powerful concluding section • **Organization** Capably arranges reasons and evidence; effectively uses transitions to show relationships among ideas • **Language** Consistently maintains a formal style and tone; shows a strong command of conventions
5	• **Development** Presents a strong claim; supports the claim with clear reasons and relevant evidence; has a strong concluding section • **Organization** Clearly arranges reasons and evidence; uses transitions to show relationships among ideas • **Language** Maintains a formal style and tone; has a few errors in conventions
4	• **Development** States a sufficient claim; supports the claim with reasons and evidence; has an adequate concluding section • **Organization** Arranges the reasons and evidence clearly with some exceptions; uses transitions adequately, but could use more • **Language** Mostly maintains a formal style and tone; includes a few distracting errors in conventions
3	• **Development** States a claim; provides some reasons and evidence, but needs more; has a somewhat weak concluding section • **Organization** Arranges the reasons and evidence in ways that can be confusing at times; needs more transitions • **Language** Often lapses into an informal style and tone; has several errors in conventions
2	• **Development** Has a weak claim; offers some unclear reasons and needs more evidence; has a weak concluding section • **Organization** Arranges reasons and evidence in a confusing way; uses few transitions • **Language** Uses an informal style and tone; has many errors in conventions
1	• **Development** Lacks a clear claim; offers unclear reasons and not enough evidence; has no concluding section • **Organization** Has no overall organization; lacks transitions • **Language** Lacks a formal style and tone; has major problems with conventions

Preparing for Timed Writing

COMMON CORE

W 10 Write routinely over shorter time frames for a range of tasks, purposes, and audiences.

1. ANALYZE THE TASK   5 MIN

Read the writing task carefully. Then, underlines words that tell the type of writing, the topic, the audience, and the purpose. Circle the type of writing you are asked to do.

WRITING TASK ~Type of Writing~

Your school is sponsoring an essay contest to celebrate "Movie Week." Contestants will write an (essay) on a film they have seen for the title of "best movie ever made." Write an essay convincing the panel of teachers and students that your movie deserves this honor. Use clear reasons and relevant evidence from the movie to support your claim.

~Purpose~   ~Audience~   ~Topic~

2. PLAN YOUR RESPONSE   10 MIN

Jot down the titles of your top five favorite movies. List a few reasons why you like each one. To help identify reasons, ask yourself which elements are key—the plot, the characters, the setting, the special effects, or the conflicts. Choose the film with the most or strongest reasons. Then, gather your evidence, thinking of specific scenes or dialogue to support each reason.

Movie Title:	
Reason 1	Evidence
Reason 2	Evidence
Reason 3	Evidence

3. RESPOND TO THE TASK   20 MIN

After identifying your reasons and evidence, draft your essay. As you write, keep these guidelines in mind:

- In the introduction, grab your audience's attention, provide necessary background information about the film, and state a strong claim.
- In each body paragraph, provide a reason and evidence to support it.
- Develop a concluding section that flows logically from your previous paragraphs and restates your claim and reasons.

4. IMPROVE YOUR RESPONSE   5–10 MIN

Revising Review key aspects of your essay. Is your claim clearly stated and supported with clear reasons? Do you end with a powerful concluding section?
Proofreading Neatly correct any errors in grammar, spelling, and mechanics.
Checking Your Final Copy Before you turn in your essay, read it once more to catch any errors you may have missed and to make any finishing touches.

Participating in a Discussion

When you and your friends discuss your favorite music, you're having an informal **discussion**. You listen to each other and support and defend your opinions. You can do the same when discussing literature.

 Complete the workshop activities in your **Reader/Writer Notebook**.

SPEAK WITH A PURPOSE

TASK

Participate in a **discussion** about an unforgettable story or novel. You will state and support a claim that one particular element—plot, setting, or conflict—is responsible for making the story unforgettable.

COMMON CORE TRAITS

PARTICIPANTS IN AN EFFECTIVE DISCUSSION . . .

- state a clear claim supported by reasons and evidence
- present ideas in a logical order
- show understanding by reviewing and paraphrasing key points, and by posing and asking questions
- delineate, or trace, a speaker's argument, identifying claims that are supported and those that are not

COMMON CORE

SL 1a–d Engage effectively in collaborative discussions.
SL 3 Delineate a speaker's argument and specific claims.
SL 4 Present claims and findings, sequencing ideas logically; use appropriate eye contact, adequate volume, and clear pronunciation.

Planning the Discussion

A group discussion is a good way to practice expressing your ideas clearly. Follow these planning suggestions:

- **Define Roles** As a group, choose a recorder and a moderator. The recorder will take notes on important ideas that come up in discussion. The moderator will keep the discussion moving by posing questions and making sure that each member has a chance to speak.

- **Agree on Rules** Determine the order in which members will speak and the length of time that they have. Clarify the importance of listening carefully and responding respectfully. Remind each other to use appropriate eye contact, adequate volume, and clear pronunciation.

- **Set Goals for the Discussion** Decide ahead of time what your group wants to accomplish. You might keep track of the different elements group members choose and reflect about the patterns you see. Or you might review multiple perspectives and ask how the discussion has led members to view literature in new ways. Your group should set goals together.

- **Prepare for the Discussion** Make sure group members all know the topic and goals of the discussion. Encourage members to prepare by outlining brief discussion notes to help them express and support their claims clearly.

Speaking & Listening Online

THINK central

Go to **thinkcentral.com**.
KEYWORD: HML6N-180

Holding the Discussion

In an effective discussion, group members listen and respond respectfully, and build on other's ideas.

GETTING STARTED

The moderator will begin by introducing the group and stating the goal of the discussion. Participants should follow the instructions from the moderator concerning whose turn it is to speak and how much time each speaker has.

Use these guidelines to hold your discussion:

Strategies for Speakers	Strategies for Listeners
• Clearly present claims, reasons, and evidence in a logical order and within the time allowed.	• Listen carefully to each speaker. Ask yourself: Do I agree or disagree with this speaker's claim? Why?
• Respond to questions with elaboration and detail. For example, if someone challenges your claim, you might say, "I understand why you might think that, but...."	• Jot down important ideas.
	• Take notes so you can keep track of the speaker's specific claim and reasons. Distinguish reasons that are supported with evidence from those reasons that are not. Also, think about the strength and weakness of the evidence.
• Maintain eye contact with listeners.	
• Speak so everyone can hear you, not too softly or loudly. Keep a friendly, positive expression and body posture.	• Ask probing questions, such as, "You keep talking about the exciting action. So, are you saying that plot is the most important element?"
• Pronounce your words clearly.	

YOUR TURN

As a Speaker Present your claim, reasons, and evidence to your group, using the strategies on these pages. Pause to reflect on and answer questions. Then follow up with your own questions.

As a Listener Focus on the evidence presented by each speaker to support his or her claim. Add your own insights to build on each speaker's ideas.

Assessment Practice

DIRECTIONS **Read this selection and answer the questions that follow.**

The Fish Story   *by Mary Lou Brooks*

1   I know what I'm going to be when I grow up—unemployed. "Face it, Ernie," my dad always says. "The way you mess up every job, you have a great future—as a bum."

2   He's probably right. My first summer job was cutting the neighbor's lawn. The mower got away from me and ate ten tomato plants. Another time, I forgot to close the windows when I washed Mr. Hammer's car. The weeds I pulled out of Mrs. Miller's garden turned out to be flowers.

3   So I was really surprised when the Bensons asked me to look after their house while they were away on vacation. The Bensons are new on the block. I guess they hadn't heard about me yet.

4   "We're leaving on Monday," explained Mrs. Benson. "You'll start on Tuesday. Just bring in the newspaper and the mail." That didn't sound too hard. Even *I* could probably handle this job.

5   "And feed Jaws once a day," Mrs. Benson added.

6   "*Jaws?*" I gulped. Did they have a pet shark or something?

7   Mrs. Benson laughed. "That's what the twins named their goldfish."

8   On Tuesday, I had baseball practice. So I was late getting to the Bensons'. I put the mail and the newspaper on the hall table. Then I headed for the fishbowl. Jaws was floating on top of the water.

9   I moaned. My first day on the job, and I killed the dumb fish! Not even the Army would want me now. That's what my dad would say—after he stopped yelling.

10   Now wait a minute, Ernie, I said to myself. This little fellow *could* still be alive. His eyes are open. He could be in a coma. I bent down very close to the water.

11   "Jaws!" I yelled. "It's me, Ernie, your babysitter. If you can hear me, blink once." He didn't.

12   I touched him with my finger. He was cold, stiff, and very slimy. "Face it, Ernie," I said out loud. "This is one dead fish you have here."

13   That night, I lay awake a long time trying to figure out why that dumb fish died. I didn't overfeed him. I never had a chance to feed him at all.

14   When I finally fell asleep, I had a nightmare. The shark from *Jaws* was chasing me. He was wearing a six-shooter. "You bumped off my kinfolk," he yelled. "Draw!"

15 I didn't tell my parents about Jaws. Every day, I went over to the Bensons' as though nothing was wrong. I had until Sunday. That's when the Bensons were coming home. Why rush things?

16 On Saturday, I remembered that Jaws was still in the fishbowl. I was about to toss him into the garbage. Suddenly, I had a great idea. I slipped Jaws into a baggie and ran to the nearest pet store.

17 "I'd like another goldfish exactly like this one," I told the owner. Then I held up the baggie.

18 The owner glared at me. Half an hour later, he was still glaring. That's how long it took to find a perfect match. I paid the owner and headed back to the Bensons' house.

19 When I got there, I cleaned the fishbowl and added fresh water. Soon, Jaws II was in his new home. But instead of swimming around, he just stared at me.

20 "What you did was wrong," those tiny black eyes seemed to say.

21 The Bensons arrived home at 1:55 Sunday afternoon. I watched from my bedroom window as they piled out of their car. At 2:13, my mom called up the stairs.

22 "Ernie," she said, "Mrs. Benson is here." Caught! I trudged down the stairs to face the music.

23 Mrs. Benson was sitting at the kitchen table with my parents. "Here's the boy behind the Great Goldfish Switch," she said.

24 I felt like running. But Mrs. Benson put her arm around my shoulder.

25 "That was very thoughtful, Ernie," she said. "Monday was so crazy I didn't have time to pick up another fish. I've been dreading telling the twins that Jaws died. Thanks to you, I won't have to."

26 She handed me money in an envelope. "This is for house-sitting," she said. "There's something extra for the new Jaws. You hear so many wild stories about kids these days. It's nice to know one who is responsible."

27 Mom looked so proud I thought she might cry. But Dad had a funny look on his face. I think he was trying not to laugh.

Reading Comprehension

Use "The Fish Story" to answer questions 1–12.

1. The conflict, or problem, begins when Ernie —
   A. forgets to feed Jaws
   B. mows over ten tomato plans
   C. finds Jaws floating on top of the water
   D. meets the Bensons when they return from vacation

2. What event happens first in the story?
   A. Ernie has a nightmare about the shark from the movie *Jaws.*
   B. Ernie runs to the pet store to buy a new fish.
   C. Ernie learns how the fish got his name.
   D. The Bensons go away for their vacation.

3. The setting of the story is —
   A. the Bensons' vacation home
   B. a neighborhood
   C. a fishing village
   D. a local pet store

4. In the climax, or turning point, of the story —
   A. Ernie goes downstairs to see Mrs. Benson and "face the music"
   B. the new fish stares at Ernie
   C. Ernie dreams about "the shark from *Jaws*"
   D. the weeds Ernie pulled up "turned out to be flowers"

5. After Ernie buys the fish, he faces a new conflict because —
   A. he feels guilty about replacing Jaws
   B. the new fish doesn't look like Jaws
   C. he is sorry he took the job at the Bensons
   D. he wants to keep the new fish for himself

6. In the beginning of the story, the reader learns that Ernie —
   A. does not want to work when he grows up
   B. has messed up several jobs
   C. would like to go on a vacation
   D. loves to take care of fish

7. During what time of year does the story take place?
   A. Fall
   B. Spring
   C. Summer
   D. Winter

8. You can infer that Mrs. Benson dreads telling the twins that the goldfish died because they might —
   A. refuse to believe her
   B. figure it out for themselves
   C. get upset at the news
   D. blame Ernie for its death

9. When does Ernie run to the pet store?

    A. When he sees the Bensons returning

    B. The day before the Bensons return

    C. As soon as he finds Jaws dead

    D. After Mrs. Benson pays him

10. Ernie's conflicts are resolved when —

    A. he buys a new fish

    B. Mrs. Benson thanks him for replacing the fish

    C. the Bensons offer him a job

    D. he accepts the death of the fish

11. From Ernie's thoughts and feelings you can infer that he —

    A. is proud of his reputation

    B. is unsure of himself

    C. wants to impress Mrs. Benson

    D. feels lucky to have a job

12. Which phrases in the story help you identify the order of events?

    A. Wait a minute, once a day, headed for

    B. On Tuesday, on Saturday at 2:13

    C. Blink once, long time, nearest pet store

    D. Going to be coming home, getting up

SHORT CONSTRUCTED RESPONSE
Write two or three sentences to answer each question.

13. What important events in the story lead up to Ernie's nightmare about the shark from the movie *Jaws*?

14. Identify two clues that show the story takes place in modern times.

Write a paragraph to answer this question.

15. Describe the conflict Ernie feels in paragraphs 1–4. With what thoughts or choices does he struggle?

GO ON

Vocabulary

Use context clues and your knowledge of synonyms to answer the following questions.

1. Which word is a synonym for *dreading* in paragraph 25?

   A. Anticipating

   B. Avoiding

   C. Fearing

   D. Planning

2. Which word is a synonym for *slimy* in paragraph 12?

   A. Bumpy

   B. Oily

   C. Spongy

   D. Squashy

3. Which word is synonym for *glared* in paragraph 18?

   A. Gawked

   B. Gazed

   C. Looked

   D. Scowled

4. Which word is a synonym for *trudged* in paragraph 22?

   A. Clumped

   B. Crept

   C. Galloped

   D. Stole

Use context clues and your knowledge of base words and suffixes to answer the following questions.

5. What is the meaning of the word *probably* in paragraph 2?

   A. In a certain way

   B. Not at all

   C. In all likelihood

   D. At some point

6. What is the meaning of the word *exactly* in paragraph 17?

   A. In every way

   B. Greater than

   C. Somewhat

   D. Almost

7. What is the meaning of the word *thoughtful* in paragraph 25?

   A. Acting with a strong purpose

   B. Having many thoughts on a topic

   C. Performing a task carelessly

   D. Showing concern for others

8. What is the meaning of the word *responsible* in paragraph 26?

   A. Able to be relied upon

   B. Likely to give an answer

   C. Forced to carry out a duty

   D. Ready to react to suggestions

Revising and Editing

1. What change, if any, should be made in the following sentence?

> The Smiths stayed in Orlando Florida, with their friends.

    A. Change *Smiths* to **Smith's**.

    B. Change *friends* to **friends'**.

    C. Add a comma after *Orlando*.

    D. Make no change.

2. What change, if any, should be made in the following sentence?

> Benjamin Franklin was born in Boston on January 17 1706.

    A. Add a comma after *17*.

    B. Put quotation marks around *Boston*.

    C. Add a comma after *January*.

    D. Make no change.

3. What is the BEST way to revise the following sentence?

> Big cars are nice they are expensive to own.

    A. Big cars are nice, they are expensive to own.

    B. Big cars are nice, but they are expensive to own.

    C. Big cars are nice, But they are expensive to own.

    D. Big cars are nice and they are expensive to own.

4. What is the BEST way to revise the following sentence?

> Some apples are red some apples are green.

    A. Some apples are red, some apples are green.

    B. Some apples are red, and, some apples are green.

    C. Some apples are red, and some apples are green.

    D. Some apples are red and green.

5. Which pair of pronouns completes the following sentences?

> No one wanted to spend _____ time doing homework. The students wanted to leave _____ time free for other things.

    A. their; his

    B. his; their

    C. his; his

    D. their; their

6. Which pair of pronouns completes the following sentences?

> In the math contest, everybody had to turn in _____ answers. If a student didn't do this, _____ test would be disqualified.

    A. her; her

    B. their; their

    C. her; their

    D. their; her

STOP

Ideas for Independent Reading

Which questions from Unit 1 made an impression on you?
Continue exploring them with these books.

COMMON CORE

RL 10 Read and comprehend literature. **RI 10** Read and comprehend literary nonfiction.

What do you fear most?

Before We Were Free
by Julia Alvarez

Anita's father is plotting to overthrow their country's cruel dictator. Now Anita has become a prisoner in her own house. Not even her diary is safe! What will happen now that everything has gone wrong?

Coraline
by Neil Gaiman

Coraline is bored in her family's huge old house. But then she finds a door that leads to another world. There she finds parents who look just like hers, but with some very scary differences.

Trouble Don't Last
by Shelley Pearsall

Eleven-year-old Samuel has been a slave all his life. Late one night, a slave named Harrison pulls Samuel from his bed. Together, they run north— to Canada and freedom. Their journey is one of joy and fear.

Can first impressions be trusted?

The Kidnapped Prince: Life of Olaudah Equiano
by Olaudah Equiano

Olaudah Equiano was just a little boy when he was stuffed into a sack and made a slave. Eleven years later he had won his freedom and gone on to write an autobiography that helped end slavery.

The View from Saturday
by E. L. Koningsburg

Nobody knows how Mrs. Olinski chose the four students on her sixth-grade academic bowl team, or what the secret to their success is. What connects these four students' lives and helps them unite as a real team?

When Zachary Beaver Came to Town
by Kimberly Willis Holt

When Zachary Beaver, the world's fattest boy, stops in Antler, Texas, Toby lines up to gawk at him. Zachary is snobby and rude and huge but there's something else about him that will change Toby forever.

How powerful is loyalty?

The Incredible Journey
by Sheila Burnford

When the Hunters left their pets with a friend, they never suspected one of the dogs would get so homesick that he would try to return home. Can two dogs and a cat survive a 250-mile trek through the wilderness to get back to the family they love?

Tae's Sonata
by Haemi Balgassi

Taeyoung, an eighth-grade Korean American, wants to be like everyone else. She's embarrassed when she's assigned to work on a South Korea report with Josh, the most popular boy in school. Can she find a way to fit in while being loyal to her culture?

The Wee Free Men
by Terry Pratchett

Tiffany's little brother has been kidnapped by an evil queen. Armed with only a frying pan and a lot of common sense, Tiffany marches into Fairyland to fight its monsters, rescue her brother, and save her world.

Get Novel Wise **THINK central**

Go to **thinkcentral.com**.
KEYWORD: HML6-188

UNIT 2

Person to Person

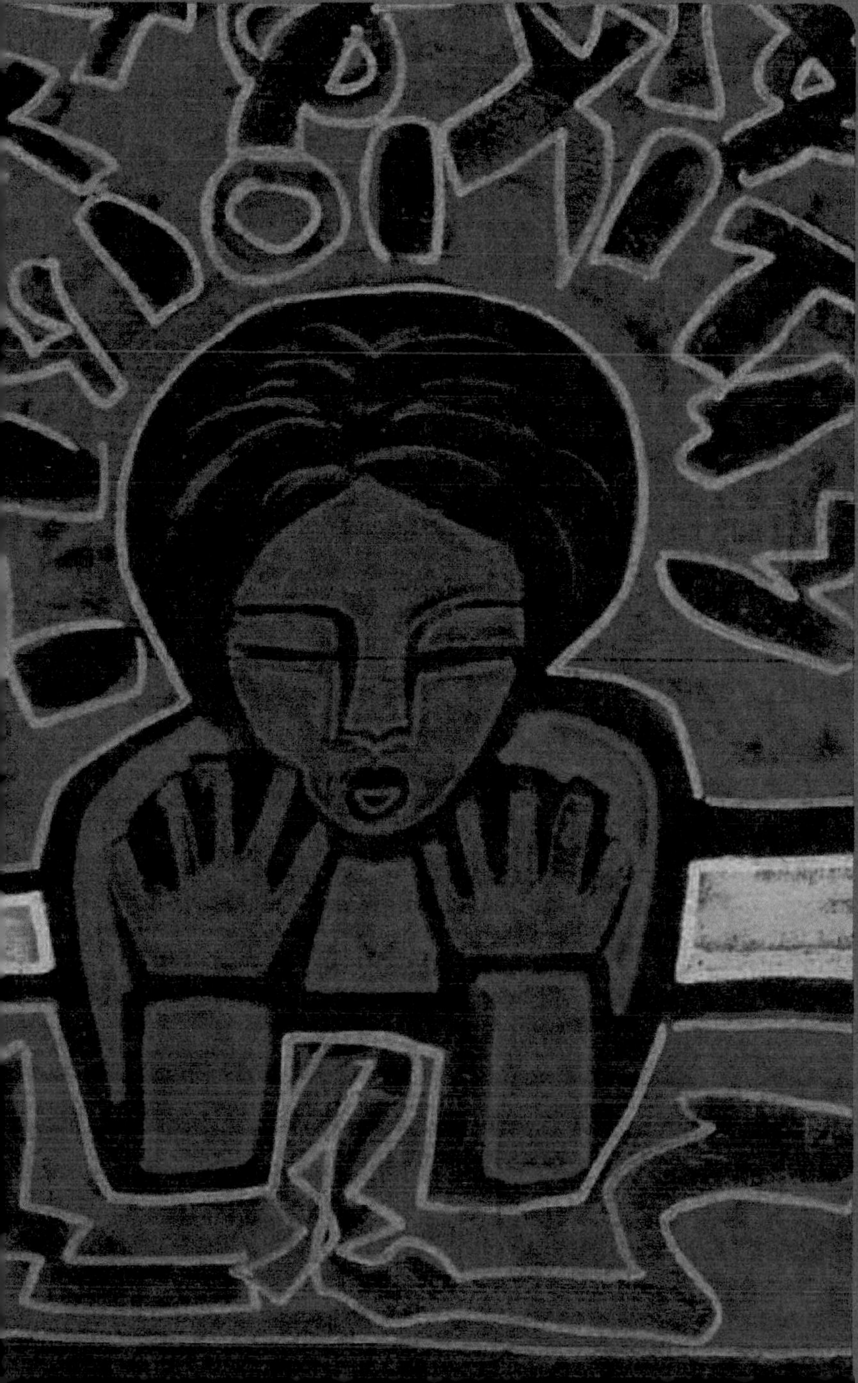

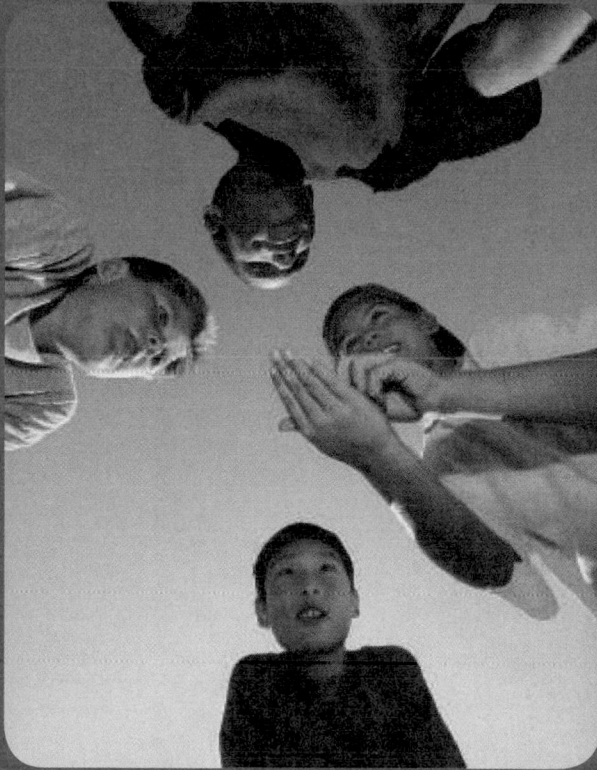

ANALYZING CHARACTER AND POINT OF VIEW

- In Fiction
- In Nonfiction
- In Poetry
- In Media

Which CHARACTERS are unforgettable?

Some of the characters we meet in books and movies are so powerful that they become part of our culture. Think about fictional characters such as Little Red Riding-Hood, Aladdin, or Zorro. Their stories are told again and again, entertaining each new generation.

ACTIVITY In a small group, make a list of unforgettable characters from TV shows, books, or movies. Describe the appearance and behavior of each one. Then consider the following questions:

- What was your first impression of the character?

- Did your opinion of the character change as you learned more about him or her? If so, in what way?

- What makes a character unforgettable?

Find It Online! **THINK** central

Go to **thinkcentral.com** for the interactive version of this unit.

Preview Unit Goals

TEXT ANALYSIS	• Analyze character and character traits as well as how a character responds or changes as the plot moves toward a resolution
	• Explain how an author develops the point of view of the narrator in a text
	• Compare and contrast one author's presentation of events with that of another
READING	• Determine figurative and connotative meanings of words and phrases as they are used in texts
	• Develop reading strategies including monitoring, predicting, setting a purpose for reading, and connecting
WRITING AND LANGUAGE	• Write a comparison-contrast essay
	• Use correct pronoun case and adjectives and adverbs correctly
SPEAKING AND LISTENING	• Ask questions and paraphrase ideas
VOCABULARY	• Explain the meaning of word roots and affixes
	• Use a glossary to determine syllabication and pronunciation
	• Use context clues to help determine the meaning of words
ACADEMIC VOCABULARY	• convey • influence • qualities
	• create • interact
MEDIA AND VIEWING	• Analyze techniques that establish characters in television

Media Smart DVD-ROM

Characters on Television

View the scenes from *Smallville* to see
how characters are developed for television.
Page 260

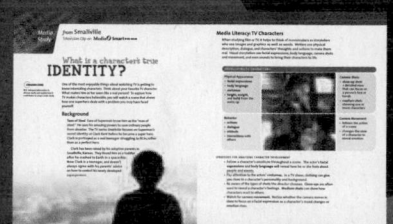

Character and Point of View

Characters in literature can be just as fascinating as people in your own life. Like real people, characters can be painfully shy, rude, or courageous. Some characters instantly draw you in, while others get on your nerves. Why do you react so strongly to the people you meet on the page? When writers use the elements of character and point of view skillfully, they create believable characters. Read on to learn more about character and point of view.

Part 1: Who Tells the Story?

COMMON CORE

Included in this workshop:
RL 3 Describe how a story's characters respond or change as the plot moves toward a resolution. **RL 6** Explain how an author develops the point of view of the narrator in a text.

Suppose two of your closest friends got into a heated argument. You heard about the argument from each friend and from an innocent bystander who overheard every word. How would the three accounts differ? As this example shows, *who* tells a story is just as important as *what* that story is about. In literature, the **narrator** is the voice that tells the story. A writer's choice of narrator is known as **point of view.** This chart explains two points of view.

FIRST-PERSON POINT OF VIEW	THIRD-PERSON POINT OF VIEW
The narrator • is a character in the story • uses the pronouns *I, me,* and *my* to refer to himself or herself • tells his or her own thoughts and feelings in his or her own voice • does not know what other characters are thinking and feeling	*The narrator* • is not a character in the story • uses the pronouns *he, she,* and *they* to refer to the characters • can reveal the thoughts, opinions, and feelings of one or more characters

▼

▼

Example

I was flying along when I spotted sparks exploding on the street below. The evil ShockBlaster was attacking innocent people! Time for me to come to the rescue again. Angry and annoyed, I realized that talented superheroes like me *never* get the day off.

Example

As Dynamyte zoomed toward the explosion, a billion thoughts raced through his mind. He wondered why villains always started trouble on his day off.

From a roof above the panicked crowd, ShockBlaster saw Dynamyte swooping across the sky toward him. "Him again?" ShockBlaster muttered.

MODEL 1: FIRST-PERSON POINT OF VIEW

The novel *Walk Two Moons* is about a 13-year-old girl named Salamanca. People call her Sal for short. One day, her mother leaves home forever, prompting Sal to deal with some confusing feelings.

from WALK TWO MOONS

Novel by **Sharon Creech**

When my mother left for Lewiston, Idaho, that April, my first thoughts were, "How could she do that? How could she leave me?"

As the days went on, many things were harder and sadder, but some things were strangely easier. When my mother had been there, I was like
5 a mirror. If she was happy, I was happy. If she was sad, I was sad. For the first few days after she left, I felt numb, non-feeling. I didn't know how to feel. I would find myself looking around for her, to see what I might want to feel.

Close Read

1. Reread the boxed sentences. Find the pronouns that show the first-person point of view.

2. How does her mother's departure initially affect Sal? Find two details that reveal Sal's feelings.

MODEL 2: THIRD-PERSON POINT OF VIEW

Becky believes she was born to play golf. After practice one day, she encounters an elderly neighbor named Doña Carmen Maria. Notice what the third-person narrator reveals about Becky's thoughts.

from How Becky Garza Learned Golf

Short story by **Gary Soto**

Doña Carmen Maria reached for one of the clubs in the bag. She said it was like a sword. She poked the air and laughed to herself.

Becky didn't smile. She was hot, thirsty, and uneasy with the old woman who again started to play with the mole on her throat. But
5 Becky's parents had always taught her to respect elders. And she had to respect Doña Carmen Maria because, if not, Becky feared the old woman would walk down the street and report her incivility. Becky could see herself grounded until she was as old as Doña Carmen Maria herself.

Close Read

1. How can you tell that this story is told from the third-person point of view? Support your answer.

2. Does Becky seem to like Doña Carmen Maria? Find details that describe Becky's thoughts and feelings about her neighbor.

Part 2: The People on the Page

When you meet someone, you form an impression based on certain clues, such as how the person looks, talks, or acts. Similar clues can help you get to know characters in literature. By noticing important details, you can infer a character's **traits,** or qualities, like shyness or friendliness. These traits can be seen in a character's behavior throughout a story in the way he or she responds or changes as the plot moves toward a resolution.

Writers use four methods to develop their characters. Use the questions and examples shown to help you understand one superhero's personality.

METHODS OF CHARACTERIZATION	EXAMPLES
 **CHARACTER'S PHYSICAL APPEARANCE** **A character's look can influence your first impression of him or her. Ask:** • What does the character look like? • What facial expressions or gestures does he or she make?	Sparks of fire sizzled in Dynamyte's hair whenever he was getting ready to show off. He smiled confidently and flexed his muscles for the crowd.
 **CHARACTER'S THOUGHTS, SPEECH, AND ACTIONS** **A character's own words and actions can reflect his or her personality. Ask:** • Does the character speak in a dialect that reflects the community in which he or she lives? • What kinds of things worry him or her? • How does he or she act toward others?	Dynamyte forgot about his day off when he realized how important he was to the city. "This is what happens when you're the *only* one capable of saving the world," he boasted as he prepared to show off some more.
 **OTHER CHARACTERS' REACTIONS** **The words or actions of other characters can tell you about a character. Ask:** • How do others treat the character? • What do they say about him or her?	ShockBlaster cringed in fear as he saw Dynamyte speeding toward him. "I must escape! I'll never win a battle against him."
NARRATOR'S DIRECT COMMENTS **The narrator may directly tell you about a character's personality. Ask:** • What qualities does the narrator say the character has? • Does the narrator admire the character?	Dynamyte's talent and skill made up for his bad attitude. He made saving the world look so easy!

METHOD 1: PHYSICAL APPEARANCE

In this fable, three princes compete for the love of a princess named Meliversa. As you read, look for descriptions of Meliversa's appearance.

from The Fable of the
Three Princes

Short story by **Isaac Asimov**

That night there was a great feast, and the three princes were the guests of honor.

The emperor, seated on a splendid throne at the head of the table, greeted them. Next to him was the princess Meliversa, and she was
5   indeed as beautiful as the sun. Her hair was long and the color of corn silk. Her eyes were blue and reminded everyone of the sky on a bright spring day. Her features were perfectly regular and her skin was flawless.

But her eyes were empty, and her face was expressionless.

Close Read

1. Find three details that describe Meliversa's beauty. One detail has been boxed.

2. Reread line 8. What do you learn about Meliversa from this description?

METHOD 2: SPEECH AND ACTIONS

Writers may use dialect to convey information about the community in which a character lives. **Dialect** is a form of language spoken in a particular place by a particular group of people. It features unique pronunciations and vocabulary. The narrator in "Jeremiah's Song" uses informal speech and grammar. Read the following passage aloud to hear the dialect.

from  Short story by **Walter Dean Myers**

I knowed my cousin Ellie was gonna be mad when Macon Smith come around to the house. She didn't have no use for Macon even when things was going right, and when Grandpa Jeremiah was fixing to die I just knowed she wasn't gonna be liking him hanging around. Grandpa
5   Jeremiah raised Ellie after her folks died and they used to be real close. Then she got to go on to college and when she come back the first year she was different. She didn't want to hear all them stories he used to to tell her anymore. Ellie said the stories wasn't true, and that's why she didn't want to hear them.

Close Read

1. Read the boxed text aloud. Then, restate the sentence using formal language. What do you learn about the characters from the writer's use of dialect?

2. Why do you think Ellie doesn't want to hear Grandpa Jeremiah's stories any more? How might college have changed her?

METHOD 3: OTHER CHARACTERS

In this excerpt, Cammy is listening to her cousin Patty Ann play the piano. As you read, notice how Cammy reacts to Patty Ann.

from COUSINS
Novel by **Virginia Hamilton**

She [Cammy] couldn't sit still. Being there with her cousin made her as angry as she could be.

Good at everything, Cammy thought to Patty Ann's back. In school, at home, at her piano. Miss Goody-goody. . . .

5   The music stopped abruptly. Patty Ann turned the page of a small notebook next to her music. The page was blank. She'd come to the end of her lessons. She closed the book. Closed her music books, too. She closed the piano top over the piano keys. To Cammy, everything she did was like chalk scraping on a blackboard.

Close Read

1. Does Cammy like Patty Ann? How can you tell?

2. Reread the boxed text. What impression of Patty Ann do you get from Cammy's reaction to her?

METHOD 4: NARRATOR'S COMMENTS

Sometimes, the narrator directly tells readers what a character is like. As you read this excerpt, think about how you would describe the soldier based on what the narrator tells you about him.

from *The King's Dragon*
Short story by **Jane Yolen**

There was once a soldier who had fought long and hard for his king. He had been wounded in the war and sent home for a rest.

Hup and one. Hup and two. He marched down the long, dusty road, using a crutch.

5   He was a member of the Royal Dragoons. His red-and-gold uniform was dirty and torn. And in the air of the winter's day, his breath plumed out before him like a cloud.

Hup and one. Hup and two. Wounded or not, he marched with a proud step. For the Royal Dragoons are the finest soldiers in the land and—they always obey orders.

Close Read

1. Look at the narrator's comments in the boxed sentences. Which word would you say does *not* describe the soldier?
   a. loyal
   b. lazy
   c. proud

2. Does the narrator seem to respect the soldier? Explain.

Part 3: Analyze the Text

Meet Anastasia Krupnik, one of Lois Lowry's most memorable characters. For homework last night, Antastasia had to write a poem. Now, she must read it in front of her entire class. Use what you've learned to analyze this excerpt.

from ANASTASIA KRUPNIK

Novel by **Lois Lowry**

Anastasia had begun to feel a little funny, as if she had ginger ale inside of her knees. But it was her turn. She stood up in front of the class and read her poem. Her voice was very small, because she was nervous.

> *hush   hush   the sea-soft night is aswim*
> 5   *with wrinklesquirm creatures*
> *listen (!)*
> *to them   move   smooth   in the moistly dark*
> *here in the   whisperwarm   wet*

That was Anastasia's poem.

10 "Read that again, please, Anastasia, in a bigger voice," said Mrs. Westvessel.

So Anastasia took a deep breath and read her poem again. She used the same kind of voice that her father did when he read poetry to her, drawing some of the words out as long as licorice sticks, and making

15 some others thumpingly short.

The class laughed.

Mrs. Westvessel looked puzzled. "Let me see that, Anastasia," she said. Anastasia gave her the poem.

Mrs. Westvessel's ordinary, everyday face had about one hundred

20 wrinkles in it. When she looked at Anastasia's poem, her forehead and nose folded up so that she had two hundred new wrinkles all of a sudden.

"Where are your capital letters, Anastasia?" asked Mrs. Westvessel.

Anastasia didn't say anything.

"Where is the rhyme?" asked Mrs. Westvessel. "It doesn't rhyme at *all*."

25 Anastasia didn't say anything.

"What kind of poem *is* this, Anastasia?" asked Mrs. Westvessel. "Can you explain it, please?"

Anastasia's voice had become very small again, the way voices do, sometimes. "It's a poem of sounds," she said. "It's about little things that

30 live in tidepools, after dark, when they move around. It doesn't have sentences or capital letters because I wanted it to look on the page like small creatures moving in the dark."

Close Read

1. Is this story told from the first-person or the third-person point of view? How can you tell?

2. Is Anastasia someone who feels comfortable in front of large crowds? Cite details to support your answer.

3. Give your impression of Mrs. Westvessel from the boxed details. Do you think she is a believable character? Explain.

4. Reread lines 24 and 26 where Mrs. Westvessel talks to Anastasia. Why are certain words italicized? What does the author's use of conversational voice tell you about Mrs. Westvessel's character?

Eleven
Short Story by Sandra Cisneros

VIDEO TRAILER THiNK central | KEYWORD: HML6-198

Is AGE more than a number?

COMMON CORE

RL 4 Determine the meaning of words and phrases as they are used in a text, including figurative and connotative meanings. **RL 6** Explain how an author develops the point of view of the narrator in a text.

For some people, a birthday is an exciting, festive event. With each increase in age, they feel more mature. For others, a birthday is just the day they were born. Inside, they may not feel any different than they did the day before. In "Eleven," a young girl struggles with what it means to grow older.

WEB IT Think about what your age means to you. Create a web that shows the things that matter to you now. Consider how the web would change if you were one year older or younger.

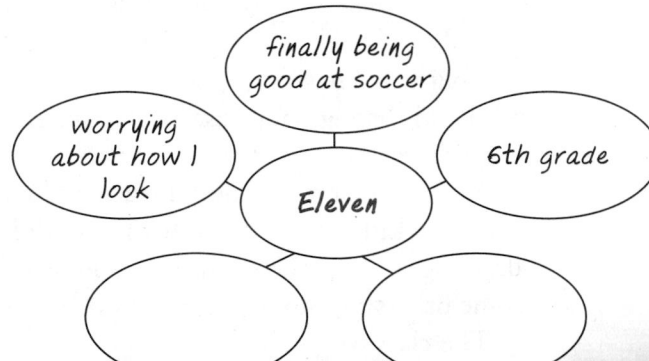

- finally being good at soccer
- worrying about how I look
- Eleven
- 6th grade

TEXT ANALYSIS: FIRST-PERSON POINT OF VIEW

This story lets you into the mind of its main character, Rachel, who is also the narrator. Rachel uses the **first-person point of view**, speaking as "I." As she tells her story, Rachel reveals the qualities of her character through her words, thoughts, and feelings. Because Rachel is telling the story herself, you won't know for sure what other characters are thinking and feeling. You'll only know what Rachel tells you.

As you read, notice how the author develops Rachel's personality by giving her a unique conversational voice. Look for phrases and descriptions that convey Rachel's very individual point of view.

READING STRATEGY: CONNECT

Authors often express an idea or a feeling with **imagery,** words and phrases that appeal to the senses of sight, taste, touch, smell, and hearing. The imagery in a story may remind you of feelings and experiences you've had or read about in other stories. When you connect through sensory imagery, you use your feelings, experiences, and imagination to help you understand what you are reading.

As you read, record imagery from the story in a chart like the one shown. Then describe connections that you can make between those images and your own experiences.

Imagery	My Connections
"underneath the year that makes you eleven"	I remember still feeling 10 on my 11th birthday.

▲ VOCABULARY IN CONTEXT

Sandra Cisneros uses the words in the list below to help tell the story of a young girl's difficult experience in school. Complete each phrase with the appropriate word from the list.

WORD LIST	alley	except	invisible	raggedy

1. _____ for math, the girl did well in school.
2. She felt _____ among the crowds of students.
3. Her old, _____ clothes embarrassed her.
4. After school, she ran home through the back _____.

 Complete the activities in your **Reader/Writer Notebook.**

Meet the Author

Sandra Cisneros
born 1954

Love of Language
Sandra Cisneros was born in Chicago where she grew up in a bilingual home, speaking English to her mother and Spanish to her father. For that reason, different aspects of language became more noticeable to her.

Escaping Through Fairy Tales
As a child, Cisneros enjoyed reading fairy tales. She loved the style of language used, and in time she began writing her own stories and poems. Cisneros's mother made sure that her daughter had the space and quiet that she needed in order to write, even in a house with six brothers.

Writing to Be Heard
In much of her writing, Cisneros explores the feeling of being out of place. As a child, Cisneros was shy, much like Rachel in "Eleven." She notes, "I am finding that with words I have the power to make people listen, to make them think in a new way. . . . It's a powerful thing to make people listen to you."

Author Online
THINK central
Go to **thinkcentral.com.**
KEYWORD: HML6-199

199

ELEVEN

Sandra Cisneros

W hat they don't understand about birthdays and what they never tell you is that when you're eleven, you're also ten, and nine, and eight, and seven, and six, and five, and four, and three, and two, and one. And when you wake up on your eleventh birthday you expect to feel eleven, but you don't. You open your eyes and everything's just like yesterday, only it's today. And you don't feel eleven at all. You feel like you're still ten. And you are—underneath the year that makes you eleven.

Like some days you might say something stupid, and that's the part of you that's still ten. Or maybe some days you might need to sit on your
10 mama's lap because you're scared, and that's the part of you that's five. And maybe one day when you're all grown up maybe you will need to cry like if you're three, and that's okay. That's what I tell Mama when she's sad and needs to cry. Maybe she's feeling three.

Because the way you grow old is kind of like an onion or like the rings inside a tree trunk or like my little wooden dolls that fit one inside the other, each year inside the next one. That's how being eleven years old is.

You don't feel eleven. Not right away. It takes a few days, weeks even, sometimes even months before you say Eleven when they ask you. And you don't feel smart eleven, not until you're almost twelve. That's the way
20 it is.

Detail of *Room 13, Los Estudiantes* (2004), José Ramirez. Mixed media on canvas, 47″ × 19″.

Analyze Visuals ▶

Based on the colors and details in this painting, how do you think the girl is feeling?

◌ COMMON CORE RL 4

Language Coach

Figurative Language When Rachel says that growing older is "like an onion," she is using a **simile,** a type of figurative language. A simile is a comparison of unlike things that uses a word such as *like* or *as*. What other similes does she use in lines 14–16?

Only today I wish I didn't have only eleven years rattling inside me like pennies in a tin Band-Aid box. Today I wish I was one hundred and two instead of eleven because if I was one hundred and two I'd have known what to say when Mrs. Price put the red sweater on my desk. I would've known how to tell her it wasn't mine instead of just sitting there with that look on my face and nothing coming out of my mouth.

"Whose is this?" Mrs. Price says, and she holds the red sweater up in the air for all the class to see. "Whose? It's been sitting in the coatroom for a month."

30 "Not mine," says everybody. "Not me."

"It has to belong to somebody," Mrs. Price keeps saying, but nobody can remember. It's an ugly sweater with red plastic buttons and a collar and sleeves all stretched out like you could use it for a jump rope. It's maybe a thousand years old and even if it belonged to me I wouldn't say so. **A**

Maybe because I'm skinny, maybe because she doesn't like me, that stupid Sylvia Saldívar says, "I think it belongs to Rachel." An ugly sweater like that, all **raggedy** and old, but Mrs. Price believes her. Mrs. Price takes the sweater and puts it right on my desk, but when I open my mouth nothing comes out.

40 "That's not, I don't, you're not . . . Not mine," I finally say in a little voice that was maybe me when I was four.

"Of course it's yours," Mrs. Price says. "I remember you wearing it once." Because she's older and the teacher, she's right and I'm not. **B**

Not mine, not mine, not mine, but Mrs. Price is already turning to page thirty-two, and math problem number four. I don't know why but all of a sudden I'm feeling sick inside, like the part of me that's three wants to come out of my eyes, only I squeeze them shut tight and bite down on my teeth real hard and try to remember today I am eleven, eleven. Mama is making a cake for me for tonight, and when Papa comes home everybody

50 will sing Happy birthday, happy birthday to you.

But when the sick feeling goes away and I open my eyes, the red sweater's still sitting there like a big red mountain. I move the red sweater to the corner of my desk with my ruler. I move my pencil and books and eraser as far from it as possible. I even move my chair a little to the right. Not mine, not mine, not mine.

In my head I'm thinking how long till lunchtime, how long till I can take the red sweater and throw it over the schoolyard fence, or leave it hanging on a parking meter, or bunch it up into a little ball and toss it in the **alley**. **Except** when math period ends Mrs. Price says loud and in

60 front of everybody, "Now, Rachel, that's enough," because she sees I've shoved the red sweater to the tippy-tip corner of my desk and it's hanging all over the edge like a waterfall, but I don't care.

A CONNECT
Reread lines 31–34. How does the imagery describing the sweater help you understand how Rachel feels?

raggedy (răg′ĭ-dē) *adj.* tattered or worn out

COMMON CORE RL 6

B FIRST-PERSON POINT OF VIEW
Writers use **dialogue**— a conversation between characters—to develop the characters' viewpoints, or attitudes. As the words come tumbling out, Cisneros reveals Rachel's anxious and uncomfortable reaction to the red sweater. Suppose the teacher were trying to give Rachel a beautiful new red sweater. How might Rachel react? How might a positive response from Rachel change your understanding of this narrator and the story?

alley (ăl′ē) *n.* a narrow street behind or between buildings

except (ĭk-sĕpt′) *prep.* but; however

"Rachel," Mrs. Price says. She says it like she's getting mad. "You put that sweater on right now and no more nonsense."

"But it's not—"

"Now!" Mrs. Price says. **C**

This is when I wish I wasn't eleven, because all the years inside of me—ten, nine, eight, seven, six, five, four, three, two, and one—are pushing at the back of my eyes when I put one arm through one sleeve of the sweater that smells like cottage cheese, and then the other arm through the other and stand there with my arms apart like if the sweater hurts me and it does, all itchy and full of germs that aren't even mine.

That's when everything I've been holding in since this morning, since when Mrs. Price put the sweater on my desk, finally lets go, and all of a sudden I'm crying in front of everybody. I wish I was **invisible** but I'm not. I'm eleven and it's my birthday today and I'm crying like I'm three in front of everybody. I put my head down on the desk and bury my face in my stupid clown-sweater arms. My face all hot and spit coming out of my mouth because I can't stop the little animal noises from coming out of me, until there aren't any more tears left in my eyes, and it's just my body shaking like when you have the hiccups, and my whole head hurts like when you drink milk too fast. **D**

But the worst part is right before the bell rings for lunch. That stupid Phyllis Lopez, who is even dumber than Sylvia Saldívar, says she remembers the red sweater is hers! I take it off right away and give it to her, only Mrs. Price pretends like everything's okay. **E**

Today I'm eleven. There's a cake Mama's making for tonight, and when Papa comes home from work we'll eat it. There'll be candles and presents and everybody will sing Happy birthday, happy birthday to you, Rachel, only it's too late.

I'm eleven today. I'm eleven, ten, nine, eight, seven, six, five, four, three, two, and one, but I wish I was one hundred and two. I wish I was anything but eleven, because I want today to be far away already, far away like a runaway balloon, like a tiny *o* in the sky, so tiny-tiny you have to close your eyes to see it. ❧

C FIRST-PERSON POINT OF VIEW
What impression of Mrs. Price does Rachel give the reader?

invisible (ĭn-vĭz'ə-bəl) *adj.* not able to be seen

D CONNECT
Reread lines 67–82. Which **images** help you understand Rachel's feelings?

E FIRST-PERSON POINT OF VIEW
Reread lines 83–86. How does the first-person point of view affect what you know about Sylvia and Phyllis?

Comprehension

1. **Recall** Rachel uses many different comparisons to describe what it is like to grow older. Name one of the comparisons she makes.

2. **Recall** What thoughts does Rachel have about the sweater as she is putting it on?

3. **Clarify** How is the issue of the sweater finally settled?

Text Analysis

4. **Make Inferences** What is it about growing older that Rachel finds disappointing? Use examples from the story to support your answer.

5. **Connect** Review your imagery chart. How do the connections you made through imagery help you understand Rachel's experience?

6. **Analyze Conversational Voice** Reread lines 35–41. Imagine that Rachel is bold instead of timid. What might she have said when Mrs. Price put the sweater on her desk? Describe the characteristics of a bold Rachel.

7. **Analyze a Minor Character** Minor characters help carry out the action of a story. Mrs. Price is a minor character in "Eleven," but she plays an important part in the story. How do you think Mrs. Price would describe the incident with the sweater? Use details to support your answer.

8. **Evaluate First-Person Point of View** As the narrator of the story, Rachel shares many of her thoughts and feelings. However, she is not able to tell us the thoughts and feelings of the other characters. Using a chart like the one shown, note what you learned through the story's first-person point of view and what you would still like to know.

What I Learned from Rachel	What I Would Like to Know

Extension and Challenge

9. **Creative Project: Art** The red sweater is an important part of "Eleven." How did you picture it in your mind as you read the story? Create a picture of the sweater as you imagined it.

Is AGE more than a number?

Revisit the activity on page 198. This time, think about how Rachel might have filled out a web about her age. Use details from the story to complete Rachel's web.

COMMON CORE

RL 4 Determine the meaning of words and phrases as they are used in a text, including connotative meanings.
RL 6 Explain how an author develops the point of view of the narrator in a text.

Vocabulary in Context

▲ VOCABULARY PRACTICE

Choose the letter of the word or phrase that is most closely related to the boldfaced word.

1. **except:** (a) not including, (b) with, (c) as well as, (d) plus
2. **invisible:** (a) impossible, (b) white, (c) unseen, (d) unwell
3. **alley:** (a) highway, (b) narrow path, (c) parking lot, (d) freeway
4. **raggedy:** (a) shabby, (b) tidy, (c) elegant, (d) beautiful

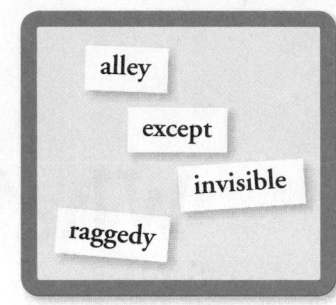

ACADEMIC VOCABULARY IN WRITING

• convey   • create   • influence   • interact   • qualities

What surprised you most about the way Mrs. Price and Rachel **interacted?** What does each character say to **convey** her feelings? Write a paragraph about what you think. Use at least two of the Academic Vocabulary words in your response.

VOCABULARY STRATEGY: SPANISH WORDS FREQUENTLY USED IN ENGLISH

American English has borrowed words from Spanish for centuries. You can sometimes figure out the meaning of an unfamiliar Spanish word by thinking of English words that it resembles.

PRACTICE Use an English dictionary that includes the origins of words, including the language they came from. Look up each of the words below and record their Spanish origins and meanings, as well as their English meanings. Then, use each word in a sentence. The first word has been done for you.

COMMON CORE

L 4c Consult dictionaries to determine or clarify a word's precise meaning.

Five Words From Spanish			
Word	Spanish Word and Spanish Meaning	English Meaning	Sentence
tornado	tornar; "to turn"	whirlwind; rapidly rotating column of air	The tornado ripped the roof off the house.
cafeteria			
chocolate			
patio			
stampede			

Interactive Vocabulary
THINKcentral
Go to **thinkcentral.com**.
KEYWORD: HML6-205

Ghost of the Lagoon

Short Story by Armstrong Sperry

Video link at
thinkcentral.com

What makes a HERO?

COMMON CORE

RL 6 Explain how an author develops the point of view of the narrator in a text.

Many different people can be considered heroes. A person's heroes might include well-known sports figures, firefighters, survivors of disaster, teachers, or respected friends and relatives. A hero, with his or her bravery, inner strength, or kindness, gives us inspiration for our everyday lives. In "Ghost of the Lagoon," a boy faces a difficult situation with heroic skill and courage.

CHART IT Think of three heroic people you know. Write their names in a chart like the one shown. Then identify the actions and personal qualities that make them heroes to you.

Heroes		
Person	Actions	Qualities
1. Aunt Gwen	helps injured animals	kind, funny
2.		

● TEXT ANALYSIS: THIRD-PERSON POINT OF VIEW

When a story is told in the **third-person point of view,** the narrator is not a character in the story. Instead, the narrator is an outside observer who zooms in on the thoughts, feelings, and actions of just one character. The narrator talks about that character in the third-person, using the pronouns *he* and *she.*

As you read "The Ghost of the Lagoon," look for details the narrator provides about the main character.

● READING STRATEGY: PREDICT

Writers often give their readers clues to help them **predict,** or make a reasonable guess about, what might happen in a story. As a reader, you combine details from the story with your own knowledge and experience to help you make predictions about what you are reading.

As you read, use a chart like the one shown to write down your predictions and the clues from the story that helped you make them.

My Prediction	Clues in Story
Mako will use his harpoon during the story.	Mako is clever, the harpoon he made is sharp and has five iron spears.

▲ VOCABULARY IN CONTEXT

Armstrong Sperry uses the boldfaced words to help tell an adventure story. Use context clues to figure out the meaning of each of the boldfaced words in the items below.

1. The boy ran off in **pursuit** of a frightening sea creature.
2. It had always made the calm, watery **lagoon** its home.
3. Creatures would sometimes hide in gaps in the **reef.**
4. The hunter was feeling **tense** from stress.
5. Mako had spent a **restless** night worrying.
6. He felt very **vulnerable** in his small, flimsy boat.

Complete the activities in your **Reader/Writer Notebook.**

Armstrong Sperry
1897–1976

Story Lover
As a boy growing up in Connecticut, Armstrong Sperry loved listening to his grandfather's wonderful tales of the South Sea Islands. In 1925, after studying art in college and working as an illustrator, Sperry headed to the South Pacific. He spent several months on the island of Bora Bora, charmed by the island's beauty and culture. He was inspired by its brave people, who rebuilt their island after it was destroyed by a hurricane during Sperry's time there.

World Traveler
Sperry returned to the United States and settled in Vermont, but he couldn't resist going back to sea. He set sail again, traveling the world in search of ideas for stories. The books and stories Sperry wrote often have characters who, like the people of Bora Bora, overcome a great challenge with strength and courage.

BACKGROUND TO THE STORY
Pacific Island
Bora Bora, where this story takes place, is one of more than 100 small islands in French Polynesia in the southern Pacific Ocean. The island is almost completely surrounded by coral reefs and is known for the crystal clear waters of its lagoon.

Author Online
THINK central
Go to thinkcentral.com.
KEYWORD: HML6-207

GHOST of the LAGOON

Armstrong Sperry

Analyze Visuals ▶

What sense does this painting give you of the story's setting?

The island of Bora Bora, where Mako lived, is far away in the South Pacific. It is not a large island—you can paddle around it in a single day—but the main body of it rises straight out of the sea, very high into the air, like a castle. Waterfalls trail down the faces of the cliffs. As you look upward, you see wild goats leaping from crag to crag.

Mako had been born on the very edge of the sea, and most of his waking hours were spent in the waters of the **lagoon,** which was nearly enclosed by the two outstretched arms of the island. He was very clever with his hands; he had made a harpoon that was as straight as an arrow and tipped with
10 five pointed iron spears. He had made a canoe, hollowing it out of a tree. It wasn't a very big canoe—only a little longer than his own height. It had an outrigger, a sort of balancing pole, fastened to one side to keep the boat from tipping over. The canoe was just large enough to hold Mako and his little dog, Afa. They were great companions, these two. **A**

lagoon (lə-gōōn′) *n.* a shallow body of water separated from a larger body of water by sandbars or other barriers

A THIRD-PERSON POINT OF VIEW
Reread lines 6–14. What does the narrator reveal about Mako?

Detail of *New Moon Rising*, Peter Sickles. © Peter Sickles/SuperStock.

One evening Mako lay stretched at full length on the pandanus mats,[1] listening to Grandfather's voice. Overhead, stars shone in the dark sky. From far off came the thunder of the surf on the **reef.**

The old man was speaking of Tupa, the ghost of the lagoon. Ever since the boy could remember, he had heard tales of this terrible
20 monster. Frightened fishermen, returning from the reef at midnight, spoke of the ghost. Over the evening fires, old men told endless tales about the monster.

Tupa seemed to think the lagoon of Bora Bora belonged to him. The natives left presents of food for him out on the reef: a dead goat, a chicken, or a pig. The presents always disappeared mysteriously, but everyone felt sure that it was Tupa who carried them away. Still, in spite of all this food, the nets of the fishermen were torn during the night, the fish stolen. What an appetite Tupa seemed to have!

Not many people had ever seen the ghost of the lagoon. Grandfather
30 was one of the few who had.

"What does he really look like, Grandfather?" the boy asked, for the hundredth time.

The old man shook his head solemnly. The light from the cook fire glistened on his white hair. "Tupa lives in the great caves of the reef. He is longer than this house. There is a sail on his back, not large but terrible to see, for it burns with a white fire. Once, when I was fishing beyond the reef at night, I saw him come up right under another canoe—"

"What happened then?" Mako asked. He half rose on one elbow. This was a story he had not heard before.

40 The old man's voice dropped to a whisper. "Tupa dragged the canoe right under the water—and the water boiled with white flame. The three fishermen in it were never seen again. Fine swimmers they were, too." **B**

Grandfather shook his head. "It is bad fortune even to speak of Tupa. There is evil in his very name."

"But King Opu Nui has offered a reward for his capture," the boy pointed out.

"Thirty acres of fine coconut land, and a sailing canoe as well," said the old man. "But who ever heard of laying hands on a ghost?"

Mako's eyes glistened. "Thirty acres of land and a sailing canoe.
50 How I should love to win that reward!"

Grandfather nodded, but Mako's mother scolded her son for such foolish talk. "Be quiet now, son, and go to sleep. Grandfather has told you that it is bad fortune to speak of Tupa. Alas, how well we have learned that lesson! Your father—" She stopped herself.

---

1. **pandanus** (păn-dā′nəs) **mats:** mats made from the fiber of leaves from a palmlike tree.

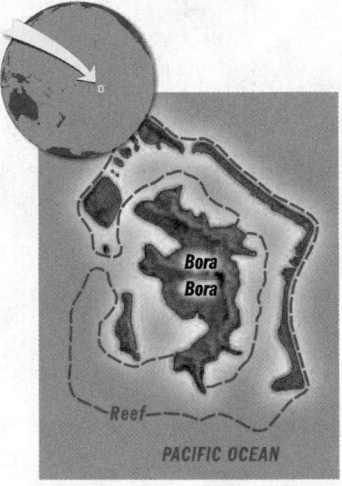

reef (rēf) *n.* a ridge of rocks, sand, or coral that rises to the surface of a body of water

SOCIAL STUDIES CONNECTION

Bora Bora

Reef

PACIFIC OCEAN

Only six miles long, Bora Bora is one of the "Society Islands" of French Polynesia in the South Pacific.

B PREDICT
Reread lines 31–42. What kind of creature do you think Tupa is? Note this information on your chart.

Detail of *Fishermen, Finisterre* (1951), Keith Vaughan. Oil on canvas, 91.4 cm × 71.1 cm. Private collection.
© Bridgeman Art Library. © 2008 Artists Rights Society (ARS), New York/DACS, London.

◀ **Analyze Visuals**

What do the **details** in this painting tell you about the three men?

"What of my father?" the boy asked quickly. And now he sat up straight on the mats.

"Tell him, Grandfather," his mother whispered.

The old man cleared his throat and poked at the fire. A little shower of sparks whirled up into the darkness.

60 "Your father," he explained gently, "was one of the three fishermen in the canoe that Tupa destroyed." His words fell upon the air like stones dropped into a deep well.

Mako shivered. He brushed back the hair from his damp forehead. Then he squared his shoulders and cried fiercely, "I shall slay Tupa and win the king's reward!" He rose to his knees, his slim body **tense**, his eyes flashing in the firelight. **C**

"Hush!" his mother said. "Go to sleep now. Enough of such foolish talk. Would you bring trouble upon us all?"

Mako lay down again upon the mats. He rolled over on his side
70 and closed his eyes, but sleep was long in coming.

The palm trees whispered above the dark lagoon, and far out on the reef the sea thundered.

tense (tĕns) *adj.* nervous; feeling strain

C PREDICT
Consider the conversation between the characters and what you know so far about Mako. What do you think is going to happen? Add this information to your chart.

The boy was slow to wake up the next morning. The ghost of Tupa had played through his dreams, making him **restless.** And so it was almost noon before Mako sat up on the mats and stretched himself. He called Afa, and the boy and his dog ran down to the lagoon for their morning swim. **D**

When they returned to the house, wide-awake and hungry, Mako's mother had food ready and waiting.

80 "These are the last of our bananas," she told him. "I wish you would paddle out to the reef this afternoon and bring back a new bunch."

The boy agreed eagerly. Nothing pleased him more than such an errand, which would take him to a little island on the outer reef, half a mile from shore. It was one of Mako's favorite playgrounds, and there bananas and oranges grew in great plenty.

"Come, Afa," he called, gulping the last mouthful. "We're going on an expedition." He picked up his long-bladed knife and seized his spear. A minute later, he dashed across the white sand, where his canoe was drawn up beyond the water's reach.

90 Afa barked at his heels. He was all white except for a black spot over each eye. Wherever Mako went, there went Afa also. Now the little dog leaped into the bow of the canoe, his tail wagging with delight. The boy shoved the canoe into the water and climbed aboard. Then, picking up his paddle, he thrust it into the water. The canoe shot ahead. Its sharp bow cut through the green water of the lagoon like a knife through cheese. And so clear was the water that Mako could see the coral gardens, forty feet below him, growing in the sand. The shadow of the canoe moved over them.

A school of fish swept by like silver arrows. He saw scarlet rock cod 100 with ruby eyes and the head of a conger eel[2] peering out from a cavern in the coral. The boy thought suddenly of Tupa, ghost of the lagoon. On such a bright day it was hard to believe in ghosts of any sort. The fierce sunlight drove away all thought of them. Perhaps ghosts were only old men's stories, anyway!

Mako's eyes came to rest upon his spear—the spear that he had made with his own hands—the spear that was as straight and true as an arrow. He remembered his vow of the night before. Could a ghost be killed with a spear? Some night, when all the village was sleeping, Mako swore to himself that he would find out! He would paddle out to the reef and 110 challenge Tupa! Perhaps tonight. Why not? He caught his breath at the thought. A shiver ran down his back. His hands were tense on the paddle. **E**

---

2. **rock cod . . . conger eel:** Rock cod is a type of saltwater fish, and a conger eel is a large eel.

restless (rĕst'lĭs) adj. unable to sleep or rest

D THIRD-PERSON POINT OF VIEW
Reread lines 73–77. What is the narrator able to reveal about Mako that the other characters in the story wouldn't know?

VISUAL VOCABULARY

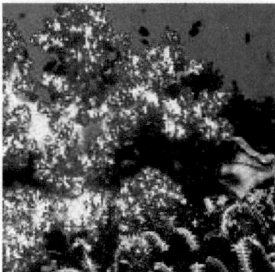

coral (kôr'əl) n. a type of marine animal, the skeletons of which build up a rocklike underwater structure called a reef

E THIRD-PERSON POINT OF VIEW
Reread lines 105–111. How do you learn what Mako is thinking even though he hasn't spoken?

As the canoe drew away from shore, the boy saw the coral reef that, above all others, had always interested him. It was of white coral—a long slim shape that rose slightly above the surface of the water. It looked very much like a shark. There was a ridge on the back that the boy could pretend was a dorsal fin, while up near one end were two dark holes that looked like eyes!

Times without number the boy had practiced spearing this make-believe shark, aiming always for the eyes, the most **vulnerable**
120 spot. So true and straight had his aim become that the spear would pass right into the eyeholes without even touching the sides of the coral. Mako had named the coral reef Tupa.

This morning, as he paddled past it, he shook his fist and called, "Ho, Mister Tupa! Just wait till I get my bananas. When I come back, I'll make short work of you!"

Afa followed his master's words with a sharp bark. He knew Mako was excited about something.

The bow of the canoe touched the sand of the little island where the bananas grew. Afa leaped ashore and ran barking into the jungle, now
130 on this trail, now on that. Clouds of sea birds whirled from their nests into the air with angry cries.

Mako climbed into the shallow water, waded ashore, and pulled his canoe up on the beach. Then, picking up his banana knife, he followed Afa. In the jungle the light was so dense and green that the boy felt as if he were moving underwater. Ferns grew higher than his head. The branches of the trees formed a green roof over him. A flock of parakeets fled on swift wings. Somewhere a wild pig crashed through the undergrowth while Afa dashed away in **pursuit**. Mako paused anxiously. Armed only with his banana knife, he had no desire to meet the wild pig.
140 The pig, it seemed, had no desire to meet him, either.

Then, ahead of him, the boy saw the broad green blades of a banana tree. A bunch of bananas, golden ripe, was growing out of the top.

At the foot of the tree he made a nest of soft leaves for the bunch to fall upon. In this way the fruit wouldn't be crushed. Then with a swift slash of his blade he cut the stem. The bananas fell to the earth with a dull thud. He found two more bunches.

Then he thought, "I might as well get some oranges while I'm here. Those little rusty ones are sweeter than any that grow on Bora Bora."

So he set about making a net out of palm leaves to carry the oranges.
150 As he worked, his swift fingers moving in and out among the strong green leaves, he could hear Afa's excited barks off in the jungle. That was just like Afa, always barking at something: a bird, a fish, a wild pig. He never caught anything, either. Still, no boy ever had a finer companion.

The palm net took longer to make than Mako had realized. By the time it was finished and filled with oranges, the jungle was dark and gloomy. Night comes quickly and without warning in the islands of the tropics.

Mako carried the fruit down to the shore and loaded it into the canoe. Then he whistled to Afa. The dog came bounding out of the bush, wagging his tail.

160 "Hurry!" Mako scolded. "We won't be home before the dark comes."

The little dog leaped into the bow of the canoe, and Mako came aboard. Night seemed to rise up from the surface of the water and swallow them. On the distant shore of Bora Bora, cook fires were being lighted. The first star twinkled just over the dark mountains. Mako dug his paddle into the water, and the canoe leaped ahead.

The dark water was alive with phosphorus.[3] The bow of the canoe seemed to cut through a pale liquid fire. Each dip of the paddle trailed streamers of light. As the canoe approached the coral reef, the boy called, "Ho, Tupa! It's too late tonight to teach you your lesson. But I'll come 170 back tomorrow." The coral shark glistened in the darkness.

And then, suddenly, Mako's breath caught in his throat. His hands felt weak. Just beyond the fin of the coral Tupa, there was another fin—a huge one. It had never been there before. And—could he believe his eyes? It was moving. **G**

The boy stopped paddling. He dashed his hand across his eyes. Afa began to bark furiously. The great white fin, shaped like a small sail, glowed with phosphorescent light. Then Mako knew. Here was Tupa—the real Tupa—ghost of the lagoon! **H**

His knees felt weak. He tried to cry out, but his voice died in his throat. 180 The great shark was circling slowly around the canoe. With each circle, it moved closer and closer. Now the boy could see the phosphorescent glow of the great shark's sides. As it moved in closer, he saw the yellow eyes, the gill slits in its throat.

Afa leaped from one side of the canoe to the other. In sudden anger Mako leaned forward to grab the dog and shake him soundly. Afa wriggled out of his grasp as Mako tried to catch him, and the shift in weight tipped the canoe on one side. The outrigger rose from the water. In another second they would be overboard. The boy threw his weight over quickly to balance the canoe, but with a loud splash Afa fell over into 190 the dark water. ◆

Mako stared after him in dismay. The little dog, instead of swimming back to the canoe, had headed for the distant shore. And there was the great white shark—very near.

---

3. **phosphorus** (fŏs′fər-əs): a substance that glows with a yellowish or white light.

COMMON CORE RL 6

G **NARRATOR**
You can tell that this story is told from the **third-person limited point of view** because the narrator's observations are limited to the thoughts, feelings, and actions of one character, Mako. Narrators who are all knowing tell stories from an **omniscient point of view,** meaning they are able to tell readers everything about every character, including how each one thinks and feels. Reread lines 171–174. How would this paragraph change if the narrator were telling this story from an omniscient point of view?

H **PREDICT**
What do you think Mako will do next? Write your prediction on your chart.

◆ **GRAMMAR IN CONTEXT**
Reread lines 184–190. Notice the writer correctly uses the object pronoun *him* in this paragraph. Here, the pronoun is part of a **compound object,** that is two or more connected subjects (Mako and Afa).

"Afa! Afa! Come back! Come quickly!" Mako shouted.

The little dog turned back toward the canoe. He was swimming with all his strength. Mako leaned forward. Could Afa make it? Swiftly the boy seized his spear. Bracing himself, he stood upright. There was no weakness in him now. His dog, his companion, was in danger of instant death.

Afa was swimming desperately to reach the canoe. The white shark had
200 paused in his circling to gather speed for the attack. Mako raised his arm, took aim. In that instant the shark charged. Mako's arm flashed forward. All his strength was behind that thrust. The spear drove straight and true, right into the great shark's eye. Mad with pain and rage, Tupa whipped about, lashing the water in fury. The canoe rocked back and forth. Mako struggled to keep his balance as he drew back the spear by the cord fastened to his wrist. **❶**

He bent over to seize Afa and drag him aboard. Then he stood up, not a moment too soon. Once again the shark charged. Once again Mako threw his spear, this time at the other eye. The spear found its mark.
210 Blinded and weak from loss of blood, Tupa rolled to the surface, turned slightly on his side. Was he dead?

▲ **Analyze Visuals**

How does the shark shown **compare** with your mental picture of Tupa?

❶ THIRD-PERSON POINT OF VIEW
Reread lines 194–206. What does the narrator know about the emotions of Mako? What does the narrator observe about the emotions of Tupa?

Mako knew how clever sharks could be, and he was taking no chances. Scarcely daring to breathe, he paddled toward the still body. He saw the faintest motion of the great tail. The shark was still alive. The boy knew that one flip of that tail could overturn the canoe and send him and Afa into the water, where Tupa could destroy them.

Swiftly, yet calmly, Mako stood upright and braced himself firmly. Then, murmuring a silent prayer to the shark god, he threw his spear for the last time. Downward, swift as sound, the spear plunged into a white
220 shoulder. **J**

Peering over the side of the canoe, Mako could see the great fish turn over far below the surface. Then slowly, slowly, the great shark rose to the surface of the lagoon. There he floated, half on one side.

Tupa was dead.

Mako flung back his head and shouted for joy. Hitching a strong line about the shark's tail, the boy began to paddle toward the shore of Bora Bora. The dorsal fin, burning with the white fire of phosphorus, trailed after the canoe.

Men were running down the beaches of Bora Bora, shouting as they
230 leaped into their canoes and put out across the lagoon. Their cries reached the boy's ears across the water.

"It is Tupa—ghost of the lagoon," he heard them shout. "Mako has killed him!"

That night, as the tired boy lay on the pandanus mats listening to the distant thunder of the sea, he heard Grandfather singing a new song. It was the song which would be sung the next day at the feast which King Opu Nui would give in Mako's honor. The boy saw his mother bending over the cook fire. The stars leaned close, winking like friendly eyes. Grandfather's voice reached him now from a great distance, "Thirty acres
240 of land and a sailing canoe . . ." ❧

J PREDICT
Review your log of predictions and clues. How do you predict the story will end?

Comprehension

1. **Recall** Where does Mako spend most of his time?

2. **Recall** What weapon does Mako use in his battle with Tupa?

3. **Clarify** What makes Mako so determined to kill Tupa?

Text Analysis

4. **Predict** Look at the chart you made while reading. Match the predictions you made with what happened in the story. Which of your predictions were correct?

5. **Understand Cause and Effect** A story's events are related by cause and effect when one event becomes the cause of another. Reread lines 147–156. What effect does Mako's decision to gather oranges have on the story?

6. **Examine Conflict** Mako's battle with the shark is an example of **external conflict,** the struggle between a character and an outside force. What **internal conflict,** or struggle within a character's mind, does Mako face when Afa falls into the water?

7. **Analyze Third-Person Point of View** Skim through the story, focusing on descriptions of Mako. Use a chart like the one shown to note information provided by the narrator that Mako might not have included if he were telling the story.

Mako's Thoughts	Mako's Feelings	Mako's Actions

Extension and Challenge

8. **SOCIAL STUDIES CONNECTION** Bora Bora is one of more than 25,000 islands in the South Pacific. These islands are broken up into three major groups: Melanesia, Micronesia, and Polynesia. Do some research to learn more about the islands in one of these groups. Look for information about how the islands were formed, their climate and vegetation, and the cultural history of the people who live there.

What makes a HERO?

What qualities does Mako share with the heroes you listed on your chart?

COMMON CORE

RL 6 Explain how an author develops the point of view of the narrator in a text. **W7** Conduct short research projects, drawing on several sources.

Vocabulary in Context

▲ **VOCABULARY PRACTICE**

Show that you understand the vocabulary words by deciding if each statement is true or false.

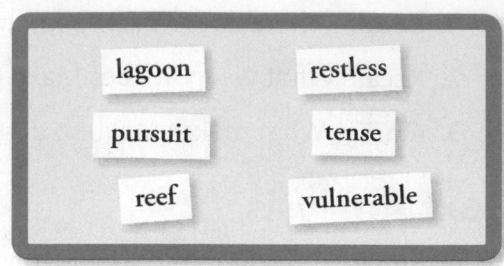

1. A person who is **restless** has a hard time relaxing.
2. A **lagoon** is an enormous body of water.
3. A fragile vase is **vulnerable** to being damaged.
4. The leader in a race is the one in **pursuit** of the other racers.
5. A **reef** is a parking lot for cars.
6. A **tense** moment is one that makes people laugh.

ACADEMIC VOCABULARY IN SPEAKING

> • convey   • create   • influence   • interact   • qualities

Imagine you are Mako. With a partner discuss how you felt when you were fighting Tupa. Use at least two Academic Vocabulary words in your response. Here is a sample of how you might begin.

> **EXAMPLE DISCUSSION**
>
> *Although I was frightened during the struggle, I tried to __convey__ a sense of bravery.*

VOCABULARY STRATEGY: SYLLABICATION AND PRONUNCIATION

Syllables are the units of sound that make up a word. When you come across a word that is difficult to pronounce, it can be helpful to break the word into syllables and sound them out loud. Once you feel comfortable pronouncing the syllables, try to pronounce the entire word. Keep in mind that some words have only one syllable and cannot be divided.

You can use a glossary like the one in the back of this book to find the syllabication guides for most words. Look at the example below. The word *lagoon* has two syllables. The raised dot shows the division between syllables. Can you say the word out loud?

○ **COMMON CORE**

L 4c Consult glossaries to find the pronunciation of a word.

la·goon

PRACTICE Use a glossary to look up the syllabication of each of the following vocabulary words and record them in your notebook. Then, practice the pronunciation of each word by sounding the syllables out loud. When you are comfortable pronouncing a word, use it in a sentence.

pursuit   reef   restless   tense   vulnerable

Language

◆ **GRAMMAR IN CONTEXT:** Use Correct Pronoun Case

COMMON CORE

L 1a Ensure that pronouns are in the proper case (subjective, objective). **W 3** Write narratives to develop imagined events.

Personal pronouns have subject and object cases, and the two are often used incorrectly, especially in compound subjects and compound objects. Use a **subject pronoun** (*I, she, he, we,* or *they*) if the pronoun is part of a compound subject. Use an **object pronoun** (*me, her, him, us,* or *them*) if the pronoun is part of a compound object. (*You* and *it* function as both subject and object pronouns.)

> *Original:*   Afa and me are going to the island to get bananas.
>
> *Revised:*   Afa and I are going to the island to get bananas.
> *(The pronoun is part of a compound subject, so it should be I, not me.)*

PRACTICE Choose the correct pronoun to complete each sentence.

1. (They, Them) and their families lived in fear of the "monster."
2. (He, Him) and Afa found Tupa that night.
3. The men shouted to Mako and (he, him).
4. (We, Us) and our families were glad that the monster was gone.

For more help with pronoun cases, see page R53 in the **Grammar Handbook.**

READING-WRITING CONNECTION

YOUR TURN Broaden your understanding of "Ghost of the Lagoon" by responding to this prompt. Then use the **revising tip** to improve your response.

WRITING PROMPT	REVISING TIP
Extended Constructed Response: Scene How would the story have been different if it had focused on the thoughts and feelings of a character other than Mako? Choose a scene in the story. Write it as a **narrative** or a **short story** as seen through the eyes of Mother, Grandfather, or even Afa.	Review your response. Have you used subject and object pronouns correctly? If not, revise your writing.

Interactive Revision

THINK central

Go to thinkcentral.com.
KEYWORD: HML6-219

Jeremiah's Song

Short Story by Walter Dean Myers

VIDEO TRAILER **THINK** central KEYWORD: HML6-220

When is a story a
TREASURE?

COMMON CORE

RL 1 Cite textual evidence to support analysis of what the text says explicitly. **RL 6** Explain how an author develops the point of view of the narrator in a text.

Some stories are forgotten as soon as the words leave the storyteller's lips. Other stories are passed from one generation to the next. Think about what makes a story a treasure—something worth remembering and sharing with others. Does it matter if the story is funny, sad, or scary? Does the story have to teach you something? In "Jeremiah's Song," the young characters consider the value of an older man's stories.

QUICKWRITE In a journal entry, briefly describe a story that is meaningful to you. The story can be one you have heard, read, or seen. Explain why this story is important to you.

● TEXT ANALYSIS: DIALECT AND CONVERSATIONAL VOICE

Writers often use dialect to bring their characters to life. In fact, you can learn a lot about a character simply by paying attention to the way he or she speaks. In "Jeremiah's Song," you experience the story through a young first-person narrator who is characterized by his use of informal speech and grammar. The narrator uses a **conversational voice** that makes it seem as though he is speaking directly to you. You can guess a little bit about the narrator's character because he speaks in a **dialect,** a way of speaking that is common in the particular region and community in which he lives.

As you read the story, think about how the narrator's voice and way of speaking helps you understand his character.

● READING STRATEGY: MONITOR

To avoid becoming confused as you read, it is good to occasionally **monitor,** or check, your understanding. One way to monitor is to **clarify** what you've read. This means you stop and make sure that you can clearly explain what has happened in the story. If not, reread and look for clues in the selection to help you restate the information in your own words.

As you read, pause to clarify meaning. It may help to use a chart like the one shown below.

This Confuses Me	My Own Words

▲ VOCABULARY IN CONTEXT

Myers uses the boldfaced words to help tell the story of an older man. To see how many you know, restate each sentence using a different word or phrase in place of the boldfaced word.

1. Grandpa has a serious **condition,** but it can be treated.
2. The doctor made a **diagnosis** about what was wrong.
3. He couldn't move his arm after he had a **stroke.**
4. Getting a cold was only a small **setback** in his recovery.

 Complete the activities in your **Reader/Writer Notebook.**

Meet the Author

Walter Dean Myers
born 1937

Role Models
Walter Dean Myers once said that people should have role models with whom they can identify. Myers's foster father and grandfather were his role models. Both were gifted storytellers, and Myers has followed in their footsteps. Throughout his writing career, Myers has introduced his readers to fictional and real African-American role models.

Getting to Know His Characters
Pictures are important to Myers's writing experience. When working on a story, he cuts out pictures of people who look the way he imagines his characters should look. His wife creates a collage of the pictures, and he hangs it over his computer. When Myers sits down to write, he feels as if he is getting to know his characters better all the time.

BACKGROUND TO THE STORY
Storytelling has a long history in the African-American community. Stories of family ties, folklore, and struggles for civil rights create strong bonds from one generation to the next. In "Jeremiah's Song," Grandpa Jeremiah shares the stories of his ancestors with the young people in his life.

Author Online

THINKcentral
Go to **thinkcentral.com.**
KEYWORD: HML6-221

Jeremiah's SONG

Walter Dean Myers

Analyze Visuals ▶

What kind of music do you think this person is playing? Explain your answer.

I knowed my cousin Ellie was gonna be mad when Macon Smith come around to the house. She didn't have no use for Macon even when things was going right, and when Grandpa Jeremiah was fixing to die I just knowed she wasn't gonna be liking him hanging around. Grandpa Jeremiah raised Ellie after her folks died and they used to be real close. Then she got to go on to college and when she come back the first year she was different. She didn't want to hear all them stories he used to tell her anymore. Ellie said the stories wasn't true, and that's why she didn't want to hear them.

10   I didn't know if they was true or not. Tell the truth I didn't think much on it either way, but I liked to hear them stories. Grandpa Jeremiah said they wasn't stories anyway, they was songs.

    "They the songs of my people," he used to say.

    I didn't see how they was songs, not regular songs anyway. Every little thing we did down in Curry seemed to matter to Ellie that first summer she come home from college. You couldn't do nothin' that was gonna please her. She didn't even come to church much. 'Course she come on Sunday or everybody would have had a regular fit, but she didn't come on Thursday nights and she didn't come on Saturday even though she used 20 to sing in the gospel choir. **Ⓐ**

    "I guess they teachin' her somethin' worthwhile up there at Greensboro," Grandpa Jeremiah said to Sister Todd. "I sure don't see what it is, though."

Ⓐ MONITOR
Reread lines 1–20. Clarify the relationship between Grandpa Jeremiah and Ellie. When and how did it change? Record your answer in your chart.

Howling Duet (Musical Interlude) (1998), Benny Andrews. Oil and collage on paper, 29⅝" × 22½". Courtesy of ACA Galleries, New York. © Estate of Benny Andrews/Licensed by VAGA, New York.

"You ain't never had no book learning, Jeremiah," Sister Todd shot back. She wiped at where a trickle of sweat made a little path through the white dusting powder she put on her chest to keep cool. "Them old ways you got ain't got nothing for these young folks."

"I guess you right," Grandpa Jeremiah said.

He said it but I could see he didn't like it none. He was a big man with a big head and had most all his hair even if it was white. All that summer, instead of sitting on the porch telling stories like he used to when I was real little, he would sit out there by himself while Ellie stayed in the house and watched the television or read a book. Sometimes I would think about asking him to tell me one of them stories he used to tell but they was too scary now that I didn't have nobody to sleep with but myself. I asked Ellie to sleep with me but she wouldn't.

"You're nine years old," she said, sounding real proper. "You're old enough to sleep alone."

I *knew* that. I just wanted her to sleep with me because I liked sleeping with her. Before she went off to college she used to put cocoa butter on her arms and face and it would smell real nice. When she come back from college she put something else on, but that smelled nice too.

It was right after Ellie went back to school that Grandpa Jeremiah had him a **stroke** and Macon started coming around. I think his mama probably made him come at first, but you could see he liked it. Macon had always been around, sitting over near the stuck window at church or going on the blueberry truck when we went picking down at Mister Gregory's place. For a long time he was just another kid, even though he was older'n me, but then, all of a sudden, he growed something fierce. I used to be up to his shoulder one time and then, before I could turn around good, I was only up to his shirt pocket. He changed too. When he used to just hang around with the other boys and play ball or shoot at birds he would laugh a lot. He didn't laugh so much anymore and I figured he was just about grown. When Grandpa got sick he used to come around and help out with things around the house that was too hard for me to do. I mean, I could have done all the chores, but it would just take me longer. **B**

When the work for the day was finished and the sows[1] fed, Grandpa would kind of ease into one of his stories and Macon, he would sit and listen to them and be real interested. I didn't mind listening to the stories when Grandpa told them to Macon because he would be telling them in the middle of the afternoon and they would be past my mind by the time I had to go to bed. **C**

---

1. **sows:** adult female hogs.

Macon had an old guitar he used to mess with, too. He wasn't too bad on it, and sometimes Grandpa would tell him to play us a tune. He could play something he called "the Delta Blues" real good, but when Sister Todd or somebody from the church come around he'd play "Precious Lord" or "Just a Closer Walk With Thee."

Grandpa Jeremiah had been feeling poorly from that stroke, and one of his legs got a little drag to it. Just about the time Ellie come from school the next summer he was real sick. He was breathing loud so you could

70 hear it even in the next room, and he would stay in bed a lot even when there was something that needed doing or fixing.

"I don't think he's going to make it much longer," Dr. Crawford said. "The only thing I can do is to give him something for the pain."

"Are you sure of your **diagnosis?**" Ellie asked. She was sitting around the table with Sister Todd, Deacon[2] Turner, and his little skinny wife.

Dr. Crawford looked at Ellie like he was surprised to hear her talking. "Yes, I'm sure," he said. "He had tests a few weeks ago and his **condition** was bad then."

"How much time he got?" Sister Todd asked.

80 "Maybe a week or two at best," Dr. Crawford said.

When he said that, Deacon Turner's wife started crying and goin' on and I give her a hard look but she just went on. I was the one who loved Grandpa Jeremiah the most and she didn't hardly even know him so I didn't see why she was crying.

Everybody started tiptoeing around the house after that. They would go in and ask Grandpa Jeremiah if he was comfortable and stuff like that or take him some food or a cold glass of lemonade.

Sister Todd come over and stayed with us. Mostly what she did is make supper and do a lot of praying, which was good because I figured that

90 maybe God would do something to make Grandpa Jeremiah well. When she wasn't doing that she was piecing on[3] a fancy quilt she was making for some white people in Wilmington.

Ellie, she went around asking everybody how they felt about Dr. Crawford and then she went into town and asked about the tests and things. Sister Jenkins asked her if she thought she knowed more than Dr. Crawford, and Ellie rolled her eyes at her, but Sister Jenkins was reading out her Bible and didn't make no notice of it.

Then Macon come over.

He had been away on what he called "a little piece of a job" and hadn't

100 heard how bad off Grandpa Jeremiah was. When he come over he talked

SOCIAL STUDIES CONNECTION

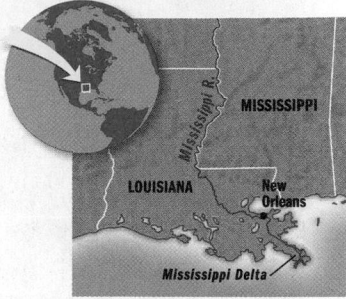

The type of music known as the Delta Blues originated in the Delta region of Mississippi. Musicians performed soulful songs accompanied only by a guitar or harmonica. This style of music soon spread across the country.

diagnosis (dī′əg-nō′sĭs) *n.* the identification of a disease through examination of a patient

condition (kən-dĭsh′ən) *n.* a disease or state of health

---

2. **Deacon:** a term used for church members who assist their church's priest or minister.

3. **piecing on:** mending or adding blocks of fabric.

Detail of *Cookin Hog Cracklin* (1995), Jessie Coates. Acrylic on masonite. Private collection.
© Jessie Coates/SuperStock.

◀ **Analyze Visuals**
What can you **infer** about the people in this painting?

to Ellie and she told him what was going on and then he got him a soft drink from the refrigerator and sat out on the porch and before you know it he was crying. **D**

You could look at his face and tell the difference between him sweating and the tears. The sweat was close against his skin and shiny and the tears come down fatter and more sparkly. **E**

Macon sat on the porch, without saying a word, until the sun went down and the crickets started chirping and carrying on. Then he went in to where Grandpa Jeremiah was and stayed in there for a long time.

110   Sister Todd was saying that Grandpa Jeremiah needed his rest and Ellie went in to see what Macon was doing. Then she come out real mad.

"He got Grandpa telling those old stories again," Ellie said. "I told him Grandpa needed his rest and for him not to be staying all night."

He did leave soon, but bright and early the next morning Macon was back again. This time he brought his guitar with him and he went on in to Grandpa Jeremiah's room. I went in, too.

Grandpa Jeremiah's room smelled terrible. It was all closed up so no drafts could get on him and the whole room was smelled down with disinfect[4] and

D MONITOR
Reread lines 88–103. In your chart, record how Sister Todd, Ellie, and Macon deal with Grandpa Jeremiah's illness.

E CONVERSATIONAL VOICE
Reread lines 104–106 and think about the words the narrator uses to describe Macon sitting on the porch. How do you think the narrator feels?

---

4. **disinfect:** short for *disinfectant*, a chemical that destroys germs and bacteria.

medicine. Grandpa Jeremiah lay propped up on the bed and he was so
120 gray he looked scary. His hair wasn't combed down and his head on the
pillow with his white hair sticking out was enough to send me flying if
Macon hadn't been there. He was skinny, too. He looked like his skin got
loose on his bones, and when he lifted his arms, it hung down like he was
just wearing it instead of it being a part of him. **F**

Macon sat slant-shouldered with his guitar across his lap. He was
messin' with the guitar, not making any music, but just going over the
strings as Grandpa talked.

"Old Carrie went around out back to where they kept the pigs penned up
and she felt a cold wind across her face. . . ." Grandpa Jeremiah was telling
130 the story about how a old woman out-tricked the Devil and got her son
back. I had heard the story before, and I knew it was pretty scary. "When
she felt the cold breeze she didn't blink nary⁵ an eye, but looked straight
ahead. . . ."

All the time Grandpa Jeremiah was talking I could see Macon fingering
his guitar. I tried to imagine what it would be like if he was actually
plucking the strings. I tried to fix my mind on that because I didn't like
the way the story went with the old woman wrestling with the Devil.

We sat there for nearly all the afternoon until Ellie and Sister Todd
come in and said that supper was ready. Me and Macon went out and ate
140 some collard greens, ham hocks, and rice. Then Macon he went back in
and listened to some more of Grandpa's stories until it was time for him to
go home. I wasn't about to go in there and listen to no stories at night.

Dr. Crawford come around a few days later and said that Grandpa
Jeremiah was doing a little better.

"You think the Good Lord gonna pull him through?" Sister Todd asked.

"I don't tell the Good Lord what He should or should not be doing,"
Dr. Crawford said, looking over at Sister Todd and at Ellie. "I just said
that *my* patient seems to be doing okay for his condition."

"He been telling Macon all his stories," I said.

150 "Macon doesn't seem to understand that Grandpa Jeremiah needs his
strength," Ellie said. "Now that he's improving, we don't want him to have
a **setback**."

"No use in stopping him from telling his stories," Dr. Crawford said.
"If it makes him feel good it's as good as any medicine I can give him."

I saw that this didn't set with Ellie, and when Dr. Crawford had left
I asked her why.

"Dr. Crawford means well," she said, "but we have to get away from the
kind of life that keeps us in the past." **G**

---

5. **nary:** not one; not any.

F CONVERSATIONAL
VOICE
Reread lines 122–124.
What words and phrases
are used to describe
how skinny Grandpa
Jeremiah is?

setback (sĕt′băk′) *n.*
an unexpected stop in
progress; a change from
better to worse

G MONITOR
Reread lines 155–158.
What does Ellie mean
when she says "we have
to get away from living
in the past"?

JEREMIAH'S SONG   **227**

She didn't say why we should be trying to get away from the stories and
160 I really didn't care too much. All I knew was that when Macon was sitting
in the room with Grandpa Jeremiah I wasn't nearly as scared as I used to
be when it was just me and Ellie listening. I told that to Macon.

"You getting to be a big man, that's all," he said.

That was true. Me and Macon was getting to be good friends, too. I didn't
even mind so much when he started being friends with Ellie later. It seemed
kind of natural, almost like Macon was supposed to be there with us instead
of just visiting.

Grandpa wasn't getting no better, but he wasn't getting no worse,
either.

170 "You liking Macon now?" I asked Ellie when we got to the middle of
July. She was dishing out a plate of smothered chops[6] for him and I hadn't
even heard him ask for anything to eat.

"Macon's funny," Ellie said, not answering my question. "He's in there
listening to all of those old stories like he's really interested in them. It's
almost as if he and Grandpa Jeremiah are talking about something more
than the stories, a secret language."

I didn't think I was supposed to say anything about that to Macon, but
once, when Ellie, Sister Todd, and Macon were out on the porch shelling
butter beans after Grandpa got tired and was resting, I went into his room
180 and told him what Ellie had said.

"She said that?" Grandpa Jeremiah's face was skinny and old looking
but his eyes looked like a baby's, they was so bright.

"Right there in the kitchen is where she said it," I said. "And I don't
know what it mean but I was wondering about it."

"I didn't think she had any feeling for them stories," Grandpa Jeremiah
said. "If she think we talking secrets, maybe she don't."

"I think she getting a feeling for Macon," I said.

"That's okay, too," Grandpa Jeremiah said. "They both young."

"Yeah, but them stories you be telling, Grandpa, they about old people
190 who lived a long time ago," I said.

"Well, those the folks you got to know about," Grandpa Jeremiah said.
"You think on what those folks been through, and what they was feeling,
and you add it up with what you been through and what you been feeling,
then you got you something."

"What you got Grandpa?"

"You got you a bridge," Grandpa said. "And a meaning. Then when
things get so hard you about to break, you can sneak across that bridge
and see some folks who went before you and see how they didn't break. **H**

---

6. **smothered chops:** pork chops thickly covered with a sauce or gravy.

H MONITOR
Reread lines 189–198.
Why are the stories
important to Grandpa
Jeremiah? Add this
information to your
chart.

The Poverty of It All (1965), Benny Andrews. Oil and collage on canvas, 26″ × 22″. Courtesy of ACA Galleries, New York. © Estate of Benny Andrews/Licensed by VAGA, New York.

◀ Analyze Visuals
What do the colors in this picture suggest about how the people are feeling?

Some got bent and some got twisted and a few fell along the way, but they
200 didn't break."

"Am I going to break, Grandpa?"

"You? As strong as you is?" Grandpa Jeremiah pushed himself up on his elbow and give me a look. "No way you going to break, boy. You gonna be strong as they come. One day you gonna tell all them stories I told you to your young'uns and they'll be as strong as you."

"Suppose I ain't got no stories, can I make some up?"

"Sure you can, boy. You make 'em up and twist 'em around. Don't make no mind. Long as you got 'em."

"Is that what Macon is doing?" I asked. "Making up stories to play on
210 his guitar?"

"He'll do with 'em what he see fit, I suppose," Grandpa Jeremiah said. "Can't ask more than that from a man." ❶

It rained the first three days of August. It wasn't a hard rain but it rained anyway. The mailman said it was good for the crops over East but I didn't care about that so I didn't pay him no mind. What I did mind was when it rain like that the field mice come in and get in things like the flour bin and I always got the blame for leaving it open.

When the rain stopped I was pretty glad. Macon come over and sat with Grandpa and had something to eat with us. Sister Todd come over, too.

COMMON CORE RL 6

❶ **DIALECT**
Writers use **dialogue**—conversations between characters—to show you, rather than tell you, about their characters. One way you can learn about characters is by observing the way they speak. Notice that Grandpa Jeremiah and the narrator use a dialect that is particular to African-Americans living in the South. You can also learn about characters by paying attention to the way they speak with each other. What can you tell about the relationship between the narrator and Grandpa Jeremiah from their dialogue in lines 196–212?

220   "How Grandpa doing?" Sister Todd asked. "They been asking about him in the church."

"He's doing all right," Ellie said.

"He's kind of quiet today," Macon said. "He was just talking about how the hogs needed breeding."

"He must have run out of stories to tell," Sister Todd said. "He'll be repeating on himself like my father used to do. That's the way I *hear* old folks get." ◆

Everybody laughed at that because Sister Todd was pretty old, too. Maybe we was all happy because the sun was out after so much rain.
230 When Sister Todd went in to take Grandpa Jeremiah a plate of potato salad with no mayonnaise like he liked it, she told him about how people was asking for him and he told her to tell them he was doing okay and to remember him in their prayers.

Sister Todd came over the next afternoon, too, with some rhubarb pie with cheese on it, which is my favorite pie. When she took a piece into Grandpa Jeremiah's room she come right out again and told Ellie to go fetch the Bible.

It was a hot day when they had the funeral. Mostly everybody was there. The church was hot as anything, even though they had the window
240 open. Some yellowjacks flew in and buzzed around Sister Todd's niece and then around Deacon Turner's wife and settled right on her hat and stayed there until we all stood and sang "Soon-a Will Be Done."

At the graveyard Macon played "Precious Lord" and I cried hard even though I told myself that I wasn't going to cry the way Ellie and Sister Todd was, but it was such a sad thing when we left and Grandpa Jeremiah was still out to the grave that I couldn't help it.

During the funeral and all, Macon kind of told everybody where to go and where to sit and which of the three cars to ride in. After it was over he come by the house and sat on the front porch and played on his guitar.
250 Ellie was standing leaning against the rail and she was crying but it wasn't a hard crying. It was a soft crying, the kind that last inside of you for a long time. **J**

Macon was playing a tune I hadn't heard before. I thought it might have been what he was working at when Grandpa Jeremiah was telling him those stories and I watched his fingers but I couldn't tell if it was or not. It wasn't nothing special, that tune Macon was playing, maybe halfway between them Delta Blues he would do when Sister Todd wasn't around and something you would play at church. It was something different and something the same at the same time. I watched his fingers go over that
260 guitar and figured I could learn that tune one day if I had a mind to. ∽

◆ **GRAMMAR IN CONTEXT**
Reread lines 220–228. Notice that the author uses both **interrogative sentences** (ones that ask questions) and **declarative sentences** (ones that make a statement). The author has correctly used question marks to punctuate interrogative sentences and periods to punctuate declarative sentences.

J **CONVERSATIONAL VOICE**
Evaluate how Myers's use of a child narrator affects the way the story is told. What observations about the funeral does the narrator make that an adult might not have made?

Comprehension

1. **Recall** Which members of the community take an interest in Grandpa Jeremiah's health?

2. **Clarify** The narrator describes a younger Macon in lines 44–55. How has Macon changed?

3. **Summarize** What evidence is there that Ellie begins to have feelings for Macon?

Text Analysis

● 4. **Monitor** Review the chart you created as you read. Choose three entries and explain how the clues helped you clarify the information.

5. **Make Inferences** By the end of the story, which characters do you think treasure Grandpa Jeremiah's stories the most? Explain.

● 6. **Analyzing Dialect** Why do you think Myers chose to use dialect in "Jeremiah's Song"? Use examples from the story to explain how your understanding of the characters would be different had the author used Standard English, the kind of English you are reading right now.

● 7. **Analyzing Conversational Voice** Recall that Myers's first-person narrator is a child who speaks with a conversational voice. Find three examples of narration that seem especially typical of how a child might tell a story. Record them in a diagram like the one shown. What effect does the choice of a child narrator and voice have on the story?

> Example: "I was the one who loved Grandpa Jeremiah the most and she didn't hardly even know him so I didn't see why she was crying." (lines 82–84)

> Example:

> Example:

> Effect on the Story:

Extension and Challenge

8. **SOCIAL STUDIES CONNECTION** Research Macon's favorite type of music—the Delta Blues—and the musicians who made it famous. Focus your search on one musician, such as Muddy Waters, Robert Johnson, Son House, or Charley Patton. Share your findings with the class.

When is a story a TREASURE?

What stories do you treasure? Why are they important to you?

COMMON CORE

RL 1 Cite textual evidence to support analysis of what the text says explicitly. RL 6 Explain how an author develops the point of view of the narrator in a text.

Muddy Waters

Vocabulary in Context

▲ VOCABULARY PRACTICE

Show that you understand the vocabulary words by deciding whether each statement is true or false.

1. You usually get a **diagnosis** from a doctor.
2. A **setback** during a long project is very exciting.
3. Having a heart **condition** means that you have strong feelings.
4. After having a **stroke,** you might not be able to speak as clearly.

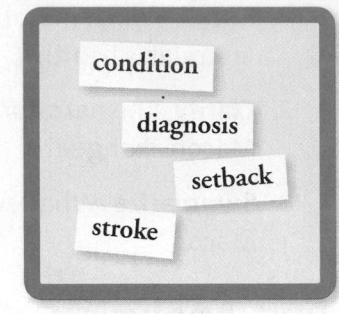

condition

diagnosis

setback

stroke

ACADEMIC VOCABULARY IN WRITING

- convey • create • influence • interact • qualities

Has anyone **influenced** your life the way that Grandpa Jeremiah touched the lives of those around him? Use at least one of the Academic Vocabulary words in your response.

VOCABULARY STRATEGY: COMPOUND WORDS

When two or more words are combined to have one meaning, they are called **compound words.** You can understand some compound words, like *firefighter,* by looking at the meanings of the combined words. For others, like the vocabulary word *setback,* you may need help from context clues to fully understand the meaning of the word.

COMMON CORE

L 4d Verify the determination of the meaning of a word by checking the inferred meaning in a dictionary. **L 6** Acquire and use accurately academic words.

PRACTICE Use context clues to figure out the meaning of each boldfaced compound word. Then write the definition. Use a dictionary if necessary.

1. It was the first time he had broken a rule, so we chose to **overlook** it.
2. She tries to pay closer attention to things, but she is still a **scatterbrain.**
3. As the **ringleader** of the neighborhood baseball team, he was responsible for gathering the players and setting the rules.
4. I became good friends with the **shopkeeper** who sold used books.
5. Once the cottage was fixed up, it was a lovely **getaway** from busy city life.

Interactive Vocabulary

THINK central

Go to **thinkcentral.com**.
KEYWORD: HML6-232

Language

◆ **GRAMMAR IN CONTEXT:** Use Correct Sentence Types and Punctuation

In order for your sentences to communicate the meaning and emotions you intend, it is important to use the correct sentence type.

Sentence Type	▶	Example
A **declarative sentence** makes a statement and ends with a period.		*Grandpa tells wonderful stories.*
An **interrogative sentence** asks a question and ends with a question mark.		*Which of grandpa's stories do you like the best?*
An **imperative sentence** makes a request or gives a command and usually ends with a period.		*Help me remember the story grandpa used to tell about living in the South.*
An **exclamatory sentence** shows strong feeling and ends with an exclamation point.		*I am so angry that you won't listen to grandpa's stories!*

PRACTICE Identify the sentence type for each of the following sentences and punctuate it correctly.

1. Oh, what a comfort that is to me
2. I cried when I heard Macon play the guitar
3. Ladies, please sit down
4. What song is Macon playing on the porch

*For more help with sentence types, see page R60 in the **Grammar Handbook.***

READING-WRITING CONNECTION

YOUR TURN

Broaden your understanding of "Jeremiah's Song" by responding to this prompt. Then use the **revising tip** to improve your response.

WRITING PROMPT	REVISING TIP
Short Constructed Response: Analysis Consider Macon's relationship with Jeremiah, Ellie, and the narrator. In **one paragraph,** summarize how Macon becomes part of the family. Include at least one example from the story to support your response.	▶ Review your response. Have you punctuated all of your sentences correctly? If not, revise your writing.

Interactive Revision THINK central

Go to **thinkcentral.com**.
KEYWORD: HML6-233

COMMON CORE

L 3a Vary sentence patterns for meaning, reader/listener interest, and style. **W 2** Write informative/explanatory texts to convey ideas.

President Cleveland, Where Are You?
Short Story by Robert Cormier

Aaron's Gift
Short Story by Myron Levoy

What would you do
for your FAMILY?

The word *family* means different things to different people. It might mean parents, siblings, cousins, or grandparents. It can also mean close, trusted friends. Although you may not always understand or agree with the people you call family, you are there for them in times of need, and they are there for you. In each of the two stories you are about to read, a boy does something nice for someone in his family.

QUICKWRITE Think of a time when you helped someone through a hard time or when someone did something special for you. Write a few sentences about that experience.

234

● TEXT ANALYSIS: CULTURAL AND HISTORICAL SETTING

A work's **cultural and historical setting** is not only the particular time and place in which a work takes place, but also refers to the **customs** of the period, or the way people lived at that time. When an author writes about a historical period, the characters will behave, confront issues, and speak in a way that reflects the customs and history of the times.

As you read, look for details that reflect a story's cultural and historical periods. Ask yourself "What situation do the characters face?" Notice the way the cultural and historical setting influences the story.

● READING STRATEGY: SET A PURPOSE FOR READING

Your **purpose,** or reason, for reading the following two stories is to find the similarities and differences between their cultural and historical settings. After reading the first story, begin filling in a chart like the one below.

	"President Cleveland, Where Are You?"	"Aaron's Gift"
Time and Place		
Details of Historical Period		
Characters' Behavior		

Review: Connect

▲ VOCABULARY IN CONTEXT

Cormier and Levoy use the listed words to help tell the stories of two boys. To see which words you already know, fill in the chart. Then write a sentence using each word you know.

WORD LIST		
allot	divulge	obsess
assassinate	incredulous	skirmish
contempt	massacre	stalemate

Know Well	Think I Know	Don't Know

Complete the activities in your **Reader/Writer Notebook.**

Robert Cormier
1925–2000

Young Poet
Robert Cormier was published for the first time at age 12, when a local paper printed some of his poems. Cormier later wrote for a newspaper before becoming one of the first writers to create literature for young adult readers. In his novels, young heroes who find themselves isolated from friends and adults must struggle with difficult problems on their own.

Myron Levoy
born 1930

Inspired Writer
When Myron Levoy was a teenager, he worked at the New York Public Library. There he came across the original manuscript of the poem "Miniver Cheevy" by Edward Arlington Robinson. Levoy had just read the poem in school, and seeing it written in the author's own hand amazed him. He was inspired to become a writer himself.

Authors Online
Go to thinkcentral.com. KEYWORD: HML6-235

THINK central

235

PRESIDENT CLEVELAND,
Where Are You?
Robert Cormier

That was the autumn of the cowboy cards—Buck Jones and Tom Tyler and Hoot Gibson and especially Ken Maynard.[1] The cards were available in those five-cent packages of gum: pink sticks, three together, covered with a sweet white powder. You couldn't blow bubbles with that particular gum, but it couldn't have mattered less. The cowboy cards were important—the pictures of those rock-faced men with eyes of blue steel. **A**

On those wind-swept, leaf-tumbling afternoons, we gathered after school on the sidewalk in front of Lemire's Drugstore, across from
10 St. Jude's Parochial School, and we swapped and bargained and matched for the cards. Because a Ken Maynard serial[2] was playing at the Globe every Saturday afternoon, he was the most popular cowboy of all, and one of his cards was worth at least ten of any other kind. Rollie Tremaine had a treasure of thirty or so, and he guarded them jealously. He'd match you for the other cards, but he risked his Ken Maynards only when the other kids threatened to leave him out of the competition altogether.

You could almost hate Rollie Tremaine. In the first place, he was the only son of Auguste Tremaine, who operated the Uptown Dry Goods Store, and he did not live in a tenement but in a big white birthday cake of a house on
20 Laurel Street. He was too fat to be effective in the football games between

---

1. **Buck Jones . . . Kent Maynard:** well-known movie cowboys who developed their skills in rodeos and Wild West shows or as stuntmen.

2. **serial** (sîr´ē-əl): a movie appearing in weekly parts.

A CULTURAL AND HISTORICAL SETTING
Reread lines 1–7. What do you learn about the cultural and historical setting in this paragraph?

Analyze Visuals ▶
Examine the photograph. What can you **infer** about the boys?

the Frenchtown Tigers and the North Side Knights, and he made us constantly aware of the jingle of coins in his pockets. He was able to stroll into Lemire's and casually select a quarter's worth of cowboy cards while the rest of us watched, aching with envy.

Once in a while I earned a nickel or dime by running errands or washing windows for blind old Mrs. Belander, or by finding pieces of copper, brass, and other valuable metals at the dump and selling them to the junkman. The coins clutched in my hand, I would race to Lemire's to buy a cowboy card or two, hoping that
30 Ken Maynard would stare boldly out at me as I opened the pack. At one time, before a disastrous matching session with Roger Lussier (my best friend, except where the cards were involved), I owned five Ken Maynards and considered myself a millionaire, of sorts.

One week I was particularly lucky; I had spent two afternoons washing floors for Mrs. Belander and received a quarter. Because my father had worked a full week at the shop, where a rush order for fancy combs had been received, he **allotted** my brothers and sisters and me an extra dime along with the usual ten cents for the Saturday-afternoon movie. Setting aside the movie fare, I found myself with a bonus of thirty-five cents, and I then
40 planned to put Rollie Tremaine to shame the following Monday afternoon.

Monday was the best day to buy the cards because the candy man stopped at Lemire's every Monday morning to deliver the new assortments. There was nothing more exciting in the world than a fresh batch of card boxes. I rushed home from school that day and hurriedly changed my clothes, eager to set off for the store. As I burst through the doorway, letting the screen door slam behind me, my brother Armand blocked my way. **B**

He was fourteen, three years older than I, and a freshman at Monument High School. He had recently become a stranger to me in many ways—indifferent to such matters as cowboy cards and the
50 Frenchtown Tigers—and he carried himself with a mysterious dignity that was fractured now and then when his voice began shooting off in all directions like some kind of vocal fireworks.[3]

"Wait a minute, Jerry," he said. "I want to talk to you." He motioned me out of earshot of my mother, who was busy supervising the usual after-school **skirmish** in the kitchen.

I sighed with impatience. In recent months Armand had become a figure of authority, siding with my father and mother occasionally. As the oldest son, he sometimes took advantage of his age and experience to issue rules and regulations.

allot (ə-lŏt′) *v.* to parcel out; distribute

B CULTURAL AND HISTORICAL SETTING
Reread lines 25–40. What details in these lines reveal that cowboy cards and movies were important?

skirmish (skûr′mĭsh) *n.* a minor battle or conflict

---

3. **his voice . . . vocal fireworks:** Because Armand's voice is changing, its pitch varies unexpectedly from high to low.

60 "How much money have you got?" he whispered.

"You in some kind of trouble?" I asked, excitement rising in me as I remembered the blackmail plot of a movie at the Globe a month before.

He shook his head in annoyance. "Look," he said, "it's Pa's birthday tomorrow. I think we ought to chip in and buy him something . . ."

I reached into my pocket and caressed the coins. "Here," I said carefully, pulling out a nickel. "If we all give a nickel, we should have enough to buy him something pretty nice."

He regarded me with **contempt.** "Rita already gave me fifteen cents, and I'm throwing in a quarter. Albert handed over a dime—all that's left 70 of his birthday money. Is that all you can do—a nickel?"

"Aw, come on," I protested. "I haven't got a single Ken Maynard left, and I was going to buy some cards this afternoon."

"Ken Maynard!" he snorted. "Who's more important—him or your father?"

His question was unfair because he knew that there was no possible choice—"my father" had to be the only answer. My father was a huge man who believed in the things of the spirit. . . . He had worked at the Monument Comb Shop since the age of fourteen; his booming laugh—or grumble—greeted us each night when he returned from the factory. 80 A steady worker when the shop had enough work, he quickened with gaiety on Friday nights and weekends . . . and he was fond of making long speeches about the good things in life. In the middle of the Depression,[4] for instance, he paid cash for a piano, of all things, and insisted that my twin sisters, Yolande and Yvette, take lessons once a week. **C**

I took a dime from my pocket and handed it to Armand.

"Thanks, Jerry," he said. "I hate to take your last cent."

"That's all right," I replied, turning away and consoling myself with the thought that twenty cents was better than nothing at all.

When I arrived at Lemire's, I sensed disaster in the air. Roger Lussier 90 was kicking disconsolately at a tin can in the gutter, and Rollie Tremaine sat sullenly on the steps in front of the store.

"Save your money," Roger said. He had known about my plans to splurge on the cards.

"What's the matter?" I asked.

"There's no more cowboy cards," Rollie Tremaine said. "The company's not making any more."

contempt (kən-tĕmpt´) *n.* the feeling produced by something disgraceful or worthless; scorn

C CULTURAL AND HISTORICAL SETTING
This story takes place during the Great Depression of the 1930s, when many businesses failed and many people were out of work. Reread lines 75–84. How does the description of Jerry's father reflect the issues families confronted during the Great Depression?

---

4. **Depression:** During the 1930s, the United States suffered an economic crisis known as the Great Depression. Banks and businesses all over the country were forced to close, and poverty and unemployment were widespread.

"They're going to have President cards," Roger said, his face twisting with disgust. He pointed to the store window. "Look!"

A placard in the window announced: "Attention, Boys. Watch for the New Series. Presidents of the United States. Free in Each 5-Cent Package of Caramel Chew."

"President cards?" I asked, dismayed.

I read on: "Collect a Complete Set and Receive an Official Imitation Major League Baseball Glove, Embossed with Lefty Grove's[5] Autograph."

Glove or no glove, who could become excited about Presidents, of all things?

Rollie Tremaine stared at the sign. "Benjamin Harrison, for crying out loud," he said. "Why would I want Benjamin Harrison when I've got twenty-two Ken Maynards?"

I felt the warmth of guilt creep over me. I jingled the coins in my pocket, but the sound was hollow. No more Ken Maynards to buy.

"I'm going to buy a Mr. Goodbar," Rollie Tremaine decided.

I was without appetite, indifferent even to a Baby Ruth, which was my favorite. I thought of how I had betrayed Armand and, worst of all, my father.

"I'll see you after supper," I called over my shoulder to Roger as I hurried away toward home. I took the shortcut behind the church, although it involved leaping over a tall wooden fence, and I zigzagged recklessly through Mr. Thibodeau's garden, trying to outrace my guilt. I pounded up the steps and into the house, only to learn that Armand had already taken Yolande and Yvette uptown to shop for the birthday present.

I pedaled my bike furiously through the streets, ignoring the indignant horns of automobiles as I sliced through the traffic. Finally I saw Armand and my sisters emerge from the Monument Men's Shop. My heart sank when I spied the long, slim package that Armand was holding.

"Did you buy the present yet?" I asked, although I knew it was too late.

"Just now. A blue tie," Armand said. "What's the matter?"

"Nothing," I replied, my chest hurting.

Whelan's Drug Store, 44th Street and Eighth Avenue, Manhattan (February 7, 1936), Berenice Abbott.

D CONNECT

Reread lines 123–132. Jerry is suddenly concerned about finding his brother. Do you think Jerry's feelings are those that a real-life person would have in the same situation? Explain your answer.

---

5. **Lefty Grove's:** belonging to Lefty Grove, a Hall of Fame pitcher for the Philadelphia A's (Athletics) and the Boston Red Sox between 1925 and 1941.

He looked at me for a long moment. At first his eyes were hard, but then they softened. He smiled at me, almost sadly, and touched my arm. I turned away from him because I felt naked and exposed.

"It's all right," he said gently. "Maybe you've learned something." 140 The words were gentle, but they held a curious dignity, the dignity remaining even when his voice suddenly cracked on the last syllable.

I wondered what was happening to me, because I did not know whether to laugh or cry.

Sister Angela was amazed when, a week before Christmas vacation, everybody in the class submitted a history essay worthy of a high mark—in some cases as high as A minus. (Sister Angela did not believe that anyone in the world ever deserved an A.) She never learned—or at least she never let on that she knew—we all had become experts on the Presidents because of the cards we purchased at Lemire's. Each card contained a picture 150 of a President and, on the reverse side, a summary of his career. We looked at those cards so often that the biographies imprinted themselves on our minds without effort. Even our street-corner conversations were filled with such information as the fact that James Madison was called "The Father of the Constitution," or that John Adams had intended to become a minister.

The President cards were a roaring success, and the cowboy cards were quickly forgotten. In the first place, we did not receive gum with the cards, but a kind of chewy caramel. The caramel could be tucked into a corner of your mouth, bulging your cheek in much the same manner as wads of tobacco bulged the mouths of baseball stars. In the second place, 160 the competition for collecting the cards was fierce and frustrating—fierce because everyone was intent on being the first to send away for a baseball glove and frustrating because although there were only thirty-two Presidents, including Franklin Delano Roosevelt,[6] the variety at Lemire's was at a minimum. When the deliveryman left the boxes of cards at the store each Monday, we often discovered that one entire box was devoted to a single President—two weeks in a row the boxes contained nothing but Abraham Lincolns. One week Roger Lussier and I were the heroes of Frenchtown. We journeyed on our bicycles to the North Side, engaged three boys in a matching bout, and returned with five new Presidents, 170 including Chester Alan Arthur, who up to that time had been missing.

Perhaps to sharpen our desire, the card company sent a sample glove to Mr. Lemire, and it dangled, orange and sleek, in the window. I was half sick with longing, thinking of my old glove at home, which I had inherited from

COMMON CORE **L 4b**

Language Coach

Word Origins Many English words contain roots and affixes that are derived from older languages. The word *biography* (line 151) comes from the Greek words *bio*, meaning "life," and *graphein*, meaning "to write." How does this word origin give you a clue to the meaning of the word *biography*?

---

6. **Franklin Delano Roosevelt:** president of the United States from 1933 to 1945; president at the time of this story.

Armand. But Rollie Tremaine's desire for the glove outdistanced my own. He even got Mr. Lemire to agree to give the glove in the window to the first person to get a complete set of cards, so that precious time wouldn't be wasted waiting for the postman.

We were delighted at Rollie Tremaine's frustration, especially since he was only a substitute player for the Tigers. Once, after spending fifty
180 cents on cards—all of which turned out to be Calvin Coolidge—he threw them to the ground, pulled some dollar bills out of his pocket, and said, "The heck with it. I'm going to buy a glove!"

"Not that glove," Roger Lussier said. "Not a glove with Lefty Grove's autograph. Look what it says at the bottom of the sign."

We all looked, although we knew the words by heart: "This Glove Is Not For Sale Anywhere."

Rollie Tremaine scrambled to pick up the cards from the sidewalk, pouting more than ever. After that he was quietly **obsessed** with the Presidents, hugging the cards close to his chest and refusing to tell us how
190 many more he needed to complete his set. **E**

I too was obsessed with the cards, because they had become things of comfort in a world that had suddenly grown dismal. After Christmas, a layoff at the shop had thrown my father out of work. He received no paycheck for four weeks, and the only income we had was from Armand's after-school job at the Blue and White Grocery Store—a job he lost finally when business dwindled as the layoff continued.

Although we had enough food and clothing—my father's credit had always been good, a matter of pride with him—the inactivity made my father restless and irritable. . . . The twins fell sick and went to the hospital to
200 have their tonsils removed. My father was confident that he would return to work eventually and pay off his debts, but he seemed to age before our eyes. **F**

When orders again were received at the comb shop and he returned to work, another disaster occurred, although I was the only one aware of it. Armand fell in love.

I discovered his situation by accident, when I happened to pick up a piece of paper that had fallen to the floor in the bedroom he and I shared. I frowned at the paper, puzzled.

"Dear Sally, When I look into your eyes the world stands still . . ."

The letter was snatched from my hands before I finished reading it.
210 "What's the big idea, snooping around?" Armand asked, his face crimson. "Can't a guy have any privacy?"

obsess (əb-sĕs') *v.*
to occupy the mind of

E CONNECT
Think about a time when you were competing for something you really wanted. In what way does that experience help you understand how Jerry and his friends are feeling?

F CULTURAL AND HISTORICAL SETTING
Reread lines 191–201. How does the situation described in these lines reflect the historical setting?

◀ **Analyze Visuals**

How does this photograph compare with your mental picture of Jerry and his friends?

He had never mentioned privacy before. "It was on the floor," I said. "I didn't know it was a letter. Who's Sally?"

He flung himself across the bed. "You tell anybody and I'll muckalize you," he threatened. "Sally Knowlton."

Nobody in Frenchtown had a name like Knowlton.

"A girl from the North Side?" I asked, **incredulous**.

He rolled over and faced me, anger in his eyes, and a kind of despair, too.

"What's the matter with that? Think she's too good for me?" he asked.

220 "I'm warning you, Jerry, if you tell anybody . . ."

"Don't worry," I said. Love had no particular place in my life; it seemed an unnecessary waste of time. And a girl from the North Side was so remote that for all practical purposes she did not exist. But I was curious. "What are you writing her a letter for? Did she leave town or something?"

"She hasn't left town," he answered. "I wasn't going to send it. I just felt like writing to her."

I was glad that I had never become involved with love—love that brought desperation to your eyes, that caused you to write letters you did not plan to send. Shrugging with indifference, I began to search in the closet for the

230 old baseball glove. I found it on the shelf, under some old sneakers. The webbing was torn and the padding gone. I thought of the sting I would feel when a sharp grounder slapped into the glove, and I winced.

incredulous
(ĭn-krĕj'ə-ləs) *adj.*
unbelieving

"You tell anybody about me and Sally and I'll—"

"I know. You'll muckalize me."

I did not **divulge** his secret and often shared his agony, particularly when he sat at the supper table and left my mother's special butterscotch pie untouched. I had never realized before how terrible love could be. But my compassion was short-lived, because I had other things to worry about: report cards due at Eastertime; the loss of income from old Mrs. Belander, who had gone to live with a daughter in Boston; and, of course, the Presidents. **G**

Because a **stalemate** had been reached, the President cards were the dominant force in our lives—mine, Roger Lussier's and Rollie Tremaine's. For three weeks, as the baseball season approached, each of us had a complete set—complete except for one President, Grover Cleveland. Each time a box of cards arrived at the store, we hurriedly bought them (as hurriedly as our funds allowed) and tore off the wrappers, only to be confronted by James Monroe or Martin Van Buren or someone else. But never Grover Cleveland, never the man who had been the twenty-second and the twenty-fourth President of the United States. We argued about Grover Cleveland. Should he be placed between Chester Alan Arthur and Benjamin Harrison as the twenty-second President, or did he belong between Benjamin Harrison and William McKinley as the twenty-fourth President? Was the card company playing fair? Roger Lussier brought up a horrifying possibility—did we need two Grover Clevelands to complete the set?

Indignant, we stormed Lemire's and protested to the harassed storeowner, who had long since vowed never to stock a new series. Muttering angrily, he searched his bills and receipts for a list of rules.

"All right," he announced. "Says here you only need one Grover Cleveland to finish the set. Now get out, all of you, unless you've got money to spend."

Outside the store, Rollie Tremaine picked up an empty tobacco tin and scaled it across the street. "Boy," he said. "I'd give five dollars for a Grover Cleveland."

When I returned home, I found Armand sitting on the piazza[7] steps, his chin in his hands. His mood of dejection mirrored my own, and I sat down beside him. We did not say anything for a while.

"Want to throw the ball around?" I asked.

He sighed, not bothering to answer.

GROVER CLEVELAND

AMERICAN HEROES CARAMEL

---

7. **piazza** (pē-ăz′ə): a porch or balcony, usually with a roof.

divulge (dĭ-vŭlj′) *v.* to reveal, especially something private or secret

G CONNECT
Reread lines 235–240. Are Jerry's concerns similar or different to concerns of boys his age today? Explain.

stalemate (stāl′māt′) *n.* a situation in which no one playing a game is able to win

"You sick?" I asked.

He stood up and hitched up his trousers, pulled at his ear, and finally told me what the matter was—there was a big dance next week at the high school, the Spring Promenade, and Sally had asked him to be her escort.

I shook my head at the folly of love. "Well, what's so bad about that?"

"How can I take Sally to a fancy dance?" he asked desperately. "I'd have to buy her a corsage . . . And my shoes are practically falling apart. Pa's got too many worries now to buy me new shoes or give me money for 280 flowers for a girl."

I nodded in sympathy. "Yeah," I said. "Look at me. Baseball time is almost here, and all I've got is that old glove. And no Grover Cleveland card yet . . ."

"Grover Cleveland?" he asked. "They've got some of those up on the North Side. Some kid was telling me there's a store that's got them. He says they're looking for Warren G. Harding."

"Holy smoke!" I said. "I've got an extra Warren G. Harding!" Pure joy sang in my veins. I ran to my bicycle, swung into the seat—and found that the front tire was flat.

290 "I'll help you fix it," Armand said.

Within half an hour I was at the North Side Drugstore, where several boys were matching cards on the sidewalk. Silently but blissfully I shouted: President Grover Cleveland, here I come! Ⓗ

After Armand had left for the dance, all dressed up as if it were Sunday, the small green box containing the corsage under his arm, I sat on the railing of the piazza, letting my feet dangle. The neighborhood was quiet because the Frenchtown Tigers were at Daggett's Field, practicing for the first baseball game of the season.

I thought of Armand and the ridiculous expression on his face when 300 he'd stood before the mirror in the bedroom. I'd avoided looking at his new black shoes. "Love," I muttered.

Spring had arrived in a sudden stampede of apple blossoms and fragrant breezes. Windows had been thrown open and dust mops had banged on the sills all day long as the women busied themselves with housecleaning. I was puzzled by my lethargy. Wasn't spring supposed to make everything bright and gay?

I turned at the sound of footsteps on the stairs. Roger Lussier greeted me with a sour face.

"I thought you were practicing with the Tigers," I said.

310 "Rollie Tremaine," he said. "I just couldn't stand him." He slammed his

COMMON CORE RL 5

Ⓗ **CULTURAL AND HISTORICAL SETTING**
Setting is not simply a mention of the time and place. To make a setting believable, writers include details that reflect the ways people actually behaved during that time. For instance, Armand writes a letter to Sally, a romantic interest (line 208). This detail is representative of the cultural setting at the time. In modern-day stories, characters in a similar situation may call each other on their cell phones or communicate via e-mail or text message. Reread lines 269–292. Which details in these lines help develop the cultural setting of the story? Identify at least two details that would be out of the place in a story with a modern setting. Give reasons for your response.

fist against the railing. "Jeez, why did he have to be the one to get a Grover Cleveland? You should see him showing off. He won't let anybody even touch that glove. . . ."

I felt like Benedict Arnold[8] and knew that I had to confess what I had done.

"Roger," I said, "I got a Grover Cleveland card up on the North Side. I sold it to Rollie Tremaine for five dollars."

"Are you crazy?" he asked.

"I needed that five dollars. It was an—an emergency."

320 "Boy!" he said, looking down at the ground and shaking his head. "What did you have to do a thing like that for?"

I watched him as he turned away and began walking down the stairs.

"Hey, Roger!" I called.

He squinted up at me as if I were a stranger, someone he'd never seen before.

"What?" he asked, his voice flat.

"I had to do it," I said. "Honest."

He didn't answer. He headed toward the fence, searching for the board we had loosened to give us a secret passage.

330 I thought of my father and Armand and Rollie Tremaine and Grover Cleveland and wished that I could go away someplace far away. But there was no place to go.

Roger found the loose slat in the fence and slipped through. I felt betrayed: Weren't you supposed to feel good when you did something fine and noble? ⓘ

A moment later, two hands gripped the top of the fence and Roger's face appeared. "Was it a real emergency?" he yelled.

"A real one!" I called. "Something important!"

His face dropped from sight and his voice reached me across the yard:

340 "All right."

"See you tomorrow!" I yelled.

I swung my legs over the railing again. The gathering dusk began to soften the sharp edges of the fence, the rooftops, the distant church steeple. I sat there a long time, waiting for the good feeling to come. ⌒

Language Coach

Oral Fluency Jerry and Roger do not follow all the rules of formal English in their speech. With a partner, read the conversation in lines 308–326 aloud. Use an appropriate, casual tone.

ⓘ **CONNECT**
What connection can you make that helps you understand how Jerry is feeling?

---

8. **Benedict Arnold:** an American general who became a traitor to his country during the Revolutionary War.

Comprehension

1. **Recall** Why is each of the boys eager to gather a complete set of President cards?

2. **Recall** What is the name of the drugstore where the Frenchtown boys usually buy the President cards?

3. **Clarify** How does Jerry get the Grover Cleveland card?

Text Analysis

4. **Make Inferences** When Jerry finds that his brother and sisters already bought their father's gift, Armand says to Jerry, "It's all right. Maybe you've learned something." What might Jerry have learned?

5. **Connect** Think about a time when you were looking forward to something. Why do you think the narrator is so excited about the new Cowboy cards?

6. **Draw Conclusions** At the end, Jerry says "I sat there for a long time, waiting for the good feeling to come." Why doesn't he feel good right away? Do you think he eventually will feel good about what he did?

7. **Analyze Cultural and Historical Setting** How does this story portray the lives of people who lived during the Great Depression? What kinds of difficulties did people face at that time?

8. **Analyze Cultural and Historical Setting** Think about the way members of Jerry's family relate to and interact with one another. What characteristics of Jerry's family seem unique to the time period? Back up your response with examples from the text.

COMMON CORE

RL 5 Analyze how a particular sentence fits into the structure of a text and contributes to the development of the setting.

Comparing Cultural and Historical Settings

Now that you have read the story, start filling in your chart. Add information that the author uses to develop the cultural and historical setting.

	"President Cleveland, Where Are You?"	"Aaron's Gift"
Time and Place	1930s, during the Great Depression	
Details of Historical Period		
Characters' Behavior		

Aaron's Gift

Myron Levoy

Aaron Kandel had come to Tompkins Square Park to roller-skate, for the streets near Second Avenue were always too crowded with children and peddlers and old ladies and baby buggies. Though few children had bicycles in those days, almost every child owned a pair of roller skates. And Aaron was, it must be said, a Class A, triple-fantastic roller skater. **A**

Aaron skated back and forth on the wide walkway of the park, pretending he was an aviator in an air race zooming around pylons,[1] which were actually two lampposts. During his third lap around the racecourse, he noticed a pigeon on the grass, behaving very strangely. 10 Aaron skated to the line of benches, then climbed over onto the lawn.

The pigeon was trying to fly, but all it could manage was to flutter and turn round and round in a large circle, as if it were performing a frenzied dance. The left wing was only half open and was beating in a clumsy, jerking fashion; it was clearly broken.

Luckily, Aaron hadn't eaten the cookies he'd stuffed into his pocket before he'd gone clacking down the three flights of stairs from his apartment, his skates already on. He broke a cookie into small crumbs and tossed some toward the pigeon. "Here pidge, here pidge," he called. The pigeon spotted the cookie crumbs and, after a moment, stopped 20 thrashing about. It folded its wings as best it could, but the broken wing still stuck half out. Then it strutted over to the crumbs, its head bobbing forth-back, forth-back, as if it were marching a little in front of the rest of the body—perfectly normal, except for that half-open wing which seemed to make the bird stagger sideways every so often.

---

1. **pylons** (pī'lŏnz'): towers marking turning points for airplanes in a race.

A **CULTURAL AND HISTORICAL SETTING**
"Aaron's Gift" is set in the early 1900s in a New York City neighborhood populated with immigrants who had fled to the United States. Reread lines 1–5. What details about the cultural and historical setting can you identify in these lines?

Analyze Visuals ▶

Examine the painting. What can you **infer** about the people and their location?

Detail of *The Rockefeller Center, New York* (1941), Israel Litwak. Oil on canvas. © Museum of the City of New York/Bridgeman Art Library.

The pigeon began eating the crumbs as Aaron quickly unbuttoned his shirt and pulled it off. Very slowly, he edged toward the bird, making little kissing sounds like the ones he heard his grandmother make when she fed the sparrows on the back fire escape.

Then suddenly Aaron plunged. The shirt, in both hands, came down
30 like a torn parachute. The pigeon beat its wings, but Aaron held the shirt to the ground, and the bird couldn't escape. Aaron felt under the shirt, gently, and gently took hold of the wounded pigeon.

"Yes, yes, pidge," he said, very softly. "There's a good boy. Good pigeon, good."

The pigeon struggled in his hands, but little by little Aaron managed to soothe it. "Good boy, pidge. That's your new name. Pidge. I'm gonna take you home, Pidge. Yes, yes, *ssh*. Good boy. I'm gonna fix you up. Easy, Pidge, easy does it. Easy, boy." **B**

Aaron squeezed through an opening between the row of benches and
40 skated slowly out of the park, while holding the pigeon carefully with both hands as if it were one of his mother's rare, precious cups from the old country. How fast the pigeon's heart was beating! Was he afraid? Or did all pigeons' hearts beat fast?

It was fortunate that Aaron was an excellent skater, for he had to skate six blocks to his apartment, over broken pavement and sudden gratings and curbs and cobblestones. But when he reached home, he asked Noreen Callahan, who was playing on the stoop, to take off his skates for him. He would not chance going up three flights on roller skates this time.

"Is he sick?" asked Noreen.

50 "Broken wing," said Aaron. "I'm gonna fix him up and make him into a carrier pigeon[2] or something."

"Can I watch?" asked Noreen.

"Watch what?"

"The operation. I'm gonna be a nurse when I grow up."

"OK," said Aaron. "You can even help. You can help hold him while I fix him up."

Aaron wasn't quite certain what his mother would say about his newfound pet, but he was pretty sure he knew what his grandmother would think. His grandmother had lived with them ever since his
60 grandfather had died three years ago. And she fed the sparrows and jays and crows and robins on the back fire escape with every spare crumb she could find. In fact, Aaron noticed that she sometimes created crumbs

B **CONNECT**
Think of a time you saw an animal in need. Why do you think Aaron decides to help Pidge?

VISUAL VOCABULARY

cobblestone
(kŏb'əl-stōn') *n.* a type of stone used to pave roads or walkways

2. **carrier pigeon:** a pigeon trained to carry messages from place to place.

where they didn't exist, by squeezing and tearing pieces of her breakfast roll when his mother wasn't looking.

Aaron didn't really understand his grandmother, for he often saw her by the window having long conversations with the birds, telling them about her days as a little girl in the Ukraine. And once he saw her take her mirror from her handbag and hold it out toward the birds. She told Aaron that she wanted them to see how beautiful they were. Very strange. But
70 Aaron did know that she would love Pidge, because she loved everything.

To his surprise, his mother said he could keep the pigeon, temporarily, because it was sick, and we were all strangers in the land of Egypt,[3] and it might not be bad for Aaron to have a pet. *Temporarily.*

The wing was surprisingly easy to fix, for the break showed clearly and Pidge was remarkably patient and still, as if he knew he was being helped. Or perhaps he was just exhausted from all the thrashing about he had done. Two Popsicle sticks served as splints, and strips from an old undershirt were used to tie them in place. Another strip held the wing to the bird's body.

80 Aaron's father arrived home and stared at the pigeon. Aaron waited for the expected storm. But instead, Mr. Kandel asked, "Who *did* this?"

"Me," said Aaron. "And Noreen Callahan."

"Sophie!" he called to his wife. "Did you see this! Ten years old and it's better than Dr. Belasco could do. He's a genius!" **C**

As the days passed, Aaron began training Pidge to be a carrier pigeon. He tied a little cardboard tube to Pidge's left leg and stuck tiny rolled-up sheets of paper with secret messages into it: The Enemy Is Attacking at Dawn. Or: The Guns Are Hidden in the Trunk of the Car. Or: Vincent DeMarco Is a British Spy. Then Aaron would set Pidge down
90 at one end of the living room and put some popcorn at the other end. And Pidge would waddle slowly across the room, cooing softly, while the ends of his bandages trailed along the floor.

At the other end of the room, one of Aaron's friends would take out the message, stick a new one in, turn Pidge around, and aim him at the popcorn that Aaron put down on his side of the room.

And Pidge grew fat and contented on all the popcorn and crumbs and corn and crackers and Aaron's grandmother's breakfast rolls.

Aaron had told all the children about Pidge, but he only let his very best friends come up and play carrier pigeon with him. But telling
100 everyone had been a mistake. A group of older boys from down the block

SOCIAL STUDIES CONNECTION

Now a country in eastern Europe, Ukraine was under the rule of Russia during the late nineteenth and early twentieth centuries.

C CULTURAL AND HISTORICAL SETTING
What differences have you noticed between Aaron's family and Jerry's family in "President Cleveland, Where Are You?"

---

3. **we were all . . . Egypt:** a Bible reference: "Love ye therefore the stranger: for ye were strangers in the land of Egypt" (Deuteronomy 10:19).

had a club—Aaron's mother called it a gang—and Aaron had longed to join as he had never longed for anything else. To be with them and share their secrets, the secrets of older boys. To be able to enter their clubhouse shack on the empty lot on the next street. To know the password and swear the secret oath. To belong. **D**

About a month after Aaron had brought the pigeon home, Carl, the gang leader, walked over to Aaron in the street and told him he could be a member if he'd bring the pigeon down to be the club mascot. Aaron couldn't believe it; he immediately raced home to get Pidge. But 110 his mother told Aaron to stay away from those boys, or else. And Aaron, miserable, argued with his mother and pleaded and cried and coaxed. It was no use. Not with those boys. No. **E**

Aaron's mother tried to change the subject. She told him that it would soon be his grandmother's sixtieth birthday, a very special birthday indeed, and all the family from Brooklyn and the East Side would be coming to their apartment for a dinner and celebration. Would Aaron try to build something or make something for Grandma? A present made with his own hands would be nice. A decorated box for her hairpins or a crayon picture for her room or anything he liked.

120 In a flash Aaron knew what to give her: Pidge! Pidge would be her present! Pidge with his wing healed, who might be able to carry messages for her to the doctor or his Aunt Rachel or other people his grandmother seemed to go to a lot. It would be a surprise for everyone. And Pidge would make up for what had happened to Grandma when she'd been a little girl in the Ukraine, wherever that was.

130 Often, in the evening, Aaron's grandmother would talk about the old days long ago in the Ukraine, in the same way that she talked to the birds on the back fire escape. She had lived in a village near a place called Kishinev[4] with hundreds of other poor peasant families like her own. Things hadn't been too bad under someone called Czar Alexander the Second,[5] whom Aaron always pictured as a tall handsome man in a gold uniform. But Alexander

D CONNECT
Reread lines 98–105. What connection can you make to the desire Aaron expresses?

E CULTURAL AND HISTORICAL SETTING
Reread lines 106–112. Who advises Jerry in "President Cleveland, Where Are You?" What difference do you find in the cultural and historical settings of the stories from these details?

La Colombe, Pablo Picasso. Embossed, cut out and painted copper, pencil strokes, 15¾″ × 10¾″. © 2008 Estate of Pablo Picasso/Artists Rights Society (ARS), New York.

---

4. **Kishinev** (kĭsh′ə-nĕf′): a city that is now the capital of the country of Moldova and is known today as Chisinau.

5. **Czar** (zär) **Alexander the Second:** emperor of Russia from 1855 to 1881.

the Second was **assassinated,** and Alexander the Third,[6] whom Aaron pictured as an ugly man in a black cape, became the czar. And the Jewish people of the Ukraine had no peace anymore.

140　　One day, a thundering of horses was heard coming toward the village from the direction of Kishinev. "The Cossacks! The Cossacks!" someone had shouted. The czar's horsemen! Quickly, quickly, everyone in Aaron's grandmother's family had climbed down to the cellar through a little trap door hidden under a mat in the big central room of their shack. But his grandmother's pet goat, whom she'd loved as much as Aaron loved Pidge and more, had to be left above, because if it had made a sound in the cellar, they would never have lived to see the next morning. They all hid under the wood in the woodbin and waited, hardly breathing.

　　Suddenly, from above, they heard shouts and calls and screams at a
150 distance. And then the noise was in their house. Boots pounding on the floor, and everything breaking and crashing overhead. The smell of smoke and the shouts of a dozen men.

　　The terror went on for an hour, and then the sound of horses' hooves faded into the distance. They waited another hour to make sure, and then the father went up out of the cellar and the rest of the family followed. The door to the house had been torn from its hinges, and every piece of furniture was broken. Every window, every dish, every stitch of clothing was totally destroyed, and one wall had been completely bashed in. And on the floor was the goat, lying quietly. Aaron's grandmother, who was
160 just a little girl of eight at the time, had wept over the goat all day and all night and could not be consoled. **F**

　　But they had been lucky. For other houses had been burned to the ground. And everywhere, not goats alone, nor sheep, but men and women and children lay quietly on the ground. The word for this sort of **massacre,** Aaron had learned, was *pogrom*. It had been a pogrom. And the men on the horses were Cossacks. Hated word. Cossacks.

　　And so Pidge would replace that goat of long ago. A pigeon on Second Avenue where no one needed trap doors or secret escape passages or woodpiles to hide under. A pigeon for his grandmother's sixtieth
170 birthday. *Oh wing, heal quickly so my grandmother can send you flying to everywhere she wants!*

　　But a few days later, Aaron met Carl in the street again. And Carl told Aaron that there was going to be a meeting that afternoon in which a map was going to be drawn up to show where a secret treasure lay buried on

---

6.　Alexander the Third: emperor of Russia from 1881 to 1894.

assassinate
(ə-săs′ə-nāt′) *v.*
to murder by surprise attack for political reasons

Ⓕ CULTURAL AND HISTORICAL SETTING
Why are the details about Aaron's grandmother important to the historical setting of the story?

massacre (măs′ə-kər)
n. the act of killing a number of helpless humans or animals

Head with a Bird II (1971), Pablo Picasso. Oil on canvas, 55 cm × 46 cm. Private collection.
© Bridgeman Art Library © 2008 Estate of Pablo Picasso/Artists Rights Society (ARS), New York.

◀ **Analyze Visuals**

Compare this painting to your mental picture of Aaron and Pidge.

the empty lot. "Bring the pigeon and you can come into the shack. We got a badge for you. A new kinda membership badge with a secret code on the back."

Aaron ran home, his heart pounding almost as fast as the pigeon's. He took Pidge in his hands and carried him out the door while his
180 mother was busy in the kitchen making stuffed cabbage, his father's favorite dish. And by the time he reached the street, Aaron had decided to take the bandages off. Pidge would look like a real pigeon again, and none of the older boys would laugh or call him a bundle of rags. **G**

G CONNECT
Reread lines 167–183. Recall a time when you were invited to join something. Why do you think Aaron chooses to join the boys?

Gently, gently he removed the bandages and the splints and put them in his pocket in case he should need them again. But Pidge seemed to hold his wing properly in place.

When he reached the empty lot, Aaron walked up to the shack, then hesitated. Four bigger boys were there. After a moment, Carl came out and commanded Aaron to hand Pidge over.

190 "Be careful," said Aaron. "I just took the bandages off."

"Oh sure, don't worry," said Carl. By now Pidge was used to people holding him, and he remained calm in Carl's hands.

"OK," said Carl. "Give him the badge." And one of the older boys handed Aaron his badge with the code on the back. "Now light the fire," said Carl.

"What . . . what fire?" asked Aaron.

"The fire. You'll see," Carl answered.

"You didn't say nothing about a fire," said Aaron. "You didn't say nothing to—"

"Hey!" said Carl. "I'm the leader here. And you don't talk unless I tell
200 you that you have p'mission. Light the fire, Al."

The boy named Al went out to the side of the shack, where some wood and cardboard and old newspapers had been piled into a huge mound. He struck a match and held it to the newspapers.

"OK," said Carl. "Let's get 'er good and hot. Blow on it. Everybody blow."

Aaron's eyes stung from the smoke, but he blew alongside the others, going from side to side as the smoke shifted toward them and away.

"Let's fan it," said Al.

In a few minutes, the fire was crackling and glowing with a bright yellow-orange flame.

210 "Get me the rope," said Carl.

One of the boys brought Carl some cord and Carl, without a word, wound it twice around the pigeon, so that its wings were tight against its body.

"What . . . what are you *doing!*" shouted Aaron. "You're hurting his wing!"

"Don't worry about his wing," said Carl. "We're gonna throw him into the fire. And when we do, we're gonna swear an oath of loyalty to—"

"No! *No!*" shouted Aaron, moving toward Carl. **H**

"Grab him!" called Carl. "Don't let him get the pigeon!"

220 But Aaron had leaped right across the fire at Carl, taking him completely by surprise. He threw Carl back against the shack and hit out at his face with both fists. Carl slid down to the ground, and the pigeon rolled out of his hands. Aaron scooped up the pigeon and ran, pretending he was on roller skates so that he would go faster and faster. And as he ran across the lot he

---

Language Coach

Derivations A new word formed by adding an affix to a base word is called a **word derivation**. *Careful* (line 190) is a word derivation of the word *care*. Name two other words derived from the word *care*.

H CONNECT
Do you find Aaron's reaction to the boys' plan believable? Explain.

pulled the cord off Pidge and tried to find a place, *any* place, to hide him. But the boys were on top of him, and the pigeon slipped from Aaron's hands.

"Get him!" shouted Carl.

Aaron thought of the worst, the most horrible thing he could shout at the boys. "Cossacks!" he screamed. "You're all Cossacks!"

230 Two boys held Aaron back while the others tried to catch the pigeon. Pidge fluttered along the ground just out of reach, skittering one way and then the other. Then the boys came at him from two directions. But suddenly Pidge beat his wings in rhythm, and rose up, up, over the roof of the nearest tenement, up over Second Avenue toward the park.

With the pigeon gone, the boys turned toward Aaron and tackled him to the ground and punched him and tore his clothes and punched him some more. Aaron twisted and turned and kicked and punched back, shouting "Cossacks! Cossacks!" And somehow the word gave him the strength to tear away from them. ❶

240 When Aaron reached home, he tried to go past the kitchen quickly so his mother wouldn't see his bloody face and torn clothing. But it was no use; his father was home from work early that night and was seated in the living room. In a moment Aaron was surrounded by his mother, father, and grandmother, and in another moment he had told them everything that had happened, the words tumbling out between his broken sobs. Told them of the present he had planned, of the pigeon for a goat, of the gang, of the badge with the secret code on the back, of the shack, and the fire, and the pigeon's flight over the tenement roof.

And Aaron's grandmother kissed him and thanked him for his present
250 which was even better than the pigeon.

"What present?" asked Aaron, trying to stop the series of sobs.

And his grandmother opened her pocketbook and handed Aaron her mirror and asked him to look. But all Aaron saw was his dirty, bruised face and his torn shirt.

Aaron thought he understood, and then, again, he thought he didn't. How could she be so happy when there really was no present? And why pretend that there was?

Later that night, just before he fell asleep, Aaron tried to imagine what his grandmother might have done with the pigeon. She would have fed
260 it, and she certainly would have talked to it, as she did to all the birds, and . . . and then she would have let it go free. Yes, of course Pidge's flight to freedom must have been the gift that had made his grandmother so happy. Her goat has escaped from the Cossacks at last, Aaron thought, half dreaming. And he fell asleep with a smile. ✺

❶ **CULTURAL AND HISTORICAL SETTING**
Reread lines 228–239. How does Aaron's calling the gang "Cossacks" relate to the cultural and historical setting of the work?

Comprehension

1. **Recall** What is Aaron doing when he finds the wounded pigeon?

2. **Recall** How do Aaron's parents react when he brings the pigeon home?

3. **Summarize** What happens when Aaron goes to the shack?

COMMON CORE

RL 5 Analyze how a particular sentence fits into the structure of a text and contributes to the development of the setting.

Text Analysis

4. **Interpret** What does Aaron's grandmother consider his gift to be? How does she communicate this view?

5. **Connect** Aaron rejects the chance to join the club. Explain whether you find this rejection believable.

6. **Analyze Cultural and Historical Setting** How do the details about Aaron's grandmother's past contribute to the cultural and historical setting of the story?

7. **Analyze Cultural and Historical Setting** How can you tell that family members looked to each other for support during this time? Support your response with examples from the text.

Comparing Cultural and Historical Settings

Now that you have read "Aaron's Gift," finish filling in your chart. Then, compare the cultural and historical settings of the two works.

	"President Cleveland, Where Are You?"	"Aaron's Gift"
Time and Place	1930s, during the Great Depression	Early 1900s in New York City
Details of Historical Period		
Characters' Behavior		

In what ways are the cultural and historical settings of the two works similar and different?

What would you do for your FAMILY?

In what ways do friends and relatives help you through difficult situations?

Vocabulary in Context

▲ **VOCABULARY PRACTICE**

Synonyms are two or more words that have the same meaning. **Antonyms** are words that have opposite meanings. Decide whether the words in each pair are synonyms or antonyms.

1. skirmish/fight
2. massacre/slaughter
3. stalemate/progress
4. incredulous/believing
5. divulge/expose
6. contempt/admiration
7. allot/dispense
8. assassinate/kill
9. obsess/worry

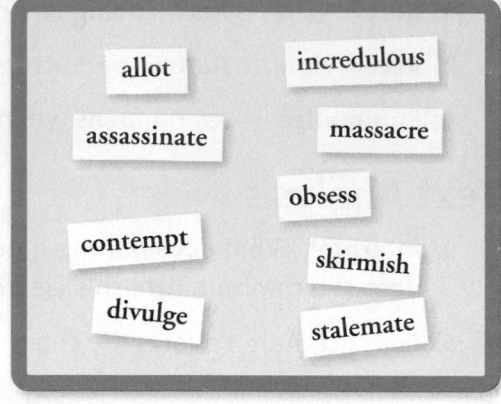

allot   incredulous
assassinate   massacre
obsess
contempt   skirmish
divulge   stalemate

ACADEMIC VOCABULARY IN WRITING

• convey   • create   • influence   • interact   • qualities

Think about the details you noted in your chart. How do the details in each story **create** a believable setting? Use at least two Academic Vocabulary words in your response.

VOCABULARY STRATEGY: CONTEXT CLUES

Context clues may be found in the words, sentences, and paragraphs that surround an unknown word. These clues can help you interpret unfamiliar words and ideas in stories that you read. **Examples** are one type of context clue. Example clues are introduced by signal words like *such as, especially, including, like,* and *for example.*

PRACTICE Use the example clue to help you define each boldfaced word.

1. Look for a **periodical,** such as a weekly or monthly magazine.
2. He was guilty of many **peccadillos,** including letting the screen door slam shut.
3. She was fond of quoting **maxims** like "Haste makes waste."
4. Elena loves **crudités,** especially celery sticks and baby carrots.

COMMON CORE

L 4a Use context as a clue to the meaning of a word or phrase.

Interactive Vocabulary **THiNK** central
Go to **thinkcentral.com**.
KEYWORD: HML6-258

Writing for Assessment

COMMON CORE W 2, W 4, W 10

1. READ THE PROMPT

You've just read two stories set in the early twentieth century. In writing assessments, you will often be asked to compare and contrast two works in some way, such as two short stories set in the past.

> In three paragraphs, compare the settings of "President Cleveland, Where Are You?" and "Aaron's Gift." Consider the time and place the stories are set and the details that are distinct to that cultural and historical period. Use details from the story that support your response.

◀ **STRATEGIES IN ACTION**

1. I need to identify the similarities and differences between the two boys.

2. I should include examples from the stories about the **cultural and historical setting** to support my ideas.

2. PLAN YOUR WRITING

Using the chart you filled in as you read, identify the ways in which the cultural and historical settings are alike and different. Then think about how to present these similarities and differences.

- Decide on a main idea for your response.

- Review the stories to find details that support your ideas.

- Create an outline to organize your response. This sample outline shows one way to organize your paragraphs.

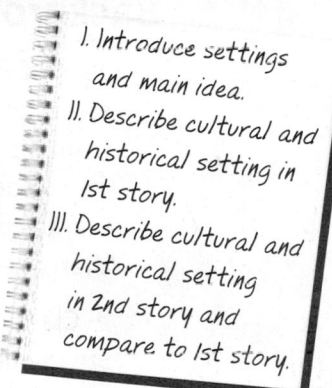

I. Introduce settings and main idea.
II. Describe cultural and historical setting in 1st story.
III. Describe cultural and historical setting in 2nd story and compare to 1st story.

3. DRAFT YOUR RESPONSE

Paragraph 1 Include the title and author of each story. State whether the cultural and historical settings of the stories are similar or different.

Paragraph 2 Describe the cultural and historical setting of the first story. Identify the details that convey the cultural and historical period.

Paragraph 3 Describe the cultural and historical setting of the second story. Identify the details that convey the cultural and historical period. Explain how the cultural and historical setting in the second story is similar to and different from the setting of the first story.

Revision Make sure you use correct verb tenses and pronoun cases throughout your writing.

What is a character's true
IDENTITY?

COMMON CORE

SL 2 Interpret information in diverse media and explain how it contributes to a topic under study.

One of the most enjoyable things about watching TV is getting to know interesting characters. Think about your favorite TV character. What makes him or her seem like a real person? To explore how TV makes characters believable, you will watch a scene that shows how one superhero deals with a problem you may have faced yourself.

Background

Teen of Steel Fans of Superman know him as the "man of steel." He uses his amazing powers to save ordinary people from disaster. The TV series *Smallville* focuses on Superman's secret identity as Clark Kent before he became a super hero. Clark is portrayed as a real teenager struggling to fit in, rather than as a perfect hero.

Clark has been raised by his adoptive parents in Smallville, Kansas. They found him as a toddler after he crashed to Earth in a spaceship. Now Clark is a teenager, and doesn't always agree with his parents' advice on how to control his newly developed superpowers.

Media Literacy: TV Characters

When studying film or TV, it helps to think of moviemakers as storytellers who use images and graphics as well as words. Writers use physical description, dialogue, and characters' thoughts and actions to make them real. Visual storytellers use facial expressions, body language, camera shots and movement, and even sounds to bring their characters to life.

DEVELOPING TV CHARACTERS

Physical Appearance
- **facial expressions**
- **body language**
- **costumes**
- **height, weight,** and **build** from the waist up

Camera Shots
- **close-up shot:** a detailed view that can focus on a person's face or hands
- **medium shot:** showing one or more characters

Behavior
- **actions**
- **dialogue**
- **attitude**
- **interactions** with others

Camera Movement
- follows the action of a scene
- changes the view of a character to reveal emotion

STRATEGIES FOR ANALYZING CHARACTER DEVELOPMENT

- Follow a character's emotions throughout a scene. The actor's **facial expressions** and **body language** will reveal how he or she feels about people and events.
- Pay attention to the actors' **costumes.** In a TV show, clothing can give you clues to a character's personality and background.
- Be aware of the types of shots the director chooses. **Close-ups** are often used to reveal a character's feelings. **Medium shots** can show how characters react to others.
- Watch for **camera movement.** Notice whether the camera moves in close to focus on a facial expression as a character's mood changes or emotion rises.

- **TV Series:** *Smallville*
- **Director:** Greg Beeman
- **Genre:** Sci-fi adventure
- **Running Time:** 4 minutes

Viewing Guide for
Smallville

The *Smallville* series begins when Clark Kent is just starting to develop the superpowers that will make him Superman. He struggles to control his powers and act like a normal teenager. His parents have decided that the best thing for him is to keep his gifts a secret, so that he can grow up to live a normal life.

   As you watch the scene, pay attention to changes in Clark's emotions. Watch his facial expressions and body language. Notice when he stands tall and proud, and when he slouches. Watch the scene several times, and keep these questions in mind.

NOW VIEW

FIRST VIEWING: Comprehension

1. **Clarify** Why doesn't Clark's father want him to join the football team?

2. **Recall** What causes Clark to use his powers to score the touchdown the second time he gets the ball?

CLOSE VIEWING: Media Literacy

3. **Interpret Body Language** When Clark runs onto the football field, he stands tall, with his chest puffed out. How do you think he feels at this moment?

4. **Interpret Emotion** In the barn with his father, Clark goes through many emotions. How do you know what he is feeling? How do the **acting** and the **camera shots** and **movement** help convey his emotions?

5. **Analyze Character** Even though they are in an argument, it is clear that Clark loves and respects his father. How is that meaning conveyed in the scene? Think about these points:

   • the actors' **body language** and **tone of voice** when they argue
   • Clark's **facial expressions** when he talks to his father
   • the reason the coach yells at Clark

Write or Discuss

Evaluate Character You've read that the creators of *Smallville* set out to make Clark Kent a real teen with real problems. Think about the scene you viewed. Use what you learned about **appearance, behavior,** and **camera work** to write a brief evaluation of Clark's character. Do you think the show's creators succeeded in making Clark seem like a real teen? Did he react the way you would have in his situation? Think about

- changes in Clark's emotions
- Clark's relationship with his dad
- Clark's decision to play football

Produce Your Own Media

Create a Character Gallery Imagine you've been hired to cast the actors for a new TV show. You will need actors who can show many different emotions. Create a photo gallery using a classmate as the star of the new show. Take four different pictures of a classmate, showing four different emotions.

HERE'S HOW Use these tips as you create and present your gallery:

- Have your actors use the **facial expressions** and **body language** techniques you noticed in the *Smallville* scene.
- Think about **close-ups** and **medium shots.** Close-ups are perfect for capturing facial expressions. Medium shots work better for posture and other body language.
- Have the rest of the class try to guess the actors' emotions.

COMMON CORE

SL 5 Include visual displays in presentations.

Media Tools — THINK central

Go to **thinkcentral.com**.
KEYWORD: HML6-263

Tech Tip

Try using a computer graphics program to present your photo gallery as a slideshow.

STUDENT MODEL

 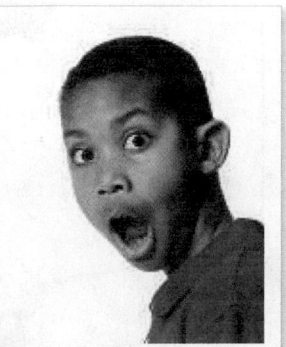  

Role-Playing and Discovery
Personal Essay by Jerry Pinkney

HISTORY Video link at
thinkcentral.com

The Life and Adventures of Nat Love
Autobiography by Nat Love

What makes a MEMORY last?

When you look back on your life, what events will you remember most clearly, and why? For some people, favorite memories come from weekend activities, family outings, or adventures. For others, memories come from a specific event which made a lasting impression on their lives. Read "Role-Playing and Discovery" and the excerpt from "The Life and Adventures of Nat Love" to see how two different authors write about their lives.

DISCUSS With your classmates, talk about your favorite activities. Take turns explaining why each activity is important to you and why you might include it in your own life story.

● TEXT ANALYSIS: NARRATIVE NONFICTION

Like fiction, narrative nonfiction tells a story. However, in nonfiction, characters, plots, and settings are real, not imaginary. Autobiography and personal narrative are two types of nonfiction. An **autobiography** is a book-length story of the writer's own life. A **personal narrative** is an essay in which the writer presents his or her thoughts and feelings about a topic.

As you read the nonfiction narratives by Pinkney and Love, look for the ways the authors express their thoughts and feelings.

● READING SKILL: IDENTIFY LANGUAGE AND TONE

Nonfiction writers use **descriptive language** to help readers imagine someone or something, usually by appealing to the senses of sight, hearing, smell, touch, or taste. Descriptive language often conveys tone. **Tone** refers to the writer's attitude—the way the writer feels about his or her topic.

As you read each selection, use a chart like the one below to record examples of the descriptive language that each writer uses to create imagery and tone.

Title	Descriptive Language	Tone
"Role-Playing and Discovery"		
"The Life and Adventures of Nat Love"		

▲ VOCABULARY IN CONTEXT

In "Role-Playing and Discovery," Jerry Pinkney uses the boldfaced words to help him write about his childhood. To see which ones you know, substitute a word with a similar meaning for each boldfaced term.

1. The **impressionable** child was easily convinced.
2. The crowd's **intensity** increased with each touchdown.
3. She answered his question with a **resounding** "No!"
4. The blizzard had a **profound** effect on the small town.

 Complete the activities in your **Reader/Writer Notebook**.

Jerry Pinkney
born 1939

Artist and Illustrator
As one of six children growing up in Philadelphia, Jerry Pinkney had to search for places where he could draw. When he was 11, he worked at a newsstand. To pass the time, he would make sketches of people passing by. One of those people happened to be a cartoonist who encouraged Pinkney to pursue a career in art. Today, Pinkney is best known as an illustrator of children's books.

Nat Love
1854–1921

Cowboy and Author
Nat Love was born into slavery in 1854. By age fifteen, he left his family in Tennessee to search for adventure and eventually joined a gang of cowboys near Dodge City, Kansas. He was a champion cowboy, earning the nickname "Deadwood Dick" after winning a shooting contest in Deadwood, South Dakota. In 1907, he wrote and published his own life story called *The Life and Adventures of Nat Love, Better Known in the Cattle Country as "Deadwood Dick."*

Authors Online
Go to **thinkcentral.com**. KEYWORD: HML6-265

THINK central

Role-Playing and Discovery

JERRY PINKNEY

On Saturdays, after household chores were finished, I would meet up with my best friends. Off we would rush to the movies. Tickets were ten cents, and there was always a double feature. I was most excited when there were westerns. As a young boy growing up in Philadelphia, Pennsylvania, I dreamed of exploring the early frontier.

My friends and I played at being cowboys and explorers. With much enthusiasm and **intensity,** we inhabited the characters portrayed on the silver screen. We fashioned our costumes and gear from what we could find at home or purchase from the local five-and-dime store. I would
10 whittle out of wood a bowie knife modeled after the one Jim Bowie had at his side while defending the Alamo. I would then take my turn at being Roy Rogers, the cowboy, or Daniel Boone,[1] the famous pioneer, journeying through the rugged wilderness. **A**

Analyze Visuals ▶

What can you **infer** about Bill Pickett from this poster?

intensity (ĭn-tĕn′sĭ-tē) *n.* extreme amount of energy or feeling

A IDENTIFY LANGUAGE
Notice the details the author provides. What picture does he convey of himself and his friends?

---

1. **Jim Bowie . . . Roy Rogers . . . Daniel Boone:** Bowie (1796–1836) and Boone (1734–1820) were famous historical figures of the American West. Roy Rogers (1911–1998) was a movie and television cowboy from the 1930s through the 1960s.

footer

The Bull-dogger (1923), Ritchey Lithography Corporation. Library of Congress.

266 UNIT 2: ANALYZING CHARACTER AND POINT OF VIEW

THE NORMAN FILM MFG. CO.
PRESENTS

BILL PICKETT
'THE BULL-DOGGER'
in Death Defying Feats of Courage and Skill.
THRILLS! LAUGHS TOO!
Produced by NORMAN FILM MFG. CO.
JACKSONVILLE, FLA.

If anyone had asked at that time if my excitement was due to an early interest in history, my answer would have been a **resounding,** "No!" However, looking back, I realize that answer would not have been entirely true. Yes, we did have fun, and yes, our flights into the past seemed to be more about action than about learning history, but that role-playing seeded my interest in discovery. When 20 I learned as an adult that one out of three cowboys was black or Mexican, that discovery was moving and **profound.**

I do wonder, though, how we would have been affected as young boys if, at that **impressionable** time, we had known about Nat Love, a cowboy; Bill Pickett, a rodeo cowboy; Jim Beckwourth, a fur trader; or Jean Baptiste Du Sable, the explorer—all persons of African descent. ∿ **B**

resounding
(rĭ-zound′ĭng) *adj.*
unmistakable; loud

profound (prə-found′)
adj. very deep or great

impressionable
(ĭm-prĕsh′ə-nə-bəl) *adj.*
easily influenced

B **PERSONAL NARRATIVE**
Reread lines 22–26. Why did Pinkney save such a strong statement for the last paragraph?

NAT LOVE
(1854–1921)
Love became famous for his skill as a range rider and marksman. He was also fluent in Spanish, and he had his autobiography published in 1907.

JEAN BAPTISTE POINTE DU SABLE
(1745–1818)
Du Sable, a trapper and trader, was born in Haiti. He is credited as being the founder of the city of Chicago.

JIM BECKWOURTH
(1800–1866)
Beckwourth worked as a trapper and fur trader, as well as a scout and mule driver for the U.S. Army.

The Life and Adventures of Nat Love

Nat Love

Having now fairly begun my life as a cowboy, I was fast learning the many ins and outs of the business, while my many roamings over the range country gave me a knowledge of it not possessed by many at that time. Being of a naturally observant disposition, I noticed many things to which others attached no significance. This quality of observance proved of incalculable benefit to me in many ways during my life as a range rider in the western country. My employment with the Pete Gallinger company took me all over the Pan Handle country, Texas, Arizona, and New Mexico with herds of
10 horses and cattle for market and to be delivered to other ranch owners and large cattle breeders. Naturally I became very well acquainted with all the many different trails and grazing ranges located in the stretch of country between the north of Montana and the Gulf of Mexico, and between the Missouri state line and the Pacific Ocean. This whole territory I have covered many times in the saddle, sometimes at the rate of eighty or one hundred miles a day. These long rides and much traveling over the country were of great benefit to me, as it enabled me to meet so many different people connected with the cattle business and also to learn the different trails and the
20 lay of the country generally. **A**

A IDENTIFY LANGUAGE
What duties does Love describe in this paragraph? How are these details different from the details Pinkney provides on page 266?

Among the other things that I picked up on my wanderings, was a knowledge of the Spanish language, which I learned to speak like a native. I also became very well acquainted with the many different brands[1] scattered over this stretch of country, consequently it was not long before the cattle men began to recognize my worth and the Gallinger Company made me their chief brand reader, which duties I performed for several years with honor to myself and satisfaction to my employers. In the cattle country, all the large cattle raisers had their squad of brand readers whose duty it was to attend all the big round-ups[2] and cuttings throughout the country, and to pick out their own brands and to see that the different brands were not altered or counterfeited. They also had to look to the branding of the young stock. **B**

B **IDENTIFY TONE**
Love uses words like *honor, satisfaction,* and *duty* in lines 20–32. What word or phrase would you use to describe the tone of this autobiography?

1. **brands:** marks indicating ownership put on animals with a hot iron. Each ranch had a specific brand to identify its animals.

2. **round-ups:** gatherings of livestock.

During the big round-ups it was our duty to pick out our brand, and then send them home under the charge of our cowboys, likewise the newly branded stock. After each brand was cut out and started homeward, we had to stay with the round up to see that strays from the different herds from the surrounding country did not again get mixed up, until the different home ranges were reached. This work employed 40 a large number of cowboys, who lived, ate and often slept in the saddle, as they covered many hundreds of miles in a very short space of time… After the general round up was over, cowboy sports and a good time generally was in order for those engaged in it. The interest of nearly all of us centered in the riding of what was known as the 7 Y-L steer. A big long horn wild steer, generally the worst in the herd, was cut out and turned loose on the open prairie. The cowboy who could rope and ride him would get the steer as his reward, and let me assure you, dear reader, that it was not so easy as it sounds. The steer separated from its fellows would become extremely ferocious and wild, and the man 50 who attempted to rope and ride him would be in momentary danger of losing his life if he relaxed in the least his vigilance and caution, because a wild steer is naturally ferocious. Even in cutting them out of the round up I have known them to get mad and attack the cowboys who only saved themselves by the quickness of their horses, or the friendly intervention of a comrade who happened to be near enough to rope the maddened long horn, and thus divert his attention to other things. But in the case of the 7 Y-L steer such intervention is against the rules, and the cowboy who attempts to rope and ride the steer must at all times look out for himself…. **C**

60 The cowboy who is successful in roping the steer must then mount and ride him. If he does that successfully the steer becomes his personal property to do with as he will—only a slight reward for the risking of his life and the trouble of accomplishing the feat. But it is done more for sport's sake than anything else, and the love of showing off, a weakness of all cowboys more or less. But really it takes a high class of horsemanship to ride a long horn, to get on his back and stay there as he runs, jumps, pitches side ways, backwards, forward, up and down, then over the prairie like a streak of lightning. I have had the experience and I can assure you it is no child's play. More than one 7 70 Y-L steer has fallen to my lot, but I had to work for it, and work hard. After all it was only part of the general routine of the cowboy's life, in which danger plays so important a part. . . . Above all things, the test of a cowboy's worth is his gameness and his nerve. He is not supposed to know what fear means, and I assure you there are very few who know the meaning of that word. ∿ **D**

Language Coach

Multiple-Meaning Words The word *charge* can mean "a fee" or "a duty or responsibility." How is the word used in line 35 of this selection?

C IDENTIFY LANGUAGE
Reread Love's description of roping the steer in lines 42–58. What vivid verbs and adjectives help you picture the scene? Do you think this was something Jerry Pinkney and his friends might have role-played? Explain.

D AUTOBIOGRAPHY
Reread lines 71–74. What insight does Love share about cowboys? How do his examples of the life of a cowboy support his conclusion?

Comprehension

1. **Recall** Who did Jerry Pinkney and his friends pretend to be?

2. **Recall** What was Jean Baptiste Du Sable most famous for?

3. **Clarify** What were Nat Love's duties as a cowboy?

Text Analysis

4. **Make Inferences** Reread lines 22–26 of "Role-Playing and Discovery." If, as a young boy, Pinkney had known about the men "of African descent" he mentions, how do you think it might have affected him?

5. **Identify Language** In most personal narratives, the author uses an informal, conversational style to express his or her thoughts or feelings. Do you think Jerry Pinkney does this in "Role-Playing and Discovery"? How does his language compare to the language Nat Love uses?

6. **Analyze Narrative Nonfiction** What differences do you find between the two forms of narrative nonfiction you just read? How does a personal narrative differ from an autobiography?

7. **Identify Author's Purpose** What do you think was Jerry Pinkney's purpose for writing his personal narrative? Why do you think Nat Love wrote his autobiography? Record reasons or clues to each author's purpose in a chart like the one shown.

Purpose	
To Inform or Explain	
To Express Thoughts or Feelings	
To Persuade	
To Entertain	

COMMON CORE

RI 4 Determine the meaning of words and phrases as they are used in a text, including figurative and connotative meanings.
RI 9 Compare and contrast one author's presentation of events with that of another. RI 10 Read and comprehend literary nonfiction.

Extension and Challenge

8.  **SOCIAL STUDIES CONNECTION** Nat Love was only one of several famous African-American cowboys from the American West. Do some research to learn more about the roles of cowboys and cowgirls in the settling of the American West. Share your findings with the rest of the class.

What makes a MEMORY last?

What kinds of events leave you with a lasting impression?

Annie Oakley, cowgirl

Vocabulary in Context

▲ VOCABULARY PRACTICE

Choose the letter of the phrase that best connects with each boldfaced word.

1. **impressionable:** (a) an old woman sewing, (b) a van filled with camping supplies, (c) an eager young student
2. **intensity:** (a) a severe thunderstorm, (b) a relaxing piece of music, (c) a tired factory worker
3. **profound:** (a) a very noisy crowd, (b) a very moving story, (c) a very mild infection
4. **resounding:** (a) a nervous speaker, (b) a loud cheer, (c) a peaceful walk

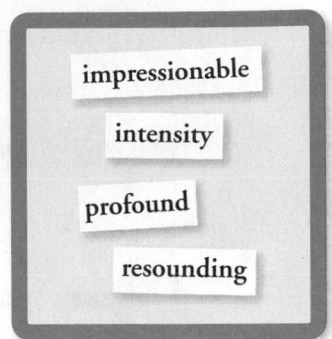

ACADEMIC VOCABULARY IN WRITING

• convey   • create   • influence   • interact   • qualities

What **qualities** of Nat Love's life as a cowboy might Jerry Pinkney have admired? How might reading Nat Love's autobiography have **influenced** Jerry Pinkney? Write a few sentences to answer these questions. Use at least one Academic Vocabulary word in your response.

VOCABULARY STRATEGY: THE LATIN ROOT *press*

The vocabulary word *impressionable* contains the Latin root *press*, which means "to push down." This root is used to form a large number of English words. Use your knowledge of what this root means, along with context clues in the sentence or paragraph, to infer the meaning of unfamiliar words.

PRACTICE Choose the word from the web that best completes each sentence. Consider what you know about the Latin root and the other word parts shown. Refer to a dictionary if you need help.

1. The _____ policies of the government caused the people to rebel.
2. Many students _____ themselves to excel in both school and sports.
3. The lawyer got in trouble for trying to _____ important evidence.
4. If a(n) _____ is punctured, air or gas may leak out.
5. After his father's death, he suffered from severe _____.

COMMON CORE

L 4b Use Latin roots as clues to the meaning of a word.

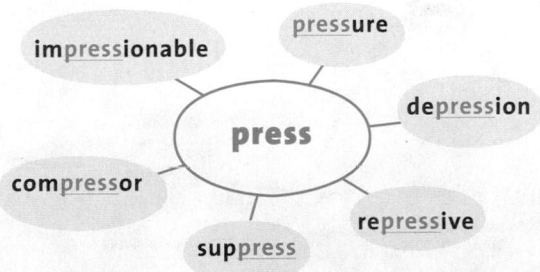

Interactive Vocabulary **THINK**central

Go to **thinkcentral.com**.
KEYWORD: HML6-273

The Red Guards

From the Memoir *Red Scarf Girl*
by Ji-li Jiang

What happens when
FREEDOM vanishes?

COMMON CORE

RI 1 Cite textual evidence to support inferences drawn from the text. **RI 4** Determine the meaning of words and phrases as they are used in text, including connotative meanings. **RI 6** Determine an author's point of view in a text and explain how it is conveyed in text. **L 3a** Vary sentence patterns for meaning, reader/listener interest, and style.

The United States is known as "the land of the free." Its laws state that citizens can travel where they like, worship as they wish, and enjoy whatever music and books they choose. What if those laws suddenly changed? In "The Red Guards," you'll read about a girl struggling with the loss of freedoms she once took for granted.

DISCUSS With a group of classmates, talk about the freedoms that you cherish most. Do you read a newspaper every day? Do you watch the television programs you want to? Can you go into a bookstore and buy any book you choose? Talk about what it means to be able to do these things—and what it would mean to not be able to.

● TEXT ANALYSIS: AUTHOR'S PERSPECTIVE

An author's personal feelings about a subject affect the way he or she writes about it. The combination of ideas, values, feelings, and beliefs that shape the way an author looks at a topic is called the **author's perspective**. In nonfiction, you can identify the author's perspective by paying attention to

- direct statements by the author that tell what he or she thinks, feels, or cares about
- words he or she uses to describe people, events, and things

As you read "The Red Guards," look for ways the author shows her perspective on events in her childhood.

● READING STRATEGY: IDENTIFY SYMBOL

A **symbol** is a person, place, or thing that stands for something else. A sunrise, for example, might be a symbol of hope or a new beginning. To identify symbols, look for

- things that the author mentions over and over
- objects that seem to have great importance to the author

As you read "The Red Guards," look for objects that serve as symbols. Think about the ideas each symbol represents. Record your thoughts in a chart like the one shown.

Symbol	Stands For
butterfly	freedom, beauty

Review: Make Inferences

▲ VOCABULARY IN CONTEXT

The words in Column A help tell about a frightening event. To see how many you know, match each word in Column A with the word in Column B that is closest in meaning.

Column A	Column B
1. zealous	a. sharp
2. leniency	b. threateningly
3. aggressively	c. take
4. acrid	d. mercy
5. confiscate	e. enthusiastic

 Complete the activities in your **Reader/Writer Notebook**.

Meet the Author

Ji-li Jiang
born 1954

Tough Times
Ji-li Jiang's (jē-lē jyäng) happy childhood in Shanghai, China, became one of fear when Mao Zedong (mou' dzǔ'dǒng') took over China. Because of their wealth, Jiang and her family were treated harshly by supporters of the Chinese government for years.

Bridging the Gap
Jiang moved to the United States in 1984. She wrote *Red Scarf Girl* to share her childhood memories of the Cultural Revolution. "By telling my story," Jiang says, "I hope that people will learn about the Cultural Revolution and make sure that such a terrible event will never happen again."

BACKGROUND TO THE MEMOIR
The Cultural Revolution
In 1966 Communist Chairman Mao Zedong began to transform China's government. He enlisted the help of teenage students known as the Red Guards. Squads of Red Guards went from house to house seeking to get rid of all "fourolds"— anything that represented old ideas, old culture, old customs, and old habits. These searches went on for several years and destroyed millions of lives.

Author Online
THINK central
Go to thinkcentral.com.
KEYWORD: HML6-275

THE RED GUARDS

Ji-li Jiang

In the following excerpt, Ji-li Jiang is 12 years old, and the Cultural Revolution is underway. At first a loyal follower of Chairman Mao, Ji-li's perspective changes after her late grandfather's status as a wealthy landlord becomes known. Mao's government considers landlords and their families possible enemies of the people. Now classified by the Red Guards as having "suspicious status," the Jiang family lives in fear.

M om got home from work that evening looking nervous. She whispered to Dad and Grandma, and as soon as we finished dinner, she told us to go outside and play.

"We have something to take care of," she said. I knew this had something to do with the Cultural Revolution. I wished she would just say so. We were too old to be fooled like little children. But I didn't say anything and went outside with the others. **A**

When it was nearly dark, Ji-yun and I went back home, leaving Ji-yong[1] with his friends.

10   As we entered the apartment, I smelled smoke, **acrid** and choking. I looked around in alarm. But Grandma was sitting alone in the main room, showing no sign of worry.

"Grandma, is there a fire?" we shouted anxiously. "Don't you smell the smoke?"

Analyze Visuals ▶

What **mood,** or feeling, do the colors in this painting help create?

A AUTHOR'S PERSPECTIVE
The author is an adult but she writes the events as a young girl. Why might a child narrator help the reader understand the author's perspective better than an adult narrator would?

acrid (ăk′rĭd) *adj.* harsh and sharp in taste or odor

---

1. **Ji-yun** (jē-yŭn) . . . **Ji-yong** (jē-yŏng): the author's younger sister and brother.

September (2003), Hung Liu. Oil on canvas, 66″ × 66″. © Hung Liu.

"Hush, hush!" Grandma pulled us to her quickly. "It's nothing. They're just burning some pictures." We looked puzzled. "Your mother heard today that photos of people in old-fashioned long gowns and mandarin jackets are considered fourolds.[2] So your parents are burning them in the bathroom."

20 "Can we go watch?" I loved looking at pictures, especially pictures of all those uncles and aunts I had never met.

Grandma shook her head. I winked at Ji-yun, and we both threw ourselves into her arms, begging and pleading. As always, she gave in, and went to the bathroom door to ask Mom and Dad.

Mom opened the door a crack and let us in.

The bathroom was filled with thick smoke that burned our eyes and made us cough. Dad passed us a glass of water. "We can't open the window any wider," he said. "The neighbors might notice the smoke and report us."

30 Mom and Dad were sitting on small wooden stools. On the floor was a tin washbowl full of ashes and a few pictures disappearing into flames. At Dad's side was a stack of old photo albums, their black covers stained and faded with age. Dad was looking through the albums, page by page, tearing out any pictures that might be fourolds. He put them in a pile next to Mom, who put them into the fire.

I picked up one of the pictures. It was of Dad, sitting on a camel, when he was about six or seven years old. He was wearing a wool hat and pants with suspenders, and he was laughing. Grandma, looking very young and beautiful and wearing a fur coat, was standing beside him. **B**

40 "Mom, this one doesn't have long gowns or anything," Ji-yun said. "Can't we keep it?"

"The Red Guards might say that only a rich child could ride a camel. And besides, Grandma's wearing a fur coat." She threw it into the fire.

Mom was right, I thought. A picture like that was fourolds.

The flames licked around the edges of the picture. The corners curled up, then turned brown. The brown spread quickly toward the center, swallowing Grandma, then the camel, and finally Dad's woolen hat.

Picture after picture was thrown into the fire. Each in turn curled, melted, and disappeared. The ashes in the washbowl grew deeper. Finally 50 there were no more pictures left. Mom poured the ashes into the toilet and flushed them away. **C**

That night I dreamed that the house was on fire. . . .

---

2. **mandarin jackets . . . fourolds:** Mandarin jackets are fancy jackets with narrow, stand-up collars. They were one of the "fourolds"—old ideas, old culture, old customs, and old habits—that were forbidden during the Cultural Revolution.

B MAKE INFERENCES
An **inference** is a kind of guess. When you make inferences as you read, you look for clues in the text, and then you relate them to your own experience. You try to fill in gaps by guessing about things that the writer doesn't tell you directly. Reread lines 36–39. What does this information suggest about the way Ji-li's father used to live? Why does the author include these descriptive details in her memoir?

C IDENTIFY SYMBOL
Consider what the photographs symbolize to the Red Guards. What might the photographs symbolize to the Jiang family? Record this information in your chart.

Early in the morning Song Po-po[3] rushed upstairs to tell us the news. All the neighbors were saying that a knife had been found in the communal[4] garbage bin. The Neighborhood Dictatorship Group had declared this to be an illegal weapon, so the entire bin had been searched and some incompletely burned pictures found. In one of them they recognized my Fourth Aunt.[5] Because my Fourth Uncle had fled to Hong Kong right before Liberation, her family was on the Neighborhood

60 Party Committee's list of black families.[6] The weapon was automatically associated with the pictures, and that was enough for Six-Fingers[7] to report to the powerful Neighborhood Party Committee.[8]

All day we were terrified. Grandma and the three of us went to the park immediately after breakfast. This time none of us wanted to play. We just sat together on Grandma's bench.

"Will the Red Guards come?" Ji-yun asked.

"Maybe they will, sweetie," Grandma answered. "We just don't know."

She took out her knitting. I tried to to do the same, but I kept finding myself staring into space with no idea of where I was in the pattern. Ji-yun

70 and Ji-yong ran off to play but always came back to the bench after a few minutes. At four o'clock Grandma sent me to see if anything was happening at home.

I cautiously walked into the alley, alert for anything unusual, but there was no sound of drums or gongs or noise at all. The mop was still on the balcony.[9] I looked into our lane. There were no trucks. Everything seemed calm, and I told Grandma it was safe to go home. **D**

Mom and Dad both came home earlier than usual. Dinner was short and nearly silent. Soon after dinner we turned the lights off and got into bed, hoping that the day would end peacefully after all. I lay for a long

80 while without sleeping but finally drifted into a restless doze. When I heard pounding on the door downstairs, I was not sure whether it was real or a dream.

It was real.

I heard my cousin You-mei ask bravely, "Who's there?"

COMMON CORE RI 4

D MEMOIR
A **memoir** is a nonfiction narrative—a story about real people and events. It is like an autobiography because the writer shares his or her own observations, feelings, and perspective about important events and people. However, memoirs usually focus on a specific aspect or period in the writer's life, rather than chronicling the writer's entire life. In this case the writer focuses on her childhood during the Cultural Revolution. Reread lines 63–76. What words and phrases convey the intense feeling the author experienced that day?

---

3. **Song Po-po** (sông pō-pō): Jiang family's downstairs neighbor, friend, and former housekeeper.

4. **communal:** used by everyone in the building.

5. **Fourth Aunt:** Ji-li Jiang's aunt. "Fourth" means the fourth child born to the parents.

6. **Because my . . . black families:** The author's uncle had gone to Hong Kong (at that time independent from China) just before Chairman Mao established his government. Because of this, the Communist Party officers in charge of the neighborhood listed the family as opponents of Communism.

7. **Six-Fingers:** the nickname for Mr. Ni, chairman of the Neighborhood Dictatorship Group, who had six fingers on one of his hands.

8. **Neighborhood Party Committee:** the Communist Party officers in charge of a neighborhood.

9. **The mop . . . balcony:** a signal used by the Jiangs to indicate to family members returning home that the Red Guards were not in the house.

Detail of *Women Warriors I* (2004), Hung Liu. Oil on canvas, 24″ × 42″. © Hung Liu.

◀ **Analyze Visuals**

Does this painting portray a positive or negative impression of the Red Guards?

Six-Fingers's voice replied, "The Red Guards. They're here to search your house. Open up!"

They rushed into Fourth Aunt's apartment downstairs.

At first we could not hear much. Then we heard more: doors slamming, a cry from Hua-hua,[10] crash after crash of dishes breaking 90 overhead, and the indistinct voices of the Red Guards.

By this time we were all awake, but no one turned on a light or said anything. We all lay and held our breaths and listened, trying to determine what was going on downstairs. No one even dared to turn over. My whole body was tense. Every sound from my Fourth Aunt's room made me stiffen with dread.

Thirty minutes passed, then an hour. In spite of the fear I began to feel sleepy again.

I was jolted awake by shouts and thunderous knocks. Someone was shouting Dad's name. "Jiang Xi-reng![11] Get up! Jiang Xi-reng!"

COMMON CORE L 3a

Language Coach

Imperatives An **imperative sentence** gives a command or makes a request and is usually followed by a period. Strong commands are followed by exclamation points. Find the imperative sentence in line 86. Why do you think the writer chose to use an exclamation point to punctuate the guard's command?

---

10. **Hua-hua** (hwä-hwä): You-mei's daughter; Fourth Aunt's granddaughter.

11. **Jiang Xi-reng** (jyäng shē-rĕng): Ji-li's father, like other people in China, is called by his surname first.

100   Dad went to the door. "What do you want?"

"Open up!" Six-Fingers shouted. "This is a search in passing! The Red Guards are going to search your home in passing."

We often asked somebody to buy something in passing or get information in passing, but I had never heard of searching a house in passing.

Dad opened the door.

The first one in was Six-Fingers, wearing an undershirt and dirty blue shorts and flip-flops. Behind him were about a dozen teenaged Red Guards. Though the weather was still quite warm, they all wore tightly belted army uniforms. Their leader was a **zealous,** loud-voiced girl with
110 short hair and large eyes. **E**

"What's your relationship with the Jiangs living downstairs?" the girl yelled, her hand **aggressively** on her hip.

"He is her brother-in-law," Six-Fingers answered before Dad could open his mouth.

"Oh, so you're a close relative," she said, as if she only now realized that. "**Leniency** for confession, severity for resistance! Hand over your weapons now, or we will be forced to search the house." She stood up straight and stared at Dad.

"What weapons?" Dad asked calmly. "We have no—"

120   "Search!" She cut Dad off with a shouted order and shoved him aside. At the wave of her arm the Red Guards behind her stormed in. Without speaking to each other, they split into three groups and charged toward our drawers, cabinets, and chests. The floor was instantly strewn with their contents.

They demanded that Mom and Dad open anything that was locked, while we children sat on our beds, staring in paralyzed fascination. To my surprise, it was not as frightening as I had imagined through the weeks of waiting. Only Little White[12] was panicked by the crowd and the noise. She scurried among the open chests until she was kicked by a Red Guard. Then
130 she ran up into the attic and did not come down. **F**

I watched one boy going through the wardrobe. He took each piece of clothing off its hanger and threw it onto the floor behind him. He went carefully through a drawer and unrolled the neatly paired socks, tossing them over his shoulder one by one.

I turned my head and saw another boy opening my desk drawer. He swept his hand through it and jumbled everything together before removing the drawer and turning it upside down on the floor. Before he could examine the contents, another one called him away to help move a chest.

---

12. **Little White:** the Jiang family's cat.

zealous (zĕl'əs) *adj.* eager and enthusiastic

E MAKE INFERENCES
Reread lines 106–110. Why do you think the Red Guard is made up mostly of teenagers?

aggressively (ə-grĕs'ĭv-lē) *adv.* in a manner showing readiness to attack

leniency (lē'nē-ən-sē) *n.* tolerance; gentleness

F MAKE INFERENCES
Reread lines 125–130. Jiang stares "in paralyzed fascination." Why isn't the experience as frightening as she had imagined it would be?

140   All my treasures were scattered on the floor. The butterfly fell out
of its glass box; one wing was crushed under a bottle of glass beads.
My collection of candy wrappers had fallen out of their notebook and
were crumpled under my stamp album.

My stamp album! It had been a birthday gift from Grandma when
I started school, and it was my dearest treasure. For six years I had been
getting canceled stamps from my friends, carefully soaking them to get
every bit of envelope paper off. I had collected them one by one until I
had complete sets. I had even bought some inexpensive sets with my own
allowance. I loved my collection, even though I knew I should not. With
150 the start of the Cultural Revolution all the stamp shops were closed down,
because stamp collecting was considered bourgeois.[13] Now I just knew
something terrible was going to happen to it. ◆

I looked at the Red Guards. They were still busy moving the chest.
I slipped off the bed and tiptoed across the room. If I could hide it before
they saw me . . . I stooped down and reached for the book. **G**

"Hey, what are you doing?" a voice demanded. I spun around in alarm.
It was the Red Guard leader.

"I . . . I didn't do anything," I said guiltily, my eyes straying toward the
stamp album.
160 "A stamp album." She picked it up. "Is this yours?"
I nodded fearfully.

"You've got a lot of fourolds for a kid," she sneered as she flipped
through it. "Foreign stamps too," she remarked. "You little xenophile."[14]

"I . . . I'm not . . ." I blushed as I fumbled for words.

The girl looked at Ji-yong and Ji-yun, who were still sitting on their
beds, watching, and she turned to another Red Guard. "Get the kids into
the bathroom so they don't get in the way of the revolution." She threw
the stamp album casually into the bag of things to be **confiscated** and
went back downstairs. She didn't even look at me. **H**
170   Inside the bathroom we could still hear the banging of furniture and
the shouting of the Red Guards. Ji-yun lay with her head in my lap,
quietly sobbing, and Ji-yong sat in silence.

After a long time the noise died down. Dad opened the bathroom door,
and we fearfully came out.

The apartment was a mess. The middle of the floor was strewn with
the contents of the overturned chests and drawers. Half of the clothes had
been taken away. The rest were scattered on the floor along with some old

---

◆ **GRAMMAR IN CONTEXT**
In line 145, the writer correctly uses the superlative form, *dearest*, to compare her stamp album to all the other things she treasures.

G AUTHOR'S PERSPECTIVE
Reread lines 140–155. What do you learn about the author's attitude toward the Cultural Revolution?

confiscate (kŏn′fĭ-skāt′) *v.* to take and keep something that belongs to someone else

H IDENTIFY SYMBOL
The stamp album symbolizes something different to Jiang than it does to the leader of the Red Guards. In your chart, record what it symbolizes to each of them.

---

13. **bourgeois** (bŏŏr-zhwä′): related to members of the middle class—that is, to people like merchants or professionals. Those labeled *bourgeois* were considered suspicious by the Communist Party.

14. **xenophile** (zĕn′ə-fīl′): person who loves foreigners and foreign objects.

copper coins. The chests themselves had been thrown on top of each other when the Red Guards decided to check the walls for holes where weapons could be hidden. Grandma's German clock lay upside down on the floor with the little door on its back torn off.

I looked for my things. The wing of the butterfly had been completely knocked off the body. The bottle holding the glass beads had smashed, and beads were rolling all over the floor. The trampled candy wrappers looked like trash.

And the stamp album was gone forever. ∾ 🄸

🄸 **IDENTIFY SYMBOL**
How does the stamp album act as a symbol here, not only for Jiang, but also for the reader?

Wildflower (2003), Hung Liu. Five-color lithograph with gold leaf and collage, Ed. 20, 25″ × 19″. © Hung Liu.

◂ **Analyze Visuals**
What **details** in this piece of art are also mentioned in the memoir?

INTERVIEW In "The Red Guards," you read about some of Ji-li Jiang's experiences during the Cultural Revolution. In the following interview, she explains her reasons for sharing her story with young readers.

AN INTERVIEW WITH JI-LI JIANG

Why did you write *Red Scarf Girl* for young people instead of adults?

In 1984 I moved to the States. The first year, I lived with an American family. They were very interested in my life in China. Using my limited English, I shared some of my stories with them. One day they gave me a present, a book, The Diary of Anne Frank. Inside they wrote: "In the hope that one day we will read the diary of Ji-li Jiang." Of course, I was very moved by the story, and also, I was inspired to write my own story through a little girl's eyes, instead of as an adult looking back. Honestly speaking, I didn't target my readers before I wrote it, but I am glad it turned out to be a children's book. I used to be a teacher in China. If my book has an impact on the kids who read it, I will feel most rewarded . . .

Why did you leave China?

After the Cultural Revolution, things didn't change much. Rigid policies and restrictions kept me from achieving my dream: to enter the Shanghai Drama Institute. I was not allowed to audition. When the universities re-opened, I passed the exam, but because of my family's political situation, I was only accepted into a less prestigious university. After frustration upon frustration, when America opened the door to students from China, I decided to go to the United States. At that time, my only option was to go overseas and study in America. . . .

Ji-li means "lucky and beautiful," a name your parents carefully selected for you. Do you consider yourself lucky?

Yes, I consider myself quite lucky. Despite everything I experienced in China, I have never lacked for love from my family, my friends, and also God. After surviving the Cultural Revolution, I find myself more sensitive to the beauty of nature and the human spirit. I am grateful for having my mind in peace, grateful to have experienced other cultures and lifestyles, and especially grateful that I have been able to do something meaningful and enjoyable to me.

Comprehension

1. **Recall** Why do Ji-li Jiang's mother and father burn the photographs?

2. **Recall** What are the author, her grandmother, and her brother and sister worrying about while they're at the park?

3. **Clarify** Why do the Red Guards search Fourth Aunt's apartment?

Text Analysis

4. **Make Inferences** The lives of Ji-li Jiang and her family have changed because of the Cultural Revolution. What personal rights and freedoms have they lost?

5. **Examine Author's Purpose** Reread the interview with Ji-li Jiang on page 284. Was Ji-li Jiang's reason for writing her memoir to inform, to persuade, to entertain, or a combination of these? Support your answer with information from the selection.

6. **Identify Author's Perspective** On a chart like the one shown, describe the author's perspective on each topic. How does identifying author's perspective help you understand the experiences Ji-Li Jiang shares in her memoir?

Topic	Perspective
Her Family's Experience	
The Cultural Revolution	

7. **Analyze Symbol** Look at the diagram you completed while reading "The Red Guards." Explain how the symbols and their meanings help you understand the events that Jiang is writing about.

Extension and Challenge

8. **Inquiry and Research** In her memoir, Ji-li Jiang calls her stamp collection her "dearest treasure." Stamp collecting is a common pastime, but people collect all sorts of items. Do research to find out some of the other items that people collect. Present your findings to the class.

9. **SOCIAL STUDIES CONNECTION** The Cultural Revolution began in China in 1966. Conduct research to find out more about how the Revolution began, who the Red Guards were, and how it affected the Chinese population. Present your report to your classmates.

Street in modern-day Shanghai, China

What happens when FREEDOM vanishes?

How do you think Ji-li Jiang would answer this question? Think about what she says in the last sentence of the interview on page 284.

COMMON CORE

RI 1 Cite textual evidence to support inferences drawn from the text. **RI 4** Determine the meaning of words and phrases as they are used in text, including connotative meanings. **RI 6** Determine an author's point of view in a text and explain how it is conveyed in text. **W 7** Conduct short research projects to answer a question.

Vocabulary in Context

▲ VOCABULARY PRACTICE

Choose the word in each item that is not related in meaning to the other words.

1. (a) sharp, (b) bitter, (c) acrid, (d) bland
2. (a) leniency, (b) displeasure, (c) patience, (d) forgiveness
3. (a) calmly, (b) aggressively, (c) coolly, (d) peacefully
4. (a) excited, (b) eager, (c) zealous, (d) prejudiced
5. (a) correct, (b) confiscate, (c) seize, (d) claim

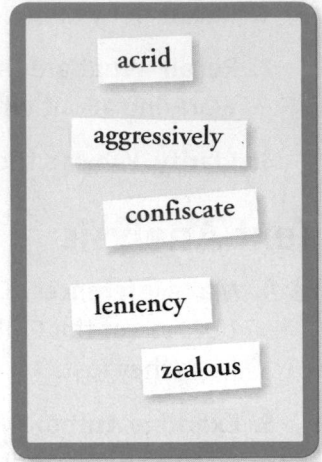

acrid

aggressively

confiscate

leniency

zealous

ACADEMIC VOCABULARY IN WRITING

| • convey | • create | • influence | • interact | • qualities |

Why is Ji-li Jiang's family afraid to **interact** with the Red Guards? What are the Red Guards' frightening **qualities**? Use at least one of the Academic Vocabulary words in your response.

VOCABULARY STRATEGY: PREFIXES THAT MEAN "NOT"

The English language uses a great many words from Latin, the language of Ancient Rome. The Latin words in the English language have come from many sources. In the box at the right are some prefixes from the Latin language. A **prefix** is a word part that appears at the beginning of a base word to form a new word. One example is the vocabulary word *indistinct* (*in* + distinct). The prefix *in-* is one of several prefixes that can mean "not." Look at the chart to see other prefixes that can mean "not," and to see what other meanings these prefixes may have. To figure out the meaning of a word that contains a prefix and a base word, think of the meaning of each word part separately. Then use this information, as well as any context clues that might be available, to define the word.

○ **COMMON CORE**

L 4b Use Latin affixes as clues to the meaning of a word.

Prefix	Meanings
dis-	not; opposite of
in-	not; in
un-	not
mis-	not; incorrectly or badly
non-	not; opposite of

PRACTICE Use these strategies to determine the meaning of each numbered word. Then use each word in a sentence that shows its meaning.

1. disagree
2. nonfiction
3. unlikely
4. incurable
5. misunderstand

Interactive Vocabulary **THINK** central

Go to thinkcentral.com.
KEYWORD: HML6-286

Language

◆ **GRAMMAR IN CONTEXT:** Compare Correctly

Adjectives and adverbs have special forms that are used to make comparisons. Use the **comparative form** to compare two people or things. Use the **superlative form** to compare three or more people or things. For most one-syllable adjectives and adverbs, add *er* to form the comparative and *est* to form the superlative. For most two-syllable adjectives and adverbs, use *more* instead of *er* and *most* instead of *est*.

> *Original:* Ji-yun was the youngest of the two girls.
>
> *Revised:* Ji-yun was the younger of the two girls.

PRACTICE Complete the following sentences with the correct form of the adjective or adverb.

1. Of all her cousins, You-mei was the (braver, bravest).
2. Ji-yun and Ji-yong were both sleeping, but Ji-li was (more, most) restless.
3. One girl yelled (more loudly, loudlier) than the other.
4. Out of all her possessions, the stamp album was what Ji-li was (sadder, saddest) about losing.

For more help with comparative and superlative forms, see page R58 in the ***Grammar Handbook.***

READING-WRITING CONNECTION

Deepen your understanding of "The Red Guards" by responding to the prompt. Then use the **revising tip** to improve your writing.

WRITING PROMPT	REVISING TIP
Extended Constructed Response: News Article The author's description of events in her childhood is full of emotion. The description would be different if a journalist from the United States, for example, were writing about it years later. Write a **two- or three-paragraph** news article about the Red Guards searching the Jiang family home.	Review your writing. Have you correctly used comparative and superlative forms? If not, revise your writing.

COMMON CORE

L 1 Demonstrate command of the conventions of grammar.
W 4 Produce explanatory writing in which the organization and style is appropriate to the task and purpose.

Life Doesn't Frighten Me
Poem by Maya Angelou

On Turning Ten
Poem by Billy Collins

How do we know we're GROWN UP?

COMMON CORE

RL 5 Analyze how a particular stanza fits into the structure of a text. **RL 6** Explain how an author develops the point of view of the speaker in the text.

When we hear someone described as "grown up," we know it refers to more than just the person's age. Along with age come new responsibilities, greater independence, and, sometimes, greater challenges. The poems you're about to read explore the excitement—and challenges—that growing up can present.

QUICKWRITE What are some ways you think you've grown up over the last few years? Consider any responsibilities you've taken on, such as caring for a pet or doing certain chores. Write these down in your journal. Then describe how you feel in general about growing up.

TEXT ANALYSIS: SPEAKER

Just as a short story has a **narrator**, a poem has a **speaker**, or voice that "talks" to the reader. The speaker may be the poet or a fictional character. (Be aware that even when a poem uses the pronouns *I* or *me*, it does not always mean that the poet is the speaker.) Identifying the speaker, and understanding his or her situation, is an essential part of discovering the meaning of a poem.

As you read each poem that follows, look for clues in the title and in individual lines that help you determine who the speaker is and what his or her situation is like.

READING STRATEGY: READING POETRY

A poem can tell a tale or provide a message, just as a short story can. To gain a better understanding of the meaning of a poem, use these strategies:

- **Reread the poem.** Each time you read a poem, you may discover new images or ideas. Look for clues to a poem's meaning in the sentence structure as well as in the words.

- **Read the poem aloud.** Reading a poem aloud will help you hear its song-like qualities and understand the importance of line breaks.

- **Take notes.** Record any words, phrases, or lines you find particularly interesting. Jot down comments or questions about the speaker or the poem's meaning.

Read "Life Doesn't Frighten Me" and "On Turning Ten" three times. Use a chart like this one to record images or ideas that help you understand the speaker and the poem's meaning.

	"Life Doesn't Frighten Me"	"On Turning Ten"
1st Reading	The speaker seems pretty brave.	
2nd Reading		
3rd Reading		

Complete the activities in your **Reader/Writer Notebook**.

Maya Angelou
born 1928

Universal Voice
Though best known for her writing, Maya Angelou (ăn'jə-loo') has also worked as a dancer, a singer, an actress, a cook, and even a streetcar conductor. Although her writing is shaped by her experiences as an African American, the topics and issues Angelou deals with remain universal. Her ability to identify with a wide range of people has led to Angelou's popularity. She notes, "In all my work, what I try to say is that as human beings we are more alike than we are unalike."

Billy Collins
born 1941

Champion of Poetry
Known for his sense of humor and entertaining poetry readings, Billy Collins is loved by critics and readers alike. He has won numerous awards for his poetry and has served as United States Poet Laureate (2001–2003). Collins thinks that poetry should be everywhere, not just in the classroom: "I believe poetry belongs in unexpected places—in elevators and on buses and subways," he once said.

Authors Online
Go to **thinkcentral.com**. KEYWORD: HML6-289

THINK central

Life Doesn't Frighten Me

MAYA ANGELOU

Shadows on the wall
Noises down the hall
Life doesn't frighten me at all
Bad dogs barking loud
5 Big ghosts in a cloud
Life doesn't frighten me at all.

Mean old Mother Goose
Lions on the loose
They don't frighten me at all **A**
10 Dragons breathing flame
On my counterpane[1]
That doesn't frighten me at all,

---

1. **counterpane:** a bedspread.

Analyze Visuals ▶

Does the girl in this photograph look frightened? Explain.

A SPEAKER
Reread lines 1–9. What **details** give clues about the speaker's age?

I go boo
Make them shoo
15 I make fun
Way they run
I won't cry
So they fly
I just smile
20 They go wild **B**
Life doesn't frighten me at all.

Tough guys in a fight
All alone at night
Life doesn't frighten me at all.

25 Panthers in the park
Strangers in the dark
No, they don't frighten me at all.

That new classroom where
Boys all pull my hair
30 (Kissy little girls
With their hair in curls)
They don't frighten me at all.

Don't show me frogs and snakes
And listen for my scream,
35 If I'm afraid at all
It's only in my dreams.

I've got a magic charm
That I keep up my sleeve,
I can walk the ocean floor
40 And never have to breathe. **C**

Life doesn't frighten me at all
Not at all
Not at all.
Life doesn't frighten me at all.

B **READING POETRY**
Read lines 13–20 aloud.
Notice how the poem's
structure changes in this
stanza, with the lines
becoming shorter. What
effect does this change
have on your reading?

C **SPEAKER**
Reread lines 37–40.
What do the lines in this
stanza tell you about the
speaker's personality?

On Turning Ten
Billy Collins

The whole idea of it makes me feel
like I'm coming down with something,
something worse than any stomach ache
or the headaches I get from reading in bad light—
5 a kind of measles of the spirit,
a mumps of the psyche,[1]
a disfiguring chicken pox[2] of the soul. **D**

D SPEAKER
Reread the title and
lines 1–7. What emotions
is the speaker feeling,
and why?

---

1. **psyche** (sī'kē): the spirit or soul.

2. **disfiguring chicken pox:** Like measles and mumps, chicken pox was once
    a common childhood disease. It caused pockmarks to appear on the skin,
    sometimes leaving scars behind.

You tell me it is too early to be looking back,
but that is because you have forgotten
10 the perfect simplicity of being one
and the beautiful complexity introduced by two. **E**
But I can lie on my bed and remember every digit.
At four I was an Arabian wizard.
I could make myself invisible
15 by drinking a glass of milk a certain way.
At seven I was a soldier, at nine a prince.

But now I am mostly at the window
watching the late afternoon light.
Back then it never fell so solemnly
20 against the side of my tree house,
and my bicycle never leaned against the garage
as it does today,
all the dark blue speed drained out of it. **F**

This is the beginning of sadness, I say to myself,
25 as I walk through the universe in my sneakers.
It is time to say good-bye to my imaginary friends,
time to turn the first big number.

It seems only yesterday I used to believe
there was nothing under my skin but light.
30 If you cut me I would shine.
But now when I fall upon the sidewalks of life,
I skin my knees. I bleed. **G**

E SPEAKER
To whom do you think the speaker is talking in lines 8–11?

F READING POETRY
Reread lines 17–23. What feelings do these lines convey?

G SPEAKER
Reread lines 31–32. What does the speaker learn about himself?

Comprehension

1. **Recall** In "Life Doesn't Frighten Me," what are three things the **speaker** isn't afraid of?

2. **Recall** In the first **stanza,** or group of lines, in "On Turning Ten," what is turning ten being compared to?

3. **Summarize** How does the speaker of "On Turning Ten" feel about turning one year older?

COMMON CORE

RL 5 Analyze how a particular stanza fits into the structure of a text. RL 6 Explain how an author develops the point of view of the speaker in the text.

Text Analysis

4. **Interpret Lines** The speaker in "On Turning Ten" says, "At four I was an Arabian wizard" and "At seven I was a soldier, at nine a prince." What is the speaker referring to in these lines?

5. **Reading Poetry** Look at the structure of the first stanza (lines 1–7) in "On Turning Ten." Explain how the sentence structure and line lengths help convey the meaning of these lines.

6. **Reading Poetry** Review the chart of your readings of the poems. Explain how your understanding of the poems and their speakers changed with each reading. Which words, or phrases had the greatest effect on you?

7. **Compare and Contrast Speakers**
Think about the situation each speaker faces and the attitude each one expresses. In what ways are the speakers alike and different? Use a chart like the one shown to record your thoughts.

8. **Make Judgments** Do you think the speaker of "Life Doesn't Frighten Me" is truly not afraid? Use examples from the poem to support your answer.

	"Life Doesn't Frighten Me"	"On Turning Ten"
Who is the speaker?	I think the speaker is a girl.	
What situation does he or she face?		
How does he or she feel about the situation?		

Extension and Challenge

9. **Listening and Speaking** Think about the poems' speakers. How do you think their voices would sound? Perform a reading of one of the poems for your class. Use a tone of voice that allows the speaker's attitude to come across in your reading.

How do we know we're GROWN UP?

How would the speaker of each poem answer this question?

Writing Workshop

INFORMATIVE TEXT

Comparison-Contrast Essay

Whether you're comparing and contrasting blockbuster movies, brands of jeans, or best-selling novels, exploring the similarities and differences between any two subjects can help you understand them better. In this workshop, you will write a comparison-contrast essay to deepen your understanding of literature.

 Complete the workshop activities in your **Reader/Writer Notebook.**

WRITE WITH A PURPOSE

WRITING TASK

Write a **comparison-contrast essay** in which you inform your audience of the similarities and differences between two literary texts, two characters, or two settings.

Idea Starters
- two poems with similar themes
- two myths, fables, or folk tales from different cultures
- two characters with similar conflicts
- the approaches to similar topics or themes in different forms or genres

THE ESSENTIALS

Here are some common purposes, audiences, and formats for comparison-contrast writing.

PURPOSES	AUDIENCES	FORMATS
• to explain how two subjects are similar and different • to show why the comparison is meaningful	• classmates and teacher • readers of a school literary magazine • consumers • Web users	• essay for class • oral presentation • literary magazine article • consumer product review • blog posting

COMMON CORE TRAITS

1. DEVELOPMENT OF IDEAS
- identifies the subjects in an **informative introduction**
- has a **controlling idea** that highlights the points of comparison or contrast
- develops ideas with **relevant** and **concrete details, quotations,** and **examples**
- provides a **concluding section** that supports the information

2. ORGANIZATION OF IDEAS
- effectively **organizes** ideas to compare and contrast
- uses **appropriate transitions** to connect ideas

3. LANGUAGE FACILITY AND CONVENTIONS
- establishes and maintains a **formal style** and **tone**
- includes **precise language** and **domain-specific vocabulary**
- uses **comparative** and **superlative forms** correctly
- uses correct **grammar, usage,** and **spelling**

Writing Online

Go to **thinkcentral.com.**
KEYWORD: HML6N-296

Planning/Prewriting

COMMON CORE
W 2a–e Write informative/explanatory texts to examine and convey ideas, concepts, and information. **W 5** Develop and strengthen writing as needed by planning.

Getting Started

CHOOSE YOUR SUBJECTS

To get ideas for your essay, first look through the selections in this unit or refer to the Idea Starters on page 296. List stories, poems, characters, or settings that have significant similarities and differences. Choose the two subjects that are most compelling to you, and jot down all the similarities and differences you can identify. Can you come up with enough similarities and differences to discuss in your essay? If not, try again with two different subjects.

▶ WHAT DOES IT LOOK LIKE?

Subjects: "Earth" by Oliver Herford and "Earth" by John Hall Wheelock

— *Main Similarity: Both poems are about the destruction of Earth.*

— *Main Difference: Each speaker has a different attitude and perspective on the event.*

DECIDE ON YOUR POINTS

Review your notes and reread the texts you have chosen. Which points of comparison and contrast will be most interesting?

- If you chose two short stories, compare plot, characters, or theme in each story.
- If you chose two characters, focus on each one's physical traits, actions, thoughts, and feelings. Describe their main conflicts and how they resolve them.
- If you chose two poems, think about examining elements such as subject, theme, speaker, and style.

▶ WHAT DOES IT LOOK LIKE?

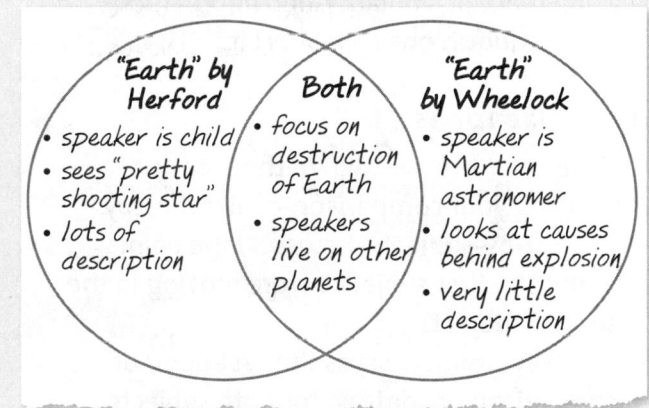

THINK ABOUT AUDIENCE AND PURPOSE

As you explore your subjects in greater depth, be sure to consider your purpose and audience. Your **purpose** is to give readers information about how your two subjects are similar and different. Your **audience** must know enough about the subjects to understand your points of comparison and contrast. If your two subjects are familiar to your audience, then you will not need much background information.

▶ TIPS:

- Survey your classmates to see how many of them are familiar with the subjects you plan to compare. This will give you an idea of how much background information and **domain specific,** or specialized, **vocabulary** you need to provide.
- Take brief notes about what the audience must know in order to understand your comparison. You can use this information when drafting your essay.

Planning/Prewriting *continued*

Getting Started

DEVELOP A CONTROLLING IDEA

Review the similarities and differences you plan to write about. What new understanding do they give you? Express this understanding in a **controlling idea,** or thesis statement. Your controlling idea should summarize the similarities and differences and tell why they are important.

▶ **ASK YOURSELF:**

- What are the key similarities and differences I need to mention in my controlling idea?
- Why are these similarities and differences important?
- How does thinking about the similarities and differences affect my understanding?

GATHER SUPPORTING DETAILS

It is not enough just to tell your audience the similarities and differences. You must also show them through **relevant information, concrete details,** and **quotations** from the texts. For each key difference or similarity, find information, details, or quotations to support it.

▶ **WHAT DOES IT LOOK LIKE?**

Key difference: Herford's speaker thinks that the destruction of Earth is beautiful. Wheelock's speaker views it scientifically.

Support: One is amazed by a beautiful shooting star rushing through the sky. The other shows no emotion.

ORGANIZE IDEAS

Choose one of these two methods for organizing your comparison-contrast essay.

- **Subject-by-subject:** Discuss all the points about the first subject before moving to the second subject.
- **Point-by-point:** Discuss the first point of comparison or contrast for both subjects before moving to the second. For example, you might discuss the topics of both poems, and then move on to the speakers.

▶ **WHAT DOES IT LOOK LIKE?**

Subject-by-subject method:

Poem A	Poem B
• Topic	• Topic
• Speaker	• Speaker
• Speaker's attitude	• Speaker's attitude

Point-by-point method:

Topic	Speaker	Speaker's attitude
• Poem A	• Poem A	• Poem A
• Poem B	• Poem B	• Poem B

PEER REVIEW Describe to a peer the focus of your essay. Then discuss which method of organization might help you present your comparison more effectively.

 **YOUR TURN** After identifying the key differences and similarities, write a working controlling idea. Then find concrete details, quotations, and examples that develop each point. In your *Reader/Writer Notebook,* create a chart like one of those shown on this page to help you organize your ideas.

Drafting

COMMON CORE **W 2c** Use appropriate transitions. **W 4** Produce clear and coherent writing. **W 9a (RL 1, 9)** Cite textual evidence; compare and contrast different texts with similar themes and topics.

The following chart shows how to organize your draft to create a clear, coherent, and informative comparison-contrast essay.

Organizing a Comparison-Contrast Essay

INTRODUCTION

- "Hook" your audience with an interesting detail, question, or quotation.
- Identify your subjects and express your **controlling idea.**
- Establish a **formal style** and **tone** by avoiding contractions and choosing precise language.

▼

BODY

- Include **relevant information, concrete details,** and **quotations** to support each point of comparison or contrast.
- Use a consistent **organizational strategy**: either subject-by-subject or point-by-point.
- Use appropriate **transitions** to clarify the relationships among ideas.

▼

CONCLUDING SECTION

- Summarize your controlling idea, but avoid restating it exactly.
- Tell why your subjects are meaningful to you.

GRAMMAR IN CONTEXT: ADVERBIAL PHRASES AS TRANSITIONS

Another useful kind of transition is the **adverbial phrase**—a prepositional phrase used as an adverb. Adverbial phrases answer the questions *when? where? how? why? how often? how long?* and *to what extent?* When used at the beginning of a sentence, an adverbial phrase is usually followed by a comma.

Example	*How You Know It's an Adverbial Phrase*
<u>From space</u>, the explosion appears beautiful.	▶ It tells from *where* the explosion appears beautiful.
<u>After the explosion</u>, Earth falls through space.	▶ It tells *when* Earth falls through space.

YOUR TURN Following the structure outlined above, write a first draft of your essay. Rework your controlling idea as needed based on the support you find. Signal similarities and differences with appropriate transitions. Try to use adverbial phrases to add description and flow.

Revising

When revising, look closely at your draft and evaluate its content, organization, and style. Make sure you achieve your purpose of identifying key similarities and differences between your subjects. The questions, tips, and strategies in the following chart can help you revise, rewrite, and improve your draft.

COMPARISON-CONTRAST ESSAY

Ask Yourself	Tips	Revision Strategies
1. Does the introduction identify two subjects and compare and contrast them in a controlling idea?	▶ **Circle** the two subjects of the essay. **Underline** the controlling idea.	▶ **Add** titles, authors, or other specific words identifying the subjects. **Add** a controlling idea if one is missing.
2. Does the essay analyze several similarities and differences?	▶ **Put a star** next to each point of comparison or contrast.	▶ If necessary, **rework** to add points of comparison and contrast. **Delete** any statements that do not belong.
3. Does the body of the essay have a clear organizational strategy—either subject-by-subject or point-by-point?	▶ **Write 1** above each point about the first subject and **2** above each point about the second subject.	▶ If necessary, **rearrange** statements into either subject-by-subject order or point-by-point order.
4. Do concrete details and examples support points of comparison and contrast?	▶ **Circle** concrete details and examples. **Draw an arrow** to points they support.	▶ **Add** details and examples for points that don't have arrows.
5. Are the style and tone consistent throughout the essay?	▶ **Underline** words and phrases that are too informal or vague, or that stand out from the rest of the text.	▶ **Replace** underlined text with more formal and precise language.
6. Does the concluding section restate the controlling idea and tell why the subjects are important?	▶ **Bracket** the controlling idea. **Underline** statements that tell why the subjects matter.	▶ **Summarize** your controlling idea. **Add** sentences that tell why the subjects are meaningful.

YOUR TURN **PEER REVIEW** Working with a classmate, review each other's drafts and trade revision suggestions. Answer each question in the chart to identify areas to improve or sections that need a new approach.

COMMON CORE

W 2a Organize ideas, concepts, and information using comparison/contrast strategies. **W 5** Develop and strengthen writing by revising, rewriting, or trying a new approach. **L 3b** Maintain consistency in style and tone.

ANALYZE A STUDENT DRAFT

Read this student's draft and the comments about it as a model for revising your own comparison-contrast essay.

Oh No! The Earth Is Exploding!

by Erica Graham, Owasso Sixth-Grade Center

❶ "Earth" by Oliver Herford and "Earth" by John Hall Wheelock are two poems about the destruction of Earth as viewed by a creature on another planet. Although the topics are identical, the poems differ greatly in description and point of view.

❷ In Herford's poem, the explosion of Earth is a beautiful sight to an innocent child who simply sees lights and color. Herford describes in great detail how the child from a planet far away witnesses the explosion as a beautiful shooting star rushing through the sky. Lines 6–12 paint a picture of what happens to the planet's creatures as Earth falls through space.

❸ In Wheelock's poem, on the other hand, a Martian astronomer watches the destruction of Earth and states that it was bound to happen. His adult point of view is that the catastrophe means nothing to the Martians. The Martian astronomer dryly says the explosion proves that highly intelligent beings had been living there. He thinks that they are responsible for destroying their own planet.

> Erica's introductory paragraph identifies the two **subjects** and states a **clear controlling idea.**

> Erica supports key points with **concrete details** from the poem.

> Erica is using the **subject-by-subject method.** However, in her discussion of Wheelock's poem, she has covered only one of her two points.

LEARN HOW Use Subject-by-Subject Method Since Erica has chosen the subject-by-subject method of organization, she needs to discuss all her points about the first poem and then discuss all the same points about the second poem. Her controlling idea presents two points of comparison: description and point of view. She covers both of these in paragraph 2 about Herford's poem. However, in her paragraph about Wheelock's poem, she covers only point of view. Erica revised her draft to include information about the description in Wheelock's poem.

ERICA'S REVISION TO PARAGRAPH ❸

He thinks they are responsible for destroying their own planet. *Even though the astronomer is watching the event, he does not describe it at all. The lack of description emphasizes how unimportant this event is to the Martian astronomer.*

❹   Both Oliver Herford's "Earth" and John Hall Wheelock's "Earth" are poems that view Earth's destruction through the eyes of a creature on another planet. The child in Herford's poem may be more easier to relate to than Wheelock's Martian astronomer, but their responses to Earth's destruction are equally surprising.

> Erica restates some of her major points and makes a connection to the audience. However, she could make her **concluding section** more effective by developing it further.

LEARN HOW **Strengthen Your Concluding Section** The concluding section of a comparison-contrast essay must restate the key points introduced in the controlling idea. It must also clearly show why the subjects are important. When Erica reread her essay, she saw that she had summarized only one of the differences she explored in her essay. In her revision, she included the second difference. She also expanded upon her controlling idea, explaining the important message at the heart of each poem.

ERICA'S REVISION TO PARAGRAPH ❹

     Both Oliver Herford's "Earth" and John Hall Wheelock's "Earth" are poems that view Earth's destruction through the eyes of a creature

Herford's poem provides a vivid description of the event, while Wheelock's lacks description and emotion.

on another planet. The child in Herford's poem may be more easier to relate to than Wheelock's Martian astronomer, but their responses to Earth's destruction are equally surprising. *Readers may be shocked that neither the child nor the astronomer views Earth's destruction as such a bad thing. Of course, the tone of both poems is ironic and slightly humorous. However, both poems force readers to consider that Earth is fragile. These poems send the strong message that Earth must be protected and cared for if it is to survive.*

YOUR TURN Use guidance and support from your peers and your teacher as well as the two "Learn How" lessons to revise your essay, rewriting when necessary. Consider whether you have achieved your purpose. Will reading your comparison-contrast essay deepen your audience's understanding of your subjects?

Editing and Publishing

W 5 Strengthen writing by editing. **L 1** Demonstrate command of the conventions of standard English grammar and usage. **L 2b** Spell correctly.

The editing stage is when you focus on correcting minor errors in grammar, usage, and punctuation. You should also read your essay to correct any misspelled words that your word-processing spell-check did not catch. Don't let mistakes keep your audience from appreciating the ideas you've worked hard to communicate.

GRAMMAR IN CONTEXT: COMPARATIVE FORMS

Writers often use adjectives and adverbs to compare two or more things. The form of the adjective or adverb shows the type of comparison the writer is making.

> Wheelock's astronomer is **wiser** than Herford's child, who views events **more simply**.
>
> [The **comparative form** compares only two things, groups, or actions.]

> Although books about space creatures are not the **biggest** sellers, I think they are the **most exciting**.
>
> [The **superlative form** compares three or more things, groups, or actions.]

When Erica reviewed her essay, she corrected a mistake people often make with comparatives.

> The child in Herford's poem may be ~~more~~ easier to relate to than Wheelock's Martian astronomer.
>
> [Never use *more* with *-er* to form a comparative.]

PUBLISH YOUR WRITING

Share your comparison-contrast essay with an audience in one of the following ways:

- Include your essay in a study guide for classmates reading the same texts.
- Post parts of your essay on a blog and ask your classmates to respond.
- Develop your essay into an oral presentation that you deliver to your audience.
- Adapt your essay into a power presentation. Develop slides that show key similarities and differences. Use graphics to enhance your main points.

YOUR TURN Proofread your essay, paying special attention to your use of comparative and superlative forms. Correct any errors you find. Then publish your essay for an audience.

Scoring Rubric

Use the rubric below to evaluate your comparison-contrast essay from the
Writing Workshop or your response to the on-demand task on the next page.

COMPARISON-CONTRAST ESSAY

SCORE	COMMON CORE TRAITS
6	• **Development** Has an engaging introduction with an informative controlling idea; is well-developed with relevant evidence; ends powerfully • **Organization** Logically organizes ideas to signal comparisons and contrasts; effectively uses transitions to clarify relationships • **Language** Consistently maintains a formal style and objective tone; ably uses precise words; demonstrates a strong command of conventions
5	• **Development** Has an informative introduction and controlling idea; includes relevant evidence; has a strong concluding section • **Organization** Organizes ideas effectively; uses appropriate transitions to clarify relationships • **Language** Maintains a formal style and objective tone; uses precise words; has a few errors in conventions
4	• **Development** Has a sufficient introduction and controlling idea; offers mostly relevant evidence; has an adequate concluding section • **Organization** Logically organizes comparisons and contrasts, with a few exceptions; uses transitions clarify relationships • **Language** Mostly maintains a formal style and objective tone; needs more precise words at times; has a few distracting errors in conventions
3	• **Development** Has an adequate, but unmemorable, introduction; states a controlling idea; lacks sufficient support; has a routine ending • **Organization** Reflects some flaws in organization; needs more transitions to clarify relationships • **Language** Has frequently lapses in style and tone; uses some vague words; has some significant errors in conventions
2	• **Development** Has a weak introduction and controlling idea; lacks (or includes unrelated) evidence; has a weak concluding section • **Organization** Has organizational flaws; lacks transitions throughout • **Language** Uses an informal style, vague language, and an inappropriate tone; has many distracting errors in conventions
1	• **Development** Has no introduction or controlling idea; offers unrelated points as details and examples; ends abruptly • **Organization** Has no overall organization • **Language** Has an inappropriate style and tone and uses incorrect language; has major problems in conventions

Preparing for Timed Writing

COMMON CORE

W 10 Write routinely over shorter time frames for a range of tasks, purposes, and audiences.

1. ANALYZE THE TASK   5 MIN

Read the task carefully. Then read it again, underlining the words that tell the type of writing, the topic, and the purpose.

> **WRITING TASK** *Topic*
>
> Think of <u>two literary characters that have major similarities or differences.</u> Write a <u>comparison-contrast essay</u> that <u>explores these similarities and differences,</u> using specific relevant examples and concrete details to develop your essay.
>
> *Type of writing*   *Purpose*

2. PLAN YOUR RESPONSE   10 MIN

List all the characters that might work for your response. Choose two characters that you know well and that have important similarities or differences. Make a chart to record their key similarities and differences and the concrete details that support each point.

Similarity or Difference	Concrete Details

3. RESPOND TO THE TASK   20 MIN

Start drafting your response. Don't worry too much about your introduction for now. You can always come back and revise it later. Keep these points in mind:
- In the introduction, identify two characters, along with the titles and authors of the text(s). Also include a controlling idea, or a thesis statement.
- In the body, discuss the most important similarities and differences. Use subject-by-subject or point-by-point organization.
- In the concluding section, summarize your controlling idea and tell why the characters are meaningful to you.

4. IMPROVE YOUR RESPONSE   5–10 MIN

Revising Review key parts of your essay. Are your ideas logically organized? Did you use concrete details, quotations, and examples to support your points?
Proofreading Proofread your essay to correct errors in grammar, usage, and spelling. Make sure all your edits are neat and your paper is easy to read.
Checking Your Final Copy Before you turn in your essay, read it one more time to catch any errors you may have missed.

Asking Questions and Paraphrasing Ideas

When you listen to a presentation, you do not have the option of rereading information you missed the first time. You can, however, ask specific questions and **paraphrase,** or restate the information in your own words, to make sure you understand the speaker's message.

 Complete the workshop activities in your **Reader/Writer Notebook.**

LISTEN WITH A PURPOSE	COMMON CORE TRAITS
TASK **Listen** carefully to a formal presentation. After the speech, **paraphrase** the major ideas. Then **ask specific questions** to clarify the information presented and the speaker's purpose and perspective on the topic.	**AN ACTIVE LISTENER . . .** • sets a purpose for listening • takes notes by paraphrasing major ideas • follows up with questions to clarify information • explores the speaker's purpose and perspective, or point of view • participates in a discussion about the speech

COMMON CORE

SL 1a, c, d Refer to evidence to probe and reflect on ideas under discussion; pose and respond to specific questions by making comments; demonstrate understanding of multiple perspectives through reflection and paraphrasing.

Listen Actively

When you listen actively, you receive, interpret, evaluate, and respond to what you're hearing. The following strategies can help you understand a speaker's message and participate effectively in a group discussion.

- **Learn about the topic.** Before the speech, read any background information that the speaker provides, or do some independent research to find out more about the topic. Look up specialized terms that relate to the topic.

- **Set a purpose for listening.** Consider your reasons for listening to the speech. Ask yourself: What do I want to learn from this presentation?

- **Identify the message.** As the speech begins, listen for the speaker's purpose, or reason for speaking. Then determine the main points that he or she wants to convey. These ideas will be repeated throughout the speech and sometimes signaled by word cues such as *to begin with, in addition, most important, finally,* and *in conclusion.*

- **Determine organizational patterns.** Look for organizational patterns such as problem-solution, comparison-contrast, or cause-and-effect. Knowing how the speech is organized can help you understand the speaker's purpose.

- **Take notes.** Make sure you have a pen and paper. You may want to create a chart to organize your notes. Record only the major ideas and supporting evidence. This will help you understand and discuss different perspectives, or viewpoints, on the issue.

**Speaking &
Listening Online**

THINK central

Go to **thinkcentral.com.**
KEYWORD: HML6N-306

Respond to What You Hear

PARAPHRASE MAJOR IDEAS

As soon as the speech is over, review your notes to make sure you have understood the speaker's message and perspective. One good strategy is to write a paraphrase that states the main ideas and important details in your own words.

Paraphrasing a Speech

Step 1	Review your notes.
Step 2	Write the main idea of the speech in your own words.
Step 3	Write supporting details and evidence in your own words.
Step 4	Simplify the vocabulary.
Step 5	Compare your paraphrase with a classmate's. Add any important details that you missed.

ASK QUESTIONS

Many speakers allow time for a question-and-answer period at the end of a speech. Keep these points in mind:

- Review your notes to identify confusing parts that you want to clarify. Contribute to the discussion by posing questions about these ideas. Then ask for more information on points that you find interesting.

- Ask open-ended questions rather than "yes or no" questions.

- Begin a question by stating your understanding of the speaker's purpose or perspective. For example: "I think you are saying that the character of Jerry is more heroic than the character of Aaron. If that is correct, could you explain your reasons to me again?"

- Be polite and respectful. Thank the speaker for answering your questions.

- Use your paraphrase to reflect on the discussion and to review key ideas and perspectives.

YOUR TURN

As a Speaker Prepare an informative speech to give to a partner. Together, think of possible questions that audience members might ask. Generate answers to these questions by referring to evidence you have gathered from your preparations.

As a Listener Listen to an oral presentation given by a classmate or teacher. Take notes during the speech. After the speech, write a paraphrase of the major ideas. Then ask two questions that clarify your understanding.

Assessment Practice

DIRECTIONS Read these selections and answer the questions that follow.

from Phoenix Farm   *by Jane Yolen*

1   So we got ready to head for Grandma's farm up in the valley, with only the clothes we'd been wearing; our cat, Tambourine; and Mama's track medals, all fused together. She found them when the firefighters let us go back upstairs to sort through our things. Nicky grabbed a souvenir, too. His old basketball. It was flat and blackened, like a pancake someone left on the stove too long.

2   I looked around and there was nothing I wanted to take. Nothing. All that I cared about had made it through the fire: Mama, Nicky, and Tam. It was as if we could start afresh and all the rest of it had been burned away. But as we were going down the stairs—the iron stairs, not the wooden ones inside, which were all gone—I saw the most surprising thing. On the thirteenth step up from the bottom, tucked against the riser, was a nest. It was unburnt, unmarked, the straw that held it the rubbed-off gold of a wheat field. A piece of red string ran through it, almost as if it had been woven on a loom. In the nest was a single egg.

3   It didn't look like any egg I'd ever seen before, not dull white or tan like the eggs from the store. Not even a light blue like the robin's egg I'd found the one summer we'd spent with Grandma at the farm. This was a shiny, shimmery gray-green egg with a red vein—the red thread—cutting it in half.

4   "Look!" I called out. But Mama and Nicky were already in the car, waiting. So without thinking it all the way through—like, what was I going to do with an egg, and what about the egg's mother, and what if it broke in the car or, worse, hatched—I picked it up and stuck it in the pocket of my jacket. Then, on second thought, I took off the jacket and made a kind of nest of it, and carefully carried the egg and my jacket down the rest of the stairs.

5   When I got into the car, it was the very first time I had ever ridden in the back all alone without complaining. And all the way to the farm, I kept the jacket-nest and its egg in my lap. All the way.

Dallas and Florida, a brother and sister, have come from an orphanage where they were badly treated. They are staying in the home of Sairy and Tiller.

from Ruby Holler *by Sharon Creech*

1   "Look at this place!" Dallas said. "You ever seen anything so amazing? All these trees? All these hills? Is that a creek over there?"

2   "Dallas, don't you go falling for sweet talk and trees and creeks. We've got to be ready to flee for the hills and catch that train, you hear?"

3   "I hope you don't mind the sleeping arrangements," Sairy said, as they stepped onto the front porch.

4   "Where are you putting us?" Florida asked. "In the hog pen?"

5   "The hog pen?" Tiller said. "I'm afraid we don't have a cockamamie hog pen. I suppose we could build you one though, if you wanted."

6   "You got a snake pit?"

7   "A snake pit?" Tiller said. "You hankering after a slimy snake pit?"

8   "No," Florida said.

9   "Don't mind that sagging porch," Sairy said, leading the way inside. "And our place is kind of small, I know." She paused to smooth a quilt covering a chair. "You'll be upstairs."

10   "In the attic?" Florida said. "You got a dusty cobwebby attic up there?"

11   Sairy motioned to the wooden ladder. "It's a loft. See? Up there—it's kind of open to everything down below. I hope you don't mind. All our kids slept up there together. I'm sorry we don't have separate rooms for you."

12   Florida and Dallas scrambled up the ladder into the light, airy loft. Windows overlooked the trees outside and the deep blue mountains beyond. There were four beds in the room, each covered with a brightly colored quilt: hundreds of patches of red and orange and yellow and brilliant green stitched together.

13   Dallas gazed out at the trees. *It's like a treehouse up here. A treehouse with beds.*

14   "Up here? Is this where you mean?" Florida called down to Sairy. "In this big huge place? Or is there a cupboard? You going to put us in a cupboard?"

15   "I thought you might sleep in those beds. Well, not all of them. Two of them. I hope that's okay," Sairy said. "I hope you'll be comfortable up there."

GO ON ➡

16   Dallas sank onto one soft bed. "Florida, this is like floating on a cloud. Try one."

17   Florida stretched out on another bed. "Probably has bugs in it," she said, jumping up again. "What's the catch? Are they going to fatten us up like Hansel and Gretel and stick us in the oven?"

18   "Dallas, Florida, could you please come down here?"

19   "See?" Florida said. "I bet they're going to put us to work now. We're probably going to have to dig a well or something."

20   Downstairs, Sairy and Tiller had laid the table with a yellow tablecloth. Spread across it was a sliced ham, warm applesauce sprinkled with cinnamon, hot corn bread, and green beans. Four places were set.

21   *It's a feast,* Dallas thought. *For kings and queens and very important people.*

22   "You having company? We have to go outside now?" Florida said.

23   "This is for us," Sairy said. "For the four of us. Two of us and two of you."

Reading Comprehension

> **Use "Phoenix Farm" to answer questions 1–4.**

1. You can tell that this story is told from the first-person point of view because the narrator —
   A. calls herself "I"
   B. does not take part in the story's action
   C. knows what other characters are feeling
   D. is not a character in the story

2. What might change if this story were told from the third-person point of view?
   A. The characters would show more emotion.
   B. The fire would be described rather than the effects of the fire.
   C. Each character would be described in detail.
   D. The reader would learn what each character saved.

3. The narrator shows that she values life more than objects by —
   A. not complaining in the backseat of the car
   B. stating that she only cared about her mother, brother, and cat
   C. noticing an unburned nest on the thirteenth step from the bottom
   D. calling out to show her mother and brother the nest

4. When the narrator makes a nest for the egg, she shows that she —
   A. loves her home
   B. acts before she thinks
   C. needs a pet to care for
   D. has a gentle and caring nature

Use the excerpt from *Ruby Holler* to answer questions 5–9.

5. What does the third-person point of view do that first-person does not?

   A. Allows the reader to learn information about each character

   B. Gives the thoughts of several characters, not just the main character

   C. Tells what the characters look like

   D. States the exact words of the characters

6. The questions Florida asks Sairy show that she and Dallas —

   A. have had problems in life

   B. are alike in many ways

   C. have a close relationship

   D. have learned to trust people

7. What is Sairy like, based on the way she treats the children?

   A. Gruff

   B. Kind

   C. Selfish

   D. Timid

8. In which example of Florida's speech are her words most conversational?

   A. *Dallas, don't you go falling for sweet talk and trees and creeks.*

   B. *'Where are you putting us?' Florida asked.*

   C. *Is this where you mean?*

   D. *We're probably going to have to dig a well or something.*

9. What impression do words like "cockamamie" and "hankering" give the reader about Tiller and Sairy?

   A. They are very young people.

   B. Their house is not very well built.

   C. They probably live in the country.

   D. Food is important to them.

Use both selections to answer question 10.

10. In *Ruby Holler,* Florida is getting a nice new home, while the girl in "Phoenix Farm" has lost her home. Why is Florida more unhappy?

    A. The girl in "Phoenix Farm" did not like her home anyway.

    B. Florida's only experiences in living with adults were unpleasant.

    C. The girl in "Phoenix Farm" wanted to visit her grandmother anyway.

    D. Florida could tell that Sairy and Tiller were mean people by their actions.

SHORT CONSTRUCTED RESPONSE
Write two or three sentences to answer this question.

11. Give two examples of Florida's use of dialect in *Ruby Holler.*

Write a paragraph to answer this question.

12. In *Ruby Holler,* how do Dallas and Florida react to their new home? Use examples from the story to support your answer.

311

Vocabulary

Use context clues to answer the following questions.

1. What does the word *fused* mean in paragraph 1 of "Phoenix Farm"?

   A. Knotted

   B. Melted

   C. Nailed

   D. Tied

2. What does the word *shimmery* mean in paragraph 3 of "Phoenix Farm"?

   A. Fragile

   B. Gleaming

   C. Precious

   D. Shaky

3. What does the word *flee* mean in paragraph 2 of *Ruby Holler*?

   A. Climb

   B. Hide

   C. March

   D. Run

4. What does the word *scrambled* mean in paragraph 12 of *Ruby Holler*?

   A. Climbed quickly

   B. Shouted loudly

   C. Walked clumsily

   D. Crawled slowly

Use context clues and your knowledge of compound words to answer the following questions.

5. What does the word *firefighter* mean in paragraph 1 of "Phoenix Farm"?

   A. Someone who starts fires

   B. A worker who puts out fires

   C. A person who captures criminals

   D. An officer in a large company

6. What does the word *pancake* mean in paragraph 1 of "Phoenix Farm"?

   A. A pan used to bake cakes

   B. A frying pan

   C. A flat, thin cake

   D. A type of clown makeup

7. What does the word *overlooked* mean in paragraph 12 of *Ruby Holler*?

   A. Forgot to do something

   B. Was taller than

   C. Failed to see something

   D. Provided a view from above

8. What does the word *treehouse* mean in paragraph 13 of *Ruby Holler*?

   A. A place to play in a tree

   B. A very tall house

   C. A house with leaves instead of windows

   D. A tree shaped like a house

Revising and Editing

DIRECTIONS **Read this passage and answer the questions that follow.**

(1) I had a horrible week. (2) On Monday, my sister and I were the sadder girls in school. (3) A car hit our dog, Ziggy—my parents and I rushed him to the vet. (4) The next day he was better, but me and my friends got in trouble for talking in class. (5) I am cheerfuller today than my friends and I were yesterday, though. (6) Ziggy can wag his tail again—my sister and I think he's much better? (7) After school, him and me will go to the park—he is the greatest dog ever!

1. What change, if any, should be made in sentence 2?

   A. Change *sadder* to **saddest**

   B. Change *my sister and I* to **my sister and me**

   C. Change **.** to **?**

   D. Make no change

2. What change, if any, should be made in sentence 3?

   A. Change *my parents and I* to **my parents and me**

   B. Change **.** to **?**

   C. Change **.** to **!**

   D. Make no change

3. What change, if any, should be made in sentence 4?

   A. Change *better* to **best**

   B. Change *me and my friends* to **my friends and I**

   C. Change **.** to **?**

   D. Make no change

4. What change, if any, should be made in sentence 5?

   A. Change *cheerfuller* to **more cheerful**

   B. Change *my friends and I* to **my friends and me**

   C. Change **.** to **!**

   D. Make no change

5. What change, if any, should be made in sentence 6?

   A. Change *my sister and I* to **my sister and me**

   B. Change *better* to **best**

   C. Change *?* to **.**

   D. Make no change

6. What change, if any, should be made in sentence 7?

   A. Change *him and me* to **he and I**

   B. Change *greatest* to **greater**

   C. Change *!* to **.**

   D. Make no change

313

Ideas for Independent Reading

Which questions from Unit 2 made an impression on you?
Continue exploring them with these books.

COMMON CORE

RL 10 Read and comprehend
literature.

What makes a hero?

The Breadwinner
by Deborah Ellis

Parvana is only 11 when
the Taliban orders all
the girls and women in
Afghanistan to stay in
their houses. When her
father is arrested, someone
must feed her family. Will
Parvana be able to do it?

Heck, Superhero
by Martine Leavitt

Heck's mom needs a
hero to help her out. But
Heck is only a kid, and
sometimes even the most
wonderful good deed in
the world can't change a
boy into a superhero—or
can it?

A Single Shard
by Linda Sue Park

Tree-ear, an orphan in
12th-century Korea, is a
potter's apprentice. When
something goes wrong
on a journey to the King's
Court, Tree-ear must learn
that there's more than one
way to show true courage.

How do we know when we're grown up?

Lupita Mañana
by Patricia Beatty

Lupita's family enters
California illegally and she
tries to support her family
by finding a job. Lupita's
search is full of obstacles
as she struggles toward
maturity in a place where
simply growing up is a
difficult, uncertain process.

The Heart of a Chief
by Joseph Bruchac

Chris Nicola, an eleven-
year-old Pennacook boy,
has a harsh life on a
reservation. Despite the
conditions Chris must deal
with, his inner qualities
and family traditions
help him to recognize his
potential.

The True Confessions of
Charlotte Doyle
by Avi

When Charlotte boards
a ship bound for Rhode
Island, she has no idea that
she'll be the only female
on board. She soon finds
herself caught up in a
conflict between a ship
captain and his bitter crew.

What would you do for your family?

Artemis Fowl
by Eoin Colfer

Twelve-year-old Artemis is
the genius son of a criminal
mastermind. He decides
to steal the fairies' gold to
restore his family's fortune
and finance his father's
rescue operation—if his
father is still alive.

Bird
by Angela Johnson

What would you do to
get your father back?
Bird leaves her mother
and takes a bus to Acorn,
Alabama, to hide out in
a shed and spy on her
stepfather. Will she get
him to come home?

The Mouse and His Child
by Russell Hoban

Does a wind-up mouse
need a mother? This one
thinks he does. Follow a
toy mouse and his father
as they hide from the evil
Manny Rat and search for
a family all their own.

**Get Novel
Wise** THINK central

Go to **thinkcentral.com**.
KEYWORD: HML6-314

UNIT 3

The Big Idea

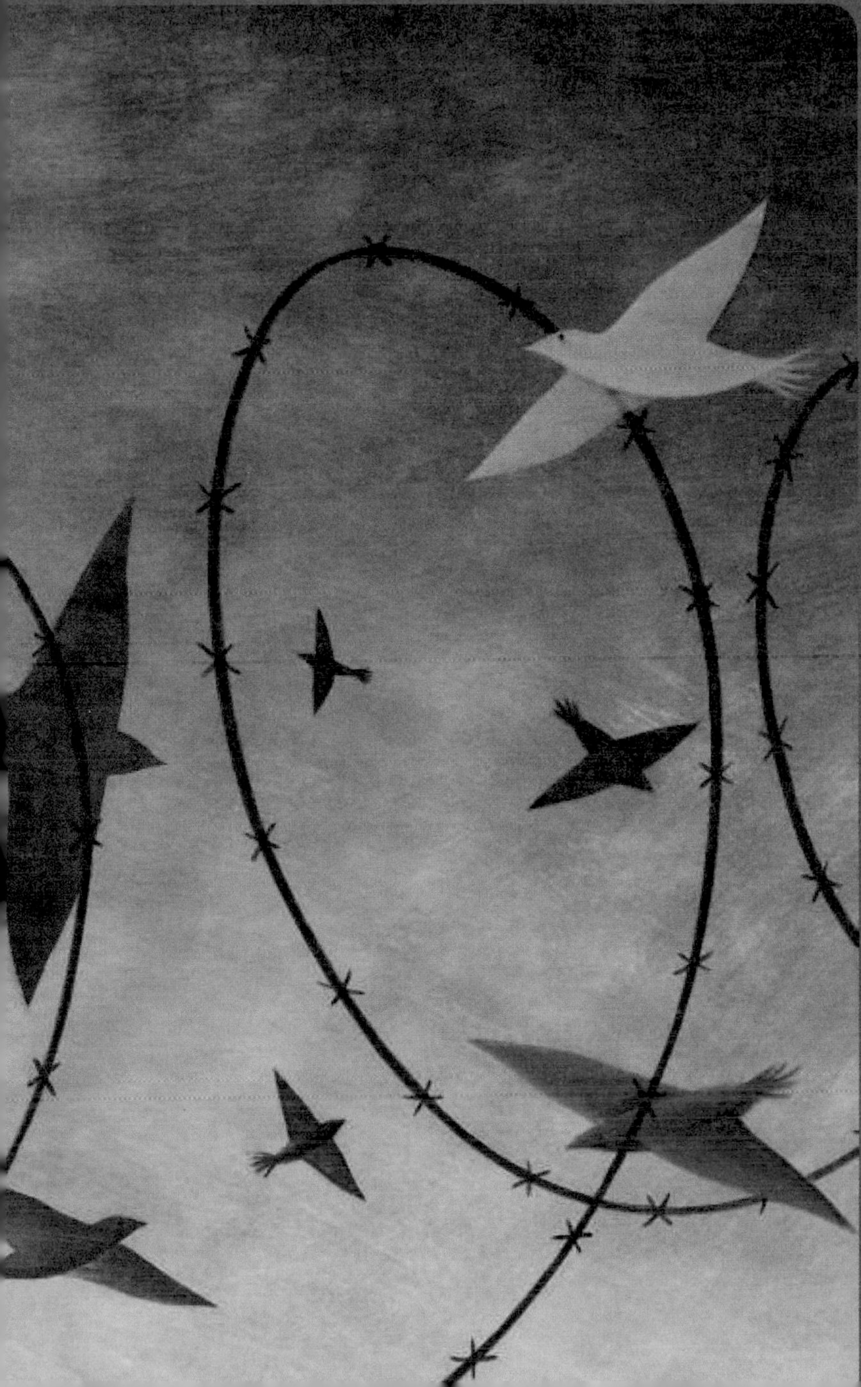

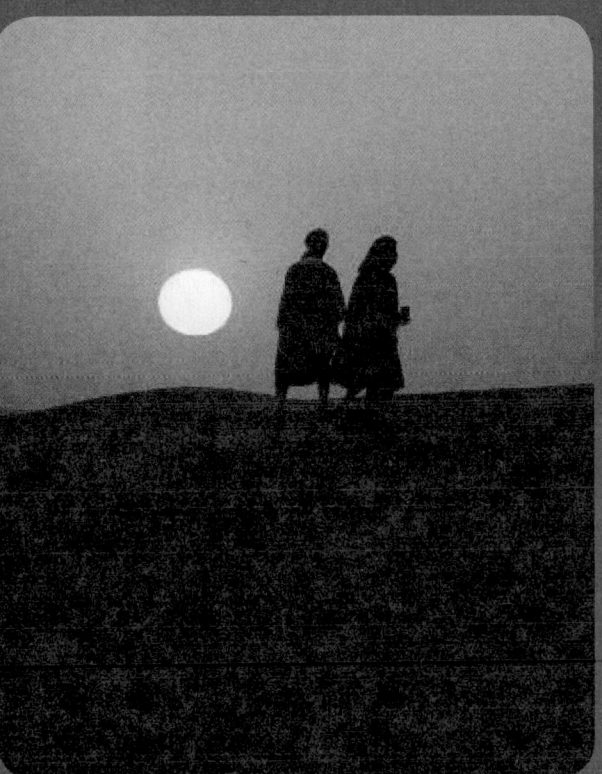

UNDERSTANDING THEME

- In Fiction
- In Poetry

What are life's big LESSONS?

What do you think of when you hear the word *lessons*? You might picture a chalkboard and a textbook, or start sweating at the thought of a quiz. But it is also possible to learn valuable lessons on a Saturday while hanging out with your friends. For instance, you might learn the importance of nurturing a friendship in order to help it grow. You can even learn lessons while reading a powerful book or watching a gripping movie. The messages about life and human nature that writers and directors convey through their work are called themes. The themes they share can keep you from having to learn lessons the hard way.

ACTIVITY Choose a book, poem, or movie that taught you one of life's big lessons. Share your choice with a small group and talk about why this lesson is important to you. Have other members of the group learned similar lessons?

Find It Online! THINK central
Go to thinkcentral.com for the interactive version of this unit.

COMMON CORE

Preview Unit Goals

TEXT ANALYSIS

- Determine a theme or central idea of a text and how it is conveyed through particular details
- Analyze how a particular sentence fits into the structure of a text and contributes to the development of the theme
- Analyze the impact of a specific word choice on meaning
- Determine an author's purpose in a text

READING

- Integrate information presented in different media or formats to develop a coherent understanding of a topic
- Develop strategies for reading, including monitoring, predicting, visualizing, and setting a purpose

WRITING AND LANGUAGE

- Write a short story
- Vary sentence patterns
- Demonstrate command of the conventions of punctuation

VOCABULARY

- Use context as a clue to the meaning of a word or phrase
- Use roots and affixes as clues to the meaning of a word
- Complete analogies

ACADEMIC VOCABULARY

- attitude
- context
- implicit
- communicate
- illustrate

MEDIA AND VIEWING

- Create a class blog

Understanding Theme

"Winning isn't everything." "Follow your heart." You've probably learned lessons like these at one time or another. Your own experience is usually the best teacher, but literature can also communicate important truths, or themes. A **theme** is a message about life or human nature that a writer wants readers to understand. In this workshop, you'll learn how to figure out what the stories, poems, and plays you read *really* mean.

COMMON CORE

Included in this workshop:
RL 2 Determine a theme or central idea of a text and how it is conveyed through particular details.

Part 1: Topic Versus Theme

Have you heard the fairy tale about the duckling who doesn't fit in? His siblings call him the "ugly duckling" because he looks different from them. In the end, the duckling discovers that he is actually a beautiful swan.

The story of the ugly duckling is about being different. But this is not the theme of the story. It is simply a **topic**—one or two words that sum up what the story is about. The **theme** is the writer's central idea or message *about* the topic. Two possible themes of the story are "It's important to accept people for who they are" or "Differences are what make people special."

While a topic can be described in a word or two, it takes a complete sentence to describe a theme, as you'll notice in the following example.

EXAMPLE

The Drum

Poem by Nikki Giovanni

daddy says the world is
a drum tight and hard
and i told him
i'm gonna beat
out my own rhythm

TOPICS
- individuality
- being yourself

THEME STATEMENTS
- It's important to be yourself.
- People should march to their own rhythm.
- Individuality is about doing your own thing.

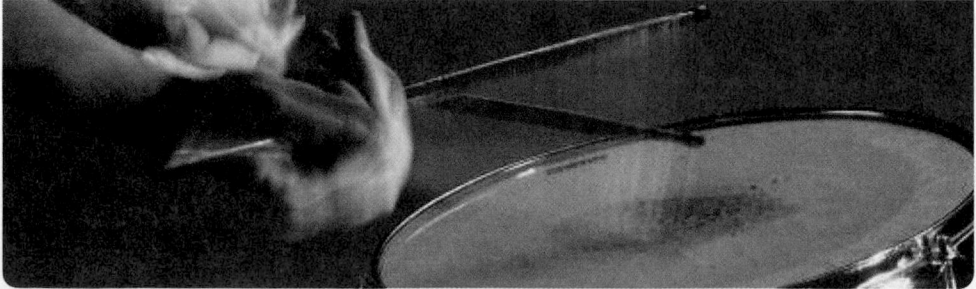

MODEL 1: THEME IN A STORY

Fables are stories that teach lessons about human nature through the actions of animal characters. These lessons communicate important themes. As you read this fable, notice the mistake the dog makes.

The Dog and His Reflection

Fable by **Aesop**

A dog who thought he was very clever stole a steak from a butcher shop. As he ran off with it in his teeth, he crossed a bridge that spanned a small, still river.

As he looked over the side of the bridge and into the water, he saw his
5 own reflection, but he thought it was another dog.

"Hmm," thought the dog, "that other dog has a nice, juicy steak almost as good as the one I have. He's a stupid-looking dog. If I can scare him, perhaps he'll drop his steak and run."

This seemed to the dog to be a perfect plan. But as he opened his
10 mouth to bark, he dropped his steak into the water and lost it.

Close Read

1. Explain how the dog loses the steak he stole from the butcher.

2. What lesson can readers learn from the dog's failed plan to get another steak when he already had one? State the theme of this fable in a sentence.

MODEL 2: THEME IN A POEM

This contemporary poem has a message about the topic of beauty.

The Stray Cat

Poem by **Eve Merriam**

It's just an old alley cat
that has followed us all the way home.

It hasn't a star on its forehead,
or a silky satiny coat.

5 No proud tiger stripes, no dainty tread,
no elegant velvet throat.

It's a splotchy, blotchy
city cat, not a pretty cat,
a rough little tough little bag of old bones.

10 "Beauty," we shall call you.
"Beauty, come in."

Close Read

1. Notice the way the cat is described. Would most people consider this cat beautiful? Explain.

2. Reread the boxed lines. Choose the statement that best expresses this poem's theme.
   a. Beauty is something that everyone can agree on.
   b. Different people have different ideas about what is beautiful.

Part 2: Clues to Theme

In some folk tales and stories, the theme is directly stated by a character or the narrator. In most works of literature, though, the theme is not usually revealed in the form of a direct statement but is conveyed through particular details. The theme is **implicit,** or not directly expressed. As a reader, you need to **infer,** or guess, the theme. To make a reasonable guess, you have to consider certain clues. The elements in the chart can all serve as clues.

THE CLUES

TITLE

The title may hint at a theme by highlighting an important idea, setting, image, or character. Ask:
- To what in the story does the title refer?
- What ideas does the title emphasize?

PLOT AND CONFLICT

A story's plot often focuses on a conflict that is important to the theme. Ask:
- What conflicts do the characters face?
- How are the conflicts resolved?

CHARACTERS AND ACTIONS

Characters can reflect a theme through their actions, thoughts, and words. Ask:
- What do the main characters do and say?
- How do the characters deal with the conflicts?
- What lessons do the characters learn?

SETTING, IMAGES, AND STYLISTIC ELEMENTS

The setting, images, and stylistic elements an author uses can suggest a theme. Ask:
- What aspects of the setting does the author emphasize?
- What stylistic elements, such as traditional motifs, or recurring ideas, does the author include? (Ideas and characters such as the trickster, the young fool, and the quest are all examples of motifs.)
- What images stand out as especially memorable?
- What conflicts does the setting create?

Part 3: Analyze the Text

As you read this folk tale, use the clues you just learned about to help you uncover the theme. The **Close Read** questions will guide you.

Gombei
and the
Wild Ducks

Japanese folk tale retold by **Yoshiko Uchida**

Once long ago, in a small village in Japan, there lived a man whose name was Gombei. He lived very close to a wooded marsh where wild ducks came each winter to play in the water for many long hours. Even when the wind was cold and the marsh waters were frozen, the ducks
5　came in great clusters, for they liked Gombei's marsh, and they often stayed to sleep on the ice.

Just as his father had done before him, Gombei made his living by trapping the wild ducks with simple loops of rope. When a duck stepped into a loop, Gombei simply pulled the rope tight and the duck was
10　caught. And like his father before him, Gombei never trapped more than one duck each day.

"After all, the poor creatures come to the marsh never suspecting that they will be caught," Gombei's father had said. "It would be too cruel to trap more than one at a time."
15　And so for all the years that Gombei trapped, he never caught more than one duck a day.

One cold winter morning, however, Gombei woke up with a dreary ache in his bones. "I am growing too old to work so hard, and there is no reason to continue as my father did for so many years," he said
20　to himself. "If I caught one hundred ducks all at once, I could loaf for ninety-nine days without working at all."

Gombei wondered why he hadn't done this sooner. "It is a brilliant idea," he thought.

The very next morning, he hurried out to the marsh and discovered
25　that its waters were frozen. "Very good! A fine day for trapping," he murmured, and quickly he laid a hundred traps on the icy surface. The sun had not yet come up and the sky was full of dark clouds. Gombei knelt behind a tree and clutched the ends of the hundred rope traps as he shivered and waited for the ducks to come.

Close Read

1. Which character does the title suggest is important to the story? As you read, look for details that show what this character is like and how he changes.

2. Reread the boxed text. What impression do you have of Gombei? Explain whether you see any problems with his plan.

30   Slowly the sky grew lighter and Gombei could see some ducks flying toward his marsh. He held his breath and watched eagerly as they swooped down onto the ice. They did not see his traps at all and gabbled noisily as they searched for food. One by one as the ducks stepped into his traps, Gombei tightened his hold on the ropes.

35   "One—two—three—" he counted, and in no time at all, he had ninety-nine ducks in his traps. The day had not even dawned and already his work was done for the next ninety-nine days. Gombei grinned at his cleverness and thought of the days and weeks ahead during which he could loaf.

40   "One more," he said patiently, "just one more duck and I will have a hundred."

The last duck, however, was the hardest of all to catch. Gombei waited and waited, but still there was no duck in his last trap. Soon the sky grew bright for the sun had appeared at the rim of the wooded 45   hills, and suddenly a shaft of light scattered a rainbow of sparkling colors over the ice. The startled ducks uttered a shrill cry and almost as one they fluttered up into the sky, each trailing a length of rope from its legs.

Gombei was so startled by their sudden flight, he didn't let go of the 50   ropes he held in his hands. Before he could even call for help, he found himself swooshed up into the cold winter sky as the ninety-nine wild ducks soared upward, pulling him along at the end of their traps. . . .

Soon one hand began to slip, a little at first, and then a little more. He was losing his grip on the ropes! Slowly Gombei felt the ropes slide 55   from his numb fingers and finally, he was unable to hold on any longer. He closed his eyes tight and murmured a quick prayer as he plummeted pell-mell down to earth. The wild ducks, not knowing what had happened, flew on trailing their ropes behind like ribbons in the sky.

As Gombei tumbled toward the ground, however, a very strange 60   thing began to take place. First, he sprouted a bill, and then feathers and wings, and then a tail and webbed feet. By the time he was almost down to earth, he looked just like the creatures he had been trying to trap. Gombei wondered if he were having a bad dream. But no, he was flying and flapping his wings, and when he tried to call out, the only 65   sound that came from him was the call of the wild duck. He had indeed become a wild duck himself. Gombei fluttered about frantically, trying to think and feel like a duck instead of a man. At last, he decided there was only one thing to do.

"If I am to be a wild duck, I must live like one," he thought, and he 70   headed slowly toward the waters of a marsh he saw glistening in the sun.

Close Read

3. What happens to Gombei as a result of his actions?

4. In lines 69–70, Gombei returns to a familiar setting—a marsh—but there is nothing familiar about the situation he's in. What conflict do you think he's about to have?

He was so hungry he simply had to find something to eat, for he had not even had breakfast yet. He swooped down to the marsh and looked about hungrily. But as he waddled about thinking only of his empty stomach, he suddenly felt a tug at his leg. He pulled and pulled, but he could not get away. Then he looked down, and there wound around his leg was the very same kind of rope trap that he set each day for the wild ducks of his marsh.

"I wasn't harming anything. All I wanted was some food," he cried. But the man who had set the trap could not understand what Gombei was trying to say. He had been trapped like a wild animal and soon he would be plucked and eaten.

"Oh-h-h-h me," Gombei wailed, "now I know how terrible it is for even one wild duck to be trapped, and only this morning I was trying to trap a hundred poor birds. I am a wicked and greedy man," he thought, "and I deserve to be punished for being so cruel."

As Gombei wept, the tears trickled down his body and touched the rope that was wound tightly about his leg. The moment they did, a wonderful thing happened. The rope that was so secure suddenly fell apart and Gombei was no longer caught in the trap.

"I'm free! I'm free!" Gombei shouted, and this time he wept tears of joy. "How good it is to be free and alive! How grateful I am to have another chance," he cried.

As the tears rolled down his face, and then his body, another strange and marvelous thing happened. First, his feathers began to disappear, and then his bill, and then his tail and his webbed feet. Finally he was no longer a duck, but had become a human being once more. . . .

"Never again will I ever trap another living thing," Gombei vowed when he reached home safely. Then he went to his cupboard and threw out all his rope traps and burned them into ash.

"From this moment on, I shall become a farmer," he said. "I will till the soil and grow rice and wheat and food for all the living creatures of the land." And Gombei did exactly that for the rest of his days.

As for the wild ducks, they came in ever-increasing numbers, for now they found grain and feed instead of traps laid upon the ice, and they knew that in the sheltered waters of Gombei's marsh they would always be safe.

Close Read

5. Examine the boxed text. What does Gombei realize about himself and his plan? Explain what has caused the change in his attitude.

6. Think about the lesson that Gombei has learned. Choose a topic from the list below and write a statement that expresses a theme or central idea of the story. Explain whether the theme is directly stated or **implied** (suggested indirectly).
   - freedom
   - treatment of others
   - understanding others' problems

The Dog of Pompeii

Short Story by Louis Untermeyer

Video link at
thinkcentral.com

VIDEO TRAILER THINK central   KEYWORD: HML6-324

What would you RISK for someone else?

COMMON CORE

RL 2 Determine a theme or central idea of a text and how it is conveyed through particular details. **RL 5** Analyze how a particular sentence fits into the structure of a text and contributes to the development of the theme, setting, or plot. **L 4a** Use context as a clue to the meaning of a word or phrase.

Some people take risks for the excitement of it, whether they are trying a new skateboarding trick or auditioning for a play. Others, such as a student entering a spelling bee, take risks hoping to gain a reward. In "The Dog of Pompeii," one character risks his life simply to help someone else.

LIST IT Brainstorm a list of situations in which you would be willing to take a risk for another person. Compare your lists with those of your classmates. What differences and similarities do you see?

● TEXT ANALYSIS: THEME VERSUS TOPIC

Most stories center around a **theme** or **central idea** about life that the writer shares with readers. A story's theme is different from its **topic,** or what the story is about.

	Length	Example
Topic	can usually be stated in a word or two	love
Theme	more complex than a topic; usually described in a sentence	Love can help people solve their differences.

One topic of "The Dog of Pompeii" is friendship. As you read, look for the larger message the author wants to share. Remember, a theme is **implicit,** or not stated directly. Characters, actions, and images can all be clues to the theme.

● READING STRATEGY: READING HISTORICAL FICTION

Writers of **historical fiction** use both real and made-up settings, events, and characters from the past. The story you are about to read is set in a real place, the town of Pompeii, Italy. It also describes a real event—a volcanic eruption. The setting and events create a cultural and historical context that directly affects the story's theme. As you read, list the details that make the story's setting and events come alive. Then, try to draw conclusions about how the historical and cultural context of the story helps build the theme.

Review: Monitor

▲ VOCABULARY IN CONTEXT

Complete each phrase with a word from the story.

WORD LIST	agonize	dislodge	ponder
	corrupt	emerge	

1. The shaking helped to _____ huge boulders.
2. The citizens _____ over what is happening in their town.
3. They wonder when they can _____ from hiding.
4. The lava begins to _____ the soil, making it unusable.
5. Modern archaeologists _____ the town's ruins.

 Complete the activities in your **Reader/Writer Notebook.**

Meet the Author

Louis Untermeyer
1885–1977

Passion for Poetry
Though as a young man he worked several jobs within his family's jewelry business, Louis Untermeyer was also constantly writing. He eventually retired from the jewelry business in order to devote more time to writing. Although Untermeyer wrote many stories, poetry was his true passion. During his lifetime, he published more than 100 books and developed friendships with famous poets such as Robert Frost and E. E. Cummings.

BACKGROUND TO THE STORY
Mount Vesuvius Erupts
In the year A.D. 79, the volcanic mountain Vesuvius (vĭ-sōō′vē-əs) erupted in southern Italy. It poured burning lava and ashes over the countryside and buried the nearby cities of Pompeii (pŏm-pā′) and Herculaneum (hûr′kyə-lā′nē-əm). Of Pompeii's estimated population of 20,000, at least 2,000 were killed. After the eruption, Pompeii lay undisturbed for almost 1,700 years, until its ruins were discovered in the late 1500s. The remains of the city, preserved by volcanic ash, present a picture of life in the Roman Empire, as if it had been frozen in time.

Author Online

THiNK central

Go to **thinkcentral.com.**
KEYWORD: HML6-325

The DOG *of* POMPEII

Louis Untermeyer

Analyze Visuals ▶

Make inferences about life in Pompeii based on the details in this image.

Tito and his dog Bimbo lived (if you could call it living) under the wall where it joined the inner gate. They really didn't live there; they just slept there. They lived anywhere. Pompeii was one of the gayest of the old Latin towns, but although Tito was never an unhappy boy, he was not exactly a merry one. The streets were always lively with shining chariots and bright red trappings;[1] the open-air theaters rocked with laughing crowds; sham battles and athletic sports were free for the asking in the great stadium. Once a year the Caesar[2] visited the pleasure city, and the fireworks lasted for days; the sacrifices in the forum[3] were better than a

10 show. But Tito saw none of these things. He was blind—had been blind from birth. He was known to everyone in the poorer quarters. But no one could say how old he was, no one remembered his parents, no one could tell where he came from. Bimbo was another mystery. As long as people could remember seeing Tito—about twelve or thirteen years—they had seen Bimbo. Bimbo had never left his side. He was not only dog but nurse, pillow, playmate, mother, and father to Tito. **A**

---

1. **trappings:** ornamental coverings or decorations.
2. **the Caesar:** the Roman emperor.
3. **forum:** the public square or marketplace of an ancient Roman city.

A **HISTORICAL FICTION**
Reread lines 3–10. Which details in this passage tell you that this story takes place in the past?

Illustrations © 1997 by Greg Ruhl.

Did I say Bimbo never left his master? (Perhaps I had better say comrade, for if anyone was the master, it was Bimbo.) I was wrong. Bimbo did trust Tito alone exactly three times a day. It was a fixed
20 routine, a custom understood between boy and dog since the beginning of their friendship, and the way it worked was this: Early in the morning, shortly after dawn, while Tito was still dreaming, Bimbo would disappear. When Tito woke, Bimbo would be sitting quietly at his side, his ears cocked, his stump of a tail tapping the ground, and a fresh-baked bread— more like a large round roll—at his feet. Tito would stretch himself; Bimbo would yawn; then they would breakfast. At noon, no matter where they happened to be, Bimbo would put his paw on Tito's knee, and the two of them would return to the inner gate. Tito would curl up in the corner (almost like a dog) and go to sleep, while Bimbo, looking quite
30 important (almost like a boy), would disappear again. In half an hour he'd be back with their lunch. Sometimes it would be a piece of fruit or a scrap of meat; often it was nothing but a dry crust. But sometimes there would be one of those flat, rich cakes, sprinkled with raisins and sugar, that Tito liked so much. At suppertime the same thing happened, although there was a little less of everything, for things were hard to snatch in the evening with the streets full of people. Besides, Bimbo didn't

COMMON CORE L 4a

Language Coach

Nouns Used as Verbs
Many English words started out as nouns and then became verbs, a process sometimes called "verbing." *Breakfast* (line 26) is usually a noun, but sometimes it is used as a verb, as in "to breakfast," a formal and somewhat old-fashioned way of saying "eat breakfast." Many common words, such as *mail, dance,* and *drink,* have meanings as both nouns and verbs. Name three other words that have meanings as both nouns and verbs.

◄ **Analyze Visuals**

Compare and contrast this image with your mental picture of the city of Pompeii.

approve of too much food before going to sleep. A heavy supper made boys too restless and dogs too stodgy—and it was the business of a dog to sleep lightly with one ear open and muscles ready for action. **B**

40   But whether there was much or little, hot or cold, fresh or dry, food was always there. Tito never asked where it came from and Bimbo never told him. There was plenty of rainwater in the hollows of soft stones; the old egg-woman at the corner sometimes gave him a cupful of strong goat's milk; in the grape season the fat winemaker let him have drippings of the mild juice. So there was no danger of going hungry or thirsty. There was plenty of everything in Pompeii if you knew where to find it—and if you had a dog like Bimbo.

As I said before, Tito was not the merriest boy in Pompeii. He could not romp with the other youngsters and play hare and hounds and I 50 spy and follow-your-master and ball-against-the-building and jackstones and kings and robbers with them. But that did not make him sorry for himself. If he could not see the sights that delighted the lads of Pompeii, he could hear and smell things they never noticed. He could really see more with his ears and nose than they could with their eyes. When he and Bimbo went out walking, he knew just where they were going and exactly what was happening.

"Ah," he'd sniff and say as they passed a handsome villa, "Glaucus Pansa is giving a grand dinner tonight. They're going to have three kinds of bread, and roast pigling, and stuffed goose, and a great stew—I think 60 bear stew—and a fig pie." And Bimbo would note that this would be a good place to visit tomorrow.

Or, "H'm," Tito would murmur, half through his lips, half through his nostrils. "The wife of Marcus Lucretius is expecting her mother. She's shaking out every piece of goods in the house; she's going to use the best clothes—the ones she's been keeping in pine needles and camphor[4]—and there's an extra girl in the kitchen. Come, Bimbo, let's get out of the dust!"

Or, as they passed a small but elegant dwelling opposite the public baths,[5] "Too bad! The tragic poet is ill again. It must be a bad fever this time, for they're trying smoke fumes instead of medicine. Whew! I'm glad 70 I'm not a tragic poet!"

Or, as they neared the forum, "Mm-m! What good things they have in the macellum today!" (It really was a sort of butcher-grocer-marketplace, but Tito didn't know any better. He called it the macellum.) "Dates from

4. **camphor** (kăm′fər): a strong-smelling substance used to keep moths away.

5. **public baths:** large public complexes with locker rooms, steam rooms, and bathing pools kept at different temperatures. In many parts of the Roman Empire, a trip to the public baths was a daily ritual for many people.

B **THEME VERSUS TOPIC**
How does Bimbo show his loyalty to Tito?

SOCIAL STUDIES CONNECTION

The city of Pompeii was located in what is now southern Italy. In the year A.D. 79, this region was part of the Roman Empire.

Africa, and salt oysters from sea caves, and cuttlefish, and new honey, and sweet onions, and—ugh!—water-buffalo steaks. Come, let's see what's what in the forum." And Bimbo, just as curious as his comrade, hurried on. Being a dog, he trusted his ears and nose (like Tito) more than his eyes. And so the two of them entered the center of Pompeii. **C**

80 The forum was the part of the town to which everybody came at least once during each day. It was the central square, and everything happened here. There were no private houses; all was public—the chief temples, the gold and red bazaars, the silk shops, the town hall, the booths belonging to the weavers and jewel merchants, the wealthy woolen market, the shrine of the household gods. Everything glittered here. The buildings looked as if they were new—which, in a sense, they were. The earthquake of twelve years ago had brought down all the old structures, and since the citizens of Pompeii were ambitious to rival Naples and even Rome, they had seized the opportunity to rebuild the whole town. And they had done it all within a dozen years. There was scarcely a building that was older than Tito.

90 Tito had heard a great deal about the earthquake, though being about a year old at the time, he could scarcely remember it. This particular quake had been a light one—as earthquakes go. The weaker houses had been shaken down; parts of the outworn wall had been wrecked; but there was little loss of life, and the brilliant new Pompeii had taken the place of the old. No one knew what caused these earthquakes. Records showed they had happened in the neighborhood since the beginning of time. Sailors said that it was to teach the lazy city folk a lesson and make them appreciate those who risked the dangers of the sea to bring them luxuries and protect their town from invaders. The priests said that the gods took

100 this way of showing their anger to those who refused to worship properly and who failed to bring enough sacrifices to the altars and (though they didn't say it in so many words) presents to the priests. The tradesmen said that the foreign merchants had **corrupted** the ground and it was no longer safe to traffic in imported goods that came from strange places and carried a curse with them. Everyone had a different explanation—and everyone's explanation was louder and sillier than his neighbor's.

They were talking about it this afternoon as Tito and Bimbo came out of the side street into the public square. The forum was the favorite promenade[6] for rich and poor. What with the priests arguing with the

110 politicians, servants doing the day's shopping, tradesmen crying their wares, women displaying the latest fashions from Greece and Egypt, children playing hide-and-seek among the marble columns, knots of

---

6. **promenade** (prŏm'ə-nād'): a public place for walking and socializing.

COMMON CORE L 4a

Language Coach

Idioms The phrase "seized the opportunity" (lines 87–88) means "took advantage of a situation." This phrase is an example of an idiom, an expression or saying that is specific to a certain language or group. Like other languages, English has many colorful idioms, most of which are based on figures of speech. Explain why "seized the opportunity" cannot be taken literally.

corrupt (kə-rŭpt') v. to cause something to change from good to bad

soldiers, sailors, peasants from the provinces—to say nothing of those who merely came to lounge and look on—the square was crowded to its last inch. His ears even more than his nose guided Tito to the place where the talk was loudest. It was in front of the shrine of the household gods that, naturally enough, the householders were arguing. **D**

"I tell you," rumbled a voice which Tito recognized as bath master Rufus's, "there won't be another earthquake in my lifetime or yours. There
120 may be a tremble or two, but earthquakes, like lightnings, never strike twice in the same place."

"Do they not?" asked a thin voice Tito had never heard. It had a high, sharp ring to it, and Tito knew it as the accent of a stranger. "How about the two towns of Sicily that have been ruined three times within fifteen years by the eruptions of Mount Etna? And were they not warned? And does that column of smoke above Vesuvius mean nothing?"

"That?" Tito could hear the grunt with which one question answered another. "That's always there. We use it for our weather guide. When the smoke stands up straight, we know we'll have fair weather; when it
130 flattens out, it's sure to be foggy; when it drifts to the east—"

"Yes, yes," cut in the edged voice. "I've heard about your mountain barometer.[7] But the column of smoke seems hundreds of feet higher than usual, and it's thickening and spreading like a shadowy tree. They say in Naples—"

"Oh, Naples!" Tito knew this voice by the little squeak that went with it. It was Attilio, the cameo[8] cutter. "*They* talk while we suffer. Little help we got from them last time. Naples commits the crimes, and Pompeii pays the price. It's become a proverb with us. Let them mind their own business."

"Yes," grumbled Rufus, "and others, too."

140 "Very well, my confident friends," responded the thin voice, which now sounded curiously flat. "We also have a proverb—and it is this: Those who will not listen to men must be taught by the gods. I say no more. But I leave a last warning. Remember the holy ones. Look to your temples. And when the smoke tree above Vesuvius grows to the shape of an umbrella pine, look to your lives."

Tito could hear the air whistle as the speaker drew his toga about him, and the quick shuffle of feet told him the stranger had gone.

"Now what," said the cameo cutter, "did he mean by that?"

"I wonder," grunted Rufus. "I wonder." ◆

150 Tito wondered, too. And Bimbo, his head at a thoughtful angle, looked as if he had been doing a heavy piece of **pondering**. By nightfall the

D HISTORICAL FICTION
Reread lines 108–115. Note important details about the forum. What does the description tell you about life in Pompeii?

◆ GRAMMAR IN CONTEXT
One way that writers make **dialogue,** or the words characters speak, sound natural is by skillfully using punctuation. Punctuation—which includes commas, periods, and dashes—can help the reader "hear" when there are pauses, full stops, and interruptions in the words the characters speak. The punctuation in lines 122–149 helps the dialogue sound natural and realistic.

ponder (pŏn'dər) *v.* to think seriously about; reflect on

---

7. **mountain barometer:** A barometer is an instrument for measuring the pressure of air and predicting weather changes. The people of Pompeii used the smoke from the volcano as a sort of barometer.

8. **cameo:** a shell or gem with a picture carved on it.

argument had been forgotten. If the smoke had increased, no one saw it in the dark. Besides, it was Caesar's birthday, and the town was in holiday mood. Tito and Bimbo were among the merrymakers, dodging the charioteers who shouted at them. A dozen times they almost upset baskets of sweets and jars of Vesuvian wine, said to be as fiery as the streams inside the volcano, and a dozen times they were cursed and cuffed. But Tito never missed his footing. He was thankful for his keen ears and quick instinct—most thankful of all for Bimbo.

160   They visited the uncovered theater, and though Tito could not see the faces of the actors, he could follow the play better than most of the audience, for their attention wandered—they were distracted by the scenery, the costumes, the by-play, even by themselves—while Tito's whole attention was centered in what he heard. Then to the city walls, where the people of Pompeii watched a mock naval battle in which the city was attacked by the sea and saved after thousands of flaming arrows had been exchanged and countless colored torches had been burned. Though the thrill of flaring ships and lighted skies was lost to Tito, the shouts and cheers excited him as much as any, and he cried out with the loudest of them.

170   The next morning there were *two* of the beloved raisin and sugar cakes for his breakfast. Bimbo was unusually active and thumped his bit of a tail until Tito was afraid he would wear it out. The boy could not imagine whether Bimbo was urging him to some sort of game or was trying to tell him something. After a while, he ceased to notice Bimbo. He felt drowsy. Last night's late hours had tired him. Besides, there was a heavy mist in the air—no, a thick fog rather than a mist—a fog that got into his throat and scraped it and made him cough. He walked as far as the marine gate to get a breath of the sea. But the blanket of haze had spread all over the bay, and even the salt air seemed smoky. **E**

180   He went to bed before dusk and slept. But he did not sleep well. He had too many dreams—dreams of ships lurching in the forum, of losing his way in a screaming crowd, of armies marching across his chest, of being pulled over every rough pavement of Pompeii.

He woke early. Or, rather, he was pulled awake. Bimbo was doing the pulling. The dog had dragged Tito to his feet and was urging the boy along. Somewhere. Where, Tito did not know. His feet stumbled uncertainly; he was still half asleep. For a while he noticed nothing except the fact that it was hard to breathe. The air was hot. And heavy. So heavy that he could taste it. The air, it seemed, had turned to powder, a warm
190 powder that stung his nostrils and burned his sightless eyes.

Then he began to hear sounds. Peculiar sounds. Like animals under the earth. Hissings and groanings and muffled cries that a dying creature might make **dislodging** the stones of his underground cave.

E THEME VERSUS TOPIC
Reread lines 170–174. Notice the way Tito reacts to Bimbo's behavior. In what way does his reaction suggest that something has changed?

dislodge (dĭs-lŏj′) v. to move from a settled position

There was no doubt of it now. The noises came from underneath. He not only heard them—he could feel them. The earth twitched; the twitching changed to an uneven shrugging of the soil. Then, as Bimbo half pulled, half coaxed him across, the ground jerked away from his feet and he was thrown against a stone fountain.

200 The water—hot water—splashing in his face revived him. He got to his feet, Bimbo steadying him, helping him on again. The noises grew louder; they came closer. The cries were even more animal-like than before, but now they came from human throats. A few people, quicker of foot and more hurried by fear, began to rush by. A family or two—then a section—then, it seemed, an army broken out of bounds. Tito, bewildered though he was, could recognize Rufus as he bellowed past him, like a water buffalo gone mad. Time was lost in a nightmare. **F**

▲ **Analyze Visuals**
What kind of **mood,** or feeling, do the colors and facial expressions of the people in this illustration create?

F **MONITOR**
Reread lines 196–199. Clarify why the water in the fountain is so hot.

It was then the crashing began. First a sharp crackling, like a monstrous snapping of twigs; then a roar like the fall of a whole forest of trees; then an explosion that tore earth and sky. The heavens, though Tito could not see them, were shot through with continual flickerings of fire. Lightnings above were answered by thunders beneath. A house fell. Then another. By a miracle the two companions had escaped the dangerous side streets and were in a more open space. It was the forum. They rested here awhile—how long he did not know.

Tito had no idea of the time of day. He could *feel* it was black—an unnatural blackness. Something inside—perhaps the lack of breakfast and lunch—told him it was past noon. But it didn't matter. Nothing seemed to matter. He was getting drowsy, too drowsy to walk. But walk he must. He knew it. And Bimbo knew it; the sharp tugs told him so. Nor was it a moment too soon. The sacred ground of the forum was safe no longer. It was beginning to rock, then to pitch, then to split. As they stumbled out of the square, the earth wriggled like a caught snake, and all the columns of the temple of Jupiter came down. It was the end of the world—or so it seemed. **G**

G HISTORICAL FICTION
Reread lines 207–224. Which details show you how the eruption has affected the forum and the town?

◄ **Analyze Visuals**
What do the actions of the people in this illustration suggest about the eruption?

To walk was not enough now. They must run. Tito was too frightened to know what to do or where to go. He had lost all sense of direction. He started to go back to the inner gate; but Bimbo, straining his back to the last inch, almost pulled his clothes from him. What did the creature want? Had the dog gone mad?

230   Then, suddenly, he understood. Bimbo was telling him the way out— urging him there. The sea gate,[9] of course. The sea gate—and then the sea. Far from falling buildings, heaving ground. He turned, Bimbo guiding him across open pits and dangerous pools of bubbling mud, away from buildings that had caught fire and were dropping their burning beams. Tito could no longer tell whether the noises were made by the shrieking sky or the **agonized** people. He and Bimbo ran on—the only silent beings in a howling world.

    New dangers threatened. All Pompeii seemed to be thronging toward the marine gate; and, squeezing among the crowds, there was the chance
240 of being trampled to death. But the chance had to be taken. It was growing harder and harder to breathe. What air there was choked him. It was all dust now—dust and pebbles, pebbles as large as beans. They fell on his head, his hands—pumice stones[10] from the black heart of Vesuvius. The mountain was turning itself inside out. Tito remembered a phrase that the stranger had said in the forum two days ago: "Those who will not listen to men must be taught by the gods." The people of Pompeii had refused to heed the warnings; they were being taught now—if it was not too late.

    Suddenly it seemed too late for Tito. The red hot ashes blistered his
250 skin; the stinging vapors tore his throat. He could not go on. He staggered toward a small tree at the side of the road and fell. In a moment Bimbo was beside him. He coaxed. But there was no answer. He licked Tito's hands, his feet, his face. The boy did not stir. Then Bimbo did the last thing he could—the last thing he wanted to do. He bit his comrade, bit him deep in the arm. With a cry of pain, Tito jumped to his feet, Bimbo after him. Tito was in despair, but Bimbo was determined. He drove the boy on, snapping at his heels, worrying his way through the crowd; barking, baring his teeth, heedless of kicks or falling stones. Sick with hunger, half dead with fear and sulphur[11] fumes, Tito pounded on, pursued by Bimbo. How long he never
260 knew. At last he staggered through the marine gate and felt soft sand under him. Then Tito fainted. . . .

agonize (ăg′ə-nīz′) v. to suffer extreme physical or mental pain

SCIENCE CONNECTION

Mount Vesuvius is a type of volcano called a composite volcano. When composite volcanoes erupt, they release not only pieces of rock but also clouds of hot ash and toxic gases.

H MONITOR
Clarify why Bimbo bites Tito in lines 254–255.

---

9. **sea gate:** a gate in the city wall, leading to the sea.

10. **pumice** (pŭm′ĭs) **stones:** lightweight rocks formed from lava.

11. **sulphur** (sŭl′fər): a pale yellow substance that produces a choking fume when burned.

Someone was dashing seawater over him. Someone was carrying him toward a boat.

"Bimbo," he called. And then louder, "Bimbo!" But Bimbo had disappeared.

Voices jarred against each other. "Hurry—hurry!" "To the boats!" "Can't you see the child's frightened and starving!" "He keeps calling for someone!" "Poor boy, he's out of his mind." "Here, child—take this!"

They tucked him in among them. The oarlocks creaked; the oars 270 splashed; the boat rode over toppling waves. Tito was safe. But he wept continually.

"Bimbo!" he wailed. "Bimbo! Bimbo!"

He could not be comforted. **ⓘ**

Eighteen hundred years passed. Scientists were restoring the ancient city; excavators were working their way through the stones and trash that had buried the entire town. Much had already been brought to light—statues, bronze instruments, bright mosaics,[12] household articles; even delicate paintings had been preserved by the fall of ashes that had taken over two thousand lives. Columns were dug up, and the forum was 280 beginning to **emerge.**

It was at a place where the ruins lay deepest that the director paused.

"Come here," he called to his assistant. "I think we've discovered the remains of a building in good shape. Here are four huge millstones that were most likely turned by slaves or mules—and here is a whole wall standing with shelves inside it. Why! It must have been a bakery. And here's a curious thing. What do you think I found under this heap where the ashes were thickest? The skeleton of a dog!"

"Amazing!" gasped his assistant. "You'd think a dog would have had sense enough to run away at the time. And what is that flat thing he's 290 holding between his teeth? It can't be a stone."

"No. It must have come from this bakery. You know it looks to me like some sort of cake hardened with the years. And, bless me, if those little black pebbles aren't raisins. A raisin cake almost two thousand years old! I wonder what made him want it at such a moment." **Ⓙ**

"I wonder," murmured the assistant. ❧

---

12. **mosaics** (mō-zā′ĭks): designs formed from inlaid pieces of stone or glass.

ⓘ THEME VERSUS TOPIC
Reread lines 262-273. What does Tito realize? How do you know? What does the fact that Tito is safe but unable to be comforted suggest about the story's theme? How would you state the theme or central idea?

emerge (ĭ-mûrj′) v. to come into view

Ⓙ HISTORICAL FICTION
Starting on line 274, what abrupt change has occurred in the story? Why do think the author did this? Explain how this final passage helps you draw conclusions about how the cultural and historical setting of the story helped to build the theme and make it more powerful.

Comprehension

1. **Recall** When does Bimbo leave Tito alone?

2. **Recall** Why is the stranger in the forum worried about the column of smoke coming from Vesuvius?

3. **Clarify** What is the source of the fumes and ashes that hurt Tito?

Text Analysis

● 4. **Monitor** Reread lines 288–290. Why didn't Bimbo have "sense enough to run away" when Mount Vesuvius erupted?

● 5. **Understand Historical Fiction** Look back at the list of details you recorded as you read. Explain why the setting is so important in the story. How does the cultural and historical context of the story contribute to the story's theme?

● 6. **Infer Theme** Keeping the topic of friendship in mind, note details about Tito and Bimbo's thoughts and actions in a web like the one shown. Then, write a sentence expressing the story's implicit theme.

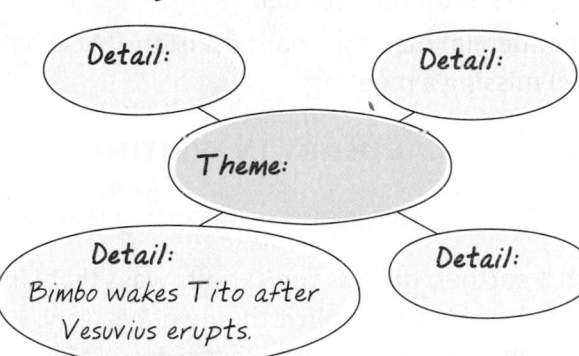

Detail:

Detail:

Theme:

Detail: Bimbo wakes Tito after Vesuvius erupts.

Detail:

7. **Analyze Foreshadowing** A clue or hint about something that will happen later on in a story is called **foreshadowing.** Reread the conversation between Rufus and the stranger in the forum in lines 118–134. What events are foreshadowed in this passage?

● 8. **Evaluate Historical Fiction** Although historical fiction can contain made-up details and characters, the characters and plot should seem realistic. Consider the use of fact and fantasy in this story. Is Bimbo's behavior, before and after the volcano erupts, believable? Support your answer.

Extension and Challenge

9. **SCIENCE CONNECTION** There are many famous volcanoes in the world with long and vivid histories. Many are at risk of erupting again in the near or distant future. Research one of these volcanoes, and prepare a brief description of one eruption and its effects.

What would you RISK for someone else?

Look back at the list you made of situations in which you'd be willing to take a risk. What do you think about the risk Bimbo took for Tito? Would you do the same for someone you care about? Why or why not?

COMMON CORE

RL 2 Determine a theme or central idea of a text and how it is conveyed through particular details. **RL 5** Analyze how a particular sentence fits into the structure of a text and contributes to the development of the theme, setting, or plot. **W 7** Conduct short research projects to answer a question, drawing on several sources.

Vocabulary in Context

▲ VOCABULARY PRACTICE

Choose the letter of the situation you would connect with each boldfaced word.

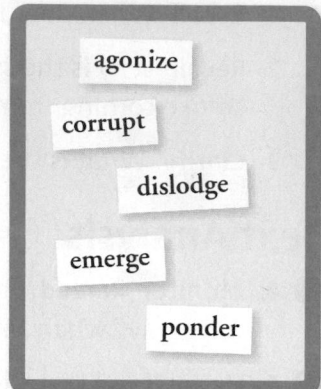

1. **agonize:** (a) sleeping in on a weekend, (b) suffering through a death in the family, (c) listening to an amusing speaker
2. **corrupt:** (a) a dad working overtime, (b) a politician taking bribes, (c) a child swimming
3. **dislodge:** (a) visit a national park, (b) loosen a stone from a wall, (c) lend a friend cash
4. **emerge:** (a) birds building nests, (b) tulips growing in spring, (c) cars entering a tunnel
5. **ponder:** (a) making a hard decision, (b) canoeing in a lake, (c) missing a meeting

ACADEMIC VOCABULARY IN WRITING

• attitude	• communicate	• context	• illustrate	• implicit

With a partner, discuss the various ways that Untermeyer, the author, helps you to discover the **implicit** theme of his story. How do Bimbo's actions throughout the story **illustrate** the depth of his devotion to his master, Tito? Use at least two Academic Vocabulary words in your discussion.

⋯COMMON CORE

L 4b Use Latin roots as clues to the meaning of a word.

VOCABULARY STRATEGY: THE LATIN ROOT *rupt*

The vocabulary word *corrupt* contains the Latin root *rupt,* which means "to break." (This root is also found in the story in the word *eruption.*) The root *rupt* is used to form a number of English words. To understand the meaning of words with *rupt,* use your knowledge of what this root means. If you need more help, look for context clues in the sentence or paragraph.

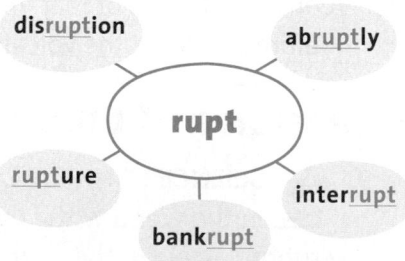

PRACTICE Choose a word from the web that best completes each sentence. Use context clues or, if necessary, a dictionary.

1. He got so far into debt that he went _____.
2. Because she was angry, she ended the conversation _____.
3. They would not stop talking, so finally I had to _____ them.
4. The _____ in the water pipe caused liquid to leak out.
5. A bee flew in the open window, causing a(n) _____ in the classroom.

Interactive Vocabulary **THINK** central
Go to **thinkcentral.com**.
KEYWORD: HML6-338

Language

◆ **GRAMMAR IN CONTEXT:** Punctuate Dialogue Correctly

COMMON CORE

L 2 Demonstrate command of the conventions of punctuation.
W 3 Write narratives to develop imagined events.

Correctly punctuated **dialogue** helps readers know which character in a story is speaking. Dialogue is set off from the rest of the text with **quotation marks.** It is often preceded or followed by phrases like *he said* or *she asked,* and is separated from the quotations by a **comma.** A **period** or comma at the end of a sentence of dialogue should be placed inside the end quotation marks.

> *Original:* Tito said I don't want you to go, Bimbo.
>
> *Revised:* Tito said, "I don't want you to go, Bimbo."

PRACTICE Rewrite the following sentences. Correct the misplaced punctuation marks and insert any missing marks.

1. "Bimbo, I need you to be my eyes said Tito."
2. Bimbo said, "You will make other friends".
3. Tito said "You are my best friend."
4. I will always be your friend, Bimbo replied.

*For more help with punctuating dialogue, see page R50 in the **Grammar Handbook.***

READING-WRITING CONNECTION

YOUR TURN Show your understanding of "The Dog of Pompeii" by responding to the prompt. Then use the **revising tip** to improve your writing.

WRITING PROMPT	REVISING TIP
Short Constructed Response: Dialogue Suppose Bimbo had the ability to speak and had told Tito about his plan to risk another trip into Pompeii. What kind of conversation would he and Tito have had? Think about the characters' friendship and the story's theme. Then write a **brief dialogue** in which the two friends share their thoughts at that moment.	Review your response. Have you punctuated your dialogue using commas, quotation marks, and periods correctly? If not, revise your writing.

Interactive Revision **THINK** central

Go to thinkcentral.com.
KEYWORD: HML6-339

Pompeii and Vesuvius

- Nonfiction Book Excerpt, page 341
- Online Article, page 346

Use with "The Dog of Pompeii," page 326.

COMMON CORE

RI 2 Determine a central idea of a text. **RI 6** Determine an author's purpose and explain how it is conveyed in the text. **RI 7** Integrate information presented in different media or formats to develop a coherent understanding of a topic.

What's the Connection?

You've just read "The Dog of Pompeii," a story that takes place on the day that Mount Vesuvius erupts and buries Pompeii in ash. Now you will learn more about this historical event and what the future may hold for those currently living in the shadow of Mount Vesuvius.

Standards Focus: Author's Purpose and Main Idea

In nonfiction, the most important idea that a writer communicates is the **main idea.** The main idea can be stated directly in the form of a **topic sentence,** which is sometimes the first sentence in a paragraph. Usually, though, you have to determine the main idea of a selection by noting the smaller ideas developed in sections of the selection.

To really understand the central idea a nonfiction writer wants to communicate, you need to determine the **author's purpose,** or the reason the author is writing. The author's purpose is often not stated directly. Instead, it is implied, or suggested by evidence in the text that you must find and analyze. You should ask yourself questions so you can make inferences and draw conclusions about the author's purpose: *Why* is the writer telling me this? *What* does the writer want me to think about this topic?

Different writers will likely have different purposes and main ideas, even when they are writing about the same topic. You will read two nonfiction selections about Pompeii and identify a central idea for each selection. You will also discover evidence that identifies the author's purpose for writing about each topic. Later, you will compare and contrast the main ideas and authors' purposes of the selections.

Source	Main Ideas	Author's Purpose (include evidence)
"In Search of Pompeii" Section 1 "Pompeii: The Evidence" Section 2 "Uncovering Pompeii" Section 3 "A Tragic Day"		
"Italians Trying to Prevent a Modern Pompeii"		

from IN SEARCH OF POMPEII
BY GIOVANNI CASELLI

Pompeii: The Evidence

Much of our knowledge of Roman life comes from the evidence uncovered at Pompeii. Splendid houses, beautiful paintings, sculptures of bronze and marble, fine glass, metal, and pottery bear witness not only to a city that perished in one day, but also to a long-vanished civilization.

A visit to Pompeii is like entering a time machine: you can see wide streets still with the ruts cut in the paving stones by the wheels of chariots, the entrance to a shop with graffiti on the wall beside it, the baths and grand houses with their wall paintings and colonnaded gardens. But, above all, there are the people of Pompeii, overwhelmed as they tried to escape the horror that overtook their city. Across nearly 2,000 years, their twisted bodies are vivid witnesses of what happened on August 24, A.D. 79. **A**

10

F OCUS ON FORM
An **informational text** is written material that provides factual information. News articles, encyclopedia entries, timelines, and nonfiction books are examples of informational texts. **Text features**, such as titles, subheadings, photos, captions, maps, and diagrams, often appear in informational texts.

A MAIN IDEA
What is the main idea of this first section? Look at the subheading and the topic sentence in the first paragraph to help you identify it. Record this information in your chart.

B INFORMATIONAL TEXT

Writers of informational texts often support their main ideas with visual information in the form of charts, photographs, timelines, illustrations, diagrams, maps, tables, and graphs. These visuals can present information more effectively than text alone. This diagram shows the layout of Pompeii. What do you learn about Pompeii by studying this diagram? What do you think is the author's purpose in presenting these details in visual form? Explain what this information adds to your understanding of the text.

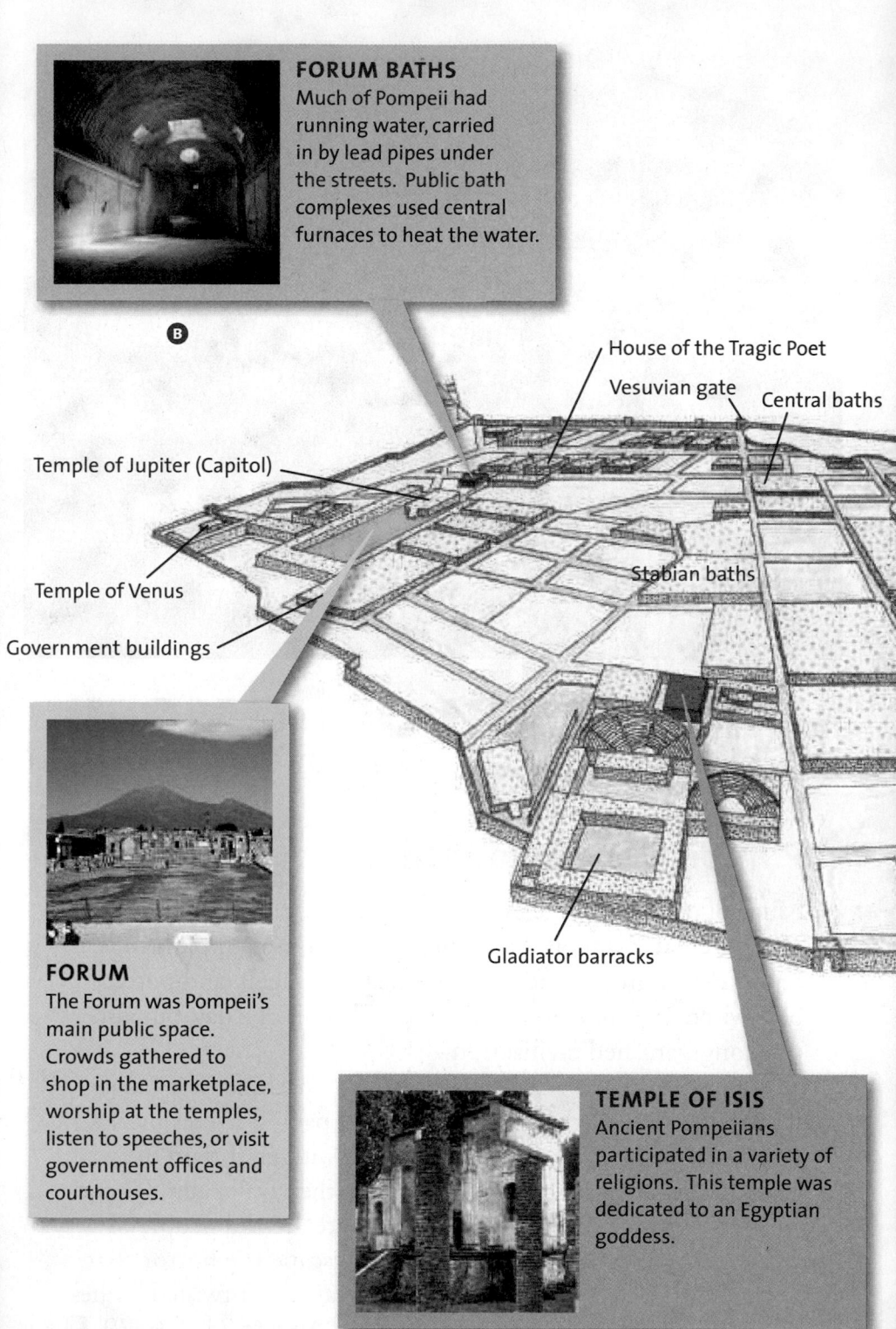

FORUM BATHS
Much of Pompeii had running water, carried in by lead pipes under the streets. Public bath complexes used central furnaces to heat the water.

House of the Tragic Poet

Vesuvian gate

Central baths

Temple of Jupiter (Capitol)

Temple of Venus

Government buildings

Stabian baths

Gladiator barracks

FORUM
The Forum was Pompeii's main public space. Crowds gathered to shop in the marketplace, worship at the temples, listen to speeches, or visit government offices and courthouses.

TEMPLE OF ISIS
Ancient Pompeiians participated in a variety of religions. This temple was dedicated to an Egyptian goddess.

Uncovering Pompeii

In December 1860, Victor Emmanuel II, king of the newly united Italy, appointed Giuseppe Fiorelli Director of the Excavations at Pompeii. The era of scientific excavation had begun.

Fiorelli divided the city into quarters, or regions, and gave every block and building a number—a system which is still used today. Archaeologists from all over the world came to see Fiorelli's work at
20 Pompeii.

Slowly and carefully, soil and volcanic debris were removed. The position of every fragment of plaster and brickwork was recorded and then restored to its original place. Charred wood was replaced by fresh timber. **C**

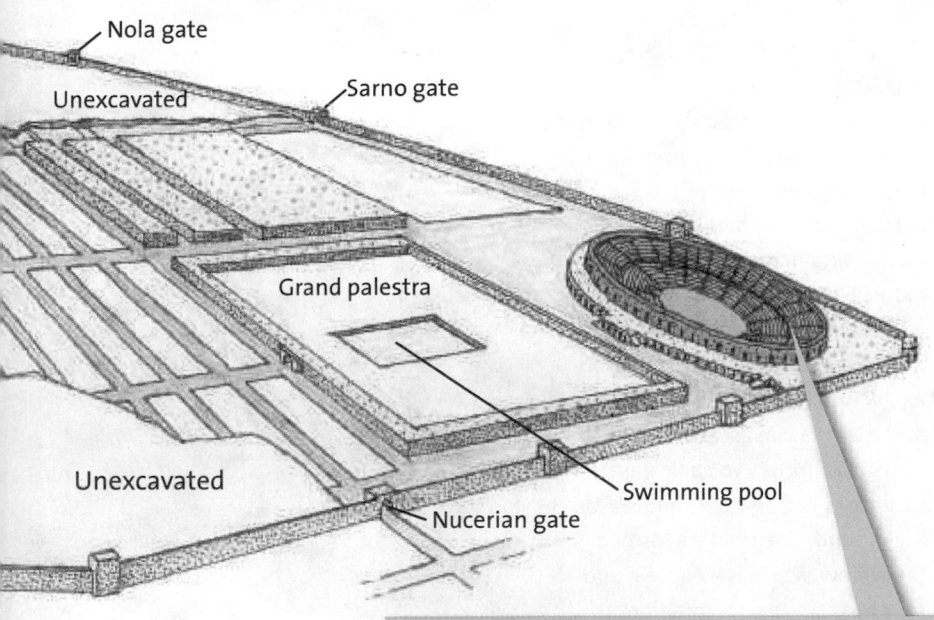

Nola gate
Unexcavated
Sarno gate
Grand palestra
Swimming pool
Unexcavated
Nucerian gate

C MAIN IDEA
The topic of this second section is the excavation of Pompeii. Look at the topic sentence in the last paragraph to help you identify the main idea about the excavation. Record this information in your chart.

AMPHITHEATER
The amphitheater was where thousands of Pompeiians gathered to see gladiators, athletic competitions, and other forms of entertainment.

A Tragic Day

When the volcano Vesuvius erupted on August 24, A.D. 79, it destroyed a rich and thickly populated part of southern Italy. We know this from the archaeological discoveries at Herculaneum and Pompeii. But, more remarkably, we know what the disaster was actually like for the people who lived in the region.

30   The young Roman nobleman Pliny the Younger witnessed the eruption and wrote a letter that is the earliest known account of such a tragedy. As people screamed and struggled to escape the horror, Pliny described the eruption as looking like "a pine tree, for it shot up to a great height in the form of a trunk, which extended itself at the top into several branches." **D**

COMPOSITE VOLCANO

A composite volcano is a cone-shaped volcano built up of layers of lava and layers of rock fragments. Composite volcanoes have violent eruptions for two reasons. First, expanding gases trapped in rising magma tend to cause explosions. Second, hardened lava from earlier eruptions often plugs openings in these volcanoes. This rock must be blown out of the way before any more magma can escape.

During an eruption, volcanic gases can mix with rock fragments and stay near the ground. The mixture forms a pyroclastic flow, which is a dense cloud of superhot gases and rock fragments that races downhill. **E**

Magma Core

A Survivor's Letter

"Ashes now fall upon us, though as yet not in great quantity. I looked behind me; gross darkness pressed upon our rear, and came rolling over the land after us like a torrent . . . darkness overspread us, not like that of a moonless or cloudy night, but of a room when it is shut up, and the lamp is put out. You could hear the shrieks of women, the crying of children, and the shouts of men; some were seeking their children, others their parents, others their wives or husbands . . . one lamenting his own fate, another that of his family . . . many lifting their hands to the gods; but the greater part imagining that there were no gods left and that the last and eternal night was come upon the world." **F**

This description from Pliny the Younger's letter to Tacitus is as vivid now as when he wrote it almost 2,000 years ago.

F AUTHOR'S PURPOSE
Why does the author include this ancient letter from Pliny the Younger? What do you learn from the letter that you can't learn from other sources?

File   Edit   View   Tools   Help

Back   Forward   Stop   Refresh   Home   Search   Favorites   Mail   Print

Italians
Trying to Prevent
a **Modern Pompeii** **G**

by Ellen Hale, USA TODAY

SAN SEBASTIANO AL VESUVIO, Italy — Concerned that too many
people now crowd the sides of the active volcano, authorities here
have launched a bold plan to prevent a repeat of the catastrophic
explosion that wiped out Pompeii and smothered thousands of its
residents nearly 2,000 years ago.

Authorities hope to thin the ranks of residents so they can be
evacuated when Mount Vesuvius erupts again. They are doing this
by offering cash incentives to move, demolishing the illegal buildings
that have sprouted on its flanks, and establishing a national park at
10 its top.

It's only a matter of time before the volcano does erupt, scientists say.

"It won't be tomorrow, it won't be next month, and maybe it
won't be next year. But it is overdue," says Giovanni Macedonio,
director of Vesuvius Observatory, the institute responsible for
monitoring the volcano. When it blows, Macedonio warns, it could
be with the power of "tens of hundreds of atomic bombs."

Vesuvius last erupted in 1944. Lava destroyed some orchards and
homes and 26 people were killed. . . . Residents put pots on their
heads to protect against rocks shooting through the air, but the
20 rumblings soon stilled. Vesuvius has been quiet since. . . .

During the volcano's 60-year slumber, however, sprawl from
nearby Naples has spilled out; nearly 600,000 people now live in
the 18 towns in the shadow of the volcano. **H**

Internet

Comprehension

1. **Recall** According to the online article, how many people could be affected by an eruption of Mount Vesuvius today?

2. **Clarify** Reread page 343. Describe the system Fiorelli used for labeling Pompeii during its excavation.

3. **Summarize** Write a brief summary of the events Pliny the Younger describes in his letter on page 345.

Text Analysis

4. **Make Inferences** Reread the description of composite volcanoes on page 344. What part of the volcano's eruption might Pliny have been describing in his letter? Explain, using details from the text.

5. **Compare Texts** Think about the cultural, historical, and contemporary contexts of "The Dog of Pompeii," *In Search of Pompeii*, and "Italians Trying to Prevent a Modern Pompeii." Then explain why these three texts appear together.

COMMON CORE

RI 2 Determine a central idea of a text. **RI 6** Determine an author's purpose and explain how it is conveyed in the text. **RI 7** Integrate information presented in different media or formats to develop a coherent understanding of a topic. **W 2** Write explanatory texts to examine a topic and convey information through analysis of relevant content.

Read for Information: Author's Purpose and Main Idea

WRITING PROMPT

Write a paragraph that explains the connection between the main ideas of the two selections you just read. Then, explain how each author's purpose for writing is similar or different.

To answer this prompt, take the information you wrote in your chart from page 340 and use it to create two Venn diagrams: one showing similarities and differences in main idea, and the other showing similarities and differences in author's purpose. Follow this example.

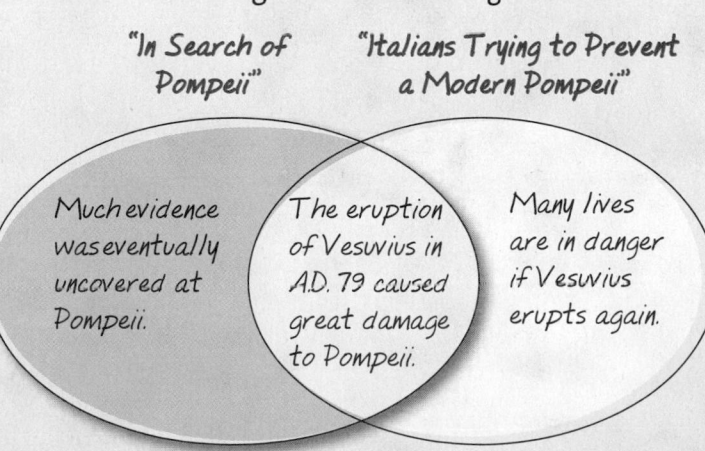

"In Search of Pompeii"

"Italians Trying to Prevent a Modern Pompeii"

Much evidence was eventually uncovered at Pompeii.

The eruption of Vesuvius in A.D. 79 caused great damage to Pompeii.

Many lives are in danger if Vesuvius erupts again.

Nadia the Willful
Short Story by Sue Alexander

Can MEMORIES
keep the past alive?

COMMON CORE

RL 2 Determine a theme or central idea of a text and how it is conveyed through particular details. **RL 3** Describe how the characters change as the plot moves toward a resolution.

Memories are how we hold on to people we have known, places we have been, and things we have done. As time goes by, those memories can fade unless we find ways to keep them fresh. In "Nadia the Willful," a character takes action to make sure that a precious memory will last.

QUICKWRITE Think about a happy or important occasion you want to remember. It might be a wedding, a birthday, or a day spent with friends. Write down some ideas about how you can preserve this memory.

Keeping Memories Alive
1. Take photos
2. Make a scrapbook

TEXT ANALYSIS: CONFLICT AND THEME

Most stories are built around a **conflict,** a struggle between opposing forces. The struggle might be with someone else, with nature, or even within the character, such as overcoming a fear. Writers often use the actions of their characters to communicate theme. To see how conflict relates to a story's theme, ask yourself the following questions:

- What conflicts does the character face?
- How does the character respond to these conflicts?
- How are the conflicts resolved?

As you read "Nadia the Willful," notice these conflicts and what they help you infer about the story's theme.

READING SKILL: COMPARE AND CONTRAST CHARACTERS

Comparing and contrasting characters can help you better understand a story. For example, in "Nadia the Willful," Nadia shares some traits with her family and members of her community. Other parts of Nadia's personality are unique.

As you read the story, use a graphic organizer like the one shown to record similarities and differences between Nadia, Tarik, and Hamed.

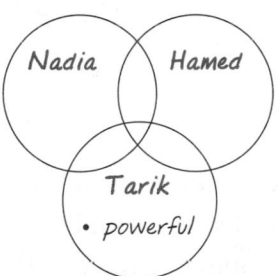

▲ VOCABULARY IN CONTEXT

Sue Alexander uses the following words to help tell how one family deals with sorrow. To see how many words you know, rewrite each sentence using a different word or phrase in place of the boldfaced vocabulary word.

WORD LIST	banish	clan	console	graciousness

1. Nadia lives in a close-knit family **clan.**
2. Her father's **graciousness** fades away in his sorrow.
3. She wants someone to **console** her after her brother's death.
4. Nadia does not want her father to **banish** anyone.

 Complete the activities in your **Reader/Writer Notebook.**

Meet the Author

Sue Alexander
1933–2008

Writing from Life
Sue Alexander wrote "Nadia the Willful" to express her sadness about the death of her own brother. She was afraid that if she set the story in the present day, it would be too painful to write. She knew that it "would have to take place somewhere far away, preferably in another culture." The story took about four months to write, except for the first paragraph, which took much longer. Alexander says, "I must have rewritten it 50 times before I found the right words for that paragraph."

BACKGROUND TO THE STORY
The Sahara Desert
The Sahara, which is the setting for this story, is the largest desert in the world. It is located in northern Africa and covers about 3.5 million square miles—an area about as large as the United States. It is sometimes called "the sea without water." Food and water are scarce, sandstorms are common, and temperatures can reach 130° Fahrenheit during the day. Despite its harsh climate, the Sahara supports approximately 2.5 million people, as well as many different kinds of plants and animals.

Author Online

THINK central

Go to **thinkcentral.com.**
KEYWORD: HML6-349

349

NADIA
the Willful

Sue Alexander

In the land of the drifting sands where the Bedouin move their tents to follow the fertile grasses, there lived a girl whose stubbornness and flashing temper caused her to be known throughout the desert as Nadia the Willful.

Nadia's father, the sheik[1] Tarik, whose kindness and **graciousness** caused his name to be praised in every tent, did not know what to do with his willful daughter.

Only Hamed, the eldest of Nadia's six brothers and Tarik's favorite son, could calm Nadia's temper when it flashed.

10 "Oh, angry one," he would say, "shall we see how long you can stay that way?" And he would laugh and tease and pull at her dark hair until she laughed back. Then she would follow Hamed wherever he led.

One day before dawn, Hamed mounted his father's great white stallion and rode to the west to seek new grazing ground for the sheep. Nadia stood with her father at the edge of the oasis[2] and watched him go.

Hamed did not return.

---

1. **sheik** (shēk): a leader of an Arab family or village.
2. **oasis:** a fertile or green spot in a desert or wasteland, made so by the presence of water.

Analyze Visuals ▶

What can you **infer** about the girl in this image?

graciousness
(grā'shəs-nəs) *n.* the condition of being pleasant, courteous, and generous

A **COMPARE AND CONTRAST**
Reread lines 8–12. What do you learn about the personalities of Nadia and Hamed?

Nadia rode behind her father as he traveled across the desert from oasis to oasis, seeking Hamed.

20 Shepherds told them of seeing a great white stallion fleeing before the pillars of wind that stirred the sand. And they said that the horse carried no rider.

Passing merchants, their camels laden with spices and sweets for the bazaar,[3] told of the emptiness of the desert they had crossed.

Tribesmen, strangers, everyone whom Tarik asked, sighed and gazed into the desert, saying, "Such is the will of Allah."[4]

At last Tarik knew in his heart that his favorite son, Hamed, had been claimed, as other Bedouin before him, by the drifting sands. And he told Nadia what he knew—that Hamed was dead.

30 Nadia screamed and wept and stamped the sand, crying, "Not even Allah will take Hamed from me!" until her father could bear no more and sternly bade her to silence.

Nadia's grief knew no bounds. She walked blindly through the oasis, neither seeing nor hearing those who would **console** her. And Tarik was silent. For days he sat inside his tent, speaking not at all and barely tasting the meals set before him.

Then, on the seventh day, Tarik came out of his tent. He called all his people to him, and when they were assembled, he spoke. "From this day forward," he said, "let no one utter Hamed's name. Punishment shall be swift for those who would remind me of what I have lost."

40 Hamed's mother wept at the decree. The people of the **clan** looked at one another uneasily. All could see the hardness that had settled on the sheik's face and the coldness in his eyes, and so they said nothing. But they obeyed.

Nadia, too, did as her father decreed, though each day held something to remind her of Hamed. As she passed her brothers at play, she remembered games Hamed had taught her. As she walked by the women weaving patches for the tents and heard them talking and laughing, she remembered tales Hamed had told her and how they had made her laugh. And as she watched the shepherds with their flock, she remembered the 50 little black lamb Hamed had loved.

Each memory brought Hamed's name to Nadia's lips, but she stilled the sound. And each time that she did so, her unhappiness grew until, finally, she could no longer contain it. She wept and raged at anyone and anything that crossed her path. Soon everyone at the oasis fled at her approach. And she was more lonely than she had ever been before. **C**

---

3. **bazaar** (bə-zär′): in Middle Eastern countries, an outdoor market of small shops.

4. **Allah** (ăl′ə): the name for God in the Islamic religion.

SOCIAL STUDIES CONNECTION

The Bedouin are a tribe of people who live in the deserts of Africa and the Middle East. They are nomads, or wanderers, who live in tents and move from place to place seeking pasture for their livestock.

console (kən-sōl′) *v.* to ease someone's sorrow; to comfort

B COMPARE AND CONTRAST
Note the similarities and differences between how Nadia and Tarik react to Hamed's death.

clan (klăn) *n.* a family group; a group united by common interests or qualities

C CONFLICT AND THEME
Reread lines 51–55. What conflict does Tarik's decree cause for Nadia?

One day, as Nadia passed the place where her brothers were playing, she stopped to watch them. They were playing one of the games that Hamed had taught her. But they were playing it wrong.

Without thinking, Nadia called out to them. "That is not the way!
60 Hamed said that first you jump this way and then you jump back!"

Her brothers stopped their game and looked around in fear. Had Tarik heard Nadia say Hamed's name? But the sheik was nowhere to be seen.

"Teach us, Nadia, as our brother taught you," said her smallest brother.

And so she did. Then she told them of other games and how Hamed had taught her to play them. And as she spoke of Hamed, she felt an easing of the hurt within her. ◆

So she went on speaking of him.

She went to where the women sat at their loom⁵ and spoke of Hamed.

---

5. **loom:** a tool used for making thread or yarn into cloth by weaving strands together at right angles.

◆ GRAMMAR IN CONTEXT
Reread lines 64–66. Although the author could have combined the sentences in this paragraph, she chose not to. This is part of her unique style. Why else do you think the author has chosen not to combine sentences that share the same subject?

She told them tales that Hamed had told her. And she told how he had
70 made her laugh as he was telling them.

At first the women were afraid to listen to the willful girl and covered
their ears, but after a time, they listened and laughed with her.

"Remember your father's promise of punishment!" Nadia's mother
warned when she heard Nadia speaking of Hamed. "Cease, I implore you!"

Nadia knew that her mother had reason to be afraid, for Tarik, in his
grief and bitterness, had grown quick-tempered and sharp of tongue. But
she did not know how to tell her mother that speaking of Hamed eased
the pain she felt, and so she said only, "I will speak of my brother! I will!"
And she ran away from the sound of her mother's voice. **D**

80 She went to where the shepherds tended the flock and spoke of Hamed.
The shepherds ran from her in fear and hid behind the sheep. But Nadia
went on speaking. She told of Hamed's love for the little black lamb and
how he had taught it to leap at his whistle. Soon the shepherds left off
their hiding and came to listen. Then they told their own stories of
Hamed and the little black lamb.

COMMON CORE RL 2

D **CONFLICT AND THEME**
Writers often use conflict to **imply,** or hint at a story's theme. Reread lines 69–79. How has Nadia changed her response to Tarik's order?

The more Nadia spoke of Hamed, the clearer his face became in her mind. She could see his smile and the light in his eyes. She could hear his voice. And the clearer Hamed's voice and face became, the less Nadia hurt inside and the less her temper flashed. At last, she was filled with peace.

90 But her mother was still afraid for her willful daughter. Again and again she sought to quiet Nadia so that Tarik's bitterness would not be turned against her. And again and again Nadia tossed her head and went on speaking of Hamed.

Soon, all who listened could see Hamed's face clearly before them.

One day, the youngest shepherd came to Nadia's tent, calling, "Come, Nadia! See Hamed's black lamb; it has grown so big and strong!"

But it was not Nadia who came out of the tent.

It was Tarik.

On the sheik's face was a look more fierce than that of a desert hawk, 100 and when he spoke, his words were as sharp as a scimitar.[6]

"I have forbidden my son's name to be said. And I promised punishment to whoever disobeyed my command. So shall it be. Before the sun sets and the moon casts its first shadow on the sand, you will be gone from this oasis—never to return."

"No!" cried Nadia, hearing her father's words.

"I have spoken!" roared the sheik. "It shall be done!" **E**

Trembling, the shepherd went to gather his possessions.

And the rest of the clan looked at one another uneasily and muttered among themselves.

110 In the hours that followed, fear of being **banished** to the desert made everyone turn away from Nadia as she tried to tell them of Hamed and the things he had done and said.

And the less she was listened to, the less she was able to recall Hamed's face and voice. And the less she recalled, the more her temper raged within her, destroying the peace she had found. **F**

By evening, she could stand it no longer. She went to where her father sat, staring into the desert, and stood before him.

"You will not rob me of my brother Hamed!" she cried, stamping her foot. "I will not let you!"

120 Tarik looked at her, his eyes colder than the desert night.

But before he could utter a word, Nadia spoke again. "Can you recall Hamed's face? Can you still hear his voice?"

Tarik started in surprise, and his answer seemed to come unbidden to his lips. "No, I cannot! Day after day I have sat in this spot where I last

Language Coach
Pronouncing mb
When you say the word *lamb* (line 96), the *b* is silent. This is true of any word that ends in *mb*. When the letters *mb* are in the middle of a word, such as *crumble*, you hear the sounds of both letters. Try pronouncing the following words aloud: *bombard, comb, combine.*

E COMPARE AND CONTRAST
Reread lines 101–106. Note Tarik's attitude in this passage. In what way does Tarik's response remind you of Nadia?

banish (băn'ĭsh) v. to send away; to exile

F CONFLICT AND THEME
What effect does the shepherd's punishment have on the clan and on Nadia?

---

6. **scimitar** (sĭm'ĭ-tər): an Asian sword with a curved cutting edge.

saw Hamed, trying to remember the look, the sound, the happiness that was my beloved son—but I cannot."

And he wept.

Nadia's tone became gentle. "There is a way, honored father," she said. "Listen."

130 And she began to speak of Hamed. She told of walks she and Hamed had taken and of talks they had had. She told how he had taught her games, told her tales, and calmed her when she was angry. She told many things that she remembered, some happy and some sad.

And when she was done with the telling, she said gently, "Can you not recall him now, Father? Can you not see his face? Can you not hear his voice?"

Tarik nodded through his tears, and for the first time since Hamed had been gone, he smiled. **G**

"Now you see," Nadia said, her tone more gentle than the softest of the
140 desert breezes, "there is a way that Hamed can be with us still."

The sheik pondered what Nadia had said. After a long time, he spoke, and the sharpness was gone from his voice.

"Tell my people to come before me, Nadia," he said. "I have something to say to them."

When all were assembled, Tarik said, "From this day forward, let my daughter Nadia be known not as willful, but as wise. And let her name be praised in every tent, for she has given me back my beloved son."

And so it was. The shepherd returned to his flock, kindness and graciousness returned to the oasis, and Nadia's name was praised in
150 every tent. And Hamed lived again—in the hearts of all who remembered him. ❧

G COMPARE AND CONTRAST
Reread lines 130–138. Does this passage show more of Nadia and Tarik's similarities or their differences? Explain.

Comprehension

1. **Recall** What is Hamed doing when he disappears?

2. **Clarify** Why does Tarik forbid his people to talk about Hamed?

3. **Summarize** What happens to make Tarik send the shepherd away?

Text Analysis

4. **Make Inferences** Reread lines 145–147. What does Tarik mean when he says that Nadia "has given me back my beloved son"?

5. **Compare and Contrast Characters** Look again at the graphic organizer you filled in as you read. Think about Nadia's and Tarik's personalities, attitudes, reactions, and roles in the story. Are they more similar or more different? Support your conclusions with examples from the story.

6. **Analyze Conflict and Theme** Recall that conflict often helps express a story's implicit theme. Use a chart like the one shown to explore the conflict in "Nadia the Willful." Then write a theme statement for the story.

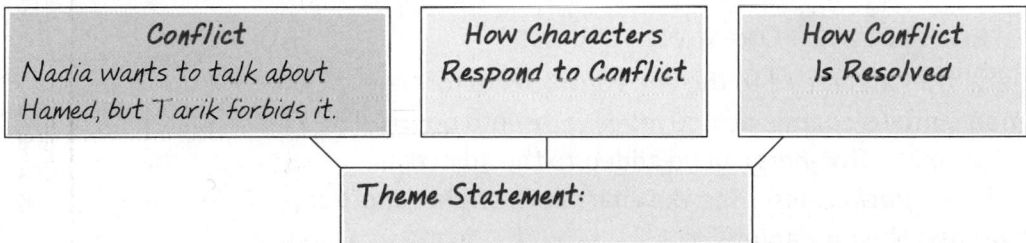

Conflict	How Characters	How Conflict
Nadia wants to talk about	Respond to Conflict	Is Resolved
Hamed, but Tarik forbids it.		

Theme Statement:

7. **Evaluate Theme** A theme is more than just the author's opinion. It should also express an idea about human nature. Does Sue Alexander's message about memories work well as a theme? Explain why or why not.

Extension and Challenge

8. **Speaking and Listening** Nadia found that the best way to keep her brother's memory alive was to tell stories about him. With a partner, create your own memorable stories. Take turns interviewing each other about interesting parts of your lives. Then choose two stories to share with the class.

9. **SOCIAL STUDIES CONNECTION** Modern life threatens the traditional lifestyle of the nomadic Bedouin. Research how the Bedouin way of life has changed over time. What traditions have they been able to keep?

Can MEMORIES keep the past alive?

What memories do you cherish? Why are they special to you?

COMMON CORE

RL 2 Determine a theme or central idea of a text and how it is conveyed through particular details. **RL 3** Describe how the characters change as the plot moves toward a resolution. **W7** Conduct short research projects to answer a question.

Vocabulary in Context

▲ VOCABULARY PRACTICE

Choose the letter of the word or phrase that means about the same as each boldfaced vocabulary word.

1. member of the **clan**: (a) neighborhood, (b) troop, (c) club, (d) family
2. **console** the sad child: (a) punish, (b) comfort, (c) praise, (d) tease
3. the host's **graciousness**: (a) idea, (b) kindness, (c) schedule, (d) memory
4. **banish** the traitor: (a) force out, (b) catch, (c) trick, (d) ignore

ACADEMIC VOCABULARY IN WRITING

| • attitude | • communicate | • context | • illustrate | • implicit |

Write a paragraph in which you state whether you agree or disagree with Nadia's decision to defy Tarik's order never to speak Hamed's name. Do you think she was justified in disobeying her father? Use at least two Academic Vocabulary words in your response.

VOCABULARY STRATEGY: NOUN-FORMING SUFFIXES

Suffixes are word parts that are added to the ends of words to form new words. Many common suffixes change adjectives or verbs into nouns. For example, the noun-forming suffix *-ness* can be added to the adjective *gracious* to form the noun *graciousness*. See the chart at the right for other noun-forming suffixes and their meanings.

When you read words with these suffixes, use their base words to figure out their meanings. Remember that when a suffix is added sometimes a final *e* is dropped from the base word, or a final letter is changed. For instance, *y* may change to *i*.

PRACTICE Identify the base word and noun-forming suffix in each boldfaced word. Then write a definition of the word.

1. People in charge of **security** in an airport seldom stand out from the crowd.
2. The coach told me not to worry if the **accuracy** of my fastball was a little off.
3. The principal made an **announcement** about the school's new lunchroom policy.
4. Jack's **outrageousness** caused the teacher to punish our whole class.
5. Their **partnership** lasted for many years.

⁙ **COMMON CORE**

L 4b Use common affixes as clues to the meaning of a word.

Suffixes	Meanings
-cy	state of; quality of being
-dom	
-ity	
-ment	
-ness	
-ship	

Interactive Vocabulary

THINK central

Go to **thinkcentral.com**.
KEYWORD: HML6-358

Language

COMMON CORE

L 3a Vary sentence patterns for style. **W 2** Write informative/explanatory texts to convey ideas.

◆ **GRAMMAR IN CONTEXT:** Combine Sentences

If your sentences seem choppy or repetitious, you may want to try combining them. Look for two sentences that have the same subject or **predicate** (what the subject does). If the sentences share a subject, delete the subject from the second sentence. Then insert a word such as *and, or,* or *but* to combine the two predicates. If the sentences share a predicate, delete the predicate from the second sentence. Then combine the two subjects.

> *Original:* Hamed made me happy. Hamed calmed my temper.
>
> *Revised:* Hamed made me happy and calmed my temper. (*Use and to form one sentence with two predicates.*)

PRACTICE Combine the sentences in each item.

1. "Nadia the Willful" discusses the topic of grief. "Nadia the Willful" demonstrates the power of memory.
2. Nadia cried when Hamed died. Her mother cried when Hamed died.
3. Nadia often behaves stubbornly. Nadia treats people nicely sometimes.
4. She traveled in the desert. Tarik traveled in the desert.

*For more help with compound subjects and predicates, see page R60 in the **Grammar Handbook.***

READING-WRITING CONNECTION

YOUR TURN

Broaden your understanding of "Nadia the Willful" by responding to this prompt. Then use the **revising tip** to improve your writing.

WRITING PROMPT	**REVISING TIP**
Short Constructed Response: Analysis Hamed's death begins a long chain of events that results in changes for the entire clan. In **one paragraph,** explain the effect that each event after Hamed's death has on the members of his clan.	Review your response. Can you combine any sentences? If so, revise your writing.

Interactive Revision

Go to **thinkcentral.com**.
KEYWORD: HML6-359

Scout's Honor
Short Story by Avi

VIDEO TRAILER **THINK** central KEYWORD: HML6-360

When is a trip an ADVENTURE?

COMMON CORE

RL 2 Determine a theme or central idea of a text and how it is conveyed through particular details. **RL 3** Describe how the characters change as the plot moves toward a resolution.

When we think of an adventure, we usually think of something big, like an African safari. But even a trip across town can be an adventure if you're going somewhere you've never been before. In the short story "Scout's Honor," three boys get more adventure than they bargained for when they try to earn a merit badge from their Boy Scout troop.

SKETCH IT How could a simple trip—a visit to a distant relative or friend, for example—become an adventure? Think about what might happen and who you might meet along the way. Sketch a timeline with labels to show how you imagine your potential adventure.

● TEXT ANALYSIS: CHARACTER AND THEME

When you read a story, you often feel as though you are experiencing the events along with its **characters.** Characters can often help reveal the **theme,** or implict message about life, that a writer wishes to share with the reader. You can find clues to the theme in

- what the characters say and do
- what lessons the characters learn
- whether the characters change in any way

As you read "Scout's Honor," study the characters to see how they help express the story's theme or central idea.

● READING STRATEGY: PREDICT

Predicting what will happen next is one of the things that makes reading exciting. When you **predict,** you use details and clues from a story to make a reasonable guess about events in the story that haven't happened yet.

As you read, use a graphic organizer like the one shown to record important details and clues. Use the clues to make predictions about that will happen next in the story.

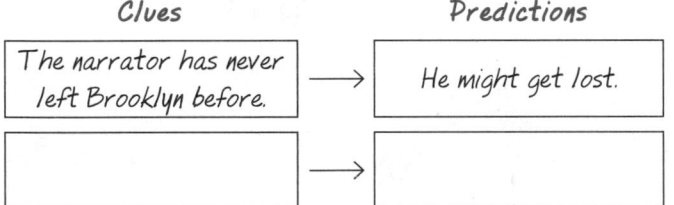

Clues	Predictions
The narrator has never left Brooklyn before. →	He might get lost.
→	

▲ VOCABULARY IN CONTEXT

Avi uses the words listed here to help tell the story of a camping adventure. To see how many you know, place each word under the heading "Know Well," "Think I Know," or "Don't Know." Then, write a brief definition of each word you know.

WORD	congeal	khaki	retrieve
LIST	discard	retort	simultaneously

Know Well	Think I Know	Don't Know

 Complete the activities in your **Reader/Writer Notebook.**

Avi
born 1937

A Struggle to Write
From an early age, Avi loved reading. Writing, however, was difficult for him. He had trouble with English classes in school, and some of his teachers thought he was not intelligent. Avi received failing grades at his first high school, but when he switched schools he was given a writing tutor. Avi recalls that the tutor told him, "You know, you're really very interesting. If you wrote better, people would know about it." From that point on, Avi says, "I wanted to write."

Learning from His Mistakes
As an adult, Avi discovered that his problems with writing were partially caused by a learning disability called *dysgraphia* (dĭs-grăf'ē-ə). People with dysgraphia reverse letters, misspell words, and confuse left and right. Now, Avi often shows his book manuscripts, "which are covered in red marks," to students with learning disabilities. He hopes that by showing students that even a best-selling author makes mistakes, he might inspire them to believe that they, too, can write. He discovered his true audience when he became a father and started writing for children and young adults.

Author Online
THINK central
Go to **thinkcentral.com.**
KEYWORD: HML6-361

Scout's Honor

Avi

Back in 1946, when I was nine, I worried that I wasn't tough enough. That's why I became a Boy Scout. Scouting, I thought, would make a man of me. It didn't take long to reach Tenderfoot rank. You got that for joining. To move up to Second Class, however, you had to meet three requirements. Scout Spirit and Scout Participation had been cinchy. The third requirement, Scout Craft, meant I had to go on an overnight hike in the *country*. In other words, I had to leave Brooklyn, on my own, for the first time in my life.

Since I grew up in Brooklyn in the 1940s, the only grass I knew was in
10 Ebbets Field[1] where the Dodgers played. Otherwise, my world was made of slate pavements, streets of asphalt (or cobblestone), and skies full of tall buildings. The only thing "country" was a puny pin oak tree at our curb, which was noticed, mostly, by dogs. **A**

---

1. **Ebbets Field:** The Los Angeles Dodgers were the Brooklyn Dodgers until the late 1950s. They played in the Ebbets Field stadium.

Analyze Visuals ▶

What sense do you get of Brooklyn from the **details** in this painting?

A PREDICT
Reread lines 7–13. Make a prediction about how easy camping will be for the narrator.

11th Floor Water Towers Looking East (2005), Sonya Sklaroff. Oil on panel, 48″ × 48″. Private Collection. © 2005 Sonya Sklaroff. www.goartonline.com.

I asked Scoutmaster Brenkman where I could find some country. Now, whenever I saw Mr. Brenkman, who was a church pastor, he was dressed either in church black or Scout **khaki.** When he wore black, he'd warn us against hellfire. When he wore khaki, he'd teach us how to build fires.

"Country," Scoutmaster Brenkman said in answer to my question, "is
20 anywhere that has lots of trees and is not in the city. Many boys camp in the Palisades."

"Where's that?"

"Just north of the city. It's a park in Jersey."

"Isn't that a zillion miles from here?"

"Take the subway to the George Washington Bridge, then hike across."

I thought for a moment, then asked, "How do I prove I went?"

Mr. Brenkman looked deeply shocked. "You wouldn't *lie,* would you? What about Scout's honor?"

30 "Yes, sir," I replied meekly.

My two best friends were Philip Hossfender, whom we nicknamed Horse, and Richard Macht, called Max because we were not great spellers. They were also Scouts, Tenderfoots like me.

Horse was a skinny little kid about half my size whose way of arguing was to ball up his fist and say, "Are you saying . . . ?" in a threatening tone.

Max was on the pudgy side, but he could talk his way out of a locked room. More importantly, he always seemed to have pocket money, which gave his talk real power.

40 I wasn't sure why, but being best friends meant we were rivals too. One of the reasons for my wanting to be tougher was a feeling that Horse was a lot tougher than I was, and that Max was a little tougher.

"I'm going camping in the Palisades next weekend," I casually informed them.

"How come?" Max challenged.

"Scout Craft," I replied.

"Oh, *that,*" Horse said with a shrug.

"Look," I said, "I don't know about you, but I don't intend to be a Tenderfoot all my life. Anyway, doing stuff in the city is for sissies.
50 Scouting is real camping. Besides, I like roughing it."

"You saying I don't?" Horse snapped.

"I'm not saying nothing," I said.

khaki (kăk′ē) *n.* cloth made of light yellowish brown cotton or wool

SOCIAL STUDIES CONNECTION

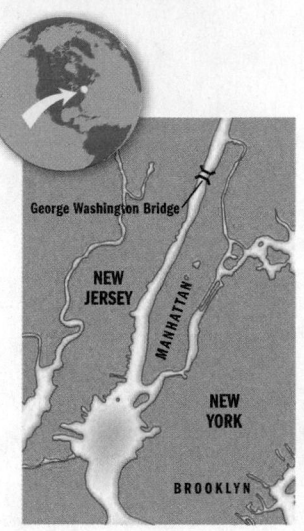

Brooklyn is one of New York City's five major sections, or boroughs. It is located south of Manhattan.

B PREDICT
What do you predict will happen? Record this and your other predictions in your graphic organizer.

Lafayette Street Morning (2005), Lisbeth Firmin. Oil on panel, 16″ × 16″. Courtesy of Klaudia Marr Gallery, Santa Fe, New Mexico.

◀ **Analyze Visuals**

Explain in what ways this painting does or does not match your mental picture of the narrator leaving for his camping trip.

They considered my idea. Finally, Horse said, "Yeah, well, I was going to do that, but I didn't think you guys were ready for it." **C**

"I've been ready for *years*," Max protested.

"Then we're going, right?" I said.

They looked around at me. "If you can do it, I can do it," Max said.

"Yeah," Horse said thoughtfully.

The way they agreed made me nervous. Now I really was going to have
60 to be tough.

We informed our folks that we were going camping overnight (which was true) and that the Scoutmaster was going with us—which was a lie. We did remember what Mr. Brenkman said about honesty, but we were baseball fans too, and since we were prepared to follow Scout law—being loyal, helpful, friendly, courteous, kind, obedient, cheerful, thrifty, brave, clean, *and* reverent—we figured a 900 batting average[2] was not bad. **D**

C **CHARACTER AND THEME**

Avi uses a conversational voice that makes the dialogue in lines 31–54 seem realistic. What do you learn about Horse and Max based on what they say?

D **PREDICT**

Why do the boys think it is okay that they are telling a lie? What does this lead you to predict about how the adventure will turn out? Why?

---

2. **900 batting average:** In baseball, a batting average is the number of times a batter gets a hit compared to the number of times he bats. A batting average of .900 is nearly perfect, since it means the batter gets a hit 90% of the time. The boys use this term to mean that since they have followed most of Scout law, they are above-average Scouts, even if they tell a lie.

So Saturday morning we met at the High Street subway station. I got there first. Stuffed in my dad's army surplus knapsack was a blanket, a pillow, and a paper bag with three white-bread peanut-butter-and-jelly sandwiches—that is, lunch, supper, and Sunday breakfast. My pockets were full of stick matches. I had an old flashlight, and since I lived by the Scout motto—Be Prepared—I had brought along an umbrella. Finally, being a serious reader, I had the latest Marvel Family comics.

Horse arrived next, his arms barely managing to hold on to a mattress that seemed twice his size. As for food, he had four cans of beans jammed into his pockets.

Max came last. He was lugging a new knapsack that contained a cast-iron frying pan, a packet of hot dogs, and a box of saltine crackers—plus two bottles. One bottle was mustard, the other, celery soda. He also had a bag of Tootsie Rolls and a shiny hatchet. "To build a lean-to,"[3] he explained.

Max's prize possession, however, was an official Scout compass. "It's really swell," he told us. "You can't ever get lost with it. Got it at the Scout store."

"I hate that place," Horse informed us. "It's all new. Nothing real."

"This compass is real," Max **retorted.** "Points north all the time. You can get cheaper ones, but they point all different directions."

"What's so great about the north?" Horse said.

"That's always the way to go," Max insisted. **E**

"Says who?" I demanded.

"Mr. Brenkman, dummy," Horse cried. "Anyway, there's always an arrow on maps pointing the way north."

"Cowboys live out west," I reminded them. They didn't care.

On the subway platform, we realized we did not know which station we were heading for. To find out, we studied the system map, which looked like a noodle factory hit by a bomb. The place we wanted to go (north) was at the top of the map, so I had to hoist Horse onto my shoulders for a closer look. Since he refused to let go of his mattress—or the tin cans in his pockets—it wasn't easy. I asked him—in a kindly fashion—to put the mattress down.

No sooner did he find the station—168th Street—than our train arrived. We rushed on, only to have Horse scream, "My mattress!" He had left it on the platform. Just before the doors shut, he and I leaped off. Max, however, remained on the train. Helplessly, we watched as his

VISUAL
VOCABULARY

compass *n.* a device used to determine geographic direction

retort (rĭ-tôrt′) *v.* to reply, especially in a quick or unkind way

E PREDICT
The boys feel that they are prepared with enough food and supplies for their trip. How effective do you predict the boys' camping gear will be?

---

3. **lean-to:** a shelter with a flat, sloping roof.

horror-stricken face slid away from us. "Wait at the next station!" I bellowed. "Don't move!"

The next train took forever to come. Then it took even longer to get
110 to the next stop. There was Max. All around him—like fake snow in a glass ball—were crumbs. He'd been so nervous he had eaten all his crackers.

"Didn't that make you thirsty?"

"I drank my soda."

I noticed streaks down his cheeks. Horse noticed them too. "You been crying?" he asked.

"Naw," Max said. "There was this water dripping from the tunnel roof. But, you said don't move, right? Well, I was just being obedient."

By the time we got on the next train—with all our possessions—we
120 had been traveling for an hour. But we had managed to go only one stop.

During the ride, I got hungry. I pulled out one of my sandwiches. With the jelly soaked through the bread, it looked like a limp scab.

Horse, envious, complained *he* was getting hungry.

"Eat some of your canned beans," I suggested.

He got out one can without ripping his pocket too badly. Then his face took on a mournful look.

"What's the matter?" I asked.

"Forgot to bring a can opener."

Max said, "In the old days, people opened cans with their teeth."
130 "You saying my teeth aren't strong?"

"I'm just talking about history!"

"You saying I don't know history?"

Always kind, I plopped half my sandwich into Horse's hand. He squashed it into his mouth and was quiet for the next fifteen minutes. It proved something I'd always believed: The best way to stop arguments is to get people to eat peanut butter sandwiches. They can't talk.

Then we became so absorbed in our Marvel Family comics we missed our station. We got to it only by coming back the other way. When we reached street level, the sky was dark.
140 "I knew it," Max announced. "It's going to rain."

"Don't worry," Horse said. "New Jersey is a whole other state. It probably won't be raining there."

"I brought an umbrella," I said smugly, though I wanted it to sound helpful.

As we marched down 168th Street, heading for the George Washington Bridge, we looked like European war refugees.[4] Every few paces, Horse

Language Coach

Regionalisms When Max refers to his drink as a *soda* in line 114, he is using a **regionalism**—a word or phrase that is used mainly by people from a certain region, or part of the country. Bubbly soft drinks are called *sodas* in northeastern United States and California, *pop* in most states north of Texas and west of New York, *Cokes* in Texas and most parts of the South, and *tonics* in Boston. What other regionalisms can you think of?

---

4. **European war refugees:** people who fled Europe to escape World War II (1939–1945) and its effects.

cried, "Hold it!" and adjusted his arms around his mattress. Each time we paused, Max pulled out his compass, peered at it, then announced, "Heading north!"

150   I said, "The bridge goes from east to west."

"Maybe the bridge does," Max insisted with a show of his compass, "but guaranteed, *we* are going north."

About then, the heel of my left foot, encased in a heavy rubber boot over an earth-crushing Buster Brown shoe, started to get sore. Things weren't going as I had hoped. Cheerfully, I tried to ignore the pain.

The closer we drew to the bridge, the more immense it seemed. And the clouds had become so thick, you couldn't see the top or the far side.

Max eyed the bridge with deep suspicion. "I'm not so sure we should go," he said. **F**

160   "Why?"

"Maybe it doesn't have another side."

We looked at him.

"No, seriously," Max explained, "they could have taken the Jersey side away, you know, for repairs."

F PREDICT
What do you predict the boys will do at this point?

Detail of *The George Washington Bridge Seen from the Upper West Side,* (ca. 1940), Louis Aston Knight. Oil on board, 10.8″ × 17″. Photo courtesy of Spanierman Gallery, LLC, New York.

▲ **Analyze Visuals**

What **mood**, or feeling, do the colors in this painting create?

"Cars are going across," I pointed out.

"They could be dropping off," he suggested.

"You would hear them splash," Horse argued.

"I'm going," I said. Trying to look brave, I started off on my own. My bravery didn't last long. The walkway was narrow. When I looked down, 170 I saw only fog. I could feel the bridge tremble and sway. It wasn't long before I was convinced the bridge was about to collapse. Then a ray of hope struck me: Maybe the other guys had chickened out. If they had, I could quit because of *them*. I glanced back. My heart sank. They were coming. **G**

After they caught up, Horse looked me in the eye and said, "If this bridge falls, I'm going to kill you."

A quarter of a mile farther across, I gazed around. We were completely fogged in.

"I think we're lost," I announced.

180 "What do we do?" Horse whispered. His voice was jagged with panic. That made me feel better.

"Don't worry," Max said. "I've got my compass." He pulled it out.

"North is that way," he said, pointing in the direction we had been going.

G CHARACTER AND THEME

Reread lines 158–174. In what ways do the boys try to hide their fear from one another?

Horse said, "You sure?"

"A Scout compass never lies," Max insisted.

"*We* lied," I reminded him.

"Yeah, but this is an *official* Scout compass," Max returned loyally.

"Come on," Max said and marched forward. Horse and I followed. In moments, we crossed a metal bar on the walkway. On one side, a sign
190 proclaimed: NEW YORK; on the other, it said: NEW JERSEY.

"Holy smoke,"[5] Horse said with reverence as he straddled the bar. "Talk about being tough. We're in two states at the same time."

It began to rain. Max said, "Maybe it'll keep us clean."

"You saying I'm not clean?" Horse shot back.

Ever friendly, I put up my umbrella.

We went on—Max on one side, Horse on the other, me in the middle—trying to avoid the growing puddles. After a while, Max said, "Would you move the umbrella? Rain is coming down my neck."

"We're supposed to be roughing it," I said.
200 "Being in the middle isn't roughing it," Horse reminded me.

I folded the umbrella up so we all could get soaked equally. **H**

"Hey!" I cried. "Look!" Staring up ahead, I could make out tollbooths[6] and the dim outlines of buildings.

---

5. **Holy smoke:** an old slang expression meaning "My goodness."

6. **tollbooths:** booths at which drivers must stop to pay a toll, or small fee.

H **CHARACTER AND THEME**
Reread lines 195–201. What do the boys' definitions of "roughing it" tell you about them?

▼ **Analyze Visuals**
What **details** do you notice in this depiction of a campsite?

Tent (1984), Christopher Brown. Oil on canvas, 72″ × 96″. Private collection.

"Last one off the bridge is a rotten egg!" Horse shouted and began to run. The next second, he tripped and took off like an F-36 fighter plane. Unfortunately, he landed like a Hell-cat dive-bomber[7] as his mattress unspooled before him and then slammed into a big puddle.

Max and I ran to help. Horse was damp. His mattress was soaked. When he tried to roll it up, water cascaded like Niagara Falls. ◆

210 "Better leave it," Max said.

"It's what I sleep on at home," Horse said as he slung the soaking, dripping mass over his shoulder.

When we got off the bridge, we were in a small plaza. To the left was the roadway, full of roaring cars. In front of us, aside from the highway, there was nothing but buildings. Only to the right were there trees.

"North is that way," Max said, pointing toward the trees. We set off.

"How come you're limping?" Horse asked me. My foot *was* killing me. All I said, though, was, "How come you keep rubbing your arm?"

220 "I'm keeping the blood moving."

We approached the grove of trees. "Wow," Horse exclaimed. "Country." But as we drew closer, what we found were **discarded** cans, bottles, and newspapers—plus an old mattress spring.

"Hey," Max cried, sounding relieved, "this is just like Brooklyn." ❶

I said, "Let's find a decent place, make camp, and eat."

It was hard to find a campsite that didn't have junk. The growing dark didn't help. We had to settle for the place that had the least amount of garbage.

Max said, "If we build a lean-to, it'll keep us out of the rain." He and

230 Horse went a short distance with the hatchet.

Seeing a tree they wanted, Max whacked at it. The hatchet bounced right out of his hand. There was not even a dent in the tree. Horse **retrieved** the hatchet and checked the blade. "Dull," he said.

"Think I'm going to carry something sharp and cut myself?" Max protested. They contented themselves with picking up branches.

I went in search of firewood, but everything was wet. When I finally gathered some twigs and tried to light them, the only thing that burned was my fingers.

Meanwhile, Horse and Max used their branches to build a lean-to

240 directly over me. After many collapses—which didn't help my work— they finally got the branches to stand in a shaky sort of way.

◆ **GRAMMAR IN CONTEXT**
Skillful writers often use different sentence structures to create particular effects. Notice that in line 208 Avi uses three very short sentences in a row: "Max and I ran to help. Horse was damp. His mattress was soaked." How would the effect of these sentences be changed if Avi had combined them like this: "Max and I ran to help Horse, who was damp, his mattress soaked"? Which version do you prefer, and why?

discard (dĭ-skärd') *v.* to throw away

❶ **CHARACTER AND THEME**
Max is relieved to find the campsite is full of garbage. Why?

retrieve (rĭ-trēv') *v.* to get back again

---

7. **Hell-cat dive-bomber:** a World War II plane that took off from and returned to an aircraft carrier.

"Uh-oh," Horse said. "We forgot to bring something for a cover."

Max eyed me. "Didn't you say you brought a blanket?"

"No way!" I cried.

"All in favor of using the blanket!"

Horse and Max both cried, "Aye."

Only after I built up a mound of partially burned match sticks and lit *them,* did I get the fire going. It proved that where there's smoke there doesn't have to be much fire. The guys meanwhile draped my blanket over
250 their branch construction. It collapsed twice.

About an hour after our arrival, the three of us were gathered inside the tiny space. There was a small fire, but more light came from my flickering flashlight.

"No more rain," Horse said with pride.

"Just smoke," I said, rubbing my stinging eyes.

"We need a vent hole," Horse pointed out.

"I could cut it with the hatchet," Max said.

"It's my mother's favorite blanket."

"And you took it?" Max said.

260 I nodded.

"You *are* tough," Horse said.

Besides having too much smoke in our eyes and being wet, tired, and in pain, we were starving. I almost said something about giving up, but as far as I could see, the other guys were still tough. **J**

Max put his frying pan atop my smoldering smoke. After dumping in the entire contents of his mustard bottle, he threw in the franks. Meanwhile, I bolted down my last sandwich.

"What am I going to eat?" Horse suddenly said.

"Your beans," I reminded him.

270 Max offered up his hatchet. "Here. Just chop off the top end of the can."

"Oh, right," Horse said. He selected a can, set it in front of him, levered himself onto his knees, then swung down—hard. There was an explosion. For a stunned moment, we just sat there, hands, face, and clothing dripping with beans.

Suddenly Max shouted, "Food fight! Food fight!" and began to paw the stuff off and fling it around.

Having a food fight in a cafeteria is one thing. Having one in the middle of a soaking wet lean-to with cold beans during a dark, wet New

J PREDICT
Reread lines 262–264. Make a prediction about whether the narrator's statement will turn out to be true.

280　Jersey night is another. In seconds, the lean-to was down, the fire kicked over, and Max's frankfurters dumped on the ground.

"The food!" Max screamed, and began to snatch up the franks. Coated with mustard, dirt, grass, and leaves, they looked positively prehistoric. Still, we wiped the franks clean on our pants then ate them—the franks, that is. Afterward, we picked beans off each other's clothes—the way monkeys help friends get rid of lice.

For dessert, Max shared some Tootsie Rolls. After Horse swallowed his sixteenth piece, he announced, "I don't feel so good."

The thought of his getting sick was too much. "Let's go home," I said,
290　ashamed to look at the others. To my surprise—and relief—nobody objected.

Wet and cold, our way lit by my fast-fading flashlight, we gathered our belongings—most of them, anyway. As we made our way back over the bridge, gusts of wind-blown rain pummeled us until I felt like a used-up punching bag. By the time we got to the subway station, my legs were melting fast. The other guys looked bad too. Other riders moved away from us. One of them murmured, "Juvenile delinquents." To cheer us up, I got out my comic books, but they had **congealed** into a lump of red, white, and blue pulp.

300　With the subways running slow, it took hours to get home. When we emerged from the High Street Station, it was close to midnight.

Before we split up to go to our own homes, we just stood there on a street corner, embarrassed, trying to figure out how to end the day gracefully. I was the one who said, "Okay, I admit it. I'm not as tough as you guys. I gave up first."

Max shook his head. "Naw. I wanted to quit, but I wasn't tough enough to do it." He looked to Horse.

Horse made a fist. "You saying I'm the one who's tough?" he demanded. "I hate roughing it!" **K**

310　"Me too," I said quickly.

"Same for me," Max said.

Horse said, "Only thing is, we just have to promise not to tell Mr. Brenkman."

Grinning with relief, we **simultaneously** clasped hands. "No matter what," Max reminded us.

To which I added, "Scout's Honor." ◕

congeal (kən-jēl′) *v.* to make into a solid mass

K **CHARACTER AND THEME**
Reread lines 302–309. Pay attention to how Horse and Max react to the narrator's confession. In what ways have their attitudes changed? What does this change suggest about the story's implicit theme?

simultaneously (sī′məl-tā′nē-əs-lē) *adv.* at the same time

HANDBOOK EXCERPT The characters in "Scout's Honor" find that meeting the Scout Craft requirement isn't as easy as it seems. Read the following excerpt to find out what today's Boy Scouts must do to earn a similar merit badge.

Wilderness Survival

1. From memory, describe the priorities for survival in a backcountry or wilderness location.

2. Describe ways to (a) avoid panic and (b) maintain a high level of morale when lost.

3. Show that you know first aid for injuries or illnesses likely to occur in backcountry outings, including hypothermia, hyperthermia, heat stroke, heat exhaustion, frostbite, dehydration, sunburn, stings, ticks, snakebite, blisters, and hyperventilation.

4. Tell what you would do to survive in the following environments:
   a. Cold and snowy
   b. Wet (forest)
   c. Hot and dry (desert)
   d. Windy (mountains or plains)
   e. Water (ocean or lake)

5. Make up a small survival kit and be able to explain how each item in it is useful.

6. Show that you can start fires using three methods other than matches.

7. Do the following:
   a. Tell five different ways of attracting attention when lost.
   b. Show how to use a signal mirror to attract attention when lost.
   c. From memory, describe five international ground-to-air signals and tell what they mean.

8. Show that you can find and improvise a natural shelter minimizing the damage to the environment.

9. Spend a night in your shelter.

10. Explain how to protect yourself against insects, reptiles, rodents, and bears.

11. Show three ways to purify water.

12. Show that you know the proper clothing to be worn in your area on an overnight in extremely hot weather and extremely cold weather.

13. Explain why it usually is not wise to eat edible wild plants or wildlife in a wilderness survival situation.

Comprehension

1. **Recall** Why do the boys need to take a camping trip?

2. **Recall** What makes the narrator decide it is time to go home?

3. **Represent** Create a diagram of the boys' route to their campsite. Be sure to include all of the important places mentioned in the story.

Text Analysis

4. **Predict** Review the graphic organizer you made as you read. Which events in the story were you able to predict? Which events were surprises?

5. **Examine Character's Impact** The narrator exhibits many different qualities: ambition, fear (of being thought a coward), and courage. Explain how these qualities affect the theme of the story.

6. **Analyze Character and Theme** Fill in a chart like the one shown. Record each character's important statements and actions, what lessons he learns, and how he changes. Then, write a theme statement.

	Narrator	Horse	Max
Statements/ Actions	"I like roughing it."		
What He Learns			
How He Changes			

Theme Statement:

7. **Draw Conclusions About Theme and Genre** How does the author, Avi, use the genre of the short story to explore his theme? Consider how his characters and their often humorous actions and statements bring the theme to life in an entertaining way.

Extension and Challenge

8. **SOCIAL STUDIES CONNECTION** Read the requirements for earning the Wilderness Survival Merit Badge on page 374. Choose three of the requirements. For each one, state whether the boys in "Scout's Honor" met that requirement. Explain why or why not.

When is a trip an ADVENTURE?

Was the trip the boys in this story took a true adventure, or was it something else? Explain.

COMMON CORE

RL 2 Determine a theme or central idea of a text and how it is conveyed through particular details. RL 3 Describe how the characters change as the plot moves toward a resolution.

Vocabulary in Context

▲ VOCABULARY PRACTICE

Synonyms are words that mean the same thing, while **antonyms** are words that mean the opposite. Examine the words in each pair and identify whether they are synonyms or antonyms.

1. retrieve/lose
2. retort/reply
3. discard/keep
4. khaki/cloth
5. congeal/separate
6. simultaneously/together

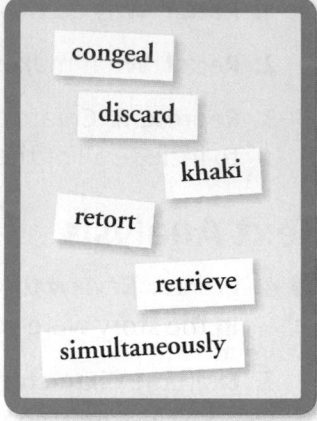

congeal

discard

khaki

retort

retrieve

simultaneously

ACADEMIC VOCABULARY IN SPEAKING

- attitude
- communicate
- context
- illustrate
- implicit

With a partner, discuss how historical **context** influences the theme of Avi's story. (Remember that the story takes place in 1946.) How would the events of the story and the characters' **attitudes** be different if the story were set in a contemporary context? Use at least two Academic Vocabulary words in your response.

VOCABULARY STRATEGY: PART-TO-WHOLE ANALOGIES

An **analogy** presents a relationship between pairs of words. A typical analogy begins with a pair of items that are related in some way. Two of the most common relationships are part to whole (for example, "Finger is to hand as toe is to foot") or whole to part (for example, "Hand is to finger as foot is to toe"). Analogies are often written in special way:

> sentence : paragraph :: paragraph : essay

You would read the analogy above like this: "A sentence is to a paragraph as a paragraph is to an essay." (The relationship of a sentence to a paragraph is of a part to a whole, since a sentence is part of a paragraph. A paragraph is part of an essay just as a sentence is part of a paragraph.)

Complete these analogies by choosing the letter of the best answer.

1. building : city ::
   tree : _____
   A. soil
   B. flower
   C. neighborhood
   D. forest

2. bed : mattress ::
   _____ : cushion
   A. curtain
   B. sofa
   C. table
   D. rug

COMMON CORE

L 5b Use the relationship between particular words to better understand each of the words.
L 6 Acquire and use accurately academic words.

Interactive Vocabulary **THINK**central

Go to **thinkcentral.com**.
KEYWORD: HML6-376

Language

◆ **GRAMMAR IN CONTEXT:** Combine Sentences

COMMON CORE

L 3a Vary sentence patterns for style. **W 3** Write narratives to develop imagined events.

On page 359, you learned how to join two subjects or two predicates to combine sentences. Another way to connect two sentences is to use a **comma** and a **coordinating conjunction,** such as *and, but, or, nor, yet, so,* or *for.* Here is an example:

> *Original:* Max was a fast talker. He always had pocket money.
>
> *Revised:* Max was a fast talker, and he always had pocket money.

PRACTICE Join these sentences by inserting a comma and the correct coordinating conjunction.

1. Horse could carry his mattress. He could leave it behind.
2. It was raining when we reached the bridge. We crossed it anyway.
3. Our stomachs were growling. We ate all of our food.
4. Horse used his hatchet to open the beans. The can exploded.

For more help with coordinating conjunctions, see page R47 in the **Grammar Handbook.**

READING-WRITING CONNECTION

Increase your understanding of "Scout's Honor" by responding to the prompt. Then use the **revising tip** to improve your writing.

WRITING PROMPT	REVISING TIP
Short Constructed Response: Narrative Consider how the characters in "Scout's Honor" might describe their camping trip to others. Would they tell about it truthfully or change the details to make it sound better? Choose either Horse or Max and write a brief **narrative** or **letter** in which he describes the adventure to a friend or family member.	Review your response. Does your narrative or letter lack sentence variety? Have you found places where you can join two subjects or two predicates to combine sentences? If so, revise your writing.

Interactive Revision THINKcentral

Go to **thinkcentral.com.** KEYWORD: HML6-377

How to Build a Bat House
Instruction Manual

What's the Connection?

In "Scout's Honor," you saw how three boys made a disastrous and comical attempt to earn a Boy Scout merit badge. To earn merit badges today, Boy Scouts can choose from many activities. All of these activities require the ability to follow instructions. A Scout might even want to try building a house for bats, using the how-to instructions in the following instruction manual.

Use with "Scout's Honor," page 362.

COMMON CORE

RI 5 Analyze how a particular sentence or section fits into the structure and contributes to the development of ideas.
RI 7 Integrate information presented in different formats to develop a coherent understanding of a topic.

Standards Focus: Follow Instructions

Instructions are a type of **procedural text,** a text that tells you how to do something. Good instructions consist of multi-step directions that explain how to complete a task, solve a problem, or perform a procedure, such as repairing a bicycle, downloading music files, or building a bookcase. Well-written instructions communicate information in a logical order, using very few words. To follow instructions successfully, follow these strategies in order:

- Preview the task by reading all the directions carefully so that you know the scope of the project. Make sure you have everything you'll need before you begin. If there are any safety precautions, work with adult supervision.

- Study any illustrations, diagrams, or charts that show the materials you'll need, recommended methods of working, or examples of the finished product.

- Follow the steps in order, and do exactly what the instructions say.

As you read "How to Build a Bat House," make a chart like the one below to keep notes about what you'll need to consider for each step of the process.

How to Build a Bat House	
Step	Things to Consider
1	I'll need to get enough plywood to cut into pieces the exact size of these measurements before I begin. I live in a cold climate, so read Step 7 now.
2	

How to Build a BAT HOUSE

Bats have gotten a bad name from horror stories and movies. That's too bad, because bats can be great little guys to have around. Give a bat a nice place to live, and it will help you cut down on mosquitoes and other insect nuisances. These tiny creatures, the world's only flying mammals, don't ask for much in the way of shelter. They want a warm, enclosed space where they can "hang" out. Yes, bats do sleep upside-down, and they also climb the walls, which means they need a surface they can grip with their tiny claws. They also like a place that stays dark at night and is near water.

This easy-to-build structure will welcome a small colony of bats. (Caution: Do not build a bat house if you have pets. Never touch a bat, alive or dead, in case the bat is sick. Report dead bats in case they carry rabies.)

Steps to Building a Bat House

1 Start with 1 sheet of ½" exterior-grade untreated plywood, at least 2' x 4'. Cut the plywood into 3 pieces of the following measurements:
a) 26 ½" x 24" (1 back)
b) 26" x 24" (1 front-top)
c) 5" x 24" (1 front-bottom)
(See Step 7 for measurements if you live in a cold climate.) **A**

2 Use 1 piece of untreated pine (1" x 2" x 8') for the sides. Cut the pine into 3 pieces as follows:
a) 24" (1 ceiling)
b) 20 ½" (2 side walls)

3 Paint or stain the wood with a dark-colored, water-based stain or paint. The dark color will absorb the sunlight and keep the bat house warm.

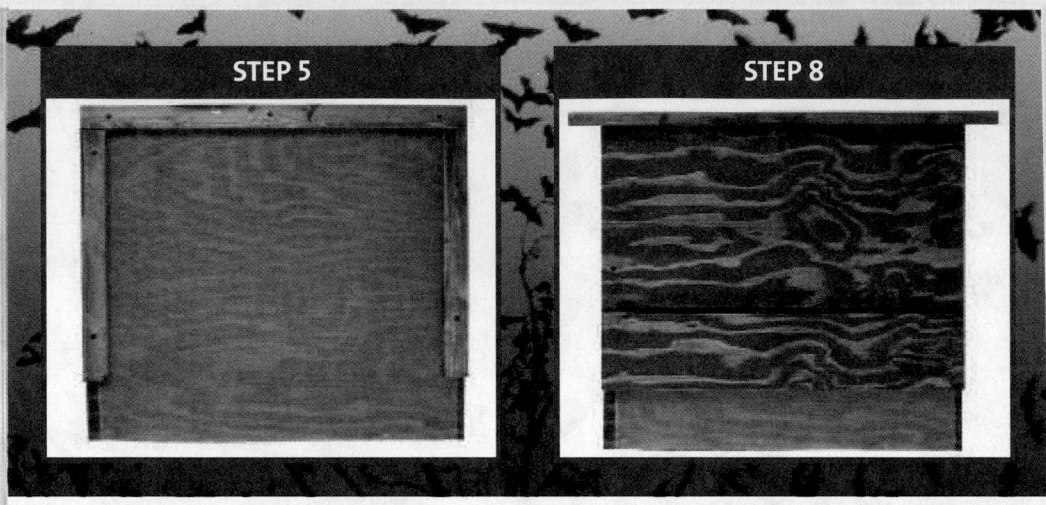

STEP 5

STEP 8

4 To give the bats a way to grab onto a wall of their house, use a staple gun to secure window screen or mesh to one side of the back panel.

5 Use exterior-grade 1" screws (you'll need 20–30) to attach the side walls to the longer sides of the back panel. Line up the walls and sides correctly. There will be 1/2" of extra back panel at the bottom for the bats to land on.

6 Place the ceiling at the top of the back panel, between the side walls. Screw into place.

7 Place the top front panel on the house. Line it up with the ceiling and screw into place. Place the bottom front panel on the house, leaving a ½" vent space between the top and bottom front panels. If you live in a cold climate, you can eliminate this vent. Simply cut a single front piece that is 23" long. **B**

8 Using 1" nails (you'll need a small box), carefully nail the roof over the top.

9 For best results, use a caulk gun to apply caulk to the joints.

10 When your bat house is ready, look for a place to hang it that faces south or east and has a nearby water source. Using heavy-duty hanging hooks and wire, hang your bat house at least 12 feet off the ground (to help keep other critters out). Choose an area that's away from lighting, such as porch lights or street lights.

B INSTRUCTIONS
If you lived in a warm climate, why would you be sure to include this vent?

Comprehension

1. **Recall** What should you do if you find a bat near your house?

2. **Clarify** Why should you paint or stain the wood a dark color?

3. **Summarize** What could be some consequences of not following these instructions precisely?

Text Analysis

4. **Analyze Characteristics of Form** What elements of this document make it a procedural text?

5. **Evaluate a Procedural Text** Were the instructions in this document clear? If you followed the steps, do you think you could construct a bat house? Why or why not?

COMMON CORE

RI 5 Analyze how a particular sentence or section fits into the structure and contributes to the development of ideas.
RI 7 Integrate information presented in different formats to develop a coherent understanding of a topic.
W 2 Write explanatory texts to convey information.

Read for Information: Create Instructions

WRITING PROMPT

Write a set of instructions explaining how to make or do something you know well. For example, you might explain how to crochet a scarf, organize a study area, or create a playlist of music files. Organize your instructions into specific steps that will enable someone else to successfully follow the procedure.

To answer this prompt, you will need to do the following:

1. First, write down everything you can think of that you do to accomplish the task. You don't need to have the steps laid out in order yet; simply write down what it takes to carry out the task or procedure.

2. Next, make a list of all the things a person would need to carry out the procedure. Are specific tools or materials needed? What are the quantities and measurements? How important is it to have exact measurements? Are there any hints, safety warnings, or options that you should include?

3. Now make a chart that captures what is involved in each step.

Step	Materials, Tools, or Ingredients Needed	What Actions Are Involved

4. Finally, write your "how-to" instructions.
   You may begin and end your instructions with a short paragraph, but the body of the instructions should be presented as numbered steps.

Ant and Grasshopper
Classical Fable by Aesop
Retold by James Reeves

The Richer, the Poorer
Modern Fable by Dorothy West

Should you LIVE for the present or the future?

Throughout the world and over the centuries, people have had different ideas about saving and spending. Some people prefer to save as much as possible, so the money will be there when they really need it. Others prefer to spend what they have right away, so that they can enjoy it. In the fables you are about to read, four characters—two from a story told more than 2,500 years ago and two from a story published in 1995—struggle with their decisions to save or spend.

DISCUSS Is it better to save for the future or enjoy yourself in the present? Discuss your opinion with a partner. Provide reasons to support your response.

TEXT ANALYSIS: FABLE

Fables teach us lessons about life. A **classical fable** like "Ant and Grasshopper" often features animals who act like human beings and ends with a clear **moral,** or message about life. Aesop's fable is an example of classical literature and comes from the classical civilization of ancient Greece.

A **modern fable** like "The Richer, the Poorer" is more likely to use human characters. It has a lesson that readers have to interpret on their own.

READING STRATEGY: SET A PURPOSE FOR READING

When you read a fable, you gain insight into the **cultural and historical setting** it comes from. Fables often reflect the concerns of the people who lived at the time the fables were written. Your purpose for reading is to compare and contrast the historical and cultural settings of two fables. As you read, think about the choices characters make and the consequences of those choices. Then think about how the fables speak to the **cultural values**—the ideas and beliefs—of the people at that time.

	"Ant and Grasshopper"		"The Richer, the Poorer"	
	Ant	Grass-hopper	Lottie	Bess
Actions	worked hard			
Consequences				

▲ VOCABULARY IN CONTEXT

West uses the words below to tell her fable. To see how many you know, match each word with the term closest in meaning.

WORD	clarity	frugal	intolerable
LIST	enhance	inefficient	lean

1. thin
2. wasteful
3. clearness
4. improve
5. unbearable
6. thrifty

 Complete the activities in your **Reader/Writer Notebook**.

Meet the Authors

Aesop
620?–560 B.C.

Ancient Storyteller
Aesop, who became known as one of the Seven Wise Men of Greece, was famous for his clever fables. Little is known about who Aesop was. Early writers of history agree that he came from Africa and was held in slavery in Greece, but was eventually given his freedom. Aesop told his fables aloud. Others repeated what they'd heard him tell, and in that way his fables survived over the centuries until they were published around 300 B.C.

Dorothy West
1907–1998

Writer from the Start
The daughter of a freed slave, Dorothy West was just 16 years old when she first received recognition as a writer. She won second prize in a contest put on by a literary magazine. As an adult, West moved to New York City, where she became a key literary figure. West wrote two novels and numerous short stories.

Authors Online
Go to **thinkcentral.com**. KEYWORD: HML6-383

THINK central

Ant *and* Grasshopper

Aesop
Retold by James Reeves

All summer the ant had been working hard, gathering a store of corn for the winter. Grain by grain she had taken it from the fields and stowed it away in a hole in the bank, under a hawthorn bush.

One bright, frosty day in winter Grasshopper saw her. She was dragging out a grain of corn to dry it in the sun. The wind was keen, and poor Grasshopper was cold. **A**

"Good morning, Ant," said he. "What a terrible winter it is! I'm half dead with hunger. Please give me just one of your corn grains to eat. I can find nothing, although I've hopped all over the farmyard. There isn't a
10 seed to be found. Spare me a grain, I beg."

"Why haven't you saved anything up?" asked Ant. "*I* worked hard all through the summer, storing food for the winter. Very glad I am too, for as you say, it's bitterly cold."

"I wasn't idle last summer, either," said Grasshopper.

"And what did you do, pray?"

"Why, I spent the time singing," answered Grasshopper. "Every day from dawn till sunset I jumped about or sat in the sun, chirruping to my heart's content."

"Oh you did, did you?" replied Ant. "Well, since you've sung all
20 summer to keep yourself cheerful, you may dance all winter to keep yourself warm. Not a grain will I give you!"

And she scuttled off into her hole in the bank, while Grasshopper was left cold and hungry.

IN GOOD TIMES PREPARE FOR WHEN THE BAD TIMES COME. ❧ **B**

From *Aesop's Fables.* © 2000 by Jerry Pinkney. Used with permission of Chronicle Books LLC, San Francisco.

Analyze Visuals ▶

What can you **infer** about these two illustrations by viewing them next to each other?

A FABLE
Reread lines 1–6. What clues tell you that this is a fable?

B FABLE
The **moral,** or lesson, is a stylistic element of a classical fable. Restate the moral in your own words. Which character's behavior does the moral support?

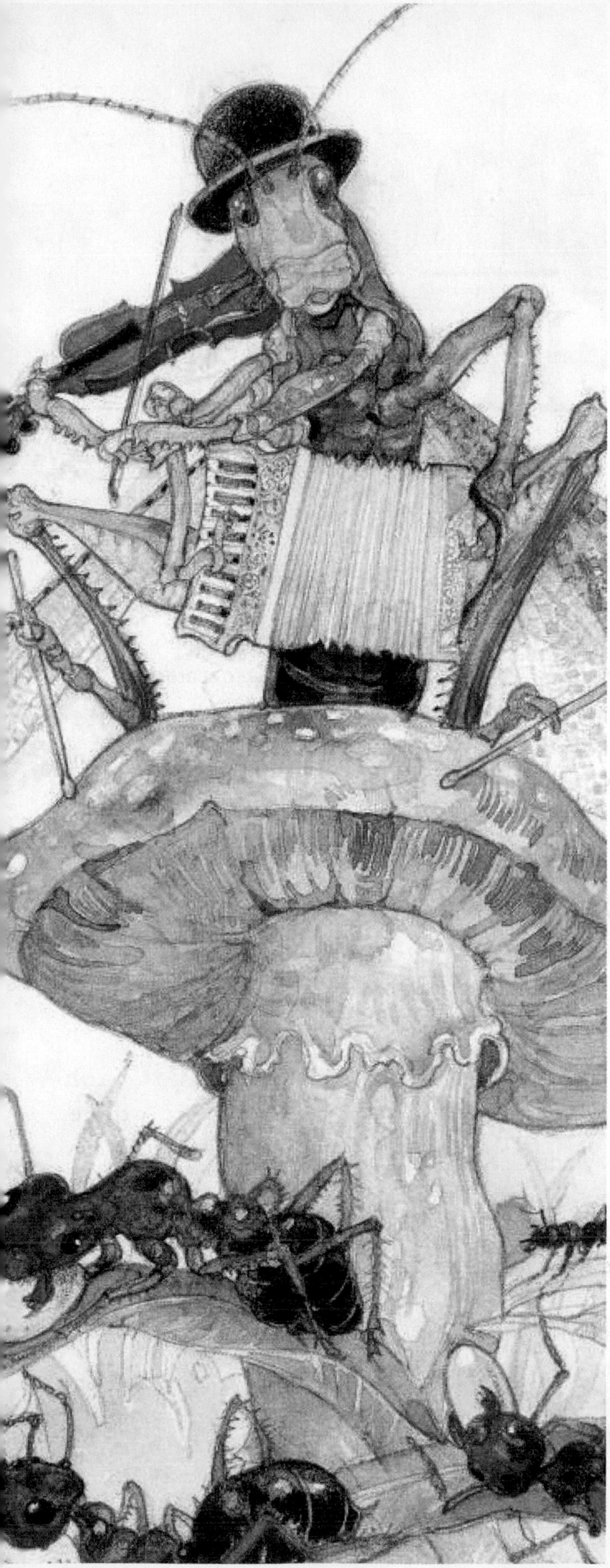

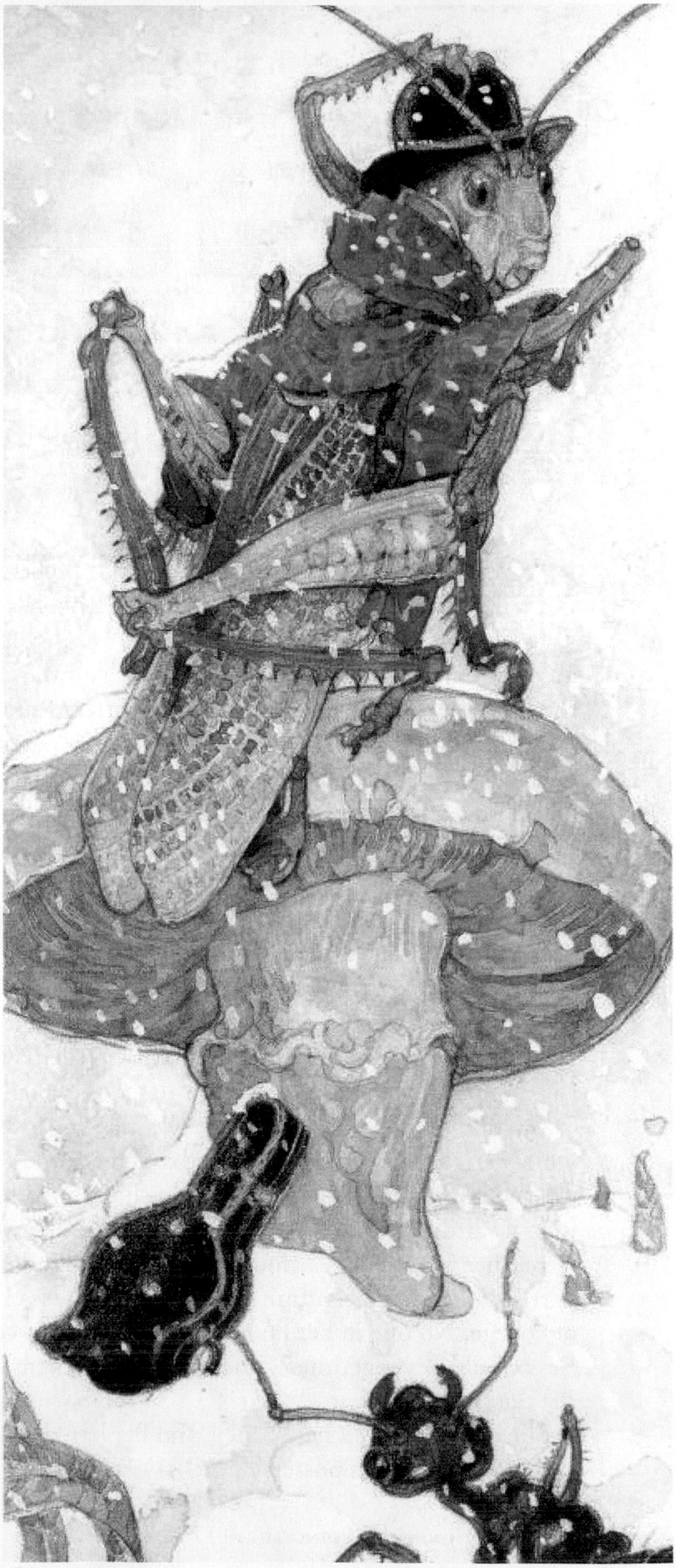

The Richer,
the Poorer

Dorothy West

Over the years Lottie had urged Bess to prepare for her old age. Over the years Bess had lived each day as if there were no other. Now they were both past sixty, the time for summing up. Lottie had a bank account that had never grown **lean**. Bess had the clothes on her back, and the rest of her worldly possessions in a battered suitcase. **C**

Lottie had hated being a child, hearing her parents' skimping and scraping. Bess had never seemed to notice. All she ever wanted was to go outside and play. She learned to skate on borrowed skates. She rode a borrowed bicycle. Lottie couldn't wait to grow up and buy herself the best
10 of everything.

As soon as anyone would hire her, Lottie put herself to work. She minded babies; she ran errands for the old.

She never touched a penny of her money, though her child's mouth watered for ice cream and candy. But she could not bear to share with Bess, who never had anything to share with her. When the dimes began to add up to dollars, she lost her taste for sweets.

By the time she was twelve, she was clerking after school in a small variety store. Saturdays she worked as long as she was wanted. She decided to keep her money for clothes. When she entered high school, she would
20 wear a wardrobe that neither she nor anyone else would be able to match.

But her freshman year found her unable to indulge so frivolous a whim, particularly when her admiring instructors advised her to think seriously of college. No one in her family had ever gone to college, and certainly Bess would never get there. She would show them all what she could do, if she put her mind to it.

She began to bank her money, and her bankbook became her most private and precious possession.

lean (lēn) *adj.* having little to spare; thin

C COMPARE AND CONTRAST
Reread lines 1–5. Consider the ways this passage is similar to the first two paragraphs of "Ant and Grasshopper." What do you think will happen in the rest of the story?

Language Coach

Word Forms To create an adverb from an adjective form, you can add the ending *-ly* to the adjective. In line 22, adding *-ly* to the adjective *serious* creates the adverb *seriously*. What other adverb in this paragraph is created by adding *-ly* to an adjective form?

In her third year in high school she found a job in a small but expanding restaurant, where she cashiered from the busy hour until closing. In her
30 last year in high school the business increased so rapidly that Lottie was faced with the choice of staying in school or working full time.

She made her choice easily. A job in hand was worth two in the future. **D**
Bess had a beau[1] in the school band, who had no other ambition except to play a horn. Lottie expected to be settled with a home and family while Bess was still waiting for Harry to earn enough to buy a marriage license.

That Bess married Harry straight out of high school was not surprising. That Lottie never married at all was not really surprising either. Two or three times she was halfway persuaded, but to give up a job that paid well for a homemaking job that paid nothing was a risk she was incapable of taking.
40 Bess's married life was nothing for Lottie to envy. She and Harry lived like gypsies,[2] Harry playing in second-rate bands all over the country, even getting himself and Bess stranded in Europe. They were often in rags and never in riches.

D COMPARE AND CONTRAST
Reread lines 26–32. In what ways is Lottie similiar to Ant in "Ant and Grasshopper"?

▼ Analyze Visuals
Describe the **mood,** or feeling, that each of these paintings conveys.

---

1. **beau:** boyfriend.
2. **gypsies:** people who move from place to place.

Woman in Calico (1944), William H. Johnson. © Smithsonian American Art Museum, Washington, D.C./Art Resource, New York.

Mom and Dad (1944), William H. Johnson. Oil on paperboard, 31″ × 25³/₈″. Gift of the Harmon Foundation. © Smithsonian American Art Museum, Washington, D.C./Art Resource, New York.

Street Life, Harlem (1940), William H. Johnson. © Smithsonian American Art Museum, Washington, D.C./Art Resource, New York.

◀ **Analyze Visuals**

Which of the sisters would you be more likely to **connect** to the woman in this painting?

Bess grieved because she had no child, not having sense enough to know she was better off without one. Lottie was certainly better off without nieces and nephews to feel sorry for. Very likely Bess would have dumped them on her doorstep.

That Lottie had a doorstep they might have been left on was only because her boss, having bought a second house, offered Lottie his first 50 house at a price so low and terms so reasonable that it would have been like losing money to refuse.

She shut off the rooms she didn't use, letting them go to rack and ruin.[3] Since she ate her meals out, she had no food at home, and did not encourage callers, who always expected a cup of tea. **E**

Her way of life was mean and miserly, but she did not know it. She thought she lived **frugally** in her middle years so that she could live in comfort and ease when she most needed peace of mind.

E FABLE
Reread lines 48–54. What do you think of Lottie's behavior?

frugal (frōōʹgəl) *adj.* avoiding waste; thrifty

---

3. **go to rack and ruin:** become shabby or wrecked.

The years, after forty, began to race. Suddenly Lottie was sixty, and retired from her job by her boss's son, who had no sentimental feeling 60 about keeping her on until she was ready to quit.

She made several attempts to find other employment, but her dowdy appearance made her look old and **inefficient.** For the first time in her life Lottie would gladly have worked for nothing, to have some place to go, something to do with her day.

Harry died abroad, in a third-rate hotel,[4] with Bess weeping as hard as if he had left her a fortune. He had left her nothing but his horn. There wasn't even money for her passage home.

Lottie, trapped by the blood tie, knew she would not only have to send for her sister, but take her in when she returned. It didn't seem fair that 70 Bess should reap the harvest of Lottie's lifetime of self-denial. **F**

It took Lottie a week to get a bedroom ready, a week of hard work and hard cash. There was everything to do, everything to replace or paint. When she was through the room looked so fresh and new that Lottie felt she deserved it more than Bess.

She would let Bess have her room, but the mattress was so lumpy, the carpet so worn, the curtains so threadbare that Lottie's conscience pricked her. She supposed she would have to redo that room, too, and went about doing it with an eagerness that she mistook for haste.

When she was through upstairs, she was shocked to see how dismal 80 downstairs looked by comparison. She tried to ignore it, but with nowhere to go to escape it, the contrast grew more **intolerable.**

She worked her way from kitchen to parlor, persuading herself she was only putting the rooms to rights to give herself something to do. At night she slept like a child after a long and happy day of playing house. She was having more fun than she had ever had in her life. She was living each hour for itself.

There was only a day now before Bess would arrive. Passing her gleaming mirrors, at first with vague awareness, then with painful **clarity,** Lottie saw herself as others saw her, and could not stand the 90 sight.

She went on a spending spree from specialty shops to beauty salon, emerging transformed into a woman who believed in miracles. **G**

inefficient (ĭn'ĭ-fĭsh'ənt) *adj.* not able to produce without wasting time or energy

F COMPARE AND CONTRAST
Note Lottie's reaction to sharing her home with Bess. How is this similar to or different from what happens in "Ant and Grasshopper"?

intolerable (ĭn-tŏl'ər-ə-bəl) *adj.* unbearable; too much to be endured

clarity (klăr'ĭ-tē) *n.* the quality of being clear

G FABLE
Reread lines 75–92. What has Lottie learned about herself? How is this lesson affecting her behavior?

---

4. **third-rate hotel:** a hotel of poor quality.

She was in the kitchen basting a turkey when Bess rang the bell. Her heart raced, and she wondered if the heat from the oven was responsible.

She went to the door, and Bess stood before her. Stiffly she suffered Bess's embrace, her heart racing harder, her eyes suddenly smarting from the onrush of cold air.

"Oh, Lottie, it's good to see you," Bess said, but saying nothing about
100 Lottie's splendid appearance. Upstairs Bess, putting down her shabby suitcase, said, "I'll sleep like a rock tonight," without a word of praise for her lovely room. At the lavish table, top-heavy with turkey, Bess said, "I'll take light and dark, both," with no marveling at the size of the bird, or that there was turkey for two elderly women, one of them too poor to buy her own bread.

With the glow of good food in her stomach, Bess began to spin stories. They were rich with places and people, most of them lowly, all of them magnificent. Her face reflected her telling, the joys and sorrows of her remembering, and above all, the love she lived by that **enhanced** the
110 poorest place, the humblest person.

Then it was that Lottie knew why Bess had made no mention of her finery, or the shining room, or the twelve-pound turkey. She had not even seen them. Tomorrow she would see the room as it really looked, and Lottie as she really looked, and the warmed-over turkey in its second-day glory. Tonight she saw only what she had come seeking, a place in her sister's home and heart. **H**

She said, "That's enough about me. How have the years used you?"

"It was me who didn't use them," said Lottie wistfully. "I saved for them. I saved for them. I forgot the best of them would go without my
120 ever spending a day or a dollar enjoying them. That's my life story in those few words, a life never lived.

"Now it's too near the end to try."

Bess said, "To know how much there is to know is the beginning of learning to live. Don't count the years that are left us. At our time of life it's the days that count. You've too much catching up to do to waste a minute of a waking hour feeling sorry for yourself."

Lottie grinned, a real wide-open grin, "Well, to tell the truth I felt sorry for you. Maybe, if I had any sense, I'd feel sorry for myself, after all. I know I'm too old to kick up my heels, but I'm going to let you show me how. If I land
130 on my head, I guess it won't matter. I feel giddy already, and I like it." ∾ **I**

---

enhance (ĕn-hăns′) v. to increase in value or quality

H FABLE
What do you learn about Bess from these lines? Based on the description, what type of behavior is the author recommending?

I FABLE
Reread lines 127–130. Consider Lottie's attitude in this passage with her attitude at the beginning of the fable. What lesson does this change in attitude hint at?

Comprehension

1. **Recall** Why does Grasshopper need to ask Ant for food?

2. **Recall** Why does Bess come to live with her sister Lottie?

3. **Summarize** What does Lottie do to prepare for Bess's arrival?

Text Analysis

● 4. **Analyze Fables** In "Ant and Grasshopper," the characters are animals who talk and act like people. What do these animal characters tell you about human nature?

● 5. **Analyze Fables** Think about which of the characters in the two fables changed and which ones did not. Identify who changed and explain in what ways he or she changed.

6. **Compare and Contrast** In what way is Grasshopper's situation similar to Bess's? In what way is it different?

● 7. **Examine Cultural and Historical Settings** Fables often reflect the concerns of a particular culture. What details from "Ant and Grasshopper" tell you that self-reliance was an important value to ancient Greeks?

COMMON CORE

RL 1 Cite textual evidence to support analysis of what the text says explicitly as well as inferences drawn from the text.
RL 2 Determine a theme or central idea of a text and how it is conveyed through particular details.

Compare and Contrast Fables

Now that you've read both fables, add a new row to the chart you filled out as you read. Use the answers to the questions in the selection to help you identify the moral of "The Richer, the Poorer." How does this moral reflect a different attitude toward saving and spending than the attitude in "Ant and Grasshopper"?

| | "Ant and Grasshopper" | | "The Richer, the Poorer" | |
	Ant	Grasshopper	Lottie	Bess
Actions	worked hard during the summer			
Consequences				

Moral: In good times prepare for when the bad times come.

Moral:

Should you LIVE for the present or the future?

Has either fable changed the way you think about living for the present or the future? Support your response with details from the text.

Vocabulary in Context

▲ VOCABULARY PRACTICE

In each item below, choose the letter of the word that has a different meaning from the other words.

1. (a) enable, (b) enhance, (c) improve, (d) increase
2. (a) wasteful, (b) disorganized, (c) unfair, (d) inefficient
3. (a) quick, (b) sparing, (c) frugal, (d) thrifty
4. (a) lean, (b) sparse, (c) little, (d) lengthy
5. (a) generosity, (b) kindness, (c) charity, (d) clarity
6. (a) impractical, (b) unenjoyable, (c) intolerable, (d) terrible

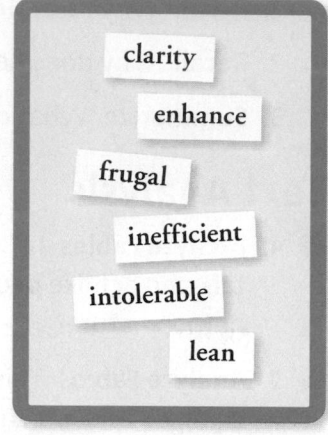

clarity
enhance
frugal
inefficient
intolerable
lean

ACADEMIC VOCABULARY IN SPEAKING

- attitude - communicate - context - illustrate - implicit

With a partner, discuss the moral of each fable. Do you find a direct statement of a moral to be effective? Or is it more convincing if a moral is **implicit**? Use at least two Academic Vocabulary words in your discussion.

VOCABULARY STRATEGY: MULTIPLE MEANING WORDS

Many English words have more than one meaning. You may have known, for example, that *lean* can mean "rest the body against something for support." But you may not have been familiar with its use in "The Richer, the Poorer," where the word means "having little to spare; thin."

If a word does not seem to make sense in context, look at the rest of the sentence to figure out what other meaning the word might have. If you are still not sure of the meaning, check a dictionary.

PRACTICE Use context clues or a dictionary to define the boldfaced words.

1. She **cast** her hat and scarf aside when she got home.
2. The golfer used an **iron** to make the shot.
3. Instead of making a decision, she chose to **hedge** for a while longer.
4. To swing the bat better, **plant** your feet solidly yet comfortably.

COMMON CORE

L 4a Use context as a clue to the meaning of a word or phrase.

Interactive Vocabulary **THINK**central

Go to **thinkcentral.com**.
KEYWORD: HML6-392

Writing for Assessment

COMMON CORE W 2, W4, W 10

1. READ THE PROMPT

The two fables you've just read present a similar idea in very different ways. In writing assessments, you will often be asked to compare and contrast similar characters or themes in two stories, poems, or fables.

In three paragraphs, compare and contrast the traditional fable "Ant and Grasshopper" with the modern fable "The Richer, the Poorer." Consider the moral of each fable and the actions of each character. Support your ideas using details from the fables.

◀ **STRATEGIES IN ACTION**

1. I have to identify the **similarities and differences** between the fables.

2. I need to describe how the **characters** behave, and any **lessons** they learn.

3. I need to include **details and examples** from the fables to support my ideas.

2. PLAN YOUR WRITING

Using the chart you filled in as you read, identify the ways in which the fables are alike and different. Then think about how to present these similarities and differences.

- Decide on a main idea, or position statement, for your response.

- Review the fables to find examples and details that support your position.

- Create an outline to organize your response. This sample outline shows one way to organize your paragraphs.

I. Introduce Fables
  and Main Idea
II. Compare
  Characters in
  Two Fables
III. Compare Moral
  of each Fable

3. DRAFT YOUR RESPONSE

Paragraph 1 Provide the titles and authors of both fables, as well as a sentence telling what each fable is about. Also include your main idea.

Paragraph 2 Explain how the four characters are similar or different. Support your position with examples of what they say, do, or think.

Paragraph 3 Provide the moral of each fable. Explain how the messages are similar or different. Use supporting details from the fables.

Revision Make sure you've used transition words such as *similarly, also, however, instead,* or *unlike* to show similarities and differences.

Esperanza Rising

COMMON CORE

RL 10 Read and comprehend literature.

Novel by Pam Muñoz Ryan

Other Books by Pam Muñoz Ryan

- *Becoming Naomi León*
- *Riding Freedom*
- *California, Here We Come!*

Meet Pam Muñoz Ryan

Award-winning author Pam Muñoz Ryan grew up in a family with a rich tradition of storytelling. Ryan inherited some of the family's most interesting stories from her grandmother, with whom she spent a lot of time. Her grandmother's own life story—leaving behind wealth and luxury in Mexico for a life of hard work in the United States during the Great Depression—inspired Ryan to write *Esperanza Rising*.

Even without the family history, Ryan would have no problem sympathizing with a young girl who feels out of place. When Ryan entered middle school, her family moved and she had to change schools. Feeling like an outsider, Ryan found comfort in books.

Try a Coming-of-Age Novel

When a novel centers on a young person becoming more mature as a result of a challenging experience, it is often called a **coming-of-age novel.** *Esperanza Rising* is an example of this type of novel.

Reading Fluency refers to how easily and well you read. When fluent readers read aloud, they sound natural and expressive. They don't read each word as an individual unit but know how to string words and phrases together so that they sound natural, like conversation. They stress the right words and use punctuation to guide them in pausing or stopping in the right places. When a fluent reader reads a character's dialogue, it sounds the way a real person would talk.

Use this selection to improve your fluency by pairing off with a classmate and taking turns reading the selection aloud. Try to capture the very real-sounding voice of the narrator and the natural-sounding dialogue.

Esperanza Rising tells the story of Esperanza Ortega, a rich, pampered girl who must give up her carefree life in Mexico for a life of hardship in the United States. After Esperanza's father is murdered, her devious uncle, Tío Luis, demands that her mother marry him. By marrying her, he hopes to gain control of the family's riches. In the excerpt you are about to read, you'll discover the extremes to which Tío Luis will go to make Esperanza's mother accept his proposal.

from

Esperanza Rising

The wind blew hard that night and the house moaned and whistled. Instead of dreaming of birthday songs, Esperanza's sleep was filled with nightmares. An enormous bear was chasing her, getting closer and closer and finally folding her in a tight embrace. Its fur caught in her mouth, making it hard to breathe. Someone tried to pull the bear away but couldn't. The bear squeezed harder until it was smothering Esperanza. Then when she thought she would suffocate, the bear grabbed her by the shoulders and shook her until her head wagged back and forth.

10   Her eyes opened, then closed again. She realized she was dreaming and for an instant, she felt relieved. But the shaking began again, harder this time.

Someone was calling her.

"Esperanza!"

She opened her eyes.

"Esperanza! Wake up!" screamed Mama. "The house is on fire!" Smoke drifted into the room.

"Mama, what's happening?"

"Get up, Esperanza! We must get Abuelita!"

20 Esperanza heard Alfonso's deep voice yelling from somewhere downstairs.

"Señora Ortega! Esperanza!"

"Here! We are here!" called Mama, grabbing a damp rag from the washbowl and handing it to Esperanza to put over her mouth and nose. Esperanza swung around in a circle looking for something, anything, to save. She grabbed the doll. Then she and Mama hurried down the hall toward Abuelita's room, but it was empty.

"Alfonso!" screamed Mama. "Abuelita is not here!"

30 "We will find her. You must come now. The stairs are beginning to burn. Hurry!"

Esperanza held the towel over her face and looked down the stairs. Curtains flamed up the walls. The house was enveloped in a fog that thickened toward the ceiling. Mama and Esperanza crouched down the stairs where Alfonso was waiting to lead them out through the kitchen.

In the courtyard, the wooden gates were open. Near the stables, the *vaqueros* were releasing the horses from the corrals. Servants scurried everywhere. Where were they going?

40 "Where's Abuelita? Abuelita!" cried Mama.

Esperanza felt dizzy. Nothing seemed real. Was she still dreaming? Was this her own imagination gone wild?

Miguel grabbed her. "'Where's your mother and Abuelita?"

Esperanza whimpered and looked toward Mama. He left her, stopped at Mama, then ran toward the house.

The wind caught the sparks from the house and carried them to the stables. Esperanza stood in the middle of it all, watching the outline of her home silhouetted in flames against the night sky.

Someone wrapped a blanket around her. Was she cold? She did
50 not know.

Miguel ran out of the burning house carrying Abuelita in his
arms. He laid her down and Hortensia screamed. The back of his
shirt was on fire. Alfonso tackled him, rolling him over and over on
the ground until the fire was out. Miguel stood up and slowly took
off the blackened shirt. He wasn't badly burned.

Mama cradled Abuelita in her arms.

"Mama," said Esperanza, "Is she . . . ?"

"No, she is alive, but weak and her ankle . . . I don't think she
can walk," said Mama.

60 Esperanza knelt down.

"Abuelita, where were you?"

Her grandmother held up the cloth bag with her crocheting
and after some minutes of coughing, whispered, "We must have
something to do while we wait."

The fire's anger could not be contained. It spread to the grapes.
The flames ran along the deliberate rows of the vines, like long
curved fingers reaching for the horizon, lighting the night sky.

Esperanza stood as if in a trance and watched El Rancho de las
Rosas burn.

❧

70 Mama, Abuelita, and Esperanza slept in the servants' cabins.
They really didn't sleep much, but they didn't cry either. They were
numb, as if encased in a thick skin that nothing could penetrate.
And there was no point in talking about how it happened. They all
knew that the uncles had arranged the fire.

At dawn, still in her nightgown, Esperanza went out among
the rubble. Avoiding the smoldering piles, she picked through the
black wood, hoping to find something to salvage. She sat on an
adobe block near what used to be the front door, and looked over
at Papa's rose garden. Flowerless stems were covered in soot. Dazed
80 and hugging herself, Esperanza surveyed the surviving victims: the

twisted forms of wrought-iron chairs, unharmed cast-iron skillets, and the mortars and pestles from the kitchen that were made from lava rock and refused to burn. Then she saw the remains of the trunk that used to sit at the foot of her bed, the metal straps still intact. She stood up and hurried toward it, hoping for *un milagro,* a miracle. She looked closely, but all that remained were black cinders.

There was nothing left inside, for someday.

❧

90 Esperanza saw her uncles approaching on horseback and ran to tell the others. Mama waited on the steps of the cabin with her arms crossed, looking like a fierce statue. Alfonso, Hortensia, and Miguel stood nearby.

"Ramona," said Tío Marco, remaining on his horse. "Another sadness in so short a time. We are deeply sorry."

"I have come to give you another chance," said Tío Luis. "If you reconsider my proposal, I will build a bigger, more beautiful house and I will replant everything. Of course, if you prefer, you can live here with the servants, as long as another tragedy does not happen to their homes as well. There is no main house or fields 100 where they can work, so you see that many people's lives and jobs depend upon you. And I am sure you want the best for Esperanza, do you not?"

Mama did not speak for several moments. She looked around at the servants who had gathered. Now, her face did not seem so fierce and her eyes were damp. Esperanza wondered where the servants would go when Mama told Tío Luis no.

Mama looked at Esperanza with eyes that said, "forgive me." Then she dropped her head and stared at the ground. "I will consider your proposal," said Mama.

110 Tío Luis smiled. "I am delighted! I have no doubt that you will make the right decision. I will be back in a few days for your answer." ❧

Keep Reading

You have just been introduced to three generations of Ortega women. Whose behavior surprised you the most, and why? As you continue to read *Esperanza Rising,* you will follow the Ortega family through hardship, injustice, and serious illness. Esperanza learns to triumph over the challenges she and her family face, while the strength of her mother and grandmother helps her grow into a remarkable young woman.

Words Like Freedom
Dreams
Poems by Langston Hughes

How do POSSIBILITIES
become realities?

COMMON CORE

RL 2 Determine a theme or central idea of a text and how it is conveyed through particular details. **RL 4** Analyze the impact of a specific word choice on meaning.

You've probably heard the saying "The sky's the limit." It means that anything is possible if we try hard enough. Even if we have unlimited possibilities, though, achieving our goals may require more than hard work. We may also need a strong desire to succeed and the help of people around us. In his poems "Words Like Freedom" and "Dreams," Langston Hughes describes some of the difficulties involved in living up to our potential.

WEB IT Think of a person who, in your opinion, is very successful. It could be a celebrity or someone you know. What helps this person to achieve his or her goals? Record your thoughts in an idea web like the one shown.

He has friends who support him.

My Uncle Steven

● TEXT ANALYSIS: THEME IN POETRY

Although a poem looks very different from a short story, it often contains a **theme,** or message about life. To identify a poem's theme, keep the following clues in mind:

- A poem's **title** sometimes helps you determine the theme by suggesting what the poem will focus on.
- A poet's use of **images** often helps to convey a poem's theme.
- Repeated words and phrases tell you how the **speaker,** or voice of the poem, feels.

Remember that there is a difference between a topic and a theme. Hughes's poems are about topics such as freedom, liberty, and dreams. The theme is Hughes's message or central idea *about* a topic like liberty.

As you read "Words Like Freedom" and "Dreams," look for images and the repeated words and phrases that help you determine the theme in each poem.

● READING STRATEGY: VISUALIZE

When you **visualize,** you form a mental picture based on a written description. Since poets often use images to express a poem's meaning, it is important for readers to visualize those images from key words and phrases.

As you read each poem, use a chart like the one shown to record the words and phrases that help you form specific mental pictures.

	Words and Phrases	Mental Picture
"Words Like Freedom"	1. "On my heartstrings freedom sings" (line 3)	1. someone singing out "freedom" with great feeling
"Dreams"		

 Complete the activities in your **Reader/Writer Notebook.**

Meet the Author

Langston Hughes
1902–1967

Writer from Harlem
In 1925, Langston Hughes left three of his poems with a famous author who was eating in the restaurant where Hughes worked. Sharing those poems led to his first book, *The Weary Blues.* Much of Hughes's writing focuses on the experiences of the people who lived around him in Harlem. "I knew only the people I had grown up with," he once said, "and they weren't people whose shoes were always shined.... But they seemed to me good people, too."

The Music of Poetry
Growing up, Hughes fell in love with jazz and the blues. He expressed this love by using blues themes, images, and rhythms in his poetry. In the 1950s, Hughes made a recording of his poems set to jazz.

Renaissance Man
Langston Hughes was one of the strongest voices of a cultural movement called the Harlem Renaissance, which took its name from the Harlem neighborhood in New York City and the time period called the Renaissance, which means "rebirth." During this period, which lasted for most of the 1920s, African-American artists, writers, and musicians worked to establish a proud and vibrant cultural identity.

Author Online **THINK** central

Go to **thinkcentral.com.**
KEYWORD: HML6-401

Words Like FREEDOM

Langston Hughes

There are words like *Freedom*
Sweet and wonderful to say.
On my heartstrings freedom sings
All day everyday.

5 There are words like *Liberty* **A**
That almost make me cry.
If you had known what I know
You would know why.

A THEME
Why does the speaker
choose to repeat the
words in lines 1 and 5?

La Grande Famille (1947), René Magritte. Oil on canvas, 100 cm × 81 cm. Private collection. © 2008 C. Herscovici, Brussels/Artists Rights Society (ARS), New York.

Dreams

Langston Hughes

Hold fast[1] to dreams
For if dreams die
Life is a broken-winged bird
That cannot fly.

5 Hold fast to dreams
For when dreams go
Life is a barren field
Frozen with snow.

B VISUALIZE
How does the mental picture of "a barren field frozen with snow" add to your understanding of the poem?

---

1. **Hold fast:** grasp tightly; stick firmly.

Comprehension

1. **Identify** In "Words Like Freedom", what do words like *liberty* make the speaker do?

2. **Recall** What line is repeated in "Dreams"?

Text Analysis

3. **Make Inferences** Reread the last two lines of "Words Like Freedom." What can you infer about the people the speaker is addressing?

● 4. **Visualize** Review the chart you filled in as you read. Then underline the words and phrases that had the strongest effect on you. Which poem was more effective at helping you visualize?

● 5. **Analyze Theme in Poetry** As you read, you looked for ways in which titles, images, and repeated words hinted at a poem's theme. Use a diagram like the one shown to write theme statements for Hughes's poems.

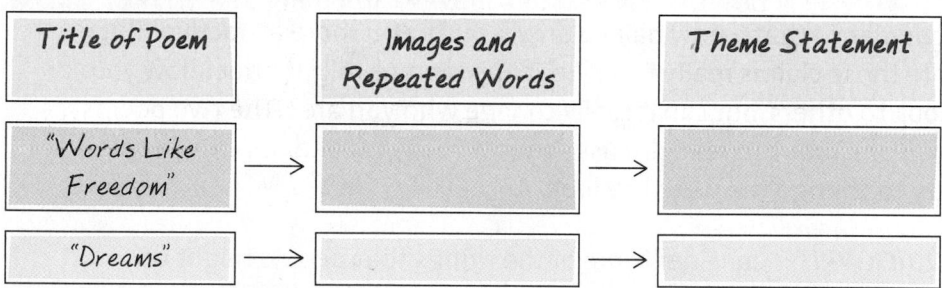

Title of Poem	Images and Repeated Words	Theme Statement
"Words Like Freedom"	→	→
"Dreams"	→	→

6. **Compare Theme** Compare the themes in "Words Like Freedom" and "Dreams." What message do you think Hughes is trying to convey?

Extension and Challenge

7. **Creative Project: Art** Like a piece of literature, a piece of visual art can mean different things to different people. Choose either "Words Like Freedom" or "Dreams" and create an original work of art to go with the poem. For inspiration, think about the poem's subject, details, and most of all, how the poem made you feel.

8. **Inquiry and Research** Research the civil rights movement to create a timeline of the important civil rights rulings and events that happened during Langston Hughes's lifetime (1902–1967). How might these events have affected Hughes's view of his possibilities?

How do POSSIBILITIES become realities?

What possibilities lie ahead for you in the future? What steps can you take to turn them into realities?

COMMON CORE

RL 2 Determine a theme or central idea of a text and how it is conveyed through particular details. **RL 4** Analyze the impact of a specific word choice on meaning. **W 7** Conduct short research projects to answer a question.

Same Song
Poem by Pat Mora

Without Commercials
Poem by Alice Walker

Can changing the way you LOOK change who you are?

COMMON CORE

RL 2 Determine a theme or central idea of a text and how it is conveyed through particular details. **RL 4** Analyze the impact of a specific word choice on meaning. **RL 5** Analyze how a particular stanza contributes to the development of the theme.

Advertisers suggest that a new pair of jeans will make you more popular or that a new hair color will make you more attractive. But are those claims really true? Your appearance might affect how you look to others, but can it really change who you are? The two poems you are about to read discuss some of the ways and reasons people try to change the way they look.

QUICKWRITE Consider some of the things that people might do when they want a new appearance. This could mean getting a haircut or a new sweater. Are there times, however, when changes to someone's appearance can be harmful? Write a brief paragraph to answer that question, including examples of harmful changes.

TEXT ANALYSIS: RECURRING THEME

The lessons learned from common life experiences are often expressed as themes in literature. When the same theme appears in more than one piece of literature, it is called a **recurring theme.**

Some themes recur (or occur over and over) for centuries. When you interpret these themes, it helps to notice the time and place in which the piece is written. The poems you are about to read were written in our time, so you will analyze them in a contemporary context. When you consider **contemporary context,** you think about how the poems reflect they way we live today. Both of the poems express a recurring theme about the importance of appearance in our society. However, each poet expresses her message in a different way. To get at the poets' shared theme, ask yourself the following questions as you read the poems:

- What is the subject being presented?
- What words tell you how the speaker feels?
- What images stand out in your mind as you read?
- What aspect of our society is the poet writing about?

READING SKILL: MAKE INFERENCES

When you **make inferences,** you make logical guesses based on two things: clues in the selection and what you already know from reading or from your own experience. As you read "Same Song" and "Without Commercials," use a chart like the one shown to record your inferences.

My Inferences	Clues from the Poems	What I Know
The girl in "Same Song" spends a lot of time getting ready each morning.	"stumbles into the bathroom at six a.m.," "curls," "strokes," "smoothes," "outlines"	It takes my sister a long time to do her hair and makeup.

Complete the activities in your **Reader/Writer Notebook.**

Meet the Authors

Pat Mora
born 1942

Beyond Borders
Pat Mora grew up feeling as though she didn't belong to either Mexican or American culture. She was born in El Paso, Texas, near the Mexican border. She later wrote in a poem that she was "an American to Mexicans / a Mexican to Americans." Mora has said that she writes to help give Hispanic ideas and issues a larger place in American literature and because she is "fascinated by the pleasure and power of words."

Alice Walker
born 1944

Solitary Observer
At the age of eight, Alice Walker was blinded in one eye by a shot from her brother's BB gun. The accident left horrible scars, but Walker later said that the emotions she went through during that time helped her to become a writer. Walker went on to become a highly influential author. In 1983, she became the first African-American woman to win the Pulitzer Prize in fiction for her novel *The Color Purple.*

Same Song

Pat Mora

While my sixteen-year-old son sleeps,
my twelve-year-old daughter
stumbles into the bathroom at six a.m.
plugs in the curling iron
5 squeezes into faded jeans
curls her hair carefully
strokes Aztec Blue shadow on her eyelids
smoothes Frosted Mauve blusher on her cheeks
outlines her mouth in Neon Pink
10 peers into the mirror, mirror on the wall
frowns at her face, her eyes, her skin,
not fair. **A**

At night this daughter
stumbles off to bed at nine
15 eyes half-shut while my son
jogs a mile in the cold dark
then lifts weights in the garage
curls and bench presses[1]
expanding biceps, triceps, pectorals,
20 one-handed push-ups, one hundred sit-ups
peers into that mirror, mirror and frowns too. **B**

for Libby

---

1. **curls and bench presses:** weight-lifting activities. Curls are done with the hands, wrists, and forearms. Bench presses involve lifting a weight with both arms while lying face-up.

A MAKE INFERENCES
Reread lines 10–12.
What does the speaker's daughter think is unfair?

B RECURRING THEME
Notice the phrase "mirror, mirror" in lines 10 and 21. What fairy tale does this phrase remind you of?

Lipsticks II, Philip Le Bas. Enamel paints on panel, 20 cm × 20 cm. Portal Gallery. © Bridgeman Art Library.

WITHOUT COMMERCIALS

Alice Walker

Listen,
stop tanning yourself
and talking about
fishbelly
5 white.
The color white
is not bad at all.
There are white mornings
that bring us days.
10 Or, if you must,
tan only because
it makes you happy
to be brown,
to be able to see
15 for a summer
the whole world's
darker
face
reflected
20 in your own. **C**

Stop unfolding
your eyes. **D**
Your eyes are
beautiful.
25 Sometimes
seeing you in the street
the fold zany[1]
and unexpected
I want to kiss
30 them
and usually
it is only
old
gorgeous
35 black people's eyes
I want
to kiss.

---

1. **zany:** silly in an outrageous sort of way.

C **RECURRING THEME**
Consider the title and first stanza of this poem in **contemporary context,** in terms of life today. What aspect of our society is the poet writing about?

D **MAKE INFERENCES**
Reread lines 21–22. What is meant by "unfolding your eyes"?

Stop trimming
your nose.
40 When you
diminish
your nose
your songs
become little
45 tinny, muted
and snub.
Better you should
have a nose
impertinent[2]
50 as a flower,
sensitive
as a root;
wise, elegant,
serious and deep.
55 A nose that
sniffs
the essence
of Earth. And knows
the message
60 of every
leaf. **E**

Stop bleaching
your skin
and talking
65 about
so much black
is not beautiful.
The color black
is not bad
70 at all.
There are black nights
that rock
us
in dreams.
75 Or, if you must,
bleach only
because it pleases you

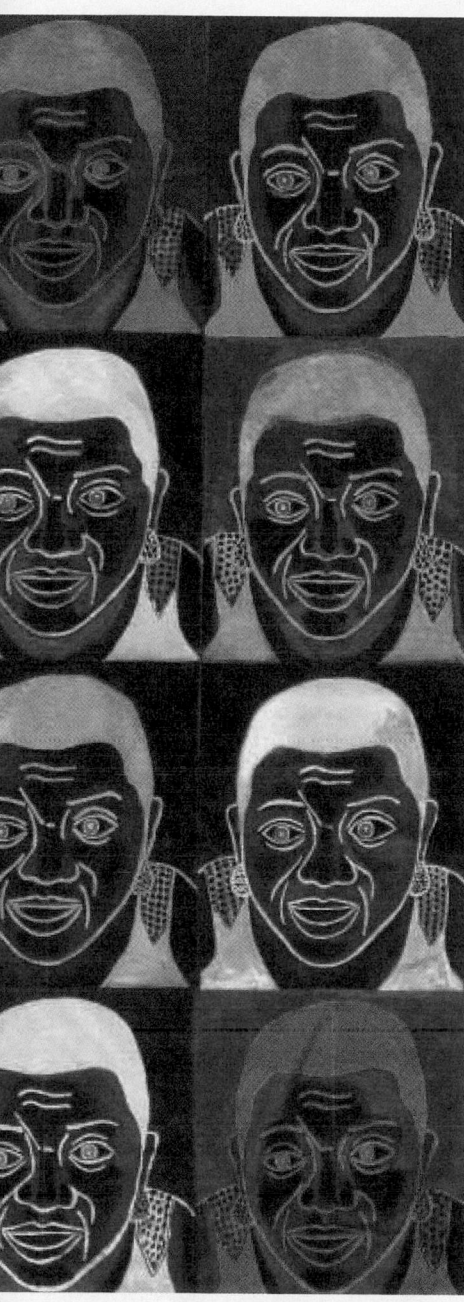

Detail of *Bessie's Blues: The American Collection #5* (1997), Faith Ringgold. Acrylic on canvas, painted, tie-dyed, and pieced fabric, 76⅞″ × 79¼″. Robert Allerton Endowment, 2002.381, The Art Institute of Chicago. Faith Ringgold © 1997.

E RECURRING THEME
What words and images in this stanza tell you how the speaker feels about the desire to change one's appearance?

2. **impertinent:** bold; beyond what is proper.

to be brown,
to be able to see
80 for as long
as you can bear it
the whole world's
lighter face
reflected
85 in your own. **F**

As for me,
I have learned
to worship
the sun
90 again.
To affirm
the adventures
of hair. **G**

For we are all
95 *splendid*
descendants
of Wilderness,
Eden:[3]
needing only
100 to see
each other
without
commercials
to believe.

105 Copied skillfully
as Adam.

Original

as Eve. **H**

F **RECURRING THEME**
According to lines 75–85, what would be the only good reason to bleach one's skin?

G **MAKE INFERENCES**
Reread lines 86–93. What does this stanza tell you about the speaker's attitude toward her own appearance?

H **THEME**
What is the poet saying about the world in which we live?

---

3. **Eden:** reference to the biblical Garden of Eden, the first home of the first humans.

Comprehension

1. **Clarify** In "Same Song," why does the daughter "stumble off to bed at nine" with her "eyes half shut"?

2. **Recall** To whom does the speaker compare everyone in "Without Commercials"?

3. **Paraphrase** Rewrite lines 94–108 of "Without Commercials" in your own words. Include a statement that paraphrases the poet's message about the world in which we live.

COMMON CORE

RL 2 Determine a theme or central idea of a text and how it is conveyed through particular details. RL 4 Analyze the impact of a specific word choice on meaning. RL 5 Analyze how a particular stanza contributes to the development of the theme.

Text Analysis

4. **Make Inferences** Look again at the inferences you recorded in your chart as you read. Which were most helpful in understanding each poem?

5. **Analyze Word Choice** Does "Without Commercials" present a mostly negative or mostly sympathetic view of people who try to change their natural appearance? Cite specific words and phrases as examples.

6. **Analyze Recurring Theme** Use a chart like the one below to gather information about the two poems. Then state in your own words the recurring theme both poems share about appearance.

	"Same Song"	"Without Commercials"
Subject Presented		
How Speaker Feels		
Images That Stand Out		

Theme About Appearance:

7. **Analyze Theme** How well do the poems reflect our society? Use examples from the poems to support your answer.

Extension and Challenge

8. **Creative Project: Writing** Keeping the recurring theme in mind, write an extra stanza for "Without Commercials" in which the speaker addresses the children from "Same Song." What advice would she give them?

Can changing the way you LOOK change who you are?

Do you believe the way we look makes us who we are, or does who we are determine how we look? Explain.

How was your day

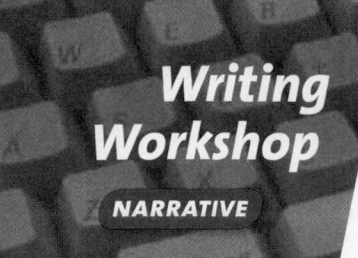

Writing Workshop

NARRATIVE

Short Story

What exciting places did the stories in this unit transport you to? What strange characters did you meet there, and what conflicts did you find? In this workshop, you'll use techniques such as dialogue and description to write an imaginative story with a plot, setting, and characters that you invent.

 Complete the workshop activities in your **Reader/Writer Notebook.**

WRITE WITH A PURPOSE

WRITING TASK

Write a **short story** set in an interesting place that will appeal to your audience. Make sure that your story has a plot, a conflict, and one or more characters.

Idea Starters
- a time-travel adventure
- a conflict among people your age
- a news story that could be fictionalized
- a "what if" situation

THE ESSENTIALS

Here are some common purposes, audiences, and formats for fictional writing.

PURPOSES	AUDIENCES	FORMATS
• to entertain your audience • to explore thoughts and feelings through characters	• classmates and teacher • friends • community members • Web users	• story for class • story for school literary magazine • classroom anthology • audio recording • Web page posting

COMMON CORE TRAITS

1. DEVELOPMENT OF IDEAS
- introduces and develops a **narrator** and/or **characters**
- introduces, develops, and resolves a **conflict**
- uses techniques such as **dialogue** and **description** to develop the plot and characters
- provides a satisfying **conclusion** that follows from the events

2. ORGANIZATION OF IDEAS
- presents an **event sequence** that unfolds naturally and logically
- uses effective **pacing** to advance the plot
- uses **transitions** to convey sequence and to indicate changes in time or setting

3. LANGUAGE FACILITY AND CONVENTIONS
- establishes and maintains a **point of view**
- includes **precise words** and **phrases,** relevant descriptive **details,** and **sensory language**

SEE OVERSET BELOW

Planning/Prewriting

COMMON CORE

W 3a–e Write narratives to develop real or imagined experiences or events using effective technique, descriptive details, and well-structured event sequences. W 5 Develop and strengthen writing as needed by planning.

Getting Started

CHOOSE A STORY IDEA

Use the Idea Starters on page 414 to help you identify possible subjects for your story. Ideas for short stories often begin with the question "What if?" Make a long list of "what if?" questions—on your own or with a friend. Put a star next to the one you like best.

▶ **WHAT DOES IT LOOK LIKE?**

> What if a character got on a bus or train and got off on a strange island?
>
> * What if a boy wanted to become the sacred medicine man of his tribe?
>
> What if I took a trip to the center of the Earth and found something new there?

THINK ABOUT AUDIENCE AND PURPOSE

As you begin to plan your story, keep your **purpose** in mind. To entertain your **audience,** you can make your story funny, scary, thrilling, mysterious, tragic, or hilarious. Think about the audience you want to reach and consider what kind of story would interest them.

▶ **ASK YOURSELF:**

- Who is my audience? What types of characters would they relate to?
- What kinds of stories keep readers interested until the very last page?
- What background information will my audience need to understand my story?

IDENTIFY CHARACTERS, CONFLICT, AND SETTING

Once you have a basic story idea, define your **characters** and the **conflict,** or problem, they will face. Your characters should be both appealing and realistic. Think about the kinds of characters you like to read about. Then make sure that the conflict they will face in your story is realistic and logical.

You'll also need to define the **setting** of your story—the time and place in which events happen. Your setting must be specific and believable, so think about the sensory and descriptive details you could include. Use a chart to list ideas for your story's characters, conflict, and setting.

As you plan your story, think about **pacing.** In a well-paced story, each event flows naturally to the next. The writer doesn't include unimportant or confusing details.

▶ **WHAT DOES IT LOOK LIKE?**

Characters	Setting
Little Bear Little Bear's father the elders Mon-o-La (the earth) the Great Spirit	long ago, near a Cherokee village

Conflict
Little Bear wants to become the tribe's medicine man, but the elders think he is too wild and young

Planning/Prewriting *continued*

Getting Started

DEVELOP THE PLOT

Your story's **plot**—the events in the story—should have five main stages: exposition, rising action, climax, falling action, and resolution. Review these stages on page 30. Then use a chart to plan the stages of your story's plot, or sequence of events.

The graphic on page 26 shows how events build to a **climax,** the most exciting point in a story. Your readers should experience **suspense**—a feeling of growing tension and excitement as they wonder what will happen next. As you plan your plot, remember to keep your readers guessing about how the story will turn out.

▶ **WHAT DOES IT LOOK LIKE?**

> **Exposition**: Introduce Little Bear and his conflict with the elders.
>
> ↓
>
> **Rising action**: The elders send Little Bear into the hills to find apples. Finally, he dreams about them.
>
> ↓
>
> **Climax:** He finds golden apple tree.
>
> ↓
>
> **Falling action**: He collects apples and returns home.
>
> ↓
>
> **Resolution**: The elders make him sacred medicine man.

CHOOSE A POINT OF VIEW

One of your characters can tell your story, using *I* and *me* to refer to himself or herself. This **first-person narrator** draws your readers in but doesn't always know everything about other characters or events. A **third-person narrator** is outside the story and refers to characters as *she, he,* and *they.* This type of narrator often shares the thoughts and feelings of the characters. Once you've decided on a point of view, be sure to keep it consistent throughout your story.

▶ **WHAT DOES IT LOOK LIKE?**

> **First-person point of view**
>
> For as long as I could remember, I had wanted to be the sacred medicine man of my tribe.

> **Third-person point of view**
>
> Little Bear longed to become the sacred medicine man of his tribe.

PEER REVIEW Briefly describe to a classmate what happens in each stage of your plot. Then ask: Do these events form a logical story? Do the events flow naturally, without distraction? How can I create more suspense for my readers?

 **YOUR TURN** In your Reader/Writer Notebook, plan your short story. Use a chart like the one on page 415 to record your characters, setting, and conflict. Then list the stages of your plot and decide whether a first-person or a third-person narrator would be better for the story.

Drafting

COMMON CORE W 4 Produce clear and coherent writing appropriate to task, purpose, and audience. **L1** Demonstrate command of standard English grammar and usage. **L2** Demonstrate command of standard English capitalization, punctuation, and spelling.

The following chart shows how to organize your draft to create a good short story.

Developing a Short Story

EXPOSITION

- Introduce the **setting,** the **main character,** and the **conflict** he or she faces.
- Engage and orient your readers in the first few lines. For example, if you start with some exciting action, they'll want to find out what happens next.
- Introduce a clear **narrator,** or the voice that tells the story.

▼

RISING ACTION AND CLIMAX

- Make the sequence of events clear by using **transitions** (such as *then, later that day,* and *the next week*). Use **pacing** to keep the action moving.
- Use **dialogue,** or the exact words characters say to each other, to show what the characters are like, to describe plot events and setting, or to create suspense.
- Make sure the conflict leads to an exciting climax. Readers should feel suspense building.
- Use **precise words** and **phrases, descriptive details,** and **sensory language** to create a vivid picture of the setting, events, and characters.

▼

FALLING ACTION AND RESOLUTION

- Show how the main character or characters resolve the conflict.
- Make sure your readers are not left with any unanswered questions.

GRAMMAR IN CONTEXT: PUNCTUATING DIALOGUE

Good dialogue brings characters to life. A speaker's exact words should be enclosed in quotation marks. Punctuation marks such as commas, question marks, and periods also belong inside quotes. Speaker tags, such as *she said,* may occur before, after, or within the quotation. They are separated from the dialogue by a comma.

Speaker Tag	Example
before the quotation ▶	*Finally,* **the elders said,** *"Go out into the hills."*
after the quotation ▶	*"Father, I have passed all the tests for a young warrior in the Cherokee nation,"* **Little Bear said** *humbly.*
within the quotation ▶	*"Your name,"* **said the elder,** *"is now Snow Child."*

Revising

When you revise, put yourself in the place of your audience. Read your draft to determine whether you have created an entertaining, suspenseful story. The questions, tips, and strategies in the following chart can help you rewrite where necessary, and revise and improve your draft.

SHORT STORY

Ask Yourself	Tips	Revision Strategies
1. Is the setting specific and believable?	▶ **Put a check mark** next to details about the setting.	▶ **Add** precise details about time and place, if needed.
2. Do the characters seem real? Does dialogue bring them to life for readers?	▶ **Highlight** character details, description, and dialogue.	▶ **Elaborate** as needed by adding descriptive and sensory details and dialogue.
3. Is the story's main conflict clear?	▶ **Underline** sentences that reveal the conflict.	▶ **Add** dialogue or action that makes the conflict clear for readers.
4. Are events arranged in sequential order and connected with transitions? Does the plot move forward and keep readers in suspense?	▶ **Number** each event and check that events are in the correct order. **Bracket** words or sentences that help create suspense.	▶ **Reorganize** events and **add** transitions if necessary. **Add** details to heighten suspense. **Cut or rearrange** details that slow down the pacing.
5. Is the first-person or the third-person point of view used consistently?	▶ **Circle** pronouns that establish the point of view in the opening paragraphs.	▶ **Replace** pronouns or details that shift the point of view.
6. Is the conflict resolved in a satisfying way? Does the resolution make sense?	▶ **Draw a star** next to the story's climax and resolution.	▶ **Add** a climax, or high point, if necessary. **Add** details to show how the conflict is resolved.

YOUR TURN **PEER REVIEW** Exchange stories with a partner and review each other's drafts. Answer each question in the chart to decide how your stories can be improved. If your partner has a lot of questions or is confused, consider trying a new approach. Take notes about each other's suggestions so that you can refer to them later, when you revise or rework your drafts.

ANALYZE A STUDENT DRAFT

Read this student's draft and the comments about it as a model for revising your own short story.

COMMON CORE **W 3b** Use narrative techniques, such as dialogue. **W 5** Develop and strengthen writing as needed by revising, editing, rewriting, or trying a new approach.

Apples in the Snow
by Jane Caflisch, Kensington Intermediate

1   Little Bear longed to become the sacred medicine man of his tribe.

2   The elders thought it unwise for him to become the medicine man. They said that he was too wild and young. But Little Bear persisted. Finally, the elders said, "Go out into the hills. If you can find apples in the snow, it will be a sign that the Great Spirit wills you to become our medicine man."

3   Little Bear fasted all day. Then he set out into the hills. He climbed and searched to no avail for that day and the next. He stopped often to pray to Mon-o-La, the earth, and to the Great Spirit.

> In the **exposition,** Jane introduces her **main character** and hints at the **conflict** he faces. She could use some **dialogue** to tell readers more about Little Bear's thoughts and feelings.

> The **rising action** is a sequence of events set in motion by the elders' test for Little Bear.

LEARN HOW   **Use Dialogue to Develop the Story**   Jane's first paragraph does little to help readers get to know Little Bear or understand the conflict he faces. When she revised her story, she decided to add a few lines of dialogue between Little Bear and his father. **Dialogue,** or the exact words spoken by characters, is an excellent way to provide information about characters and to advance the action of the plot. In this case, Jane used dialogue to reveal why Little Bear longs to be the sacred medicine man and why the elders might not let him to do it.

JANE'S REVISION TO PARAGRAPH 1

Little Bear longed to become the sacred medicine man of his tribe.

∧"Father, I have passed all tests for a young warrior in the Cherokee nation," Little Bear said humbly. "But I seek more challenge and more responsibility. I want to be our tribe's sacred medicine man."

"Little Bear," his father replied, "you have my permission to address the elders. Since you are only fourteen, they will surely reject your petition."

4   Then, on the third night, Little Bear had a dream. He dreamed that he was standing by a golden apple tree. Around it the snow had melted. Then from inside the tree came a musical voice. "Come pick my apples. I grow them for you, for you, for you. . . ." Little Bear awoke. He tried to think of what the dream meant. While he thought, he walked up the hill.

5   Thinking and walking, he soon reached the top. There he began to pray. When he opened his eyes, there was the golden apple tree of his dream. He waited for the voice to come, but when it did not, he decided that it had spoken in his dream and that was enough. So he picked the apples and started down the mountain thanking the goodness of the spirits. When he turned to look at the tree, it was gone.

6   When he reached his village, there was great feasting. The elders told him that the golden tree was the tree of Mon-o-La. So Little Bear became Snow Child and assumed the role of the tribe's sacred medicine man.

> Jane builds **suspense** by making readers wonder what Little Bear's dream means.

> The story reaches a **climax** as the main character achieves his goal.

> Jane's **resolution** shows how the conflict ends, but the **sequence of events** is confusing and paced unnaturally.

LEARN HOW Use a Logical Sequence of Events In Jane's draft, the feasting occurs *before* the elders accept Little Bear as the tribe's medicine man. A confusing detail like this can distract readers from a story's plot. Jane decided to revise her ending to make her resolution more logical, natural, and powerful. She knew that by rearranging the sequence of events and giving more details about the elders' decision, she would leave her readers with a well-paced ending and a lasting image.

JANE'S REVISION TO PARAGRAPH 6

~~When he reached his village, there was great feasting. The elders told him that the golden tree was the tree of Mon-o-La. So Little Bear became Snow Child and assumed the role of the tribe's sacred medicine man.~~

When Little Bear reached the village, he humbly presented the golden apple to the elders. Smiling broadly, the chief elder raised the apple high above his head and proclaimed Little Bear the tribe's sacred medicine man: "You are now Snow Child." The entire village feasted in his honor.

YOUR TURN Use feedback from your peers and your teacher as well as the two "Learn How" lessons to revise your short story. Does it fulfill the purpose of presenting the action of the story in a dramatic way? How could you revise or rework your resolution to leave a more lasting impression on your audience?

W 5 Strengthen writing by editing.
L 1 Demonstrate command of standard English grammar and usage. **L 2** Demonstrate command of standard English capitalization, punctuation, and spelling. **L 2b** Spell correctly.

Editing and Publishing

In the editing stage, you check your essay to make sure it is free of any errors in usage, punctuation, and sentence structure. You should also read carefully to catch any spelling errors, even if you do a spell-check on your computer. Edit your writing carefully, using proofreading marks to make the necessary corrections.

GRAMMAR IN CONTEXT: USING PARTICIPIAL PHRASES

A **participle** is a verb form that is being used as an adjective to describe something. **Participial phrases** provide action and movement in writing. When used at the beginning or end of a sentence, a participial phrase is separated from the main clause by a comma. For example, study the following sentence from Jane's short story:

> *Thinking and walking, he soon reached the top.*
>
> [*Thinking and walking* is a **participial phrase** made up of two participles. A comma separates it from the rest of the sentence.]

As Jane was proofreading her story, she found another participial phrase, this one at the end of a sentence. She had forgotten to use a comma, so she added one.

> *So he picked the apples and started down the mountain ‸ thanking the goodness of the spirit.*

PUBLISH YOUR WRITING

Share your short story with an audience.
- Present your story to your class as a dramatic reading.
- Turn the story into a graphic novel, with illustrations and speech balloons for dialogue.
- Make an audio recording of your story for listeners to enjoy.
- Share copies of your story with a small group. Then meet with the group to discuss your story.
- Create a class blog that describes the plot of your story and encourages your audience to read it.

YOUR TURN Correct any errors in your short story by carefully proofreading it. Add action, movement, and variety by using participial phrases and punctuating them correctly. Then publish your final story so that others can enjoy it.

Scoring Rubric

Use the rubric below to evaluate your short story from the Writing Workshop or your response to the on-demand prompt on the next page.

SHORT STORY

SCORE	COMMON CORE TRAITS
6	• **Development** Skillfully introduces, develops, and resolves a conflict; develops compelling, believable characters; effectively uses dialogue and descriptive details • **Organization** Has a smooth, logical event sequence that builds to a strong conclusion; uses effective transitions and pacing • **Language** Skillfully uses precise words and phrases; weaves in sensory language; shows a strong command of conventions
5	• **Development** Effectively introduces, develops, and resolves a conflict; develops interesting, believable characters; ably uses dialogue and descriptive details • **Organization** Has a logical event sequence that builds to a conclusion; uses mostly effective transitions and pacing • **Language** Effectively uses precise words and phrases; includes sensory language; has a few errors in conventions
4	• **Development** Introduces, develops, and resolves a conflict; has interesting characters; could use some more dialogue or descriptive details • **Organization** Includes some unimportant events, resulting in ineffective transitions and pacing • **Language** Mostly uses precise words and phrases; needs more sensory language; has a few distracting errors in conventions
3	• **Development** Introduces and resolves a conflict, but it needs more development; has some weak characters; needs more dialogue or descriptive details • **Organization** Has a confusing sequence at times; has a slow pace at times; needs more transitions • **Language** Uses some precise words and phrases; lacks enough sensory language; has some significant errors in conventions
2	• **Development** Has ineffective conflict, characters, dialogue, and details • **Organization** Has an unclear sequence and uneven pacing; lacks transitions • **Language** Mostly lacks precise words and phrases; mostly lacks sensory language; has many distracting errors in conventions
1	• **Development** Lacks conflict, developed characters, dialogue, and details • **Organization** Has no apparent organization • **Language** Lacks precise words and phrases; lacks sensory language; has major problems with conventions

Preparing for Timed Writing

COMMON CORE

W 10 Write routinely over shorter time frames for a range of tasks, purposes, and audiences.

---

1. ANALYZE THE TASK 5 MIN

Read the task carefully. Then read it again, underlining the words that tell the type of writing, the audience, and the purpose.

> **WRITING TASK** *Purpose* *Type of writing* *Audience*
>
> Write an <u>entertaining</u> <u>short story</u> for your <u>classmates</u> about a boy or girl your age who wants to play a team sport but whose parents are against it. Use precise language to establish a vivid setting and use dialogue to develop a believable plot and characters.

---

2. PLAN YOUR RESPONSE 10 MIN

Think about the boy or girl who will be the main character of your story. What precise details can you use to describe this person? The prompt has given you a conflict, but you need to decide what events happen as a result of the conflict and how the conflict is resolved. Use a chart, such as the one shown, to plan these events. Also think about the setting and whether you will use a first-person or a third-person narrator.

Conflict:	
	Event 1:
	Event 2:
	Event 3:
Resolution:	

---

3. RESPOND TO THE TASK 20 MIN

Use your notes to draft your short story. Follow these guidelines:

- Establish the setting, introduce the main character, and reveal the conflict the character faces. Include obstacles that make the conflict hard to resolve.
- As your story develops, use realistic dialogue to show what your characters are like and to advance the plot. Use effective pacing to keep the action moving.
- Be sure to end your story with a clear resolution of the conflict.

---

4. IMPROVE YOUR RESPONSE 5–10 MIN

Revising Review key aspects of your story. Did you explain the conflict? Did you describe the setting? Are your characters and resolution believable?

Proofreading Correct errors in grammar, spelling, punctuation, and capitalization. Make sure your edits are neat. Erase any stray marks.

Checking Your Final Copy Before you turn in your story, read it one more time to catch any errors you may have missed.

Technology Workshop

Creating a Class Blog

Have you or your friends ever posted a question or comment on a blog? A blog is a Web site with regular entries of text and other materials. On a class blog, you and your classmates can post short stories you have written. Then you can use your posts as a springboard to discuss topics related to your stories.

 Complete the workshop activities in your **Reader/Writer Notebook**.

PRODUCE WITH A PURPOSE	COMMON CORE TRAITS
TASK	**A SUCCESSFUL SHORT STORY BLOG . . .**
Create a **blog** in which you and your classmates share and discuss short stories. Your discussions may focus on a story's content, its elements, or its use of techniques. Plan and produce the blog with your group. Then add posts to spark discussion among your online community.	• focuses on discussing short stories • uses a structure that allows for easy navigation • has an appealing home page with easy-to-read text and multimedia components, such as graphics, images, and sound • includes posts that are clear and respectful • is updated regularly by all group members

COMMON CORE

W 6 Use technology, including the Internet, to produce and publish writing as well as to interact and collaborate with others; demonstrate sufficient command of keyboarding skills. **SL 1a–d** Engage effectively in collaborative discussions.

Plan and Produce Your Blog

The following guidelines include multiple action steps. Discuss them with your classmates as you create your blog.

- **Organize Stories and Topics** Read all of the stories for your blog in preparation for the planning discussion. Work with your team to create topics, or categories, that will lead to interesting posts and discussions. For example, you might organize your stories according to their forms or genres, such as adventure stories, historical fiction, and fantasy. Respectfully consider each suggestion a group member makes.

- **Agree on Your Discussion Threads** Include a separate discussion thread, or chain of posts, for each story and topic or category. Consider starting with two or three discussion threads. Later, you can add more. Remember, you have to update your blog regularly.

- **Design Your Home Page** Decide what text and multimedia features to include, and make a sketch of your home page. Remember to state the purpose of your blog and provide rules for participation.

- **Define Roles** A successful team works productively by collaborating. Assign roles to each group member, and set specific goals and deadlines for each task.

- **Build Your Blog** With the help of your school technology coordinator, create your blog using the Web site you chose.

Speaking & Listening Online

Go to thinkcentral.com.
KEYWORD: HML6N–424

Participate in an Online Discussion

A good online discussion can generate excitement and enthusiasm among the participants. Here are some tips for having interesting and meaningful online discussions:

- **Clearly State Your Idea or Purpose** Identify your purpose in your subject line and at the beginning of your post. Make it clear what story, or what post from another blogger, you are discussing. Remember to support what you are saying with specific details from the story or post.

- **Use the Language of Literature** Set a good example for other bloggers by using the correct terms when talking about story elements or narrative techniques. For example, refer to setting, plot, characters, dialogue, pacing, description, purpose, and audience.

- **Keep Your Post Short and to the Point** The most effective blog entries are brief and focused. Most bloggers don't want to scroll through too much text; some might skip over an entry that is too long.

- **Use a Respectful Tone** Some topics or stories might cause people to disagree. For example, comments on a story about a current event or a complicated issue might show multiple perspectives. Remember that your audience can't see you and observe your reactions to what they are writing. That's why it's important to use a polite tone, even if you disagree with another post.

- **Keep the Discussion Going** Remember that participation is what makes a blog discussion a success. Pose and respond to questions regularly with elaboration and detail. If a thread isn't generating much discussion, add comments that contribute to the topic, text, or issue.

- **Invite Other Classmates to Your Story Blogosphere** Send other classmates an e-mail with a link to your blog to encourage greater participation.

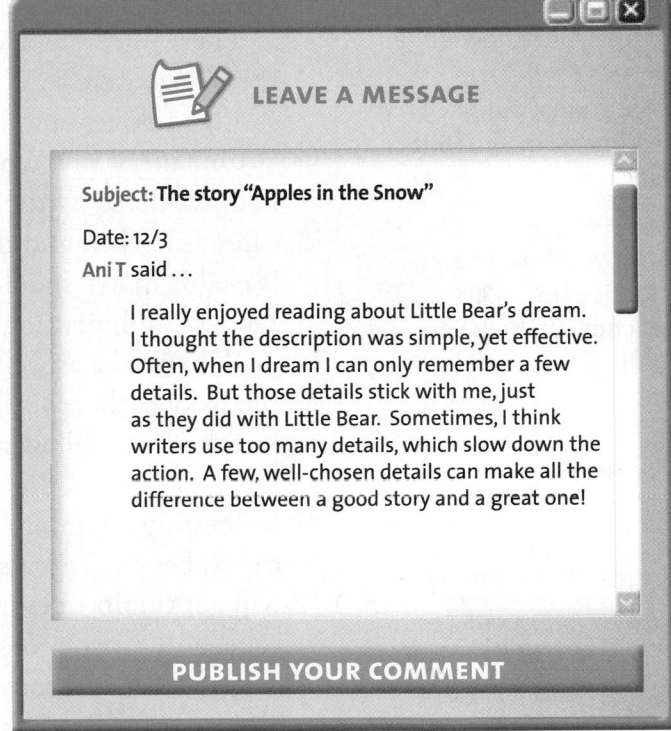

LEAVE A MESSAGE

Subject: **The story "Apples in the Snow"**

Date: 12/3

Ani T said . . .

I really enjoyed reading about Little Bear's dream. I thought the description was simple, yet effective. Often, when I dream I can only remember a few details. But those details stick with me, just as they did with Little Bear. Sometimes, I think writers use too many details, which slow down the action. A few, well-chosen details can make all the difference between a good story and a great one!

PUBLISH YOUR COMMENT

YOUR TURN Plan and produce a class blog using the instructions on these pages. Once you've launched your blog, visit it and post messages several times each week. Respond to a message in an existing thread or start a new thread. As a team, plan to add a new thread every few weeks.

Assessment Practice

DIRECTIONS Read these selections and answer the questions that follow.

The Wolf and the House Dog

by Aesop

1   There once was a Wolf who got very little to eat because the Dogs of the village were so wide awake and watchful. He was really nothing but skin and bones, and it made him very downhearted to think of it.

2   One night this Wolf happened to fall in with a fine fat House Dog who had wandered a little too far from home. The Wolf would gladly have eaten him then and there, but the House Dog looked strong enough to leave his marks should he try it. So the Wolf spoke very humbly to the Dog, complimenting him on his fine appearance.

3   "You can be as well fed as I am if you want to," replied the Dog. "Leave the woods; there you live miserably. Why, you have to fight hard for every bite you get. Follow my example and you will get along beautifully."

4   "What must I do?" asked the Wolf.

5   "Hardly anything," answered the House Dog. "Chase people who carry canes, bark at beggars, and fawn on the people of the house. In return you will get tidbits of every kind, chicken bones, choice bits of meat, sugar, cake, and much more besides, not to speak of kind words and caresses."

6   The Wolf had such a beautiful vision of his coming happiness that he almost wept. But just then he noticed that the hair on the Dog's neck was worn and the skin was chafed.

7   "What is that on your neck?"

8   "Nothing at all," replied the Dog.

9   "What! Nothing!"

10   "Oh, just a trifle!"

11   "But please tell me."

12   "Perhaps you see the mark of the collar to which my chain is fastened."

13   "What! A chain!" cried the Wolf. "Don't you go wherever you please?"

14   "Not always! But what's the difference?" replied the Dog.

15   "All the difference in the world! I don't care a rap for your feasts and I wouldn't take all the tender young lambs in the world at that price." And away ran the Wolf to the woods.

There is nothing worth so much as liberty.

Your World

by Georgia Douglas Johnson

Your world is as big as you make it
I know, for I used to abide
In the narrowest nest in a corner
My wings pressing close to my side.

5 But I sighted the distant horizon
Where the sky-line encircled the sea
And I throbbed with a burning desire
To travel this immensity.

I battered the cordons around me
10 And cradled my wings on the breeze
Then soared to the uttermost reaches
With rapture, with power, with ease!

Reading Comprehension

Use "The Wolf and the House Dog" to answer questions 1–7.

1. Which statement compares the way the Wolf and the House Dog feel at the beginning of the fable?

   A. Both want to change the way they live.

   B. The House Dog is lonely; the Wolf is scared.

   C. The House Dog is satisfied; the Wolf is unhappy.

   D. The House Dog is angry; the Wolf is friendly.

2. You can infer the House Dog probably avoids talking about the mark on his neck because he —

   A. does not know he has a mark

   B. is vain about his appearance

   C. feels ashamed to wear a collar

   D. thinks the Wolf will hurt him

3. The topic of this fable is —

   A. freedom

   B. friendship

   C. greed

   D. vanity

4. At the end of the fable, you can infer that the Wolf —

   A. feels sad that the House Dog has to wear a collar

   B. envies the House Dog, even though he wouldn't want to be him

   C. is glad he found out about the chain before moving into a house

   D. is sure he will find something to eat soon

5. What is the main difference between the attitude of the House Dog and that of the Wolf?

   A. The House Dog is boastful; the Wolf is humble.

   B. The House Dog prefers to be cared for; the Wolf prefers to be on his own.

   C. The House Dog likes people; the Wolf dislikes them.

   D. The House Dog is a good hunter; the Wolf is not.

6. What comparison can you make between the Wolf and the House Dog based on their physical appearance?

   A. The Wolf has a hard life; the House Dog has an easy life.

   B. The Wolf has a good life; the House Dog is mistreated.

   C. The Wolf is gray; the House Dog is spotted.

   D. The Wolf lives outdoors; the House Dog lives indoors.

7. The Wolf doesn't eat the House Dog because —

    A. the Wolf isn't hungry that day

    B. the Dog looks stronger than the Wolf

    C. other good food is available nearby

    D. the Dog's owners chase the Wolf away

> **Use "Your World" to answer questions 8–12.**

8. The topic of the poem is —

    A. leaving home

    B. choosing independence

    C. enjoying nature

    D. making friends

9. From the description in lines 2–4 you can infer that the speaker's life used to be —

    A. safe and predictable

    B. happy and comfortable

    C. lonely and harsh

    D. busy and exciting

10. The description in lines 11–12 suggests that the speaker has —

    A. become an important person

    B. experienced new adventures

    C. lived a life of luxury

    D. decided to return home

11. Which statement best describes the theme of this poem?

    A. Sometimes it is good to live alone.

    B. Happiness comes from traveling.

    C. Experience is the best teacher.

    D. You are as free as you want to be.

12. Reread line 9.

> "I battered the cordons around me."

You can infer that the speaker —

    A. did not want to change

    B. needed to feel safe in life

    C. had to overcome obstacles

    D. traveled around the world

> **Use both selections to answer question 13.**

13. What theme, or message about life, is found in both of these selections?

    A Being well fed is the key to survival.

    B. Liberty is more important than security.

    C. The truth will come out in the end.

    D. Some things are too good to be true.

SHORT CONSTRUCTED RESPONSE
Write three or four sentences to answer this question.

14. "The Wolf and the House Dog" and "Your World" are both about making choices. Compare the choices that the characters and the speaker make in these selections.

Write a paragraph to answer this question.

15. In what way is the speaker in "Your World" like the Wolf in Aesop's fable? Use details from the selections to support your answer.

Vocabulary

Use context clues and your knowledge of suffixes to answer the following questions.

1. What is the meaning of the word *immensity* in line 8 of "Your World"?

   A. Bigger

   B. Growing

   C. Hugeness

   D. Largely

2. What is the meaning of the word *rapture* in line 12 of "Your World"?

   A. Bliss

   B. Ecstatic

   C. Enchant

   D. Happily

3. What is the meaning of the word *appearance* in paragraph 2 of "The Wolf and the House Dog"?

   A. Groomed

   B. Handsome

   C. Looks

   D. Nicely

4. What is the meaning of the word *miserably* in paragraph 3 of "The Wolf and the House Dog"?

   A. Crying

   B. Depress

   C. Sadness

   D. Unhappily

Use context clues and your knowledge of multiple meaning words to answer the following questions.

5. Which meaning of the word *rap* is used in paragraph 15 of "The Wolf and the House Dog"?

   "I don't care a rap for your feasts…"

   A. Discussion

   B. Punishment

   C. Tap

   D. Bit

6. Which meaning of the word *trifle* is used in paragraph 10 of "The Wolf and the House Dog"?

   "Oh, just a trifle!"

   A. Small thing

   B. Custard dessert

   C. Tiny amount

   D. Shiny trinket

7. Which meaning of the word *abide* is used in lines 2–3 of "Your World"?

   "I know, for I used to abide
   In the narrowest nest in a corner"

   A. Await

   B. Comply

   C. Live

   D. Tolerate

Revising and Editing

DIRECTIONS Read this passage and answer the questions that follow.

---

(1) Call me when you get to Sue's my mom said nervously. (2) This was my first train trip on my own. (3) It was a big event in our family. (4) I was leaving Chicago. (5) I was going to my aunt's house in New York.

(6) My parents had said You're too young to travel alone. (7) They didn't want me to go by myself. (8) I convinced them to let me go, anyway. (9) I knew this would be a journey worth taking.

---

1. What is the BEST way to punctuate the dialogue in sentence 1?

   A. "Call me when you get to Sue's", my mom said nervously.

   B. "Call me when you get to Sue's" my mom said nervously.

   C. Call me when you get to Sue's, my mom said nervously.

   D. "Call me when you get to Sue's," my mom said nervously.

2. What is the BEST coordinating conjunction to combine sentences 2 and 3?

   A. Or   **C.** For

   B. So   **D.** But

3. What is the BEST way to combine sentences 4 and 5 by using one subject and two predicates?

   A. I was leaving Chicago; I was going to my aunt's house in New York.

   B. I was leaving Chicago and going to my aunt's house in New York.

   C. I was leaving Chicago, and I was going to my aunt's house in New York.

   D. My aunt and I were leaving Chicago and going to her house in New York.

4. What is the BEST way to punctuate the dialogue in sentence 6?

   A. My parents had said "You're too young to travel alone."

   B. My parents had said, You're too young to travel alone.

   C. My parents had said, "You're too young to travel alone."

   D. My parents had said "You're too young to travel alone".

5. What is the BEST coordinating conjunction to combine sentences 7 and 8?

   A. Or   **C.** But

   B. For   **D.** So

COMMON CORE

RL 10 Read and comprehend literature.

Ideas for Independent Reading

Which questions from Unit 3 made an impression on you? Continue exploring them with these books.

Can memories keep the past alive?

The Color of My Words
by Lynn Joseph

Anna Rosa is only 12, but she knows she's a writer. She soon learns that writing is powerful as well as dangerous. She also realizes that writing someone's story will help keep his memory alive.

Locomotion
by Jacqueline Woodson

Lonnie's parents are dead and he can't live with his sister. Everything seems bad—but every day, in Ms. Marcus's class, he writes poems about the people he loves so he'll never forget them. Slowly, things begin to get better.

Up on Cloud Nine
by Anne Fine

Stolly is in a coma and Ian can't help him, so Ian sits next to his friend's bed and starts writing down everything he remembers about Stolly's life. Will Ian's memories help Stolly understand his past when he wakes up?

When is a trip an adventure?

Gregor the Overlander
by Suzanne Collins

Gregor is so bored that a trip to the laundry room in the basement seems exciting. Before their clothes are dry, however, he and his sister are sucked into the Underland and have to fight their way back home.

Hatchet
by Gary Paulsen

Brian is on a small plane going to visit his father the summer after his parents' divorce. Suddenly, the pilot has a heart attack and Brian finds himself alone in the Canadian wilderness. How will he survive?

Journey to the River Sea
by Eva Ibbotson

Maia is nervous and excited when she sets off from England to live with relatives in Brazil. She doesn't realize that her sea voyage and a trip on the Amazon are only the beginning of a bigger adventure.

Should you live for the present or the future?

The Fire-Eaters
by David Almond

Bobby's life has just gone bad: He has cruel teachers, a sick father, and the United States is about to enter a nuclear war. Then Bobby meets McNulty, a fire-eater. Can believing in miracles help Bobby see hope for the future?

Gentle's Holler
by Kerry Madden

Dreaming of the future, Livy sees herself standing on the Great Wall of China, not up in a tree in North Carolina watching her little sisters. After a terrible accident, Livy has to decide if her dreams are more important than her family.

Listening for Lions
by Gloria Whelan

When her parents die during an epidemic in Africa, Rachel's deceitful neighbors send her to England in their dead daughter's place. Will Rachel be stuck living a lie or will she be able to return to the country she loves?

Get Novel Wise

THINK central

Go to **thinkcentral.com**.
KEYWORD: HML6-432

UNIT 4

Writer's Craft

SENSORY LANGUAGE, IMAGERY, AND STYLE

- In Fiction
- In Nonfiction
- In Poetry
- In Drama
- In Media

Who has STYLE?

Picture some people you know. How do they look? What are they wearing? Perhaps one person has neatly trimmed hair and wears a button-down shirt. Another is dressed in an old T-shirt and flip-flops, and has ten bracelets on each wrist. However these people look or act, each is displaying a personal style—the choices that make him or her unique. Writers, filmmakers, and artists also have a unique style. They display this style through the way they choose to tell their stories or express their ideas.

ACTIVITY Think of a television or movie character who has a distinct personal style. Get together with a few classmates and describe your character's style without naming him or her. Can the others guess your choice?

Reader (1999), William Wegman. Color Polaroid, 24″ × 20″.

Lion King (1999), William Wegman. Color Polaroid, 24″ × 20″.

Glamour Puss (1999), William Wegman. Color Polaroid, 24″ × 20″.

Preview Unit Goals

TEXT ANALYSIS
- Determine the meaning of words and phrases as they are used in the text, including figurative and connotative meanings
- Analyze the impact of a specific word choice on meaning and tone
- Analyze how a particular sentence, paragraph, or section fits in the overall structure and contributes to the development of ideas
- Describe how a story's plot unfolds in a series of episodes

READING
- Cite textual evidence to support what the text says explicitly as well as inferences drawn from the text

WRITING AND LANGUAGE
- Write a literary analysis
- Demonstrate command of the conventions of grammar

SPEAKING AND LISTENING
- Present a literary analysis

VOCABULARY
- Verify the preliminary determination of the meaning of a word by checking the inferred meaning in a dictionary
- Use context clues and affixes as clues to the meaning of a word

ACADEMIC VOCABULARY
- aspect
- interpret
- sensory
- distinctive
- perceive

MEDIA AND VIEWING
- Integrate information presented in different media to develop a coherent understanding of a topic

Media Smart DVD-ROM

Artists and Style

Discover how artists and illustrators create style in their works. Page 552

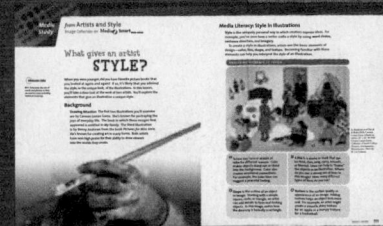

Sensory Language, Imagery, and Style

Every story has its own unmistakable personality—one that you respond to positively or negatively. Here, you'll learn about the elements that make up a story's personality. These elements are sensory language, imagery, and style.

Part 1: Imagery and Sensory Language—Words That Create Pictures

COMMON CORE

Included in this workshop:
RL 4 Determine the meaning of words and phrases as they are used in a text, including figurative and connotative meanings; analyze the impact of a specific word choice on meaning and tone.

To help readers share their experiences of the world, writers create images. **Imagery** is language that creates pictures. An **image** is a single word or phrase that appeals to our senses. Writers hope their images will unlock storehouses of memory and stir our imaginations. They hope their images will make us say "Oh, yes, I see what you mean."

Writers use **sensory language** to describe things they've experienced or imagined. Sensory language and imagery are part of a writer's style. They represent the writer's own way of seeing the world. An image or description can be so fresh, so powerful that it can speak to our deepest feelings. It can be phrased in a way that it makes us feel joy or grief, wonder or horror, love or disgust. Take a close look at the imagery and sensory language in the examples below. Which of your senses do they appeal to?

IMAGERY

Imagery is language that appeals to the senses.

Example: Vivid Imagery

Vivid imagery helps us see, smell, and feel the scene. The highlighted phrases help put you right in the midst of the field.

They were standing in a sunlit field, and the air about them was moving with the delicious fragrance that comes only on the rarest of spring days when the sun's touch is gentle . . .

—from *A Wrinkle in Time* by Madeleine L'Engle

SENSORY LANGUAGE

Sensory language is the words writers use to create images.

Example: Sensory Language

Paulsen's descriptive words make fun of his clumsiness and help you see what kind of carpenter he was.

. . . I worked in construction, mostly hitting my fingers with a hammer and making serious attempts at cutting something off my body with power saws while I tried to build houses. . . .

—from *My Life in Dog Years* by Gary Paulsen

MODEL 1: IMAGERY

In his memoir, author Jerry Spinelli shares his memories of growing up in Pennsylvania. Read on to find out what Spinelli remembers about one important subject—his family's garbage can!

from # Knots in My Yo-Yo String
Memoir by **Jerry Spinelli**

To lift the lid off the garbage can was to confront all the horrors of the creepiest movie: dead, rotting matter; teeming colonies of pale, slimy creeping things; and a stench that could be survived only in the smallest whiffs.

5   Ironically, the garbage can was never more disgusting than the day *after* garbage collection—for the collection was never quite complete. The garbage man would snatch the can from our curbside and overturn it into the garbage truck's unspeakable trough. He would bang it once, maybe twice, against the trough wall. This would dislodge most of the

10   garbage, including a rain of maggots, but not the worst of it, not the very bottom of it, the most persistent, the oldest, the rottenest, the vilest.

Close Read

1. Many details, including the one in the box, help you to see or smell the garbage. Identify three other images.

2. Review the imagery in this description of a garbage can. Which senses does Spinelli appeal to?

MODEL 2: SENSORY LANGUAGE

A young Chinese immigrant named Moon Shadow comes to San Francisco to join his father. Shortly after Moon Shadow arrives, he follows his father on a mysterious nighttime mission. As you read, notice the sensory language used to describe the setting.

from # DRAGONWINGS
Novel by **Laurence Yep**

I counted to ten before I followed him outside. It was a night when the thick fog drifted through the streets and I could not see more than an arm's length before me, and everything seemed unreal, as if I were asleep and dreaming. The gaslights showed in the fog only as dull spots of

5   light—like ghosts hovering. A building would appear out of the grayness and then disappear. The whole world seemed to have become unglued. If ever there was a night for monsters to be out, this was the night.

Close Read

1. The boxed detail helps readers to picture the nighttime setting. Find three more sensory details that describe the setting.

2. Review the sensory details you found. If you were painting a picture of this setting which details would you include?

Part 2: What Is Style?

You've seen how sensory language and imagery can affect your reaction to a story. Style, though, is what really gives a story its one-of-a-kind personality. **Style** refers to a writer's unique way of communicating ideas. It is the result of many literary elements and devices, including word choice, sentence structure, imagery, point of view, tone, and voice. You'll learn about some of these elements as you examine two excerpts by authors with different styles.

E. L. KONIGSBURG'S STYLE

Claudia and Jamie awoke very early the next morning. It was still dark. Their stomachs felt like tubes of toothpaste that had been all squeezed out. Giant economy-sized tubes. They had to be out of bed and out of sight before the museum staff came on duty.

—from *From the Mixed-up Files of Mrs. Basil E. Frankweiler*

JEAN CRAIGHEAD GEORGE'S STYLE

Miyax pushed back the hood of her seal-skin parka and looked at the Arctic sun. It was a yellow disc in a lime-green sky, the colors of six o'clock in the evening and the time when the wolves awoke. Quietly she put down her cooking pot and crept to the top of a dome-shaped frost heave, one of the many earth buckles that rise and fall in the crackling cold . . .

—from *Julie of the Wolves*

WORD CHOICE

Word choice, or a writer's use of language, is a basic element of style.

- Konigsburg: Uses casual, informal language like *giant* and *squeezed out*.
- George: Uses precise, descriptive adjectives, such as *lime-green* and *dome-shaped*.

SENTENCE STRUCTURE

Sentence structure refers to the lengths and types of sentences a writer uses.

- Konigsburg: Writes in short, simple sentences, creating a straightforward style.
- George: Uses longer, complex sentences that are packed with descriptions.

IMAGERY

Some writers are known for their use of **imagery,** language that appeals to readers' senses.

- Konigsburg: Includes a humorous image— stomachs *like tubes of toothpaste*. This creates a playful style.
- George: Uses vivid images like *yellow disc in a lime-green sky*.

MODEL 1: COMPARING STYLES

Buried riches, greedy pirates, and wild adventures are all part of Robert Louis Stevenson's novel *Treasure Island*. In this excerpt, a boy and his mother open a sea chest that once belonged to a ship captain. An evil blind man is in pursuit of the chest. As you read, you'll examine the elements that help to create Stevenson's dramatic and formal style.

from # Treasure Island

Novel by **Robert Louis Stevenson**

When we were about half-way through, I suddenly put my hand upon her arm; for I had heard in the silent, frosty air, a sound that brought my heart into my mouth—the tap-tapping of the blind man's stick upon the frozen road. It drew nearer and nearer, while we sat
5 holding our breath. Then it struck sharp on the inn door, and then we could hear the handle being turned, and the bolt rattling as the wretched being tried to enter; and then there was a long time of silence both within and without.

Close Read

1. One element of Stevenson's style is his use of sensory language and imagery. Find three images that help you to hear what's happening. One example has been boxed.

2. Would you describe Stevenson's sentences as short and simple or as long and complex? Support your answer.

MODEL 2: COMPARING STYLES

The characters in this modern story are also startled by a sound at their door. As you read, you'll look closely at the elements that make Bruce Coville's style lighter and more informal than Stevenson's.

from # Duffy's Jacket

Short story by **Bruce Coville**

"There's something at the door," I said frantically. "Maybe it's been lurking around all day, waiting for our mothers to leave. Maybe it's been waiting for years for someone to come back here."
Scratch, scratch.
5 "I don't believe it," said Duffy. "It's just the wind moving a branch. I'll prove it."
He got up and headed for the door. But he didn't open it. Instead he peeked through the window next to it. When he turned back, his eyes looked as big as the hard-boiled eggs we had eaten for supper.

Close Read

1. How do the boxed sentences compare with the sentences in *Treasure Island*?

2. Informal dialogue is one element of Coville's style. Reread the dialogue in lines 1–6. Which words or phrases make this sound like an everyday conversation?

Part 3: Analyze the Text

Now, you'll apply what you've learned by analyzing two excerpts. Both excerpts describe summer days, but they are strikingly different. Read on to see how sensory language, imagery, and style help to create these differences.

The first excerpt is from the beginning of the novel *Tuck Everlasting*. Don't worry if you don't know exactly what's happening. This is an intentional choice by the author, and it's meant to draw you into the story.

from

Tuck Everlasting

Novel by **Natalie Babbitt**

The first week of August hangs at the very top of summer, the top of the live-long year, like the highest seat of a Ferris wheel when it pauses in its turning. The weeks that come before are only a climb from balmy spring, and those that follow a drop to the chill of autumn, but the first
5   week of August is motionless, and hot. It is curiously silent, too, with blank white dawns and glaring noons, and sunsets smeared with too much color. Often at night there is lightning, but it quivers all alone. There is no thunder, no relieving rain. These are strange and breathless days, the dog days, when people are led to do things they are sure to be
10 sorry for after.

One day at that time, not so very long ago, three things happened and at first there appeared to be no connection between them.

At dawn, Mae Tuck set out on her horse for the wood at the edge of the village of Treegap. She was going there, as she did once every ten
15 years, to meet her two sons, Miles and Jesse.

At noontime, Winnie Foster, whose family owned the Treegap wood, lost her patience at last and decided to think about running away.

And at sunset a stranger appeared at the Fosters' gate. He was looking for someone, but he didn't say who.
20 No connection, you would agree. But things can come together in strange ways. The wood was at the center, the hub of the wheel. All wheels must have a hub. A Ferris wheel has one, as the sun is the hub of the wheeling calendar. Fixed points they are, and best left undisturbed, for without them, nothing holds together. But sometimes people find
25 this out too late.

Close Read

1. One aspect of Babbitt's style is her use of colorful imagery. What images in lines 1–10 tell you what the first week of August is like? To which senses do these images appeal?

2. The writer's style might be described as both conversational and secretive. What words and phrases in lines 11–12 and 20–25 contribute to this style?

3. Reread the boxed detail, in which the narrator delivers a strange warning. Also review the images you found in lines 1–10. Which other examples of sensory language and imagery in the excerpt reinforce this strange warning?

The summer days that Jewell Parker Rhodes describes in "Block Party" are ones that she herself experienced as a child. As you read this excerpt, you'll analyze some of the elements that make Rhodes's description so different from Babbitt's.

from

BLOCK PARTY

Memoir by **Jewell Parker Rhodes**

Summer block parties were the best. We'd close off traffic and sometimes the Fire Department would open the hydrants and we'd dance and sing while water gushed at us. A spray of wet beneath the moon and stars. Tonie, Aleta, and I pushed boxes together to make a stage and lipsynched to the record player, pretending we were The Supremes. *"Stop, in the name of love! Before you break my heart. Think it o-o-over! . . ."* and we'd giggle as the grown-ups clapped and the other children squealed, and everyone danced, even fat Charlie who could boogie so well you'd swear there was magic in his shoes.

The best block parties happened for no reason. Anyone—even a child—could wake up one day and call for "Block Party Day." And we'd share ribs, corn, chicken, tater pie, and collard greens, and Miss Sarah who never married always made punch with vanilla ice cream and it would melt into a swishy mess. Finally, when legs wouldn't move another dance step, then the record player was taken away, the street was swept. There were cries and whispers of good night. My real family and I, we'd go into the house. Grandma, Grandpa, Aunt, and Daddy would tuck us in bed and kiss me, Tonie, and Aleta good night. And I would wait until Tonie and Aleta were asleep in the small twin beds (I didn't want them to think I was off my head) and I'd go to the window. Then, peeking over the ledge, I'd whisper my own private "G'night" to the rest of my family, tucked in their beds inside the tall houses all along my street, there in the city where the three rivers meet.

Close Read

1. What images in lines 1–14 help to establish the joyful mood of the summer scene?

2. Reread the boxed text. Notice that Rhodes packs many thoughts into one long sentence, using a series of *and*'s. Identify another sentence that reflects this style.

3. Words like *G'night* in line 21 help to create a conversational style. Find two other informal words or phrases.

4. How would you describe Rhodes's feelings about block parties? Use examples of her sensory language and imagery to support your response.

The All-American Slurp

HISTORY Video link at thinkcentral.com

Short Story by Lensey Namioka

Are people more ALIKE or different?

COMMON CORE

RL 4 Determine the meaning of words and phrases as they are used in a text, including figurative and connotative meanings; analyze the impact of a specific word choice on meaning and tone.

Have you ever been somewhere and found that the language, food, or customs were different than what you were used to? You may have felt out of place. Or perhaps you discovered that you actually had a lot in common with the people you met. In "The All-American Slurp," a Chinese-American girl learns that people can share similarities even when they appear very different at first.

SURVEY Complete the survey below. Then form a group with two or three people you don't know well. Share your surveys to see how much you do (or don't) have in common.

Survey:

Choose Your Favorites

Choose your favorite from each grouping. Then find out how your classmates answered.

Music
- Rock 'n' Roll
- Country
- Classical

Food
- Desserts
- Spicy Foods
- Salty Snacks

Holidays
- Thanksgiving
- Halloween
- Valentine's Day
- Fourth of July

Movies
- Dramas
- Comedies
- Musicals
- Sci-Fi

Seasons
- Winter
- Spring
- Summer
- Fall

● TEXT ANALYSIS: TONE AND IMAGERY

Have you ever been embarrassed? Sometimes people use humor to make light of an embarrassing experience. Lensey Namioka writes about a series of awkward situations one family faces after immigrating to a new country. Having gone through a similar experience, she makes light of the situation by using a humorous tone and memorable imagery.

A writer's **tone** is his or her attitude towards a subject. Tone can often be described in a single word, such as angry, playful, or admiring. Namioka establishes a humorous tone toward her subject through her characters' thoughts, words, and actions. She also uses strong **imagery**—words and phrases that appeal to one or more of our senses—to help you imagine the funny scenarios in her story. Most sensory images are visual, but images can often appeal to several senses at once.

● READING STRATEGY: VISUALIZING

Details in a story help you **visualize,** or picture in your mind, what takes place. Record the ways in which the writer's sensory images help you visualize the events in the story.

Details	What I Visualize
Mother combs June's hair.	a mother combing her daughter's hair in front of a mirror and smiling

▲ VOCABULARY IN CONTEXT

Namioka uses the listed words in her story. To see how many you know, complete each sentence with a word from the list.

WORD	consumption	etiquette	mortified
LIST	cope	lavishly	revolting

1. Follow proper _____ when you meet someone new.
2. I'm _____ when I can't remember someone's name.
3. Their sofa was _____ decorated with fancy pillows.
4. That weird stew was absolutely _____!
5. The waiter had to _____ with the loud guests.
6. _____ of too many spicy foods makes me feel ill.

 Complete the activities in your **Reader/Writer Notebook.**

Meet the Author

Lensey Namioka
born 1929

Outsiders' Stories
Lensey Namioka says that her stories tell about people who feel like "outsiders." This is true whether the story is set in present-day Seattle or 16th-century Japan. To write these stories, she draws upon her own experiences.

Growing Up on the Outside
Namioka grew up in China. When war broke out in 1937, her family moved to western China, where the food was very spicy and the dialect (regional form of a language) was hard to understand. This made her feel like an outsider in her own country. Before the war ended, her family moved to the United States. The strange customs, food, and language of her new country made her feel even more like an outsider.

Living in Two Worlds
At first, Namioka's father charged everyone in the family a fine for each English word used at home. He did so because he did not want his family to forget the Chinese language. Namioka's mother ended the fines when she refused to pay. "Besides," says Namioka, "there were words that just had no Chinese translation. How do you say 'cheeseburger' in Chinese, for instance?"

Author Online **THINK** central
Go to thinkcentral.com.
KEYWORD: HML6-443

443

The All-American Slurp

Lensey Namioka

The first time our family was invited out to dinner in America, we disgraced ourselves while eating celery. We had emigrated to this country from China, and during our early days here we had a hard time with American table manners.

In China we never ate celery raw, or any other kind of vegetable raw. We always had to disinfect the vegetables in boiling water first. When we were presented with our first relish tray, the raw celery caught us unprepared.

We had been invited to dinner by our neighbors, the Gleasons. After
10 arriving at the house, we shook hands with our hosts and packed ourselves into a sofa. As our family of four sat stiffly in a row, my younger brother and I stole glances at our parents for a clue as to what to do next. **A**

Mrs. Gleason offered the relish tray to Mother. The tray looked pretty, with its tiny red radishes, curly sticks of carrots, and long, slender stalks of pale green celery. "Do try some of the celery, Mrs. Lin," she said. "It's from a local farmer, and it's sweet."

Mother picked up one of the green stalks, and Father followed suit. Then I picked up a stalk, and my brother did too. So there we sat, each with a stalk of celery in our right hand.

20 Mrs. Gleason kept smiling. "Would you like to try some of the dip, Mrs. Lin? It's my own recipe: sour cream and onion flakes, with a dash of Tabasco sauce."

Analyze Visuals ▶

What emotion or attitude does the girl's facial expression convey?

A **TONE AND IMAGERY**
Reread lines 1–12. What words and images help create a humorous tone toward the subject of the story?

Most Chinese don't care for dairy products, and in those days I wasn't even ready to drink fresh milk. Sour cream sounded perfectly **revolting**. Our family shook our heads in unison.

Mrs. Gleason went off with the relish tray to the other guests, and we carefully watched to see what they did. Everyone seemed to eat the raw vegetables quite happily.

Mother took a bite of her celery. *Crunch.* "It's not bad!" she whispered.

30 Father took a bite of his celery. *Crunch.* "Yes, it *is* good," he said, looking surprised.

I took a bite, and then my brother. *Crunch, crunch.* It was more than good; it was delicious. Raw celery has a slight sparkle, a zingy taste that you don't get in cooked celery. When Mrs. Gleason came around with the relish tray, we each took another stalk of celery, except my brother. He took two.

There was only one problem: long strings ran through the length of the stalk, and they got caught in my teeth. When I help my mother in the kitchen, I always pull the strings out before slicing celery.

40 I pulled the strings out of my stalk. *Z-z-zip, z-z-zip.* My brother followed suit. *Z-z-zip, z-z-zip, z-z-zip.* To my left, my parents were taking care of their own stalks. *Z-z-zip, z-z-zip, z-z-zip.* **B**

Suddenly I realized that there was dead silence except for our zipping. Looking up, I saw that the eyes of everyone in the room were on our family. Mr. and Mrs. Gleason, their daughter Meg, who was my friend, and their neighbors the Badels—they were all staring at us as we busily pulled the strings of our celery.

That wasn't the end of it. Mrs. Gleason announced that dinner was served and invited us to the dining table. It was **lavishly** covered with
50 platters of food, but we couldn't see any chairs around the table. So we helpfully carried over some dining chairs and sat down. All the other guests just stood there.

Mrs. Gleason bent down and whispered to us, "This is a buffet dinner. You help yourselves to some food and eat it in the living room."

Our family beat a retreat back to the sofa as if chased by enemy soldiers. For the rest of the evening, too **mortified** to go back to the dining table, I nursed[1] a bit of potato salad on my plate. **C**

Next day Meg and I got on the school bus together. I wasn't sure how she would feel about me after the spectacle[2] our family made at the party.
60 But she was just the same as usual, and the only reference she made to the party was, "Hope you and your folks got enough to eat last night. You certainly didn't take very much. Mom never tries to figure out how

---

1. **nursed:** very slowly ate.
2. **spectacle:** public display of bad behavior.

revolting (rĭ-vōl'tĭng) *adj.* causing disgust
revolt v.

B TONE AND IMAGERY
Using a word that sounds like what it means is called **onomatopoeia** (ŏn'ə-măt'ə-pē'ə). Notice the word *crunch* in lines 29–30 and the word *z-z-zip* in lines 40–42. How do these words add humor to the story? Which senses do these images of eating celery appeal to?

lavishly (lăv'ĭsh-lē) *adv.* in a rich or plentiful way; abundantly

mortified (môr'tə-fīd') *adj.* ashamed, humiliated
mortify v.

C VISUALIZE
In line 55, what picture does the description of the family beating "a retreat back to the sofa as if chased by enemy soldiers" create in your mind?

◀ **Analyze Visuals**
Based on the food shown, what can you **infer** about the event pictured here?

much food to prepare. She just puts everything on the table and hopes for the best."

I began to relax. The Gleasons' dinner party wasn't so different from a Chinese meal after all. My mother also puts everything on the table and hopes for the best. **D**

Meg was the first friend I had made after we came to America. I eventually got acquainted with a few other kids in school, but Meg
70 was still the only real friend I had.

My brother didn't have any problems making friends. He spent all his time with some boys who were teaching him baseball, and in no time he could speak English much faster than I could—not better, but faster.

I worried more about making mistakes, and I spoke carefully, making sure I could say everything right before opening my mouth. At least I had a better accent than my parents, who never really got rid of their Chinese accent, even years later. My parents had both studied English in school before coming to America, but what they had studied was mostly written English, not spoken.

D TONE
The tone of lines 65–67 is different from the tone the author used to describe the dinner party. Choose one word to describe the tone of this paragraph.

80 Father's approach to English was a scientific one. Since Chinese verbs have no tense, he was fascinated by the way English verbs changed form according to whether they were in the present, past imperfect, perfect, pluperfect, future, or future perfect tense. He was always making diagrams of verbs and their inflections,[3] and he looked for opportunities to show off his mastery of the pluperfect and future perfect tenses, his two favorites. "I shall have finished my project by Monday," he would say smugly.[4]

Mother's approach was to memorize lists of polite phrases that would cover all possible social situations. She was constantly muttering things
90 like "I'm fine, thank you. And you?" Once she accidentally stepped on someone's foot, and hurriedly blurted, "Oh, that's quite all right!" Embarrassed by her slip, she resolved to do better next time. So when someone stepped on *her* foot, she cried, "You're welcome!"

In our own different ways, we made progress in learning English. But I had another worry, and that was my appearance. My brother didn't have to worry, since Mother bought him blue jeans for school, and he dressed like all the other boys. But she insisted that girls had to wear skirts. By the time she saw that Meg and the other girls were wearing jeans, it was too late. My school clothes were bought already, and we didn't have money
100 left to buy new outfits for me. We had too many other things to buy first, like furniture, pots, and pans.

The first time I visited Meg's house, she took me upstairs to her room, and I wound up trying on her clothes. We were pretty much the same size, since Meg was shorter and thinner than average. Maybe that's how we became friends in the first place. Wearing Meg's jeans and T-shirt, I looked at myself in the mirror. I could almost pass for an American—from the back, anyway. At least the kids in school wouldn't stop and stare at me in the hallways, which was what they did when they saw me in my white blouse and navy blue skirt that went a couple of inches below the knees.
110 When Meg came to my house, I invited her to try on my Chinese dresses, the ones with a high collar and slits up the sides. Meg's eyes were bright as she looked at herself in the mirror. She struck several sultry poses, and we nearly fell over laughing.

The dinner party at the Gleasons' didn't stop my growing friendship with Meg. Things were getting better for me in other ways too. Mother finally bought me some jeans at the end of the month, when Father got his paycheck. She wasn't in any hurry about buying them at first, until

---

3. **inflections** (ĭn-flĕk′shənz): different tenses.
4. **smugly:** with self-satisfaction; self-righteously.

Language Coach

Verb Forms Mr. Lin is studying verb tenses, the time of action or state of being expressed by a verb. If you struggle with verb tenses, follow the rules below.

Tense	Use	Example
Present	To express an action or state of being that is occurring now	Father **makes** diagrams of verbs.
Past	To express an action or state of being that occurred in the past	Father **made** diagrams of verbs.
Future	To express an action or state of being that will occur in the future	Father **will make** diagrams of verbs tomorrow.

Scan pages 448–449 for examples of present, past, and future verb tenses.

 SOCIAL STUDIES CONNECTION

The Chinese dress Meg tries on is a *cheongsam* (chông′säm′) or *qipao* (kĭ′pä-ō′). *Cheongsam* is from the Cantonese dialect and translates as "long dress." *Qipao* is Mandarin for "banner gown."

I worked on her. This is what I did. Since we didn't have a car in those days, I often ran down to the neighborhood store to pick up things for her. The groceries cost less at a big supermarket, but the closest one was many blocks away. One day, when she ran out of flour, I offered to borrow a bike from our neighbor's son and buy a ten-pound bag of flour at the big supermarket. I mounted the boy's bike and waved to Mother. "I'll be back in five minutes!"

Before I started pedaling, I heard her voice behind me. "You can't go out in public like that! People can see all the way up to your thighs!"

"I'm sorry," I said innocently. "I thought you were in a hurry to get the flour." For dinner we were going to have pot-stickers (fried Chinese dumplings), and we needed a lot of flour.

"Couldn't you borrow a girl's bicycle?" complained Mother. "That way your skirt won't be pushed up."

"There aren't too many of those around," I said. "Almost all the girls wear jeans while riding a bike, so they don't see any point buying a girl's bike."

We didn't eat pot-stickers that evening, and Mother was thoughtful. Next day we took the bus downtown and she bought me a pair of jeans. In the same week, my brother made the baseball team of his junior high school, Father started taking driving lessons, and Mother discovered rummage sales. We soon got all the furniture we needed, plus a dart board and a 1,000-piece jigsaw puzzle (fourteen hours later, we discovered that it was a 999-piece jigsaw puzzle). There was hope that the Lins might become a normal American family after all. **E**

Then came our dinner at the Lakeview Restaurant.

The Lakeview was an expensive restaurant, one of those places where a headwaiter dressed in tails conducted you to your seat, and the only light came from candles and flaming desserts. In one corner of the room a lady harpist played tinkling melodies.

Father wanted to celebrate, because he had just been promoted. He worked for an electronics company, and after his English started improving, his superiors decided to appoint him to a position more suited to his training. The promotion not only brought a higher salary but was also a tremendous boost to his pride.

Up to then we had eaten only in Chinese restaurants. Although my brother and I were becoming fond of hamburgers, my parents didn't care much for Western food, other than chow mein.[5]

E VISUALIZE
Try to visualize the narrator's image of a "normal American family" (line 142). Which of the narrator's descriptions stand out to you the most? Record them in your chart.

---

5. **chow mein** (chou´ mān´): Chinese-American dish of vegetables and meat served over fried noodles.

But this was a special occasion, and Father asked his coworkers to recommend a really elegant restaurant. So there we were at the Lakeview, stumbling after the headwaiter in the murky dining room.

At our table we were handed our menus, and they were so big that to read mine I almost had to stand up again. But why bother? It was mostly in French, anyway. **F**

Father, being an engineer, was always systematic. He took out a pocket French dictionary. "They told me that most of the items would be in French, so I came prepared." He even had a pocket flashlight, the size of a marking pen. While Mother held the flashlight over the menu, he looked up the items that were in French.

"*Pâté en croûte,*" he muttered. "Let's see . . . *pâté* is paste . . . *croûte* is crust . . . hmm . . . a paste in crust."

The waiter stood looking patient. I squirmed and died at least fifty times.

At long last Father gave up. "Why don't we just order four complete dinners at random?" he suggested.

"Isn't that risky?" asked Mother. "The French eat some rather peculiar things, I've heard."

"A Chinese can eat anything a Frenchman can eat," Father declared.

The soup arrived in a plate. How do you get soup up from a plate? I glanced at the other diners, but the ones at the nearby tables were not on their soup course, while the more distant ones were invisible in the darkness.

Fortunately my parents had studied books on Western **etiquette** before they came to America. "Tilt your plate," whispered my mother. "It's easier to spoon the soup up that way."

She was right. Tilting the plate did the trick. But the etiquette book didn't say anything about what you did after the soup reached your lips. As any respectable Chinese knows, the correct way to eat your soup is to slurp. This helps to cool the liquid and prevent you from burning your lips. It also shows your appreciation.

We showed our appreciation. *Shloop,* went my father. *Shloop,* went my mother. *Shloop, shloop,* went my brother, who was the hungriest.

The lady harpist stopped playing to take a rest. And in the silence, our family's **consumption** of soup suddenly seemed unnaturally loud. You know how it sounds on a rocky beach when the tide goes out and the water drains from all those little pools? They go *shloop, shloop, shloop.* That was the Lin family, eating soup.

At the next table a waiter was pouring wine. When a large *shloop* reached him, he froze. The bottle continued to pour, and red wine flooded the tabletop and into the lap of a customer. Even the customer didn't notice anything at first, being also hypnotized by the *shloop, shloop, shloop.*

160

170

180

190

COMMON CORE RL 4

F HYPERBOLE
One way a writer can add humor to a story is to use **hyperbole,** an exaggeration of the truth for emphasis or humorous effect. The use of hyperbole adds to the humorous tone of this story. Lines 159–160 contain an example of hyperbole. The narrator says the menu was was so big "I almost had to stand up" to read it. Read ahead to lines 170–197 and find at least two more examples of hyperbole.

etiquette (ĕt′ĭ-kĕt′) *n.* the practice of social manners

consumption (kən-sŭmp′shən) *n.* the act of taking in, eating, or drinking **consume** *v.*

It was too much. "I need to go to the toilet," I mumbled, jumping to my feet. A waiter, sensing my urgency, quickly directed me to the ladies' room.

I splashed cold water on my burning face, and as I dried myself with a paper towel, I stared into the mirror. In this perfumed ladies' room, with its pink-and-silver wallpaper and marbled sinks, I looked completely out of place. What was I doing here? What was our family doing in the Lakeview Restaurant? In America? **G**

The door to the ladies' room opened. A woman came in and glanced curiously at me. I retreated into one of the toilet cubicles and latched the door.

Time passed—maybe half an hour, maybe an hour. Then I heard the door open again, and my mother's voice. "Are you in there? You're not sick, are you?"

There was real concern in her voice. A girl can't leave her family just because they slurp their soup. Besides, the toilet cubicle had a few drawbacks as a permanent residence. "I'm all right," I said, undoing the latch.

Mother didn't tell me how the rest of the dinner went, and I didn't want to know. In the weeks following, I managed to push the whole thing into the back of my mind, where it jumped out at me only a few times a day. Even now, I turn hot all over when I think of the Lakeview Restaurant. **H**

COMMON CORE RL 4

G SENSORY LANGUAGE
Writers use **sensory language** to help you imagine what their characters see, feel, hear, smell, and taste. Reread lines 201–205. Write down the phrases in this paragraph that include sensory language and identify which of the five senses each phrase appeals to.

H VISUALIZE
Many events embarrass the narrator during the dinner at the Lakeview Restaurant. Record the details and what you visualized in your chart.

◀ **Analyze Visuals**
Does this meal look inviting or intimidating? Explain.

But by the time we had been in this country for three months, our family was definitely making progress toward becoming Americanized. I remember my parents' first PTA[6] meeting. Father wore a neat suit and tie, and Mother put on her first pair of high heels. She stumbled only once. They met my homeroom
230 teacher and beamed as she told them that I would make honor roll soon at the rate I was going. Of course Chinese etiquette forced Father to say that I was a very stupid girl and Mother to protest that the teacher was showing favoritism toward me. But I could tell they were both very proud.

The day came when my parents announced that they wanted to give a
240 dinner party. We had invited Chinese friends to eat with us before, but this dinner was going to be different. In addition to a Chinese-American family, we were going to invite the Gleasons.

"Gee, I can hardly wait to have dinner at your house," Meg said to me. "I just *love* Chinese food."

That was a relief. Mother was a good cook, but I wasn't sure if people who ate sour cream would also eat chicken gizzards[7] stewed in soy sauce.

Mother decided not to take a chance with chicken gizzards. Since we had Western guests, she set the table with large dinner plates, which we never used in Chinese meals. In fact we didn't use individual plates at all, but
250 picked up food from the platters in the middle of the table and brought it directly to our rice bowls. Following the practice of Chinese-American restaurants, Mother also placed large serving spoons on the platters. ◆

The dinner started well. Mrs. Gleason exclaimed at the beautifully arranged dishes of food: the colorful candied fruit in the sweet-and-sour pork dish, the noodle-thin shreds of chicken meat stir-fried with tiny peas, and the glistening pink prawns[8] in a ginger sauce.

◆ **GRAMMAR IN CONTEXT**
A **clause** is a group of words that has a subject and a verb. An **independent clause** can stand alone as a sentence, but a **dependent clause,** such as *"Following the practice of Chinese-American restaurants"* in lines 251–252, cannot. Notice that the writer avoids using sentence fragments by joining all dependent clauses with independent clauses.

---

6. **PTA:** Parent Teacher Association.

7. **gizzards:** A gizzard is the muscular pouch behind a bird's stomach that helps with its digestion.

8. **prawns** (prônz): large seafood, similar to shrimp.

At first I was too busy enjoying my food to notice how the guests were doing. But soon I remembered my duties. Sometimes guests were too polite to help themselves and you had to serve them with more food.

260   I glanced at Meg, to see if she needed more food, and my eyes nearly popped out at the sight of her plate. It was piled with food: the sweet-and-sour meat pushed right against the chicken shreds, and the chicken sauce ran into the prawns. She had been taking food from a second dish before she finished eating her helping from the first!

   Horrified, I turned to look at Mrs. Gleason. She was dumping rice out of her bowl and putting it on her dinner plate. Then she ladled prawns and gravy on top of the rice and mixed everything together, the way you mix sand, gravel, and cement to make concrete.

   I couldn't bear to look any longer, and I turned to Mr. Gleason. He was
270 chasing a pea around his plate. Several times he got it to the edge, but when he tried to pick it up with his chopsticks, it rolled back toward the center of the plate again. Finally he put down his chopsticks and picked up the pea with his fingers. He really did! A grown man! ❶

   All of us, our family and the Chinese guests, stopped eating to watch the activities of the Gleasons. I wanted to giggle. Then I caught my mother's eyes on me. She frowned and shook her head slightly, and I understood the message: the Gleasons were not used to Chinese ways, and they were just **coping** the best they could. For some reason I thought of celery strings.

   When the main courses were finished, Mother brought out a platter of
280 fruit. "I hope you weren't expecting a sweet dessert," she said. "Since the Chinese don't eat dessert, I didn't think to prepare any."

   "Oh, I couldn't possibly eat dessert!" cried Mrs. Gleason. "I'm simply stuffed!"

   Meg had different ideas. When the table was cleared, she announced that she and I were going for a walk. "I don't know about you, but I feel like dessert," she told me, when we were outside. "Come on, there's a Dairy Queen down the street. I could use a big chocolate milkshake!"

   Although I didn't really want anything more to eat, I insisted on paying for the milkshakes. After all, I was still hostess.

290   Meg got her large chocolate milkshake and I had a small one. Even so, she was finishing hers while I was only half done. Toward the end she pulled hard on her straws and went *shloop, shloop.*

   "Do you always slurp when you eat a milkshake?" I asked, before I could stop myself.

   Meg grinned. "Sure. All Americans slurp." ∿ ❿

❶ **TONE**
Reread lines 257–273. Is it the Gleasons' actions, the narrator's responses, or both that add humor to the story? Explain.

cope (kōp) *v.* to struggle to overcome difficulties

❿ **TONE AND IMAGERY**
What does the tone and imagery in lines 290–295 tell you about how the narrator feels after her parents' dinner party?

Comprehension

1. **Recall** What two types of food served at the Gleasons' dinner party are unusual for the Lin family?

2. **Recall** How does each member of the Lin family learn English?

3. **Clarify** Why do the Lins slurp their soup in the French restaurant?

COMMON CORE

RL 2 Provide a summary of the text distinct from personal opinions or judgments. **RL 4** Determine the meaning of words and phrases, including connotative meanings; analyze the impact of a specific word choice on tone.

Text Analysis

4. **Visualize** Review the chart you created while reading. Which sensory details helped you picture the story events most vividly in your mind? How do these details help you understand the Lin's experiences?

5. **Analyze Imagery** Look back through the story and list some of the images the author uses to describe the events that take place, noting which sense—sight, sound, smell, touch, and taste—each image appeals to. Then explain how the use of imagery adds humor to the story.

6. **Compare and Contrast Characters** Find examples of similarities and differences between the Lins and the Gleasons. Do you think the narrator feels more like or different from her neighbors by the end of the story? Support your answer with evidence from the story.

7. **Evaluate Tone** Find examples of characters' thoughts, words, and actions that contribute to the humorous tone of "The All-American Slurp." Record the examples in a chart like the one shown. Which details do you think have the strongest effect on the tone of the story?

Thoughts	Words	Actions

Extension and Challenge

8. **SOCIAL STUDIES CONNECTION** Imagine that you are preparing the Lin family for their dinner at the Gleasons' house. Write a **summary,** or a brief retelling, of the article on page 457 for the Lins. Remember that your summary should only include information from the article, and not your personal opinions.

Are people more ALIKE or different?

Namioka seems to think people are more alike than different. Do you agree?

Vocabulary in Context

▲ VOCABULARY PRACTICE

Choose the letter of the item you would associate with each vocabulary word as it is used in "The All-American Slurp."

1. **revolting:** (a) a borrowed sweater, (b) a spoiled sandwich, (c) an old car
2. **lavishly:** (a) a generous amount, (b) a large classroom, (c) a crowded train station
3. **mortified:** (a) playing a trick, (b) going to a meeting, (c) falling down in public
4. **etiquette:** (a) fixing a bicycle, (b) writing a thank-you note, (c) baking a dessert
5. **consumption:** (a) taking an elevator, (b) finding a lost hat, (c) eating lunch
6. **cope:** (a) get angry, (b) finish a project, (c) manage stress

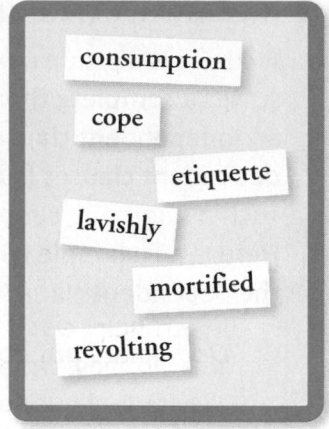

ACADEMIC VOCABULARY IN WRITING

> • aspect • distinctive • interpret • perceive • sensory

Write a paragraph in which you discuss how the writer's **distinctive** use of **sensory** language and hyperbole in "The All-American Slurp" added to your enjoyment of the story. Use at least two Academic Vocabulary words in your response.

VOCABULARY STRATEGY: SIMILES AS CONTEXT CLUES

When writers want to compare two things, they sometimes use figurative language called similes. **Similes** are comparisons that use the words *like* or *as*. In "The All-American Slurp," the narrator's family leaves the buffet table at a party "as if chased by enemy soldiers." The simile here is humorous and helps you understand how quickly the family left.

Similes can also give you context clues to help you figure out the meanings of unfamiliar words. If you can form a mental picture of the comparison, you understand the meaning of the unfamiliar word.

PRACTICE Use the simile in each sentence as a context clue to help you define the boldfaced word.

1. She was stepping as **gingerly** as the parent of a sleeping baby.
2. Storm clouds **loomed** like Friday's spelling test.
3. He felt like a caged bird in the house's **confining** guest room.
4. Her sloppy handwriting was as **cryptic** as any secret code.
5. The awkward fit of his clothes made him feel **gawky,** like a newborn giraffe.

COMMON CORE

L 4a Use context as a clue to the meaning of a word or phrase.
L 5a Interpret figures of speech in context.

Interactive Vocabulary **THiNK** central
Go to **thinkcentral.com**.
KEYWORD: HML6-455

Language

◆ **GRAMMAR IN CONTEXT:** Avoid Clauses As Fragments

A clause is a group of words that has a subject and a verb. If a clause states a complete thought and can stand alone as a sentence, it is called an **independent clause.** Fragments, or incomplete sentences, occur when **dependent clauses** (subordinate clauses) are used on their own. To correct such a fragment, simply join the dependent clause to an independent clause. Here is an example with the independent clause highlighted in yellow and the dependent clause highlighted in green:

> *Original:*   I put down my chopsticks. Because everyone was staring.
>
> *Revised:*   I put down my chopsticks because everyone was staring.

PRACTICE Find four fragments in the following paragraph. Then fix the fragments by correctly combining independent and dependent clauses.

> The Lins invited us to a Chinese dinner at their house. Because we had them over for dinner. I wasn't expecting any surprises. Since we ate at Chinese restaurants all the time. I piled a heap of the sweet-and-sour meat on my plate with all the other food. As Mrs. Lin passed the dish around. Most of the food was pretty good. Dad didn't embarrass me. Although he picked up a pea with his fingers.

For more help with independent and dependent clauses, see page R62 in the ***Grammar Handbook.***

READING-WRITING CONNECTION

YOUR TURN   Broaden your understanding of "The All-American Slurp" by responding to this prompt. Then use the **revising tip** to improve your writing.

WRITING PROMPT	REVISING TIP
Extended Constructed Response: Explanation The Lin family learned American etiquette the hard way. Read "American Lifestyles and Habits" on page 457. In **two or three paragraphs,** explain what information from the article would have helped the Lins.	Review your response. Have you used any fragments, or incomplete sentences? If so, revise your writing.

Interactive Revision

Go to <u>thinkcentral.com</u>.
KEYWORD: HML6-456

COMMON CORE

L1 Demonstrate command of the conventions of grammar.
W 2 Write informative/ explanatory texts to examine a topic.

ONLINE ARTICLE In "The All-American Slurp," you read about a Chinese family adjusting to customs in the United States. The following article offers advice to visitors and immigrants about American etiquette.

American Lifestyles & Habits Project Harmony

Etiquette and traditions for guests in an American family

There are some significant differences between cultures concerning etiquette and hospitality. The role of the guest is quite different in America than it is in other countries. In America, guests are generally urged to "make themselves at home." Americans believe that both guests and hosts are most comfortable when neither is anxious about being too polite or reserved. For instance, if you are hungry you should not wait for your host to offer you food. It's perfectly normal to ask for a snack, or to make one yourself! . . .

The types of food that Americans eat shock many people and it sometimes takes time to adjust. If you are longing for some "normal" food, you should offer to cook a national meal. Americans are almost always interested in trying new foods and would be honored if their guest(s) offered to cook a dinner.

When you are sitting at the table, you will generally have to help yourself. You may be offered food once, and if you refuse, it will not be offered again. As mentioned before, Americans tend to give honest, straightforward answers rather than feign politeness. While in your country it may be considered polite to answer "no" when food is first offered, American hosts will take "no" as exactly that and will not offer you the food again. If there is something additional that you would like at the table, you should ask for it or just take it.

When it comes to food, you may find that Americans

- Love vegetarian, low-fat salads with different salad dressings

- Eat most of their food quickly, and often take a meal with them to eat en route somewhere

- Put ice in almost all beverages—one American favorite is ICED tea!

- Use lots of spices and often like ethnic foods

- Eat dinner as the main meal of the day

- Often eat little or no breakfast—so be sure to ask for food in the morning

The True Story of the Three Little Pigs
Folk Tale Retelling by Jon Scieszka

Are there TWO SIDES to every story?

COMMON CORE

RL 3 Describe how a story's plot unfolds in a series of episodes. **L 4d** Verify the preliminary determination of the meaning of a word by checking the inferred meaning in a dictionary.

"That's not how it happened. Let me tell it!" When you hear two sides to a story, the differences between the two often outweigh the similarities. Because people often view events differently, the details in each version will vary depending on which person is telling the story. In "The True Story of the Three Little Pigs," you'll discover what happens when someone clearly stretches the truth.

QUICKWRITE Think about a time when you either read or heard two sides to the same story, either in real life, in a book, or in a movie. How did the versions differ? Write a brief summary of each side. Then explain why you think there were two sides to the story.

● TEXT ANALYSIS: STYLE—RULE OF THREE

"The True Story of the Three Little Pigs" is a retelling of the popular traditional tale. In this version, the Big Bad Wolf is the narrator. He gives a different view of what you know from the original story. As you read, you will notice that the writer has given the tale a humorous twist.

Though this is a recent retelling, the author keeps the stylistic elements of traditional literature. One of these elements is the **rule of three.** In many traditional works, including folk tales, if an event happens once, it will happen two more times. For example, a king might test his daughters three times to find out who is loyal to him. Like other repeated elements in storytelling, the frequent use of the number three is called a **motif.** In literature, the function of the rule of three is to build suspense and anticipation for what happens next. As you read, notice similar events that occur three times. Also, look for the small differences each time the event occurs.

● READING SKILL: IDENTIFY CAUSE AND EFFECT

As in real life, events in a plot are often linked by cause and effect. A **cause** is an event that makes something happen. An **effect** is what happens as a result of a cause. Many times, an effect then causes another event, creating a cause-and-effect chain.

The cause-and-effect chain below shows how a seemingly harmless event from the original "Three Little Pigs" story causes a heap of trouble for one of the three pigs. As you read "The True Story of the Three Little Pigs," use a graphic organizer like this one to identify the cause-and-effect relationships in the story.

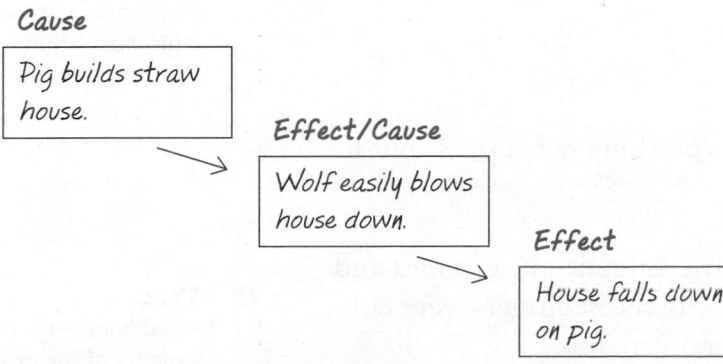

Cause

Pig builds straw house.

Effect/Cause

Wolf easily blows house down.

Effect

House falls down on pig.

 Complete the activities in your **Reader/Writer Notebook.**

Meet the Author

Jon Scieszka
born 1954

Tales with a Twist
Jon Scieszka (chĕs´kä) originally had trouble getting "The True Story of the Three Little Pigs" published because its humor was considered too grown up. But Scieszka knew young people would appreciate it, saying that "nothing cracks them up like a joke that turns stuff upside down."

Friends and Partners
Scieszka and illustrator Lane Smith have been friends and work partners for many years. Sharing a similar sense of humor and love for the absurd made the two a natural fit. "The True Story of the Three Little Pigs" was their first book.

BACKGROUND TO THE FOLK TALE
The Original "Three Little Pigs"
In the classic tale, the first and second little pigs built their houses from straw and sticks. When the pigs wouldn't let the wolf in, he blew their houses down and ate the pigs. The third little pig built his house from bricks. When the wolf couldn't blow the house down, he went down the chimney. The pig had a pot of boiling water waiting for him, so the third little pig had wolf stew for dinner.

Author Online THINK central
Go to thinkcentral.com.
KEYWORD: HML6-459

THE TRUE STORY OF THE THREE LITTLE PIGS

A. Wolf
As Told to Jon Scieszka

Everybody knows the story of the Three Little Pigs. Or at least they think they do. But I'll let you in on a little secret. Nobody knows the real story, because nobody has ever heard *my* side of the story.

I'm the wolf. Alexander T. Wolf.

You can call me Al.

I don't know how this whole Big Bad Wolf thing got started, but it's all wrong.

Maybe it's because of our diet.

Hey, it's not my fault wolves eat cute little animals like bunnies and
10 sheep and pigs. That's just the way we are. If cheeseburgers were cute, folks would probably think you were Big and Bad, too.

But like I was saying, the whole Big Bad Wolf thing is all wrong. The real story is about a sneeze and a cup of sugar. **Ⓐ**

Analyze Visuals ▶

What **details** do you notice about the wolf in this illustration?

Ⓐ STYLE
Reread lines 1–13. What elements of the original folk tale do you find in this passage?

Illustrations by Lane Smith.

THIS IS THE REAL STORY.

Way back in Once Upon a Time time, I was making a birthday cake for my dear old granny.

I had a terrible sneezing cold.

I ran out of sugar.

So I walked down the street to ask my neighbor for a cup of sugar.

20 Now this neighbor was a pig.

And he wasn't too bright, either.

He had built his whole house out of straw.

Can you believe it? I mean who in his right mind would build a house of straw?

So of course the minute I knocked on the door, it fell right in. I didn't want to just walk into someone else's house. So I called, "Little Pig, Little Pig, are you in?" No answer.

I was just about to go home without the cup of sugar for my dear old granny's birthday cake.

30 That's when my nose started to itch.

I felt a sneeze coming on.

Well I huffed.

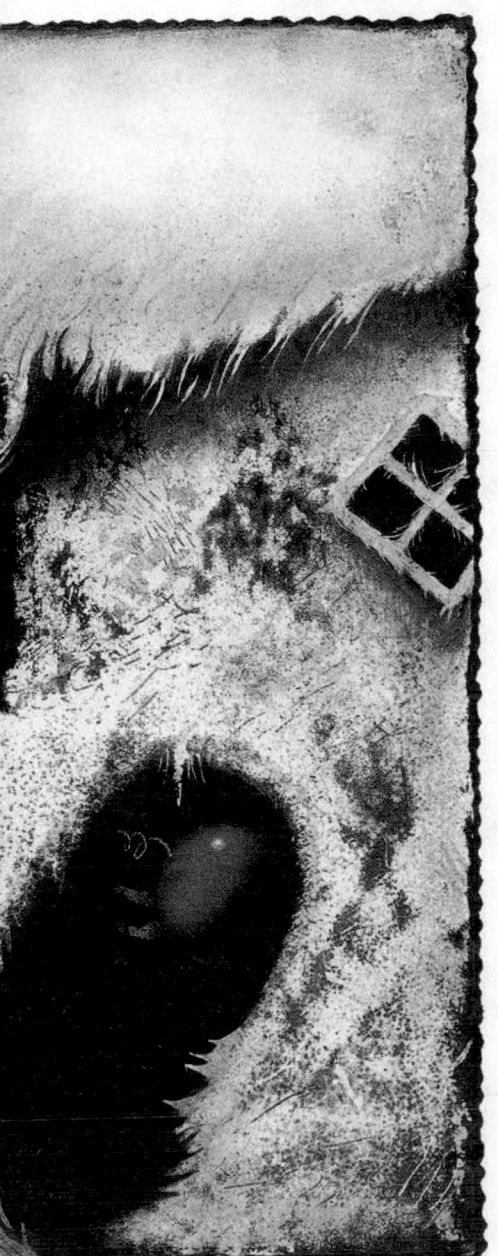

And I snuffed.

And I sneezed a great sneeze.

And you know what? That whole darn straw house fell down. And right in the middle of the pile of straw was the First Little Pig—dead as a doornail. **B**

He had been home the whole time.

40 It seemed like a shame to leave a perfectly good ham dinner lying there in the straw. So I ate it up.

Think of it as a big cheeseburger just lying there.

I was feeling a little better. But I still didn't have my cup of sugar. So I went to the next neighbor's house.

This neighbor was the First Little Pig's brother.

50 He was a little smarter, but not much.

He had built his house of sticks.

I rang the bell on the stick house.

Nobody answered.

I called, "Mr. Pig, Mr. Pig, are you in?"

He yelled back, "Go away wolf. You can't come in. I'm shaving the hairs on my chinny chin chin."

COMMON CORE L 4d

Language Coach

Definitions The word *right* has different meanings in lines 23, 25, and 36. In which instance does *right* mean "precisely"? In which instance does the word mean "healthy"? In which instance does it mean "completely"? Use a dictionary to help you decide.

B **CAUSE AND EFFECT** According to the wolf, what causes the death of the first pig? Create a cause-and-effect chain that shows the series of events.

I had just grabbed the doorknob when I felt another sneeze coming on.
I huffed. And I snuffed. And I tried to cover my mouth, but I sneezed
60 a great sneeze.

And you're not going to believe it, but this guy's house fell down just
like his brother's.

When the dust cleared, there was the Second Little Pig—dead as a doornail. Wolf's honor.

Now you know food will spoil if you just leave it out in the open.

So I did the only thing there was to do. I had dinner again.

Think of it as a second helping.

I was getting awfully full.

But my cold was feeling a little better.

70 And I still didn't have that cup of sugar for my dear old granny's birthday cake. **C**

So I went to the next house.

This guy was the First and Second Little Pigs' brother.

He must have been the brains of the family.

He had built his house of bricks.

I knocked on the brick house. No answer.

I called, "Mr. Pig, Mr. Pig, are you in?"

And do you know what that rude little porker answered?

"Get out of here, Wolf. Don't bother me again."

80 Talk about impolite!

He probably had a whole sackful of sugar.

And he wouldn't give me even one little cup for my dear sweet old granny's birthday cake.

What a pig!

I was just about to go home and maybe make a nice birthday card instead of a cake, when I felt my cold coming on.

I huffed.

And I snuffed.

And I sneezed once again.

90 Then the Third Little Pig yelled, "And your old granny can sit on a pin!"

Now I'm usually a pretty calm fellow. But when somebody talks about my granny like that, I go a little crazy. **D**

When the cops drove up, of course I was trying to break down this Pig's door. And the whole time I was huffing and puffing and sneezing and making a real scene.

The rest, as they say, is history.

C STYLE
Reread lines 48–71. How is the wolf's visit to the second pig similar to his visit to the first? How is it different? What words or phrases make the wolf's reasons for eating the pigs funny?

D CAUSE AND EFFECT
Reread lines 90–93. What are the cause and effect identified in these lines? Use the graphic organizer to show this relationship.

◀ **Analyze Visuals**

In what way does the illustration of the newspaper page add to the Wolf's tale?

The news reporters found out about the two pigs I had for dinner. They figured a sick guy going to borrow a cup of sugar didn't sound very
100 exciting.

So they jazzed up the story with all of that "Huff and puff and blow your house down."

And they made me the Big Bad Wolf.

That's it.

The real story. I was framed. **ⓔ**

But maybe you could loan me a cup of sugar. ∾

COMMON CORE RL 3

ⓔ STYLE
In traditional literature, the rule of three helps build anticipation about how a story will end. The first two episodes advance the plot. The third episode usually leads to the resolution. In the original version, the third pig's house is made of bricks. When the wolf fails to blow this last house down, he climbs down the chimney and falls into a pot of boiling water. What stylistic elements of the original story did the writer keep? What elements did he change? Why do you think the writer revised events in the third episode?

Comprehension

1. **Recall** Why is the wolf telling his story?

2. **Recall** At the beginning of the story, what two things does the wolf say the "real story" is about?

3. **Clarify** Why does the wolf think it's the first pig's fault that the straw house fell down?

4. **Summarize** What happens at the house of the third pig?

COMMON CORE

RL 3 Describe how a story's plot unfolds in a series of episodes.
RL 7 Compare and contrast the experience of reading a story to viewing a live version of the text.

Text Analysis

5. **Analyze Cause-and-Effect Relationships** While reading the story, you recorded cause-and-effect relationships. Recall what you know about the original "Three Little Pigs" story. Explain how the cause-and-effect relationships in this version are different from those in the original tale.

6. **Analyze Style** How does the **rule of three** build suspense in this tale? Using a chart like the one shown, note the details in the story that build suspense during each story event. What differences do you notice in each of the visits?

Story Event	Details
Wolf visits first pig	
Wolf visits second pig	
Wolf visits third pig	

7. **Analyze Style** What new details does the writer add to the original "Three Little Pigs"? How do these details add humor to the tale?

8. **Make Judgments** How convincing is the wolf as a narrator? Explain why you do or do not trust his retelling of the story.

Extension and Challenge

9. **Creative Project: Drama** With a group of classmates, perform for your class a traditional version of "The Three Little Pigs," followed by "The True Story of the Three Little Pigs." Consider how the characters' voices and behavior might change between the two performances.

Are there TWO SIDES to every story?

Think of another classic tale like "The Three Little Pigs" that could be told from two sides. Select a character who might tell the story differently and write a new version with that character acting as narrator.

Tuesday of the Other June
Short Story by Norma Fox Mazer

VIDEO TRAILER THINK central KEYWORD: HML6-468

How do you deal with a
BULLY?

A bully can turn your life into a nightmare. All your thoughts become focused on the next awful encounter. Advice for dealing with a bully is often to "walk away." When actually dealing with a bully, however, many people dream of standing up for themselves. In "Tuesday of the Other June," you'll read about a girl who becomes the target of a bully.

LIST IT Imagine that your best friend is being bothered by a bully and has come to you for help. What advice would you give? Prepare a short list of suggestions.

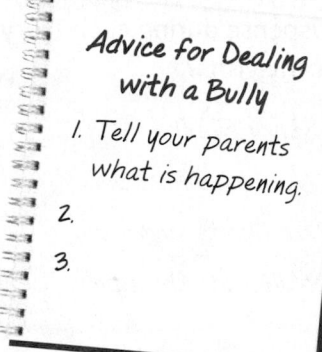

Advice for Dealing with a Bully
1. Tell your parents what is happening.
2.
3.

SECTION C   THE STAR JOURNAL   C5

For Better or For Worse   **by Lynn Johnston**

For Better or For Worse © 1983 Lynn Johnston Productions. Distributed by Universal Press Syndicate. Reprinted with permission. All rights reserved.

TEXT ANALYSIS: SENSORY LANGUAGE AND IMAGERY

Authors use many techniques to bring their characters and conflicts alive for their readers. For example, an author might use **sensory language,** words or phrases that appeal the reader's senses of sight, hearing, touch, smell, and taste. These sensory details create **imagery** that helps the reader imagine how things look, feel, or taste. As you read, pay attention to specific details which help you picture what is happening and how a character feels.

READING STRATEGY: CONNECT

When you read a story, you might find characters or events similar to those you know in real life. You may even find two texts that focus on similar themes. As you read this story and the poem that follows, think about connections you can make based on your own personal experiences, current events, and other texts. Use a diagram like the one shown.

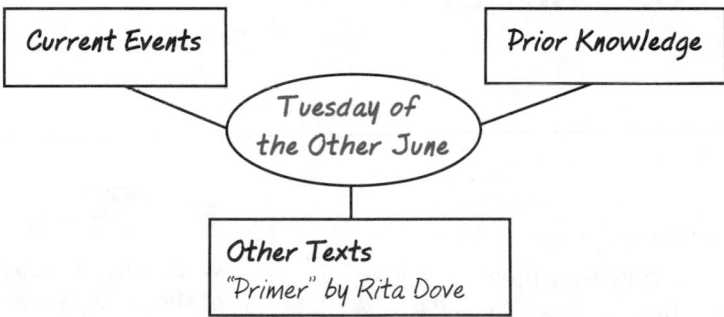

VOCABULARY IN CONTEXT

The boldfaced words help to tell the story of a girl's encounter with a bully. Restate each sentence using a different word or words for the boldfaced term.

1. The scary situation put her in a **daze.**
2. Her enemy loved to **torment** her.
3. Fear was reflected in her **emerald** eyes.
4. June had no **devoted** friends to help her out.
5. The young girl's body went **rigid** with terror.
6. Finally, she put on a **dazzling** display of courage.

Complete the activities in your **Reader/Writer Notebook.**

Meet the Author

Norma Fox Mazer
born 1931

Writing for Pleasure
By the age of 13, Norma Fox Mazer knew that she wanted to become a writer. With that goal in mind, she became editor of her high school newspaper and served as a correspondent for her town's newspaper as well.

Success
Mazer went on to write fiction, and after the success of her first book, she continued writing novels for young people. Today she is a well-known prize-winning writer of fiction for young adults. Viewing literature as a way of making sense of the world, she writes about the real problems teenagers face.

Building Characters
Mazer carefully develops her characters before introducing them to her readers. She says, "There comes a time when I understand my characters so well that I know exactly how they will act and react at any moment, and that's wonderful." Mazer's sense of her characters helps them come alive in her writing.

Author Online
THINK central
Go to **thinkcentral.com.**
KEYWORD: HML6-469

469

Tuesday of the Other June

Norma Fox Mazer

Analyze Visuals ▶

What sense do you get of the personalities of the two girls in this painting?

"Be good, be good, be good, be good, my Junie," my mother sang as she combed my hair; a song, a story, a croon, a plea. "It's just you and me, two women alone in the world, June darling of my heart, we have enough troubles getting by, we surely don't need a single one more, so you keep your sweet self out of fighting and all that bad stuff. People can be little-hearted, but turn the other cheek, smile at the world, and the world'll surely smile back."

We stood in front of the mirror as she combed my hair, combed and brushed and smoothed. Her head came just above mine, she said when

10 I grew another inch she'd stand on a stool to brush my hair. "I'm not giving up this pleasure!" And she laughed her long honey laugh. **A**

My mother was April, my grandmother had been May, I was June. "And someday," said my mother, "you'll have a daughter of your own. What will you name her?"

"January!" I'd yell when I was little. "February! No, November!" My mother laughed her honey laugh. She had little **emerald** eyes that warmed me like the sun.

A IMAGERY
Reread lines 8–11. What details help you form a mental picture of what is happening?

emerald (ĕm′ər-əld) *adj.* of a rich green color

Detail of *Fire and Ice* (2004), Brian Calvin. Acrylic on canvas, 48″ × 60″. Courtesy of Anton Kern Gallery, New York. © Brian Calvin.

Every day when I went to school, she went to work. "Sometimes
I stop what I'm doing," she said, "lay down my tools, and stop everything,
20 because all I can think about is you. Wondering what you're doing and
if you need me. Now, Junie, if anyone ever bothers you—"

"—I walk away, run away, come on home as fast as my feet will take
me," I recited.

"Yes. You come to me. You just bring me your trouble, because I'm here
on this earth to love you and take care of you."

I was safe with her. Still, sometimes I woke up at night and heard
footsteps slowly creeping up the stairs. It wasn't my mother, she was asleep
in the bed across the room, so it was robbers, thieves, and murderers,
creeping slowly . . . slowly . . . slowly toward my bed.

30 I stuffed my hand into my mouth. If I screamed and woke her, she'd
be tired at work tomorrow. The robbers and thieves filled the warm
darkness and slipped across the floor more quietly than cats. **Rigid**
under the covers, I stared at the shifting dark and bit my knuckles
and never knew when I fell asleep again. **B**

In the morning we sang in the kitchen. "Bill Grogan's goat! Was feelin'
fine! Ate three red shirts, right off the line!" I made sandwiches for our
lunches, she made pancakes for breakfast, but all she ate was one pancake
and a cup of coffee. "Gotta fly, can't be late."

I wanted to be rich and take care of her. She worked too hard; her
40 pretty hair had gray in it that she joked about. "Someday," I said, "I'll buy
you a real house, and you'll never work in a pot factory again." **C**

"Such delicious plans," she said. She checked the windows to see if they
were locked. "Do you have your key?"

I lifted it from the chain around my neck.

"And you'll come right home from school and—"

"—I won't light fires or let strangers into the house, and I won't tell
anyone on the phone that I'm here alone," I finished for her.

"I know, I'm just your old worrywart mother." She kissed me
twice, once on each cheek. "But you are my June, my only June, the
50 only June."

She was wrong; there was another June. I met her when we stood next
to each other at the edge of the pool the first day of swimming class
in the Community Center.

"What's your name?" She had a deep growly voice.

"June. What's yours?"

She stared at me. "June."

"We have the same name."

"No we don't. June is my name, and I don't give you permission to use it. Your name is Fish Eyes." She pinched me hard. "Got it, Fish Eyes?"

60　　The next Tuesday, the Other June again stood next to me at the edge of the pool. "What's your name?"

"June."

"Wrong. Your—name—is—Fish—Eyes."

"June."

"Fish Eyes, you are really stupid." She shoved me into the pool.

The swimming teacher looked up, frowning, from her chart. "No one in the water yet."

Later, in the locker room, I dressed quickly and wrapped my wet suit in the towel. The Other June pulled on her jeans. "You guys see that

70　bathing suit Fish Eyes was wearing? Her mother found it in a trash can."

Analyze Visuals ▼

How do the details in this work of art connect with the story?

Left panel of *Le Plongeur (Paper Pool 18)* (1978), David Hockney. Colored and pressed paper pulp. 72″x171″.
© David Hockney/Bradford Art Galleries and Museums, West Yorkshire, United Kingdom/Bridgeman Art Library.

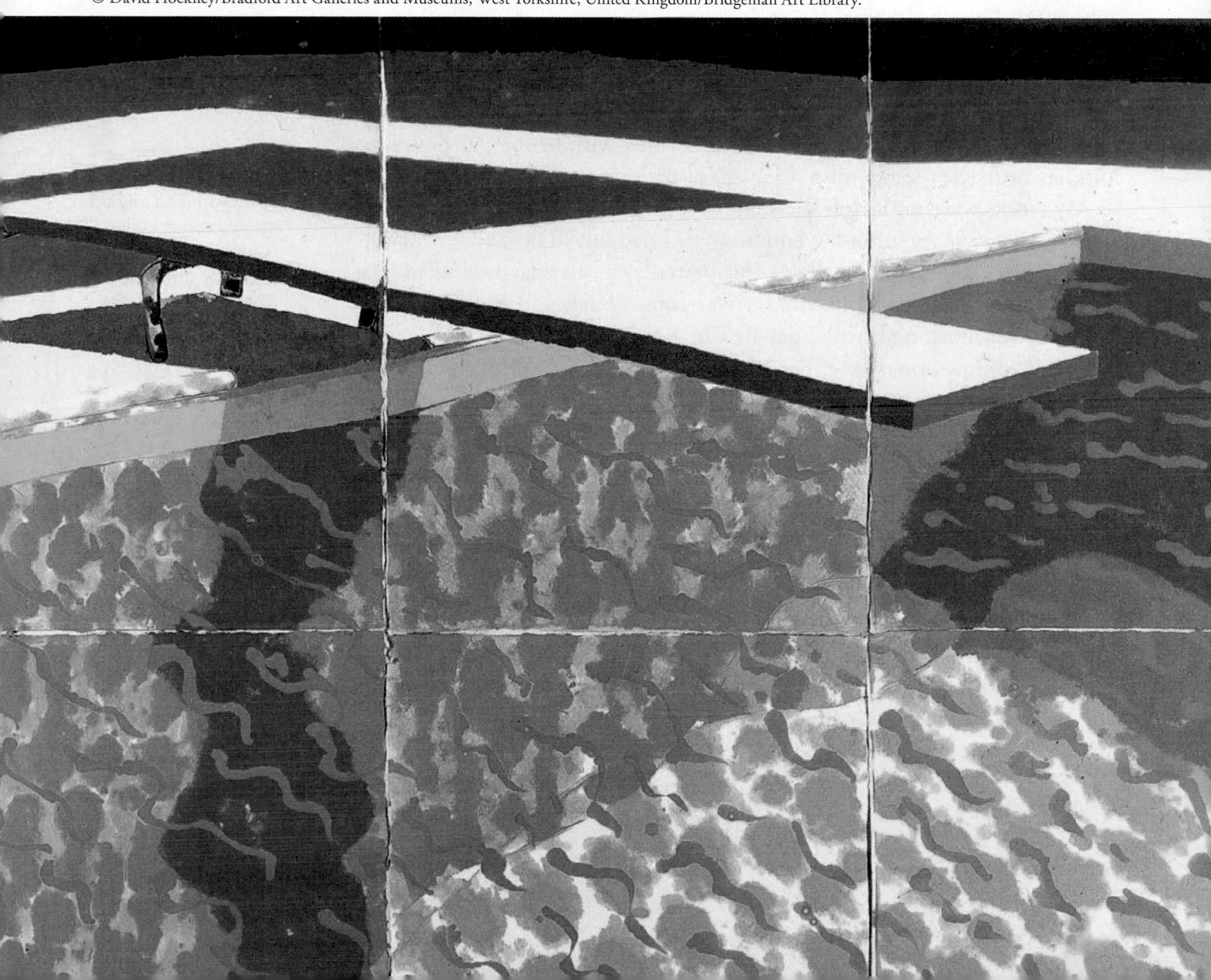

"She did not!"

The Other June grabbed my fingers and twisted. "Where'd she find your bathing suit?"

"She bought it, let me go."

"Poor little stupid Fish Eyes is crying. Oh, boo hoo hoo, poor little Fish Eyes."

After that, everyone called me Fish Eyes. And every Tuesday, wherever I was, there was also the Other June—at the edge of the pool, in the pool, in the locker room. In the water, she swam alongside me, blowing and huffing, knocking into me. In the locker room, she stepped on my feet, pinched my arms, hid my blouse, and knotted my braids together. She had large square teeth; she was shorter than I was, but heavier, with bigger bones and square hands. If I met her outside on the street, carrying her bathing suit and towel, she'd walk toward me, smiling a square, friendly smile. "Oh well, if it isn't Fish Eyes." Then she'd punch me, blam! her whole solid weight hitting me. **D**

I didn't know what to do about her. She was training me like a dog. After a few weeks of this, she only had to look at me, only had to growl, "I'm going to get you, Fish Eyes," for my heart to slink like a whipped dog down into my stomach. My arms were covered with bruises. When my mother noticed, I made up a story about tripping on the sidewalk. **E**

My weeks were no longer Tuesday, Wednesday, Thursday, and so on. Tuesday was Awfulday. Wednesday was Badday. (The Tuesday bad feelings were still there.) Thursday was Betterday and Friday was Safeday. Saturday was Goodday, but Sunday was Toosoonday, and Monday— Monday was nothing but the day before Awfulday.

I tried to slow down time. Especially on the weekends, I stayed close by my mother, doing everything with her, shopping, cooking, cleaning, going to the laundromat. "Aw, sweetie, go play with your friends."

"No, I'd rather be with you." I wouldn't look at the clock or listen to the radio (they were always telling you the date and the time). I did special magic things to keep the day from going away, rapping my knuckles six times on the bathroom door six times a day and never, ever touching the chipped place on my bureau. But always I woke up to the day before Tuesday, and always, no matter how many times I circled the worn spot in the living-room rug or counted twenty-five cracks in the ceiling, Monday disappeared and once again it was Tuesday. **F**

The Other June got bored with calling me Fish Eyes. Buffalo Brain came next, but as soon as everyone knew that, she renamed me Turkey Nose.

D IMAGERY
What sensory language does the author use to help you imagine the bully's behavior towards June?

E CONNECT
Have you read any other stories about bullies? Is June's reaction to her bully similar or different from what has happened in other stories?

F IMAGERY
Reread lines 100–107. What images help you understand how June feels about her situation?

110 Now at night it wasn't robbers creeping up the stairs, but the Other June, coming to **torment** me. When I finally fell asleep, I dreamed of kicking her, punching, biting, pinching. In the morning I remembered my dreams and felt brave and strong. And then I remembered all the things my mother had taught me and told me.

Be good, be good, be good; it's just us two women alone in the world . . . Oh, but if it weren't, if my father wasn't long gone, if we'd had someone else to fall back on, if my mother's mother and daddy weren't dead all these years, if my father's daddy wanted to know us instead of being glad to forget us—oh, then I would have punched the Other June with a frisky
120 heart, I would have grabbed her arm at poolside and bitten her like the dog she had made of me. **G**

One night, when my mother came home from work, she said, "Junie, listen to this. We're moving!"

Alaska, I thought. Florida. Arizona. Someplace far away and wonderful, someplace without the Other June.

"Wait till you hear this deal. We are going to be caretakers, trouble-shooters for an eight-family apartment building. Fifty-six Blue Hill Street. Not janitors; we don't do any of the heavy work. April and June, Trouble-shooters, Incorporated. If a tenant has a complaint
130 or a problem, she comes to us and we either take care of it or call the janitor for service. And for that little bit of work, we get to live rent free!" She swept me around in a dance. "Okay? You like it? I do!"

So. Not anywhere else, really. All the same, maybe too far to go to swimming class? "Can we move right away? Today?"

"Gimme a break, sweetie. We've got to pack, do a thousand things. I've got to line up someone with a truck to help us. Six weeks, Saturday the fifteenth." She circled it on the calendar. It was the Saturday after the last day of swimming class.

Soon, we had boxes lying everywhere, filled with clothes and towels
140 and glasses wrapped in newspaper. Bit by bit, we cleared the rooms, leaving only what we needed right now. The dining-room table staggered on a bunched-up rug, our bureaus inched toward the front door like patient cows. On the calendar in the kitchen, my mother marked off the days until we moved, but the only days I thought about were Tuesdays—Awfuldays. Nothing else was real except the too fast passing of time, moving toward each Tuesday . . . away from Tuesday . . . toward Tuesday. . . . **H**

torment (tôr′mĕnt′) *v.* to cause severe distress to the body or mind

G CONNECT
In line 115, June remembers her mother's advice to be good. Do you think it's better advice to "be good" or to take revenge on the Other June? Explain.

COMMON CORE RL 4

H PERSONIFICATION
Personification occurs when an author gives human qualities to an animal, object, or idea. Reread lines 141–147. What objects or ideas are personified in these lines? What effect does this have on you as a reader? As you read the rest of the story, look for other examples of personification.

And it seemed to me that this would go on forever, that Tuesdays would
come forever and I would be forever trapped by the side of the pool, the
150 Other June whispering Buffalo Brain Fish Eyes Turkey Nose into my ear,
while she ground her elbow into my side and smiled her square smile
at the swimming teacher.

And then it ended. It was the last day of swimming class. The last
Tuesday. We had all passed our tests, and, as if in celebration, the Other
June only pinched me twice. "And now," our swimming teacher said, "all
of you are ready for the Advanced Class, which starts in just one month.
I have a sign-up slip here. Please put your name down before you leave."
Everyone but me crowded around. I went to the locker room and pulled on
my clothes as fast as possible. The Other June burst through the door
160 just as I was leaving. "Goodbye," I yelled, "good riddance to bad trash!"
Before she could pinch me again, I ran past her and then ran all the way
home, singing, "Goodbye . . . goodbye . . . goodbye, good riddance
to bad trash!" ◆

Later, my mother carefully untied the blue ribbon around my swimming
class diploma. "Look at this! Well, isn't this wonderful! You are on
your way, you might turn into an Olympic swimmer, you never know
what life will bring."

"I don't want to take more lessons."

"Oh, sweetie, it's great to be a good swimmer." But then, looking into
170 my face, she said, "No, no, no, don't worry, you don't have to."

The next morning, I woke up hungry for the first time in weeks.
No more swimming class. No more Baddays and Awfuldays. No more
Tuesdays of the Other June. In the kitchen, I made hot cocoa to go with
my mother's corn muffins. "It's Wednesday, Mom," I said, stirring the
cocoa. "My favorite day."

"Since when?"

"Since this morning." I turned on the radio so I could hear the
announcer tell the time, the temperature, and the day.

Thursday for breakfast I made cinnamon toast, Friday my mother made
180 pancakes, and on Saturday, before we moved, we ate the last slices of
bread and cleaned out the peanut butter jar.

"Some breakfast," Tilly said. "Hello, you must be June." She shook
my hand. She was a friend of my mother's from work; she wore big hoop
earrings, sandals, and a skirt as **dazzling** as a rainbow. She came
in a truck with John to help us move our things.

John shouted cheerfully at me, "So you're moving." An enormous man
with a face covered with little brown bumps. Was he afraid his voice
wouldn't travel the distance from his mouth to my ear? "You looking

◆ GRAMMAR IN
CONTEXT
The **tense** of a verb
indicates the time of
an action or a state of
being. An action can
happen in the present,
the past, or the future.
The verbs *ended, was,
had,* and *pinched* in lines
153–155 tell you that
these actions take place
in the past.

dazzling (dăz′lĭng) *adj.*
beautiful; amazing
dazzle *v.*

at my moles?" he shouted, and he heaved our big green flowered chair
190 down the stairs. "Don't worry, they don't bite. Ha, ha, ha!" Behind him
came my mother and Tilly balancing a bureau between them, and behind
them I carried a lamp and the round, flowered Mexican tray that was my
mother's favorite. She had found it at a garage sale and said it was as close
to foreign travel as we would ever get.

    The night before, we had loaded our car, stuffing in bags and boxes
until there was barely room for the two of us. But it was only when we
were in the car, when we drove past Abdo's Grocery, where they always
gave us credit,[1] when I turned for a last look at our street—it was only
then that I understood we were truly going to live somewhere else, in
200 another apartment, in another place mysteriously called Blue Hill Street. **I**

    Tilly's truck followed our car.

    "Oh, I'm so excited," my mother said. She laughed. "You'd think
we were going across the country."

    Our old car wheezed up a long steep hill. Blue Hill Street. I looked from
one side to the other, trying to see everything.

    My mother drove over the crest of the hill. "And now—ta da!—our
new home."

COMMON CORE L 4c

Language Coach

Synonyms The word
bureau (line 191) means
a chest of drawers. Use
a thesaurus to find other
words that describe a
chest of drawers.

I CONNECT
As they are driving away
from their home, June
suddenly realizes that
her life is going to start
anew elsewhere. Have
you ever had to move?
How did you feel about
moving to a new place?

---

1. **credit:** an agreement to trust in someone's ability and intention to pay for something at a later date.

"Which house? Which one?" I looked out the window and what I saw was the Other June. She was sprawled on the stoop of a pink house, lounging back on her elbows, legs outspread, her jaws working on a wad of gum. I slid down into the seat, but it was too late. I was sure she had seen me.

My mother turned into a driveway next to a big white building with a tiny porch. She leaned on the steering wheel. "See that window there, that's our living-room window. . . and that one over there, that's your bedroom. . . ."

We went into the house, down a dim, cool hall. In our new apartment, the wooden floors clicked under our shoes, and my mother showed me everything. Her voice echoed in the empty rooms. I followed her around in a **daze.** Had I imagined seeing the Other June? Maybe I'd seen another girl who looked like her. A double. That could happen. **J**

"Ho yo, where do you want this chair?" John appeared in the doorway. We brought in boxes and bags and beds and stopped only to eat pizza and drink orange juice from the carton.

"June's so quiet, do you think she'll adjust all right?" I heard Tilly say to my mother.

"Oh, definitely. She'll make a wonderful adjustment. She's just getting used to things."

But I thought that if the Other June lived on the same street as I did, I would never get used to things.

That night I slept in my own bed, with my own pillow and blanket, but with floors that creaked in strange voices and walls with cracks I didn't recognize. I didn't feel either happy or unhappy. It was as if I were waiting for something.

Monday, when the principal of Blue Hill Street School left me in Mr. Morrisey's classroom, I knew what I'd been waiting for. In that room full of strange kids, there was one person I knew. She smiled her square smile, raised her hand, and said, "She can sit next to me, Mr. Morrisey."

"Very nice of you, June M. OK, June T, take your seat. I'll try not to get you two Junes mixed up."

I sat down next to her. She pinched my arm. "Good riddance to bad trash," she mocked.

I was back in the Tuesday swimming class, only now it was worse, because every day would be Awfulday. The pinching had already started. Soon, I knew, on the playground and in the halls, kids would pass me, grinning. "Hiya, Fish Eyes."

daze (dāz) *n.* a condition in which one cannot think clearly

J SENSORY LANGUAGE
Reread lines 217–221. Which details help you picture what it looks like inside the house and how it feels to be there?

Analyze Visuals ▶
How does this painting compare with your mental picture of June's new neighborhood?

The Other June followed me around during recess that day, droning in my ear, "You are my slave, you must do everything I say, I am your master, say it, say, 'Yes, master, you are my master.'"

250 I pressed my lips together, clapped my hands over my ears, but without hope. Wasn't it only a matter of time before I said the hateful words?

"How was school?" my mother said that night.

"OK."

She put a pile of towels in a bureau drawer. "Try not to be sad about missing your old friends, sweetie; there'll be new ones."

The next morning, the Other June was waiting for me when I left the house. "Did your mother get you that blouse in the garbage dump?" She butted me, shoving me against a tree. "Don't you speak anymore, Fish Eyes?" Grabbing my chin in her hands, she pried open my mouth.

260 "Oh, ha ha, I thought you lost your tongue."

We went on to school. I sank down into my seat, my head on my arms. "June T, are you all right?" Mr. Morrisey asked. I nodded. My head was almost too heavy to lift.

The Other June went to the pencil sharpener. Round and round she whirled the handle. Walking back, looking at me, she held the three sharp pencils like three little knives.

Someone knocked on the door. Mr. Morrisey went out into the hall. Paper planes burst into the air, flying from desk to desk. Someone turned on a transistor radio. And the Other June, coming closer, smiled and

270 licked her lips like a cat sleepily preparing to gulp down a mouse.

I remembered my dream of kicking her, punching, biting her like a dog.

Then my mother spoke quickly in my ear: Turn the other cheek, my Junie; smile at the world, and the world'll surely smile back.

But I had turned the other cheek and it was slapped. I had smiled and the world hadn't smiled back. I couldn't run home as fast as my feet would take me, I had to stay in school—and in school there was the Other June. Every morning, there would be the Other June, and every afternoon, and every day, all day, there would be the Other June. **K**

She frisked down the aisle, stabbing the pencils in the air toward me.

280 A boy stood up on his desk and bowed. "My fans," he said, "I greet you." My arm twitched and throbbed, as if the Other June's pencils had already poked through the skin. She came closer, smiling her Tuesday smile.

"No," I whispered, "no." The word took wings and flew me to my feet, in front of the Other June. "Noooooo." It flew out of my mouth into her surprised face.

The boy on the desk turned toward us. "You said something, my **devoted** fans?"

COMMON CORE L 4c

Language Coach

Multiple-Meaning Words The word *recess* (line 247) means a temporary pause or break from work. Students usually have recess to relax and play. However, *recess* can also be used to describe a hollow space in a wall. Use a dictionary to find out what *recess* means when used as a verb instead of a noun.

K CONNECT
Knowing what you do about bullies, what do you think June is going to do if the Other June attacks her?

devoted (dĭ-vō'tĭd) *adj.* very loyal; faithful
devote *v.*

Detail of *Fire and Ice* (2004), Brian Calvin. Acrylic on canvas, 48″ × 60″. Courtesy of Anton Kern Gallery, New York. © Brian Calvin.

"No," I said to the Other June. "Oh, no! No. No. No. No more." I pushed away the hand that held the pencils.

290 The Other June's eyes opened, popped wide like the eyes of somebody in a cartoon. It made me laugh. The boy on the desk laughed, and then the other kids were laughing, too.

"No," I said again, because it felt so good to say it. "No, no, no, no." I leaned toward the Other June, put my finger against her chest. Her cheeks turned red, she squawked something—it sounded like "Eeeraaghyou!"—and she stepped back. She stepped away from me.

The door banged, the airplanes disappeared, and Mr. Morrisey walked to his desk. "OK. OK. Let's get back to work. Kevin Clark, how about it?" Kevin jumped off the desk and Mr. Morrisey picked up a piece

300 of chalk. "All right, class—" He stopped and looked at me and the Other June. "You two Junes, what's going on there?"

I tried it again. My finger against her chest. Then the words. "No—more." And she stepped back another step. I sat down at my desk.

"June M," Mr. Morrisey said.

She turned around, staring at him with that big-eyed cartoon look. After a moment she sat down at the desk with a loud slapping sound.

Even Mr. Morrisey laughed.

And sitting at my desk, twirling my braids, I knew this was the last Tuesday of the Other June. ∾ ❶

❶ SENSORY LANGUAGE
How do the sensory language and details in lines 302–309 help you imagine the scene? What does the author mean by "the last Tuesday of the Other June"?

PRIMER
Rita Dove

In the sixth grade I was chased home by
the Gatlin Kids, three skinny sisters
in rolled-down bobby socks.[1] Hissing
Brainiac! And *Mrs. Stringbean!*, they trod my heel.
5 I knew my body was no big deal
but never thought to retort:[2] who's
calling *who* skinny? (Besides, I knew
they'd beat me up.) I survived
their shoves across the schoolyard
10 because my five-foot-zero mother drove up
in her Caddie[3] to shake them down to size.
Nothing could get me into that car.
I took the long way home, swore
I'd show them all: I would grow up.

---

1. **bobby socks:** 1940s and 1950s term for socks reaching just above the ankle.

2. **retort:** answer back in a sharp way.

3. **Caddie:** Cadillac, a type of car.

Comprehension

1. **Recall** What is June's mother's approach to dealing with life's difficulties?

2. **Recall** What unpleasant discovery does June make on moving day?

3. **Represent** Reread lines 92–96. Create a weekly calendar showing the days of the week and June's nickname for each.

Text Analysis

4. **Identify Imagery** June, the narrator of the story, uses **sensory details** to describe the house she shares with her mother. Review the story and find examples of these details. Then, write a sentence describing the house.

5. **Analyze Sensory Language** Go back to the story and look for descriptions of the narrator. How does the author create a full picture of June, including her inner feelings? Find examples of words and phrases that help you identify how June looks and feels.

6. **Analyze Character** Think about the type of person June's mother is. How does her personality and behavior affect June? Does she give June good advice? Use evidence from the story to support your response.

7. **Connect** Review the chart that you filled out as you read the story. Does the story remind you of any other events, personal or fictional? Explain.

8. **Connect** Reread Rita Dove's poem on page 482. How is the **speaker,** or voice, of the poem like June the narrator? Use examples from each selection to support your answer.

Current Events		Prior Knowledge
	Tuesday of the Other June	
	Other Texts "Primer" by Rita Dove	

Extension and Challenge

9. **Readers' Circle** With a small group, discuss the way June deals with the Other June. In what other way could she have responded? Did June do the right thing?

How do you deal with a BULLY?

Write a list of options for someone dealing with a bully. Think about June from "Tuesday of the Other June" and the speaker in "Primer."

COMMON CORE

RL 4 Determine the meaning of words and phrases as they are used in a text, including connotative meanings. **RL 9** Compare and contrast texts in different forms in terms of their approaches to similar topics. **SL 1** Engage in collaborative discussions (in groups).

Vocabulary in Context

▲ **VOCABULARY PRACTICE**

Choose the letter of the word or phrase you would associate with each boldfaced vocabulary word.

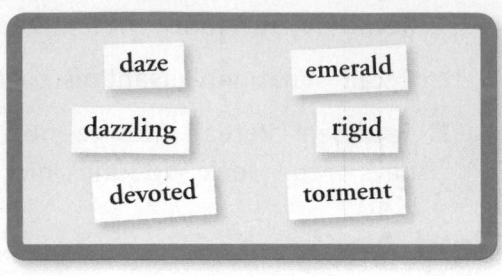

1. **Emerald** is a shade of (a) gray, (b) blue, (c) green.
2. A person in a **daze** is (a) excited, (b) confused, (c) good at sports.
3. (a) An enemy, (b) A vacation, (c) A prize might **torment** you.
4. The **rigid** flagpole (a) sways in the wind, (b) does not move, (c) falls over.
5. A **dazzling** light is (a) dim, (b) harsh, (c) bright.
6. Someone who is **devoted** to you is (a) very fond of you, (b) confused by your decisions, (c) unwilling to stick up for you.

ACADEMIC VOCABULARY IN WRITING

• aspect   • distinctive   • interpret   • perceive   • sensory

Norma Fox Mazer uses **sensory** language to create a **distinctive** bully in the character of the "Other June." What is your **interpretation** of this character? Write a paragraph describing the Other June and try to explain her behavior. Use at least two Academic Vocabulary words in your response.

VOCABULARY STRATEGY: FIGURATIVE LANGUAGE IN CONTEXT

Figurative language is language used to express ideas in an imaginative way. Often, one idea or thing is being compared to another. In this story, a character's skirt is said to be "as dazzling as a rainbow." This figurative comparison helps you see the skirt in a new and interesting way. At the same time, thinking of the qualities of a rainbow—its brightness and beauty—can help you understand what the word *dazzling* means. The comparison provides context clues to help you interpret the meaning of an unknown word.

PRACTICE Explain the comparison being made in each sentence. Then write a definition for each boldfaced word.

1. Jeremy was as **pugnacious** as a boxer preparing for a championship bout.
2. His dog was as **recalcitrant** as a child who refused to go to sleep.
3. The three young children were **loquacious,** like chattering monkeys.
4. That volcano is as **dormant** as a hibernating bear.

COMMON CORE

L 4a Use context as a clue to the meaning of a word or phrase.
L 5a Interpret figures of speech in context.

Interactive Vocabulary
THINK central

Go to **thinkcentral.com**.
KEYWORD: HML6-484

Language

◆ **GRAMMAR IN CONTEXT:** Use Correct Verb Tense

COMMON CORE

L1 Demonstrate command of the conventions of grammar. **W 3** Write narratives to develop imagined events.

Verb tenses are used to show that events or actions occur at certain times. The **past tense** is used for an event or action that has already occurred. The **present tense** is used for an event or action that occurs in the moment or regularly. The **future tense** is used to refer to an event or action that has not yet occurred. When you write, it is important to use the correct tense and not switch it inappropriately.

Original: When the mother went to work, she thinks about June.

Revised: When the mother went to work, she thought about June.
(*The second part of the sentence needs a past tense verb.*)

PRACTICE Choose the correct verb tense to complete each sentence.

1. June wakes up every night worrying about robbers, but in the morning she and her mother (sing, sang) together.

2. June dreaded Tuesdays because she (has, had) to go to swimming class.

3. As her mother (drives, drove) over the hill, June sees the Other June.

4. June will meet up with the Other June soon, and she (handles, will handle) the situation differently.

*For more help with verb tenses, see page R56 in the **Grammar Handbook.***

READING-WRITING CONNECTION

YOUR TURN Deepen your understanding of "Tuesday of the Other June" by responding to this prompt. Then use the **revising tip** to improve your writing.

WRITING PROMPT	REVISING TIP
Extended Constructed Response: Description "Tuesday of the Other June" focuses on the main character's feelings of helplessness and anxiety. Imagine how June might feel after finally standing up to the Other June. Write **two or three paragraphs** describing June's thoughts, feelings, and actions after the encounter.	Review your paragraphs. Have you used verbs in the correct tense? If not, revise your writing.

Interactive Revision **THINK** central

Go to **thinkcentral.com**.
KEYWORD: HML6-485

The Problem with Bullies
Feature Article

Use with "Tuesday of the Other June," page 470.

COMMON CORE

RI 1 Cite textual evidence to support what the text says explicitly. **RI 5** Analyze how a particular section fits into the overall structure of a text.

What's the Connection?

In the short story you just read, a young girl becomes the target of a bully. In the **feature article** you are about to read, Sean Price takes a closer look at the problem of bullying.

Standards Focus: Take Notes

When you **take notes,** you record the most important information from whatever you are reading. **Previewing** the article—looking at its title, subheadings, topic sentences, and graphic aids—can help you determine its **main idea,** the central or most important idea that the writer conveys. For example, by previewing "The Problem with Bullies," you can see that this article covers the following information

- statistics about bullying
- forms of bullying
- the roots of bullying
- the effects of bullying
- programs for stopping bullying

Use a graphic organizer like the one below to help you record the supporting details and facts that develop the main idea. After you read, you will use your notes to write a summary.

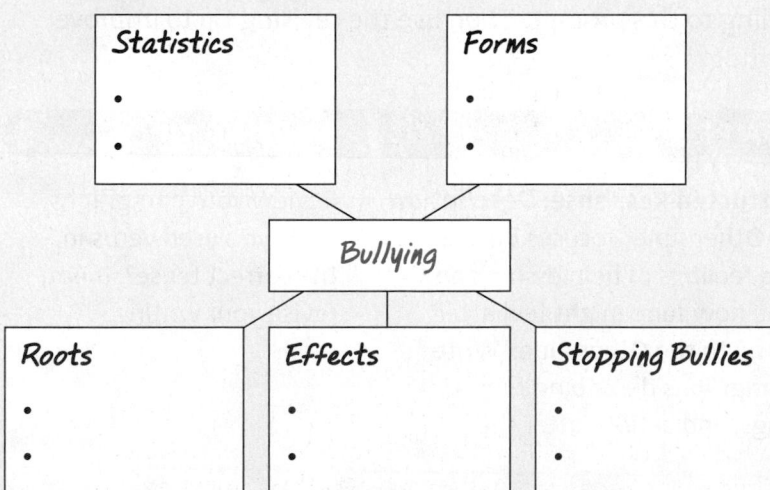

FOCUS ON FORM

"The Problem with Bullies" is a **feature article,** a nonfiction article found in a newspaper or magazine. This article gives readers information on a specific problem and offers some solutions.

COMMON CORE RI 5

A **ORGANIZATIONAL PATTERNS**
Understanding how an author organizes an article can help you locate and understand the information the author includes to support the main idea. One way to organize information is by problem-and-solution: the author identifies a problem and then provides one or more possible solutions. From the title of this article, you can tell the author is going to write about the problem of bullies. As you read, use your graphic organizer to note details about possible solutions.

The PROBLEM with BULLIES by Sean Price

B y sixth grade, Karen had experienced her share of hardships. She had just been adopted by a family in Chattanooga, Tennessee, after spending six years in foster care. Naturally shy and quiet, Karen also struggled with a slight speech impediment.[1] She had only one good friend. **A**

---

1. **speech impediment:** a physical condition that makes it difficult for a person to speak clearly.

All this made Karen (not her real name) an easy target for a bully. Her tormentor,[2] a popular girl at school, loved to taunt Karen about the way she spoke and about her home life.

"She made fun of the fact that I was a foster kid and that my mother didn't take care of me," says Karen.

Sometimes the abuse was physical. The bully might shove Karen or throw one of her shoes in the toilet. Even after the other girl received several suspensions and detentions for her bullying, she refused to give Karen a break.

Millions of U.S. teens understand what Karen went through. A study by the National Institute of Children's Health and Human Development found that more than 16 percent of students in grades 6–12 say that they have been bullied. Nineteen percent said that they had been bullies themselves. **B**

It's not just the victims who are hurt by bullying. Another study found that 60 percent of the bullies in grades 6–9 will be convicted of a criminal act by age 24!

At one time, bullying was considered just a natural part of growing up. Today, authorities see it as a serious health crisis. It is estimated that bullying keeps 160,000 kids out of school each day.

What Is Bullying? **C**

Bullying takes many forms: gossip, snubbing, put-downs, threats, and violent attacks. Its roots lie in the difference of power between the bullies and their victims. Bullies tend to be confident, impulsive, and popular. Victims tend to be withdrawn and have few friends. Many bullies come from homes where they are neglected or abused. Bullying allows them to exercise power that's denied to them at home.

Boys and girls bully differently. Boys tend to use threats and physical violence. Girl bullies rely more on backbiting (cruel comments), social exclusion, and spreading false rumors. Cyberbullying, a newer form of harassment, allows bullies to humiliate[3] their peers with e-mail and blog postings.

---

2. **tormentor:** a person who is the source of harassment, annoyance, or pain.
3. **humiliate:** to lower the pride, dignity, or self-respect of another.

B FEATURE ARTICLE
Reread lines 15–19. Then reread the **Focus on Form** on page 487. Why is bullying an appropriate topic for a feature article? Explain.

C TAKE NOTES
"What Is Bullying?" is a subhead. What kinds of information do you think this section will contain? Take notes in your graphic organizer as you read.

For victims, being bullied damages self-esteem. Bullying expert
40 Marlene Snyder says that fear of bullies also makes class time much
more trying for the victims. "They're sitting there trying to survive, not
being able to really learn," she says.

Karen's frequent complaints about the bullying finally brought her
some relief. She and her tormentor were given separate class
schedules for eighth grade.

Karen believes the other girl may have been threatened with
expulsion. Whatever happened, the bully now ignores Karen. Life is
easier to handle. And yet the bullying has left its mark.

"School's still stressful," Karen says. "I'm always on the watch to
50 see who's coming toward me." **D**

D **TAKE NOTES**
In your graphic
organizer, note the
effects of bullying that
are included in this
section.

COMMON CORE RI 5

E ORGANIZATIONAL PATTERNS
In this feature article, the writer identifies bullying as a problem. In lines 51–61, he details a possible solution. How would you describe the author's viewpoint on bullying? How does the problem-and-solution organizational pattern help develop this viewpoint?

Stopping Bullies

In recent years, many schools have implemented⁴ effective antibullying programs. Denny Middle School in Seattle, Washington, launched such a program recently. Already there have been signs of progress. Craig Little, a student, saw a new student being taunted by a group of fellow seventh-graders. The lead bully wouldn't let the boy pass.

Instead of standing by, Craig acted. He said, "You guys leave him alone, and let him go." Craig then escorted the boy away from the group. The lead bully and the new student have since made up. "I talked to both of them [later], and they're all right with each other," Craig said. "They're kind of becoming friends." **E**

---

4. **implemented:** put into effect or carried out.

Comprehension

1. **Recall** How many students do authorities estimate are out of school each day because of bullying?

2. **Clarify** Why was Karen a target of bullying?

Text Analysis

3. **Improve Your Notes** Go back to the graphic organizer you created as you read this article. Using the organizer, write a statement summing up the writer's main idea. Then, highlight the details that help support this idea.

4. **Evaluate a Feature Article** A strong feature article explores a topic of high interest and develops new ideas or useful information about a topic. Do you think the author organizes the information in a way that makes sense, or would you present the information differently? Think about the main idea, headings, details, and statistics the article provides. How could you organize the article to make the main idea and supporting details more accessible or easier to read? Explain.

COMMON CORE

RI 2 Determine a central idea of a text and how it is conveyed through particular details; provide a summary of the text distinct from personal opinions or judgments. **RI 5** Analyze how a particular section fits into the overall structure of a text. **W 2** Write explanatory texts to convey information.

Read for Information: Write a Summary

WRITING PROMPT

A **summary** is a brief retelling of the main ideas of a piece of writing. Write a two-paragraph summary of "The Problem with Bullies." Be sure to include only information from the article. Remember that a summary should not include your own opinions or judgments.

To answer this prompt, do the following:

1. Review your graphic organizer. If necessary, go back to the article to find details you might have missed the first time. Add any new details to your lists.

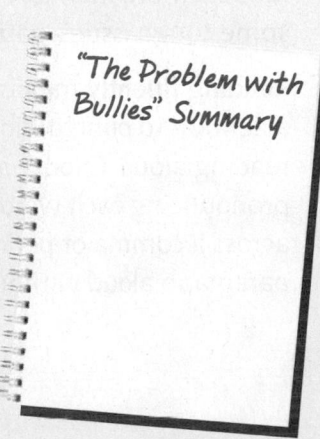

"The Problem with Bullies" Summary

2. Restate each piece of information in your own words. You should not copy anything word for word from the article.

3. Decide how you will organize your summary. Make sure you maintain the same meaning and logical order as in the original article.

4. Combine the information to write a summary.

Maniac Magee

Novel by Jerry Spinelli

COMMON CORE

RL 10 Read and comprehend literature.

Other Books by Jerry Spinelli

- *Knots in My Yo-Yo String*
- *Milkweed*
- *Report to the Principal's Office!*
- *Space Station Seventh Grade*
- *Stargirl*

Meet Jerry Spinelli

Growing up, Jerry Spinelli dreamed of being a major league baseball player. Luckily for his readers, by the time Spinelli finished high school, his dream had changed: He wanted to become a writer. He wrote four novels in 12 years while also working as a magazine editor. All four novels were rejected, but Spinelli was not about to give up. He wrote another novel, *Space Station Seventh Grade*. This time, children's publishers loved it. Spinelli's career as a published writer had begun.

What has Spinelli learned from his many years of writing? For one thing, he says that if you "write what you care about,... you stand the best chance of doing your best writing." Spinelli takes his own advice. "The first 15 years of my life turned out to be one big research project," Spinelli explains. "I thought I was simply growing up in Norristown, Pennsylvania; looking back, now I can see that I was also gathering material that would one day find its way into my books."

Try a Humorous Novel

Like many other **humorous novels,** *Maniac Magee* offers its readers more than just a great laugh. It uses humor to address some tough issues, particularly racism.

Reading fluently means you read each word carefully and pay attention to punctuation. To increase your fluency, practice reading aloud. Choose a paragraph to read aloud and practice pronouncing each word correctly and pausing when you come across a comma or period. When you are able to read the entire paragraph aloud without any errors, move on to the next one.

Read a Great Book

Not many homeless 12-year-olds end up becoming legends; but then again, there is only one Jeffrey Lionel Magee. As Jerry Spinelli writes, "The history of a kid is one part fact, two parts legend, and three parts snowball." Part tall tale, part novel, *Maniac Magee* follows the many adventures of Jeffrey as he searches for a place to call home. In the excerpt you are about to read, Jeffrey begins a new life in Two Mills, Pennsylvania.

from

Maniac Magee

Everybody knows that Maniac Magee (then Jeffrey) started out in Hollidaysburg and wound up in Two Mills. The question is: What took him so long? And what did he do along the way?

Sure, two hundred miles is a long way, especially on foot, but the year that it took him to cover it was about fifty-one weeks more than he needed—figuring the way he could run, even then.

The legend doesn't have the answer. That's why this period is known as The Lost Year.

And another question: Why did he stay here? Why Two Mills?

10 Of course, there's the obvious answer that sitting right across the Schuylkill is Bridgeport, where he was born. Yet there are other theories. Some say he just got tired of running. Some say it was the butterscotch Krimpets. And some say he only intended to pause here but that he stayed because he was so happy to make a friend.

If you listen to everybody who claims to have seen Jeffrey-Maniac Magee that first day, there must have been ten thousand people and a parade of fire trucks waiting for him at the town limits. Don't believe it. A couple of people truly remember, and here's what
20 they saw: a scraggly little kid jogging toward them, the soles of both sneakers hanging by their hinges and flopping open like dog tongues each time they came up from the pavement.

But it was something they heard that made him stick in their minds all these years. As he passed them, he said, "Hi." Just that— "Hi"—and he was gone. They stopped, they blinked, they turned, they stared after him, they wondered: *Do I know that kid?* Because people just didn't say that to strangers, out of the blue.

❧

As for the first person to actually stop and talk with Maniac, that would be Amanda Beale. And it happened because of a
30 mistake.

It was around eight in the morning, and Amanda was heading for grade school, like hundreds of other kids all over town. What made Amanda different was that she was carrying a suitcase, and that's what caught Maniac's eye. He figured she was like him, running away, so he stopped and said, "Hi."

Amanda was suspicious. Who was this white stranger kid? And what was he doing in the East End, where almost all the kids were black? And why was he saying that?

But Amanda Beale was also friendly. So she stopped and said
40 "Hi" back.

"Are you running away?" Jeffrey asked her.

"Huh?" said Amanda.

Jeffrey pointed at the suitcase.

Amanda frowned, then thought, then laughed. She laughed so hard she began to lose her balance, so she set the suitcase down and sat on it so she could laugh more safely. When at last she could speak, she said, "I'm not running away. I'm going to school."

She saw the puzzlement on his face. She got off the suitcase and opened it up right there on the sidewalk.

50 Jeffrey gasped. "Books!"

Books, all right. Both sides of the suitcase crammed with them. Dozens more than anyone would ever need for homework.

Jeffrey fell to his knees. He and Amanda and the suitcase were like a rock in a stream; the school-goers just flowed to the left and right around them. He turned his head this way and that to read the titles. He lifted the books on top to see the ones beneath. There were fiction books and nonfiction books, who-did-it books and let's-be-friends books and what-is-it books and how-to books and how-not-to books and just-regular-kid books. On the bottom was a 60 single volume from an encyclopedia. It was the letter A.

"My library," Amanda Beale said proudly.

Somebody called, "Gonna be late for school, girl!"

Amanda looked up. The street was almost deserted. She slammed the suitcase shut and started hauling it along. Jeffrey took the suitcase from her. "I'll carry it for you."

Amanda's eyes shot wide. She hesitated; then she snatched it back. "Who *are* you?" she said.

"Jeffrey Magee."

"Where are you from? West End?"

70 "No."

She stared at him, at the flap-soled sneakers. Back in those days the town was pretty much divided. The East End was blacks, the West End was whites. "I know you're not from the East End."

"I'm from Bridgeport."

"Bridgeport? Over there? *That* Bridgeport?"

"Yep."

"Well, why aren't you there?"

"It's where I'm from, not where I am."

80 "Great. So where do you *live?*"

Jeffrey looked around. "I don't know . . . maybe . . . here?"

"*Maybe?*" Amanda shook her head and chuckled. "*Maybe* you better go ask your mother and father if you live here or not."

She speeded up. Jeffrey dropped back for a second, then caught up with her. "Why are you taking all these books to school?"

Amanda told him. She told him about her little brother and sister at home, who loved to crayon every piece of paper they could find, whether or not it already had type all over it. And about the dog, 90 Bow Wow, who chewed everything he could get his teeth on. And that, she said, was why she carried her whole library to and from school every day.

First bell was ringing; the school was still a block away. Amanda ran. Jeffrey ran.

"Can I have a book?" he said.

"They're mine," she said.

"Just to read. To borrow."

"No."

"Please. What's your name?"

100 "Amanda."

"Please, Amanda. Any one. Your shortest one."

"I'm late now and I'm not gonna stop and open up this thing again. Forget it."

He stopped. "Amanda!"

She kept running, then stopped, turned, glared. What kind of kid was this, anyway? All grungy. Ripped shirt. Why didn't he go back to Bridgeport or the West End, where he belonged? Bother some white girl up there? And why was she still standing here?

"So what if I loaned you one, huh? How am I gonna get it back?"

110 "I'll bring it back. Honest! If it's the last thing I do. What's your address?"

"Seven twenty-eight Sycamore. But *you* can't come there. You can't even be *here*."

Second bell rang. Amanda screamed, whirled, ran.

"Amanda!"

She stopped, turned. "*Ohhhh,*" she squeaked. She tore a book from the suitcase, hurled it at him—"*Here!*"—and dashed into school.

The book came flapping like a wounded duck and fell at 120 Jeffrey's feet. It was a story of the Children's Crusade. Jeffrey picked it up, and Amanda Beale was late to school for the only time in her life.

❧

Jeffrey made three other appearances that first day.

The first came at one of the high school fields, during eleventh-grade gym class. Most of the students were playing soccer. But about a dozen were playing football, because they were on the varsity, and the gym teacher happened to be the football coach. The star quarterback, Brian Denehy, wound up and threw a sixty-yarder to his favorite receiver, James "Hands" Down, who was streaking a

130 fly pattern down the sideline.

But the ball never quite reached Hands. Just as he was about to cradle it in his big brown loving mitts, it vanished. By the time he recovered from the shock, a little kid was weaving upfield through the varsity football players. Nobody laid a paw on him. When the kid got down to the soccer field, he turned and punted the ball. It sailed back over the up-looking gym-classers, spiraling more perfectly than anything Brian Denehy had ever thrown, and landed in the outstretched hands of still stunned Hands Down. Then the kid ran off.

140 There was one other thing, something that all of them saw but no one believed until they compared notes after school that day: up until the punt, the kid had done everything with one hand. He had to, because in his other hand was a book. ❧

Keep Reading

Jeffrey seems like an unusual boy the minute he hits town, so why do you think Amanda lets him borrow her book? To find out how Jeffrey turns into the legendary Maniac Magee, read the rest of the novel. As the hilarious plot unfolds, Maniac continues to search for a home—and for a way to heal the conflicts he finds in Two Mills.

The Jacket
Personal Narrative by Gary Soto

VIDEO TRAILER **THINK** central KEYWORD: HML6-498

What builds
CONFIDENCE?

If you have confidence, that means you believe in yourself and in what you can accomplish. Confidence can help you speak in front of a group, meet new people, or make difficult choices. Real confidence comes from within. Still, as Gary Soto expresses in "The Jacket," outside pressures can sometimes bring you down.

LIST IT Brainstorm with a small group of classmates to make a list of the kinds of experiences that can build confidence. Then identify some ways that a person's confidence can be damaged.

Confidence Builders	Confidence Busters
doing well on a test	

TEXT ANALYSIS: SIMILES AND METAPHORS

Personal narratives allow writers to share their experiences with readers. As in fiction, nonfiction writers use descriptive language and literary devices such as similes and metaphors. A **simile** is a comparison of two things that uses the word *like* or *as*. A **metaphor** is a comparison of two things that does not use *like* or *as*. Writers often use such comparisons to reveal their emotions and attitudes toward the subjects they are writing about. For example, look at the following simile from "The Jacket":

I stared at the jacket, like an enemy, thinking bad things . . .

The simile "like an enemy" reveals Soto's anger toward the jacket. Look for other similes and metaphors as you read and notice what they help you understand.

READING STRATEGY: SUMMARIZE

One way to check your understanding of a work is to summarize it. A good **summary** provides a brief retelling of the main ideas. It uses your own words, but does not include your opinions, or personal views, about the subject. As you read "The Jacket," record the key events of the story in a log like the one below. Make sure you maintain the same meaning and a logical order in your notes.

> **Key Events**
>
> • *The narrator asks his mother for a black leather jacket.*

▲ VOCABULARY IN CONTEXT

Gary Soto uses the boldfaced words to help tell about a jacket he hated. To see how many you know, replace each boldfaced word with a word or phrase that means the same thing.

1. Gary Soto remembers looking at his **profile** in the mirror, hoping to look cool in his new jacket.
2. He spun each arm like a **propeller** to see how silly the jacket looked.
3. Eventually the jacket began to **shrivel** and no longer fit.
4. Soto remembers the **vicious** thoughts he had about it.

 Complete the activities in your **Reader/Writer Notebook**.

Meet the Author

Gary Soto
born 1952

Discovering Writing
Gary Soto was planning to study geography in college. Then, while browsing in the poetry section of his school library, he discovered a collection of modern poetry. "I thought, wow, wow, wow," Soto recalls. "I wanted to do this thing."

Poetry of His Own
Soto published his first book of poetry in 1976. Many of his poems are about Mexican Americans living and working in U.S. cities or working as migrant farm laborers. To create the lively, poetic images in his writing, he often draws upon childhood memories of growing up in a Mexican-American community in Fresno, California.

Fresno Boy
Soto understands the effect of poverty on children. His father died in a work accident when Soto was five, and the family's small income improved only a little when his mother remarried. Soto's personal experiences of having to do without many things comes through in much of his writing, including "The Jacket."

The Jacket

Gary Soto

M y clothes have failed me.
   I remember the green coat that I wore in fifth and sixth grades when you either danced like a champ or pressed yourself against a greasy wall, bitter as a penny toward the happy couples.
   When I needed a new jacket and my mother asked what kind I wanted, I described something like bikers wear: black leather and silver studs[1] with enough belts to hold down a small town. We were in the kitchen, steam on the windows from her cooking. She listened so long while stirring dinner that I thought she understood for sure the kind I wanted. The
10 next day when I got home from school, I discovered draped on my bedpost a jacket the color of day-old guacamole.[2] I threw my books on the bed and approached the jacket slowly, as if it were a stranger whose hand I had to shake. I touched the vinyl sleeve, the collar, and peeked at the mustard-colored lining. ◆

Analyze Visuals ▶

Examine the facial expression of the boy in this photograph. What kind of attitude does he seem to have?

◆ **GRAMMAR IN CONTEXT**
Reread lines 13–14. Notice that Soto correctly uses commas to separate his list of the different parts of the jacket that the narrator touched.

---

1. **studs:** small ornamental metal buttons mounted on fabric.

2. **guacamole** (gwä′kə-mō′lē): a thick paste made from avocados, citrus juice, onions, and seasoning, often served as a dip.

From the kitchen mother yelled that my jacket was in the closet. I closed the door to her voice and pulled at the rack of clothes in the closet, hoping the jacket on the bedpost wasn't for me but my mean brother. No luck. I gave up. From my bed, I stared at the jacket. I wanted to cry because it was so ugly and so big that I knew I'd have to wear it a long time. I was a
20 small kid, thin as a young tree, and it would be years before I'd have a new one. I stared at the jacket, like an enemy, thinking bad things before I took off my old jacket whose sleeves climbed halfway to my elbow.

I put the big jacket on. I zipped it up and down several times, and rolled the cuffs up so they didn't cover my hands. I put my hands in the pockets and flapped the jacket like a bird's wings. I stood in front of the mirror, full face, then **profile,** and then looked over my shoulder as if someone had called me. I sat on the bed, stood against the bed, and combed my hair to see what I would look like doing something natural. I looked ugly. I threw it on my brother's bed and looked at it for a long time before I slipped it on
30 and went out to the backyard, smiling a "thank you" to my mom as I passed her in the kitchen. With my hands in my pockets I kicked a ball against the fence, and then climbed it to sit looking into the alley. I hurled orange peels at the mouth of an open garbage can and when the peels were gone I watched the white puffs of my breath thin to nothing. **Ⓐ**

I jumped down, hands in my pockets, and in the backyard on my knees I teased my dog, Brownie, by swooping my arms while making bird calls. He jumped at me and missed. He jumped again and again, until a tooth sunk deep, ripping an L-shaped tear on my left sleeve. I pushed Brownie away to study the tear as I would a cut on my arm. There was no blood,
40 only a few loose pieces of fuzz. Dumb dog, I thought, and pushed him away hard when he tried to bite again. I got up from my knees and went to my bedroom to sit with my jacket on my lap, with the lights out.

That was the first afternoon with my new jacket. The next day I wore it to sixth grade and got a D on a math quiz. During the morning recess Frankie T., the playground terrorist, pushed me to the ground and told me to stay there until recess was over. My best friend, Steve Negrete, ate an apple while looking at me, and the girls turned away to whisper on the monkey bars.[3] The teachers were no help: they looked my way and talked about how foolish I looked in my new jacket. I saw their heads bob with
50 laughter, their hands half-covering their mouths. **Ⓑ**

Even though it was cold, I took off the jacket during lunch and played kickball in a thin shirt, my arms feeling like braille[4] from goose bumps. But when I returned to class I slipped the jacket on and shivered until I

Ⓐ SIMILES AND METAPHORS
Identify the simile in line 25. How does this comparison tell you how Soto feels?

Ⓑ SUMMARIZE
How do other people treat the narrator now that he is wearing the jacket? Record key events in your log.

---

3. **monkey bars:** a structure of poles and bars for climbing, often found in playgrounds.
4. **braille** (brāl): a system of writing or printing for blind people, made up of arrangements of raised dots representing letters and numbers.

◄ **Analyze Visuals**
What can you **infer** about the two girls in this image and the secret they are sharing?

was warm. I sat on my hands, heating them up, while my teeth chattered like a cup of crooked dice. Finally warm, I slid out of the jacket but a few minutes later put it back on when the fire bell rang. We paraded out into the yard where we, the sixth graders, walked past all the other grades to stand against the back fence. Everybody saw me. Although they didn't say out loud, "Man, that's ugly," I heard the buzz-buzz of gossip and even
60 laughter that I knew was meant for me.

And so I went, in my guacamole-colored jacket. So embarrassed, so hurt, I couldn't even do my homework. I received Cs on quizzes, and forgot the state capitals and the rivers of South America, our friendly neighbor. Even the girls who had been friendly blew away like loose flowers to follow the boys in neat jackets. **C**

I wore that thing for three years until the sleeves grew short and my forearms stuck out like the necks of turtles. All during that time no love came to me—no little dark girl in a Sunday dress she wore on Monday.

C SIMILES AND METAPHORS
Identify the simile in lines 64–65. How does this simile help you understand Soto's frustration?

At lunchtime I stayed with the ugly boys who leaned against the chainlink
70 fence and looked around with **propellers** of grass spinning in our mouths.
We saw girls walk by alone, saw couples, hand in hand, their heads like
bookends pressing air together. We saw them and spun our propellers so
fast our faces were blurs.

propeller (prə-pĕl′ər) *n.*
a spinning blade used to
move a boat or airplane
forward **propel** *v.*

I blame that jacket for those bad years. I blame my mother for
her bad taste and her cheap ways. It was a sad time for the heart. With
a friend I spent my sixth-grade year in a tree in the alley, waiting for
something good to happen to me in that jacket, which had become the
ugly brother who tagged along wherever I went. And it was about that
time that I began to grow. My chest puffed up with muscle and, strangely,
80 a few more ribs. Even my hands, those fleshy hammers, showed bravely
through the cuffs, the fingers already hardening for the coming fights.
But that L-shaped rip on the left sleeve got bigger, bits of stuffing coughed
out from its wound after a hard day of play. I finally Scotch-taped it
closed, but in rain or cold weather the tape peeled off like a scab and more
stuffing fell out until that sleeve **shriveled** into a palsied arm.[5] That
winter the elbows began to crack and whole chunks of green began to fall
off. I showed the cracks to my mother, who always seemed to be at the
stove with steamed-up glasses, and she said that there were children in
Mexico who would love that jacket. I told her that this was America and
90 yelled that Debbie, my sister, didn't have a jacket like mine. I ran outside,
ready to cry, and climbed the tree by the alley to think bad thoughts and
watch my breath puff white and disappear.

shrivel (shrĭ′vəl) *v.* to
shrink or wrinkle

But whole pieces still casually flew off my jacket when I played hard,
read quietly, or took **vicious** spelling tests at school. When it became so
spotted that my brother began to call me "camouflage," I flung it over the
fence into the alley. Later, however, I swiped the jacket off the ground and
went inside to drape it across my lap and mope. **D**

vicious (vĭsh′əs) *adj.*
severe or fierce

D **SUMMARIZE**
What does the narrator
blame the jacket for? Use
your log to summarize
the key events that
contributed to his
feelings about the jacket.

I was called to dinner: steam silvered my mother's glasses as she said
grace;[6] my brother and sister with their heads bowed made ugly faces at
100 their glasses of powdered milk. I gagged too, but eagerly ate big rips of
buttered tortilla that held scooped-up beans. Finished, I went outside with
my jacket across my arm. It was a cold sky. The faces of clouds were piled
up, hurting. I climbed the fence, jumping down with a grunt. I started up
the alley and soon slipped into my jacket, that green ugly brother who
breathed over my shoulder that day and ever since. ↜ **E**

E **SIMILES AND
METAPHORS**
Reread lines 104–105.
What does the
metaphor there help
Soto to convey?

---

5. **palsied** (pôl′zēd) **arm:** a paralyzed or weakened arm.

6. **grace:** a short prayer or blessing said before or after a meal.

Comprehension

1. **Recall** How did the jacket become ripped?

2. **Clarify** Reread lines 104–105. What does Soto mean when he calls his jacket an "ugly brother who breathed over my shoulder"?

3. **Summarize** Why is Soto disappointed by his sixth-grade year?

Text Analysis

4. **Compare and Contrast** What are the similarities and differences between the jacket Soto asked for and the one he received? Explain how what he wanted affected his attitude toward what he got.

5. **Summarize** Use your log to write a one paragraph summary of the events in Soto's personal narrative. Remember that summaries do not include **opinions,** or personal views. Make sure you maintain the same order and meaning as the original text.

6. **Identify Symbol** A **symbol** is a person, place, thing, or activity that stands for something beyond itself. What might Soto's jacket symbolize? Use details from the essay to support your answer.

7. **Analyze the Effects of Simile and Metaphor** Create a chart like the one shown to gather similes and metaphors Soto uses in "The Jacket." What overall **tone,** or attitude toward the jacket, do these comparisons convey? What else do they contribute to the essay?

Simile	Basic Description	Positive or Negative
"I stared at the jacket, like an enemy" (line 21)	he stared meanly or cautiously at it	negative

8. **Evaluate** Reread lines 61–74. Do you agree with Soto that the jacket is responsible for his "bad years"? Give examples from the essay to support your answer.

Extension and Challenge

9. **Reader's Circle** In a small group, discuss the ways in which Soto's attitude might have made wearing the jacket seem worse than it actually was. What could he have done to overcome the effects of the jacket?

What builds CONFIDENCE?

With a group of classmates, reread lines 43–50. Take turns discussing the effect the jacket had on Soto's confidence.

COMMON CORE

RI 2 Provide a summary of the text distinct from personal opinions and judgments.
RI 4 Determine the meaning of words and phrases as they are used in a text, including figurative and connotative meanings.

Vocabulary in Context

▲ VOCABULARY PRACTICE

Use context clues to choose the vocabulary word that best completes each sentence.

1. The airplane made an emergency landing when its _____ broke.
2. It was sad to see my favorite sweater _____ and shrink with each wash.
3. I know he was upset, but he didn't need to be so _____.
4. Many portraits show only the person's _____, not the whole face.

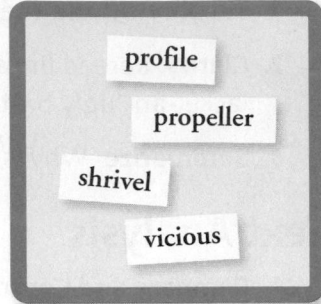

profile

propeller

shrivel

vicious

ACADEMIC VOCABULARY IN WRITING

• aspect • distinctive • interpret • perceive • sensory

Write a paragraph discussing Soto's use of personification and descriptive language in "The Jacket." Look for **distinctive** phrases such as "day-old guacamole" and "green ugly brother," and vivid verbs such as "paraded" and "silvered." How does Soto's use of memorable words and phrases affect the way you **perceive** the jacket? Use at least two Academic Vocabulary words in your response.

VOCABULARY STRATEGY: THE LATIN ROOT *pro*

The vocabulary words *profile* and *propellers* both contain the Latin root *pro*, which means "forth" or "forward." You can find the word root *pro* combined with other roots and base words in many English words. When you come across an unfamiliar word containing *pro*, use context clues, as well as your knowledge of the root, to figure out the meaning.

PRACTICE Choose the word from the web that best completes each sentence. Use a dictionary if necessary. Then explain how the root *pro* helps give meaning to each word.

1. After five years, the company decided to _____ him from assistant to manager.
2. We couldn't see the movie because the _____ wasn't working.
3. His _____ and detailed thank-you note was four pages long!
4. They were pleased to make such good _____ on their report.
5. He has become a very _____ man since running for town mayor.

COMMON CORE

L 4b Use Latin roots as clues to the meaning of a word.

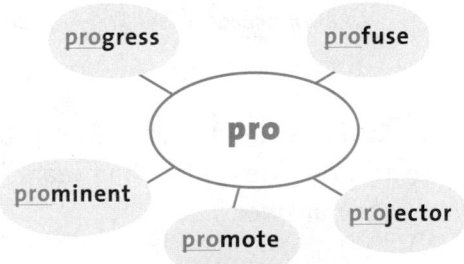

progress   profuse

pro

prominent   projector

promote

Interactive Vocabulary   THINK central

Go to thinkcentral.com.
KEYWORD: HML6-506

Language

◆ **GRAMMAR IN CONTEXT:** Use Commas Correctly

When writing a sentence that includes a list of three or more items, use **commas** to help make the sentence's meaning clear. Place commas after every **item in a series** except the last item. To separate two or more **adjectives** describing the same noun, use a comma after all but the last adjective.

> *Original:* Soto remembers the embarrassment sadness and awkwardness of having an ugly jacket.
>
> *Revised:* Soto remembers the embarrassment, sadness, and awkwardness of having an ugly jacket.

PRACTICE Insert commas where needed in the following sentences.

1. His mother bought cheap sturdy and practical clothes for the kids.
2. He uses humorous vivid familiar images to describe the jacket's ugliness.
3. The jacket resulted in poor grades no girlfriend and ugly friends for Soto.
4. Thinking of the jacket brings back memories of poverty disappointments and loneliness.

*For more help with commas, see page R49 in the **Grammar Handbook.***

READING-WRITING CONNECTION

YOUR TURN Broaden your understanding of "The Jacket" by responding to this prompt. Then use the **revising tip** to improve your writing.

WRITING PROMPT	REVISING TIP
Extended Constructed Response: Evaluation "The Jacket" tells about a time in Soto's life when he lacked confidence. Does he seem to have more confidence as an adult looking back? In **two or three paragraphs,** explain the ways in which Soto has or hasn't changed since the years when he wore the green jacket.	Review your response. Have you used commas correctly? If not, revise your writing.

◝ COMMON CORE

L 2 Demonstrate command of the conventions of punctuation.
W 2 Write informative/ explanatory texts to convey ideas.

Interactive Revision

THINK central

Go to **thinkcentral.com.**
KEYWORD: HML6-507

The First Skateboard in the History of the World
Memoir by Betsy Byars

How strong is
PEER PRESSURE?

Friends and classmates can have a strong influence on you. They may encourage you to make decisions—good or bad. The pressure you feel to please or fit in with people your age is called peer pressure. Standing up to peer pressure can be difficult, but giving in to it can cause trouble. In "The First Skateboard in the History of the World," Betsy Byars recalls her bumps and bruises from a time when peer pressure was too hard to resist.

WEB IT Think about the different ways peer pressure affects us. What things might a person do in order to fit in? Create a word web to gather your ideas.

wear a certain style of clothing

Fitting In

accept a dare

SECTION C   THE STAR JOURNAL   C4

LOOK, IF YOU'RE GOING TO HANG OUT WITH US, FIRST THING YOU GOTTA' DO IS LOSE THE BELL. —Hagen.

© Ralph Hagen/www.CartoonStock.com.

● TEXT ANALYSIS: STYLE IN NONFICTION

A writer's **style** is the distinctive way he or she uses language. When you read a nonfiction work such as a memoir, you will recognize some of the literary language and devices you find in fiction.

In her memoir, Byars creates a casual, friendly style through

- **word choice,** the distinctive way she uses language to express her ideas
- **sentence structure,** including short, direct sentences and fragments, or parts of sentences
- realistic **dialogue,** or conversations

As you read, notice how Byars uses these elements to create a specific style.

● READING STRATEGY: ANALYZE AUTHOR'S PURPOSE

An author may have many purposes for writing. An author typically writes a **memoir,** or true account of personal experiences, for one or more of these reasons:

- to inform the reader about his or her life
- to share his or her own thoughts and feelings
- to entertain readers with a good story

Use a chart like the one shown to analyze the author's purposes for writing this excerpt from her memoir. Record details from the text that support each purpose.

Inform	Share Thoughts or Feelings	Entertain

▲ VOCABULARY IN CONTEXT

Betsy Byars uses the boldfaced words to help tell a story about risk taking. To see how many you know, substitute a different word or phrase for each one.

1. Riding a skateboard requires **agility** as well as bravery.
2. The neighborhood kids never **protest** anything Bee says.
3. Betsy didn't get any **acclaim** for her tremendous efforts.
4. No one offered to **administer** first aid to the injured rider.

 Complete the activities in your **Reader/Writer Notebook.**

Meet the Author

Betsy Byars
born 1928

Reader on Wheels
Betsy Byars learned to roller-skate about the same time she started to read. She often roller-skated to the local library. She says she was a "good reader but a poor skater," so she unfortunately spent much of her childhood with bandages on her knees.

Adventurous Life
Adventure has always played a huge role in the way Byars lives her life. She and her husband are pilots and live on an airstrip in South Carolina. The bottom floor of their house is an airplane hangar where they park their own airplane. From their front yard, they can taxi down the runway and take flight.

BACKGROUND TO THE MEMOIR
Sidewalk Surfing

The first skateboards were made with boards and roller-skate wheels. Skateboarding became a craze in California in the 1950s. On days when the water or weather wasn't good for surfing, people would "sidewalk surf" using homemade skateboards.

Author Online
THINK central
Go to **thinkcentral.com.**
KEYWORD: HML6-509

THE FIRST SKATEBOARD
IN THE HISTORY OF THE WORLD

Betsy Byars

Since none of my friends knew I was scared of anything, I was thought to be a tough little kid.

My bravery (and the rest of me) was about seven years old when I was selected by the neighborhood to test ride The First Skateboard in the History of the World. **A**

I didn't even know what a skateboard was. This was the summer of 1935. Skateboards hadn't been invented back then. But that did not stop our neighborhood from making one.

Here's what went into The First Skateboard in the History of the World:

10   One board.

Forty-two assorted nails.

One roller skate.

Back then, roller skates were made out of metal and could be adjusted to stretch waaaay out for long feet, which a lot of us had. We stretched this skate out so far that it came apart. This suited us just fine. We nailed the front half of the skate to the front of the board and the back half to the back.

A AUTHOR'S PURPOSE
Reread lines 1–5. What purpose or purposes has the writer revealed so far? Record details in the appropriate column of your chart.

Analyze Visuals ▶

Describe as many **details** in this illustration as you can.

Illustrations by Juliette Borda.

Then we turned the board over and hammered the tips of the nails (which had come through the board) down—hard. We had a deep respect for nails. We had all stepped on nails at one time or another, and even though we **protested** all the way to the doctor's office, "It wasn't rusty! I swear it wasn't rusty! If you don't believe me ask Skrunky! He'll tell you it wasn't rusty!" we still got a shot. We also had a deep respect for shots. **B**

The whole construction took less than five minutes, and the skateboard was ready to go. By this time we knew it was a skateboard because the leader of the neighborhood—a sixth grade girl named Bee—said, "Who wants to go first on the skateboard?"

There was a silence.

Then Bee answered her own question. "Betsy will."

There was a sort of echo from the rest, "Betsy will-ill-ill-ill-ill."

And that was how I—seven-year-old Betsy Alice Cromer—got the honor of testing The First Skateboard in the History of the World.

At the time it didn't seem like an honor, more like a military duty.

protest (prə-tĕst´) v. to argue about or object to something

B STYLE IN NONFICTION
Reread lines 18–23. Which words or phrases in this paragraph contribute to the casual style of the piece?

The FIRST Skateboard

ONE BOARD

42 assorted nails

one Hammer

One Roller Skate

However, we always did what Bee told us to do. The explanation "Bee told me to" often made my mother explode with, "And if Bee told you to stick your head in a lion's mouth, would you?" "If Bee told you to jump off the Empire State Building,[1] would you?" Well . . . I was glad it never came to those things. **C**

40 We took the skateboard to the top of Magnolia Avenue, which was the street I lived on. Magnolia Avenue was not a steep hill, but the sidewalk had been buckled by the roots of old trees, and it was considered challenging for a skater.

We put the skateboard down on the sidewalk.

Bee said, "Go ahead, Betsy."

I said, "I will."

Fortunately we were unfamiliar with skateboards, and we didn't know you were supposed to stand up on them, so I sat down. Otherwise I wouldn't be alive today.

I sat, put my feet up on the skateboard, and held on to the sides with
50 both hands.

Somebody gave me a push.

I rolled a few inches but came to a stop at the first wide crack in the sidewalk.

They pushed again—harder.

Same disappointing ride. **D**

"This hill isn't steep enough," Bee complained, "I vote we take it to Red Hill."

"Red Hill-ill-ill-ill," came the echo.

The echo had a scary ring to it this time because Red Hill was the Alps,
60 the Himalayas, and Mount Everest[2] all rolled into one.

We weren't allowed to roller-skate down Red Hill. We weren't even allowed to ride our bikes down it. But nobody had told us we couldn't *skateboard* down it.

We set off in a silence, tense with excitement. My throat was dry. I had recently recovered from a broken arm—the result of a daring feat on the monkey bars in Dilworth Park.

See, we had been having a contest to see who could hang on to the bars by one hand the longest, and I held on so long that my body began to angle out to the side, as if I were doing a gymnastic display of **agility**,

---

1. **Empire State Building:** a skyscraper in New York City, once the world's tallest building.
2. **the Alps, the Himalayas, and Mount Everest:** The Alps and the Himalayas are mountain ranges located in Europe and Asia, respectively. Mount Everest, located on the border between Nepal and Tibet, is the highest mountain in the world.

70 which I wasn't. When I finally let go, I was horizontal to the ground and landed on my left elbow, which showed its displeasure by snapping in two. (I did win the contest, but neither of my parents congratulated me on the win.) **E**

E STYLE IN NONFICTION
Reread lines 68–73. What words and phrases in these lines add humor to the episode?

By the time we reached the top of Red Hill, my left arm was throbbing a warning like jungle drums.

And we reached the top of Red Hill very quickly.

"Sit down," Bee said.

I didn't want to, but I had to. Bee had told me to. I sat down on the skateboard. I said, "Now don't push me till I'm ready and I'm not ready 80 yet so don't push me till I say I'm ready, till I say 'Go.' Then when I say 'Go,' I only want Wilma to push me"—Wilma was the weak link in the gang—"and until I say 'Go,' everybody stay back and leave me—"

The neighborhood gang heard only the "Go" and they pushed. And I went.

The first thing that happened was that all the skin was scraped off my knuckles. (I was holding onto the sides of the board and my weight in the center of the board brought it closer to the road than anticipated.)

The next thing that happened was a three-part miracle.

The skate broke off the back of the board, the back of the board acted 90 as a brake, and The First Skateboard in the History of the World ground to a halt twenty feet down Red Hill.

There were cries of disappointment and of determination to renail the skate and start all over again, but these cries were drowned out by my own.

"I knew it wasn't going to work! Look what it did to my fingers! If you don't know how to make skateboards, don't make skateboards! Anyway, there is no such thing as a skateboard and there never will be!"

I stormed down the hill. My shouts of outrage turned to whimpers of pain as I got out of the gang's earshot and saw the damage to my knuckles. 100 I grew silent as I got within earshot of 915 Magnolia Avenue, my home. I liked to **administer** my own first-aid treatments because I was the only one who would stop administering if it hurt.

"What have you done now?" my mother asked, seeing me at the bloodied basin.

I gave my usual answer. "Nothing."

"What—have—you—done—now?" My mother always added the word *now* to give the impression that I did a lot of things.

Language Coach

Idioms An idiom is an expression specific to a language that means something beyond its literal meaning. In line 81, the writer calls Wilma the "weak link" of her group. What is the meaning of this idiom?

administer
(ăd-mĭn′ĭ-stər) *v.* to give or apply

"I went down Red Hill on a skateboard."

"A what?"

110 "A board with a skate on the bottom."

"I suppose Bee told you to."

Silence.

"And if Bee told you to catch a train to Timbuktu,[3] would you?"

Probably. **F**

So the test ride of the skateboard came and went without notice, without **acclaim.** I never got on another one. I never will.

But when I see kids on skateboards doing 180 ollies, ollie impossibles, lipslides, and G-turns,[4] I think to myself, You guys would never believe it to look at me now, but I actually test rode The First Skateboard in the
120 History of the World. ❧ **G**

F STYLE IN NONFICTION
Reread lines 103–114. How does Byars's use of realistic dialogue reveal that her mother is upset?

acclaim (ə-klām') *n.* enthusiastic praise

G AUTHOR'S PURPOSE
Read lines 115–120. What does Byars want her readers to know about her?

---

3. **Timbuktu** (tĭm'bŭk-tōō'): a city located in central Mali, in West Africa.

4. **180 ollies . . . G-turns:** a series of complicated and even dangerous tricks and jumps done by experienced skateboarders.

Comprehension

1. **Recall** Who is the leader of the neighborhood?

2. **Recall** Why did the group decide to take the skateboard to Red Hill?

3. **Clarify** Do the other kids know Betsy is afraid to ride the skateboard?

Text Analysis

4. **Make Inferences** Reread lines 24–38. What is Betsy's reason for riding the skateboard? What words and phrases reveal that bravery is not her only reason for being daring?

● 5. **Examine Style** Reread lines 39–73. Find examples of Byars's casual, friendly style by looking at her use of short sentences, fragments, realistic dialogue, and word choice. What effect do these elements have on you as the reader? Record your answers in a chart like the one shown.

	Example	Effect on Reader
Short Sentences or Fragments		
Realistic Dialogue		
Word Choice	Lines 72–73: " .. neither of my parents congratulated me on the win."	Helps me laugh as Byars looks back on the foolish things she did as a child.

6. **Analyze Memoir** Authors write memoirs to share important personal experiences. Why is this episode significant to the writer? Support your response with details from the text.

● 7. **Analyze Author's Purpose** Review the chart you completed as you read. What do you think was the author's main purpose for writing her memoir? Support your answer with details from the text.

Extension and Challenge

8. **Inquiry and Research** Research the history of skateboarding. Create a timeline that traces trends in skateboarding, changes in the design of skateboards, and the development of skateboarding tricks.

> ### How strong is PEER PRESSURE?
>
> Review the word web you created before your read. How has reading this memoir changed your ideas about wanting to fit in?

COMMON CORE

RI 6 Determine an author's purpose and explain how it is conveyed in the text. **RI 10** Read and comprehend literary nonfiction. **W 7** Conduct short research projects to answer a question, drawing on several sources.

Vocabulary in Context

▲ VOCABULARY PRACTICE

Choose the vocabulary word that best completes each sentence.

1. The diver proved his _____ by doing a backflip.
2. I continually _____ against my early bedtime.
3. Our Neighborhood Watch program received _____ for its success.
4. It is a superhero's job to _____ justice.

acclaim
administer
agility
protest

ACADEMIC VOCABULARY IN WRITING

> • aspect • distinctive • interpret • perceive • sensory

How do you **perceive** Betsy's decision to ride the skateboard? Which **aspects** of her behavior seem brave and which seem reckless? Use at least two Academic Vocabulary words in your response.

VOCABULARY STRATEGY: USE A DICTIONARY TO DETERMINE PART OF SPEECH

Many English words have more than one meaning. You can begin to determine what a word means in a sentence by identifying its part of speech. A **part of speech** describes how a word is used. In a dictionary entry, a word's part of speech appears after its pronunciation. In line 52, Byars writes that she stopped at a "crack in the sidewalk." The word *crack* has more than one meaning. If you were to look up *crack* in a dictionary, you might find these two entries:

> **crack** [krak] *n.:* a split or opening made by breaking without separating into parts.

> **crack** [krak] *v.:* to break without separating into parts.

The first entry is a **noun**, which names a person, place, or thing. The second entry is a **verb**, which shows action. Byars is using the word *crack* as a noun. She is writing about something she encountered, not an action she performed.

PRACTICE Read each sentence below. Determine whether the boldfaced word is used as a noun or a verb. Then, define the word in your *Reader/Writer Notebook*. Use a dictionary if you need help.

1. The kids would **protest** when they were sent to the doctor.
2. Hammering the **skate** into the board was not easy.
3. Betsy won the **contest**, but her parents were not impressed.
4. Betsy's mother was not satisfied with Betsy's **answer**.

Interactive Vocabulary THINK central

Go to **thinkcentral.com**.
KEYWORD: HML6-517

Skateboard Science

Science Article

What's the Connection?

When Betsy Byars test rode "The First Skateboard in the History of the World," she had two simple goals: stay on the board and don't get hurt. Today, skateboarders perform acrobatic leaps, dizzying mid-air spins, and other tricks that look nearly impossible. In this lesson, you will read a **science article** that explains one of these moves.

Use with "The First Skateboard in the History of the World," page 510.

COMMON CORE

RI 5 Analyze how a particular sentence, paragraph, or section fits into the overall structure and contributes to the development of ideas.
RI 6 Determine an author's purpose and explain how it is conveyed in the text.
RI 7 Integrate information presented in different formats as well as in words to develop a coherent understanding of a topic. **L 4c** Consult glossaries to determine or clarify a word's precise meaning.

Standards Focus: Follow Multi-Tasked Instructions

The skateboarding trick described on the next few pages is usually completed in one fluid motion. The writers divide it into steps to give a scientific explanation of how the skateboarder is able to complete the trick. Use these strategies to follow the instructions:

• **Preview** the instructions to get an idea of what they are about. Look at titles, subheadings, and graphics such as photos or illustrations.

• Read the steps in **numerical order.** Don't skip around.

• Notice **transitional words and phrases** such as *during, as,* and *meanwhile.* These words connect ideas between and within each step.

• Focus on the vivid verbs, adverbs, and adjectives that **describe** what happens in each step.

• Pay attention to **illustrations.** Illustrations enhance your understanding of instructions. Be sure you understand the factual information they present.

Finally, to make certain you truly understand these steps, restate each one in your own words in a chart like the one shown.

***Review:* Take Notes**

	My Own Words
Before the Ollie	Three forces are acting on the rider and his board. Weight and gravity pull the board and rider down. The ground pushes them up. These forces cancel each other out, so nothing speeds up the skateboard or stops it from rolling.
Step 1	
Step 2	

Skateboard Science

by Pearl Tesler and Paul Doherty

In the Beginning, Skateboarding Was Simple. . . . Ⓐ

With nothing more than a two-by-four on roller-skate wheels, the sidewalk surfers of the 30s, 40s, and 50s had a straightforward mission: Start at the top of a hill and ride down. The primary goal was just to stay on and avoid collisions; given the humble equipment and rough road conditions, it was no small challenge. Now, thanks in part to improvements in design and materials, skateboarders have a higher calling.

In a blur of flying acrobatics, skaters leap and skid over and onto obstacles, executing flips and turns of ever increasing
10 complexity—all at top speeds. For onlookers and beginners, it can be hard to follow the action, let alone answer the question that springs naturally to mind: How on earth do they do that? While it may seem that modern skateboarders are defying the laws of physics, the truth is that they're just using them to their advantage. Let's take a closer look at a fundamental skateboarding move and the physics principles behind it.

Internet

Ⓕ **OCUS ON FORM**
A **science article** is an informational text on a scientific subject. The author's purpose for writing a science article is usually to inform or explain. Science articles often use illustrations to convey factual information and clarify ideas.

Ⓐ **TAKE NOTES**
Preview the article's title and subheadings. Use the subheadings as topics for notes, leaving space beneath them. Then, as you read, record key information about the topics in the appropriate spaces.

B TAKE NOTES
Reread lines 18–20.
What are two pieces of
background information
about the ollie that you
can add to your notes?

C SCIENCE ARTICLE
How does the
illustration clarify
the information in
lines 30–36?

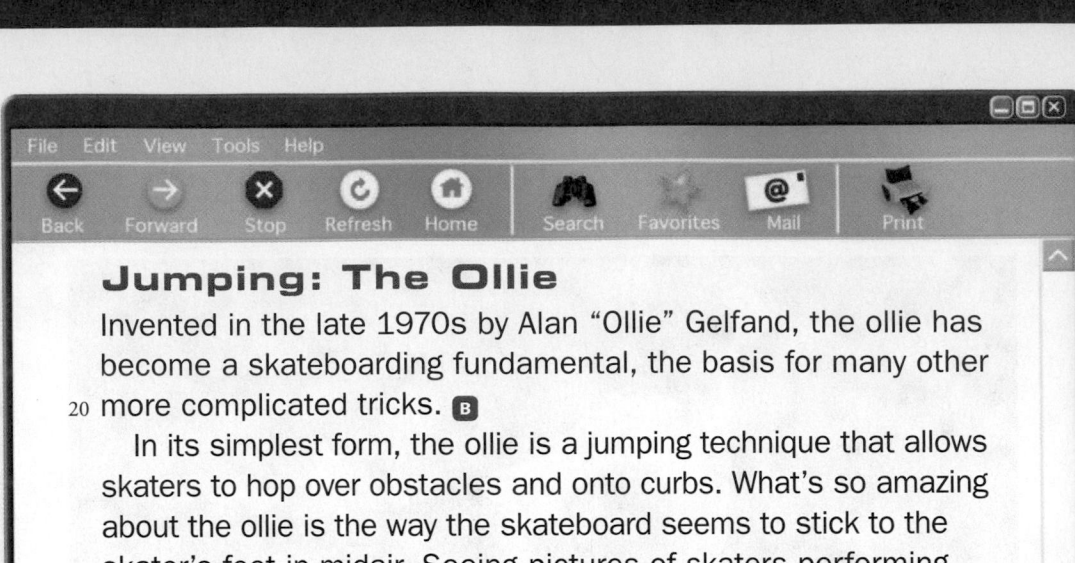

Jumping: The Ollie

Invented in the late 1970s by Alan "Ollie" Gelfand, the ollie has become a skateboarding fundamental, the basis for many other
20 more complicated tricks. **B**

In its simplest form, the ollie is a jumping technique that allows skaters to hop over obstacles and onto curbs. What's so amazing about the ollie is the way the skateboard seems to stick to the skater's feet in midair. Seeing pictures of skaters performing soaring four-foot ollies, many people assume that the board is somehow attached to a skater's feet. It's not. What's even more amazing about the ollie is that to get the skateboards to jump up, the skaters push down on the board! . . . Let's take a closer look.

Forces in the Ollie

30 Imagine a skater rolling along a flat surface. As he does so, there are three forces acting on the skateboard. One of these forces is the weight of the rider. Another is the force of gravity on the board itself. The third is the force of the ground pushing up on the skateboard. Since these three forces balance out to zero, the skateboard doesn't speed up or slow down. It rolls along at a constant speed. **C**

As the skater gets ready to perform an ollie, he crouches down. This will help him jump
40 high when the time comes. (Don't believe it? Stand perfectly straight and try jumping without crouching . . . you didn't get very high, did you?) Now let's follow the changing forces that go into making an ollie.

File   Edit   View   Tools   Help

Back   Forward   Stop   Refresh   Home   Search   Favorites   Mail   Print

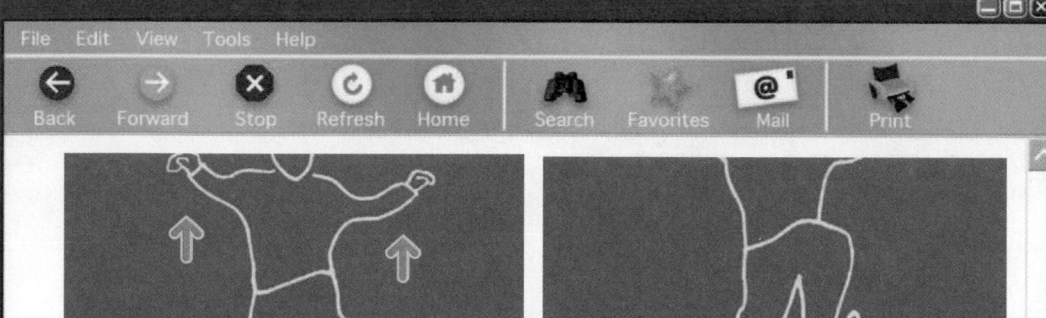

1 The skater pushes himself upward by explosively straightening his legs and raising his arms. During the jump, his rear foot exerts a much greater force on the tail of the board than his front foot does on the nose. This causes the board to pivot counterclockwise about the rear wheel, which means the tail of the board touches the ground. **D**

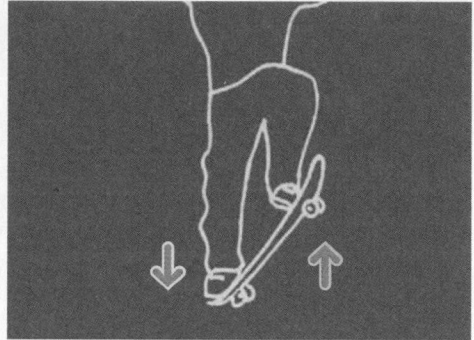

2 As the tail strikes the ground, the ground pushes back. The result of this upward force is that the board bounces up and begins to pivot clockwise, this time around its center of mass, which is the center of the board.

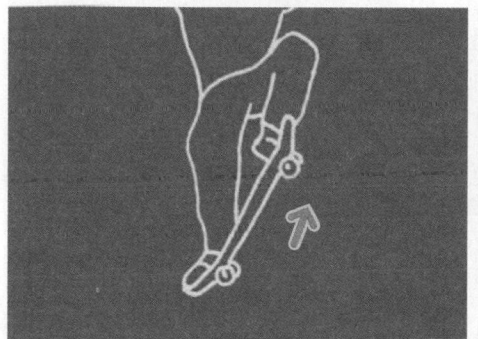

3 With the board now completely in the air, the skater slides his front foot forward, using the friction between his foot and the rough surface of the board to drag the board upward even higher.

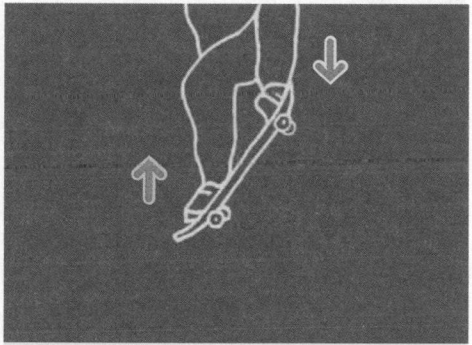

4 The skater then begins to push his front foot down, raising the rear wheels and leveling out the board. Meanwhile, he lifts his rear leg to get it out of the way of the rising tail of the board. If he times this motion perfectly, his rear foot and the rear of the board rise in perfect unison, seemingly "stuck" together. **E**

Internet

COMMON CORE   RI 6

D AUTHOR'S PURPOSE
Authors writing on the same topic may write for very different purposes. In her memoir, Betsy Byars tells about the first time she rode a skateboard. In her description, she includes her thoughts and feelings about what happens. This science article also discusses riding a skateboard. However, the writer includes mostly factual information about how to ride a skateboard. Why does the memoir include thoughts and feelings while the science article focuses on facts? What is the difference in the implied purpose of each work?

E FOLLOW INSTRUCTIONS
Why does the illustrator include arrows in these illustrations? What factual information do they convey?

F **FOLLOW INSTRUCTIONS**
Notice how many steps there are in an ollie according to this article. Be sure to restate the same number of steps in your chart.

COMMON CORE L 4c

G **SCIENCE ARTICLE**
When you read a science article, you may come across familiar words that have unfamiliar meanings. For example, the writer of this article frequently refers to the "nose" of a skateboard. In this context, the word *nose* does not mean "the part of the face above the mouth." The writer has included a **glossary** of skateboarding terms to help you determine the meanings of unusual or difficult words. You can use the glossary to find out that, in this context, *nose* means "the front end of a skateboard." Why is a glossary like this one especially helpful when you read a science article?

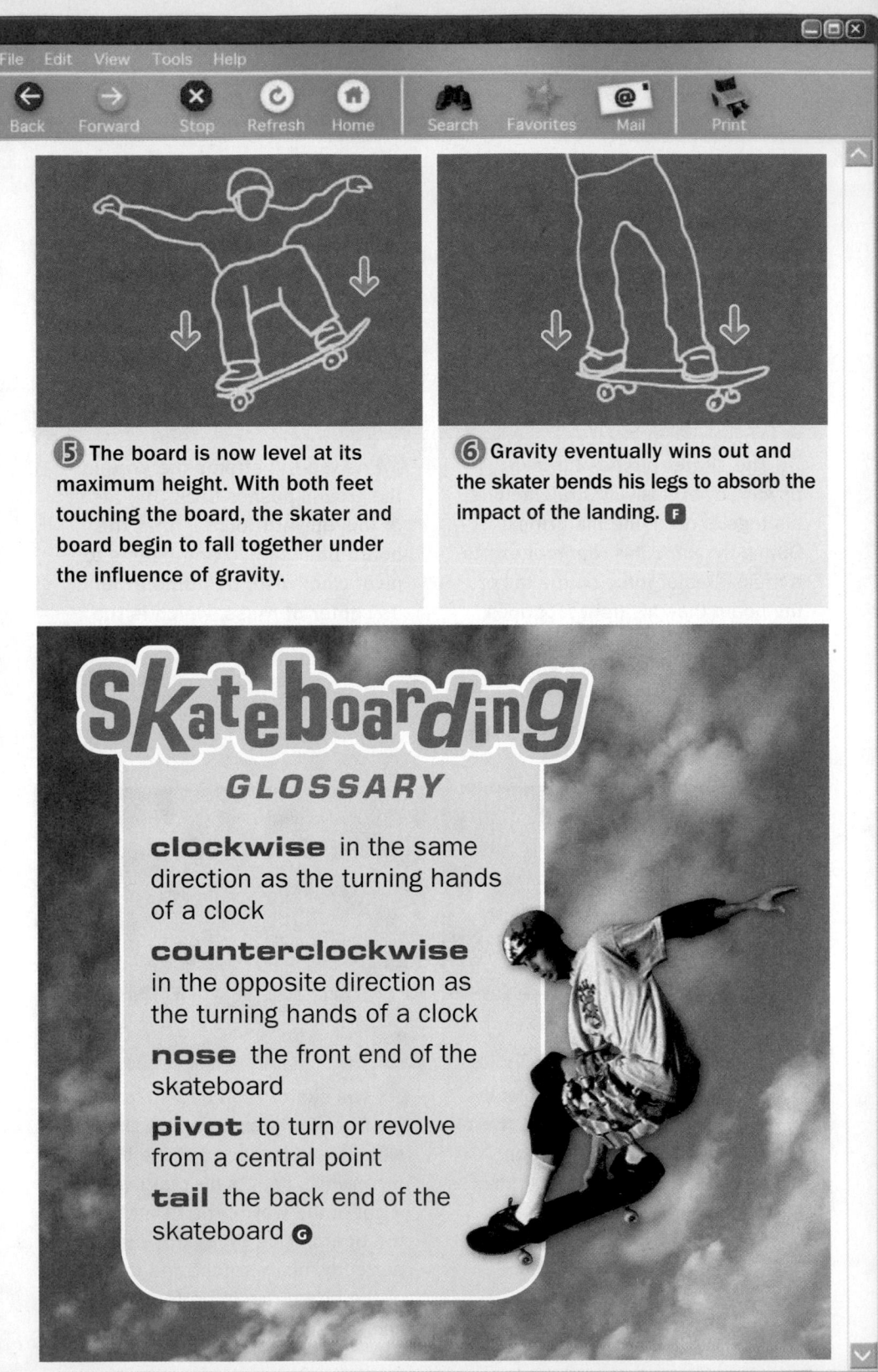

5 The board is now level at its maximum height. With both feet touching the board, the skater and board begin to fall together under the influence of gravity.

6 Gravity eventually wins out and the skater bends his legs to absorb the impact of the landing. **F**

Skateboarding
GLOSSARY

clockwise in the same direction as the turning hands of a clock

counterclockwise in the opposite direction as the turning hands of a clock

nose the front end of the skateboard

pivot to turn or revolve from a central point

tail the back end of the skateboard **G**

Comprehension

1. **Recall** How did the ollie get its name?

2. **Clarify** What are some of the ways skateboarding has changed since the 1930s, 1940s, and 1950s?

Text Analysis

● 3. **Follow Multi-Tasked Instructions** How do the transitional words and phrases in the article help a reader perform a procedure correctly? Support your response with an example from the instructions.

4. **Evaluate a Science Article** How did the factual information presented in the illustrations help you understand the instructions? Provide a specific example from the text in your response.

COMMON CORE

RI 5 Analyze how a particular sentence, paragraph, or section fits into the overall structure and contributes to the development of ideas.
RI 6 Determine an author's purpose and explain how it is conveyed in the text.
RI 7 Integrate information presented in different formats as well as in words to develop a coherent understanding of a topic. **W 2** Write informative/expository texts.
W 2a Organize ideas, concepts, and information, using strategies such as comparison/contrast.

Read for Information: Compare and Contrast Author's Purpose

WRITING PROMPT

Betsy Byars's memoir and the science article you just read are about skateboarding. While both texts are on the same topic, the authors probably wrote them for very different purposes. Write a paragraph in which you **compare** and **contrast** each author's purpose for writing a text on skateboarding. Keep in mind that an author's purpose is usually implied, so you must infer it using details in the text. Remember too that authors often have more than one purpose for writing.

To answer this prompt, you will need to do the following:

1. Review the chart you completed as you read "The First Skateboard in the History of the World."

2. Create a similar chart for "Skateboard Science." Record details from the text that reveal the purpose of the text.

Inform	Share Thoughts or Feelings	Entertain

3. In a paragraph, contrast each author's purpose for writing a text on the topic of skateboarding. First, state how each author's purpose is different. Then, support your statement with details from the text.

Poem: The Morning Walk
Poem by Mary Oliver

Video link at thinkcentral.com

There Is No Word for Goodbye
Poem by Mary Tall Mountain

When are WORDS not enough?

◌ **COMMON CORE**

RL 1 Cite textual evidence to support inferences drawn from the text. **RL 4** Analyze the impact of a specific word choice on meaning.

Sometimes what you *do* is more important than what you *say*. Saying "good game" may mean more if you also shake your opponent's hand. Saying "hello" may mean more if you also smile. Actions often add deeper meaning to simple words. In "The Morning Walk" and "There Is No Word for Goodbye," two poets explore the limitations of language.

QUICKWRITE Think of a time when using an electronic form of communication, such as e-mail or instant messaging, led to a misunderstanding. Explain briefly how talking in person could have made your meaning clearer.

● TEXT ANALYSIS: IMAGERY AND MOOD

Whenever you read a poem, you should ask yourself, "How does this poem make me feel?" A poem can make you feel many different ways, such as sad, joyful, thoughtful, or even frightened. The feeling readers get from a poem is called the poem's **mood.** Poets take great care to create mood in their poems. Often they use **imagery,** or description that appeals to the reader's sense of sight, touch, taste, smell, or hearing, to create a poem's mood.

• "the dark blanket of sky" (sense of sight)

• "leaves crunched under Jeb's feet" (sense of hearing)

The two poems you are about to read focus on the meanings of words. However, the feeling the reader gets from each poem is different. As you read each poem, look for examples of imagery and any other interesting words and phrases to help you identify the mood.

● READING STRATEGY: SET A PURPOSE FOR READING

In this lesson, your **purpose for reading** is to compare and contrast the moods of two poems. To help you do this, pay attention to your feelings as you read. Then, reread the poems and fill in a chart like the one shown.

	"The Morning Walk"	"There Is No Word for Goodbye"
Which descriptions appeal to your sense of sight?		
Which descriptions appeal to your sense of hearing?		
Which descriptions appeal to your sense of touch?		
What other words or phrases stand out?		

Review: **Make Inferences**

 Complete the activities in your **Reader/Writer Notebook.**

Mary Oliver
born 1935

Nature Guide
Walking in the woods near her Massachusetts home often provides inspiration for Mary Oliver's poetry. But one day, Oliver forgot to bring a pencil on her walk and was frustrated that she could not write down her ideas. To make sure this didn't happen again, she later returned to the woods and hid pencils among the trees. Oliver has said that a writer's duty begins with "the powers of observing."

Mary Tall Mountain
1918–1997

Divided Poet
Through her poetry, Mary Tall Mountain rediscovered the home and heritage she lost as a child, bringing her two worlds together. Tall Mountain was only six years old when her mother died, an event that caused her to be adopted by white Americans and taken away from her village. From then on, she felt torn between her new home and her Native-American community in Alaska. She once said, "Wherever I can find a place to sit down and write, that is my home."

Authors Online
Go to **thinkcentral.com.** KEYWORD: HML6-525

Poem: The
Morning Walk
Mary Oliver

Analyze
Visuals ▶

Notice the colors in this painting. What effect do they have on the **mood** of the painting?

There are a lot of words meaning *thanks*.
Some you can only whisper.
Others you can only sing.
The pewee whistles instead.
5 The snake turns in circles,
the beaver slaps his tail
on the surface of the pond.
The deer in the pinewoods stamps his hoof.
Goldfinches shine as they float through the air. Ⓐ
10 A person, sometimes, will hum a little Mahler.[1]
Or put arms around old oak tree.
Or take out lovely pencil and notebook to find a few
touching, kissing words.

Ⓐ **MOOD**
Reread lines 4–9. What mood do the descriptions of the animals create?

---

1. **Mahler:** Gustav Mahler (gōōs′täf mä′lər) (1860–1911); composer and conductor of classical music.

Detail of *Stag on Alert, In Wooded Clearing*, Rosa Bonheur. © SuperStock.

There Is No Word for Goodbye

Mary Tall Mountain

Sokoya,[1] I said, looking through
the net of wrinkles into
wise black pools
of her eyes. **B**

5 What do you say in Athabaskan[2]
when you leave each other?
What is the word
for goodbye?

A shade of feeling rippled
10　　the wind-tanned skin.
Ah, nothing, she said,
watching the river flash. **C**

B IMAGERY
Try to imagine the speaker's aunt. What feelings do you get from the description?

C MAKE INFERENCES
What might the aunt be experiencing in lines 9–12?

---

1. **Sokoya** (sə-koi'yə): word meaning "aunt on the mother's side."
2. **Athabaskan** (ăth'ə-băs'kən): a language spoken by Native American tribes in parts of Canada, Alaska, Oregon, and California.

Detail of *Bluebells in Shakespeare's Wood* (2004), Timmy Mallett. Acrylic. © Timmy Mallett.

She looked at me close.
    We just say, Tlaa. That means,
15   See you.
    We never leave each other.
    When does your mouth
    say goodbye to your heart? **D**

She touched me light
20   as a bluebell.
    You forget when you leave us,
    You're so small then.
    We don't use that word.

We always think you're coming back,
25   but if you don't,
    we'll see you some place else.
    You understand.
    There is no word for goodbye. **E**

D **MAKE INFERENCES**
Reread lines 14–18. What does the aunt mean by the question she asks at the end of this section?

E **MOOD**
Reread the poem to find other places where the word *goodbye* appears. How does the repetition of *goodbye* affect the mood of the poem?

Comprehension

1. **Recall** In Mary Oliver's poem, what are the different animals expressing through their sounds and actions?

2. **Clarify** In Mary Tall Mountain's poem, why doesn't the aunt tell the poem's speaker how to say *goodbye* in her language?

3. **Clarify** What does the word *tlaa* mean?

Text Analysis

4. **Make Inferences** Explain why Mary Oliver might have decided to call her poem "The Morning Walk." Support your response with textual evidence.

5. **Analyze Imagery** Which images in "The Morning Walk" are most vivid? What feeling do they create?

6. **Analyze Mood** Would you describe the mood of "There Is No Word for Goodbye" as angry, hopeful, sad, joyful, or thoughtful? You may choose more than one word. Support your choices with details from the poem.

7. **Draw Conclusions** In "There Is No Word for Goodbye," what do you learn about Athabaskan people and how they view one another?

Comparing Mood

Now that you have read both poems and answered some questions about them, fill in a chart like the one shown. Then, write a paragraph in which you compare the two poems. Start by briefly summarizing each poem.

	"The Morning Walk"	"There Is No Word for Goodbye"
Which descriptions appeal to your sense of sight?	The snake turns in circles	
Which descriptions appeal to your sense of hearing?	whisper, sing	
Which descriptions appeal to your sense of touch?	none	
What other words or phrases stand out?	thanks	
What is the mood of the poem?	joyful	

COMMON CORE

RL 1 Cite textual evidence to support inferences drawn from the text. **RL 4** Analyze the impact of a specific word choice on meaning.

Writing for Assessment

COMMON CORE　　W 2, W 4, W 10

1. READ THE PROMPT

Poems usually include words that are full of emotion. Recognizing these feelings and how the poet created them is an important part of appreciating poems. In writing assessments, you will often be asked to **compare and contrast** the mood or feeling created in two poems or stories.

> In three paragraphs, compare "The Morning Walk" and "There Is No Word for Goodbye." Describe the mood of each poem and tell whether the moods are more similar or different. Be sure to include a comparison of how each poet uses imagery to create mood. Support your ideas using details from the poems.

◀ **STRATEGIES IN ACTION**

1. I need to describe the **similarities and differences** between the poems.

2. I need to describe the **feeling** I get from each poem and decide if the feelings are more alike or different.

3. I need to include **examples** of words and images from the poems that help support my ideas.

2. PLAN YOUR WRITING

Study the chart you filled in to review your ideas about the mood of each poem. Then think about how to present your ideas.

- Decide on the main idea, or focus, for your response.
- Reread the poems to find more examples and details.
- Create an outline to organize your paragraphs. This sample outline shows one way you might organize them.

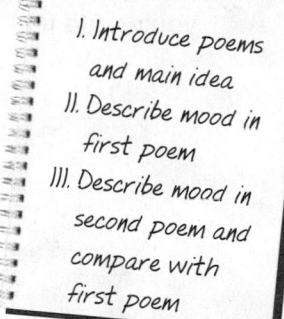

I. Introduce poems and main idea
II. Describe mood in first poem
III. Describe mood in second poem and compare with first poem

3. DRAFT YOUR RESPONSE

Paragraph 1 Include the titles of the poems and the names of the poets. Summarize what happens in each poem. Then state your opinion about whether the moods are mostly similar or different.

Paragraph 2 Describe the mood in the first poem. Explain which words and images create the mood.

Paragraph 3 Describe the mood in the second poem. Explain which words and images create the mood. Tell how the mood in this poem is similar to or different from the mood in the first poem.

Revision Double check that you have included enough details as support.

The Phantom Tollbooth, Act One
Novel by Norton Juster

Dramatized by Susan Nanus

When is logic not
LOGICAL?

COMMON CORE

RL 4 Determine the meaning of words and phrases as they are used in a text, including figurative and connotative meanings; analyze the impact of a specific word choice on meaning and tone. **RL 5** Analyze how a particular scene fits into the overall structure of a text. **RL 7** Compare and contrast a drama to a video version of the text.

Has there ever been a time when you thought you were making sense, but no one understood what you meant? In *The Phantom Tollbooth*, a boy travels to a land where nothing makes sense. There he finds that what he thinks is logical really isn't.

QUICKWRITE Imagine that one day you arrive at school to find everyone behaving differently and nothing as it normally is. What kinds of changes do you imagine taking place? Write one or two paragraphs describing people's behavior, how things look, and how you would feel.

DANGER
SOFT SAND

● TEXT ANALYSIS: HUMOR

Writers often use **humor** to increase interest and entertain readers. Writers add humor in a number of ways. They may

- have the characters speak and act in funny ways. Playwrights may use **personification,** the technique of giving human qualities to an animal or object. In this play you will meet several personified characters, including a Spelling Bee and a Watchdog named Tock.
- create events that lead to funny situations.
- add puns for comic effect. A **pun** is a deliberate confusion of similar-sounding words or phrases that have different meanings. For example, in *The Phantom Tollbooth*, the Whether Man says that "it's more important to know whether there will be weather than what the weather will be." (pun: *whether* and *weather*)

As you read Act One of *The Phantom Tollbooth,* notice how these elements add humor to the play.

● READING STRATEGY: VISUALIZE

Details that tell you how something looks, sounds, smells, feels, or tastes help you **visualize,** or form a mental picture, as you read. In plays, sensory details are often provided in stage directions, which give information about the setting, characters' speech and behavior, sound effects, and lighting.

As you read, create a log like the one shown to record the stage directions that help you visualize what's happening.

See	Hear	Smell	Touch	Taste
	ticking			

▲ VOCABULARY IN CONTEXT

Match the words from the play with their definitions.

1. crag
2. dejectedly
3. destination
4. ferocious
5. leisurely
6. surmise

a. unhurried
b. where a person is going
c. make a guess
d. fierce
e. cliff
f. unhappily

 Complete the activities in your **Reader/Writer Notebook.**

Meet the Author

Norton Juster
born 1929

Architect of Words
After spending many years working as an architect, Norton Juster turned from constructing buildings to constructing elaborate wordplay. Juster traces his love of puns back to his childhood, saying that "as a child you have a feeling you're being oppressed by puns, though after a while you realize they're a lot of fun." He compares playing with words to "drawing outside of the lines" and encourages others to experiment with wordplay and "follow an idea wherever it goes."

BACKGROUND TO THE NOVEL
Words Versus Numbers
Just as Norton Juster balances words and numbers in his life, so, too, does the fantasy land featured in *The Phantom Tollbooth*. One king rules Dictionopolis, the kingdom of words, and another rules Digitopolis, the kingdom of numbers. A long-standing feud divides the two: Are words or numbers more important?

Juster wrote *The Phantom Tollbooth* as a novel. Susan Nanus later adapted the story as a play. In 1970, Juster's book was made into an animated film. Some images from the movie are used to illustrate the play in the pages that follow.

THE PHANTOM TOLLBOOTH

Norton Juster
Dramatized by Susan Nanus

CAST

(*in order of appearance*)

The Clock

Milo, a boy

The Whether Man

Six Lethargarians

Tock, the Watchdog (same as The Clock)

Azaz the Unabridged, King of Dictionopolis

The Mathemagician, King of Digitopolis

Princess Sweet Rhyme

Princess Pure Reason

Gatekeeper of Dictionopolis

Three Word Merchants

The Letterman (Fourth Word Merchant)

Spelling Bee

The Humbug

The Duke of Definition

The Minister of Meaning

The Earl of Essence

The Count of Connotation

The Undersecretary of Understanding

A Page

The Set

It is recommended that the setting be either a platform set, employing vertical pipes from which banners, etc., are hung for various scenes, or a book set, with the spine UC, the leaves of the book being painted drops[1] which are turned like book leaves whenever the scene changes.

The settings should be impressionistic rather than realistic:

1. **Milo's bedroom:** *With shelves, pennants, pictures on the wall, as well as suggestions of the characters of the Land of Wisdom.*

2. **The road to the Land of Wisdom:** *A forest, from which the* Whether Man *and the* Lethargarians *emerge.*

3. **Dictionopolis:** *A marketplace full of open air stalls as well as little shops. Letters and signs should abound. There may be street signs and lampposts in the shapes of large letters (large O's and Q's) and all windows and doors can be in the shape of H's and A's.*

Act One Scene 1

The stage is completely dark and silent. Suddenly the sound of someone winding an alarm Clock *is heard, and after that, the sound of loud ticking is heard.*

Lights up on the Clock, *a huge alarm clock. The* Clock *reads 4:00. The lighting should make it appear that the* Clock *is suspended in mid-air (if possible). The* Clock *ticks for 30 seconds.*

Clock. See that! Half a minute gone by. Seems
10 like a long time when you're waiting for something to happen, doesn't it? Funny thing is, time can pass very slowly or very fast, and sometimes even both at once. The time now? Oh, a little after four, but what that means should depend on you. Too often, we do something simply because time tells us to. Time for school, time for bed, whoops, 12:00, time to be hungry. It can get a little silly, don't you think? Time is important, but it's what you do
20 with it that makes it so. So my advice to you is to use it. Keep your eyes open and your ears perked. Otherwise it will pass before you know it, and you'll certainly have missed something!

Things have a habit of doing that, you know. Being here one minute and gone the next. In the twinkling of an eye. In a jiffy. In a flash!

I know a girl who yawned and missed a
30 whole summer vacation. And what about that caveman who took a nap one afternoon, and woke up to find himself completely alone. You see, while *he* was sleeping, someone had invented the wheel and everyone had moved to the suburbs. And then of course, there is Milo. (*Lights up to reveal* Milo's *bedroom. The* Clock *appears to be on a shelf in the room of a young boy—a room filled with books, toys, games, maps, papers, pencils, a bed, a desk. There*
40 *is a dartboard with numbers and the face of the* Mathemagician, *a bedspread made from* King Azaz's *cloak, a kite looking like the* Spelling Bee, *a punching bag with the* Humbug's *face, as well as records, a television, a toy car, and a large box that is wrapped and has an envelope taped to the top. The sound of footsteps is heard, and then enter* Milo **dejectedly**. *He throws down his books and coat, flops into a chair, and sighs loudly.*) Who never knows what to do
50 with himself—not just sometimes, but always. When he's in school, he wants to be out, and when he's out, he wants to be in. (*During the following speech,* Milo *examines the various toys, tools, and other possessions in the room, trying*

---

1. **painted drops:** cloths that are painted to look like scenery, or, in this case, the pages of a book.

them out and rejecting them.) Wherever he is, he wants to be somewhere else—and when he gets there, so what. Everything is too much trouble or a waste of time. Books—he's already read them. Games—boring. T.V.—dumb. So what's
60 left? Another long, boring afternoon. Unless he bothers to notice a very large package that happened to arrive today.

Milo. (*Suddenly notices the package. He drags himself over to it, and disinterestedly reads the label.*) "For Milo, who has plenty of time." Well, that's true. (*sighs and looks at it*) No. (*walks away*) Well . . . (*Comes back. Rips open envelope and reads.*)

Voice. "One genuine turnpike tollbooth, easily
70 assembled at home for use by those who have never traveled in lands beyond."

Milo. Beyond what? (*continues reading*)

Voice. "This package contains the following items:" (Milo *pulls the items out of the box and sets them up as they are mentioned.*) "One (*1*) genuine turnpike tollbooth to be erected according to directions. Three (*3*) precautionary signs to be used in a precautionary fashion. Assorted coins for paying tolls. One (*1*) map,
80 strictly up to date, showing how to get from here to there. One (*1*) book of rules and traffic regulations which may not be bent or broken. Warning! Results are not guaranteed. If not perfectly satisfied, your wasted time will be refunded."

Milo (*skeptically*). Come off it, who do you think you're kidding? (*walks around and examines tollbooth*) What am I supposed to do with this? (*The ticking of the* Clock *grows loud
90 and impatient.*) Well . . . what else do I have to do. (Milo *gets into his toy car and drives up to the first sign. NOTE: The car may be an actual toy car propelled by pedals or a small motor, or simply*

a cardboard imitation that Milo *can fit into, and move by walking.*)

Voice. "HAVE YOUR **DESTINATION** IN MIND."

Milo (*pulls out the map*). Now, let's see. That's funny. I never heard of any of these places.
100 Well, it doesn't matter anyway. Dictionopolis. That's a weird name. I might as well go there. (*Begins to move, following map. Drives off.*)

Clock. See what I mean? You never know how things are going to get started. But when you're bored, what you need more than anything is a rude awakening.

(*The alarm goes off very loudly as the stage darkens. The sound of the alarm is transformed into the honking of a car horn, and then is joined
110 by the blasts, bleeps, roars and growls of heavy highway traffic. When the lights come up, Milo's bedroom is gone and we see a lonely road in the middle of nowhere.*)

Act One **Scene 2**
The Road to Dictionopolis

Enter Milo *in his car.*

Milo. This is weird! I don't recognize any of this scenery at all. (*A sign is held up before* Milo, *startling him.*) Huh? (*reads*) WELCOME TO EXPECTATIONS. INFORMATION, PREDICTIONS AND ADVICE
120 CHEERFULLY OFFERED. PARK HERE AND BLOW HORN. (Milo *blows horn.*)

Whether Man (*A little man wearing a long coat and carrying an umbrella pops up from behind the sign that he was holding. He speaks very fast and excitedly*). My, my, my, my, my, welcome, welcome, welcome, welcome to the Land of Expectations, Expectations, Expectations! We don't get many travelers these days; we certainly don't get many travelers. Now what can I do for you? I'm the Whether Man.

Milo (*referring to map*). Uh . . . is this the right road to Dictionopolis?

Whether Man. Well now, well now, well now, I don't know of any *wrong* road to Dictionopolis, so if this road goes to Dictionopolis at all, it must be the right road, and if it doesn't, it must be the right road to somewhere else, because there are no wrong roads to anywhere. Do you think it will rain?

Milo. I thought you were the Weather Man.

Whether Man. Oh, no, I'm the Whether Man, not the weather man. (*pulls out a sign or opens a flap of his coat, which reads: "WHETHER"*) After all, it's more important to know whether there will be weather than what the weather will be.

Milo. What kind of place is Expectations?

Whether Man. Good question, good question! Expectations is the place you must always go to before you get where you are going. Of course, some people never go beyond Expectations, but my job is to hurry them along whether they like it or not. Now what else can I do for you? (*opens his umbrella*)

Milo. I think I can find my own way.

Whether Man. Splendid, splendid, splendid! Whether or not you find your own way, you're bound to find some way. If you happen to find my way, please return it. I lost it years ago. I imagine by now it must be quite rusty. You did say it was going to rain, didn't you? (*escorts Milo to the car under the open umbrella*) I'm glad you made your own decision. I do so hate to make up my mind about anything, whether it's good or bad, up or down, rain or shine. Expect everything, I always say, and the unexpected never happens. Goodbye, goodbye, goodbye, good . . . (*A loud clap of thunder is heard.*) Oh dear! (*He looks up at the sky, puts out his hand to feel for rain, and runs away. Milo watches puzzledly and drives on.*)

Milo. I'd better get out of Expectations, but fast. Talking to a guy like that all day would get me nowhere for sure. (*He tries to speed up, but finds instead that he is moving slower and slower.*) Oh, oh, now what? (*He can barely move. Behind Milo, the Lethargarians[2] begin to enter from all parts of the stage. They are dressed to blend in with the scenery and carry small pillows that look like rocks. Whenever they fall asleep, they rest on the pillows.*) Now I really am getting nowhere. I hope I didn't take a wrong turn. (*The car stops. He tries to start it. It won't move. He gets out and begins to tinker with it.*) I wonder where I am.

Lethargarian 1. You're . . . in . . . the . . . Dol . . . drums[3] . . . (Milo *looks around.*)

Lethargarian 2. Yes . . . the . . . Dol . . . drums . . . (*A yawn is heard.*)

Milo (*yelling*). WHAT ARE THE DOLDRUMS?

Lethargarian 3. The Doldrums, my friend, are where nothing ever happens and nothing ever changes. (*Parts of the scenery stand up or six people come out of the scenery colored in the same colors of the trees or the road. They move very slowly and as soon as they move, they stop to rest again.*) Allow me to introduce all of us. We are the Lethargarians at your service.

---

2. **Lethargarians** (lĕth′ər-jär′ē-ənz): a made-up name based on the word *lethargy*. A *Lethargarian* would thus be dull, inactive, or uncaring.

3. **in the doldrums** (dōl′drəmz′): the condition of being depressed or listless; here, *the Doldrums* refers to an imaginary land.

Milo (*uncertainly*). Very pleased to meet you. I think I'm lost. Can you help me?

Lethargarian 4. Don't say think. (*He yawns.*) It's against the law.

Lethargarian 1. No one's allowed to think in the Doldrums. (*He falls asleep.*)

Lethargarian 2. Don't you have a rule book? It's local ordinance[4] 175389-J. (*He falls asleep.*)

Milo (*pulls out rule book and reads*). Ordinance 175389-J: "It shall be unlawful, illegal and unethical to think, think of thinking, **surmise**, presume, reason, meditate or speculate while in the Doldrums. Anyone breaking this law shall be severely punished." That's a ridiculous law! Everybody thinks.

All the Lethargarians. We don't!

Lethargarian 2. And most of the time, you don't, that's why you're here. You weren't thinking and you weren't paying attention either. People who don't pay attention often get stuck in the Doldrums. Face it, most of the time, you're just like us. (*Falls, snoring, to the ground.* Milo *laughs.*)

Lethargarian 5. Stop that at once. Laughing is against the law. Don't you have a rule book? It's local ordinance 574381-W.

Milo (*opens the rule book and reads*). "In the Doldrums, laughter is frowned upon and smiling is permitted only on alternate Thursdays." Well, if you can't laugh or think, what can you do?

Lethargarian 6. Anything as long as it's nothing, and everything as long as it isn't anything. There's lots to do. We have a very busy schedule . . .

Lethargarian 1. At 8:00 we get up and then we spend from 8 to 9 daydreaming.

Lethargarian 2. From 9:00 to 9:30 we take our early midmorning nap . . .

Lethargarian 3. From 9:30 to 10:30 we dawdle and delay . . .

Lethargarian 4. From 10:30 to 11:30 we take our late early morning nap . . .

Lethargarian 5. From 11:30 to 12:00 we bide our time[5] and then we eat our lunch.

Lethargarian 6. From 1:00 to 2:00 we linger and loiter . . .

Lethargarian 1. From 2:00 to 2:30 we take our early afternoon nap . . .

Lethargarian 2. From 2:30 to 3:30 we put off for tomorrow what we could have done today . . .

Lethargarian 3. From 3:30 to 4:00 we take our early late afternoon nap . . .

Lethargarian 4. From 4:00 to 5:00 we loaf and lounge until dinner . . .

Lethargarian 5. From 6:00 to 7:00 we dilly-dally . . .

Lethargarian 6. From 7:00 to 8:00 we take our early evening nap and then for an hour before we go to bed, we waste time.

Lethargarian 1 (*yawning*). You see, it's really quite strenuous doing nothing all day long, and so once a week, we take a holiday and go nowhere.

Lethargarian 5. Which is just where we were going when you came along. Would you care to join us?

Milo (*yawning*). That's where I seem to be going, anyway. (*stretching*) Tell me, does everyone here do nothing?

Lethargarian 3. Everyone but the terrible Watchdog. He's always sniffing around to see that nobody wastes time. A most unpleasant character.

---

4. **ordinance:** a rule or law designed to control or govern behavior.

5. **bide our time:** an expression that means "to wait for further developments."

Milo. The Watchdog?

Lethargarian 6. THE WATCHDOG!

All the Lethargarians (*yelling at once*). RUN! WAKE UP! RUN! HERE HE COMES! THE WATCHDOG! (*They all run off. Enter a large dog with the head, feet, and tail of a dog, and*
280 *the body of a clock, having the same face as the character the* Clock.)

Watchdog. What are you doing here?

Milo. Nothing much. Just killing time. You see . . .

Watchdog. KILLING TIME! (*His alarm rings in fury.*) It's bad enough wasting time without killing it. What are you doing in the Doldrums, anyway? Don't you have anywhere to go?

Milo. I think I was on my way to Dictionopolis
290 when I got stuck here. Can you help me?

Watchdog. Help you! You've got to help yourself. I suppose you know why you got stuck.

Milo. I guess I just wasn't thinking.

Watchdog. Precisely. Now you're on your way.

Milo. I am?

Watchdog. Of course. Since you got here by not thinking, it seems reasonable that in order to get out, you must *start* thinking. Do you mind if I get in? I love automobile rides. (*He gets in.*
300 *They wait.*) Well?

Milo. All right. I'll try. (*screws up his face and thinks*) Are we moving?

Watchdog. Not yet. Think harder.

Milo. I'm thinking as hard as I can.

Watchdog. Well, think just a little harder than that. Come on, you can do it.

Milo. All right, all right. . . . I'm thinking of all the planets in the solar system, and why water

expands when it turns to ice, and all the words
310 that begin with "q," and . . . (*The wheels begin to move.*) We're moving! We're moving!

Watchdog. Keep thinking.

Milo (*thinking*). How a steam engine works and how to bake a pie and the difference between Fahrenheit and Centigrade . . .[6]

Watchdog. Dictionopolis, here we come.

Milo. Hey, Watchdog, are you coming along?

Tock. You can call me Tock, and keep your eyes on the road.

320 **Milo.** What kind of place is Dictionopolis, anyway?

Tock. It's where all the words in the world come from. It used to be a marvelous place, but ever since Rhyme and Reason[7] left, it hasn't been the same.

Milo. Rhyme and Reason?

Tock. The two princesses. They used to settle all the arguments between their two brothers who rule over the Land of Wisdom. You see,
330 Azaz is the king of Dictionopolis and the Mathemagician is the king of Digitopolis and they almost never see eye to eye on anything. It was the job of the Princesses Sweet Rhyme and Pure Reason to solve the differences between the two kings, and they always did so well that both sides usually went home feeling very satisfied. But then, one day, the kings had an argument to end all arguments. . . .

(*The lights dim on* Tock *and* Milo, *and come up*
340 *on* King Azaz *of Dictionopolis on another part of the stage. Azaz has a great stomach, a grey beard reaching to his waist, a small crown and a long robe with the letters of the alphabet written all over it.*)

---

6. **Fahrenheit** (făr′ən-hīt′) **and Centigrade** (sĕn′tĭ-grād′): *Fahrenheit* is a temperature scale on which water freezes at 32° and boils at 212°. On the *Centigrade* (or *Celsius*) scale, water freezes at 0° and boils at 100°.

7. **Rhyme and Reason:** sense or explanation. The princesses try to establish order. When they disappear, there is "neither Rhyme nor Reason in this kingdom."

THE PHANTOM TOLLBOOTH © Turner Entertainment Co.
A Warner Bros. Entertainment Company. All Rights Reserved.

Azaz. Of course, I'll abide by the decision of Rhyme and Reason, though I have no doubt as to what it will be. They will choose *words,* of course. Everyone knows that words are more important than numbers any day of the week.

350 (*The* Mathemagician *appears opposite* Azaz. *The* Mathemagician *wears a long flowing robe covered entirely with complex mathematical equations, and a tall pointed hat. He carries a long staff with a pencil point at one end and a large rubber eraser at the other.*)

Mathemagician. That's what you think, Azaz. People wouldn't even know what day of the week it is without *numbers.* Haven't you ever looked at a calendar? Face it, Azaz. It's numbers

360 that count.

Azaz. Don't be ridiculous. (*to audience, as if leading a cheer*) Let's hear it for WORDS!

Mathemagician (*to audience, in the same manner*). Cast your vote for NUMBERS!

Azaz. A, B, C's!

Mathemagician. 1, 2, 3's! (*A fanfare*[8] *is heard.*)

Azaz and Mathemagician (*to each other*). Quiet! Rhyme and Reason are about to announce their decision.

370 (Rhyme *and* Reason *appear.*)

Rhyme. Ladies and gentlemen, letters and numerals, fractions and punctuation marks—may we have your attention, please. After careful consideration of the problem set before us by King Azaz of Dictionopolis (Azaz *bows.*) and the Mathemagician of Digitopolis (Mathemagician *raises his hands in a victory salute.*) we have come to the following conclusion:

380 **Reason.** Words and numbers are of equal value, for in the cloak of knowledge, one is the warp and the other is the woof.[9]

Rhyme. It is no more important to count the sands than it is to name the stars.

---

8. **fanfare:** a loud blast of trumpets.

9. **warp and . . . woof:** In weaving, the *warp* is made of parallel threads stretched on a loom. The *woof* is made of threads that wind between the warp threads to make cloth.

Rhyme and Reason. Therefore, let both kingdoms, Dictionopolis and Digitopolis, live in peace. (*The sound of cheering is heard.*)

Azaz. Boo! is what I say. Boo and Bah and Hiss!

390 **Mathemagician.** What good are these girls if they can't even settle an argument in anyone's favor? I think I have come to a decision of my own.

Azaz. So have I.

Azaz and Mathemagician (*to the* Princesses). You are hereby banished from this land to the Castle-in-the-Air. (*to each other*) And as for you, KEEP OUT OF MY WAY! (*They stalk off in opposite directions.*)

400 (*During this time, the set has been changed to the Market Square of Dictionopolis. Lights come up on the deserted square.*)

Tock. And ever since then, there has been neither Rhyme nor Reason in this kingdom. Words are misused and numbers mismanaged. The argument between the two kings has divided everyone and the real value of both words and numbers has been forgotten. What a waste!

Milo. Why doesn't somebody rescue the
410 Princesses and set everything straight again?

Tock. That is easier said than done. The Castle-in-the-Air is very far from here, and the one path which leads to it is guarded by **ferocious** demons. But hold on, here we are. (*A man appears, carrying a gate and a small tollbooth.*)

Gatekeeper. AHHHHREMMMM! This is Dictionopolis, a happy kingdom, advantageously located in the foothills of Confusion and caressed by gentle breezes
420 from the Sea of Knowledge. Today, by royal proclamation, is Market Day. Have you come to buy or sell?

Milo. I beg your pardon?

Gatekeeper. Buy or sell, buy or sell. Which is it? You must have come here for a reason.

Milo. Well, I . . .

Gatekeeper. Come now, if you don't have a reason, you must at least have an explanation or certainly an excuse.

430 **Milo** (*meekly*). Uh . . . no.

Gatekeeper (*shaking his head*). Very serious. You can't get in without a reason. (*thoughtfully*) Wait a minute. Maybe I have an old one you can use. (*pulls out an old suitcase from the tollbooth and rummages through it*) No . . . no . . . no . . . this won't do . . . hmmm . . .

Milo (*to* Tock). What's he looking for? (*Tock shrugs.*)

Gatekeeper. Ah! This is fine. (*Pulls out a*
440 *medallion on a chain. Engraved in the medallion is: "WHY NOT?"*) Why not. That's a good reason for almost anything . . . a bit used, perhaps, but still quite serviceable. There you are, sir. Now I can truly say: Welcome to Dictionopolis.

(*He opens the gate and walks off.* Citizens *and* Merchants *appear on all levels of the stage, and* Milo *and* Tock *find themselves in the middle of a noisy marketplace. As some people buy and sell their*
450 *wares, others hang a large banner which reads:* WELCOME TO THE WORD MARKET.)

Milo. Tock! Look!

Merchant 1. Hey-ya, hey-ya, hey-ya, step right up and take your pick. Juicy tempting words for sale. Get your fresh-picked "if's," "and's" and "but's"! Just take a look at these nice ripe "where's" and "when's."

Merchant 2. Step right up, step right up, fancy, best-quality words here for sale. Enrich your vocabulary and expand your speech with such elegant items as "quagmire,"[10] "flabbergast,"[11] or "upholstery."

Merchant 3. Words by the bag, buy them over here. Words by the bag for the more talkative customer. A pound of "happy's" at a very reasonable price . . . very useful for "Happy Birthday," "Happy New Year," "happy days," or "happy-go-lucky." Or how about a package of "good's," always handy for "good morning," "good afternoon," "good evening," and "goodbye."

Milo. I can't believe it. Did you ever see so many words?

Tock. They're fine if you have something to say. (*They come to a Do-It-Yourself Bin.*)

Milo (*to* Merchant 4 *at the bin*). Excuse me, but what are these?

Merchant 4. These are for people who like to make up their own words. You can pick any assortment you like or buy a special box complete with all the letters and a book of instructions. Here, taste an "A." They're very good. (*He pops one into* Milo's *mouth.*)

Milo (*tastes it hesitantly*). It's sweet! (*He eats it.*)

Merchant 4. I knew you'd like it. "A" is one of our best-sellers. All of them aren't that good, you know. The "Z," for instance—very dry and sawdusty. And the "X"? Tastes like a trunkful of stale air. But most of the others aren't bad at all. Here, try the "I."

Milo (*tasting*). Cool! It tastes icy.

Merchant 4 (*to* Tock). How about the "C" for you? It's as crunchy as a bone. Most people

are just too lazy to make their own words, but take it from me, not only is it more fun, but it's also *de*-lighting, (*holds up a "D"*) e-lating,[12] (*holds up an "E"*) and extremely *u*seful! (*holds up a "U"*)

Milo. But isn't it difficult? I'm not very good at making words.

(*The* Spelling Bee, *a large colorful bee, comes up from behind.*)

Spelling Bee. Perhaps I can be of some assistance . . . a-s-s-i-s-t-a-n-c-e. (*The three turn around and see him.*) Don't be alarmed . . . a-l-a-r-m-e-d. I am the Spelling Bee. I can spell anything. Anything. A-n-y-t-h-i-n-g. Try me. Try me.

Milo (*backing off,* Tock *on his guard*). Can you spell goodbye?

Spelling Bee. Perhaps you are under the misapprehension[13] . . . m-i-s-a-p-p-r-e-h-e-n-s-i-o-n that I am dangerous. Let me assure you that I am quite peaceful. Now, think of the most difficult word you can, and I'll spell it.

Milo. Uh . . . o.k. (*At this point,* Milo *may turn to the audience and ask them to help him choose a word or he may think of one on his own.*) How about . . . "Curiosity"?

Spelling Bee (*winking*). Let's see now . . . uh . . . how much time do I have?

Milo. Just ten seconds. Count them off, Tock.

Spelling Bee (*as* Tock *counts*). Oh dear, oh dear. (*just at the last moment, quickly*) C-u-r-i-o-s-i-t-y.

Merchant 4. Correct! (*All cheer.*)

Milo. Can you spell anything?

---

10. **quagmire** (kwăg'mīr'): has two meanings: land with a soft, muddy surface; a difficult situation.

11. **flabbergast:** to cause to be overcome with astonishment; astound.

12. **elating** (ĭ-lā'tĭng): making a person proud or joyful.

13. **misapprehension** (mĭs-ăp'rĭ-hĕn'shən): the misunderstanding of something.

Spelling Bee (*proudly*). Just about. You see, years ago, I was an ordinary bee minding my own business, smelling flowers all day, occasionally picking up part-time work in people's bonnets. Then one day, I realized that I'd never amount to anything without an education, so I decided that . . .

Humbug (*coming up in a booming voice*). BALDERDASH![14] (*He wears a lavish coat, striped pants, checked vest, spats and a derby hat.*) Let me repeat . . . BALDERDASH! (*swings his cane and clicks his heels in the air*) Well, well, what have we here? Isn't someone going to introduce me to the little boy?

Spelling Bee (*disdainfully*). This is the Humbug. You can't trust a word he says.

Humbug. NONSENSE! Everyone can trust a Humbug. As I was saying to the king just the other day . . .

Spelling Bee. You've never met the king. (*to Milo*) Don't believe a thing he tells you.

Humbug. Bosh, my boy, pure bosh. The Humbugs are an old and noble family, honorable to the core. Why, we fought in the Crusades with Richard the Lionhearted,[15] crossed the Atlantic with Columbus, blazed trails with the pioneers. History is full of Humbugs.

Spelling Bee. A very pretty speech . . . s-p-e-e-c-h. Now, why don't you go away? I was just advising the lad of the importance of proper spelling.

Humbug. BAH! As soon as you learn to spell one word, they ask you to spell another. You can never catch up, so why bother? (*puts his arm around* Milo) Take my advice, boy, and forget about it. As my great-great-great-grandfather George Washington Humbug used to say . . .

Spelling Bee. You, sir, are an impostor i-m-p-o-s-t-o-r who can't even spell his own name!

Humbug. What? You dare to doubt my word? The word of a Humbug? The word of a Humbug who has direct access to the ear of a King? And the king shall hear of this, I promise you . . .

Voice 1. Did someone call for the king?

Voice 2. Did you mention the monarch?

Voice 3. Speak of the sovereign?

Voice 4. Entreat the emperor?

Voice 5. Hail his highness?

(*Five tall, thin gentlemen regally dressed in silks and satins, plumed hats and buckled shoes appear as they speak.*)

Milo. Who are they?

Spelling Bee. The King's advisors. Or in more formal terms, his cabinet.

Minister 1. Greetings!

Minister 2. Salutations!

Minister 3. Welcome!

Minister 4. Good afternoon!

Minister 5. Hello!

Milo. Uh . . . Hi.

(*All the* Ministers, *from here on called by their numbers, unfold their scrolls and read in order.*)

Minister 1. By the order of Azaz the Unabridged[16] . . .

Minister 2. King of Dictionopolis . . .

---

14. **balderdash:** nonsense.

15. **Crusades with Richard the Lionhearted:** The Crusades were journeys undertaken by European Christians in the eleventh through thirteenth centuries to fight the Muslims for control of the Holy Land. Richard the Lionhearted was an English king who led the Third Crusade (1190–1192).

16. **unabridged:** containing the original content; not shortened.

Minister 3. Monarch of letters . . .

Minister 4. Emperor of phrases, sentences, and miscellaneous figures of speech . . .

Minister 5. We offer you the hospitality of our 600 kingdom . . .

Minister 1. Country

Minister 2. Nation

Minister 3. State

Minister 4. Commonwealth

Minister 5. Realm

Minister 1. Empire

Minister 2. Palatinate

Minister 3. Principality.

Milo. Do all those words mean the same thing?

610 **Minister 1.** Of course.

Minister 2. Certainly.

Minister 3. Precisely.

Minister 4. Exactly.

Minister 5. Yes.

Milo. Then why don't you just use one? Wouldn't that make a lot more sense?

Minister 1. Nonsense!

Minister 2. Ridiculous!

Minister 3. Fantastic!

620 **Minister 4.** Absurd!

Minister 5. Bosh!

Minister 1. We're not interested in making sense. It's not our job.

Minister 2. Besides, one word is as good as another, so why not use them all?

Minister 3. Then you don't have to choose which one is right.

Minister 4. Besides, if one is right, then ten are ten times as right.

630 **Minister 5.** Obviously, you don't know who we are. (*Each presents himself and* Milo *acknowledges the introduction.*)

Minister 1. The Duke of Definition.

Minister 2. The Minister of Meaning.

Minister 3. The Earl of Essence.

Minister 4. The Count of Connotation.

Minister 5. The Undersecretary of Understanding.

All Five. And we have come to invite you to the 640 Royal Banquet.

Spelling Bee. The banquet! That's quite an honor, my boy. A real h-o-n-o-r.

Humbug. DON'T BE RIDICULOUS! Everybody goes to the Royal Banquet these days.

Spelling Bee (*to the* Humbug). True, everybody does go. But some people are invited and others simply push their way in where they aren't wanted.

Humbug. HOW DARE YOU? You buzzing 650 little upstart, I'll show you who's not wanted . . . (*raises his cane threateningly*)

Spelling Bee. You just watch it! I'm warning w-a-r-n-i-n-g you! (*At that moment, an ear-shattering blast of trumpets, entirely off-key, is heard, and a* Page *appears.*)

Page. King Azaz the Unabridged is about to begin the Royal Banquet. All guests who do not appear promptly at the table will automatically lose their place. (*A huge table* 660 *is carried out with* King Azaz *sitting in a large chair, carried out at the head of the table.*)

Azaz. Places. Everyone take your places. (*All the characters, including the* Humbug *and the* Spelling Bee, *who forget their quarrel, rush to take their places at the table.* Milo *and* Tock *sit near the* King. Azaz *looks at* Milo.) And just who is this?

Milo. Your Highness, my name is Milo and this is Tock. Thank you very much for inviting 670 us to your banquet, and I think your palace is beautiful!

Minister 1. Exquisite.

Minister 2. Lovely.

Minister 3. Handsome.

Minister 4. Pretty.

Minister 5. Charming.

Azaz. SILENCE! Now tell me, young man, what can you do to entertain us? Sing songs? Tell stories? Juggle plates? Do tumbling tricks? 680 Which is it?

Milo. I can't do any of those things.

Azaz. What an ordinary little boy. Can't you do anything at all?

Milo. Well . . . I can count to a thousand.

Azaz. AARGH, numbers! Never mention numbers here. Only use them when we absolutely have to. Now, why don't we change the subject and have some dinner? Since you are the guest of honor, you may 690 pick the menu.

Milo. Me? Well, uh . . . I'm not very hungry. Can we just have a light snack?

Azaz. A light snack it shall be!

(Azaz *claps his hands. Waiters rush in with covered trays. When they are uncovered, shafts of light pour out. The light may be created through the use of battery-operated flashlights which are secured in the trays and covered with a false bottom. The guests help themselves.*)

700 **Humbug.** Not a very substantial meal. Maybe you can suggest something a little more filling.

Milo. Well, in that case, I think we ought to have a square meal . . .

Azaz (*claps his hands*). A square meal it is! (*Waiters serve trays of colored squares of all sizes. People serve themselves.*)

Spelling Bee. These are awful. (*Humbug coughs and all the guests do not care for the food.*)

Azaz (*claps his hands and the trays are removed*).
710 Time for speeches. (*to Milo*) You first.

Milo (*hesitantly*). Your Majesty, ladies and gentlemen, I would like to take this opportunity to say that . . .

Azaz. That's quite enough. Musn't talk all day.

Milo. But I just started to . . .

Azaz. NEXT!

Humbug (*quickly*). Roast turkey, mashed potatoes, vanilla ice cream.

Spelling Bee. Hamburgers, corn on the cob,
720 chocolate pudding p-u-d-d-i-n-g. (*Each guest names two dishes and a dessert.*)

Azaz (*the last*). Pate de fois gras, soupe a l'oignon, salade endives, fromage et fruits et demi-tasse.[17] (*He claps his hands. Waiters serve each guest his words.*) Dig on. (*to Milo*) Though I can't say I think much of your choice.

Milo. I didn't know I was going to have to eat my words.

---

17. **pate de fois gras . . . demi-tasse:** *French: pâté de fois gras* (pä-tä də fwä grä′): a paste made from goose liver; *soupe a l'oignon* (sōōp ä läɴ′nôn): onion soup; *salade endives* (sä-läd′ ĕn′dīv′): lettuce salad; *fromage et fruits* (frō′mäj ĕ frōō′ē): cheese and fruit; *demitasse* (dĕm′ē-täs′): a small cup of strong, black coffee.

Azaz. Of course, of course, everybody here does. 730 Your speech should have been in better taste.

Minister 1. Here, try some somersault. It improves the flavor.

Minister 2. Have a rigamarole.[18] (*offers breadbasket*)

Minister 3. Or a ragamuffin.[19]

Minister 4. Perhaps you'd care for a synonym bun.

Minister 5. Why not wait for your just desserts?

Azaz. Ah yes, the dessert. We're having a special 740 treat today . . . freshly made at the half-bakery.

Milo. The half-bakery?

Azaz. Of course, the half-bakery! Where do you think half-baked ideas come from? Now, please don't interrupt. By royal command, the pastry chefs have . . .

Milo. What's a half-baked idea?

(*Azaz gives up the idea of speaking as a cart is wheeled in and the guests help themselves.*)

Humbug. They're very tasty, but they don't 750 always agree with you. Here's a good one. (Humbug *hands one to* Milo.)

Milo (*reads*). "The earth is flat."

Spelling Bee. People swallowed that one for years. (*picks up one and reads*) "The moon is made of green cheese." Now, there's a half-baked idea.

(*Everyone chooses one and eats. They include: "It Never Rains but Pours," "Night Air Is Bad Air," "Everything Happens for the Best," "Coffee* 760 *Stunts Your Growth."*)

Azaz. And now for a few closing words. Attention! Let me have your attention! (*Everyone leaps up and exits, except for* Milo, Tock *and the* Humbug.) Loyal subjects and friends, once again on this gala occasion, we have . . .

Milo. Excuse me, but everybody left.

Azaz (*sadly*). I was hoping no one would notice. It happens every time.

770 **Humbug.** They've gone to dinner, and as soon as I finish this last bite, I shall join them.

Milo. That's ridiculous. How can they eat dinner right after a banquet?

Azaz. SCANDALOUS! We'll put a stop to it at once. From now on, by royal command, everyone must eat dinner before the banquet.

Milo. But that's just as bad.

Humbug. Or just as good. Things which are equally bad are also equally good. Try to look 780 at the bright side of things.

Milo. I don't know which side of anything to look at. Everything is so confusing, and all your words only make things worse.

Azaz. How true. There must be something we can do about it.

Humbug. Pass a law.

Azaz. We have almost as many laws as words.

Humbug. Offer a reward. (Azaz *shakes his head and looks madder at each suggestion.*) Send for 790 help? Drive a bargain? Pull the switch? Lower the boom?[20] Toe the line? (*As* Azaz *continues to scowl, the* Humbug *loses confidence and finally gives up.*)

---

18. **rigamarole** (rĭg′ə-mə-rōl′): has two meanings: confused or rambling conversation; a complicated set of procedures. Here, the writer is playing off the word *roll*, as in *dinner roll*.

19. **ragamuffin** (răg′ə-mŭf′ĭn): a shabbily dressed, dirty child. Here, the writer is playing off the word *muffin*.

20. **lower the boom:** a sailing term that refers to the *boom* of a sailboat, the long poll that extends from the mast and holds or extends the foot of the sail. To *lower the boom* is to put the boom of the sailboat down. The phrase can also be slang for "scold harshly."

Milo. Maybe you should let Rhyme and Reason return.

Azaz. How nice that would be. Even if they were a bother at times, things always went so well when they were here. But I'm afraid it can't be done.

800 **Humbug.** Certainly not. Can't be done.

Milo. Why not?

Humbug (*now siding with* Milo). Why not, indeed?

Azaz. Much too difficult.

Humbug. Of course, much too difficult.

Milo. You could, if you really wanted to.

Humbug. By all means, if you really wanted to, you could.

Azaz (*to* Humbug). How?

810 **Milo** (*also to* Humbug). Yeah, how?

Humbug. Why . . . uh, it's a simple task for a brave boy with a stout heart, a steadfast dog and a serviceable small automobile.

Azaz. Go on.

Humbug. Well, all that he would have to do is cross the dangerous, unknown countryside between here and Digitopolis, where he would have to persuade the Mathemagician to release the Princesses, which we know to be

820 impossible because the Mathemagician will never agree with Azaz about anything. Once achieving that, it's a simple matter of entering the Mountains of Ignorance from where no one has ever returned alive, an effortless climb up a two-thousand-foot stairway without railings in a high wind at night to the Castle-in-the-Air. After a pleasant chat with the Princesses, all that remains is a **leisurely** ride back through those chaotic **crags** where the frightening

830 fiends have sworn to tear any intruder from limb to limb and devour him down to his belt buckle. And finally after doing all that, a triumphal parade! If, of course, there is anything left to parade . . . followed by hot chocolate and cookies for everyone.

Azaz. I never realized it would be so simple.

Milo. It sounds dangerous to me.

Tock. And just who is supposed to make that journey?

840 **Azaz.** A very good question. But there is one far more serious problem.

Milo. What's that?

Azaz. I'm afraid I can't tell you that until you return.

Milo. But wait a minute, I didn't . . .

Azaz. Dictionopolis will always be grateful to you, my boy and your dog. (Azaz *pats* Tock *and* Milo.)

Tock. Now, just one moment, sire . . .

850 **Azaz.** You will face many dangers on your journey, but fear not, for I can give you something for your protection. (Azaz *gives* Milo *a box*.) In this box are the letters of the alphabet. With them you can form all the words you will ever need to help you overcome the obstacles that may stand in your path. All you must do is use them well and in the right places.

Milo (*miserably*). Thanks a lot.

860 **Azaz.** You will need a guide, of course, and since he knows the obstacles so well, the Humbug has cheerfully volunteered to accompany you.

Humbug. Now, see here . . . !

Azaz. You will find him dependable, brave, resourceful and loyal.

COMPARE A PLAY AND A FILM
The illustrations for this play come from the film version of *The Phantom Tollbooth*. What similarities and differences in the setting, plot, and characters do you recognize between the play and the film?

THE PHANTOM TOLLBOOTH © Turner Entertainment Co. A Warner Bros. Entertainment Company. All Rights Reserved.

Humbug (*flattered*). Oh, Your Majesty.

Milo. I'm sure he'll be a great help. (*They approach the car.*)

870 **Tock.** I hope so. It looks like we're going to need it.

(*The lights darken and the King fades from view.*)

Azaz. Good luck! Drive carefully! (*The three get into the car and begin to move. Suddenly a thunderously loud noise is heard. They slow down the car.*)

Milo. What was that?

Tock. It came from up ahead.

Humbug. It's something terrible, I just know it.
880 Oh, no. Something dreadful is going to happen to us. I can feel it in my bones. (*The noise is repeated. They all look at each other fearfully as the lights fade.*)

(*end Act One*)

Comprehension

1. **Recall** Why does Milo receive the unusual package?

2. **Recall** What forbidden activity does Milo perform in order to get himself out of the Doldrums?

3. **Summarize** Briefly explain the events that led to the banishment of Rhyme and Reason.

Text Analysis

● 4. **Visualize** Review your log of stage directions. Use the details you listed to visualize the characters or settings they describe. Which details are most effective at helping you visualize?

5. **Examine a Character** How has Milo's life changed from the beginning of Act One to the end of Act One?

● 6. **Analyze Humor** Review the definition of a **pun** on page 533. Then use a chart to record examples of puns that appear in the play. For each, explain the different meanings the word or words can have.

Pun	Real Meaning	Humorous Meaning
watchdog	a dog that watches over people or a place	a dog that has the body of a clock (like a watch)

7. **Analyze Personification** Choose one of the personified characters in the play. Which traits made that character human? Explain.

8. **Compare and Contrast** Review the play's illustrations. How well do you think the images from the animated film represent the humorous spirit of the play? Cite examples of characters, plot, and settings from the play in your response.

Extension and Challenge

9. **Creative Project: Art** Sketch a character or a setting in the play based on the details you used earlier to help you visualize.

10. **Readers' Circle** Literature that contains at least one unreal or impossible element is called fantasy. In a small group, make a list of elements that show why *The Phantom Toolbooth* is a work of fantasy.

When is logic not LOGICAL?

What amused you about the unusual circumstances in the play? Would you have reacted in a logical way if you had been in Milo's situation?

COMMON CORE

RL 4 Determine the meaning of words and phrases as they are used in a text, including figurative and connotative meanings; analyze the impact of a specific word choice on meaning and tone. **RL 5** Analyze how a particular scene fits into the overall structure of a text. **RL 7** Compare and contrast a drama to a video version of the text.

from **Artists and Style**

Image Collection on **Media Smart** DVD-ROM

What gives an artist
STYLE?

COMMON CORE

RI 4 Determine the meaning of words and phrases as they are used in a text, including technical meanings.

When you were younger, did you have favorite picture books that you looked at again and again? If so, it's likely that you admired the style, or the unique look, of the illustrations. In this lesson, you'll take a close look at the work of two artists. You'll explore the elements that give an illustration a unique style.

Background

Drawing Attention The first two illustrations you'll examine are by Carmen Lomas Garza. She's known for portraying the joys of everyday life. The book in which these images first appeared is entitled *In My Family*. The third illustration is by Benny Andrews from the book *Pictures for Miss Josie*. He's known for creating art in many forms. Both artists have won high praise for their ability to draw viewers into the worlds they create.

Media Literacy: Style in Illustrations

Style is the uniquely personal way in which creators express ideas. For example, you've seen how a writer crafts a style by using **word choice**, **sentence structure**, and **imagery**.

   To create a style in illustrations, artists use the basic elements of design—**color, line, shape,** and **texture.** Becoming familiar with these elements can help you interpret the style of an illustration.

ANALYZING ELEMENTS OF DESIGN

La Bendición en el Día de la Boda (1993), Carmen Lomas Garza. Alkyds on canvas, 24″ × 32″. © 1993 Carmen Lomas Garza. Collection of Smith College Museum, Northampton, Massachusetts. Photo by M. Lee Fatheree.

❶ Artists use hues or shades of **color** for different reasons. Color makes objects stand out or blend into the background. Color also creates emotional connections. For example, the color blue can suggest a peaceful feeling.

❸ A **line** is a stroke or mark that can be thick, thin, long, curvy, smooth, or blurred. Lines can help to "frame" the objects in an illustration. Where do you see a strong use of lines in this image? How many different types of lines do you see?

❷ **Shape** is the outline of an object or image. Starting with a simple square, circle, or triangle, an artist can add details to form real-looking objects. In this image, notice how the doorway is basically a rectangle.

❹ **Texture** is the surface quality or appearance of an image. Adding texture helps an object look more real. For example, an artist might create a smooth, shiny texture for an apple or a bumpy texture for a basketball.

La Llorona (1989), Carmen Lomas Garza. Gouache, 18″ × 26″. © 1989 Carmen Lomas Garza. Collection of Sonia Saldivar-Hull and Felix Hull, Austin, Texas. Photo by Wolfgang Dietze.

Illustration by Benny Andrews. © 2003 Benny Andrews.

Viewing Guide for

Artists and Style

Use the DVD to look at each illustration at a larger size. Each illustration presents a scene of family or friends. On this page you see another illustration by Carmen Lomas Garza and one by Benny Andrews.

In looking at each image, think about what first catches your eye. Record any words or phrases that describe what you see. Then study each image carefully. Examine the smaller details. Look for the use of **color, line, shape,** and **texture.** Answer these questions to help you understand each illustrator's style.

NOW VIEW

FIRST VIEWING: Comprehension

1. **Identify** What is the subject of each painting?

2. **Clarify** In this illustration, how do you know that what the mother is saying is interesting?

CLOSE VIEWING: Media Literacy

3. **Analyze Color** In this illustration, children listen as a mother tells a mysterious tale. What colors give the illustration a mood of mystery?

4. **Analyze Shape** Focus on the illustration on page 553. Where do you see objects that are shaped like triangles?

5. **Analyze Texture** In the illustration of a father and son, identify any part of the image that seems to have a rough texture.

6. **Interpret the Style** Choose one of the illustrations from this lesson. In your own words, write a statement that describes anything you can about the artist's style. Think about

   - the subject matter of the image
   - the design elements that you see
   - the feelings you think the image expresses

Write or Discuss

Compare Styles Carmen Lomas Garza says most of her illustrations "are from my recollections of my childhood in south Texas where I was born and raised." The illustrations of Benny Andrews are often based on his early life in Georgia. Look closely at the illustrations that appear in this lesson. In a few sentences, compare the styles of each artist. Think about

- the special ways each illustrator uses **color, line, shape,** or **texture**
- the feeling or feelings each illustration communicates to you

COMMON CORE

SL 2 Interpret information in diverse media and explain how it contributes to a topic under study.

Produce Your Own Media

Create an Illustration Plan and create your own illustration, in any style you would like to try. You might create an illustration that fits the subject of "family and friends" or base your creation on any topic that inspires you.

HERE'S HOW Follow these suggestions to create the illustration.

- What colors will you choose? Will you draw shapes using bold lines or soft? Decide what design elements will work best for you.
- Choose your paint, pencils, crayons, chalk, or markers. You might even form images out of pieces of cut up paper or fabric.
- Show your illustration to a partner. Imagine that your illustration is part of a larger picture book, and tell the story that the images would tell.

Media Tools — **THINK** central

Go to thinkcentral.com.
KEYWORD: HML6-555

STUDENT MODEL

Tech Tip

Use a drawing program to make an illustration or to add a new style.

Writing Workshop

INFORMATIVE TEXT

Literary Analysis

Through the literature in this unit, you have entered other lives and other worlds. In this workshop, you'll learn how to write a literary analysis. You'll share your reaction to a literary work by analyzing one of the literary elements that made the work memorable or enjoyable for you.

 Complete the workshop activities in your **Reader/Writer Notebook**.

WRITE WITH A PURPOSE

WRITING TASK

Write a **literary analysis** in which you analyze and interpret a literary work that you find especially memorable. Discuss one literary element that helps explain your reaction to the work.

Idea Starters
- an unforgettable setting
- a character you respect
- a conflict that reminds you of a real-life problem
- a plot that keeps you on the edge of your seat
- a theme that relates to your own life

THE ESSENTIALS

Here are some common purposes, audiences, and formats for literary analysis.

PURPOSES	AUDIENCES	FORMATS
• to explore a work of fiction and share insights with others • to analyze the use of a literary element and its effect on readers	• classmates and teacher • readers of a literary magazine • book groups • Web users	• essay for class • book review for a magazine • book group presentation • Web page posting

COMMON CORE TRAITS

1. DEVELOPMENT OF IDEAS
- presents an **engaging introduction**
- develops a **controlling idea** that offers an **analysis** of one literary element and how it affects readers
- supports main points of analysis with **concrete details** and **quotations from the text**
- concludes with a **summary of main points** and **insights**

2. ORGANIZATION OF IDEAS
- **organizes** ideas in a logical way
- uses **transitions** appropriately to **clarify relationships** among ideas and concepts

3. LANGUAGE FACILITY AND CONVENTIONS
- establishes and maintains a **formal style** and **tone**
- includes **precise language**
- avoids **run-on sentences**
- uses **capitalization** correctly
- employs correct **grammar, mechanics**, and **spelling**

Writing Online

THINK central

Go to **thinkcentral.com**.
KEYWORD: HML6N-556

Planning/Prewriting

COMMON CORE

W 2a–f Write informative/explanatory texts to examine a topic and convey ideas through the selection, organization, and analysis of content. **W 5** Develop and strengthen writing as needed by planning.

Getting Started

CHOOSE A LITERARY WORK

Your first step is to choose a literary work to write about. It might be a story, a novel, or a poem. Since your analysis will explain why you appreciated the work, pick a selection that you feel strongly about. Also make sure that the work you choose is complex enough to give you something to analyze.

▶ **ASK YOURSELF:**

- What are some of my favorite stories, novels, and poems?
- What is it about each work that made a strong impression on me?
- Which work would I most enjoy analyzing and sharing my thoughts about?

THINK ABOUT LITERARY ELEMENTS

Reread your selected work (or skim it if it's a novel) to recall the details that you found most interesting or meaningful. Then use the Idea Starters on page 556 to help you focus your analysis. Make a chart listing some of the **literary elements** you might analyze, such as setting, characters, conflict, theme, or plot. Then put a star next to one element that you think is most important.

▶ **WHAT DOES IT LOOK LIKE?**

Characters	Conflict	Theme*
Iqbal Masih Fatima Hussain Khan	Iqbal and the other children battle for their freedom against the master.	The courage of one person can make a difference in the lives of others.

THINK ABOUT AUDIENCE AND PURPOSE

As you plan your essay, keep in mind your **audience** and **purpose.** Since your audience may not have read the work you are analyzing, you must provide enough background information for them to understand your essay. Your purpose is to explain your analysis of the work and to persuade readers that your analysis is valid.

▶ **ASK YOURSELF:**

- Who will read my essay?
- What are the most important ideas about the work that I want my readers to understand?
- What basic facts must my readers know to understand my ideas?
- What **domain-specific,** or specialized, **vocabulary** should I include or define to help my audience better understand my ideas?

DEVELOP A CONTROLLING IDEA

Write a sentence that states the most important idea you want to convey about the literary element you starred. This sentence will serve as the **controlling idea,** or thesis statement, for your essay. You can revise your controlling idea later, but writing it down now will help you focus your writing.

▶ **WHAT DOES IT LOOK LIKE?**

Controlling Idea: In the novel Iqbal, the character Iqbal shows that one person's actions can improve the lives of many others.

Planning/Prewriting *continued*

Getting Started

GATHER SUPPORTING EVIDENCE

You'll need to provide **evidence** to support your controlling idea. Most of this evidence will come from the work itself. The following kinds of evidence are especially useful in a literary analysis:

WHAT DOES IT LOOK LIKE?

- **Detail:** a specific fact or idea from the text of the literary work ▶ *Iqbal was forced to work twelve hours a day at a carpet factory, chained to his loom.*

- **Historical fact:** a fact from the real world that provides background for the literature ▶ *More than 700,000 children at that time in Pakistan were bonded into labor to pay off their parents' debts.*

- **Paraphrase:** a restatement of a brief section of text, using your own words ▶ *Iqbal once took a knife and sliced down the middle of a beautiful carpet he had just completed.*

- **Quotation:** words taken directly from the text and enclosed in quotation marks ▶ *Fatima remembers, "Iqbal had been the first brave enough to say loud and clear that the debt is never cancelled."*

- **Summary:** a brief retelling of the main ideas in a longer section of text ▶ *Iqbal eventually escaped from the carpet factory and returned with the Bonded Labor Liberation Front of Pakistan to rescue his friends.*

PEER REVIEW Share with a peer your controlling idea and the evidence you have gathered to support it. Which pieces of evidence provide the strongest support for your controlling idea? If your peer has read the work, ask him or her to suggest other evidence you might include. If you can't provide enough support, consider reworking your controlling idea.

 **YOUR TURN** In your *Reader/Writer Notebook*, use a chart like the one on page 557 to collect information about the literary elements you might analyze in your literary analysis. Narrow your focus to one of these elements. Then write a controlling idea and gather details, quotations, and other evidence to support it.

Drafting

The following chart shows how to organize your draft effectively.

COMMON CORE

W 4 Produce clear and coherent writing. **W 9a (RL 1, 5)** Draw evidence from literary texts; cite evidence to support analysis; analyze how a particular scene contributes to theme, setting, or plot. **L 3b** Maintain consistency in style and tone.

Organizing Your Literary Analysis

INTRODUCTION

- Identify the title and author of the work you are analyzing.
- Clearly state your **controlling idea,** the most important idea you want to communicate.
- Provide any **background information** readers may need to understand your essay.

▼

BODY

- Provide several reasons to support your controlling idea. Discuss each in a separate paragraph.
- Provide supporting **evidence** from the text, such as **quotations** and **concrete details.**
- Use **precise language** to explain your ideas clearly.
- Organize your essay in a **logical sequence.** Use **transitions,** such as *next* or *in addition to,* to connect related ideas.
- Maintain a **formal style** and **tone,** or attitude. Avoid contractions and use unbiased, clear language.

▼

CONCLUDING SECTION

- Restate your controlling idea and briefly summarize your main points.
- Conclude by providing an **insight** about the literary element and its effects on readers.

GRAMMAR IN CONTEXT: CAPITALIZING PROPER NOUNS

A literary analysis uses many proper nouns—titles of works, names of authors and characters, names of places described in the work. A **proper noun** names a particular person, place, or thing. Each word in a proper noun begins with a capital letter.

	Common Nouns	*Proper Nouns*
Person ▶	*boy, character, factory owner, author*	*Iqbal Masih, Fatima, Hussain Khan, Francesco D'Adamo*
Place ▶	*city, country, river*	*Lahore, Pakistan, Ravi River*
Thing ▶	*organization, month, novel*	*Bonded Labor Liberation Front, April, Iqbal*

YOUR TURN

Develop a first draft of your essay, following the structure outlined in the chart above. Make sure you correctly capitalize all proper nouns.

Revising

Evaluate your draft for content, organization, and style. You want to make sure your audience will understand your literary analysis. This chart can help you revise, rewrite, and improve your draft to achieve your purpose.

LITERARY ANALYSIS

Ask Yourself	Tips	Revision Strategies
1. Are the title and author of the literary work identified in the introduction?	▶ **Highlight** the author and the title.	▶ **Add** a sentence or phrase naming the author and the title.
2. Does the controlling idea identify one literary element and the writer's main point about it?	▶ **Underline** the controlling idea. **Circle** the literary element and the main point about it.	▶ **Add** a sentence that clearly states your controlling idea.
3. Are examples presented in a logical way? Do transitions clarify the relationships among ideas?	▶ **Number** the examples in the order they appear in your essay. **Circle** transitional words.	▶ **Rearrange** ideas, such as putting them in sequential order. **Add** transitions to connect ideas as needed.
4. Is each idea supported by relevant evidence?	▶ **Draw a box** around each piece of evidence, such as details and quotations.	▶ **Add** details, examples, or quotations to support ideas. **Explain** the significance of each piece of evidence.
5. Does the concluding section restate the controlling idea?	▶ **Put a star** above the restatement.	▶ **Add** a restatement of the controlling idea, if necessary.
6. Does the concluding section provide an insight into the work?	▶ **Circle** sentences in the concluding section that state your insight.	▶ **Add** sentences that tell about your insight into the work.

YOUR TURN **PEER REVIEW** Use these suggestions as you rework and revise with a partner:
- Does your partner understand your analysis? Why or why not?
- Is the controlling idea clear? Ask your partner where it would be helpful to explain a key idea or to add more supporting evidence.
- What additional background information might help your partner understand the literary work?

ANALYZE A STUDENT DRAFT

COMMON CORE **W 2a** Introduce a topic. **W 5** Strengthen writing as needed by revising, editing, rewriting, or trying a new approach.

Read this student's draft and the comments about it as a model for revising your own literary analysis.

Literary Review of the Novel *Iqbal*
by Reid Cline, Murchison Middle School

1 When children are abused, the only way their lives can be saved is if someone intervenes and fights for their rights. *Iqbal,* a novel by Francesco D'Adamo, is based on the true story of a young boy living in Pakistan.

2 Iqbal Masih was forced to work twelve hours a day at a carpet factory, chained to his loom in unimaginable conditions. His parents bonded him into child labor to pay off a debt they owed to moneylenders, a fate shared by more than 700,000 children at that time in Pakistan.

3 Courageous and unwilling to accept his situation, Iqbal once took a knife and sliced down the middle of a beautiful carpet he had just completed. For his defiance, he was imprisoned in the "tomb," an underground cistern filled with snakes, scorpions, and suffocating heat. The other children were also brutally punished for Iqbal's rebellion. Iqbal's bravery, however, showed the other children that they could fight back.

> Reid's introduction gives the **title** and **author** of the literary work, but there is no clear **controlling idea**.

> A **vivid detail** helps provide background information about Iqbal's situation in the novel.

> Reid **paraphrases** an event in the novel to show that Iqbal was courageous.

LEARN HOW Develop a Controlling Idea A **controlling idea** tells readers the main idea of an essay. When this statement is unclear or missing, readers will be confused about the purpose of the essay. Reid wanted to clarify his controlling idea in his introduction, so he reviewed the writing task and his prewriting notes. His prewriting controlling idea related to the main character and to a theme of the novel: *The character Iqbal shows that one person's actions can improve the lives of many others.* He rewrote his introduction to clearly state his controlling idea.

REID'S REVISION TO PARAGRAPH **1**

~~When children are abused, the only way their lives can be saved is if someone intervenes and fights for their rights. *Iqbal,* a novel by Francesco D'Adamo, is based on the true story of a young boy living in Pakistan.~~

The novel Iqbal is memorable for me because it shows how one person's act of courage can improve the lives of many other people. The main character in Francesco D'Adamo's novel is a perfect example of this theme. As a young boy living in Pakistan, Iqbal showed selfless courage that helped free thousands of children from slavery.

---

4   The narrator of the novel is Fatima, a ten-year-old girl imprisoned with Iqbal and hundreds of other children by their cruel master, Hussain Khan. It is through her voice that we learn how Iqbal's courage affected the other children. They learned the master was tricking them with lies. Iqbal convinced the children that the master was cheating them by changing the marks counting their debt payment.

5   Iqbal vowed never to give up the fight for the children of Pakistan. He eventually escaped from the carpet factory and returned with the Bonded Labor Liberation Front of Pakistan to rescue his friends. He continued to work with the Bonded Labor Liberation Front to free children from slave labor. He became the voice and face for the liberation of bonded child laborers working in the factories, fields, kilns, and mines of Pakistan. Sadly, Iqbal was gunned down by the "carpet mafia" on April 16, 1995.

6   Iqbal's example encouraged other oppressed children to stand up against the wrong done to them. This courageous and unforgettable character showed them that if they stood together, they could influence change in the society, they could bring this terrible injustice to the attention of the world.

> This **summary** of events shows how Iqbal's actions affected others. Reid could strengthen this paragraph by adding a **quotation**.

> Reid includes **historical facts** to develop his ideas.

> In his **concluding section,** Reid restates his controlling idea in a fresh and forceful way.

LEARN HOW Add Quotations as Evidence Direct quotations from the text can provide relevant and sufficient evidence to support your ideas. Reid decided to show, rather than just describe, Iqbal's effect on Fatima and the other children by adding a direct quotation from the novel.

REID'S REVISION TO PARAGRAPH 4

Iqbal convinced the children that the master was cheating them by changing the marks counting their debt payment.

Fatima remembers, "Iqbal had been the first brave enough to say loud and clear that the debt is never cancelled. And he was the only one to talk concretely about the future."

YOUR TURN Use feedback from your peers as well as the two "Learn How" lessons to revise your literary analysis. Evaluate how well your essay supports your controlling idea with evidence such as concrete details, definitions, examples, and quotations from the work.

Editing and Publishing

COMMON CORE

W 5 Strengthen writing by editing. **L 1** Demonstrate command of conventions of standard English grammar and usage. **L 2** Demonstrate command of conventions of standard English capitalization, punctuation, and spelling.

Your audience won't be able to appreciate your essay if it is full of grammar, usage, spelling, capitalization, and punctuation errors. In the editing stage, you fix mistakes like these to make your literary analysis clear.

GRAMMAR IN CONTEXT: CORRECTING RUN-ON SENTENCES

A **run-on sentence** is two or more sentences incorrectly written as one sentence. As Reid was checking his draft, he noticed a run-on sentence in the last paragraph. To correct it, he rewrote the run-on sentence as two sentences.

> *This courageous and unforgettable character showed them that if they stood together, they could influence change in the society they could bring this terrible injustice to the attention of the world.*

Here are two other ways Reid could have corrected the run-on:

> *This courageous and unforgettable character showed them that if they stood together, they could influence change in the society, and they could bring this terrible injustice to the attention of the world.*
>
> [A **conjunction** such as *and, but,* or *or* can be added to form a compound sentence.]

> *This courageous and unforgettable character showed them that if they stood together, they could influence change in the society; they could bring this terrible injustice to the attention of the world.*
>
> [A **semicolon** can be used to make a compound sentence.]

PUBLISH YOUR WRITING

Share your literary analysis with an audience.

- Make copies of your essay and distribute them to others who might be interested in reading the work you analyzed.
- Ask the school librarian if you may post a copy of your essay on a bulletin board or display in the library.
- Develop your literary analysis into an oral presentation that you deliver to your audience.
- Submit your essay to a school literary magazine or Web site.

YOUR TURN
Correct any errors in your literary analysis by carefully proofreading it. Make sure there are no run-on sentences. Then publish your final essay where it is most likely to reach your audience.

Scoring Rubric

Use the rubric below to evaluate your literary analysis from the Writing Workshop or your response to the on-demand task on the next page.

LITERARY ANALYSIS

SCORE	COMMON CORE TRAITS
6	• **Development** Has a thorough introduction with an insightful controlling idea; supports main points with relevant evidence; has a powerful concluding section • **Organization** Arranges ideas in an effective, logical order; effectively uses transitions to show relationships among ideas • **Language** Consistently maintains a formal style and tone; uses precise language; shows a strong command of conventions
5	• **Development** Has a capable introduction with an effective controlling idea; supports main points with evidence; has a strong concluding section • **Organization** Arranges ideas logically; uses transitions to connect ideas • **Language** Maintains a formal style and tone; uses precise language; has a few errors in conventions
4	• **Development** Has an introduction that could use stronger information and a more insightful controlling idea; needs more relevant evidence; has an adequate concluding section • **Organization** Arranges ideas logically with some exceptions; could use transitions more effectively • **Language** Mostly maintains a formal style and tone; needs more precise language; has a few distracting errors in conventions
3	• **Development** Has an introduction lacking in information; has an adequate controlling idea; provides some evidence; has a somewhat weak concluding section • **Organization** Reflects some flaws in organization; needs more transitions • **Language** Sometimes uses an informal style and tone; uses some vague word choices; has some significant errors in conventions
2	• **Development** Has a weak introduction and a controlling idea that does not relate to the writing task; lacks sufficient evidence; has a weak concluding section • **Organization** Arranges ideas and evidence in a confusing way; uses few transitions • **Language** Uses an informal style and tone; uses many vague word choices; has many distracting errors in conventions
1	• **Development** Has no introduction or controlling idea; offers little or no evidence; ends abruptly • **Organization** Lacks an overall organization; lacks transitions • **Language** Lacks a formal style and tone; has few precise words; has major problems with grammar, mechanics, and spelling

Preparing for Timed Writing

COMMON CORE

W 10 Write routinely over shorter time frames for a range of tasks, purposes, and audiences.

1. ANALYZE THE TASK   5 MIN

Read the task carefully. Then read it again, underlining the words that tell the type of writing, the audience, and the purpose.

WRITING TASK *Type of writing*   *Audience*

Write a literary analysis in which you analyze a story for your classmates and teacher. Select a short story that you know well and use relevant evidence to support a controlling idea about a literary element in the story, such as character, plot, mood, or theme. *Purpose*

2. PLAN YOUR RESPONSE   10 MIN

Choose a short story you know well. Decide which literary element you will write about. Then write a sentence stating the main idea you want to communicate to your audience. Consider any background information your readers might need. In a chart, list the ideas and details you will include in your analysis.

Thesis: _____

Main Points	Evidence

3. RESPOND TO THE TASK   20 MIN

Begin drafting your literary analysis. You may want to start by simply stating your controlling idea. As you write, keep the following points in mind.

- **Introduction** Grab your readers' attention with a lively opening. Provide the title and author and include a clear controlling idea.
- **Body** Present the main points that support your controlling idea and include evidence for each main point.
- **Concluding Section** Restate your controlling idea and give your overall impression of the work.

4. IMPROVE YOUR RESPONSE   5–10 MIN

Revising Review the key aspects of your essay. Did you state your controlling idea clearly? Did you provide supporting evidence for each main point?

Proofreading Correct any errors in grammar, spelling, punctuation, and capitalization. Watch out for run-on sentences. Mark your edits neatly.

Checking Your Final Copy Before you turn in your essay, read it one more time to catch any errors you may have missed.

Giving an Oral Response to Literature

You and your friends probably share your analyses of books, movies, songs, and video games every day. An oral response to literature has the same basic purpose: to communicate your ideas about a work in a way that engages listeners.

 Complete the workshop activities in your **Reader/Writer Notebook.**

SPEAK WITH A PURPOSE	COMMON CORE TRAITS
TASK Adapt your literary analysis into a well-organized **oral presentation.** Practice your presentation, and then give it to the class.	**A STRONG ORAL RESPONSE . . .** • presents the speaker's claim on a specific literary work • provides necessary background information for the audience • offers a variety of evidence to support the claim • uses verbal and nonverbal techniques effectively

COMMON CORE

SL 4 Present claims and findings, sequencing ideas logically and using pertinent descriptions, facts, and details; use appropriate eye contact, volume, and pronunciation.
SL 6 Adapt speech to a variety of contexts, demonstrating command of formal English.

Adapt Your Essay

Your oral presentation will communicate the same points as your written essay. However, you'll need to adapt it so that listeners will be able to follow along easily. Keep these ideas in mind as you adapt your analysis:

- **Purpose** Your purpose is to present your claim about a literary work. State your controlling idea or claim at the beginning of your speech. Then repeat the controlling idea in slightly different words to make sure everyone understands and remembers it.

- **Audience** Consider what your audience members already know about your subject and what they need to know. You may need to insert some background information to help them understand your speech.

- **Effective Language** As you adapt your written analysis into a speech, use shorter sentences that get right to the point. Don't be afraid to repeat key ideas. Listeners can't go back and reread the text, so it's helpful to remind them of important points. Your tone should be friendly, but remember to use formal English. Avoid slang and expressions that sound very casual.

- **Organization** Stick to the same logical sequence you used in your analysis, but remember to engage your listeners at all times. In your introduction, grab their attention with a striking detail from the work. As you illustrate your main points with pertinent descriptions, facts, and other evidence, guide listeners with transitions such as *first, second,* and *finally.* In your conclusion, restate your controlling idea and leave your audience with something to think about.

THINK central

Speaking & Listening Online

Go to <u>thinkcentral.com</u>.
KEYWORD: HML6-566

Deliver Your Presentation

USE VERBAL TECHNIQUES

These verbal techniques can make your presentation more effective:

- **Enunciation** Speak clearly and pronounce words correctly. When you practice your speech, note any words that you tend to stumble over. Substitute different words or rearrange sentences so that you can deliver your speech smoothly.

- **Voice Modulation** Don't speak in a monotone, a dull voice with no change in expression. Instead, show enthusiasm through your voice so your audience will become enthusiastic about your response.

- **Pitch** Your voice rises and falls naturally when you speak. If you are nervous, your voice may get higher. Control your pitch by taking deep breaths and staying calm. Change the pitch of your voice to emphasize key points.

- **Speaking Rate** In informal conversations, you may speak very quickly. When you deliver a speech, you need to speak more slowly to help listeners understand you. Pause now and then so that important points can sink in.

- **Volume** If you normally speak quietly, you will need to raise your volume when giving your speech. You shouldn't yell, but listeners at the back of the room must be able to hear you clearly.

USE NONVERBAL TECHNIQUES

Nonverbal communication, or body language, adds appeal to your message. Practice using these techniques when you give an oral presentation:

- **Eye Contact** Look audience members in the eyes to keep their attention. Try to let your eyes rest on each member of the audience at least once.

- **Facial Expression** Smile, frown, or raise an eyebrow to show your feelings or to emphasize parts of your message.

- **Gestures** Give a thumbs up, shrug, nod, or shake your head to emphasize a point or to add meaning to your speech.

- **Posture** Be sure to stand tall but not too rigidly. If you are relaxed, your audience will be, too.

 **YOUR TURN**

As a Speaker Practice giving your speech to a partner. Then ask him or her to comment on how clearly you communicated your main points and whether your voice, facial expressions, and gestures seemed natural and appropriate.

As a Listener Listen to your partner's presentation. Paraphrase the major ideas and supporting evidence you heard in the speech. If necessary, ask questions to clarify the speaker's purpose and point of view.

Assessment Practice

DIRECTIONS Read these selections and answer the questions that follow.

from Alan Mendelsohn, the Boy from Mars
by Daniel Pinkwater

1   I got off to a bad start at Bat Masterson Junior High School. My family had moved from my old school district during the summer, and I didn't know a single kid at the school. On top of that, it turned out that kids at Bat Masterson put a lot of emphasis on how you look. This created a problem—I am a short, portly kid, and I wear glasses. Every other kid in the school was tall, had a suntan, and none of them wore glasses. Also clothes wrinkle up on me. I don't know why this should be—five minutes after I get dressed in the morning, everything is wrinkled. It looks like I slept in my clothes.

2   Not only did I not know anybody on my first day, not only did I find out that a short, portly, wrinkled kid with glasses is an outcast in that school, but I also sat down on somebody's half-finished Good Humor bar in the school yard. That reduced my confidence. Then it turned out that the school was not expecting me. My records, and grades, and whatever the old school was supposed to send, they had not sent—or they had sent them to the wrong place—or they had gotten lost.

3   So I had to sit on this bench in the office for most of the morning, sort of sticking to the bench because of the leftover Good Humor on the seat of my pants. Finally they gave me this big pile of cards to fill out. Then I had to run all over the school getting teachers to sign the cards. Three or four times I had to go back to the office with notes from teachers saying that their class was full, or it was the wrong class, or it conflicted with another class I was supposed to take.

4   And each time I entered a classroom, the class would giggle at me. Then the teacher would ask my name. It was written at the top of every one of the cards—but the teacher would ask me to say it anyway. "Leonard Neeble," I would say, and the kids in the class would just go wild. I don't know why, but my name gets them every time.

5   At lunchtime I walked around the school yard. All the kids looked sort of grown-up and unwrinkled. Some of the girls even had lipstick on. The kids stood around in groups, talking and laughing. Some guys were showing off, walking on top of benches, and chasing each other, and

hollering. Nobody looked at me or said anything to me. I had the feeling that if I tried to talk to anybody, they wouldn't have been able to hear me. I looked for a quiet spot to eat my tuna fish sandwich.

Sparky *by Earl Nightingale*

1   I came across a story about a boy named Sparky. School was all but impossible for Sparky. He failed every subject in the eighth grade. He flunked physics in high school. Receiving a flat zero in the course, he distinguished himself as the worst physics student in the school's history. He also flunked Latin and algebra and English. He didn't do much better in sports. Although he did manage to make the school golf team, he promptly lost the only important match of the year. There was a consolation match. He lost that too.

2   Throughout his youth Sparky was awkward socially. He was not actually disliked by the other students; no one cared that much. He was astonished if a classmate ever said hello to him outside school hours. No way to tell how he might have done at dating. In high school, Sparky never once asked a girl out. He was too afraid of being turned down.

3   Sparky was a loser. He, his classmates—everyone knew it. So he rolled with it. Sparky made up his mind early in life that if things were meant to work out, they would. Otherwise he would content himself with what appeared to be his inevitable mediocrity.

4   But one thing was important to Sparky: drawing. He was proud of his own artwork. Of course, no one else appreciated it. In his senior year of high school, he submitted some cartoons to the editors of his class yearbook. They were turned down. Despite this particularly painful rejection, Sparky was so convinced of his ability that he decided to become a professional artist.

5   Upon graduating from high school, he wrote a letter to Walt Disney Studios. He was told to send some samples of his artwork, and the subject matter for a cartoon was suggested. Sparky drew the proposed cartoon. He spent a great deal of time on it and on the other drawings. Finally the reply from Disney Studios came—he had been rejected once again. Another loss for the loser.

6   So Sparky wrote his own autobiography in cartoons. He described his childhood self, a little-boy loser and chronic underachiever. The cartoon character would soon become famous all over the world. For Sparky, the boy who failed every subject in the eighth grade and whose work was rejected again and again, was Charles Schulz. He created the "Peanuts" comic strip and the little cartoon boy whose kite would never fly and who never succeeded in kicking the football—Charlie Brown.

Reading Comprehension

> **Use the excerpt from *Alan Mendelsohn, the Boy from Mars* (pp. 568–569) to answer questions 1–4.**

1. The author's main purpose in this excerpt is to —
   A. persuade readers to be kind to new students
   B. explain how to be popular in a new school
   C. entertain readers by describing a situation they can understand
   D. give information about Bat Masterson Junior High School

2. Which imagery does the author use to create a humorous tone?
   A. Girls wearing lipstick
   B. Leonard sitting on an ice cream bar
   C. Teachers signing a pile of cards
   D. Boys showing off in the schoolyard

3. What statement in paragraph 1 gives details that tell the reader what Leonard looks like?
   A. *I got off to a bad start*
   B. *I didn't know a single kid at school*
   C. *clothes wrinkle up on me*
   D. *Every other kid in the school was tall*

4. Paragraph 5 creates an image of —
   A. a boy all alone in a crowded schoolyard
   B. students standing around a boy, teasing him
   C. a boy laughing a some other boys
   D. a classroom full of giggling students

> **Use "Sparky" (p. 569) to answer questions 5–9.**

5. What events happen three times to Sparky?
   A. Three different girls turn him down for dates.
   B. He fails at three areas of his life: school, dating, and art.
   C. His art work is rejected by three different people.
   D. His school gives him failing grades three times.

6. Which phrase from the selection helps you "see" Sparky's failure?

A. *a boy named Sparky*

B. *in the eighth grade*

C. *a flat zero*

D. *the worst physics student*

7. Which statement BEST expresses the author's purpose in telling Sparky's story?

A. *He was not actually disliked by the other students; no one cared that much.*

B. *Sparky made up his mind early in life that if things were meant to work out, they would.*

C. *Finally the reply from Disney Studios came—he had been rejected once again.*

D. *For Sparky, the boy who failed every subject in the eighth grade and whose work was rejected again and again, was Charles Schulz.*

8. The author tells the story of Sparky's failures mainly in —

A. sentences with flowery words

B. sentence fragments

C. short, direct sentences

D. realistic dialogue

9. Which words in the selection help to create a casual style?

A. distinguished, mediocrity

B. awkward, underachiever

C. chronic, inevitable

D. flunked, loser

> **Use both selections to answer question 10.**

10. Which statement is true about the tone of both selections?

A. Poetic language is used to create a formal tone.

B. The tone changes from playful to gloomy.

C. Vivid details add a mysterious tone to the narrative.

D. The author has a sympathetic tone toward the person he writes about.

SHORT CONSTRUCTED RESPONSE
Write two or three sentences to answer this question.

11. Write three examples of sensory language that create imagery in the selections. Tell what imagery each example of language creates.

Write a paragraph to answer this question.

12. Why do you think Earl Nightingale waits until the end to reveal Sparky's identity? As you write your answer, think about the author's purpose in telling Sparky's story.

GO ON ➡

Vocabulary

Use figurative language as context clues to answer the following questions.

When she tripped in front of the class, Carmen felt as <u>awkward</u> as a ballerina in boots.

1. The word *awkward* means —
   A. clumsy
   B. comfortable
   C. special
   D. unhappy

For city drivers, traffic jams are as <u>inevitable</u> as the sunrise.

2. The word *inevitable* means —
   A. early in the day
   B. sure to happen
   C. hard to handle
   D. far away

His <u>mediocrity</u> made him feel as common as a weed along the roadside.

3. The word *mediocrity* means —
   A. average ability
   B. great strength
   C. artistic skills
   D. sense of humor

Use context clues and your knowledge of Latin roots to answer these questions.

4. The Latin root *duct* means "lead." What does the word *reduced* mean in paragraph 2?

". . . but I also sat down on somebody's half-finished Good Humor bar in the school yard. That <u>reduced</u> my confidence."

   A. Made lower
   B. Gained in numbers
   C. Kept the same
   D. Changed for the better

5. The Latin root *cord* means "heart." What does the word *records* mean in paragraph 2?

"My <u>records</u>, and grades, and whatever the old school was supposed to send, they had not sent. . ."

   A. Musical selections
   B. Story of one's life
   C. History of one's achievements
   D. Favorite songs

6. The Latin root *flict* means "strike." What does the word *conflicted* mean in paragraph 3?

". . . their class was full, or it was the wrong class, or it <u>conflicted</u> with another class I was supposed to take."

   A. Taught hard material
   B. Happened at the same time
   C. Was not very interesting
   D. Was the same as

Revising and Editing

DIRECTIONS Read this passage and answer the questions that follow.

(1) Everyone has felt uncomfortable unhappy or awkward at some time in the past. (2) Maybe you have low grades, no friends, or uncool clothes when the school year started. (3) However, your situation probably changed when you made a good solid friend. (4) A friend makes life better. (5) A friend will help you study and even shared clothes with you. (6) In short, if you find a friend, you will have more than just a kind helpful person. (7) You had a new, better, happier life!

1. What change, if any, should be made in sentence 1?
   A. Change *uncomfortable unhappy or awkward* to **uncomfortable, unhappy or awkward**
   B. Change *uncomfortable unhappy or awkward* to **uncomfortable, unhappy, or awkward**
   C. Change *has felt* to **will feel**
   D. Make no change

2. What change, if any, should be made in sentence 2?
   A. Change *low grades, no friends, or uncool clothes* to **low grades no, friends or, uncool clothes**
   B. Change *have* to **will have**
   C. Change *have* to **had**
   D. Make no change

3. What change, if any, should be made in sentence 3?
   A. Change *will change* to **changed**
   B. Change *good solid* to **good solid,**
   C. Change *good solid* to **good, solid**
   D. Make no change

4. What change, if any, should be made in sentence 5?
   A. Change *will help* to **helped**
   B. Change *shared* to **will share**
   C. Change *shared clothes* to **shared, clothes**
   D. Make no change

5. What change, if any, should be made in sentence 6?
   A. Change *find* to **found**
   B. Change *will have* to **had**
   C. Change *kind helpful* to **kind, helpful**
   D. Make no change

6. What change, if any, should be made in sentence 7?
   A. Change *had* to **will have**
   B. Change *new, better, happier* to **new, better happier**
   C. Change *new, better, happier* to **new better happier**
   D. Make no change

STOP

COMMON CORE

RL 10 Read and comprehend literature.

Ideas for Independent Reading

Which questions from Unit 4 made an impression on you? Continue exploring with these books.

What builds confidence?

Becoming Naomi León
by Pam Muñoz Ryan

Naomi is shy. She's only comfortable when she's carving soap. When Naomi's mother tries to take her away from her grandmother and brother, the three run away to Mexico, where Naomi finally learns about her father's legacy and herself.

The Bicycle Man
by David L. Dudley

Carissa, a 12-year-old in rural Georgia in 1927, can't seem to do anything right. One day, old Bailey stops in front of her house with his bicycle. He teaches Carissa and her mother how to find their balance, which helps them move forward on their own.

Surviving the Applewhites
by Stephanie S. Tolan

Jake's last chance before juvenile hall is a home school run by the chaotic and eccentric Applewhite family. Jake thinks he'll be out of there in a week. Can a group of self-involved artists help a "bad" boy discover who he really is?

How strong is peer pressure?

I Walk in Dread
by Lisa Rowe Fraustino

In the winter of 1691, four girls in Salem, Massachusetts, accuse people of being witches and a trial begins. As more and more people are accused, more girls claim to be victims. Who is telling the truth?

Sixth-Grade Glommers, Norks, and Me
by Lisa Papademetriou

Allie is starting sixth grade at a new school. When her best friend, Tamara, wants Allie to change so she can be popular, Allie questions her own choices. Will she be able to survive middle school alone?

Stitches
by Glen Huser

Travis wants to be a puppeteer, and his best friend is a girl who walks with a limp. Neither of these things makes life easy at his junior high, where boys are expected to take shop class and play sports. Will Travis change?

When are words not enough?

Missing May
by Cynthia Rylant

Six months after Aunt May's death, 12-year-old Summer worries that sadness will pull her little family apart. Together, she and Uncle Ob search for a message from May, some sign that will tell them how they can live without her.

Pictures of Hollis Woods
by Patricia Reilly Giff

Hollis always wanted to be part of a family. But when she got one, she messed it up. She only has her drawings to remember how happy she was. Now she has a second chance, and she'll do anything to make it work.

Samir and Yonatan
by Daniella Carmi

Samir, a Palestinian, lies in an Israeli hospital waiting for an operation. All day long he's angry, homesick, and lonely. But every night, Yonatan, an Israeli in the next bed, whispers stories to him about Mars. Will the stories bring Samir peace?

Get Novel Wise

THiNK central

Go to **thinkcentral.com**.
KEYWORD: HML6-574

Word Pictures

**THE LANGUAGE
OF POETRY**

What makes a POEM a poem?

Is a jump-rope rhyme a poem? What about the lyrics of your favorite song, or even a song that parents sing to children? Once you start looking for poems, you'll find that they are all around you. You may even have written some yourself.

ACTIVITY Write down the words to two poems you already know. Remember that you might choose a rhyme from a children's game or the verses to a favorite song. Then, in a group, discuss these questions:

- Compare your poems with the ones chosen by other students. What do all your poems have in common?

- What do you think makes a group of words a "poem"? How is a poem different from prose, from a news article, or a short story, or a play?

Find It Online!

Go to **thinkcentral.com** for the interactive version of this unit.

I asked my mother
for fifty cents
To see the elephant
jump the fence.
He jumped so high
he touched the sky,
And didn't come back
'til the Fourth of July.

COMMON CORE

Preview Unit Goals

TEXT ANALYSIS
- Analyze sound devices, including rhyme, rhythm, meter, refrain, alliteration, and onomatopoeia
- Determine the meaning of words and phrases as they are used in a text, including figurative and connotative meanings
- Analyze the impact of a specific word choice on meaning and tone
- Determine a central idea of a text and how it is conveyed through particular details; provide a summary of the text distinct from personal opinions or judgments

READING
- Cite textual evidence to support analysis of what the text says explicitly as well as inferences drawn from the text
- Develop reading strategies, including paraphrasing

WRITING AND LANGUAGE
- Write an online feature article
- Use compound-complex sentences

SPEAKING AND LISTENING
- Update an online feature article

VOCABULARY
- Use Greek and Latin affixes and roots as clues to the meaning of a word

ACADEMIC VOCABULARY
- associations
- device
- insight
- reaction
- specific

MEDIA AND VIEWING
- Maintain an online feature article

Reading Poetry

Poetry is everywhere, not just within the pages of this book. Song lyrics, greeting-card messages, and commercial jingles can all be considered poetry. You might describe some poems as clever, others as inspiring, and still others as sappy. Every so often, though, you might encounter a poem that gets inside your heart and mind. How does a poem do that? Read on to find out.

Part 1: What Makes Poetry Different?

COMMON CORE

Included in this workshop:
RL 4 Determine the meaning of words and phrases as they are used in a text, including figurative meanings; analyze the impact of a specific word choice on meaning.
RL 5 Analyze how a particular stanza fits into the overall structure of a text.

One difference between poetry and prose has to do with **structure,** or the way a poem looks on the page. While short stories and news articles consist of sentences and paragraphs, poems are made up of lines. A **line** can be a single word, a sentence, or part of a sentence. In many poems, lines are arranged into groups called **stanzas.** The way a poet chooses to arrange lines and stanzas can affect a poem's meaning.

Poetry is different from prose in another way. Poetry *sounds* different from prose, as you'll see when you read the poem below, with all of its rhymes and bouncy rhythms. As you will also see, poems have speakers and the speaker may not be the poet.

A Fine Head of Lettuce
Poem by **Jack Prelutsky**

I'm a fine head of lettuce,
a handsome romaine.
I haven't a cranium
made for a brain.

I'm simple and shy.
I remain on my own.
I'm known in the garden
as lettuce alone.

STUDY THE POEM
- Who is the **speaker?**
- How many **stanzas** does the poem have?
- How many **lines** are in each stanza?
- What words rhyme in this poem? Is there a pattern to the rhymes?
- Poets like playing with words. What verbal joke do you find in the last line?

MODEL: STRUCTURE, SPEAKER, AND SOUNDS

The poem "Losing Face" is more serious than "A Fine Head of Lettuce." The poem sounds different too—more like conversation. It doesn't have the bouncy rhythm and comic rhymes of the lettuce poem. Read Wong's poem aloud.

LOSING FACE

Poem by **Janet S. Wong**

Finally Mother is proud
of something
I have done.
"My girl won
5   the art contest,"
she tells the world,
smiling so big
and laughing so loud
her gold tooth
10   shows.

I'm the only one
who knows
how I drew so well,
erasing the perfect lines
15   I traced,
drawing worse ones
on purpose
in their place.
I feel awful.
20   I want to tell.

But I don't want to lose
Mother's glowing
proud face.

Close Read

1. Who is the speaker of this poem? Describe the conflict she is having.

2. Where does Wong use rhyme in the first stanza?

3. The poem is structured so that each stanza helps you understand the speaker's feelings. In your own words, summarize what each stanza is about.

4. Reread the boxed section. It is the only place where each line contains a complete sentence. Why might the poet have chosen to emphasize these lines?

5. Reread the last stanza. Why doesn't the speaker want to admit what she's done?

Part 2: What Are the Elements of Poetry?

Think about the comforting melody of a lullaby, the contagious beat of a certain song, or those few words in a poem that perfectly capture how you're feeling. The power of a poem comes from more than its structure and its speaker. Sound devices, imagery, and figurative language are the elements that can make a poem unforgettable.

SOUND DEVICES

Most poems are meant to be heard, not just read. A poem's sounds are often as carefully chosen as its words. Poets use sound devices to make music and to emphasize ideas.

SOUND DEVICES	EXAMPLES
RHYME Rhyme is the repetition of accented vowel sounds, as in *thing* and *sing*, *cry* and *sky*. **METER AND RHYTHM** Meter is a more or less regular pattern of stressed and unstressed syllables. Rhythm is a musical quality created by the alternation of accented and unaccented syllables.	**The rhyme and meter in this poem help to create a singsong sound.** Some people talk and talk and never say a thing Some people look at you and birds begin to sing. Some people laugh and laugh and yet you want to cry. Some people touch your hand and music fills the sky. —"People" by Charlotte Zolotow
ALLITERATION Alliteration is the repetition of consonant sounds in words that are close together, such as the *s* in makes **s**till pools, and **s**leep-**s**ong. **REFRAIN** Refrain is a word or line that is repeated in a poem to create a certain effect, such as the phrase *the rain*.	**The refrain in these lines suggests the steady downpour. The alliteration mimics the rain's soothing sounds.** The rain makes still pools on the sidewalk. The rain makes running pools in the gutter. The rain plays a little sleep-song on our roof at night— And I love the rain. —from "April Rain Song" by Langston Hughes

MODEL 1: RHYME, RHYTHM, AND REFRAIN

In "Pete at the Zoo," a young speaker considers an important question: Do zoo animals ever get lonely? Read the poem aloud, paying particular attention to the use of rhymes and rhythms.

PETE AT THE ZOO

Poem by **Gwendolyn Brooks**

Ĭ wónдĕr ĭf thĕ élĕphănt
Ĭs lónĕly ĭn hĭs stáll
When all the boys and girls are gone
And there's no shout at all,
5   And there's no one to stamp before,
No one to note his might.
Does he hunch up, as I do,
Against the dark of night?

Close Read

1. Which words rhyme at the ends of the lines?

2. Stressed and unstressed syllables are marked in lines 1–2. Read these lines aloud, emphasizing the stressed words.

3. What does the repetition of words and phrases in the boxed lines help to emphasize about nighttime at the zoo?

MODEL 2: METER AND ALLITERATION

What kinds of sounds do you associate with fireworks? In this poem, meter and alliteration help you to hear some of these sounds. Read the poem aloud to get the full effect.

Fireworks

Poem by **Valerie Worth**

First
A far thud,
Then the rocket
Climbs the air,
5   A dull red flare,
To hang, a moment,
Invisible, before
Its shut black shell cracks
And claps against the ears,
10 Breaks and billows into bloom,
Spilling down clear green sparks, gold spears,
Silent sliding silver waterfalls and stars.

Close Read

1. Does this poem sound like conversation, or is it written in **meter**—a regular pattern of stressed and unstressed syllables?

2. What sounds are repeated in the boxed line to create alliteration? Where does the poet use **onomatopoeia**—words that sound like what they mean—to help you hear the fireworks?

FIGURATIVE LANGUAGE AND IMAGERY

Figurative language is the use of imaginative comparisons to help you see the world in new ways. Figurative language is not literally true. Four common figures of speech are **simile, metaphor, personification,** and **hyperbole.** Review these figures of speech in the examples below. What comparison is each figure of speech built on? How does each figure of speech help you see a part of the world in a new imaginative way?

Images use sensory language to appeal to your senses of sight, hearing, smell, taste, and touch. Most images are visual. Figures of speech often create images, as they do in each of the examples below. What do you see or hear in each figure of speech?

SIMILE

Simile is a comparison between two unlike things that includes the word *like* or *as*.

In a high wind the
leaves don't
fall but fly
straight out of the
tree like birds

—"Poem" by A. R. Ammons

METAPHOR

Metaphor is a comparison between two unlike things that does not include the word *like* or *as*.

The fallen leaves are cornflakes
That fill the lawn's wide dish,

—from "December Leaves" by
Kaye Starbird

PERSONIFICATION

Personification is a description of an object, an animal, or an idea as if it were human or had human qualities.

New sounds to
walk on
today,

dry
leaves
talking
in hoarse
whispers
under bare trees.

—"New Sounds" by Lilian Moore

HYPERBOLE

Hyperbole is a figure of speech that uses exaggeration to create a special effect.

He turns and drags half the lake out
after him

—"Mooses" by Ted Hughes

Part 3: Analyze the Text

Eve Merriam transports you to a familiar scene—a dinner table. Merriam uses many of the techniques you just learned about to help you visualize the scene and understand the speaker's relationship with his or her parents.

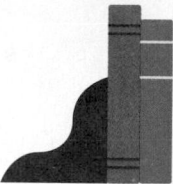 

LIKE BOOKENDS

Poem by **Eve Merriam**

Like bookends
my father at one side
my mother at the other

propping me up
5   but unable to read
what I feel.

Were they born with clothes on?
Born with rules on?

When we sit at the dinner table
10   we smooth our napkins into polite folds.
How was your day dear
             Fine
And how was yours dear
             Fine
15   And how was school
             The same

Only once in a while
when we're not trying so hard
when we're not trying at all
20   our napkins suddenly whirl away
and we float up to the ceiling
where we sing and dance until it hurts from laughing

and then we float down
with our napkin parachutes
25   and once again spoon our soup
and pass the bread please.

Close Read

1. Notice the simile in lines 1–6. How are the mother and father like bookends?

2. Examine the two boxed images. What contrasting dinner scenes do they help you visualize?

3. Reread lines 17–20. What sounds are repeated to create alliteration?

4. **Hyperbole** is a kind of figure of speech that uses exaggeration to make a point. What hyperbole do you find in lines 20–21?

5. Lines 23–24 contain a metaphor. What two things does the metaphor compare?

Analysis of Baseball
Poem by May Swenson

Video link at
thinkcentral.com

Alone in the Nets
Poem by Arnold Adoff

What can SPORTS teach us?

COMMON CORE

RL 5 Analyze how a particular sentence or stanza fits into the structure of a text. **RL 7** Compare and contrast the experience of reading a poem to listening to the text.

Many people consider sports an important part of their life, whether they play sports or just watch. Athletes enjoy being part of a team and competing with their peers. Fans enjoy watching games to see the skill and endurance of the athletes. The following poems present two views of sports.

LIST IT Think about the sports that are part of your life. With a small group, pick one sport and come up with a list of what the sport teaches you about life. Compare your list with the lists of other groups in the class.

● TEXT ANALYSIS: THE STRUCTURE OF A POEM

One of the first things you will notice about poems is that they are made up of lines. A **line** of poetry can be a complete sentence, part of a sentence, or even a single word.

- Short lines might give a poem a fast, choppy **rhythm,** or beat. Long lines might give it a smoother, slower rhythm.

- Poets use **line breaks,** or the places where lines of poetry end, to add emphasis to certain words or phrases.

- Some poets use other stylistic elements for effect—unusual punctuation, unusual word breaks, and unusual spacing.

● READING STRATEGY: READING POETRY ALOUD

Usually, poetry is meant to be heard as well as read. Many poems have **rhyming words,** or repeated sounds at the ends of words, that are easier to notice when the poem is **read aloud.** The emphasis on certain words or phrases is also easier to notice when you use the poet's punctuation and line breaks to pace your reading and choose your **intonation,** or pitch. Poets might also include **onomatopoeia,** words that sound like what they mean, such as *bang* or *thump.* In addition to helping you hear sounds, these elements can emphasize a poem's meaning.

Read "Analysis of Baseball" and "Alone in the Nets" aloud. In a chart like the one shown, record places in the poems where you notice rhyming words or repeated words and phrases. Also record any onomatopoeia, or "noise" words, you find.

	"Analysis of Baseball"	"Alone in the Nets"
Rhyming Words	hits/it/mitt	
Repeated Sounds, Words, and Phrases		
Onomatopoeia		

 Complete the activities in your **Reader/Writer Notebook.**

Meet the Authors

May Swenson
1919–1989

Poet of Daily Life
May Swenson has been praised for her ability to make readers "see what they had only glanced at before." A native of Utah, Swenson moved to New York City after college. In New York, she worked as a secretary and an editor to make ends meet while writing poetry. She won many awards for her writing, including a MacArthur Foundation "genius grant." Most of Swenson's poems focus on everyday life.

Arnold Adoff
born 1935

Word Musician
At the age of 16, Arnold Adoff took up two new hobbies: writing poetry and listening to jazz. The free forms of jazz influence much of his poetry. "Writing a poem," he says, "is making music with words and space." Adoff is known for writing in unusual forms, arranging his words in unique ways on the page, and using punctuation creatively. He was married to writer Virginia Hamilton before her death in 2002.

Authors Online
THINK central
Go to **thinkcentral.com.** KEYWORD: HML6-585

ANALYSIS OF BASEBALL

May Swenson

It's about
the ball,
the bat,
and the mitt.
5 Ball hits
bat, or it
hits mitt.
Bat doesn't
hit ball, bat
10 meets it.
Ball bounces
off bat, flies
air, or thuds
ground (dud)
15 or it
fits mitt.

Bat waits
for ball
to mate.
20 Ball hates
to take bat's
bait. Ball
flirts, bat's
late, don't
25 keep the date.
Ball goes in
(thwack) to mitt,
and goes out
(thwack) back
30 to mitt. **A**

Ball fits
mitt, but
not all
the time.
35 Sometimes
ball gets hit
(pow) when bat
meets it,
and sails
40 to a place
where mitt
has to quit
in disgrace.
That's about
45 the bases
loaded,
about 40,000
fans exploded.

It's about
50 the ball,
the bat,
the mitt,
the bases
and the fans. **B**
55 It's done
on a diamond,
and for fun.
It's about
home, and it's
60 about run.

A **READING POETRY ALOUD**
What noise words, or **onomatopoeia**, are used in the poem so far? Find at least five rhymes. Find at least five lines in the poem that use alliteration.

B **STRUCTURE**
What is the effect of all these short lines?

Alone
in the Nets
Arnold Adoff

I
am
alone   of   course,
    in the nets, on this cold and raining afternoon,
5   and our best defending fullback[1]
    is lying on the wet ground   out of position.
    Half the opposition is pounding
                        down the field,
            and their lead forward[2] is gliding
10   so fast, she can just barely keep
            the ball in front of her   sliding
                        foot.

Her cleats[3] are expensive,
and her hair bounces
15   neatly
like the   after
        girls   in the shampoo commercials.
            There   is   a   big   grin
                    on her face.

20 Now: In This Frozen Moment   On This Moving World Through Space

        is the right time to ask   why am I here just standing
                        in my frozen place?
Why   did I get up on time this morning?
Why   did I get up at all?
25 Why   did I listen to the coach and agree to play
        this strange position in a   r e a l   game
        in a strange town   on this   wet   and   moving world?

---

1. **defending fullback:** In soccer, this refers to a player whose position is near the defensive goal or goal line.
2. **lead forward:** the primary, or main, player on the offensive line in the game of soccer.
3. **cleats:** shoes with pieces of metal or hard rubber sticking out from the soles.

C STRUCTURE
Reread lines 1–4. Why do you think the poet chose to place the first two words of the poem on their own lines?

D READING POETRY ALOUD
What words or phrases would you emphasize if you were to read lines 1–12 aloud? Explain.

Why   is it raining?
Why   is it raining so h a r d?
30 Where
           are all of _{our} defenders?
Why   do all of _{our} players
           do all of the falling
                               down?

                                        Why am I here? **E**

But Frozen Moments Can Unfreeze   And I Can Stretch

and reach for the ball   flying to the corner of
                                                      our
                                                      goal.

40 I can reach   and jump
                     and d i v e   into the s p a c e
                                        between my out
                                               stretched
                                                    hands
45 and the outside poles
              of the nets.

My fears evaporate   like my sweat in this chilling
                                                      breeze,
and I can move with this moving world
50 and pace my steps
like that   old
                 movie
             high
             noon sheriff in his just
55   right
                                  time.

That grinning forward gets her shot away too soon,
and I am there, on my own time, in the air,
                              to meet the ball,
60 and fall on it
  for the save.

I wave my happy ending wave and get up.
            The game goes on. **F**

E STRUCTURE
Reread lines 28–35. How does the arrangement of the words and letters help convey the meaning in these lines?

F READING POETRY ALOUD
What words are repeated in this poem? Find at least three places in the poem where words or lines are spaced to enforce meaning. How would you read the poem aloud?

MAGAZINE ARTICLE The poems "Analysis of Baseball" and "Alone in the Nets" give you a sense of two different sports. In the following article, you will read about the challenges and benefits of becoming a professional athlete.

TEEN ATHLETES:

Many Kids Dream of Playing in the Big Leagues. But at What Cost?

Victor Landauro

Becoming a famous athlete may look easy, but it's not. Just ask an Olympic gold medalist or a pro soccer player. They will tell you that playing sports well means hard work and discipline.

"I've made a lot of sacrifices," gymnast Carly Patterson told *Junior Scholastic.*

The 16-year-old won Olympic gold in the all-around competition, her sport's premier event. Despite achieving Olympic glory, Carly is actually jealous of her 14-year-old sister's "regular" life. "[Jordan] goes to public school, has sleepovers with friends, and eats junk food," says Carly. "I can't do that because I need to rest and eat healthy."

Freddy Adu, who plays forward for the D.C. United soccer team, knows firsthand what Carly is talking about. "I love playing, but I work very hard at soccer," the 15-year-old told *JS.* "I hear fans cheer for me, and it definitely makes me train harder.". . .

Not Fun Anymore

Almost everyone agrees that athletics are good for most kids. Several studies show that playing sports can lead to better physical and emotional health. Through athletics, children learn important lessons in sportsmanship, discipline, teamwork, and leadership.

But critics worry that those benefits are getting lost in the chase to become the next star. Too many kids are either pushing—or being pushed by coaches and parents—to reach the top of their sport.

"Many kids who quit sports typically say, 'It's not fun anymore,'" says Avery Faigenbaum, a professor of exercise science and physical education at the College of New Jersey. "They would rather play on a losing team than sit on the bench of a winning team.". . .

Life Beyond Sports

Upon retirement, many professional athletes seek new challenges. There is even a Baseball Hall of Famer on Capitol Hill: Kentucky Senator Jim Bunning. Other athletes have become judges, lawyers, business leaders, and teachers.

"It's important to have multiple dreams," says Jay Coakley, a sociologist who studies sports. "Dream of a life that is outside of sports, too."

That advice weighs heavily on Carly Patterson. "I want to go to college, and maybe become a singer," she says. "I'm going to keep on working and see what happens."

Comprehension

1. **Clarify** According to lines 49–60 of "Analysis of Baseball," what is baseball about?

2. **Clarify** What happens to the forward's shot at the end of "Alone in the Nets"?

COMMON CORE

RL 5 Analyze how a particular sentence or stanza fits into the structure of a text. **RL 7** Compare and contrast the experience of reading a poem to listening to the text.

Text Analysis

3. **Make Inferences** Could these poems be about more than baseball and soccer? Support your interpretations with evidence from the texts.

4. **Evaluate Structure** In a chart like the one shown, record places in "Alone at the Nets" where the poet arranges letters and words in unusual ways. How do these arrangements contribute to the meaning of the poem?

Word, Phrase, or Line	Shape	Effect of the Shape
a r e a l game	stretched out, made to be long	makes me read the line more slowly and put emphasis on **real**

5. **Read Poetry Aloud** Look at the chart you completed as you read aloud to find places where you noticed sound effects in these poems, including rhyming words, repeated words and phrases, and onomatopoeia. How do the sound effects connect with the action in the poems?

Extension and Challenge

6. **Creative Project: Writing** Rewrite "Alone at the Nets" as an article for your school newspaper. You may want to review the magazine article on page 590 to see an example of sports writing. Be sure to include team names, player names, the date of the game, and the final score.

What can SPORTS teach us?

According to these poems, what can sports teach us about life? Do you share these feelings?

Sea-Fever

Video link at
thinkcentral.com

Poem by John Masefield

The Village Blacksmith
Poem by Henry Wadsworth Longfellow

VIDEO TRAILER **THINK** central KEYWORD: HML6-592

How can WORK
affect our lives?

COMMON CORE

RL 5 Analyze how a particular sentence contributes to the development of the theme.

What do you think of when you hear the word work? If your experience with projects or chores hasn't been pleasant, then words like *boring* and *dull* might come to mind. When you love what you do, however, work can become more than just a job. For the people in the following two poems, the work they do each day becomes a part of who they are.

DISCUSS What jobs might be interesting enough to build your life around? With a small group, discuss the characteristics that would make a job mean more to you than just a paycheck.

● TEXT ANALYSIS: RHYME

Rhyme is the repetition of sounds at the ends of words. A poet may use rhyme loosely, or develop a pattern of rhyme throughout a poem. In this example from "The Village Blacksmith," lines that rhyme are labeled with the same letter:

Under a spreading chestnut-<u>tree</u>	a
The village smithy <u>stands</u>;	b
The smith, a mighty man is <u>he</u>,	a
With large and sinewy <u>hands</u>;	b

As you read "Sea-Fever" and "The Village Blacksmith," record rhyming words in a log like the one shown.

"Sea-Fever"	"The Village Blacksmith"
	tree/he

Review: **Refrain**

■ READING SKILL: RECOGNIZE METER

Poems and songs often have a regular rhythm, which is called meter. Meter creates a pattern of stressed (ˊ) and unstressed (˘) syllables. Read aloud this first line of "Sea-Fever" to hear its regular beat:

˘ ˊ ˘ ˊ ˘ ˊ ˘ ˘ ˊ ˘ ˊ ˘ ˊ ˘ ˊ ˘
I must go down to the seas again, to the lonely sea and
˘ ˘ ˊ
   the sky,

As you read the following poems, notice how the poets have arranged their words to create regular patterns of stressed and unstressed syllables.

▲ VOCABULARY IN CONTEXT

Guess the meanings of the words below that are used in the Masefield poem that follows. Match each definition to the word you think it defines. After you have read the poem, check to see how close you came to the correct definitions.

WORD LIST	brawny	repose	sinewy

1. strong and muscular
2. lean and tough
3. freedom from work

 Complete the activities in your **Reader/Writer Notebook.**

John Masefield
1878–1967

Poet of the Sea
John Masefield's love of the sea began in childhood. He received part of his education at a floating school, on a ship. His first job was a position on the crew of an ocean liner. Illness eventually forced him to leave the sea, but his love of water continued to play an important role in his life.

Henry Wadsworth Longfellow
1807–1882

Best Seller
Longfellow got an early start on college—at age 14. By graduation, he had published nearly 40 poems. Poems such as "The Song of Hiawatha" and "Paul Revere's Ride" made Longfellow one of the most popular American poets of his time.

BACKGROUND TO THE POEM
The Village Smith
Years ago in America, each village had a blacksmith. Using the roaring fire in his forge, the blacksmith would shape iron into things like horseshoes, weapons, and tools.

Authors Online
Go to **thinkcentral.com.** KEYWORD: HML6-593

Sea-Fever

John Masefield

I must go down to the seas again, to the lonely sea and
    the sky,
And all I ask is a tall ship and a star to steer her by,
And the wheel's kick and the wind's song and the white
    sail's shaking,
And a grey mist on the sea's face and a grey dawn breaking. **A**

5 I must go down to the seas again, for the call of the
    running tide
Is a wild call and a clear call that may not be denied;
And all I ask is a windy day with the white clouds flying, **B**
And the flung spray and the blown spume,[1] and the
    sea-gulls crying.

I must go down to the seas again to the vagrant[2] gypsy life,
10 To the gull's way and the whale's way where the wind's like
    a whetted[3] knife;
And all I ask is a merry yarn[4] from a laughing fellow-rover,
And a quiet sleep and a sweet dream when the long
    trick's[5] over.

A RHYME
Reread lines 1–4, paying
attention to the pattern
of rhyming words.
Record any rhyming pairs
or groups in your log.

COMMON CORE RL 5

B REFRAIN
The most obvious sound
effect used in poetry is
the refrain. A **refrain** is a
repeated word, phrase,
or line in a poem. What
lines do you notice
working as refrains in
this poem? What do the
refrains reveal about the
speaker's frame of mind?

---

1. **spume** (spyōōm): foam or froth on a liquid.
2. **vagrant** (vā′grənt): wandering from place to place; unrestrained.
3. **whetted** (hwĕt-ĭd): sharpened.
4. **yarn**: long, entertaining tale.
5. **trick**: term of work or duty.

Unnamed clipper ship, Claude Marks. Private
collection. Photo © Bridgeman Art Library.

THE VILLAGE BLACKSMITH

Henry Wadsworth Longfellow

The Blacksmith, (1909), James Carroll Beckwith. Oil on canvas, 52¼″ × 32¼″. Photo © Smithsonian American Art Museum, Washington, D.C./Art Resource, New York.

Under a spreading chestnut-tree
    The village smithy stands;
The smith, a mighty man is he,
    With large and **sinewy** hands;
5 And the muscles of his **brawny** arms
    Are strong as iron bands.

His hair is crisp, and black, and long,
    His face is like the tan;
His brow is wet with honest sweat,
10   He earns whate'er he can,
And looks the whole world in the face,
    For he owes not any man. **C**

Week in, week out, from morn till night,
    You can hear his bellows[1] blow;
15 You can hear him swing his heavy sledge,
    With measured beat and slow,
Like a sexton[2] ringing the village bell,
    When the evening sun is low.

sinewy (sĭn′yōō-ē) *adj.*
lean and tough

brawny (brô′nē) *adj.*
strong and muscular

C RHYME
Reread the first two stanzas. What pattern of rhyming words do you hear?

---

1. **bellows:** a device for providing air to feed a fire.
2. **sexton:** an employee of a church, responsible for maintaining the building and ringing the church bells.

And children coming home from school
20   Look in at the open door;
They love to see the flaming forge,
      And hear the bellows roar,
And catch the burning sparks that fly
      Like chaff from a threshing-floor.[3]

25 He goes on Sunday to the church,
      And sits among his boys;
He hears the parson pray and preach,
      He hears his daughter's voice,
Singing in the village choir,
30   And it makes his heart rejoice. **D**

It sounds to him like her mother's voice,
      Singing in Paradise!
He needs must think of her once more,
      How in the grave she lies;
35 And with his hard, rough hand he wipes
      A tear out of his eyes.

Toiling, —rejoicing, —sorrowing,
      Onward through life he goes;
Each morning sees some task begin,
40   Each evening sees it close;
Something attempted, something done,
      Has earned a night's **repose.**

Thanks, thanks to thee, my worthy friend,
      For the lesson thou hast taught!
45 Thus at the flaming forge of life
      Our fortunes must be wrought;
Thus on its sounding anvil[4] shaped
      Each burning deed and thought.

D RECOGNIZE METER
Write out lines 25–28
and label each syllable
with a stressed or
unstressed mark. What
do you notice about the
pattern of the rhythm?

repose (rĭ-pōz′) n.
freedom from work or
worry; rest

---

3. **chaff from a threshing-floor:** Chaff is the dry coating on grains
   of wheat. It is discarded during threshing, when the wheat and
   straw are separated.

4. **sounding anvil:** An anvil is a heavy block of iron on which metals
   are hammered into shape. *Sounding* refers to the ringing noise
   the hammering makes.

Comprehension

1. **Clarify** What "call" is the **speaker,** or voice of the poem, answering in "Sea-Fever"?

2. **Clarify** In the last line of "Sea-Fever," what is the "long trick"?

3. **Clarify** Explain what the blacksmith thinks about when he hears his daughter sing.

Text Analysis

4. **Analyze Similes** What simile describes the wind in line 10 of "Sea-Fever"? What similes in "The Village Blacksmith" describe the smith and his work?

● 5. **Analyze Refrain** Note which words and phrases are repeated in each stanza in "Sea-Fever." In each case, why do you think the poet chose to repeat those words?

● 6. **Analyze Meter** Write down a few lines from each poem and mark the stressed and unstressed syllables, as shown on page 593. Now read the lines aloud. What effect does the rhythm have on each line?

● 7. **Evaluate Rhyme** In addition to creating a pattern of sound, rhyme helps emphasize important ideas or words in a poem. Look back at the chart you filled in as you read. Consider the groups of rhyming words that appear in "Sea-Fever." Why might the poet have chosen to emphasize these words in his poem about sailing?

8. **Draw Conclusions** How does the speaker in "The Village Blacksmith" feel about the blacksmith? In the center of a web like the one shown, record whether you think the speaker's view of the blacksmith is positive or negative. Then fill out the web with words and phrases from the poem that support your opinion.

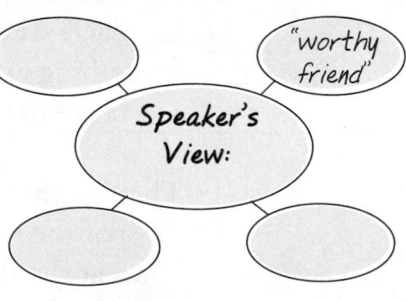

Extension and Challenge

9. **Research Project** What is your ideal job? Research the career on the Internet and write a paragraph on your findings. Be sure to include information on the specific educational or training requirements. Then explain why the job would be worthwhile or fulfilling to you.

How can WORK affect our lives?

What jobs would mean more to you than just a paycheck? What does the way we feel about work reveal about our values?

COMMON CORE

RL 4 Determine the meaning of words and phrases as they are used in a text, including figurative meanings. **RL 5** Analyze how a particular sentence contributes to the development of the theme. **W 7** Conduct short research projects to answer a question, drawing on several sources.

Vocabulary in Context

▲ VOCABULARY PRACTICE

Answer the following questions about the vocabulary words.

1. If you wanted a day's **repose**, would you go to a cabin in the woods or a busy train station?
2. Who would more likely be described as **sinewy**, a pie-eating champion or a track star?
3. Does a **brawny** person have a slender build or large muscles?

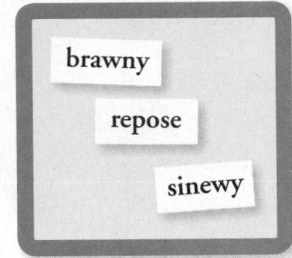

brawny

repose

sinewy

ACADEMIC VOCABULARY IN WRITING

> • associations   • device   • insight   • reaction   • specific

What **associations** do you make with the life of a sailor and the life of a blacksmith? What **insights** into these occupations do you get from the poems? Use at least two Academic Vocabulary words in your response.

VOCABULARY STRATEGY: GREEK ROOTS

The histories of many English words go back to the Greek language. For example, Longfellow says that the blacksmith thinks of his wife in Paradise. The word *Paradise* is built in part on the Greek word *-peri-* meaning "around, about." In Greek the word *paradeisos* means a park enclosed by a wall.

PRACTICE In column A below is a list of English words. In column B is a list of Greek roots that the English words are built on. Match each English word with its Greek root (or roots). Then write a definition of the English word. When you have finished, see how many other English words you can think of that are built on these Greek roots.

A	B
1. audio	**a.** *-audio-* "hear"
2. Bible	**b.** *-vid-* "see"
3. dinosaur	**c.** *-philos-* "loving"
4. Philadelphia	**d.** *-sauros-* "lizard"
5. video	**e.** *-bibl-* "book"

Interactive Vocabulary   **THINK** central

Go to **thinkcentral.com**.
KEYWORD: HML6-599

Fall
Poem by Sally Andresen Stolte

Change
Poem by Charlotte Zolotow

How do we respond to NATURE'S mysteries?

COMMON CORE

RL 4 Determine the meaning of words and phrases as they are used in a text. **RL 10** Read and comprehend literature.

How do we respond to the mysteries and beauties of the natural world? Many times, we try to find a connection between the natural world and our own human world. We look at animals and see some of our own traits. We look at the mysterious changes that take place in the world of nature and we think of changes that take place in our own lives. In the poems you are about to read, two poets look at nature and let their imaginations go to work.

QUICKWRITE What aspect of the natural world do you find amazing or puzzling or even frightening or disgusting? Think of an animal or a plant or a natural event that you are curious about, or in awe of. Write a paragraph telling what it is, how it makes you feel, and what it makes you think of.

● TEXT ANALYSIS: IMAGERY

Imagery is created by the use of **sensory language**—words and phrases that appeal to the senses of sight, hearing, touch, smell, and taste. Poets use imagery to create vivid descriptions or express a strong idea in only a few words.

The winter
still stings
clean and cold and white

In these lines from "Change," the word *white* appeals to your sense of sight, while the words *stings* and *cold* appeal to your sense of touch. As you read "Fall" and "Change," record examples of imagery and note the sense or senses each example appeals to.

	Taste	Sight	Touch	Smell	Hearing
"Fall"					
"Change"		"white"	"stings", "cold"		

● READING SKILL: UNDERSTAND REFRAIN

When you read a poem, you will sometimes come across a **refrain,** the same word, phrase, or line repeated several times. Poets often use refrains to emphasize a particular word or idea or to establish a mood. Refrain can also help develop a poem's rhythm, or beat. In "Change," for example, the second line of most stanzas repeats the word *still*. This repetition emphasizes that the seasons are always the same from year to year.

The summer
still hangs (lines 1–2)

The autumn
still comes (lines 6–7)

The winter
still stings (lines 10–11)

The spring
still comes (lines 14–15)

As you read, look for repeated words, phrases, and lines. Consider why the poet might have chosen to repeat them.

 Complete the activities in your **Reader/Writer Notebook.**

Meet the Authors

Sally Andresen Stolte
born 1947

Lifelong Inspiration
Sally Stolte was raised on a farm in Iowa and remembers watching the geese fly over the fields each fall. It was this scene that she captured in the haiku poem you are about to read, which she wrote for a high school English assignment. Today, Stolte lives in Minnesota. Her interests include reading, quilting, and, birdwatching.

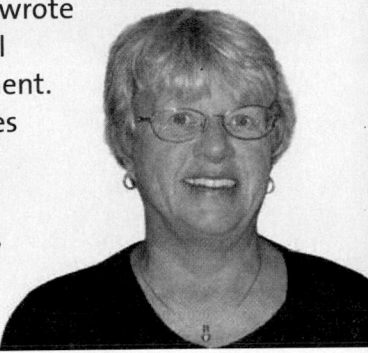

Charlotte Zolotow
born 1915

Natural Observer
As a young woman, Charlotte Zolotow worked for a publishing company. Walking to work each day, she passed a park, and saw how the park changed with the seasons. She told her boss that it might be a good topic for a children's book. Zolotow ended up writing that book, the first of many in a writing career that has lasted more than 70 years.

Authors Online
Go to **thinkcentral.com**. KEYWORD: HML6-601

THINK central

Fall

Sally Andresen Stolte

The geese flying south
In a row long and V-shaped
Pulling in winter. **Ⓐ**

Ⓐ IMAGERY
Which of the five senses (sight, hearing, taste, touch, and smell) do the details in this poem appeal to? Record your answers in your chart.

Analyze Visuals ▶
Do the geese in this image seem to be coming or going? Explain.

Change

Charlotte Zolotow

The summer
still hangs
heavy and sweet
with sunlight
5 as it did last year.

The autumn
still comes
showering gold and crimson
as it did last year.

10 The winter
still stings
clean and cold and white
as it did last year. **B**

The spring
15 still comes
like a whisper in the dark night. **C**

It is only I
who have changed.

The Farewell (1952), Bernard Perlin. Photo © Smithsonian American Art Museum, Washington, D.C./Art Resource, New York.

Comprehension

1. **Clarify** What event in nature is the speaker observing in the poem "Fall"?

2. **Recall** According to the speaker in "Change," which season comes "like a whisper in the dark night"?

3. **Represent** Divide a piece of paper into fourths and sketch the mental picture you get of each season based on the descriptions in "Change."

Text Analysis

● 4. **Examine Imagery** Line 3 of "Fall" describes the geese "Pulling in winter." Think about why the poet might have chosen to use the word *pulling*. What image does this create in your mind? Be specific in your description.

● 5. **Understand Refrain** What is the refrain in "Change"? How does the refrain remind us that the speaker's life is different from the yearly cycle of the seasons?

● 6. **Analyze Imagery** Look back at the chart you completed as you read these poems. Note which of your five senses the poems appeal to most often. Which seasons in the poems seem to appeal most to the sense of touch, and which ones appeal more to the sense of sight?

Extension and Challenge

7. **Creative Project: Poem** A **lyric poem** is a short poem in which a speaker expresses personal thoughts and feelings. Write a lyric poem about your favorite or least favorite season. Include imagery that appeals to the senses. Try also to use a simile that tells what the season reminds you of.

8. **Inquiry and Research** Do some research on the science behind why birds such as wild geese migrate. Why do some kinds of birds migrate while others do not? Present your findings to the class.

How do we respond to NATURE'S mysteries?

One of these poets looks at geese flying south. The other thinks of the four seasons. What other mysteries of nature could be the subject of poems?

COMMON CORE

RL 4 Determine the meaning of words and phrases as they are used in a text. **RL 10** Read and comprehend literature. **W 7** Conduct short research projects to answer a question.

Language

◆ **GRAMMAR IN CONTEXT:** Maintain Subject-Verb Agreement

The verb in a sentence must always **agree in number** with the subject of the sentence. This means that if a subject is singular, its verb must have a singular form. If the subject is plural, its verb must have a plural form. Be especially careful when forming sentences that begin with *here* or *there*, and when forming questions.

> *Original:* There was too many leaves to count.
>
> *Revised:* There were too many leaves to count. (*The subject* leaves *is plural, so the verb should be plural too.*)

PRACTICE Choose the verb form that agrees in number with the subject in each of the following sentences.

1. Here (comes, come) the new season.
2. (Is, Are) the leaves starting to change color?
3. My sister (rakes, rake) the leaves in the yard.
4. There (is, are) no colors prettier than autumn's colors.

*For more help with subject-verb agreement, see page R65 in the **Grammar Handbook.***

READING-WRITING CONNECTION

YOUR TURN

Increase your understanding of the poems "Fall" and "Change" by responding to this prompt. Then use the **revising tip** to revise your writing.

WRITING PROMPT	REVISING TIP
Short Constructed Response: Analysis Write at least **one paragraph** in which you present and explain your response to one of these poems, or to both of them. First, cite clearly how you felt about the poem—did you like it, dislike it, feel confused by it? Then explain your response using details from the poem.	Do the verbs in your sentences agree in number with their subjects? If not, revise your writing so that your verbs and subjects are in agreement.

COMMON CORE

L1 Demonstrate command of the conventions of grammar.
W 2 Write informative/explanatory texts to convey ideas.

Interactive Revision

THINK central

Go to **thinkcentral.com**.
KEYWORD: HML6-607

Message from a Caterpillar
Poem by Lilian Moore

Fog
Poem by Carl Sandburg

Two Haiku
Poems by Bashō

How much can one WORD say?

COMMON CORE

RL 4 Determine the meaning of words and phrases as they are used in a text, including figurative meanings; analyze the impact of a specific word choice on meaning.

Sometimes a single word can pack a powerful punch. Words like *peace, freedom, friendship,* and *love* represent strong feelings, ideas, and memories. In each of the following short poems, the poet has worked as much meaning as possible into the smallest number of words.

WEB IT What are some small words that are big on meaning? Choose a word that you find expressive. Create a web with the word at the center. In the outer part of the web, write the feelings, ideas, and memories that you connect to that word.

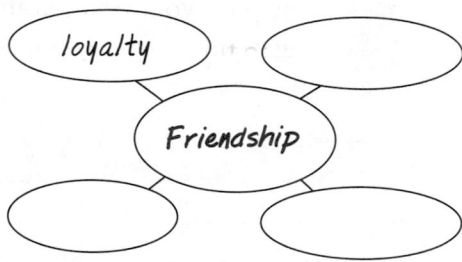

● TEXT ANALYSIS: IMAGERY AND METAPHOR

Imagery is the use of sensory language—language that appeals to our senses of sight, hearing, smell, taste, and touch. Imagery is one of the central elements of poetry. Images in poetry help us see the world in a fresh light.

Another important element in poetry is **metaphor**—the use of language in which one thing is compared to another, very different thing. Metaphors can work as sensory language too: in comparing one thing to another, different thing, metaphors often help us to see, hear, smell, taste, or touch something in a brand new way.

"The road was a ribbon of moonlight," a line from a poem by Alfred Noyes, presents a vivid visual image to us. It also contains a metaphor: the road at night, flooded with moonlight, is compared to a ribbon.

● READING STRATEGY: PARAPHRASE

Paraphrasing means restating someone else's ideas in your own words. A paraphrase often helps clarify ideas that are expressed in complicated terms. Putting someone else's words into your own words can help you understand a poem.

As you read each of the following poems, take the time to paraphrase the ideas in your own familiar vocabulary. Then, in a chart like the one below, jot down your paraphrase of ideas in each poem. List the ideas in the order they appear in the poem so that you maintain the meaning and order of each poem.

Poem	Paraphrase
"Message from a Caterpillar"	
"Fog"	
"Two Haiku"	

Complete the activities in your **Reader/Writer Notebook**.

Lilian Moore
1909–2004

Lifelong Writer
Some of Lilian Moore's earliest memories were of hanging out in her neighborhood and making up stories to tell her friends. Writing simple, vivid stories and poems for young readers eventually became her life's work.

Carl Sandburg
1878–1967

Informal Poet
Carl Sandburg adopted an informal style in his poetry, believing that formal poetry had "the skill of a solved crossword puzzle." He thought of poetry as a glimpse, leaving readers "to guess about what is seen during a moment."

Matsuo Bashō
1644–1694

Wandering Poet
Matsuo Bashō is considered one of Japan's greatest poets. He set the rules for haiku, poems that describe a single moment of discovery, or enlightenment, using only 17 syllables.

Authors Online
THINK central
Go to **thinkcentral.com**. KEYWORD: HML6-609

Message from a Caterpillar

Lilian Moore

Don't shake this
bough.
Don't try
to wake me
5 now.

In this cocoon
I've work to
do.
Inside this silk
10 I'm changing
things.

I'm worm like now
but in this
dark
15 I'm growing
wings. **A**

A PARAPHRASE
Reread lines 12–16.
Restate what is going on
inside the cocoon.

FOG

Carl Sandburg

The fog comes
on little cat feet. **B**

It sits looking
over harbor and city
5 on silent haunches[1]
and then moves on. **C**

B METAPHOR
What is the fog
compared to?

C IMAGERY
What does this poem
help you see and even
hear?

---

1. **haunches:** the hind legs of a
   four-legged animal.

Two Haiku

Bashō

Winter solitude—
in a world of one color
the sound of the wind.

A field of cotton—
as if the moon
had flowered. **D**

D PARAPHRASE
Explain in your own
words the images in
these haiku that appeal
to your senses of sight
and sound.

Comprehension

1. **Clarify** Why doesn't the caterpillar in "Message from a Caterpillar" want to be awakened?

2. **Clarify** In the first haiku, what does "a world of one color" refer to?

3. **Represent** Sketch the image the second haiku creates in your mind.

Text Analysis

4. **Make Inferences** What larger meaning could be found in the last two lines of "Message from a Caterpillar"?

5. **Analyze Metaphor** Carl Sandburg bases his poem "Fog" on a single **metaphor,** or comparison of two things, stated on lines 1–2. How does Sandburg extend the metaphor through the entire poem?

6. **Analyze Haiku** A traditional haiku written in Japanese has only three lines and 17 syllables. The first and third lines have five syllables, and the second line has seven. (Haiku translated into English may not follow this pattern exactly.) Within these strict rules, the poet tries to capture a moment in time, a kind of discovery. What moment of discovery is revealed in each haiku here?

7. **Analyze Imagery** Most haiku contain seasonal imagery. What season is the focus of each of these haiku? What words give you clues?

8. **Compare and Contrast Poems** Compare and contrast "Fog" with the first haiku by Bashō. In what ways are they similar and different? Record your responses in a Venn diagram.

9. **Paraphrase** Review your chart, and write a paraphrase of each poem. In a paraphrase you express every idea, line by line, in your own words. Follow the order of the ideas used in each poem.

"Fog" has a title | Both | Haiku no title

COMMON CORE

RL 4 Determine the meaning of words and phrases as they are used in a text, including figurative meanings; analyze the impact of a specific word choice on meaning.

Extension and Challenge

10. **Inquiry and Research** From 1912 to 1917, a group of poets formed and called themselves "Imagists." Do research to find out how they were influenced by Japanese poetry such as haiku. Share your findings with the class.

How much can one WORD say?

Look back at the word web you created on page 608. Using the web for ideas, write a haiku of your own. Use seasonal imagery. Try to express as much as you can in three short lines.

Windshield Wiper

HISTORY Video link at
thinkcentral.com

Poem by Eve Merriam

Night Journey

Poem by Theodore Roethke

How do you SEE the world?

COMMON CORE

RL 1 Cite textual evidence to support inferences drawn from the text.

When you stand on your head, the world looks very different, even unfamiliar. Turning upside down is one way of changing your perspective, or your way of seeing something. Perspective can also be a mental outlook, or a way of responding to things that happen. The poems you are about to read involve both physical and mental perspective. Both poems are written from the perspective of looking out a window, but they capture two very different responses.

LIST IT To get a sense of perspective, try looking a little differently at something you see every day. Roll a piece of paper to form a tube, and look through it at what's around you. Make a list of everything you see. Did you notice anything that you hadn't noticed before?

● TEXT ANALYSIS: SOUND DEVICES

You may have heard or read poems that sound almost like songs. Poetry gets many of its musical qualities from **sound devices.** Sound devices can reinforce meaning or add emphasis. Three commonly used sound devices are

- **refrain,** the repetition of a word, phrase, or line (*Example: It was a good song, a sad song, a sweet song.*)

- **onomatopoeia** (ŏn′ə-măt′ə-pē′ə), the use of words that sound like their meanings (*Examples: buzz, zap*)

- **alliteration,** the repetition of the same consonant sound, usually at the beginning of words (*Example: magical mountain mist*)

A poet might use these devices to draw attention to a particular line or idea. As you read "Windshield Wiper" and "Night Journey," record examples of these devices.

Repetition and Refrain	Onomatopoeia	Alliteration
fog smog / fog smog		

● READING SKILL: MAKE INFERENCES

You have to make inferences when you read almost any text. An **inference** is an educated guess about some detail in a text that is not clear, or that seems to suggest a meaning well beyond its surface meaning.

Poetry usually uses fewer words than a short story or a novel, so making inferences is one of the skills essential to understanding a poem. When you read a poem, ask yourself:

- Why has the poet chosen to structure the poem this way? How does the structure of the poem support its meaning?

- What do the images suggest about the way the writer feels about the subject?

- What do the metaphors mean? What is the significance of the comparisons the poet is making?

- How does the rhythm or meter of the poem support its meaning?

 Complete the activities in your **Reader/Writer Notebook.**

Meet the Authors

Eve Merriam
1916–1992

Lover of Language
Eve Merriam's advice on how to appreciate poetry was "Eat it, drink it, enjoy it, and share it." Merriam began writing poetry at age seven. She loved rhythm and rhyme and the way poems came to life when read aloud. After college, she continued to write poetry while working as a writer in advertising and radio. Merriam particularly enjoyed sharing her love of poctry with young readers.

Theodore Roethke
1908–1963

Reluctant Poet
Theodore Roethke spent his childhood reading and longed to write beautifully, but he struggled with the idea of becoming a poet. Worried about fitting in, he went to law school—but quickly decided to become a poet after all. Roethke eventually won a Pulitzer Prize for his poetry. Much of his work explores the natural world and memories of his childhood.

Authors Online
Go to **thinkcentral.com.** KEYWORD: HML6-615

THiNK central

Windshield Wiper

Eve Merriam

fog smog
tissue paper
clear the blear

fog more
5   splat splat

rubber scraper
overshoes
bumbershoot[2]
slosh through

10   drying up
sky lighter
nearly clear

fog smog
tissue paper
clear the smear **A**

fog more
downpour

rubber scraper
macintosh[1]
muddle on
slosh through

drying up
sky lighter
nearly clear
clearing clearing veer **B**
clear here clear

A MAKE INFERENCES
Why do you think the poet chooses to set the poem up in this way—with this unusual spacing?

B SOUND DEVICES
How does the repetition in these lines reflect the subject of the poem?

---

1. **macintosh:** raincoat.
2. **bumbershoot:** umbrella.

Night Journey

Theodore Roethke

Now as the train bears west, **C**
Its rhythm rocks the earth,
And from my Pullman berth[1]
I stare into the night
5 While others take their rest.
Bridges of iron lace, **D**
A suddenness of trees,
A lap of mountain mist
All cross my line of sight,
10 Then a bleak wasted place,
And a lake below my knees.
Full on my neck I feel
The straining at a curve;
My muscles move with steel,
15 I wake in every nerve.
I watch a beacon swing
From dark to blazing bright;
We thunder through ravines
And gullies washed with light.
20 Beyond the mountain pass
Mist deepens on the pane;
We rush into a rain
That rattles double glass. **E**
Wheels shake the roadbed stone,
25 The pistons jerk and shove,
I stay up half the night
To see the land I love.

C SOUND DEVICES
One sound device poets use is **rhythm,** the repetition of stressed and unstressed syllables. Read this poem aloud to feel its rhythm. How do the short rhythmic lines remind you of the motion of the train?

D MAKE INFERENCES
A **metaphor** is a comparison between two unlike things, which helps you see something in a new way. What is the metaphor in line 6? How does it help you visualize the bridge?

E SOUND DEVICES
What sound device appears in lines 18, 23, and 25? Record your answer in your chart.

---

1. **Pullman berth:** A Pullman is a type of railroad car invented by George Pullman (1831–1897). The sleeping car featured private beds called berths.

Comprehension

1. **Clarify** What kinds of weather are described in "Windshield Wiper"?

2. **Recall** Name three things that the speaker sees in "Night Journey."

Text Analysis

3. **Understand Structure** Take another look at the unusual way in which "Windshield Wiper" is arranged on the page. What does it mean when that space in the center disappears in lines 13 and 14?

4. **Make Inferences** Why does the poet arrange "Windshield Wiper" in an unusual way? How does the structure of the poem support its meaning?

5. **Examine Word Choice** Skim "Night Journey" and list all the words you can find that convey movement. Compare lists with a partner.

6. **Analyze Sound Devices** What sound devices did you find in each poem? Review your chart to see where each poet uses refrain, onomatopoeia, and alliteration. Which sound device is used most often in each poem?

7. **Analyze Rhyme** Create a chart like the one shown, and list the rhyming words or phrases in each poem. In which poem does rhyme have a more important role? Explain.

	"Windshield Wiper"	"Night Journey"
Rhyming Words and Phrases	blear / smear	

COMMON CORE

RL1 Cite textual evidence to support analysis of what the text says explicitly as well as inferences drawn from the text.

Extension and Challenge

8. **SOCIAL STUDIES CONNECTION** Read the excerpt from *A Long Hard Journey* that begins on page 623. What further information does the excerpt provide about the speaker's trip in "Night Journey"?

How do you SEE the world?

Reread the list of observations you made for the activity on page 614. Now look at the same scene again, without the paper tube. Did your observations change when you changed your perspective?

Language

◆ **GRAMMAR IN CONTEXT:** Maintain Subject-Verb Agreement

You have already learned that a verb must agree with its subject in number. A **compound subject** is made up of two or more subjects joined by a **conjunction,** such as *and* or *or.* This conjunction is the clue that tells you whether to use a singular or plural verb in the sentence. A compound subject joined by *and* usually takes a plural verb. If a compound subject is joined by *or,* the verb should agree with the part of the subject closer to it.

Original:	Bells or the train whistle mean the train is arriving.
Revised:	Bells or the train whistle means the train is arriving.

PRACTICE Choose the verb form that agrees with each compound subject.

1. A dining car or comfortable seats (makes, make) the trip more enjoyable.
2. My mother and I (plays, play) board games to pass the time.
3. My uncle and my grandparents (was, were) there to meet the train.
4. The conductor or the engineer (rings, ring) the whistle as the train leaves.

*For more help with subject-verb agreement with compound subjects, see page R65 in the **Grammar Handbook**.*

READING-WRITING CONNECTION

YOUR TURN Broaden your understanding of "The Windshield Wiper" and "Night Journey" by responding to the prompt. Then use the **revising tip** to improve your writing.

WRITING PROMPT	REVISING TIP
Extended Constructed Response: Analysis "Windshield Wiper" and "Night Journey" differ greatly in their structure—even in the way they look on the page. The poems also differ in their messages—in what they say to you. In a **three-paragraph essay** analyze each poem, paying particular attention to the structure of each poem and to the message the poet is sending you. Use one paragraph to talk about "Windshield Wiper," use another paragraph to talk about "Night Journey," and use the final paragraph to tell how you responded to each poem and why.	Review your essay. Make sure each sentence has correct subject-verb agreement. If you find an error, correct it when you revise your essay.

COMMON CORE

L 1 Demonstrate command of the conventions of grammar.
W 2 Write informative/explanatory texts to examine a topic.

Interactive Revision **THINK** central

Go to **thinkcentral.com.**
KEYWORD: HML6-621

from **A Long Hard Journey: The Story of the Pullman Porter**

Informational Text

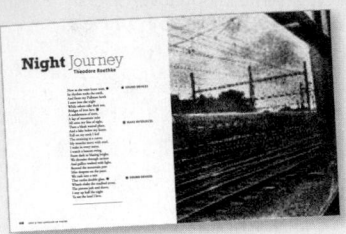

Use with "Night Journey,"
page 618.

COMMON CORE

RI 1 Cite textual evidence to support what the text says explicitly. **RI 2** Determine a central idea of a text and how it is conveyed through particular details; provide a summary of the text distinct from personal opinions or judgments.
RI 10 Read and comprehend literary nonfiction.

What's the Connection?

In the poem "Night Journey," the speaker describes the American landscape through the window of a Pullman car. In 1867, George Pullman's Palace Car Company began employing men who had formerly been held in slavery as porters. Porters worked on luxury trains and provided services to passengers. The Pullman Company operated successfully into the mid-1900s. During that time, porters were almost exclusively African Americans.

Standards Focus: Find Main Ideas and Supporting Details

As you read this excerpt from *A Long Hard Journey*, look for the main points the writer makes about porters and the trains they served on. You may notice that there is more than one main idea in this informational text. It takes practice to identify all the main ideas, but you can find them by taking notes in a chart like the one shown. Your notes should include

- facts (information that can be proved true)
- descriptive details
- other important information from the selection

	Details	Main Ideas
Porters		
Furnishings		
Conveniences		
Passengers		

In most texts a main idea is not stated directly. You have to infer it, or figure it out from clues in the text. Study the details in your completed chart and ask yourself, "What is the writer saying about each of these topics?" Later you will use your chart to summarize the main ideas and supporting details in this text.

A Long Hard Journey: The Story of the Pullman Porter

by Patricia and Fredrick McKissack

When Pullman cars first became popular, steam locomotives like this one were used to pull the cars.

F OCUS ON FORM
An **informational text** provides factual information. Newspaper articles, encyclopedia articles, and nonfiction books are all considered informational texts.

The early porters were called "Travelin' Men." They were highly respected, even revered by their contemporaries.[1] A young woman considered herself fortunate to be courted by a porter, and with good reason. They were pillars of their community; they made a decent living and had experiences other men only dreamed about. As a popular song of that day indicated, some women preferred a railroad husband over all others. **A**

A MAIN IDEA AND DETAILS
What do you learn about Pullman porters from this introduction? Add details to your chart.

---

1. **contemporaries:** other people who were living in that time period.

A railroader, a railroader
A railroader for me.
10   *If ever I marry in this wide world,*
A railroader's bride I'll be. . . .

Nineteenth-century porters traveled to faraway places, mingled with wealthy, well-educated travelers, and worked in elegant surroundings. In 1867, the *Western World* magazine described the Pullman porter's work environment:

> The furniture is of black walnut, handsomely carved and ornamented and upholstered with royal purple velvet plush imported from England expressly for this purpose. The finest Axminster carpets cover the floor. The night curtains for the
> 20   berths are of heaviest silk; splendid chandeliers are pendent overhead; elegant mirrors grace the walls. Luxurious beds invite repose by night and when made up for the day the cars betray no trace of the eating or sleeping uses to which they can be put. The total cost of each car is $30,000. . . . **B**

Since most of their neighbors had never seen such luxury, the porters formed an almost exclusive brotherhood bonded by their common experiences. It has been said they had more in common with each other than they did with family, friends, and neighbors. Fathers did so well that they encouraged their sons to become porters.
30 Uncles helped nephews, and brothers spoke for brothers.

Porters saw in their travels what most of their neighbors could only dream about. But on a more realistic level, having a steady job allowed them to marry, buy homes, and raise their children with dignity. . . . **C**

Meanwhile, George Pullman continued to make it possible for ordinary passengers to experience some of the pleasures and privileges generally reserved for the wealthy. His "Hotel Cars" were designed to give passengers the benefits of fine hotel food, service, and a comfortable bed, all on wheels. Pullman later designed and built the dining car which boasted "every variety of meats, vegetables, and pastry" that could be
40 "cooked on the cars, according to the best style of culinary art."[2]

The *Delmonico* was the first Pullman dining car, introduced in 1868. All passengers, whether using Pullman sleeping-car arrangements or not, could now eat in the diners. That also meant the hiring of more

---

2. **culinary art:** cooking of high quality and skill.

B MAIN IDEA AND DETAILS
Reread lines 12–24. Note any information about furnishings in the appropriate row of your chart.

C MAIN IDEA AND DETAILS
Reread lines 25–33. Which benefits of the job can you infer were important to the porters? Record notes in your chart.

Pullman lounge cars offered elegant furniture, carved ceilings, and all the comforts of home.

blacks as waiters, cooks, and stewards—although these positions were not exclusively black, as porter jobs were.

In 1870, the first all-Pullman train, called the *Board of Trade Special*, made its run from Boston to California. A baggage car contained iceboxes to keep the wines cool and the vegetables fresh. There was even a printing press on board that issued a daily newspaper, the *Trans-Continental*. It is
50 no wonder James Norman Hall, author of *The Caine Mutiny*, said, "I can no more conceive of a world without railroads and trains to run on them than I can imagine wishing to live in such a world." **D**

In spite of his plush surroundings, the porter's job was anything but glamorous. He was viewed as a servant. At first these travelin' men didn't mind playing the role George Pullman had cast for them. They wore the mask very well.

Dressed in well-tailored blue uniforms,[3] the Pullman porters adhered to very specific rules of conduct issued by the Pullman Company. Although a pleasant "good morning" or "good afternoon" when greeting each boarding
60 passenger was all that was originally required, many porters took the time to learn the names of their regular passengers and greeted them by name—"Good morning, Mr. Smith"—and *always* with a broad smile. . . .

---

3. **well-tailored blue uniforms:** According to the Pullman Company rule book, porters were required to wear navy blue uniform coats, along with hats, ties, and polished black shoes, whenever they helped passengers outside the train. Inside the train, porters wore starched white jackets. In warmer weather, an all-white uniform was often worn.

COMMON CORE RI 2

D MAIN IDEA AND DETAILS
Recall that you include only the writer's main ideas and most important details in a summary. Reread lines 46–52. You would probably include the detail that iceboxes were added to baggage cars in your summary. This detail supports the writer's main idea about conveniences on Pullman cars. Would you include the quote from James Norman Hall in your summary? Explain why or why not.

Once the passengers were comfortably seated and their bags were stored, the porter attended to special requests. He might be handing out newspapers, 70 helping a mother with restless children, or pointing out geographic points of interest to first-time travelers or foreign visitors.

The Pullman porter's primary focus was the customer's welfare. He was instructed—and 80 very often tested—to answer all calls promptly and courteously, no matter what time the calls were made. **E**

Porters were expected to follow numerous rules for dress and behavior. On the train, a spotless white coat was required at all times. From the moment a train pulled into the station, a porter was "on call" to meet the passengers' every need.

When it was time to make the beds, the porter was expected to move with speed and agility. The company rule book was precise. According to Nathaniel Hall, a porter, the rule book specified "the proper handling of the linen closet—the proper method of folding and putting away clean linen and blankets, the correct way of stacking laundry bags and dirty, 90 discarded bedding. A sheet, towel, or pillowcase once unfolded cannot be used again, although it may be spotless. Technically, it is dirty and must make a round trip to the laundry before it can reenter the service."

Porters were not allowed to make noise. "Noise was tabooed," reported Hall. "And even a soft knock on the top of the berth [was] forbidden. A porter must gently shake the curtains on the bedding from without."

Pullman demanded that all passengers were made to feel special. . . . Porters' salaries were deliberately kept low so they'd be dependent upon the tip to make ends meet.

The public knew that on a Pullman coach, the customer was always 100 right. No exceptions. **F**

E MAIN IDEA AND DETAILS
In your chart, note how the porters were expected to act. What kinds of conveniences did these rules make possible?

F INFORMATIONAL TEXT
Review the facts in this informational text. Do you think most of them can be verified? Why or why not?

Comprehension

1. **Recall** Who was allowed to eat in the *Delmonico* dining car?

2. **Clarify** Reread line 56. What does this line mean?

Text Analysis

3. **Ask Questions** Review the chart you created as you read this informational text. Record any questions you have about specific details in the text. Then discuss your questions in class.

4. **Evaluate an Informational Text** Would you describe this selection as well-researched and balanced? Use examples to support your answer.

COMMON CORE

RI 1 Cite textual evidence to support what the text says explicitly. **RI 2** Determine a central idea of a text and how it is conveyed through particular details; provide a summary of the text distinct from personal opinions or judgments. **RI 10** Read and comprehend literary nonfiction. **W 2** Write explanatory texts to convey information.

Read for Information: Summarize Main Ideas and Supporting Details

WRITING PROMPT

What are the main ideas in this informational text about Pullman porters, and what details do the writers use to support the main ideas? How would you state the overall main idea of this text?

To answer this prompt, refer to the chart you created as you read the article. Then follow these steps in planning, writing, and revising your essay.

1. First, write a brief summary of the article. A **summary** is a brief restatement of the most important points in a text. Write three or four sentences summing up the main ideas of the text.

2. Refer to your chart and jot down at least three specific details that support the main points.

3. Review your summary of the most important points in the article and the details that support those points. Then write a statement in your own words that expresses the main idea of the article. Remember that a summary should not include your own opinions or personal beliefs about the topic. Here, in graphic form, is how your essay should be structured:

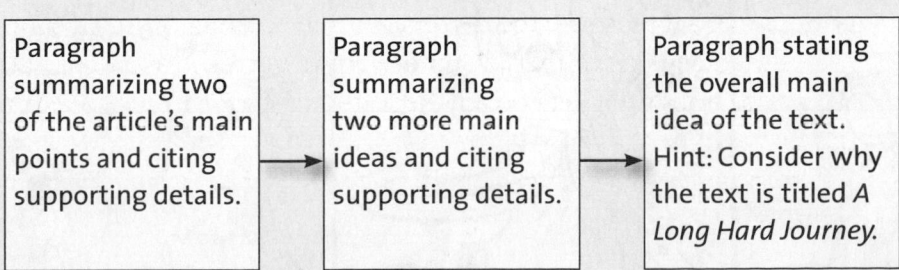

| Paragraph summarizing two of the article's main points and citing supporting details. | Paragraph summarizing two more main ideas and citing supporting details. | Paragraph stating the overall main idea of the text. Hint: Consider why the text is titled *A Long Hard Journey*. |

I'm Nobody! Who are You?

Poem by Emily Dickinson

Is the Moon Tired?

Poem by Christina Rossetti

Mooses

Poem by Ted Hughes

VIDEO TRAILER THINK central KEYWORD: HML6-628

How can POETRY surprise you?

Have you ever read a story that completely surprised you? Perhaps you were surprised by what happened to its characters or the feeling it gave you when you finished reading. Poetry can also surprise us because the poet uses language in an especially original way. Figures of speech (similes, metaphors, personification, and hyperbole), images, and sounds can make a poem totally surprising—and memorable.

DISCUSS In this section you will find three poems. One is about being a nobody, one is about the moon, and one is about a moose. Discuss for a few minutes what aspect of each subject you imagine each poem will focus on. After you read the poems, see if they surprised you.

SECTION C   THE STAR JOURNAL   C9

Garfield

● TEXT ANALYSIS: FIGURATIVE LANGUAGE

Figurative language is language based on imaginative comparisons. Writers use figurative language to describe a part of life in memorable and original ways. As you read, look for the following types of figurative language.

- A **simile** is a comparison of two things, using the words *like* or *as*. (*Her eyes were like green emeralds.*)
- A **metaphor** is a comparison of two things without the words *like* or *as*. (*Her eyes were green emeralds.*)
- **Personification** is the giving of human qualities to something that is not human. (*The sun smiled down on us.*)
- **Hyperbole** is the use of exaggeration for effect. (*The sun burned us to a crisp.*)

Review: Sound Devices

■ READING SKILL: MAKE INFERENCES

When you read poetry, you will have to **make inferences**, or educated guesses, about the poem's meaning. To make an inference, you use details from the text, plus what you know from your own experience. As you read, record each inference you make in a graphic organizer like the one shown.

Lines in Poem		My Knowledge		Inference
"I'm Nobody!" (line 1)	+	When someone is called a "nobody," it could mean "nobody special."	=	The speaker is very ordinary.

▲ VOCABULARY IN CONTEXT

In two of the poems you are about to read, the following words are used to create images or metaphors. Use the correct word to complete the sentences that follow.

WORD LIST	blunder	cackle	dreary	lectern

1. It would be _____, not fun, to be a somebody.
2. The moose is tall and sturdy like a high wooden _____.
3. The dry underbrush seems to _____ at the ugly moose.
4. Clumsy and lost, he will _____ on through the woods.

 Complete the activities in your **Reader/Writer Notebook**.

Meet the Authors

Emily Dickinson
1830–1886

Famous Nobody
Emily Dickinson kept to herself and rarely left home. Only seven of her poems were published before her death. After Dickinson died, her family discovered a collection of nearly 1,800 other poems and had them published. Today she is considered one of the greatest American poets.

Christina Rossetti
1830–1894

Quiet Artist
Christina Rossetti came from a talented family of poets, writers, and painters. She resisted fame, however, and "went very little into society." Poor health was one reason for her solitary life.

Ted Hughes
1930–1998

Natural Poet
Ted Hughes grew up hunting in the woods of rural England. Later he avoided hunting, preferring to write poetry about the "aliveness of animals in their natural states."

Authors Online
Go to **thinkcentral.com**. KEYWORD: HML6-629

THINK central

Detail of *The Son of Man* (1964), René Magritte.
© 2008 C. Herscovici, Brussels/Artists Rights Society
(ARS), New York. Photo © Christie's Images/Corbis.

I'M NOBODY!
WHO ARE YOU?
Emily Dickinson

I'm Nobody! Who are you?
Are you—Nobody—Too?
Then there's a pair of us!
Don't tell! they'd advertise—you know!

5　How **dreary**—to be—Somebody!
How public—like a Frog—
To tell one's name—the livelong June—
To an admiring Bog![1] **Ⓐ**

dreary (drîr'ē) *adj.*
dismal, bleak, or boring

Ⓐ FIGURATIVE LANGUAGE
In lines 5–8, the speaker uses a simile to compare a public person— "Somebody"—to a frog, and uses a metaphor to compare the public to a "Bog." Are these flattering comparisons? Explain why or why not.

---

1. **bog:** an area of soft, waterlogged ground.

Detail of *The Masterpiece on the Mysteries* (1955), René Magritte. Oil on canvas. © 2008 C. Herscivici, Brusssels/Artists Rights Society (ARS), New York. Photo © Christie's Images/SuperStock.

Is the Moon Tired?

Christina Rossetti

Is the moon tired? she looks so pale
Within her misty veil: **B**
She scales the sky from east to west,
And takes no rest.

5 Before the coming of the night
The moon shows papery white;
Before the dawning of the day
She fades away. **C**

B MAKE INFERENCES
What is the "misty veil" mentioned in line 2?

C FIGURATIVE LANGUAGE
What words does Rossetti use to personify the moon?

MOOSES
Ted Hughes

The goofy Moose, the walking-house frame, **D**
Is lost
In the forest. He bumps, he **blunders,** he stands.

With massy bony thoughts sticking out near his ears—
5 Reaching out palm upwards, to catch whatever might be
    falling from heaven—
He tries to think,
Leaning their huge weight
On the **lectern** of his front legs.

10 He can't find the world!
Where did it go? What does a world look like?
The Moose
Crashes on, and crashes into a lake, and stares at the
    mountain and cries
15 "Where do I belong? This is no place!"

He turns and drags half the lake out after him **E**
And charges the **cackling** underbrush—

He meets another Moose.
He stares, he thinks "It's only a mirror!"

D FIGURATIVE LANGUAGE
Reread line 1. Explain why you think the poet uses this metaphor to describe the moose.

blunder (blŭn′dər) v. to move clumsily

lectern (lĕk′tərn) n. a stand that holds papers for someone standing up to deliver a speech or lecture

E FIGURATIVE LANGUAGE
What **hyperbole**—or exaggeration—can you find in line 16?

cackle (kăk′əl) v. to make a sound of shrill laughter or chatter

Splash, Nancy Glazier. Oil, 26″ × 34″.

20 "Where is the world?" he groans, "O my lost world!
And why am I so ugly?
And why am I so far away from my feet?"

He weeps.
Hopeless drops drip from his droopy lips. **F**

25 The other Moose just stands there doing the same.

Two dopes of the deep woods. **G**

F SOUND DEVICES
How does the **alliteration** in line 24—the repetition of consonant sounds in words close together—help you to picture the moose?

G MAKE INFERENCES
Who might the speaker be referring to in the last line?

Comprehension

1. **Recall** In "I'm Nobody! Who are You?" why doesn't the speaker want to be a "somebody"?

2. **Clarify** What does the speaker in "Is the Moon Tired?" think made the moon tired and pale?

3. **Clarify** In "Mooses," what does the speaker think of mooses?

Text Analysis

4. **Make Inferences** What does the speaker in "I'm Nobody! Who are You?" think about the public? How does the poem connect with Dickinson's own experiences as a poet?

5. **Draw Conclusions** Do you think the speaker in "I'm Nobody! Who are You?" means what she says about fame? Explain.

6. **Understand Figurative Language** Find the metaphors used to describe the moose in lines 1 and 9 of "Mooses." What does the metaphor in line 4 describe?

7. **Evaluate Inferences** Look back at the chart you completed as you read the poems. Compare your charts in class. Do you all agree on the inferences you made about each poem's meaning?

8. **Make Judgments** Reread "Mooses" and use a web like the one shown to record details in the poem that are funny or sad. Is "Mooses" a mostly sad poem or a mostly humorous one? Support your judgments with details from the poem.

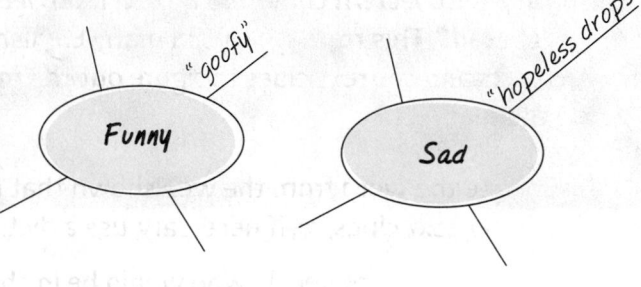

Extension and Challenge

9. **Creative Project: Writing** We often think of the things around us, such as cars, computers, or pets, as having personalities of their own. Choose an animal or object. Using **personification,** write a poem that shows the animal or object you chose with human qualities. Share your poem with the class.

How can POETRY surprise you?

Discuss in class the element of surprise in these poems: Did each poem include something that you did not expect? Think of language as well as message.

COMMON CORE

RL 1 Cite textual evidence to support inferences drawn from the text. RL 4 Determine the meaning of words and phrases as they are used in a text, including figurative meanings. RL 6 Explain how an author develops the point of view of the speaker in a text.

Vocabulary in Context

▲ VOCABULARY PRACTICE

To show your understanding of the vocabulary words, choose the letter of the term that is most closely related to the boldfaced word.

1. **blunder:** (a) dance, (b) cook, (c) stumble, (d) mumble
2. **lectern:** (a) voter, (b) guide, (c) desk, (d) chair
3. **cackle:** (a) laugh, (b) gather, (c) cry, (d) punish
4. **dreary:** (a) heavy, (b) gloomy, (c) ready, (d) old

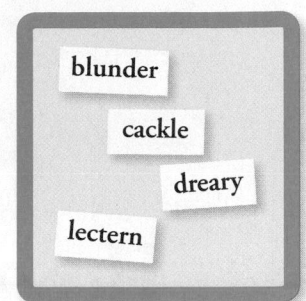

ACADEMIC VOCABULARY IN SPEAKING

> • associations   • device   • insight   • reaction   • specific

Poets use figurative language to describe aspects of life in a unique way. With a partner, discuss a **specific** example of figurative language from one of the poems. What is your **reaction** to the poet's use of figurative language? What **insight** about life did the poet hope to make? Use at least two Academic Vocabulary words in your discussion.

VOCABULARY STRATEGY: THE LATIN ROOT *lect*

The vocabulary word *lectern* contains the Latin root *lect,* which means "to choose" or "to read." This root appears in many English words. You can use other word parts and context clues to figure out the meaning of words containing the root *lect*.

> **COMMON CORE**
>
> **L 4b** Use Latin roots as clues to the meaning of a word.

PRACTICE Choose the word from the web shown that best completes each sentence. Use context clues, or, if necessary, use a dictionary.

1. We held a(n) _____ to decide who would be in charge of the Student Council.
2. People in other parts of the country may speak a different _____ of English.
3. Since this store has such a great _____, you can buy nearly anything here.
4. The teacher's _____ on literature was long, but interesting.
5. The house had been abandoned for years and showed signs of _____.

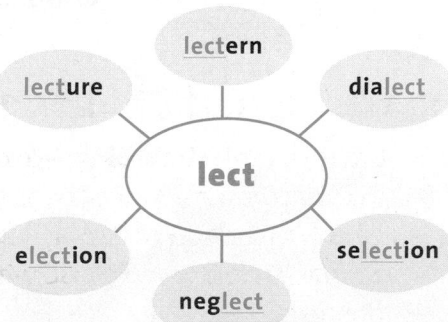

Interactive Vocabulary **THINK**central

Go to **thinkcentral.com**.
KEYWORD: HML6-635

who knows if the moon's
Poem by E. E. Cummings

Two Limericks
Poems by Edward Lear and Ogden Nash

How can LANGUAGE
be used to surprise you?

COMMON CORE

RL 4 Determine the meaning of words and phrases as they are used in a text.

Language can be used to inform you, to entertain you, and to try to change your mind about something. Language can also be used to surprise you, to develop your imagination, so that you can imagine worlds you might never actually experience.

WEB IT Try using language in an unexpected way. Think of something to describe, such as the sky. Instead of writing about the way it looks, try to describe how it sounds, feels, tastes, or smells. Create a web like the one shown to organize your response. Let your imagination go to work.

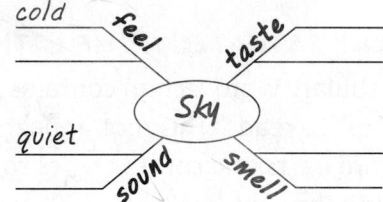

TEXT ANALYSIS: FORM IN POETRY

The way a poem uses the elements of poetry to express meaning is called the poem's **form.** Form can be the way the poem looks on the page. Form can be the way the poet uses sound and figures of speech. Form can be the way the poet uses rhymes and rhythms. The poems you are about to read are written in very different forms.

- The poem by E. E. Cummings is written in free verse. **Free verse** does not have a pattern of rhymes (in fact it may have no rhymes at all). Free verse is not written in meter and the lines may vary in length. "Alone in the Nets" (page 588) is written in free verse.

- The poems by Edward Lear and Ogden Nash are **limericks,** poems about very silly subjects. Despite their silly subject matter, limericks are written in a rigid form. They have five lines, a regular de-dum-de-dum meter, and a regular rhyme scheme.

READING STRATEGY: PARAPHRASE

Paraphrasing means restating a line or a stanza in your own words. Paraphrasing is a good way to see if you understand something you have read, especially if it's difficult or uses unfamiliar language. As you read the Cummings poem (the limericks are very easy) jot down your thoughts and try paraphrasing sections you have trouble understanding.

- When you come across a word or idea that you don't understand, **reread** the passage.

- To **clarify** a confusing detail, or make it more understandable, **paraphrase** the lines; that is, try to restate them in your own words.

As you read the poems that follow, use a graphic organizer like the one shown to record phrases or lines that give you trouble. Also note what meanings become clearer as you reread or paraphrase them.

Phrases or Lines	Why It's Confusing	Paraphrase
"coming out of a keen city" (line 2)	How can a city be "keen"?	leaving a grand city

 Complete the activities in your **Reader/Writer Notebook.**

Meet the Authors

E.E. Cummings
1894–1962

A New Kind of Poet
From age 8 to age 22, E. E. Cummings wrote one poem a day. While in college, he began to experiment with his writing. He ignored "proper" grammar and punctuation to write in a way that he felt best expressed his feelings.

Edward Lear
1812–1888

An Accidental Poet
Edward Lear considered himself an artist, and he first became famous for his drawings. Then he began writing limericks to entertain his employer's grandchildren. Lear's skill at writing these five-line nonsense poems was key to his lasting fame.

Ogden Nash
1902–1971

A Humorous Success
Odgen Nash's early serious poems were rarely published. When he started writing humorous verse, however, Nash quickly found success.

Authors Online
Go to **thinkcentral.com.** KEYWORD: HML6-637

THINK
central

who knows if the moon's

E. E. Cummings

who knows if the moon's
a balloon,coming out of a keen city
in the sky—filled with pretty people? **Ⓐ**
(and if you and i should

5 get into it,if they
should take me and take you into their balloon,
why then
we'd go up higher with all the pretty people

than houses and steeples and clouds:
10 go sailing
away and away sailing into a keen
city which nobody's ever visited,where

always
       it's
15   Spring)and everyone's
in love and flowers pick themselves **Ⓑ**

Ⓐ PARAPHRASE
Reread lines 1–3. What
words or phrases
in these lines are
confusing? Add them to
your chart.

Ⓑ FORM IN POETRY
Reread lines 13–16. Why
do you think Cummings
broke these lines the
way he did?

Two Limericks

There was an Old Man with a beard,
Who said, "It is just as I feared!—
Two Owls and a Hen,
Four Larks and a Wren,
5 Have all built their nests in my beard!"

— Edward Lear

A bugler named Dougal MacDougal
Found ingenious ways to be frugal.
He learned how to sneeze
In various keys,
5 Thus saving the price of a bugle. **C**

— Ogden Nash

C FORM IN POETRY
What do you notice about the rhymes in each **limerick?**

Comprehension

1. **Clarify** What does the speaker in "who knows if the moon's" imagine will happen if you go up in the balloon with him?

2. **Recall** In the first limerick, what does the Old Man find in his beard?

3. **Clarify** In the second limerick, why doesn't Dougal need a bugle?

⟨COMMON CORE⟩

RL 4 Determine the meaning of words and phrases as they are used in a text.

Text Analysis

4. **Paraphrase** Look back at the graphic organizer you completed as you read. What parts of "who knows if the moon's" were you able to understand better after paraphrasing? Explain.

5. **Compare and Contrast Form** Using a chart like the one shown, compare and contrast the form of the limericks with the form of "who knows if the moon's."

	"who knows if the moon's"	Two Limericks
Rhythm and Rhyme	no regular rhythm or rhyme	regular rhythm, regular rhyme pattern (aabba)
Lines and Stanzas		
Shape		

6. **Analyze Imagery** What images does the speaker in "who knows if the moon's" create to help you imagine what the city in the sky will be like?

7. **Analyze Free Verse** Cummings' poem is written in free verse but it still has rhymes and a kind of rhythm. What rhyming words can you find? What examples of **alliteration**—consonant sounds repeated in words close together—can you find? Read the poem aloud to see how the lines of different lengths create a rhythm.

8. **Visualize** What funny images, or pictures, do the limericks put in your mind?

Extension and Challenge

9. **Creative Project: Writing** Write a few limericks of your own using silly rhymes. Imitate the beat and rhyme scheme of the limericks you read. Often limericks, like the one here by Lear, open with the words "There was" or "There once was."

How can LANGUAGE be used to surprise you?

Look back at the web you completed on page 636. Using the words you recorded there, or new words, write a free verse poem about what you imagine a city above the sky would be like. Try to use sound effects, figures of speech, and unusual graphic elements, as Cummings does.

Good Hotdogs / Ricos hot dogs
Poem by Sandra Cisneros

Ode to an Artichoke
Poem by Pablo Neruda

When is FOOD more than fuel?

COMMON CORE

RL 4 Determine the meaning of words and phrases as they are used in a text, including figurative meanings; analyze the impact of a specific word choice on tone.

If food were only useful for keeping us alive, people would probably just eat the same thing day after day. However, food serves many purposes. Sitting down to eat allows us to spend time with family and friends, celebrate important events, and build traditions. For the two writers whose poems you are about to read, food sparks memories—and their imagination.

DISCUSS How do you feel about certain foods? Do some foods really comfort you and make you feel happy? What associations do you have with those foods that make you happy? Are there any foods you could write a poem about?

TEXT ANALYSIS: TONE

Imagine a friend said to you, "Hey, nice shoes." You would know whether this comment was honest or sarcastic based on the tone of your friend's voice.

Recognizing tone is also important when you think about the meaning of a poem. The **tone** of a poem is the poet's attitude toward the subject. Tone can usually be described with a single word, such as *humorous, respectful,* or *sarcastic.* Poets create tone mainly through word choice.

The two poems in this lesson are about food. As you read, use these clues to identify each poet's attitude:

- Identify the **subject.** Ask, "Is the poet writing about something more than food?"

- Notice the **images** and descriptions. Are they serious, silly, frightening, or something else?

- Decide how the **speaker** feels about the subject. Does the speaker seem happy, sad, angry, or amused?

Review: **Personification**

READING STRATEGY: SET A PURPOSE FOR READING

Your **purpose for reading** "Good Hotdogs" and "Ode to an Artichoke" is to identify the tone of each poem and then compare and contrast the tones. Read the poems twice. First read them to understand what they are about. The second time you read, look for images and descriptions that are clues to tone. Record the clues in a chart like the one shown. You will be asked to do more with this chart later.

	"Good Hotdogs"	"Ode to an Artichoke"
What is the subject of the poem?	memories of sharing hot dogs with a friend	the life of an artichoke
Which images stand out?	"... the store that smelled like steam"	

Complete the activities in your **Reader/Writer Notebook.**

Meet the Authors

Sandra Cisneros
born 1954

Doubly Rich Writer
As a young child, Sandra Cisneros spoke English to her mother and Spanish to her father. Cisneros says bilingual speakers are "doubly rich. You have two ways of looking at the world."

Pablo Neruda
1904–1973

Poet from the Start
Growing up in Chile, Ricardo Basoalto was inspired by his country's plants and trees. By age ten, he was already thinking of himself as a poet. At age 13, he published his poetry— after renaming himself Pablo Neruda. In 1971 Neruda received the Nobel Prize for literature.

BACKGROUND TO THE POEMS

Reading Poetry in Translation
Sometimes a poem written in one language is translated into another one so that more readers can enjoy it. A translation will not always have the same rhyme or rhythm as the original poem, but it should re-create the same tone.

Authors Online
Go to **thinkcentral.com.** KEYWORD: HML6-643

Good Hotdogs

Sandra Cisneros

for Kiki

Fifty cents apiece
To eat our lunch
We'd run
Straight from school
5 Instead of home
Two blocks Ⓐ
Then the store
That smelled like steam
You ordered
10 Because you had the money
Two hotdogs and two pops for here
Everything on the hotdogs
Except pickle lily[1]
Dash those hotdogs
15 Into buns and splash on
All that good stuff
Yellow mustard and onions
And french fries piled on top all

Ⓐ **TONE**
Reread lines 1–6. Which words in these lines show that the speaker and her friend are eager to eat hot dogs together?

---

1. **pickle lily:** or piccalilli, a type of relish.

Ricos hot dogs

Sandra Cisneros

para Kiki

Cincuenta centavos cada uno
Para almorzar
Corríamos
Directo de la escuela
5 Sin pasar por la casa
Dos cuadras
Y a la tienda
Que olía a vapor
Tú los pedías
10 Porque traías el dinero
Dos *hot dogs* y dos sodas
Los *hot dogs* con todo
Menos pepinillos
Pon de volada las salchichas
15 En los panes y échales
Todo lo rico
Mostaza y cebolla
Y papas fritas encima todo

Rolled up in a piece of wax
20 Paper for us to hold hot
In our hands
Quarters on the counter
Sit down
Good hotdogs
25 We'd eat
Fast till there was nothing left
But salt and poppy seeds even
The little burnt tips
Of french fries
30 We'd eat
You humming
And me swinging my legs **B**

B **TONE**
Which words and descriptions in lines 19–32 might hint at a joyful attitude?

Envuelto en papel
20 Encerado para agarrarlo calientito
En las manos
Pesetas en el mostrador
Y a sentarnos
Ricos *hot dogs*
25 Nos los comíamos
Rápido hasta que no quedaba nada
Más que sal y semillas hasta
Las puntitas quemadas
De las papas
30 Nos las comíamos
Tú tarareando
Y yo columpiando las piernas

Translated into Spanish by Liliana Valenzuela

ODE TO AN ARTICHOKE

Pablo Neruda

The soft-hearted
artichoke
put on armor,
stood at attention, raised
5 a small turret[1]
and kept itself
watertight
under
its scales. **G**
10 Beside it,
the fertile plants
tangled,
turned into
tendrils, cattails,
15 moving bulbs.

G PERSONIFICATION AND TONE
Reread lines 1–9. What words compare the artichoke to a soldier? How does the speaker feel about the artichoke?

---

1. **turret:** a small tower.

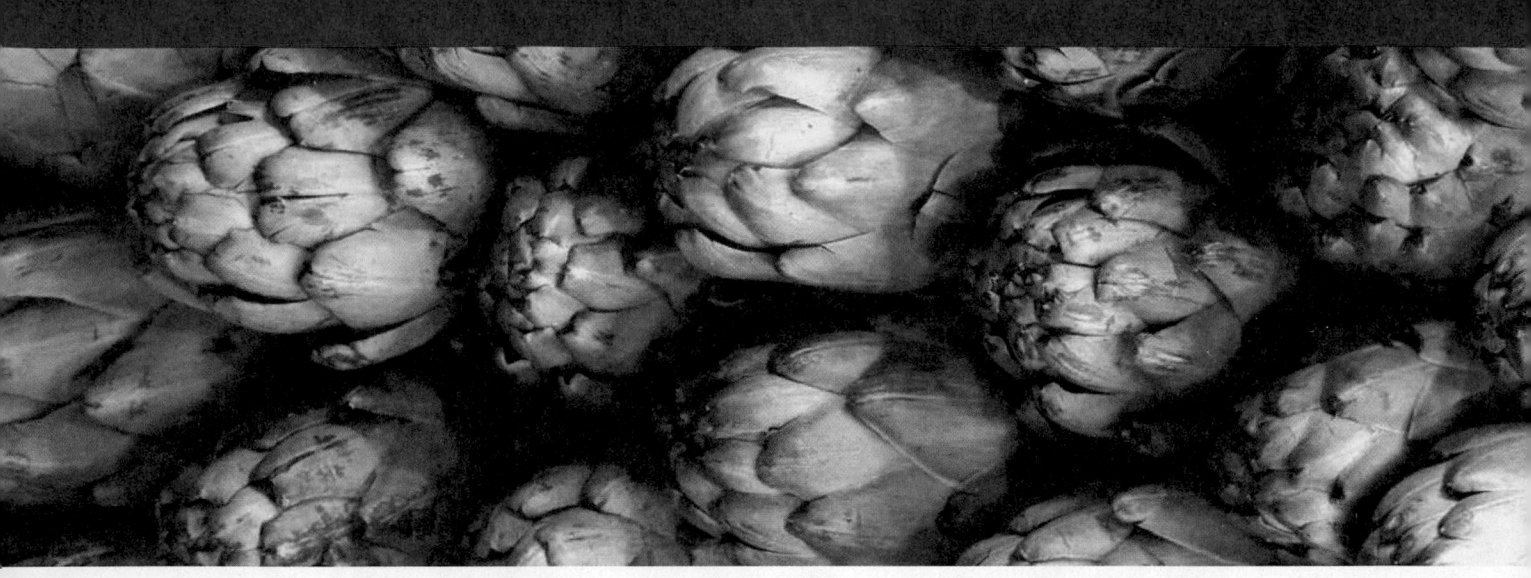

In the subsoil
the red-whiskered
carrot slept,
the grapevine
20 parched the shoots
that wine climbs up,
the cabbage
busied itself
with trying on skirts,
25 the marjoram[2]
with making the world smell sweet, **D**
and the gentle
artichoke
in the kitchen garden,
30 equipped like a soldier,
burnished[3]
like a grenade,
was full of itself.
And one day,
35 packed with others,
in big willow
baskets, it marched
through the market
to act out its dream—

---

2. **marjoram** (mär'jər-əm): a sweet herb used in cooking.

3. **burnished:** polished.

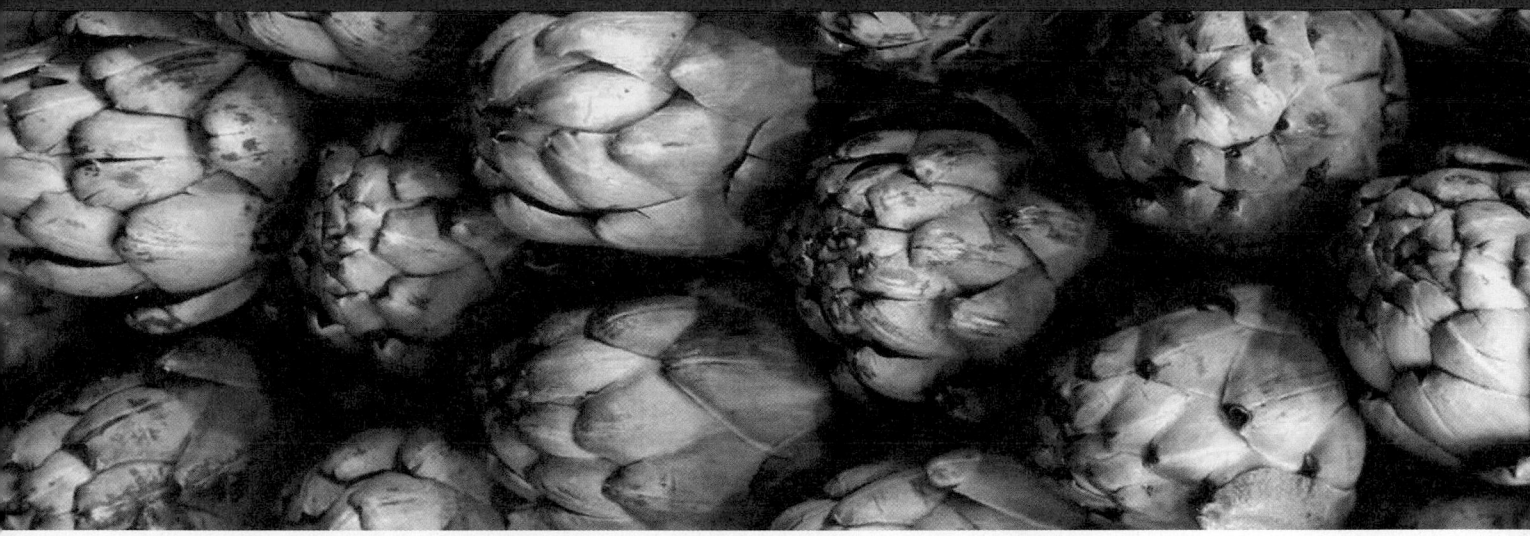

40 the militia.[4]
It was never as martial[5]
in rows
as at the fair.
Among the vegetables,
45 men in white shirts
were
the artichokes'
marshals,
closed ranks,
50 commands, **E**
the explosion
of a falling crate;
but
then
55 Maria
shows up
with her basket,
fearlessly
chooses
60 an artichoke,
studies it, squints at it
against the light like an egg,
buys it,

E **FIGURATIVE LANGUAGE AND TONE**
Which metaphors and similes in lines 27–50 compare the artichoke to a soldier going into battle? How does the speaker feel about these "soldiers"?

---

4. **militia** (mə-lǐsh′ə): military force used in emergencies.

5. **martial** (mär′shəl): relating to the armed forces.

dumps it
65 into her bag
with a pair of shoes,
a white cabbage and
a bottle
of vinegar
70 till
she enters the kitchen
and drowns it
in the pot. **F**
And so
75 this armored vegetable
men call an artichoke
ends its career
in peace.
Later,
80 scale by scale,
we strip
this delight
and dine on
the peaceful pulp
85 of its green heart. **G**

Translated into English by Cheli Durán

F IMAGES AND TONE
Which images in lines
55–73 convey the
speaker's attitude
toward the artichoke?

G TONE
Reread lines 74–85. How
can you tell that the
speaker feels sympathy
and respect for the
artichoke?

Comprehension

1. **Clarify** What do you know about the speaker in "Good Hotdogs"? Who do you think Kiki is—the person the poem is dedicated to?

2. **Recall** In "Ode to an Artichoke," what happens to the artichoke after Maria buys it?

Text Analysis

● 3. **Analyze Imagery** Which words and phrases in "Good Hotdogs" help you taste and smell the girls' lunch?

● 4. **Analyze Personification** How is the artichoke personified? How are the other foods in the garden personified? (Are any of the images of the foods humorous? Look at the cabbage.)

5. **Analyze an Ode** A traditional **ode** is a serious poem written to praise a person, an event, or something in nature in a dignified way. How is "Ode to an Artichoke" like a traditional ode? How is it different?

Comparing Tone

Now that you have read both poems, you can finish filling in your chart. Be sure to add the final question to your chart.

	"Good Hotdogs"	"Ode to an Artichoke"
What is the subject of the poem?	memories of sharing hot dogs with a friend	the life of an artichoke
Which images stand out?	"The store/That smelled like steam"	
What is the tone, or the poet's attitude toward the subject of the poem?		

When is FOOD more than fuel?

Has either poem changed the way you think about food? Support your response with examples from the poems.

COMMON CORE

RL 4 Determine the meaning of words and phrases as they are used in a text, including figurative meanings; analyze the impact of a specific word choice on tone.

Language

◆ **GRAMMAR IN CONTEXT: Combine Sentences**

COMMON CORE

L 3a Vary sentence patterns for meaning, reader/listener interest, and style. **W 3** Write narratives to develop real experiences.

To make your writing read more smoothly and to show relationships between your ideas, try using compound-complex sentences. A **compound-complex sentence** is a compound sentence (made up of two or more independent clauses) with one or more subordinate clauses added. The relationship between details is made clear in the compound-complex sentence below.

Three Simple Sentences: We played in the park for hours. We were frightened. The shadows looked like lurking monsters.

Compound-Complex Sentence: Though we played in the park for hours, we were frightened because the shadows looked like lurking monsters.

PRACTICE Add the subordinate clause to each compound sentence to create a compound-complex sentence.

1. I was seven, and I had just started second grade. (when I first met Eva)
2. She had moved in next door, but I was too shy to talk to her. (until I found out she was in my class)
3. We found out we had a lot in common, and soon we became best friends. (Though she was from a different country,)
4. One day it was very cold outside, yet we decided to play in the park. (since we didn't have much homework)

READING-WRITING CONNECTION

YOUR TURN Add to your appreciation of "Good Hotdogs" and "Ode to an Artichoke" by responding to this prompt. Then use the **revising tip** to make your sentences read more smoothly and clearly.

WRITING PROMPT	REVISING TIP
Extended Constructed Response: Narrative In **two or three paragraphs** tell a story about an experience in your life in which food played an important role. Perhaps the experience with food was good; perhaps it was not so good. Try to use images to help your reader share your experience. What tone will you aim for in your narrative? How did you feel about the food and that experience?	Review your writing. Can you combine any simple sentences into compound-complex sentences to make your writing clearer? If you read your writing aloud, you might find some sentences that will read more smoothly if they are combined.

Interactive Revision **THINK** central

Go to thinkcentral.com. KEYWORD: HML6-654

Writing for Assessment

 **COMMON CORE** W 2, W 4, W 10

1. READ THE PROMPT

Tone is an important element in any piece of writing. In writing assessments, you may be asked to compare and contrast the tone of two poems, stories, or essays.

> Although "Good Hotdogs" and "Ode to an Artichoke" both touch on the subject of food, their tones are not exactly the same. In three paragraphs, compare and contrast the two poems. Describe the tone of each poem, and explain whether the tones are more similar or different. Support your response by using details from the poems.

◀ **STRATEGIES IN ACTION**

1. I need to identify the **similarities and differences** between the poems.

2. I need to describe each poet's **attitude** toward the subject and decide if those attitudes are more alike or different.

3. I need to include **examples** of images, descriptions, and the speaker's feelings to support my ideas.

2. PLAN YOUR WRITING

Using the chart you filled out for the two poems, consider how the tones of the poems are similar and different. Then think about how to set up your response.

- Decide on a main idea for your response.
- Reread the poems and your chart to make sure you have enough examples to support your ideas.
- Make an outline to help organize your response. This sample outline shows one way you might organize your three paragraphs.

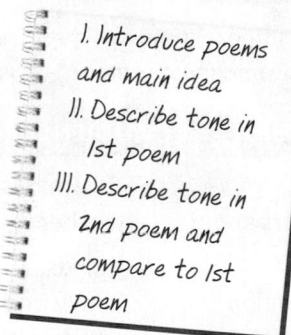

I. Introduce poems and main idea
II. Describe tone in 1st poem
III. Describe tone in 2nd poem and compare to 1st poem

3. DRAFT YOUR RESPONSE

Paragraph 1 Include the titles of the poems and the names of the poets. State whether the tones of the poems are more similar or different.

Paragraph 2 Describe the subject and tone of the first poem. Identify the images, descriptions, and speaker's feelings that help develop the tone.

Paragraph 3 Describe the subject and tone of the second poem. Explain which images, descriptions, and speaker's feelings help develop the tone. Tell how the tone is similar to and different from the tone of the first poem.

Revision Ask two classmates to read your response and look for errors such as sentence fragments and run-on sentences. Revise your writing as needed.

Writing Workshop
INFORMATIVE TEXT

Online Feature Article

The World Wide Web has given people around the world the opportunity to share their thoughts about all sorts of topics. In this workshop you will learn how to write your own article for the Web. Your article will focus on a topic, person, event, or place that interests you. Using a variety of online resources, you will enrich your writing and make it appealing to a broad range of readers.

 Complete the workshop activities in your **Reader/Writer Notebook.**

WRITE WITH A PURPOSE

WRITING TASK

Write an **online feature article** about a topic, person, event, or place that interests you.

Idea Starters
- tourist guide for a favorite city or town
- profile of a musician, writer, or athlete
- analysis of an event in the news
- explanation of a hobby or activity

THE ESSENTIALS

Here are some common purposes, audiences, and formats for informative online writing.

PURPOSES	AUDIENCES	FORMATS
• to inform readers about a topic • to develop and maintain an online readership	• classmates and teacher • friends, family, and community members • Web users with interests in the topic • fans of your person or place	• news or magazine article • encyclopedia article • wiki article • electronic brochure • podcast

COMMON CORE TRAITS

1. DEVELOPMENT OF IDEAS
- introduces a topic and states a **controlling idea**
- supports the topic with evidence, such as **relevant facts, details,** and **quotations**
- provides a **concluding section** that follows from the information

2. ORGANIZATION OF IDEAS
- **logically organizes** information
- includes **formatting, links,** and **multimedia**
- uses appropriate **transitions** to connect ideas

3. LANGUAGE FACILITY AND CONVENTIONS
- uses **precise language** and **domain-specific vocabulary**
- maintains a **formal style**
- uses correct **pronouns**
- reflects correct **grammar, mechanics,** and **spelling**

Writing Online

THINK central

Go to **thinkcentral.com**.
KEYWORD: HML6N-656

Planning/Prewriting

COMMON CORE — **W 2a–f** Write informative/explanatory texts to examine a topic. **W 5** Develop and strengthen writing by planning. **W 6** Use technology to produce and publish writing. **W 8** Gather relevant information from multiple print and digital sources.

Getting Started

CHOOSE A TOPIC

Think about all the topics that interest you. Try to come up with at least three ideas and then do some quick research. Your goal is to find out how much information is available on each possible topic. Choose a topic that has plenty of available information but not so much that you can't cover it well. To help guide your research, write each topic or idea as a clearly-worded **research question** that you are trying to answer.

THINK ABOUT AUDIENCE AND PURPOSE

Think about why you are writing your article and who might read it. For example, if you write about your favorite kind of music, your audience would probably be people who also enjoy that music. Your **purpose** might be to tell your **audience** about a new group you discovered or to review a concert you've just attended.

FIND PRINT AND DIGITAL SOURCES

As you begin to research your ideas, look for both print and digital sources. Choose sources that provide unbiased, up-to-date information. Reliable sources include newspapers and magazines, university Web sites, and government sites.

Keep a record of all your sources. For print sources, write down the author and title. For online sources, note the correct Web address, or URL. Briefly summarize the information from each source.

For additional research strategies, see pages 1010–1027.

▶ **TIPS FOR FINDING A FOCUS:**

- Look for topics in local, national, or international news.
- Review your class notes for topics that relate to an interest you have.
- Read blogs or wikis that your teachers or classmates recommend.
- Consider your interests outside of school as a source of possible topics.

▶ **ASK YOURSELF:**

- Who would be most interested in my topic?
- What does my audience probably already know about my topic?
- What **background information** should I provide?
- Will I need to add and define any **domain-specific,** or specialized, **vocabulary** terms?
- Where might I post my article?

▶ **WHAT DOES IT LOOK LIKE?**

Sources	Comments
Book: <u>We're There! Boston</u> by Elizabeth Skinner Grumbach	interactive tourist guidebook; has games, photos, and historical events
Web site: www.boston.com	has travel guide; includes info about Boston neighborhoods and activities
Web site: www.thefreedomtrail.org	describes all the historic places on Boston's Freedom Trail

Planning/Prewriting *continued*

Getting Started

GATHER EVIDENCE

Use a graphic organizer to record evidence—quotations, facts, examples, or multimedia—that is relevant to your topic. Evidence is **relevant** is if it strongly related to the ideas you want to present.

▶ **WHAT DOES IT LOOK LIKE?**

From a Print Source	From a Digital Source
A statue of Mary Dyer sits on Beacon Hill. She worked hard for religious freedom. But in 1660 she was executed on Boston Common because she refused to give up her beliefs. <u>Mary Dyer: Biography of a Rebel Quaker</u>	The Shaw Memorial "serves as a reminder of … the Civil War. In particular, it serves as a memorial to the group of men who were among the first African Americans to fight in that war." www.nps.gov/boaf/ historyculture/shaw.htm

DRAFT A CONTROLLING IDEA

Think of the **controlling idea** as the best answer to your **research question.** Your controlling idea, or thesis statement, states what you want your audience to understand about your topic. As you develop your article, you may need to revise your controlling idea or try a new approach.

▶ **WHAT DOES IT LOOK LIKE?**

Boston is not just about great sports teams such as the Red Sox and the Celtics. The capital of Massachusetts has a rich history that goes all the way back to even before the Puritans.

CREATE A STORYBOARD

A **storyboard** shows how you want to organize and present the information you have collected. Your storyboard should note where you want to include **links** to other Web sites, **graphics,** and **multimedia.** Use **titles, headings, bullet points,** and other types of **formatting** to make it easier for your audience to understand and navigate your article.

▶ **WHAT DOES IT LOOK LIKE?**

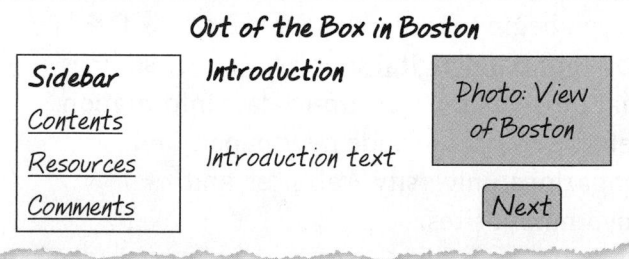

PEER REVIEW Share your controlling idea with a classmate. Describe the research you gathered. Ask: How well do you think this information supports my controlling idea? Then exchange storyboards and ask: Do you think it will be easy for my audience to follow my article?

YOUR TURN List possible research questions in your *Reader/Writer Notebook.* Choose one and gather information about it. Draft a controlling idea and create a storyboard, or plan, for your online article.

Drafting

This chart shows a structure for developing a well-organized online feature article.

 **COMMON CORE** **W 4** Produce clear, coherent writing appropriate to task, purpose, and audience. **L 2a** Use punctuation to set off nonrestrictive/parenthetical elements.

Organizing Your Online Feature Article

INTRODUCTION

- Grab your audience's attention with a **question, quotation,** or **anecdote** (brief story).
- Provide your audience with enough **background** to understand the topic.
- Establish a **formal writing style** by using **precise language** and avoiding slang.
- Include the **controlling idea** you drafted earlier.

▼

BODY

- Develop your controlling idea with **relevant facts, details,** and **examples.**
- Use appropriate **transitions,** such as *also* and *even though,* to connect ideas.
- Incorporate **multimedia** and **links** to give more depth and interest to your article.
- Use **formatting,** such as **headings** and **titles,** to help your audience navigate your article.

▼

CONCLUDING SECTION

- Write a **concluding section** that builds on what you have written and summarizes the main ideas of your article.

GRAMMAR IN CONTEXT: NONRESTRICTIVE/PARENTHETICAL ELEMENTS

A **nonrestrictive phrase** or clause adds information that is not essential to the meaning of a sentence. When writing, you can include nonrestrictive phrases and clauses to add interesting details. Use commas, parentheses, or dashes to set off nonrestrictive elements from the rest of the sentence. The highlighted words in this example show how one student used nonrestrictive phrases and clauses in her draft. Notice how each nonrestrictive element is punctuated.

> After breakfast, we decided to walk Boston's Freedom Trail, which is marked in red bricks and runs for about 2.5 miles. The Trail leads to 16 major historical sites. Each site, as we soon discovered, has something to do with the American Revolution. The last stop on the Trail is the USS Constitution (also called Old Ironsides).

 YOUR TURN Write a draft of your article, using your storyboard as a guide. Use commas, parentheses, or dashes to set off nonrestrictive elements. Add appropriate multimedia and links.

Revising

As you revise your article, make sure your information supports your controlling idea. The following chart will help you revise and rewrite the parts of your article that need reworking.

ONLINE FEATURE ARTICLE

Ask Yourself	Tips	Revision Strategies
1. Does my introduction grab the reader's attention?	▶ **Highlight** attention-grabbing questions, quotations, or anecdotes.	▶ **Add** a compelling question, quotation, or anecdote to capture your audience.
2. Is my controlling idea clear and suitable for my audience and purpose?	▶ **Circle** the controlling idea of your article.	▶ **Add** a controlling idea if one is missing. **Rewrite** the existing one to more clearly state the main idea of your article.
3. Have I organized information in a clear, logical way?	▶ **Underline** links, headings, bulleted lists, and menu options.	▶ **Reorganize** the text, links, and menu options to make information easier to find and read.
4. Does my evidence support my controlling idea?	▶ **Draw a box** around text or multimedia that doesn't support your controlling idea.	▶ **Delete** unrelated text or multimedia. **Add** details, definitions, quotations, or facts for any ideas that are not supported.
5. Have I maintained a formal writing style?	▶ **Highlight** words or phrases that seem too casual.	▶ **Delete** words or phrases that are too informal for your audience and purpose.
6. Does my concluding section follow from the body of my article?	▶ **Put a check mark** next to the sentences in your concluding section that best summarize what your article is all about.	▶ **Add** sentences that summarize your main ideas.

YOUR TURN

PEER REVIEW Have a peer use this chart to evaluate your online article. Ask: Which ideas need more support? Is my use of multimedia helpful or distracting? What other links could I include?

ANALYZE A STUDENT DRAFT

COMMON CORE

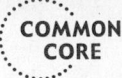

W 2a Use multimedia to aid comprehension. **W 5** Develop and strengthen writing by revising, rewriting, or trying a new approach. **SL 5** Include multimedia components to clarify information.

Read this draft, paying attention to the comments about its strengths and the suggestions for improvement.

Out of the Box in Boston
by Daria P.

▼ Contents

- Introduction
- Boston's Puritan Past
- Hiking the Freedom Trail
- Italy Rules! (Boston's North End)
- The Lady in Black and other Boston Legends
- The Harbor and Beyond

▼ **Additional Resources**

- Boston's Best Ice Cream
- Video Tours
- Feedback

Introduction

"Just as they were getting ready to start on their way, a strange enormous bird came by." That's a line from *Make Way for Ducklings*, a famous children's book written by Robert McCloskey. He was a New England writer who lived in Boston for several years. The "strange enormous bird" in his story is actually a swan boat. If you ever go to Boston's Public Garden, you can take a ride in one of these paddle-wheel boats. In the stern of each boat there is a giant swan made of fiberglass. The boats slowly glide around a lagoon in the Public Garden, which was the first of its kind in the United States.

For over 130 years, the Swan Boats have been carrying passengers. That might seem like a long time, but Boston's history goes back much further than the city's swan boats. This summer my uncle and I spent a whole day checking out the sites in Boston. Before our visit, the only thing I knew about Boston was that it had some great teams, such as the Celtics and the Red Sox. But now I realize that sports is just one small part of the city's past and present.

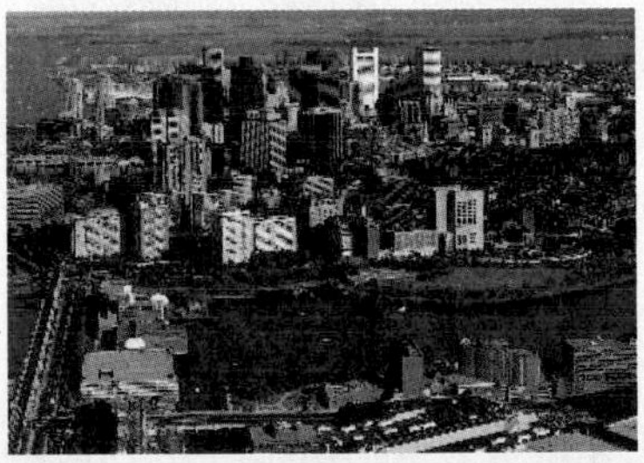

Daria begins with an **interesting quotation** from a children's book set in Boston.

The **sidebar** shows a clear, easy-to-navigate organization.

By making better use of text and multimedia features, Daria could turn her article into an interactive experience.

LEARN HOW **Use Text and Multimedia Features** In the first paragraph, Daria embeds links to external Web sites to add dimension to her article. However, she needs to take the same approach in her second paragraph. By adding more links to multimedia features, photographs, and video clips, she can take advantage of the online medium and help her audience better understand her topic.

DARIA'S REVISION TO *INTRODUCTION* ❷

That might seem like a long time, but Boston's history goes back much further than the city's swan boats. *link to site with video clips about Boston's colonial and revolutionary past, and to more information about the swan boats*

YOUR TURN Use the revision chart, the "Learn How" lesson, and the feedback you received to revise your article. Evaluate your use of multimedia and online text features. Try a new approach is something is not working.

Editing and Publishing

 **COMMON CORE**

W 5 Strengthen writing by editing. **L 1c–d** Recognize and correct inappropriate shifts in pronoun number and person; recognize and correct vague pronouns

In the editing stage, you correct any grammar, spelling, and punctuation mistakes. Also check to make sure all your online features and multimedia elements work before you publish your article. Be sure that your pages are easy to read and navigate.

GRAMMAR IN CONTEXT: AVOID PRONOUN PROBLEMS

A **pronoun** is a word used in place of one or more nouns or pronouns. An **antecedent** is the noun or pronoun that a pronoun refers to. Even for the most experienced writers, pronouns can be challenging to use correctly. These two rules can help you avoid common problems.

Rule	*Problems*
A pronoun must agree with its antecedent in number, person, and gender.	The **video game** has ~~their~~ flaws. [The antecedent video game is singular, so the pronoun its should be used] **You** write ~~their~~ own detective stories. [You is a second-person antecedent. Your is the correct pronoun] **Lucy** called ~~his~~ friend. [The feminine pronoun her should be used to describe Lucy]
Be sure that each pronoun refers clearly to only one person, place, or thing.	**Tony and Fred** want to become veterinarians. ~~He~~ now works at an animal shelter. [To be clear, the writer should replace He with the name Tony or Fred]

As Daria proofread her essay, she caught a few pronoun problems. Here is how she corrected them:

> After the trolley tour, we took a shortcut through the Boston Common back to the hotel. ~~It~~ had a lot of visitors. There was a street musician performing and a guy on stilts who nearly lost ~~their~~ balance. If tourists are looking for interesting sights in Boston, ~~you~~ just have to keep ~~your~~ eyes open.
>
> The Common   they   his   their

PUBLISH YOUR WRITING

After you have finished editing your article, you are ready to publish it. Consider these ideas to help you attract readers:

- E-mail your friends. Tell them about your article and how to find it.
- Post a link to your article in forums or online communities that you and your peers frequently visit.
- Create an interactive Web page to share your article with classmates.

Scoring Rubric

Use this rubric to evaluate your online feature article.

ONLINE FEATURE ARTICLE

SCORE	COMMON CORE TRAITS
6	• **Development** Effectively introduces a topic; clearly states an interesting controlling idea; offers varied and relevant evidence; ends powerfully • **Organization** Is effectively and logically organized; includes helpful text features or multimedia; uses varied transitions throughout • **Language** Ably uses precise words; maintains a formal style; shows a strong command of conventions
5	• **Development** Competently introduces a topic; states a clear controlling idea; offers relevant evidence; has a strong concluding section • **Organization** Is logically organized; includes text features or multimedia; effectively uses transitions • **Language** Uses precise words; generally maintains a formal style; has a few errors in conventions
4	• **Development** Introduces a topic; states a controlling idea; offers mostly relevant evidence; has an adequate concluding section • **Organization** Is mostly logically organized; could use some more text features or multimedia; needs more transitions • **Language** Uses some vague words; mostly maintains a formal style; includes a few distracting errors in conventions
3	• **Development** States a controlling idea, but the introduction could be more interesting; lacks enough evidence; has a somewhat weak concluding section • **Organization** Has some flaws in organization; needs more text features; uses multimedia that does not relate to the purpose; lacks many transitions • **Language** Needs more precise words; has frequent changes in style; has some critical errors in conventions
2	• **Development** Has a weak controlling idea; does not support most ideas; ends unexpectedly • **Organization** Has organizational flaws; lacks text features to guide readers; uses too much multimedia or not enough; lacks transitions throughout • **Language** Lacks precise words or uses them incorrectly; uses an informal style; has many errors in conventions
1	• **Development** Lacks a controlling idea, development, and a concluding section • **Organization** Has no organization, text features, or transitions; uses distracting multimedia • **Language** Uses vague words; has an inappropriate style; has major problems in conventions

Updating an Online Feature Article

As the author of an online feature article, your job now is to keep your published work updated. This may mean adding new information, replacing dead (broken) links, or even reorganizing the article to make it easier for readers to navigate. In this workshop, you will learn how to update and improve your online article.

 Complete the workshop activities in your **Reader/Writer Notebook**.

PRODUCE WITH A PURPOSE

TASK

Update your online feature article to provide new information on your topic, fix any navigation problems, and replace dead links. Be sure to obtain permission to use any multimedia elements that are covered by copyright laws.

COMMON CORE TRAITS

A STRONG UPDATE . . .

- replaces dead links and out-of-date information
- responds to readers' feedback in a respectful way
- adds or revises content to address new information about the topic
- changes design or navigation if necessary
- attracts new readers and holds the interest of returning readers

COMMON CORE

W 6 Use technology to publish writing and interact with others. **SL 1c–d** Pose and respond to questions by making comments; review key ideas and demonstrate understanding of multiple perspectives. **SL 5** Include multimedia components.

Maintaining Your Article

After publishing your article online, visit the site as often as you can to maintain it. Use these guidelines to help you:

- **Update Your Links** Check each link to make sure the Web address, or URL, is still working and connects to the information you intended. If you find any incorrect or dead links, update them to reflect the correct URL, find suitable replacements, or remove the links from the article.

- **Respond to Comments** If you have provided a way for readers to give feedback on your article, make sure to read everything that's posted. Address comments or requests for information promptly and politely. Remove inappropriate comments as quickly as possible.

- **Add a *Last Updated* Date** Include a line of text that gives the date you last updated your article. This lets your readers know how recent the information is and that you are committed to keeping it current.

Media Tools

THINK central

Go to **thinkcentral.com**.
KEYWORD: HML6N-664

Modifying and Improving Your Article

As you learn more about your topic and read user feedback, modify and improve your online feature article. You might modify your article for a variety of reasons, such as:

- **To Add Content** As new information about your topic becomes available, revise your article to include updated content and delete out-of-date information. If you have chosen a topic with aspects that change frequently (such as schedules for walking tours of city neighborhoods), you might consider adding a Recent News or Updates section.

- **To Address User Feedback** Readers may offer feedback on the accuracy of your facts, your navigational features, or your site design. Be willing to revise your work, or even try a new approach, to address helpful reader feedback.

- **To Redesign Your Article** Aim to make your article as visually attractive and reader-friendly as possible. To accomplish this, consider reorganizing the menu or navigational features, adding new images or multimedia, or changing fonts and backgrounds.

- **To Increase Your Readership** Whenever you make changes to your article, consider posting a status update on your social networking site. Send e-mail updates to your readers or post a link to your article on a related site. Your goal is to attract new readers and prompt former readers to return.

Matt76 (reader) said . . .

Your choice of video clips really made me understand what makes Boston such a special place. Did you get to go aboard the *USS Constitution* in Boston Harbor? I made a model of that ship when I was in fourth grade.

August 17, 3:30 PM

DariaP (site administrator) said . . .

Thanks for the comment. I wanted to go aboard the *USS Constitution* (nicknamed *Old Ironsides*), but there wasn't enough time. Besides, we had already taken a cruise around the Harbor. Keep your eye out for updates!

August 18, 9:15 AM

NEWS FEED

 **DariaP** Hello, fellow travelers. I finally got back to Boston on a field trip to the science museum. We had a blast. You can read all about this amazing museum in my **updated feature article**. Check it out!

 **YOUR TURN** Regularly visit your online feature article. Check if your links are still working, and then update, replace, or delete any dead links. Keep your content up-to-date and consider trying new approaches to engage your current readers and attract new ones.

Assessment Practice

DIRECTIONS Read these poems and answer the questions that follow.

Rain Sizes *by John Ciardi*

Rain comes in various sizes.
Some rain is as small as a mist.
It tickles your face with surprises,
And tingles as if you'd been kissed.

5 Some rain is the size of a sprinkle
And doesn't put out all the sun.
You can see the drops sparkle and twinkle,
And a rainbow comes out when it's done.

Some rain is as big as a nickle[1]
10 And comes with a crash and a hiss.
It comes down too heavy to tickle.
It's more like a splash than a kiss.

When it rains the right size and you're wrapped in
Your rainclothes, it's fun out of doors.
15 But run home before you get trapped in
The big rain that rattles and roars.

---

1. **nickle:** a spelling variation of the word *nickel*.

Rain in Ohio *by Mary Oliver*

The robin cries: *rain!*
The crow calls: *plunder!*

The blacksnake climbing
in the vines halts
5 his long ladder of muscle

while the thunderheads whirl up
out of the white west,

their dark hooves nicking
the tall trees as they come.

10 *Rain, rain, rain!* sings the robin
frantically, then flies for cover.

The crow hunches.
The blacksnake

pours himself swift and heavy
15 into the ground.

Reading Comprehension

Use "Rain Sizes" to answer questions 1–6.

1. Which statement describes the pattern of rhyme in this poem?

   A. The first and third and the second and fourth lines in each stanza rhyme.

   B. The first and second lines in each stanza rhyme.

   C. All four lines in each stanza have the same rhyme.

   D. The first and second and the third and fourth lines in each stanza rhyme.

2. Which description of rain is a simile?

   A. *Rain comes in various sizes.* (line 1)

   B. *Some rain is the size of a sprinkle* (line 5)

   C. *And a rainbow comes out when it's done.* (line 8)

   D. *Some rain is as big as a nickle* (line 9)

3. In line 4, the speaker uses a simile to compare the misty rain to —

   A. someone's face

   B. a kiss

   C. a surprise

   D. rainbows

4. Which phrase from the poem is an example of onomatopoeia?

   A. *Tickles your face* (line 3)

   B. *Put out all the sun* (line 6)

   C. *Run home before* (line 15)

   D. *Rattles and roars* (line 16)

5. Which image appeals to your sense of hearing?

   A. *Some rain is as small as a mist.*

   B. *You can see the drops sparkle and twinkle.*

   C. *And comes with a crash and a hiss.*

   D. *It comes down too heavy to tickle.*

6. You can infer that the speaker in "Rain Sizes" —

   A. does not notice the rain

   B. enjoys all types of rain

   C. stays indoors when it rains

   D. wishes the sun would come out

Use "Rain in Ohio" to answer questions 7–11.

7. In line 5, the speaker uses the metaphor "his long ladder of muscle" to emphasize the snake's —

   A. length and power

   B. speed and cunning

   C. size and dangerousness

   D. scaly skin and strong back

8. Read lines 6–9.

> "while the thunderheads whirl up
> out of the white west,
>
> their dark hooves nicking
> the tall trees as they come."

What are the thunderheads being compared to?

A. Tumbleweeds rolling

B. Wagons rumbling

C. Horses galloping

D. Trees swaying

9. Read lines 10–11.

> *"Rain, rain, rain!* sings the robin
> frantically, then flies for cover."

You can infer that when the robin sings "Rain, rain, rain!" it is —

A. expressing joy

B. sounding a warning

C. signaling its location

D. looking for a mate

10. The metaphor in lines 13–15 compares the blacksnake's movement to —

A. flowing liquid

B. distant thunder

C. heavy rains

D. the still air

11. What can you infer about how the birds and the snake feel about the approaching storm?

A. Curious

B. Confused

C. Fearful

D. Happy

> **Use both selections to answer question 12.**

12. In both poems, the descriptions of rain —

A. are scientific

B. include vivid imagery

C. use the same metaphors

D. have rhyming words

SHORT CONSTRUCTED RESPONSE
Write two or three sentences to answer each question.

13. In "Rain Sizes," what idea does the speaker emphasize by repeating the phrase "some rain is"?

14. Do you think "Rain in Ohio" describes the approach of a wild thunderstorm or a gentle rain? Give two examples from the poem to support your idea.

Write a paragraph to answer this question.

15. Find three images in "Rain in Ohio" that describe how the robin, the crow, and the blacksnake react to the storm. Are their reactions the same or different? Explain.

GO ON

Vocabulary

Use context clues and the definitions
of Latin or Greek words to answer the
following questions.

1. The Latin word *prendere* means "to seize."
   What word in the poems comes from the
   word *prendere*?

   A. Drop

   B. Fun

   C. Ladder

   D. Surprise

2. The Greek word *phrēn* means "the mind."
   What word in the poems comes from the
   word *phrēn*?

   A. Flies

   B. Frantically

   C. Home

   D. Whirls

3. The Latin word *pūrus* means "pure." What
   word in the poems comes from the word
   pūrus?

   A. Down

   B. Pours

   C. Put

   D. Rain

4. The Latin word *quiritare* means "to shriek
   or scream." What word in the poems
   comes from the word *quiritare*?

   A. Calls

   B. Cries

   C. Rattles

   D. Roars

5. The Latin word *assisa* means "a fixed
   quantity." What word in the poems comes
   from the word *assisa*?

   A. Long

   B. Plunder

   C. Size

   D. Swift

6. The prefix *co-* means "with," and the
   Latin word *operire* means "to close
   completely." What word in the poems
   comes from the Latin word *cooperire*?

   A. Cover

   B. Crow

   C. Ground

   D. Home

Revising and Editing

1. What is the BEST way to show correct subject-verb agreement?

   A. My cousin play a midfield position in lacrosse.

   B. My cousins plays a midfield position in lacrosse.

   C. My cousin do play a midfield position in lacrosse.

   D. My cousin plays a midfield position in lacrosse.

2. What is the BEST way to show correct subject-verb agreement?

   A. There are stars out tonight.

   B. There are star out tonight.

   C. There is stars out tonight.

   D. There was stars out tonight.

3. What is the BEST way to show correct subject-verb agreement?

   A. Is the boat at the dock?

   B. Are the boat at the dock?

   C. Is the boats at the dock?

   D. Was the boats at the dock?

4. What is the BEST way to show correct subject-verb agreement?

   A. A coin and shells was in his pocket.

   B. A coin and shells is in his pocket.

   C. Coins and shells was in his pocket.

   D. A coin and shells are in his pocket.

5. What is the BEST way to show correct subject-verb agreement?

   A. Either the guides or the teacher explain the owl's diet.

   B. Either the guide or the teacher explain the owl's diet.

   C. Either the guide or the teacher explains the owl's diet.

   D. Either the guide or the teachers explains the owl's diet.

6. What is the BEST way to show correct subject-verb agreement?

   A. My brother and sisters sings in the chorus.

   B. My brother and sisters is singing in the chorus.

   C. My brother and sisters sing in the chorus.

   D. My brothers and sister sings in the chorus.

7. What is the BEST way to show correct subject-verb agreement?

   A. Was there empty seats on the bus?

   B. Are there empty seats on the bus?

   C. Are there an empty seat on the bus?

   D. Is there empty seats on the bus?

671

Ideas for Independent Reading

Which questions from Unit 5 made an impression on you? Continue exploring with these books.

COMMON CORE

RL 10 Read and comprehend literature.

What can sports teach us?

Crash
by Jerry Spinelli

Sports can bring out the best or the worst in people. Crash Coogan, seventh-grade football star and part-time bully, is no different from anyone else—that is, until his grandfather, Scooter, comes for a visit and decides to stay.

Slam Dunk: Poems About Basketball
edited by Lillian Morrison

Forty-two poems describe such things as the brush of the ball as it leaves the tips of the fingers, the tension as the ball circles the rim, and the way the ball looks clinging to the side of the net as it goes in.

Strike Two
by Amy Goldman Koss

Gwen and Jess are ready for a summer of softball, but when the staff at the town newspaper goes on strike, things get ugly. Can Gwen hatch a plan that will bring the town and her team together again?

How do we respond to nature's mysteries?

Airborn
by Kenneth Oppel

A year after Matt pulled a dying balloonist onto his airship, he meets the man's granddaughter, Kate. Now he has to choose between loyalty to his captain and the desire to help Kate find proof of the fantastic creatures in her grandfather's journal.

Carver: A Life in Poems
by Marilyn Nelson

George Washington Carver was born a slave in 1864. His curiosity about nature pushed him to go to places African Americans had never been. By the time of his death in 1943, he had become an artist, an educator, and a world-renowned scientist.

Fossil Fish Found Alive: Discovering the Coelacanth
by Sally M. Walker

In 1938, Marjorie Courtenay-Latimer discovers a strange blue fin in a pile of specimens for her museum in South Africa. She thinks it is from a fish that was believed to be extinct.

How can poetry surprise you?

The Crow-Girl
by Bodil Bredsdorff

Before the Crow-Girl's grandmother died, she told the girl that some people feed you by looking at you, but others leave you ice-cold even in front of a roaring fire. Now that the girl is alone, will her grandmother's advice help her survive?

Technically, It's Not My Fault: Concrete Poems
by John Grandits

Robert is an ordinary boy with extraordinary ideas. One time he re-created Galileo's gravity experiment by using a tomato and a concrete block. It really wasn't his fault that the experiment went wrong.

The Penderwicks
by Jeanne Birdsall

When four eccentric sisters, their naturalist father, a canine escape-artist, two rabbits, a boy, and a gardening competition all come together, it's a summer no one can forget—even if Mrs. Tifton wishes she could.

6

Timeless Tales

MYTHS, LEGENDS, AND TALES

6 Share What You Know

Why do we tell STORIES?

Think of a movie that taught you about a historical event, a television program that inspired you in some way, or a novel that kept you laughing from the first page to the last. Stories are told for many reasons—some simply entertain us, while others teach us a lesson. Many stories are told year after year to pass on cultural values and traditions from one generation to the next.

ACTIVITY Recall an experience you've had or a story you've heard that you'd like to share with others. Now get together with a small group. As you take turns telling stories, consider these questions:

- Why do you think each person decided to tell the story he or she did?

- Which story do you think you will remember and retell? Why?

COMMON CORE

Preview Unit Goals

TEXT ANALYSIS
- Analyze characteristics of myths, legends, tall tales, and folk tales
- Determine a central idea of a text and how it is conveyed through particular details
- Provide a summary of the text distinct from personal opinions and judgments
- Analyze in detail how a key idea is introduced, illustrated, and elaborated in a text

READING
- Cite textual evidence to support analysis of what the text says explicitly as well as inferences drawn from the text
- Integrate information presented in different formats as well as in words to develop a coherent understanding of a topic

WRITING AND LANGUAGE
- Write a how-to explanation
- Write a compare-contrast essay
- Use capitalization and punctuation conventions correctly
- Vary sentence patterns for meaning

SPEAKING AND LISTENING
- Give and follow oral instructions

VOCABULARY
- Use Greek or Latin affixes as clues to the meaning of a word
- Gather vocabulary knowledge when considering a word or phrase important to comprehension
- Use the relationship between particular words to better understand each of the words

ACADEMIC VOCABULARY
- circumstance
- contribute
- element
- significant
- tradition

Myths, Legends, and Tales

A young girl lives happily ever after, thanks to a fairy godmother and a glass slipper. A lion learns the value of a small friend. A knight defeats a hideous monster. Many stories that are still popular today, such as Aesop's fables and medieval legends, were first told hundreds, even thousands of years ago. Handed down by word of mouth and later recorded in writing, these stories do more than entertain. They help us to understand and appreciate other times and cultures.

COMMON CORE

Included in this workshop:
RL 1 Cite textual evidence to support analysis of what the text says explicitly as well as inferences drawn from the text.
RL 2 Determine a central idea of a text and how it is conveyed through particular details.

Part 1: What Stories Live On?

In this unit, you will read many traditional stories that have stood the test of time, such as myths, legends, and several kinds of folk tales. Each of these types of traditional tales has specific characteristics, or stylistic elements, that you will see again and again. Examine this graphic to discover some of these stylistic elements.

STYLISTIC ELEMENTS OF CLASSICAL AND TRADITIONAL STORIES

MYTH
Classical story created to explain mysteries of the universe

- Often explains how something connected with humans or nature came to be
- Usually features gods, goddesses, and other beings with supernatural powers as well as human flaws

LEGEND
Traditional story believed to be based on real people and events

- Tells about a hero or heroine with special powers and admirable qualities
- Describes the hero's or heroine's struggle against a powerful force

TALL TALE
Humorous story about events and characters that are exaggerated

- Often features a character who is "larger than life"—stronger, louder, or more extraordinary than a regular person
- Uses **hyperboles**—figures of speech that use exaggeration for effect: "My dog weighs a ton."

MODEL 1: MYTH

This myth comes from the Creek, a Native American tribe from the southern United States. What mysteries of the natural world does the myth explain?

How Day and Night Came

Creek myth retold by **Virginia Pounds Brown** and **Laurella Owens**

The question was: how shall day and night be divided? Some wanted it always to be daytime; others wanted it always to be night.

After much talk, the chipmunk said: "I see that the raccoon has rings on his tail divided equally, first a dark color and then a light color. I
5   think day and night should be divided like the rings on the raccoon's tail."

The animals were surprised at the wisdom of the chipmunk. They adopted his plan and divided day and night like the rings on the raccoon's tail, one succeeding the other in regular order.

10   The bear was so envious of the chipmunk's wisdom and of the attention given that small creature, that he attacked him. He scratched the chipmunk's back so deeply that even today chipmunks have stripes on their backs.

Close Read

1. Describe the plan the chipmunk devises to divide day and night.

2. One stylistic element that most traditional stories share is repetition. Events occur in threes, for example, or specific words and phrases are repeated. What examples of repetition do you see here?

3. In addition to the origin of day and night, what other mystery of the natural world does this myth explain?

MODEL 2: TALL TALE

Now read this excerpt from a tall tale about a character named Sal Fink.

from **SAL FINK** *Hi-i-i-i-i-i-ow-ow-ow-who-whooh!*

Tall tale retold by **Robert D. San Souci**

. . . Mississippi River boatman Mike Fink had one daughter, Sal, who was a "ring-tailed roarer" in her own right. In fact, she became known far and wide as the "Mississippi Screamer," because of the way she would bellow "*Hi-i-i-i-i-i-ow-ow-ow-who-whooh!*" when she was feeling high-
5   spirited or ready for a fight. Up and down the river she was known for fighting a duel with a thunderbolt, riding the river on the back of an alligator while "standen upright an' dancing 'Yankee Doodle,'" and even outracing a steamboat poling her own keelboat with a hand-picked crew.

Close Read

1. What qualities make Sal Fink "larger than life"?

2. The boxed detail describes one unbelievable feat that Sal has accomplished. What else has Sal done that seems unbelievable or exaggerated?

Part 2: What Can Stories Teach Us?

The Creek myth you just read does more than explain two mysteries of the natural world. It also teaches readers about the qualities that mattered most to the Creek. One such quality is wisdom. Did you notice that all the animals, except for the jealous bear, respected the chipmunk? Read between the lines of traditional stories from various cultures and you can draw conclusions about the **cultural values**—ideas and beliefs—that were honored by that culture.

Consider this Vietnamese folk tale about two brothers named Kim and De. Kim is a hard-working man who is embarrassed by De's laziness. Notice how asking yourself a few questions about this traditional story can help you make inferences about Vietnamese cultural values.

from The Beggar in the Blanket

Vietnamese folk tale retold by **Gail B. Graham**

. . . Kim's wife was a gentle and thoughtful woman, and she felt sorry for De.

"It's been more than a month since we've seen your brother," she said to Kim one night. "Why don't you ask him to come and have dinner
5   with us?"

Kim was surprised. "What would Nguyen and Ton and Cao and Duc and all my other friends think if they came in and found that good-for-nothing brother of mine sitting at our table?" he asked. "They would be insulted! They would never come to my house again!"

10   "So much the worse for them," replied his wife. "Friends are not the same as a brother."

"And it's a good thing they're not!" Kim retorted. "The whole village would starve if all my friends were as lazy as De."

Kim's wife could see that it was no use arguing with her stubborn
15   husband. Nevertheless she vowed that she would make Kim understand the value of a brother, even a poor and lazy brother like De.

QUESTIONS TO ASK

Which characters have admirable qualities, and which have flaws?
Kim's "thoughtful" wife is described positively, while her husband is "stubborn," and De is "lazy."

What lessons do the characters learn?
Kim's wife vows to teach her husband a lesson about the importance of family.

What can you infer about this culture's values?
The people who told this tale valued family and believed in the value of hard work.

MODEL 1: CULTURAL VALUES IN A MYTH

In this ancient Greek myth, two gods disguise themselves as humans and travel from door to door in search of food and shelter. Baucis and Philemon, a poor couple, welcome the strangers into their home. Find out what happens when the gods reveal their identity to their hosts.

from BAUCIS AND PHILEMON
Greek myth retold by **Olivia E. Coolidge**

"Philemon, you have welcomed us beneath your roof this day when richer men refused us shelter. Be sure those shall be punished who would not help the wandering stranger, but you shall have whatever reward you choose. Tell us what you will have."

5   The old man thought for a little with his eyes bent on the ground, and then he said: "We have lived together here for many years, happy even though the times have been hard. But never yet did we see fit to turn a stranger from our gate or to seek reward for entertaining him. To have spoken with the immortals face to face is a thing few men can
10 boast of. . . ."

Close Read

1. Consider how the gods respond to Philemon's actions. What can you infer about the kinds of behavior that were rewarded in ancient Greek culture?

2. Reread the boxed text. What does it tell you about how the Greeks felt about their gods?

MODEL 2: CULTURAL VALUES IN A LEGEND

Many movies and novels tell about the daring deeds of Robin Hood, a hero of medieval legend. Though he was an outlaw, Robin Hood was celebrated by many because he fought to help the helpless.

from Robin Hood *of* Sherwood Forest
Legend retold by **Ann McGovern**

Life in those olden days was oftentimes cruel and unjust for the good yeomen and poor folk who were made to pay large sums of money to the nobles and the rich. High taxes, outrageous rents, and fines made the poor even poorer as they tried to scratch a life out of the fields and forests.

5   Indeed, the laws of the rich were such that whosoever stepped into the King's forest to kill a deer to keep their families from starving or cut wood to keep from freezing were guilty of crime and, if caught, could be hanged.

So it was that men, such as Robin Hood, Will Stutely, Midge the
10 Miller's son, and others as honest as these, were called outlaws through no wish or fault of their own.

Close Read

1. Which details suggest that the people who first told this legend were fed up with the unfair laws of the rich?

2. Reread the boxed details, noting how the characters are described. What qualities do you think were valued in medieval times?

Part 3: Analyze the Text

Classical Greek myths are more than 3,000 years old, so why are we still drawn to them? With their mighty heroes, flawed gods and goddesses, and supernatural events, ancient Greek myths still have the power to entertain. At the same time, they help us to understand the values and beliefs of the people who first told them. Use what you've learned in this workshop to analyze "Orion," one of several Greek myths that you will read in this unit.

ORION

Greek myth retold by **Alice Low**

Orion was a giant and a brave hunter. He could walk on water, a gift given him by his father, Poseidon, god of the sea.

One day Orion walked across the water to the island of Chios. There he fell in love with the king's daughter, Merope.

5 Orion said to the king, "I wish to marry your daughter, for I have fallen deeply in love with her. Tell me what I must do to gain her hand."

"Very well," said the king. "Since you are famous as a mighty hunter, you must rid my island of lions and bears and wolves. Only then will I give you my precious daughter's hand in marriage."

10 Orion strode through the hills and killed all the wild animals with his sword and his club. Then he brought their skins to the king and said, "Now I have finished my task. Let us set a day for the wedding."

But the king did not want to part with his daughter and kept putting off the wedding date. This angered Orion, and he tried to carry off

15 Merope.

Close Read

1. Reread the boxed details. What qualities and powers make Orion special?

2. Here is a common stylistic element in the traditional tales of many cultures: A king or other powerful man sets difficult, even impossible, tasks for a young man who wants to marry his daughter. Why do you think the king in this myth gives Orion such a challenge?

Her father retaliated.¹ He called on the god of wine, Dionysus, to put Orion into a deep sleep. Then the king blinded Orion and flung him onto the sand by the sea.

When Orion awoke sightless, he cried out, "I am blind and helpless. How shall I ever hunt again or win Merope for my bride?"

In his despair, Orion consulted an oracle,² which answered him, "O Orion, you shall regain your sight if you travel east to the place where the sun rises. The warm rays of the sun shall heal your eyes and restore their power."

But how could a blind man find his way to that distant place? Orion followed the sound of the Cyclopes'³ hammers to the forge of the god Hephaestus.⁴ When the god saw the blind hunter, he took pity on him and gave him a guide to lead him to the sun, just as it was rising.

Orion raised his eyes to the sun and, miraculously, he could see again. After thanking the sun, Orion set off for the island of Chios to take revenge on the king. But the king and his daughter had fled, possibly to Crete, and Orion went there to look for them. He never found them, but he met up with Artemis, goddess of the hunt, and spent days hunting with her. They were a happy pair, roving through the woods, until Artemis's brother, Apollo, became jealous.

Apollo sent a scorpion to attack Orion. Orion could not pierce the scorpion's tough body with his arrows, but he dodged the poisonous insect and strode far out to sea.

Apollo was bent on destroying Orion, and he called to Artemis, "See that rock way out there in the sea? I challenge you to hit it."

Artemis loved a challenge. She drew her bow and aimed carefully. Her first arrow hit the mark, and Apollo congratulated her on her skill.

But when the waves brought Orion's body to the shore, Artemis moaned with grief. "I have killed my beloved companion. I shall never forget him. And the world shall never forget him, either."

She lifted his body up into the sky, where he remains among the stars to this day—the mighty hunter, one of the most brilliant constellations,⁵ with his sword and his club and three bright stars for his belt.

---

1. **retaliated:** got revenge.
2. **oracle:** in ancient Greece, a wise person who was said to be able to communicate with the gods and predict the future.
3. **Cyclopes:** one-eyed monsters.
4. **Hephaestus:** the god of fire, responsible for creating armor, sculptures, and other objects by shaping hot metal with a hammer.
5. **constellations:** groupings of stars in the sky.

Close Read

3. Whom does Orion turn to for help with his problem? Explain what his actions in lines 21–27 suggest about ancient Greek beliefs.

4. Review lines 16–18 and 25–28. What role do the gods play in Orion's life?

5. Reread lines 34–44. What human qualities or emotions do Apollo and Artemis display?

6. How does Apollo trick Artemis into "destroying Orion"?

7. What mystery of the universe does this myth explain?

The Story of Ceres and Proserpina
Classical Myth Retold by Mary Pope Osborne

How powerful is LOVE?

COMMON CORE

RL 2 Determine a central idea of a text and how it is conveyed through particular details.
RL 3 Describe how a story's plot unfolds in a series of episodes.

Love can be a powerful force in people's lives, shaping the decisions they make and the actions they take. In this myth, you'll read about a mother's deep affection for her daughter and how it affects the people and places around her.

LIST IT Make a list of three people you care about deeply. You can include relatives, friends, or other special people who have been meaningful in your life. Under each name, note at least one way in which the person has shown his or her love.

Ways People
Show Love

1. Mom Always tells me that she is proud of me.

2.

3.

● TEXT ANALYSIS: CLASSICAL MYTHS

Classical myths are ancient stories that were used to explain the world and the gods and goddesses who ruled over it, shaping the lives of all humans. Passed down by word of mouth for generations, these myths have recurring, or repeating, themes and stylistic elements, such as:

- They explain how something in the world, such as the seas or the mountains, came to be.
- They feature gods, goddesses, and other beings with extraordinary powers. However, these beings often have the same emotions and weaknesses as humans.

As you read "The Story of Ceres and Proserpina," notice what it explains about the natural world and the behavior of the gods.

● READING SKILL: RECOGNIZE CAUSE AND EFFECT

The events of a story are often linked by cause-and-effect relationships. That is, one event acts as a **cause,** directly bringing about another event, or **effect.** The effect might, in turn, be the cause of another effect, creating a chain of events. As you read "The Story of Ceres and Proserpina," look for cause-and-effect relationships. Record them in a graphic organizer like the one shown.

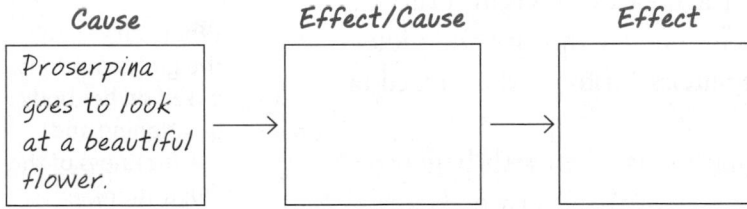

▲ VOCABULARY IN CONTEXT

Osborne uses the listed words to create a vivid setting for this myth. Which word best completes each sentence?

WORD LIST	barren	chariot	fertile	shrouded

1. The _____ field produced an enormous crop of corn.
2. Two horses pulled a golden _____.
3. The _____ mountain was difficult to see.
4. The sandy desert was dry and _____.

 Complete the activities in your **Reader/Writer Notebook.**

Mary Pope Osborne
born 1949

Adventure Seeker

Mary Pope Osborne grew up in a military family. By the time she was 15, she had lived in Austria, as well as a number of places in the United States. She continued to travel as an adult and once spent many months traveling through Asia. "I craved the adventure and changing scenery of our military life," Osborne said.

Time Travel

As children, Osborne and her brothers sought adventures everywhere they went. These adventures became the basis for Osborne's most popular fiction series, *The Magic Tree House,* about a brother and sister who find books that transport them to distant times and places.

BACKGROUND TO THE MYTH

Classical Mythology

The myths told by the ancient Greeks and Romans are known as classical mythology. The earliest Greek myths appeared almost 3,000 years ago. When Rome conquered Greece around 178 B.C., the Romans adopted the Greek myths but changed the names of the gods to Roman names.

Author Online **THINK**central

Go to **thinkcentral.com.**
KEYWORD: HML6-683

THE STORY OF CERES AND PROSERPINA

Retold by Mary Pope Osborne

One day Proserpina, the young maiden of spring, was picking wildflowers with her mother, Ceres, the goddess of grain. Entering the cool moist woods, Proserpina filled her basket with lilies and violets. But when she spied the white petals of the narcissus flower, she strayed far from her mother.

Just as Proserpina picked a beautiful narcissus, the earth began to rumble. Suddenly the ground cracked open, splitting fern beds and ripping flowers and trees from their roots. Then out of the dark depths sprang Pluto, god of the underworld. **Ⓐ**

10 Standing up in his black **chariot,** Pluto ferociously drove his stallions toward Proserpina. The maiden screamed for her mother, but Ceres was far away and could not save her.

Pluto grabbed Proserpina and drove his chariot back into the earth. Then the ground closed up again, leaving not even a seam.

When the mountains echoed with Proserpina's screams, her mother rushed into the woods, but it was too late—her daughter had disappeared.

Beside herself with grief, Ceres began searching for her kidnapped daughter in every land. For nine days the goddess did not rest, but carried two torches through the cold nights, searching for Proserpina.

Analyze Visuals ▶

What can you tell about the girl's emotions, based on her body positioning and the fuzziness of the illustration?

Ⓐ CLASSICAL MYTHS
Reread lines 6–9. What extraordinary power is Pluto exhibiting?

chariot (chăr′ē-ət) *n.* a two-wheeled vehicle used in ancient times

Illustrations by Leonid Gore.

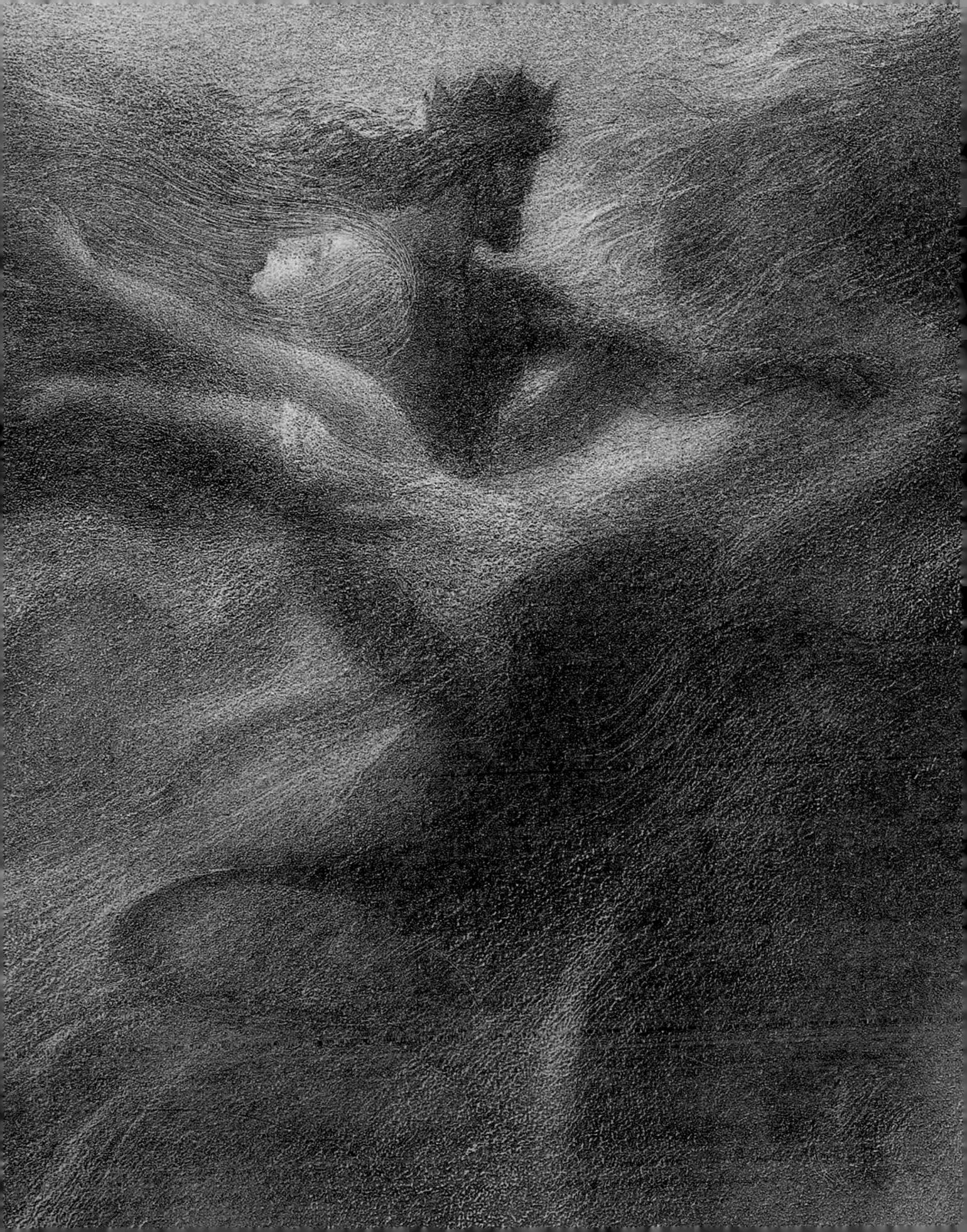

20   On the tenth day, Hecate, goddess of the dark of the moon, came to Ceres. Holding up a lantern, the **shrouded** goddess said, "I also heard your daughter's screams, but I didn't see her. Let us fly to Helios, the sun god, and ask him what happened."

    Ceres and Hecate flew to Helios, the sun god; and weeping, Ceres asked Helios if he'd seen her daughter while he was shining down upon the woods.

    "I pity you, Ceres," said Helios, "for I know what it is to lose a child. But I know the truth. Pluto wanted Proserpina for his wife, so he asked his brother, Jupiter, to give him permission to kidnap her. Jupiter gave
30 his consent, and now your daughter reigns over the land of the dead with Pluto."

    Ceres screamed in rage and thrust her fist toward Mount Olympus,[1] cursing Jupiter for aiding in the kidnapping of his own daughter. Then she returned to earth, disguised as an old woman, and began wandering from town to town.

    One day as she rested by a well, Ceres watched four princesses gathering water. Remembering her own daughter, she began to weep.

    "Where are you from, old woman?" one princess asked. ◆

    "I was kidnapped by pirates, and I escaped," said Ceres. "Now I know
40 not where I am."

    Feeling pity for her, the princesses brought Ceres home to their palace. At the palace, their mother, the queen, took an immediate liking to Ceres when she noticed how good she was with her baby son the prince. When she asked Ceres if she would live with them and be his nurse, the goddess gladly consented.

    Ceres grew deeply fond of the child. The thought that he would someday grow old and die was too much for her to bear. So she decided to change him from a mortal to a god. Every night, when everyone else was asleep, she poured a magic liquid on the body of the baby prince and
50 held him in a fire. Soon the prince began to look like a god; everyone was amazed at his beauty and strength. The queen, disturbed by the changes in her child, hid in the nursery and watched Ceres and the boy. And when she saw Ceres place the child into the fire, she screamed for help.

    "Stupid woman!" shouted Ceres, snatching the baby from the fire. "I was going to make your son a god! He would have lived forever! Now he'll be a mere mortal and die like the rest of you!"

    The king and queen then realized that the boy's nurse was Ceres, the powerful goddess of grain, and they were terrified. **B**

---

shrouded (shroud′əd) *adj.* concealed or hidden

Language Coach

Word Roots The word root *wander* comes from the Old English word meaning "to travel." How does knowing this root give you a clue to the meaning of the word *wandering* (line 34)?

◆ **GRAMMAR IN CONTEXT**
Titles used for royalty—king, queen, prince, princess (as in line 38), duke, etc.—are only capitalized when they are used as a name or directly before a name, as in *Queen Elizabeth* or *Prince William*.

B CLASSICAL MYTHS
Myths and other classical stories have **motifs,** or recurring story elements, such as magical transformations and wicked stepmothers. This passage features a common motif: a god or goddess takes a human form, but the disguise is ruined when people see the god do something extraordinary. Look for other motifs in this myth, and ask yourself how they affect the story.

---

1. **Mount Olympus** (ə-lĭm′pəs)**:** the highest point in Greece and home of the gods and goddesses.

"I will only forgive you," said Ceres, "if you build a great temple
in my honor. Then I will teach your people the secret rites to help the
corn grow." **C**

At dawn the king ordered a great temple be built for the goddess.
But after the temple was completed, Ceres did not reveal the secret
rites. Instead she sat by herself all day, grieving for her kidnapped daughter.
She was in such deep mourning that everything on earth stopped growing.
It was a terrible year—there was no food, and people and animals began
to starve. **D**

Jupiter grew worried—if Ceres caused the people on earth to die, there
would be no more gifts and offerings for him. Finally he sent gods from
Mount Olympus to speak with her.

The gods came to Ceres and offered her gifts and pleaded with her to
make the earth **fertile** again.

"I never will," she said, "not unless my daughter is returned safely to me."

Jupiter had no choice but to bid his son, Mercury, the messenger god,
to return Proserpina to her mother.

Wandering the underworld, Mercury passed through dark smoky
caverns filled with ghosts and phantoms, until he came to the misty

60

70

C CAUSE AND EFFECT
Reread lines 46–61.
What are the effects
of the queen's scream?

D CLASSICAL MYTHS
What extraordinary
abilities has Ceres
displayed?

fertile (fûr′tl) *adj.*
able to produce farm
crops or other vegetation

▼ **Analyze
Visuals**
What **mood,** or feeling,
is conveyed through this
illustration?

throne room of Pluto and Proserpina. Though the maiden was still frightened, she had grown accustomed to her new home and had almost forgotten her life on earth.

"Your brother, Jupiter, has ordered you to return Proserpina to her mother," Mercury told Pluto. "Otherwise, Ceres will destroy the earth."

Pluto knew he could not disobey Jupiter, but he didn't want his wife to leave forever, so he said, "She can go. But first, we must be alone."

When Mercury left, Pluto spoke softly to Proserpina: "If you stay, you'll be queen of the underworld, and the dead will give you great honors."

As Proserpina stared into the eyes of the king of the dead, she dimly remembered the joy of her mother's love. She remembered wildflowers in the woods and open sunlit meadows. "I would rather return," she whispered.

Pluto sighed, then said, "All right, go. But before you leave, eat this small seed of the pomegranate fruit. It is the food of the underworld—it will bring you good luck."

Proserpina ate the tiny seed. Then Pluto's black chariot carried her and Mercury away. The two stallions burst through the dry ground of earth—then galloped over the **barren** countryside to the temple where Ceres mourned for her daughter.

When Ceres saw her daughter coming, she ran down the hillside, and Proserpina sprang from the chariot into her mother's arms. All day the two talked excitedly of what had happened during their separation, but when Proserpina told Ceres about eating the pomegranate seed, the goddess hid her face and moaned in anguish.

"What have I done?" cried Proserpina.

"You have eaten the sacred food of the underworld," said Ceres. "Now you must return for half of every year to live with Pluto, your husband." **E**

And this is how the seasons began—for when fall and winter come, the earth grows cold and barren because Proserpina lives in the underworld with Pluto, and her mother mourns. But when her daughter comes back to her, Ceres, goddess of grain, turns the world to spring and summer: The corn grows, and everything flowers again. ❧

barren (bărʹən) *adj.* unable to produce or without vegetation

E CAUSE AND EFFECT
What are the effects of the trick Pluto plays on Proserpina?

Comprehension

1. **Recall** How long does Ceres search for Proserpina before Hecate visits her?

2. **Summarize** How does the myth explain the changing of the seasons?

3. **Represent** Ceres, Pluto, Hecate, Helios, and Mercury are each the god or goddess of something. Create a chart or diagram showing what each controls.

Text Analysis

4. **Draw Conclusions** The gods in mythology are not equal in rank or power. Make a chart like the one shown. Using details from the myth, note the powers that each of the three gods has. Then explain which god in this myth has the greatest power.

Jupiter	Ceres	Pluto

5. **Identify Cause and Effect** Look at the cause-effect chains you created while reading "The Story of Ceres and Proserpina." Think about how the events in the plot are connected to each other. Which events in the plot create cause-effect chains?

6. **Analyze Classical Myths** In what ways does this myth demonstrate the gods' influence over people on Earth? Explain.

7. **Evaluate Theme** Why might a story about the power of love and loss be used to help explain the change of seasons?

Extension and Challenge

8. **Creative Project: Writing** Imagine that the gods and goddesses used the same methods of communication that we use today. Compose a few of the e-mails that Ceres and Proserpina might have sent to each other during Proserpina's second visit to the underworld.

9. **Inquiry and Research** Research one of the gods or goddesses from "The Story of Ceres and Proserpina." What additional information did you find about that character? Share your findings with the class.

How powerful is LOVE?

Look back at your list of the ways people you know have shown their love. How convincing is this myth in showing the power of a mother's love for her child?

COMMON CORE

RL 2 Determine a central idea of a text and how it is conveyed through particular details.
RL 3 Describe how a story's plot unfolds in a series of episodes.
W 7 Conduct short research projects to answer a question.

Vocabulary in Context

▲ VOCABULARY PRACTICE

Show that you understand the vocabulary words by deciding if each statement is true or false.

1. A **barren** hillside is covered with trees and flowers.
2. If there is a **shrouded** opening to a castle, it is easy to see it clearly.
3. In **fertile** soil, crops usually grow easily.
4. A **chariot** has four wheels and a powerful engine.

barren

chariot

fertile

shrouded

ACADEMIC VOCABULARY IN WRITING

• circumstance • contribute • element • significant • tradition

Retell the most **significant** events in this myth. Which **circumstance** surprises you most? Use at least one of the Academic Vocabulary words in your response.

VOCABULARY STRATEGY: WORDS DERIVED FROM LATIN AND GREEK

The ancient Romans and Greeks gave us more than just classical mythology. They also gave us words and word parts that have greatly expanded and enriched the English vocabulary. Some of these Latin (Roman) and Greek words and word parts are connected to the classical myths. For example, we get the word *martial,* as in "martial arts," from the name of the Roman god of war and warriors, Mars. (In Greek myths, Mars is called Ares.)

PRACTICE Match the words from Greek and Roman mythology on the left with the modern English words derived from them on the right.

1. Helios, Roman god of the sun
2. Ceres, Roman goddess of grain
3. Olympus, home of the Greek and Roman gods
4. Pluto, Roman god of the underworld
5. Jupiter, Roman king of the gods (also known as Jove)

a. cereal (grain-based food)
b. Olympics (world athletic competition)
c. jovial (happy)
d. helium (a naturally occurring element in the atmosphere)
e. plutonium (a radioactive element)

COMMON CORE

L 4b Use Greek or Latin roots as clues to the meaning of a word.
L 6 Acquire and use accurately academic words.

Interactive Vocabulary **THINK** central

Go to **thinkcentral.com**.
KEYWORD: HML6-690

Language

◆ **GRAMMAR IN CONTEXT: Capitalize Correctly**

Be sure to capitalize a family relationship word, such as *mother, father,* or *uncle,* when it is used as a name or directly before a name. Do not capitalize a family relationship word when it follows a possessive pronoun like *her* or *my* or an article like *a, an,* or *the.*

> Original: Proserpina and her Mother were very close.
>
> Revised: Proserpina and her mother were very close.

PRACTICE Correct the capitalization errors in each sentence.

1. Proserpina said, "I long for the days when mother and I were together."
2. It was clear that Ceres missed her Daughter.
3. "I'll find an Aunt to look after you," Jupiter said.
4. Mercury said, "I'd be happy to send a message for you, father."

*For more help with capitalization, see page R51 in the **Grammar Handbook.***

READING-WRITING CONNECTION

YOUR TURN Demonstrate your understanding of "The Story of Ceres and Proserpina" by responding to the following prompt. Then use the **revising tip** to improve your writing.

WRITING PROMPT	REVISING TIP
Extended Constructed Response: Analysis Why was Ceres unable to go to the underworld and bring Proserpina back? In **two or three paragraphs,** explain why Ceres's power to rescue her daughter was limited.	Review your response. Have you used correct capitalization in describing Ceres's powers and limits as a goddess? Pay particular attention to how you have handled family relationship words like *mother* and *daughter*.

Interactive Revision | **THINK** central

Go to thinkcentral.com. KEYWORD: HML6-691

COMMON CORE

L 2 Demonstrate command of the conventions of capitalization.
W 2 Write explanatory texts to convey information through analysis of content.

Apollo's Tree: The Story of Daphne and Apollo
Classical Myth Retold by Mary Pope Osborne

Video link at
thinkcentral.com

Arachne
Classical Myth Retold by Olivia E. Coolidge

VIDEO TRAILER **THINK** central KEYWORD: HML6-692

Can PRIDE ever hurt you?

COMMON CORE

RL 2 Determine a central idea of a text and how it is conveyed through details. **RL 3** Describe how the characters respond or change as the plot moves toward a resolution. **RL 10** Read and comprehend literature.

It's good to have pride in yourself as well as in your accomplishments. But when pride turns to conceit and boasting, it can get you into trouble. Some classical myths, such as the two you are about to read, serve as warnings about the dangers of being overly sure of yourself.

DISCUSS With a group of classmates, discuss a time when you or someone you know witnessed the dangers of pride. What were the consequences? Take turns discussing the effect it had on those involved.

● TEXT ANALYSIS: CULTURAL VALUES IN MYTHS

Cultural values are the standards of behavior that a society expects from its people. Myths and their themes reflect the cultural values of the societies in which they were first told. Some values often taught in Greek and Roman myths are

- respecting your elders
- respecting and obeying the gods, who are often involved in humans' everyday lives
- knowing your place

As you read "Apollo's Tree" and "Arachne," notice what happens to the characters who do not maintain these values. Then determine what lessons are being taught by the myths.

● READING STRATEGY: PREDICT

When you **predict,** you make reasonable guesses about what will happen next based on clues in a story and your own experiences. As you read each of the myths that follow, create a chart like the one shown to record your predictions.

Myth	My Predictions	Clues in Story	What Really Happens
"Apollo's Tree"	Cupid will shoot Apollo with an arrow.		

▲ VOCABULARY IN CONTEXT

These words help tell the stories of people trapped by pride. Make a chart like the one shown. Put each vocabulary word in the appropriate column. Then write a brief definition of each word you know or think you know.

WORD LIST		
distorted	indignantly	ominous
exquisite	obscure	sacred
immensely	obstinacy	

Know Well	Think I Know	Don't Know at All

 Complete the activities in your **Reader/Writer Notebook.**

Mary Pope Osborne
born 1949

Inspired Traveler
While on an extended journey through Asia, Mary Pope Osborne became ill and ended up in a hospital in Nepal. During her stay, she read J. R. R. Tolkien's trilogy *The Lord of the Rings.* Osborne has said that in those three books, she "encountered worlds of light and worlds of darkness." Reading them "planted seeds of the imagination that led directly to my being an author of children's books." (For more information about Mary Pope Osborne, see page 683.)

Olivia E. Coolidge
1908–2006

Historical Writer
Born in England, Olivia E. Coolidge eventually became a U.S. citizen. After World War II, she began writing biographical and historical books for young people. "My general purpose," Coolidge once explained about her writing, "...is to give a picture of life." She went on to add that "a good book should excite, amuse, and interest."

Authors Online
Go to thinkcentral.com. KEYWORD: HML6-693

APOLLO'S TREE
The Story of Daphne and Apollo

Retold by Mary Pope Osborne

One day when Apollo, the god of light and truth, was a young man, he came upon Cupid, the god of love, playing with one of his bows. "What are you doing with my bow?" Apollo asked angrily. "Don't try to steal my glory, Cupid! I've slain a great serpent with that weapon. Play with your own little bow and arrows!"

"Your arrows may slay serpents, Apollo," said the god of love, "but *my* arrows can do worse harm! Even you can be wounded by them!"

With that **ominous** threat, Cupid flew into the sky and landed on top of a high mountain. Then he pulled two arrows from his quiver:[1] One had
10 a blunt tip filled with lead. Whomever was hit by this arrow would run from anyone professing love. The second arrow was sharp and made of gold. Whomever was hit with this arrow would instantly fall in love. **A**

Cupid aimed his first arrow at Daphne, a beautiful nymph[2] hunting deep in the woods. Daphne was a follower of Diana, Apollo's twin sister and the goddess of wild things. Like Diana, Daphne loved her freedom, as she roamed the woods and fields with her hair in wild disarray and her limbs bare to the sun and rain.

Cupid pulled the bowstring back and shot the blunt-tipped arrow at Daphne. When the arrow flew through the air, it became invisible. And
20 when it pierced Daphne's heart, she felt a sharp pain, but knew not why.

Holding her hands over her wound, Daphne rushed to her father, the river god. "Father!" she shouted. "You must make me a promise!"

"What is it?" called the god who stood in the river, surrounded by water nymphs.

ominous (ŏm′ə-nəs) *adj.* threatening; frightening

A PREDICT
Reread lines 1–12. What do you think Cupid is going to do? Add your prediction to your chart.

Analyze
Visuals ▶
Examine the painting of Cupid. What **details** do you notice?

---

1. **quiver** (kwĭv′ər): a portable case for holding arrows.

2. **nymph** (nĭmf): any of a number of minor gods represented as beautiful maidens in Greek and Roman mythology.

Detail of *Cupid,* manner of Jean-Baptiste Greuze.
Oil on canvas. © Christie's Images/SuperStock.

"Promise I will never have to get married!" Daphne cried.

The river god, confused by his daughter's frantic request, called back, "But I wish to have grandchildren!"

"No, Father! No! I *never* want to get married! Please, let me always be as free as Diana!"

30 "But I want you to marry!" cried the god.

"No!" screamed Daphne. And she beat the water with her fists, then rocked back and forth and sobbed.

"All right!" shouted the river god. "Do not grieve so, Daphne! I promise I'll never make you marry!" **B**

"And promise you'll help me escape my suitors!" cried the huntress.

"I promise, I will!" called the river god.

After Daphne secured this promise from her father, Cupid aimed his second arrow—the sharp, gold-tipped one—at Apollo, who was wandering in the woods. Just as the young god came 40 upon Daphne, Cupid pulled back the tight string of his bow and shot the golden arrow into Apollo's heart.

The god instantly fell in love with Daphne. Even though the huntress's hair was wild and she wore only rough animal skins, Apollo thought she was the most beautiful woman he'd ever seen.

"Hello!" he cried. But Daphne gave him a startled look, then bolted into the woods like a deer.

Apollo ran after her, shouting, "Stay! Stay!" But Daphne fled as fast as the wind.

"Don't run, please!" cried Apollo. "You flee like a dove flees an eagle. 50 But I'm not your enemy! Don't run from me!"

Daphne continued to run.

"Stop!" Apollo cried.

Daphne did not slow down. ◆

"Do you know who I am?" said the god. "I am not a farm boy or a shepherd. I am Lord of Delphi! Son of Jupiter! I've slain a great serpent with my arrow! But alas, I fear Cupid's weapons have wounded me worse!"

Daphne continued to run, her bare limbs lit by the sun and her soft hair wild in the wind.

Apollo grew tired of begging her to stop, so he began to pick up 60 speed. On the wings of love, running more swiftly than he'd ever run before, the god of light and truth gave the girl no rest, until soon he was close upon her. **C**

Her strength gone, Daphne could feel Apollo's breath on her hair. "Help me, Father!" she cried to the river god. "Help me!"

B CULTURAL VALUES
Reread lines 25–34. In what way does Daphne's behavior show disrespect toward elders?

◆ GRAMMAR IN CONTEXT
The author uses a variety of sentence structures in this passage. What is the effect of the very short simple sentences in lines 51 and 53? Why are these simple sentences more effective than compound sentences would have been?

C PREDICT
How do you think the myth will end?

Apollo and Daphne (1565–1570), Paolo Veronese. Oil on canvas, 109.4 cm × 113.3 cm.
© San Diego Museum of Art, San Diego, California/Bridgeman Art Library.

◀**Analyze Visuals**
How do the people in this painting compare with your mental picture of Apollo and Daphne?

No sooner had she spoken these words, than her arms and legs grew heavy and turned to wood. Then her hair became leaves, and her feet became roots growing deep into the ground. She had become a laurel tree;[3] and nothing was left of her, but her **exquisite** loveliness.

Apollo embraced the tree's branches as if they were Daphne's arms.
70 He kissed her wooden flesh. Then he pressed his hands against the tree's trunk and wept.

"I feel your heart beating beneath this bark," Apollo said, tears running down his face. "Since you can't be my wife, you'll be my **sacred** tree. I'll use your wood for my harp and for my arrows. I'll weave your branches into a wreath for my head. Heroes and scholars will be crowned with your leaves.[4] You'll always be young and green—my first love, Daphne." ꙮ **D**

exquisite (ĕk´skwĭ-zĭt) *adj.* of extraordinary beauty or charm

sacred (sā´krĭd) *adj.* worthy of great respect; holy

D CULTURAL VALUES
Think about what happens to Apollo. What lessons does the myth teach?

3. **laurel tree:** a Mediterranean evergreen tree with fragrant leaves and small, blackish berries.

4. **Heroes and scholars . . . your leaves:** In ancient times, a wreath of laurel leaves was often given to poets, heroes, and victors in athletic contests as a mark of honor.

ARACHNE

Retold by Olivia E. Coolidge

Arachne was a maiden who became famous throughout Greece,
though she was neither wellborn nor beautiful and came from
no great city. She lived in an **obscure** little village, and her father was
a humble dyer of wool. In this he was very skillful, producing many varied
shades, while above all he was famous for the clear, bright scarlet which
is made from shellfish and which was the most glorious of all the colors
used in ancient Greece. Even more skillful than her father was Arachne.
It was her task to spin the fleecy wool into a fine, soft thread and to weave
it into cloth on the high-standing loom within the cottage. Arachne
10 was small and pale from much working. Her eyes were light and her
hair was a dusty brown, yet she was quick and graceful, and her fingers,
roughened as they were, went so fast that it was hard to follow their
flickering movements. So soft and even was her thread, so fine her cloth,
so gorgeous her embroidery,[1] that soon her products were known all over
Greece. No one had ever seen the like of them before.

obscure (ŏb-skyŏŏr′)
adj. far from cities
or other areas of
human population

Analyze Visuals ▶

What can you **infer**
about the woman in
this illustration?

---

1. **embroidery:** the decoration of fabric with needlework.

Illustrations by Blair Drawson.

At last Arachne's fame became so great that people used to come from far and wide to watch her working. Even the graceful nymphs would steal in from stream or forest and peep shyly through the dark doorway, watching in wonder the white arms of Arachne as she stood at the
20 loom and threw the shuttle[2] from hand to hand between the hanging threads or drew out the long wool, fine as a hair, from the distaff[3] as she sat spinning. "Surely Athena herself must have taught her," people would murmur to one another. "Who else could know the secret of such marvelous skill?"

Arachne was used to being wondered at, and she was **immensely** proud of the skill that had brought so many to look on her. Praise was all she lived for, and it displeased her greatly that people should think anyone, even a goddess, could teach her anything. Therefore, when she heard them murmur, she would stop her work and turn round **indignantly** to say,
30 "With my own ten fingers I gained this skill, and by hard practice from early morning till night. I never had time to stand looking as you people do while another maiden worked. Nor if I had, would I give Athena credit because the girl was more skillful than I. As for Athena's weaving, how could there be finer cloth or more beautiful embroidery than mine? If Athena herself were to come down and compete with me, she could do no better than I." **E**

One day when Arachne turned round with such words, an old woman answered her, a grey old woman, bent and very poor, who stood leaning on a staff and peering at Arachne amid the crowd of onlookers.
40 "Reckless girl," she said, "how dare you claim to be equal to the immortal gods themselves? I am an old woman and have seen much. Take my advice and ask pardon of Athena for your words. Rest content with your fame of being the best spinner and weaver that mortal eyes have ever beheld."

"Stupid old woman," said Arachne indignantly, "who gave you a right to speak in this way to me? It is easy to see that you were never good for anything in your day, or you would not come here in poverty and rags to gaze at my skill. If Athena resents my words, let her answer them herself. I have challenged her to a contest, but she, of course, will not come.
50 It is easy for the gods to avoid matching their skill with that of men." **F**

At these words the old woman threw down her staff and stood erect. The wondering onlookers saw her grow tall and fair and stand clad in long robes of dazzling white. They were terribly afraid as they realized

VISUAL VOCABULARY

loom *n.* a device for making cloth by weaving strands of yarn or thread together

immensely (ĭ-mĕns′lē) *adv.* extremely; very

indignantly (ĭn-dĭg′nənt-lē) *adv.* angrily; in annoyance

E PREDICT
Reread lines 16–36. Based on Arachne's boasting, what do you predict will happen next?

F CULTURAL VALUES
Reread lines 37–50. What value does Arachne fail to show respect for? Explain.

that they stood in the presence of Athena. Arachne herself flushed red for a moment, for she had never really believed that the goddess would hear her. Before the group that was gathered there she would not give in; so pressing her pale lips together in **obstinacy** and pride, she led the goddess to one of the great looms and set herself before the other. Without a word both began to thread the long woolen strands that hung from
60 the rollers and between which the shuttle would move back and forth. Many skeins[4] lay heaped beside them to use, bleached white, and gold, and scarlet, and other shades, varied as the rainbow. Arachne had never thought of giving credit for her success to her father's skill in dyeing, though in actual truth the colors were as remarkable as the cloth itself. **G**

Soon there was no sound in the room but the breathing of the onlookers, the whirring of the shuttles, and the creaking of the wooden frames as each pressed the thread up into place or tightened the pegs by which the whole was held straight. The excited crowd in the doorway began to see that the skill of both in truth was very nearly
70 equal but that, however the cloth might turn out, the goddess was the quicker of the two. A pattern of many pictures was growing on her loom. There was a border of twined branches of the olive, Athena's favorite tree, while in the middle, figures began to appear. As they looked at the glowing colors, the spectators realized that Athena was weaving into her pattern a last warning to Arachne. The central figure was the goddess herself, competing with Poseidon[5] for possession of the city of Athens; but in the four corners were mortals who had tried to strive with gods and pictures of the awful fate that had overtaken them. The goddess ended a little before Arachne and stood back from
80 her marvelous work to see what the maiden was doing.

Never before had Arachne been matched against anyone whose skill was equal, or even nearly equal, to her own. As she stole glances from time to time at Athena and saw the goddess working swiftly, calmly, and always a little faster than herself, she became angry instead of frightened, and an evil thought came into her head. Thus, as Athena stepped back a pace to watch Arachne finishing her work, she saw that the maiden had taken for her design a pattern of scenes which showed evil or unworthy actions of the gods, how they had deceived fair maidens, resorted to trickery, and appeared on earth from time to time in the form of poor and humble
90 people. When the goddess saw this insult glowing in bright colors on Arachne's loom, she did not wait while the cloth was judged but stepped forward, her grey eyes blazing with anger, and tore Arachne's work across.

obstinacy
(ŏb'stə-nə-sē) *n.* the act of being stubborn or disobedient

G PREDICT
Who do you think will win the weaving contest? Add this prediction to your chart.

Language Coach

Comparison of Modifiers In lines 70–71 the author writes "the goddess was the quicker of the two." When two things, groups, or actions are being compared, use the comparative form: "Athena was quicker than Arachne." Since *quick* is a one-syllable word, and since it has a regular comparison form, you simply add –er to make the comparative form. Do not add the word *more* to the comparative form of a one-syllable word; it's incorrect to say "more quicker."

---

4. **skeins** (skānz): lengths of thread or yarn wound in long, loose coils.

5. **Poseidon** (pō-sīd'n): in Greek mythology, the god of waters, earthquakes, and horses.

◀ **Analyze Visuals**

What human qualities do you see in this illustration of Arachne as a spider?

Then she struck Arachne across the face. Arachne stood there a moment, struggling with anger, fear, and pride. "I will not live under this insult," she cried, and seizing a rope from the wall, she made a noose and would have hanged herself. Ⓗ

The goddess touched the rope and touched the maiden. "Live on, wicked girl," she said. "Live on and spin, both you and your descendants.[6] When men look at you, they may remember that it is not wise to strive 100 with Athena." At that the body of Arachne shriveled up; and her legs grew tiny, spindly, and **distorted**. There before the eyes of the spectators hung a little dusty brown spider on a slender thread.

All spiders descend from Arachne, and as the Greeks watched them spinning their thread wonderfully fine, they remembered the contest with Athena and thought that it was not right for even the best of men to claim equality with the gods. ༄

Ⓗ **CULTURAL VALUES**
In what ways does Arachne's behavior show disrespect for the gods?

distorted (dĭ-stôrt′əd) *adj.* twisted out of shape; misshapen

---

6. **descendants** (dĭ-sĕn′dənts): persons whose ancestry can be traced to a particular individual.

Comprehension

1. **Recall** In "Apollo's Tree," what is special about each of Cupid's two arrows?

2. **Recall** In addition to her skill as a weaver, what makes Arachne's work so beautiful?

3. **Clarify** What final warning does Athena try to give Arachne through the designs she weaves into her cloth?

Text Analysis

4. **Interpret** Reread lines 1–12 and 54–56 of "Apollo's Tree." What does Apollo mean when he says that the wounds from Cupid's weapons are worse than those from his own arrows? Explain your answer.

● 5. **Identify Cultural Values in Myths** People living in ancient Greece didn't always behave as expected. Make a chart like the one shown. Under each of the three values, list details that show how characters in each myth demonstrate or disregard the value.

Ancient Greek Values		
Respect Elders	Respect the Gods	Know Your Place

● 6. **Analyze Predictions** Look at the chart you filled in while reading "Apollo's Tree" and "Arachne." Complete the chart by noting what actually happened in the story. Which of your predictions were correct?

7. **Draw Conclusions About Theme** In what ways does Arachne's pride bring about her downfall? What does this tell you about how the ancient Greeks viewed pride?

Extension and Challenge

8. **Creative Project: Art** In "Arachne," Athena and Arachne include designs in their weavings that are intended as messages for each other. Sketch how you imagine these designs look, using the descriptions in the myth as your guide.

Can PRIDE ever hurt you?

Recall your discussion with classmates about the dangers of pride. How did the examples of the negative effects of too much pride compare with the events of this myth? Explain whether you think the myth of Arachne is a powerful warning against the dangers of pride.

COMMON CORE

RL 2 Determine a central idea of a text and how it is conveyed through details. **RL 3** Describe how the characters respond or change as the plot moves toward a resolution. **RL 10** Read and comprehend literature.

Vocabulary in Context

▲ VOCABULARY PRACTICE

Choose the vocabulary word that best completes each sentence.

1. The funhouse mirror made her body look strangely____.
2. The ____ town couldn't be found on her map.
3. Her positive attitude made Kiana ____ popular.
4. The site of the grave was considered ____ by the mourners.
5. When asked if she was lying, Lola denied it ____.
6. The ____ diamond sparkled brightly.
7. Kyle's ____ often got him in trouble at school.
8. The ____ clouds carried with them a terrible thunderstorm.

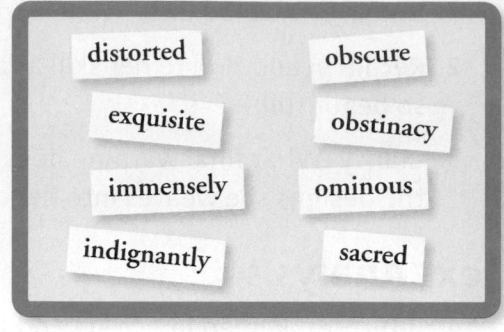

distorted   obscure

exquisite   obstinacy

immensely   ominous

indignantly   sacred

ACADEMIC VOCABULARY IN SPEAKING

• circumstance   • contribute   • element   • significant   • tradition

What **circumstances contribute** to Athena's treatment of Arachne? In a small group discuss whether Arachne deserves the punishment she receives. Use at least two of the Academic Vocabulary words in your response.

VOCABULARY STRATEGY: GREEK AND LATIN AFFIXES

Many English words and word parts come from ancient Greek and Latin. Knowing the meanings of Greek and Latin affixes helps you recognize and understand related words and build your vocabulary. Look at these **prefixes**—affixes that appear at the beginning of a word. Fill in the final column of the chart with other examples of words that use each prefix.

COMMON CORE

L 4b Use Greek or Latin affixes as clues to the meaning of a word.

Prefix	Meaning	Example	Your Examples
anti- (Greek)	against	antidote	
de- (Latin)	from; away; down	decline	
multi- (Latin)	many	multiply	
uni- (Latin)	one	universe	
re- (Latin)	again; back	rewind	
in-, im- (Latin)	not	impossible	
sub- (Latin)	under	submarine	
dia- (Greek)	through, across	diameter	
inter- (Latin)	between; among	interweave	
micro- (Greek)	very small	microscope	

Interactive Vocabulary **THINK** central

Go to **thinkcentral.com**.
KEYWORD: HML6-704

Language

◆ **GRAMMAR IN CONTEXT:** Form Compound Sentences

An **independent clause** contains a subject and a verb and can stand alone as a sentence. A **simple sentence** contains one independent clause. A **compound sentence** contains two or more independent clauses. The clauses are joined either by a comma and a coordinating conjunction such as *and, or, but,* or *so,* or by a semicolon.

> *Original:* Cupid played with Apollo's bows. Apollo became angry. (*Each simple sentence contains one independent clause.*)

> *Revised:* Cupid played with Apollo's bows, and Apollo became angry. (*The compound sentence contains two independent clauses joined by a comma and a coordinating conjunction.*)

PRACTICE Combine each pair of simple sentences to form a compound sentence. Use the coordinating conjunction that most clearly shows the relationship between the two ideas.

1. The arrow hits Daphne. She feels a sharp pain.
2. Apollo falls in love with Daphne. Daphne runs away from him.
3. Arachne is a skillful weaver. Athena is a better weaver.
4. Arachne is rude to Athena. The goddess turns her into a spider.

For more help with simple and compound sentences, see page R63 in the **Grammar Handbook.**

READING-WRITING CONNECTION

Increase your understanding of "Apollo's Tree" and "Arachne" by responding to this prompt. Then use the **revising tip** to improve your writing.

WRITING PROMPT	REVISING TIP
Short Constructed Response: Letter or Speech Imagine that you are a friend of Arachne and you are concerned that her behavior will get her into trouble. Write a **letter** or **speech** in which you urge her to be less boastful.	Review your response. Does your letter or speech use compound sentences? If not, revise your writing.

Interactive Revision **THINK** central

Go to thinkcentral.com.
KEYWORD: HML6-705

Spider Webs
Online Science Article

What's the Connection?

One of the two Greek myths you've just read was about the origin of spiders and their webs. You will now read a science article to learn about the different kinds of webs spiders weave.

Standards Focus: Organizational Patterns—Classification

Expository text is informational text written to explain, define, persuade, or inform. Newspaper, magazine, and Web site articles are examples of expository texts. Expository text is built on text features and organizational patterns. **Text features** are the physical design of an expository text: headings, layout, graphics, and captions. **Organizational patterns** are patterns writers use to organize the information they present. Comparison-and-contrast, cause-and-effect, and proposition-and-support are examples of organizational patterns. Writers carefully choose the best organizational pattern to introduce, illustrate, and elaborate their key ideas and effectively present their viewpoint. You can more easily understand the information in an expository text when you can identify its organizational pattern.

Classification is an organizational pattern you'll often find in scientific writing. In classification, the writer organizes the text by sorting related information into categories. As you read "Spider Webs," make an outline of the article's structure so that you can better understand the organizational pattern of classification. Start by writing what the article is about (its main idea), and then list the parts into which the article is divided.

Main Idea of Article
I. Subheading
A. Detail
B. Detail
II. Subheading
A. Detail
B. Detail
III. Subheading
A. Detail
B. Detail

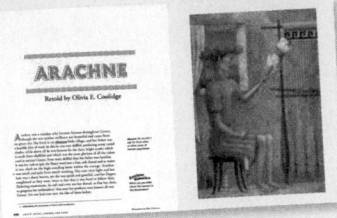

Use with "Apollo's Tree: The Story of Daphne and Apollo" and "Arachne," pages 694 and 698.

COMMON CORE

RI 3 Analyze in detail how a key idea is introduced, illustrated, and elaborated in a text. **RI 7** Integrate information presented in different media or formats to develop a coherent understanding of a topic.

Back   Forward   Stop   Refresh   Home   Search   Favorites   Mail   Print

SPIDER WEBS

You know there are many kinds of spiders, but did you know there are also many kinds of spider webs? In fact, a spider web can be a big clue to the kind of spider that made it. When you know the different kinds of webs that spiders commonly make, you can make a pretty accurate guess about the kind of spider that created it. **A**

▲ The kind of web that you are probably most familiar with is made by **ORB SPIDERS** (*Araneidae* family). Their webs are shaped like spirals on lines and are often very beautiful. To maintain that beauty, orb spiders have to repair their webs at least once every day. As the web loses its stickiness, the spider will eat it as it spins new threads. **B**

Internet

A CLASSIFICATION
What is the writer's purpose? How does the organizational pattern of classification support the writer's purpose?

B CLASSIFICATION
Why do you think the writer begins with the kind of spider web readers are most likely to be familiar with?

File   Edit   View   Tools   Help

Back   Forward   Stop   Refresh   Home   Search   Favorites   Mail   Print

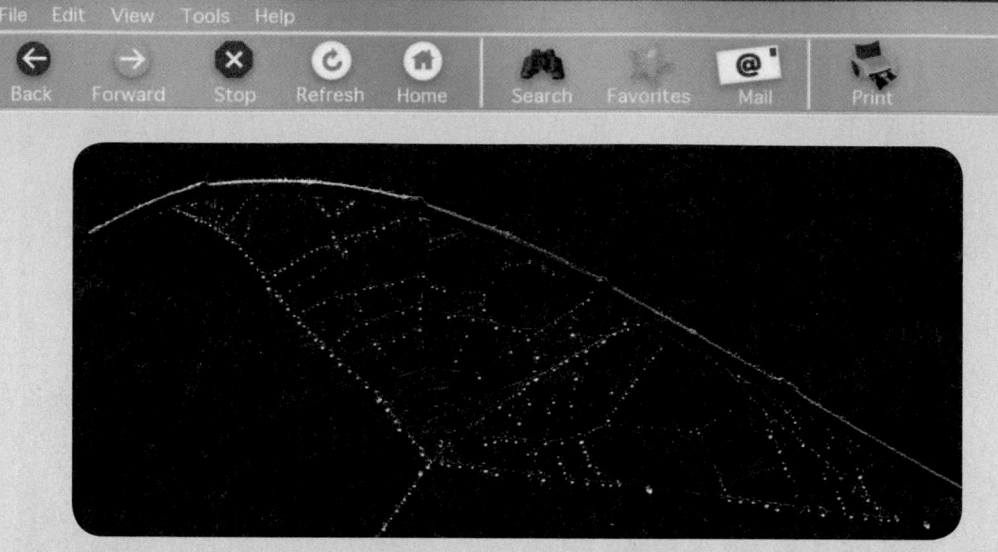

▲ **TRIANGLE SPIDERS** (*Uloboridae* family) make triangular webs. These webs resemble a slice of the webs made by orb spiders. **C**

C **CLASSIFICATION**
Why does it help to have the names of the spiders, such as "triangle spiders," boldfaced?

▲ **FUNNEL SPIDERS** (*Agelenidae* family) make webs that might look like a bird's nest made of silk. The spiders make sheets of silk and shape them into funnels. The funnels have one big opening to catch prey. They also have one small opening in the back in case the spider needs to escape. These webs are not actually sticky. The spiders that make them are just better at moving around in the smooth funnel shape than their prey.

Sometimes, funnel spider webs aren't cupped. Instead, spiders may make flat sheets with a small funnel-shaped retreat off to one side. **D**

D **SCIENCE ARTICLE**
How do the photographs help you understand the text? Explain whether the text would still be effective without visuals.

 Internet

File   Edit   View   Tools   Help

Back   Forward   Stop   Refresh   Home   Search   Favorites   Mail   Print

▲ **Cobweb spiders** (*Theriidae* family) make small, random messes of silk string that are attached to their surroundings by long strings. Cobweb spiders are also called comb-footed spiders. **E**

▲ **Meshweb spiders** (*Dictynidae* family) make webs that are similar to those of cobweb spiders but have a little more structure. The spiders are usually found in small, messy webs at the tips of vegetation, especially in grassy fields. They can also be found under stones and dead leaves. **F**

Internet

COMMON CORE RI 7

E ILLUSTRATIONS
Notice that each photograph has a description beneath it that presents information about the web and the spider that created it. This kind of description with an illustration is called a **caption**. What supplies more information: the photograph or the caption? Could you have one without the other? What information does the photograph present that the caption does not provide?

F CLASSIFICATION
What comparison does the writer make between the meshweb spiders and the cobweb spiders above? Why might such comparisons be helpful in a text that uses the classification organizational pattern?

G CLASSIFICATION
How many different kinds of sheetweb spiders does the author describe? What are the similarities and differences between them? Why do you think the author presents the spiders in this particular order?

H SCIENCE ARTICLE
How does the photograph help you understand what the author describes? In addition to photographs, what other kinds of visuals could the writer have included in this article, and how would they have helped you?

I CLASSIFICATION
How did the classification organizational pattern introduce, illustrate, and elaborate the writer's key idea? What would you say is the author's viewpoint throughout the article—how did he or she feel about the topic? How did the organizational pattern support that viewpoint?

File   Edit   View   Tools   Help

Back   Forward   Stop   Refresh   Home   Search   Favorites   Mail   Print

▶ **SHEETWEB SPIDERS**
(*Linyphiidae* family) make many kinds of webs that are formed out of sheets of silk. The sheets are a maze of threads, and don't have many large gaps.

There are several kinds of sheetweb spiders. *Platform spiders* make thickly interwoven sheets of silk. *Filmy dome spiders* make dome-shaped sheets that are secured by a network of silk strings. *Bowl and doily¹ spiders* make unusual webs. The tops look like bowls that are secured by strings to something above them. The bowl appears to be sitting on a doily that is the second part of the web and is attached horizontally. These kinds of webs make very effective booby-traps for unsuspecting insects. **G**

H

▲ Spider webs are a sign that spiders have been nearby, but they aren't the only sign. Spiders also spin webs to protect their eggs and developing young. These **EGG CASES** look like eggs but actually contain hundreds of tiny spider eggs.

Some spiders don't make webs at all. However, these spiders do use silk to make a little hiding place for themselves, especially females with eggs. **I**

---

1. **doily** (doi′lē): a small mat, often round and made of lace, that is used as a protective or decorative cover on furniture.

Internet

Comprehension

1. **Recall** What is another name for a cobweb spider?

2. **Recall** What are the three kinds of sheetweb spiders mentioned in the article?

Text Analysis

3. **Make Inferences** From the information in this article, what inference can you make about how spiders get their names?

4. **Evaluate a Science Article** How did the text features (headings, boldface type, captions, and photographs) help you understand the information as you read? What information did text features provide that the text did not?

5. **Evaluate Organizational Patterns** Why did the author choose the organizational pattern of classification for this article? How did this organizational pattern affect the development of the article's main idea and the author's viewpoint—how the writer feels about the subject matter?

COMMON CORE

RI 2 Provide a summary of the text distinct from personal opinions and judgments.
RI 3 Analyze in detail how a key idea is introduced, illustrated, and elaborated in a text.
RI 7 Integrate information presented in different media or formats to develop a coherent understanding of a topic.
W 2 Write explanatory texts to convey information.

Read for Information: Outline and Summarize

WRITING PROMPT

Write a summary of the science article "Spider Webs." Use the outline you created to help you write your summary. Summarize the article's main ideas and supporting details in your own words.

To answer this prompt, do as follows:

1. Review the outline you made. Does it include a subheading for each type of spider? Have you listed details about each spider under each subheading?

2. Title your summary with a statement of the article's main idea.

3. Remember that a summary is a short restatement of the main idea and the most important details in a text. You must decide which ideas to include and which to leave out.

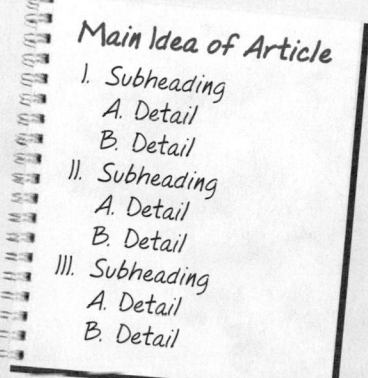

Main Idea of Article
I. Subheading
   A. Detail
   B. Detail
II. Subheading
   A. Detail
   B. Detail
III. Subheading
   A. Detail
   B. Detail

4. Recall that a summary does not include your own opinions and ideas, but it is told in your own words.

For more help with outlining, see page R4 in the **Reading Handbook.**

The Chenoo

Native American Legend Retold by Joseph and James Bruchac

VIDEO TRAILER THINK central KEYWORD: HML6-712

Is FEAR ever fun?

COMMON CORE

RL 1 Cite textual evidence to support inferences drawn from the text. **L 6** Gather vocabulary knowledge when considering a word or phrase important to comprehension or expression.

What do scary movies, amusement park haunted houses, and roller coasters have in common? Though they cause chills, screams, and fear, we turn to them again and again because they are fun. In the following Native American legend, you'll meet a monster—so prepare yourself for some fearful fun.

CHART IT Make a chart listing the fearful activities you've experienced. Then rate their fear and fun levels on a scale of 1 to 5 (with 5 being the highest). Compare your answers with those of your classmates.

Activity	Fun Level	Fear Level
roller coaster	4	3
reading a scary story		

● TEXT ANALYSIS: CHARACTERISTICS OF LEGENDS

A **legend** is a traditional tale about heroes and heroines and their deeds. While many legends are based on real people and events from history, they also contain certain stylistic elements that make them exciting. One stylistic element of most legends is that everyday objects or events take on extraordinary meanings, becoming **symbols** of something else. Another such element is a hero or heroine that shows uncommon courage and cleverness in the face of danger. You will also notice that many events in legends could not actually occur in the real world. Be sure to note these stylistic elements as you read "The Chenoo."

● READING SKILL: MAKE INFERENCES

When you **make inferences** as you read, you make educated guesses about the events or characters in a story. For example, you might infer that a character is kind and considerate if that character helps someone in need. Often, these inferences will help you identify a story's **theme,** or message about life or human nature.

As you read "The Chenoo," record the inferences you make about Nolka based on her words and actions.

Nolka's Words and Actions	Inferences About Nolka
cleans an elk hide and heats rocks for a sweat lodge	She is hard-working and takes good care of her brothers.

▲ VOCABULARY IN CONTEXT

The Bruchacs use the listed words to help tell the story of an encounter with a monster. Choose the word that best completes each sentence.

WORD LIST	clearing	inspect	proceed	sibling

1. The brothers were worried about their _____, Nolka.
2. They walked through the forest into a _____.
3. She wanted to _____, but she was frozen by fear.
4. Awasos bent down to _____ the tracks on the ground.

 Complete the activities in your **Reader/Writer Notebook.**

Meet the Authors

Joseph Bruchac III
born 1942

Keeper of Culture
Joseph Bruchac (brōō'shăk) has devoted his life to educating people about Native American culture. Bruchac, who is part Abenaki, has produced more than 70 books and is well known as a storyteller.

James Bruchac
The Next Generation
James Bruchac felt lucky to grow up as the son of storyteller Joseph Bruchac. Of the many Native American legends he heard as a child, his favorites were monster stories. James works with his father and younger brother to help preserve Native American culture.

BACKGROUND TO THE LEGEND
Scary Stories
Monster stories are a popular type of legend passed down in Native American culture. In many monster stories, a hero or heroine defeats a foe by using his or her wits and courage. Often, the lesson of these stories is that bravery and intelligence can triumph over evil.

Authors Online
Go to **thinkcentral.com**. KEYWORD: HML6-713

THINK central

The Chenoo

Retold by Joseph and James Bruchac

Long ago, during the Moon of Falling Leaves,[1] a woman and her two brothers traveled to the north to set up a hunting camp. Hoping to bring back enough furs and meat for the winter, they went far away from their village, much farther than anyone had gone in a long time.

During the first two days after making camp the hunting was very good. Each day the two brothers would go hunting. The sister, whose name was Nolka, would stay behind to tend their camp and prepare any game caught the day before. On the third day, however, while out hunting, the brothers came across a very large set of footprints. Those
10 footprints were over two feet long and ten feet apart. Kneeling down, Awasos, the older of the two brothers, carefully **inspected** each track. **A**

"Great-grandfather told me of a creature that makes tracks like this. It is called a Chenoo."[2] Awasos lifted his head to scan the forest around them.

"Yes, I remember," answered Kasko, Awasos's younger brother. "He said they were giant cannibals[3] with sharp teeth and hearts made of ice. Consuming the spirit of a human being makes them stronger."

---

1. **Moon of Falling Leaves:** In many Native American cultures, the Moon of Falling Leaves is the name given to the tenth of the thirteen cycles of the moon each year. The Moon of Falling Leaves usually begins in October.

2. **Chenoo** (chā'nōō)

3. **cannibals:** people or animals that feed on others of their own kind.

inspect (ĭn-spĕkt') v. to examine carefully

A **MAKE INFERENCES**
What inference can you make about the footprints?

Looking closer at the tracks, the two men realized the huge footprints were headed in the direction of their camp.

"We must return and check on our sister," said Awasos. Both men
20 began to run back toward camp.

Meanwhile, back at camp, unaware of any danger, Nolka was busy cleaning an elk hide. Several yards away, in a large fire pit, a pile of rocks was being heated up for her brothers' evening sweat lodge.

Having finished the hide, Nolka slowly stood up to add more wood to the fire. As she did so, she heard a sudden sound of breaking branches. She turned and looked up. There stood a huge Chenoo. Its large gray body was covered with pine pitch[4] and leaves, and it wore a necklace of human skulls. Its legs and arms were as thick as tree stumps. Its open mouth revealed a sharp set of teeth, and its eyes were darker than a starless
30 night. The Chenoo raised its arms, preparing to grasp Nolka in its long, bony fingers. **B**

Knowing there was nowhere to hide, Nolka thought quickly.

"Grandfather!" she said with a smile. "Where have you been?"

"GRANDFATHER?" the Chenoo growled. It stopped in its tracks and looked confused. No human being had ever dared to speak to it this way before. **C**

"Yes, Grandfather. I have been waiting here all day for you. Don't you even remember me?" Nolka said. There was a long pause. Nolka did her best to appear calm.

40 "GRANDDAUGHTER?!" roared the Chenoo. "I HAVE A GRANDDAUGHTER?!"

"Yes, of course you do. I have been preparing this sweat lodge for you all day," Nolka said, motioning toward the large pile of rocks glowing in the fire. She hoped to delay the Chenoo from trying to eat her until her brothers returned from hunting. So far the plan was working. **D**

"Grandfather, please come into the lodge," she said, lifting up the door flap.

"THANK YOU, GRANDDAUGHTER," the Chenoo rumbled as it walked over to the sweat lodge and bent down. Crawling in on its hands and knees, the giant squeezed through the door. Sitting down, his legs
50 around the fire pit, the Chenoo filled the entire lodge.

Walking over to the fire, Nolka picked up a large forked stick and carried one hot rock after another and began placing them in the center of the lodge. She was just pulling another rock out of the fire when she heard someone coming.

---

4. **pine pitch:** the thick, sticky sap of a pine tree.

SOCIAL STUDIES CONNECTION

A sweat lodge, or sweathouse, is a structure used by many Native Americans to induce sweating as a cleansing ritual. It is heated by pouring water over hot stones.

B LEGENDS
What details show how powerful the Chenoo is?

C LEGENDS
Reread lines 32–36. A common stylistic element in traditional stories is the cleverness of a young hero, who may quickly come up with a trick or a plan to deal with an enemy that seems impossible to defeat. Is the Chenoo really Nolka's grandfather? What is Nolka trying to accomplish here?

D MAKE INFERENCES
Reread lines 37–44. Though Nolka appears calm and in control, what feelings is she probably experiencing?

"Sister, what are you doing?" called Awasos as he and Kasko, both completely out of breath, came running into the **clearing.**

"We saw huge tracks headed toward our camp," Kasko said. "We were afraid that you—"

Nolka held up a hand to her mouth, and her brothers stopped talking. 60 She looked over toward the lodge.

"Our grandfather has finally arrived!" Nolka said. "Come and greet him." Then she picked up another glowing rock. As she walked over to the lodge, her brothers, totally confused, followed her. **E**

"Grandfather, your grandsons have returned to greet you," said Nolka to the Chenoo, through the door of the lodge.

"Grandsons? I have grandsons?" roared the Chenoo. Looking into the lodge, Awasos and Kasko could not believe it. There sat the very same monster whose tracks they had seen headed toward camp.

"Hello, my grandsons!" the Chenoo rumbled.

70 "Oh, ah, yes. Hello, grandfather . . . it is good to see you," Kasko said, after being nudged in the ribs by Nolka.

"This lodge feels good. Bring me more rocks!"

"Yes, Grandfather," Kasko said.

The two men and their sister piled one glowing rock after another in the center of the lodge. Then, after placing a large birch-bark bucket

clearing (klîr′ ĭng) *n.*
an open area of land, as
in the middle of a forest

E **LEGENDS**
What courageous
qualities does
Nolka show?

◄ **Analyze
Visuals**

In what way is this
photograph like the
Chenoo's necklace?

full of water just inside the door of the lodge, they closed the flap. Moments later, a loud hissing sound came from inside the lodge as the Chenoo began to pour water on the rocks.

"Now is our chance to make a run for it," Nolka whispered to her 80 brothers. The three of them began to quietly sneak out of camp. But they had not moved quickly enough.

"MORE ROCKS! BRING ME MORE ROCKS! OPEN THE DOOR!" roared the Chenoo.

Nolka ran over and swung open the flap of the lodge. Awasos and Kasko **proceeded** to bring in four more loads of rocks. Then, after the fourth load, the flap to the lodge was again closed. As soon as the door was closed, the sound of hissing steam came again from within the lodge. And just as before, just when they began to sneak away, the Chenoo shouted for them again.

90 "OPEN THE DOOR. MORE ROCKS, MORE WATER!"

"Yes, Grandfather. We are coming!"

Quickly Awasos and Kasko brought more rocks as Nolka ran to a nearby stream to refill the birch-bark bucket. When they opened the door to the lodge, huge gusts of steam flowed out so thickly that the only thing in the lodge they could see was the Chenoo's huge arm as it reached out to grab the freshly filled bucket of water.

Closing the flap again, all three **siblings** agreed it was no use trying to run. The Chenoo would only call for them again. And sure enough, it did.

"OPEN THE DOOR. MORE ROCKS. MORE WATER."

100 This time, they brought in every rock from the fire, even the rocks from the fire circle. They hoped the heat would be so great that the Chenoo would pass out. Standing by the lodge, they listened closely. But, to their surprise, as the hissing sound of the water hitting the rocks got louder and louder, the Chenoo began to sing.

"WAY-YAA, way-yaa, way-yaa, HOOO!!
WAY-YAA, way-yaa, way-yaa, HOOO!!"

Then it paused to pour more water on the rocks before it sang again.

"WAY-YAA, way-yaa, way-yaa, HOOO!!
WAY-YAA, way-yaa, way-yaa, HOOO!!"

110 This time, as the Chenoo sang, they noticed that its voice did not seem as loud. Again they heard the sounds of steam rising as water was poured on the stones.

"WAY-YAA, way-yaa, way-yaa, HOOO!!
WAY-YAA, way-yaa, way-yaa, HOOO!!"

That voice was much softer now, so soft that it sounded like the voice of an old man.

"WAY-YAA, way-yaa, way-yaa, HOOO!!

proceed (prō-sēd′) *v.* to go forward or onward; continue

sibling (sĭb′lĭng) *n.* a brother or sister

COMMON CORE L 6

Language Coach

Onomatopoeia When writers want to create "sounds" in their work, they use **onomatopoeia**—a word or group of words that imitate the sound being described. The word *hissing* in lines 87 and 103 sounds like what it is describing—the sound of water as it hits fire. Onomatopoetic words like *boom* and *meow* are sometimes similar in different languages, but often they are very different. For example, in English the words *drip drop* might be used to describe the sound of water dripping. In French, however, it would be *plic ploc*; in Korean *tok tok*; and in Tamil *sottu-sottu*.

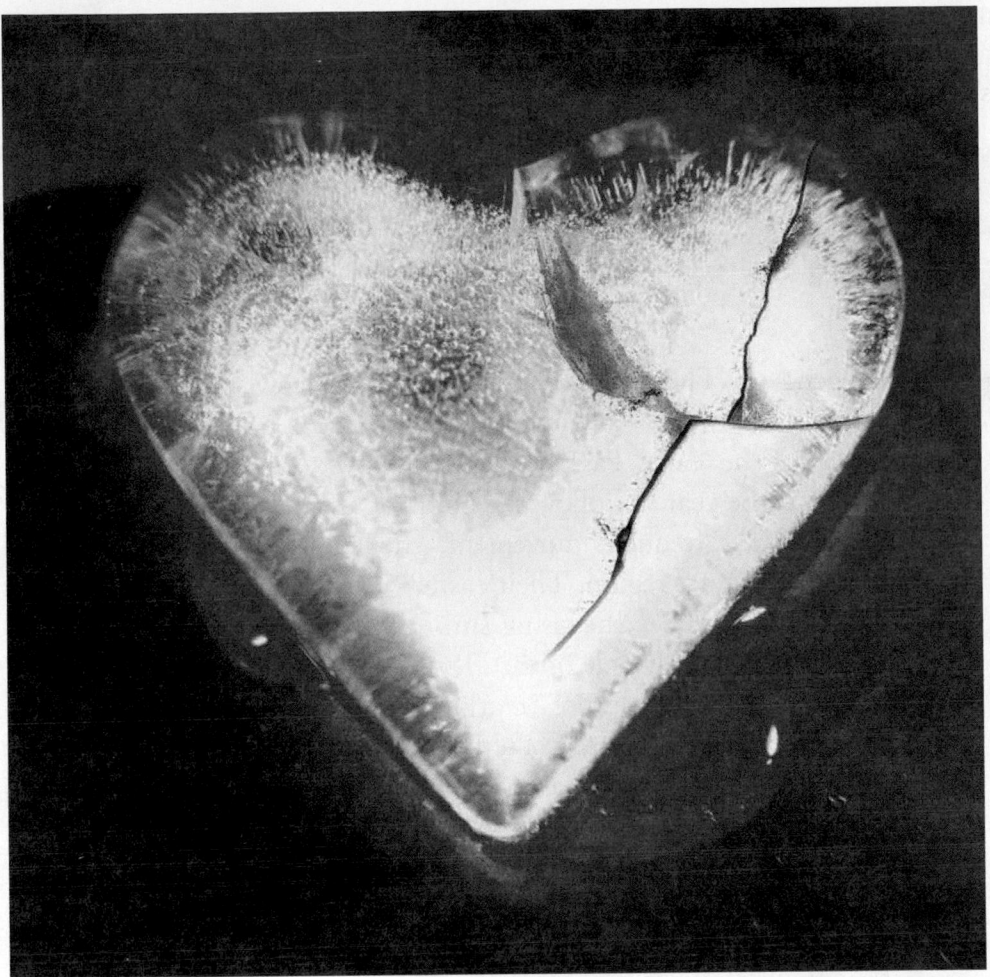

◀ **Analyze Visuals**
What part of the legend does this photograph represent?

WAY-YAA, WAY-YAA, WAY-YAA, HOOO!!"

Then it was silent.

120   "Grandchildren, open the door," a little voice called from inside the sweat lodge.

   Awasos lifted up the door flap. A huge gust of steam blew out from the lodge, knocking him backward. As the steam rose into the air, a little old man crawled out from the lodge. As he stood up, the little old man began to cough. He coughed and coughed until he coughed up a huge piece of ice in the shape of a human heart. Falling to the ground, the heart-shaped piece of ice that was the bad spirit of the Chenoo shattered on a rock.

   "Thank you, my grandchildren. You have saved me. I am no longer a monster. Now I am truly your grandfather," said the old man with

130 a smile. **F**

So Nolka and her two brothers took the old man who had been a Chenoo as their grandfather. They brought him back to their village, where he quietly and peacefully lived out the rest of his days. ∽

F **LEGENDS**
Startling transformations are a stylistic element in many traditional stories. In what other myths, legends, or folk tales have you seen similar transformations, in which a monster becomes human? What theme might such stories express?

ARTICLE "The Chenoo" is a legend from the Passamaquoddy, a northeast American Indian people. This brief article presents information about the Passamaquoddy. Note the information the map and timeline convey.

The PASSAMAQUODDY

The legend of "The Chenoo" has been passed down from generation to generation by the Passamaquoddy people of northeastern North America. The early Passamaquoddy moved from place to place throughout the year to follow the herds of animals they hunted.

Despite their frequent movement, the Passamaquoddy remained within one general region. Their eastern location allowed them to be among the first to see the rising sun each day. Because of this, they became known as "People of the Dawn."

10 Today, Passamaquoddy reservations are located in eastern Maine in two locations: Pleasant Point and Indian Township. These reservations are within the same region where previous generations of Passamaquoddy people lived and traveled.

COMMON CORE RI 7

A INTERPRET MAPS
Physical maps illustrate the natural landscape of an area. They often use shading to indicate **relief** (mountains, hills, and valleys). Maps often include a **legend,** or key, that explains symbols, lines, and shadings used on the map. They also often include a **compass rose,** or directional indicator, showing north, south, east, and west. Which of these features does this map include? What information from the article does this map illustrate? What else do you learn about the lands of the Passamaquoddy from this map?

A

Map showing CANADA, VERMONT, NEW HAMPSHIRE, MAINE, with Indian Township and Pleasant Point reservations and the ATLANTIC OCEAN. Legend: Traditional homeland, Present-day reservation.

Timeline of Passamaquoddy History **B**

1400 ▣ Passamaquoddy are part of 20,000 Native Americans living in the area now known as Maine.

1604 ▣ French explorer Samuel de Champlain makes contact with Passamaquoddy, opening up period of trade with Europe. Passamaquoddy population is about 2,000.

1616 ▣ European diseases spread among Passamaquoddy and other Maine tribes, causing a pandemic called the "Great Dying." Passamaquoddy population goes down to about 150.

1701 ▣ Passamaquoddy join with other Maine tribes to form Wabanaki Confederacy, a protection against enemies.

1776 ▣ Many Passamaquoddy fight alongside American Colonists against the British in the Revolutionary War.

1820 ▣ Maine becomes a state; Passamaquoddy reservations are created at Indian Township and Pleasant Point.

1954 ▣ Passamaquoddy are granted right to vote in national elections.

1972 ▣ Passamaquoddy, together with Penobscot Nation, file a lawsuit against the Federal government, claiming that over 12 million acres of their land were taken in treaties that violated the law.

1980 ▣ President Jimmy Carter signs Maine Indian Land Claims Settlement Act. Penobscots and Passamaquoddys are given a 27 million dollar trust fund and 300,000 acres of land.

Present ▣ Passamaquoddy number about 3,500 and own more than 200,000 acres of land in Maine. A strong cultural revival seeks to keep alive the language, stories, and customs of the people.

⬭ COMMON CORE RI 7

B INTERPRET TIMELINES

A **timeline** lists events according to their **chronological order** (the order in which they happened). Timelines present a lot of information in a small amount of space. This timeline places events alongside the time period in which they occur. What does this timeline tell you about the Passamaquoddy that you don't learn from the article itself? What important information would you miss if you did not read this timeline?

Comprehension

1. **Recall** What does Nolka do while her brothers are hunting?

2. **Recall** Why do the brothers rush back to camp when they see a set of large footprints?

3. **Clarify** How do the three siblings plan to escape from the Chenoo?

COMMON CORE

RL 1 Cite textual evidence to support inferences drawn from the text.

Text Analysis

4. **Make Inferences** Look at the chart you created as you read. In what ways does Nolka demonstrate the qualities of a heroine?

5. **Examine Characteristics of Legends** Which details about the characters and events in "The Chenoo" seem real, and which do not? Make a chart like the one shown. Fill in each square using details from the legend.

	Character	Event
Real		
Not Real		

6. **Identify Theme** In many legends, the hero slays a monster, but in this legend, the hero saves a monster. What lessons about human nature and behavior does this story teach?

7. **Analyze Characteristics of Legends** What other **stylistic elements** common to traditional stories did you find in this legend? How did they contribute to the theme?

8. **Analyze Symbol** Reread lines 122–127. What might the heart of ice that the Chenoo coughs up symbolize?

Extension and Challenge

9. **SOCIAL STUDIES CONNECTION** Storytelling has always been an important part of Native American culture. Review the article on 720 about the people who first told the story of the Chenoo. Then choose another Native American legend to read. Share a summary of the story with the class.

Is FEAR ever fun?

What was creepy or scary about this story? What made it fun to read? Why do you think people get pleasure from reading stories about monsters and other scary things?

Vocabulary in Context

▲ VOCABULARY PRACTICE

Choose the letter of the word or phrase that is most closely related to the boldfaced word.

1. **proceed:** (a) continue, (b) halt, (c) pause
2. **sibling:** (a) friend, (b) father, (c) brother
3. **inspect:** (a) ignore, (b) refuse, (c) examine
4. **clearing:** (a) grove of trees, (b) open land, (c) thick jungle

clearing

inspect

proceed

sibling

ACADEMIC VOCABULARY IN SPEAKING

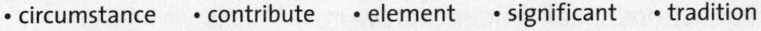

• circumstance   • contribute   • element   • significant   • tradition

"The Chenoo" contains some realistic **elements** and others that are not as believable. Which parts **contribute** to your understanding of the theme of the story? Use at least two Academic Vocabulary words in your discussion.

VOCABULARY STRATEGY: USE REFERENCE AIDS

To express ideas clearly and correctly, you need to choose your words carefully. Sometimes this means that you need to replace a vague or general word with a more specific synonym. **Synonyms** are words with similar meanings. For example, *gorgeous* is a synonym for *exquisite*. To find a synonym for a word, look in a **reference aid,** or information resource.

• A **dictionary** often lists synonyms after the definition(s) of a word.

> **exquisite** (ĕk′skwĭ-zĭt) *adj.* of extraordinary beauty or charm: *They watched the exquisite sunset.* **syn** beautiful, gorgeous, flawless, superb

• A reference book of synonyms, such as a **thesaurus** or a synonym finder lists synonyms of words. Many word processing programs feature an electronic thesaurus tool.

> **exquisite** *adjective* beautiful, gorgeous, flawless, superb

PRACTICE Use a dictionary or thesaurus to find a synonym for each word. Note the synonym as well as the reference aid you used to find it.

1. bravery   2. battle   3. naughty   4. calm

COMMON CORE

L 4c Consult dictionaries and thesauruses, both print and digital, to clarify meaning.

Interactive Vocabulary **THINK** central

Go to **thinkcentral.com.**
KEYWORD: HML6-723

Damon and Pythias
Greek Legend Dramatized by Fan Kissen

What is true
FRIENDSHIP?

COMMON CORE

RL 3 Describe how a drama's plot unfolds as well as how the characters respond or change as the plot moves toward a resolution. **RL 5** Analyze how a particular scene contributes to the development of the theme. **RL 7** Compare and contrast a drama to a video version of the text.

It's often said that actions speak louder than words. This is certainly the case when it comes to friendship. It's important for people to *show* that they're your friends and not just *say* it. In *Damon and Pythias*, you'll read about a man who is willing to pay the ultimate price to help a friend.

WEB IT Think about what types of behavior reflect true friendship—the ways people prove to each other that they're loyal and trustworthy. Then use a web diagram like the one shown to record your thoughts.

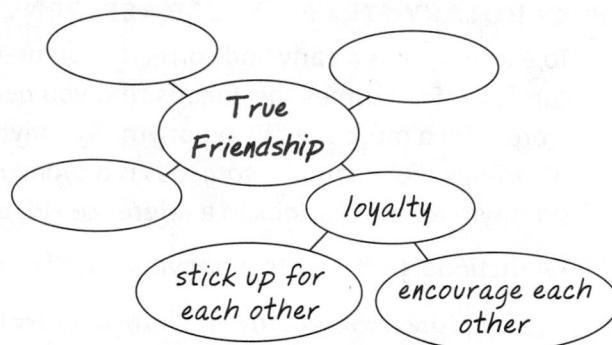

True Friendship

loyalty

stick up for each other

encourage each other

● TEXT ANALYSIS: CULTURAL VALUES IN LEGENDS

What does it take to be a hero? In many cases, a hero is someone who shows great bravery. In legends and other traditional stories, though, a hero is expected not only to be brave but also to uphold the **cultural values** of a society. These are the behaviors a society wants its people to have. In ancient Greece, two important cultural values were

- loyalty, or devotion to friends and family
- honesty

As you read *Damon and Pythias,* look for examples of how the main characters demonstrate these values. Then notice their effect on the plot and the conflict resolution.

● READING STRATEGY: READING A PLAY

In some plays, a **narrator,** or teller of the story, helps guide the audience through the action. The narrator supplies background information, explains what's happening, and tells about conversations and events not included in the dialogue. The narrator might also explain characters' thoughts and feelings and why they act as they do.

As you read, use a chart to summarize the narrator's information and how it helps you understand the play.

Narrator's Information	How It Helps
lines 10–12: The king is cruel and shows no mercy for anyone.	tells me what kind of person the king is

▲ VOCABULARY IN CONTEXT

Fan Kissen uses the words in Column A to help tell the story of two men fighting a cruel king. Match the words in Column A with their meanings in Column B.

Column A
1. desperately
2. harsh
3. persuade
4. proclaim
5. tyrant

Column B
a. convince
b. dictator
c. urgently
d. rough
e. announce

 Complete the activities in your **Reader/Writer Notebook.**

Meet the Author

Fan Kissen
1904–1978

Radio Writer
From the 1940s to the 1960s, Fan Kissen had a radio series called *Tales from the Four Winds.* Kissen dramatized world folk tales and legends, such as *Damon and Pythias,* for the series. Though the majority of her writing consists of plays written in radio script format, Kissen also produced several biographies of little-known historical figures for young people.

BACKGROUND TO THE LEGEND

Legendary Friendship
Damon and Pythias is an ancient Greek legend, adapted here as a radio play. The events in this story take place in Greece around the 4th century B.C. The relationship between Damon and Pythias has remained a model of true friendship throughout the centuries.

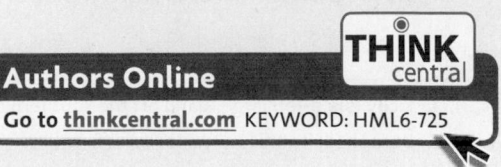

Authors Online

THINK central

Go to **thinkcentral.com** KEYWORD: HML6-725

Damon
and Pythias

Dramatized by Fan Kissen

CAST OF CHARACTERS

Narrator	**Pythias**	**Mother**
First Voice	**King**	**First Robber**
Second Voice	**Damon**	**Second Robber**
Soldier	**Third Voice**	

Narrator. Long, long ago there lived on the island of Sicily[1] two young men named Damon and Pythias.[2] They were known far and wide for the strong friendship each had for the other. Their names have come down to our own times to mean true friendship. You may hear it said of two persons:

First Voice. Those two? Why, they're like Damon and Pythias!

10 **Narrator.** The king of that country was a cruel **tyrant**. He made cruel laws, and he showed no mercy toward anyone who broke his laws. Now, you might very well wonder:

Second Voice. Why didn't the people rebel?

Narrator. Well, the people didn't dare rebel because they feared the king's great and powerful army. No one dared say a word against the king or his laws—except Damon and Pythias. One day a soldier overheard 20 Pythias speaking against a new law the king had **proclaimed.**

Soldier. Ho, there! Who are you that dares to speak so about our king?

Pythias (*unafraid*). I am called Pythias.

Soldier. Don't you know it is a crime to speak against the king or his laws? You are under

---

1. **Sicily** (sĭs′ə-lē): large island off the southern tip of Italy.
2. **Damon** (dā′mən) . . . **Pythias** (pĭth′ē-əs).

arrest! Come and tell this opinion of yours to the king's face!

(*music: a few short bars in and out*)

30 **Narrator.** When Pythias was brought before the king, he showed no fear. He stood straight and quiet before the throne.

King (*hard, cruel*). So, Pythias! They tell me you do not approve of the laws I make.

Pythias. I am not alone, Your Majesty, in thinking your laws are cruel. But you rule the people with such an iron hand that they dare not complain.

King (*angry*). But you have the daring to 40 complain for them! Have they appointed you their champion?

Pythias. No, Your Majesty. I speak for myself alone. I have no wish to make trouble for anyone. But I am not afraid to tell you that the people are suffering under your rule. They want to have a voice in making the laws for themselves. You do not allow them to speak up for themselves.

King. In other words, you are calling me a tyrant! Well, you shall learn for yourself how 50 a tyrant treats a rebel! Soldier! Throw this man into prison!

Soldier. At once, Your Majesty! Don't try to resist, Pythias!

Pythias. I know better than to try to resist a soldier of the king! And for how long am I to remain in prison, Your Majesty, merely for speaking out for the people?

King (*cruel*). Not for very long, Pythias. Two weeks from today, at noon, you shall be put 60 to death in the public square as an example to anyone else who may dare to question my laws or acts. Off to prison with him, soldier!

(*music: in briefly and out*)

Narrator. When Damon heard that his friend Pythias had been thrown into prison and the severe punishment that was to follow, he was heartbroken. He rushed to the prison and **persuaded** the guard to let him speak to his friend.

70 **Damon.** Oh, Pythias! How terrible to find you here! I wish I could do something to save you!

Pythias. Nothing can save me, Damon, my dear friend. I am prepared to die. But there is one thought that troubles me greatly.

Damon. What is it? I will do anything to help you.

Pythias. I'm worried about what will happen to my mother and my sister when I'm gone.

Damon. I'll take care of them, Pythias, as if 80 they were my own mother and sister.

Pythias. Thank you, Damon. I have money to leave them. But there are other things I must arrange. If only I could go to see them before I die! But they live two days' journey from here, you know.

Damon. I'll go to the king and beg him to give you your freedom for a few days. You'll give your word to return at the end of that time. Everyone in Sicily knows you for a man who 90 has never broken his word.

Pythias. Do you believe for one moment that the king would let me leave this prison, no matter how good my word may have been all my life?

Damon. I'll tell him that I shall take your place in this prison cell. I'll tell him that if you do not return by the appointed day, he may kill me in your place!

Pythias. No, no, Damon! You must not do 100 such a foolish thing! I cannot—I will not—let you do this! Damon! Damon! Don't go! (*to himself*) Damon, my friend! You may find yourself in a cell beside me!

(*music: in briefly and out*)

Damon (*begging*). Your Majesty! I beg of you! Let Pythias go home for a few days to bid farewell to his mother and sister. He gives his word that he will return at your appointed time. Everyone knows that his word can be trusted.

110 **King.** In ordinary business affairs—perhaps. But he is now a man under sentence of death. To free him even for a few days would strain his honesty—any man's honesty—too far. Pythias would never return here! I consider him a traitor, but I'm certain he's no fool.

Damon. Your Majesty! I will take his place in the prison until he comes back. If he does not return, then you may take my life in his place.

King (*astonished*). What did you say, Damon?

120 **Damon.** I'm so certain of Pythias that I am offering to die in his place if he fails to return on time.

King. I can't believe you mean it!

Damon. I do mean it, Your Majesty.

King. You make me very curious, Damon, so curious that I'm willing to put you and Pythias to the test. This exchange of prisoners will be made. But Pythias must be back two weeks from today, at noon.

130 **Damon.** Thank you, Your Majesty!

King. The order with my official seal shall go by your own hand, Damon. But I warn you, if your friend does not return on time, you shall surely die in his place! I shall show no mercy!

(*music: in briefly and out*)

Narrator. Pythias did not like the king's bargain with Damon. He did not like to leave his friend in prison with the chance that he might lose his life if something went wrong. But

140 at last Damon persuaded him to leave, and Pythias set out for his home. More than a week went by. The day set for the death sentence drew near. Pythias did not return. Everyone in the city knew of the condition on which the king had permitted Pythias to go home. Everywhere people met, the talk was sure to turn to the two friends.

First Voice. Do you suppose Pythias will come back?

150 **Second Voice.** Why should he stick his head under the king's axe, once he's escaped?

Third Voice. Still, would an honorable man like Pythias let such a good friend die for him?

First Voice. There's no telling what a man will do when it's a question of his own life against another's.

Second Voice. But if Pythias doesn't come back before the time is up, he will be killing his friend.

Third Voice. Well, there's still a few days' time.

160 I, for one, am certain that Pythias will return in time.

Second Voice. And I am just as certain that he will *not*. Friendship is friendship, but a man's own life is something stronger, I say!

Narrator. Two days before the time was up, the king himself visited Damon in his prison cell.

(*sound: iron door unlocked and opened*)

King (*mocking*). You see now, Damon, that you were a fool to make this bargain. Your friend

170 has tricked you! He will not come back here to be killed! He has deserted you!

Damon (*calm and firm*). I have faith in my friend. I know he will return.

King (*mocking*). We shall see!

(*sound: iron door shut and locked*)

Narrator. Meanwhile, when Pythias reached the home of his family, he arranged his business affairs so that his mother and sister would be able to live comfortably for the rest of their

180 years. Then he said a last farewell to them before starting back to the city.

Mother (*in tears*). Pythias, it will take you only two days to get back. Stay another day, I beg you!

Pythias. I dare not stay longer, Mother. Remember, Damon is locked up in my prison cell while I'm gone. Please don't make it harder for me! Farewell! Don't weep for me. My death may help to bring better days for all our people.

Narrator. So Pythias began his return journey in plenty of time. But bad luck struck him on the very first day. At twilight,[3] as he walked along a lonely stretch of woodland, a rough voice called:

First Robber. Not so fast there, young man! Stop!

Pythias (*startled*). Oh! What is it? What do you want?

Second Robber. Your money bags.

Pythias. My money bags? I have only this small bag of coins. I shall need them for some last favors, perhaps, before I die.

First Robber. What do you mean, before you die? We don't mean to kill you, only to take your money.

Pythias. I'll give you my money, only don't delay me any longer. I am to die by the king's order three days from now. If I don't return to prison on time, my friend must die in my place.

First Robber. A likely story! What man would be fool enough to go back to prison, ready to die?

Second Robber. And what man would be fool enough to die for you?

First Robber. We'll take your money, all right. And we'll tie you up while we get away.

Pythias (*begging*). No! No! I must get back to free my friend! (*fade*) I must go back!

Narrator. But the two robbers took Pythias' money, tied him to a tree, and went off as fast as they could. Pythias struggled to free himself. He cried out for help as loud as he could for a long time. But no one traveled through that lonesome woodland after dark. The sun had been up for many hours before he finally managed to free himself from the ropes that had tied him to the tree. He lay on the ground, hardly able to breathe.

(*music: in briefly and out*)

Narrator. After a while Pythias got to his feet. Weak and dizzy from hunger and thirst and his struggle to free himself, he set off again. Day and night he traveled without stopping, **desperately** trying to reach the city in time to save Damon's life.

(*music: up and out*)

Narrator. On the last day, half an hour before noon, Damon's hands were tied behind his back, and he was taken into the public square. The people muttered[4] angrily as Damon was led in by the jailer. Then the king entered and seated himself on a high platform.

(*sound: crowd voices in and hold under single voices*)

Soldier (*loud*). Long live the king!

First Voice (*low*). The longer he lives, the more miserable our lives will be!

King (*loud, mocking*). Well, Damon, your lifetime is nearly up. Where is your good friend Pythias now?

Damon (*firm*). I have faith in my friend. If he has not returned, I'm certain it is through no fault of his own.

King (*mocking*). The sun is almost overhead. The shadow is almost at the noon mark. And still your friend has not returned to give you back your life!

Damon (*quiet*). I am ready, and happy, to die in his place.

---

3. **twilight:** the time of day between sunset and dark. The darker stage of twilight is often called dusk.

4. **mutter:** to speak in low tones, especially to complain.

Reception in the Senate, detail from the Arch of Trajan (100s). Marble. Benevento, Campania, Italy. © Bridgeman Art Library.

King (*harsh*). And you shall, Damon! Jailer, lead the prisoner to the—

(*sound: crowd voices up to a roar, then under*)

First Voice (*over noise*). Look! It's Pythias!

260 **Second Voice** (*over noise*). Pythias has come back!

Pythias (*breathless*). Let me through! Damon!

Damon. Pythias!

Pythias. Thank the gods I'm not too late!

Damon (*quiet, sincere*). I would have died for you gladly, my friend.

Crowd Voices (*loud, demanding*). Set them free! Set them both free!

King (*loud*). People of the city! (*crowd voices out*)
270 Never in all my life have I seen such faith and friendship, such loyalty between men. There are many among you who call me **harsh** and cruel. But I cannot kill any man who proves such strong and true friendship for another. Damon and Pythias, I set you both free. (*roar of approval from crowd*) I am king. I command a great army. I have stores[5] of gold and precious jewels. But I would give all my money and my power for one friend like Damon or Pythias!

280 (*sound: roar of approval from crowd up briefly and out*)

(*music: up and out*)

---

5. **stores:** great quantities.

MOVIE REVIEW Read the following review and summary of a modern animated film that takes part of its inspiration—and its plot—from the ancient story of Damon and Pythias.

DAMON and PYTHIAS Meet the ARABIAN NIGHTS

A friendship so powerful that two people are willing to sacrifice their lives for each other is one reason the Greek legend of Damon and Pythias has lasted for centuries. Now this classic legend is the story at the heart of an animated film—one about another legendary hero, the Persian/ Arabic seafaring adventurer Sinbad. **A**

10 *Sinbad: Legend of the Seven Seas* (2003), an animated feature from the Dreamworks company, mixes the legends and stories of the *Arabian Nights* with classical Greek and Roman mythology. Sinbad is portrayed as a successful thief, pirate, and adventurer who grew up in Syracuse (a Greek kingdom in southern Italy). As a child, his best friend was the prince of that land, Proteus. Sinbad and Proteus parted ways over the years, but they reunite accidentally as Sinbad is trying to overtake and rob Proteus' ship. It is obvious that the two men still have regard for each other. In fact, the old friendship is still very important to Prince Proteus, who sees something in Sinbad that no one else seems to see. Sinbad is so affected by the reunion with his childhood friend that he

20 abandons his goal to steal what Proteus's powerful Book of Peace, a supernatural object that protects Syracuse. **B**

The plot goes into full swing when the tricky and sly Greek goddess Eris, who rules chaos and discord, disguises herself as Sinbad and steals the valuable book. Because Sinbad is a famous thief, no one believes that he did not steal the Book of Peace—no one except his boyhood friend Proteus. Sinbad is about to be placed in prison to await execution, but Proteus takes on the Damon role, agreeing to stay in prison in his friend's place until Sinbad (the Pythias of the story) returns with the Book of Peace. Sinbad will have to do the impossible to regain the Book of Peace:

30 go to Tartarus, the underworld. If Sinbad does not return with the book in time, Proteus will be executed. Proteus has unquestioning faith in Sinbad.

A COMPARE AND CONTRAST
What differences between *Damon and Pythias* and *Sinbad* are introduced in this first paragraph?

B COMPARE AND CONTRAST
How are the characters in *Sinbad* similar to those in *Damon and Pythias*? How are the characters different?

It's hard to see why, since Sinbad at first (and for some time afterward) wants to do nothing more than simply run off to an island paradise and forget the whole thing.

It is a woman who redeems the rough-around-the edges hero: Proteus's fiancé Marina has stowed away on Sinbad's ship and uses all her powers of persuasion to make sure Sinbad does the right thing and goes to Tartarus. Over the course of several life-and-death adventures, Sinbad and Marina fall in love. Not surprisingly, it is Marina's influence and love
40 that transform Sinbad into a truly brave and unselfish hero, someone not unlike Pythias. **C**

Sinbad almost recovers the Book of Peace, but he is tricked by Eris, who says she will only give him the book if he can tell the truth: Will he go back to Syracuse to die in Proteus's place if he cannot get the Book of Peace from her? She believes that Sinbad will never go back to Syracuse without the book, for that will mean death. She wants Proteus's execution to throw Syracuse into total chaos—which she loves. When Sinbad tells Eris that he will go back to Syracuse with or without the book, Eris accuses him of lying. Eris throws Sinbad and Marina out of Tartarus and
50 keeps the Book of Peace herself.

Eris, however, has underestimated the new Sinbad. Love has made him stronger and nobler. He realizes he cannot abandon Proteus, no matter the cost. In a dramatic last-minute rescue, Sinbad saves Proteus from a beheading. When Proteus finds out that Sinbad has come back without the book, he realizes that Sinbad has done something utterly heroic and completely unselfish. This brave self-sacrifice defeats Eris, and she gives up the Book of Peace. (This all happens, of course, just as the executioner's blade is about to come down on Sinbad's neck.) With the return of the Book of Peace, all is well in Syracuse. Proteus—who is as
60 understanding, self-sacrificing, and heroic as Damon and Pythias put together—lets Marina go, realizing that she loves Sinbad and the adventurous life at sea. **D**

It's good to see classic works like *Damon and Pythias* show up in some form in popular culture, even if few people will recognize it. Still, one wonders if the modern world could accept—and believe—an idealistic story of unselfish friendship closer to the original legend. Would audiences be as entertained if the story of flawless heroes who readily risk their lives for each other lacked the spunky heroines to cheer them on and make them do the right thing?

C COMPARE AND CONTRAST
Reread lines 35–41. What differences in the plot can you identify between this film and the story of *Damon and Pythias?*

D COMPARE AND CONTRAST
What is the resolution of *Sinbad: Legend of the Seven Seas?* Is it similar to or different from the resolution of *Damon and Pythias?* Explain.

Comprehension

1. **Recall** Why is Pythias arrested?

2. **Clarify** Why is the king willing to strike such an unusual bargain with Damon?

3. **Summarize** What causes Pythias to return so late?

Text Analysis

4. **Make Inferences** Reread lines 168–173. What does Damon's response to the king's mockery tell you about the nature of his friendship with Pythias?

5. **Reading a Play** Look at the chart you filled in while reading. Explain how the play would be different without the **narrator's** comments. What key pieces of information would be missing?

6. **Identify Cultural Values in a Legend** How do Damon and Pythias prove their honesty and their loyalty to each other? Make a list of their important words and actions, and explain what they reveal about ancient Greek cultural values.

> **Examples of Honesty and Loyalty**
>
> 1. Damon immediately rushes to prison to see Pythias.
>
> 2.

7. **Make Judgments** Throughout Sicily, Pythias was known for being a trustworthy person. Why do you think some people still doubted that he would return in time to save Damon?

8. **Compare a Play and a Film** Read the review of the animated film *Sinbad: Legend of the Seven Seas*. Explain how the story of Damon and Pythias was adapted to form a central plot line in this movie. How is the film like the story of Damon and Pythias, and how is it different?

Extension and Challenge

9. **Creative Project: Drama** In a small group, record your own "radio broadcast" of *Damon and Pythias*. Include any music or sound effects mentioned in the play. Then play the recording for the class.

What is true FRIENDSHIP?

Look back at the web diagram you used to record your thoughts about the kinds of behaviors that prove friends are loyal and trustworthy. After reading *Damon and Pythias*, what new insights do you have into the kinds of behaviors that reflect true friendship?

COMMON CORE

RL 3 Describe how a drama's plot unfolds as well as how the characters respond or change as the plot moves toward a resolution. **RL 5** Analyze how a particular scene contributes to the development of the theme. **RL 7** Compare and contrast a drama to a video version of the text.

Language

◆ **GRAMMAR IN CONTEXT:** Form Complex Sentences

COMMON CORE

L 3a Vary sentence patterns for meaning, reader/listener interest, and style. **W 3** Write narratives to develop imagined events.

An **independent clause** can stand alone as a sentence. A **dependent clause** is a group of words that contains a subject and a verb but cannot stand alone as a sentence. Dependent clauses begin with words and phrases such as *because, even though, if, since, that*, and *when*. When a dependent clause and an independent clause are combined, they form a **complex sentence.**

Original: Pythias criticizes the king. Even though he knows he will be punished for it. (*The first clause is independent. The second clause is dependent and cannot stand alone.*)

Revised: Pythias criticizes the king even though he knows he will be punished for it. (*Together, the clauses form a complex sentence.*)

PRACTICE Form a complex sentence by combining the two clauses in each of the following sentences.

1. Pythias promises to return. After he visits his family.
2. Most people probably wouldn't return. If they were in his position.
3. Damon never gave up his faith. Because he completely trusted Pythias.
4. The crowd was happy. That Damon and Pythias would both be free.

*For more help with dependent clauses and complex sentences, see page R63 in the **Grammar Handbook.***

READING-WRITING CONNECTION

YOUR TURN Expand your knowledge of *Damon and Pythias* by responding to this prompt. Then use the **revising tip** to improve your writing.

WRITING PROMPT	REVISING TIP
Extended Constructed Response: Dialogue Imagine the conversation Damon and Pythias have after Pythias agrees to let him take his place in prison. Write the conversation between the two characters as a **full-page dialogue**. (Use the play for examples of how to write dialogue.)	Reread your dialogue to see if it sounds realistic. In speech, people use all kinds of sentence structures, from simple to compound and complex. Be sure that you have included a good amount of sentence variety to make your dialogue sound natural. Include a few complex sentences, which combine a dependent with an independent clause. Try beginning some sentences with a dependent clause.

Interactive Revision

Go to **thinkcentral.com**.
KEYWORD: HML6-735

Uncle Septimus's Beard

Tall Tale by Herbert Shippey

Why do we EXAGGERATE?

⋯⋯ **COMMON CORE**

RL 4 Determine the meaning of words and phrases as they are used in a text, including figurative meanings. L 6 Gather vocabulary knowledge when considering a word or phrase important to comprehension.

Have you ever claimed you were hungry enough to eat a horse, or said that you waited in the rain until you were soaked to the bone? Sometimes, in order to express feelings or describe adventures, people exaggerate. As you will see in the tale that follows, exaggeration can add humor to a story and make everyday experiences sound more interesting.

QUICKWRITE Think of a time when you or someone you know exaggerated in order to make a point or make a story more exciting. Then write a brief version of each—the real story, and the exaggerated version. Share your writing with your classmates.

● TEXT ANALYSIS: CHARACTERISTICS OF A TALL TALE

A **tall tale** is a humorous story in which the characters and events are exaggerated. This means that the characters and events are made to seem bigger, louder, or greater in some way than they really are. For example:

Eventually the beard reached down to his toes and began to drag on the ground. Then he had to wash it out every evening to get rid of the dust and grit that would collect during the day.

As you read "Uncle Septimus's Beard," look for other examples of exaggeration. Look especially for the use of a kind of figurative language called **hyperbole**—a phrase or statement that is wildly exaggerated. Often, a hyperbole involves a comparison. Common hyperboles include "I nearly died laughing" and "That cat ran like his tail was on fire."

● READING STRATEGY: VISUALIZE

Tall tales are often so full of exaggerated action and description that you can **visualize,** or picture in your mind, many of their characters and scenes. As you read "Uncle Septimus's Beard," make a list of strong sensory images, descriptive words and phrases that help you create a strong mental picture of the tale's events.

> Vivid Descriptions
> 1. Beard used to sweep floor
> 2. Beard used as a jump rope

▲ VOCABULARY IN CONTEXT

Herbert Shippey uses the boldfaced words to help tell the story of a man's unbelievable beard. Try to figure out what each boldfaced word means within its sentence.

WORD LIST	assert	imposing	incident	inspiration

1. Everyone remembers an **incident** involving the beard.
2. No one knew Septimus's **inspiration** for growing it.
3. People **assert** that it was the greatest beard ever.
4. The **imposing** beard was the talk of the town.

 Complete the activities in your **Reader/Writer Notebook.**

Meet the Author

Herbert Shippey
born 1944

Weeding and Reading
As a teenager, it was Herbert Shippey's job to weed his family's garden. He would often take rests from his work in the hot Georgia sun to read Henry David Thoreau's *Walden.* He says that reading opened his mind to "imaginative possibilities." Later, when deciding upon a career, Shippey chose to combine work with pleasure by becoming an English teacher.

BACKGROUND TO THE TALL TALE
Campfire Stories
Folk tales are traditional stories that have been handed down from one generation to the next and are about common people, or folk. When a folk tale is about extraordinary events and characters, it is called a **tall tale.** Some of the first tall tales were told around campfires in the American West of the 1800s.

Humorous Tales
To help cope with their difficult lives, some early American settlers created and told humorous stories. Some of the heroes and heroines of these stories were imaginary characters. Others were real people who were known for their strength and courage. As the stories of these people's deeds were retold, they often became exaggerated, and the people became larger than life.

Author Online
THINK central
Go to **thinkcentral.com.**
KEYWORD: HML6-737

UNCLE SEPTIMUS'S BEARD

Herbert Shippey

No one knows exactly why Uncle Septimus began growing a beard. Aunt Rachel always said that she admired a man with hair on his chin. Her grandfather, a circuit-riding Methodist preacher, was noted for having a long beard. Whenever he stood at the pulpit,[1] pounding his fists and preaching hellfire and brimstone, some people thought he looked like Moses in their Bible pictures. So maybe this **imposing** image, recalled so vividly by Aunt Rachel, was the **inspiration** for Uncle Septimus's decision. Or maybe one day he just got tired of shaving.

Moreover, no one knew why everyone—including his grandchildren—
10 called him "Uncle." Perhaps his blue eyes sparkled with such good humor and he did so many neighborly deeds that he seemed like an uncle to half the county.

When his beard extended to his waist, Uncle Septimus tucked it beneath the bib of his overalls to keep from dribbling milk, gravy, or cane syrup on it when he sat down to eat. Sometimes, though, he'd forget, and after a meal he'd have to walk to the back porch to shake out the crumbs and bacon rinds. The shakings alone were enough to keep his bird dogs and chickens fat and happy. **A**

Illustrations by Joel Priddy.

---

1. **pulpit:** raised platform or stand used in preaching or leading a religious service.

Analyze Visuals ▶

In what ways does the illustration add humor to the tall tale?

imposing (ĭm-pō′zĭng)
adj. impressive; grand

inspiration
(ĭn′spə-rā′shən)
n. something that motivates or influences

A TALL TALE
Reread lines 9–18. What details about Septimus and his beard seem exaggerated?

Eventually the beard reached down to his toes and began to drag
20 on the ground. Then he had to wash it out every evening to get rid
of the dust and grit that would collect during the day. Aunt Rachel
was rather pleased with this new development, because she no longer
had to sweep the floor, except under the beds.

The beard grew longer and longer. It became so long that it dragged
several feet behind Uncle Septimus, but he refused to trim it. Sometimes
at family dinners he fell asleep in his favorite chair beneath the pecan tree
in the front yard. Then the grandchildren took the beard and used it as
a jump rope. They swung it round and round and took turns jumping,
but Uncle Septimus never seemed to notice. On other occasions, he
30 looped the beard up in his own hands and let the children swing on it.

The grandchildren all loved the beard, and they enjoyed examining it
while he slept, because they found marvelous surprises. Since the beard
was so long, all kinds of things became entangled in it. One summer
morning two of the grandchildren pulled out a robin's egg, a broken
arrowhead made from caramel-colored flint, six chicken feathers, two
swirled marbles, a silver dollar, and two green lizards that had set up
housekeeping, not to mention tons of cockleburs and beggar lice.[2] **B**

Later that same day Uncle Septimus went fishing at the creek with his
sons. He sat on a log and carefully removed his beard from beneath the
40 bib of his overalls. Handful by handful, he drew the beard out, letting
the end down into the water and then allowing the current to carry
it downstream. It steadily unreeled the way a harpoon rope uncoils when
it has stuck firmly in a sounding whale. Septimus's sons watched the long
gray strand floating downstream until the whole mass was quivering
underwater like seaweed.

Uncle Septimus sat still for several minutes, and then the sons waded
into the creek and began drawing the beard in. Coil after dripping coil
fell upon the sand, and the fish tangled in the beard flopped onto the
bank. Soon there were catfish, bluegills, largemouth bass, pike, jack, gar,
50 snapping turtles, and even a water moccasin.[3] There were so many fish
that Uncle Septimus gave a fish fry for the whole community.

Oftentimes on a cold winter night Uncle Septimus wrapped his beard
around himself to keep warm in bed. If Aunt Rachel wanted to wake him
up, she just asked one of her hefty sons to jerk the end of the beard, and
out he would come, rolling like a bolt of fabric tossed on a store counter.

B VISUALIZE
What specific sensory
images about the uses
of the beard most help
you picture the beard
in your mind? Add this
information to your list.

---

2. **cockleburs and beggar lice:** any of several plants having small, prickly fruits that cling to clothing
   or animal fur.

3. **catfish . . . water moccasin:** catfish, bluegills, largemouth bass, pike, jack, and gar are all types
   of freshwater fish. The water moccasin, also known as a cottonmouth, is a poisonous water snake
   found in the southeastern and south central United States.

Sometimes Uncle Septimus wrapped the beard round and round himself when he sat at his deer stand before daybreak on a frosty winter morning. In the uncertain predawn light, it looked as if a large, gray boa constrictor had attacked him. Uncle Septimus claimed, though, that winding the
60 beard around himself allowed him to walk through the woods without getting it tangled in the branches and briars. But there was a drawback. It took him most of the night just to entwine⁴ himself, and he had to be careful to leave openings for his arms so that he could shoot. Needless to say, going to the bathroom was a problem. So most of the time he preferred just to let the beard drag behind him on the ground. **C**

You could always tell where Uncle Septimus had been. Old man Marchant said that one time he went to Drothers's store, hoping to find Uncle Septimus. He needed to see him about a hog that had broken out. So he said to Bill Drothers, "I see Septimus has just left because yonder goes
70 his beard dragging out the front door. If I run, maybe I can catch him."

But Bill Drothers, sitting by the stove and reading the weekly paper, didn't even look up. "You needn't bother," he said. "Septimus left over an hour ago, and his beard's been unwinding ever since. Most likely he's home now, sitting on his front porch and chewing tobacco while one of his boys hauls in the beard."

The beard did create problems. One time Uncle Septimus walked several times around the yard raking leaves, and the beard got all fouled up. It had wrapped around a tree several times, and you could no longer see the well for the beard. And the chicken coop was completely
80 covered. It took his boys three days to untangle him, and all that time the chickens didn't lay a single egg because they thought it was night. Uncle Septimus sat there the whole time, complaining about how he missed his fried eggs.

Aunt Rachel kept saying, "Septimus, if you don't cut off that beard, it's going to be the death of you! One of these days you're going to get so tangled up, ain't nobody going to be able to get to you." **D**

After that **incident,** Septimus's sons rigged up a windlass⁵ and wrapped the beard around it. That way he could work around the yard, and his boys could wind the beard back up after he was finished. The beard didn't
90 completely unwind unless he went a long ways. Aunt Rachel also found the windlass useful. Whenever she needed her husband, all she had to do was start turning the handle, and eventually she'd see him coming down the road, led by his beard. **E**

---

4. **entwine** (ĕn-twīn′): to twist or coil together.
5. **windlass:** a machine used for pulling and lifting, usually on ships.

C TALL TALE
Reread lines 52–65. In what way does the simile "rolling like a bolt of fabric tossed on a store counter" create a humorous effect? What other strong sensory images add to the humor here?

D TALL TALE
Reread lines 76–86. How many examples of hyperbole do you find here? Explain how hyperbole and sensory images add to the meaning of the story. What does the skillful use of hyperbole add to the effectiveness of a tall tale?

incident (ĭn′sĭ-dənt) n. a single event or occurrence

E VISUALIZE
Reread lines 87–93. What sensory details do you find amusing when you visualize this scene?

◄ **Analyze Visuals**

What similarities do you see between the tornado and Uncle Septimus's beard in this illustration?

COMMON CORE L 6

Language Coach

Jargon Specialized language used by a group of people who share a profession or interest is called **jargon.** The term *funnel cloud* in line 105 is an example of jargon used by scientists and weather reporters. A funnel cloud is a kind of whirlwind. When a funnel cloud touches land, it is a tornado. When it touches water, it is a waterspout. Some other kinds of whirlwinds are dust devils, gustnados, fire whirls, and landspouts. What are some other examples of jargon that you might hear in a weather report?

Late one March afternoon, Uncle Septimus was plowing in the back field. The wind had been blowing all day, and the beard went streaming off downwind. Everything worked all right for a while. Uncle Septimus simply plowed upwind, and the beard didn't get in his way. It was a big field, and the beard had plenty of room to swish back and forth. But not quite enough room. There was a fence at the edge of the field, and the beard 100 backed up behind the fence and didn't go flowing off into the next county.

Well, Uncle Septimus got nearly forty acres plowed that afternoon, but the wind was blowing so hard he couldn't hear Aunt Rachel standing on the back porch calling him to supper. The boys came out and yelled to get their daddy's attention. But to their horror, the family saw a funnel cloud form over the woods beyond the field and start moving in Uncle Septimus's direction.

That tornado was twisting around, pulling up trees and stumps by the roots and tossing them in the air, and Uncle Septimus, not noticing

anything, just kept on plowing. At first it seemed the twister would miss
110 him. But though it had passed Uncle Septimus by, it was heading straight
for the beard pile behind the fence.

What happened next was simply amazing. The tornado caught that beard
and began winding it up round and round until Uncle Septimus himself
shot off into the cloud like a yo-yo snatched up by a child. That twister
began to roar louder and louder, and the lightning flashed all around.
Hail the size of hen eggs fell. Then the twister began to make a peculiar
high-pitched noise that gradually dwindled to a low hum. Finally, the thing
squeaked once and fell silent, like a man who's choked on a piece of tobacco.
That cloud swelled out like it would bust. It turned green and then gray and
120 purple and black. It swayed back and forth, uncertain which way to go.
And then the thing just blew up. Rain, hail, and clouds flew off in all
directions, leaving a clear evening sky with the full moon shining through.
Even a rip-snorting tornado couldn't deal with that much beard. **F**

Nobody knows what happened to Uncle Septimus. He just disappeared.
Some folks say he was carried up into heaven like the prophet Elijah.
Others say he was blown clean to Texas or some other place out West.
They speculate that even now he's trying to find his way back home.
Others say that he got blown to the Great Smoky Mountains and that he's
living up there today on top of Clingman's Dome,[6] and that a lot of times
130 when we look up and see a jet contrail,[7] it's not really vapor but Uncle
Septimus's beard. On windy days, they say, he goes up to the highest peak
and lets the wind catch that beard and stretch it out across the sky, just
to give it a good airing. Other people **assert** that what we take to be
Spanish moss hanging on the oaks in southern Georgia and northern
Florida may really be pieces of Uncle Septimus's beard.

Aunt Rachel preferred to take that view. She'd ride down the road beneath
the oak trees and say, "You know, it's kind of comforting to see the Spanish
moss. In a way it's kind of like Septimus never really left home. Seems all I'd
have to do is start tugging on one of those moss tips, and pretty soon here
140 would come Septimus back from Texas or Tennessee or wherever he's gone."

You may take whichever view you prefer. But one thing is for certain.
Uncle Septimus's beard was the most wonderful ever, and it's unlikely
people in this part of the country will ever stop talking about it. Probably
in the future they'll say he was kidnapped by aliens and that the tail of
Halley's comet[8] is really just his beard stretching across the night sky. ∿ **G**

---

6. **Clingman's Dome:** a mountain located on the border of North Carolina and Tennessee. It is the highest
peak in the Great Smoky Mountains.

7. **jet contrail:** a visible trail of water vapor or ice crystals that sometimes forms behind a jet plane.

8. **Halley's comet:** a bright, heavenly body with a cloudy tail that is visible from Earth about every 76 years.

Comprehension

1. **Recall** Reread lines 24–30. How do Uncle Septimus's grandchildren make use of his beard?

2. **Clarify** What are some of the advantages and disadvantages of the beard?

3. **Summarize** What happens to the beard during the tornado?

Text Analysis

● 4. **Visualize** Look at the list of vivid descriptions you made while reading. Which sensory images made it easiest for you to visualize the beard? Explain.

● 5. **Identify Characteristics of a Tall Tale** As Septimus's beard grows, so does the unbelievability of details and events. Draw a picture of a long beard. List examples of sensory imagery and figurative language, such as hyperbole, that the author uses to describe the beard as it grows. (Put the earliest descriptions at the top of the beard and the last examples at the bottom.) How does the increasing exaggeration add to the meaning and effect of this tall tale?

6. **Examine a Character** Aunt Rachel has both positive and negative feelings about Septimus's beard. Skim through the story and note her reactions to the beard. Are her feelings about Septimus and his beard more positive or negative overall? Explain your answer.

7. **Analyze a Character** Uncle Septimus was not a hero in the usual sense, yet he was a much-celebrated character. What made him special to the people around him? Cite examples from the story.

Extension and Challenge

8. **Creative Project: Music** Many American folk heroes, such as John Henry and Pecos Bill, had songs written about them. With a group of classmates, write a song about Uncle Septimus and his incredible beard. Present your song to the rest of the class.

9. **Inquiry and Research** Some characters who appear in tall tales were real people. Research American folk literature and find a character from a tall tale who was based on a real person. Why did he or she become the subject of a tale? Share your findings with your classmates.

COMMON CORE

RL 4 Determine the meaning of words and phrases as they are used in a text, including figurative meanings. **W 7** Conduct short research projects to answer a question, drawing on several sources.

Why do we EXAGGERATE?

Look back at the two versions of a story you wrote—the real story and the exaggerated version. After reading "Uncle Septimus's Beard," what new ideas do you have about the reasons people exaggerate the things that happen to them?

Vocabulary in Context

▲ VOCABULARY PRACTICE

Choose the vocabulary word that best completes each sentence.

1. Len's unusual height and large build made him an ____ figure.
2. The winner of the race was an ____ to her fans.
3. In one embarrassing ____, Stella tripped on the stairs.
4. Lisa's parents ____ that she is a gifted pianist.

assert

imposing

incident

inspiration

ACADEMIC VOCABULARY IN SPEAKING

• circumstance   • contribute   • element   • significant   • tradition

The **traditions**, customs, and stories passed down within a culture are known as its folklore. With a small group, decide which **elements** of "Uncle Septimus's Beard" make it a good example of folklore. Use at least two of the Academic Vocabulary words in your discussion.

VOCABULARY STRATEGY: ANALOGIES

In tests, you may encounter test items called analogies. An **analogy** describes a relationship between two different things. It is expressed using two groups of words. The relationship between the first pair of items is the same as the relationship between the second pair of words. For example,

> whisper : shout :: soft : loud (*Read this as "whisper is to shout as soft is to loud."*)

In this case, you are comparing degrees, or qualities, of things: A whisper is soft; a shout is loud. Another common kind of analogy asks you to compare whole to part or part to whole: "pizza : slice :: cheese : wedge" (*A pizza is divided into slices; cheese is divided into wedges.*)

PRACTICE Choose the word that correctly completes each analogy.

1. strings : guitar :: keys : ____
   a. car   **b.** piano   **c.** door   **d.** chain
2. face : beard :: head : ____
   a. wig   **b.** hat   **c.** hair   **d.** scarf
3. engine : car :: ____ : flashlight
   a. lens   **b.** bulb   **c.** switch   **d.** battery
4. teachers : school :: ____ : hospital
   a. doctors   **b.** interns   **c.** patients   **d.** visitors

COMMON CORE

L 5b Use the relationship between particular words to better understand each of the words.

Interactive Vocabulary   **THINK** central

Go to **thinkcentral.com**.
KEYWORD: HML6-745

The Crane Maiden
Japanese Folk Tale Retold by Rafe Martin

Aunty Misery
Puerto Rican Folk Tale Retold by Judith Ortiz Cofer

When is it time to
LET GO?

COMMON CORE

RL 2 Provide a summary of the text distinct from personal opinions or judgments.
L 6 Gather vocabulary knowledge when considering a word or phrase important to comprehension or expression.

There are times when we have to say goodbye—to someone or something we love, or to feelings that are no longer helpful. There may also be times when we have to choose to release someone from a promise or sense of responsibility. The following two folk tales demonstrate different kinds of letting go.

DISCUSS With a group of classmates, make a list of stories or movies in which a character has to give up someone or something. Discuss which situation was the most difficult, and why.

Story or Movie	Character	What Character Lets Go Of
1.		
2.		

TEXT ANALYSIS: CHARACTERISTICS OF FOLK TALES

Folk tales are traditional stories that have been passed down from one generation to the next by being told aloud. No matter what culture they come from, folk tales usually have similar characteristics.

- Characters may be human or animal and represent one or more broad qualities, such as greed, honesty, or cleverness.
- Similar stylistic elements, or motifs, occur again and again, such as magic helpers, transformations, and events that are repeated three times (the "rule of three").
- A wise lesson or message about life is presented at the end.

Look for these characteristics listed as you read the folk tales.

READING STRATEGY: SUMMARIZE

When you **summarize,** you retell the main ideas and most important details of something you've read or heard. A summary uses fewer words than the original and doesn't include your own opinions. However, you do need to decide which ideas and information are most important to include.

Create a chart like the one shown to record key information from each folk tale. This will help you maintain meaning and logical order when you summarize the folk tales later.

Setting	Characters	Key Events

VOCABULARY IN CONTEXT

These boldfaced words are used to help convey the messages in these two folk tales. To see how many of the words you already know, write a definition of each.

WORD	hospitality	mournful	taunt
LIST	inevitable	snare	

1. Neighborhood children **taunt** and tease the old woman.
2. Her **hospitality** made the visitor feel welcome in her home.
3. He found the poor animal trapped in a **snare.**
4. It was **inevitable** that the girl would have to leave.
5. They were **mournful** about the loss of their daughter.

 Complete the activities in your **Reader/Writer Notebook.**

Rafe Martin
born 1946

Writer and Storyteller
Rafe Martin started out as a writer. But after he had children and began reading aloud to them, he discovered the full power of storytelling: "I began to get a sense that the telling of stories was really how they were passed on, and the power lay in finding voice and sharing stories." Martin continues to write and has produced over 20 books based on traditional tales.

Judith Ortiz Cofer
born 1952

Writer from Two Cultures
As a child, Judith Ortiz Cofer moved back and forth between her family's native Puerto Rico and their home in Paterson, New Jersey. In Puerto Rico, Cofer learned traditional storytelling from her grandmother. In Paterson, she spent much of her free time at the public library. Cofer read the library's entire section of folk literature. In her own stories, Cofer blends her love of language with her experience of growing up in two cultures.

Authors Online
Go to **thinkcentral.com**. KEYWORD: HML6-747

The Crane Maiden

Retold by Rafe Martin

Once, long ago, an old couple lived all alone near the edges of a marsh.[1] They were hard-working but poor.

One day the man had been gathering marsh plants, cattails, and such for his wife to cook. As he walked back along the trail, he heard a sharp cry and the sounds of someone—or something—struggling. Parting the long grasses by the trail's edge, he walked carefully into the marsh. The sounds—a clacking and a flapping, whirring noise—came from up ahead. Frightened but still curious, he stepped forward and looked. There on the ground before him lay a great white crane. Its leg was trapped
10 in a **snare** and it was flapping desperately about trying to get free. Its beak was clacking open and shut. Its eye was wild with pain and fear. Its wings were muddied. Never had the man seen such desperation in a wild creature. His heart was moved. Speaking soothingly he drew closer. Somehow the crane seemed to sense his intent and grew calm. Gentle and slow were the man's movements as he approached. Then, bending down, he loosened the snare from the crane's leg and backed away. **A**

Analyze Visuals ▶

What is the **mood** of this painting? Identify the **details** that create the mood.

snare (snâr) *n.* a trap for catching small animals and birds

A SUMMARIZE
What have you learned so far about the setting and characters? Record this information in your chart.

1. **marsh:** a wet, low-lying area, often thick with tall grasses.

Crane (about 1800), Kano Yosen'in Korenobu. Hanging scroll.
Photo © 2007 Museum of Fine Arts, Boston.

The crane stood up. Flexing its injured leg, it stood there gazing directly at the man. Then opening its wings, it flapped once, twice, lifted up off the muddy ground, and flew away. ◆

20   The man stood gazing after the great white bird as it made its way across the sky. Tears came to his eyes with the beauty of it. "I must see this clearly, and remember it, every detail," he said to himself. "How my wife will enjoy hearing of this adventure. I shall weave every detail into words for her, so she too will see."

   "You are late," his wife said when her husband returned. "I have been worried. Are you all right?"

   "I am better than all right, dear wife. I have had an adventure. I have seen such a sight. Wait, let me remove my sandals and sit down. I shall tell you all."

30   Then he told her of his finding the trapped crane, of the bird's panic and pain, and of the great joy he felt as he watched the white bird fly away.

   "Dear husband, I am so glad you helped that wild creature. Truly it must have been a wondrous sight to see the crane rise up from the muddied ground and soar into the heavens."

   "It was. It was. I have told it to you as best I could. For when I saw it fly I knew it was a sight you would have loved. And I wanted to share it with you." **B**

   "Thank you, husband." Then she steamed the plants he had gathered and they ate their rice and drank their tea and, when it grew late and
40 the moon rose up in the blackness and sailed across the night sky, they let the fire sink down and they slept. **C**

T he next morning they heard a knocking at the door. The woman opened the door and there stood a young girl.

   "I am lost," she said. "May I come in?"

   "Of course. Come in, dear child," the old woman said. "Have a cup of tea. Sit down."

   So the girl came in. She was alone in this world, she said, "Let me confess," she added, after drinking the tea and eating the rice the old couple gave her, "I would like to stay here with you. I am a hard worker.
50 I no longer wish to be alone. You are kind people. Please let me stay."

   The old couple had always wanted a daughter, and so it was agreed.

   "Thank you," the girl said. "I do not think you will regret it." She peered curiously around the house. She looked into an adjoining room. Her face lit up. "I see you have a loom.[2] May I use it from time to time?"

2. **loom:** a device for making cloth by weaving strands of yarn or thread together.

◆ **GRAMMAR IN CONTEXT**
Reread lines 18–20. Two sentences in a row open with an introductory phrase: "Flexing its injured leg" and "Then opening its wings." Each introductory phrase is followed by a comma. Be sure to insert a comma after an introductory word (*however, yet*) or introductory phrase (*on the other hand, the next day, after football practice*) that begins a sentence. Otherwise, your readers might be confused. (Try reading the sentences aloud without a comma to hear why.)

B FOLK TALES
What quality or qualities have the old man and his wife demonstrated?

C SUMMARIZE
What has happened in the story so far? Record the key events in your chart.

Young Woman in a Summer Kimono (1920), Hashiguchi Goyo. © Christie's Images/Corbis.

◄ **Analyze Visuals**

How does the girl in this work of art **compare** with your image of the young girl in the story?

"Daughter," the woman said, "all that we have is yours. Of course you may use the loom."

"I am a shy weaver," the girl said. "Please, Mother, please, Father, when I am weaving do not look into the room until I am done. Will you promise me this?" **D**

60 "It will be as you wish, child."

The next day their new daughter said she would go into the weaving room. The door was to be shut and neither her father nor her mother were to look in until her work was completed.

All day the girl sat at the loom. And all day the old couple heard the clacking and the whirring of the shuttle, the spinning of the bobbins[3] of thread.

When the sun was setting the girl emerged, pale and worn. But in her hands she held the most splendid cloth the old couple had ever seen. The pattern was perfect, the colors glowing. Images of the marsh, the sun, 70 the flight of cranes flowed elegantly through the finely woven material.

"Mother, Father, please take this cloth to the market and sell it. With the money your life will become easier. I want to do this for you."

The old people were astonished at their daughter's skill. The next day the man brought the cloth to the town. Immediately people began to bid for the beautiful cloth, which was sold at last for three ryo[4] of gold—an unheard of sum.

That night the old couple and their daughter, dressed in new kimonos, ate a wonderful meal—all bought with a small bit of the gold. For several months life was easy. But then the money was gone.

80 Once more the daughter entered the room, closed the door, and began to weave. *Clack clack clack, whirr whirr whirr.* Hours later she emerged, pale and worn. In her arms was a cloth that shone like silver, filled with patterns of the moon and stars, patterns of sunlight and moonlight shining on water. The old couple had never imagined a material of such stunning beauty.

But once again the girl said, "Mother, Father, do not keep the cloth. I can make more. Please sell it and use the money to care for your old age."

So again the man took the cloth to town. The merchants were astonished. They bid furiously, one against the other, until the cloth 90 had been sold for six ryo of gold. **E**

---

3. **shuttle . . . bobbins:** A shuttle is a device used in loom weaving to carry thread back and forth between other threads held lengthwise. A bobbin is a spool that holds thread or yarn for weaving.

4. **ryo** (ryō): a gold piece used as currency in Japan until the mid-1800s.

D FOLK TALES
Pay attention to what the girl requests in lines 57–59. A common stylistic element in traditional tales is the "binding promise," in which a mysterious character requests that others do (or do not do) something. Based on your experience with folk tales, what is usually the outcome when a character asks others to keep a promise like this?

COMMON CORE L 6
Language Coach

Foreign Words in English In the twentieth century, a number of words came into English from Japanese. *Kimono* (line 77) is a combination of the Japanese words *ki*, which means "wearing," and *mono*, which means "thing." In English, *kimono* refers to a long wide-sleeved Japanese robe worn most often by women.

E SUMMARIZE
In your chart, summarize what has happened in the story since the young girl arrived at the old couple's home.

For many months the family lived happily together. But in time, that money too was gone. The daughter went once again to the loom. But this time her mother and father were curious. Why must they not look? They couldn't bear it. They decided that they would take just a peek through a crack in the wall. If their daughter could not see them, they reasoned, it would not disturb her at all. **F**

Clack clack clack, whirr whirr whirr. The man and the woman walked softly along the wall, knelt down, and peered through a thin crack in the paper wall. At the loom sat a white crane pulling feathers from its own breast and wings with its long bill. It was weaving with those feathers. The crane turned toward the crack and looked with a great black **mournful** eye. The man and the woman tumbled backward. But it was too late. They had been seen.

Later, when the door of the room opened, their daughter emerged, pale and worn. In her arms she held a most magnificent cloth. On it were images of the setting sun, the rising moon, the trees in autumn, the long migrations of the cranes. On it too were the images of a man and a woman watching a white crane fly away.

"Father, Mother," she said, "I had hoped to stay with you always. But you have seen me as I truly am. I am the crane you saved, Father, from the trap. I wanted to repay you for your kindness. I shall never forget you, but now that you know this truth, I cannot stay with you." **G**

The man and the woman wept. They begged and pleaded, "We love you. Do not leave us. We do not care that you are a crane! You are our daughter. We shall tell no one."

"It is too late," whispered the girl. "The marshes call to me. The sky calls to me. The wind in the trees whispers my name. And I must follow. Perhaps all is as it should be. The debt has been repaid. I shall never forget you. Farewell."

She walked from the hut and stood out in the open air. The man and the woman watched in wonder as before their eyes their beautiful pale daughter became a beautiful white crane. Flapping her wings once, twice, three times, the great crane rose slowly up off the ground and, circling the hut, flew away. **H**

"Farewell," said the man and the woman, watching the crane disappear over the marsh. "We shall miss you, daughter. But we are glad that you are free." **I**

After that, every year when the cranes migrated, the old couple left a silver dish of grain out before their door. And every year a beautiful crane came to eat that grain.

So the story goes. ❧

Aunty Misery

Retold by Judith Ortiz Cofer

This is a story about an old, very old woman who lived alone in her little hut with no other company than a beautiful pear tree that grew at her door. She spent all her time taking care of her pear tree. But the neighborhood children drove the old woman crazy by stealing her fruit. They would climb her tree, shake its delicate limbs, and run away with armloads of golden pears, yelling insults at "Aunty Misery," as they called her.

One day, a pilgrim[1] stopped at the old woman's hut and asked her permission to spend the night under her roof. Aunty Misery saw that he had an honest face and bade the traveler come in. She fed him and made a bed for him in front of her hearth. In the morning while he was getting ready to leave, the stranger told her that he would show his gratitude for her **hospitality** by granting her one wish.

"There is only one thing that I desire," said Aunty Misery.

"Ask, and it shall be yours," replied the stranger, who was a sorcerer[2] in disguise.

"I wish that anyone who climbs up my pear tree should not be able to come back down until I permit it."

20 "Your wish is granted," said the stranger, touching the pear tree as he left Aunty Misery's house. **J**

---

1. **pilgrim:** a traveler.
2. **sorcerer:** a wizard or magician.

Analyze Visuals ▶
What **mood** does this painting suggest?

hospitality
(hŏs′pĭ-tăl′ĭ-tē) *n.*
the friendly, generous treatment of guests

J FOLK TALES
Which characteristics of folk tales are in the story so far?

Detail of *Windy Day Gribun, Isle of Mull,* John Lowrie-Morrison.
© John Lowrie-Morrison/Getty Images.

And so it happened that when the children came back to **taunt** the old woman and to steal her fruit, she stood at her window watching them. Several of them shimmied[3] up the trunk of the pear tree and immediately got stuck to it as if with glue. She let them cry and beg her for a long time before she gave the tree permission to let them go, on the condition that they never again steal her fruit or bother her. **K**

Time passed and both Aunty Misery and her tree grew bent and gnarled with age. One day another traveler stopped at her door. This one looked suffocated and exhausted, so the old woman asked him
30 what he wanted in her village. He answered her in a voice that was dry and hoarse, as if he had swallowed a desert: "I am Death, and I have come to take you with me."

Thinking fast, Aunty Misery said, "All right, but before I go I would like to pluck some pears from my beloved pear tree to remember how much pleasure it brought me in this life. But, I am a very old woman and cannot climb to the tallest branches where the best fruit is; will you be so kind as to do it for me?"

With a heavy sigh like wind through a catacomb,[4] Death climbed the pear tree. Immediately he became stuck to it as if with glue. And no
40 matter how much he cursed and threatened, Aunty Misery would not give the tree permission to release Death.

Many years passed and there were no deaths in the world. The people who make their living from death began to protest loudly. The doctors claimed no one bothered to come in for examinations or treatments anymore, because they did not fear dying; the pharmacists' business suffered too because medicines are, like magic potions, bought to prevent or postpone the **inevitable**; the priests and undertakers[5] were unhappy with the situation also, for obvious reasons. There were also many old folks tired of life who wanted to pass on to the next world
50 to rest from the miseries of this one.

Aunty Misery realized all this, and not wishing to be unfair, she made a deal with her prisoner, Death: if he promised not ever to come for her again, she would give him his freedom. He agreed. And that is why so long as the world is the world, Aunty Misery will always live. ∿ **L**

taunt (tônt) v.
to mock or insult

K SUMMARIZE
How does Aunty Misery solve her problem? Add these events to your chart.

inevitable
(ĭn-ĕv'ĭ-tə-bəl) adj.
impossible to avoid or prevent

L FOLK TALES
What qualities does Aunty Misery demonstrate through her actions?

---

3. **shimmied:** shinnied, or scooted.

4. **catacomb** (kăt'ə-kōm'): an underground cemetery made up of tunnels full of graves.

5. **undertakers:** funeral directors.

Comprehension

1. **Recall** In "The Crane Maiden," what does the old man do to help the crane?

2. **Recall** What does the man do with the cloth the girl makes?

3. **Clarify** In "Aunty Misery," how does the old woman save her own life?

Text Analysis

4. **Make Inferences** Why do you think the crane, once discovered, needs to leave the man and woman?

5. **Analyze a Character** In the second folk tale, why do the children name the woman Aunty Misery? Explain whether the name is appropriate for her.

● 6. **Summarize** Look at the chart you filled out while you read the folk tales. Choose one of the stories and, using your chart, retell the tale in your own words. Be sure to maintain meaning and logical order in your summary.

● 7. **Identify Characteristics of Folk Tales** Use a chart to list the characteristics of folk tales found in the stories you just read, including stylistic elements like the rule of three, transformations, and magic helpers.

	"The Crane Maiden"	*"Aunty Misery"*
Qualities characters represent		
Stylistic elements		
Story lesson		

8. **Examine Figurative Language** **Personification** is a kind of figurative language in which an animal, an object, or an idea is given the qualities of a human. What human qualities does Death have in "Aunty Misery"?

Extension and Challenge

9. **Creative Project: Drama** Choose either "The Crane Maiden" or "Aunty Misery" and, with a group of classmates, write it as a play. Perform your play for the rest of the class.

> ## When is it time to LET GO?
>
> Think back to your discussion about stories and movies that involve a character's difficult decision to let go of someone or something. Which character in the tales you just read had to give up the most? Explain.

COMMON CORE

RL 2 Provide a summary of the text distinct from personal opinions or judgments. **RL 7** Compare the experience of reading a story to viewing a live version of the text.

Vocabulary in Context

▲ VOCABULARY PRACTICE

Decide whether the words in each pair are **synonyms**—words with similar meanings—or **antonyms**—words with opposite meanings.

1. hospitality/rudeness
2. inevitable/expected
3. mournful/cheerful
4. snare/trap
5. taunt/defend

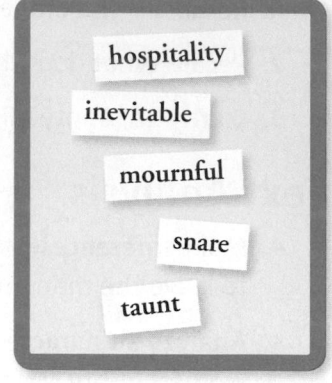

hospitality

inevitable

mournful

snare

taunt

ACADEMIC VOCABULARY IN WRITING

> • circumstance   • contribute   • element   • significant   • tradition

In a paragraph, consider whether Aunty Misery makes the right choice when she decides to release death. What **circumstances contribute** to her decision? Use at least two Academic Vocabulary words in your response.

VOCABULARY STRATEGY: GENERAL CONTEXT CLUES

When you come across an unfamiliar word in your reading, try rereading what's around the word to figure out its meaning. Context clues may be found in the same sentence as the unfamiliar word or in one or more other sentences in the paragraph. For example, "its leg was trapped in a snare" is a clue to the meaning of the vocabulary word *snare* in "The Crane Maiden." From this context clue, we know that a snare is a type of trap.

PRACTICE Use context clues to write the definition of each boldfaced word in the sentences below.

1. After the crime, the **malefactor** was sent to prison.
2. The dark, heavy curtains will **occlude** all light from coming through the window.
3. Isabel's **propensity** to talk out of turn often got her in trouble.
4. I was **ravenous** because I hadn't eaten since yesterday.
5. The sickly child was **susceptible** to frequent colds and other illnesses.

·········· **COMMON CORE**

L 4a Use context as a clue to the meaning of a word or phrase.

Interactive Vocabulary **THINK** central

Go to **thinkcentral.com**.
KEYWORD: HML6-758

Language

◆ **GRAMMAR IN CONTEXT: Use Commas Correctly**

COMMON CORE

L 2 Demonstrate command of the conventions of punctuation.
W 2a Organize ideas using comparison/contrast.

To avoid confusing your readers, be sure to use a comma after an **introductory word,** such as *finally* or *meanwhile*. Also, insert a comma after an **introductory phrase,** such as *on the other hand* or *the next day*.

> *Example:* On his way home, the old man found a trapped crane.

PRACTICE In each sentence, insert a comma where it is needed.

1. Until then the old man had been gathering cattails.
2. Through the crack the old couple saw a crane sitting at the loom.
3. Eventually their time together would have to end.
4. After saying goodbye the crane flew away.

*For more help with punctuating introductory words and phrases, see page R49 in the **Grammar Handbook.***

READING-WRITING CONNECTION

YOUR TURN Demonstrate your understanding of "The Crane Maiden" and "Aunty Misery" by responding to these prompts. Then use the **revising tip** to improve your writing.

WRITING PROMPT	REVISING TIP
Extended Constructed Response: Comparison The old couple in "The Crane Maiden" and main character in "Aunty Misery" face situations in which they have to let go of something. Write **three paragraphs** in which you compare and contrast the conflicts and resolutions in "Aunty Misery" and "The Crane Maiden." In your first paragraph, briefly summarize the situation the old couple faces in "The Crane Maiden," and describe how they deal with having to "let go." In the second paragraph, describe the situation in "Aunty Misery," explaining what Aunty Misery has to let go of and how she deals with it. In your final paragraph, sum up the differences between the conflicts and resolutions in the two stories.	Introductory words and phrases that serve as transitions (*on the other hand, however, in contrast to*) are very important when you are trying to keep your ideas clear in comparison-contrast writing. Be sure that you use a comma after every introductory phrase you use in your response.

Interactive Revision **THINK** central

Go to **thinkcentral.com**.
KEYWORD: HML6-759

Yeh-Shen: A Cinderella Story from China

Folk Tale Retold by Ai-Ling Louie

Video link at
thinkcentral.com

Sootface: An Ojibwa Cinderella Story

Folk Tale Retold by Robert D. San Souci

Is GOODNESS always rewarded?

COMMON CORE

RL 2 Determine a theme or central idea of a text and how it is conveyed through particular details. **L 1a** Ensure that pronouns are in the proper case (possessive).

Have you ever heard someone being accused of living in a "fairy-tale world"? In this kind of world, everything works out for the best and goodness triumphs over evil. Unfortunately, life often doesn't turn out this way in the real world. Stories with happy endings, however, can give comfort and hope. They can encourage people to be kind even when life is cruel. The following tales from two cultures present different versions of a familiar story.

LIST IT Get together with a small group and make a list of as many classic tales as you can think of. How many have an ending in which goodness is rewarded? Compare lists with other groups in your class.

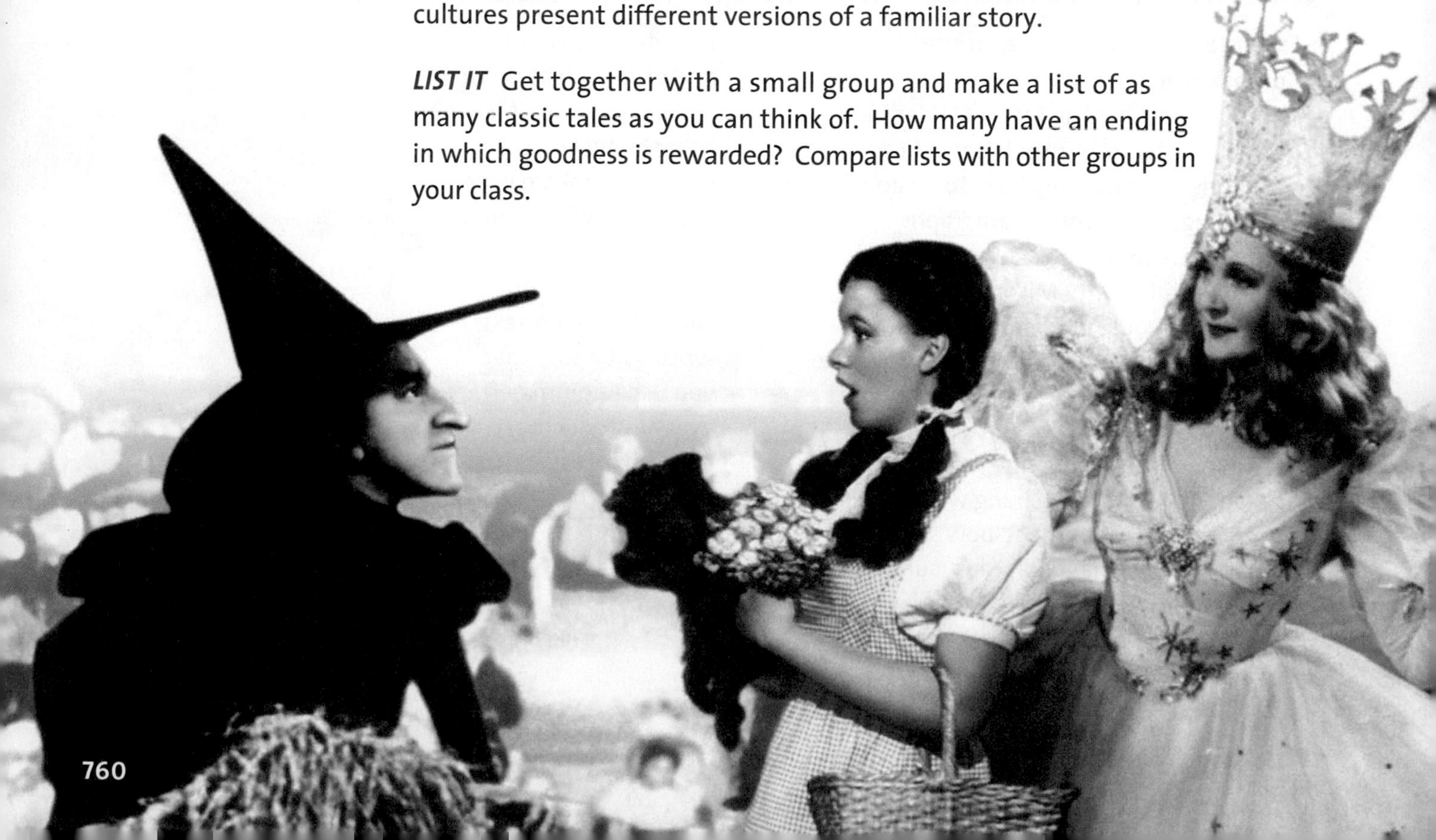

TEXT ANALYSIS: UNIVERSAL THEME

A **universal theme** is a message that is meaningful to people in any culture and in any time. The themes in folk tales are often universal because they state truths about human life.

There are more than 900 different versions of the Cinderella story from cultures all over the world. Although the versions of the tale are not identical, they share similar plots and themes, as well as some of the same stylistic elements, such as a jealous stepmother or stepsisters. As you read the following two versions of the Cinderella story, think about the characters and events, as well as the lessons each teaches. Why is the basic storyline of Cinderella common the world over? What theme does the tale express?

READING STRATEGY: SET A PURPOSE FOR READING

In this lesson, your purpose for reading is to compare and contrast two folk tales and identify the universal theme they share. To do this, take notes in a chart like the one shown.

	"Yeh-Shen"	"Sootface"
Characters	Yeh-Shen, pet fish, stepmother	
Key Events		
Lesson		

Review: Compare and Contrast

▲ VOCABULARY IN CONTEXT

These words help tell two Cinderella stories. See how many you already know. Make a chart like the one shown, and put each vocabulary word in the appropriate column.

WORD LIST	banquet	eldest	glistening
	collapse	embrace	

Know Well	Think I Know	Don't Know at All

Complete the activities in your **Reader/Writer Notebook.**

Meet the Authors

Ai-Ling Louie
born 1949

Storyteller
The grandmother of Ai-Ling Louie (ī-lǐng lōō'ē) heard the tale of Yeh-Shen in China and passed it down within her family. While working as a teacher, Louie wrote the story down to share it with her class and other readers.

Robert D. San Souci
born 1946

Voice of Many Cultures
Through his retellings of traditional tales, award-winning author Robert D. San Souci (săn sōō'sē) helps his readers "discover how much we share in common with people around the world."

BACKGROUND TO THE FOLK TALES

In the version of the Cinderella story most Americans know, Cinderella goes to the prince's ball, where she loses a glass slipper. The prince seeks out the owner of the slipper, eventually returning it to Cinderella, and the two marry.

Authors Online
Go to **thinkcentral.com.** KEYWORD: HML6-761

Yeh-Shen
A Cinderella Story from China

Retold by Ai-Ling Louie

*I*n the dim past, even before the Ch'in and the Han dynasties,[1] there lived a cave chief of southern China by the name of Wu. As was the custom in those days, Chief Wu had taken two wives. Each wife in their turn had presented Wu with a baby daughter. But one of the wives sickened and died, and not too many days after that Chief Wu took to his bed and died too.

Yeh-Shen, the little orphan, grew to girlhood in her stepmother's home. She was a bright child and lovely too, with skin as smooth as ivory and dark pools for eyes. Her stepmother was jealous of all this beauty and goodness, for her own daughter was not pretty at all. So in her displeasure, she gave
10 poor Yeh-Shen the heaviest and most unpleasant chores.

The only friend that Yeh-Shen had to her name was a fish she had caught and raised. It was a beautiful fish with golden eyes, and every day it would come out of the water and rest its head on the bank of the pond, waiting for Yeh-Shen to feed it. Stepmother gave Yeh-Shen little enough food for herself, but the orphan child always found something to share with her fish, which grew to enormous size. **Ⓐ**

Analyze Visuals ▶

This painting shows a scene and its reflection in the water. **Identify** where the water begins and ends.

Ⓐ UNIVERSAL THEME
Reread lines 11–16. What do you learn about Yeh-Shen from the way she treats her friend? What kind of person is Yeh-Shen?

---

1. **Ch'in** (chĭn) **and the Han** (hän) **dynasties** (dī'nə-stēz): groups that held power in China. The Ch'in dynasty ruled from 221 to 206 B.C., and the Han dynasty ruled from 206 B.C. to A.D. 220.

Somehow the stepmother heard of this. She was terribly angry to discover that Yeh-Shen had kept a secret from her. She hurried down to the pond, but she was unable to see the fish, for Yeh-Shen's pet wisely hid itself.
20 The stepmother, however, was a crafty woman, and she soon thought of a plan. She walked home and called out, "Yeh-Shen, go and collect some firewood. But wait! The neighbors might see you. Leave your filthy coat here!" The minute the girl was out of sight, her stepmother slipped on the coat herself and went down again to the pond. This time the big fish saw Yeh-Shen's familiar jacket and heaved itself onto the bank, expecting to be fed. But the stepmother, having hidden a dagger[2] in her sleeve, stabbed the fish, wrapped it in her garments, and took it home to cook for dinner. **B**

When Yeh-Shen came to the pond that evening, she found her pet had disappeared. Overcome with grief, the girl **collapsed** on the ground and
30 dropped her tears into the still waters of the pond.

"Ah, poor child!" a voice said.

Yeh-Shen sat up to find a very old man looking down at her. He wore the coarsest of clothes, and his hair flowed down over his shoulders.

"Kind uncle, who may you be?" Yeh-Shen asked.

"That is not important, my child. All you must know is that I have been sent to tell you of the wondrous powers of your fish."

"My fish, but sir . . ." The girl's eyes filled with tears, and she could not go on.

The old man sighed and said, "Yes, my child, your fish is no longer
40 alive, and I must tell you that your stepmother is once more the cause of your sorrow." Yeh-Shen gasped in horror, but the old man went on. "Let us not dwell on things that are past," he said, "for I have come bringing you a gift. Now you must listen carefully to this: The bones of your fish are filled with a powerful spirit. Whenever you are in serious need, you must kneel before them and let them know your heart's desire. But do not waste their gifts."

Yeh-Shen wanted to ask the old sage[3] many more questions, but he rose to the sky before she could utter another word. With heavy heart, Yeh-Shen made her way to the dung heap to gather the remains of her friend.
50 Time went by, and Yeh-Shen, who was often left alone, took comfort in speaking to the bones of her fish. When she was hungry, which happened quite often, Yeh-Shen asked the bones for food. In this way, Yeh-Shen managed to live from day to day, but she lived in dread that her stepmother would discover her secret and take even that away from her. **C**

---

2. **dagger:** a short, pointed weapon.

3. **sage:** someone known for his or her wisdom.

B UNIVERSAL THEME
Why does the stepmother kill the fish?

collapse (kə-lăps') *v.*
to fall down

C COMPARE AND CONTRAST
Like other folk tales, the Cinderella story contains recurring stylistic elements that serve an important function in the story. One recurring element in folk tales is the magic helper. Who is the magic helper here? How is this magic helper different from the ones in the Cinderella stories you know?

So the time passed and spring came. Festival time was approaching: It was the busiest time of the year. Such cooking and cleaning and sewing there was to be done! Yeh-Shen had hardly a moment's rest. At the spring festival young men and young women from the village hoped to meet and to choose whom they would marry. How Yeh-Shen 60 longed to go! But her stepmother had other plans. She hoped to find a husband for her own daughter and did not want any man to see the beauteous Yeh-Shen first. When finally the holiday arrived, the stepmother and her daughter dressed themselves in their finery and filled their baskets with sweetmeats.[4] "You must remain at home now, and watch to see that no one steals fruit from our trees," her stepmother told Yeh-Shen, and then she departed for the **banquet** with her own daughter. **D**

As soon as she was alone, Yeh-Shen went to speak to the bones of her fish. "Oh, dear friend," she said, kneeling before the precious bones, "I long to go to the festival, but I cannot show myself in these rags. 70 Is there somewhere I could borrow clothes fit to wear to the feast?" At once she found herself dressed in a gown of azure blue,[5] with a cloak of kingfisher feathers draped around her shoulders. Best of all, on her tiny feet were the most beautiful slippers she had ever seen. They were woven of golden threads, in a pattern like the scales of a fish, and the **glistening** soles were made of solid gold. There was magic in the shoes, for they should have been quite heavy, yet when Yeh-Shen walked, her feet felt as light as air.

"Be sure you do not lose your golden shoes," said the spirit of the bones. Yeh-Shen promised to be careful. Delighted with her transformation, she bid a fond farewell to the bones of her fish as she slipped off to join 80 in the merrymaking. **E**

That day Yeh-Shen turned many a head as she appeared at the feast. All around her people whispered, "Look at that beautiful girl! Who can she be?"

But above this, Stepsister was heard to say, "Mother, does she not resemble our Yeh-Shen?"

Upon hearing this, Yeh-Shen jumped up and ran off before her stepsister could look closely at her. She raced down the mountainside, and in doing so, she lost one of her golden slippers. No sooner had the shoe fallen from her foot than all her fine clothes turned back to rags. Only one thing remained—a tiny golden shoe. Yeh-Shen hurried to the 90 bones of her fish and returned the slipper, promising to find its mate. But now the bones were silent. Sadly Yeh-Shen realized that she had lost her only friend. She hid the little shoe in her bedstraw, and went outside to cry. Leaning against a fruit tree, she sobbed and sobbed until she fell asleep. **F**

---

4. **sweetmeats:** sweet food, such as candy.

5. **azure blue** (ăzh'ər blōō): a light purplish blue.

banquet (băng'kwĭt) *n.* a dinner honoring a particular guest or occasion

D COMPARE AND CONTRAST
Reread lines 55–66. Why doesn't Yeh-Shen's stepmother allow her to go to the festival?

glistening (glĭs'ən-ĭng) *adj.* sparkling

E UNIVERSAL THEME
Reread the warning in line 77. What do you predict will happen to the golden slippers?

F COMPARE AND CONTRAST
What effect does losing the slipper have on Yeh-Shen? How is this like or unlike other Cinderella stories you have read?

Celebration (1996), Pang Gui Chen. Watercolor. Red Lantern Folk Art, Mukashi Collection.
© The Mukashi Collection/SuperStock.

▲ **Analyze Visuals**

Choose a figure from this painting that reminds you of one of the story's characters. Which character does the figure remind you of, and why?

The stepmother left the gathering to check on Yeh-Shen, but when she returned home she found the girl sound asleep, with her arms wrapped around a fruit tree. So thinking no more of her, the stepmother rejoined the party. Meantime, a villager had found the shoe. Recognizing its worth, he sold it to a merchant, who presented it in turn to the king of the island kingdom of T'o Han.

100   The king was more than happy to accept the slipper as a gift. He was entranced by the tiny thing, which was shaped of the most precious of metals, yet which made no sound when touched to stone. The more he marveled at its beauty, the more determined he became to find the woman to whom the shoe belonged. A search was begun among the ladies of his

own kingdom, but all who tried on the sandal found it impossibly small. Undaunted, the king ordered the search widened to include the cave women from the countryside where the slipper had been found. Since he realized it would take many years for every woman to come to his island and test her foot in the slipper, the king thought of a way
110 to get the right woman to come forward. He ordered the sandal placed in a pavilion[6] by the side of the road near where it had been found, and his herald announced that the shoe was to be returned to its original owner. Then from a nearby hiding place, the king and his men settled down to watch and wait for a woman with tiny feet to come and claim her slipper. **G**

*A*ll that day the pavilion was crowded with cave women who had come to test a foot in the shoe. Yeh-Shen's stepmother and stepsister were among them, but not Yeh-Shen—they had told her to stay home. By day's end, although many women had eagerly tried to put on the slipper, it still had not been worn. Wearily, the king continued his vigil[7]
120 into the night. **H**

It wasn't until the blackest part of night, while the moon hid behind a cloud, that Yeh-Shen dared to show her face at the pavilion, and even then she tiptoed timidly across the wide floor. Sinking down to her knees, the girl in rags examined the tiny shoe. Only when she was sure that this was the missing mate to her own golden slipper did she dare pick it up. At last she could return both little shoes to the fish bones. Surely then her beloved spirit would speak to her again.

Now the king's first thought, on seeing Yeh-Shen take the precious slipper, was to throw the girl into prison as a thief. But when she turned
130 to leave, he caught a glimpse of her face. At once the king was struck by the sweet harmony of her features, which seemed so out of keeping with the rags she wore. It was then that he took a closer look and noticed that she walked upon the tiniest feet he had ever seen. **I**

With a wave of his hand, the king signaled that this tattered creature was to be allowed to depart with the golden slipper. Quietly, the king's men slipped off and followed her home.

All this time, Yeh-Shen was unaware of the excitement she had caused. She had made her way home and was about to hide both sandals in her bedding when there was a pounding at the door. Yeh-Shen went to see
140 who it was—and found a king at her doorstep. She was very frightened at first, but the king spoke to her in a kind voice and asked her to try the

---

6. **pavilion** (pə-vĭl′yən): a decorated tent.

7. **vigil** (vĭj′əl): a period of observing.

G COMPARE AND CONTRAST
How is the king's plan to find the owner of the slipper similar to and different from the way the prince or king in other Cinderella stories looks for the shoe's owner?

H UNIVERSAL THEME
How does the king react when he receives Yeh-Shen's missing slipper as a gift?

I UNIVERSAL THEME
Reread lines 121–133. Why does the king first think Yeh-Shen is a thief?

golden slippers on her feet. The maiden did as she was told, and as she stood in her golden shoes, her rags were transformed once more into the feathered cloak and beautiful azure gown.

Her loveliness made her seem a heavenly being, and the king suddenly knew in his heart that he had found his true love.

Not long after this, Yeh-Shen was married to the king. But fate was not so gentle with her stepmother and stepsister. Since they had been unkind to his beloved, the king would not permit Yeh-Shen to bring them 150 to his palace. They remained in their cave home, where one day, it is said, they were crushed to death in a shower of flying stones. ∾ Ⓙ

Ⓙ **UNIVERSAL THEME**
How is Yeh-Shen rewarded in the story?

Shadow Puppets, Chen Lian Xing. Watercolor. Red Lantern Folk Art, Mukashi Collection.
© The Mukashi Collection/SuperStock.

◄ **Analyze Visuals**
Notice how the figures in this painting are dressed. **Compare** them with how you imagined Yeh-Shen and the king looked.

Comprehension

1. **Recall** Who is Yeh-Shen's only friend?

2. **Recall** What does Yeh-Shen's stepmother do to trick the fish?

3. **Summarize** How does the king find the owner of the golden slipper?

Text Analysis

4. **Analyze Characters** In the beginning of the story, Yeh-Shen is described as having "beauty and goodness." What details about her thoughts and actions show her goodness?

5. **Make Judgments** Reread lines 147–151. Do the stepmother and Yeh-Shen get what they deserve at the end of the story? Support your ideas with details from the folk tale.

6. **Analyze Cultural Context** Cinderella stories from around the world share certain stylisitic elements. However, each version of the tale expresses the values and characteristics of the culture it comes from. What qualities might you infer the ancient Chinese valued in women? Support your response with evidence from the text.

● 7. **Evaluate Universal Theme** What **universal theme,** or truth about life, does this folk tale express about how people should treat each other. Is this message still important today? Explain.

Comparing Theme

Now that you have read the first folk tale, finish filling in the "Yeh-Shen" column of your chart.

	"Yeh-Shen"	"Sootface"
Characters	Yeh-Shen, pet fish, stepmother	
Key Events		
Lesson		

COMMON CORE

RL 2 Determine a theme or central idea of a text and how it is conveyed through particular details.

Sootface
An Ojibwa Cinderella Story

Retold by Robert D. San Souci

Once, an Ojibwa man whose wife had died raised three daughters alone. They lived in a village beside a lake, deep in a forest of birch.

The sisters were supposed to share the work of gathering firewood, cooking food, and sewing clothes from skins their father provided.

The two older girls, though pretty enough, were lazy and bad-tempered. When their father was away hunting, they gave most of the work to their youngest sister. The flames from the cooking fire singed her hair and burned her skin. Sometimes her sisters beat her and smeared her face with ashes. Then they made fun of her and called her Sootface.

10 Poor Sootface's eyes were always sad and tired, but her sisters only gave her more work. At evening her **eldest** sister cried, "Hurry, lazy Sootface! Fetch some wood to make a fire. Cook the deer meat, for we are hungry."

In the morning, her middle sister said, "Hurry, lazy Sootface! Clean the ashes from last night's fire. Brush the mats, gather berries, and bring fresh water. Our father will soon return from hunting." **A**

Analyze Visuals ▶

What do the **details** in this illustration help you to **infer** about the girl?

eldest (ĕl'dĭst) *adj.* oldest

A UNIVERSAL THEME
What terrible situation is Sootface in?

Illustrations by Daniel San Souci.

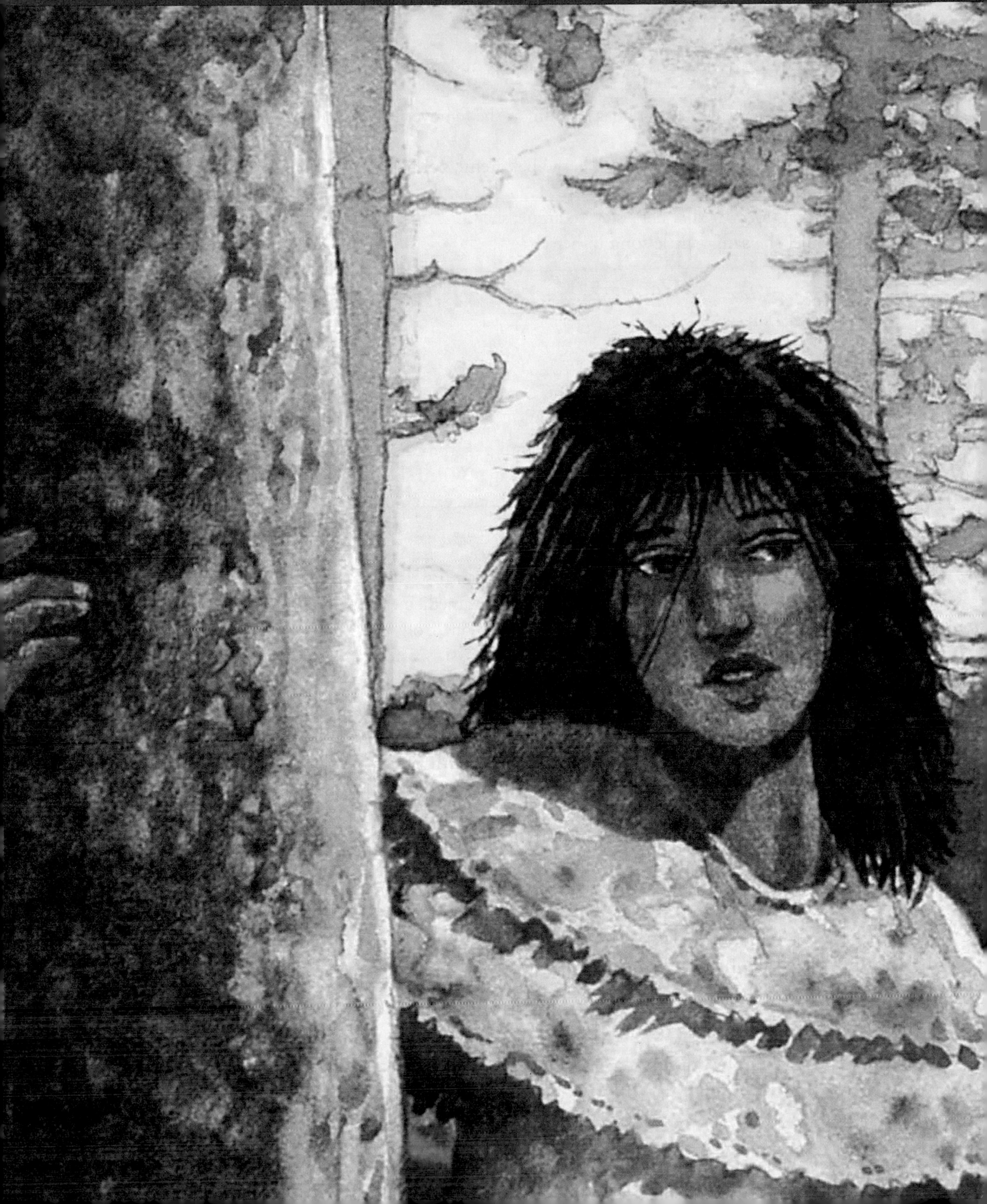

When the hunter returned, he saw poor Sootface and asked, "What has happened to my youngest child?"

The eldest sister said, "That one is so clumsy, she fell over her own feet and rolled through the ashes."

20 And the middle sister said, "We tell her to be careful, not to go too near the fire, but she will not heed us."

Sootface was too afraid of her sisters to argue; she just kept on working. All the while, she sang a little song to herself:

Oh, I am thinking,
Oh, I am dreaming,
That even ugly as I am,
I will someday find a husband. **B**

Her sisters took the best skins to make dresses and moccasins for themselves. Sootface had only scraps to sew into a skirt and a worn-out
30 pair of her father's moccasins, grown stiff with age. When she walked to the lake to fetch water, the young men would nudge each other and point and laugh.

Now, there was a mighty warrior who lived with his sister in a wigwam across the lake from the village. A great medicine man had given him the power to make himself invisible. No one from the village had ever seen him, though they saw his white moccasins when his sister hung them beside the door flap. They saw the flap rise and fall when he entered or left his wigwam.

The villagers knew he was a great hunter, for they watched his sister
40 skin and dry all the deer, elk, and other game that her brother brought her. Though no one but his sister could see him, the women of the village were sure that he was very handsome.

One day, the invisible warrior told his sister, "Go to the village across the water, and say that I will marry the woman who can see me. This means that she has a kind and honest heart. Each day I will carry my magic bow. The woman who tells you what my bow and bowstring are made of will be my bride." **C**

His sister brought this message to the village people. One by one the young women came to visit the lone wigwam. Each carefully
50 braided her hair, dressed in her softest deerskin skirt and moccasins, and wore her finest necklaces of shells or beads.

The invisible hunter's sister greeted each young woman kindly. But when she asked them to tell her what her brother looked like,

B UNIVERSAL THEME
Reread lines 16–27. Why doesn't Sootface's father help her?

VISUAL VOCABULARY

wigwam (wĭg′wŏm′) *n.* a Native American dwelling, usually having an arched or conelike shape

C UNIVERSAL THEME
Reread lines 43–47. Based on your knowledge of other Cinderella stories, who do you predict will pass this test?

and what his bow and bowstring were made of, each young woman failed the test, and was sent home.

This went on for a long time. At last, Sootface's eldest sister said that she was going to visit the invisible hunter.

She brushed her hair until it gleamed, and had Sootface braid it for her. Then she went on her way, wrapped in her best deerskin robe and wearing
60 her finest beaded moccasins. She met the hunter's sister beside the lake. Soon they saw white moccasins approaching.

"Can you see my brother?" asked his sister.

"Oh, yes," lied the eldest sister.

"Of what is his bow made?"

"Birch."

"And with what is it strung?"

"Rawhide."

"You did not see my brother," the other woman said.

The eldest sister went home in a bad temper. She yelled at Sootface
70 and gave her more work to do.

The middle sister, who thought herself clever, decided to try her luck. She hung strings of pale shells at her throat and had Sootface weave some into her long braids. Off she went, sure she would become the lucky bride.

As she walked with the hunter's sister, she saw the white moccasins approaching. Quickly, she said, "Here comes your brother now."

"Of what is his bow made?" asked the hunter's sister.

> **Language Coach**
>
> **Speaker Tags** Notice that in some lines of dialogue, the speaker is not directly identified. In dialogue, *he said, she yelled, the eldest sister asked,* and other identifying phrases are called speaker tags. Speaker tags tell you immediately who is talking. At times, though, too many **speaker tags** in a running dialogue become repetitive and annoying, so the writer leaves them out. Reread lines 62–68. Who is speaking in the lines without speaker tags? How can you tell?

◄**Analyze Visuals**

What do you notice about the shadows in this illustration?

"Horn," said the middle sister, thinking of the finest bow she could imagine.

"And with what is it strung?"

"Braided horsehair," said the middle sister, pleased at her own cleverness. But the other woman shook her head. "You have not seen my brother." **D**

The middle sister arrived home in a fury. She scolded Sootface and smeared more ashes on her face.

The next day, Sootface decided to visit the hunter's lodge as her sisters had done. She begged her eldest sister, "Sister, let me wear your white shell necklace, softest skirt, and moccasins. I want to go and seek a husband."

But her sister refused, saying, "You would only make my clothes as sooty as yourself."

Then Sootface begged her second sister, "Sister, help me wash and braid my hair, so I may go and seek a husband."

But her sister said, "The fire has burned your hair too short to braid. And I do not want my hands dirtied by the ash that clings to you."

Sootface was stung by their unkindness. But she was determined to present herself to the warrior and his sister. She went alone into the woods. There she said, "Sister birch tree, share your soft white skin with me. Then I can wear a new skirt when I go to seek a husband."

Sootface took strips of birch bark and sewed them together to make a skirt. She wove herself a necklace of wildflowers, and soaked her old, stiff moccasins in a spring until they grew softer. Next, she washed her face and hair as best she could. Her hair was too short to braid, so she added flowers to it, all the while singing:

Soon, I am thinking,
Soon, I am dreaming,
That I will find a husband.
I am sure it will be so.

But when she passed through the village, dressed in the finery the forest had provided, her eldest sister cried, "You are so ugly and foolish-looking, go inside at once!"

"You will shame us before the hunter and his sister," called Sootface's middle sister.

But Sootface walked on as though they were no more than chattering birds in the trees. **E**

D UNIVERSAL THEME
Why can't the two sisters see the warrior's bow and bowstrings?

COMMON CORE L 1a

Language Coach

Possessive Pronouns
A possessive pronoun shows ownership. Some possessive pronouns are used before nouns. In line 89, the pronoun *her* is a possessive pronoun; it tells you the sister in the sentence is Sootface's sister. What other word in this paragraph is a possessive pronoun? What does this word indicate ownership of?

E COMPARE AND CONTRAST
Reread lines 93–112. Based on what you have read so far, how would you describe Sootface? How is she similar to and different from other Cinderella characters you know?

◄ **Analyze Visuals**
Based on her facial expression in the illustration, how would you describe Sootface's reaction to her sisters' comments?

When her sisters saw that she would not listen to them, they began to laugh at her. To friends and neighbors, the eldest sister said, "Come, see little Sootface. Her clothes are birch bark and weeds. Her moccasins are stiff and cracked. Yet she goes to find a husband!"

Next the middle sister shouted, "Look at little Sootface! Her hair is burned too short for braids. The smell of cook fires clings to her. Still she hopes to find a husband!"

120   Soon all the village was laughing at her. But the young woman continued on her way, never once looking back. **F**

After a time Sootface met the hunter's sister, who was drawing water from the lake. She greeted Sootface kindly, and they began talking.

Suddenly, Sootface said, "There is a handsome man walking toward us. Do you know him?"

The hunter's sister said, "You can see him?"

"Yes, he is carrying a beautiful bow."

"Of what is his bow made?"

"A rainbow!"

F COMPARE AND CONTRAST
What stylistic elements—such as the magic helper, the rule of three, and supernatural transformations— have you seen in this Cinderella story so far? What elements have you not seen?

130 "And how is it strung?"

"With white fire, like the Milky Way, the Path of Souls."

The hunter's sister **embraced** Sootface, crying, "You are going to be my brother's bride and my own sister!"

She led Sootface to the wigwam. There she poured water into a big pot and mixed in sweet-smelling herbs. Sootface found her hurt and sadness washed away as easily as the ashes from her face.

The hunter's sister gave her a dress of soft white buckskin decorated with beads and quillwork. Then she combed Sootface's hair with a magic comb that made it long and thick and shiny as a blackbird's wing. This
140 she plaited[1] into braids.

"You have made me beautiful," said Sootface when she looked at her reflection in the pot of water.

"Your beauty was merely hidden beneath the scars and ashes," said the other woman kindly. Then she called her brother into the lodge.

"What is your name?" the young man asked gently.

"Sootface," the girl said, blushing.

He smiled and shook his head. "Your eyes shine with such joy that I will call you Dawn-Light. Today I will carry a gift of game to your family as a sign of our betrothal."[2]

150 Then his sister said, "Come, radiant Dawn-Light, and sit beside my brother. Claim the wife's place by the door flap. From now on this is your home."

At these words, Dawn-Light exclaimed:

Now, I am happy,
Now, I am certain,
That I have found my husband,
My new sister and new home.

They were married soon after. Everyone was pleased, except Dawn-Light's two older sisters, who had to do all the cooking and
160 cleaning themselves now. ∾ Ⓖ

The Milky Way is the galaxy that contains our solar system. In the night sky, it can be seen as a broad band of light.

embrace (əm-brās') *v.* to hold close

Ⓖ **CINDERELLA STORY**
How is Sootface rewarded in the story?

---

1. **plaited:** folded or braided.

2. **betrothal:** a promise to marry.

Comprehension

COMMON CORE

RL 2 Determine a theme or central idea of a text and how it is conveyed through particular details.

1. **Recall** Why do the older sisters mistreat Sootface?

2. **Recall** What are the warrior's bow and bowstring made of?

3. **Clarify** What kind of woman does the warrior want to marry?

Text Analysis

4. **Analyze History and Culture** What details in "Sootface" tell you that it takes place in the distant past? What details reveal aspects of American Indian Culture?

5. **Analyze Characters** Which qualities of Sootface and Yeh-Shen help them resolve their dilemmas? Explain your answer.

● 6. **Analyze Universal Theme** "Sootface" is an Ojibwa folk tale. Which traits do you think are more important to the Ojibwa: kindness and honesty, or beauty and cleverness? What traits seem to be important to the Chinese, based on "Yeh-Shen"? How are the values of the two cultures alike and different? Use story details to support your ideas.

Comparing Theme

Fill in your chart with information from "Sootface." Then add the final row to your chart and state the universal theme you identify in both folk tales.

	"Yeh-Shen"	"Sootface"
Characters	Yeh-Shen, pet fish, stepmother	Sootface, invisible warrior, sisters
Key Events		
Lesson		
Universal Theme		

Is GOODNESS always rewarded?

Review the list you and classmates made of classic tales that end with goodness being rewarded. Now that you have read two versions of the Cinderella story, do you have any further insights into the popularity of stories that end with good people being rewarded for their kindness?

Vocabulary in Context

▲ VOCABULARY PRACTICE

Choose the letter of the word or words that have a meaning similar to the boldfaced word.

1. a wedding **banquet:** (a) performance, (b) tuxedo, (c) dinner, (d) ring
2. the **eldest** sibling: (a) prettiest, (b) loudest, (c) smartest, (d) oldest
3. **embrace** the child: (a) hold, (b) feed, (c) reward, (d) scold
4. a **glistening** dress: (a) sparkling, (b) fading, (c) hanging, (d) flowing
5. it might **collapse:** (a) rebuild, (b) fall down, (c) dance, (d) wave

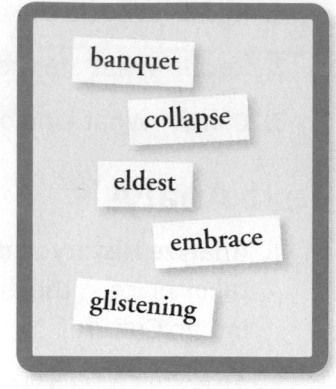

ACADEMIC VOCABULARY IN SPEAKING

| • circumstance | • contribute | • element | • significant | • tradition |

You've considered the common **elements** of Cinderella stories from two cultures. Does each story teach similar **traditions** and values? What **significant** differences, if any, do you notice between the cultures? Talk it over with a classmate. Use at least two Academic Vocabulary words in your response.

VOCABULARY STRATEGY: RECOGNIZING BASE WORDS

You've already learned that it's easier to understand an unfamiliar word that has **affixes**—word parts added to the beginning (prefix) or end (suffix) of a **base word**—if you first identify the base word. However, sometimes the base word is spelled differently when affixes are added. For example, the word *reception* contains the base word *receive* and the suffix *-tion*. If you're having problems recognizing the base word, try using context clues to figure out the meaning of the unfamiliar word.

PRACTICE For each boldfaced word, identify the base word and the suffix. Then define the word. Use a dictionary if necessary.

1. Mr. Stine made a large **contribution** to the school.
2. She had a **considerable** advantage over the other players.
3. He had a negative **perception** of what she was trying to say.
4. Lily's **remembrance** of her vacation brought a smile to her face.
5. She received **recognition** for her accomplishments at work.

⬤ **COMMON CORE**

L 4b Use Latin affixes as clues to the meaning of a word.

Suffixes	Meanings
-able	capable of being
-ance	state of being
-ion, -tion	result of being

Interactive Vocabulary THINK central

Go to **thinkcentral.com**.
KEYWORD: HML6-778

Writing for Assessment

1. READ THE PROMPT

The two Cinderella stories you've just read express the same universal theme. In writing assessments, you often will be asked to compare and contrast two works that are similar in some way, such as these two folk tales.

The folk tales "Yeh-Shen" and "Sootface" express the same universal theme. However, each tale expresses the theme in a different way. In three paragraphs, compare and contrast the way in which the two tales express their message about life. Support your response by using details from each tale.

◄ **STRATEGIES IN ACTION**

1. I need to make sure I understand the **message** both folk tales express.

2. I need to identify the **similarities and differences** in how the tales express the message.

3. I need to include **specific information** from the tales to help support my ideas.

2. PLAN YOUR WRITING

Review the compare-and-contrast chart you filled in as you read. Add any missing information about characters, events, or lessons. Use the chart to determine how each tale expresses the universal theme. Then think about how you will set up your response.

- Decide what your main idea will be.

- On your chart, mark the most important similarities and differences between the two tales.

- Create an outline to organize your ideas. This sample outline shows one way to organize your paragraphs.

I. Introduce Tales and Main Idea
II. How 1st Tale Expresses Theme
III. How 2nd Tale Expresses Theme and Compares to 1st Tale

3. DRAFT YOUR RESPONSE

Paragraph 1 Include the titles of the folk tales and the names of the authors who retold them. Tell what universal theme is expressed in the tales. Then state your main idea, which should say something about the similarities or the differences in how the tales present the theme.

Paragraph 2 Describe how the theme is expressed in the first folk tale through characters, events, and lessons.

Paragraph 3 Describe how the theme is expressed in the second folk tale and how it is similar to or different from the first tale.

Revision Make sure you vary sentence patterns for meaning, reader interest, and style. For example, try to create compound sentences to keep your writing interesting.

"How-To" Explanation

In this unit, you have encountered characters who must deal with a variety of problems. Sometimes solving a problem requires a clear explanation of how to do something. In this workshop, you will write a how-to explanation that will help others complete a task.

 Complete the workshop activities in your **Reader/Writer Notebook**.

WRITE WITH A PURPOSE

WRITING TASK

Write a **"how-to" explanation** in which you give step-by-step instructions for how to do something or make something.

Idea Starters
- folding a paper swan
- sending an instant message
- putting a new seat on a bicycle
- making your favorite cookies

THE ESSENTIALS

Here are some common purposes, audiences, and formats for how-to explanations.

PURPOSES	AUDIENCES	FORMATS
• to teach someone how to do or make something • to share your expertise with others • to give directions to a place	• classmates and teacher • friends • consumers • younger students • travelers • Web users	• essay for class • recipe • instruction manual or video • driving directions • feature article in a newspaper or newsletter • blog posting

COMMON CORE TRAITS

1. DEVELOPMENT OF IDEAS
- presents an attention-grabbing **introduction** that identifies the topic
- has a **purpose** that states what will be explained and why
- develops ideas with **relevant definitions, concrete details,** and **examples**
- provides a **concluding section** that summarizes and restates the importance of the topic

2. ORGANIZATION OF IDEAS
- effectively **organizes** steps of the process in correct order
- uses **appropriate transitions** to clarify the order of steps

3. LANGUAGE FACILITY AND CONVENTIONS
- establishes and maintains a **formal style and tone**
- includes **precise language** and **domain-specific vocabulary**
- uses **subordinating conjunctions** correctly
- demonstrates command of correct **grammar, usage,** and **spelling**

Writing Online

THINK central

Go to **thinkcentral.com**.
KEYWORD: HML6N-780

Planning/Prewriting

COMMON CORE

W 2a–f Write informative/explanatory texts to examine and convey ideas, concepts, and information. **W 5** Develop and strengthen writing as needed by planning.

Getting Started

CHOOSE A TOPIC

Use the Idea Starters on page 780 to help you identify possible topics for your "how-to" explanation. List items that you have made or processes that you know how to complete. For each topic, think about whether you can explain the process in a manageable number of steps. Then review your topics. Choose a familiar process that can be explained in three to five steps.

▶ WHAT DOES IT LOOK LIKE?

Topic	Do I know this process well?	Can I describe it in 3–5 steps?
building a soapbox car	No. I helped my older brother build one.	No. There are more than five steps.
instant messaging	Yes. I send lots of messages every day.	Yes. Sending a message takes about four steps.
folding laundry	Yes. I fold my own laundry once a week	Yes. Folding a shirt takes about three steps.

Notes: Both instant messaging and folding a shirt have the right number of steps for my essay, and I know how to do both well. However, instant messaging is a more engaging topic for my audience.

THINK ABOUT AUDIENCE AND PURPOSE

Since your **purpose** is to teach someone how to do something, make sure that you can successfully complete this process yourself. You need to be certain that your instructions are accurate and complete. Also, think about **domain-specific,** or specialized, **vocabulary** you will be using and whether the terms will need to be defined for your **audience.**

▶ ASK YOURSELF:

- Who will read my "how-to" explanation? How familiar is my audience with my topic?
- What terms might I need to define so that my audience will understand the process?
- Which steps in the process will I need to support with **definitions, concrete details,** and **examples**?

CHOOSE AN ORGANIZATIONAL STRATEGY

One of the most important parts of writing an effective "how-to" explanation is presenting the steps in the correct order. Most "how-to" explanations are written in chronological order, or the order in which the steps should be carried out. This organizational strategy gives the explanation coherence—that is, all the parts fit together in a way that makes sense to the reader.

▶ TIPS

- Imagine making the product or completing the process. Think about what you do first, next, and last.
- Write down each step using **precise** verbs and adjectives. Then visualize each step. Does your mental picture match your description? If not, reread the text to find what you have missed.

Planning/Prewriting *continued*

Getting Started

LIST THE MATERIALS

Make a list of all the materials that are needed to create the product or complete the process. Be sure to use **precise language** to describe each item. For example, "a two-inch length of black yarn" is more precise than "a piece of yarn."

ORGANIZE YOUR IDEAS

Creating a planning chart is a good way to organize ideas for a "how-to" explanation. You can then use the chart to guide your writing. Format your chart using numbers to show the order of the steps. Later, when you begin drafting, you will use **transitional words** such as *first, next, then,* and *finally* in place of the numbers to clarify the relationships between steps.

▶ TIPS

- In some "how-to" explanations, the materials are included within the paragraphs that describe the steps. Readers learn about the materials as they are used in each step.
- In other cases, such as recipes and craft project instructions, all the materials are presented in a list, before the steps.

▶ WHAT DOES IT LOOK LIKE?

Planning Chart for "How to Instant Message"

Purpose (state in introduction)	To explain how to use instant messaging, a fun and simple form of communication
Materials	A computer or other IM device with an Internet connection
Steps in order	1. Get registered. 2. Sign on. 3. Fill the buddy list. 4. Select a buddy, type a message, and click "send."
Why this skill is valuable (state in conclusion)	You are instantly connected with buddies.

PEER REVIEW Select a peer who is familiar with the topic of your "how-to" explanation. Explain who your audience is. Then ask your peer to review your planning chart. Ask: Have I left out any materials or steps in the process? Which steps do you think might be confusing? What terms might be unfamiliar to a reader? What details can I provide to help clarify the steps? Do I need to try a new approach to better explain the process?

YOUR TURN After you have chosen the topic of your "how-to" explanation, create a planning chart like the one above in your *Reader/Writer Notebook*. Then, keeping in mind your purpose, audience, and task, think about concrete details and precise language you can use to describe the steps you have listed. Ask yourself questions such as *when? where? what kind? which one? how?* and *how much?*

Drafting

COMMON CORE

W 2c Use appropriate transitions to clarify the relationships among ideas and concepts. **W 4** Produce clear and coherent writing in which the development, organization, and style are appropriate to task, purpose, and audience.

The following chart shows how to organize your draft to create a clear, coherent, and informative "how-to" explanation.

Organizing a "How-To" Explanation

INTRODUCTION

- Begin with an attention-grabbing opener. You might engage readers by posing a question, or by stating a fact that shows why your topic is interesting to your audience.
- State your purpose. If you begin with a question, your purpose statement should answer it. Tell readers what you are going to explain and why.
- Establish a **formal style** and **tone** by choosing precise, unbiased language and avoiding slang.

▼

BODY

- Determine how you will present the steps of your process. You might describe one step per paragraph. Some steps might be made up of a series of smaller steps.
- Present the steps in the correct order. Use appropriate **transitions** such as *first*, *then*, and *next* to clarify the relationships between the steps.

▼

CONCLUDING SECTION

- Restate the reason for making the product or completing the process.
- If appropriate, briefly summarize the steps.

GRAMMAR IN CONTEXT: TRANSITIONS THAT SHOW SEQUENCE

As you draft your "how-to" explanation, using appropriate **transitions** will help you clearly explain the process in the order in which steps occur. These transitions may be single words or phrases. They usually come at the beginning of a sentence.

Type of Transition	Examples
phrase	▶ *The first thing you need to do is get registered.*
single word	▶ *Next, fill in all of the information that's requested.* *Now you need to fill your buddy list.* *Once you get some specific names in your list, you can . . .*

YOUR TURN Develop a first draft of your "how-to" explanation using the planning chart you created. Remember to use transitions that show the sequence of steps.

Revising

As you reread and rework the draft of your "how-to" explanation, think about whether you have achieved your purpose. Also, make sure your explanation will be clear to your audience. This chart can help you revise, rewrite, and improve your draft.

"HOW-TO" EXPLANATION

Ask Yourself	Tips	Revision Strategies
1. Does the introduction catch readers' attention and state why they would want to complete the process? Does it state a clear purpose?	▶ **Put a star** next to the reason readers would want to complete the process. **Put brackets** around the statement of purpose.	▶ If needed, **add** a more powerful statement of the reason. If needed, **add** a statement of purpose.
2. Are all of the required materials listed or mentioned?	▶ **Circle** all the materials needed to complete the process.	▶ **Add** any materials that have been left out.
3. Are the steps of the process in the correct order?	▶ **Number** each step to show the order in which it occurs in the process.	▶ If necessary, **rearrange** the steps so they are in the correct order. **Add** any steps that have been left out.
4. Do transitional words clarify the relationships between steps in the process?	▶ **Highlight** transitions such as *first, second, after, next,* and *last*.	▶ **Add** transitions where needed.
5. Is each step described with precise language? Is a formal style and tone maintained throughout the explanation?	▶ **Underline** precise verbs, nouns, and adjectives. **Draw an arrow** next to vague words and informal language.	▶ If necessary, **elaborate** on the steps by adding precise words and specific details. **Replace** vague and informal language with precise, formal terms.
6. Does the concluding section restate the reason for completing the process?	▶ **Put a star** beside the sentence that restates the reason.	▶ **Add** a sentence that restates the reason, if necessary.

YOUR TURN

PEER REVIEW Ask a classmate to read your "how-to" explanation. Then ask how confident he or she feels about being able to complete the process. Take notes on any questions your partner has and decide if you need to take a new approach to help describe the process for your audience. Then review your partner's essay in the same way.

ANALYZE A STUDENT DRAFT

Read this student's draft and the comments about it. Use it as a model for revising your own "how-to" explanation.

COMMON CORE

W 2b Develop the topic with relevant, concrete details. **W 5** Develop and strengthen writing by revising, rewriting, or trying a new approach. **L 3b** Maintain consistency in style and tone.

How to Instant Message
by Christopher Cultrara, Queen of Peace Elementary School

1 Today, people use many different forms of communication, from letters to e-mail. Instant messaging is quickly becoming a favorite of people of all ages. In this essay I'll explain how to get started with instant messaging.

2 The first thing you need to do is get registered and get a screen name. Most people use a common instant messaging engine, so that's where you should start. Go to the instant messaging Web site and click on the "get a new screen name" link. Next, fill in all of the information that's requested. Then, enter the screen name you want to use, and enter a password. Your screen name and password can be anything you want. I always write my password and screen name in a safe place. I might forget them. Finally, click on "submit" to submit all of the information. You should then have your screen name and be able to sign on.

> In his **introduction,** Christopher makes a comment on instant messaging. More specific details would help engage his audience.

> Christopher presents steps of the process in **chronological order,** using appropriate **transitions.** He also gives a piece of **personal advice** for keeping track of passwords.

LEARN HOW **Write an Engaging Introduction** In his first paragraph, Christopher notes that instant messaging is very popular with people of all ages. When revising his essay, he decided he could do a better job of explaining why this topic is interesting and important. So, he added concrete details to the introduction that would make a more direct and personal connection with his audience.

CHRISTOPHER'S REVISION TO PARAGRAPH **1**

~~Today, people use many different forms of communication, from letters to e-mail.~~ Instant messaging is quickly becoming a favorite of people of all ages. ~~In this essay I'll explain how to get started with instant messaging.~~

I use this fun and simple form of communication every day. I stay in constant contact with everyone and never miss important events or parties any more. If you are looking for a quick way to stay in immediate contact with your family and friends, then instant messaging is for you. Read this essay, and then get ready for flying fingers!

❸   Now you need to fill your buddy list. To get your buddy list, you must sign on using your screen name. Once you are signed on and your buddy list comes up, you can begin to enter your friends' screen names. Insert them into your buddy list by typing them in under "new buddy."

❹   Once you get some specific names in your list, you can arrange them into groups, such as "friends" or "family." You can also make up new groups and call them anything you want.

❺   Now that you are set up, instant messaging itself is very simple. Just click on the buddy you want to instant message. That will display the instant message window. Type in your message and hit "send." That's all there is to it. You and your "buddies" are connected in an instant! Enjoy!

> Christopher uses **precise language** and **examples** to help readers visualize the process. He could improve this section by adding some **personal advice**.

> The **concluding section** restates, in an upbeat way, why readers would want to complete this process.

LEARN HOW **Add Personal Advice** A "how-to" essay can be dry and impersonal if the writer does not include some personal advice or tips throughout. Christopher offered a tip earlier, in paragraph 2. When he revised paragraph 3, he decided to add another tip.

CHRISTOPHER'S REVISION TO PARAGRAPH ❸

Now you need to fill your buddy list. To get your buddy list, you must sign on using your screen name. Once you are signed on and your buddy list comes up, you can begin to enter your friends' screen names. Insert them into your buddy list by typing them in under "new buddy."

When you're sending a message, be careful to select your intended buddy. I once sent a message to an entire group of friends, and I meant to send it only to my brother—extremely embarrassing!

YOUR TURN Using guidance and support from your peers and teacher as well as the two "Learn How" lessons, evaluate and revise your essay to make sure you have engaged your audience and accomplished your purpose. As you reread your "how-to" explanation, look for places where you could revise to add personal advice or experience that is concrete and useful. Add at least one tip that could help your reader be more successful with the task.

COMMON CORE **W 5** Strengthen writing by editing. **L 1** Demonstrate command of the conventions of standard English grammar and usage. **L 2b** Spell correctly.

Editing and Publishing

If your "how-to" essay contains grammar, spelling, and punctuation errors, your audience may have trouble understanding your instructions. In the editing stage, you proofread your work to fix any minor errors in grammar, usage, and punctuation that remain in your draft. If you used your word-processing spell-checker, reread your essay to correct any remaining misspelled or incorrectly used words.

GRAMMAR IN CONTEXT: SUBORDINATING CONJUNCTIONS

Using subordinating conjunctions can make your "how-to" explanation clearer and easier to follow. A **subordinating conjunction** links a dependent clause to an independent clause in a sentence. Subordinating conjunctions can show various kinds of relationships between ideas. Subordinating conjunctions such as *after, as soon as, before, now that, once, when,* and *while* are transitions that show the order in which things happen.

Read this sentence from Christopher's draft:

Once you are signed on and your buddy list comes up, you can begin to enter your friends' screen names.

[*Once* is a **subordinating conjunction.** It begins a dependent clause that tells "when" you can begin to enter the screen names. The next clause in the sentence is an independent clause.]

As Christopher was proofreading his essay, he noticed two sentences that would be clearer if he joined them with a subordinating conjunction.

I always write my password and screen name in a safe place. ⌐in case⌐ *I might forget them.*

[The phrase *in case* is a subordinating conjunction that shows how forgetting the password and screen name is related to writing them in a safe place.]

PUBLISH YOUR WRITING

Share your "how-to" explanation with an audience in one of the following ways:

- Make copies of your essay and distribute them to others who would like to learn your process.
- Post your essay on a blog used by students interested in the process.
- Develop your essay into a set of oral instructions you will give to a group of students.

 **YOUR TURN** Carefully proofread your essay to correct any errors. Use subordinating conjunctions where they can clarify the process you are explaining. Then publish your final essay where it is most likely to reach your audience.

Scoring Rubric

Use the rubric below to evaluate your "how-to" explanation from the Writing Workshop or your response to the on-demand task on the next page.

"HOW-TO" EXPLANATION

SCORE	COMMON CORE TRAITS
6	• **Development** Has an engaging introduction focused on task, purpose, and audience; clearly states a purpose; supports steps with concrete details and definitions; has a powerful concluding section • **Organization** Organizes steps in correct order; uses appropriate transitions to clarify process • **Language** Consistently maintains a formal style and tone; uses precise language; demonstrates a strong command of conventions
5	• **Development** Has an effective and focused introduction; states a purpose; supports steps with concrete details and definitions; has a strong concluding section • **Organization** Steps are in order; uses effective transitions to clarify process • **Language** Maintains a formal style and tone; uses precise language; demonstrates a fairly strong command of conventions
4	• **Development** Has an engaging but unfocused introduction; states a purpose; needs more support for steps; has an adequate concluding section • **Organization** Organizes most steps in order; uses some transitions to clarify process • **Language** Mostly maintains a formal style and tone; needs more precise language; has a few errors in conventions
3	• **Development** Has an adequate introduction that needs focus; suggests a purpose but does not state it clearly; lacks sufficient support for steps; has a routine concluding section • **Organization** Some steps are out of order; needs more transitions to link steps • **Language** Frequently lapses into an informal style and tone; uses some vague word choices; has some distracting errors in conventions
2	• **Development** Has an introduction unrelated to the task; states no purpose; lacks details and definitions; has a weak concluding section • **Organization** Has organizational flaws; lacks transitions • **Language** Uses an informal style and tone; uses mostly vague language; has many distracting errors in conventions
1	• **Development** Has no introduction or purpose; offers few details or definitions; ends abruptly • **Organization** Includes steps in incorrect order • **Language** Uses an inappropriate style and tone; uses tired language; has major problems with conventions

Preparing for Timed Writing

COMMON CORE **W 10** Write routinely over shorter time frames for a range of tasks, purposes, and audiences.

1. ANALYZE THE TASK   5 MIN

Read the task carefully. Then read it again, underlining the words that tell the audience and the purpose. Circle the type of writing.

WRITING TASK *Audience*

Suppose a student a few years younger than you asks for your help in using a cell phone or other device. Write a "how-to" explanation to teach the student how to use the device. Use precise language, and present the steps in chronological order.

Purpose

2. PLAN YOUR RESPONSE   10 MIN

Decide which device you are going to write about. Think about the steps you follow when you use the device. Record the steps in a chart. As you review the steps, think about how you will explain them to younger readers. Will you use simpler words, shorter sentences, or engaging personal advice?

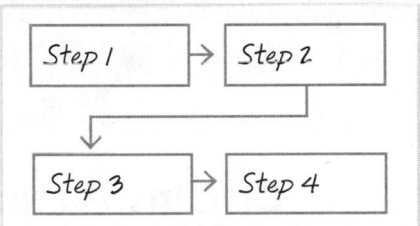

3. RESPOND TO THE TASK   20 MIN

Using the notes you've made, draft your essay. Keep these guidelines in mind:

- In the introduction, make clear the process you are explaining and why readers should want to learn the task. Capture readers' attention with an interesting question or a fact.
- In the body, use precise language and accurate definitions as you present the steps in chronological order. Describe any materials required to complete the task.
- In the concluding section, restate the reason for completing the task.

4. IMPROVE YOUR RESPONSE   5–10 MIN

Revising Go back over key aspects of the explanation. Did you explain why your topic is useful or important to readers? Did you organize your explanation clearly, giving the steps in the correct order?

Proofreading Find and correct errors in grammar, spelling, punctuation, and capitalization. Make sure all your edits are neat, and erase any stray marks.

Checking Your Final Copy Before you turn in your explanation, read it one more time to catch any errors you may have missed.

Giving and Following Oral Instructions

When you teach a friend to play a new game or explain how to enter a contest, you are giving oral instructions. Almost every day we give—and follow—oral instructions.

 Complete the workshop activities in your **Reader/Writer Notebook**.

SPEAK WITH A PURPOSE	COMMON CORE TRAITS
TASK Adapt your "how-to" explanation as a set of **oral instructions**. Your goal is to teach your classmates to perform a task or process that will be useful to them. Practice your presentation, and then give it to the class.	**STRONG ORAL INSTRUCTIONS . . .** • state the topic and purpose in a way that captures listeners' interest • present action steps in chronological order • use precise language and offer tips • use effective verbal and nonverbal techniques • close with a restatement of the purpose • use visual displays to clarify information

COMMON CORE

SL 1d Review key ideas through paraphrasing. **SL 2** Interpret and explain information presented in diverse media and formats. **SL 4** Sequence ideas logically with descriptions, facts, and details. **SL 5** Include visual displays in presentations.

Give Instructions

Here are some tips to keep in mind as you adapt and deliver your instructions:

- **Use note cards.** Your presentation will be more effective if you make eye contact with your listeners. For this reason, you should avoid reading directly from your essay. Instead, write key words and phrases from your essay on index cards. You might create one card for your introduction, a card for each step in the process, and one card for your concluding section.

- **Speak clearly and naturally.** Speak at a slower rate and at a louder volume than you do in normal conversation. Pause briefly after giving each action step. This gives listeners a chance to take in the information. Also pause after transition words such as *first* and *next*. This tells the audience that you are about to introduce a new action step.

- **Use nonverbal techniques.** In addition to your speech, you can use "body language" to communicate ideas to your audience. For example, use facial expressions (a smile, a raised eyebrow) and gesture with your arms and hands to help illustrate what you are saying.

- **Pay attention to your audience.** When speaking to a group, it's important to make sure that all of your listeners are following along. If someone in the audience looks confused, take a moment and define confusing terms or even repeat a whole step. For example, you could write the steps of the instructions on the board and then do quick illustrations to help explain the concepts with visuals.

Speaking & Listening Online

Go to **thinkcentral.com**.
KEYWORD: HML6-790

Follow Instructions

When oral instructions have multiple action steps, you must listen carefully. Learning some simple techniques can help you improve your listening skills.

PAY ATTENTION TO CUES

Good listeners listen *actively*. This means that they reflect on the meaning of the speaker's words as they listen. They try to interpret and connect the speaker's main points. Speakers usually give verbal and nonverbal cues to convey messages to their listeners. Picking up on these cues and interpreting any visual displays the speaker uses will help you follow oral instructions.

Verbal and Nonverbal Cues Used by Speakers

VERBAL CUES	NONVERBAL CUES
• Words such as *first, next,* and *finally* that tell the order of events	• Movements or facial expressions that show the speaker's attitude
• Repetition of words, phrases, or statements to clarify ideas	• Hand, arm, or other body movements that emphasize or illustrate a point
• Emphasizing important ideas by speaking more loudly or slowly or by pausing before or after key words	• Facial expressions that invite listeners to ask questions or take part in some other way

FOCUS AND TAKE NOTES

A good way to focus on what a speaker is saying is to take notes. When you listen to instructions with multiple action steps, try these strategies:

- Jot down the topic and why it is important.
- When you hear a cue word that signals a new step in the process, sum up the previous step in a few words.
- When the speaker is finished, try to paraphrase, or restate, key ideas in your own words. If you cannot paraphrase the speaker's major ideas, ask questions to improve your understanding.

YOUR TURN

As a Speaker Present your oral instructions to a partner, incorporating both verbal and nonverbal techniques. Make sure your process follows a logical sequence with supportive examples and ideas. Remember to include a visual display if it will help your listeners understand the instructions. Use your partner's feedback to improve your delivery.

As a Listener Listen to your partner's presentation carefully. Take notes and paraphrase key ideas. After the presentation, review your notes with your partner to make sure you understand the process clearly. Then evaluate how your partner used verbal, nonverbal, and visual techniques to make the speech effective.

Assessment Practice

DIRECTIONS Read this selection and answer the questions that follow.

Cassiopeia *Retold by Alice Low*

1   Cassiopeia, wife of King Cepheus of Ethiopia, boasted to the sea nymphs, "I and my daughter, Andromeda, are far more beautiful than you. You are plain next to us."

2   The lovely sea nymphs swam to Poseidon, god of the sea, to tell him about Cassiopeia's insult. "You must punish Cassiopeia," they said. "She must not get away with such boasting."

3   Poseidon acted quickly. He sent a huge and hungry sea monster to Ethiopia to devour scores of King Cepheus's people.

4   King Cepheus was distraught, and he asked an oracle,[1] "What must I do to rid my country of this ferocious monster?"

5   The oracle replied, "Chain your daughter, Andromeda, to a rock by the sea. Leave her there for the sea monster to feast upon. Only in this way shall you be rid of it."

6   To his wife's despair, King Cepheus did as he was told, and poor Andromeda awaited her fate, chained and helpless. But as the sea monster was about to devour her, the hero Perseus flew overhead in Hermes' winged sandals. Just in time, he landed on the monster's back and thrust his sword into it repeatedly. After a raging battle, Perseus killed the monster and carried away the lovely Andromeda, who became his bride.

7   Perseus and Andromeda lived happily together, but the sea nymphs never forgot Cassiopeia's insult. Many years later, when Cassiopeia died, the sea nymphs again begged Poseidon to punish her.

8   This time Poseidon did so by setting Cassiopeia in the north sky in a most uncomfortable position. She sits in a high-backed chair that looks like a *W*—but during the part of the year, the chair hangs upside down.

9   Near Cassiopeia, Athena placed the constellation Andromeda, and Andromeda's brave husband, Perseus, stands not far from her in the Milky Way. Cepheus is there, too, though dimmer, and so is Cetus, the sea monster, also called the Whale.

---

1. **oracle:** a person through whom a god is believed to speak.

Reading Comprehension

Use "Cassiopeia" to answer questions 1–6.

1. Cassiopeia shows disrespect for a cultural value when she —
   A. disobeys Poseidon's orders
   B. becomes upset with King Cepheus
   C. rewards Andromeda with lavish gifts
   D. insults the sea nymphs by bragging

2. King Cepheus chains his daughter, Andromeda, to a rock by the sea in order to —
   A. save Cassiopeia
   B. help Perseus save Andromeda
   C. get rid of the sea monster
   D. punish Andromeda

3. Which statement best summarizes paragraph 6?
   A. Cassiopeia is sad because Cepheus chains Andromeda to a rock.
   B. Perseus rescues Andromeda just as the sea monster is about to eat her.
   C. Hermes gives his winged sandals to Perseus.
   D. Andromeda happily marries Perseus.

4. Why does Poseidon set Cassiopeia in an uncomfortable position in the sky?
   A. The sea monster will stop eating people if Cassiopeia is upside down.
   B. Poseidon wants to punish her for insulting the sea nymphs.
   C. Cassiopeia will be able to see her family from that position.
   D. King Cepheus needs a warning for his false statements.

SHORT CONSTRUCTED RESPONSE
Write two or three sentences to answer this question.

5. Classical myths often explain how something in the universe came to be. What natural wonder does this myth explain?

Write a paragraph to answer this question.

6. Summarize what happens to Andromeda in this myth.

Castor and Pollux   *Retold by Alice Low*

1   Castor and Pollux were inseparable twin brothers. Their father was Zeus, and their mother was a mortal, Leda of Sparta.

2   They were strong, athletic young men. Castor was renowned as a soldier and tamer of horses, and Pollux was an outstanding boxer. Both entered the Olympic games and won many competitions. They were worshipped as gods by athletes, soldiers, and sailors.

3   Castor and Pollux were among the Argonauts, who aided Jason in his quest for the Golden Fleece. But after their return, they had a dispute with two young men. A terrible battle followed, and Castor, who was mortal, was killed. Pollux, who was immortal, wept over the body of his twin. He cried to his father, Zeus, "Please let me kill myself and follow my brother to the underworld. I feel that half of myself is gone, and the half that remains is but a shadow."

4   Zeus took pity on Pollux and said, "Though I cannot enable you to die, for you are immortal, I shall allow you and Castor to be together always. Together you shall spend alternate days in the underworld and on Olympus. And because of your great love for your brother, I shall raise your images into the sky. There you shall shine next to each other forever."

5   And Castor and Pollux became the twin stars, forming the constellation Gemini.

Reading Comprehension

> Use "Castor and Pollux" to answer questions 7–13.

7. Castor and Pollux become separated because —

 A. they participate in different Olympic sports

 B. Zeus decides that they must spend days apart

 C. Castor is killed in a battle, but Pollux is immortal

 D. Pollux is unhappy about decisions Castor makes

8. Which human emotion does the god Zeus feel toward the troubled Pollux?

 A. Adoration

 B. Affection

 C. Compassion

 D. Jealousy

9. In this myth, Zeus has the power to —

 A. help Castor and Pollux win many Olympic competitions

 B. make it possible for Castor and Pollux to remain together forever

 C. let Pollux become human so that he can join his brother

 D. give Castor immortality so that he can always live on Olympus with his brother

10. What cultural value does Pollux honor?

 A. Brotherly love

 B. Obedience to the gods

 C. Respect for his elders

 D. Honorable living

11. What happens when Zeus agrees to help Pollux?

 A. The constellation Gemini appears in the sky.

 B. Castor loses his life in a fierce battle.

 C. Pollux suffers through a time of great sadness.

 D. Everyone praises the Argonauts who looked for the Golden Fleece.

SHORT CONSTRUCTED RESPONSE
Write two or three sentences to answer this question.

12. Reread paragraph 2. Identify two cultural values in this myth that seem to be important to the Greeks.

Write a short paragraph to answer this question.

13. According to the myth, how was the Gemini constellation formed?

GO ON ➡

Vocabulary

Use your knowledge of context clues to answer the following questions.

1. In the last paragraph of each selection, what is a *constellation*?

   A. A group of stars named for someone

   B. Several famous, important characters

   C. The god of the sea

   D. A cruel sea monster

2. What does *renowned* mean in paragraph 2 of "Castor and Pollux"?

   A. Devoted to one's brother

   B. Good at sports and athletics

   C. Well known; easily recognized

   D. Having fame; widely honored

3. What does *immortal* mean in paragraphs 3 and 4 of "Castor and Pollux"?

   A. Having the same injury

   B. Always loyal

   C. Never dying

   D. Wishing for life

4. What does *alternate* mean in paragraph 4 of "Castor and Pollux"?

   A. Occurring all the time

   B. Happening in turns

   C. Waiting for each other

   D. Taking all day to happen

Use your knowledge of context clues and thesaurus entries to answer the following questions.

> **boast** *verb.* brag, possess, feature, display, claim

5. Which word is the BEST synonym for *boast* in paragraph 1 of "Cassiopeia"?

   A. brag

   B. claim

   C. display

   D. possess

> **poor** *adjective.* deprived, broke, needy, penniless, weak, bad, humble, pitiable

6. Which word is the BEST synonym for *poor* in paragraph 6 of "Cassiopeia"?

   A. bad

   B. broke

   C. needy

   D. pitiable

> **strong** *adjective.* muscular, sturdy, tough, stout, solid, tough, spicy, hot, sharp, biting, bright, intense, convincing, effective

7. Which word is the BEST synonym for *strong* in paragraph 2 of "Castor and Pollux"?

   A. effective

   B. intense

   C. muscular

   D. spicy

Revising and Editing

DIRECTIONS **Read this passage and answer the questions that follow.**

(1) Every year, my brothers and my mom help uncle Harry and aunt Lea make maple syrup. (2) "Sugaring" takes place in the early spring. (3) The whole season lasts only one or two months. (4) My uncle and my brother Seth drill holes into the trees, and mom and aunt Lea attach buckets to them. (5) The buckets then collect the sap. (6) Every day, Seth brings the sap to the sugarhouse. (7) I boil off the water. (8) Maple syrup is a treat. (9) We must work very hard to make just a small batch of it. (10) It takes about 40 gallons of maple sap to produce one gallon of maple syrup!

1. Two more words that should be capitalized in sentence 1 are —

    A. brothers, mom **C.** uncle, aunt

    B. mom, uncle **D.** mom, aunt

2. How might you combine sentences 2 and 3 to form one compound sentence?

    A. "Sugaring" takes place in the early spring, and the whole season lasts only one or two months.

    B. "Sugaring" takes place in the early spring, when the whole season lasts only one or two months.

    C. "Sugaring" takes place in the early spring, the whole season lasts only one or two months.

    D. "Sugaring" takes place in the early spring the whole season lasts only one or two months.

3. Two more words that should be capitalized in sentence 4 are —

    A. brother, uncle **C.** mom, aunt

    B. uncle, aunt **D.** brother, mom

4. How might you combine sentences 6 and 7 to form one compound sentence?

    A. Every day, Seth brings the sap to the sugarhouse, I boil off the water.

    B. Every day, Seth brings the sap to the sugarhouse, and I boil off the water.

    C. Every day, Seth brings the sap to the sugarhouse, where I boil off the water.

    D. Every day, Seth brings the sap to the sugarhouse I boil off the water.

5. How might you combine sentences 8 and 9 to form one compound sentence?

    A. Maple syrup is a treat, but we must work very hard to make just a small batch of it.

    B. Maple syrup is a treat we must work very hard to make just a small batch of it.

    C. Maple syrup is a treat that we must work very hard to make just a small batch of it.

    D. Maple syrup is a treat, we must work very hard to make just a small batch of it.

STOP

Ideas for Independent Reading

Which questions from Unit 6 made an impression on you? Continue exploring with these books.

Why do we exaggerate?

American Tall Tales
by Mary Pope Osborne

Davy Crockett carries thunder in his fist and lightning flies from his fingers. Paul Bunyan carves the Grand Canyon with his pickax. Stories of these larger-than-life characters captured the adventurous spirit of early American pioneers.

Montmorency: Thief, Liar, Gentleman
by Eleanor Updale

Montmorency, a thief who wants to be a gentleman, copies the manners and clothing of the rich when he gets out of jail. But that isn't enough. He must become a member of the group he once hated.

Ruby Electric
by Theresa Nelson

Ruby writes screenplays to escape her life. In her movies, dads are part of their daughters' lives and moms don't have secrets. Then, suddenly, her father reappears, and Ruby has to cope with the truth about her family.

When is it time to let go?

Dybbuk: A Version
by Barbara Rogasky

Konin, a poor scholar, is in love with Leah. When Leah's father decides she must marry a rich man, Konin searches for a way to make his fortune. Can Konin and Leah's love endure the trials they will face?

Home Is East
by Many Ly

Everyone in St. Petersburg's small Cambodian community told Amy Lin her mother would run away, but it still hurt when she left. Now Amy and her father live in California, and Amy keeps hoping her mother will return.

The Liberation of Gabriel King
by K. L. Going

Gabriel is scared of 38 things, including moving up to the fifth grade. His best friend, Frita, comes up with a plan to free him of his fears before school starts. Will he be able to let his fears go?

Is goodness always rewarded?

Goddess of Yesterday
by Caroline B. Cooney

Anaxandra pretends to be a princess when she is rescued by King Menelaus. Now she is trapped within the walls of Troy as Menelaus's army arrives to reclaim his wife, Helen. Anaxandra soon finds that the lives of many people depend on her.

Stand Tall
by Joan Bauer

At six feet three inches tall, Tree is the tallest 12-year-old most people have met. Because of his size, many people expect too much of him. But when disaster strikes his family and town, Tree surprises everyone, even himself.

The Sea of Trolls
by Nancy Farmer

Jack is only 11 when Norse warriors called the beserkers kidnap him and his sister. After they are taken to a cruel, half-troll queen, Jack sets out on a dangerous quest in order to save his sister's life.

Get Novel Wise

THINK central

Go to thinkcentral.com.
KEYWORD: HML6-798

UNIT 7

Life Stories

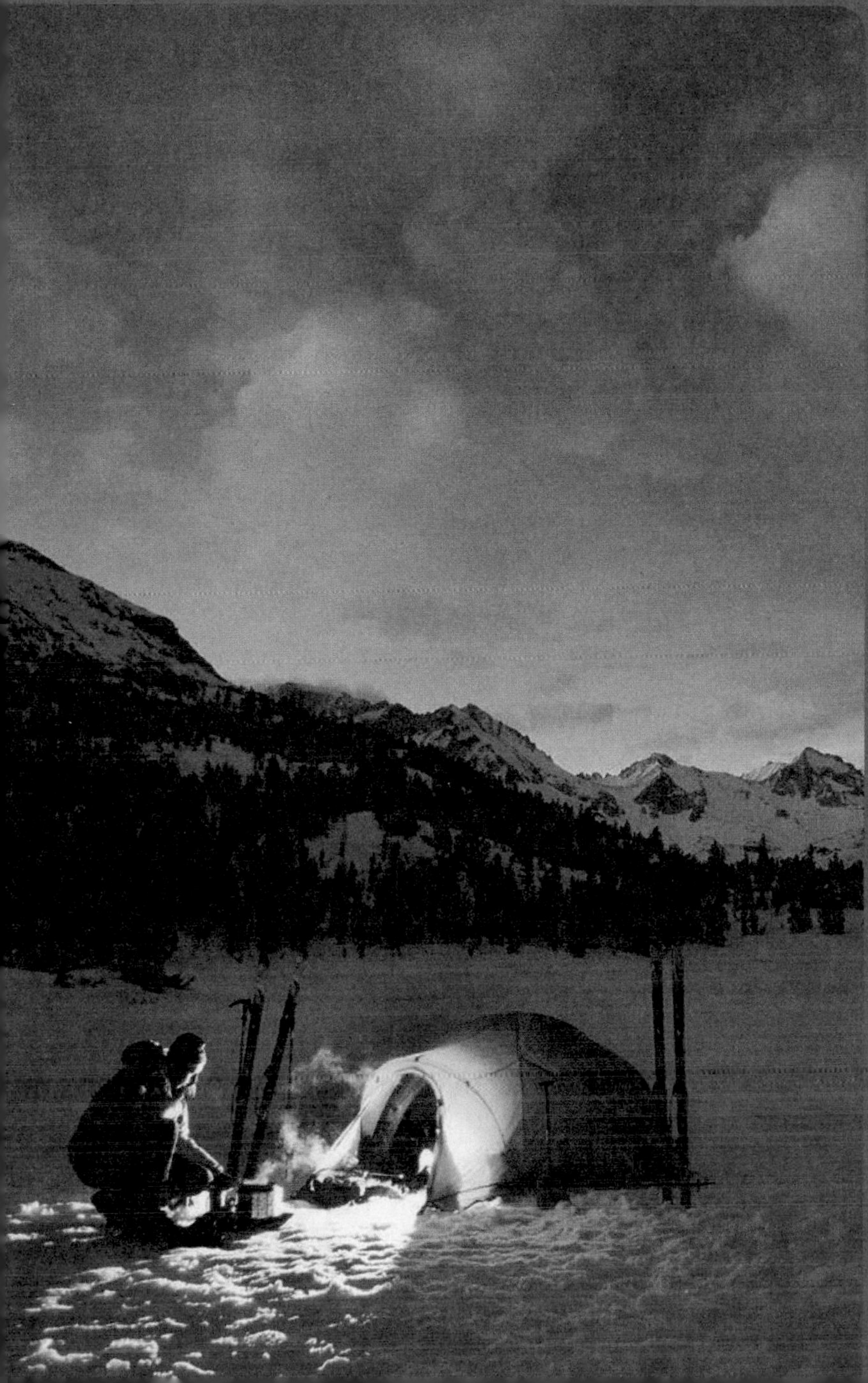

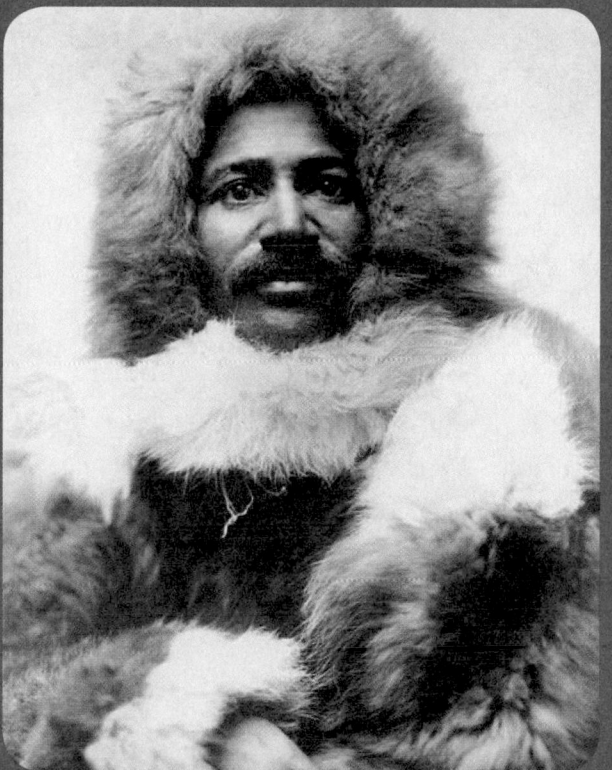

BIOGRAPHY AND AUTOBIOGRAPHY

- In Nonfiction
- In Poetry
- In Media

What makes a person larger than LIFE?

Martin Luther King Jr., Anne Frank, George Washington—why are these people remembered? Each person comes from a very different time and place. Yet they are alike in that their words and actions shaped the lives of the people of their time, and continue to influence people today. Each one is larger than life.

ACTIVITY Think of someone who has had a strong impact on you. It might be a historical figure, a celebrity, or someone you know. In a small group, discuss the following questions to decide what makes this person larger than life:

• What is the person best known for?

• How has he or she influenced your life, or the lives of others?

• Might his or her words and actions affect the future? How?

Find It Online!  **THINK** central

Go to **thinkcentral.com** for the interactive version of this unit.

Preview Unit Goals

TEXT ANALYSIS
- Analyze in detail how a key individual, event, or idea is introduced, illustrated, and elaborated in a text
- Determine an author's point of view in a text
- Compare and contrast one author's presentation of events with that of another

READING
- Determine the meaning of words and phrases as they are used in a text, including figurative meanings
- Trace chronological order using signal words

WRITING AND LANGUAGE
- Write a personal narrative
- Use colons correctly
- Capitalize proper nouns correctly

VOCABULARY
- Use affixes as clues to the meaning of a word.
- Use the relationship between particular words to better understand each of the words
- Verify the preliminary determination of the meaning of a word or phrase.

ACADEMIC VOCABULARY
- achieve
- appreciate
- characteristics
- conclude
- obvious

MEDIA AND VIEWING
- Integrate information presented in different media as well as in words to develop a coherent understanding of a topic
- Produce a documentary

Media Smart DVD-ROM

Messages in a Documentary

Discover how documentaries present information about a subject in a scene from *Houdini: The Great Escape.* Page 860

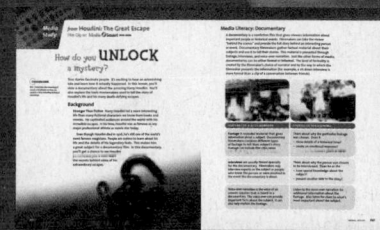

Biography and Autobiography

How did Harry Houdini develop his tricks? How did Helen Keller feel when she learned to communicate? Most people are curious about the lives of others, from historical figures to today's athletes and stars. Biographies and autobiographies can let you in on the lives of many fascinating people.

COMMON CORE

Included in this workshop:
RI 4 Determine the meaning of words and phrases as they are used in a text, including figurative meanings. **RI 6** Determine an author's point of view in a text. **RI 9** Compare and contrast one author's presentation of events with that of another.

Part 1: Life Stories

Biographies, autobiographies, memoirs, journals, and personal narratives all tell the true stories of people's lives. What makes each type of nonfiction narrative unique? One important difference has to do with *who* does the writing. Study the chart below to discover other differences—as well as important similarities.

MEMOIR	PERSONAL NARRATIVE	AUTOBIOGRAPHY	BIOGRAPHY
*Writer **IS** the Subject*	*Writer **IS** the Subject*	*Writer **IS** the Subject*	*Writer is **NOT** the Subject*
	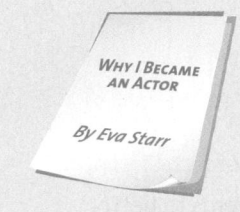		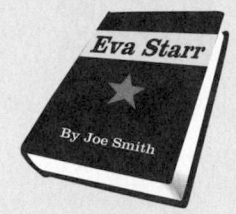
Characteristics	*Characteristics*	*Characteristics*	*Characteristics*
• autobiographical account written from the first-person point of view • describes the subject's experiences and observations about important people or events • often includes the **historical context** of the subject—information about the society and culture of the time	• autobiographical essay written from the first-person point of view • tells a story about real people and events • a short work of nonfiction that usually deals with a single subject	• autobiographical account written from the first-person point of view • describes the subject's thoughts, feelings, and opinions about his or her life • is based primarily on details that come from the subject's own memories	• is written from the third-person point of view • is based on information from many sources, including books about the subject, the subject's journals and letters, and interviews • sometimes includes details provided by the subject

MODEL 1: BIOGRAPHY

Years ago, readers worldwide first fell in love with the wizard Harry Potter. Soon after, J. K. Rowling became a household name. This excerpt is from a biography of Rowling, the author of the *Harry Potter* series.

from J. K. Rowling

Biography by **Bradley Steffens**

J. K. Rowling, as she was becoming known to the world, was pretty well prepared to handle life's ups and downs. She had equipped herself with a good education, traveled and lived abroad, been married and divorced, given birth to a child, and lost a parent. She had struggled
5 through grim poverty and realized a lifelong dream of publishing a book. Yet nothing could have prepared her for what was about to happen. Within five years she would become one of the richest and most recognizable women in the world. The media would report on her every move. . . . Most important, hundreds of millions of people—children
10 and adults alike—would read and reread her books.

Close Read

1. How can you tell that this excerpt is from a biography rather than an autobiography?

2. What was Rowling's life like before she became famous? Name two specific things you learn about her from this excerpt.

MODEL 2: MEMOIR

As a Jew growing up in Poland, Anita Lobel was only five when World War II began. At that time, Nazi Germany had invaded Poland with the intent of imprisoning and killing Jewish people. Lobel and her brother spent days in hiding from German soldiers before they were captured.

from No Pretty Pictures: *A Child of War*

Memoir by **Anita Lobel**

Walking as we did down the middle of the bridge, I hoped that we were hidden from view. Under our feet this short, solid stone walkway felt like a tightrope. I held my brother's hand. We will get across, I thought. We will. We had squeaked by in other situations. This was just
5 another adventure. Already, with every step, the distance to the safe side was shrinking. The guards were not looking in our direction. Not yet.

Close Read

1. From what point of view is this paragraph told? How can you tell?

2. In the boxed text, Lobel describes what she was thinking when she was crossing the bridge. Where else does she share her thoughts or feelings?

Part 2: Literary Language and Devices in Nonfiction Narratives

You probably associate **literary language and devices,** such as imagery and metaphors, with poetry, but writers of nonfiction narratives, including autobiographies, memoirs, and personal narratives, also use such devices. Writers use literary devices as tools to reach our emotions, appeal to our imaginations, and convey meaning. Literary devices give life to a work. They also help convey a **tone** that reveals the writer's attitude toward his or her subject. All of these devices work together to create an overall impression of the subject and his or her life.

LITERARY LANGUAGE AND DEVICES	EXAMPLES
Imagery is language that appeals to our senses. Imagery creates pictures in our minds and can also help us hear, smell, or taste something and feel its textures and temperature. **Ask:** • To what sense or senses does the image appeal? • What is the effect of using this imagery?	The afternoon sun penetrated the mass of honeysuckle that covered the porch, and fell on my upturned face. —from *The Story of My Life* by Helen Keller
There are many kinds of figurative language, or language that makes an imaginative comparison and is not meant to be taken literally. In a **simile** a writer compares two unlike things using words such as *like, as, then,* and *resembles*. In a **metaphor** a writer directly compares two things without a comparison word. **Ask:** • Is the author using a simile or metaphor? How do I know? • What point is the writer making with this comparison?	Like a jewel under a bright light, Houdini responded to attention by revealing brilliant new facets. —from *Spellbinder: The Life of Harry Houdini* by Tom Lalicki
Tone refers to the writer's attitude—the way the writer feels about the subject he or she is writing about. When you talk to people, you can tell how they feel from their expressions and voices. When you read, however, you have to depend on words and the way the writer uses language to understand how a writer feels about the subject. Tone can be playful or serious, joyous or sad, and so on. **Ask:** • What words and details in the text convey the writer's tone? • What word or words would you use to describe the way the writer feels about the subject?	The most important day I remember in all my life is the one in which my teacher, Anne Mansfield Sullivan, came to me. I am filled with wonder when I consider the immeasurable contrasts between the two lives which it connects. —from *The Story of My Life* by Helen Keller

MODEL 1: READING A BIOGRAPHY

Tony Hawk is a professional skateboarder. By the time he was 16, Hawk was taking the skateboarding world by storm and winning all kinds of competitions. This article was published in 1986, when Hawk was 18.

from **Chairman of the Board**

Sports Illustrated magazine article by **Armen Keteyian**

When Hawk swoops down from the top of a U-shaped bowl and starts digging into his bag of tricks—720s, 360 varial inverts, finger flips—he's a sight to see, an aerialist who is equal parts gymnast, acrobat and ballet dancer. He often concludes his show with an
5 electrifying 720 aerial; Hawk is the only skater in the world who can complete two midair somersaults and somehow still land on a 31- by 10-inch hunk of hardwood.

Close Read

1. If you knew nothing about Tony Hawk except for what you've just read, how would you describe him?

2. Examine the boxed details. Do they give you a positive or negative impression of Hawk?

MODEL 2: READING AN AUTOBIOGRAPHY

In 1999 Hawk retired from competitive skateboarding. However, he has managed to stay involved in the sport that brought him fame. Hawk has developed his own line of skateboards and even has video games named after him. In this autobiography, Hawk looks back on his childhood and his career.

from **TONY HAWK: PROFESSIONAL SKATEBOARDER**

Autobiography by **Tony Hawk** with Sean Mortimer

I got picked on. I was less than five feet tall when I entered eighth grade, and weighed less than eighty pounds. I was so skinny that I resembled a set of toothpicks walking awkwardly down the hallway. Only my legs had a hint of muscle on them. If I flexed my bicep
5 nothing would pop up—muscle or fat. And, I was short. If I had to be skinny, at least someone could have given me height. I was a seriously late bloomer and in school nothing is more noticeable than that.

Close Read

1. Nonfiction writers use literary language and devices to make their writing lively and interesting. Reread lines 1–3. What simile does Hawk use to describe himself?

2. In what way does this excerpt change your impression of the champion skater described in the magazine article?

Part 3: Analyze the Text

Marian Anderson, an African-American singer, rose to fame in the 1930s. She performed for audiences across the country. However, she was banned from singing at Constitution Hall because she was black. Outraged, some people arranged for Anderson to give a free concert at the Lincoln Memorial in Washington, D.C. On April 9, 1939, Anderson performed for 75,000 people.

Author Russell Freedman writes about Anderson's life in *The Voice That Challenged a Nation,* published 11 years after her death.

from

The Voice That Challenged a Nation

Marian Anderson and the Struggle for Equal Rights

Biography by **Russell Freedman**

Marian Anderson never expected to become an activist in the struggle for equal rights. Away from the concert stage she valued her privacy and preferred a quiet family life. She disliked confrontations. And she never felt comfortable as the center of a public controversy.

5 "I would be fooling myself to think that I was meant to be a fearless fighter," she said in her autobiography. "I was not, just as I was not meant to be a soprano instead of a contralto."[1]

Actually, Anderson had to fight hard to win her place in American music history. As she pursued her career, she was forced to challenge
10 racial barriers simply to succeed as a singer. . . .

It was only after she toured Europe to great acclaim in the early 1930s that her artistry was recognized in her own homeland. And even then, Anderson's fame could not easily overcome the racial prejudice that she confronted as a black singer touring America. Well into her career, she
15 was turned away from restaurants and hotels.

Anderson's exceptional musical gifts and her uncompromising artistic standards made it possible for her to break through racial barriers. She became a role model, inspiring generations of African American performers who followed her. But it was the strength of her character,
20 her undaunted[2] spirit and unshakable dignity, that transformed her from a singer to an international symbol of progress in the advancement of human rights.

---

1. **soprano . . . contralto:** terms used to describe a singer's vocal range.
2. **undaunted:** courageously determined, especially during difficult times.

Close Read

1. How can you tell that this excerpt is from a biography?

2. What do you learn about Anderson's personality in lines 1–4?

3. What source of information does the biographer cite in this excerpt?

4. What details does the writer include to give you a positive impression of Anderson? One detail is boxed. What word would you use to describe the tone of this paragraph?

Now read this excerpt from Anderson's autobiography, which was published in 1956. In the excerpt, Anderson remembers that April day in 1939 when she sang at the Lincoln Memorial.

from

My Lord, What a Morning

Autobiography by **Marian Anderson**

There seemed to be people as far as the eye could see. The crowd stretched in a great semicircle from the Lincoln Memorial around the reflecting pool on to the shaft
5 of the Washington Monument. I had a feeling that a great wave of good will poured out from these people, almost engulfing me. And when I stood up to sing our National Anthem I felt for a moment as though I were choking. For a desperate second I thought that the words, well
10 as I know them, would not come.

I sang, I don't know how. There must have been the help of professionalism I had accumulated over the years. Without it I could not have gone through the program. I sang—and again I know because I consulted a newspaper clipping—"America," the aria "O mio Fernando,"
15 Schubert's "Ave Maria," and three spirituals—"Gospel Train," "Trampin'," and "My Soul Is Anchored in the Lord."

I regret that a fixed rule was broken, another thing about which I found out later. Photographs were taken from within the Memorial, where the great statue of Lincoln stands, although there was a tradition
20 that no pictures could be taken from within the sanctum.[1]

It seems also that at the end, when the tumult[2] of the crowd's shouting would not die down, I spoke a few words. I read the clipping now and cannot believe that I could have uttered another sound after I had finished singing. "I am overwhelmed," I said. "I just can't talk.
25 I can't tell you what you have done for me today. I thank you from the bottom of my heart again and again."

It was the simple truth. But did I really say it?

---

1. **sanctum:** a sacred place.
2. **tumult:** commot on.

Close Read

1. Reread lines 1–10. What sensory images help you picture the scene Anderson faced that day?

2. In lines 13–14 and 22–24, Anderson admits that she consulted a newspaper for help with remembering details about the day. Why might she have had trouble recalling a day she experienced firsthand?

3. What picture of Anderson do you have after reading both excerpts? Explain how this picture would be different if you had not read her autobiography.

Matthew Henson at the Top of the World

Biography by Jim Haskins

VIDEO TRAILER **THiNK** central | KEYWORD: HML6-808

Why attempt the
IMPOSSIBLE?

Sailing across the ocean. Taking a walk on the moon. Once, these things were thought to be impossible. Then someone had the courage to try what had never been done. In the following selection, you will see how a young explorer's determination helped him go where nobody had gone before.

WEB IT What do you want to accomplish in your lifetime? Write down one of your biggest ambitions in the center of a word web like the one shown. Then brainstorm different things you could do to make that achievement possible.

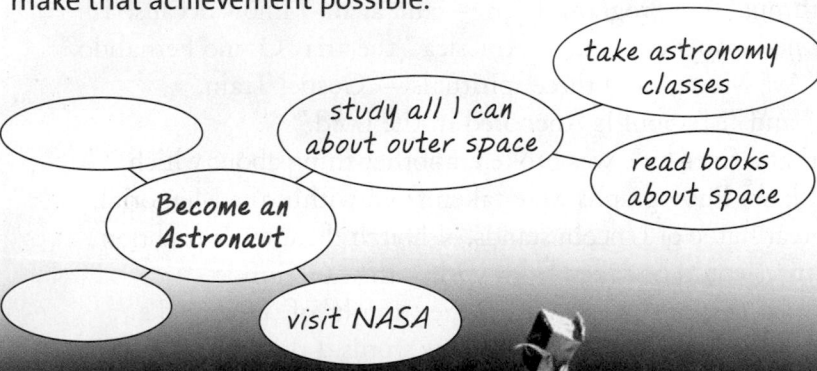

take astronomy classes

study all I can about outer space

read books about space

Become an Astronaut

visit NASA

TEXT ANALYSIS: BIOGRAPHY

A **biography** is the true account of a person's life, written by another person. No two writers are the same, so every biography is unique—even if many are about the same person. Still, all biographies share a few characteristics.

- They are written from the third-person point of view.
- They explain how events, people, and experiences shaped the person's life.
- They include quotations from people who knew him or her.

As you read this biography of Matthew Henson, look for these elements.

READING SKILL: COMPARE AND CONTRAST

When you **compare and contrast,** you identify the ways in which two or more subjects are alike or different. As you read the following biography, use a Venn diagram to compare and contrast the explorers Matthew Henson and Robert Peary. Some points you may want to consider are family background, education, and personal motivation.

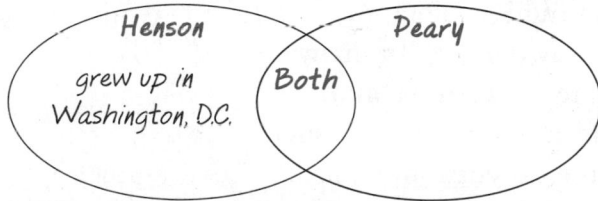

Review: Recognize Cause-and-Effect Relationships

▲ VOCABULARY IN CONTEXT

Jim Haskins uses the following boldfaced words to tell about a journey. To see how many you know, try to substitute a different word or phrase for each one.

1. Matthew Henson was an **ardent** adventurer.
2. His difficult early years taught him **resourcefulness.**
3. His lack of money was a **manifestation** of prejudice.
4. Their **expedition** to the North Pole began in 1908.
5. First, Henson studied the **feasibility** of the expedition.
6. If they succeeded, they would win **prestige** and fame.

 Complete the activities in your **Reader/Writer Notebook.**

Meet the Author

Jim Haskins
1941–2005

Bringing History to Light
Jim Haskins attended a segregated school in his Alabama hometown. Although the school did not have the best facilities or the latest books, Haskins received a good education. He recalled that his teachers acted "as if it were their mission in life to educate us." They emphasized the contributions African Americans had made to society. When Haskins became a children's book writer, he wanted to do the same thing for his readers. He wrote biographies of Martin Luther King Jr., Hank Aaron, and Stevie Wonder, among others.

BACKGROUND TO THE BIOGRAPHY

Arctic Exploration
The Arctic is the area north of the Arctic Circle, 66° north latitude. The Dutch and the English began exploring the Arctic in the early 1500s. They hoped to find a trade route to Asia. In early Arctic exploration, ships often became trapped in the ice, and many sailors lost their lives.

By the late 1800s, nearly all of the Arctic had been explored. Groups began to set records, pushing farther north each time. The race to reach the North Pole became an international competition.

Author Online **THINK** central
Go to thinkcentral.com.
KEYWORD: HML6-809

Matthew Henson
AT THE TOP OF THE WORLD

Jim Haskins

While the explorers of the American West faced many dangers in their travels, at least game and water were usually plentiful; and if winter with its cold and snow overtook them, they could, in time, expect warmth and spring. For Matthew Henson, in his explorations with Robert Peary at the North Pole, this was hardly the case. In many ways, to forge ahead into the icy Arctic took far greater stamina[1] and courage than did the earlier explorers' travels, and Henson possessed such hardiness. As Donald MacMillan, a member of the **expedition,** was later to write: "Peary knew Matt Henson's real worth. . . . Highly respected by the Eskimos, he was easily the most popular man on board ship. . . . Henson . . . was of more real value to our Commander than [expedition members] Bartlett, Marvin, Borup, Goodsell and myself all put together. Matthew Henson went to the Pole with Peary because he was a better man than any one of us." **A**

Matthew Henson was born on August 8, 1866, in Charles County, Maryland, some forty-four miles south of Washington, D.C. His parents were poor, free tenant farmers[2] who barely eked a living from the sandy soil. The Civil War had ended the year before Matthew was born, bringing with it a great deal of bitterness on the part of former slave-owners. One **manifestation** of this hostility was the terrorist activity on the part of the Ku Klux Klan in Maryland. Many free and newly freed blacks had suffered at the hands of this band of night riders. Matthew's

Analyze Visuals ▶

Based on the **details** in this photograph, what can you **infer** about Matthew Henson?

expedition
(ĕk'spĭ-dĭsh'ən) *n.* a journey taken by a group with a definite goal

A COMPARE AND CONTRAST
According to the quote from Donald MacMillan, how did Henson compare to other expedition members?

manifestation
(măn'ə-fĕ-stā'shən) *n.* evidence that something is present

---

1. **stamina** (stăm'ə-nə): physical strength or endurance.
2. **tenant farmers:** farmers who rent the land they work and live on and pay rent in cash or crops.

father, Lemuel Henson, felt it was only a matter of time before the Klan turned its vengeful eyes on his family. That, and the fact that by farming he was barely able to support them, caused him to decide to move north to Washington, D.C. **B**

At first, things went well for the Henson family, but then Matthew's mother died and his father found himself unable to care for Matthew. The seven-year-old boy was sent to live with his uncle, a kindly man
30 who welcomed him and enrolled him in the N Street School. Six years later, however, another blow fell; his uncle himself fell upon hard times and could no longer support Matthew. The boy couldn't return to his father, because Lemuel had recently died. Alone, homeless, and penniless, Matthew was forced to fend for himself.

Matthew Henson was a bright boy and a hard worker, although he had only a sixth-grade education. Calling upon his own **resourcefulness,** he found a job as a dishwasher in a small restaurant owned by a woman named Janey Moore. When Janey discovered that Matthew had no place to stay, she fixed a cot for him in the kitchen; Matthew had found a home again.

40 Matthew Henson didn't want to spend his life waiting on people and washing dishes, however, no matter how kind Janey was. He had seen enough of the world through his schoolbooks to want more, to want adventure. This desire was reinforced by the men who frequented the restaurant—sailors from many ports, who spun tales of life on the ocean and of strange and wonderful places. As Henson listened, wide-eyed, to their stories, he decided, as had so many boys before him, that the life of a sailor with its adventures and dangers was for him. Having made up his mind, the fourteen-year-old packed up what little he owned, bade good-bye to Janey, and was off to Baltimore to find a ship. **C**

50 Although Matthew Henson's early life seems harsh, in many ways he was very lucky. When he arrived in Baltimore, he signed on as a cabin boy on the *Katie Hines,* the master of which was a Captain Childs. For many sailors at that time, life at sea was brutal and filled with hard work, deprivation, and a "taste of the cat": whipping. The captains of many vessels were petty despots,[3] ruling with an iron hand and having little regard for a seaman's health or safety. Matthew was fortunate to find just the opposite in Childs.

Captain Childs took the boy under his wing. Although Matthew of course had to do the work he was assigned, Captain Childs took a
60 fatherly interest in him. Having an excellent private library on the ship, the captain saw to Matthew's education, insisting that he read widely in geography, history, mathematics, and literature while they were at sea.

B RECOGNIZE CAUSE-AND-EFFECT RELATIONSHIPS
Why does Henson's father move his family to Washington, D.C.?

resourcefulness (rĭ-sôrsʹfəl-nĕs) *n.* the ability to act effectively, even in difficult situations

C BIOGRAPHY
What inspired Matthew Henson to become an explorer?

---

3. **petty despots** (dĕsʹpəts): leaders who insist on absolute power and mistreat people.

◀ **Analyze Visuals**
Compare and contrast the ship in this photograph with what you know about modern ships.

The years on the *Katie Hines* were good ones for Matthew Henson. During that time he saw China, Japan, the Philippines, France, Africa, and southern Russia; he sailed through the Arctic to Murmansk. But in 1885 it all ended; Captain Childs fell ill and died at sea. Unable to face staying on the *Katie Hines* under a new skipper, Matthew left the ship at Baltimore and found a place on a fishing schooner bound for Newfoundland. **D**

Now, for the first time, Henson encountered the kind of unthinking 70 cruelty and tyranny so often found on ships at that time. The ship was filthy, the crew surly and resentful of their black shipmate, and the captain a dictator. As soon as he was able, Matthew left the ship in Canada and made his way back to the United States, finally arriving in Washington, D.C., only to find that things there had changed during the years he had been at sea.

Opportunities for blacks had been limited when Henson had left Washington in 1871, but by the time he returned they were almost nonexistent. Post–Civil War reconstruction had failed, bringing with its failure a great deal of bitter resentment toward blacks. Jobs were scarce, and the few available were menial ones. Matthew finally found a job as 80 a stock clerk in a clothing and hat store, B. H. Steinmetz and Sons, bitterly wondering if this was how he was to spend the rest of his life. But his luck was still holding. **E**

Steinmetz recognized that Matthew Henson was bright and hardworking. One day Lieutenant Robert E. Peary, a young navy officer, walked into the store, looking for tropical hats. After being shown a number of hats, Peary unexpectedly offered Henson a job as his personal servant. Steinmetz had recommended him, Peary said, but the job wouldn't be easy. He was bound for Nicaragua to head an engineering survey team. Would Matthew be willing to put up with the discomforts and hazards of such a trip?

D BIOGRAPHY
Reread lines 63–68. What details does the author provide about Henson's first job on a ship?

E BIOGRAPHY
Why does the author emphasize Henson's luck? When was he lucky before? Explain why Henson's character may have contributed to his luck.

90 Thinking of the adventure and opportunities offered, Henson eagerly said yes, little realizing that a partnership had just been formed that would span years and be filled with exploration, danger, and fame.

Robert E. Peary was born in Cresson, Pennsylvania, in 1856, but was raised in Maine, where his mother had returned after his father's death in 1859. After graduating from Bowdoin College, Peary worked as a surveyor[4] for four years and in 1881 joined the navy's corps of civil engineers. One result of his travels for the navy and of his reading was an **ardent** desire for adventure. "I shall not be satisfied," Peary wrote to his mother, "until my name is known from one end of the earth to the other." 100 This was a goal Matthew Henson could understand. As he later said, "I recognized in [Peary] the qualities that made me willing to engage myself in his service." In November 1887, Henson and Peary set sail for Nicaragua, along with forty-five other engineers and a hundred black Jamaicans. **F**

Peary's job was to study the **feasibility** of digging a canal across Nicaragua (that canal that would later be dug across the Isthmus of Panama). The survey took until June of 1888, when the surveying party headed back to the United States. Henson knew he had done a good job for Peary, but, even as they started north, Peary said nothing to him about continuing on as his servant. It was a great surprise, then, when 110 one day Peary approached Henson with a proposition. He wanted to try to raise money for an expedition to the Arctic, and he wanted Henson to accompany him. Henson quickly accepted, saying he would go whether Peary could pay him or not.

"It was in June, 1891, that I started on my first trip to the Arctic regions, as a member of what was known as the 'North Greenland Expedition,'" Matthew Henson later wrote. So began the first of five expeditions on which Henson would accompany Peary.

During this first trip to Greenland, on a ship named *Kite,* Peary discovered how valuable Henson was to any expedition. He reported 120 that Henson was able to establish "a friendly relationship with the Eskimoes, who believed him to be somehow related to them because of his brown skin. . . ." Peary's expedition was also greatly aided by Henson's expert handling of the Eskimoes, dogs, and equipment. Henson also hunted with the Eskimoes for meat for the expedition and cooked under the supervision of Josephine Peary, Robert's wife. On the expedition's return to New York, September 24, 1892, Peary wrote, "Henson, my faithful colored boy, a hard worker and apt at anything, . . . showed himself . . . the equal of others in the party." **G**

ardent (är′dnt) *adj.* having strong enthusiasm or devotion

F COMPARE AND CONTRAST
Reread lines 97–103. Compare and contrast the reasons that Peary and Henson wanted to become explorers. Record your answers in your Venn diagram.

feasibility
(fē′zə-bĭl-ə-tē′) *n.* the possibility of something's being accomplished

G BIOGRAPHY
According to Robert Peary, what qualities made Henson a valuable member of the expedition team?

---

4. **surveyor:** one who measures the boundaries of lands, areas, or surface features.

This first expedition to the Arctic led to several others, but it was with
130 the 1905 expedition that Peary first tried to find that mystical[5] point, the
North Pole, the sole goal of the 1908 expedition.

On July 6, 1908, the *Roosevelt* sailed from New York City. Aboard
it were the supplies and men for an expedition to reach the North
Pole. Accompanying Peary were Captain Robert Bartlett and Ross
Marvin, who had been with Peary on earlier expeditions; George Borup,
a young graduate from Yale and the youngest member of the group;
Donald MacMillan, a teacher; and a doctor, J. W. Goodsell. And, of
course, Matthew Henson. In Greenland the group was joined by forty-one
Eskimos and 246 dogs, plus the supplies. "The ship," Henson wrote, "is
140 now in a most perfect state of dirtiness." On September 5, the *Roosevelt*
arrived at Cape Sheridan and the group began preparing for their journey,
moving supplies north to Cape Columbia by dog sled to establish a base
camp. Peary named the camp Crane City in honor of Zenas Crane, who
had contributed $10,000 to the expedition.

The plan was to have two men, Bartlett and Borup, go ahead of the rest
of the group to cut a trail stretching from the base camp to the North Pole.
On February 28, the two men set out, and on March 1, the remainder of
the expedition started north, following the trail Bartlett and Borup had cut
the day before. At first, trouble seemed to plague them. On the first day,
150 three of the sledges broke, Henson's among them. Fortunately, Henson was
able to repair them, despite the fact that it was nearly 50 degrees below zero.

As the days passed, further trouble came the way of the expedition. Several
times they encountered leads—open channels of water—and were forced
to wait until the ice closed over before proceeding. On March 14, Peary
decided to send Donald MacMillan and Dr. Goodsell back to the base camp.
MacMillan could hardly walk, because he had frozen a heel when his foot had
slipped into one of the leads. Dr. Goodsell was exhausted. As the expedition
went on, more men were sent back due to exhaustion and frostbite. George
Borup was sent back on March 20, and, on the 26th, so was Ross Marvin.
160 Although the expedition had encountered problems with subzero
temperatures, with open water, and in handling the dogs, they had had
no real injuries. On Ross Marvin's return trip to the base camp, however,
he met with tragedy. On his journey, Marvin was accompanied by two
Eskimos. He told them that he would go ahead to scout the trail. About
an hour later, the Eskimos came upon a hole in the ice; floating in it was
Marvin's coat. Marvin had gone through thin ice and, unable to save
himself, had drowned or frozen. The Peary expedition had suffered its
first—and fortunately its last—fatality.

---

5. **mystical:** associated with a sense of wonder or mystery.

SCIENCE
CONNECTION

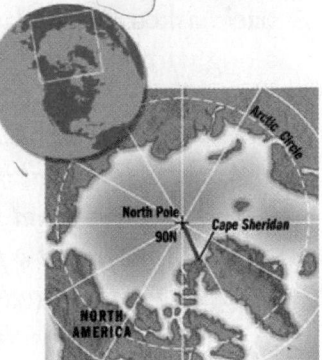

Peary and Henson were
looking for the North
Pole, or the top point of
the axis on which Earth
rotates. The red line
represents the route
they traveled. The pole
is located on the Arctic
ice cap, a layer of ice
approximately ten feet
thick and floating on the
ocean's surface.

COMMON CORE L 4b

Language Coach

Prefixes A **prefix** is a
word part added to the
beginning of a word.
Knowing the meanings
of common prefixes will
help you determine the
meanings of unfamiliar
words. *Sub-* is a prefix
derived from Latin
meaning "below,"
"under," or "beneath."
How does knowing the
meaning of this prefix
help you define the
meaning of *subzero*
(line 160)?

By April 1, Peary had sent back all of the original expedition except for
170 four Eskimos and Matthew Henson. When Bartlett, the last man to be sent
back, asked Peary why he didn't also send Henson, Peary replied, "I can't get
along without him." The remnant of the original group pushed on. **H**

> *We had been travelling eighteen to twenty hours out of every twenty-four.*
> *Man, that was killing work! Forced marches all the time. From all our other*
> *expeditions we had found out that we couldn't carry food for more than fifty*
> *days, fifty-five at a pinch. . . .*
> *We used to travel by night and sleep in the warmest part of the day. I was*
> *ahead most of the time with two of the Eskimos.*

So Matthew Henson described the grueling[6] journey. Finally, on the
180 morning of April 6, Peary called a halt. Henson wrote: "I was driving ahead
and was swinging around to the right. . . . The Commander, who was about
50 feet behind me, called to me and said we would go into camp. . . ." In
fact, both Henson and Peary felt they might have reached the Pole already.
That day, Peary took readings with a sextant and determined that they were
within three miles of the Pole. Later he sledged ten miles north and found
he was traveling south; to return to camp, Peary would have to return north
and then head south in another direction—something that could only
happen at the North Pole. To be absolutely sure, the next day Peary again
took readings from solar observations. It was the North Pole, he was sure. ◆

---

6. **grueling** (grōō′ə-lĭng): physically or mentally demanding; exhausting.

H BIOGRAPHY
Why do you think the
writer quotes Peary's
exact words?

**VISUAL
VOCABULARY**

sextant (sĕk′stənt) *n.* a
tool that measures one's
location based on the
position of the sun, the
moon, or a star

◆ **GRAMMAR IN
CONTEXT**
The colon is used in
a variety of ways.
Often a colon is used
to introduce a direct
quotation, as in line 180.
Colons are also used to
introduce a list of items.

Explorers hold the flags of their countries as they stand on the Arctic ice.

◀ **Analyze
Visuals**

What do the **details** in
this illustration suggest
about Artic exploration
in Henson's time?

190 On that day Robert Peary had Matthew Henson plant the American flag at the North Pole. Peary then cut a piece from the flag and placed it and two letters in a glass jar that he left at the Pole. The letters read:

> *90 N. Lat., North Pole*
> *April 6, 1909*
> *Arrived here today, 27 marches from C. Columbia.*
> *I have with me 5 men, Matthew Henson, colored, Ootah, Egingwah, Seegloo, and Ooqueah, Eskimos; 5 sledges and 38 dogs. My ship, the S.S. Roosevelt, is in winter quarters at Cape Sheridan, 90 miles east of Columbia.*
> *The expedition under my command which has succeeded in reaching the*
200 *Pole is under the auspices[7] of the Peary Arctic Club of New York City, and has been fitted out and sent north by members and friends of the Club for the purpose of securing this geographical prize, if possible, for the honor and* **prestige** *of the United States of America.*
> *The officers of the Club are Thomas H. Hubbard of New York, President; Zenus Crane, of Mass., Vice-president; Herbert I. Bridgman, of New York, Secretary and Treasurer.*
> *I start back for Cape Columbia tomorrow.*
>
> Robert E. Peary
United States Navy

210 *90 N. Lat., North Pole*
> *April 6, 1909*
> *I have today hoisted the national ensign[8] of the United States of America at this place, which my observations indicate to be the North Polar axis of the earth, and have formally taken possession of the entire region, and adjacent,[9] for and in the name of the President of the United States of America.*
> *I leave this record and United States flag in possession.*
>
> Robert E. Peary
United States Navy

Having accomplished their goal, the small group set out on the return
220 journey. It was, Matthew Henson wrote, "17 days of haste, toil, and misery. . . . We crossed lead after lead, sometimes like a bareback rider in the circus, balancing on cake after cake of ice." Finally they reached the *Roosevelt,* where they could rest and eat well at last. The Pole had been conquered! ❶

During the return trip to New York City, Henson became increasingly puzzled by Peary's behavior. "Not once in [three weeks]," Henson wrote,

prestige (prĕ-stēzh′) *n.* recognition; fame

COMMON CORE RI 4

❶ **FIGURATIVE LANGUAGE**
A **simile** is an imaginative comparison between two things that seem to have very little in common. A simile says that something is *like* something else. Writers use similes to stir our imagination and to help us see things in unexpected ways. A simile can sometimes make a point as well as a hundred words can. Reread lines 219–223. What surprising simile does Henson use to describe the trip back? Why is it surprising?

---

7. **auspices** (ô′spĭ-sĭz): protection or support.
8. **hoisted the national ensign:** raised the flag.
9. **adjacent** (ə-jā′sənt): close to or next to.

"did he speak a word to me. Then he . . . ordered me to get to work. Not a word about the North Pole or anything connected with it." Even when the *Roosevelt* docked in New York in September of 1909, Peary remained withdrawn and silent, saying little to the press and quickly withdrawing to 230 his home in Maine.

The ostensible reason for his silence was that when the group returned to New York, they learned that Dr. Frederick A. Cook was claiming that *he* had gone to the North Pole—and done so before Peary reached it. Peary told his friends that he wished to wait for his own proofs to be validated by the scientific societies before he spoke. He felt sure that Cook would not be able to present the kinds of evidence that he could present, and so it proved. **J**

On December 15, Peary was declared the first to reach the North Pole; Cook could not present adequate evidence that he had made the discovery. Peary and Bartlett were awarded gold medals by the National Geographic 240 Society; Henson was not. Because Henson was black, his contributions to the expedition were not recognized for many years.

After 1909, Henson worked in a variety of jobs. For a while, he was a parking-garage attendant in Brooklyn, and at the age of forty-six, he became a clerk in the U.S. Customs House in Lower Manhattan. In the meantime, friends tried again and again to have his contributions to the expedition recognized. At last, in 1937, nearly thirty years after the expedition, he was invited to join the Explorers Club in New York, and in 1944, Congress authorized a medal for all of the men on the expedition, including Matthew Henson. **K**

250 After his death in New York City on March 9, 1955, another lasting tribute was made to Henson's endeavors. In 1961, his home state of Maryland placed a bronze tablet in memory of him in the State House. It reads, in part:

MATTHEW ALEXANDER HENSON
Co-Discoverer of the North Pole
with
Admiral Robert Edwin Peary
April 6, 1909

Son of Maryland, exemplification of courage, fortitude[10] and patriotism,
260 *whose valiant deeds of noble devotion under the command of Admiral Robert Edwin Peary, in pioneer arctic exploration and discovery, established everlasting prestige and glory for his State and Country. . . .* ❧

J RECOGNIZE CAUSE-AND-EFFECT RELATIONSHIPS
Reread the explanation Peary gives for being "withdrawn and silent" on the trip back to New York. What other reasons might he have had for behaving this way toward Henson?

K COMPARE AND CONTRAST
Compare and contrast the way Peary treated Henson during the expedition and the way the public treated him upon their return.

---

10. **fortitude:** strength of mind; courage.

Comprehension

1. **Recall** Why was Henson forced to take care of himself at age 13?

2. **Clarify** Why didn't Frederick Cook get credit for discovering the Pole?

Text Analysis

3. **Make Inferences** Reread lines 109–113. What does this passage tell you about Henson's goals as an explorer?

4. **Compare and Contrast** Review the diagram you completed as you read. Notice the ways in which Peary and Henson are similar and different. Why do you think they made a good team as they attempted the impossible?

5. **Identify Cause-and-Effect Relationships** What events in Matthew Henson's life helped him become an explorer? In a cause-and-effect chain like the one shown, trace the events that led to Henson's career.

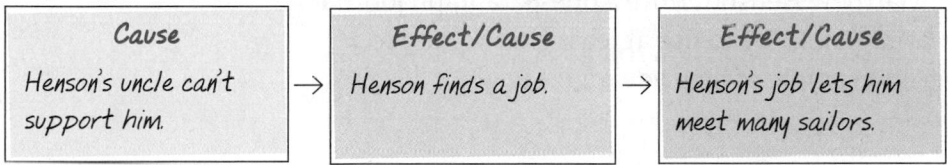

Cause		Effect/Cause		Effect/Cause
Henson's uncle can't support him.	→	Henson finds a job.	→	Henson's job lets him meet many sailors.

6. **Analyze Biography** Biographies draw their information from a variety of reliable sources. These sources may include diaries, letters, reference books, or even photographs. List some of the sources Jim Haskins uses in "Matthew Henson at the Top of the World." In what ways do they add to the picture of Henson's life? Use examples to support your answer.

7. **Analyze Tone** Biographers reveal their feelings toward their subjects through the words they use to describe their personalities and actions. Skim Haskin's descriptions of Henson. What word or phrase would you use to describe Haskin's **tone**, or attitude, toward Henson? Explain whether you think his tone reflects the tone of the statement cited in lines 259–262.

Extension and Challenge

8. **SCIENCE CONNECTION** Use the Internet and Will Steger's journal entries on pages 823–826 to write a report about modern North Pole expeditions. Discuss how explorers travel there, what their goals are, and what they do once they're there.

Why attempt the IMPOSSIBLE?

How do you think Matthew Henson would answer this question?

COMMON CORE

RI 3 Analyze in detail how a key individual, event, or idea is introduced, illustrated, and elaborated in a text. RI 6 Determine an author's point of view and explain how it is conveyed in the text.

Vocabulary in Context

▲ **VOCABULARY PRACTICE**

Choose the word that best completes each sentence.

1. After getting lost three times, we abandoned our _____ to the lake.
2. Bill is a(n) _____ fan of that writer and has read all of her books.
3. Lucy's _____ helped her find her way back to the camp.
4. Fame and _____ are not the only reasons to be ambitious.
5. The project's _____ depends upon how much time is available.
6. The time she gives to her students is one _____ of her love of teaching.

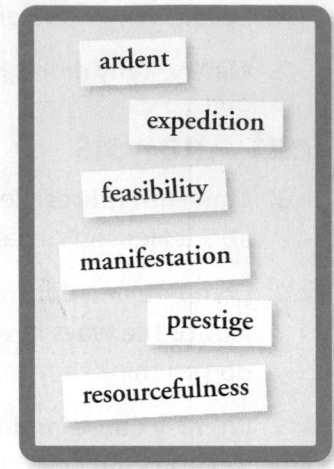

ardent

expedition

feasibility

manifestation

prestige

resourcefulness

ACADEMIC VOCABULARY IN WRITING

> • achieve • appreciate • characteristics • conclude • obvious

From the point of view of Matthew Henson, write a one-paragraph journal entry about a day on the *Katie Hines*. Try to use at least two Academic Vocabulary words. Here is an example of how you might begin.

EXAMPLE SENTENCE

*Today I am excited, because we **achieved** our goal of beginning a new expedition.*

VOCABULARY STRATEGY: IDIOMS

In the selection you have just read, the phrase "took the boy under his wing" (line 58) doesn't mean that Captain Childs had wings. It means that Captain Childs took care of Matthew Henson. Expressions like these are called **idioms.** Though the words in an idiom do not have the meaning you might expect, you often can figure out what the expression means by looking at context clues. Otherwise, a dictionary will help. You may also want to search online dictionaries of idioms for the meaning of these and other idioms. Consulting a dictionary of idioms may be more helpful than using a conventional dictionary because an idiom needs to be understood as a phrase, not by defining each word individually.

PRACTICE Write a brief definition for the boldfaced idiom in each sentence.

1. I don't know anything else about it now, but I'll **keep you posted**.
2. She's good at **breaking the ice** when she meets someone new.
3. Arnold **hit the roof** when someone stole his bicycle.
4. I can't make any definite plans—can we just **play it by ear**?
5. That exam next week is **nothing to sneeze at**, so you'd better study.

: COMMON CORE

L 4a Use context as a clue to the meaning of a word or phrase.
L 6 Acquire and use accurately academic words.

Interactive Vocabulary THINK central

Go to **thinkcentral.com.**
KEYWORD: HML6-820

Language

◆ **GRAMMAR IN CONTEXT:** Use Colons Correctly

A **colon** is a punctuation mark used to introduce a list of items. If a list follows a verb or preposition, however, do not use a colon.

> *Example:* On the expedition, they took the following items: sleds, dogs, and food.

> *Example:* On the expedition, they took sleds, dogs, and food.

PRACTICE Rewrite the following sentences, inserting or deleting colons as needed.

1. The only things he could see were: snow, ice, and his companions.
2. Henson was: ambitious, helpful, and skilled at repairs.
3. They were confronted with: a broken sled, thin ice, and frostbite.
4. Those who were sent back included the following Borup, Marvin, and Bartlett.

*For more help with colons, see page R50 in the **Grammar Handbook**.*

READING-WRITING CONNECTION

YOUR TURN

Increase your understanding of "Matthew Henson at the Top of the World" by responding to these prompts. Then use the **revising tips** to improve your writing.

WRITING PROMPTS	REVISING TIPS
Short Constructed Response: Analysis What do you think was Matthew Henson's most important contribution? In a **one-paragraph response,** explain your opinion using examples from the biography. Include at least one list in your response.	Review your response. Have you used colons correctly? If not, revise your writing.
Extended Constructed Response: Business Letter Write a **two-or-three paragraph letter** to the National Geographic Society, persuading its members to honor Matthew Henson for his accomplishments. Discuss his willingness to try the impossible and great skill in helping others on the expedition to the North Pole.	Review your letter. Have you used colons correctly? If not, revise your writing

COMMON CORE

L2 Demonstrate command of the conventions of punctuation. **W1** Write arguments to support claims. **W2** Write informative/explanatory texts to convey ideas.

Interactive Revision

THINK central

Go to **thinkcentral.com**.
KEYWORD: HML6-821

Over the Top of the World

• Journal Entries, page 823

Video link at
thinkcentral.com

Up and Over the Top

• Personal Narrative, page 827

Use with "Matthew Henson at the Top of the World," page 810.

COMMON CORE

RI 1 Cite textual evidence to support analysis of what the text says explicitly as well as inferences drawn from the text.
RI 3 Analyze in detail how a key individual, event, or idea is introduced, illustrated, and elaborated in a text.
RI 6 Determine an author's purpose and explain how it is conveyed in the text.

What's the Connection?

You just learned about the hardships and challenges that faced Arctic explorers in the early 1900s. In the journal entries you are about to read you will learn how **contemporary,** or present day, explorers led by Will Steger, tackle the same journey. Then you will read a personal narrative by Bill Cosby about a challenge he set for himself when he was in middle school. Authors often write about conquering challenges. As you study these selections, try to determine each author's purpose in writing about the topic of facing challenges.

Standards Focus: Analyzing an Author's Purpose

Authors write for a number of reasons: An **author's purpose** may be to inform, to describe, to entertain, to persuade, to reveal a truth about life, or to share an experience. Authors often write nonfiction narratives, such as biographies, journals, and personal narratives, for more than one purpose—to share an experience and to persuade, for example. One purpose is usually more important than the others.

Authors rarely directly state their reason for writing. To help you figure out an author's purpose, create a chart like the one below for each of the following selections: "Matthew Henson at the Top of the World," "Over the Top of the World," and "Up and Over the Top." Record the author's purpose in different parts of the nonfiction narrative in your chart. Then, in a sentence, state the author's main purpose in writing.

Author's Purpose	Details
Inform	
Describe	
Entertain	
Persuade	
Reveal a Truth About Life	
Share an Experience	
Author's Main Purpose _____	

F **OCUS ON FORM**
A **journal** is a personal record of thoughts, activities, and feelings. While a journal reveals a lot about the person writing, it can also give information about the time and place in which it was written.

from Over the Top of the World by Will Steger

APRIL 10

Here are the conditions we face most days: The ice is more than three years old and thick, so leads are usually less than three feet wide. Each time we come to one we have to decide whether to try to cross over it or find a way around. There's roughly two feet of snow covering the ice, and we're traveling through an area filled with 10-to-15-foot-tall pressure ridges. . . .

APRIL 16

The temperatures continue to drop, and today was a very cold,
10 difficult day. . . . By day's end, we and the dogs were all very tired.
     Our goal now is to reach land in Canada sometime in July.
That will mean another 100 days living in tents, eating the same
frozen food, rarely bathing or changing clothes. I see why some
people can't understand why we do these expeditions! **A**

A AUTHOR'S PURPOSE
What difficult conditions does Steger cite in lines 11–15? Why does the author include these details? Add the details to your chart.

APRIL 17

We passed 89 degrees north latitude, which means we are less than 60 miles from the pole! Unlike explorers who traveled to the North Pole at the turn of the century, we are able to find out exactly where we are at any moment using a handheld computer called a Global
20 Positioning System, or GPS. By communicating with a satellite orbiting Earth, in just minutes it can tell us our exact latitude and longitude. We use it every night to see how far we've traveled—and every morning to see how far we've drifted. . . . **B**

APRIL 22

We have reached the North Pole exactly as planned, on Earth Day. It's been nine years since I first dogsledded here, and I've seen and learned a lot since then. I've now traveled to both poles, North and South, and find something calm and peaceful about being at the top, or the bottom, of the world. . . .
30   We were greeted by a small group of friends who had flown up for the occasion with our resupply. We spent the morning having our pictures taken while our fingers and toes nearly froze. . . .
    Our friends have brought supplies with them, including letters and small gifts from our families, whom we haven't seen for two months. In addition, they carried with them 15 more days of food and fuel, a half-dozen waterproof bags, and some boards and plastic necessary for repairing our sleds, which have been quite punished by the rough ice. . . . But I got the best present—an apple pie baked by my mother back in Minneapolis.

40 APRIL 24

So far, the most surprising aspect of the whole trip is all the snow. Most years the Arctic is like a desert, with very little precipitation. This year is different. It snows almost every day! Even when the skies are

B AUTHOR'S PURPOSE
What do you learn in the April 17 entry? Why does Steger provide this information? Add the details to your chart.

clear, there is a light sprinkling. Some storms dump five or six
50 inches overnight. On top of that, the winds have been incredible.
Temperatures have gone as low as −40°F, but the average is −20°F.
Since we left Siberia, the warmest temperature was 0°F. . . . **C**

MAY 3

Outside this morning it's clear, −20°F, with a north wind, which is
good because it is at our back. I'm looking forward to the days now,
as are the dogs, who are strong and excited. It's a very simple existence
we lead when we're traveling like this. . . .

One of the reasons we're here is to draw attention to the
environmental problems that affect the Arctic. We are collecting
60 snow samples along the way for scientists back home to test.
On most days it's hard to believe there's pollution out here in the
middle of the Arctic Ocean. But there is. In the air, the water,
and the ice and, unfortunately, in the wildlife.

The pollution problems that scientists study in the Arctic are
created in big industrial cities and on farms in North America,
Asia, and Europe. Pollution travels through the air and water,
carried by wind, river, and ocean currents. Once in the Arctic,
pollutants "live" longer because of the cold conditions. Studies
have shown that man-made pollutants are starting to show up
70 in Arctic animals, like seals and polar bears. So we're not affecting
just the air and the water, but the animals, too. . . . **D**

MAY 13

Early this morning, at 4 o'clock, we were awakened by the sound
of dogs howling. All 22 of them in unison. They don't howl for no
reason, so I was sure there was a polar bear nearby.

They soon quieted down, though, and I fell back asleep—only
to be awakened again a half-hour later when a gigantic snap in
the ice sent a shockwave rolling through camp. A tremor lifted
our tents, like an earthquake rolling right beneath our sleeping
80 bags. The air was filled with a thundering, grinding, rumbling
roar, a very frightening sound, one we had not heard before. I shot
out of my bag and quickly unzipped the tent door, ready to jump
out in my long underwear to pull the tent to safety.

C AUTHOR'S PURPOSE
Reread lines 48–52.
Which author's purpose
do these details
support? Add them to
your chart.

D AUTHOR'S PURPOSE
Reread lines 58–71.
Which author's purpose
do these details
support? How are these
details different from
those presented in
earlier journal entries?
Add these details to
your chart.

What I saw amazed me. A wall of ice, 20 feet tall and as long as a football field, was moving our way as if being pushed by the blade of a giant bulldozer. Blocks of ice as big as cars were falling off the top of the moving wall and being crushed beneath it. It moved toward us, threatening to crush us, too.

The dogs were in shock, standing perfectly still and quiet. All five
90 of us were out of our tents, and we, too, were in shock. All we could do was watch, helplessly. Just as suddenly as it began, the wall of ice stopped, only 100 feet from our tents.

Julie has compared traveling on the Arctic Ocean to traveling on a big, floating jigsaw puzzle. This morning we watched as some of the bigger pieces shifted around. It was very powerful, and very beautiful, too. And, I admit, quite frightening. . . . **E**

JUNE 24

Another miserable day of hauling. It snowed throughout the day, dumping more than a foot, resulting in deep drifts coming up over
100 our knees. All day long we slaved in a complete whiteout, pulling the sleds forward just inches at a time. In six hours, we made only three miles. No one is saying it out loud, but we're all wondering if we'll ever make it to land. . . .

JULY 3

Our last morning was spent pulling the canoe-sleds up a 200-foot ridge and then riding them down the other side like toboggans. I was on the front, pushing with one leg as if I were riding a scooter, and Victor was sitting in the back, pushing with his ski poles and yelling like a little boy. It was a perfect way to end the trip—slipping and sliding and
110 laughing.

As we pulled the last couple of miles, I could feel all the tension of the past months lift off my shoulders. I picked up the first stones I saw and rolled them in my hand, feeling their smooth hardness. When we finally saw dirt and small flowers, we kneeled and pulled them to our faces. It was perhaps the best smell I have ever had! We made it! We were all safe, finally on solid ground.

E JOURNAL
Reread lines 89–96. What are Steger's thoughts and feelings about the event described in the May 13 entry?

UP
AND OVER THE
TOP
BY BILL COSBY

F **OCUS ON FORM**
A **personal narrative** is an autobiographical essay written from the first-person point of view. It reflects the writer's experiences, feelings, and personality. It usually deals with a single subject and offers a snapshot of a moment in the writer's life. Personal narratives often appear in magazines and newspapers.

When I was in junior high school in Philadelphia, I wasn't really interested in any other activity than watching this fellow named Sporty. That was his nickname.

One day after school I saw Sporty high-jumping. He had both high-jump stands up, three old mats to break his fall, and a bamboo pole. Sporty was jumping at 4'6". Well, at the time I was only about 5'3" and very wiry. I watched him jump, and it looked simple enough. I wanted to do it.

Now, the way Sporty jumped and the way I jumped were two
10 different styles. Let's say my style was a sort of running-away-from-the-scene-of-the-crime jump. Sporty's was the classic Eastern Roll.

Sporty approached his target with a certain number of steps, planted his right foot (because he was left-footed) and threw the left leg up. Then as he began to clear the bar, he flattened his body out and kicked his back leg up to keep from knocking the bar off. He also landed smoothly on his back.

So now I tried my style. Coming from the side of the bar, I ran up, stopped, planted both legs and jumped straight up. Then, bringing my knees to my chin, I came down with my behind crashing the bamboo
20 pole. One broken pole!

This, of course, made Sporty very upset. So, I apologized and asked him if he would show me how to do it right. **F**

At that particular point, Mr. Richard Lister came over and offered to teach us. Mr. Lister was our gym teacher, a very kind gentleman, who had high-jumped for Temple University. I think his record was 6'9". Of course, to Sporty and me that was out of this world.

F **COMPARE AUTOBIOGRAPHY AND PERSONAL NARRATIVE**
An **autobiography** is a writer's account of his or her own life, told from the first-person point of view. An autobiography focuses on the most important people and events in the writer's life over a period of many years, if not a lifetime. In what ways is Cosby's personal narrative similar to an autobiography? In what ways is it different?

I notified my mother I would be home late because Sporty and I were high-jumping. My mother wanted to know if there was a high-jumping team. I said, "No, but Sporty and I have a great time just jumping over this bamboo pole." Then she asked me whether I had
30 finished my homework.

I showed up after school, quickly changed my clothes, came out and saw Sporty in a gray sweat suit. First thing: Warm up! Mr. Lister gave us this set of exercises, showing us how we must bend over and do the same things we had done in gym class earlier that day. I notified Mr. Lister that I had done these exercises. Mr. Lister said, "You're going to have to do them again. You have to warm up properly. Get the blood flowing. Loosen up." This, he said, was warning the body that it was about to get involved in something special.

Mr. Lister decided to work on my style, because the school couldn't afford any more broken poles. I had a lot of energy and drive. This was
40 something I really wanted to do, and I enjoyed doing it.

I knew I had the coordination, because I was one of the top gym-class athletes. Mr. Lister said, "Son, the thing you are going to have to learn is that in order to do anything well, you must start from lesson one. Then we go to lessons two, three, four, and five. After you have learned these, it may come to you that this is not necessarily the right way for you. You may then, perhaps, make some adjustments. But in the meantime, you are fighting yourself." **G**

So Mr. Lister and I worked on a very smooth approach to the bar at the very embarrassing height of two feet. I made my five-step approach,
50 stopped, lifted my leg, threw my arms up, cleared the bar, and fell on my back.

Mr. Lister said, "Good." And I protested, "Yes, but look! A two-foot bar!" He said, "It is better for you to miss at two feet than to break another bar at four feet two. Look how many bars we've saved. You jump twenty times, you save twenty bars."

As the months passed, Sporty and I were both jumping at 4'6". Then Sporty moved the bar to 4'9". This was indeed a challenge. At 5'3", you may be looking eye-to-eye with a 4'9" bar. I made the approach, and as I approached I became frightened. Not that I would hurt myself,
60 not that I would break the bar—I became frightened because this looked like something I couldn't do.

G AUTHOR'S PURPOSE
Why is Cosby telling you what his teacher said? Add this detail to your chart.

The closer I got to the bar, the more I realized I couldn't do it. The more I accepted the fact I couldn't, the more I didn't prepare myself physically. In other words, as my mind said no, it allowed certain things to happen so my body would not give its all.

And I did exactly what I thought. I knocked the bar off.

As a matter of fact, the first time I tried it, I remember running up, planting my foot, starting to do it, and then snatching the bar off with my left hand. I never left the ground.

70   I put the bar back up. Sporty ran at it, jumped, and his trail leg nicked the bar. But it stayed up. He made 4'9". Of course, Sporty and I were now competing against each other, and I figured, if Sporty can do it, I *better* do it.

I stood on my mark, started with the right foot, and took three steps. Then came that thought again: "Awfully high. You can't make it." Again as I finished the last two steps, I grabbed the bar with my left hand and put it back up. Sporty approached again, made his jump, but knocked the bar over. I felt better.

H AUTHOR'S PURPOSE
Reread lines 62–69. Why does Cosby tell you about his thoughts and their effect on him? Add these details to your chart.

AUTHOR'S PURPOSE
Reread lines 79–81. Why is Cosby telling you about his thoughts? Add these details to your chart.

After talking to myself, I decided I could do it now. Suddenly, I realized that in being afraid to fail I was making a halfhearted attempt. **I**

So I tried to block all negative thoughts and remembered everything positive about myself.

I approached the bar, and for some reason none of the negative thoughts came into play. I found myself looking down on the bar, six inches over it. I had cleared that bar, and I was happy.

(What I am doing now is freezing this moment so you can get the actual feeling of what happened: I approached the bar, I planted that foot, jumped with all my might, went up and went over. I am six inches over, and I say to myself, "I'm up. I'm over. I've actually done it." Hear the great burst of applause, the cheers from all those little people in my brain. "Yea! We've done it!")

However, I had forgotten to complete the jump, so as I sailed across the bar my trail leg hit and knocked the bar off. Still, I had made the height, and I had cleared it by a good six inches!

I put the bar up quickly, came back around, and Sporty said, "You know, you really made that." We were both excited, both talking fast, and Sporty, for some reason, felt very good about what I had done.

Again I made my approach with no negative thoughts. Up. Over. Six inches over. This time I remembered to kick and clear that leg. So 4'9" was no longer a problem. I felt secure. Now I began to think about the next height. If I could do 4'9", looking down on it, how high could I go? 5'2"? Impossible! I'm 5'3". How could I jump my height? Wouldn't it be wonderful if I could?

That was a great day for me because I learned something about myself. I learned to talk to myself, reason with myself, believe in myself.

Self-confidence has a lot to do with one's performance—how well you perform, how much success you have and, even if you do not succeed, how much progress you are making.

You can become successful at whatever you choose to do, but first you must have some sort of feeling for it. How do you get a feeling for it? Sometimes the answer is simply "try." If you don't, you'll never know. **J**

AUTHOR'S PURPOSE
Reread lines 111–114. Paraphrase Cosby's advice. What was his main purpose in writing this personal narrative?

Comprehension

1. **Clarify** Reread the May 3 entry in "Over the Top of the World." What are the sources of Arctic pollution?

2. **Summarize** What goal does Cosby set for himself in "Up and Over the Top"? What steps does he take to attain this goal?

Text Analysis

3. **Compare and Contrast Author's Purpose** Compare and contrast the author's purposes for writing. What similarities and differences do you find among the reasons each author had for writing? What surprises you about your findings? Support your response with details from your chart.

COMMON CORE

RI 1 Cite textual evidence to support analysis of what the text says explicitly as well as inferences drawn from the text. **RI 3** Analyze in detail how a key individual, event, or idea is introduced, illustrated, and elaborated in a text. **RI 6** Determine an author's point of view or purpose and explain how it is conveyed in the text. **W 2** Write explanatory texts to examine a topic and convey information through analysis of relevant content.

Read for Information: Synthesize Ideas Across Texts

WRITING PROMPT

Toward the end of his personal narrative, Bill Cosby writes "Self-confidence has a lot to do with one's performance—how well you perform, how much success you have and, even if you do not succeed, how much progress you are making." Explain whether you think Henson and Steger would agree with Cosby. Begin to synthesize ideas across the selections by thinking about the accomplishments of each man.

The following steps can help you synthesize ideas:

1. Jot down ideas and information about the topic.

2. Use this information to make connections across the texts.

3. Pick out specific evidence from the biography, journal, and the personal narrative for support.

4. State your conclusion in a topic sentence. Then present reasons and evidence that support your conclusion.

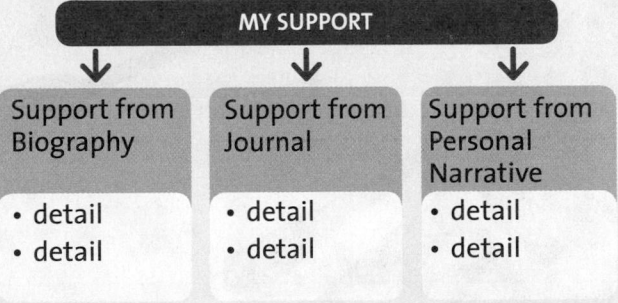

MY SUPPORT		
Support from Biography	**Support from Journal**	**Support from Personal Narrative**
• detail • detail	• detail • detail	• detail • detail

5. Be sure to present your evidence clearly by maintaining meaning and logical order within and across the texts.

from **The Story of My Life**
Autobiography by Helen Keller

Video link at
thinkcentral.com

VIDEO TRAILER **THINK** central KEYWORD: HML6-832

Do we have to accept our LIMITS?

COMMON CORE

RI 4 Determine the meaning of words and phrases as they are used in a text, including figurative meanings. **RI 6** Determine an author's point of view and explain how it is conveyed in the text. **RI 10** Read and comprehend literary nonfiction.

Sometimes the things we most want to do are the hardest to accomplish. It can be discouraging to discover our limits and frustrating to find ourselves facing unexpected challenges. Fortunately, many serious obstacles can be overcome with creativity and determination. In this excerpt from *The Story of My Life*, Helen Keller describes triumphing over her limitations.

QUICKWRITE Helen Keller found a way to succeed despite being both blind and deaf. Think of someone else—from your life, a book, or a movie—who also had to deal with some type of limitation. Write a brief paragraph describing this person and his or her efforts to conquer a major difficulty.

TEXT ANALYSIS: AUTOBIOGRAPHY

The most personal kind of nonfiction writing is **autobiography**—a writer's account of his or her own life. In biographies, the subject is a person other than the writer. In autobiographies, the writer is the subject. Autobiographies

- are told from the first-person point of view, using first-person pronouns (*I, me, we, us, our, my, mine*)
- include literary language and devices to provide descriptions of people and events that have influenced the writer
- share the writer's personal thoughts and feelings about his or her experiences

As you read *The Story of My Life*, think about the information the author decides to include about herself.

READING STRATEGY: MONITOR

Monitoring is the process of checking your understanding as you read. One way to do this is to **ask questions** about what you have just read.

As you read Helen Keller's autobiography, note any passages that you find confusing. Record them in a chart like the one shown. Next to each passage, write what you think it means.

Keller's Words	My Questions
"Anger and bitterness had preyed upon me" (line 14)	Why is Helen Keller so bitter and angry?

VOCABULARY IN CONTEXT

Helen Keller uses the following words to tell how she came to understand the world around her. To see how many you know, match each vocabulary word from the Word List with the numbered word or phrase closest in meaning.

WORD LIST	consciousness	sensation	uncomprehending
	repentance	tangible	

1. not understanding
2. awareness
3. feeling
4. touchable
5. regret

Complete the activities in your **Reader/Writer Notebook.**

Meet the Author

Helen Keller
1880–1968

Overcoming All Obstacles

Before Helen Keller was two years old, she developed a fever that left her blind and deaf. The young girl was highly intelligent, but her parents did not know how to communicate with her properly. Anne Sullivan, a teacher from the Perkins Institution for the Blind, became Keller's tutor.

Lifetime of Learning

Sullivan taught Keller sign language and Braille, a system of raised dots that enables blind people to read. When Keller was ten, she learned about a blind and deaf child who had learned to speak by studying the movements of people's lips. Keller was determined to do the same. She eventually learned to speak aloud in English, French, and German. Keller graduated from Radcliffe College in 1904.

Teaching Others

As an adult, Keller became a spokesperson for people with disabilities. She helped stop deaf and blind people from being placed in hospitals for the mentally ill. She also spoke about preventing the diseases that caused childhood blindness. In 1964, Keller received the Presidential Medal of Freedom, the highest honor that can be given to an American civilian.

Author Online

THINK central

Go to **thinkcentral.com.**
KEYWORD: HML6-833

The Story of My Life

Helen Keller

The most important day I remember in all my life is the one on which my teacher, Anne Mansfield Sullivan, came to me. I am filled with wonder when I consider the immeasurable contrasts between the two lives which it connects. It was the third of March, 1887, three months before I was seven years old.

On the afternoon of that eventful day, I stood on the porch, dumb,[1] expectant. I guessed vaguely from my mother's signs and from the hurrying to and fro in the house that something unusual was about to happen, so I went to the door and waited on the steps. The afternoon
10 sun penetrated the mass of honeysuckle that covered the porch, and fell on my upturned face. My fingers lingered almost unconsciously on the familiar leaves and blossoms which had just come forth to greet the sweet southern spring. I did not know what the future held of marvel or surprise for me. Anger and bitterness had preyed upon me continually for weeks and a deep languor had succeeded[2] this passionate struggle. **A**

Have you ever been at sea in a dense fog, when it seemed as if a **tangible** white darkness shut you in, and the great ship, tense and

Analyze Visuals ▶

What can you **infer** about the relationship between Helen Keller and Anne Sullivan by looking at this photograph of them?

A AUTOBIOGRAPHY
Reread lines 6–15. In what way does the first-person point of view help show Keller's thoughts and feelings?

tangible (tăn′jə-bəl) *adj.* possible to touch; real

---

1. **dumb:** unable to speak; mute.
2. **deep languor had succeeded:** a complete lack of energy had followed.

anxious, groped her way toward the shore with plummet and sounding-line,[3] and you waited with beating heart for something to happen? I was like that ship before my education began, only I was without compass or sounding-line, and had no way of knowing how near the harbor was. "Light! Give me light!" was the wordless cry of my soul, and the light of love shone on me in that very hour. **B**

I felt approaching footsteps. I stretched out my hand as I supposed to my mother. Someone took it, and I was caught up and held close in the arms of her who had come to reveal all things to me, and, more than all things else, to love me.

The morning after my teacher came she led me into her room and gave me a doll. The little blind children at the Perkins Institution had sent it and Laura Bridgman[4] had dressed it; but I did not know this until afterward. When I had played with it a little while, Miss Sullivan slowly spelled into my hand the word "d-o-l-l." I was at once interested in this finger play and tried to imitate it. When I finally succeeded in making the letters correctly I was flushed with childish pleasure and pride. Running downstairs to my mother I held up my hand and made the letters for *doll*. I did not know that I was spelling a word or even that words existed; I was simply making my fingers go in monkey-like imitation. In the days that followed I learned to spell in this **uncomprehending** way a great many words, among them *pin, hat, cup* and a few verbs like *sit, stand* and *walk*. But my teacher had been with me several weeks before I understood that everything has a name. **C**

One day, while I was playing with my new doll, Miss Sullivan put my big rag doll into my lap also, spelled "d-o-l-l" and tried to make me understand that "d-o-l-l" applied to both. Earlier in the day we had had a tussle over the words "m-u-g" and "w-a-t-e-r." Miss Sullivan had tried to impress it upon me that "m-u-g" is *mug* and that "w-a-t-e-r" is *water*, but I persisted in confounding the two. In despair she had dropped the subject for the time, only to renew it at the first opportunity. I became impatient at her repeated attempts and, seizing the new doll, I dashed[5] it upon the floor. I was keenly delighted when I felt the fragments of the broken doll at my feet. Neither sorrow nor regret followed my passionate outburst. I had not loved the doll. In the still, dark world in which I lived there was no strong sentiment or tenderness. I felt my teacher sweep the fragments to one side of the hearth, and I had a sense of satisfaction that the cause of

3. **plummet and sounding-line:** a weighted rope used to measure the depth of water.

4. **Perkins Institution . . . Laura Bridgman:** The Perkins Institution was a school for the blind, located in Massachusetts. Laura Bridgman (1829–1889), a student at the Perkins Institution, was the first deaf and blind child to be successfully educated. Like Keller, Bridgman became quite famous for her accomplishments.

5. **dashed:** threw or knocked with sudden violence.

B AUTOBIOGRAPHY
What literary devices does Keller use in this paragraph? How does she describe her experience of being blind?

uncomprehending
(ŭn'kŏm-prĭ-hĕn'dĭng)
adj. not understanding

C MONITOR
What does Keller not understand about the words she is spelling?

my discomfort was removed. She brought me my hat, and I knew I was going out into the warm sunshine. This thought, if a wordless 60 **sensation** may be called a thought, made me hop and skip with pleasure.

We walked down the path to the well-house, attracted by the fragrance of the honeysuckle with which it was covered.

This house on the Keller property was where Sullivan often took Helen for lessons.

70 Someone was drawing water and my teacher placed my hand under the spout. As the cool stream gushed over one hand she spelled into the other the word *water*, first slowly, then rapidly. I stood still, my whole attention fixed upon the motions of her fingers. Suddenly I felt a misty **consciousness** as of something forgotten—a thrill of returning thought; and somehow the mystery of language was revealed to me. I knew then that "w-a-t-e-r" meant the wonderful cool something that was flowing over my hand. That living word awakened my soul, gave it light, hope, joy, set it free! There were barriers still, it is true, but barriers that could in time be swept away. **D**

I left the well-house eager to learn. Everything had a name, and each 80 name gave birth to a new thought. As we returned to the house every object which I touched seemed to quiver with life. That was because I saw everything with the strange, new sight that had come to me. On entering the door I remembered the doll I had broken. I felt my way to the hearth and picked up the pieces. I tried vainly[6] to put them together. Then my eyes filled with tears; for I realized what I had done, and for the first time I felt **repentance** and sorrow. **E**

I learned a great many new words that day. I do not remember what they all were; but I do know that *mother, father, sister, teacher* were among them— words that were to make the world blossom for me, "like Aaron's rod, with 90 flowers."[7] It would have been difficult to find a happier child than I was as I lay in my crib at the close of that eventful day and lived over the joys it had brought me, and for the first time longed for a new day to come. ❧

◀ **Analyze Visuals**

Compare Helen's description of the well-house (lines 64–69) to this photograph of it. What do you learn from each source?

sensation (sĕn-sā'shən) *n.* a feeling

consciousness (kŏn'shəs-nĭs) *n.* awareness of one's own thoughts

D **AUTOBIOGRAPHY** Reread lines 64–78. Which literary language in this passage might not have been included in a biography?

repentance (rĭ-pĕn'təns) *n.* sorrow or regret

E **MONITOR** Reread lines 79–86. Why does Keller suddenly feel sorry for breaking the doll?

---

6. **vainly:** without success.

7. **like Aaron's rod, with flowers:** a reference to a story in the Bible in which a wooden staff suddenly sprouts flowers.

Comprehension

1. **Recall** How does Helen Keller know that something unusual is happening on the day Anne Sullivan arrives?

2. **Recall** What is the first word Sullivan tries to teach Keller?

3. **Summarize** How does Keller's world change once she begins to understand the connection between language and meaning?

Text Analysis

● 4. **Monitor** Look back at the chart you used to ask questions as you read. Choose one passage that you found difficult to understand, and explain what clues helped you answer your questions.

5. **Identify Sensory Details** Although Keller lacked the senses of sight and hearing, she was able to observe many things using her remaining senses. In a graphic organizer like the one shown, record words and phrases that Keller used to help her readers understand what she was describing.

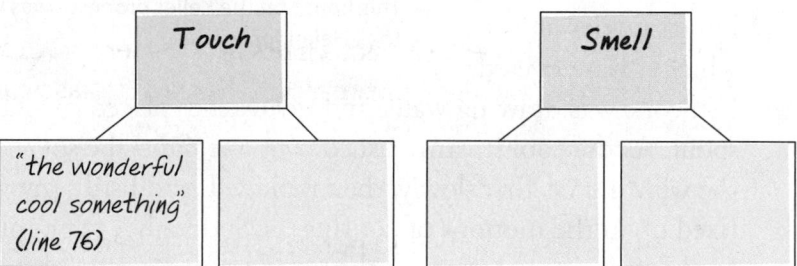

● 6. **Analyze Autobiography** Consider what Keller shares about her experiences. How would the story of Keller's life be different if Anne Sullivan had written it?

7. **Evaluate Literary Devices** Keller was aware that many of her readers would never experience the challenge of missing one or more senses. Reread lines 16–23, focusing on the **analogy,** or point-by-point comparison, in which Keller describes herself as a ship lost in the fog. Is this an effective way for her to share her feelings? Explain.

Extension and Challenge

8. **Inquiry and Research** In the 1800s, blind and deaf people had few resources. Many were confined to hospitals. Fortunately, this is no longer the case. Research two or three of the technological advances that now help people overcome their physical limits. Share your discoveries with the class.

> ## Do we have to accept our LIMITS?
> How was Helen Keller able to overcome her disabilities?

COMMON CORE

RI 4 Determine the meaning of words and phrases as they are used in a text, including figurative meanings. **RI 6** Determine an author's point of view and explain how it is conveyed in the text. **RI 10** Read and comprehend literary nonfiction.

Vocabulary in Context

▲ VOCABULARY PRACTICE

Complete each sentence using the appropriate vocabulary word.

1. After the ride ended, he still had the _____ of being upside-down.
2. Her happiness was _____, like a warm blanket wrapped around her.
3. The teacher looked at him in a(n) _____ way, so he repeated himself.
4. A feeling of _____ is natural after you do something hurtful or wrong.
5. When I hit my head, I lost _____ and my mind went blank.

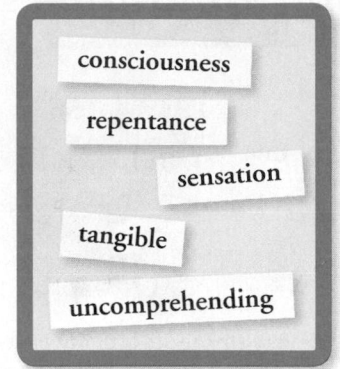

consciousness

repentance

sensation

tangible

uncomprehending

ACADEMIC VOCABULARY IN WRITING

- achieve
- appreciate
- characteristics
- conclude
- obvious

Which of Helen Keller's **characteristics** helped her overcome her limits? What can you **conclude** about Keller based on what she has **achieved**? Use at least two Academic Vocabulary words in your discussion.

VOCABULARY STRATEGY: ANALOGIES

An **analogy** is a kind of word puzzle. You are given two words and can complete the analogy by identifying another pair of words with a similar relationship. You may be asked to complete analogies that describe a whole to part relationship. Here is an example of such an analogy.

foot : toe :: _____ : finger

Consider that something whole consists of more than one part. A foot is made up of toes, so the correct answer is *hand,* which is made up of fingers.

You may also be asked to complete analogies that describe a part to whole relationship. Here's is an example.

petal : flower :: _____ : tree

A petal is a part of a flower, so the correct answer is *branch* which is a part of a tree.

PRACTICE First, determine whether each analogy describes a part to whole or whole to part relationship. Then, complete each analogy.

1. beach : sand :: lawn : _____
2. continent : country :: _____ : city
3. corn : cob :: _____ : pod
4. article : newspaper :: chapter : _____
5. letter : word :: word : _____

COMMON CORE

L 5b Use the relationship between particular words to better understand each of the words. **L 6** Acquire and use accurately academic words.

Interactive Vocabulary **THINK** central

Go to **thinkcentral.com**.
KEYWORD: HML6-839

American Sign Language
Procedural Text

What's the Connection?

You've just read an excerpt from Helen Keller's autobiography *The Story of My Life,* in which she describes what it was like to be deaf and blind. She also explains how she learned the concept of words from her teacher Annie Sullivan. Now you will learn about a method of communication used by deaf people called sign language.

Use with *The Story of My Life,* page 834.

COMMON CORE

RI 5 Analyze how a particular sentence or section fits in the overall structure and contributes to the development of ideas. **RI 7** Integrate information presented in different media or formats to develop a coherent understanding of a topic.

Standards Focus: Interpret Information in Procedural Texts

Information on how to complete a task, or procedure, can be presented in a variety of ways. **Procedural information** may include

- a statement of the task to be performed
- a list of materials or tools needed
- a series of numbered or sequenced instructions
- a diagram or an illustration

By reading a procedural document and following the steps it outlines, you should be able to complete the task it describes. To be effective, a procedural text should be written in simple, imperative sentences, such as "do this, do that." The steps must be conveyed in chronological order, from the first to the last step in the procedure. Sometimes, a procedural text may be a simple chart containing illustrations or diagrams that show you what to do with some accompanying text. Sometimes, all the information you need is in the visuals, and the illustrations or diagrams may contain no additional text. If this is the case, you need to **glean,** or gather information from the visuals to complete the task.

When reading procedural texts, first scan the text to identify the type of information presented. Then, focus on the specific content of that information. You might use a chart like the one below to list types of information and notes on what you learn from each.

Type of Information	Notes on Content
Title	
Introductory or explanatory text	
Diagrams or illustrations	
Numbered or sequenced items	

AMERICAN SIGN LANGUAGE

F OCUS ON FORM
A **procedural text** is written to describe how something is done. Recipes, repair manuals, and how-to instructions are all examples of procedural texts. To aid comprehension, many procedural texts include visuals, such as illustrations or diagrams. Procedural texts may also include titles, numbered or sequenced steps, and lists of materials.

American Sign Language (ASL) is a visual language that incorporates gestures, facial expressions, head movements, body language, and even the space around the speaker. Hand signs are the foundation of the language. Many signs are **iconic**, meaning the sign uses a visual image that resembles the concept it represents. For instance, to express the concept of "deer" in ASL, you would hold your hands up to either side of your head, fingers spread, to represent antlers. Actions are often expressed through hand signals that mimic the action being communicated—if you wished to
10 sign the concept "eat," you would bring your fingers and thumb of your dominant hand together as if holding food and then move your hand toward your mouth. **A**

COMMON CORE RI 7

A INTERPRET INFORMATION
A **procedural text** is a text that explains how to complete a task. Text and illustrations work together to convey information in a procedural text. Lines 8–12 describe how to sign the word *eat*. The accompanying diagram shows you how to sign the words *eat* and *deer*. Use the information in the text and diagrams to sign the word *eat*. Then, use the information in the diagram to sign the word *deer*.

EAT DEER

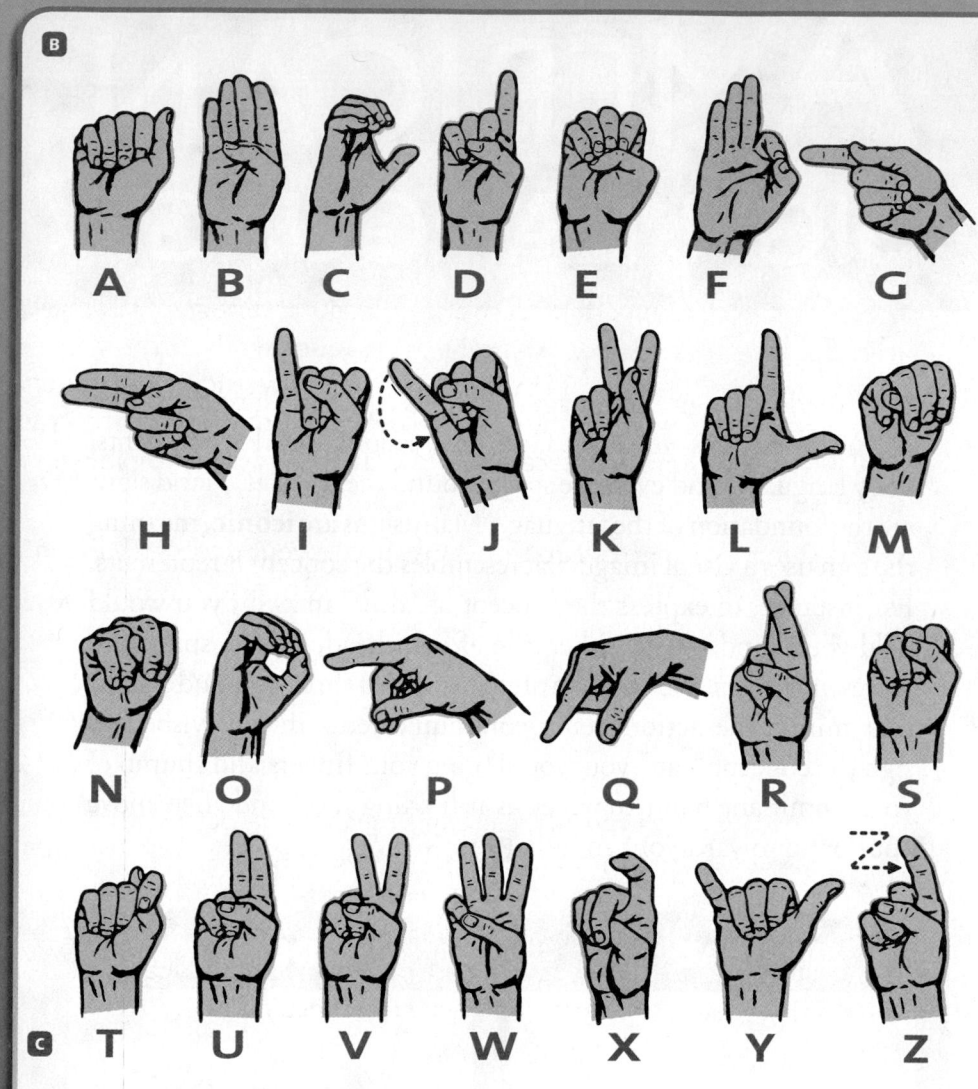

C **INTERPRET INFORMATION**
What do you think the arrows that accompany the "J" and the "Z" illustration represent?

D **PROCEDURAL TEXT**
What is the purpose of this procedural document?

The alphabet is an important series of signs. Some hand signs for letters resemble the written form of the respective letter. When you use the hand signs for letters to spell out a word, you are **finger spelling**. Finger spelling is useful to convey names or to ask someone the sign for a particular concept. ASL uses one-handed signals for each letter of the alphabet (some other sign languages use both hands for some letters). Many people find finger spelling 20 the most challenging hurdle when learning to sign, as accomplished speakers are very fast finger spellers. **D**

Comprehension

1. **Recall** What is American Sign Language?

2. **Clarify** How is American Sign Language different from other some other sign languages?

3. **Summarize** What is finger spelling?

Text Analysis

4. **Evaluate a Procedural Text** A strong procedural text gives clear, detailed instructions on how to do something. How do you think the information given with the chart could be improved? What would you add or change to make the instruction more clear? Look at the chart you filled in as you read to see if there are places where additional information might improve the text.

5. **Analyzing Visuals** How do the visuals add to your understanding of the text? Explain.

COMMON CORE

RI 5 Analyze how a particular sentence or section fits in the overall structure and contributes to the development of ideas.
RI 7 Integrate information presented in different media or formats to develop a coherent understanding of a topic.
W 2 Write explanatory texts to convey information through the selection and organization of relevant content.

Read for Information: Create a Procedural Text

WRITING PROMPT

The procedural text you just read explains what American Sign Language is and explains the process of fingerspelling. Use the information from the article and do some more research on American Sign Language to create instructions for students to sign "My name is [Jennifer]." Write directly to the reader, and think about what type of information should be included in your final document.

To answer this prompt, follow these steps:

1. First, do some research in the library or on the Internet to find out more about American Sign Language. You need to find the signs for the words "My name is." Write down the information you find, and determine if you need to include a visual along with a written description.

2. Write instructions for fingerspelling a person's name.

3. Review your instructions to see if they are clear. Do you need to add numbered steps to the process? What visuals will make the task more clear?

4. Have groups of students work together to follow your instructions to sign "My name is. . . ." If your instructions are clear, they should be able to follow them. If not, ask the students what information might make the instructions easier to follow and revise your work.

Under the Royal Palms: A Childhood in Cuba

Memoir by Alma Flor Ada

COMMON CORE

RI 10 Read and comprehend literary nonfiction.

Meet Alma Flor Ada

By the time she was three, Alma Flor Ada had already learned to read. She had also learned that she was born into a family of storytellers. It is no surprise, then, that she would grow up to become a storyteller herself.

Ada writes to share some of "the joy, the excitement, the surprise" she felt reading books and hearing stories as a child. Seeing her books in the hands of readers is one of her greatest joys.

Other Books by Alma Flor Ada

- *Alma Flor Ada and YOU*
- *Choices and Other Stories from the Caribbean*
- *The Gold Coin*
- *Where the Flame Trees Bloom*

Try a Memoir

A **memoir** is a form of nonfiction in which a person tells about significant events in his or her life. Unlike an autobiography, which generally covers a person's entire life, a memoir may describe just one particular time period or experience. Alma Flor Ada's memoir describes the experiences that shaped her childhood in Cuba during the 1940s.

Reading Fluency When you read fluently, you read each word carefully and pay attention to punctuation. To increase your fluency, practice reading aloud. Choose a paragraph to read aloud and practice pronouncing each word correctly and pausing when you come across a comma or period. When you are able to read the entire paragraph aloud without any errors, move on to the next paragraph.

Read a Great Book

The award-winning memoir *Under the Royal Palms* paints a vivid picture of growing up in Cuba. Alma Flor Ada grew up on her family's ranch, which was called *La Quinta Simoni*. In the excerpt you are about to read, Alma and her cousins are led by their imaginations to explore an unfamiliar area. They quickly find themselves lost in their "jungle" playground. What will happen to them?

from

Under the Royal Palms:

A Childhood in Cuba

Life at *La Quinta Simoni* provided constant invitations for adventure. One morning I met my cousins Jorge and Virginita by the fallen tree. It was a huge poplar, possibly uprooted by a hurricane. But the tree had refused to die and, although fallen, had sprouted new branches. These new branches, covered with heart-shaped leaves, projected upward like spears pointed at the sky. The tree was an excellent place for playing. Sometimes it became our pirate ship: On it, we crossed the Caribbean while the wind filled our green sails. At other times it was a castle, and
10 from its turrets we defended our fortress from invading warriors. Or perhaps it was a covered wagon crossing the plains, or a sleigh racing across the Russian steppes pursued by a wolf pack.

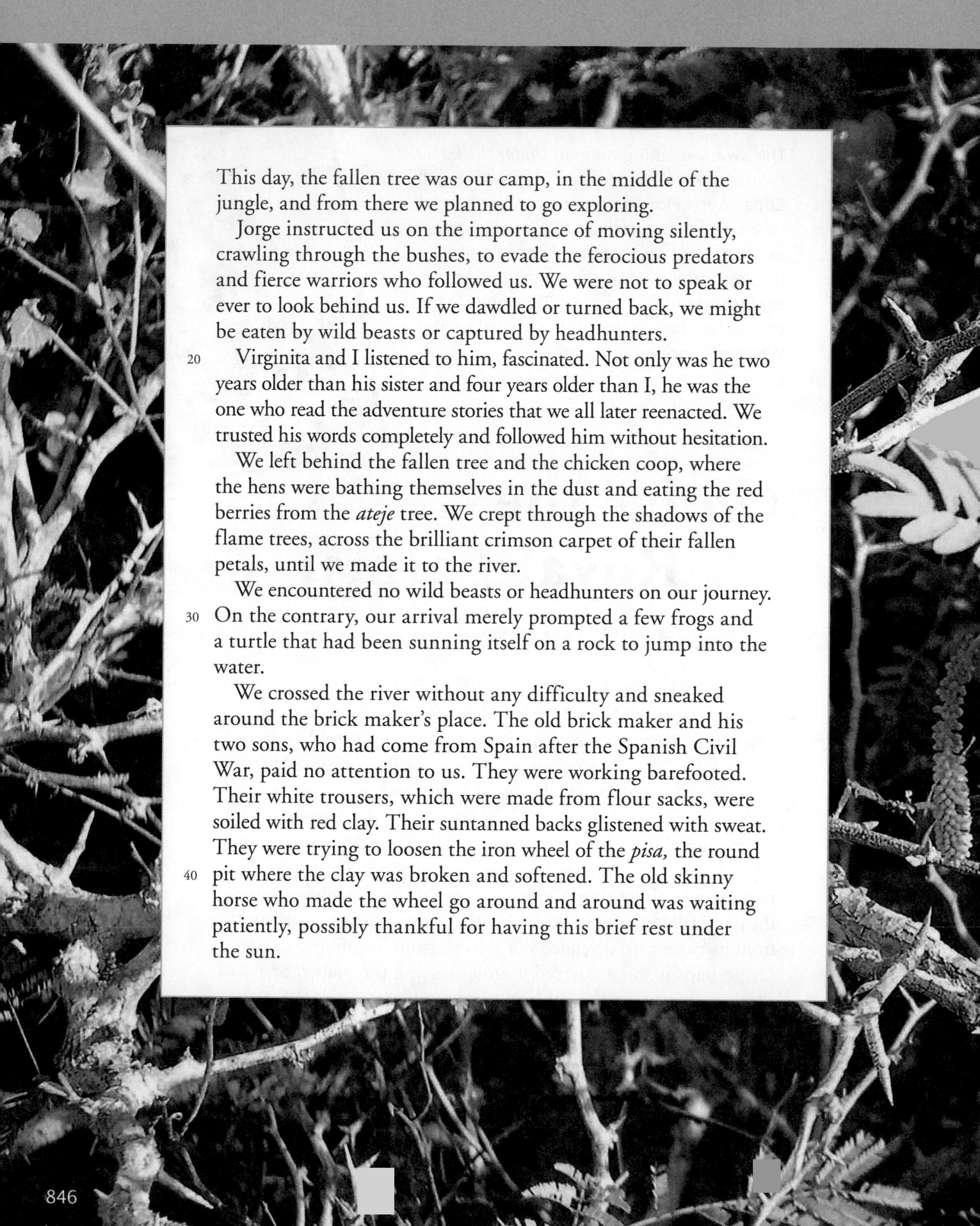

This day, the fallen tree was our camp, in the middle of the jungle, and from there we planned to go exploring.

Jorge instructed us on the importance of moving silently, crawling through the bushes, to evade the ferocious predators and fierce warriors who followed us. We were not to speak or ever to look behind us. If we dawdled or turned back, we might be eaten by wild beasts or captured by headhunters.

20   Virginita and I listened to him, fascinated. Not only was he two years older than his sister and four years older than I, he was the one who read the adventure stories that we all later reenacted. We trusted his words completely and followed him without hesitation.

We left behind the fallen tree and the chicken coop, where the hens were bathing themselves in the dust and eating the red berries from the *ateje* tree. We crept through the shadows of the flame trees, across the brilliant crimson carpet of their fallen petals, until we made it to the river.

We encountered no wild beasts or headhunters on our journey.
30 On the contrary, our arrival merely prompted a few frogs and a turtle that had been sunning itself on a rock to jump into the water.

We crossed the river without any difficulty and sneaked around the brick maker's place. The old brick maker and his two sons, who had come from Spain after the Spanish Civil War, paid no attention to us. They were working barefooted. Their white trousers, which were made from flour sacks, were soiled with red clay. Their suntanned backs glistened with sweat. They were trying to loosen the iron wheel of the *pisa,* the round
40 pit where the clay was broken and softened. The old skinny horse who made the wheel go around and around was waiting patiently, possibly thankful for having this brief rest under the sun.

Beyond the brick maker's place, the thorny bushes began. They say that the *marabú* plant was brought to Cuba by a countess who loved its flowers, which resemble pink powder puffs. But the bush did not want to remain locked up in a garden, so it slowly spread out across the fields.

Once *marabú* takes hold of a field, it is difficult to clear it.
50 Its roots intertwine under the soil, forming a net that is almost impossible to pull out. One must plow the field to turn over the earth and then rake it, making sure that every last piece of root is removed. Otherwise, it will sprout again.

A *marabú* field is impenetrable unless a path is opened with a machete. The thorny branches form a barrier open only at ground level.

And it was at that level that we began to cross the *marabú* field. Jorge showed us how easy it could be if we simply crawled between and around the thin trunks. It was easy enough, indeed.
60 But soon we had lost him. Because it was impossible to stand up or even to turn, we did not stop. Virginita and I continued, trying to follow the route plotted by our chief explorer, who was by now far ahead and out of sight. . . .

As we moved farther into the *marabú* field, the trees seemed to grow closer and closer together, the branches more intertwined. The thorns caught on our dresses, tore at our hair. But there was nothing we could do. With Jorge's order never to turn back still fresh in our minds, and with a desperate desire to escape the *marabú* jungle, we struggled on, hoping to find our leader at some
70 turn of the maze. . . .

For hours, Virginita and I crawled through the *marabú,* avoiding when we could the dead thorny branches that had fallen on the ground, leaving behind pieces of our dresses and strands of our hair.

Meanwhile, at home, everyone was alarmed. The girls were lost! Jorge, who had returned a long time ago, had moved on to other pastimes. Nobody knew where to find us.

My parents went to the river. They talked to the brick makers. But not for a minute did they imagine we would have entered the *marabú* field. Jorge, to avoid a scolding, said only that he had left us playing at the other side of the river.

Late in the afternoon, with our clothes in tatters and our faces covered with muddy tears, we finally emerged at the other end of the *marabú* field. We were immediately surrounded by a group of children, half naked and as dirty as we were by then, who invited us to play hide-and-seek. Of course we were much too exhausted to accept.

Hearing us crying, the parents of the children appeared at the doors of their huts.

"Poor little ones," one of the women said kindly. "They are lost." She took me in her arms and asked Virginita to follow her.

With water from an old tin basin, she washed our faces and arms, all covered with scratches. Then she opened an old lard can, which she used as her cupboard, and took out two crackers— thick, large sailors' crackers. She sprinkled them with coarse brown sugar—poor people's way of fooling their bodies into believing they had eaten when there was no more substantial food to be had. Then she gave one to each of us.

"Eat, little ones, eat," she said, coaxing us. "Don't worry. We'll take you home."

And from the doorway, the children looked at us with big, open eyes, trying to imagine what we possibly could have done to merit such a generous and unexpected treat. ॰

Keep Reading

How do you think Alma's parents will react when she and her cousin return home? As you continue reading her memoir, you'll meet the rest of her extended family and share in her adventures, her joys, and her sorrows. Most of all, you will have the chance to see how every event shapes Alma, as she grows from a child into a young woman.

from Spellbinder: The Life of Harry Houdini

Biography by Tom Lalicki

Can you BELIEVE your eyes?

COMMON CORE

RI 1 Cite textual evidence to support what the text says explicitly. **RI 2** Determine a central idea of a text and how it is conveyed through particular details. **RI 3** Analyze in detail how a key individual, event, or idea is introduced, illustrated, and elaborated in a text.

If you've ever watched a movie full of incredible stunts and outrageous special effects, then you know you can't always believe what you see. Still, sometimes it's fun to play along with an illusion, even when we know the truth. In the following biography, you will read about Harry Houdini, an entertainer who thrilled audiences with his daring tricks—some of which weren't illusions at all.

DISCUSS Sometimes it's simple to figure out how a trick is done. When an illusion is really impressive, however, it can be hard to convince yourself that it isn't real. With a small group, talk about some illusions you've seen that you just can't explain.

● TEXT ANALYSIS: MAIN IDEA AND DETAILS

Much of what we know about famous or historical figures comes from their **biographies,** or the stories of their lives written by another person. Biographers cover the main events of a person's life and often reveal their own ideas about what kind of person the subject was. Writers back up their main ideas with supporting details such as the following:

- **anecdotes,** or brief stories from the person's life that reveal something about his or her character

- **examples** of the person's thoughts, feelings, or behavior

- **statements** made by or about the person

- **descriptions** of life-changing experiences and events

As you read *Spellbinder,* look for Tom Lalicki's main ideas about Houdini and the details he includes to back up his views.

● READING SKILL: TRACE CHRONOLOGICAL ORDER

Many biographies present the events of a person's life in **chronological order,** or the order in which they happened. For clues to the order of events, look for words and phrases that identify specific times, such as *before, first, two years earlier,* or *meanwhile.*

As you read *Spellbinder,* track the major events in Houdini's early career on a timeline like the one shown.

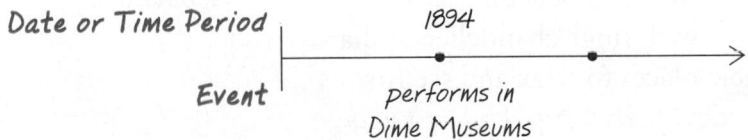

Date or Time Period | 1894

Event | performs in Dime Museums

▲ VOCABULARY IN CONTEXT

Tom Lalicki uses the following words to help tell the story of a master of illusion. To see how many you already know, place each word in the appropriate column.

WORD LIST	certify	commence	devise	obstacle

Know Well	Think I Know	Don't Know at All

 Complete the activities in your **Reader/Writer Notebook.**

Tom Lalicki
born 1949

Writing History and Mystery
Tom Lalicki (pictured below) started out as a filmmaker, but a love of history eventually led him to become a writer. Lalicki's work includes biographies of scientists Dian Fossey, who dedicated her life to studying gorillas, and Alexander Graham Bell, inventor of the telephone. He has also written a mystery novel featuring Harry Houdini.

BACKGROUND TO THE BIOGRAPHY

Escape Artist
Harry Houdini (1874–1926), whose real name was Erich Weisz, was born in Hungary. His family immigrated to the United States when he was a child. As a young man, Weisz changed his name to Houdini and began performing as an escape artist. Houdini mostly used his strength and skill to open locks, though on occasion he hid tools on his body or in his clothes. Houdini often boasted about his strength, but this boast may have contributed to his death. After a tiring performance, Houdini allowed a young man to punch him in the stomach to challenge his strength. Unfortunately, Houdini did not know he was suffering from an infected appendix, which the punches may have made worse. He died of the infection shortly afterward.

Author Online **THINK** central
Go to **thinkcentral.com.**
KEYWORD: HML6-851

SPELLBINDER: THE LIFE OF

HARRY HOUDINI

Tom Lalicki

Vaudeville, the variety stage show, was the premier family
entertainment at the end of the 19th century. Singers, comedians,
dancers, impersonators,[1] comedy singers, comedy dancers, and magicians
filled out affordable three-hour shows for growing audiences. . . .

Promoters built lavish theaters, decorated with huge chandeliers, pillars,
and murals that gave audiences comfortable places to relax and see first-
rate shows. There were several tiers[2] of vaudeville theaters. The best acts
played the Keith-Albee Circuit of theaters on the East Coast and the
Orpheum Circuit on the West. But in 1894, the husband-and-wife team
10 of Bess and Harry Houdini were far from prime-time players.

Ranked below vaudeville were the Dime Museums, an outgrowth of
P. T. Barnum's Museums.[3] There magicians, jugglers, and puppeteers were
jumbled together with curiosity, or "curio," acts like sword swallowers,
fire eaters, midgets, giants, and fat ladies. Performers did from twelve to
twenty shows a day for very low wages. Even recent immigrants could
understand and afford these shows. **Ⓐ**

---

1. **impersonators:** performers who mimic the voices or appearances of other people, usually famous
   people.

2. **tiers:** ranks or levels.

3. **P. T. Barnum's Museums:** The stage promoter P. T. Barnum (1810–1891) ran a series of traveling
   museums that featured performers and "oddities"—including the fake mummified body of a mermaid.
   Barnum's exhibitions eventually became the Barnum and Bailey Circus.

Analyze Visuals ▶

What information does
this poster provide
about Houdini?

**Ⓐ MAIN IDEA AND
DETAILS**
Reread lines 1–16. What
do these details about
vaudeville and the Dime
Museums help you
understand about Bess
and Harry Houdini?

Handcuff King Poster, 1906. The
Granger Collection, New York.

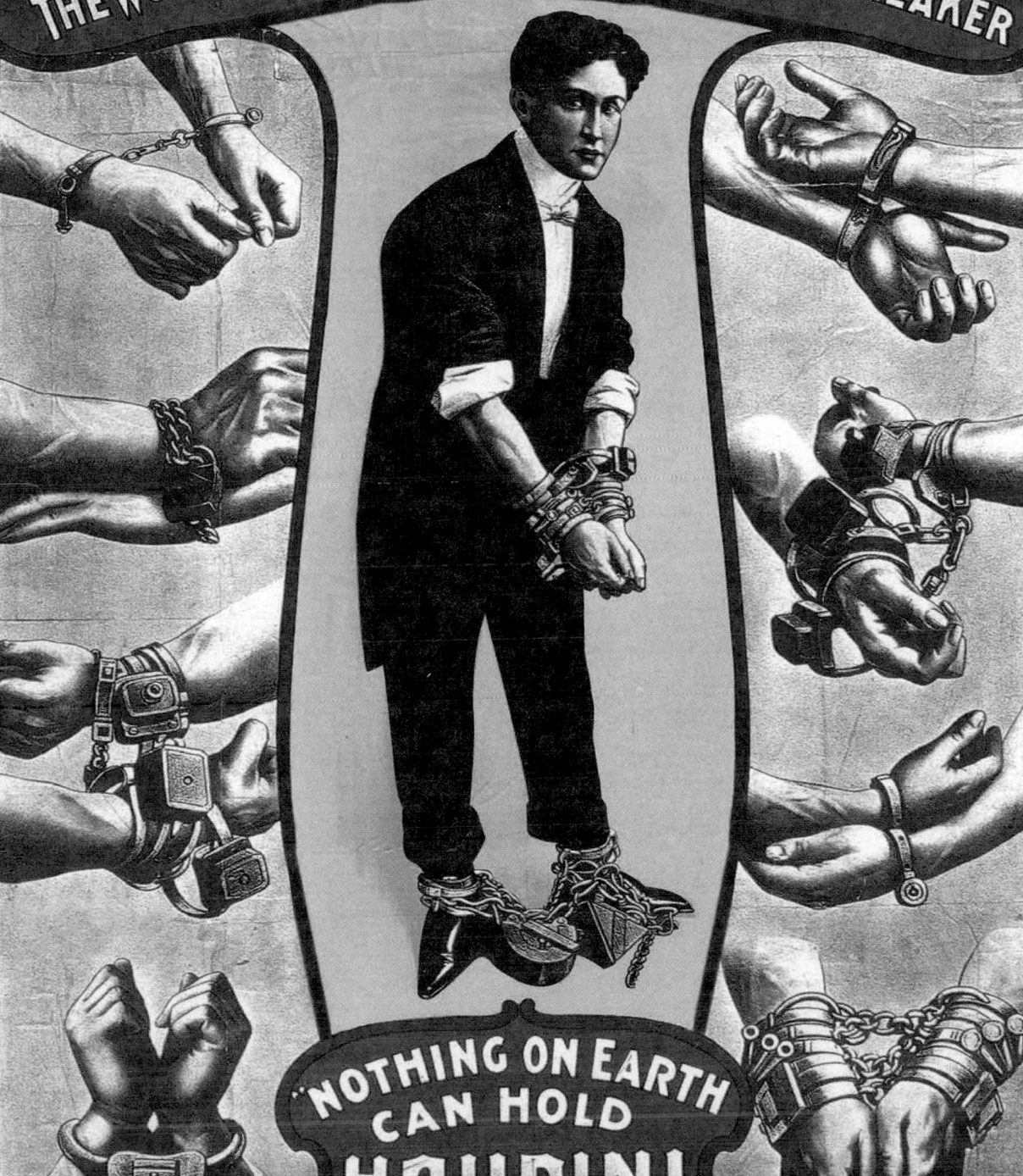

The bottom rung of urban entertainment was the beer hall, where noisy and not very interested patrons enjoyed corny one-act plays and sentimental songs. Small-town folk needed entertainment, too, and that was offered by circuses and medicine shows.[4]

Between 1894 and 1899, the Houdinis learned the craft of showmanship by performing in all these arenas, struggling to make ends meet the whole time. To get bookings, they did a song-and-dance act and appeared in very bad plays. Houdini performed as "Projea, the Wild Man" in an animal cage and did a mind-reading act and onstage séances.[5] . . .

A less determined, less confident man would have given up entirely and taken a job. The closest Houdini came to that was opening a correspondence school[6] for magicians in his mother's apartment. He offered all his secrets for sale. Luckily, nobody thought the tricks worth buying.

The problem with Houdini's act was that he hadn't yet discovered the real Houdini. He performed as "The King of Cards," "The King of Billiard Balls," even as "The Paper Tearing King," without much success. Audiences loved the Metamorphosis escape[7] but did not love Houdini's magic tricks. He worked constantly to develop new ones. He watched and studied hundreds of other performers to learn showmanship. He improved his grammar and stage speech. Most importantly, he invented brilliant ways to promote the act. But none of his efforts opened the door to stardom. **B**

In 1895, Houdini let audience members handcuff him (with their own handcuffs) as part of Metamorphosis. He escaped. Then he let the police of Gloucester, Massachusetts, lock him in their handcuffs. And he escaped. In Woonsocket, Rhode Island, police and newspaper reporters shackled Houdini with six sets of handcuffs and locked him in a room. He escaped in eighteen seconds. **C**

It was terrific advertising in those relatively small towns, but it went no farther. In the days before national news magazines, radio, and television, Houdini's escape from police handcuffs in Woonsocket was purely local news. . . .

Another trademark trick that Houdini developed during this time was the straitjacket escape—a stunning feat of strength and agility nobody else could match. . . .

---

4. **medicine shows:** traveling groups common in the 1800s that provided entertainment and sold "miracle cures" (usually phony) for a variety of illnesses and pains.

5. **séances** (sā′än-səz′): meetings at which people attempt to receive messages from ghosts or spirits.

6. **correspondence school:** a school that sends lessons and exams to students by mail.

7. **Metamorphosis escape:** In this trick, Bess would lock Harry, handcuffed, inside a trunk. On the count of three, Houdini would free himself and Bess would be locked inside the trunk.

Language Coach

Connotation The feeling attached to a word is called its **connotation.** Authors consider the connotations of words they use to create a precise picture in the reader's mind. Reread the sentence in lines 17–19. Which words in this sentence have a negative connotation? How do they affect the way you perceive what is being described?

B **MAIN IDEA AND DETAILS**
Reread lines 31–38. What main idea do the details in these lines support?

C **CHRONOLOGICAL ORDER**
Reread lines 39–44. What two clues does the author use to indicate the order of Houdini's early handcuff escapes?

During a Canadian tour, Houdini visited a mental hospital and [witnessed the use of straitjackets]. Determined to escape from a straitjacket himself, Houdini borrowed one
60 and had Bess wrap him in it. She restrained him in the jacket seven times before he **devised** a technique for escaping. It left him swollen, bruised, and bloody.

Onstage, the cabinet curtain was drawn closed as the straitjacketed Houdini twisted, turned, and rolled on the floor
70 until, free, he opened the curtain holding the empty canvas coat. This stunt didn't catch on right away, either. Audiences thought it was a cheat. Nobody could escape from a real straitjacket, so they assumed Houdini's was rigged. The trick was a flop.

Houdini didn't give up on either the handcuff or the straitjacket escape. Houdini never gave up on a good idea. If audiences didn't like an escape *he* liked, he tried to improve the presentation. He had the patience and determination to keep going back over a problem until it was solved.

While playing a Minneapolis hall in the spring of 1899, lightning struck Houdini's floundering[8] career. Martin Beck, who ran the
80 entire Orpheum vaudeville circuit, liked Metamorphosis and the handcuff escape. He told Houdini to drop the card, billiard ball, and paper-tearing tricks from the act. Beck wanted Houdini to do a twenty-minute turn in the top vaudeville theaters for sixty dollars a week—more than he had ever earned before. Houdini wrote that the offer "changed my whole Life's journey." **D**

Like a jewel under a bright light, Houdini responded to attention by revealing brilliant new facets.[9] Now he played only two shows a day, not twelve. He stayed in cities for a week or more, not one night. This gave him the time and the platform to experiment with his act and impress his
90 audience. **E**

◀ **Analyze Visuals**

This photograph shows Houdini completing a straitjacket escape. Why might Houdini have chosen to perform this trick upside down?

devise (dĭ-vīz′) *v.* to plan or design

D **CHRONOLOGICAL ORDER**
When and how did Houdini meet Martin Beck? Add this information to your timeline.

E **MAIN IDEA AND DETAILS**
In what ways was meeting Martin Beck a life-changing experience for Houdini?

---

8. **floundering:** struggling or stumbling.

9. **facets:** a flat, polished surface on a jewel. The word *facets* also refers to different sides of a personality.

He constantly improved Metamorphosis. He sometimes borrowed a suit jacket from the audience, which he would put on before going into the trunk. After the switch, Bess would emerge wearing the borrowed jacket. Sometimes he took people into the trunk who escaped with him.

Responding to an accusation that he used keys to open handcuffs, Houdini went to a San Francisco police station on July 13, 1899. [His clothes were removed] and examined by a police surgeon who **certified** that he was hiding nothing. His mouth was taped shut, his wrists and ankles were shackled in ten sets of police handcuffs. For good measure, the ankle cuffs were attached to the handcuffs with an eleventh pair before he was locked into an interrogation room.[10] Five minutes later Houdini walked out, still "n——" (the way most polite newspapers spelled the word *naked* then), carrying all the cuffs in his hands. **F**

In April 1900, again [unclothed], he took just three minutes to escape from a doubly locked jail cell in Kansas City. He repeated these escapes wherever the police allowed. Each police force added new **obstacles,** almost desperate not to be embarrassed by this upstart magician. But they always were. And as Houdini knew, the stories written about him by big-city newspapers were the most valuable and cheapest advertising available.

The public commotion he caused generated massive interest in his stage act and sold tickets. His $60 salary rapidly increased to $250 a week—half the total yearly income of an average American worker.

Houdini also introduced another new trick that, like Metamorphosis, would continue to thrill audiences for his entire career. To perform the East Indian Needles, Houdini called an audience committee onstage to look into his nose and throat. Nothing hidden there. He swallowed a handful of sewing needles, loudly chewing on them and washing them down with water. Next, he swallowed a ball of sewing thread. Then he put his hand into his mouth and slowly drew out the thread with the needles threaded onto it. ◆

Although profoundly successful, Houdini needed more. The Houdini legend was started and continuously reinforced by a tireless engine churning out mountains of promotion. The engine was Houdini's mind. A 1900 flyer he sent to theater managers announced: Where the possibility ceases, the impossibility **commences**! . . . Harry Houdini, "king of handcuffs," defies duplication, explanation, imitation or contradiction. ∿

certify (sûr′tə-fī′) *v.* to confirm as true or genuine

F MAIN IDEA AND DETAILS
Reread lines 95–103. Explain what this **anecdote** reveals about Houdini's character.

obstacle (ŏb′stə-kəl) *n.* something that stands in the way or prevents progress

◆ GRAMMAR IN CONTEXT
Proper nouns, such as names, titles, countries, nationalities, and languages are always capitalized. Reread lines 113–120. Notice that the writer correctly capitalizes the name of Houdini's trick and the specific type of needles he used.

commence (kə-mĕns′) *v.* to begin

---

10. **interrogation room:** a secure room in which police officers question suspects.

Comprehension

1. **Recall** What names did Harry Houdini perform under before becoming famous as "The King of Handcuffs"?

2. **Recall** What advice did Martin Beck give Houdini?

3. **Summarize** How did Houdini try to prove that he wasn't cheating during his performances?

Text Analysis

4. **Make Inferences** Reread lines 121–127. What does Houdini's method of advertising his performances tell you about him?

5. **Identify Supporting Details** One of the author's main ideas in this selection is that "Houdini never gave up on a good idea" (line 75). Skim the selection to find supporting details that back up this statement. Record the details in a diagram like the one shown.

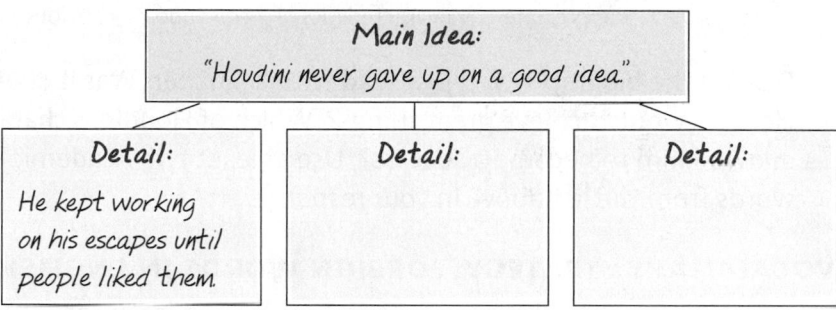

Main Idea:
"Houdini never gave up on a good idea."

Detail:
He kept working on his escapes until people liked them.

Detail:

Detail:

6. **Clarify Main Idea** What do you think is the main idea of the entire selection? List details from the selection to support your answer. Then write a brief summary of the main idea and supporting details you have chosen. You may want to organize your main idea and details in a diagram like the one shown.

7. **Evaluate Chronological Order** Look back at the timeline you made as you read. In what way does the use of chronological order help you understand the path Houdini took in order to become famous?

Extension and Challenge

8. **Readers' Circle** What was the key to Harry Houdini's success? With a small group, discuss which was most useful to Houdini during his early career—his personality, his skills, or the help of people around him. Use examples from the selection to support your opinion.

Can you BELIEVE your eyes?

What do you think made Houdini's tricks believable? Explain.

COMMON CORE

RI 1 Cite textual evidence to support what the text says explicitly. **RI 2** Determine a central idea of a text and how it is conveyed through particular details; provide a summary of the text distinct from personal opinions or judgments. **RI 3** Analyze in detail how a key individual, event, or idea is introduced, illustrated, and elaborated in a text.

Houdini prepares to escape from a locked milk can.

Vocabulary in Context

▲ **VOCABULARY PRACTICE**

Show that you understand the vocabulary words by deciding whether each statement is true or false.

1. When you **commence** a project, you are almost done.
2. When teachers **devise** homework assignments, they are grading them.
3. If someone can **certify** a claim, you ought to believe it.
4. Something that helps you achieve your goals is an **obstacle.**

certify

commence

devise

obstacle

ACADEMIC VOCABULARY IN SPEAKING

> • achieve   • appreciate   • characteristics   • conclude   • obvious

Discuss the biography you just read with a partner. Was it **obvious** that Houdini would **achieve** great things? Which of Houdini's **characteristics** allowed him to become a success? Use at least two Academic Vocabulary words from the list above in your response.

VOCABULARY STRATEGY: FOREIGN WORDS IN ENGLISH

As an English speaker, you might be surprised to learn that many of the words we regularly use actually come from other languages. For example, the word *vaudeville* comes from a French word meaning "humorous songs." Understanding how languages share words can add to your knowledge of word meanings.

PRACTICE Use a dictionary to find the original language and meaning of each of the boldfaced words. Try using these words in your own speech and writing.

1. We always have **macaroni** for dinner on Wednesday nights.
2. If you want to perform in the **ballet,** you will have to practice.
3. He prefers to eat **tofu** rather than chicken or beef.
4. I went to the **opera** with my grandparents last year.
5. She enjoys having breakfast out on the **patio.**

⋯ **COMMON CORE**

L 4d Verify the preliminary determination of the meaning of a word or phrase.

Interactive Vocabulary **THINK** central

Go to **thinkcentral.com.**
KEYWORD: HML6-858

Language

◆ **GRAMMAR IN CONTEXT: Capitalize Correctly**

Proper nouns, as well as any adjectives made from those nouns, are always capitalized. Some specific types of proper nouns to watch for are

- names and titles of people (*Dr. Jackson, Mr. Lewis Smith*)
- countries (*France, Germany*)
- nationalities and ethnicities (*Korean, my Italian-American uncle*)
- languages (*Spanish, Russian*)
- religions (*Christianity, Islam*)

   Example: Harry Houdini, who was Jewish, was born in Hungary.

PRACTICE Rewrite the following sentences, capitalizing all proper nouns.

1. Often, mrs. houdini was part of harry's act.
2. Houdini learned to use a straitjacket while on a canadian tour.
3. He worked hard to improve his english.
4. Houdini earned more than the average american worker.

*For more help with capitalization, see page R51 in the **Grammar Handbook.***

READING-WRITING CONNECTION

Increase your appreciation of *Spellbinder* by responding to these prompts. Then use the **revising tips** to improve your writing.

WRITING PROMPTS	REVISING TIPS
Short Constructed Response: Promotional Flyer As you read in lines 121–127, Harry Houdini often used flyers to promote his performances. Choose one of the illusions described in the selection and write a **one-paragraph flyer** persuading people to attend.	Review your flyer. Have you used correct capitalization? If not, revise your writing.
Extended Constructed Response: Evaluation On his deathbed, Houdini told his doctor, "I am nothing but a fake, while you do great things for your fellow man." Do you agree or disagree with Houdini's opinion of himself? Respond in **two or three paragraphs.**	Review your response. Have you capitalized proper nouns correctly? If not, revise your writing.

Interactive Revision

Go to **thinkcentral.com**.
KEYWORD: HML6-859

COMMON CORE

L 2 Demonstrate command of the conventions of capitalization.
W 2 Write informative/ explanatory texts to examine a topic.

from **Houdini: The Great Escape**
Film Clip on Media ● **Smart** DVD-ROM

How do you UNLOCK a mystery?

COMMON CORE

RI 4 Determine the meaning of words and phrases as they are used in a text, including technical meanings.

True stories fascinate people. It's exciting to hear an astonishing tale and learn how it actually happened. In this lesson, you'll view a documentary about the amazing Harry Houdini. You'll also explore the tools moviemakers used to tell the story of Houdini's life and his many death-defying escapes.

Background

Stranger Than Fiction Harry Houdini led a more interesting life than many fictional characters we know from books and movies. He captivated audiences around the world with his incredible escapes. In his time, Houdini was as famous as any major professional athlete or movie star today.

Even though Houdini died in 1926, he's still one of the world's most famous magicians. People are curious to learn about his life and the details of his legendary feats. This makes him a great subject for a documentary film. In this documentary, you'll get a chance to see Houdini perform, and you'll even learn the secrets behind some of his extraordinary escapes.

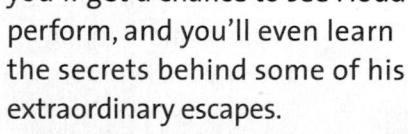

Media Literacy: Documentary

A **documentary** is a nonfiction film that gives viewers information about important people or historical events. Filmmakers can take the viewer "behind the scenes" and provide the full story behind an interesting person or event. Documentary filmmakers gather factual material about their subjects and use it to tell their stories. This material is presented through footage, interviews, and voice-over narration. Just like other forms of media, documentaries can be either **formal** or **informal.** The level of formality is created by the filmmaker's choice of narrator and by the way in which the filmmaker presents the information (for example, a sit-down interview is more formal than a clip of a conversation between friends).

FEATURES OF A DOCUMENTARY	STRATEGIES FOR VIEWING
Footage is recorded material that gives information about a subject. Documentary filmmakers combine different types of footage to tell their subject's story. Footage can include film clips, news reports, photographs and interviews.	Think about why the particular footage was chosen. Does it • show details of a historical time? • create an emotional response? • reveal the filmmakers' point of view?
Interviews are usually filmed specially for the documentary. Filmmakers may interview experts on the subject or people who knew the person or were involved in the event the documentary is about.	Think about why the person was chosen to be interviewed. Does he or she • have special knowledge about the subject? • present another side to the story?
Voice-over narration is the voice of an unseen speaker that is heard in a documentary. The voice-over can provide important facts about the subject. It can also help explain the footage.	Listen to the voice-over narration for additional information about the footage. Also listen for clues to what's most important about the subject.

- **Film:** *Houdini: The Great Escape*
- **Directors:** Kevin Burns, Lawrence Williams
- **Genre:** Documentary
- **Running Time:** 5.5 minutes

Viewing Guide for

Houdini: The Great Escape

The amazing things Harry Houdini did make many people want to know the whole story. They want to see him perform his escapes, and to learn the secrets behind them. With this documentary, you'll get to do just that.

Think about the documentary features as you view the clip. Notice how they work together to tell Houdini's story. View the clip more than once, thinking about the footage, interviews, and voice-over narration.

NOW VIEW

FIRST VIEWING: Comprehension

1. **Recall** During his performances, what did Houdini ask the audience to do just before he had himself locked in the milk can?

2. **Summarize** In your own words, describe how Houdini escaped from the packing crate lowered into the river.

CLOSE VIEWING: Media Literacy

3. **Examine Voice-Over Narration** Think about the voice-over narration that plays over the film footage of Houdini hanging upside down and escaping from the straitjacket. What details do you learn from the narration that you couldn't get from just watching the footage?

4. **Analyze Interviews** What type of people do the filmmakers interview for the documentary? Why do you think these people were chosen to talk about Houdini?

5. **Evaluate Footage** The documentary uses film clips, photographs, newspaper articles, and posters from Houdini's time. Which type of footage best helps you understand Houdini? Give a reason for your choice.

6. **Evaluate Formality** How formal or informal was the presentation of information? How did the level of formality contribute to or take away from your enjoyment of the documentary?

Write or Discuss

Compare the Film and Essay You've now read a biography of Harry Houdini and seen a documentary about him. Think about what you learned from the essay and what you learned from the film. What are the strengths of each? Write a paragraph that compares the two. Think about

- the amount of detail you learned about Houdini's life from the essay
- the footage of Houdini performing his tricks
- the descriptions of Houdini's tricks in the interviews
- the information given by the voice-over narration

Produce Your Own Media

Create a Photo Documentary Think about how you would make a documentary about an ordinary person. To keep the audience interested, you'd want to focus on the most fascinating parts of that person's life. What sets him or her apart from everyone else? You'll also need to decide whether your presentation will be formal or informal. Choose an ordinary person you know, and shoot a series of photographs to tell the behind-the-scenes story of his or her life. Attach your photographs to a bulletin board or poster board and present them to the class.

HERE'S HOW Here are a few suggestions for shooting your photo documentary:

- First, do your research. Interview your subject to find out about his or her life. Choose the most interesting parts to focus on.
- Think of your photos as documentary footage. Take shots of important people, locations, and objects in your subject's daily life.
- If you don't have a camera, take notes as you follow your subject through his or her day. Write a description of the most interesting events of the day.

STUDENT MODEL

COMMON CORE

RI 7 Integrate information presented in different media as well as in words to develop a coherent understanding of a topic. **RI 9** Compare and contrast one author's presentation of events with that of another.

Media Tools

Go to **thinkcentral.com**.
KEYWORD: HML6-863

Tech Tip

If available, use computer software to create a slideshow presentation of your photo documentary.

In a Neighborhood in Los Angeles
Poem by Francisco X. Alarcón

For Gwen, 1969
Poem by Margaret Walker

How would you like to be
REMEMBERED?

COMMON CORE

RL 1 Cite textual evidence to support analysis of what the text says explicitly as well as inferences drawn from the text.

Suppose you and your family were moving to another state. How would you want to be remembered by your friends and classmates? Would you like them to remember something you accomplished, the way you looked, or how you treated others? The writers whose poems you are about to read recall the lasting impact of a special grandmother and an important American poet.

LIST IT Divide a sheet of paper in half. Use one half to list what you remember about a person who has had a significant effect on your life. On the other half of the page, make a list of the ways you hope to be remembered.

How I Remember _____	How I Want to Be Remembered
1.	1.
2.	2.

TEXT ANALYSIS: CHARACTERIZATION IN POETRY

In just a few lines, a poem can paint a portrait of a memorable character. To create great characters, poets use four methods of **characterization** similar to those used for fiction and nonfiction. Those methods are

- describing the character's physical appearance
- presenting the character's thoughts, words, and actions
- revealing what others think and say about the character
- having the speaker of the poem comment directly on the character

As you read the following poems, record examples of these methods of characterization in a chart like the one shown.

	Grandmother	Gwen
What does the character look like?		
What does she think, say, and do?	"mijito don't cry" (lines 4–5)	
What do others say about her?		

READING SKILL: ASK QUESTIONS

Asking questions as you read helps you comprehend the meaning of a literary work. As you read, ask yourself the following kinds of questions:

- **literal** questions to identify what something is
- **interpretive** questions to explain the meaning of something
- **evaluative** questions to judge the value of something
- **universal** questions to relate the work to your own life

You'll probably discover that by the time you finish reading a poem, you'll be able to answer many of your questions. Rereading will help you strengthen your understanding and help you answer any remaining questions.

 Complete the activities in your **Reader/Writer Notebook**.

Meet the Authors

Francisco X. Alarcón
born 1954

Poet of Two Countries
When Francisco Alarcón was a child, his family moved back and forth between Mexico and the United States several times. One constant in his life was his grandmother, who helped raise him. Among his recent projects is a bilingual poetry collection for young readers.

Margaret Walker
1915–1998

Historian for the People
Margaret Walker graduated from college at the height of the Great Depression. She eventually found a writing job through the Works Progress Administration, a government job-creation agency. It was the beginning of a long career as a poet, essayist, and professor. Among her coworkers were novelist Richard Wright and poet Gwendolyn Brooks.

Authors Online
Go to **thinkcentral.com**. KEYWORD: HML6-865

THiNK central

In a Neighborhood in Los Angeles

Francisco X. Alarcón

I learned
Spanish
from my grandma

mijito[1]
5 don't cry
she'd tell me **Ⓐ**

on the mornings
my parents
would leave

10 to work
at the fish
canneries

my grandma
would chat
15 with chairs

sing them
old
songs

dance
20 waltzes with them
in the kitchen **Ⓑ**

Ⓐ CHARACTERIZATION
What do the grandmother's words in lines 4–6 tell us about her? Record this information in your characterization chart.

Ⓑ CHARACTERIZATION
Reread lines 13–21. What can you infer about the grandmother's personality from this description of her actions?

---

1. *mijito* (mē-hē′tō): Spanish for "my little child." A contraction of the phrase *mi hijito*.

when she'd say
niño barrigón[2]
she'd laugh

25 with my grandma
I learned
to count clouds

to point out
in flowerpots
30 mint leaves

my grandma
wore moons
on her dress

Mexico's mountains
35 deserts
ocean

in her eyes
I'd see them
in her braids

40 I'd touch them
in her voice
smell them

one day
I was told:
45 she went far away

but still
I feel her
with me

whispering
50 in my ear
mijito

———
2. *niño barrigón* (nēn'yō bär-rē-gōn'):
a Spanish phrase meaning
"potbellied little boy."

C **ASK QUESTIONS**
What questions could
you ask about the
narrator's relationship
with his grandmother?

Rain Slicked Avenue (2004), Lisbeth Firmin. Oil on panel, 20″ × 20″. Klaudia Marr Gallery, Santa Fe, New Mexico.

For Gwen, 1969 (Gwendolyn Brooks)

Margaret Walker

The slender, shy, and sensitive young girl
is woman now,
her words a power in the Ebon land.[1]
Outside her window on the street
5 a mass of life moves by.
Chicago is her city. **D**
Her heart flowers with its flame—
old stockyards, new beaches
all the little storefront churches
10 and the bar on the corner.
Dreamer and seer of tales
She witnesses rebellion,
struggle and sweat.
The people are her heartbeat—
15 In their footsteps pulsate daily
all her black words of fire and blood. **E**

D CHARACTERIZATION
Reread lines 1–6. What do you learn about Gwen in these lines?

E ASK QUESTIONS
What questions could you ask about the subject of this poem? Record at least two questions in your notebook.

---

1. **Ebon land:** a reference to African-American society and culture.

MAGAZINE ARTICLE In "For Gwen, 1969," Margaret Walker celebrates the successes of her friend, poet Gwendolyn Brooks. Brooks remained successful and influential for 30 years after 1969. This article traces her impressive career.

A Way with Words

James C. Hall

Gwendolyn Brooks liked to say that African-American poetry is the story of a community learning "to lift its face unashamed." Poetry's emotion and commitment to powerful, memorable language made it ideal for writers who wanted to transform how people felt about the possibilities of the future. Gwendolyn Brooks has always successfully tapped the ability of poetry to affect our sense of life's possibilities. . . .

By paying close attention to the lives of common folk in the Chicago neighborhoods around her, Brooks discovered a way to draw attention to the unjust conditions in which they lived and to celebrate the fact that they did so with courage and purpose. Keeping families together, caring for loved ones, educating, and teaching were all necessary parts of the struggle—parts that most definitely deserved celebration. . . . Yet, at the same time, Brooks's poetry did not reduce the complex nature of human beings to social problems.

Her book *Annie Allen* was granted the Pulitzer Prize in 1950, and Brooks became the first African American to win that award. Brooks's poetry was elaborate in its use of symbolism and its reference to other writing. However, she always managed to tell the story of individuals whose lives and struggles were easy to recognize and respect. Human lives were always complicated in a Brooks poem, but a reader rarely leaves her work puzzled or unaffected.

Brooks was born in 1917 and died in 2000. For most of her life, Chicago was home, and she had always been one of its model cultural ambassadors. . . .

In the final decades of Brooks's life, she worked to cultivate an interest in poetry among schoolchildren. She recognized how underserved Chicago's children were and how often poetry and the arts were the first activities to be cut in an underfunded school system. With her own resources, she sponsored a poetry contest for children of all backgrounds and creatively drew attention to the skills and ability that might be lost. As effectively as any writer in the African-American tradition, Brooks managed to model a life and create a body of work that made known the necessity of "lifting one's face unashamed."

Comprehension

1. **Clarify** What happens to the speaker's grandmother at the end of "In a Neighborhood in Los Angeles"?

2. **Recall** What is Gwen's "heartbeat" in "For Gwen, 1969"?

Text Analysis

3. **Make Inferences About Character** Reread lines 1–3 of "For Gwen, 1969." What can you infer about the speaker's feelings toward Gwen?

4. **Identify Author's Purpose** What do you think is the author's main purpose in each poem—to inform, to entertain, to persuade, or to share personal thoughts and feelings? Support your answer with details from the poems.

5. **Analyze Characterization** Look back at the chart you filled in as you read. Explain which methods of characterization the poet relies on most in "In a Neighborhood in Los Angeles." Is his characterization believable?

6. **Ask Questions** Look back at the questions you recorded while reading "Gwen, 1969." Evaluate whether Walker's characterization of Brooks is complete by considering which of those questions you could answer by reading the poem alone and which you could answer only after reading the biography on page 870.

7. **Evaluate Characterization** Which character do you think is more powerfully presented, the grandmother or Gwen? Explain.

8. **Paraphrase a Poem** A **paraphrase** is a restatement of a text in your own words. A good paraphrase maintains the meaning and logical order of the original text. To effectively paraphrase a poem, you might restate its meaning either line by line or stanza by stanza. Paraphrase one of the poems you just read. Then, compare your paraphrase to the original text to make sure you have maintained the meaning and order of the poem.

Extension and Challenge

9. **SOCIAL STUDIES CONNECTION** Reread the article about Gwendolyn Brooks on page 870, then do some research on Chicago during the 1960s. Why might Margaret Walker have chosen the year 1969 as the setting for her poem about Brooks?

How would you like to be REMEMBERED?

Compare and contrast the ways in which the poems describe their subjects. Do you think the women would be happy with the way they are remembered? Explain.

COMMON CORE

RL 1 Cite textual evidence to support analysis of what the text says explicitly as well as inferences drawn from the text. **W 7** Conduct short research projects to answer a question.

Personal Narrative

Just like Bill Cosby, Helen Keller, and other writers in this unit, you can write about events in your life. A significant experience in your life might be a great story for others to read. In this workshop, you'll find out how to create a personal narrative from one of your own experiences.

 Complete the workshop activities in your **Reader/Writer Notebook.**

WRITE WITH A PURPOSE

WRITING TASK

Write a **personal narrative** based on an important event or experience in your life. Include descriptive details and sensory language to help your readers understand what the experience was like. Be sure to explain why the event was special for you.

Idea Starters
- your first day in a new neighborhood
- the day you got a pet
- a scary or suspenseful event
- a difficult challenge you overcame
- a pleasant surprise, such as a birthday party

THE ESSENTIALS

Here are some common purposes, audiences, and formats for personal narratives.

PURPOSES	AUDIENCES	FORMATS
• to share a personal experience • to express why an experience is meaningful to you	• classmates and teacher • friends • family • Web users	• essay for class • literary magazine • classroom anthology • journal • blog • documentary film

COMMON CORE TRAITS

1. DEVELOPMENT
- presents an engaging **introduction**
- uses techniques such as **dialogue** and **description** to develop the narrative
- provides a **conclusion** that follows from the events

2. ORGANIZATION
- **organizes** events in a logical sequence
- uses **transitions** to make the **order of events** clear
- uses effective **pacing** to develop the narrative

3. LANGUAGE
- establishes and maintains a **first person point of view**
- includes **precise language, relevant details,** and **sensory language**
- uses **prepositional phrases** effectively
- employs correct **grammar, usage,** and spelling

Writing Online

THINK central

Go to **thinkcentral.com**.
KEYWORD: HML6N-872

Planning/Prewriting

**COMMON CORE** W 3a–e Write narratives to develop real or imagined events using effective technique, relevant descriptive details, and well-structured event sequences. **W 5** Develop and strengthen writing by planning, revising, editing, rewriting, or trying a new approach.

Getting Started

CHOOSE A SUBJECT

To help you identify possible subjects for your personal narrative, make a list of memorable times and events in your life. Think about why each experience was important to you. Circle your best idea—one that makes an interesting story and that also had an impact on your life.

▶ **WHAT DOES IT LOOK LIKE?**

> getting my green belt in tae kwon do
> the day we moved to our new apartment
> ⟨getting scared while walking in Chicago⟩
> going fishing with Grandma G.
> my first roller coaster ride

THINK ABOUT AUDIENCE AND PURPOSE

As you begin to plan your narrative, keep your **purpose** in mind. You want to help your **audience** understand what you have experienced. Consider the kinds of details you will need to include in order to make the experience come alive for your readers.

▶ **ASK YOURSELF:**

- Who is my audience? How do I make my writing appeal to them?
- What ideas do I want to share with my readers? What are the most important details I should include?
- How can I engage my readers' interest at the beginning of my narrative?

LIST DETAILS

Try to remember as many descriptive details as you can, and write them down. You don't need to use them all in your narrative, but writing down as many details as you can will help you remember the experience more clearly.

▶ **WHAT DOES IT LOOK LIKE?**

> **Details about the walk:**
> dark sidewalks   litter
> loud BANG!   not like Texas
> graffiti   wanting to go home
> shadows   crunchy candy canes
> the candy store   Andrew's house

USE DESCRIPTIVE LANGUAGE

Choose a person, place, or object that is important to your narrative. Use a cluster diagram to record creative, descriptive words that will help your reader understand what you are describing. Make sure your language is **precise,** or very specific. Include **sensory language** that can help convey your experience. You may wish to make diagrams on several different topics as you develop your narrative.

▶ **WHAT DOES IT LOOK LIKE?**

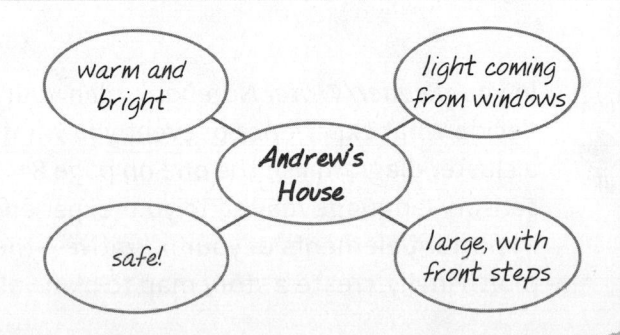

Planning/Prewriting *continued*

Getting Started

MAKE A STORY MAP

Like any great story, a personal narrative has well-developed characters and a detailed setting and plot. The **setting** is when and where the story takes place. The **plot** is the series of related events in a story. Create a story map to help you develop the elements of your narrative.

As you think about the events, keep in mind how you want to **pace** your narrative. In a well-paced narrative, the action moves smoothly, and the writer doesn't linger on events or details.

▶ WHAT DOES IT LOOK LIKE?

> **Working title:** *A Scary Walk Home*
> **Setting:** *Chicago, last October*
> **Events:**
> 1. *We go to the candy store.*
> 2. *We start walking and I get scared.*
> 3. *There's a loud bang.*
> 4. *We reach Andrew's house.*
> **Effect on me:** *It made me want to be back home.*

PLAN THE DIALOGUE

Dialogue is a conversation between two or more people. Using dialogue allows readers to "hear" the voices of the characters in a narrative. It can also build **suspense**—a feeling of growing tension and excitement. Review your story map and consider where you might use dialogue to convey key information, reveal characters' feelings or personalities, or create interest in your narrative. Write some dialogue that you think would be effective for different parts of your narrative.

▶ WHAT DOES IT LOOK LIKE?

> *To show that I was scared and Andrew was perfectly calm:*
> **Me:** *"Um . . . y-you know how to get to your house, right?"*
> **Andrew:** *"Of course I know how to get to my house."*
> **Me (shrieking):** *"What was that?"*
> **Andrew:** *"Oh, that's probably just Leo, our neighbor. He sets off a lot of fireworks."*

PEER REVIEW Review your story map with a peer. Then ask: Where are the best places to use dialogue to make my narrative lively and interesting for readers?

YOUR TURN In your *Reader/Writer Notebook*, plan your personal narrative. First, decide what experience or event you want to write about. Then use a cluster diagram like the one on page 873 to gather descriptive and sensory language related to your experience. Take notes on other important elements of your narrative—the characters, setting, and plot. Finally, create a story map to plan your narrative.

Drafting

 **COMMON CORE** **W 4** Produce clear and coherent writing in which the development, organization, and style are appropriate to task, purpose, and audience. **L 1e** Recognize variations from standard English and improve expression in conventional language.

This chart shows how to create a well-organized personal narrative.

Organizing a Personal Narrative

INTRODUCTION

- Start with a statement or a piece of dialogue that will get your readers' attention.
- Set the scene for your audience. Tell when and where your experience takes place and introduce the people who were involved.

▼

BODY

- Describe events in the order in which they take place. Use **transitions** (*first, then, afterward*) to convey the sequence of events and to show changes from one time frame to another.
- Use **dialogue** to bring your characters to life and convey important information.
- Include **descriptive details** and **sensory language** to help readers connect with your experience.
- Use effective **pacing** to keep the action moving.

▼

CONCLUDING SECTION

- Bring the narrative to a close soon after the **climax,** or moment of greatest excitement.
- Express the importance or meaning of the experience to you.

GRAMMAR IN CONTEXT: IMPROVING EXPRESSION

A personal narrative can have formal and informal language. Slang, a type of informal language, can be useful in helping readers hear a character's voice, but it can also be difficult for readers to understand. To keep your writing clear, use slang in dialogue only.

Examples of Slang Expressions	Meaning
chill out	relax
awesome	great, really interesting
be a blast	something will be a lot of fun

"Nope. We're hoofin' it," Andrew chirped.

[This quote uses the slang expression *hoofing it* which means "to walk."]

Revising

Even if you plan your first draft carefully, it can still be improved during the revising stage. The following chart can help you evaluate the content, organization, and style of your personal narrative and make changes to improve its effectiveness. You may discover that parts of your narrative need rewriting or reworking.

PERSONAL NARRATIVE

Ask Yourself	Tips	Revision Strategies
1. Does the beginning catch the attention of the audience?	▶ **Highlight** the part of the introduction that gets the reader's attention.	▶ **Add** action, dialogue, or other precise details to make the introduction more interesting.
2. Has the writer enriched the narrative with relevant details and sensory language?	▶ **Circle** each descriptive word or phrase and underline sensory language.	▶ **Add** details and language to help the reader understand the events in your narrative.
3. Are transitions used to convey the sequence of events in a logical order?	▶ **Number** each event in the order that it happened. Check that the sequence is logical.	▶ **Reorganize** events, if necessary, or **add** transitions to clarify the order of events.
4. Does the writer use formal and informal language appropriately?	▶ **Bracket** words or phrases that are too informal.	▶ **Rework** words or phrases that may be difficult for readers to understand. Use limited slang in dialogue.
5. Does the narrative convey the importance of the experience to the writer?	▶ **Underline** thoughts and feelings about the experience.	▶ **Add** information to explain the significance of the experience.

YOUR TURN

PEER REVIEW Exchange your personal narrative with a partner and review each other's drafts. As you read and comment on your classmate's narrative, be sure to highlight places where the order of events is confusing. Point out parts of the narrative that might need reworking or a new approach.

COMMON CORE

W 5 Strengthen writing by revising, rewriting, or trying a new approach. **L 3a** Vary sentence patterns.

ANALYZE A STUDENT DRAFT

Read this student's draft and the comments about it as a model for revising your own personal narrative.

There's No Place Like Home

by Veronica Alley, Rancho Santa Margarita Intermediate School

❶   My cousin Andrew and I stood outside the candy store in the chilly air. "Is your mother coming to pick us up?" I asked.

"Nope. We're hoofin' it," Andrew chirped.

> At the start of her essay, Veronica uses **dialogue** to capture readers' interest.

❷   I was alarmed to hear that we'd be walking home, in a city like this, at this time of day. My heart sank. But whatever apprehension I felt dissolved like sugar in my mouth when we entered the candy store. There were many, many different kinds of candy. We left munching on chocolate bars and crunching cherry-flavored candy canes.

> This paragraph includes some relevant descriptive details, but it could be improved by using different sentence patterns.

❸   It was dark now, and we shared the uneven sidewalks of Chicago with hordes of frightening-looking people. My anxiety returned.

"Um . . . y-you know how to get to your house, right?"

"Of course I know how to get to my house," Andrew smirked.

❹   Looking around, I saw graffiti-covered buildings, littered sidewalks, and scary-looking children. Passersby glared at me, their faces seeming to snarl at me from the shadows, as if they could smell my fear. Back home, the only things that could smell anxiety were dogs, bees, and my glitchy computer. I suddenly missed my quiet city in Texas.

> Vivid and exciting **descriptive language** helps pull readers into the narrative. Veronica's writing **style** is dramatic and suspenseful.

LEARN HOW Use a Variety of Sentence Patterns Veronica's fourth paragraph contains only **declarative sentences,** or statements that end in periods. When she revised her essay, she decided to make her narrative more lively and appealing by inserting a question and an exclamation.

VERONICA'S REVISION TO SECTION ❷

We were

~~I was alarmed to hear that we'd be~~ walking home, in a city like this, at this time of day ? My heart sank. But whatever apprehension I felt dissolved like sugar in my mouth when we entered the candy store. *Oh, the choices!* ~~There were many, many different kinds of candy.~~ We left munching on chocolate bars and crunching cherry-flavored candy canes.

⑤   After a while I decided that talking with Andrew would maybe take my mind off our surroundings. "So, how's school?" I began casually.

"Fifth grade is fun. I like my teacher."

Suddenly I heard a loud explosive BANG! I screamed and looked around frantically.

"What was that?" I shrieked at Andrew.

"Oh, that's probably just Leo, our neighbor. He sets off a lot of fireworks."

⑥   I wanted to go home. I was feeling more and more scared. I was relieved when Andrew finally announced, "We're almost at my house."

⑦   I sighed in relief. We turned the corner, and I recognized the large house, with its warm, bright windows. I dashed up the front steps, my cheeks red from the cold. Andrew followed and opened the door. A joyful choir sang in my head as I stepped into the warm, safe house.

> **Transition** words and phrases help convey sequence.

> Veronica *tells* how she feels in this part of the narrative, but she should use more **details and descriptive language** to *show* how she feels.

> The **conclusion** shows the importance of the experience—Veronica really appreciates feeling safe again.

LEARN HOW Use Details and Descriptive Language As Veronica describes her walk home from the candy store, she tells readers, "I was feeling more and more scared." She could bring this scene to life by using concrete details and descriptive language to *show* readers how she felt. When she revised her essay, Veronica added vivid language to reveal exactly how she felt at this moment.

VERONICA'S REVISION TO SECTION ⑥

I wanted to go home. ~~I was feeling more and more scared.~~ I was relieved when Andrew finally announced, "We're almost at my house."

The home I once regarded as boring suddenly seemed very appealing, not to mention safe. I imagined myself at home, sitting on my warm, comfortable sofa, watching my favorite television show. There would be no scary people snarling at me, and no explosions. I began gnawing madly at my chocolate bar.

 **YOUR TURN** Use guidance from your peers and your teacher as well as the two "Learn How" lessons to revise your personal narrative. Evaluate how well you have achieved the purpose of sharing your experience with your audience.

Editing and Publishing

COMMON CORE

W 3d Use descriptive details. **W 5** Strengthen writing as needed by editing. **L 2** Demonstrate command of the conventions of capitalization, punctuation, and spelling when writing.

In the editing stage, you check your personal narrative to make sure it is free of any errors in spelling, punctuation, and sentence structure. Edit your writing carefully to improve expression and vary sentences, using proofreading marks to make the necessary corrections.

GRAMMAR IN CONTEXT: PREPOSITIONAL PHRASES

A **preposition** shows the relationship of a noun or pronoun to another word in a sentence. The preposition, the noun that follows it, and any other words that modify the noun make up a **prepositional phrase.** Prepositional phrases can be used to give information about location, time, and direction, or to provide other important details. For instance, look at the following sentence from Veronica's draft:

> My cousin Andrew and I stood outside the candy store in the chilly air.
>
> [The two **prepositional phrases** add important details about the setting of the narrative.]

You can add variety to your writing by beginning a sentence with a prepositional phrase. A comma is used to set off a prepositional phrase when it begins a sentence. As Veronica edited her essay, she realized she had forgotten this punctuation mark in one sentence.

> After a while, I decided that talking with Andrew would maybe take my mind off our surroundings.

PUBLISH YOUR WRITING

Share your personal narrative with an audience.

- Present a dramatic reading of your narrative to a group of classmates or family members.
- Submit a copy of your personal narrative to a literary magazine.
- Conduct an interview with someone involved in the experience you wrote about. Then summarize your interview and share it with an audience.
- Add your narrative to a class Web site, or create your own blog.
- Turn your narrative into a short documentary film and share with classmates.

YOUR TURN

Correct any errors in your personal narrative by carefully proofreading it. Use prepositional phrases to add relevant details. Then publish the final version of your narrative.

Scoring Rubric

Use the rubric below to evaluate your personal narrative from the Writing Workshop or your response to the on-demand task on the next page.

PERSONAL NARRATIVE

SCORE	COMMON CORE TRAITS
6	• **Development** Has an engaging introduction; develops events with strong dialogue and description; ends powerfully • **Organization** Organizes events sequentially and logically; effectively uses transitions to convey sequence; has engaging pacing • **Language** Consistently maintains an appropriate balance between formal and informal language and style; ably uses descriptive details and sensory language; demonstrates a strong command of conventions
5	• **Development** Has an interesting introduction; uses dialogue and describes events effectively; has a strong concluding section • **Organization** Organizes ideas sequentially and logically; uses appropriate transitions to clarify sequence; has appropriate pacing • **Language** Maintains a good balance between formal and informal language and style; uses precise words; has a few errors in conventions
4	• **Development** Has a sufficient introduction; offers adequate dialogue and description; has an adequate concluding section • **Organization** Logically organizes ideas; uses transitions to convey sequence; has adequate pacing • **Language** Mostly maintains a balance between formal and informal language; lacks an interesting style; needs more descriptive details and sensory language; has a few distracting errors in conventions
3	• **Development** Has an unmemorable introduction; lacks sufficient dialogue and description; has an uninspired ending • **Organization** Reflects flaws in sequence; needs more transitions; has slow pacing • **Language** Frequently uses informal language and has a weak style; uses some vague words; has some significant errors in conventions
2	• **Development** Has a weak and uninteresting introduction; has ineffective dialogue and description; has a weak concluding section • **Organization** Has sequencing flaws; lacks transitions; has weak pacing • **Language** Uses informal and easily misunderstood language; lacks style; has many distracting errors in conventions

Preparing for Timed Writing

COMMON CORE

W 10 Write routinely over shorter time frames for a range of tasks, purposes, and audiences.

1. ANALYZE THE TASK   5 MIN

Read the task carefully. Then read it again, underlining the words that tell the type of writing, the topic, the audience, and the purpose.

WRITING TASK *Type of writing*   *Audience*   *Topic*

Write a <u>personal narrative</u> for your <u>classmates</u> based on a <u>successful experience in your life.</u> Include relevant details to <u>help your readers understand what the experience was like.</u> Conclude your narrative by explaining why the event was important to you. *Purpose*

2. PLAN YOUR RESPONSE   10 MIN

To choose your topic, think of things you have accomplished that were difficult or that made you feel happy or proud. When you have chosen your topic, consider what your audience will find interesting about it. Use a chart to list details about your actions, thoughts, and feelings. Also note why the experience was important to you.

Topic	Details	Why It's Important

3. RESPOND TO THE TASK   20 MIN

Keep these points in mind as you draft your narrative:
- In the introduction, grab your readers' attention and identify your topic. Include any necessary background information.
- In the body, include relevant details and dialogue. Use pacing to build some suspense, and remember to include your personal thoughts and feelings.
- In the concluding section, explain why the experience was important to you.

4. IMPROVE YOUR RESPONSE   5–10 MIN

Revising Check your draft against the prompt. Did you focus on a single experience? Did you include details that will help your audience connect to your experience? Did you explain the importance of the experience?
Proofreading Neatly correct any errors in grammar, spelling, and mechanics.
Checking Your Final Copy Before you turn in your essay, read it one more time to catch any errors you may have missed.

Producing a Documentary

A **documentary** is a nonfiction movie that gives viewers information about people and events. Documentary filmmakers collect material in a variety of media and organize it into a clear presentation. A good documentary uses a logical structure to tell an interesting story. In this workshop, you will learn how to produce a documentary based on your personal narrative.

 Complete the workshop activities in your **Reader/Writer Notebook.**

PRODUCE WITH A PURPOSE	COMMON CORE TRAITS
TASK Create a **documentary** that uses video, photographs, music, and narration to present information from a personal narrative to viewers.	**A SUCCESSFUL DOCUMENTARY . . .** • results from preparation and planning • integrates several sources of information and media • conveys a coherent story

Planning Your Documentary

COMMON CORE

RL 7 Compare and contrast the experience of reading a story to viewing a video version of the text. **SL 5** Include multimedia components and visual displays to clarify information. **W 6** Use technology to produce and publish writing.

Your documentary should run for about five minutes. Make sure that it presents the important characters and events of your narrative. Consider how watching a documentary differs from reading a narrative. Think of ways to illustrate the ideas and emotions that you want to express. Follow the guidelines below to plan your documentary.

- **Write a Script** Identify the parts of your narrative that best express its key events and central conflict. For a story about moving to a new city, for example, scenes that contrast your old and new neighborhoods can quickly establish context and conflict. Then choose the best ways to present your information. Will your narrator adopt a first- or third-person point of view? Will characters reenact scenes or dialogue? Will you combine live action with still images?

- **Collect Media** Research and gather all available images, sounds, and video clips related to your topic. Choose only those that help convey information and advance your plot. Locate sound effects that can add interest and meaning to still photos. Then identify the scenes, such as interviews, reenactments, or location shots that you will need to film.

- **Create a Storyboard** A storyboard shows each scene in the documentary through a series of drawings, like a comic strip. Creating a storyboard helps you decide how to present each scene. Try to vary your scenes between still and moving images.

Media Tools
THINK central

Go to **thinkcentral.com.**
KEYWORD: HML6N–882

Producing Your Documentary

Follow your script and storyboard to record and assemble the different parts of your documentary. Most documentaries contain three basic types of material: narration, footage, and interviews.

RECORDING NARRATION

Use narration to present important information and to connect scenes. A narrator can also give voice to a character by reading from a document that the character has written. Make sure that the narrator speaks slowly and clearly.

USING FOOTAGE

Your footage includes all the recorded audio and visual material in your documentary. Footage can run by itself, or you can use it to illustrate voice-over narration and interviews. Be sure to get permission for any footage you use.

RECORDING INTERVIEWS

Film any available participants, witnesses, or subject experts. For each interview, prepare a list of specific questions, each related to a scene in your storyboard. The answers to your questions should help advance the plot.

As you film your documentary:

- stick to your script and storyboard
- help your narrator and cast members rehearse their lines
- re-shoot scenes until you get them right
- create well-lit, visually interesting sets for your interviews
- ask anyone you interview to answer questions in complete sentences. For example, the answer to "When did you meet Ben?" should be "I met Ben in 2009," not "In 2009."

As you edit your documentary:

- vary the pace of your edits to reflect the mood. Short, quick cuts can emphasize action or conflict. Long clips help viewers focus on ideas.
- delete any scenes or parts of scenes that don't add information or interest
- dd music to establish tone. Think about music you've heard in movies during sad, happy, and scary moments. Music helps viewers understand what happens on screen.

 YOUR TURN Play a "rough cut" of your documentary for a few friends. Ask for feedback. Did they enjoy the documentary? Was it interesting? If not, ask them to identify parts that need improvement. Try to incorporate their suggestions into your final edit.

Assessment Practice

DIRECTIONS Read this selection and answer the questions that follow.

In 1962, the astronaut John Glenn became the first American to orbit the earth. In 1998, at age 77, he again joined the crew of a space shuttle, this time as the oldest person ever to travel in space.

from John Glenn: A Memoir
by John Glenn with Nick Taylor

1   I especially enjoyed being with my father, whom most people called Herschel, while I grew up being called Bud. He could turn very serious at times, . . . but most of the time he was lighthearted. He joked a lot and made me laugh. Part of the fun of being with him was that he was curious. He always wanted to learn about new things, and he would go out of his way to investigate them. Although the Glenn Plumbing Company grew into a successful business of which he was very proud, I think he recognized the limitations of his education. He wanted to give me the curiosity and sense of unbounded possibility that could come from learning.

2   The summer I turned eight, Dad took me along to Cambridge one day when he went to check on a plumbing job. It was the time of year when wildflowers bloomed on the roadsides and in the farm fields where cattle grazed. He checked on the job, and as we drove past a grass-field airport outside of town, he spotted a plane there and we stopped.

3   We got out of the car to look. A man had an old open-cockpit biplane—it was a WACO, but I didn't know that then—and he was taking people up. He was a Steve Canyon-type pilot, a helmet-and-goggles sort of guy right out of the comics. We were leaning against the car and watching him, and my dad said, "You want to go up, Bud?"

4   I almost died. Flying was a great adventure. Everybody knew about Charles Lindbergh's transatlantic flight two years before. When Lindy came home, the papers had chronicled his every move. Dad had read that he would be flying by Cambridge and New Concord on his way to Columbus, and soon after that we were on a farm outside of town when a silver plane flying west passed high overhead. I'd always imagined it was him. I probably was scared at the idea of going up, but there wasn't any doubt about it—I wanted to do it. I thought it would be the greatest thing that ever happened. "You mean it?" I said.

5   "I sure do," Dad replied. "In fact, if you don't want to do it, I'm going anyway. So you better come unless you want to sit down here and watch."

6   We walked over to the plane. It was bigger than I had thought, with two cockpits, one in front of the other. Dad handed the guy some money. He climbed into the backseat, and the pilot helped me up after him. Dad was big, but the seat was wide enough for the two of us, and one strap fit across us both. I could barely see out. The pilot got in front and revved the engine. We bounced down that grass strip and then we were in the air. The plane banked, and I could look straight down. We flew around Cambridge a couple of times. Dad kept trying to point things out to me, but I couldn't catch his words over the sound of the engine and the rushing air. We turned back and landed.

7   When I got out of the plane I was elated. I couldn't get the view from the air out of my mind, and the feeling of being suspended without falling. We had gone so high, and everything on the ground looked so small, like the buildings and trees in a toy train set you'd see in a store window.

8   As we drove home, Dad asked me if I'd liked the flight. I told him that I had. He said he had, too. He said he'd wanted to see what flying was like ever since he had been in France in World War I and had seen biplanes dogfighting over the lines. I realized later that it wasn't simply fun for him. Flying was progressive, just the kind of thing he would have wanted to experience so he could speak with authority about what it felt like and, just as likely, what it meant. His eagerness to experiment was one of the most important lessons of my youth.

Reading Comprehension

Use *John Glenn: A Memoir* to answer questions 1–14.

1. Which sentence tells you that the selection is an autobiography?

   A. *Flying was a great adventure.* (paragraph 4)

   B. *Everybody knew about Charles Lindbergh's transatlantic flight two years before.* (paragraph 4)

   C. *The pilot got in front and revved the engine.* (paragraph 6)

   D. *I realized later that it wasn't simply fun for him.* (paragraph 8)

2. Which detail in this excerpt might not have been included in a biography?

   A. John Glenn's childhood nickname

   B. The name of Herschel Glenn's business

   C. Information about Charles Lindbergh

   D. The description of how John Glenn felt after his first plane ride

3. Herschel Glenn's reply in paragraph 5 supports the idea that he —

   A. had a spirit of adventure

   B. was a serious person

   C. knew a lot about flying

   D. owned a successful business

4. Which phrases show the order of events?

   A. at times; where cattle grazed; around Cambridge

   B. the summer I turned eight; two years before; when I got out of the airplane

   C. out of his way; past a grass-field airport; one in front of the other

   D. his every move; my youth; got in front

5. Which quotation expresses the main idea of the excerpt?

   A. *I especially enjoyed being with my father, whom most people called Herschel, while I grew up being called Bud.* (paragraph 1)

   B. *I couldn't get the view from the air out of my mind, and the feeling of being suspended without falling.* (paragraph 7)

   C. *As we drove home, Dad asked me if I'd liked the flight. I told him that I had.* (paragraph 8)

   D. *His eagerness to experiment was one of the most important lessons of my youth.* (paragraph 8)

6. You can tell this excerpt is from a memoir rather than a biography because —

   A. it is written from a first-person point of view

   B. it includes quotations from people who knew John Glenn

   C. it explains how events shaped John Glenn's life

   D. it talks about other people who were alive at the time

7. The description of the pilot in paragaph 3 reminds the reader that —

   A. children often confuse fantasy and reality

   B. early pilots were not concerned about safety

   C. John Glenn liked to read when he was young

   D. this memory is told from a child's point of view

8. Which sentence reveals John Glenn's personal feelings?

   A. *He could turn very serious at times, … but most of the time he was lighthearted.* (paragraph 1)

   B. *He joked a lot and made me laugh.* (paragraph 1)

   C. *It was the time of year when wildflowers bloomed on the roadsides and in the farm fields where cattle grazed.* (paragraph 2)

   D. *I probably was scared at the idea of going up, but there wasn't any doubt about it—I wanted to do it.* (paragraph 4)

9. In this selection, the statement "When Lindy came home, the papers had chronicled his every move" (paragraph 4) supports the idea that —

   A. airplanes made transatlantic travel possible

   B. people were eager to learn about flying

   C. news coverage in the past was better than it is today

   D. World War II dogfighters made flying seem easy

10. Which event would come first in a timeline of John Glenn's life?

   A. John Glenn takes his first plane ride.

   B. Herschel Glenn stops his car near a biplane outside of town.

   C. John Glenn and his father drive to Cambridge.

   D. Charles Lindbergh flies across the Atlantic Ocean.

11. John Glenn's father first wondered what flying was like when he saw —

   A. biplanes dogfighting during WWI

   B. an airplane on a grass-field airport near town

   C. a newspaper article about Charles Lindbergh

   D. a silver plane flying overhead

12. If this excerpt were taken from a biography instead of an autobiography, it would be —

   A. told from the first-person point of view

   B. written by someone else

   C. based on details from Glenn's memories

   D. published during Glenn's lifetime

SHORT CONSTRUCTED RESPONSE
Write two or three sentences to answer this question.

13. Find two details to support the idea that Glenn's father was curious about flying.

Write a paragraph to answer this question.

14. Rewrite paragraph 2 as if it were from a biography instead of an autobiography.

GO ON ➡

Vocabulary

> Use context clues and your knowledge of word origins to answer the following questions.

1. The Latin word *vestigare* means "to track." In paragraph 1, what does the word *investigate* mean?

   "He always wanted to learn new things, and he would go out of his way to <u>investigate</u> them."

   A. To grab hold
   B. To give money to
   C. To examine in detail
   D. To turn upside down

2. The Latin word *līmes* means "border." In paragraph 1, what does the word *limitations* mean?

   "… I think he recognized the <u>limitations</u> of his education."

   A. Details
   B. Outlines
   C. Requirements
   D. Shortcomings

3. The Latin prefix *bi-* means "two." In paragraph 3, what does the word *biplane* mean?

   "A man had an old open-cockpit <u>biplane</u>.…"

   A. Extra-wide seats
   B. Large propellers
   C. A powerful engine
   D. A double pair of wings

4. The Greek word *khronos* means "time." In paragraph 4, what does the word *chronicled* mean?

   "When Lindy came home, the papers had <u>chronicled</u> his every move."

   A. Refused to report on
   B. Made a historical record of
   C. Questioned the reasons for
   D. Attached great importance to

5. The Latin word *pendere* means "to hang." In paragraph 7, what does the word *suspended* mean?

   "I couldn't get the view from the air out of my mind, and the feeling of being <u>suspended</u> without falling."

   A. Attached to the ground with bolts
   B. Removed from a position or team
   C. Interrupted for a period of time
   D. Held in the air without support

6. The Latin prefix *pro-* means "forward." In paragraph 8, what does the word *progressive* mean?

   "Flying was <u>progressive</u>, just the kind of thing he would have wanted to experience so he could speak with authority about what it felt like.…"

   A. Modern
   B. Changeable
   C. Popular
   D. Risky

Revising and Editing

DIRECTIONS Read this passage and answer the questions that follow.

(1) John herschel glenn was born in 1921. (2) His parents raised him and his sister jean in a small town in ohio. (3) Throughout his lifetime, Glenn has held several positions Marine pilot, astronaut, businessman, and politician. (4) In february 1962, while flying aboard the spacecraft friendship 7, he became the first american to orbit the earth. (5) He was elected and re-elected to the U.S. Senate in the following years 1976, 1980, 1986, and 1992. (6) In Congress he devoted much of his time to three causes creating a research station in space, funding scientific education, and limiting the development of nuclear weapons. (7) In 1998, at the age of 77, mr. Glenn returned to space aboard the shuttle discovery.

1. Choose the BEST way to capitalize the name in sentence 1.
   A. john Herschel Glenn
   B. John Herschel Glenn
   C. John herschel Glenn
   D. john herschel Glenn

2. Which nouns should be capitalized in sentence 2?
   A. parents, sister   C. sister, jean
   B. parents, ohio   D. jean, ohio

3. In sentence 3, a colon should be placed after the word —
   A. has   C. held
   B. Throughout   D. positions

4. Which nouns should be capitalized in sentence 4?
   A. february, spacecraft
   B. february, friendship, american
   C. spacecraft, friendship, american
   D. february, american

5. In sentence 5, a colon should be placed after the word —
   A. years
   B. in
   C. re-elected
   D. to

6. In sentence 6, a colon should be placed after the word —
   A. time
   B. devoted
   C. causes
   D. to

7. Which nouns should be capitalized in sentence 7?
   A. mr., shuttle
   B. space, shuttle
   C. mr., discovery
   D. space, discovery

STOP

Ideas for Independent Reading

Which questions from Unit 7 made an impression on you?
Continue exploring with these books.

COMMON CORE

RL 10 Read and comprehend literature. **RI 10** Read and comprehend literary nonfiction.

Why attempt the impossible?

The Man Who Went to the Far Side of the Moon
by Bea Uusma Schyffert

While Neil Armstrong and Buzz Aldrin walked on the moon, Michael Collins was alone in the team's spacecraft, separated from everyone he knew by the vast darkness of space.

Shipwreck at the Bottom of the World
by Jennifer Armstrong

Sir Ernest Shackleton sails from England to Antarctica in 1914. Almost two years later, his crew is stranded hundreds of miles from any port. Will Shackleton be able to save them all?

With Courage and Cloth
by Ann Bausum

Before 1920, most Americans thought the idea of a woman voting was ridiculous. It had taken over 70 years for activists like Alice Paul to convince the president and other lawmakers to give women the right to vote.

How do you unlock a mystery?

At Her Majesty's Request
by Walter Dean Myers

Sarah was born an African princess. After her village is destroyed, a British commander saves Sarah. He brings her to England as a gift for the queen. What will life be like for the rescued orphan?

Hana's Suitcase
by Karen Levine

When children visiting a Holocaust museum in Tokyo ask questions about a suitcase, Fumiko decides to find some answers. Two years later, she knows the suitcase belonged to a little girl—and she has found the girl's brother.

The Longitude Prize
by Joan Dash

In the 1700s, sailors die every year because they lose their way at sea. John Harrison, a carpenter and clockmaker, knows he can save them with his idea. He just has to get the Royal Society to believe that it will work.

How would you like to be remembered?

Don't Hold Me Back
by Winfred Rembert

He didn't lead marches, but Winfred Rembert was part of the Civil Rights Movement. He and his parents were farm workers and often treated like slaves. But Rembert's paintings record stories of courage and hope.

Girls Think of Everything
by Catherine Thimmesh

Mary Anderson invented the windshield wiper after a terrifying streetcar ride. Grace Hopper created the first computer language that used English. Female inventors are responsible for many of the things we use every day.

The Lost Garden
by Laurence Yep

As a boy in 1950s San Francisco, Laurence Yep didn't fit in. He felt American, but the other kids said he wasn't. He hated going to Chinatown because he couldn't speak Chinese. Writing helped him find his place.

Get Novel Wise **THINK** central

Go to **thinkcentral.com**.
KEYWORD: HML6-890

UNIT 8

Know the Facts

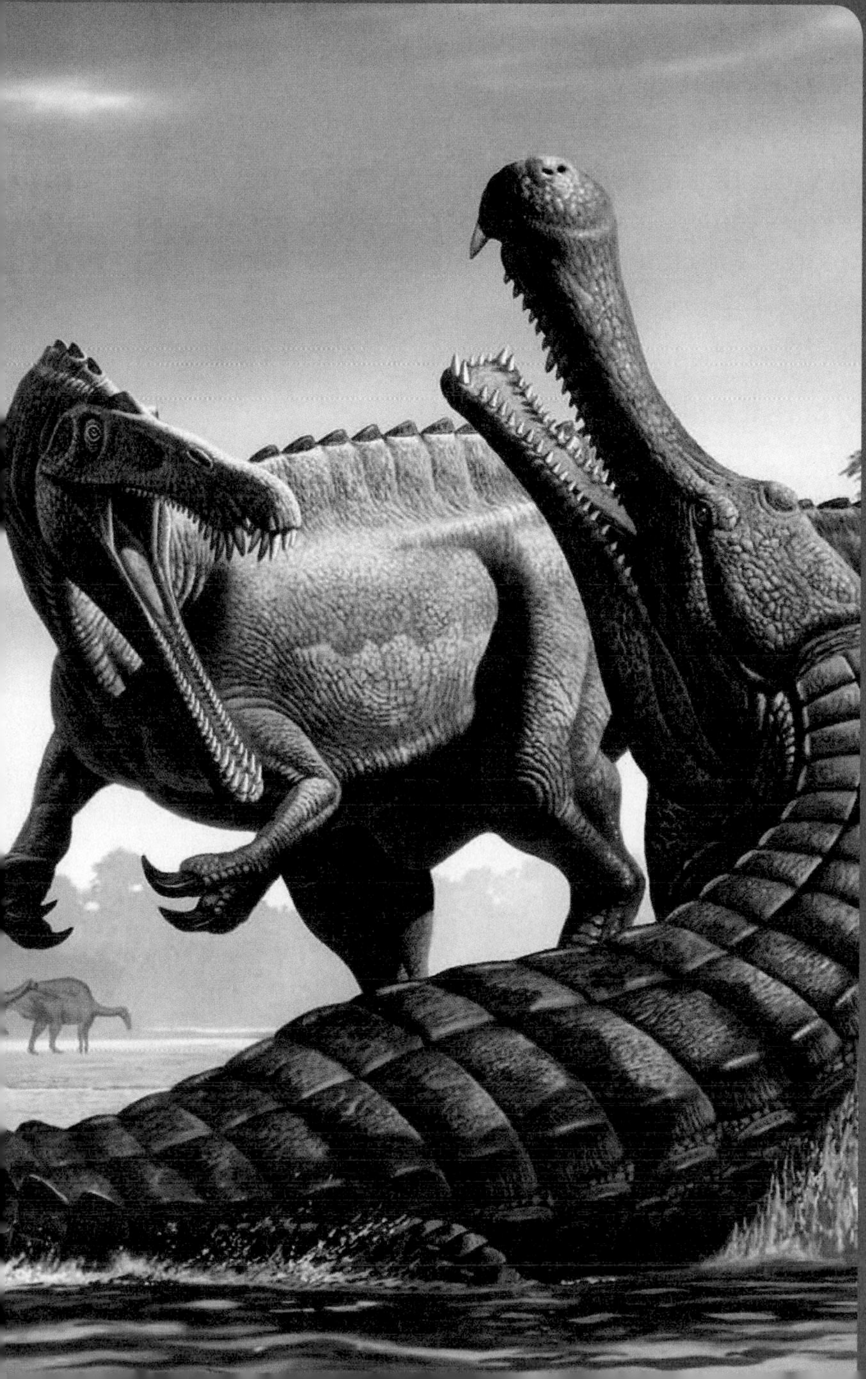

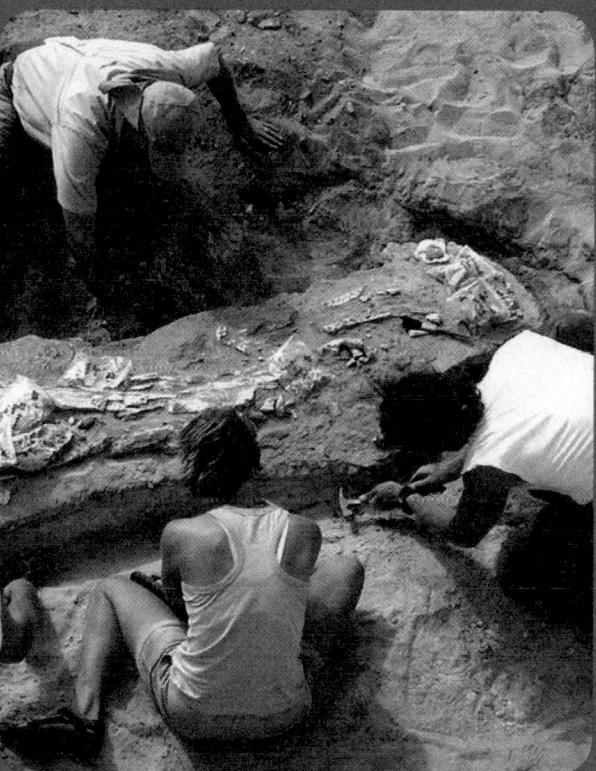

INFORMATION, ARGUMENT, AND PERSUASION

- In Nonfiction
- In Media

Can **INFORMATION** be trusted?

Newspapers, the Internet, television commercials—all of these sources and more are constantly bombarding you with information. But not all the information you receive is as reliable as a fingerprint or as trustworthy as an X-ray. How do you know when to trust what you are reading and hearing?

ACTIVITY Get together with a small group. Take turns naming sources that you use to get information. Then discuss whether you can trust each source that is mentioned. Consider the following questions:

• Who created the source? Is that person or group reliable?

• How current is the information?

• Why is the information being provided?

Find It Online! **THINK** central

Go to <u>thinkcentral.com</u> for the interactive version of this unit.

892

Preview Unit Goals

TEXT ANALYSIS	• Determine a central idea and how it is conveyed through particular details; provide a summary of the text
	• Analyze how a sentence, paragraph, or section fits into the overall structure and contributes to the development of ideas
	• Trace and evaluate the argument and specific claims in a text
	• Determine the meaning of words and phrases as they are used in a text, including connotative meanings
WRITING AND LANGUAGE	• Write a persuasive essay
	• Capitalize and punctuate titles correctly
SPEAKING AND LISTENING	• Deliver a persuasive speech
VOCABULARY	• Use Greek or Latin roots as clues to the meaning of a word
	• Use context as a clue to the meaning of a word or phrase
ACADEMIC VOCABULARY	• adequacy • concept • structural
	• authority • purpose
MEDIA AND VIEWING	• Explain messages conveyed in news reports
	• Identify and analyze persuasive techniques in advertising

Media Smart DVD-ROM

Messages in Media

Analyze the messages conveyed in news reports and the persuasive techniques used in advertisements.
Pages 932 and 984

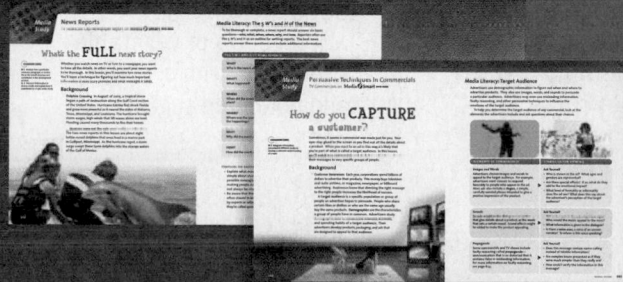

Reading for Information

People are always in search of information. With all the newspapers, magazines, and Web sites out there, how do you find the information you need? In this workshop, you'll learn how to read texts that explain and inform.

Part 1: Organizational Patterns

COMMON CORE

Included in this workshop:
RI 2 Determine a central idea and how it is conveyed through particular details; provide a summary of the text.
RI 5 Analyze how a particular sentence, paragraph, or section fits into the overall structure and contributes to the development of ideas. **RI 7** Integrate information presented in different media or formats.

Expository texts are texts that explain. When expository texts are well-written, they can clarify an issue, process, or situation. To present information in a clear and logical way, authors of expository texts use **organizational patterns,** or text structures, to develop their main ideas and express their viewpoints. For example, an author who uses a **problem-and-solution** organizational pattern states a problem and then provides a successful solution to the problem. The author may also reveal his or her feelings about the problem and its solution. Notice how a problem-and-solution organizational pattern develops the main idea of the following article.

❶ The **title** tells you the topic of the article.

❷ The **main idea** is presented as a problem and a solution.

❸ The problem-solution **organizational pattern** develops the article's main idea with examples.

❹ A **sidebar** provides more information.

Food Ad Tricks

❶

Lights! Camera! Glue?
These foods have starring roles in TV commercials. But they won't behave on the set! With a few clever tricks, advertisers can make them look mouth-watering and yummy. ❷

Ice Cream
• *Problem:* Melts under the hot lights of the movie set.
• *Solution:* Get a stand in! Mix a scoop of vegetable shortening with corn syrup and powdered sugar.

Hot Chocolate
• *Problem:* Refuses to stay bubbling hot on the set.
• *Solution:* Squirt in some dishwashing liquid.

❸ Is this hot chocolate bubbling hot or filled with soap suds? Advertisers hope you can't tell the difference.

Can They Do That? ❹
Food ad tricks are not considered false advertising—as long as the food they're actually selling you is real.

Cereal
• *Problem:* Gets mushy and soggy-looking in a bowl of milk.
• *Solution:* Pour white glue into the cereal.

Read the expository text below. What situation does the writer want to explain to readers? How do organizational patterns develop the author's important ideas?

Swimmers *Beware:*
Jellyfish Are Everywhere!

Magazine article by **Susan Jaques**

What Are Jellyfish?

Jellyfish are not fish at all. They are invertebrates, relatives of corals and sea anemones
5   (uh-NEH-muh-neez). A jelly has no head, brain, heart, eyes, or ears. It has no bones, either. . . .

To capture prey for food, jellies have a net of tentacles
10   that contain poisonous, stinging cells. When the tentacles brush against prey (or, say, a person's leg), thousands of tiny stinging cells explode, launching barbed
15   stingers and poison into the victim.

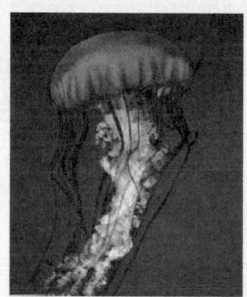

Feared by many beachgoers, bell-shaped **sea nettles** are known for their painful stings.

Where Danger Lurks

All jellies sting, but not all jellies have poison that hurts
20   humans. Of the 2,000 species of jellyfish, only about 70 seriously harm or occasionally kill people.

Listed here are the more dangerous jellies and where you
25   can find—or avoid—them.

- *Lion's mane*—Atlantic Ocean from above the Arctic Circle to Florida; Gulf of Mexico; Pacific Ocean from Alaska to southern
30   California
- *Portuguese man-of-war*— Gulf of Mexico; Caribbean Sea near the Bahamas; West Indies
- *Sea nettle*—Chesapeake Bay;
35   Pacific Ocean from Alaska to southern California; Atlantic Ocean from Massachusetts to Florida; Gulf of Mexico

DON'T GET STUNG

1. Take note of jellyfish warning signs posted on the beach.

2. Be careful around jellies washed up on the sand. Some still sting if their tentacles are wet.

3. If you are stung, wash the wound with vinegar or rubbing alcohol.

Close Read

1. Recall that expository texts are texts that explain. What does the writer explain in lines 1–5?

2. Reread the [boxed] text. The **cause-and-effect organizational pattern** shows how one event brings about, or causes, another. Why is this organizational pattern appropriate for explaining how jellyfish use their tentacles?

3. What problem does the section labeled "Don't Get Stung" address?

4. Lists are often used to sort in an organizational pattern called **classification**. What information about different kinds of jellyfish does the list in lines 26–38 provide?

Part 2: Summarizing Informational Texts

Writers use organizational patterns in the hopes of conveying their ideas clearly. However, it is up to you to identify and summarize the most important ideas of a text.

SUMMARIZING

You can create a summary of any piece of writing. When you **summarize** a text, you restate the author's main ideas and details in your own words. Creating summaries of informational texts is especially useful if you are doing research from a number of sources because your summaries will help you recognize the ways in which one source differs from another. Try to maintain the meaning and logical order of main ideas and details when you summarize across texts. It will help you evaluate how each source covers similar content. Follow these tips when you are summarizing a text.

- A summary is much shorter than the original text and includes only the most important points. In nonfiction, these are the **main ideas** and **key supporting details.**

- Stop at the end of each paragraph to restate in a sentence what the author wrote. This will help you find the main ideas and details.

- Do not include your own opinions (your personal beliefs or feelings) in a summary. A summary should only include information from the text.

Read the summary below and answer the questions. Notice what information the writer includes and what the writer leaves out.

MODEL: SUMMARY

A Summary of "Swimmers Beware: Jellyfish Are Everywhere!"

In "Swimmers Beware: Jellyfish Are Everywhere!" Susan Jaques provides an overview of how to avoid being stung by a jellyfish. The
5 writer explains how jellyfish use their tentacles to sting their victims. However, while all jellyfish sting, not all stings cause humans pain. The writer gives a list of tips to avoid being stung. She also explains how to wash the wound if you are stung. She goes on to list places where especially dangerous jellyfish, such as the lion's mane, the
10 Portuguese man-of-war, and the sea nettle, are found, and suggests being careful when you go to these places. However, I don't think the possibility of being stung is a good reason to stay away from the Gulf of Mexico.

Close Read

1. Where do you find the main idea of the article?

2. Reread the sentence in line 7. Should this detail be included in the summary? How does this detail support the main idea?

3. Reread the boxed text. Why should this sentence not be included in a good summary?

Part 3: Analyze the Text

Read this Web article, using what you've learned in this workshop to help you understand the information. The **Close Read** questions will help you determine the most important ideas.

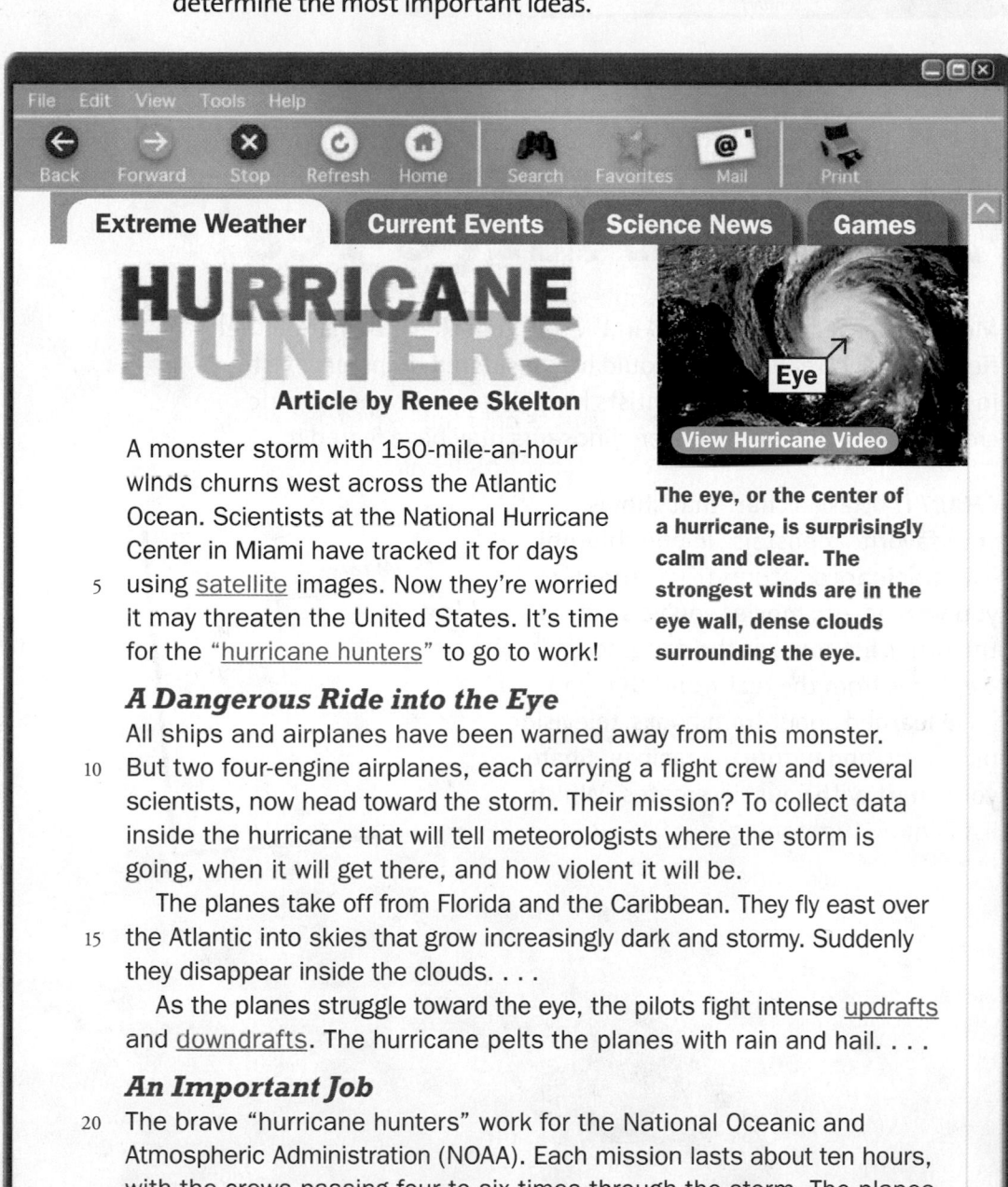

File | Edit | View | Tools | Help

Back Forward Stop Refresh Home   Search Favorites Mail   Print

Extreme Weather | Current Events | Science News | Games

HURRICANE HUNTERS
Article by Renee Skelton

A monster storm with 150-mile-an-hour winds churns west across the Atlantic Ocean. Scientists at the National Hurricane Center in Miami have tracked it for days
5 using <u>satellite</u> images. Now they're worried it may threaten the United States. It's time for the "<u>hurricane hunters</u>" to go to work!

Eye

View Hurricane Video

The eye, or the center of a hurricane, is surprisingly calm and clear. The strongest winds are in the eye wall, dense clouds surrounding the eye.

A Dangerous Ride into the Eye
All ships and airplanes have been warned away from this monster.
10 But two four-engine airplanes, each carrying a flight crew and several scientists, now head toward the storm. Their mission? To collect data inside the hurricane that will tell meteorologists where the storm is going, when it will get there, and how violent it will be.
       The planes take off from Florida and the Caribbean. They fly east over
15 the Atlantic into skies that grow increasingly dark and stormy. Suddenly they disappear inside the clouds. . . .
       As the planes struggle toward the eye, the pilots fight intense <u>updrafts</u> and <u>downdrafts</u>. The hurricane pelts the planes with rain and hail. . . .

An Important Job
20 The brave "hurricane hunters" work for the National Oceanic and Atmospheric Administration (NOAA). Each mission lasts about ten hours, with the crews passing four to six times through the storm. The planes carry sophisticated computers and weather instruments that determine characteristics such as temperature, air pressure, wind speed, and wind
25 direction inside the hurricane. . . .
       By mission's end, NOAA can warn everyone in the hurricane's path. "We love flying into hurricanes," says Philip Kenul, a pilot. "What we do helps a lot of people."

Internet

Close Read

1. Where is the eye of a hurricane located? Explain whether you would include this detail in a summary of the article.

2. Reread lines 8–18. What is the main idea of this section? Find at least two details in these lines that support this idea.

3. Which of the supporting details from lines 8–18 would you include in a summary of the article? Which details would you omit?

4. Reread lines 19–28, noting the subheading and the three boxed details. What is the main idea of this section?

SuperCroc

 HISTORY Video link at **thinkcentral.com**

Magazine Article by Peter Winkler

VIDEO TRAILER THINK central KEYWORD: HML6-898

Are MONSTERS real?

COMMON CORE

RI 2 Determine a central idea of a text and how it is conveyed through particular details; provide a summary of the text distinct from personal opinions or judgments. **RI 7** Integrate information presented in different media or formats to develop a coherent understanding of a topic. **L 4a** Use context as a clue to the meaning of a word or phrase.

Monsters have always existed in the world of the imagination. Yet fierce, deadly creatures that could be considered monsters exist in reality as well. In fact, scientists have discovered a prehistoric creature so terrifying that even dinosaurs may have feared it.

CHART IT Make a chart that shows your favorite monsters. In one column, list imaginary creatures from stories you've read and movies you've seen. In the other, list some of the dangerous creatures from the real world that you have learned about from books, television programs, and nature magazines. Share your chart with your classmates. Which list is more frightening?

Imaginary	Real
Godzilla	Komodo dragon

TEXT ANALYSIS: TEXT FEATURES

Text features are design elements that present information visually. They highlight key ideas and provide additional information. Some common text features are

- **subheadings,** or section titles, which hint at the main idea or topic of the section that follows
- **graphic aids,** such as maps, photographs, or timelines
- **captions,** which provide information about a graphic aid

As you read "SuperCroc," identify the text features it contains, and notice the information they present.

READING STRATEGY: SUMMARIZE

When you **summarize,** you use your own words to restate the main ideas and significant supporting details of a spoken or written work. A summary is generally no more than one-third the length of the original work and includes just the facts—not your personal opinions.

As you read "SuperCroc," use a chart like the one shown to record the most important information from each section of the article. You will use this information later when you write your summary.

Section	Key Information
Introduction	scientists studying dinosaur fossils in Niger
What Makes This Croc So Super?	

VOCABULARY IN CONTEXT

Peter Winkler uses the boldfaced words to help tell about the discovery of a real-life monster from the past. To see how many words you know, substitute a different word or phrase for each of the boldfaced words.

1. Paul Sereno is a dinosaur **expert.**
2. Dinosaurs have been **extinct** for millions of years.
3. His team found more than just one **fossil.**
4. This **species** of crocodile was previously unknown.
5. The **predator** could have eaten anything it wanted.

 Complete the activities in your **Reader/Writer Notebook.**

Meet the Author

Peter Winkler
born 1963

Adventure School
Peter Winkler is a freelance writer from Long Island, New York. He once realized he was in over his head—literally—when he was unable to climb back into an overturned kayak in the cold waters of the Pacific Ocean. He ended up having to swim to shore. Winkler's assignment had been to cover the Presidio Adventure Racing Academy. He realized later that although the experience was frightening, "somehow I'd still learned the key lesson of adventure school: Stretch yourself, and life will take shapes you never imagined."

National Geographic Writer
Peter Winkler has been writing for the National Geographic Society since 1987. His writings include Web features, science articles for young people, television scripts, educational materials, and three books. He has also written about movies for CineFan, an online movie database.

Author Online
Go to **thinkcentral.com.** KEYWORD: HML6-899

THINK central

SUPERCROC

PETER WINKLER

O ut of Africa comes a giant reptile that lived with dinosaurs—
and ate them.

"We're stuck again!" Scientist Paul Sereno and his team said those
words many times as they drove into a rugged part of Africa. Desert
sand kept stopping their vehicles.
It took 10 hours to go just 87 miles.

That long crawl ended at Gadoufaoua,[1]
a dry region in the country of Niger.[2]
To most eyes, the place looked empty.
10 There was sand. There was wind. There
was nothing else. Or so it seemed.

But Sereno saw much more. He saw
a chance to find dinosaurs. Sereno, a
paleontologist, knew that the region
contains countless **fossils** from ancient
dinosaurs. Gadoufaoua is one of

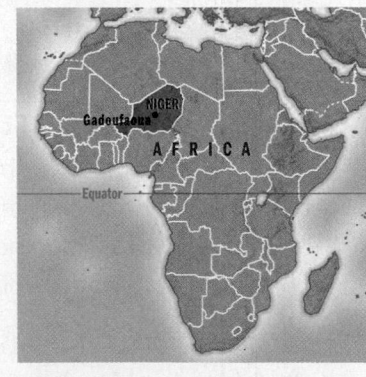

The country of Niger is in West
Africa. Ⓐ

---

1. **Gadoufaoua** (gə-dōō´fä´wŏh).

2. **Niger** (nī´jər).

fossil (fŏs´əl) *n*. the
remains of a living thing,
preserved in soil or rock

Ⓐ **TEXT FEATURES**
Identify three things
this map tells you about
Gadoufaoua. What
information does the
map present that the
text does not?

Africa's richest sources of dino fossils.

Sereno found some fossils there in 1997. He came back in 2000 to seek more. The team spent four months in the desert. Crew members woke at 6:00 each morning, then explored the sand dunes for about 12 hours. They worked even when the temperature hit 125°F.

And they found fossils. By the end of the expedition, Sereno and his team had collected 20 tons of bones. Most of the fossils came from dinosaurs, including types never seen before. Others came from turtles, fish, and crocodiles.

One of those crocodiles was *Sarcosuchus imperator*,[3] a name that means "flesh crocodile emperor." Sereno's team nicknamed it "SuperCroc."

Using SuperCroc's jaw bone and their own bodies, Sereno (fourth from front) and his team demonstrate SuperCroc's estimated length. **B**

What Makes This Croc So Super? **C**

In a word, size. The skull alone was six feet long. Sereno says it's "about the biggest I've ever seen."

Naturally, Sereno wondered how big SuperCroc was overall. The team found only part of its skeleton, so Sereno had to make an estimate. To do that, he looked at crocodiles that live today. He and other **experts** compared the animals' skull and body sizes.

Based on his research, Sereno concluded that an adult SuperCroc could grow to be 40 feet long and probably weighed as much as 10 tons. That's heavier than an African elephant.

Those measurements make SuperCroc one of the largest crocodiles ever to walk Earth. Today's biggest crocs grow to about 20 feet. **D**

---

3. *Sarcosuchus imperator* (sär′kō-sōō′kĭs ĭm-pîr′ā-tôr).

COMMON CORE RI 7

B TEXT FEATURES
Information that is related to the amount, number, or measurement of something is called **quantitative information.** For example, the fact that twelve inches equals one foot is quantitative information. Explain how the photo and its accompanying caption present quantitative information in a way that is easy to understand. In what ways is this visual presentation of SuperCroc's size more effective than simply providing the measurements in the text?

C TEXT FEATURES
Preview the article's subheadings. What do you think the article will tell you about SuperCroc?

expert (ĕk′spûrt′) *n.* one who is skilled in or knowledgeable about a particular thing

D SUMMARIZE
What is the main idea of this section of the article? What supporting details would you include in a summary of the article? Record this information in your chart.

Illustration of SuperCroc

A Different-Looking Beast

SuperCroc's long head is wider in front than in the middle. That shape is unique. No other croc—living or **extinct**—has a snout quite like it.

60 At the front of SuperCroc's head is a big hole. That's where the nose would be. That empty space may have given the ancient **predator** a keen sense of smell. Or perhaps it helped SuperCroc make noise to communicate with other members of its **species.**

SuperCroc wore serious armor. Huge plates of bone, called scutes, covered the animal's back. Hundreds of them lay just below the skin. A single scute from the back could be a foot long! **E**

When Did SuperCroc Live?

Estimating a fossil's age is a challenge. Sereno and his team looked
70 carefully at the group of fossils they had found. They compared the fossils to others whose ages the scientists did know. Based on those comparisons, Sereno believes SuperCroc lived about 110 million years ago.

Gadoufaoua looked a bit different in those days. What is now a desert was a land of
80 winding rivers. Plenty of trees grew along the banks. Huge fish swam the rivers, while various dinosaurs lived in the forests.

Five or more crocodile species lurked in the rivers. SuperCroc, Sereno says, was "the
90 monster of them all." **F**

Paul Sereno brushes sand from "sabercroc," another of several species of crocodile fossils found at Gadoufaoua.

extinct (ĭk-stĭngkt') *adj.* no longer existing

predator (prĕd'ə-tər) *n.* an animal that feeds on other animals

species (spē'shēz) *n.* a variety or type of something

E SUMMARIZE
Reread lines 55–67. What have you learned about SuperCroc's appearance? Add this information to your chart. What information would you include in a summary of the article?

F SUMMARIZE
Reread lines 68–90. Note what you learned in this section in your chart.

CROC ORIGINS G

Present
**CENOZOIC
ERA**

EXTINCTION

65 million years ago

144 Cretaceous

MESOZOIC ERA

Crocs

Pterosaurs

Dinosaurs

Birds

206 Jurassic

248 Triassic

**PERMIAN
PERIOD**

Archosaurs

—— Actual fossil record
•••• Estimate of the age of these groups

Sereno's team carves out the skulls of two giant crocs found facing each other. H

COMMON CORE RI 7

G TEXT FEATURES
Graphic aids like maps, charts, timelines, and graphs present factual, quantitative, or technical information that you have to interpret. A **timeline** shows events in chronological order (the order in which they happened). It may use symbols, lines, and numbers to explain or to display information. This timeline covers vast time periods that are expressed as eras. According to this timeline, what is one big difference between crocs and dinosaurs? What is the relationship between crocs and birds? Identify two other things you can interpret about crocodiles from the information presented in this timeline.

H TEXT FEATURES
What information does this photograph and its caption add to the article? What important factual information does the caption provide? What would you be able to interpret from the photograph if it did not have a caption?

I **SUMMARIZE**
Reread lines 91–101.
What does this section
tell you about SuperCroc?
What information would
you include in a summary
of this article?

What Did SuperCroc Eat?

"Anything it wanted," Sereno says. SuperCroc's narrow jaws held about 130 teeth. The teeth were short but incredibly strong. SuperCroc's mouth was "designed for grabbing prey[4]—fish, turtles, and dinosaurs that strayed too close."

SuperCroc likely spent most of its life in the river. Water hid the creature's huge body. Only its eyes and nostrils poked above the surface.

After spotting a meal, the giant hunter moved quietly toward the animal. Then—*wham!* That huge mouth locked onto its prey. 100 SuperCroc dragged the stunned creature into the water. There the animal drowned. Then it became food. **I**

A crowd gathers around the first life-sized model of SuperCroc at the Australian Museum in Sydney, Australia. **J**

J **TEXT FEATURES**
What does the caption
help you understand
about the photograph?

◆ **GRAMMAR IN
CONTEXT**
Look at the subheading
of this section. All of
the words in the title are
capitalized except *to*.
This is because, in titles,
prepositions of fewer
than five letters (such
as *to*, *in*, or *on*) are not
capitalized. Prepositions
such as *between* and
within are capitalized in
titles.

K **SUMMARIZE**
Why didn't SuperCroc
survive? Add this
information to your
chart.

What Happened to SuperCroc? ◆

The giant beast probably lived only a few million years. That raises a huge question: Why didn't SuperCroc survive?

Sereno suspects that SuperCrocs were fairly rare. After all, a monster that big needs plenty of room in which to live. Disease or disaster could have wiped out the species pretty quickly. But no one knows for sure what killed SuperCroc. That's a mystery for future scientists. **K**

---

4. **prey:** animals that become the food of another animal.

Comprehension

1. **Recall** Why are Paul Sereno and his team interested in Gadoufaoua?

2. **Recall** What length does Sereno estimate SuperCroc could have grown to be?

3. **Clarify** What did Sereno and his team find in Gadoufaoua other than crocodile fossils?

Text Analysis

● 4. **Summarize** Review the chart you completed as you read "SuperCroc." Clarify your understanding of the article by writing a brief summary. Remember that a summary should include only the facts, not your own personal opinions.

5. **Analyze Organizational Patterns** Notice the writer's use of the compare-and-contrast organizational pattern in lines 49–58. According to this passage, what are two ways that SuperCroc differs from crocodiles of today? Use a chart like the one shown to list your responses.

SuperCroc	Crocs Today

● 6. **Examine Text Features** Review the article's photographs and captions. What kind of information can photographs and captions provide that the regular text usually cannot?

7. **Draw Conclusions** Reread the section subtitled "When Did SuperCroc Live?" on page 902. Judging by the way Sereno and his team estimated the age of SuperCroc's fossils, what conclusions can you draw about how scientists determine the age of ancient creatures?

Extension and Challenge

8. **Inquiry and Research** Paleontologists like Paul Sereno don't just dig for fossils in the desert. Conduct some research to discover how a person becomes a paleontologist. Find out what a paleontologist might have to do in order to prepare for an expedition, and what happens after the expedition is finished. Present your findings to the class.

Are MONSTERS real?

Examine the monster chart you created before reading "SuperCroc," and look at the list of creatures you chose as the most frightening. How has reading "SuperCroc" affected your choice? Explain.

COMMON CORE

RI 2 Determine a central idea of a text and how it is conveyed through particular details; provide a summary of the text distinct from personal opinions or judgments. RI 7 Integrate information presented in different media or formats to develop a coherent understanding of a topic.

Vocabulary in Context

▲ VOCABULARY PRACTICE

Choose the letter of the word that is not related in meaning to the other words.

1. (a) skeleton, (b) fossil, (c) bone, (d) alive
2. (a) expert, (b) inexperienced, (c) authority, (d) knowledgeable
3. (a) kind, (b) species, (c) type, (d) desert
4. (a) extinct, (b) living, (c) active, (d) breathing
5. (a) slayer, (b) admirer, (c) predator, (d) killer

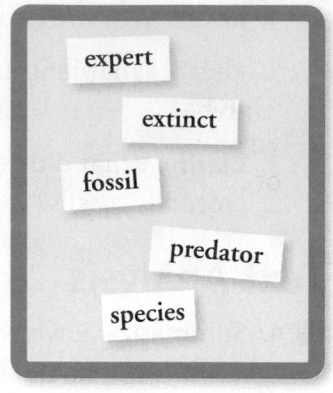

ACADEMIC VOCABULARY IN SPEAKING

- adequacy
- authority
- concept
- purpose
- structural

With a partner, decide if Sereno and his team have the necessary **authority** to declare SuperCroc "the monster of them all." Use at least two Academic Vocabulary words in your discussion.

VOCABULARY STRATEGY: WORD ORIGINS

Many common words in the English language have fascinating histories, going all the way back to ancient Greek and Latin words. You will find many words with Greek and Latin origins in scientific writing. For example, the vocabulary word *fossil* comes from the Latin word *fossilis,* which means "dug up." It makes sense, then, that a fossil is something that is uncovered, or dug up, from rock or earth.

Information about a word's origin can be found in most dictionaries. Understanding the **etymology,** or history of a word, can help you connect the word's meaning to something you already know. An example of an etymology is shown here:

> **argue** (är′gyo͞o) *v.* to disagree or quarrel [from Latin *argutare,* to babble, chatter]

PRACTICE Look up the etymology of each word in a dictionary. Write the word's origin, and explain how knowing the word's history can help you remember its meaning.

1. dinosaur
2. extinction
3. expedition
4. monster
5. predator
6. crocodile

⸛ COMMON CORE

L 4b Use Greek or Latin roots as clues to the meaning of a word.
L 6 Acquire and use accurately academic words.

Interactive Vocabulary **THINK** central

Go to **thinkcentral.com**.
KEYWORD: HML6-906

Language

◆ **GRAMMAR IN CONTEXT: Capitalize Correctly**

The **titles** of magazine articles, books, poems, and short stories must all be **capitalized** correctly. When writing a title, capitalize the first and last words, any important words, and all verbs. Do not capitalize conjunctions, articles, or prepositions of fewer than five letters.

> *Original:*   Finding Fossils In The Desert Dunes
>
> *Revised:*   Finding Fossils in the Desert Dunes

PRACTICE Rewrite each title by correcting any capitalization errors.

1. Monsters of The Past, The Present, and The Future
2. The day Godzilla met the gila monster
3. Silent Predator Of The African Waters
4. the scientist and the giant fossil

*For more help with capitalizing titles, see page R51 in the **Grammar Handbook.***

READING-WRITING CONNECTION

YOUR TURN Demonstrate your understanding of "SuperCroc" by responding to the following prompts. Then use the **revising tips** to improve your writing.

WRITING PROMPTS	REVISING TIPS
Short Constructed Response: Description Imagine that you could go back in time and see SuperCroc with your own eyes. Write a **one-paragraph description** of the prehistoric monster and his surroundings.	Check to see that you used capitalization correctly throughout your evaluation. If not, revise your writing.
Extended Constructed Response: Article Decide whether "SuperCroc" is a well-written article. Does the author present his information clearly and in a style that holds your interest? Write a **two- or- three-paragraph evaluation** of the article.	If you cited specific subheadings in the article, be sure that you did not capitalize any conjunctions, articles, or prepositions of fewer than five letters.

Interactive Revision   THINK central

Go to **thinkcentral.com**.
KEYWORD: HML6-907

COMMON CORE

L 2 Demonstrate command of the conventions of capitalization.
W 2 Write explanatory texts to examine a topic and convey information through analysis of relevant content.

Bird Brains

Online Article by Gareth Huw Davies

How SMART are animals?

○ **COMMON CORE**

RI 2 Determine a central idea of a text and how it is conveyed through particular details.
RI 3 Analyze in detail how a key event is introduced, illustrated, and elaborated in a text.

Who doesn't love watching animals? Whether they are performing tricks on command or displaying their behavior in the wild, animals continually demonstrate their unique intelligence. In the article you are about to read, you'll learn about birds who do surprisingly clever things, including playing tricks on humans.

QUICKWRITE Write an anecdote, or brief story, about a time you saw—or heard about—an animal doing something that showed its cleverness. Share the story with your classmates.

● TEXT ANALYSIS: MAIN IDEAS

In a work of nonfiction, **main ideas** are the most important ideas that a writer communicates about a topic. Authors use specific methods to organize their ideas. In the article that follows, the author uses a proposition-and-support organizational pattern. The author presents a **proposition**, an important idea, opinion, or viewpoint and **supports** the proposition with reasons.

As you read "Bird Brains," look for the author's proposition.

● READING SKILL: RECOGNIZE SUPPORT

A proposition can be supported by

- **facts**, including the results of scientific research and surveys
- **statistics**, facts in number form
- **examples**, specific instances that illustrate reasons or facts
- **expert opinions** from people who know the subject.

As you read "Bird Brains," collect support in a chart like the one below.

Types of Support
Facts:
Statistics:
Examples:
Expert Opinions:

▲ VOCABULARY IN CONTEXT

The listed words help explain birds' intelligence. Choose the word that best completes each sentence.

WORD LIST	complexity	mimic	variation
	engage	perception	

1. She found a way to ____ the bird in conversation.
2. Our ____ of birds is often not accurate.
3. A parrot isn't a ____ that only repeats what it hears.
4. The ____ of their behavior shows their intelligence.
5. Some birds play a ____ of a trick known to humans.

 Complete the activities in your **Reader/Writer Notebook.**

Meet the Author

Gareth Huw Davies
born 1948

Nature Writer
Gareth Huw Davies has been a journalist since his first article was published in London's *Sunday Times* newspaper in 1976. Though his writing specialties include wildlife and the environment, he has also written articles about technology, music, medicine, and travel. He is the author of two books and has been nominated for a number of awards for his work.

British Bird Journalist
Born in Swansea, Wales, Davies typically writes for various British newspapers and magazines. However, "Bird Brains" is one of a number of articles he wrote for *The Life of Birds*, a series that appeared on the PBS (Public Broadcasting Service) Web site.

Author Online
Go to **thinkcentral.com.** KEYWORD: HML6-909

THINK central

File   Edit   View   Tools   Help

Back   Forward   Stop   Refresh   Home   Search   Favorites   Mail   Print

A carrion crow waits for traffic before placing a walnut on the road, then enjoys a meal.

CLEVER CROWS

At a traffic light crossing on a university campus in Japan, carrion crows and humans line up patiently, waiting for the traffic to halt.

When the lights change, the birds hop in front of the cars and place walnuts, which they picked from the adjoining trees, on the road. After the lights turn green again, the birds fly away and vehicles drive over the nuts, cracking them open. Finally, when it's time to cross again, the crows join the pedestrians and pick up their meal.

If the cars miss the nuts, the birds sometimes hop back and put
10 them somewhere else on the road. Or they sit on electricity wires and drop them in front of vehicles. . . .

The crows in Japan have only been cracking nuts this way since about 1990. They have since been seen doing it in California. Researchers believe they probably noticed cars driving over nuts fallen from a walnut tree overhanging a road. The crows already knew about dropping clams from a height on the seashore to break them open. The birds found this did not work for walnuts because of their soft green outer shell. . . . **B**

Internet

A MAIN IDEAS
Look at the subheading. What do you think is the main idea of this section?

B RECOGNIZE SUPPORT
Reread lines 12–17. What details develop the main idea of this passage?

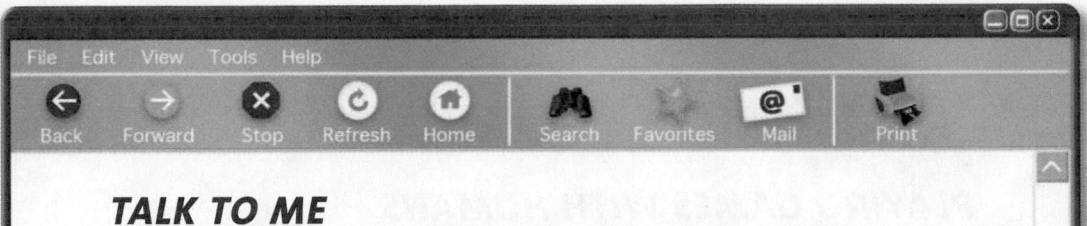

TALK TO ME

Another sign of intelligence, thought to be absent in most non-human
20 animals, is the ability to **engage** in complex, meaningful communication.
The work of Professor Irene Pepperberg of the University of Arizona, Tucson,
has now shown the general **perception** of parrots as mindless **mimics**
to be incorrect. **C**

The captive African grey parrot Alex is one of a number of parrots and
macaws now believed to have the intelligence and emotional make-up of
a 3- to 4-year-old child. Under the tutelage[1] of Professor Pepperberg, he
acquired a vocabulary of over 100 words. He could say the words for colors
and shapes and, apparently, use them meaningfully. He has learned the
labels for more than 35 different objects. He also knows when to use "no,"
30 and phrases such as "Come here," "I want X," and "Wanna go Y." . . .

---

1. **tutelage** (tōōt′l-ĭj): instruction; teaching.

Professor Irene Pepperberg interacts with her research subject, Alex.

engage (ĕn-gāj′) *v.*
to involve; participate

perception
(pər-sĕp′shən) *n.*
an impression or feeling

mimic (mĭm′ĭk) *n.* one
who imitates the speech
and gestures of others

C MAIN IDEAS
What is the main idea
of the paragraph?
What proposition, or
argument, does the
author seem to be
developing in this article
so far?

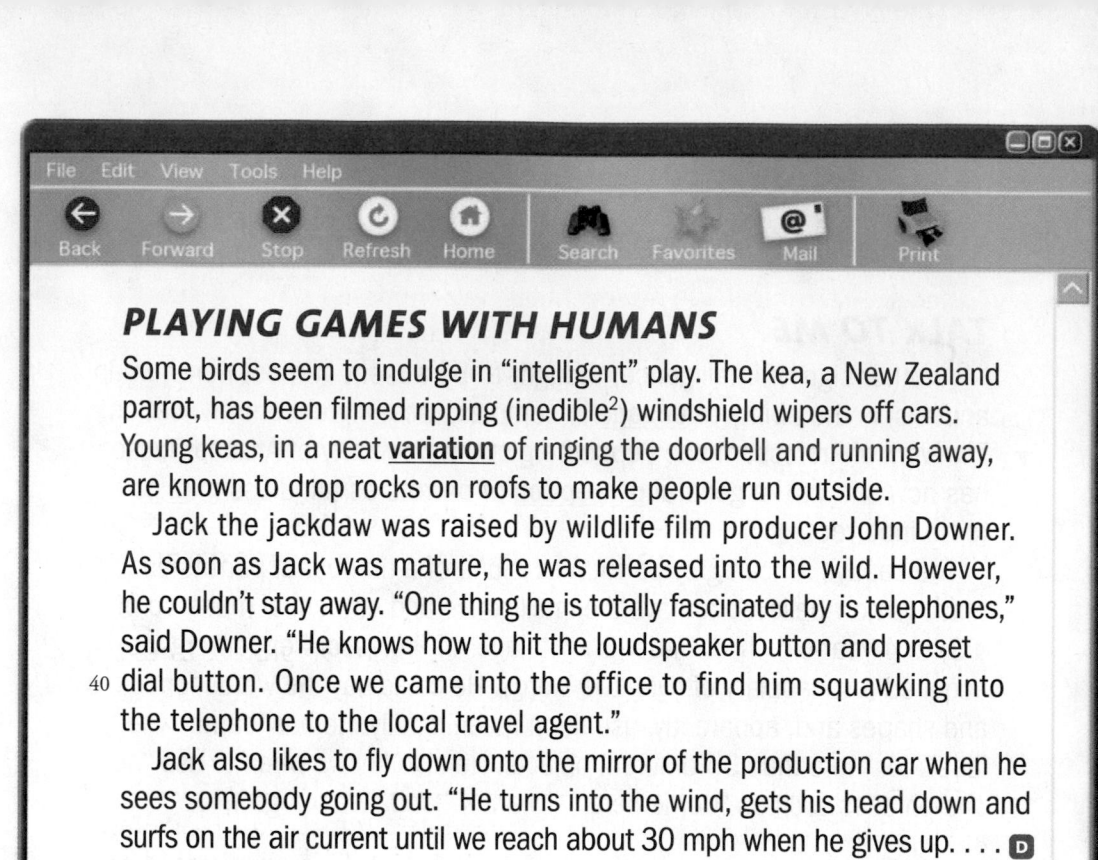

PLAYING GAMES WITH HUMANS

Some birds seem to indulge in "intelligent" play. The kea, a New Zealand parrot, has been filmed ripping (inedible[2]) windshield wipers off cars. Young keas, in a neat **variation** of ringing the doorbell and running away, are known to drop rocks on roofs to make people run outside.

Jack the jackdaw was raised by wildlife film producer John Downer. As soon as Jack was mature, he was released into the wild. However, he couldn't stay away. "One thing he is totally fascinated by is telephones," said Downer. "He knows how to hit the loudspeaker button and preset
40 dial button. Once we came into the office to find him squawking into the telephone to the local travel agent."

Jack also likes to fly down onto the mirror of the production car when he sees somebody going out. "He turns into the wind, gets his head down and surfs on the air current until we reach about 30 mph when he gives up. . . . **D**

ADJUSTING TO OTHERS

Scientists believe it is not physical need that drives creatures to become smarter, but social necessity. The **complexities** of living together require a higher level of intelligence. . . .

The African honeyguide, for example, lures badgers to bees' nests,
50 and feeds on the leftovers. To humans they offer their services as paid employees. They call and fly backward and forward to draw local tribespeoples'[3] attention to the location of honeycombs. They are then rewarded with a share of the takings for their trouble.

Of course, the bird world has its share of "bird brains." There are the birds that build three nests behind three holes under a flower pot because they can't remember which is which. There are also birds that attack their own reflections. . . .

The level of intelligence among birds may vary. But no living bird is truly stupid. Each generation of birds that leaves the protection of
60 its parents to become independent has the inborn genetic information that will help it to survive in the outside world and the skills that it has learned from its parents. It's just that some have more than others. **E**

---

2. **inedible** (ĭn-ĕd'ə-bəl): not suitable or safe for eating.
3. **tribespeople:** the people of a particular tribe, or group.

Internet

---

variation (vâr'ē-ā'shən) *n.* a slightly different form of something

D RECOGNIZE SUPPORT
What kind of support is in lines 36–44? How does this support develop the main idea in this section?

complexity (kəm-plĕk'sĭ-tē) *n.* the quality of being complicated

E MAIN IDEAS
State the main idea presented in lines 58–62. How well have the supporting details the writer included in the article convinced you that this **proposition,** or argument, about bird intelligence is true? Explain whether you think this main idea represents the author's viewpoint.

Comprehension

1. **Recall** Why do the crows drop walnuts in front of cars?

2. **Recall** How do African honeyguides help humans?

3. **Clarify** What behaviors do scientists interpret as being signs of intelligence in birds?

Text Analysis

● 4. **Identify Main Idea** Reread lines 58-62 of the article and state the main idea. Explain how the main idea presented here serves as the **proposition**, or argument, for the entire article.

● 5. **Evaluate Support** Review the support chart you completed. Does the support in this text effectively develop the writer's proposition? Back up your response with examples from the text.

6. **Evaluate Organizational Patterns** How effective is an organizational pattern in which all the support is presented before the proposition is directly stated? Do you think the writer should have reversed his approach, starting with the proposition and then presenting all the article's supporting details? Explain.

7. **Make Judgments** Which of the birds in the article seems to be the most intelligent? Make a chart like the one shown and note the activities or abilities of the various birds in the article. Then, using the information in your chart, explain which bird or type of bird you think is the most intelligent, and why.

Bird	Activity or Ability

Extension and Challenge

8. **SCIENCE CONNECTION** Crows are known for being clever. Search the Internet for information about crow habits, behaviors, and intelligence. Note any evidence that supports the conclusion that crows are especially intelligent. Present your findings in an oral report.

A clever crow takes a drink.

How SMART are animals?

Look back at the story you wrote about an animal doing something clever. How intelligent were the birds in this article compared to the animal you wrote about?

COMMON CORE

RI 2 Determine a central idea of a text and how it is conveyed through particular details.
RI 3 Analyze in detail how a key event is introduced, illustrated, and elaborated in a text.

Vocabulary in Context

▲ **VOCABULARY PRACTICE**

Show that you understand the vocabulary words by deciding if each statement is true or false.

1. The game of softball is a **variation** of baseball.
2. If you **engage** in conversation, you do not speak.
3. A **complexity** makes something more complicated or difficult.
4. A **mimic** imitates how someone moves and speaks.
5. A **perception** is based only on facts, never on feelings.

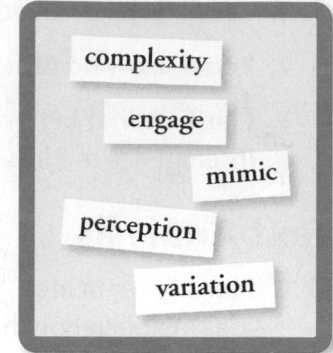

complexity

engage

mimic

perception

variation

ACADEMIC VOCABULARY IN SPEAKING

• adequacy • authority • concept • purpose • structural

With a partner, discuss the **adequacy** of the supporting details in this article. Did the supporting details convey the **concept** of bird intelligence, or are you unconvinced? Use at least two Academic Vocabulary words in your discussion.

VOCABULARY STRATEGY: ANALOGIES

An **analogy** describes a relationship, or comparison, between two different things that are alike in some way—a way that is not always obvious. There are over a dozen possible word relationships in analogies, but one of the most common is the part-to-whole relationship.

> stage : theater :: field : stadium
>
> (Read this as: *Stage is to theater as field is to stadium*.)

A stage is the part of a theater is where actors perform for an audience; a field is the part of a stadium where football players or other athletes perform for an audience. Thus, a stage and a field share an analogous, or similar, relationship.

PRACTICE Complete the following analogies.

1. dog : doghouse :: fish : _____
   a. ocean   **b.** market   **c.** lake   **d.** aquarium
2. trumpet player : band :: soldier : _____
   a. country   **b.** platoon   **c.** war   **d.** gun
3. dock : boat :: _____ : car
   a. highway   **b.** road   **c.** tires   **d.** garage
4. governor : state :: _____ : country
   a. president   **b.** mayor   **c.** senator   **d.** politician
5. paper : book :: _____ : movie
   a. theater   **b.** film   **c.** camera   **d.** actors

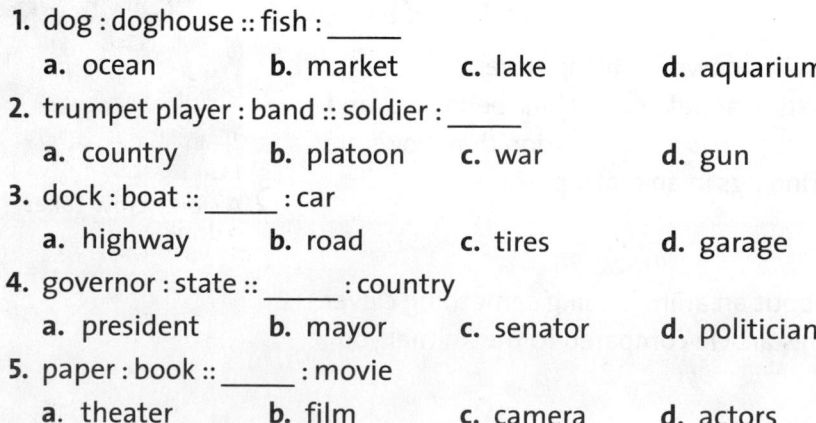

COMMON CORE

L 5b Use the relationship between particular words to better understand each of the words.

Interactive Vocabulary **THINK** central

Go to **thinkcentral.com**.
KEYWORD: HML6-914

Language

◆ **GRAMMAR IN CONTEXT: Punctuate Titles Correctly**

Be sure to punctuate titles correctly when you write. Use **quotation marks** for the titles of shorter works, such as short stories, essays, articles, songs, and poems. Use **italics** (or underlining) to set off titles of longer works, including books, plays, magazines, newspapers, movies, and TV series.

> *Examples:* The book *Are You My Mother?* is about a confused baby bird.
>
> "Kookaburra" is one of many songs about birds.

PRACTICE Rewrite each sentence, correctly punctuating the titles.

1. The TV series The Life of Birds was carefully researched.
2. This month's issue of Nature focuses entirely on birds.
3. I learned a lot from Joan Anderson's essay Cardinal Companion.
4. Robert Frost's poem A Dust of Snow mentions a crow.

For more help with punctuating titles, see page R50 in the **Grammar Handbook**.

READING-WRITING CONNECTION

YOUR TURN Increase your understanding of "Bird Brains" by responding to the following prompt. Then use the **revising tip** to improve your writing.

WRITING PROMPT	REVISING TIP
Extended Constructed Response: Letter Pretend that you are trying to persuade a publisher that its new book on animal intelligence should include a chapter about bird intelligence. Write a **two-paragraph letter** stating your case. Use a proposition-and-support organizational pattern, in which your main idea is your proposition. Your supporting details, or evidence, should be drawn from the article you have just read.	Review your letter. Have you stated your proposition as the main idea of your letter? Are your supporting details drawn from the article you have just read? Have you made a strong case for your position, or do you need to go back and add more supporting details?

Interactive Revision

Go to **thinkcentral.com**.
KEYWORD: HML6-915

COMMON CORE

L 2 Demonstrate command of the conventions of punctuation.
W 1 Write arguments to support claims with relevant evidence.

The First Emperor

Video link at
thinkcentral.com

Book Excerpt from *The Tomb Robbers* by Daniel Cohen

Digging Up the Past: Discovery and Excavation of Shi Huangdi's Tomb

Magazine Article by Helen Wieman Bledsoe

VIDEO TRAILER **THINK** central KEYWORD: HML6-916

How can we uncover the PAST?

⸰⸰⸰ **COMMON CORE**

RI 5 Analyze how a particular
sentence, paragraph, or section
fits into the overall structure and
contributes to the development of
ideas. **RI 7** Integrate information
presented in different media or
formats to develop a coherent
understanding of a topic. **L 2**
Demonstrate command of the
conventions of punctuation.

To learn about the recent past, we might ask older friends and
relatives to recall events they lived through, or to talk about the
way life used to be. To explore the very distant past, we have to dig
deeper—literally! The two selections you are about to read describe
an amazing discovery that has uncovered an important part of
China's ancient history.

QUICKWRITE Think about a time period you wish you knew more
about. It might be when your parents were children, when your
grandparents were children, or even thousands of years ago. Write
down what span of years you would like to learn more about and why.

TEXT ANALYSIS: SYNTHESIZING INFORMATION

There can be dozens, even hundreds, of resources available on the same topic. However, not every source presents the same information on a topic. When you read multiple sources on the same topic, you **synthesize information;** that is, you integrate information from different sources into a broad understanding of a topic.

As you read the texts, you'll notice that they are about the same topic. First, determine the focus of each selection. Then, make logical connections across the texts in order to come up with a synthesis, or combination, of the information that the texts convey.

READING STRATEGY: SET A PURPOSE FOR READING

Your purpose for reading these two selections is to synthesize information. A chart can help you.

What do you learn about...	"The First Emperor"	"Digging Up the Past"
...the emperor?		
...the history of the tomb?		
...the excavation of the tomb?		

▲ VOCABULARY IN CONTEXT

Make a chart like the one shown. Write each vocabulary word in the appropriate column, and then write a brief definition of each word you already know.

WORD LIST		
ancestor	disintegrate	reconstruction
archaeological	excavation	surpass
barbarian	immortality	
dedicate	preservation	

Know Well	Think I Know	Don't Know at All

Complete the activities in your **Reader/Writer Notebook.**

Meet the Authors

Daniel Cohen
born 1936

Ghost Writer
Though Daniel Cohen has written about world history, music, and nature, he is best known for his books of ghost stories. Research for these books led him to creep around houses believed by some to be haunted. He even spent "a damp and chilly night in an English churchyard."

Helen Wieman Bledsoe

Magazine Writer
Helen Wieman Bledsoe is a freelance writer whose articles have been published in more than 20 magazines. She also enjoys art, history, and travel.

BACKGROUND TO THE TEXTS

A Matter of Time
The information contained in a nonfiction work is often affected by the time period in which the piece was written. "The First Emperor" was written when the excavation of the emperor's tomb was just beginning. "Digging Up the Past" was written some years later, when more information was available.

Authors Online
Go to **thinkcentral.com.** KEYWORD: HML6-917

THINK central

**Ⓐ SYNTHESIZE
INFORMATION**
Preview the selection's
title and graphic aids.
What do you think the
selection will be about?

archaeological
(är′kē-ə-lŏj′ĭ-kəl) *adj.*
relating to the study
of past human life
and culture

Ch'in Shih Huang Ti (1700s). Chinese painting. © British Library/The Art Archive.

THE FIRST EMPEROR Ⓐ

Daniel Cohen

There is what may turn out to be the greatest **archaeological**
find of modern times, one that may ultimately outshine even
the discovery of the tomb of Tutankhamun.[1] It is the tomb of the
emperor Ch'in Shih Huang Ti.[2] Now admittedly the name Ch'in
Shih Huang Ti is not exactly a household word in the West. But
then neither was Tutankhamun until 1922. The major difference is
that while Tutankhamun himself was historically insignificant,
Ch'in Shih Huang Ti was enormously important in Chinese
history. In many respects he was really the founder of China.

---

1. **Tutankhamun** (tōōt′äng-kä′mən): Egyptian pharaoh whose tomb was found intact in 1922.
2. **Ch'in Shih Huang Ti** (chĭn shĭh hwäng′ dē): The use of the word *Ch'in* (or *Qin*) at the beginning
of the emperor's name is a formal title that refers to the place from which the emperor came.

10 The future emperor started out as the king of the small state Ch'in. At the time, the land was divided up among a number of small states, all constantly warring with one another. Ch'in was one of the smallest and weakest. Yet the king of Ch'in managed to overcome all his rivals, and in the year 221 B.C. he proclaimed himself emperor of the land that we now know as China. From that date until the revolution of 1912, China was always ruled by an emperor. The name China itself comes from the name Ch'in. **B**

Shih Huang Ti ruled his empire with ferocious efficiency. He had the Great Wall of China built to keep out the northern
20 **barbarians.** The Great Wall, which stretches some fifteen hundred miles, is a building project that rivals and perhaps **surpasses** the Great Pyramid.[3] The Great Wall took thirty years to build and cost the lives of countless thousands of laborers. Today the Great Wall remains China's number one tourist attraction.

As he grew older, Shih Huang Ti became obsessed with the prospect of his own death. He had survived several assassination attempts and was terrified of another. He traveled constantly between his 270 different palaces, so that no one could ever be sure where he was going to be. He never slept in the same room for two

---

3. **Great Pyramid:** massive four-sided monument built around a tomb by people in ancient Egypt.

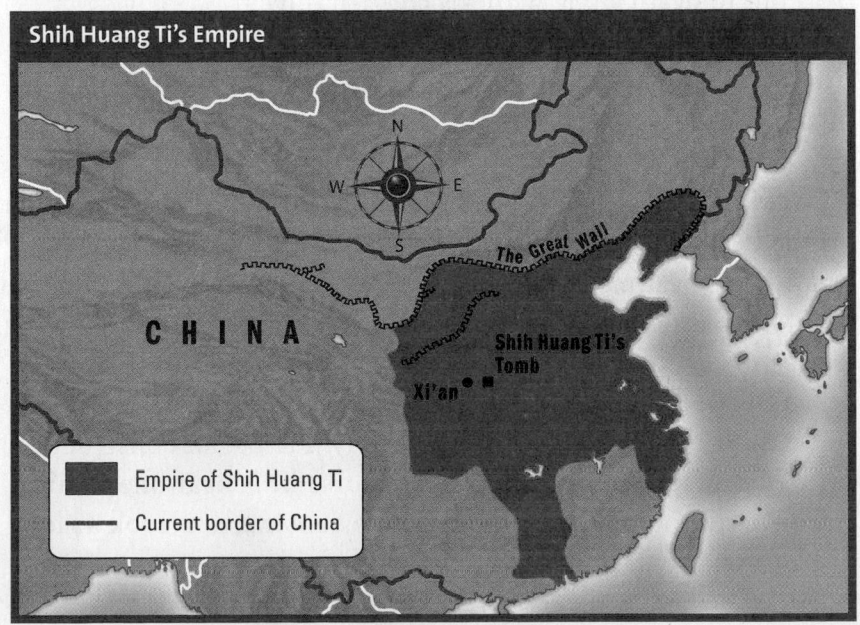

Shih Huang Ti's Empire

- Empire of Shih Huang Ti
- Current border of China

The Great Wall

CHINA

Shih Huang Ti's Tomb

Xi'an

C

B SYNTHESIZE INFORMATION
What is the focus of the information presented in lines 10–17?

barbarian (bär-bâr′ē-ən) *n.* a person considered by those of another group to have a primitive culture

surpass (sər-păs′) *v.* to become greater than; to go beyond

COMMON CORE RI 7

C ANALYZE TEXT FEATURES
Factual information is based on true statements or actual events. "Today the Great Wall remains China's number one tourist attraction" (lines 23–24) is an example of factual information. Writers will sometimes include factual information in graphic aids such as a map. What factual information does this map convey about the size of Shih Huang Ti's empire and the size of China today?

Analyze Visuals ▶

Compare the man in the carriage with your mental image of Shih Huang Ti.

Emperor Ch'in Shih Huang Ti Travelling in a Palanquin (1600s). Chinese School. Color on silk.
© Bibliothèque Nationale, Paris/Bridgeman Art Library.

immortality
(ĭm′ôr-tăl′ĭ-tē) *n.*
endless life

ancestor (ăn′sĕs′tər) *n.*
a person from whom another person or group is descended

D SET A PURPOSE FOR READING
What do you learn about Shih Huang Ti in lines 32–40? Record this information in your chart.

30 nights in a row. Anyone who revealed the emperor's whereabouts was put to death along with his entire family.

Shih Huang Ti searched constantly for the secret of **immortality**. He became prey to a host of phony magicians and other fakers who promised much but could deliver nothing.

The emperor heard that there were immortals living on some far-off island, so he sent a huge fleet to find them. The commander of the fleet knew that if he failed in his mission, the emperor would put him to death. So the fleet simply never returned. It is said that the fleet found the island of Japan and stayed there to become the
40 **ancestors** of the modern Japanese. **D**

In his desire to stay alive, Shih Huang Ti did not neglect the probability that he would die someday. He began construction of an immense tomb in the Black Horse hills near one of his favorite summer palaces. The tomb's construction took as long as the construction of the Great Wall—thirty years.

The emperor, of course, did die. Death came while he was visiting the eastern provinces.[4] But his life had become so secretive that only a few high officials were aware of his death. They contrived to keep it a secret until they could consolidate their
50 own power. The imperial procession[5] headed back for the capital. Unfortunately, it was midsummer and the emperor's body began to rot and stink. So one of the plotters arranged to have a cart of fish follow the immense imperial chariot to hide the odor of the decomposing corpse. Finally, news of the emperor's death was made public. The body, or what was left of it, was buried in the tomb that he had been building for so long. . . .

There are two contradictory stories about the tomb of Ch'in Shih Huang Ti. The first says that it was covered up with earth to make it resemble an ordinary hill and that its location
60 has remained unknown for centuries.

But a more accurate legend holds that there never was any attempt to disguise the existence of the tomb. Ch'in Shih Huang Ti had been building it for years, and everybody knew where it was. After his death the tomb was surrounded by walls enclosing an area of about five hundred acres. This was to be the emperor's "spirit city." Inside the spirit city were temples and all sorts of other sacred buildings and objects **dedicated** to the dead emperor.

Over the centuries the walls, the temples, indeed everything above ground was carried away by vandals. The top of the tomb
70 was covered with earth and eventually came to resemble a large hill. Locally the hill is called Mount Li. But still the farmers who lived in the area had heard stories that Mount Li contained the tomb of Ch'in Shih Huang Ti or of some other important person. . . . **E**

In the spring of 1974 a peasant plowing a field near Mount Li uncovered a life-sized clay statue of a warrior. Further digging indicated that there was an entire army of statues beneath the ground. Though **excavations** are not yet complete, Chinese authorities believe that there are some six thousand life-sized clay statues of warriors, plus scores of life-sized statues of horses.

---

4. **provinces:** districts, or parts, of a country.
5. **imperial procession:** a group of people traveling with an emperor.

dedicate (děd'ĭ-kāt') *v.* to set apart for a particular use

E SET A PURPOSE FOR READING
What have you learned so far about the tomb? Add this information to your chart.

excavation (ĕk'skə-vā'shən) *n.* the act or process of exposing by digging away a covering

A worker tries to piece together the broken terra-cotta statues. **F**

F ANALYZE TEXT FEATURES
What does this photograph tell you about what was involved in piecing together the terra-cotta statues?

preservation
(prĕz′ər-vā′shən) *n.* the state of being mostly unchanged or kept from harm

G SET A PURPOSE FOR READING
In your chart, note what you have learned from this selection about the excavation of the tomb.

80 Most of the statues are broken, but some are in an absolutely remarkable state of **preservation.** Each statue is finely made, and each shows a distinct individual, different from all the others.

This incredible collection is Shih Huang Ti's "spirit army." At one time Chinese kings practiced human sacrifice so that the victims could serve the dead king in the next world. Shih Huang Ti was willing to make do with models. Men and horses were arranged in a military fashion in a three-acre underground chamber. The chamber may have been entered at some point. The roof certainly collapsed. But still the delicate figures have survived surprisingly well. 90 Most of the damage was done when the roof caved in. That is why the Chinese archaeologists are so hopeful that when the tomb itself is excavated, it too will be found to have survived surprisingly well.

The Chinese are not rushing the excavations. They have only a limited number of trained people to do the job. After all, the tomb has been there for over two thousand years. A few more years won't make much difference. **G**

Though once denounced as a tyrant, Ch'in Shih Huang Ti is now regarded as a national hero. His name is a household word in China. The Chinese government knows that it may have an 100 unparalleled ancient treasure on its hands, and it wants to do the job well. Over the next few years we should be hearing much more about this truly remarkable find.

Comprehension

1. **Recall** Why did Shih Huang Ti have the Great Wall built?

2. **Recall** What steps did Shih Huang Ti take to protect himself against people who might want to harm him?

3. **Clarify** What makes Shih Huang Ti an important person from the past?

Text Analysis

● 4. **Synthesize Information** Consider the information that the author emphasizes in "The First Emperor." In one or two sentences, state the main idea of the selection.

5. **Examine Cause and Effect** Reread lines 18–24. What were the effects of building the Great Wall of China?

6. **Analyze Text Features** What information do the map and its labels on page 919 provide that the text does not?

7. **Evaluate Information** Skim through the selection, and note the evidence that supports its main idea. Then explain whether you think the author provided enough evidence to support the main idea. How has the writer made logical connections between his main idea and supporting details? Use examples from the text to support your answer.

Synthesizing Information

Review the chart you began to fill in as you read. Add notes about the information presented in "The First Emperor."

What do you learn about . . .	"The First Emperor"	"Digging Up the Past"
. . . the emperor?	He had the Great Wall of China built.	
. . . the history of the tomb?		
. . . the excavation of the tomb?	There is an army of statues in it.	

COMMON CORE

RI 5 Analyze how a particular sentence, paragraph, or section fits into the overall structure and contributes to the development of ideas. **RI 7** Integrate information presented in different media or formats to develop a coherent understanding of a topic.

DIGGING UP THE PAST:
DISCOVERY AND EXCAVATION OF SHI HUANGDI'S TOMB Ⓐ
Helen Wieman Bledsoe

Ⓐ **SYNTHESIZE INFORMATION**
Preview the article's title and graphic aids. What do you think the article will focus on?

Analyze Visuals ▶

These terra-cotta soldiers are only a small number of the thousands of statues unearthed at the sight of Shi Huangdi's tomb. What **details** do you notice in the rows of statues?

In March 1974, Chinese peasants digging a well near Xi'an in the central province of Shaanxi[1] found some unusual pottery fragments. Then, deeper down at 11 feet, they unearthed a head made of terra-cotta. They notified the authorities, and excavation of the site began immediately. To date, workers have dug up about 8,000 sculpted clay soldiers, and the site has proved to be one of the greatest archaeological discoveries of all time.

For over 2,000 years, these clay warriors have been guarding the tomb of Shi Huangdi,[2] the First Emperor of China. Tradition says that the First Emperor began building his tomb when he ascended to the throne at age 13, and that it was unfinished at his death, 36 years later. The Chinese historian Sima Qian wrote in the *Shiji,* "Historical Records," that the emperor forced 700,000 laborers to work on his elaborate tomb.

The warriors stand guard in three pits (a fourth was found to be empty) that cover five-and-a-half acres and are 16 to 24 feet deep. The largest one contains 6,000 terra-cotta soldiers marching in military formation in 11 trenches, each as long as a football field. At the western end of the formation is a vanguard[3] of archers and bowmen. At the head of six of the trenches stand the remnants of chariots, each with four life-sized horses and 18 soldiers. The wooden chariots have largely **disintegrated,** unlike the well-preserved terra-cotta horses and men. Last come row upon row of soldiers. **Ⓑ**

Despite the enormous number of men, no two faces are alike. Their expressions display dignity, steadfastness, and intelligence. Each is tall, standing five-and-a-half to six feet high. Some people think the terra-cotta soldiers portray real-life men from the vast army of the First Emperor.

The warriors' legs are solid columns of clay, with square-toed sandals on their feet. The hollow bodies are of coiled clay. The head and hands of each soldier were carefully molded and attached to the body in assembly-line fashion. Traces of pink, yellow, purple, blue, orange, green, brown, and black pigment show that the figures were once brightly painted. The horses were roan (reddish-brown), brown, or black with pink mouths.

---

1. **Xi'an** (shē'än') . . . **Shaanxi** (shän'shē'): Xi'an is a city of central China. The former capital of the Qin (also called Ch'in) dynasty, it is now the capital of China's Shaanxi province.
2. **Shi Huangdi** (also **Shih Huang Ti**): The spelling of Chinese names and places can vary.
3. **vanguard** (văn'gärd): the troops that move at the head of an army.

disintegrate
(dĭs-ĭn'tĭ-grāt') *v.*
to break down into smaller parts

Ⓑ SYNTHESIZE INFORMATION
What is the focus of the information presented in lines 14–22?

C ANALYZE TEXT FEATURES
Writers of expository texts may present quantitative information in a graph like this one. A **graph** illustrates the numerical relationship between two or more things. This graph presents information on the size of the four excavated pits. What system of measurement does its diagram use? Using this system of measurement, what are the approximate measurements of the largest pit? (Can you convert this number to feet and inches?)

D SYNTHESIZE INFORMATION
What additional information have you learned about the tomb. How does this information connect with what you learned in "The First Emperor"?

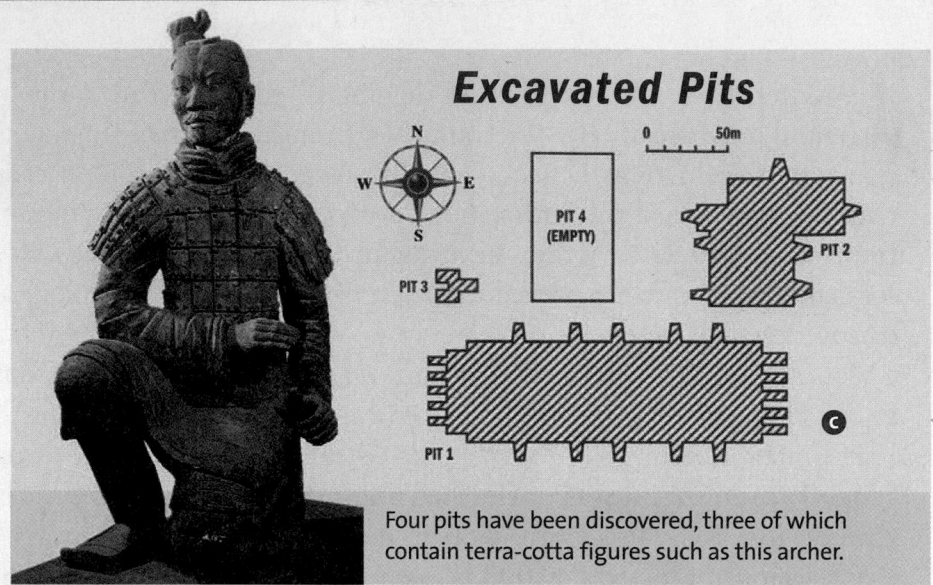

Excavated Pits

Four pits have been discovered, three of which contain terra-cotta figures such as this archer.

The warriors' hair styles and topknots, and the tassels trimming their garments, denote their military rank. Many do not wear helmets or carry shields, a mark of bravery in battle. Their armor was probably of lacquered[4] leather; some pieces look like baseball catchers' pads. The soldiers' hands are positioned to hold weapons, but most of the weapons have disappeared. Very likely they were stolen when the pits were looted after the fall of the Qin Dynasty (the Dynasty founded by Shi Huangdi). Even so, bronze spears, halberds (a combination spear and battle-ax), swords, daggers, and about 1,400 arrowheads remain. Some of the blades are still very sharp.

A second pit, only partially excavated, contains about 1,400 more soldiers. While the first pit holds mostly infantry,[5] the second has a more mobile attack force of horses and chariots. A third pit is thought to hold the high command of the army. The chariot of the Commander-in-Chief survives, with men surrounding it in protective formation. **D**

Covered by a wooden roof and ten feet of earth, these figures were not intended to be seen. When the pits were looted and burned, the roof fell in and damaged most of the sculptures. __Reconstruction__ is a slow, delicate task. Today, a visitor to the site can walk on long wooden platforms 16 feet above the pits and gaze down with astonishment at the thousands of sculptured soldiers below.

---

4. **lacquered** (lăk′ərd): covered with a glossy, protective coating.
5. **infantry:** foot soldiers.

Approximately a mile away from the pits is a gently sloping, rounded mountain covered with trees—the burial mound of the First Emperor. The four-sided, rammed-earth mound covers three
60 quarters of a square mile and is 156 feet high. It once stood at 400 feet. Of the two great walls that enclosed the funerary park[6] only rubble remains. The perimeter[7] of the outer wall is almost four miles. Set into the strong thick walls were four gates and four corner towers. Inside the walls were gardens, pavilions,[8] and a sacrificial palace, in addition to the burial mound. The burial chamber itself is still untouched, its contents as yet unknown.

Tradition based on the *Shiji* says that the emperor's body was buried in a suit of small jade pieces sewed together with gold thread and covered with a pearl and jade shroud. Also in the burial
70 mound were bronze models of Shi Huangdi's palaces and government offices. These replicas featured such details as pearls to represent the sun and moon, and pools of mercury[9] to recreate rivers and seas.

---

6. **funerary park:** the place of a burial.
7. **perimeter:** the boundary or border of something.
8. **pavilions** (pə-vĭl'yənz): open-sided buildings used for shelter or recreation.
9. **mercury:** quicksilver; a chemical element that is a silvery liquid at room temperature.

○ **COMMON CORE L 2**

Language Coach

Hyphens in Compound Modifiers Look at the compounds *four-sided* and *rammed-earth* in line 59. These are compound modifiers, which use hyphens only when they appear before a word they are modifying. What other compound modifiers do you know?

Over 1,000 of the more than 6,000 soldiers and horses in Pit 1 have been restored.

Terra-cotta archers in Pit 2 wait for restoration.

E SET A PURPOSE FOR READING
Reread lines 67–76. What do you learn about the emperor and his tomb, based on the *Shiji* and the items that have been excavated so far? Add your findings to your chart.

According to the ancient Chinese, the soul of the dead continued living and therefore required all of life's necessities within the tomb. Kings especially needed many luxuries and that is why their tombs are treasure houses of jewels, gold, silver, and bronze. **E**

The *Shiji* states that in order to prevent people from robbing the tomb, "Craftsmen built internal devices that would set off arrows should anyone pass through the tunnels." Because Sima Qian wrote
80 his history a century after the death of the First Emperor, the accuracy of his statements is questionable. In fact, grave robbers did enter and loot Shi Huangdi's tomb for 30 years after the fall of the Qin Dynasty (four years after the Emperor's death). During this time, many precious relics most likely were stolen.

In 1980, additional smaller pits were discovered. One contains pottery coffins with bones of exotic birds and animals, probably from the royal zoo. Another has vessels inscribed with the words, "Belonging to the Officials in Charge of Food at Mount Li," and must be where food and sacrifices were offered to the dead emperor.
90 Uncovered in the nearby Hall of Slumber were clothes and everyday objects for use by the soul of the Emperor. As the excavations continue, each find serves to remind us of the tremendous energy and genius of Shi Huangdi and his people.

Comprehension

1. **Recall** How was Shi Huangdi's tomb discovered?

2. **Recall** What happened to the tomb after the fall of the Qin dynasty?

Text Analysis

3. **Analyze Text Features** Look back at the graph on page 926 of "Digging Up the Past." Does the graph demonstrate what the tomb looks like more effectively than the text? What information does the graph tell you that the text does not? Explain your answer.

● 4. **Synthesize Information** Why do you think Shi Huangdi chose to have such an elaborate tomb built? Explain, using information from "The First Emperor" and "Digging Up the Past" for support.

Synthesizing Information

Now that you have read both selections, finish filling in your chart. Add the two additional questions and answer them. First, identify the focus of each selection. Then, write a brief explanation of the main idea or ideas the two selections share.

What do you learn about . . .	"The First Emperor"	"Digging Up the Past"
. . . the emperor?	He had the Great Wall of China built.	He ascended to the throne at age 13.
. . . the history of the tomb?		
. . . the excavation of the tomb?	There is an army of statues in it.	Each pit is 16 to 24 feet deep.
What do you learn the most about in each selection?		
Synthesizing Information: What main idea or ideas do the two selections share?		

How can we uncover the PAST?

Look back at the Quickwrite you wrote about a time period you'd like to know more about. Now that you have read these selections about Shi Huangdi's tomb, do you have any more ideas about time periods you'd like to "uncover"? Explain.

COMMON CORE

RI 5 Analyze how a particular sentence, paragraph, or section fits into the overall structure and contributes to the development of ideas. **RI 7** Integrate information presented in different media or formats to develop a coherent understanding of a topic.

Vocabulary in Context

▲ VOCABULARY PRACTICE

Choose the word or phrase that is closest in meaning to each boldfaced word.

1. **preservation:** (a) demolition, (b) protection, (c) destruction
2. **disintegrate:** (a) fall apart, (b) combine with, (c) match up
3. **reconstruction:** (a) elimination, (b) cancellation, (c) restoration
4. **ancestor:** (a) older sister, (b) great-grandmother, (c) youngest daughter
5. **surpass:** (a) go beyond, (b) turn around, (c) fall back
6. **dedicate:** (a) dislike, (b) devote, (c) daydream
7. **barbarian:** (a) associate, (b) brute, (c) partner
8. **immortality:** (a) everlasting life, (b) short life, (c) temporary life
9. **archaeological:** (a) historical, (b) comical, (c) mystical
10. **excavation:** (a) an injury, (b) a vehicle, (c) a dig

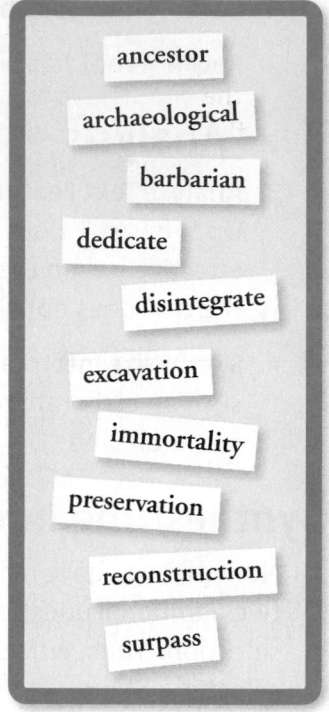

ancestor

archaeological

barbarian

dedicate

disintegrate

excavation

immortality

preservation

reconstruction

surpass

ACADEMIC VOCABULARY IN WRITING

> • adequacy   • authority   • concept   • purpose   • structural

Critique the **adequacy** of each writer's supporting details. Did he or she fully support the main ideas in his or her article? Use at least two Academic Vocabulary words in your response.

VOCABULARY STRATEGY: WORD PARTS

Sometimes you can figure out the meaning of an unfamiliar word by breaking the word into parts. For example, the vocabulary word *reconstruction* has three parts: the prefix *re-* ("again"), the base word *construct* ("to build"), and the suffix *-ion* ("action or process").

When you combine the three meanings, you will find that *reconstruction* means "the action of building again." Knowing the meaning of one or more parts of a word will help you determine the meaning of the complete word. Most word parts come from Greek, Latin, or Old English (OE).

⸬ **COMMON CORE**

L 4b Use Greek or Latin affixes as clues to the meaning of a word.

Prefixes	Meanings
dis- (Latin)	apart
micro- (Greek)	small
un- (OE)	the opposite of
hyper- (Greek)	over, excessive

Suffixes	Meanings
-ance (Latin)	condition, state
-ate (Latin)	to act upon
-logy (Greek)	study, theory
-ive (Latin)	of, relating to

PRACTICE Identify the word parts in each word. Then try to define the word. If you need help, use a dictionary.

1. unfortunate
2. disappearance
3. hyperactive
4. microbiology

Interactive Vocabulary **THINK** central

Go to **thinkcentral.com**.
KEYWORD: HML6-930

Writing for Assessment

COMMON CORE W 2, W 4, W 10

1. READ THE PROMPT

The two selections you've just read provide different kinds of information on the same topic. In writing assessments, you will often be asked to compare nonfiction selections that deal with a similar topic in different ways.

> In three paragraphs, compare the main idea of "The First Emperor" and "Digging Up the Past." Remember that the topic of each piece of writing is the same, but each presents different information. Support your comparison using details from each.

◀ **STRATEGIES IN ACTION**

1. I need to identify the **similarities and differences** in the main idea of each selection.

2. I need to determine the **type** of information in each selection.

3. I should include **examples** from the selections to support my ideas.

2. PLAN YOUR WRITING

Using the chart you filled in as you read, identify the ways in which the selections are alike and different. Then think about how to present these similarities and differences.

- Decide on a position statement for your response.

- Review the selections to find details and examples that support your comparison.

- Create an outline to organize your ideas. This sample outline shows one way to organize your three paragraphs.

> I. Introduction and main idea of 1st selection
> II. Main idea of 2nd selection
> III. Compare main ideas of selections

3. DRAFT YOUR RESPONSE

Paragraph 1 Provide the title and author of each selection, as well as a sentence explaining the topic they share. State the main idea of the first selection. Include details from the book excerpt as examples.

Paragraph 2 State the main idea of the second selection. Include details from the magazine article as examples.

Paragraph 3 Compare the types of information presented in each selection. Support your comparison with examples from each.

Revision Include transition words such as *also, however, instead,* or *unlike* to demonstrate similarities and differences.

What's the FULL news story?

Whether you watch news on TV or turn to a newspaper, you want to have all the details. In other words, you want your news reports to be thorough. In this lesson, you'll examine two news stories. You'll learn a technique for figuring out how much important information a news story provides and what messages it sends.

Background

Dolphin Crossing In August of 2005, a tropical storm began a path of destruction along the Gulf Coast section of the United States. Hurricane Katrina first struck Florida and grew more powerful as it neared the states of Alabama, Texas, Mississippi, and Louisiana. The hurricane brought storm surges, high winds that lift waves above sea level. Flooding caused many thousands to flee their homes.

Humans were not the only ones seeking a safer place. The two news reports in this lesson are about eight bottle-nosed dolphins that once lived in a marine park in Gulfport, Mississippi. As the hurricane raged, a storm surge swept these tame dolphins into the strange waters of the Gulf of Mexico.

Media Literacy: The 5 *W*'s and *H* of the News

To be **thorough** or complete, a news report should answer six basic questions—**who, what, when, where, why,** and **how.** Reporters often use the 5 *W*'s and *H* as an outline for writing reports. The best news reports answer these questions and include additional information.

THE 5 *W*'S AND *H* OF NEWS REPORTS

WHO?
Who is the report about?

WHAT?
What happened?

WHEN?
When did the event take place?

WHERE?
Where was the scene of the happenings?

WHY?
Why did the event occur?

HOW?
How did the event unfold?

SECTION E   THE STAR JOURNAL   E 5

Homeless Dolphins to Get Back Together in Bahamas

JACKSON, Miss. (AP) — Several dolphins that were swept out to sea by Hurricane Katrina will soon be reunited at a resort in the Bahamas.

A resort on Paradise Island in the Bahamas will take on 17 dolphins from the Marine Life Oceanarium—eight of which were rescued from open water in September.

"The dolphins, I think, are a symbol of everything that's happened on the Gulf Coast and to find a new home for them—that's something that we hope will happen for everybody on the coast," said Howard Karawan, president and managing director of the company that owns the resort.

STRATEGIES FOR ANALYZING THOROUGHNESS

- Explain what message the medium is conveying. Is the message simply about sharing information, or is there another purpose? (Some possible messages might be warning the public about something or making people aware of a social issue.) These media messages may not always be obvious.
- Be aware that the "why" and "how" details about an event are often shared in **interviews.** On TV, the brief statements made by experts or witnesses are called **sound bites.** In printed news, they're called **quotes.**

Viewing Guide for

News Reports

Watch an ABC network news report that was first broadcast in the weeks after Hurricane Katrina had struck. Then read a newspaper report that appeared some time later. In analyzing each report, look or listen for any details that help you answer the 5 *W*'s and the *H* questions. Record your answers. Use these questions to guide you as you examine each report.

NOW VIEW

FIRST VIEWING: Comprehension

1. **Summarize** Refer to any notes that answer the 5 *W*'s and *H* questions. Use your answers to write a brief summary of either the TV news or newspaper report.

2. **Clarify** The TV newscast report appeared in August of 2005. How much later did the newspaper report appear?

CLOSE VIEWING: Media Literacy

3. **Identifying Details** The TV newscast focuses on only two of the dolphins. In the newspaper report, what more recent news do you learn about the condition of the dolphins?

4. **Analyze Sound Bites** In your opinion, were the **interviews** in the newscast helpful to you in answering the 5 *W*'s and *H* questions? Explain. Think about

   - the introduction by the news anchor at the beginning
   - the details given by the reporter at the rescue

5. **Analyzing Levels of Formality** Another feature of print and media news reporting to keep in mind are the levels of **formality** and **informality**. When something is formal, it usually follows rules, or conventions, and seems "official." Formality usually implies an objective, unemotional, impersonal approach. When something is informal, it is more casual. An informal report may include opinions and emotional reactions and may try to get the audience to feel a certain way. Compare and contrast levels of formality and informality in the newscast and the newspaper report.

Write or Discuss

Evaluate News Reports You've analyzed two news reports. Choose either the TV news report or the newspaper report. Briefly express your opinion of how good a job the report does of providing complete information about the dolphins. Think about

- how well it answers the **5 W's and H** questions
- how easy or difficult it was to find the important details
- any additional information in the report that added interest

Produce Your Own Media

Create Nursery Rhyme News Recall the stirring events surrounding such nursery rhyme characters as Jack and Jill or Humpty Dumpty. Or think of how tales like "Little Red Riding Hood" or "The Three Little Pigs" might be reported as news. Choose any rhyme or tale that's familiar to your class. Rewrite the tale as a news story and add more imaginative details. Have a partner check that your report delivers all the necessary information. If two or more students choose the same characters, plan each additional report as a news update.

HERE'S HOW Follow these suggestions for your report.

- Write the news report by using the **5 W's and H** questions as an outline.
- Include **sound bites** or **quotes** from the characters.
- Take the role of a reporter to present your nursery news reports to the class. Each student can take turns reading aloud from a "news" desk.

STUDENT MODEL

SCIENTISTS DISCOVER STAR

NEW YORK—In a press conference this morning, scientists announced the discovery of a new star. Its common name is Twinkle, Twinkle.

The lead scientist, Dr. Ester Esteban, is still amazed. "I wonder why it has taken billions and billions of years to find this star," Dr. Esteban said. "It sparkles like a diamond in the sky."

COMMON CORE

W 3 Write narratives to develop real or imagined events using well-structured event sequences.

Media Tools — Go to **thinkcentral.com**. KEYWORD: HML6-935

Tech Tip
If available, add clip art to the news reports.

Argument and Persuasion

Think about the choices and decisions that you make in a single day. You might choose to volunteer at an animal shelter, buy a new pair of shoes, or cast your vote for student-council president. Which persuasive messages influence your decisions?

Part 1: What Is an Argument?

When you hear the word *argument,* you may think of angry people shouting heated statements. In formal speaking and writing, however, a good argument is not emotional. It is a carefully stated claim supported by reasons and evidence. An argument is made up of two important parts.

- The **claim** is a writer's position on a problem or an issue.
- The **support** is the reasons and evidence that help to prove the claim. A writer may include many kinds of evidence, including eye-opening statistics, compelling anecdotes, or examples. Support in an argument is usually *for* or *against* an issue. Study the support for the claim stated below. What is the author's **viewpoint,** or attitude toward the issue of teens using the Internet? Is the support for or against the issue?

COMMON CORE

Included in this workshop:
RI 7 Integrate information presented in different media or formats to develop a coherent understanding of a topic.
RI 8 Trace and evaluate the argument and specific claims in a text, distinguishing claims that are supported by reasons and evidence from claims that are not.

CLAIM
Teens who use the Internet for different kinds of tasks are developing important life skills.

Support 1   **Support 2**   **Support 3**

Support **1**

Using the Internet for research can help teens become experts at finding information. For example, looking up homework help and comparison-shopping online both require savvy research abilities.

Support **2**

Teens are learning how to multi-task. One study found that 30 percent of teens do more than one thing when they are on the Internet—for instance, surf the Web *and* e-mail friends at the same time.

Support **3**

The immediate responses required by e-mails and instant messages can help teens learn to type faster and to process information quickly. These abilities are critical in school and in business.

MODEL: PARTS OF AN ARGUMENT

This article is from *Humane Teen,* a Web site intended to educate students about important issues involving animal rights and the environment. As you begin reading the article, look for the author's claim.

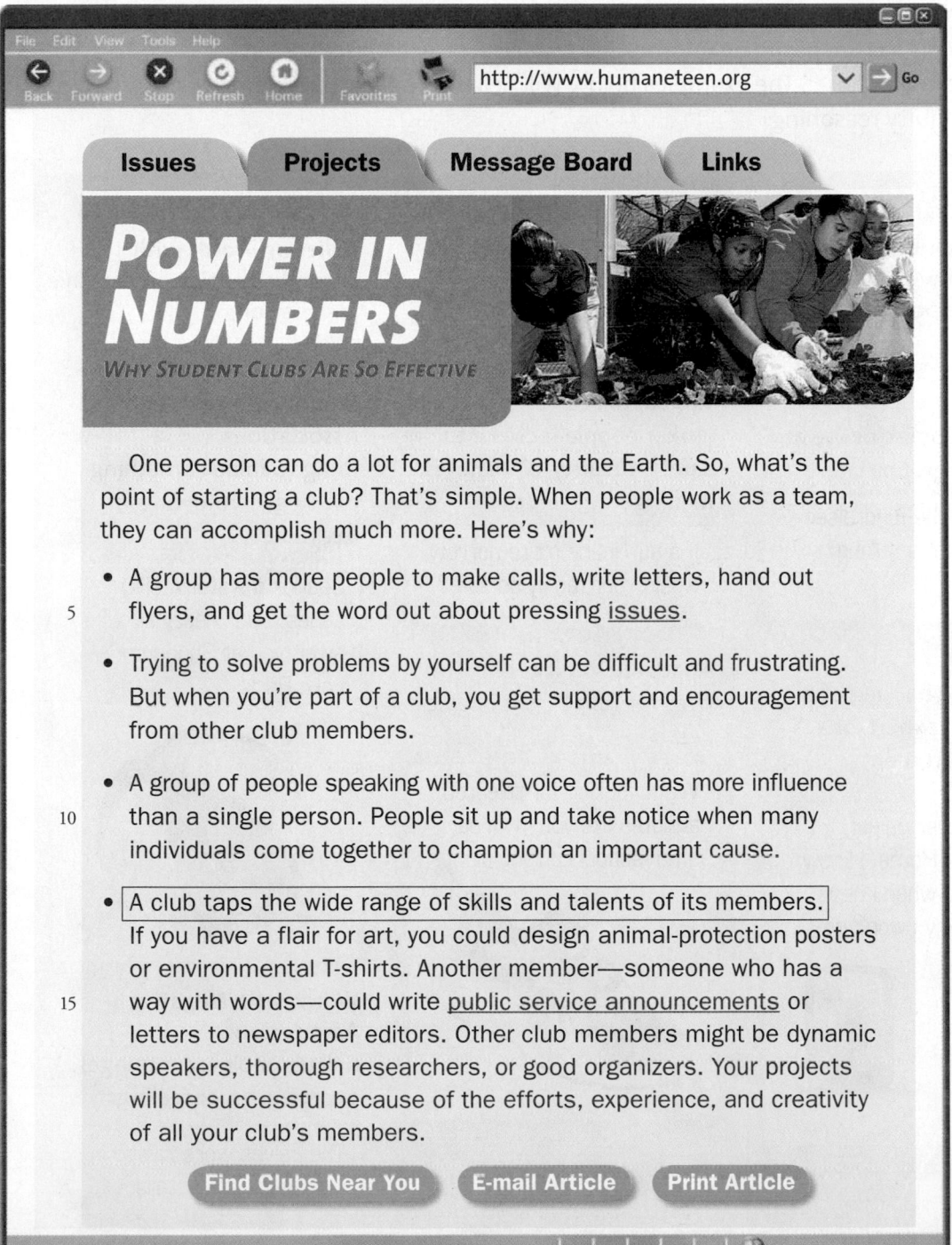

File   Edit   View   Tools   Help

http://www.humaneteen.org   Go

Issues   **Projects**   **Message Board**   **Links**

POWER IN NUMBERS
WHY STUDENT CLUBS ARE SO EFFECTIVE

One person can do a lot for animals and the Earth. So, what's the point of starting a club? That's simple. When people work as a team, they can accomplish much more. Here's why:

- A group has more people to make calls, write letters, hand out
5   flyers, and get the word out about pressing <u>issues</u>.

- Trying to solve problems by yourself can be difficult and frustrating. But when you're part of a club, you get support and encouragement from other club members.

- A group of people speaking with one voice often has more influence
10   than a single person. People sit up and take notice when many individuals come together to champion an important cause.

- A club taps the wide range of skills and talents of its members. If you have a flair for art, you could design animal-protection posters or environmental T-shirts. Another member—someone who has a
15   way with words—could write <u>public service announcements</u> or letters to newspaper editors. Other club members might be dynamic speakers, thorough researchers, or good organizers. Your projects will be successful because of the efforts, experience, and creativity of all your club's members.

Find Clubs Near You   E-mail Article   Print Article

Internet

Close Read

1. Look at the title of this article and reread the first paragraph. What is the author's claim?

2. In your own words, restate two of the reasons that the author gives to support the claim.

3. One of the author's reasons has been boxed. What examples are given to back up this reason?

4. In your opinion, does the author include enough evidence to support the claim? Is the evidence for or against the effectiveness of clubs?

Part 2: The Power of Persuasion

The persuasive messages that have made a lasting impression on you have probably been based on specific **persuasive techniques,** or methods, that were used to sway your heart and mind.

The persuasive techniques shown in the chart can make strong arguments even more powerful. However, they can also disguise flaws in weak arguments because these techniques can lead to faulty reasoning. **Faulty reasoning** is a claim based on information that is incorrect, biased, or simply does not make sense. The examples below will help you be alert to common kinds of faulty reasoning.

Appeals by Association	*Emotional Appeals*	*Loaded Language*
"Sell" a product or an idea by linking it with something or someone positive or influential	**Use strong feelings, rather than facts and evidence, to persuade**	**Relies on words with strongly positive or negative associations**

Appeals by Association

Bandwagon
Taps into people's desire to belong to a group

> Don't miss the fundraiser that everyone's talking about!

Testimonial
Relies on the backing of a celebrity, an expert, or a satisfied customer

> As the lead singer of Destination Home, I know good sound when I hear it. That's why I won't go anywhere without my FX portable music player.

Emotional Appeals

Appeal to Fear
Makes people feel as if their safety, security, or health is in danger

> If a hurricane hit tomorrow, would your family be safe?

Appeal to Vanity
Uses flattery to win people over

> We're looking for talented athletes like you. Join our after-school running club.

Loaded Language

Words with Positive Associations
Bring to mind something exciting, comforting, or desirable

> Sparkling waters, silky sands, and breezy air all await you at Shongum Lake Park.

Words with Negative Associations
Call up unpleasant images, experiences, or feelings

> The calves were raised in cramped, filthy stalls.

MODEL 1: PERSUASION IN WRITING

In this editorial, the author discusses a serious problem facing your generation. What persuasive techniques does he use to win you over?

A RECIPE FOR DISASTER
WHY TODAY'S TEENS NEED TO SHAPE UP

Magazine editorial by **Luis Frontera**

Picture this situation. You've just gotten home from a long day at school. You're not ready to start your homework, so you decide to kick back and watch TV. After seeing ads for greasy French fries, sugary soft drinks, and salty chips, you head to the kitchen to fix yourself
5 an enormous (and unhealthy) snack. With the TV blaring in the background, you then waste hours on the Web.

If you think there's nothing wrong with this lazy lifestyle, think again. Today's teens are the most overweight and inactive generation in history, largely because of poor eating habits, lack of exercise, and
10 exposure to mindless media. If teens don't break these damaging habits, they will increase their risk of developing life-threatening diseases, such as diabetes and hypertension.

Close Read

1. What is the claim in this editorial? What supporting evidence does the writer provide?

2. What emotional appeal does the author use?

3. Two examples of loaded language have been boxed. Find three additional examples.

MODEL 2: PERSUASION IN ADVERTISING

As you examine this public service ad, think about how the creators want you to react to its message.

These teens have taken their health and well-being into their own hands.

WILL YOU JOIN THEM OR SIT ON THE SIDELINES?

Campaign for Fit Teens America

Close Read

1. What claim does this ad make? What supporting evidence is provided?

2. Identify the persuasive technique that is used in this ad. Why was this technique used to target teens? Explain.

3. How does the photograph in this ad help to enhance the message? Review the messages in models 1 and 2. Compare and contrast the viewpoints in the messages, as well as the structures used to make the claims. Which message is more persuasive, and why?

Part 3: Analyze the Texts

Now, you'll apply what you've learned as you analyze two texts—an editorial and a poster. Both texts are about pit bulls, but their similarities end there. As you read each text, notice the argument that is being presented and how each author's viewpoint, or attitude toward the subject, differs.

DANGEROUS THREAT?
NO–Loving Pet!

Editorial by Lisa Epstein

Recently, pit bulls have become the targets of negative media coverage. All pit bulls have the urge to attack people, some articles state. They are a danger to children, a few experts say. And, they are just *too* violent to be household pets, some lawmakers believe. As the educated owner of a
5   pit bull, I can say that these reports are false. Pit bulls are not necessarily violent toward humans. In fact, they can make affectionate, loving pets.

So where did the misperception come from? More than 200 years ago, pit bulls were bred to compete in fights with other dogs. For that reason, pit bulls had certain qualities—such as aggression and
10 determination—that were important for fighting. Pit bulls today still have these same qualities, but they have other qualities as well: loyalty, friendliness, and a desire to please.

It's true that some pit bulls, such as those featured in news stories, *are* violent. However, this is because of bad owners, not because they're
15 a violent breed. Some irresponsible owners train their pit bulls to fight or attack, and because pit bulls want to please their owners, they act accordingly. In contrast, owners who treat pit bulls with love are rewarded with endless affection in return.

People who still need proof that pit bulls aren't violent can look at
20 recent studies. For example, the American Temperament Test Society (ATTS) is an organization that rates all breeds of dogs based on qualities like shyness and friendliness. In one study, pit bulls got a better overall rating than golden retrievers, whom many people view as the friendliest dogs around.

25 So, don't believe the unfair reports about how violent pit bulls are. In reality, they don't want to attack us; they want to curl up at our feet.

Close Read

1. Reread lines 1–6. What is the author's claim?

2. Review the persuasive techniques listed on page 938. Which technique does the author use in the boxed sentence?

3. What reason does the author give in the third paragraph to support her claim? Explain this reason in your own words.

4. Reread lines 19–24. In your opinion, does the author include enough evidence to support her claim? Why or why not?

5. Are the facts in this editorial used for or against the issue of keeping pit bulls as pets? Explain.

Not everyone agrees that pit bulls are cuddly, harmless creatures. What do the creators of this poster want viewers to know about pit bulls?

IS THIS THE KIND OF DOG THAT YOU WANT ROAMING OUR STREETS?

Pit bulls are violent creatures, capable of biting and attacking innocent children. These vicious beasts do not belong in our neighborhood. Support the law that would prohibit people from having pit bulls as pets.

Sponsored by Neighborhood Safety Watch

Close Read

1. In your own words, describe the claim that this poster makes. What supporting evidence do you find?

2. What persuasive technique is used to convince the intended audience—responsible neighbors—of the claim? How can you tell?

3. How do the photograph and the page design add to the persuasive power of the poster? Explain your answer.

4. One example of loaded language has been boxed. Find two additional examples.

5. Compare and contrast the structure and viewpoints of these two different authors writing for the same purpose—to persuade you to accept their claims about pit bulls. Which text is most convincing? Why?

What Video Games Can Teach Us
Magazine Article by Emily Sohn

The Violent Side of Video Games
Magazine Article

Can a GAME play YOU?

COMMON CORE

RI 8 Trace and evaluate the argument and specific claims in a text, distinguishing claims that are supported by reasons and evidence from claims that are not. **RI 9** Compare and contrast one author's presentation of events with that of another. **L 2** Demonstrate command of the conventions of punctuation.

How often have you heard the reminder "It's only a game"? It's meant to warn us that games shouldn't be taken too seriously. But suppose a game could help you learn, or change the way you act. Would it still be "only a game"? Many people think that video games, in particular, can have a powerful effect on their players. The following articles will show you some of the ways in which video games can be helpful or harmful.

DISCUSS Gather in a small group to discuss your video game habits. Take turns answering such questions as "How much time do you spend playing video games each week?" "What kinds of games do you play?" and "Do you think video games have a positive or negative effect on you?" When you are done, compare your answers with those of the other groups.

● TEXT ANALYSIS: ARGUMENT

An **argument** consists of a **claim,** or position on an issue or problem, supported by reasons and evidence. A basic argument might look like this.

Claim: *Dogs are smart.*

Support: *My dog knows his name and does tricks.*

The two articles that follow examine the pros and cons of playing video games. As you read them, look for facts included in each argument that are for or against the issue. Which article is in favor of playing video games and which one is opposed to them?

● READING SKILL: EVALUATE SUPPORT

To avoid being easily swayed by a weak argument, it is a good idea to evaluate the support and reasoning a writer includes. Watch for these weaknesses:

- **Vague language**—statements that are unclear
- **Irrelevant examples**—examples that do not directly relate to the claim
- **Faulty reasoning**—reasoning that includes fallacies, or errors in logic.

As you read each article, record examples of strong support and weak support in a chart like the one shown.

"What Video Games Can Teach Us"	
Strong Support	Weak Support
	Vague language: "a number of young gamers" (line 33)

▲ VOCABULARY IN CONTEXT

You'll find the following words in the articles on playing video games. To see how many you know, write definitions for the boldfaced words.

1. Video games **captivate** many people.
2. Some people worry about games that **simulate** violence.
3. Video game players learn to make **precise** movements.
4. The opinions of different experts **complicate** the issue.

 Complete the activities in your **Reader/Writer Notebook.**

Emily Sohn

A Mind for Science

A specialist in health and science, Emily Sohn has written for a number of publications, including *Health, U.S. News & World Report, Smithsonian,* and *Outside.* She has also written for the student Web site for *Science News.*

On Assignment

Though she is based in Minneapolis, Minnesota, Sohn's work as a freelance writer has taken her to faraway and fascinating places. Sohn has traveled to Cuba, Turkey, the Peruvian Amazon, and Sweden in order to research her stories. She is also the science correspondent for Project Exploration, a "living classroom" founded by paleontologist Dr. Paul Sereno and educator Gabrielle Lyon. Sohn went to the Sahara Desert in Niger to report on the project's Dinosaur Expedition 2005.

Free Time

Sohn loves being outside. When she's not writing or traveling, Sohn enjoys rock climbing, camping, and exploring.

Author Online
Go to **thinkcentral.com**. KEYWORD: HML6-943

THINK central

WHAT VIDEO GAMES CAN TEACH US

Emily Sohn

HERE'S SOME NEWS FOR YOU TO SHARE WITH YOUR PARENTS AND TEACHERS: VIDEO GAMES MIGHT ACTUALLY BE GOOD FOR YOU.

Whenever a wave of teenage violence strikes, movies, TV, or video games often take the heat. Some adults assume that movies, TV, and video games are a bad influence on kids, and they blame these media[1] for causing various problems. A variety of studies appear to support the link between media violence and bad behavior among kids.

But media don't necessarily *cause* violence, says James Gee. Gee
10 is an education professor at the University of Wisconsin, Madison. "You get a group of teenage boys who shoot up a school—of course they've played video games," Gee says. "Everyone does. It's like blaming food because we have obese people."

Video games are innocent of most of the charges against them, Gee says. The games might actually do a lot of good. Gee has written a book titled *What Video Games Have to Teach Us About Learning and Literacy.* Ⓐ

A **ARGUMENT**
Reread lines 1–17 and locate the author's claim. What **reasons** does she provide as support for her argument? What reasons does she include against it?

1. **media:** a general term that includes television, films, magazines, newspapers, and video games.

A growing number of researchers agree with Gee. If used in the right way, video and computer games have the potential to inspire learning.
20 And they can help players improve coordination[2] and visual skills.

Attention-Getting Games

A good video game is challenging, entertaining, and **complicated**, Gee says. It usually takes 50 to 60 hours of intense concentration to finish one. Even kids who can't sit still in school can spend hours trying to solve a video or computer game. . . .

The <u>captivating</u> power of video games might lie in their interactive nature. Players don't just sit and watch. They get to participate in the action and solve problems. Some games even allow players to make changes in the game, allowing new possibilities.

And kids who play computer games often end up knowing more
30 about computers than their parents do. "Kids today are natives in a culture in which their parents are immigrants," Gee says.

In his 2 to 3 years of studying the social influences of video games, Gee has seen a number of young gamers become computer science majors in college. One kid even ended up as a teaching assistant during his freshman year because the school's computer courses were too easy for him. **B**

Screen Reading

Video games can enhance reading skills too. In the game *Animal Crossing,* for instance, players become characters who live in a town full of animals. Over the course of the game, you can buy a house, travel
40 from town to town, go to museums, and do other ordinary things. All the while, you're writing notes to other players and talking to the animals. Because kids are interested in the game, they often end up reading at a level well above their grade, even if they say they don't like to read. ◆

Games can inspire new interests. After playing a game called *Age of Mythology,* Gee says, kids (like his 8-year-old son) often start checking out mythology books from the library or join Internet chat groups about mythological characters. History can come alive to a player participating in the game. . . .

---

2. **coordination:** the ability to make multiple muscle groups work smoothly together.

complicate
(kŏm′plĭ-kāt′) *v.*
to make difficult
or complex

captivate (kăp′tə-vāt′)
v. to attract and
hold interest

B **EVALUATE SUPPORT**
Reread lines 32–36.
Why might the author
have chosen to use
vague language to
make this point?

◆ **GRAMMAR IN
CONTEXT**
The second sentence
in line 37 begins with a
prepositional phrase,
"In the game," which
modifies "*Animal
Crossing.*" When you
use prepositional
phrases to modify a
word in a sentence, be
sure that you place the
prepositional phrase
close to that word, as
the author has done.
Otherwise, you can
confuse your readers.

Improved Skills

Video games might also help improve visual skills. That was what
50 researchers from the University of Rochester in New York recently found.

In the study, frequent game players between the ages of 18 and 23
were better at monitoring what was happening around them than those
who didn't play as often or didn't play at all. They could keep track
of more objects at a time. And they were faster at picking out objects
from a cluttered environment.

"Above and beyond the fact that action video games can
be beneficial," says Rochester neuroscientist[3] Daphne Bavelier,
"our findings are surprising because they show that the learning
induced by video game playing occurs quite fast and generalizes
60 outside the gaming experience." **C**

The research might lead to better ways to train soldiers or treat
people with attention problems, the researchers say, though they
caution against taking that point too far.

Says Bavelier, "We certainly don't mean to convey the message
that kids can play video games instead of doing their homework!"

If Gee gets his way, though, teachers might some day start
incorporating computer games into their assignments. Already,
scientists and the military use computer games to help **simulate**
certain situations for research or training, he says. Why shouldn't
70 schools do the same thing? . . . **D**

Researchers at the Massachusetts Institute of Technology have
started a project they describe as the "Education Arcade." The
project brings together researchers, scholars,[4] game designers and
others interested in developing and using computer games in the
classroom. . . .

Looking at the bright side of video and computer games could
also help bring kids and adults closer together. Playing games can
be a social activity, during which kids and adults learn from one
another. By opening up lines of communication and understanding,
80 maybe one day we'll praise video games for saving society, not
blame them for destroying it.

---

3. **neuroscientist** (noŏr′ō-sī′ən-tĭst): a scientist who studies the brain and the nervous system.
4. **scholars:** people who study a particular subject.

C **EVALUATE SUPPORT**
Does the support the
author provides in lines
51–60 seem strong?
Explain why or why not.

simulate (sĭm′yə-lāt′)
v. to imitate

D **EVALUATE SUPPORT**
What irrelevant example
does the author use in
lines 66–70? Record
this information in
your chart. Explain
whether you think this
is an example of faulty
reasoning.

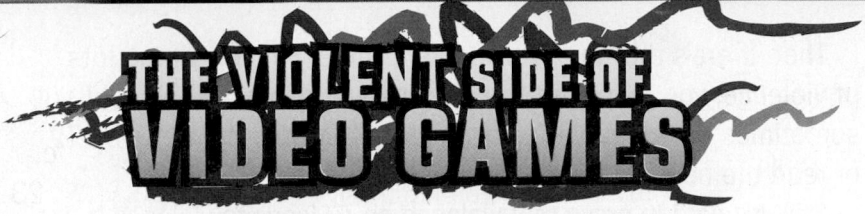

THE VIOLENT SIDE OF VIDEO GAMES

WHEN I WAS A KID, I WAS OBSESSED WITH VIDEO GAMES.

I saved my allowance to buy new games every month. I read Nintendo magazines for tips about solving the Super Mario Brothers adventures. I played so many hours of *Tetris* that I used to dream about little blocks falling perfectly into place.

There were physical effects too. My thumbs turned into machines, quick and **precise**. During especially difficult levels of play, my palms would sweat. My heart would race. I'd have knots in my stomach from anxiety. It was the same feeling I'd sometimes get from watching scary
10 movies or suspenseful TV shows.

After a while, I started to think that looking at screens and playing games all the time might be affecting me in ways I didn't even suspect. It turns out that I was probably right. **E**

Scientists are discovering that playing video and computer games and watching TV and movies can change the way we act, think, and feel. Whether these changes are good or bad has become a subject of intense debate.

Concerns About Violence

Violence is one of the biggest concerns, especially as computer graphics and special effects become more realistic. Some parents
20 and teachers blame . . . aggressive behavior on media violence—as seen in TV programs, movies, and video games.

"If you've ever watched young children watching kickboxing," says child psychologist[1] John Murray, "within a few minutes they start popping up and pushing and shoving and imitating the actions." Murray is at Kansas State University in Manhattan, Kansas.

There's also evidence that people become less sensitive to violence after a while, Murray says. In other words, you get so used to seeing it that you eventually think it's not such a big deal. **F**

---

1. **child psychologist** (sī-kŏl'ə-jĭst): a person trained to study thought and behavior patterns in children.

precise (prĭ-sīs') *adj.* exact or correct

E ARGUMENT
Reread the title of the selection, followed by lines 1–13. What claim does the author make?

F EVALUATE SUPPORT
Reread lines 22–28. Why is this support weak? Record the information in your chart.

G **EVALUATE SUPPORT**
Reread lines 29–32.
What is the irrelevant
example in these lines
meant to support?

Then there's the "mean world syndrome."[2] If you watch lots
30 of violence, you may start to think the world is a bad place. I still
sometimes have trouble falling asleep if I watch the news on TV
or read the newspaper right before going to bed. G

Still, it's hard to prove that violence on TV leads to violence in real
life. It might be possible, for example, that people who are already
aggressive for other reasons are more drawn to violent games and
TV shows. . . .

Video Power

COMMON CORE L 2

Language Coach

Indirect Quotations In
lines 37–49 the author
reports what experts
Murray and Anderson
say about video games
without using quotation
marks. These are called
indirect quotations.
Indirect quotations are
paraphrases or brief
summaries of what a
person said. They are
not in the person's exact
words. Why would it
be misleading to place
indirect quotations in
quotation marks?

Most of the research has focused on TV and movie violence, mainly
because TV and movies have been around much longer than video
games, says psychologist Craig Anderson of Iowa State University
40 in Ames, Iowa. Anderson has a Web site dedicated to looking at the
link between video games and violence.

In his own research and in analyses[3] of research by others,
Anderson says that he has detected a connection between violent
video games and violent behavior. He has found that people who
repeatedly play violent games have aggressive thoughts and become
less helpful and sociable. Physically, their heart rates accelerate.

*Video games might have an even more powerful effect on the
brain than TV does, Murray says. Players actively participate in the
violence. . . .

50 Next time you play a violent video game, Murray suggests, check
your pulse just before and after each round as one way to see how
the game affects you.

"Ninety-nine percent of the time, I'll bet your heart rate will have
increased rather dramatically while playing one," Murray says. "This
indicates that . . . you are being affected." H

Three teenagers from Puerto Rico have data to back up that
observation. With the help of a school nurse, the high school seniors
found that people of all ages showed a rise in blood pressure and
heart rate after playing a superviolent game. Playing an active,
60 nonviolent game did not have the same effect.

H **EVALUATE SUPPORT**
Reread lines 47–55.
Does the evidence in
this section provide
support for or against
the claim? Explain why
or why not.

---

2. **syndrome** (sĭn′drōm′): a group or pattern of symptoms that make up a disease or condition.

3. **analyses** (ə-năl′ĭ-sēz′): examinations of different information or experimental results.

Comprehension

1. **Recall** According to "What Video Games Can Teach Us," why is the military using computer games for training?

2. **Clarify** According to "The Violent Side of Video Games," what is the "mean world syndrome"?

3. **Summarize** Reread lines 37–46 in "The Violent Side of Video Games." Then write a summary of Craig Anderson's discoveries.

COMMON CORE

RI 8 Trace and evaluate the argument and specific claims in a text, distinguishing claims that are supported by reasons and evidence from claims that are not. **RI 9** Compare and contrast one author's presentation of events with that of another.

Text Analysis

4. **Examine Evidence** One common type of evidence is **expert testimony,** or quotes from people who are knowledgeable about whatever subject is being argued. Look over the articles to find the experts who are quoted in each one. Why might the author have chosen these particular experts?

5. **Evaluate Support** Look back at the chart you filled in as you read, reviewing the support for each article. What examples of faulty reasoning did you find?

6. **Analyze an Argument** In a graphic organizer like the one shown, list the reasons Sohn gives for her position in "What Video Games Can Teach Us." Then list the evidence she includes to support her position. Create a similar chart for the second article. Use your charts to compare and contrast the structure and viewpoints of the two articles.

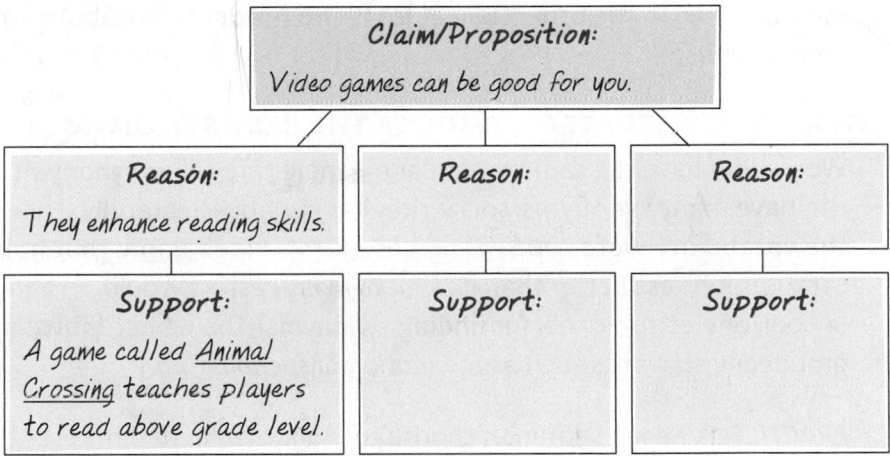

Claim/Proposition:
Video games can be good for you.

Reason: They enhance reading skills.

Reason:

Reason:

Support: A game called *Animal Crossing* teaches players to read above grade level.

Support:

Support:

Extension and Challenge

7. **Technology Connection** Research to find out what professions use computer games or simulations to train staff. What kinds of simulations or games are used? How effective are they in preparing people to do real work?

Can a GAME play YOU?

Review the results of the group activity on page 942. How have your views of the positive or negative effects of video games changed?

Vocabulary in Context

▲ VOCABULARY PRACTICE

Choose the letter of the word or phrase that best completes each sentence.

1. You **complicate** directions by (a) adding steps, (b) explaining them, (c) writing them down.
2. To **simulate** eating, you (a) buy food, (b) pretend to chew, (c) think of dinner.
3. A movie can **captivate** you, making you want to (a) get popcorn, (b) chat, (c) watch closely.
4. A **precise** measurement is (a) estimated, (b) correct, (c) unreliable.

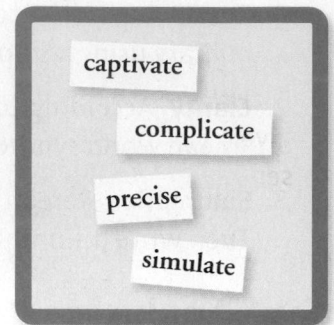

ACADEMIC VOCABULARY IN SPEAKING

• adequacy   • authority   • concept   • purpose   • structural

With a small group, discuss the **adequacy** of the supporting details and evidence in the articles on video games. Decide whether one article is more convincing than the other. Use at least two Academic Vocabulary words in your response.

VOCABULARY STRATEGY: CHOOSE THE BEST SYNONYM

Words that have the same or similar meanings are called **synonyms.** A word can have many synonyms, so a writer has to choose carefully. For example, the vocabulary word *captivating* describes a video game that holds or captures interest better than its synonym *interesting* would. In a **thesaurus** (a book or electronic tool for finding synonyms), the word *captivating* is also grouped with words such as *fascinating* or *spellbinding*.

PRACTICE For each sentence, choose the synonym in parentheses that best replaces the boldfaced word in the context provided. Consult a dictionary or thesaurus for help.

1. The abandoned factory was dark and **empty.** (deserted, unfilled)
2. After the marathon, he **drank** as much water as he could. (sipped, gulped)
3. The room was **large** and airy. (spacious, massive)
4. The kittens **hit** a ball of yarn back and forth. (batted, smacked)
5. By the end of the five-mile hike, we were all **tired.** (sleepy, exhausted)

COMMON CORE

L 4c Consult thesauruses, both print and digital, to clarify meaning.

Interactive Vocabulary **THINK** central

Go to **thinkcentral.com.**
KEYWORD: HML6-950

Language

◆ **GRAMMAR IN CONTEXT:** Avoid Misplaced Modifiers

A **prepositional phrase** begins with a preposition—such as *from, in, on, under,* or *with*—and ends with a noun or pronoun. Prepositional phrases **modify,** or give information about, another word in the sentence. For example, in the sentence "The mouse is under the table," *under the table* modifies *mouse.* If a prepositional phrase is placed too far from the word it modifies, the sentence's meaning may be unclear.

Original: Anderson connected video games with behavior in his research.

Revised: In his research, Anderson connected video games with behavior.

PRACTICE   Move each prepositional phrase to the correct position.

1. Much has been said about violent video games in the news media.
2. Video games can have a more powerful effect than TV on the brain.
3. You can learn a lot from video games with patience and concentration.
4. Emily Sohn talks about playing many video games in her article.

*For more help with misplaced modifiers, see page R59 in the **Grammar Handbook**.*

READING-WRITING CONNECTION

YOUR TURN   Show your understanding of the two articles on video games by responding to the prompt. Then use the **revising tip** to improve your writing.

WRITING PROMPT	**REVISING TIP**
Extended Constructed Response: Opinion A newspaper editorial is a short piece of writing that expresses an opinion. Write a two- or three-paragraph **editorial** or **letter to the editor** stating whether education in your school should or should not include instructional video games. Cite evidence from one or both of the articles in your editorial.	Check to see that you avoided misplaced modifiers in your editorial. Review your work to be sure that you don't confuse your readers with a prepositional phrase that is in the wrong place.

COMMON CORE

L1 Demonstrate command of the conventions of grammar. **W1** Write arguments to support claims with relevant evidence.

Interactive Revision

THINK central

Go to **thinkcentral.com**.
KEYWORD: HML6-951

Should Wild Animals Be Kept as Pets?

Video link at
thinkcentral.com

Persuasive Essay by the Humane Society of the United States

Can we ever TAME ~Help~ what's wild?

Would you like to have a wolf for a pet? How about a monkey? Owning a wild animal may sound exciting, but unfortunately, people who keep wild animals as pets often run into trouble when they are trying to tame them. In the essay you are about to read, you'll discover some of the challenges that can come with having an unusual pet.

LIST IT Is there a particular wild animal you wish you could own? Make a list of what you think might be the advantages (reasons for) and disadvantages (reasons against) of keeping that type of animal. Compare your lists with those of your classmates.

Monkey	
Advantages	Disadvantages
I could teach it to play games.	It might break things.

952

TEXT ANALYSIS: PERSUASIVE TECHNIQUES

If you make an argument for or against an issue, you persuade other people using facts and other evidence. But there are other ways to persuade people to adopt an opinion or take action. These **persuasive techniques** include

- **Emotional appeals**—messages that produce strong feelings, such as pity or fear
- **Appeals to authority**—references to people who are experts on a subject
- **Loaded language**—words with strongly positive or strongly negative connotations, or shades of meaning

As you read "Should Wild Animals Be Kept as Pets?" notice the persuasive techniques used in the essay. Record examples in a chart like the one shown.

Emotional Appeals	Appeals to Authority	Loaded Language

READING STRATEGY: PREVIEW

When you **preview** a text, you look for clues that tell you what it is about. One way to preview is to **skim text features,** quickly looking over such elements as the title, subheadings, and graphic aids. As you read, notice how previewing the text features helps you focus on the most important ideas.

VOCABULARY IN CONTEXT

The words in Column A help to explain the Humane Society's position on the issue of keeping wild animals. See how many you know by matching each vocabulary word in Column A with the word in Column B that is closest in meaning.

Column A	Column B
1. captivity	a. inborn
2. domesticate	b. tame
3. instinctive	c. confinement
4. unsuitable	d. improper

Background

Animal Protector

Founded in 1954, the Humane Society of the United States is the world's largest animal-protection organization. Members of the Humane Society are tireless in their efforts on behalf of the country's many dogs, cats, and other pets. However, the Humane Society also works to protect wildlife, animals raised for food, and animals used in research. It is also the leading disaster relief agency for animals.

Policies and a Vision

The Humane Society works to help make the public more aware of the proper treatment of animals. The Humane Society also enforces laws that help to protect animals from cruelty, exploitation, and neglect. The organization has a vision of a world in which humans and animals live in harmony. It believes that we have a moral duty to protect the animals whose habitats we share.

 Complete the activities in your **Reader/Writer Notebook.**

Ocelot

A PREVIEW
Skim the essay's title and photographs. Based on these text features, what types of information do you expect to find in the essay?

captivity (kăp-tĭv′ĭ-tē) *n.* the condition of being confined or not free

Should Wild Animals Be Kept as Pets? A

The Humane Society of the United States

The Humane Society of the United States strongly opposes keeping wild animals as pets. This principle[1] applies to both native and nonnative species, whether caught in the wild or bred in **captivity.** The overwhelming majority[2] of people who obtain these animals are unable to provide the care they require.

---

1. **principle:** a policy or rule.
2. **overwhelming majority:** most or almost all.

Caring for Wild Animals Is Difficult or Impossible B

Despite what animal sellers may say, appropriate care for wild animals requires considerable expertise,[3] specialized facilities,[4] and lifelong dedication to the animals. Their nutritional and social needs
10 are demanding to meet and, in many cases, are unknown. They often grow to be larger, stronger, and more dangerous than owners expect or can manage. Small cats such as ocelots and bobcats can be as deadly to children as lions and tigers. Wild animals also pose a danger to human health and safety through disease and parasites.[5]

Baby Animals Grow Up

Baby animals can be irresistibly adorable—until the cuddly baby becomes bigger and stronger than the owner ever imagined. The **instinctive** behavior of the adult animal replaces the dependent behavior of the juvenile, resulting in biting, scratching, or displaying
20 destructive behaviors without provocation[6] or warning. Such animals typically become too difficult to manage and are confined to small cages, passed from owner to owner, or disposed of in other ways. There are not enough reputable sanctuaries[7] or other facilities to properly care for unwanted wild animals. They can end up back in the exotic pet trade.[8] Some may be released into the wild where, if they survive, they can disrupt the local ecosystem.[9] C

Wild Animals Spread Disease

The Centers for Disease Control and Prevention[10] discourages direct contact with wild animals for a simple reason: They can carry
30 diseases that are dangerous to people, such as rabies, herpes B virus, and Salmonella. The herpes B virus commonly found among macaque monkeys can be fatal to humans. Thousands of people

---

3. **considerable expertise:** a great deal of knowledge and experience.
4. **specialized facilities:** places that are created and used for a specific function.
5. **parasites** (păr′ə-sīts′)**:** animals that live on or in other animals and feed off of them.
6. **provocation** (prŏv′ə-kā′shən)**:** something done to cause anger or irritation.
7. **reputable sanctuaries** (rĕp′yə-tə-bəl săngk′chōo-ĕr′ēz)**:** trustworthy and reliable places that provide protected areas for animals.
8. **exotic pet trade:** the business of buying and selling wild, and sometimes rare, animals.
9. **ecosystem:** a community of living things, together with their environment.
10. **The Centers . . . Prevention:** One of 13 groups that are part of the U.S. Department of Health and Human Services, which works to protect the health and safety of Americans. Also referred to by its acronym: CDC.

B PREVIEW
Preview the article's subheadings. Why do you think they have been included in the essay?

instinctive
(ĭn-stĭngk′tĭv) *adj.*
of or about the natural behaviors of a type of animal

C PERSUASIVE TECHNIQUES
Reread lines 15–26. What emotional appeals are used in this section? Add this information to your chart. What strong feelings do these emotional appeals stir up?

D ANALYZE ARGUMENT
Frequently, persuasive arguments are written to influence the way you feel about an important issue. Some arguments might try to convince you to agree with an issue; others attempt to build opposition to an issue. Regardless of the idea it supports, an argument will include facts and other forms of evidence to build its case. This persuasive text is written to influence the way readers feel about keeping wild animals as pets. Identify the facts included in lines 27–38. How do these facts strengthen the argument against keeping wild animals as pets?

domesticate
(də-mĕs′tĭ-kāt′) *v.* to tame a wild species of animal over generations

unsuitable
(ŭn-sōō′tə-bəl) *adj.* not appropriate or fitting

Long-tailed macaque monkey

get Salmonella infections each year from contact with reptiles or amphibians, causing the CDC to recommend that these animals be kept out of homes with children under five. A recent outbreak of monkeypox[11] was set in motion when small mammals carrying the disease were imported for the pet trade and infected native prairie dogs, which were also sold as pets. **D**

Domestication Takes Thousands of Years

40 Wild animals are not **domesticated** simply by being captive-born or hand-raised. It's a different story with dogs and cats, who have been domesticated by selective breeding for desired traits over thousands of years. These special animal companions depend on humans for food, shelter, veterinary care, and affection. Wild animals, by nature, are self-sufficient and fare best without our interference. The instinctive behavior of these animals makes them **unsuitable** as pets.

---

11. **monkeypox:** a virus first found in monkeys, which is harmful and sometimes fatal to both humans and animals.

Capturing Wild Animals Threatens Their Survival

When wild-caught animals are kept as pets, their suffering may begin with capture—every year millions of birds and reptiles
50 suffer and die on the journey to the pet store. Even after purchase, their lives are likely to be filled with misery. If they survive, they may languish[12] in a cramped backyard cage or circle endlessly in a cat carrier or aquarium. More often, they become sick or die because their owners are unable to care for them properly. The global wild pet trade continues to threaten the existence of some species in their native habitats. **E**

Having any animal as a pet means being responsible for providing appropriate and humane care. Where wild animals are concerned, meeting this responsibility is usually impossible.
60 People, animals, and the environment suffer the consequences.

---

12. **languish** (lăng′gwĭsh): suffer in a state of neglect or indifference.

COMMON CORE RI 4

Language Coach
Negative Connotations
This essay uses words like *suffering*, *misery*, and *languish*. These are words with strong **negative connotations**, or suggested meanings. What is the emotional effect of such strong words?

E **PERSUASIVE TECHNIQUES**
Reread lines 47–56. Record examples of the loaded language used in this section in your chart.

Prairie dog

Comprehension

1. **Recall** What three things are required to properly care for a wild animal?

2. **Clarify** Reread lines 15–26. What can happen to wild animals when their owners are no longer able to manage them?

3. **Clarify** Reread lines 40–46. Describe the process by which animals become domesticated.

Text Analysis

4. **Examine Author's Argument** Why do you think the Humane Society argues against keeping wild animals as pets? Include evidence from the text that supports your answer.

5. **Monitor Previewing** In what way did previewing the text features help you better understand the essay? Explain.

6. **Evaluate Persuasive Techniques** Review the chart that you filled in as you read. Then explain which of the three persuasive techniques used in the essay was the most convincing and why.

7. **Draw Conclusions** According to the essay, there are distinct differences between wild animals and domesticated, or tame, animals. In a chart like the one shown, note the unique traits of each type of animal. Then explain which traits make wild animals the most unsuitable as pets.

Wild	Tame

Extension and Challenge

8. **Speaking and Listening** Imagine that you have been asked to film a public service announcement explaining the responsibilities and challenges that come with having an exotic pet. With a partner, write the script for your announcement. Then present it to the class.

9. **Inquiry and Research** Research wildlife sanctuaries, rescue centers, and other facilities in your area that aid in the survival and protection of animals. Choose one and summarize the work they do. Present your findings to the class.

An alligator at an exotic animal sanctuary

Can we ever TAME what's wild?

Look back at the list you made of advantages and disadvantages of owning a particular wild animal. Now that you have read this essay, how would your list change?

COMMON CORE

RI 8 Trace and evaluate the argument and specific claims in a text, distinguishing claims that are supported by reasons and evidence from claims that are not. **W 7** Conduct short research projects.

Vocabulary in Context

▲ VOCABULARY PRACTICE

Show your understanding of the vocabulary words by deciding whether each statement is true or false.

captivity

domesticate

instinctive

unsuitable

1. An **instinctive** behavior is one that an animal learns as it grows.
2. You cannot **domesticate** an animal in a day.
3. Animals in **captivity** are never kept in cages.
4. If something meets a person's needs, it is considered **unsuitable.**

ACADEMIC VOCABULARY IN WRITING

> • adequacy • authority • concept • purpose • structural

In what sense can the "author" of the essay—the Humane Society of the United States—be seen as an **authority,** or expert on the subject? Use at least two Academic Vocabulary words in your response.

VOCABULARY STRATEGY: CONTEXT CLUES

You can sometimes figure out the meaning of an unfamiliar word by finding **context clues** in the same sentence, or within the surrounding paragraph. You may figure out what a word means because of a cause-and-effect relationship presented in the sentence: *The torch **ignited**, lighting up the entire patio.* (You can tell that *ignited* has something to do with lighting up or catching fire.) You may also discover a word's meaning through a compare and contrast structure in which the unfamiliar word is contrasted with a more familiar word or phrase: *I play video games **infrequently**, not all the time.*

PRACTICE Use context clues to write a definition of each boldfaced word.

1. Bulldozers **graded** the land so that it was smooth and level for the new road.
2. Ice will **liquefy** if the temperature is above 32 degrees.
3. A **miscellany** of tools, including satellites, radar, and barometers, help people predict the weather.
4. Over the course of the season, the basketball player has had many free throw opportunities but has scored points only **sporadically.**

COMMON CORE

L 4a Use context as a clue to the meaning of a word or phrase.
L 6 Acquire and use accurately academic words.

Interactive Vocabulary THINK central

Go to **thinkcentral.com**.
KEYWORD: HML6-959

No Thought of Reward
Speech by Mawi Asgedom

What good comes from a
GOOD DEED?

COMMON CORE

RI 6 Determine an author's point of view or purpose and explain how it is conveyed in the text.
RI 8 Trace and evaluate the argument and specific claims in a text, distinguishing claims that are supported by reasons and evidence from claims that are not.

You have probably heard the saying "It's better to give than to receive." Sometimes even the smallest good deeds can have an enormous effect on the lives of others—and on the life of the giver, as well. In the speech you are about to read, Mawi Asgedom shares what his father taught him about giving to others.

DISCUSS Is it sensible to do good deeds just for the sake of doing good, or is it reasonable to expect something good in return? Discuss this question with your classmates.

VOLUNTEERS WANTED!
Clean up Avondale Park

When: Saturday, August 7th Where: Avondale Park
(Avondale Blvd. and Maple St.) Who: Volunteers of all ages

Come help make our wonderful park a better, more beautiful environment for everyone.

Encourage your friends and neighbors to join in this fun community effort.

Bench painting and clean up begin at 10:00 A.M. Refreshments will be provided for all volunteers.

TEXT ANALYSIS: AUTHOR'S MESSAGE

An **author's message** in a persuasive text is the main point the writer wants to get across to his or her readers. An author's message is usually **implied,** meaning you have to infer it from details in the text. Often an author's message is expressed by

- the title of a work
- a statement in the introduction or conclusion
- supporting details, such as the actions or comments of people in the selection

As you read "No Thought of Reward," look at these elements to identify the author's message.

READING SKILL: ANALYZE PERSUASION

Persuasion is the art of leading others to accept a certain idea or take a specific action. To persuade someone, writers often start by building a logical, well-supported argument. Then, they might use persuasive devices to strengthen the argument.

In his persuasive speech, Mawi Asgedom supports his position with **examples** from personal experience. He also uses **rhetorical questions,** or questions that have an obvious answer, to suggest that anyone with common sense must agree with him. As you read the speech, record the personal examples and rhetorical questions Asgedom uses in a chart like the one shown.

Personal Examples	Rhetorical Questions
Tewolde supported a homeless man.	"Whom do you value: the person who takes from you or the person who gives to you?"

▲ VOCABULARY IN CONTEXT

Mawi Asgedom uses the boldfaced words to tell how he learned the value of good deeds. Restate each sentence using a different word or phrase for the boldfaced term.

1. Babay wanted his sons to **contribute** to their town.
2. At first, the boys didn't **appreciate** their father's advice.
3. They later admired his **dedication** to helping others.

 Complete the activities in your **Reader/Writer Notebook.**

Meet the Author

Mawi Asgedom
born 1976

Inspiring Others
Motivational speaker Mawi Asgedom (mou'ē ŏz'gə'dŏm) travels the country inspiring American teenagers to become successful, caring people. He has produced several CDs and books, including *Of Beetles and Angels,* a memoir of his early life.

A Young Refugee
Asgedom arrived in the United States at the age of seven. His family had escaped from civil war in their native Ethiopia, and then suffered through three years in a refugee camp. In the United States, Asgedom had to overcome the challenges of poverty, a new language, and cruel teasing. Nevertheless, he worked hard in school and was accepted to Harvard University with a full scholarship.

Little Deeds of Kindness
Asgedom is often moved by small acts of kindness. In his graduation speech at Harvard, Asgedom said, "Any one of us, however small and helpless we may feel, can spark unimagined changes.... Quite often, it will be the small things that ... will have the most impact."

Author Online

THINK central

Go to **thinkcentral.com.**
KEYWORD: HML6-961

No Thought of *Reward*

Mawi Asgedom

Language Coach

Oral Fluency In the word *neighbors* (line 15), the *gh* letter combination is silent. However, in *enough* (line 14), this letter combination is pronounced like the letter *f*. Look up the following words in a dictionary: *tough, straight, weigh, cough*. In which words is the *gh* silent? In which words does it sound like the letter *f*?

When we were kids, my brother Tewolde and I always looked forward to the weekend. Our father made us get up at 5:00 A.M. every weekday to exercise, so all we wanted to do Saturday morning was sleep late.

But our father, whom we called Babay, would have none of that. At the crack of dawn, his voice would echo all around our house.

"SELAMAWI, TEWOLDE, GET THE CLEANING BRUSHES," our father would order us. "IT'S TIME TO
10 REMOVE THE LEAVES FROM THE DRIVEWAY."

This wasn't just any driveway—the driveway that separated our house from our neighbors' must have been 100 feet long. Raking it took hours, and if that weren't bad enough, we barely even used it—it really belonged to our neighbors.

Tewolde and I would protest with every possible argument: "Come on, Babay! It's early in the morning. It's cold outside. Our family uses only a small part of the driveway. No one expects us to rake the whole thing! Why
20 can't our neighbors rake their own part?"

Our father's firm tone told us we had no choice.

"I KNOW YOU ARE MAD NOW, MY CHILDREN. BUT I AM TEACHING YOU HOW TO LIVE WELL WITH YOUR NEIGHBORS. YOU NEED TO LEARN, STARTING NOW, HOW TO GIVE TO OTHERS WITHOUT THOUGHT OF REWARD FOR YOURSELF." **A**

For a long time, we thought our father was crazy. Who in their right mind woke up early on a Saturday morning to
30 clear someone else's driveway for free?

But as we grew older, my brother Tewolde took our father's words to heart. Tewolde continued to rake the

A AUTHOR'S MESSAGE
Reread lines 22–27. Notice how the author repeats the idea stated in his title. Based on this repetition, what can you conclude is the author's message?

neighbors' leaves and also gave much more: He supported a homeless man who had no one else to turn to, gave to his classmates through kind words and actions, and even sent hundreds of dollars a year to support a child in South America—without telling anyone.

Years later, when Tewolde died, and again, when my father passed away, I was stunned by the number of folks 40 who came to honor their memories. The funeral-home directors said they had never witnessed such turnouts, not even for community leaders. **B**

How was it that my brother and father—poor, black immigrants in a wealthy, white town—had meant something special to so many folks? *It was because they had given so much without expecting anything in return.*

See, most of us walk around thinking: *How can I make myself happy? What can I get? How can I get other people to hook me up?*

50 But what if we instead thought: *What can I give to those around me? How can I **contribute** to my school, to my family, to my friends, to my neighbors?*

Wouldn't we mean something special to other people? Wouldn't other people want to give back to us, too?

Just think about your own life. Whom do you value: the person who takes from you, or the person who gives to you?

If you give your school everything you have—hard work, a great attitude, respect for others—won't your teachers and counselors[1] be more likely to **appreciate** you?

60 If you give your friends love, kindness, and support, won't they be more likely to give it back to you?

If you give your sports team effort, **dedication,** and a great attitude, won't your coaches more likely give you playing time? If you were the coach, wouldn't you want to give back to those who gave the most? I know I would. **C**

So if you want to mean something special to others, don't just focus on what you can get. Start by focusing on what you can give—without expecting any reward.

---

1. **counselors:** people responsible for giving students help and advice.

B **ANALYZE PERSUASION**
In persuasive texts, examples can be used to argue for or against an issue. Suppose you had to write an essay on the issue of using study groups. To argue for using study groups, you might write about a time when your test score improved after studying with a friend. To argue against using study groups, you might relate an example in which your group was not productive. In lines 31–42, Asgedom includes examples of his brother's actions. How do these actions—and their results—strengthen the writer's argument for performing good deeds?

contribute
(kən-trĭb′yo͞ot) *v.* to offer a gift or a service

appreciate
(ə-prē′shē-āt′) *v.* to admire or value

dedication
(dĕd′ĭ-kā′shən) *n.* commitment or devotion

C **ANALYZE PERSUASION**
Reread lines 53–65, recording any rhetorical questions in your chart. What is the effect of these questions?

Comprehension

1. **Recall** Why did Mawi Asgedom and his brother look forward to the weekend?

2. **Recall** Name two of Tewolde's good deeds.

3. **Clarify** In the author's opinion, why did large numbers of people go to Babay's and Tewolde's funerals?

COMMON CORE

RI 6 Determine an author's point of view or purpose and explain how it is conveyed in the text.
RI 8 Trace and evaluate the argument and specific claims in a text, distinguishing claims that are supported by reasons and evidence from claims that are not.

Text Analysis

● 4. **Examine Author's Message** Notice the various places in the speech where Asgedom repeats or restates his message. What reason might he have had for doing this?

5. **Identify Cause-and-Effect Relationships** Throughout his speech, Asgedom provides examples of cause-and-effect situations. Identify the cause-and-effect statements in the speech. Then, create a graphic organizer like the one shown for each example. How do these statements strengthen the writer's argument for performing good deeds without expecting any reward?

> **Cause:** Give your sports team effort. → **Effect:** Get more playing time.

● 6. **Analyze Persuasion** Look back at the chart you filled in as you read. Note the point at which Asgedom begins to include rhetorical questions. Do these questions strengthen or weaken his argument?

7. **Draw Conclusions** Reread the instructions Asgedom gives in lines 66–68 and compare them to Babay's original statement in lines 23–27. Notice that Asgedom's version begins with "if you want to mean something special to others." Why do you think he uses this approach?

● 8. **Evaluate Persuasion** Was Asgedom's speech successful in persuading you to accept his idea about good deeds? Explain why or why not.

Extension and Challenge

9. **Speaking and Listening** Develop a "Do a Good Deed for Your School" public service announcement in which you encourage students to contribute to building an atmosphere of kindness, contribution, and appreciation in your school.

What good comes from a GOOD DEED?

Now that you have read the speech, think back to the discussion activity on page 960. How has this speech affected your views? Make a list of at least five good deeds that you could do to improve the lives of others. Which of these activities do you think you would find most rewarding?

Vocabulary in Context

▲ VOCABULARY PRACTICE

Show that you understand the boldfaced vocabulary words by answering the following questions.

1. Would you **contribute** to a charity by asking for help or by donating money?
2. Which shows more **dedication,** turning in homework or coming late to class?
3. If you **appreciate** classical music, do you like to listen to it?

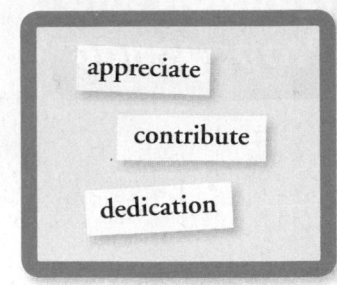

ACADEMIC VOCABULARY IN WRITING

 • adequacy   • authority   • concept   • purpose   • structural

Write about a person, group, or organization you know that has done something helpful for another person or for the community. What was the **purpose** of the good deed? Use at least two Academic Vocabulary words in your response.

VOCABULARY STRATEGY: FOREIGN WORDS AND PHRASES IN ENGLISH

Just as people have come to the United States from other countries, many of the words and phrases we use in English have also come from other lands. For example, you may have received invitations to parties or events that say you must "RSVP," which stands for *repondez s'il vous plait* (rā-pōn-dā' sēl vü plā), a French phrase that means "Please respond."

PRACTICE Use a dictionary or online source to explain the meaning of each boldfaced word or phrase. The language the word or phrase comes from is shown in parentheses.

1. Casey told her little brother a thousand times that going into her room without her permission was **verboten**. (German)
2. I know it's a **cliché,** but I really do feel like I'm between a rock and a hard place. (French)
3. Living in a beautiful forest by a creek would be Sam's idea of **la dolce vita.** (Italian)
4. Instead of brooding about your argument, you should just talk to your friend **mano a mano.** (Spanish)
5. Kaswana smiled and said **"Hakuna matata"** when I apologized for forgetting to bring the book I'd promised to loan her. (Swahili)

COMMON CORE

L 6 Gather vocabulary knowledge when considering a word or phrase important to comprehension or expression.

Go to **thinkcentral.com**.
KEYWORD: HML6-965

Start the Day Right!
Public Service Announcement Script

Shine-n-Grow: Hair Repair That Really Works!
Advertisement

Brain Breeze
Advertisement

How far will we go to IMPROVE ourselves?

COMMON CORE

RI 4 Determine the meaning of words and phrases as they are used in a text, including connotative meanings. RI 6 Determine an author's point of view or purpose and explain how it is conveyed in the text. RI 8 Trace and evaluate the argument and specific claims in a text, distinguishing claims that are supported by reasons and evidence from claims that are not.

An often-quoted motivational saying tells us that "The biggest room in the world is the room for improvement." The desire to improve can be healthy if we're eliminating bad habits, improving performance, or trying new things to broaden our experience. Sometimes, though, we may go on anxious quests to chase an illusion of perfection.

DISCUSS In a small group, brainstorm a list of ads, commercials, or posters you've seen recently that try to appeal to the drive for self-improvement. Discuss whether each advertiser's message was effective or ineffective and explain why.

Start the Day Right!
Public Service Announcement

"Start the Day Right!" is a **public service announcement**, a non-commercial media or print advertisement that seeks to generate public awareness of a social issue, such as safety, health, or education. Public service announcements are informative and educational, but they are also always **persuasive**—intended to bring about some change in people's attitudes or behaviors.

Standards Focus: Persuasive Techniques

Have you ever stopped to think about how many persuasive messages you receive from the media? Whether it's an ad in a magazine for jeans, a TV commercial for dishwashing liquid, or a billboard promoting bicycle helmet safety, you are exposed to dozens of persuasive messages each day. All of these persuasive messages attempt to win you over to a particular idea or influence you to take a specific action.

Writers will use **persuasive techniques** such as logical and emotional appeals to convince their audience. **Logical appeals** rely on facts and evidence to support a **claim,** or message. **Emotional appeals,** on the other hand, do not rely on facts and evidence. They stir the feelings of an audience, often through the use of **loaded language**—words with either positive or negative connotations, or suggested meanings.

"Start the Day Right!" is a script and storyboard for a public service announcement television commercial. As you read, notice the persuasive techniques it uses. Identify examples in a chart like the one shown.

"Start the Day Right!"	
Claim	
Logical Appeals and Evidence	
Emotional Appeals and Loaded Language	

 Complete the activities in your **Reader/Writer Notebook.**

Public Service Announcements
Public service announcements are created for government agencies, such as the Peace Corps, and non-profit organizations, such as the Red Cross. Public service announcements are usually created as ad campaigns, consisting of a variety of ads for different media. An ad campaign will usually have a strong "identity," such as a catchy saying like the Army's "Be All You Can Be."

Truth in Advertising
The Federal Trade Commission (FTC) is the part of the federal government that makes certain that advertisers do not engage in deceptive, or untruthful, practices. If an advertiser makes a claim, even an implicit one, the FTC demands that there is sufficient support to back up the claims. This support must be "competent and reliable scientific evidence," such as test results and research findings. If a company is found guilty of untruthful advertising, the FTC can take action, doing everything from fining the company to demanding that the company give refunds to consumers.

Propaganda
Propaganda generally refers to messages that are spread by governments or institutions that try to control the way people think or behave and refuse to recognize other points of view. Not all propaganda is bad. Most people would agree that a doctor who uses propaganda techniques to discourage smoking is using "good propaganda." However, most propaganda is full of misinformation and false statements.

CAMPAIGN: *Start the Day Right!*

FOR: Health for Kids and Other Important People

TV: 30-second spot

A PERSUASIVE TECHNIQUES
What loaded language do you find here? Record these words in your chart.

VIDEO

Camera opens on sunlit classroom with middle school students at desks. Most of them seem engaged, listening to a teacher at the front of the room, out of frame. The camera starts to focus on one boy, who looks like he is about to fall asleep.

AUDIO

Announcer: Every morning, in every classroom in America, students come to school without having eaten a nutritious breakfast. At most, they've eaten empty calories provided by junk foods. Maybe they haven't eaten anything at all. The result? They're tired, irritable, unable to concentrate in class. **A**

VIDEO

Boy puts his head on his desk. His classmate looks over and pokes him in the arm. He looks up, a bit dazed, and realizes he is in class and should be taking notes. He shakes his head as if to wake himself, blinks his eyes a few times, and fights to stay awake. **B**

AUDIO

Announcer: Scientific studies show that the eating habits kids learn when they're young will affect them all their lives. Poor nutrition during the school years can lead to a variety of health problems in adulthood—everything from low energy and obesity to diabetes and heart disease. **C**

B PERSUASIVE TECHNIQUES
Public service ads often show situations that most people can identify with. How effective will this sequence be with television viewers?

C PERSUASIVE TECHNIQUES
What is the logical appeal in this section? What facts support the logical appeal? Record them in your chart.

VIDEO

Camera shows same boy at kitchen table the next morning with his parents and infant brother. The boy and his parents are eating cereal; a banana is on the table. **D**

AUDIO

Announcer: You wouldn't let them go out the door without their homework—don't let them go out the door without a good breakfast. No matter how rushed you are, there's always a way to fit in a nutritious breakfast—for every member of the family. For some handy tips on how to create healthy on-the-go breakfasts, visit our Web site, Health for Kids and Other Important People, at www.hkoip.org. **E**

D PERSUASIVE TECHNIQUES
Persuasive texts often use images to make an emotional connection to people's lives. What is the effect of this image?

E PERSUASIVE TECHNIQUES
What words tell you that this section is relying on emotional appeals? Write these words in your chart.

Comprehension

1. **Recall** What is the central message of this ad?

2. **Recall** What are some of the effects of not eating a healthy breakfast?

3. **Clarify** What action do the creators of this ad want its audience to take?

Text Analysis

4. **Make Inferences** Who is the target audience for this ad? How can you tell?

5. **Draw Conclusions** Why would an organization create an ad like this? What is the advertisement's purpose?

6. **Evaluate Persuasive Techniques** Identify two examples of evidence in the ad that support its claim. Explain whether the support for the claim is convincing.

7. **Analyze Persuasive Techniques** Remember that loaded language is a way to appeal to an audience's emotions. There are degrees of loaded language—some is mild, and some is very strong. When loaded language is too strong, we may begin to doubt the message. How strong was the loaded language in this ad? How does the degree of loaded language impact the way you perceive the ad's message?

Comparing Information

Review the chart you made as you read "Start the Day Right!" How convincing was this ad? What persuasive techniques contributed to its effectiveness?

"Start the Day Right!"	
Claim	
Logical Appeals and Evidence	
Emotional Appeals and Loaded Language	

COMMON CORE

RI 4 Determine the meaning of words and phrases as they are used in a text, including connotative meanings. **RI 6** Determine an author's point of view or purpose and explain how it is conveyed in the text. **RI 8** Trace and evaluate the argument and specific claims in a text, distinguishing claims that are supported by reasons and evidence from claims that are not.

COMMON CORE

RI 6 Determine an author's point of view or purpose and explain how it is conveyed in the text.
RI 8 Trace and evaluate the argument and specific claims in a text, distinguishing claims that are supported by reasons and evidence from claims that are not.

Shine-n-Grow: Hair Repair That Really Works!

Advertisement

"Shine-n-Grow: Hair Repair That Really Works!" is a commercial advertisement intended to generate sales for a service or product. Do not assume that all the information in an advertisement is trustworthy. Sometimes, information that seems factual and based on evidence may not be.

Standards Focus: Faulty Reasoning

When you examine an advertisement, be sure not to confuse logic with faulty reasoning. **Logic** is correct reasoning backed by reasons and evidence. **Faulty reasoning** (also called fallacious reasoning) is flawed thinking. A sign of faulty reasoning is the use of **logical fallacies**, or mistaken ways of reasoning. (When you see the words *fallacy* or *fallacious*, think of the word *false*.) Here are four common logical fallacies. You will often see examples of these fallacies in advertising—especially dishonest advertising.

- **Hasty generalization**—a conclusion drawn from too little evidence
- **Overgeneralization**—a broad conclusion using all-or-nothing words like *every*, *always*, and *never*
- **Circular reasoning**—reasons that say the same thing over and over again using different words
- **False cause**—the assumption that one event caused another because it occurred earlier in time

Add a row to your chart to address faulty reasoning. Then, use your chart to identify and analyze the persuasive techniques in "Shine-n-Grow: Hair Repair That Really Works!"

"Shine-n-Grow: Hair Repair That Really Works!"	
Claim	
Logical Appeals and Evidence	
Emotional Appeals and Loaded Language	
Faulty, or Fallacious, Reasoning	

SHINE -N- GROW

Hair Repair That Really Works!

Have you ever suffered at the hands of a barber or careless hair stylist who cut your hair much shorter than you wanted? Have you ever envied your friends who have long hair? Now you no longer have to wait for weeks, months, or even years for your hair to grow back the way you want it to. With **SHINE-N-GROW** shampoo, your hair can grow faster than you ever dreamed possible. We guarantee that in no time at all, you can achieve the look everyone wants: a full head of
10 hair that's long, healthy, and shiny. **A**

A FAULTY REASONING
Explain the fallacy in lines 8–10. What assumptions does the advertiser make about the audience?

SHINE-N-GROW shampoo contains a unique combination of vitamins, minerals, and hair-growth ingredients that

- directly provide nutrients to each strand of hair to help it grow
- wash away dullness and replace it with shine
- bring life back to dry or damaged hair

SHINE-N-GROW research scientists have discovered a combination of natural ingredients that
20 helps hair grow faster. Studies have shown that the average person's hair grows at a rate of one-fourth to one-half inch or less per month. A study was conducted to determine the effects of using the **SHINE-N-GROW** formula. The results were amazing! Test subjects reported hair growth of up to **five inches in three months!** (See our Web site for results.) **B**
Bacteria and dirty oils slow down hair growth. **SHINE-N-GROW**'s natural ingredients kill bacteria, making it easier for hair to grow through the scalp.
30 Thanks to our secret combination of ingredients, the cleansing value of the shampoo is far superior to that of any other products on the market. Customers who use **SHINE-N-GROW** just once never go back to their old brands. You'll love **SHINE-N-GROW**, too.

B PERSUASIVE TECHNIQUES
Notice that the writer uses words such as "research scientists," "studies," and "test subjects" in lines 18–26. In which row of your chart would you include these phrases? Explain.

> *"My hair has never been so long before in my life. I've tried everything, but nothing has worked as well as SHINE-N-GROW to make my hair long and clean."*
>
> —Susan Steinberg, actress, Brooklyn, New York

People who use **SHINE-N-GROW** shampoo have reported that their hair has grown faster and has been cleaner, shinier, and easier to manage. Happy customers agree that their hair feels better after it's been washed. "I just feel more confident," one customer said, "and I've

40 been getting more dates ever since I started using your shampoo." **C**

SHINE-N-GROW is the only shampoo that actually speeds up hair growth while it makes your hair smooth, shiny, and spectacular! Using **SHINE-N-GROW** guarantees what no other shampoo can: that you'll always have long, shiny hair. **D**

Learn more about **SHINE-N-GROW** on our Web site at www.shine-n-grow.com, and download a coupon for 15% off your first purchase! **SHINE-N-GROW** is

50 available now at better drugstores and supermarkets.

> *"My boyfriend mentioned the shine in my hair the first time I used SHINE-N-GROW. He really noticed how it helped my dry and damaged hair."*
>
> —Christine Martinez, nurse, Tucson, Arizona

> *"My last haircut was way too short, so I tried SHINE-N-GROW, and now my hair is long again—and clean! Finally my hair looks the way I like it."*
>
> —Roger Canter, accountant, Los Angeles, California **E**

COMMON CORE RI 8

C FAULTY REASONING

Have you ever been stuck in the rain without your umbrella? You might feel like the rain started falling *because* you forgot your umbrella. However, that thought is an example of the type of faulty reasoning called false cause. **False cause** is the belief that one event caused another when they are actually unrelated. Reread the statement the customer makes on lines 35–41. Why is this an example of false cause?

D FAULTY REASONING

What type of fallacy is in lines 44–46?

E PERSUASIVE TECHNIQUES

Notice the loaded language in these testimonials and in the testimonial on page 974. Write some of the words and phrases in your chart. How do these testimonials influence your response to this product?

Comprehension

1. **Recall** What do the creators of the ad guarantee to users of "Shine-n-Grow"?

2. **Recall** Why is the shampoo called "Shine-n-Grow"?

3. **Clarify** What is the purpose of this advertisement?

Text Analysis

4. **Make Inferences** Why is the product's name printed in a different typeface from the rest of the text? Why is the name repeated so many times in the ad?

5. **Analyze Faulty Reasoning** Consider this statement from the text: "Customers who use SHINE-N-GROW just once never go back to their old brands. You'll love SHINE-N-GROW, too." Identify the type of fallacy used in this statement. Then, explain why the statement is an example of faulty reasoning.

6. **Draw Conclusions** The creators of this ad include a number of unlikely claims. Explain whether you believe Shine-n-Grow can do what it claims. Support your response with evidence from the text.

Comparing Information

Review the chart you made as you read "Shine-n-Grow: Hair Repair That Really Works!" Then, consider this question: Would you rush out to buy Shine-n-Grow shampoo for your hair? Evaluate whether the persuasive techniques used in the advertisement were convincing.

"Shine-n-Grow: Hair Repair That Really Works!"	
Claim	
Logical Appeals and Evidence	
Emotional Appeals and Loaded Language	
Faulty, or Fallacious, Reasoning	

COMMON CORE

RI 6 Determine an author's point of view or purpose and explain how it is conveyed in the text.
RI 8 Trace and evaluate the argument and specific claims in a text, distinguishing claims that are supported by reasons and evidence from claims that are not.

COMMON CORE

RI 4 Determine the meaning of words and phrases as they are used in a text, including connotative meanings. **RI 6** Determine an author's point of view or purpose and explain how it is conveyed in the text. **RI 8** Trace and evaluate the argument and specific claims in a text, distinguishing claims that are supported by reasons and evidence from claims that are not.

Brain Breeze
Advertisement

At a glance, the magazine advertisement that follows might seem to make a very strong case. But does it actually prevent you from thinking for yourself? As you read "Brain Breeze," consider the effectiveness of the advertiser's techniques.

Standards Focus: Propaganda Techniques

When persuasion is extremely one-sided and appeals to the emotions at the expense of reason, it can become propaganda. **Propaganda** is the attempt to convince an audience to accept ideas without considering other viewpoints. Advertisements can seldom be called propaganda. However, they sometimes use **propaganda techniques**, such as the ones shown below.

Propaganda Techniques	Examples
Bandwagon appeal takes advantage of people's desire to be part of a group or to be popular.	"Everyone else is doing it. Why aren't you?"
A **stereotype** presents a narrow, fixed idea about all the members of a certain group.	"No politician can be trusted."
Name-calling is the use of loaded words to create negative feelings about a person, group, or thing.	"Only a tree-hugger would try to protect that park from developers."
Snob appeal sends the message that something is valuable because only "special" people appreciate it.	"Our jeans are designed for people who insist on quality."
An **endorsement** is a recommendation made by someone who is well-known but not necessarily an authority.	Celebrities use their fame to persuade you to believe in a cause, candidate, or product.

Add a final row to your chart to track the use of propaganda techniques. As you read, use your chart to analyze the persuasive techniques in "Brain Breeze."

"Brain Breeze"	
Claim	
Logical Appeals and Evidence	
Emotional Appeals and Loaded Language	
Faulty, or Fallacious, Reasoning	
Propaganda Techniques	

BRAIN BREEZE

The FIRST and ONLY Mental Power Booster that fits in the palm of your hand!

Uses music and air movement to sharpen your concentration and clear your clouded mind!
- **Study with No Effort!**
- **Finish Big Projects While You Relax!**
- **Feel Smarter and Less Stressed!**

Do you have a big test coming up? a big project to complete? Are you so wound up with stress that you can't think straight? Time to open the windows of your mind and let *BRAIN BREEZE* in!

Businesspeople, students, the guy who lives next door—everyone is looking for that competitive mental edge. Now, getting that edge is easier than you ever thought possible with *BRAIN BREEZE*—the Mental Power Booster that uses scientifically researched music and the physics of airflow to make you more productive, less stressed—and smarter! **A**

BRAIN BREEZE is an amazing new technological breakthrough! It increases your concentration and keeps you at the top of your mental game while it soothes and relaxes you with a patented combination of moving air and music—all delivered from a device no larger than the palm of your hand! It's so easy to use that even the laziest couch potato can benefit.

A PROPAGANDA TECHNIQUES
What propaganda technique is used in this paragraph?

Only ten watts needed to power the device! Works on batteries or with a power cord (provided).

- Weighs 14.7 ounces—less than a digital camera! Completely portable! Use at home, in the library—on the road!
- Additional music tracks available through digital download. (See our Web site for details.)
- Available in five fashionable colors to reflect your lifestyle and personality: *Lively Lime, Tranquil Turquoise, Shimmering Silver, Awesome Orange,* and *Perky Pink.*
- Satisfaction guaranteed! You have fourteen days to try *BRAIN BREEZE*, risk free. Return it for a complete refund if you don't feel smarter and less stressed!
- 90-DAY WARRANTY. **B**

B **PERSUASIVE TECHNIQUES**
How does the advertiser try to make Brain Breeze seem like a desirable product to the audience? Use your chart to record some of the loaded words used in the ad.

C **PERSUASIVE TECHNIQUES**
Why is the information about the development of Brain Breeze included in the advertisement? Where on your chart will you put this information?

D **PROPAGANDA TECHNIQUES**
What is the purpose of the quote from Tony Fine? What propaganda technique is this?

BRAIN BREEZE the Mental Power Booster, was developed by Professor Gary Fract of the University of Hadleyburg and was tested for effectiveness at Right Idea Labs, a scientific center for the advancement of learning. Researchers found that in a study of one hundred people aged sixteen to sixty-nine, scores increased an average of five points overall on tests of memory and problem-solving ability among those who used *BRAIN BREEZE.* **C**

High-achieving, high-income people appreciate the *BRAIN BREEZE* advantage. After using *BRAIN BREEZE* at his desk for two weeks, financial planner Tony Fine realized he was successfully dealing with two to three more clients per day than he had been before. "There's just something about the combination of the music and the airflow. It makes me feel more focused and organized," he says, "and I was already the most organized person I know." **D**

Emery Goodson, a medical student, had been using *BRAIN BREEZE* for just a week when she realized that studying no longer felt like a chore.

Amazing, room-filling, state-of-the-art sound from one small speaker! (Or use the lightweight headphones, included.)

Airflow is silent. There's no fan and no motor, so there's nothing to make noise. Our patented technology moves air electronically.

THE DEVELOPMENT TEAM

Professor Gary Fract, specialist in cognitive advancement, is author of *The Effect of Music on Developing Thought*, a major study of the cognitive changes that individuals undergo when listening to certain types of music. Right Idea Labs pioneered important studies on the effects of indoor airflow on mental focus by testing thousands of participants in the Idea Room, a model controlled environment.

Find out more about *BRAIN BREEZE* at www.gobrainbreeze.com. **E**

"*BRAIN BREEZE* is like this little treat I give myself," she says. "Now studying is something I look forward to. It's like a mental vacation, except I'm working!"

Even elderly people can enjoy the benefits of *BRAIN BREEZE*. Studies have shown that using *BRAIN BREEZE* at least once a week can vastly improve people's memories. Imagine—no more forgetting relatives' birthdays! **F**

BRAIN BREEZE comes fully programmed with thirty-nine different music tracks, each carefully selected from a research database of music scientifically proven to enhance concentration and problem-solving abilities. Choose from five different airflow settings, from low to high, based on the complexity of the work you are doing.

For information about scientific research on *BRAIN BREEZE*, go to www.gobrainbreeze.com. Find out how you can try *BRAIN BREEZE* on a free trial basis—and order one today for overnight delivery. Don't be the last person in your office or school to act on this offer. Get the *BRAIN BREEZE* advantage now! **G**

E PERSUASIVE TECHNIQUES
Why is this information about Gary Fract included? Where will you put it on your chart?

F PROPAGANDA TECHNIQUES
Stereotyping is one of the propaganda techniques you might encounter in advertisements. What stereotype is presented in this paragraph?

G PROPAGANDA TECHNIQUES
What propaganda technique does the advertiser use in this paragraph? Do you think the audience will be responsive to this technique? Explain.

Comprehension

1. **Recall** What is Brain Breeze? Name three things the advertiser claims Brain Breeze can do.

2. **Recall** According to the advertiser, how can Brain Breeze help businesspeople? How can it help students?

3. **Clarify** What can someone do if they use Brain Breeze and are not happy with the results?

Text Analysis

● 4. **Analyze Propaganda** Consider this statement from Brain Breeze: "Don't be the last person in your office or school to act on this offer." What propaganda technique do the advertisers use in this statement? What is the intended effect on the audience?

● 5. **Evaluate Propaganda** Identify an example of snob appeal in the advertisement. How does this propaganda technique make Brain Breeze appealing to readers?

6. **Make Judgments** Propaganda techniques like stereotyping and name-calling may actually upset an audience. Are there any propaganda techniques in this ad that have the potential to make readers angry? Explain.

Comparing Information

Review the chart you made as you read "Brain Breeze." Explain whether you are persuaded to try Brain Breeze. What details in the ad helped you reach your conclusion?

"Brain Breeze"	
Claim	
Logical Appeals and Evidence	
Emotional Appeals and Loaded Language	
Faulty, or Fallacious, Reasoning	
Propaganda Techniques	

How far will we go to IMPROVE ourselves?

Think back to your discussion about ads that appeal to the drive for self-improvement. What kind of ads, if any, can really point us in the direction of self-improvement?

Writing For Assessment

COMMON CORE W 2, W 4, W 10

1. READ THE PROMPT

The three selections you've just read provide examples of persuasive techniques in media advertising. In writing assessments, you will often be asked to compare nonfiction selections that share similar characteristics.

> In a four-paragraph essay, compare the persuasive techniques used in the public service announcement script "Start the Day Right!" and the two advertisements, "Shine-n-Grow" and "Brain Breeze." Support your comparison using specific details from each selection, and conclude with as statement explaining which ad is most successful in sending a persuasive message.

◀ **STRATEGIES IN ACTION**

1. I need to identify the **similarities and differences** in the persuasive techniques used in each selection.

2. I need to include **examples** from the selections to support my ideas.

3. I need to determine which selection is most **convincing** in sending a persuasive message.

2. PLAN YOUR WRITING

Look back at the charts you made for each selection as you read. Identify persuasive techniques the selections share as well as ones that are unique to a selection. Then think about how to present the similarities and differences in the three selections.

- Decide on a thesis statement for your response.

- Review the selections to find the best examples of persuasive techniques to support your comparison.

- Create an outline to organize your ideas. The sample outline to the right shows one way to organize your essay.

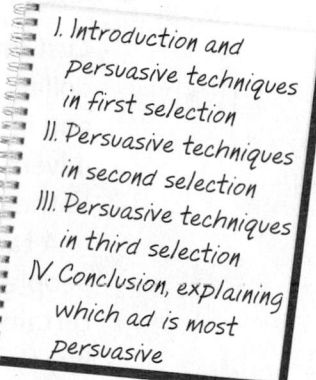

I. Introduction and Persuasive techniques in first selection
II. Persuasive techniques in second selection
III. Persuasive techniques in third selection
IV. Conclusion, explaining which ad is most Persuasive

3. DRAFT YOUR RESPONSE

Paragraph 1 Provide the title of each selection, as well as a sentence explaining what the three selections have in common. Discuss the persuasive techniques in the first selection, using specific examples taken from your chart.

Paragraphs 2 and 3 Discuss the persuasive techniques of selections two and three using specific examples taken from your chart. Use a separate paragraph for each selection.

Paragraph 4 Conclude with a statement of which selection you found most persuasive, and why.

Revision Use transition words and phrases such as *on the other hand, however, like, unlike,* and *instead* to show how the selections are alike and different.

Persuasive Techniques in Commercials
TV Commercials on **Media ● Smart** DVD-ROM

How do you CAPTURE a customer?

COMMON CORE

RI 7 Integrate information presented in different media to develop a coherent understanding of a topic.

Sometimes, it seems a commercial was made just for you. Your eyes stay glued to the screen as you find out all the details about a product. When you react to an ad in this way, it's likely that you're part of what is called a target audience. In this lesson, you'll watch two commercials and study how advertisers direct their messages to very specific groups of people.

Background

Customer Awareness Each year, corporations spend billions of dollars to advertise their products. This money buys television and radio airtime, or magazine, newspaper, or billboard advertising. Businesses know that directing the right message to the right people increases the likelihood of success.

A **target audience** is a specific population or group of people an advertiser hopes to persuade. People who share certain likes or dislikes or who are the same age usually buy the same products. **Demographics** are the characteristics a group of people have in common. Advertisers study demographic data to research the interests, activities, and spending habits of a target audience. Then advertisers develop products, packaging, and ads that are designed to appeal to that audience.

Media Literacy: Target Audience

Advertisers use demographic information to figure out when and where to advertise products. They also use images, words, and sounds to persuade a particular audience. Advertisers may even use misleading information, faulty reasoning, and other persuasive techniques to influence the emotions of the target audience.

   To help you determine the target audience of any commercial, look at the elements the advertisers include and ask questions about their choices.

ELEMENTS OF COMMERCIALS	STRATEGIES FOR VIEWING
Images and Words Advertisers choose images and words to appeal to the target audience. For example, advertisers want viewers to respond favorably to people who appear in the ad. Most ads also include a **slogan,** a simple, carefully worded phrase intended to give a positive impression of the product.	**Ask Yourself** • Who is shown in the ad? What ages and genders are represented? • Are there special effects? If so, what do they add to the emotional impact? • What level of formality or informality does the ad use? What does this say about the advertiser's perception of the target audience?
Sounds Sounds might be the **dialogue** or **narration** that give details about a product, or the **music** that sets a certain mood. Sound effects might be added to make the product appealing.	**Ask Yourself** • If there's **music** in the ad, what's the style? Who would the music appeal to the most? • What information is given in the **dialogue?** • Is there a **voice-over,** a voice of an unseen narrator? To whom is this voice speaking?
Propaganda Some commercials and TV shows include faulty reasoning called **propaganda**—communication that is so distorted that it contains false or misleading information. For more information on faulty reasoning, see page R24.	**Ask Yourself** • Does this message contain name-calling instead of reliable information? • Are complex issues presented as if they were much simpler than they really are? • How could I verify the information in this message?

Viewing Guide for
TV Commercials

Prepare to watch the Apple iPod commercial first and then the one for Microsoft Windows XP. To analyze each commercial, look or listen closely for clues that reveal the target audience. In addition, look for techniques that make the ads appealing. Take notes. Use the questions below to guide your analysis of the ads.

NOW VIEW

FIRST VIEWING: Comprehension

1. **Identify** What are the people doing in the iPod commercial?

2. **Clarify** Which ad doesn't describe the product through voice-over narration?

CLOSE VIEWING: Media Literacy

3. **Analyze Images** The iPod commercial shows outlines of people that appear against colorful backgrounds. While the people and backgrounds change, what remains the same?

4. **Analyze Target Audience** What audience do you think the makers of the iPod commercial are targeting? Explain.

5. **Draw Conclusions** The Windows XP commercial has the look and feel of a fairy tale. This might be a clue that the commercial is targeted to a young audience. Explain who else might be a target audience for this ad. Think about

   - what Windows XP allows young people to do
   - who might be inspired by the girl's qualities and abilities

6. **Compare Commercials** Both the iPod and Windows XP ads use music. How else are they alike or different? Compare and contrast the elements of these ads. Use your notes about the commercials to fill in a Venn diagram like the one below.

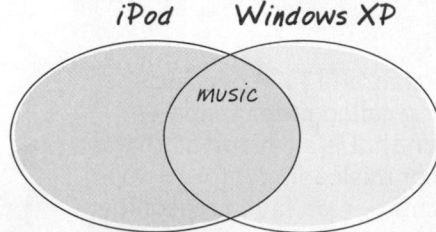

iPod   Windows XP

music

Write or Discuss

Analyze Persuasive Techniques You have analyzed two commercials to find out how advertisers appeal to a target audience. Go back to focus on one of the commercials. Decide whether it is an example of propaganda. Think about

- the **target audience** for the commercial
- whether **graphics, special effects,** or **music** help to get the message across
- whether any information is misleading, distorted, or includes faulty reasoning
- how you might prove or disprove the information the commercial presents

Produce Your Own Media

Create a Storyboard Before shooting a commercial, advertisers plan it on a **storyboard.** This device presents images and brief descriptions of a product. In small groups, create a storyboard for a commercial. Begin by brainstorming the type of product and its most important features. Determine what segment of the population you'll target as your audience. Then map out the first six frames of the storyboard. Instead of planning an entire commercial, use a few frames to highlight the product and show who would use it.

HERE'S HOW Use these suggestions as you create the storyboard.

- Use each visual to cover one main point of your ad.
- Include a graphic image that shows the product and a **slogan** to make the product memorable.
- Catch viewers' eyes by showing images from different angles.
- Keep your descriptions brief. You can even replace them by writing out spoken dialogue (or voice-over narration).

STUDENT MODEL

"When I want a deliciously healthy snack..."

"I dunk!"

"I dunk the easy way with Fruit Dunkers!"

"Fruit Dunkers is perfect for active kids like me."

"They combine yogurt with your favorite fruit!"

"Just dip and dunk!"

COMMON CORE

SL 5 Include visual displays in presentations.

Media Tools **THINK central**

Go to **thinkcentral.com**.
KEYWORD: HML6-987

Tech Tip
If available, use a camera to photograph the basic actions.

Writing Workshop
ARGUMENT

Persuasive Essay

In this unit, you read selections in which writers asserted firm **claims**, or positions, and backed them with clear reasons and relevant evidence. What are some issues that matter to you? In this workshop, you will write a persuasive essay that argues your claim on an important issue.

 Complete the workshop activities in your **Reader/Writer Notebook.**

WRITE WITH A PURPOSE

WRITING TASK

Write a **persuasive essay** that states a claim, or position, on an issue. Support your claim with reasons and evidence that will convince your audience to agree with you.

Idea Starters
- protecting endangered animals
- rules that are unfair to young people
- ways to improve your neighborhood or school
- violence in video games

THE ESSENTIALS

Here are some common purposes, audiences, and formats for persuasive writing.

PURPOSES	AUDIENCES	FORMATS
• to influence people's attitudes or actions • to persuade readers to agree with your opinion	• classmates and teacher • friends • family • neighbors • Web users • school board	• essay for class • letter to the editor • speech • blog posting • commercial or public service announcement (PSA)

COMMON CORE TRAITS

1. DEVELOPMENT OF IDEAS
- includes an **introduction** that states a **claim**
- supports the claim with **clear reasons** and **relevant evidence**
- addresses **opposing claims**
- offers a **concluding section** that follows from the claim and support

2. ORGANIZATION OF IDEAS
- **organizes** reasons and evidence in a logical way
- uses **transitions**—words, phrases, and clauses—to connect ideas

3. LANGUAGE FACILITY AND CONVENTIONS
- establishes and maintains a **formal style** and **tone**
- correctly punctuates **direct and indirect quotations**
- demonstrates correct **grammar, usage,** and **spelling**

Writing Online

THINK central

Go to **thinkcentral.com.**
KEYWORD: HML6N-988

Planning/Prewriting

COMMON CORE

W 1a–e Write arguments to support claims with clear reasons and relevant evidence. **W 4** Produce clear and coherent writing appropriate to task, purpose, and audience. **W 5** Develop and strengthen writing as needed by planning.

Getting Started

CHOOSE AN ISSUE

First, choose an issue about which you feel strongly and can write effectively. An **issue** is a topic that people disagree on. Your issue should be one that you know something about and that will also interest your audience. Use the Idea Starters on page 988 to help you identify possible topics for your persuasive essay.

▶ ASK YOURSELF:

- What are some issues that I feel strongly about?
- For each issue, what reasons can I think of to support my claim?
- What are some opposing claims that other people might have?
- Which issue would be the most interesting to my audience?

THINK ABOUT AUDIENCE AND PURPOSE

In a persuasive essay, your **purpose** is to convince readers to share your point of view on an issue and, in some cases, to take action. You'll need to determine who the **audience** is for your essay, as well as what they need to know to follow your argument.

▶ ASK YOURSELF:

- Who is my audience?
- What interest does my audience have in my issue?
- What does my audience need to know to about the issue? What aspects of it might they want to learn more about?

STATE YOUR CLAIM

Think about both sides of your issue. Which side do you feel more strongly about? Write a claim that clearly states your position on the issue.

▶ WHAT DOES IT LOOK LIKE?

Issue: *The impact that one person's actions can have*

My viewpoint: *A big impact*

My claim: *It only takes one person to change a situation and make everyone's life a lot better.*

PROVIDE REASONS

Once you establish a claim, you have to support it with clear reasons. **Reasons** are statements that justify or explain your claim to your audience. Use a chart to record some reasons that support your claim. Then discuss your reasons with a peer to find out which ones are the most appealing and convincing.

▶ WHAT DOES IT LOOK LIKE?

Claim: *It only takes one person to change a situation and make everyone's life a lot better.*

| **Reason 1:** *Some changes that seem small can actually make a big difference.* |
| **Reason 2:** *If one person does something good, other people may follow his or her example.* |
| **Reason 3:** *If everyone behaves selfishly, the overall impact on the world can be disastrous.* |

Planning/Prewriting *continued*

Getting Started

COLLECT EVIDENCE

To persuade your readers that they ought to agree with your claim, you'll need to provide relevant **evidence** to support your reasons. Consult **credible**, or trustworthy, sources to gather evidence and develop your understanding of the topic. Here are several types of evidence you might include in your essay:

WHAT DOES IT LOOK LIKE?

- **Facts:** statements that can be proven true

  ▶ *In 1976, Wangari Maathai had the idea of encouraging people to plant trees in Kenya. Her Green Belt Movement has now planted more than 20 million trees.*

- **Examples:** specific instances that illustrate a general idea

  ▶ *History has many examples of one person making a difference, such as Rosa Parks.*

- **Expert opinions:** statements made by authorities on a subject

  ▶ *Author Stephen R. Covey says individuals have enormous power to change the world.*

- **Anecdotes:** brief stories that illustrate a point

  ▶ *One class in my school began recycling. Every other class was participating by the end of the month.*

CONSIDER OPPOSING CLAIMS

Some people in your argument may disagree with the claim you present in your essay. Address their **alternate** or **opposing claims** and explain why your viewpoint is more valid. Think of arguments you could use in response. To persuade them to accept your claim, you'll need to consider alternative claims and respond to them.

WHAT DOES IT LOOK LIKE?

My Claim: One person can make a difference.	
Possible Opposing Claim: The actions of just one person can't change the world.	**Response:** History has many examples of one person making a difference, such as Rosa Parks.

PEER REVIEW Share with a peer the evidence you have gathered to support your claim. Ask: Which evidence is most convincing? What new approach could I take to strengthen my claim? What other approaches to my topic do you suggest?

Drafting

W 1c Use words, phrases, and clauses to link major sections of the text and clarify relationships between claim(s) and reasons. **W 4** Produce clear and coherent writing. **L 3** Use knowledge of language and conventions when writing.

The following chart shows how to organize your draft to create an effective persuasive essay.

Organizing Your Persuasive Essay

INTRODUCTION

- Grab the audience's attention with a memorable statement, anecdote, or fact. Be sure to establish and maintain a formal style and tone.
- State your claim in a clear claim.
- Provide any background information your audience may need to understand the issue.

▼

BODY

- Provide clear **reasons** to support your claim. Back up each reason with **relevant evidence.**
- **Organize** your essay in an effective way. Present your second strongest reason first, and then other reasons. End with your strongest reason.
- Consider **opposing claims** and address them.
- Maintain a formal **style** and **tone,** or attitude, by using a confident voice and thoughtful, persuasive words.

▼

CONCLUDING SECTION

- Restate your claim and briefly summarize your evidence.
- Conclude with a **call to action** urging your audience to do what you want them to do.

GRAMMAR IN CONTEXT: USING TRANSITIONS

Transitions are words, phrases, and clauses that show how ideas are related to one another. Because persuasive essays often present reasons in order of importance, transitions that show this order can help clarify the relationship among your claim and reasons.

Transitions That Show Order of Importance

best of all	more/most important
first	primarily
furthermore	to begin with
last	finally
mainly	ultimately

▶ *Example*

I believe that one person can make a difference. **To begin with,** *small changes that might not seem to have a big effect can have a huge impact over time.* **Furthermore,** *if everyone just acts selfishly, no good changes will come to the world.*

YOUR TURN

Develop a first draft of your persuasive essay, following the plan outlined in the chart above. Use transitional words and phrases to show how your claim and reasons are related.

Revising

Evaluate the development, organization, and style of your essay and revise it as necessary. Ask yourself if you've achieved your purpose and clearly communicated your ideas to your audience. These questions, tips, and strategies will help you revise, rewrite, and improve your draft.

PERSUASIVE ESSAY

Ask Yourself	Tips	Revision Strategies
1. Does the introduction have a clear claim that states a position?	▶ **Read** it and identify the position on the issue.	▶ Add a claim or, if necessary, replace the claim with a clearer one.
2. Are there at least two clear reasons that support the claim? Does at least one piece of relevant evidence support each reason?	▶ **Circle** the reasons that support the claim. **Highlight** evidence that supports each reason. **Draw an arrow** from the evidence to the reason.	▶ **Add** reasons that support the claim. **Add** facts and examples that support each reason. If necessary, **explain** how the evidence supports the reasons and claim.
3. Do transitions clarify the relationships among the claim and reasons?	▶ **Draw a box** around each transition word, phrase, or clause.	▶ Add transition words, phrases, or clauses that help show how your claim and reasons are related.
4. Does the argument include opposing claims and responses	▶ **Underline** opposing claims. **Circle** your responses to them.	▶ **Add** possible opposing claims and respond to them effectively.
5. Does the concluding section include a restatement of the claim, a summary of the evidence, and a call to action?	▶ **Put a check mark** next to the restatement. **Circle** the summary. **Put a box** around the call to action.	▶ **Add** a restatement of the claim, a summary of the evidence, and/or a call to action.
6. Does the argument maintain a formal style and tone?	▶ **Put a star** next to vague or informal words and phrases.	▶ **Replace** starred words and phrases with more formal language.

YOUR TURN **PEER REVIEW** Work with a peer to review your drafts, using the questions in the chart. Help each other identify sections that may need rewriting or a new approach.

ANALYZE A STUDENT DRAFT

W 5 Strengthen writing by revising, rewriting, or trying a new approach.
L 3b Maintain consistency in style and tone.

Read this student's draft and the comments about it as a model for revising your own persuasive essay.

Makx a Diffxrxncx

by Elena Chen, Ridgely Middle School

1 As I start this lxttxr, thosx who rxad it might think somxthing is wrong and stop rxading at this point. But plxasx kxxp on rxading.

2 As you can sxx, for onx lxttxr of thx alphabxt I havx substitutxd an x. Somx of you might find this strangx. Lxt mx xxplain.

3 A lot of pxoplx don't think that onx pxrson in this world can makx a diffxrxncx. But lxt mx txll you this. In history wx havx all sxxn and hxard pxoplx who havx stood up for what thxy bxlixvx in. Thxy havx indxxd madx a diffxrxncx in our livxs. It only takxs onx pxrson to changx somxthing and makx xvxryonx's lifx a lot bxttxr. Considxr rxcycling: It only takxs onx pxrson to rxcyclx; thxn xvxryonx xlsx will follow. If wx all thought only of oursxlvxs, thx world would bx a disastrous placx right now. Thx ozonx layxr would bx gonx and wx would all bx harmxd by thx sun.

> The use of the letter *x* instead of *e* **grabs readers' attention** right away.

> Elena mentions a possible **opposing claim** and responds to it.

> Elena states her **claim** and presents several **clear reasons.** Adding **a relevant anecdote** would help her appeal to her audience.

LEARN HOW **Use Relevant Anecdotes as Evidence** Elena's third paragraph makes the point that individuals can make a major difference in the lives of others. When she revised her letter, she decided to strengthen this argument by adding a relevant anecdote. **Anecdotes,** or brief stories intended to make a point, can make an argument more convincing by relating the issue to actual events.

ELENA'S REVISION TO PARAGRAPH **3**

A lot of pxoplx don't think that onx pxrson in this world can makx a diffxrxncx. But lxt mx txll you this. In history wx havx all sxxn and hxard pxoplx who havx stood up for what thxy bxlixvx in. ~~Thxy~~ havx indxxd madx a diffxrxncx in our livxs.

Onx such pxrson was Rosa Parks, an African Amxrican woman who livxd during sxgrxgation in Montgomxry, Alabama. On Dxcxmbxr 1, 1955, aftxr a long day of work shx gratxfully sxttlxd into a sxat on thx bus. Whxn ordxrxd to givx up hxr placx to a whitx man, thx xxhaustxd Parks rxfusxd. Hxr bravx act rallixd many to protxst and changx unjust laws of thx day. Rosa Parks is just onx of thx many individuals who

❹ It only takxs onx pxrson to comx right out and say hx or shx carxs. What I'm saying is to lxt go of your pridx and do what you bxlixvx is right. If you arx confidxnt, thxn you will succxxd. You should know that you can makx a diffxrxncx.

❺ Now, what doxs all this havx to do with mx writing x's instxad of e's? Did it xvxr occur to you that if onx lxttxr can makx a diffxrxncx thxn so can onx pxrson? Xvxn though this is a small xxamplx, it shows that if onx tiny lxttxr in thx alphabxt can makx such a diffxrxncx in a pixcx of writing, thxn, of coursx, onx pxrson can makx a diffxrxncx in thx world today.

> Elena includes a **call to action** to urge readers to do something.

> Elena ends by **restating her claim.** She could strengthen her conclusion by adding an **expert opinion.**

LEARN HOW **Use Expert Opinions as Evidence** In her final paragraph, Elena connects her claim with why she has written *x*'s instead of *e*'s. She wants to show that just as switching one letter of the alphabet can make a big difference, one individual can have a strong impact as well. To strengthen her conclusion even more, she decided to include an expert opinion by quoting a person who has demonstrated knowledge of the topic.

ELENA'S REVISION TO PARAGRAPH ❺

Now, what doxs all this havx to do with mx writing x's instxad of e's? Did it xvxr occur to you that if onx lxttxr can makx a diffxrxncx thxn so can onx pxrson? ~~Xvxn though this is a small xxamplx, it shows that if~~ onx tiny lxttxr in thx alphabxt can makx such a diffxrxncx in a pixcx of writing, thxn, of coursx, onx pxrson can makx a diffxrxncx in thx world today.

Stxphxn R. Covxy undxrstands thx powxr of individuals to xffxct changx. Thx bxstsxlling author of Thx 7 Habits of Highly Xffxctivx Pxoplx *has said hx bxlixvxs "that individuals havx xnormous powxr to changx thx world." Hx writxs I am pxrsonally convincxd that onx pxrson can bx a changx catalyst, a transformxr in any situation, any organizṭion. If such a small xxamplx as changing*

 **YOUR TURN** Use the two "Learn How" lessons, as well as feedback from your peers and teacher, to revise your argument. Evaluate how well it convinces your audience of your claim by including clear reasons and relevant evidence.

Editing and Publishing

W 5 Strengthen writing by revising, editing, rewriting, or trying a new approach. **L 2** Demonstrate command of the conventions of standard English capitalization, punctuation, and spelling. **L 2b** Spell correctly.

When you edit, you review your essay to make sure it contains no grammar, spelling, capitalization, and punctuation errors. Mistakes like these can take away from your essay's impact and even keep your audience from understanding your claim and support. Read your argument carefully, even after you have used an electronic spell check, to catch misspellings that the computer missed.

GRAMMAR IN CONTEXT: PUNCTUATING QUOTATIONS

Persuasive writing often cites the opinions of experts. In her letter to the editor, Elena summarizes author Stephen R. Covey's ideas about the power of individuals to change the world. Her summary is called an **indirect quotation** because she does not use the exact words of the author. Indirect quotations are not placed in quotation marks. When editing her letter, Elena corrected the punctuation of her summary.

> *Thx intxrnational lxadxrship authority and bxstsxlling author of Thx 7 Habits of Highly Xffxctivx Pxoplx has said hx bxlixvxs that individuals havx xnormous powxr to changx thx world.*

In another sentence, Elena uses Covey's exact words—a **direct quotation.** She added quotation marks around these words so readers would know they were taken directly from another writer's work. She also added a comma to set off the quotation from the rest of the sentence.

> *Hx writxs I am pxrsonally convincxd that onx pxrson can bx a changx catalyst, a transformxr in any situation, any organization.*

PUBLISH YOUR WRITING

Share your persuasive essay with an audience.

- Make copies of your persuasive essay and distribute them to others who might be interested in the issue you address.
- Develop your essay into a speech that you deliver to your audience.
- Revise your essay into a letter to the editor of a local newspaper and submit it for publication.
- Post your essay on a school or community Web site or bulletin board.

YOUR TURN Correct any errors in your argument by carefully proofreading it. Make sure direct and indirect quotations are punctuated correctly. Then publish your final argument where it is most likely to reach your intended audience.

Scoring Rubric

Use this rubric to evaluate your persuasive essay from the Writing Workshop or your response to the on-demand task on the next page.

PERSUASIVE ESSAY

SCORE	COMMON CORE TRAITS
6	• **Development** States a claim on a clearly identified issue; supports the claim with clear reasons and relevant evidence; responds to opposing claims; ends powerfully • **Organization** Is clearly organized to persuasive effect; uses transitions to clarify the relationships among the claim and reasons • **Language** Consistently maintains a formal style and tone; shows a strong command of conventions
5	• **Development** States a claim on an issue; offers clear reasons and evidence; acknowledges opposing claims; ends with a strong concluding section • **Organization** Is clearly organized; uses transitions to show relationship of ideas • **Language** Uses a formal style and tone; has a few errors in conventions
4	• **Development** States a clear claim; offers mostly valid support; needs to more fairly address opposing claims; has an adequate concluding section • **Organization** Reflects a clear organization, with one or two exceptions; could use a few more transitions to show how the claim and reasons relate • **Language** Mostly uses a formal style but the tone is somewhat inconsistent; includes a few distracting errors in conventions
3	• **Development** Needs a more precise claim; has some reasons and evidence; needs counterclaims; ends weakly • **Organization** Has some flaws in organization; needs more transitions to show how the claim and reasons relate • **Language** Often lapses into an informal style or inconsistent tone; has several errors in conventions
2	• **Development** Has a weak claim; offers unclear reasons and irrelevant evidence; fails to acknowledge opposing claims; has a very weak concluding section • **Organization** Has major organizational flaws; lacks transitions throughout • **Language** Uses an informal style and inconsistent tone; has many errors in conventions
1	• **Development** Lacks a clear claim; provides no clear reasons or relevant evidence; ignores opposing claims; ends abruptly • **Organization** Has no organization and transitions • **Language** Uses an inappropriate style and tone; has major problems with grammar, mechanics, and spelling

Preparing for Timed Writing

COMMON CORE

W 10 Write routinely over shorter time frames for a range of tasks, purposes, and audiences.

1. ANALYZE THE TASK   5 MIN

Read the task carefully. Then read it again, underlining the words that tell the type of writing, the audience, the claim you must make, and the opposing claim you must address.

> **WRITING TASK** *Claim*   *Opposing claim*
>
> You want your parents to raise your weekly allowance. They point out that they raised it only eight months ago. Write an argument in which you convince your parents to support your request. Use specific reasons and examples.
>
>   *Type of writing*   *Audience*

2. PLAN YOUR RESPONSE   10 MIN

Brainstorm a list of clear reasons why your allowance should be raised. Use a chart to list the reasons and the relevant evidence (such as examples, facts, and anecdotes) you will use to support each reason.

Reasons	Evidence

3. RESPOND TO THE TASK   20 MIN

Using your notes, begin drafting your argument letter. Keep these points in mind:
- At the beginning, clearly identify the issue and state your claim.
- In the body of your argument letter, clearly present your reasons and support each reason with relevant evidence. Don't forget to address possible opposing claims.
- In the concluding section, restate your claim, summarize the supporting evidence, and include a call to action.

4. IMPROVE YOUR RESPONSE   5–10 MIN

Revising Review key aspects of your argument. Do you identify the issue and state your claim clearly? Do you provide relevant evidence for each of your reasons? Do you include a call to action?

Proofreading Neatly correct any errors in grammar, spelling, and mechanics.

Checking Your Final Copy Before you turn in your argument, read it one more time to catch any errors you may have missed.

Giving a Persuasive Speech

If you've ever asked a friend for a favor or tried to convince someone to do something, you've given a persuasive speech. To turn your persuasive essay into a speech, you'll need to adapt it with your new audience (your listeners) in mind.

 Complete the workshop activities in your **Reader/Writer Notebook.**

SPEAK WITH A PURPOSE

TASK

Adapt your persuasive essay into a formal **persuasive speech.** Practice your speech, and then present it to your class.

COMMON CORE TRAITS

A STRONG PERSUASIVE SPEECH . . .

- presents a specific claim on an issue
- supports the claim in a logically organized way with clear reasons and relevant evidence
- addresses opposing claims
- employs verbal and nonverbal techniques, such as appropriate eye contact, adequate volume, and clear pronunciation, to communicate ideas effectively

COMMON CORE

SL 3 Delineate a speaker's argument, distinguishing claims that are supported by reasons and evidence from claims that are not. **SL 4** Present claims and findings, use appropriate eye contact, adequate volume, and clear pronunciation.

Adapt Your Essay

Giving an organized persuasive presentation may seem simple: just read aloud the persuasive essay you wrote in the Writing Workshop. But there is much more to it. Here are some guidelines for developing an effective speech:

- **Think about the audience and purpose.** Your teacher will give you details about who will be in the audience—classmates, students you don't know, or members of the community. Your purpose is to persuade members of the audience.

- **Use your essay to create a script.** Underline or highlight important points you want to include. Present your claim and findings clearly and sequence your ideas in a logical way.

- **Emphasize key ideas.** Keep your sentences brief and to the point. Choose relevant descriptions, facts, and details to highlight your main ideas. Repeat key words or phrases to emphasize their importance.

- **Include clear transitions.** To help listeners follow your presentation, you might need to add words that clarify the connections between ideas. Help your listeners by adding transitional words, phrases, and clauses.

- **Include a visual aid.** Make your message memorable by showing it on a poster, a flip chart, or a power presentation.

Speaking &
Listening Online

Go to **thinkcentral.com.**
KEYWORD: HML6N-998

Give Your Speech

Even the most persuasive ideas can fall flat if they aren't delivered well. As you practice your speech, concentrate on using **verbal techniques** (what your voice does as you speak) and **nonverbal techniques** (what your face and body do as you speak) to communicate your ideas effectively.

USE VERBAL AND NONVERBAL TECHNIQUES

- **Speaking Rate, Volume, and Pitch** Speak at a slow rate so your audience can keep up with what you are saying. Avoid shouting, but speak loudly enough so your audience can hear you. Vary your pitch—the rise and fall of your speaking voice—to help keep your audience interested in your message.
- **Pronunciation** Clearly pronounce your words to allow the audience to understand every point you make.
- **Conventions of Language** Use standard English and correct grammar. Avoid slang terms or informal style.
- **Eye Contact** Remember to look at your audience throughout your speech.
- **Gestures and Facial Expressions** Use your hands and facial expressions to emphasize key points and to engage your audience.

Evaluate a Speech

As you listen, consider whether the speaker presents a convincing argument.

- **Take notes.** As you listen to the argument, take notes on the claim and the reasons and evidence used to support it. Delineate, or trace, the argument and note any claims that are not supported by evidence.
- **Evaluate the support.** Review your notes to determine whether the speaker supports his or her claim with clear reasons and relevant evidence. Were the reasons presented logically? Did descriptions, facts, and details relate clearly to the reasons and claim? Did the evidence seem credible, or believable?

YOUR TURN

As a Speaker Deliver your persuasive speech to a partner. Be sure your speech is organized and you present a specific claim on an issue. Don't forget to use effective verbal and nonverbal techniques.

As a Listener Listen to your partner's speech. Take notes on his or her specific claim and the reasons and evidence used to support it. After the speech, share your notes to make sure you understood his or her message. Evaluate your partner's delivery and give suggestions for improvement.

Assessment Practice

DIRECTIONS Read these selections and answer the questions that follow.

Fighting Is Never a Good Solution *by Sylvia Cassedy*

1   A fight broke out on the playground yesterday because of a torn jacket. Some members of Miss Goldstein's class took José's goose-down jacket without his permission and used it for second base. When Dolores scored a double, the jacket tore and most of its feathers spilled out.

2   At first there was just a lot of arguing. Pretty soon, though, kids started hitting and punching one another. By the time the fight was over, two kids were injured, David with a bent finger and Alison with a bloody nose. Agnes had to be sent home because she has asthma and is allergic to feathers.

3   When a fight breaks out, nobody gains. José still has no jacket, Dolores's double was never counted, a lot of kids who used to be friends are now enemies, and the whole class has been punished by having to give up a week of recess.

4   We think that the damage of a fight like this is greater than a torn coat or a week spent indoors. Lots of times countries go to war with each other because their leaders don't know how to settle arguments peacefully. Ten years from now the people in this class will be grown up. If they don't learn now how to settle disagreements without hitting each other over the head, what will they be like when they are old enough to use guns and drop bombs?

Where Do You Stand?

from **The Kids' Guide to Working Out Conflicts**

by Naomi Drew

1   You may have heard teachers or other kids talk about *conflict resolution*. This is another term for solving or resolving conflicts. When it comes to conflict resolution, where do you stand right now? What are you doing to be a conflict solver? Take this quick self-test to find out. Respond yes or no to each statement:

2   **When I have a conflict . . .**
   ✓ I try to calm down before I react.
   ✓ I do my best to avoid physical fighting.
   ✓ I believe I have more to gain by working things out.
   ✓ I listen to what the other person has to say.
   ✓ I try to see how I'm responsible instead of just blaming the other person.
   ✓ I look for ways to solve the problem rather than win the argument.
   ✓ I'm willing to compromise.
   ✓ I avoid using put-downs.
   ✓ I speak my truth, but I do it respectfully.
   ✓ I try to put myself in the other person's place instead of only focusing on my own stuff.

3   **How many times did you answer yes?**
   - **Five or more?** If so, you're already a conflict solver a good part of the time. Keep at it! Also know that you'll become an even better conflict solver by working to turn your "no" answers into "yeses."
   - **Fewer than five?** You're not there yet . . . but you can get there. Choose one new idea to try and do it until it starts to come more easily. Then choose another. Also continue doing whatever you said yes to.
   - **If you answered yes to the third statement,** you've already made an important start. Being willing to work out conflicts is the first big step on the road to becoming a conflict solver.

GO ON ➤

Reading Comprehension

Use "Fighting Is Never a Good Solution" to answer questions 1–8.

1. Which statement from the article identifies the author's claim?

   A. *Fighting Is Never a Good Solution* (the title)

   B. *When Dolores scored a double, the jacket tore and most of its feathers spilled out.* (paragraph 1)

   C. *At first there was just a lot of arguing.* (paragraph 2)

   D. *Ten years from now the people in this class will be grown up.* (paragraph 4)

2. The support the author gives in paragraph 2 is BEST described as —

   A. an emotional description

   B. a factual description

   C. an irrelevant list

   D. a few overgeneralizations

3. In paragraph 3, the statement "When a fight breaks out, nobody gains" is —

   A. the author's position in the argument

   B. an example of irrelevant support

   C. a reason that supports the claim

   D. an example of faulty reasoning

4. Which phrase is a generalization that could weaken the author's argument?

   A. *most of its feathers* (paragraph 1)

   B. *At first* (paragraph 2)

   C. *We think* (paragraph 4)

   D. *Lots of times* (paragraph 4)

5. Which statement is a strongly worded opinion that supports the claim?

   A. *A fight broke out on the playground yesterday because of a torn jacket.* (paragraph 1)

   B. *At first there was just a lot of arguing.* (paragraph 2)

   C. *Agnes had to be sent home because she has asthma and is allergic to feathers.* (paragraph 2)

   D. *We think that the damage of a fight like this is greater than a torn coat or a week spent indoors.* (paragraph 4)

6. By writing that *the whole class has been punished by having to give up a week of recess* (paragraph 3), the author appeals to the reader's sense of —

   A. curiosity

   B. fairness

   C. kindness

   D. worry

7. The persuasive technique used in the last four lines is BEST characterized as —

   A. a logical appeal

   B. an emotional appeal to fear

   C. words with positive connotations

   D. an irrelevant example

8. Which statement BEST summarizes the argument in this article?

  A. Adults' arguments end up in physical fights more often than children's do.

  B. After José's jacket was used for second base, a fight broke out on the playground.

  C. Physical fighting can make an argument even worse.

  D. It isn't worthwhile to fight because you might get punished.

Use "Where Do You Stand?" to answer questions 9–12.

9. The title "Where Do You Stand?" serves to —

  A. reveal information about the topic

  B. introduce the topic in a challenging way

  C. summarize the main idea of the article

  D. argue a point with reasons and evidence

10. The subheading *When I have a conflict . . .* introduces a —

  A. caption   **C.** sidebar

  B. checklist   **D.** summary

11. Which statement BEST summarizes the article?

  A. To find out if you are good at resolving conflicts, take a test.

  B. Good conflict solvers need to tell the truth about an argument.

  C. You can work on your behavior to become a better conflict solver.

  D. If you say *yes* fewer than five times on the self-test, memorize the listed suggestions.

12. Which text feature helps you learn your score?

  A. Bullets   **C.** Checklist

  B. Caption   **D.** Drawing

Use both selections to answer question 13.

13. Which statement supports the main idea of both selections?

  A. It is better to hide my angry feelings when there is a conflict.

  B. My feelings about a conflict are more important than anyone else's.

  C. How I act when I am angry can make a situation better or worse.

  D. It is easy to get into a fight, but I can run away if it gets bad.

SHORT CONSTRUCTED RESPONSE
Write two or three sentences to answer this question.

14. Identify one persuasive technique used in "Fighting Is Never a Good Solution." Give details to support your answer.

Write a paragraph to answer this question.

15. Reread the self-test checklist from "Where Do You Stand?" Summarize the advice on how to be a good conflict solver.

GO ON

Vocabulary

Use context clues to answer the following questions about words in "Fighting Is Never a Good Solution."

1. What does *injured* mean in paragraph 2?
   A. Upset
   B. Unhappy
   C. Harmed
   D. Defeated

2. The word *allergic* in paragraph 2 means having —
   A. an illness with flu-like symptoms that is passed from person to person through the air
   B. a condition in which a rash or sickness appears after one comes into contact with something that doesn't affect most people
   C. a strong dislike of anything that is annoying or unpleasant to taste
   D. an interest in the makeup of a naturally occurring material or substance

3. What does *damage* mean in paragraph 4?
   A. Something that helps
   B. Possible cause
   C. Money paid
   D. Bad result

Use the chart to answer the following questions.

Prefix	Meaning
com-	together or with
dis-	not; absence of
in-	into; within
re-	again; in return

Suffix	Meaning
-ment	the act or result of
-ion	the act or condition of
-ful	full of
-ible	capable of; tending to

4. Which word means "the result of not having the same opinion"?
   A. Disagreement   C. Recess
   B. Instead   D. Statement

5. Which word means "to settle differences together by having each side give up something"?
   A. Already   C. Compromise
   B. Argument   D. Permission

6. Which word means "to do or say something in return"?
   A. React   C. Respectfully
   B. Resolution   D. Responsible

Revising and Editing

Use your knowledge of punctuation and capitalization to answer the following questions.

1. What is the correct way to punctuate and capitalize the following short story title?

trapped in a comic book

   A. "Trapped In A Comic Book"
   B. *Trapped in A Comic Book*
   C. "Trapped in a Comic Book"
   D. *Trapped in a comic Book*

2. What is the correct way to punctuate and capitalize the following book title?

where the sidewalk ends

   A. *Where The Sidewalk Ends*
   B. "Where the sidewalk Ends"
   C. "Where The Sidewalk ends"
   D. *Where the Sidewalk Ends*

3. What is the correct way to punctuate and capitalize the following poem title?

hector the collector

   A. "Hector the collector"
   B. *Hector the Collector*
   C. *Hector The Collector*
   D. "Hector the Collector"

4. What is the correct way to punctuate and capitalize the following magazine article title?

ways we can protect the environment

   A. *Ways we can protect the Environment*
   B. "Ways We Can Protect the Environment"
   C. *Ways We Can Protect The Environment*
   D. "Ways we can protect the environment"

5. What is the correct way to punctuate and capitalize the following book title?

the tomb robbers

   A. "The tomb robbers"
   B. *The tomb Robbers*
   C. *The Tomb Robbers*
   D. "the Tomb Robbers"

6. What is the correct way to punctuate and capitalize the following short story title?

girl at the window

   A. *Girl At the Window*
   B. "Girl at the Window"
   C. *Girl at the Window*
   D. "Girl At The Window"

Ideas for Independent Reading

Which questions from Unit 8 made an impression on you?
Continue exploring with these books.

COMMON CORE

RI 10 Read and comprehend literary nonfiction.

How smart are animals?

The Chimpanzees I Love
by Jane Goodall

Goodall has studied one community of chimpanzees in Tanzania for over 40 years. She has seen them use sticks as tools and watched as they pass on skills like hunting and child-rearing from one generation to the next.

Exploding Ants: Amazing Facts About How Animals Adapt
by Joanne Settel, PhD.

Why does a cuckoo chick push the other babies out of the nest? If an owl doesn't chew, how does it eat? Animals find all kinds of ways to survive in various circumstances.

Wild Horses I Have Known
by Hope Ryden

All horses were wild before people caught and tamed them. About 400 years ago, some horses in the United States got loose and have been roaming free ever since. How have they survived?

How can we uncover the past?

Buttons, Bones, and the Organ-Grinder's Monkey: Tales of Historical Archaeology
by Meg Greene

Some people search for clues about the past in books. Others look in old trash pits or ancient cellars to find evidence of how people really lived.

Curse of the Pharaohs
by Zahi Hawass

The mummy's curse warns that anyone who disturbs the pharaohs' tombs will be haunted by their spirits. Egyptian archeologist Zahi Hawass says he doesn't believe that, but strange things have happened to him on the job.

Secrets from the Rocks
by Albert Marrin

Roy Chapman Andrews led the first archaeological expedition into Mongolia in 1922. His team found dinosaur eggs and evidence of the first mammal, along with a large deposit of other fossils.

What's the full news story?

Phineas Gage
by John Fleischman

In 1848, an iron rod shot straight through Phineas Gage's brain. He survived, but his family said he wasn't the same man afterward. Doctors studied Phineas to find out more about how the human brain works.

Remember: The Journey to School Integration
by Toni Morrison

Imagine having to walk through an angry mob just to go to school. This is what life was like for thousands of children when the Supreme Court ended segregation in 1954.

Where the Action Was
by Penny Colman

During World War II, women weren't allowed near combat. However, 127 brave female journalists managed to get around the rules and report on some of the most important events during the war.

Get Novel Wise

THiNKcentral

Go to **thinkcentral.com**.
KEYWORD: HML6-1006

UNIT 9

The Power of Research

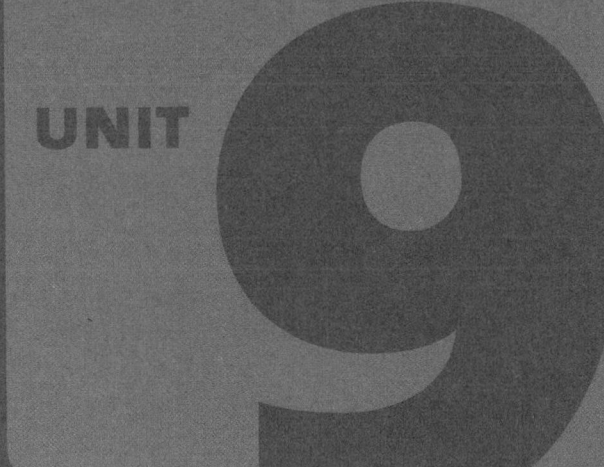

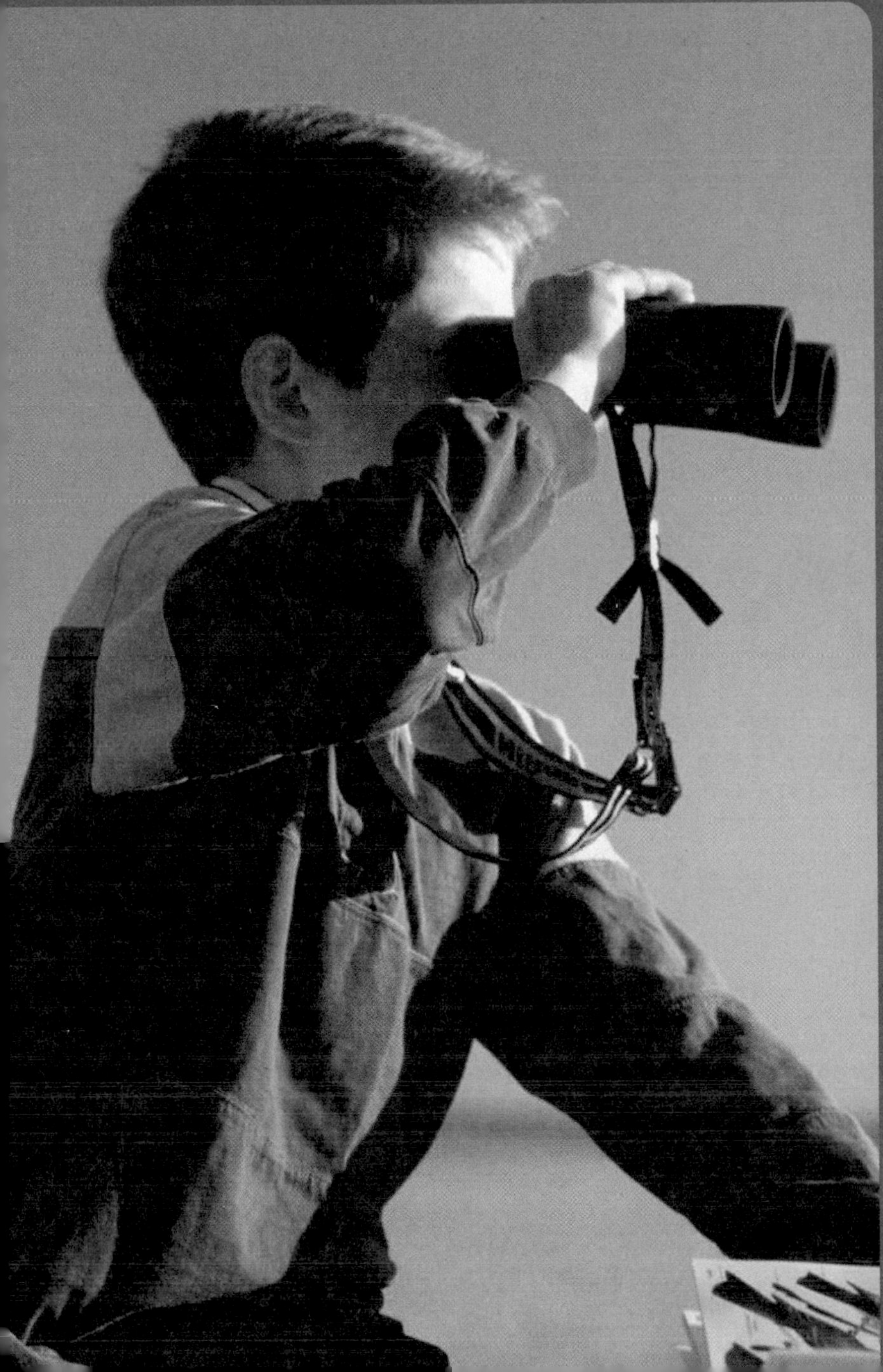

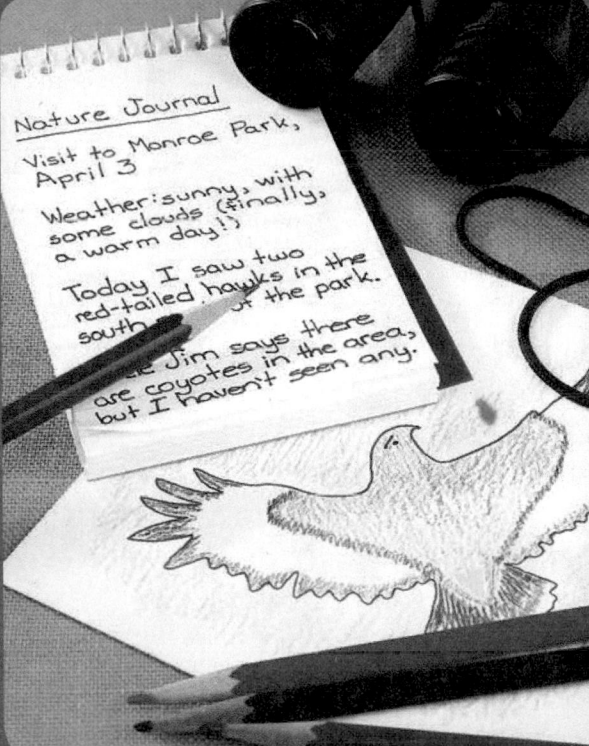

RESEARCH WORKSHOPS

- Research Strategies
- Writing Research Papers

Share What You Know

What is RESEARCH?

Research is using sources to find answers. You do research in your everyday life. For example, if you want to know what the weather will be like tomorrow, you can turn on the television or go online. However, conducting research for a report or presentation can be more of a challenge. In this unit, you will learn to locate and use sources of information to answer complex questions.

ACTIVITY Work with a partner to list some questions that you often answer by doing research, either at home or at school. Explain where you get the answers.

What I Research	Where I Find Answers

Find It Online!

Go to **thinkcentral.com** for the interactive version of this unit.

1008

Preview Unit Goals

DEVELOPING RESEARCH SKILLS	• Plan research
	• Develop research questions
	• Use library and media center resources
	• Gather information from multiple print and digital sources
	• Assess the credibility of each source
	• Collect your own data
WRITING	• Write a research paper
	• Decide on a research topic
	• Locate and evaluate sources
	• Use technology to take notes
	• Summarize and paraphrase
	• Quote directly and avoid plagiarism
	• Document sources
	• Prepare a Works Cited list
	• Format your paper
SPEAKING AND LISTENING	• Give a power presentation
ACADEMIC VOCABULARY	• formulate • reliable
	• refine • systematically
	• relevant

Writing and Research in a Digital Age

KEYWORD: HML6-1009

From online news feeds and electronic archives to podcasts and digital notebooks, technology tools can help you tackle any research project. Find out how.

UNIT 9

Research Strategies Workshop

How do I answer my QUESTIONS?

COMMON CORE

Included in this workshop:
W 6 Use technology, including the Internet, to produce writing. **W 7** Conduct short research projects to answer a question, drawing on several sources and refocusing the inquiry when appropriate.
W 8 Gather relevant information from multiple print and digital sources; assess the credibility of each source.

Questions don't always have easy answers. Sometimes you will **research** a topic and find that you have even more questions about it than when you started. This unit explains where to look for answers and how to tell which sources are reliable.

QUICKWRITE You might do research for a school assignment or just to satisfy your own curiosity. In this unit, you will follow a student who is curious about coyotes because her uncle keeps seeing them in his suburban backyard. She also saw a news program about coyotes in urban and suburban areas. If you were this student, what questions would you ask about the coyotes? Create a cluster diagram like this one but with your own questions about coyotes.

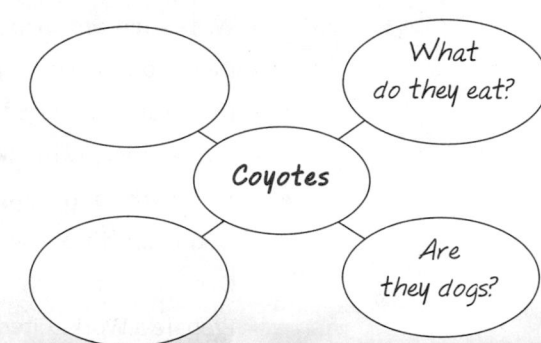

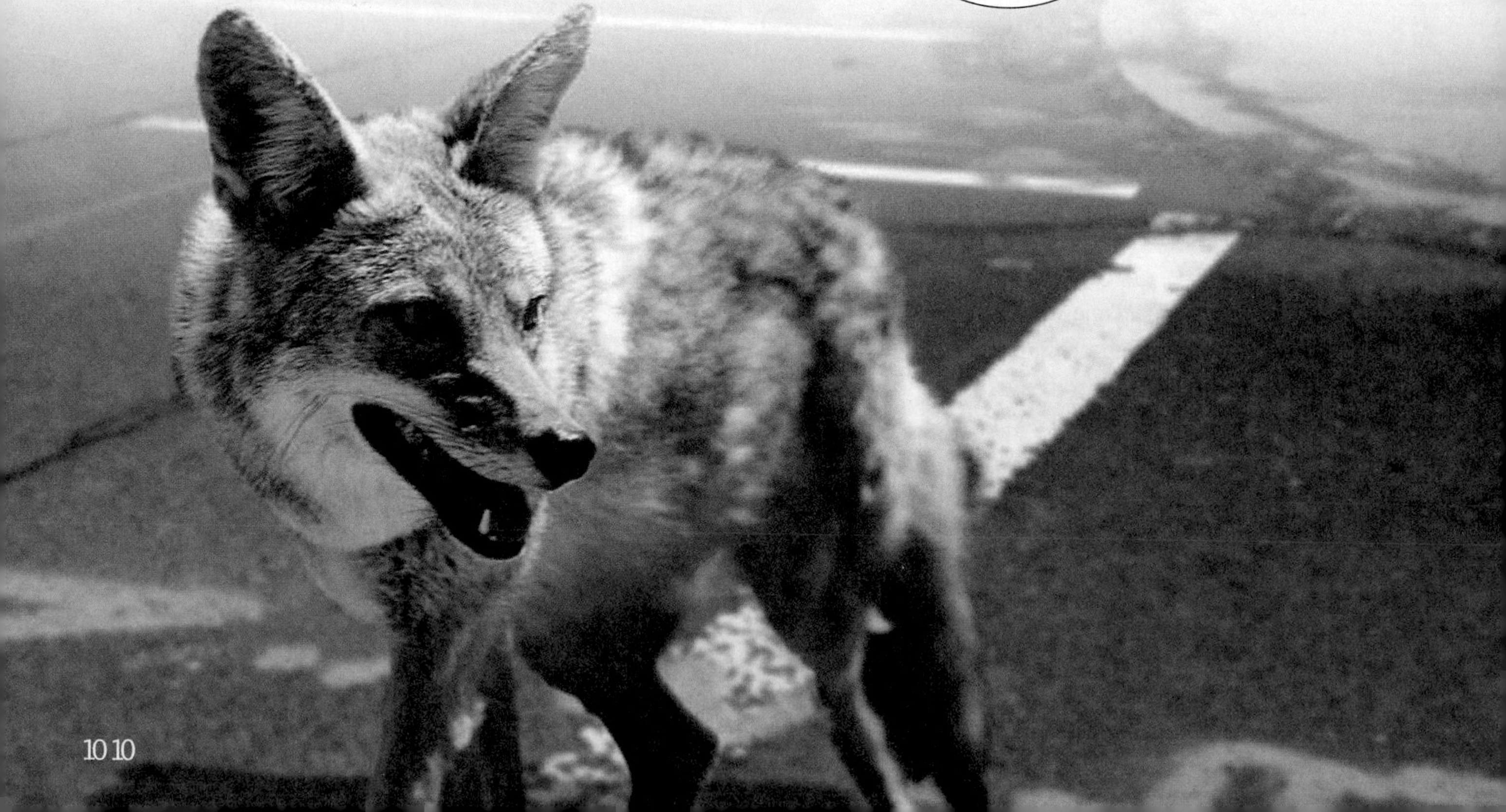

Beginning the Research Process

Good planning makes research easier and faster. Take a few minutes to think about what you want to accomplish before you dive in.

DECIDE ON A GOAL

What do you want to find out? Begin by writing down some goals—general and specific ones. Here's how one student listed her goals.

> *General goal:* I want to learn more about coyotes.
>
> *Questions:*
>
> - **Why do coyotes interest me?** It seems weird that they would live near people.
> - **What do I want to learn about them?** I wonder if lots of them live in cities and suburbs.
>
> *Specific goal:* I want to learn more about how many coyotes live in cities and suburbs, and I want to know why they live there.

FIND SOME GENERAL INFORMATION

Now that you have a specific goal in mind, it's time to start your search. Try some or all of these ideas.

- **Talk with people.** Ask someone who knows about your topic to share information with you.
- **Try the Internet.** Type the name of your topic into a search engine. Visit Web sites that seem to contain relevant information.
- **Go to the library.** Read an encyclopedia article or a magazine article on your topic, or skim a nonfiction book on the subject.
- **Talk to a librarian.** Get suggestions for books, magazines, or online sources. Use these sources to gather more information.

DECIDE ON A TOPIC

Smaller, more specific topics are easier to research than big ones. This chart shows how one student narrowed her topic as she learned more about it.

Specific Topic	More Specific	Even More Specific
coyotes that live in cities or suburbs	why coyotes have moved to my suburb	why coyotes have moved to my suburb and what people are doing about it

Research Tools

THINKcentral

Go to **thinkcentral.com**.
KEYWORD: HML6-1011

ASK OPEN-ENDED RESEARCH QUESTIONS

The next step is to formulate, or develop, open-ended research questions. An open-ended question cannot be answered with just a yes or a no. Here are some questions on the topic of coyotes in the suburbs.

> - Where do coyotes normally live? What is their habitat?
> - What do coyotes eat? What is their prey?
> - Why are coyotes moving to the suburbs now? What dangers do they pose to people or pets?

Now highlight important words in your research questions. You will type these **keywords** into library catalogs, databases, and search engines.

PREPARE TO TAKE NOTES

If you follow a plan as you research, you will get more done in less time. When you are exploring sources, it is helpful to record information systematically, or in an organized way. Sometimes simply recording information on note cards can be useful. If you are researching for a class assignment, consider using word processing programs and other available technology to keep your notes organized. By using these programs to record data, you can see the relationships between ideas in formats such as charts, graphs, and diagrams. Ask yourself which format would be the best choice to gather information. The student interested in coyotes recorded information in a chart.

Source of Information on Coyotes	Notes About Source
my uncle	He has seen coyotes in his backyard twice this spring.
newspaper article	Last week's <u>Montgomery Reporter</u> had an article about coyote sightings.
radio news story	This morning, a news reporter talked about coyotes and deer in the suburbs.
the Web	I tried a search engine and got millions of results. There's lots of information about coyotes, but how can I find exactly what I need?

In the pages that follow, you will explore a range of print and electronic sources that can help you address research questions.

Using the Internet

The World Wide Web is part of the **Internet,** a huge system of linked computers. The Web includes hundreds of millions of Web sites and billions of Web pages.

EXPLORE THE WEB

Begin by clicking on your search engine or browser. **Search engines** are Web sites that organize information based on keywords, titles, and other content. You can choose from many search engines. Because search engines select and organize information differently, no two will give you exactly the same results.

USE KEYWORDS AND ADVANCED SEARCHES

Type some of your keywords into a search engine. You will locate the most relevant sources when you combine specific keywords.

Different search engines allow you to modify your search in different ways. Click on your search engine's "Advanced Search" or "Search Tips" link to find out more. Here are some examples of search modifiers:

- Try putting a phrase in quotation marks. A search for *"coyote habitat"* finds only pages that mention both terms, in that order, right next to each other.

- Some search engines allow you to use the terms AND, NOT, and OR. For example, a search for *coyote AND suburbs* results in a list of Web pages that contain both terms, but not necessarily right next to each other. These pages may provide relevant information but may also include off-topic sites.

- Other search engines let you put a plus sign next to words or phrases that you want included and a minus sign next to words and phrases that you don't want included. If a search for *coyote* results in many Web pages about a movie with that word in the title, you may want to modify your search to *+coyote -movie*.

Notice how the more specific terms below bring more specific results.

YOU TYPE IN...	YOU GET...	THIS IS...
coyote	17,600,000 results	much too broad, so you add another keyword
+coyote +habitat	451,000 results	still too broad, so you try again
"coyotes in the suburbs"	294 results	best, because the results are specific to the topic

---

TERMS FOR THE INTERNET

You will use these terms when discussing online research:

- keyword
- Web site
- Web page
- search engine
- Web address
- home page
- hyperlink
- icon

TIP The research questions that you wrote will help you think of keywords.

EXAMINE SEARCH ENGINE RESULTS

One search can bring up many pages of results. Follow these guidelines for examining the first page of results:

1. Don't just click on the first result. It may not be the most useful one for you.

2. Read the description for each result. Pay particular attention to the Web address. Many Web addresses include the abbreviations *.com* or *.net.* Sites with these addresses are usually created by individuals or by companies that are trying to sell products. Sites created by the government or by nonprofit organizations generally have *.gov* or *.org* in their addresses.

3. If a description matches your goal or keywords, click on it. If not, go to the next result or to the next page of results. You can also think of ways to improve your search terms and try again.

4. Don't print a Web page until you have skimmed the text and looked at the images. Printing dozens of Web sites may make you feel that you have done lots of research. However, if the sites you print are off-topic or repeat the same information many times over, all you are doing is wasting paper.

TIP Because most *.gov* and *.org* sites are the work of large groups and are frequently reviewed, they are often more reliable than other sites. Be aware, however, that organizations like political parties also have *.org* addresses.

YOUR TURN

Look at Search Engine Results

These are the first results that showed up in an online search.

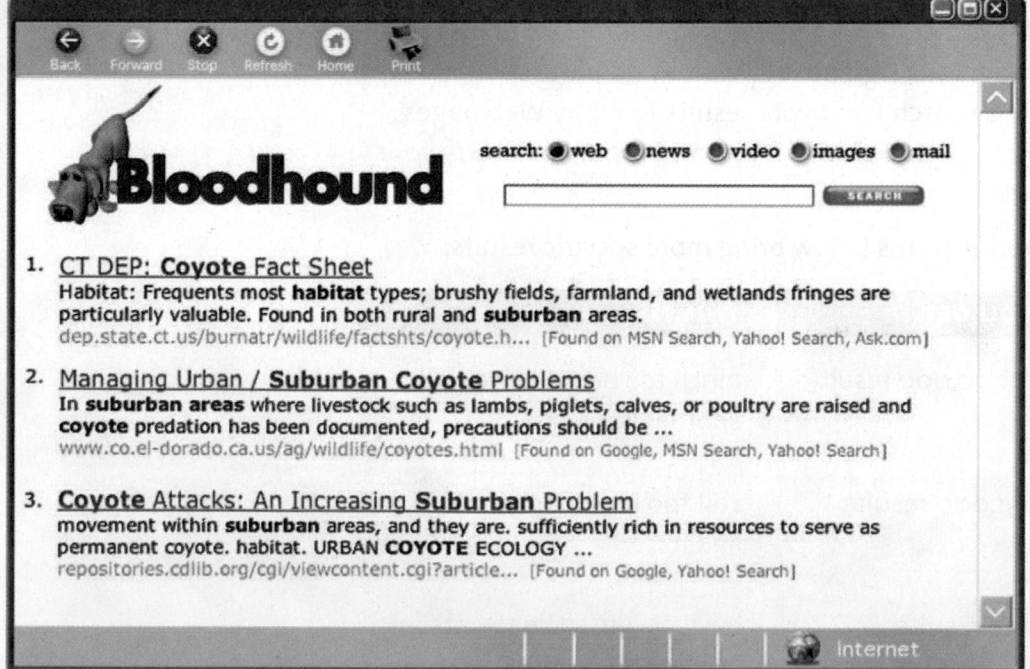

Close Read

1. Which terms did the searcher use? How do you know?

2. Which result is most relevant to the research topic of coyotes in the suburbs? Explain.

3. Is this search too broad, too narrow, or just right? Give reasons for your answer.

NAVIGATE A WEB SITE

You can use these features of Web sites to help you locate information.

A **Home page**—A **home page** is the main page or organizing page of a Web site. It welcomes you to the site, gives general information, and helps you get where you want to go.

B **Menus**— A **menu** shows the main categories of information on the site. Clicking on a menu item gives you more details about that category.

C **Hyperlinks and Icons**—Most Web sites contain **hyperlinks,** which are underlined words, terms, or Web addresses. Clicking on hyperlinks (sometimes just called links) takes you to information on another page or on a different site. **Icons** are small pictures or symbols on a Web site. Clicking on an icon takes you to information on another page.

D **Sponsor and Credits**—A **sponsor** is a company, organization, or individual that pays for and owns the site. **Credits** tell where the information on a Web site came from. Sometimes credits tell who wrote and designed the site. They might also tell when the site was last updated.

YOUR TURN

Look at Search Engine Results

Is this a useful Web site for someone who wants to learn about coyotes?

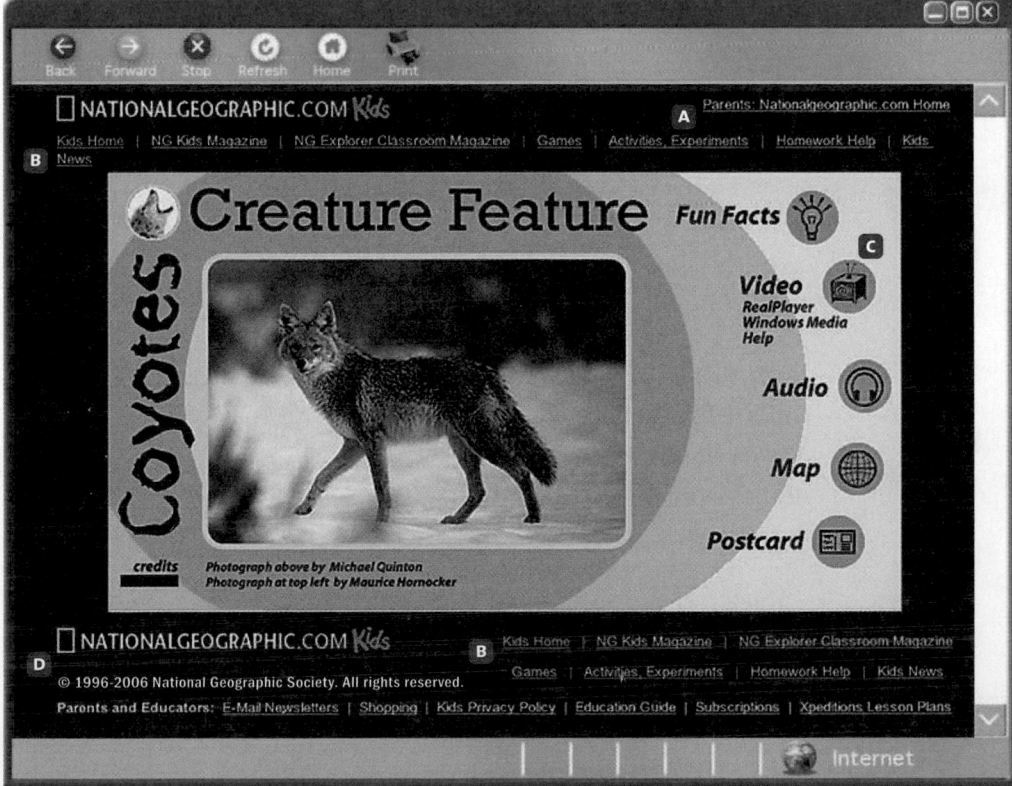

Close Read

1. Where are the icons on this page?

2. Which icon would you click to find out where in the world coyotes live?

3. Who created this site, and when was it last updated? Why is that information important?

TERMS FOR THE LIBRARY

These terms will come in handy as you use the library or media center:

- fiction
- nonfiction
- reference texts
- library catalog
- primary source
- secondary source
- table of contents
- bibliography
- glossary
- index

Using the Library or Media Center

The Internet can be an excellent source of information. However, don't forget to explore the resources available at your local public library or at your school's media center. Most libraries have different sections for adults, young adults, and children. Some libraries also have special sections, such as areas devoted to business or to family history. Computer terminals throughout the library can help you locate sources within the library, use online sources such as databases and electronic bulletin boards, send e-mails, and write reports.

LIBRARY AND MEDIA CENTER RESOURCES

BOOKS

Fiction—Novels and short stories are fiction. Works of fiction come from writers' imaginations, but they may be based on real people, places, and events.

Nonfiction—Biographies, diaries, newspaper and magazine articles, cookbooks, speeches, history books, science books, procedural manuals, and how-to books are nonfiction. Nonfiction works are about real people, places, events, and ideas.

REFERENCE

Reference desk—You can ask for help with your research here.

Reference texts—Encyclopedias, dictionaries, atlases, and almanacs are examples of reference texts. You usually cannot remove reference texts from the library.

NEWSPAPERS AND PERIODICALS

Newspapers and magazines—Your library or media center has current issues and may also have older copies in print or on microfilm.

AUDIO AND VIDEO RESOURCES

DVDs—Documentaries or instructional films may provide helpful information.

Audio—You may find music, books, plays, poems, or speeches recorded on CDs.

E-RESOURCES

Electronic collections—Ask a librarian about databases, electronic bulletin boards, CD-ROMs, e-books, e-audiobooks, podcasts, and MP3s.

USE THE LIBRARY CATALOG

The **library catalog** lists the library's or library network's holdings. The reference librarian can also show you the best and fastest ways to search it.

You can search a library catalog in a variety of ways.

- **Author**—Usually, you type the author's last name first, like this: *Soto, Gary.* If you don't get results, try the first name first: *Gary Soto.* Make sure you spell both names correctly.

- **Title**—You may be able to do a successful title search even if you don't know the full title of the book or other resource you are searching for. Try typing in a partial title and see what the results are.

- **Keyword (sometimes called Subject)**—As you learned on page 1013, you should make your keywords very specific. You may need to enter a variety of words to locate the information you need. For example, if the keywords *coyote habitat* bring you few useful results, try *coyote migration* or *coyote control.* Modify your search until you find the right results.

YOUR TURN **Look at Library Catalog Results**

A student searched for the keywords *coyote control* and found the following results.

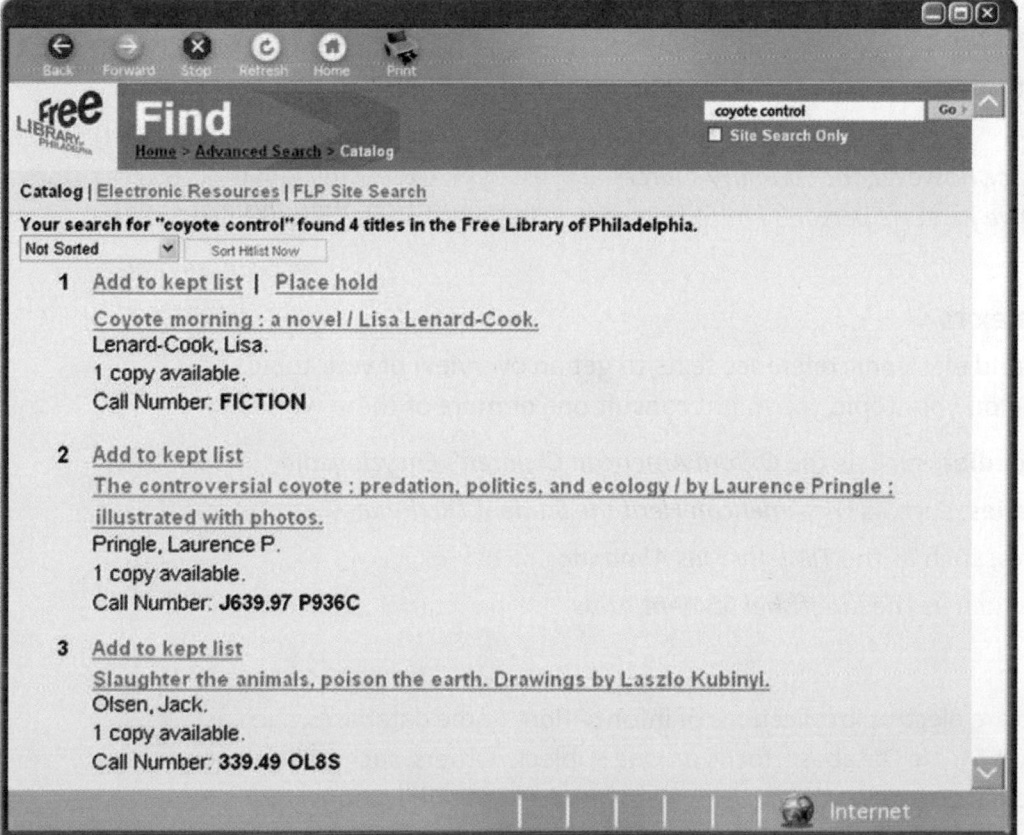

Close Read

1. Is the first choice listed a relevant source for someone who wants to learn about coyotes in the suburbs? Explain.

2. Which of the three books shown here would be most useful to someone looking for information on coyote habitats? Why?

3. How could the user find out more about each of these books?

Selecting Sources

The millions of choices on the Internet and at the library can be confusing.
Learning more about the different types of nonfiction resources can help.

PRIMARY AND SECONDARY SOURCES

Every source of information is either a primary source or a secondary source.

PRIMARY SOURCES	SECONDARY SOURCES
WHAT THEY ARE	**WHAT THEY ARE**
sources of information created by people who took part in or witnessed events	**records of events created by people who were not directly involved in or present at the events**
Examples: letters, e-mails, diaries, journals, speeches, autobiographies, advertisements, interviews, first-person newspaper and magazine articles, public documents such as birth certificates	*Examples:* textbooks, reference works, biographies, third-person newspaper and magazine articles, documentaries
▼	▼
WHEN TO USE THEM	**WHEN TO USE THEM**
• to learn about witnesses' and participants' thoughts, feelings, and reactions	• for an overview of a topic based on many sources
• to gather records and data of a time period	• to understand how a topic is perceived over time
Remember, however, that primary sources might give just one person's limited view.	*Remember, however, that secondary sources usually include a writer's interpretation or analysis of events.*

REFERENCE TEXTS

Use print and electronic reference texts to get an overview of your topic.
Depending on your topic, you might consult one or more of these works:

- **Encyclopedias,** such as the *Oxford American Children's Encyclopedia*
- **Dictionaries,** such as the *American Heritage Student Dictionary*
- **Almanacs,** such as the *TIME for Kids Almanac*
- **Atlases,** such as the *Kingfisher Student Atlas*

DATABASES

Databases are electronic collections of information. Some databases, such as
the Internet Movie Database, focus on one subject. Others, such as InfoTrac
Junior (see page 1020), gather articles from hundreds of publications.

Your school or local library offers many databases for free. Use them when you have narrowed your topic and are looking for very specific information.

NONFICTION BOOKS

Nonfiction books are good sources of in-depth information. Here's how to decide whether a specific book matches your research goal.

1. Read the **title** and **subtitle** to get a general idea of what the book is about. If there are entire books on your exact topic, you may have selected a topic that is too broad. If so, go back to page 1011 and narrow your topic. You may also need to refine your research question to make it more specific.

2. Turn to the **copyright page.** Look for the copyright date. Focus on the latest date shown, and decide if the book is up to date.

3. Look at the **table of contents.** Part and chapter headings will give you an overview of what the book covers. This page will also tell you whether the book has other useful features. For example, it may have a **bibliography** (a list of sources used), a list of **further reading,** or a **glossary** (a list of specialized terms and their definitions).

4. Check the **index** for specific topics or terms that interest you. Make sure the book has many pages on your topic rather than just a mention.

TIP Is the book that you are looking at older than you are? If so, you may want to choose a different book—unless you are researching a historical topic and want to find out what people thought of it many years ago.

YOUR TURN

Examine the Parts of a Book

Which parts of a book are shown here?

Copyright © 2008
by Darrell Madison
All rights reserved. No part of this publication may be reproduced or transmitted in any form or by any means, electronic or mechanical, without the express permission of the publisher.
10 9 8 7 6 5 4 3 2 1
Printed in the United States of America

Contents

COYOTES
Wildlife Sense and Safety

Darrell Madison

Wheeler Books
Charlottesville

Recommended Reading

Baumgartner, Will. *Wildlife in the Suburbs and City.* Denver: High Sierra Books, 2008.

Gadski, Mary Ellen. *Coyotes, Controversy, and Control.* New York: Solstice Environmental Books, 2007.

Reid, Catherine. *Coyote: Seeking the Hunter in Our Midst.* Boston: Houghton Mifflin, 2004.

Index

Close Read

1. What is the subtitle of this book? What does it tell you about the book?

2. Does this book include information about dens? How about animal control programs? How do you know?

3. When was this book published? Why is it important to note this information?

NEWSPAPERS AND PERIODICALS

Newspapers are publications that contain news and advertising. They are published daily, weekly, or very frequently. **Periodicals** are publications that are issued on a regular basis of more than one day apart. They contain news, advice, fiction, or a combination of these. Magazines are the most common type of periodical.

Recent newspaper and periodical articles can provide current information on your topic. Many articles present information briefly in a way that is easy to understand.

- **Examples of Newspapers**—*Washington Post, Los Angeles Times, Indianapolis Star, Baltimore Sun, Dallas Morning News, Arizona Republic*
- **Examples of Magazines**—*Sports Illustrated, U.S. News & World Report, Teen Ink, Next Step, HowStuffWorks Express*

You can search for magazine and newspaper articles on your topic by using a database such as InfoTrac. The page below comes from a periodical database called InfoTrac Junior. It is for students in grades 5 through 12.

YOUR TURN

Finding a Newspaper or Magazine Article

A search for *coyote population* brought up these results. Clicking on the underlined title of the article or the underlined words *Check Out* brings up the text of the article.

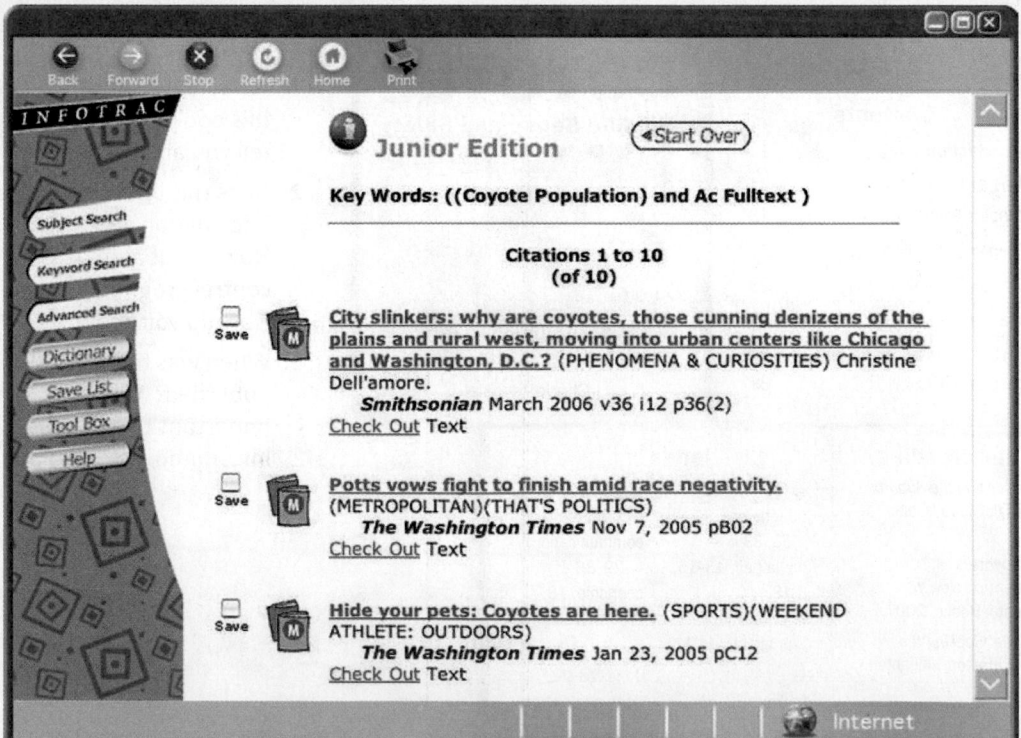

Close Read

1. What three search options does this database provide? (Hint: Look at the menu on the left.)

2. If you were searching for information on coyotes in people's backyards, which two entries would probably be most helpful? Why?

3. Which entry is not relevant to the topic of coyotes in the suburbs? How do you know?

Evaluating Sources

Some sources contain out-of-date information or errors, so make sure you evaluate every source you find. When you evaluate a source, you consider its reliability and relevance. A source is reliable if you can trust it to contain up-to-date, accurate information. A relevant source contains information directly related to your topic.

You can evaluate a source for your research by asking the following questions. On pages 1022–1024, you will find questions to ask about specific source types.

WHAT TO ASK	WHY IT MATTERS
Is the information current?	Up-to-date information is especially important when you are researching topics in rapidly changing fields such as medicine, technology, science, and sports. Even when you are researching something that happened long ago, up-to-date sources often contain the latest findings and insights.
Who is the author?	Not every author is an expert on his or her topic. Look for information on the author's other publications. You will cite sources by an author with experience related to the topic.
Who is the publisher?	Some publishers are more careful and accurate than others. For example, books published by a university press usually contain accurate information. On the other hand, popular magazines and newspapers with fads and gossip in their headlines can be unreliable. Ask a librarian for help finding valid sources. A source is valid if it is based on fact and published by recognized authorities.
What is the purpose of the information?	Some publications and Web sites may be trying to sell you a product. Others may want you to donate money or support a political idea. Look for sources that are written to inform readers. Sources focused on facts are more likely to be reliable.
Is this information relevant to my research question?	Check the table of contents or menus and links for words and phrases that relate to your research goals. If you are having difficulty locating information, you may need to refine your research question.

EVALUATE WEB SITES

The Internet is a useful research tool, but no one verifies the information on every Web site. When you visit a Web site, ask yourself these questions to evaluate the reliability and relevance of the site.

- **Who created the site?** Look for details about the author, information about a sponsoring organization, and a "last updated" reference.

- **Why was the site created?** Do the creators want to inform you about something? Do they want to entertain you? Are they trying to persuade you to support or oppose an issue? Maybe they want to sell you a product or service. Some sites are created for more than one purpose; however, the most reliable sites are created to inform.

- **Do you notice problems with the site?** Be wary if some hyperlinks lead nowhere. Avoid using sites that contain errors in grammar and spelling. The site may have been put together quickly and sloppily and should not be considered reliable.

- **Could you find more reliable information somewhere else?** Use a variety of sources, such as encyclopedias, almanacs, magazines, newspapers, interviews with experts, and documentaries.

 **YOUR TURN** **Examine a Personal Web Site**
What do you think is useful here? What errors or problems do you see?

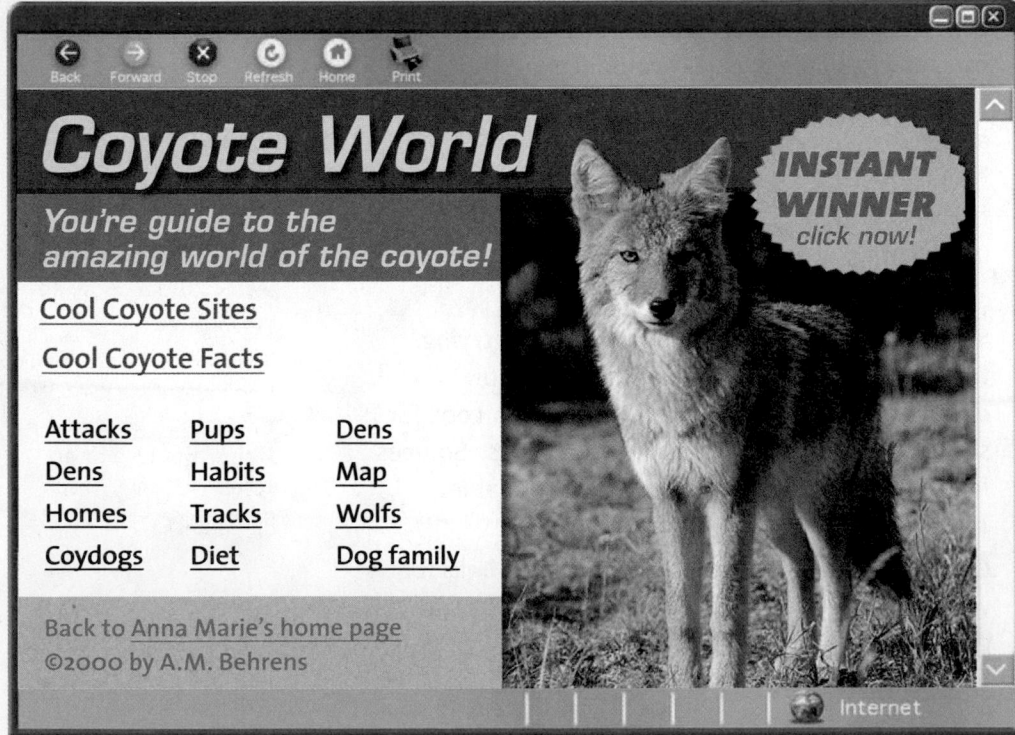

Close Read

1. Who created this site? When was it created?

2. What is the purpose of this site?

3. What problems do you notice with the site?

EVALUATE NONFICTION BOOKS

Books often provide even more information than Web sites do. To evaluate a nonfiction book for relevance and reliability ask these questions:

- **Is this book up to date?** You learned on page 1019 why the copyright page is important. Check the copyright page and the book jacket for dates and for words such as "all new" or "revised and updated." A book that has been through many updates and printings is more likely to be reliable.

- **Is the book carefully researched?** The book jacket may quote reviewers and state their qualifications. Look inside the book for **footnotes** and **end notes** that tell you where the author got information. Check the back of the book to see if there is an **appendix** with extra material, such as maps, charts, and tables.

- **What does the book say about the author?** Look for an author biography on the book jacket, at the beginning of the book, or at the end of the book. Read the biography for information about the author's education, profession, and other publications. Also, look for a **preface** near the front. This short introductory essay may provide clues to the author's background and a statement of his or her purpose.

YOUR TURN

Examine a Nonfiction Book

Use what you have learned about nonfiction books and about the parts of a book (page 1019) to decide whether this book is a good source for someone who is researching coyote habitats.

The
Coyote
Conflicts and
Conservation
Guinevere O'Brien, Ph.D.

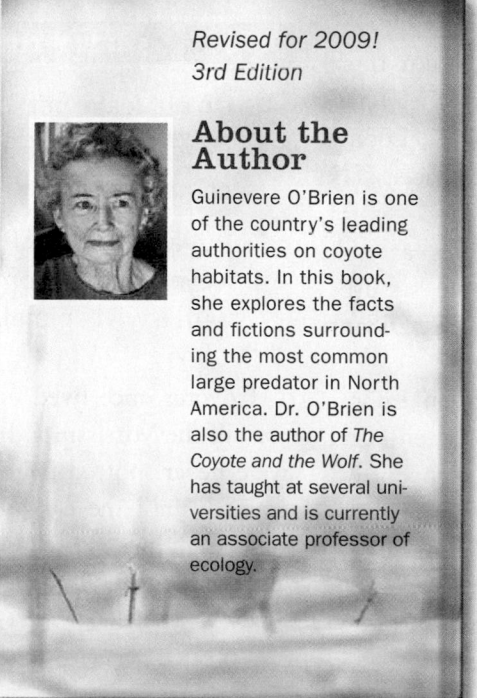

Revised for 2009!
3rd Edition

About the Author

Guinevere O'Brien is one of the country's leading authorities on coyote habitats. In this book, she explores the facts and fictions surrounding the most common large predator in North America. Dr. O'Brien is also the author of *The Coyote and the Wolf.* She has taught at several universities and is currently an associate professor of ecology.

Close Read

1. What is this book about?

2. Explain whether the author is qualified to write about this topic.

3. How up to date is this information? How do you know?

4. What other parts of this book should someone evaluate to be sure it is right for his or her research goal? (Hint: See page 1019.)

EVALUATE NEWSPAPERS AND PERIODICALS

Your library may offer some newspapers and periodicals in hard copy (in other words, printed on paper) and many others online or on microfilm. Ask these questions when evaluating an article:

- **Is this magazine or newspaper well-known and respected?** Most large-circulation newspapers and magazines are reliable. Avoid newspapers and magazines that focus on fads, space aliens, and celebrity gossip.

- **When was it published?** Usually, up-to-date sources are best. There are exceptions, however. For example, if you are researching the civil rights era, a newspaper article from 1961 could be an excellent source.

- **Who is the author?** Sometimes, magazines and newspapers provide information about the writer's qualifications and his or her other publications. Staff writers and contributing editors tend to be reliable.

- **Can the facts be verified?** Does the author say where his or her facts came from? You should be able to verify every fact in at least one other source.

YOUR TURN

Examine a Newspaper Article

Ask questions about the periodical, the author, the facts, and other content to evaluate this article.

from the **Montgomery Reporter**

Local Coyotes Are Getting Bold

BY MARTIN HERZOG, STAFF WRITER

Don't leave your food, your trash, or your house pets outside. That's the advice of Sharon DiSanti, Loomis County's animal control officer. The reason is coyotes.

"People think of coyotes as wild animals, but they're in the suburbs, and they're getting bolder," DiSanti explains.

In recent years, coyotes in Loomis County have become more bold, and, probably, more numerous. Once it was unusual to see coyotes anywhere except in rural or forested areas. Now coyotes are showing up in backyards and even in urban areas around the country.

SAFETY TIPS
1. Do not leave pet food outside.
2. Cover and secure all trash and compost.
3. Bring in cats and other pets.
4. Never try to become friendly with a wild animal.

Coyotes once lived only in regions west of the Mississippi. In fact, coyotes were never spotted in this part of the country until the early 1950s. At that time sightings were extremely rare, and the coyote's range was thought to be

See COYOTE, page B3

Close Read

1. Explain whether this article is relevant to the research topic "coyotes in the suburbs"?

2. Would you call the information in this article reliable? Why or why not?

3. The reporter's e-mail address appeared at the end of this article when it was printed. Why would having that e-mail address be useful to a researcher?

Gathering Your Own Facts

The library and the Internet are both rich sources of information, but you can collect data in other places as well. For instance, you can visit museums and historical societies. You can attend lectures by speakers who are experts in a particular topic. You can conduct interviews. You can even do field research.

INTERVIEWS

Interviews can be excellent ways to gather information. To learn whether coyotes live in your area, you might interview a neighbor who works for the local parks department or a relative who works for your community's animal control office. You can interview someone in person, by telephone, by e-mail, or by letter. The most important part of an interview is preparing for it. See page R81–R82 to learn more about preparing for and conducting an interview.

FIELD RESEARCH AND OBSERVATION

When you observe with a research goal in mind, you are doing **field research.** If you are studying coyotes, you might go to a zoo and make observations. You might take notes about what coyotes look like and how they move or sound. Also, you might make observations about a coyote's size and features by looking at a stuffed coyote in a natural history museum or a science museum.

Another way to gather your own facts about coyotes is by visiting the office of an animal control officer or a wildlife management office. Your notes might look like this.

Notes on Visit to Kaufman County Wildlife Office, 5/1/2009

- *Tracking charts show 44 coyote sightings in 2008, 32 so far in 2009.*
- *State map shows movement from rural areas to the suburbs and the city between 1999 and 2009.*
- *So far in 2009, department has received 11 calls from residents:*

  3 unconfirmed sightings
  4 confirmed sightings of coyotes in yards or near trash bins
  2 pet attacks (1 fatal)
  1 livestock attack (1 fatal)
  1 human interaction (no harm done)

Now that you have gathered all this research, what will you do with it? You could write a narrative describing why you wanted to research this topic and what you found. You could create a magazine article or a Web site to showcase your results. You could even write a research paper—to find out how, see page 1028.

Research Tips and Strategies

Library Sleuth

Two basic systems are used to classify nonfiction books. Most high school and public libraries use the Dewey decimal system; university and research libraries generally use the Library of Congress system.

DEWEY DECIMAL SYSTEM

000–099	General works
100–199	Philosophy and psychology
200–299	Religion
300–399	Social sciences
400–499	Language
500–599	Natural sciences and mathematics
600–699	Technology (applied sciences)
700–799	Arts and recreation
800–899	Literature and rhetoric
900–999	Geography and history

LIBRARY OF CONGRESS SYSTEM

A	General works	L	Education
B	Philosophy, psychology, religion	M	Music
		N	Fine arts
C	History	P	Language and literature
D	General and Old World history	Q	Science
		R	Medicine
E–F	American history	S	Agriculture
G	Geography, anthropology, recreation	T	Technology
		U	Military science
H	Social sciences	V	Naval science
J	Political science	Z	Bibliography and library science
K	Law		

Web Watch

Knowing what search tools to use is crucial to finding information on the World Wide Web.

Search Engines

Search engines differ in speed, size of database, method of searching, and other variables. Never use only one search engine.

- Google
- Yahoo!
- Ask.com

Metasearch Engines

A metasearch tool can save you time by sending a search to multiple search engines simultaneously.

- TheInfo.com
- Dogpile
- Metacrawler

Directories

Directories are useful when you are researching a general topic, because they arrange resources into subject categories.

- AOL
- About.com
- Yahoo!

Virtual Libraries

At a virtual library, you can look up information in encyclopedias, directories, and indexes.
You can even e-mail a question to a librarian.

- Internet Public Library
- Librarians' Index to the Internet

Other Web Resources

Library catalogs: Library of Congress
Encyclopedias: Encyclopaedia Britannica Online
Newspaper archives: New York Times Index
Specialized databases: Medline

Writing and Research in a Digital Age

THINK central

KEYWORD: HML6-1026 Discover a wealth of Web search tools and resources.

Checklist for Evaluating Sources

☑ The information is relevant to the topic you are researching.

☑ The information is **valid** and up-to-date. (This point is especially important when researching time-sensitive fields such as science, medicine, and sports.)

☑ The information is from someone who is an **authority** on this topic.

☑ The information is from a trusted, **reliable** source that is updated or reviewed regularly.

☑ The author's or institution's purpose for writing is clear (whether the source is **objective** or biased).

☑ The information is written at the right level for your needs. For example, a children's book is probably too simplistic, while a scientific paper may be too complex.

☑ The information has the level of detail you need—neither too general nor too specific.

☑ The facts are **accurate** and can be verified in more than one source.

Sharing Your Research

At last you have established your research goal, located sources of information, evaluated the materials, and taken notes on what you learned. Now you have a chance to share the results with the people in your world—and even beyond. Here are some options:

• Use presentation software to create a power presentation for your classmates, friends, or family.

• Publish your research findings on a wiki.

• Develop a newsletter or brochure summarizing your information.

• Explain what you learned in an oral presentation to your classmates or to people in your community.

• Write up your research in a formal research paper.
  See the following pages. ▶

See pages 1044–1045: Giving a Power Presentation

Research Paper

Once you have used research strategies to find reliable information on a topic, how can you share what you've learned? One way is by writing a short research paper. The graphic below will help you get started on writing an informative, memorable paper.

 Complete the workshop activities in your **Reader/Writer Notebook.**

WRITE WITH A PURPOSE

WRITING PROMPT

Write a **research paper** that answers a question about a topic that interests you.

Idea Starters

- What causes an earthquake?
- What is life on a space station like?
- How did the game of basketball get started?
- Why were cats important to the ancient Egyptians?
- Were there ever any female pirates?

THE ESSENTIALS

Here are some common purposes, audiences, and formats for informative/explanatory writing.

PURPOSES	AUDIENCES	FORMATS
• to inform others about your topic	• classmates and teacher	• essay for class
• to offer a unique perspective on a topic	• community members	• encyclopedia article
	• people interested in your topic	• oral report
• to learn more about a topic	• Web users	• power presentation
		• wiki
		• documentary

COMMON CORE TRAITS

1. DEVELOPMENT OF IDEAS

- clearly introduces a topic and states a **controlling idea** that answers the **research question**
- uses **several sources** to develop the topic with **relevant facts, definitions, details,** and **quotations**
- provides a **concluding section** related to the information presented

2. ORGANIZATION OF IDEAS

- **organizes** and **classifies** ideas, concepts, and information
- includes **formatting** and **graphics** when useful
- uses **appropriate transitions**

3. LANGUAGE FACILITY AND CONVENTIONS

- uses **precise language** and **domain-specific vocabulary**
- maintains a **consistent style** and **tone**
- provides basic **bibliographic information**
- reflects **correct capitalization, punctuation,** and **spelling**

Writing Online

THINK central

Go to thinkcentral.com.
KEYWORD: HML6N-1028

Planning/Prewriting

COMMON CORE — W 2a–f Write informative/explanatory texts to examine and convey ideas, concepts, and information. W 5 Develop and strengthen writing as needed by planning. W 7 Conduct short research projects to answer a question.

Getting Started

CHOOSE A TOPIC

What topic should you research? To get some ideas, look at the Idea Starters on page 1028, or think about topics or general subject areas that your teacher has assigned. When you identify a topic that interests you, start freewriting—that is, spend a few minutes writing anything that comes into your head related to the topic. Then circle the idea that most appeals to you.

▶ **TIPS FOR CHOOSING A TOPIC**

- Make a list of interesting questions, such as *Why do cats purr?* and *How do helicopters fly?* Then choose a question from your list that you think would make a good topic for research.
- Consider personal interests (for example, sports, animals, travel, or the environment) that you would like to learn more about.
- Think about historical, political, or cultural figures or events that interest you.

NARROW YOUR FOCUS

Learn about your topic by reading an encyclopedia article or by exploring Web sites. Keep in mind that your research paper will be only a few pages long. Small, specific topics are easier to research and write about than large ones. Use a graphic organizer to narrow your topic.

TIP Check library catalogs and databases such as InfoTrac to see how much information is available on your topic. If there's too little, broaden your focus. If there's too much, focus on a smaller part of the topic.

▶ **WHAT DOES IT LOOK LIKE?**

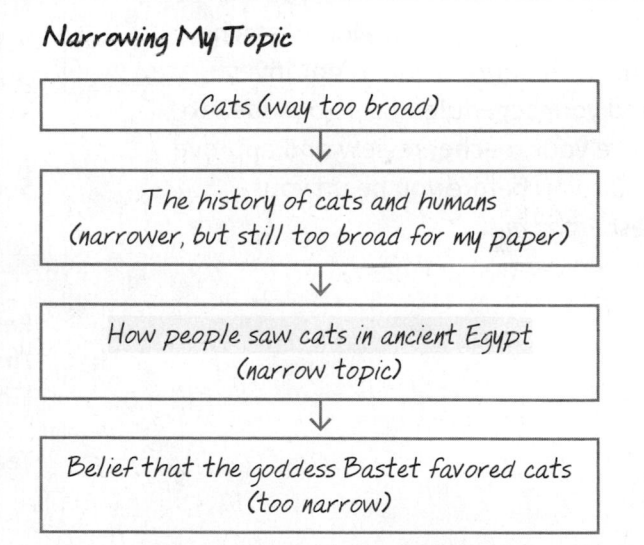

Narrowing My Topic

Cats (way too broad)
↓
The history of cats and humans (narrower, but still too broad for my paper)
↓
How people saw cats in ancient Egypt (narrow topic)
↓
Belief that the goddess Bastet favored cats (too narrow)

THINK ABOUT AUDIENCE AND PURPOSE

Before you do any further planning, make sure you identify your **audience** and your **purpose.** These two considerations will guide you throughout the research process.

▶ **ASK YOURSELF:**

- Who is my audience? What do I want the audience to learn about my topic?
- How much does my audience already know about my topic? What background information will they need?

Planning/Prewriting *continued*

Getting Started

FORMULATE A RESEARCH QUESTION

Once you have narrowed your topic, **formulate,** or develop, an open-ended question that you want to answer in your research paper. Make sure the question does not have a simple, one-word answer. Next, list some more focused questions related to your major research question. These questions will help you find the specific evidence you will need for your paper.

▶ **WHAT DOES IT LOOK LIKE?**

> **Topic:** How people saw cats in ancient Egypt
>
> **Major Research Question:** What was the role of cats in ancient Egypt?
>
> **Related Questions:**
> - How did wild cats become pets?
> - What made people start liking cats?
> - Why did ancient Egyptians make mummies out of cats?

DEVELOP A RESEARCH PLAN

Create a plan that outlines your purpose, your audience, your major research question, sources you might investigate, and your schedule. It's a good idea to have your teacher review and approve your plan before you begin your research.

▶ **TEMPLATE FOR A RESEARCH PLAN**

Name: .... **Purpose:** .... **Audience:** .... **Major Research Question:** .... **Sources to Investigate:** ....
SCHEDULE **Research Due:** .... **First Draft Due:** .... **Final Draft Due:** ....
Teacher Approval: ....

PEER REVIEW Exchange research plans with a classmate. Review each other's major research questions to decide if the questions are clear, focused, and interesting. Ask: What related questions should I answer in my paper? What sources should I investigate to find information?

YOUR TURN List four or five topic ideas in your *Reader/Writer Notebook,* and decide which one would be best for your research paper. Then narrow your topic and develop a major research question. With your purpose and audience in mind, create a research plan using the template above.

Researching

COMMON CORE

W 8 Gather information from multiple sources; assess the credibility of each source; quote or paraphrase the data and conclusions of others and avoid plagiarism. **W 9b (RI 1)** Draw evidence from informational texts to support research.

Following Your Research Plan

LOCATE SOURCES

To find answers to your research question, you'll need to gather information from a variety of sources. **Primary sources** are created by people who witnessed or took part in the events they describe. Examples include letters, diaries, autobiographies, and eyewitness accounts. **Secondary sources** are made by people not directly involved in the events described. Encyclopedia articles, biographies, textbooks, and most news articles are secondary sources.

To find relevant sources, type **keywords** (specific words and phrases related to your topic) into an Internet search engine or a library catalog. If you have trouble finding information, ask a librarian for help. He or she can suggest the best sources for your topic. Create a chart to keep track of the information you find in your sources.

See pages 1013–1017 for more information about how to search for information using research tools.

▶ **WHAT DOES IT LOOK LIKE?**

Sources	Comments
Library Encyclopedias	
"Cats," <u>World Book Encyclopedia</u>	not much about cats in Egypt
<u>New Encyclopedia of the Cat</u> (Ref 636.8 F656)	several interesting pages about cats in Egypt
Library Books	
<u>Cat Mummies</u> by Kelly Trumble (J932 T77lc)	lots on mummies and the cat goddess
<u>The Ancient Egyptians</u> by Elton LeChavre (932 LEC)	three chapters on Egyptian religion
Web Sites	
"Cool Cats of Egypt"	no information about the author, and the links don't work
"Cats in Ancient Egypt" (bookmarked on Jessica's computer)	lots of good facts, exactly on my topic, and the site was created by a museum

EVALUATE EACH SOURCE

Evaluating your sources is an important step in the research process. Ask yourself: Is this source appropriate and credible, or trustworthy? Do not use a source if

- it does not contain enough information on your topic
- it is written at a level that is too high or too low for you
- it might not be accurate (For example, Web sites without an author, a sponsor, or working links may not have been checked or updated by anyone.)

▶ **WHAT DOES IT LOOK LIKE?**

Sources I Won't Use

1. "Cats," <u>World Book Encyclopedia</u> (not enough information on my topic)
2. <u>The Ancient Egyptians</u> (too hard to understand)
3. "Cool Cats of Egypt" (information may not be correct)

Researching *continued*

Following Your Research Plan

PREPARE A SOURCE LIST

When you have decided which sources you want to use, record information about them. You may choose to record sources by writing information on index cards. If you have a computer available, you may decide to use an electronic file. One option is to use special note-taking software that is designed to guide you through the research process. (Check with your school librarian to see if this option is available to you.)

Be sure to number each source and include the following details in your source list.

Online encyclopedia
- author (if given) and title of article
- name of publisher
- date of publication or posting (if given)
- medium (Web) and date accessed

Print or CD-ROM encyclopedia
- author (if given) and title of article
- name and year of encyclopedia
- publisher and place of publication (if CD-ROM)
- medium of publication (Print or CD-ROM)

Web site
- author (if given) and title of page or article
- name of Web site
- name of the organization that sponsored or created the site (if given)
- date posted (if given)
- medium (Web) and date accessed

Book
- author or editor and title
- place of publication, publisher, and year of publication
- library call number
- medium of publication (Print)

▶ WHAT DOES IT LOOK LIKE?

Online encyclopedia

> **Source #:** 1
> **Type:** Online encyclopedia
>
> "Cat, domestic." *Encyclopaedia Britannica.* Encyclopaedia Britannica Online. 2006. Web. 6 Apr. 2009.

Print encyclopedia

> **Source #:** 2
> **Type:** Print encyclopedia
>
> "Cats." *The World Book Encyclopedia.* 2006 ed. Print.

Web site

> **Source #:** 3
> **Type:** Article on Web site
>
> Bisno, Jay. "Cats in Ancient Egypt." *Cats! Wild to Mild.* Natural History Museum of Los Angeles County. 10 May 1997. Web. 9 Apr. 2009.

Book

> **Source #:** 4
> **Type:** Book
>
> Trumble, Kelly. *Cat Mummies.* New York: Clarion, 1996. j932 T771c. Print.

Following Your Research Plan

TAKE NOTES

Consult with your teacher to determine the best method for recording information from sources. You might decide to use an electronic file for each source, or you might use a separate note card for each piece of information. For each entry, include

- the number of the source (from your source list)
- a heading that tells the main idea
- the fact, opinion, or quotation that you want to use in your paper
- the page number, the section name, or another way of locating the information

Sometimes you'll want to include the exact words used by another writer in your paper. In other cases, you'll use your own words to share information with your readers. Use these three methods to record information from your sources:

- **Quote** the source, copying the important phrase, sentence, or paragraph word for word. Put quotation marks around the passages you have copied.
- **Paraphrase** the source, that is, express what it says in your own words. Since a paraphrase is a rewording of another piece of writing, a paraphrased passage is usually around the same length as the original.
- **Summarize** the source, using your own words to record only the key ideas. A summary states an idea in fewer words than the original source.

TIP A good summary does not include your own opinions and omits less important details.

▶ **WHAT DOES IT LOOK LIKE?**

Original Source

Artisans made thousands of small bronze sculptures of cats. They sold them to people who worshiped Bastet. These worshipers offered the bronze cats at temples and shrines and hoped for an answer to their prayers.

Trumble, Kelly, Cat Mummies, page 13

Paraphrase

Source #: 4
Cat status in ancient Egypt

Artists created cat statues out of bronze. Followers of Bastet bought the statues and took them to holy places. They offered them to the goddess so that she would help them with what they asked for (13).

Summary

Source #: 4
Cat status in ancient Egypt

Visitors to holy places brought cat statues to offer to the goddess Bastet (13).

Researching *continued*

Following Your Research Plan

AVOID PLAGIARISM

Copying words and ideas from a source and presenting them as your own is called **plagiarism.** Plagiarism is the same as stealing another writer's work. How can you be sure to give credit to the sources you use? Here are some tips:

- **As you take notes, summarize and paraphrase as much as possible.** This takes longer than copying does, but it helps you think through and understand what you are reading.
- **Don't overuse one source.** Be sure to get your information from at least three sources. This way you will learn many perspectives on your topic and develop your own ideas.
- **Every time you copy something exactly, put quotation marks around it.** Even if you paraphrase most of a sentence but copy just a few key words, put quotation marks around the words from the source.
- **When you write your draft, put your sources away.** Use only your electronic notes or your note cards.
- **At the end of your paper, list your sources.** Your teacher may ask you to create a bibliography or a Works Cited list. An example of a Works Cited list appears on page 1041.

▶ WHAT DOES IT LOOK LIKE?

Original Source

Cats . . . found a good source of food living around people's homes and farms as well as affection from their human friends.

Bisno, Jay, "Cats in Ancient Egypt"

Plagiarized

> Cats found food by living near people's homes, and they also got affection from their human friends.

Correctly Documented

> Cats "found a good source of food living around people's homes," and cats and people started to have a friendly relationship (Bisno).

Original Source

Depictions of cats often show them with jewelry such as earrings and necklaces, so it is likely that Egyptians adorned their pets.

"Egypt & Domestication," Cats! Wild to Mild

Plagiarized

> Pictures of cats often show them with jewelry like earrings and necklaces, so Egyptians probably put jewelry on their pets.

Correctly Documented

> On statues and in paintings, some cats wear earrings and other jewelry ("Egypt").

Following Your Research Plan

WRITE A CONTROLLING IDEA

Consider the information you have gathered from your sources. How did you answer your research questions? What main point do these answers suggest? Write this main point in a **controlling idea,** or thesis statement to help focus your research. The controlling idea for your paper should be a sentence that answers your major research question. Everything in your paper should help explain and support your controlling idea.

TIP Don't worry if your controlling idea isn't perfect now. You can revise it later, after you write your draft.

▶ **WHAT DOES IT LOOK LIKE?**

Answers to Some of My Research Questions:
- Wild cats were useful because they killed pests.
- By 2000 B.C., many cats were pets in Egypt.
- Cats became associated with the goddess Bastet and were worshiped.
- As people with different beliefs conquered Egypt, cats gradually lost their sacred status.

Controlling Idea:
In ancient Egypt, people's ideas about cats changed over time.

CREATE AN OUTLINE

Use your notes to make a writing plan.

- Separate and classify your notes that have the same or similar headings into different groups.
- Look at your groups and decide which order best fits your controlling idea. For example, if your controlling idea is about how people's ideas about cats changed over time, you would organize your groups of notes in chronological order, or from the earliest ideas to the latest ones.
- Use your groups to write an outline of your paper. List each main point as a Roman numeral. Underneath each main point, list supporting details, facts, and examples. This outline will guide your writing as you draft.

TIP You can create a graphic organizer instead of a formal outline. Try a flowchart or a sequence chain.

▶ **WHAT DOES IT LOOK LIKE?**

Cats in Ancient Egypt
I. Changes in how people viewed cats
   A. Once were wild animals
   B. Became pets
   C. In Egypt, became sacred animals
II. Wild cats
   A. Bigger than pet cats we know today
   B. Killed mice, rats, and snakes
   C. Became important to ancient Egyptians
III. Sacred cats
   A. Bastet, the cat goddess
   B. Earrings and other jewelry for cats
   C. Cat mummies
IV. Cats no longer sacred
   A. Different rulers in Egypt
   B. Different beliefs

YOUR TURN Using your research questions as a guide, gather information about your topic. Write a controlling idea that expresses your main point. Then classify the information you have gathered in an outline. Keep your audience and purpose in mind.

Drafting

The following chart gives a framework for drafting a research paper.

Organizing Your Research Paper

INTRODUCTION

- Catch your audience's attention with an intriguing **description,** a brief and vivid **quotation**, or a thought-provoking **question.**
- Provide enough background information for readers to understand your topic.
- Include a clear controlling idea that introduces the research question.
- Establish a **formal style** and **tone,** or attitude, by avoiding contractions and choosing precise, unbiased language.

▼

BODY

- Use your outline and your notes to tell your audience what you learned about your topic. Use appropriate **transitions** to clarify the relationships between ideas.
- Focus each paragraph on a main point and support it with **facts, definitions, concrete details, quotations,** and other information.
- Mention your sources to tell your audience where you discovered information.
- Define **domain-specific,** or specialized, terms that you use to explain your topic.
- Combine ideas from different sources. Classify and organize ideas to clarify information, and add your own interpretations, conclusions, and comments. Use **transitions** to connect ideas.
- Consider creating a graphic to sum up or clarify information. For example, you might include a labeled **diagram**, a cause-effect **chart, a graph,** or a **timeline**. Be sure to include a source line that tells where you found the facts in your graphic.

▼

CONCLUDING SECTION

- **Summarize** your controlling idea and most important points.
- Consider ending with a final interesting idea, such as your own reflections on the topic, questions that remain unanswered, or suggestions for additional research.

▼

WORKS CITED LIST

- Include a **Works Cited list** as a separate page at the end of your draft.
- Use a **style manual,** such as the *Modern Language Association Handbook for Writers of Research Papers* or the *Chicago Manual of Style,* to ensure that you are correctly documenting your sources according to your teacher's preference.
- List sources in **alphabetical order** by the authors' last names (or by the title, for a work with no author listed).
- Begin each entry on a **separate line,** aligned with the left margin. Indent additional lines one-half inch.

COMMON CORE **W 4** Produce clear and coherent writing. **W 8** Provide basic bibliographic information. **L 2** Demonstrate a command of standard English punctuation.

LEARN HOW **Document Your Sources** In your research paper, tell readers where you found a fact or idea by acknowledging your sources in your sentences. Use language such as "According to Bisno,..." and "In *Cat Mummies,* Trumble explains that...." Also include **parenthetical citations:** show each source in parentheses at the end of a sentence. This chart gives some examples.

Guidelines for Citing Sources in a Research Paper

Source with one author	▶ Use the author's last name and a page number: (Fogle 21).
Web site with no page numbers	▶ Use only the author's name: (Bisno).
Author and page number unknown	▶ Use a short form of the title: ("Egypt").
More than one source supporting an idea	▶ Separate each source citation with a semicolon: (Fogle 20; Trumble 11).
Author already mentioned in the sentence	▶ Use only the page number: (21).

GRAMMAR IN CONTEXT: PUNCTUATING TITLES

Follow these rules to correctly punctuate any titles you include in your paper.

Rule	*Example*
Underline or italicize titles of books, encyclopedias, movies, magazines, newspapers, music albums, works of art, TV and radio programs, and Web sites.	▶ *Cat Mummies* contains interesting information about the cat goddess.
Use **quotation marks** for short stories, book chapters, songs, TV episodes, radio segments, single Web pages, and articles in newspapers, encyclopedias, and magazines.	▶ Bisno, Jay. "Cats in Ancient Egypt." *Cats! Wild to Mild.* Natural History Museum of Los Angeles County. 10 May 1997. Web. 9 Apr. 2009.

YOUR TURN Develop a draft of your research paper. As you draft, be sure to follow the outline you created. Remember to credit all your sources, and use the correct punctuation for any titles you include in your draft.

Revising

In this stage, you evaluate the content, structure, and style of your draft with your purpose and audience in mind. The chart below can help you revise, rewrite, or try a new approach.

RESEARCH PAPER

Ask Yourself	Tips	Revision Strategies
1. Does the introduction clearly state your controlling idea? Does it answer the major research question?	▶ **Underline** the controlling idea. **Draw a box** around the part that answers the major research question.	▶ **Add** a controlling idea, or **revise** the existing one to more clearly answer the research question.
2. Does each body paragraph develop one main point related to the controlling idea?	▶ In the margin, **label** each paragraph with the main point it develops.	▶ **Rearrange** information so that each paragraph addresses only one main point. **Delete** unrelated ideas.
3. Does each paragraph contain supporting evidence?	▶ **Highlight** the facts, examples, and quotations that support each main point.	▶ **Add** facts, examples, and quotations from your research notes.
4. Does the concluding section summarize the controlling idea and end with a final interesting idea?	▶ **Circle** the part of the concluding section that summarizes the controlling idea. **Draw a wavy line** under the sentences that give readers an interesting idea to think about.	▶ **Add** a summary of the controlling idea. **Revise** the concluding section to describe the importance of the topic, raise unanswered questions, or recommend additional research.
5. Is information properly paraphrased, summarized, or quoted?	▶ Review all the facts, examples, and quotations you included. **Underline** those missing quotations, parenthetical citations, or sound as if someone else wrote them.	▶ **Add** citations and quotation marks if necessary. Rework incorrectly paraphrased information.
6. Does a Works Cited list correctly document all sources?	▶ **Put a check mark** next to each source used in the paper and in the Works Cited list.	▶ **Add** entries that are missing from the Works Cited list. **Delete** entries that are not in the paper.

YOUR TURN **PEER REVIEW** Have a peer use the chart to evaluate your paper and suggest improvements. Take notes on what you and your partner discuss so that you can use them when you revise or rework your draft.

ANALYZE A STUDENT DRAFT

W 2d Use precise language. **W 5** Strengthen writing by revising, editing, rewriting, or trying a new approach.

Read this student's draft and the comments about it as a model for revising your own research paper.

Hensley 1

Melissa Hensley
Mrs. Weiss
English 6
14 April 2009

Cats in Ancient Egypt

❶   My paper is about cats. The dictionary says that a cat is "a small mammal domesticated for many centuries." Some people even worshiped cats. Cats became truly powerful in ancient Egypt when they went from being wild animals to useful animals to sacred animals.

❷   Before about 4000 B.C. in Egypt, cats were wild. They were also bigger than the pet cats we know today (Bisno). When Egyptians began to farm, they had to store their grain, but mice and rats got into the grain and ate it. Cats attacked the mice and rats (Bisno; Fogle 20). People realized that cats could help keep grain safe. For that reason, cats became valuable to people.

> Melissa includes a clear **controlling idea** in her **introduction.** However, her opening lines are dull and don't catch her readers' attention.

> Here Melissa supports a main point with a **relevant fact.**

LEARN HOW **Craft an Effective Introduction** Melissa's paper begins with a bland statement that is not likely to make her audience want to continue reading. To capture her readers' attention, she could replace the statement with a thought-provoking question, a powerful quotation, or a vivid image. Notice how the revision in blue improves Melissa's introduction. Why might this opening be more interesting to readers?

MELISSA'S REVISION TO PARAGRAPH ❶

Cats didn't always brush up against people's legs and purr. A long time ago, cats were fierce, wild animals. Over time, they got closer to people and became pets. Eventually, some

    ~~My paper is about cats. The dictionary says that a cat is "a small mammal domesticated for many centuries." Some~~ people even worshiped cats.

❸ Big, wild cats also killed poisonous snakes (Fogle 21). People must have noticed this and then figured out that it would be good to keep cats around their homes. People began to feed the cats to make sure that they stayed around. At some point, they probably began to pet and enjoy the cats, too. Bisno says that the cats "found a good source of food living around people's homes" and that cats and people started to have a friendly relationship. By 2000 B.C., many cats were pets instead of wild animals (Bisno).

❹ Cats and people interacted for a few thousand years before people started thinking of cats as sacred. That happened beginning about 1000 B.C. (Bisno). At that time, ancient Egyptians began to believe that cats were the special favorites of a goddess named Bastet. In fact, in some works of art, Bastet has a female body and the head of a cat ("Egypt"). According to Trumble, the cat became Bastet's "sacred animal" (11). As a result, people started to worship cats ("Egypt").

❺ Art from ancient Egypt shows the importance of the cat. In statues and paintings, some cats wear earrings and other jewelry ("Egypt"). Trumble explains that visitors to holy places brought cat statues to offer to the goddess Bastet (13). Some cats were made into mummies. This probably means that Egyptians thought cats would have an afterlife just as people would ("Egypt").

❻ Cats aren't sacred in Egypt anymore. That's because different groups of people conquered Egypt. They brought new religions that didn't include animals. For example, when the Romans conquered Egypt, they brought Christianity. Later, the Arabs brought Islam (Trumble 39–40, 48). Beliefs changed, and over time, cats were just cats once again. The timeline shows the changes between 4000 B.C. and A.D. 1000. The dates are estimates.

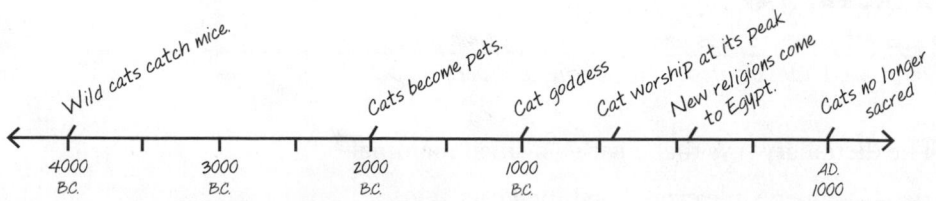

Sources: "Egypt"; Trumble 39–40; Bisno.

Melissa adds her own **original comments and ideas** based on her analysis of information from her sources. She also incorporates a **quotation** from one source.

The writer supports her point with concrete details from **multiple sources** and uses correct **parenthetical citations.**

The paper classifies and **organizes information chronologically** to describe changes over time. Melissa connects ideas with **transitions.**

This **graphic** summarizes a lot of information in a way that readers can grasp quickly.

Hensley 3

❼   Attitudes toward cats changed over time in ancient Egypt. Cats went from being wild animals to being useful friends who killed rats, mice, and snakes. Then cats became identified with a goddess, and people began to worship cats as well as the goddess. Later on, new religions helped bring cats back down to the level of friendly animals. That is where we still find cats today.

In her concluding section Melissa restates her controlling idea and summarizes her main points.

Hensley 4

Works Cited

Bisno, Jay. "Cats in Ancient Egypt." *Cats! Wild to Mild.* Natural

    9 Apr. 2009⊙

    History Museum of Los Angeles County. 10 May 1997. Web.∧

"Egypt & Domestication." *Cats! Wild to Mild.* Natural History

    Web. 9 Apr. 2009⊙

    Museum of Los Angeles County.∧

Fogle, Bruce. The New Encyclopedia of the Cat. London:

    Dorling, 2001. Print⊙
    ∧

Trumble, Kelly. *Cat Mummies.* New York: Clarion, 1996. Print⊙
    ∧

YOUR TURN Use guidance from your peers and teacher as well as the two "Learn How" lessons to revise your research paper. Consider trying a new approach if the organization of your paper isn't supporting your controlling idea or addressing your audience.

LEARN HOW **Format a Works Cited List** When writing a research paper, it's critical that you document all your sources according to the guidelines your teacher gives you. To correct her Works Cited list, Melissa needed to make the following revisions:

- End each entry with a period.
- Include the date of access for online sources.
- Italicize the titles of books.
- Use quotation marks around the titles of articles found online or in periodicals.

Notice Melissa's revisions in blue.

Editing and Publishing

In the editing stage, give your paper one final review and prepare it for publication. Edit your paper carefully, correcting any errors in grammar, spelling, punctuation, and sentence structure. Review your paper to make sure you have maintained a formal style and tone. Format your paper according to the following guidelines:

- Leave one-inch margins at the top, bottom, and sides of each page (except for page numbers).
- On the first page, at the top left, type your name, your teacher's name, the class, and the date (as shown on page 1039).
- On each page, type your last name and the page number one-half inch from the top, aligned at the right corner.
- Double-space all text, including the Works Cited list.
- Indent paragraphs one-half inch from the left margin.

GRAMMAR IN CONTEXT: VARYING SENTENCE PATTERNS

Varying your sentence patterns will make your paper easier and more interesting to read. Analyze the sentences in your draft. Have you used mostly simple sentences? If so, look for places to combine sentences.

When she proofread her paper, Melissa combined two simple sentences into a compound sentence by adding a comma and the coordinating conjunction *and*.

Cats aren't sacred in Egypt anymore. That's because different groups of people conquered Egypt. ⌃, *and* They brought new religions that didn't include animals.

PUBLISH YOUR WRITING

Here are some suggestions for sharing your research with an audience:

- E-mail your paper to a friend or relative who shares your interest.
- Have a "discovery day" in class. You and your classmates can share your research in small groups.
- Adapt your paper into a power presentation and share it with your class.
- Post your research paper on a class Web site.

YOUR TURN Proofread your draft, paying particular attention to sentence patterns. If your paper contains mostly short, simple sentences, try to vary the sentence patterns by combining some of the sentences. Then publishyour paper to share your research findings.

Scoring Rubric

Use the rubric below to evaluate your research paper.

RESEARCH PAPER	
SCORE	*COMMON CORE TRAITS*
6	• **Development** Has an engaging introduction; states insightful controlling idea; provides varied, relevant facts and details; ends powerfully • **Organization** Classifies and organizes information; enhances information with formatting and graphics; uses appropriate transitions • **Language** Ably uses precise language and domain-specific vocabulary; maintains a formal style and tone; shows a command of conventions; correctly cites sources
5	• **Development** Introduces topic competently; states strong controlling idea; provides relevant facts and details; has strong ending • **Organization** Classifies and organizes most information; has formatting and graphics; effectively uses transitions • **Language** Uses precise language and domain-specific vocabulary; generally maintains a formal style and tone; few errors in conventions; correctly cites sources
4	• **Development** Introduces topic; has a controlling idea; offers mostly relevant facts and details; has a concluding section • **Organization** Classifies and organizes some information; could use more formatting and graphics; needs more transitions • **Language** Uses vague language; maintains a formal style and tone; has distracting errors in conventions; incorrectly cites some sources
3	• **Development** Has an lackluster introduction and controlling idea; offers some relevant details; has a weak concluding section • **Organization** Has flaws in organization; needs more formatting; uses few transitions • **Language** Needs more precise words; has lapses in formal style and tone; has critical errors in conventions; incorrectly cites many sources
2	• **Development** Has a weak controlling idea and introduction; does not sufficiently support ideas; has disconnected concluding section • **Organization** Lacks organization, formatting, graphics, and transitions • **Language** Uses few precise words; lacks a formal style and tone; has many errors in conventions; incorrectly cites sources
1	• **Development** Lacks a controlling idea and support; ends abruptly • **Organization** Has no organization, formatting, graphics, or transitions • **Language** Uses vague words; has inappropriate style ignores conventions; no citations

Technology Workshop

Producing a Power Presentation

You can share your research paper with the class by turning it into a power presentation. Display computer-generated slides and graphics to give your research report an interactive aspect that will engage your audience.

 Complete the workshop activities in your **Reader/Writer Notebook**.

PRODUCE WITH A PURPOSE

PROMPT

Adapt your research paper as a **power presentation.** Create slides that use text and graphics to help you cover the main points of your research paper. Practice your presentation and then share it with your class.

COMMON CORE TRAITS

A STRONG POWER PRESENTATION . . .

- focuses on a clear <u>controlling idea</u>
- uses easy-to-read text and graphics to communicate ideas clearly
- has an appealing, appropriate design for each slide
- flows smoothly from one slide to another
- is organized logically to help the audience follow the main <u>points</u> and <u>evidence</u>
- conveys the speaker's knowledge of the topic

COMMON CORE

W 6 Use technology to produce and publish writing.
SL 2 Interpret information presented in diverse media and formats. **SL 5** Include multimedia and visual displays to clarify information.

Plan Your Presentation

Remember that your audience will be listening to your ideas instead of reading them. Keep the following tips in mind as you adapt your research paper:

- **Stick to the big ideas.** Create one slide for your introduction, one for your conclusion, and at least one for each main point. Each slide should give one idea in a headline, followed by at least two bullet points that list supporting evidence and ideas. Remember that too much text can make a slide difficult to read. Arrange your slides in a logical order.

- **Format the text.** Use only one or two fonts and one or two type sizes. Use your word processing skills to make sure that similar items have the same formatting. Make sure the type is easy to read, even from far away. Check for spelling and other errors.

- **Design the slides.** Think about the mood and message you want to convey to your audience. Select appropriate borders, pictures, or other art. Choose colors so that the type stands out against the background. You might use the same design for closely related ideas.

- **Add multimedia.** Sound and animation can clarify information and add excitement to your presentation. They can also be distracting, however, so do not use them too often. Be sure to respect copyright laws and use only elements for which you have permission.

Media Tools

Go to <u>thinkcentral.com</u>.
KEYWORD: HML6N-1044

Develop Your Presentation

Follow these guidelines to make your presentation go smoothly:

- **Practice.** Learn how to use the equipment. Instead of simply restating the words on a slide, explain and expand on your main points. (Use your research paper for ideas.) Go through your entire presentation to decide how much time you can devote to each slide and stay within your time limit.

- **Prepare your opening statement.** Begin with an opening that captures the attention and interest of your audience. Then briefly state your presentation.

- **Watch your speaking rate.** Even if you are nervous, don't race through your presentation. Pause after each slide to allow your audience time to take in the information you've presented. Ask a friend to sit at the back of the room and signal if you are talking too quickly or too slowly.

WILD CATS

- bigger than pet cats we know today
- killed mice, rats, and snakes
- became important to ancient Egyptians

- **Use effective verbal techniques.** Use formal English and avoid using slang words and clichés. Speak loudly and slowly so that everyone in your audience can hear you. Change the **modulation,** or pitch, of your voice to emphasize important points. Make sure your tone of voice reflects a neutral point of view.

- **Use nonverbal techniques.** Match your gestures and facial expressions to what you say. Raising your voice while pointing a finger, for example, can signal to the audience that you are making an important point. Maintain eye contact to hold your audience's interest.

- **Request feedback.** When you are finished, ask the audience to tell you what they liked about your presentation. Find out if they clearly understood your main points. Think about what you will do differently in your next presentation.

YOUR TURN Plan and produce a power presentation using the guidelines on these pages. Hold at least one practice session with a peer before you give your presentation to your class.

Student Resource Bank

Short stories, poems, magazine articles, newspapers, and Web pages are all different types of texts that require some different strategies to be understood. For example, you might plot the events of a short story on a diagram, whereas you may use text features to spot main ideas in a magazine article. You should also identify patterns of organization in the text. Using these strategies will help you read different kinds of texts with ease.

COMMON CORE

Included in this handbook:
RL 1, RL 10, RI 1, RI 2, RI 3, RI 5, RI 6, RI 7, RI 8, RI 10

1 Reading Literary and Nonfiction Texts

Literary and **nonfiction texts** include short stories, novels, poems, dramas, biographies, autobiographies, and essays. To appreciate and analyze literary and nonfiction texts, you will need to understand the characteristics of each type of text.

1.1 READING A SHORT STORY
Strategies for Reading

- Read the **title.** As you read the story, you may notice that the title has a special meaning.

- Keep track of **events** as they happen. Plot the events on a diagram like this one.

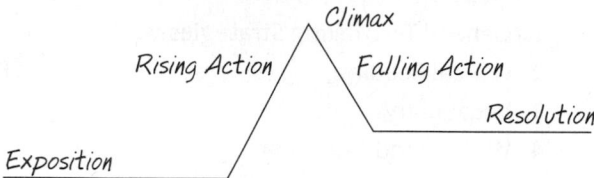

- From the details the writer provides, **visualize** the characters. **Predict** what they might do next.

- Look for specific adjectives that help you visualize the **setting**—the time and place in which events occur.

1.2 READING A POEM
Strategies for Reading

- Notice the **form** of the poem, or the number of lines and their arrangement on the page.

- Read the poem aloud a few times. Listen for **rhyme** and **rhythm.**

- **Visualize** the images and comparisons.

- **Connect** with the poem by asking yourself what message the poet is trying to send.

- Create a word web or another **graphic organizer** to record your reactions and questions.

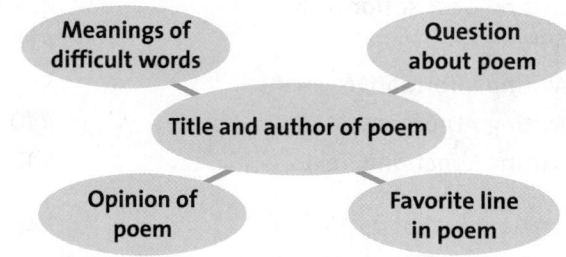

1.3 READING A PLAY
Strategies for Reading

- Read the stage directions to help you **visualize** the setting and characters.

- **Question** what the title means and why the playwright chose it.

- Identify the main conflict (struggle or problem) in the play. To **clarify** the conflict, make a chart that shows what the conflict is and how it is resolved.

- **Analyze** the characters. What do they want? How do they change during the play? You may want to make a chart that lists each character's name, appearance, and traits.

1.4 READING LITERARY NONFICTION
Strategies for Reading

- If you are reading a biography or an autobiography, a family tree or word web can help you keep track of the people mentioned.

- When reading an essay, **evaluate** the writer's ideas. Is there a clear main or central idea? Does the writer use appropriate details to support the main idea?

☑ Reading Informational Texts: Text Features

An **informational text** is writing that provides factual information. Informational materials—such as chapters in textbooks and articles in magazines, encyclopedias, and newspapers—usually contain elements that help the reader recognize their purpose, pattern of organization, and central ideas. These elements are known as **text features.**

2.1 UNDERSTANDING TEXT FEATURES

Text features are design elements of a text that indicate its pattern of organization or otherwise make its central ideas and information understandable. Text features include titles, headings, subheadings, boldface type, bulleted and numbered lists, and graphic aids, such as charts, graphs, illustrations, and photographs. Notice how the text features help you find key information on the textbook page shown.

Ⓐ The **title** or **main heading** identifies the topic.

Ⓑ A **subheading** indicates the start of a new topic or section and identifies that section's focus.

Ⓒ **Questions** may be used to focus your understanding of the text.

Ⓓ A **bulleted list** shows items of equal importance.

Ⓔ **Graphic aids,** such as illustrations, photographs, charts, diagrams, maps, and timelines, often make ideas in the text clearer.

Ⓕ A **caption,** or the text that accompanies a graphic aid, gives information about the graphic aid that isn't necessarily obvious from the image itself.

PRACTICE AND APPLY

1. What is the second subheading following the title?

2. What is a dynasty?

3. Which text feature tells you about the structures shown in the photograph?

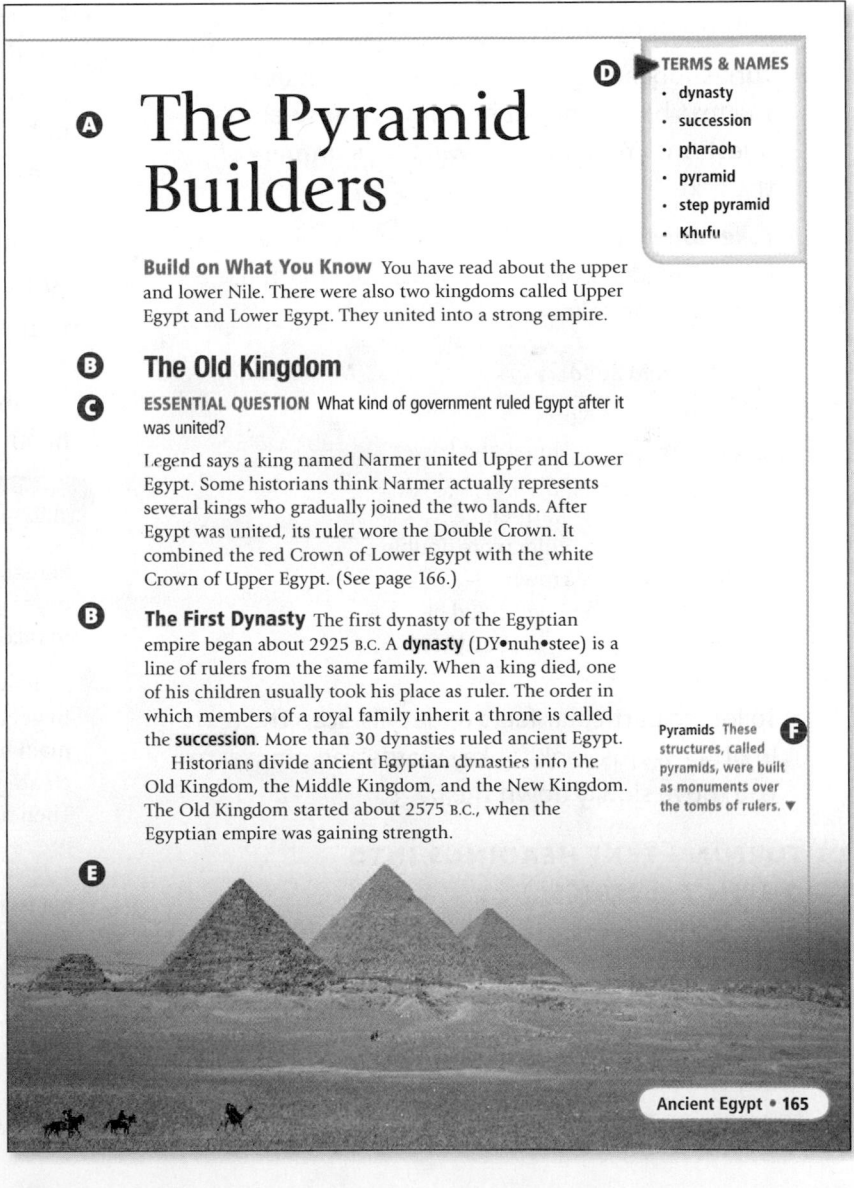

Ⓐ # The Pyramid Builders

Ⓓ ▶ TERMS & NAMES
- dynasty
- succession
- pharaoh
- pyramid
- step pyramid
- Khufu

Build on What You Know You have read about the upper and lower Nile. There were also two kingdoms called Upper Egypt and Lower Egypt. They united into a strong empire.

Ⓑ ## The Old Kingdom

Ⓒ **ESSENTIAL QUESTION** What kind of government ruled Egypt after it was united?

Legend says a king named Narmer united Upper and Lower Egypt. Some historians think Narmer actually represents several kings who gradually joined the two lands. After Egypt was united, its ruler wore the Double Crown. It combined the red Crown of Lower Egypt with the white Crown of Upper Egypt. (See page 166.)

Ⓑ **The First Dynasty** The first dynasty of the Egyptian empire began about 2925 B.C. A **dynasty** (DY•nuh•stee) is a line of rulers from the same family. When a king died, one of his children usually took his place as ruler. The order in which members of a royal family inherit a throne is called the **succession**. More than 30 dynasties ruled ancient Egypt.

Historians divide ancient Egyptian dynasties into the Old Kingdom, the Middle Kingdom, and the New Kingdom. The Old Kingdom started about 2575 B.C., when the Egyptian empire was gaining strength.

Ⓕ Pyramids These structures, called pyramids, were built as monuments over the tombs of rulers. ▼

Ⓔ

Ancient Egypt • 165

2.2 USING TEXT FEATURES

You can use text features to locate information, to help you understand it, and to take notes. Just use the following strategies when you encounter informational text.

Strategies for Reading

- **Preview** the text by looking at the title, headings, and subheadings to get an idea of the main concepts and the way the text is organized.

- Before you begin reading the text more thoroughly, **skim** it—read it quickly—to get an overview.

- Read any **questions** that appear at the end of a lesson or chapter. Doing this will help you set a purpose for your reading.

- Turn subheadings into questions. Then use the text below the subheadings to answer the questions. Your answers will be a **summary** of the text.

- **Take notes** by turning headings and subheadings into main ideas, or central ideas. You might use a chart like the following.

The Pyramid Builders	Main heading
The Old Kingdom	Notes: 1. Upper and Lower Egypt united by Narmer 2. Ruler wore double crown 3. Egypt ruled by dynasties

Subheading

- To locate particular facts or details, **scan** the text. In other words, look for key words and phrases as you move slowly down the page.

2.3 TURNING TEXT HEADINGS INTO OUTLINE ENTRIES

After you have read a selection at least once, you can use text features to take notes in outline form. The following outline shows how one student used text headings from the textbook sample on page R3. Study the outline and use the strategies that follow to create an outline based on text features.

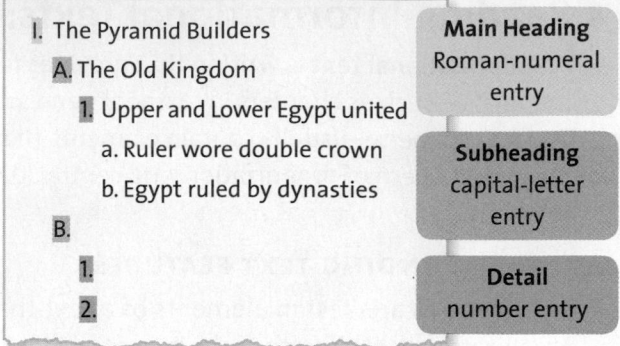

I. The Pyramid Builders — **Main Heading** Roman-numeral entry
  A. The Old Kingdom — **Subheading** capital-letter entry
    1. Upper and Lower Egypt united
      a. Ruler wore double crown — **Detail** number entry
      b. Egypt ruled by dynasties
  B.
    1.
    2.

Strategies for Using Text Headings

- Preview the headings and subheadings in the text to get an idea of what different kinds there are and what their positions might be in an outline.

- Be consistent. Note that subheadings that are the same size and color should be used consistently in Roman-numeral or capital-letter entries in the outline. If you decide that a chapter heading should appear with a Roman numeral, then that's the level at which all other chapter headings should appear.

- Write the main headings and subheadings that you will use as your Roman-numeral and capital-letter entries first. As you read, fill in numbered details from the text under the headings and subheadings in your outline.

PRACTICE AND APPLY

Reread "The Violent Side of Video Games," pages 947–948. Use text features in the selection to take notes in outline form.

Preview the headings and subheadings in the text to get an idea of the different kinds. Decide which main headings, titles, and subheadings you will use to create your Roman-numeral and capital-letter entries. Then fill in the details.

2.4 GRAPHIC AIDS

Information is communicated not only with words but also with graphic aids, such as graphs, diagrams, charts, maps, and timelines. **Graphic aids** are visual representations of verbal statements that make complex information easier to understand. For that reason, they are often used to organize, simplify, and summarize information for easy reference.

Graphs

Graphs are used to illustrate statistical information. A **graph** is a drawing that shows the relative values of numerical quantities. Different kinds of graphs are used to show different numerical relationships.

Strategies for Reading

Ⓐ Read the title.

Ⓑ Find out what is being represented or measured.

Ⓒ In a circle graph, compare the sizes of the parts.

Ⓓ In a line graph, study the slant of the line. The steeper the line, the faster the rate of change.

Ⓔ In a bar graph, compare the lengths of the bars.

A **circle graph,** or **pie graph,** shows the relationships of parts to a whole. The entire circle equals 100 percent. The parts of the circle represent percentages of the whole.

MODEL: CIRCLE GRAPH

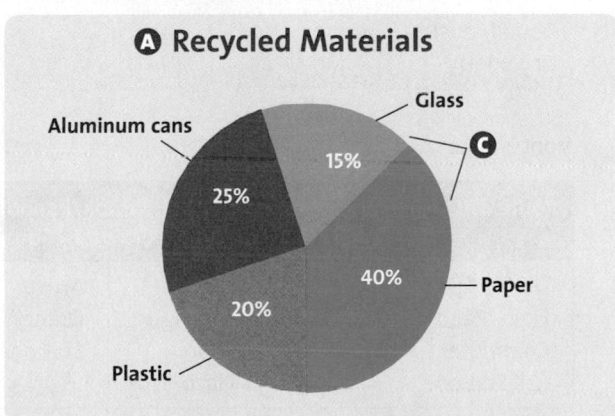

Line graphs show changes in numerical quantities over time and can be used to present trends such as global temperature change. A line graph is made on a grid. On the following line graph, the vertical axis indicates average global temperature, and the horizontal axis shows the number of years ago. The line connecting the data points shows a trend or pattern.

MODEL: LINE GRAPH

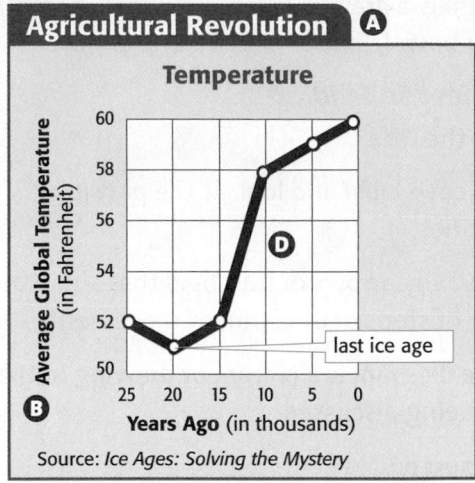

In a **bar graph,** vertical or horizontal bars are used to show or compare categories of information, such as the sizes of different empires. The lengths of the bars indicate quantities—in this case, size.

MODEL: BAR GRAPH

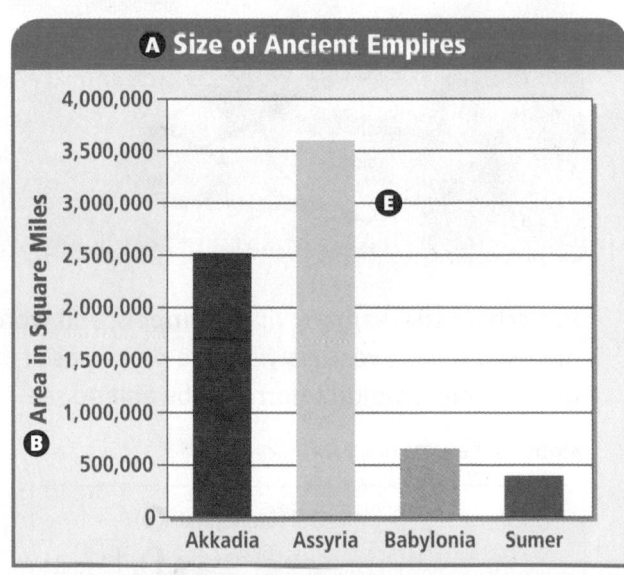

Source: *Institute for Research on World Systems*

WATCH OUT! Evaluate information presented in graphs carefully. The way you interpret the information depends on the graph form. For example, circle graphs show major differences well but tend to reduce the importance of smaller differences.

Diagrams

A **diagram** is a drawing that shows how something works or how its parts relate to one another.

Strategies for Reading

A Read the title.

B Read each label and look at the part it identifies.

C Follow any arrows or numbers that show the order of steps or direction of movement.

A **picture diagram** is a picture or drawing of the subject being discussed.

MODEL: PICTURE DIAGRAM

The Great Pyramid of Khufu **A**

King's chamber
Air shaft
Grand gallery **B**
Passage to grand gallery
Queen's chamber
Escape passage
Underground chamber

In a **schematic diagram,** lines, symbols, and words are used to help readers visualize processes or objects they wouldn't normally be able to see.

MODEL: SCHEMATIC DIAGRAM

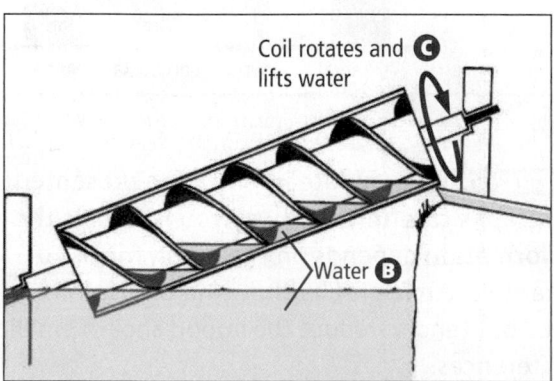

Coil rotates and **C** lifts water

Water **B**

▲ Archimedes' Water-Lifting Device **A**

Charts and Tables

A **chart** presents information, shows a process, or makes comparisons, usually in rows or columns.

A **table** is a specific type of chart that presents a collection of facts in rows and columns and shows how the facts relate to one another.

Strategies for Reading

A Read the title to learn what information the chart or table covers.

B Study column headings and row labels to determine the categories of information presented.

C Look down columns and across rows to find specific information.

MODEL: CHART

Greek and Roman Gods **A**		
Description	Greek **B**	Roman
Supreme god	Zeus	Jupiter **C**
Supreme goddess	Hera (wife of Zeus)	Juno (wife of Jupiter)
God of the sea	Poseidon	Neptune
God of music and poetry	Apollo	Apollo

MODEL: TABLE

Route 238 **A**	Quincy Center Station—Holbrook/Randolph Commuter Rail Station via Crawford Square		
Leave **B** Holb./Rand. Commuter Rail Station	Leave Crawford Square	Leave South Shore Plaza	Arrive Quincy Station
6:25 A	6:29 A	6:42 A	7:08 A
6:50	6:54	7:07	7:35 **C**
7:20	7:25	7:38	8:06
7:50	7:55	8:08	8:36
8:25	8:30	8:43	9:11
8:55	9:00	9:13	9:41
9:25	9:30	9:46	10:14

Maps

A **map** visually represents a geographic region, such as a state or country. It provides information about areas through lines, colors, shapes, and symbols. There are different kinds of maps.

- **Political maps** show political features, such as national borders.
- **Physical maps** show the landforms in an area.
- **Road or travel maps** show roads and highways.
- **Thematic maps** show information on a specific topic, such as climate, weather, or natural resources.

Strategies for Reading

Ⓐ Read the title to find out what kind of map it is.

Ⓑ Read the labels to get an overall sense of what the map shows.

Ⓒ Look at the **key** or **legend** to find out what the symbols and colors on the map stand for.

MODEL: PHYSICAL MAP

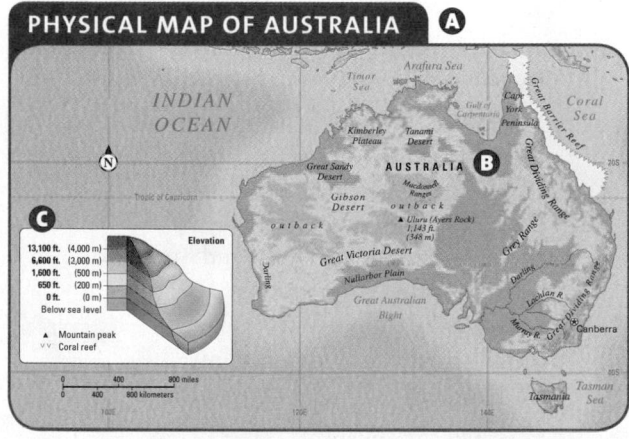

MODEL: THEMATIC MAP

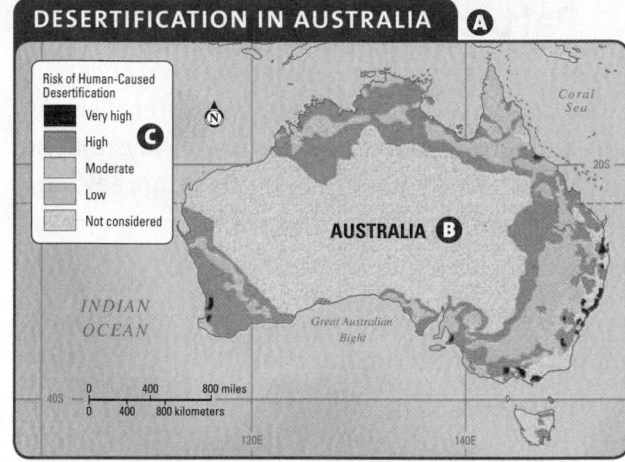

Timelines

A timeline shows events in the order in which they occurred. Events are listed along a horizontal or vertical line and are usually labeled with the year in which they happened.

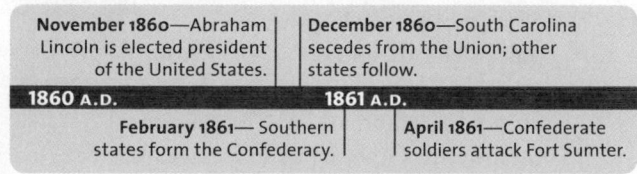

November 1860—Abraham Lincoln is elected president of the United States.

December 1860—South Carolina secedes from the Union; other states follow.

1860 A.D.   1861 A.D.

February 1861— Southern states form the Confederacy.

April 1861—Confederate soldiers attack Fort Sumter.

PRACTICE AND APPLY

Use the graphic aids shown on pages R5–R7 to answer the following questions:

1. According to the circle graph, is more glass or plastic recycled?

2. For how many years did the average global temperature decrease?

3. According to the bar graph, what was the approximate area of Babylonia?

4. How many chambers did the Great Pyramid of Khufu contain?

5. What did the coil in Archimedes' water-lifting device do?

6. Use the chart to find the name of the Roman god of the sea.

7. According to the train schedule, if you took the 7:25 A.M. train from Crawford Square, when would you arrive at Quincy Station?

8. What Australian desert is partially below sea level?

9. According to the thematic map of Australia, what part of the country has the highest risk of desertification?

10. Use information in the timeline to make a prediction about what might happen in May 1861.

3 Reading Informational Texts: Patterns of Organization

Reading any type of writing is easier once you recognize how it is organized. Writers usually arrange ideas and information in ways that best show how they are related. There are several common patterns of organization:

- main idea and supporting details
- chronological order
- cause-effect organization
- compare-and-contrast organization
- problem-solution order

Writers try to present their arguments in ways that will help readers follow their reasoning and accept their viewpoints. For more about common ways of organizing and presenting arguments, see *Analyzing Logic and Reasoning,* page R21.

3.1 MAIN IDEA AND SUPPORTING DETAILS

Main idea and supporting details is a basic pattern of organization in which a central idea about a topic is supported by details. The **main idea** is the most important idea about a topic that a particular text or paragraph conveys. **Supporting details** are words, phrases, or sentences that tell more about the main idea. The main idea may be directly stated at the beginning and then followed by supporting details, or it may merely be implied by the supporting details. It may also be stated after it has been implied by supporting details.

Strategies for Reading

- To find a stated main idea in a paragraph, identify the paragraph's topic. The topic is what the paragraph is about and can usually be summed up in one or two words. The word, or synonyms of it, will usually appear throughout the paragraph. Headings and subheadings are also clues to the topics of paragraphs.
- Ask: What is the topic sentence? The topic sentence states the most important idea, message, or information the paragraph conveys

about this topic. It is often the first sentence in a paragraph; however, it may appear at the end.

- To find an implied main idea, ask yourself: Whom or what did I just read about? What do the details suggest about the topic?
- Formulate a sentence stating this idea and add it to the paragraph. Does your sentence express the main idea?

Notice how the main idea is expressed in each of the following models.

MODEL: MAIN IDEA AS THE FIRST SENTENCE

Technology consists of all the ways in which people apply knowledge, tools, and inventions to meet their needs. Technology dates back to early humans. At least 2 million years ago, people made stone tools for cutting. Around 1,500 B.C., early humans also made carrying bags, stone hand axes, awls (tools for piercing holes in leather or wood), and drills.

> Main idea
> Supporting details

MODEL: MAIN IDEA AS THE LAST SENTENCE

In time, humans developed more complex tools, such as hunting bows made of wood. They learned to make flint spearheads and metal tools. Early humans used tools to hunt and butcher animals and to construct simple forms of shelter. Technology—these new tools—gave humans more control over their environment and set the stage for a more settled way of life.

> Supporting details
> Main idea

MODEL: IMPLIED MAIN IDEA

Prehistoric art exists in Africa, Asia, Europe, Australia, and the Americas. Cave paintings thousands of years old show lively images of bulls, stallions, and bison. Prehistoric jewelry and figurines also have been found. Early humans may have worn these items. Other items may have had religious meaning.

> Implied main idea: Early humans created art and art objects for many purposes.

Read each paragraph, and then do the following:

1. Identify the main idea in the paragraph, using one of the strategies discussed on the previous page.

2. Identify whether the main idea is stated or implied in the paragraph.

> Late on the night of April 18, 1775, Boston patriot Joseph Warren learned of a British military operation planned for the next day. To warn John Hancock and Samuel Adams, who were across the Charles River in Lexington, Warren dispatched two riders, Paul Revere and William Dawes. . . . Revere's ride has been celebrated in poems and textbooks, but Dawes' role was at least as important.
> —PBS Online, "The Other Riders"

> I passed out of the house. Day was trying to dawn through the smoke-pall. A sickly light was creeping over the face of things. Once only the sun broke through the smoke-pall, blood-red, and showing a quarter its usual size. The smoke-pall itself, viewed from beneath, was a rose color that pulsed and fluttered with lavender shades. Then it turned to mauve and yellow and dun. There was no sun. And so dawned the second day on stricken San Francisco.
> —Jack London, "The Story of an Eyewitness"

3.2 CHRONOLOGICAL ORDER

Chronological order is the arrangement of events in the order in which they happen. This type of organization is used in short stories and novels, historical writing, biographies, and autobiographies. To show the order of events, writers use order words, such as *before, after, next,* and *later,* and time words and phrases that identify specific times of day, days of the week, and dates, such as *the next morning, Friday,* and *on June 6, 2009.*

Strategies for Reading

- Look in the text for headings and subheadings that may indicate a chronological pattern of organization, such as *Early Life* or *The Later Years.*

- Look for words and phrases that identify times, such as *in a year, three weeks later, in 79 A.D.,* and *the next day.*

- Look for words that signal order, such as *first, afterward, then, during,* and *finally,* to see how events or steps are related.

- Note that a paragraph or passage in which ideas and information are arranged chronologically will have several words or phrases that indicate time order, not just one.

- Ask yourself: Are the events in the paragraph or passage presented in time order?

Notice the words and phrases that signal time in the first two paragraphs of the following model.

> The great Chinese teacher Confucius was born in 551 B.C. His father died when he was 3 years old. Although Confucius came from a very poor family, he studied hard and became well-educated.
>
> By the time he was 15, in 536 B.C., Confucius' heart was set on learning. In his 30s, Confucius started his teaching career. He later became one of the most important teachers in history. One of his teachings was that people should treat each other the way they would like to be treated. His teachings still seem wise after 2,500 years.
>
> When Confucius died in 479 B.C., he had many followers. About 100 years later, one of his followers, Mencius, began spreading Confucius' ideas. Mencius extended these ideas and added some of his own. He taught that people are basically good and that everyone has equal value. For that reason, he believed that rulers are no

Events

Time phrase

better than their subjects. A good king, he said, must treat his people well.

After Mencius died in 289 B.C., Hsun-tzu carried on Confucius' teachings. Hsun-tzu lived from about 300 to 230 B.C. He did not agree with Mencius that people were basically good. Instead, he taught that human nature was evil. He did believe that education and strong laws and governments could help people become good. Some people say that Hsun-tzu's teachings about strong government later helped the dictator Shih Huang Ti to conquer China and set up the Ch'in Dynasty in 221 B.C.

Order word

PRACTICE AND APPLY

Reread the preceding model and then do the following:

1. List at least four words or phrases in the last three paragraphs that indicate time or order.

2. List all the events in Confucius' life that are mentioned in the model.

3. Create a timeline, beginning with Confucius' birth and ending in 479 B.C., that shows all the events you listed for question 2.

3.3 CAUSE-EFFECT ORGANIZATION

Cause-effect organization is a pattern of organization that shows the relationships between events, ideas, and trends. Cause-effect relationships may be directly stated or merely implied by the order in which the information is presented. Writers often use the cause-effect pattern in historical and scientific writing. Cause-effect relationships may have several forms.

One cause with one effect

One cause with multiple effects

Multiple causes with a single effect

A chain of causes and effects

Strategies for Reading

- Look for headings and subheadings that indicate a cause-effect pattern of organization, such as "Effects of Food Allergies."

- To find the effect or effects, read to answer the question "What happened?"

- To find the cause or causes, read to answer the question "Why did it happen?"

- Look for words and phrases that help you identify specific relationships between events, such as *because, since, had the effect of, led to, as a result, resulted in, for that reason, due to, therefore, if . . . then,* and *consequently.*

- Look closely at each cause-effect relationship. Do not assume that because one event happened before another, the first event caused the second event.

- Use graphic organizers like the diagrams shown to record cause-effect relationships as you read.

Notice the words that signal causes and effects in the following model.

> **MODEL**
> **Watch Out for Mosquitoes**
>
> If you spend any time outdoors in the summer, at some point you will probably find yourself covered with mosquito bites. Mosquitoes can transmit serious diseases such as yellow fever, encephalitis, and malaria. Usually, though, mosquito bites just cause people to develop raised, red bumps that itch.
>
> This is what happens. Female mosquitoes need blood to nourish their eggs. Consequently, they zero in on living things whose blood they can suck. Once they find a likely victim, the attack begins.
>
> This attack is not really a bite, since a mosquito isn't able to open her jaws. Instead, she punctures the victim's skin with sharp stylets inside her mouth. The mosquito's saliva then flows into these puncture wounds. Because the saliva keeps the victim's blood from clotting, the mosquito can drink her fill.
>
> Meanwhile, the mosquito's saliva causes the person to have an allergic reaction. As a result, the person develops the itchy swelling we call a mosquito bite. Ironically, if the mosquito finishes eating before the victim slaps her or brushes her off, there will be less saliva left in the skin. Therefore, the redness and itching will not be so severe.

- Cause
- Effect
- Cause
- Signal word
- Effect

PRACTICE AND APPLY

1. Make a graphic organizer like the sample illustrated on page R10 to show the chain of causes and effects described in the text.

2. List three words or phrases that the writer uses to signal cause-effect relationships in the last two paragraphs.

3.4 COMPARE-AND-CONTRAST ORGANIZATION

Compare-and-contrast organization is a pattern of organization that provides a way to look at similarities and differences in two or more subjects. A writer may use this pattern of organization to compare the important points or characteristics of two or more subjects. These points or characteristics are called **points of comparison.** The compare-and-contrast pattern of organization may be developed in either of two ways:

Point-by-point organization—The writer discusses one point of comparison for both subjects, then goes on to the next point.

Subject-by-subject organization—The writer covers all points of comparison for one subject and then all points of comparison for the next subject.

Strategies for Reading

- Look in the text for headings, subheadings, and sentences that may suggest a compare-and-contrast pattern of organization, such as "Plants Share Many Characteristics," to help you identify where similarities and differences are addressed.

- To find similarities, look for words and phrases such as *like, similarly, both, all, every, also,* and *in the same way.*

- To find differences, look for words and phrases such as *unlike, but, on the other hand, more, less, in contrast,* and *however.*

- Use a graphic organizer, such as a Venn diagram or a compare-and-contrast chart, to record points of comparison and similarities and differences.

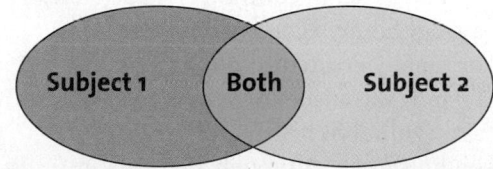

	Subject 1	Subject 2
Point 1		
Point 2		
Point 3		

Read the following models. As you read, use the signal words and phrases to identify the similarities and differences between the subjects and how the details are organized in each text.

MODEL 1

Pass the Bread, Please

There are as many varieties of bread as there are countries. Two kinds that you can enjoy today—from Paris, France, to Paris, Texas, and from Cairo, Illinois, to Cairo, Egypt—are the baguette and the bagel.

Both baguettes and bagels are made from the same basic ingredients, which may include flour, water, yeast, butter, eggs, and salt. Different methods are used to prepare them, however. In each case, bakers first mix the dough, knead it, and leave it to rise. Unlike baguettes, though, bagels are boiled in water before they are baked. This process makes them heavy and chewy and gives them a very light crust. Baguettes, on the other hand, are soft in the center and have a crisp, crunchy crust.

Another difference between the two types of bread is their shape. The word *baguette* means "wand" or "stick" in French. That describes what the bread looks like, too. Baguettes are thin and usually about two feet long. In some places, you can find shorter and fatter versions as well.

The bagel, in contrast, is shaped like a ring. Some legends say that it was originally created to honor a Polish king. It was made to look like a stirrup as a symbol of his victories in battle on horseback. Although all bagels are round, their size can vary greatly. You can choose from minibagels that are only a couple of inches in diameter to larger bagels six inches or more across.

Comparison word

Subjects

Contrast word

Standard baguettes and bagels are both made from white flour. Nowadays, you can choose from a whole universe of variations, however. Baguettes come in sourdough, rye, or whole-wheat varieties.

Bagels come in all those varieties, too. In addition, though, they are available in flavors ranging from apple and blueberry to spinach and tomato. Inside, you might find raisins, nuts, or even chocolate chips. And they might be topped with poppy seeds, sunflower seeds, or sesame seeds.

So the next time you get a craving for crispy, light bread, try a baguette. But for chewy bread with tasty flavors and fillings, choose a bagel.

MODEL 2

What Kind of Person Are You?

There are definitely two types of people in the world—cat people and dog people. About the only thing they share is the fact that they like pets. Aside from that, they are as different as the pets they favor. Comparing these pets might help you figure out what kind of person you are.

Subjects

Comparison word

Contrast word

Cat people tend to be very independent. They don't like to be controlled or to control anything else. So they don't want an animal that needs a lot of attention. Cats are their perfect pets since they almost take care of themselves.

You can leave cats alone for days at a time. Just set out bowls of food and water, and they will eat and drink only what they want.

Cats also groom themselves without your help. They can be quite affectionate, but only on their own terms. A cat will snuggle with you— when and if it feels like it.

Dog people, on the other hand, enjoy feeling needed and don't mind having a pet that is more dependent. Dogs definitely are dependent.

Unlike cats, dogs need a lot of attention daily. They can't be left alone for more than several hours because they have to be fed and walked regularly. You can't just leave food out for them, because they'll eat it all at once. Dogs also generally need a lot of interaction with people. Many of them seem to think their only purpose in life is to please their owners.

As different as cats and dogs are, the good news is that there are plenty of each to go around.

> **Contrast words and phrases**

PRACTICE AND APPLY

Refer to the preceding models to answer the following questions:

1. Which model is organized by subject? Which model is organized by points of comparison?

2. Identify two words or phrases in each model that signal a compare-and-contrast pattern of organization.

3. List two points that the writer of each model compares and contrasts.

4. For one of the two models, use a Venn diagram or a compare-and-contrast chart to identify two or more points of comparison and the similarities and differences shown.

3.5 PROBLEM-SOLUTION ORDER

Problem-solution order is a pattern of organization in which a problem is stated and analyzed and then one or more solutions are proposed and examined. This pattern of organization is often used in persuasive writing, where an author expresses a specific viewpoint, such as editorials or proposals.

Strategies for Reading

- Look for an explanation of the problem in the first or second paragraph.

- Look for words, such as *problem* and *reason*, that may signal an explanation of the problem.

- To find the solution, ask: What suggestion does the writer offer to solve the problem?

- Look for words, such as *propose, conclude,* and *answer,* that may signal a solution.

MODEL

It happened again last night. Two cars collided at the corner of West Avenue and Beach Street. This is the sixth accident that has taken place at that intersection in the past year. Luckily, no one has been seriously injured or killed so far. But we need to do something before it's too late. How many crashes do there have to be before we make the streets safer for everyone?

This intersection is so dangerous because West Avenue bends around just before it crosses Beach Street. This means that drivers or cyclists aren't able to see traffic approaching on West Avenue until they're entering the intersection. They have to just take their chances and hope they make it to the other side. Too many times, they don't.

One action that would help solve this problem would be to put a stoplight at the intersection. This would allow drivers and cyclists to move safely through the intersection in both directions. It would also slow traffic down and force people to pay more attention to their driving. Although it would cost the community some money to put in the stoplight, think how much it would save in car repairs, personal injuries, and possibly even lives.

Here's what you can do to help solve this problem. First, talk to your friends and neighbors about it. Then, go to the village hall and sign the petition!

PRACTICE AND APPLY

Reread the model and then answer the following questions:

1. According to the model, what is the cause of the problem?

2. What solution does the writer offer? What words are a clue?

4 Reading Informational Texts: Forms

Magazines, newspapers, Web pages, and consumer, public, and workplace documents are all examples of informational materials. To understand and analyze informational texts, pay attention to text features and patterns of organization.

4.1 READING A NEWSPAPER ARTICLE

Because people often skim newspapers, newspaper publishers use devices to attract attention to articles.

Strategies for Reading

A Consider whether **graphic aids** or quotations are attracting your attention. **Pull quotes**— engaging quotations pulled from the body of the text and reprinted in larger type—are often used to get readers interested in an article.

B Once you decide that you're interested in the article, read the **title** and other **headings** to find out more about its topic and organization.

C Notice whether the article has a **byline,** a line naming the author.

D A **caption,** or text accompanying a graphic aid, may provide information or examples that add to the meaning of the article and are not obvious from the graphic aid.

PRACTICE AND APPLY

1. Who wrote this article?

2. What does the pull quote tell you?

3. How does the photograph relate to the article?

MODEL: NEWSPAPER ARTICLE

Metro · Region

B Peers Talk It Out

SPECIAL REPORT

C by Janis Leibs Dworkis

At the Nathaniel Hawthorne Elementary School, sixth graders Earnestine Glosson (front left) and Rocio De Leon (front right) mediate a misunderstanding between fourth graders Laura Rios and Quaniqua Davis (back, left and right). **D**

Does a 10-year-old really know enough to help other students solve their problems? Can he understand more than one side of an issue? Can she be fair and impartial if she knows the students involved?

About 10 percent of the 85,000 schools in the United States offer some form of peer mediation. The Dallas Independent School District offers peer

A "If they had been sent to an adult, . . . they would probably just have been told not to do a fight."

mediation in about half of its almost 200 schools. And almost every school district in the Dallas–Fort Worth area offers a similar program in at least some of its schools.

The peer mediation concept is simple: two or more students who have a disagreement talk over their problem in front of one or two of their peers, with no adults present. The peer mediators, who remain neutral, help the students come to a mutually agreeable solution. . . .

Sixth-grader Rocio De Leon is serving her third year as a student mediator at Hawthorne. She says, . . . "If they had been sent to an adult, instead of coming to mediation, they would probably just have been told not to do a fight. But the adult wouldn't really understand them. It's a lot easier for a child to understand because you're talking to a person who is actually your age and having some of the same problems as you are."

Those who work with peer mediation hope that, in the long run, these problem-solving skills will lessen the occurrence of fighting—not only at school, but elsewhere, too.

4.2 READING A TEXTBOOK

Each textbook that you use has its own system of organization based on the content in the book. Often an introductory unit will explain the book's organization and special features. If your textbook has such a unit, read it first.

Strategies for Reading

A Before you begin reading a lesson or chapter, read any **questions** that appear at the beginning or end of it. Then use the questions to set your purpose for reading.

B Read slowly and carefully to better understand and remember the ideas presented in the text. When you come to an unfamiliar word, first try to figure out its meaning from **context clues.** If necessary, find the meaning of the word in a **glossary** in the textbook, or in a dictionary. Avoid interrupting your reading by constantly looking up words in a dictionary.

*For more information on context clues and glossaries, see the **Vocabulary and Spelling Handbook,** pages R68 and R72.*

C Use the book's special features, such as sidebars, to increase your understanding of the text. A **sidebar** is a short presentation of additional information. It is usually set off in a box on the page.

D Take notes as you read. Use text features such as **subheadings** and boldfaced terms to help you organize your notes. Record your notes in graphic organizers, such as cause-effect charts, to help you clarify relationships among ideas.

MODEL: TEXTBOOK PAGE

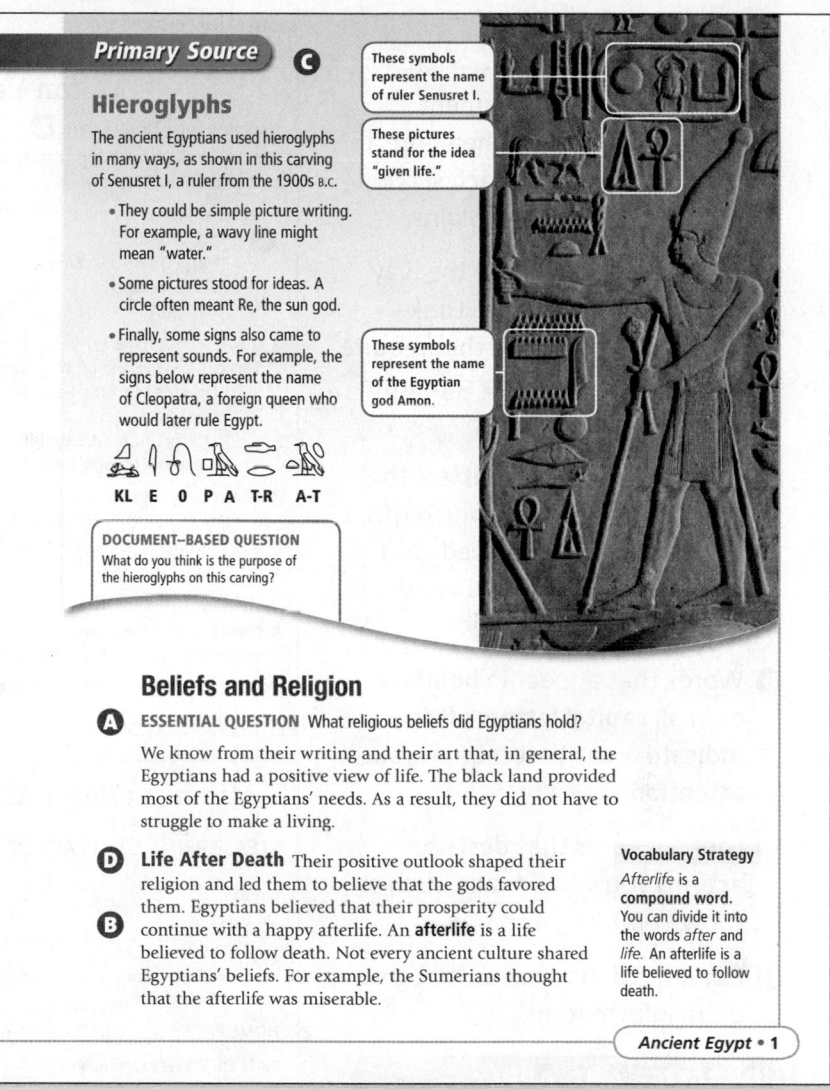

Primary Source **C**

Hieroglyphs

The ancient Egyptians used hieroglyphs in many ways, as shown in this carving of Senusret I, a ruler from the 1900s B.C.

- They could be simple picture writing. For example, a wavy line might mean "water."
- Some pictures stood for ideas. A circle often meant Re, the sun god.
- Finally, some signs also came to represent sounds. For example, the signs below represent the name of Cleopatra, a foreign queen who would later rule Egypt.

KL E O P A T-R A-T

These symbols represent the name of ruler Senusret I.

These pictures stand for the idea "given life."

These symbols represent the name of the Egyptian god Amon.

DOCUMENT–BASED QUESTION
What do you think is the purpose of the hieroglyphs on this carving?

Beliefs and Religion

A ESSENTIAL QUESTION What religious beliefs did Egyptians hold?

We know from their writing and their art that, in general, the Egyptians had a positive view of life. The black land provided most of the Egyptians' needs. As a result, they did not have to struggle to make a living.

D **Life After Death** Their positive outlook shaped their religion and led them to believe that the gods favored them. Egyptians believed that their prosperity could **B** continue with a happy afterlife. An **afterlife** is a life believed to follow death. Not every ancient culture shared Egyptians' beliefs. For example, the Sumerians thought that the afterlife was miserable.

Vocabulary Strategy
Afterlife is a **compound word.** You can divide it into the words *after* and *life.* An afterlife is a life believed to follow death.

Ancient Egypt • 1

PRACTICE AND APPLY

Reread the textbook page and answer the following questions:

1. Does the sidebar on hieroglyphic give more details about the other text on this page, or does it add new information?

2. Where do you find the definition and additional information for the word *afterlife?*

3. What is the answer to the Essential Question?

4.3 READING A CONSUMER DOCUMENT

Consumer documents are printed materials that accompany products and services. They usually provide information about the use, care, operation, or assembly of the products they accompany. Some common consumer documents are contracts, warranties, manuals, instructions, and schedules.

Strategies for Reading

A Read the **heading** to see what information the document covers. Read the **subheadings** to learn what process each section of the instructions explains.

B Read the directions all the way through at least once. Look carefully for sections that require information such as a signature or a date.

C Look for **numbers** or **letters** that indicate the order in which the steps should be followed. You can also look for signal words such as *first* and *finally*.

D Words that appear in **boldface** or in all **capital letters** often indicate areas that require your attention.

E Look for **verbs that describe actions** you should take, such as *show*, *complete*, and *sign*.

F Pay attention to **notes** that give extra information.

PRACTICE AND APPLY

Reread the library card application and the instructions for applying. Use these documents to answer the questions.

1. How might you apply for a library card if you do not have a driver's license?

2. Who is responsible for borrowed materials if the library card owner is under the age of 14?

MODEL: INSTRUCTIONS

Milton Valley Public Library **A**

Applying for a Library Card **A**

Residents of Milton Valley can apply for a library card at either the Central or South Milton branch. To apply:

1. Present two forms of identification. Acceptable forms of identification are:

C
    Student ID
    Valid Driver's License
    State ID Card
    Passport

2. If you do not have a driver's license or State ID, you must show proof of residency. This can be any one of the following:
    Driver's Learning Permit
    Bank Statement
    Utility or Credit Card Bill
    Lease or Housing Contract

3. Complete a registration form by providing the following information: name, address, telephone number, previous address (if you have lived at your current residence for less than three years), and signature.

4. If you are under the age of 14, you will need to have your parent or guardian sign **E** the application.

5. Finally, submit your application and wait to have a picture taken for your library card. Cards will be ready for pickup in half an hour.

MODEL: APPLICATION

Milton Valley Public Library Card Application

PLEASE PRINT. USE BLACK OR BLUE INK. **D**

NAME: _____

ADDRESS: _____ CITY: _____

STATE: _____ ZIP CODE/POSTAL CODE: _____

PREVIOUS ADDRESS: _____

HOME PHONE: (____)_____ MOBILE PHONE: (____)_____

DATE OF BIRTH (dd/mm/yyyy): _____

I agree to be responsible for any materials borrowed from Milton Valley Public Library in my name.

SIGNATURE:_____ DATE: _____ **B**

For cardholders under the age of 14: You must have permission of a parent or guardian along with a signature. Parents: Your signature indicates that you are responsible for any materials borrowed under your child's name. **F**

PARENT SIGNATURE: _____ DATE: _____

PLEASE PRINT NAME: _____ **B**

Office Use Only

Card No. _____ Date Issued _____ Expires _____

4.4 READING A PUBLIC DOCUMENT

Public documents are documents that are written for the public to provide information that is of public interest or concern. These documents are often free. They can be federal, state, or local government documents. They can be speeches or historical documents. They may even be laws, posted warnings, signs, or rules and regulations. Public documents, like the model shown here, often present information in tables. Facts and other important data are organized in ways that readers can grasp quickly and easily.

Strategies for Reading

Ⓐ The **title** tells you about the message of the document.

Ⓑ The **rows** and **columns** of the chart help you find the specific information you need.

- **Column 1:** Your age, situation, and special needs
- **Column 2:** When you should get your flu shot

Ⓒ The **contact information** at the bottom of the page tells you what number to call or Web site to consult if you have questions or need more information.

MODEL: PUBLIC NOTICE

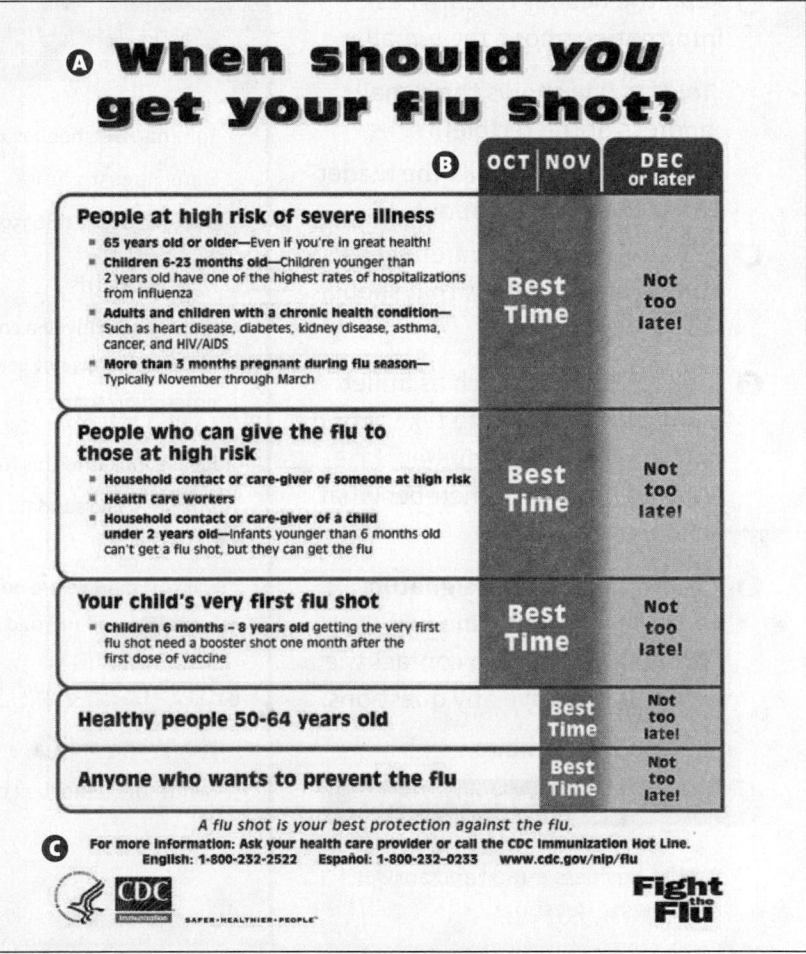

PRACTICE AND APPLY

Refer to the public notice to answer the following questions:

1. Who can't get a flu shot?

2. When is the best time for healthy people 50 to 64 years old to get their flu shots?

3. What phone number should you call to get information in Spanish?

4. What are the advantages of presenting this information in a table instead of writing it out in paragraphs?

4.5 READING A WORKPLACE DOCUMENT

Workplace documents are materials that are produced or used within a workplace, for business purposes. Some documents, such as minutes of a meeting or a sales report, may be generated by a business to monitor itself. Others may explain company policies or make requests. Workplace documents include memos, e-mails, business letters, job applications, and résumés.

Strategies for Reading

Ⓐ Read the header to learn basic information about the e-mail.

  To: This line shows the e-mail address of the recipient.

  Subject: This line tells the reader what the e-mail is about.

Ⓑ Read the document carefully, as it may contain details that should not be overlooked.

Ⓒ Look for features, such as **bullet points,** that ask you to take action or find specific information. Take notes to help you remember what actions are required.

Ⓓ Pay attention to the **signature line.** The signature line will often tell you how to contact the sender if you have any questions.

PRACTICE AND APPLY

Read the business e-mail and answer the following questions:

1. What is this e-mail about?

2. Who sent the e-mail, and who received it?

3. When did the customer order her shoes?

4. What should Mr. Harris do if the sandals are out of stock?

5. How can Mr. Harris contact Ms. Luzeka?

MODEL: BUSINESS E-MAIL

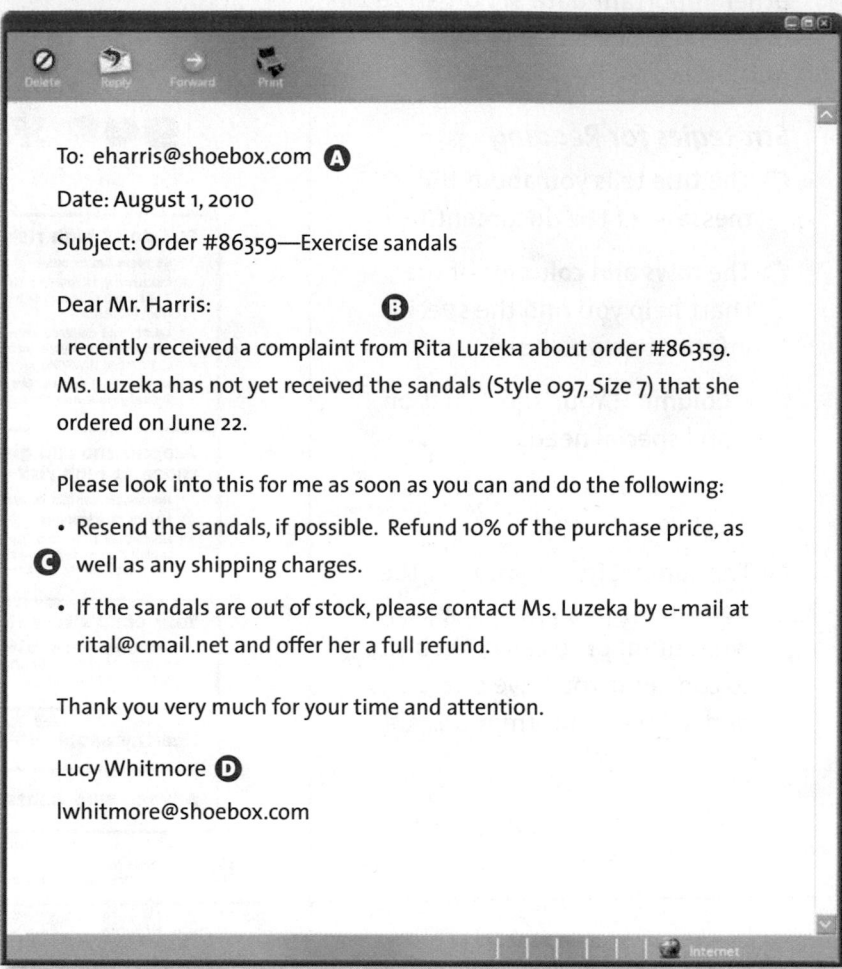

To: eharris@shoebox.com **Ⓐ**

Date: August 1, 2010

Subject: Order #86359—Exercise sandals

Dear Mr. Harris: **Ⓑ**

I recently received a complaint from Rita Luzeka about order #86359. Ms. Luzeka has not yet received the sandals (Style 097, Size 7) that she ordered on June 22.

Please look into this for me as soon as you can and do the following:

• Resend the sandals, if possible. Refund 10% of the purchase price, as
Ⓒ well as any shipping charges.

• If the sandals are out of stock, please contact Ms. Luzeka by e-mail at rital@cmail.net and offer her a full refund.

Thank you very much for your time and attention.

Lucy Whitmore **Ⓓ**

lwhitmore@shoebox.com

4.6 READING ELECTRONIC TEXT

Electronic text is any text that is in a form that a computer can store and display on a screen. Electronic text can be part of Web pages, CD-ROMs, search engines, and documents that you create with your computer software. Like books, Web pages often provide aids for finding information. However, each Web page is designed differently, so this online information is not necessarily in the same location on each page. It is important to know the functions of different parts of a Web page so that you can easily find the information you want.

Strategies for Reading

Ⓐ First look at the **title** of a page to determine what topics it covers. The title is different from the **Web address,** or URL, which usually begins with *http://*.

Ⓑ Look for a **menu bar** along the top, bottom, or side of a Web page. Clicking on an item in a menu bar will take you to another part of the Web site.

Ⓒ Notice any **hyperlinks** to related pages. Hyperlinks are often underlined or highlighted in a contrasting color. You can click on a hyperlink to get to another page—one that may or may not have been created by the same person or organization.

Ⓓ For information that you want to keep for future reference, save documents on your computer or print them. For online sources, you can pull down the **Favorites** or **Bookmarks** menu and bookmark pages so that you can easily return to them or print the information you need. Printing the pages will allow you to highlight key ideas on a hard copy.

MODEL: WEB PAGE

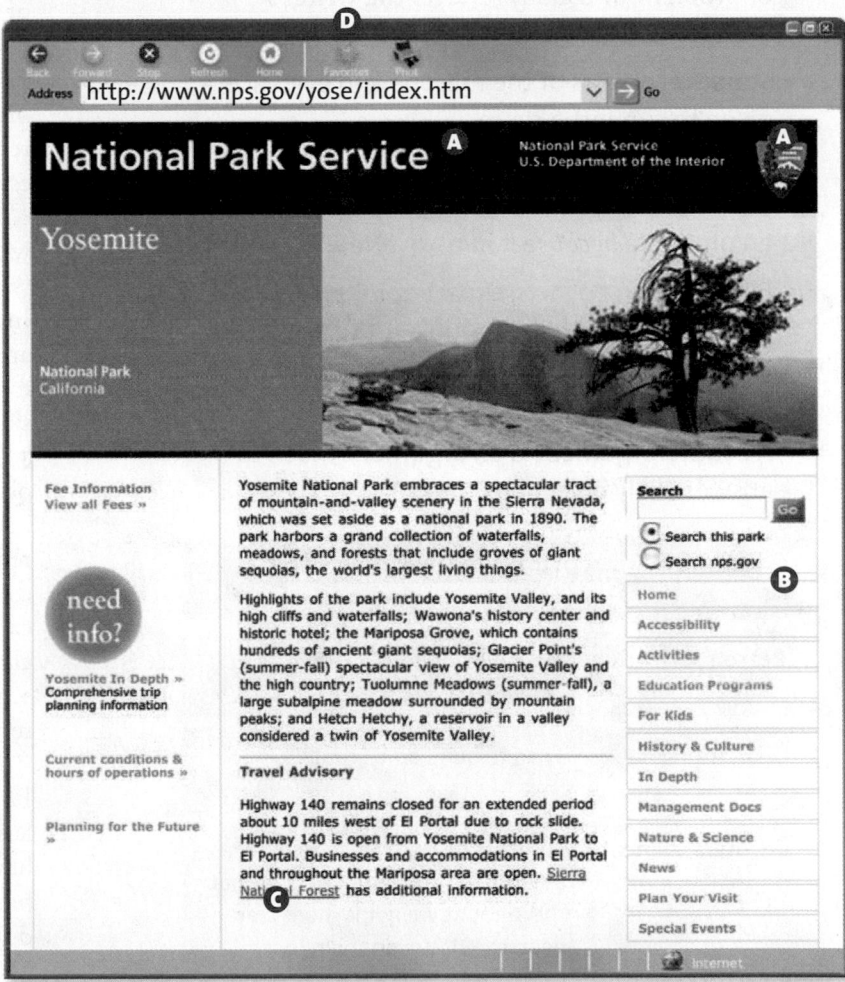

PRACTICE AND APPLY

1. What is the Web address, or URL, of this Web page?

2. Which menu items would you click on to help plan your family's visit to Yosemite?

3. How could you use this Web site to find information about another national park?

5 Reading Persuasive Texts

5.1 ANALYZING AN ARGUMENT

A **persuasive text** is writing that tries to sway its readers' feelings, beliefs, or actions. It typically makes use of an argument and persuasive devices, or tricks. An **argument** is a logical appeal that consists of the following elements:

- A **claim** is the writer's position on an issue or problem. It usually reflects the writer's viewpoint, or attitude, on the issue.

- **Support** consists of the reasons and evidence given to support a claim.

- **Reasons** are declarations made to justify an action, decision, or belief. For example, "I carry an umbrella *because it rains so often.*"

- **Evidence** can be facts, expert opinions, examples, or other details that back up a reason or a claim. For example, "This week, it has rained every day!" (fact)

- A **counterargument** is an argument made to answer likely objections.

Claim	We get too much homework.
Reason	We have no time for other activities.
Evidence	I had to quit Eagle Scouts.
Counterargument	Students do need to do a certain amount of homework to learn, but the amount we get is more than necessary. It's overwhelming.

Use a chart like the one shown to identify the claim, reasons, evidence, and counterargument in the following editorial.

Our School Needs to Get in the Swim
by Maria Lopez

This school needs a swimming pool. Swimming is an important life skill and one of the best forms of exercise there is. It is one of the few activities that won't harm the body and can actually improve circulation, breathing, and mobility. I believe it is the responsibility of the school to provide this essential part of students' lifelong education.

The school's mission is to educate the whole person—mind and body—and to prepare students to be productive citizens. In addition to our academic subjects, we are taught how to eat right and budget our money. But we don't learn the water safety skills that could someday save our lives.

The community and school board obviously don't feel the same way about this issue as I do, however. They repeatedly have refused to fund the building of a pool. In the opinion of one board member, "Students can take swimming lessons at the local health club." Other school officials think that the school has more important needs, such as repairing the sagging gym floor.

In my opinion, these reasons are not valid. First, most students cannot afford swimming lessons at the health club. Even those who have the money don't have the time. They're busy with homework and other activities during the school year and have to work or go to summer school during vacation.

I agree that the gym floor should be replaced, but I believe that educational needs should come first. Even if knowing how to swim never saves your life, it can improve its quality. Isn't that what an education is all about?

5.2 RECOGNIZING PERSUASIVE TECHNIQUES

Persuasive texts typically rely on more than just the **logical appeal** of an argument to be convincing. They also rely on ethical and emotional appeals and other **persuasive techniques**—devices that can convince you to adopt a position or take an action.

Ethical appeals establish a writer's credibility and trustworthiness with an audience. When a writer links a claim to a widely accepted value, the writer not only gains moral support for that claim but also establishes him- or herself as a reputable person readers can trust. For example, with the following appeal the writer reminds readers of a value they should accept and aligns himself with the reader: "Most of us think it's important to be informed about current events, but we don't spend much time reading newspapers."

The chart shown here explains several other methods of persuasion.

Persuasive Technique	Example
Appeals by Association	
Bandwagon appeal Suggests that a person should believe or do something because "everyone else" does	Don't be the last person in town to be connected to Neighbor Net.
Testimonial Relies on endorsements from well-known people or satisfied customers	Start your day with the vitamins recommended by four out of five doctors— Superstrength Vigorvites.
Snob appeal Taps into people's desire to be special or part of an elite group	You deserve to eat like a king. Join the distinguished diners at Marco's Palace.
Appeal to loyalty Relies on people's affiliation with a particular group	Show your support for the community by marching in our local parade!
Emotional Appeals	
Appeals to pity, fear, or vanity Use strong feelings, rather than facts, to persuade	If you don't see a dentist regularly, your teeth will rot.

PRACTICE AND APPLY

Identify the persuasive techniques used in this model.

Learn While You Sleep

Join the increasing number of with-it people who are making every hour of their day—and night—count. No matter whether they're awake or asleep, they keep going, growing, and improving themselves every minute. Impossible? Not according to college basketball superstar Jordan Navarro, whose grade-point average went from a 2.5 to a 4.0 after just one month on the program. "As amazing as it sounds, my free-throw average shot up, too," he said. Stop wasting time and start becoming the smart and effective person you always dreamed of being. Just call 555-ZZ-LEARN and sign up right now.

5.3 ANALYZING LOGIC AND REASONING

While persuasive techniques may sway you to side with a writer, they should not be enough to convince you that an argument is sound. To determine the soundness of an argument, you really need to examine the argument's claim and support and the logic or reasoning that links them. To do this, identify the writer's mode of reasoning.

The Inductive Mode of Reasoning

When a person adds up evidence to arrive at a general idea, or generalization, that person is using **inductive reasoning.** Here is an example.

EVIDENCE

Fact 1 Allison's eyes swell and she has trouble breathing when she's around cats.

Fact 2 Roses make her sister Lucy sneeze.

Fact 3 Max gets an allergic reaction from nuts.

GENERALIZATION

People can be allergic to animals, plants, and foods.

Strategies for Determining the Soundness of Inductive Reasoning

Ask yourself the following questions to evaluate inductive reasoning:

- **Is the evidence valid?** Inaccurate facts can lead to false conclusions.

- **Does the conclusion follow logically from the evidence?** From the facts listed, the conclusion that *all* animals, plants, and foods cause allergic reactions would be too broad.

- **Is the evidence drawn from a large enough sample?** These three facts are enough to support the generalization. However, if you wanted to support a conclusion that most people are allergic to something, you would need a much larger sample.

The Deductive Mode of Reasoning

When a person starts with a generally accepted idea and then applies it to a situation or problem in order to reach a conclusion, that person is using **deductive reasoning.** Here's an example.

| Many people are allergic to animals. | Generally accepted idea |

▼

| Allison's eyes swell up and she has trouble breathing when she's around cats. | Specific situation |

▼

| Allison is allergic to cats. | Conclusion |

Strategies for Determining the Soundness of Deductive Reasoning

Ask yourself the following questions to evaluate deductive reasoning:

- **What is the generally accepted idea or generalization that the conclusion is based on?** Writers don't always state this general idea. So you may need to begin your evaluation by identifying it.

- **Is the generally accepted idea or generalization something you know is true and agree with?** Sometimes it isn't. Be sure to consider whether you think it is really true.

- **Is the conclusion valid?** To be valid, the conclusion must be the only logical one you can reach by applying the general idea to the specific situation. Here is an example of flawed deductive reasoning.

| Many people are allergic to animals. | Generally accepted idea |

▼

| Allison's eyes are swollen and she's having trouble breathing. | Specific situation |

▼

| Allison is allergic to cats. | Conclusion |

While the general idea is true, there is no evidence present in this situation to suggest that Allison's symptoms are the result of an allergy to any animal. There also could be other causes for her symptoms.

PRACTICE AND APPLY

Identify the mode of reasoning used here.

> I was doing my homework in my room last night when the light went out. Going out into the hall, I saw that the lights were still on in the kitchen and in my parents' room. That told me the problem was just in my room. The lamp was still plugged in, so I tried putting in a new light bulb. Luckily, that worked.

Unsupported Inferences

An **inference** is a guess that is based on evidence and, usually, some sort of prior knowledge. The generalization based on evidence on page R21, "People can be allergic to animals, plants, and foods," is an example of an inference.

An **unsupported inference** is a guess that is not adequately supported by the evidence that has been provided. For example, as noted on page R22, there is not enough evidence provided to support the conclusion that most people are allergic to something. So that conclusion would be an unsupported inference. Likewise, the faulty conclusion in the previous example ("Allison is allergic to cats.") is an unsupported inference because no evidence at all is given to support it.

See whether you can spot the unsupported inference in the following paragraph.

MODEL

Pediatrician Dr. Alice Abrahams says, "When people make exercise a habit as youngsters, they establish a positive pattern for the rest of their lives." That was certainly true for my mom. She studied jazz dance as a child and now does aerobics as an adult. Clearly, children who exercise regularly are much more likely to become adults who exercise regularly. They are also more likely to get involved in aerobics classes as adults.

If you guessed that the last sentence in the model was an unsupported inference, you would be right. Although the writer's mother went on to take aerobics classes as an adult, there is certainly not enough evidence present to back up the last statement.

PRACTICE AND APPLY

Identify the three unsupported inferences in the following text. Give reasons for your answers.

A good education should include physical fitness classes. The exercise that children get in gym class helps make them strong. It also helps them establish the healthy habit of exercising. My cousin's gym classes have made her the healthy girl she is today. I am sure that we would be healthy, too, if we had physical education at school. We would also get along better.

Identifying Faulty Reasoning

Have you ever heard or read an argument that struck you as being wrong or faulty but been unable to say just why? If so, chances are good that the argument was based on a **logical fallacy,** or an error in logic. Becoming familiar with common fallacies will give you a better chance of detecting their presence and explaining precisely why an argument is unconvincing. This chart identifies errors in logic that most often find their way into arguments.

TYPE OF FALLACY	DEFINITION	EXAMPLE
Circular reasoning	Supporting a statement by simply repeating it in different words	I forgot my lunch because I **didn't remember to bring it.**
Either/or fallacy	A statement that suggests that there are only two choices available in a situation that really offers more than two options	**Either** you get an A in English this year **or** you'll get an F.
Oversimplification	An explanation of a complex situation or problem as if it were much simpler than it is	**Just be a good listener** and you'll have lots of friends.
Overgeneralization	A generalization that is too broad. You can often recognize overgeneralizations by the use of words such as *all, everyone, every time, anything, no one,* and *none.*	I **always** say the wrong thing.
Hasty generalization	A conclusion drawn from too little evidence or from evidence that is biased	**We all must have done badly on the test,** because Ms. Chen looked angry at the beginning of class today.
Stereotyping	A dangerous type of overgeneralization. Stereotypes are broad statements about people on the basis of their gender, ethnicity, race, or political, social, professional, or religious group.	**Boys** are better at sports than **girls** are.
Attacking the person or name-calling	An attempt to discredit an idea by attacking the person or group associated with it	Only **immature** people like animated movies.
Evading the issue	Responding to an objection with arguments and evidence that do not address its central point	I didn't tell you I broke the statue, **but you said you never liked it anyway.**
False cause	The mistake of assuming that because one event occurred after another event in time, the first event caused the second one	Ellie studied really hard for the test, **so the teacher cancelled it.**

Look for examples of logical fallacies in the following argument. Identify each one and explain why you identified it as such.

> My parents can't understand me because they just don't get it. Adults are like robots and just keep doing things the way they were taught. For example, all my friends are allowed to stay up as late as they want on weekends, but I have to be in bed by 9:00. Why? Because that's how my parents were raised. I've tried to explain to them that if I can't stay up later, I'll lose all my friends. They just say I'll understand when I'm a parent. Well, I guess I'll never understand, because I'll never have kids.

5.4 EVALUATING PERSUASIVE TEXTS

Learning how to evaluate persuasive texts and identify bias and propaganda will help you become more selective when doing research or just trying to stay informed.

Strategies for Identifying Bias

Bias is an inclination for or against a particular opinion or viewpoint. Journalists usually try to keep their personal biases from affecting their writing, but sometimes a bias shows up anyway. Here are some of the most common signs of bias.

- Presenting just one way of looking at an issue or topic
- The absence of key information
- Stacking more evidence on one side of the argument than the other
- Treating weak or unproven evidence as valid and important
- Using **loaded language,** or words with strongly positive or negative connotations

EXAMPLE: *This movie insults my intelligence. It was so ridiculous that I walked out before it was done.* (*Insults* and *ridiculous* have very negative connotations.)

Strategies for Identifying Propaganda

Propaganda is any form of communication that is so distorted that it conveys false or misleading information. When a text includes more than one of the following, it is probably propaganda.

- Signs of **bias,** such as the absence of key information
- Inflammatory images that make powerful **emotional appeals**
- **Logical fallacies,** such as name-calling, false cause, and the either/or fallacy
- Lots of **ethical appeals,** or attempts to make readers feel that they and the writer(s) of the text share the same values

EXAMPLE: *I care about you people. He doesn't. His voting record shows that he really only cares about rich businessmen.* (The candidate does not mention that he voted exactly the same way as his opponent did on the issues.)

Now take a look at another example of propaganda on page 941. Use the close read questions to help you see how it distorts the truth. How else does it mislead you? (*Hint:* Look for signs of bias in the image.)

Strategies for Evaluating Evidence

Use the questions below to critically evaluate evidence in persuasive texts.

- **Are the facts presented verifiable?** Facts can be proven by eyewitness accounts, authoritative sources, experts, or research.
- **Are the opinions well informed?** Any opinions offered as support should come from experts on the topic or eyewitnesses to the event.
- **Is the evidence sufficient?** Sufficient evidence leaves no reasonable questions unanswered. If a choice is offered, background for making the choice is provided. If taking a side is called for, all sides of the issue are presented.
- **Is the evidence relevant?** The evidence should come from sources that the text's intended audience respects and regards as suitable. For example, in a report for scientists, evidence

should come from scientific journals, experts in the field, and experiments rather than a casual poll of friends, a personal experience, or an expert in some unrelated field.

Read the argument below. Identify the facts, opinions, and elements of bias.

> Lewis Middle School doesn't care about students' needs. I know the school board voted to remove our lockers so we can't hide dangerous items there. We don't deserve this lack of respect and suspicion, though. The lockers gave us a place to store our books, jackets, lunches, and other gear when we weren't using them. It's not fair to make us haul our stuff around all day. After all, my textbooks alone weigh over 70 pounds—as much as I do. Would you board members want to carry me around on your back all day?

Strategies for Determining a Strong Argument

Make sure that all or most of the following statements are true:

- The argument presents a claim or thesis.

- The claim is connected to its support by a general principle that most readers would readily agree with. Valid general principle: *People are responsible for treating others with kindness.* Invalid general principle: *People are responsible for making other people happy.*

- The reasons make sense.

- The reasons are presented in a logical and effective order.

- The claim and all reasons are adequately supported by sound evidence.

- The evidence is adequate, accurate, and appropriate.

- The logic is sound. There are no instances of faulty reasoning.

- The argument offers counterarguments to address possible reader concerns and counterclaims.

Use the preceding criteria to evaluate the strength of the following proposal.

MODEL

Summary of Proposal

I propose that the town put trash containers at bus stops, train stations, playgrounds, parks, beaches, and all other public areas.

Need

The community is littered with paper, food and drink containers, and other garbage. This situation doesn't make us feel good about ourselves or where we live.

Proposed Solution

Making trash containers available in places where people gather will help create a cleaner environment and restore our pride in our community.

Everybody would be willing to throw their bottles, cans, newspapers, gum wrappers, bags, and other garbage in a container if there was one available. Most people aren't willing to carry their trash with them until they find a proper place to throw it, however. Many citizens are such slobs that they won't even walk across the street to throw something away rather than just dropping it on the ground.

I know that installing these trash containers will cost money. Workers also will have to be paid to empty them regularly. Another objection might be that kids sometimes overturn trash containers or enjoy rolling them around.

These objections are ridiculous, though. None of us really believe that having a clean, pleasant community wouldn't be worth the few dollars this would cost. And a simple—and cheap—way to prevent kids from playing with the containers would be to chain them to a pole or fence.

Either the town council votes to approve this proposal and put it into effect right away, or they should be voted out of office.

6 Adjusting Reading Rate to Purpose

You may need to change the way you read certain texts in order to understand them. First you need to be aware of what you want to get out of what you are reading. Then you can adjust the speed at which you read in response to your purpose and the difficulty of the material. The techniques described here can be used whether you are reading silently or aloud.

Determine Your Purpose for Reading

You read different types of materials for different purposes. You may read a novel for enjoyment. You may read a textbook unit to learn a new concept. When you read for enjoyment, you naturally read at a pace that is comfortable for you. When you read for information, you need to read material more slowly and thoroughly. When you are being tested on material, you may think you have to read fast, especially if the test is being timed. However, you can actually increase your understanding of the material if you slow down.

Determine Your Reading Rate

The rate at which you read most comfortably is called your **independent reading level.** It is the rate at which you read materials that you enjoy. To learn to adjust your reading rate to read materials for other purposes, you need to be aware of your independent reading level. You can figure out your reading level by following these steps:

1. Select a passage from a book or story you enjoy.
2. Have a friend or classmate time you as you begin reading the passage silently.
3. Read at the rate that is most comfortable for you.
4. Stop when your friend or classmate tells you one minute has passed.
5. Determine the number of words you read in that minute and write down the number.
6. Repeat the process at least two more times, using different passages.
7. Add the numbers and divide the sum by the number of times your friend timed you.

Reading Techniques for Informational Material

You can use the following techniques to adapt your reading for informational texts, to prepare for tests, and to better understand what you read:

- **Skimming** is reading quickly to get the general idea of a text. To skim, read the title, headings, graphic aids, highlighted words, and first sentence of each paragraph. Also, read any introduction, conclusion, or summary. Skimming can be especially useful when taking a test. Before reading a passage, you can skim questions that follow it in order to find out what is expected and better focus on the important ideas in the text.

  When researching a topic, skimming can help you decide whether a source has information that is related to your topic.

- **Scanning** is reading quickly to find a specific piece of information, such as a fact or a definition. When you scan, your eyes sweep across a page, looking for key words that may lead you to the information you want. Use scanning to review for tests and to find answers to questions.

- **Changing pace** is increasing or decreasing the rate at which you read parts of a particular text. When you come across explanations of familiar concepts, you might be able to speed up without misunderstanding them. When you encounter unfamiliar concepts or material presented in a new way, however, you may need to slow down to understand the information.

WATCH OUT! Reading too slowly can affect your ability to understand what you read. Make sure you aren't just reading one word at a time. Practice reading phrases.

PRACTICE AND APPLY

Find an article in a magazine or textbook. Skim the article. Then answer the following questions:

1. What did you notice about the organization of the article from skimming it?

2. What is the main idea of the article?

Writing is a process that can help you explore your thoughts, experiment with ideas, and make connections. Through writing, you can examine and record your thoughts, feelings, and ideas for yourself alone, or you can communicate them to an audience.

COMMON CORE

Included in this handbook:
W 1a–e, W 2a–f, W 3a–e, W 4, W 5, W 6

1 The Writing Process

The writing process consists of the following stages: prewriting, drafting, revising and editing, proofreading, and publishing. These are not stages that you must complete in a set order. Rather, you may return to an earlier stage at any time to improve your writing.

1.1 PREWRITING

In the prewriting stage, you explore what you want to write about, what your purpose for writing is, whom you are writing for, and what form you will use to express your ideas. Ask yourself the following questions to get started.

Topic	• Is my topic assigned, or can I choose it? • What truly interests me?
Purpose	• Am I writing to entertain, to inform, to persuade, to argue, to request, or for some combination of these purposes? • What effect do I want to have on my readers?
Audience	• Who is the audience? • What might the audience members already know about my topic? • What about the topic might interest them?
Format	• Can I choose my form of writing? If so, which format would work best—story, personal letter, letter to the editor, review, poem, report, narrative, or something else?

Find Ideas for Writing

- Browse through magazines, newspapers, and Web sites.
- Start a file or notebook of articles you want to save for future reference.
- With a group, brainstorm a list of ideas.
- Write down further ideas as they come to you.

- Interview someone who is an expert on a particular topic.
- Use graphic organizers to explore other ideas that relate to a general topic.

Organize Ideas

Once you've chosen a topic, you will need to compile and organize your ideas. If you are writing a description, you may need to gather sensory details. For an essay or a research paper, you may need to record information from different sources. To record notes from sources you read or view, use any or all of these methods:

- **Summarize**—Briefly retell the main ideas of a piece of writing in your own words.
- **Paraphrase**—Restate all of the information in your own words.
- **Quote**—Record the author's exact words.

Depending on what form your writing takes, you may also need to arrange your ideas in a certain pattern.

*For more information, see the **Writing Handbook**, pages R34–R41.*

1.2 DRAFTING

In the drafting stage, you put your ideas on paper and allow them to develop and change as you write. Don't worry about correct grammar and spelling at this stage. There are two ways that you can draft.

Discovery drafting is a good approach when you are not quite sure what you think about your subject. You just start writing and let your feelings and ideas lead you in developing the topic.

Planned drafting may work better if you know that your ideas have to be arranged in a certain way, as in a research paper. Try making a writing plan or an informal outline before you begin drafting.

1.3 REVISING AND EDITING

The revising and editing stage allows you to polish your draft and make changes to its content, organization, and style. Use the questions that follow to spot problems and determine what changes would improve your work:

- Does my writing have a **main idea** or central focus? Is my controlling idea clear?
- Have I used **precise** nouns, verbs, and modifiers?
- Have I included enough **details** and **evidence?** Where can I add details, statistics, or examples?
- Do all ideas and details support my main idea?
- Is my writing clear and **coherent?** Do sentences connect to one another smoothly and logically?
- Have I used a consistent **point of view?**
- Do I need to add **transitional words, phrases,** or **sentences** to explain relationships among ideas?
- Have I used a variety of **sentence types?** Are my sentences well constructed? Would combining sentences improve the rhythm of my writing?
- Does my **tone** fit my audience and purpose?

1.4 PROOFREADING

When you are satisfied with your revision, proofread your paper for mistakes in grammar, usage, and mechanics. Dictionaries, handbooks, and other resources will help you correct errors. You may want to do this several times, looking for a different type of mistake each time. Ask:

- Have I made any errors in **subject-verb agreement** and **pronoun-antecedent agreement?**
- Have I checked for errors in **confusing word pairs,** such as *it's/its, than/then,* and *too/to?*
- Have I corrected any **run-on sentences** and **sentence fragments?**
- Have I followed rules for **correct capitalization** and used **punctuation marks** correctly?
- Have I checked the **spellings** of unfamiliar words in the dictionary?
- Have I checked for errors in **possessive form** or in the **comparative** and **superlative forms** of adverbs and adjectives?

TIP If possible, don't begin proofreading right after you've finished writing. Put your work away for at least a few hours. When you return to it, you will find it easier to identify and correct mistakes.

*For more information, see the **Grammar Handbook** and the **Vocabulary and Spelling Handbook**, pages R46–R75.*

Use the proofreading symbols in the chart to mark changes on your draft.

Proofreading Symbols	
∧ Add letters or words.	/ Make a capital letter lowercase.
⊙ Add a period.	⌗ Begin a new paragraph.
≡ Capitalize a letter.	⌿ Delete letters or words.
⊃ Close up space.	⌒ Switch the positions of letters or words.
⋀ Add a comma.	

1.5 PUBLISHING AND REFLECTING

Always consider sharing your finished writing with a wider audience.

Publishing Ideas
- Post your writing on a blog.
- Create a multimedia presentation and share it with classmates.
- Publish your writing in a school newspaper, local newspaper, or literary magazine.
- Present your work orally in a report, speech, reading, or dramatic performance.

Reflecting on Your Writing
Think about your writing process and whether you would like to add what you have written to your writing portfolio. Ask yourself:

- What did I learn about myself and my subject during this writing project?
- What was the biggest problem I faced during the writing process? How did I solve the problem?
- Which parts of the writing process did I most and least enjoy?
- Did I design and format my work in a way that makes it easy for others to read?
- What did I learn about my own process that I can use the next time I write?

1.6 PEER RESPONSE

Peer response consists of the suggestions and comments you make about the writing of your peers and also the comments and suggestions they make about your writing. You can ask a peer reader for help at any time in the writing process.

Using Peer Response as a Writer

- Tell readers where you are in the writing process and whether you would prefer feedback about your ideas or about your writing.
- Ask questions that will help you get specific information about your writing. Open-ended questions, which require more than yes-or-no answers, are more likely to give you information that will help you revise.
- Give your readers plenty of time to respond thoughtfully to your writing.
- Encourage your readers to be honest.

Being a Peer Reader

- Respect the writer's feelings.
- Offer positive reactions first.
- Make sure you understand what kind of feedback the writer is looking for and respond accordingly.

For more information on the writing process, see the **Writing Process Workshop,** *pages 20–23.*

2 Building Blocks of Good Writing

Whatever your purpose is for writing, you need to capture your reader's interest and organize your thoughts clearly.

2.1 INTRODUCTIONS

An introduction should present a controlling idea and capture your reader's attention.

Kinds of Introductions

There are many different ways to write an introduction. The one you choose depends on who the audience is and on your purpose for writing.

Make a Surprising Statement Beginning with a startling statement or an interesting fact can stir your reader's curiosity about a subject, as in the following model.

> **MODEL**
>
> A male Kodiak bear may weigh 1,500 pounds, measure 10 feet long, and run up to 30 miles an hour. Protected within Alaska's Kodiak National Wildlife Refuge, nearly 3,000 of these bears share 100-mile-long Kodiak Island, where they feast on fish, berries, and whale and seal carcasses.

Provide a Description A vivid description sets a mood and brings a scene to life for your reader.

Here, details about running on a track set the mood for a narrative about a race.

> **MODEL**
>
> In the pale morning light, the shadowy track was still. Rounding the curve, the athlete locked her eyes on the single floodlight at the far end of the track, her every muscle straining toward it.

Ask a Question Beginning with a question can make your reader want to read on to find out the answer. The following introduction asks a question about the importance of a particular person.

> **MODEL**
>
> Why does Danielle Del Ferraro hold a special place in the history of the Soap Box Derby? Since the derby began in 1934, she has been the only participant ever to win twice.

Relate an Anecdote Beginning with an anecdote, or brief story, can hook your reader and help you make a point in a dramatic way. The following anecdote introduces a firsthand account of a memorable event.

> **MODEL**
>
> Dressed in my best clothes, I rushed outside, late for my sister's wedding. I waited impatiently for the light to change at the corner. Then, from out of nowhere came an out-of-control in-line skater. The result was a head-on collision.

Address the Reader Speaking directly to your reader establishes a friendly, informal tone and involves the reader in your topic.

> **MODEL**
>
> Find out how you can get in shape and have fun at the same time. Come to a free demonstration of Fit for Life on Friday night at 7:00 P.M.

Begin with a Controlling Idea A controlling idea expressing a main idea may be woven into both the beginning and the end of a piece of nonfiction writing.

> **MODEL**
>
> Although the names of the Greek and Roman gods were different, the things the gods did were very similar.

TIP To write the best introduction for your paper, you may want to try more than one of the methods and then decide which is the most effective for your purpose and audience.

2.2 PARAGRAPHS

A paragraph is made up of sentences that work together to develop an idea or accomplish a purpose. Whether or not it contains a topic sentence stating the main idea, a good paragraph must have unity and coherence.

Unity

A paragraph has unity when all the sentences support and develop one stated or implied idea. Use the following technique to create unity in your paragraphs:

Write a Topic Sentence A topic sentence states the main idea of the paragraph; all other sentences in the paragraph provide supporting details. A topic sentence is often the first sentence in a paragraph, as shown in the model that follows.

However, it may also appear later in a paragraph or at the end, to summarize or reinforce the main idea.

> **MODEL**
>
> The most important rule for a beginning photographer is this: check before you click. Is your subject well lighted or will you need a flash? Have you framed your picture carefully? Are you holding the camera still? Checking the basics will go a long way toward making your snapshots memorable.

TIP Paying attention to topic sentences when you read literature can help you craft your own topic sentences. Notice the use of strong topic sentences in "Matthew Henson at the Top of the World" on page 810. For example, the fourth paragraph on page 812 begins, "Although Matthew Henson's early life seems harsh, in many ways he was very lucky." The rest of the paragraph then explains some of the advantages Henson had while he was growing up.

Coherence

A paragraph is coherent when all its sentences are related to one another and each flows logically to the next. Use the following techniques to make your paragraphs more coherent:

- Present your ideas in the most logical order.

- Use pronouns, synonyms, and repeated words to connect ideas.

- Use transitional words to show relationships among ideas.

In the model shown here, the writer used several techniques to create a coherent paragraph.

> **MODEL**
>
> Most scientists believe that all of Earth's land once formed one supercontinent. Over 200 million years ago, this supercontinent began to break into two large masses of land. Since that time, the plates on which continents rest have continued to move.

2.3 TRANSITIONS

Transitions are words and phrases that show connections between details. Clear transitions help show how your ideas relate to one another.

Kinds of Transitions

The types of transitions you choose depend on the ideas you want to convey.

Time or Sequence Some transitions help to clarify the sequence of events over time. When you are telling a story or describing a process, you can connect ideas with such transitional words as *first, second, always, then, next, later, soon, before, finally, after, earlier, afterward,* and *tomorrow.*

> **MODEL**
>
> During the Revolutionary War, many of the colonists who remained loyal to the British monarchy lost their houses and land by force. After the war, between 80,000 and 100,000 of these Loyalists went to England or emigrated elsewhere.

Spatial Order Transitional words and phrases such as *in front, behind, next to, along, nearest, lowest, above, below, underneath, on the left,* and *in the middle* can help your reader visualize a scene.

> **MODEL**
>
> As I waited, I stared at the bleachers across the rink. My family was lined up in the front row. Behind this group and to the right were friends from school, and next to my friends were three of my teachers.

Degree of Importance Transitional words such as *mainly, strongest, weakest, first, second, most important, least important, worst,* and *best* may be used to rank ideas or to show degrees of importance.

> **MODEL**
>
> Why do I read mysteries? Mainly I read them because I enjoy suspense. Second, I like meeting characters who are different from anybody I know in real life. Least important, but still a reason, is that I enjoy reading about interesting places.

Compare and Contrast Words and phrases such as *similarly, likewise, also, like, as, neither . . . nor,* and *either . . . or* show similarity between details. *However, by contrast, yet, but, unlike, instead, whereas,* and *while* show difference. Note the use of transitions showing contrast in the model.

> **MODEL**
>
> Matthew Henson was not recognized as the co-discoverer of the North Pole until 1944, although he and Robert Peary had reached it together on April 9, 1909. By contrast, the achievement of Roald Amundsen's team, which made it to the South Pole in December 1911, was recognized almost immediately.

TIP Both *but* and *however* can be used to join two independent clauses. When *but* is used as a coordinating conjunction, it is preceded by a comma. When *however* is used as a conjunctive adverb, it is preceded by a semicolon and followed by a comma.

> **EXAMPLE**
>
> A greenbottle fly is small, but its eyes contain many lenses.
>
> You can try to quietly sneak up on a fly with a swatter; however, the fly, with its compound eyes, will still be able to see the motion of the swatter.

Cause-Effect When you are writing about a cause-effect relationship, use transitional words and phrases such as *since, because, thus, therefore, so, due to, for this reason,* and *as a result* to help explain that relationship and make your writing coherent.

> **MODEL**
>
> Because a tree fell across the electric wires Monday night, we lost our electricity for four hours.

2.4 CONCLUSIONS

A conclusion should leave readers with a strong final impression.

Kinds of Conclusions

Good conclusions sum up ideas in a variety of ways. Here are some techniques you might try:

Restate Your Controlling Idea A good way to conclude an essay is by restating your controlling idea, or thesis, in different words. The following conclusion restates the controlling idea introduced on page R31.

> **MODEL**
>
> It may surprise you to hear that two very different cultures might have very similar gods, but this comparison of Zeus and Jupiter shows how similar the Greek and Roman gods could be.

Ask a Question Try asking a question that sums up what you have said and gives your reader something new to think about. This question concludes a piece of persuasive writing and suggests a course of action.

> **MODEL**
>
> More and more people are biking to school and work and are riding for exercise. Doesn't it make sense to create safe bike lanes throughout our city?

Make a Recommendation When you are persuading your audience to take a position on an issue, you can conclude by recommending a specific course of action.

> **MODEL**
>
> You can make your research easier by taking advantage of the Internet. Develop a list of keywords that will help you narrow your search.

Offer an Opinion Leave your reader with something to think about by offering your personal opinion on the topic. The following model offers an opinion about draining wetlands.

> **MODEL**
>
> Even though the developers draining the wetlands hope to bring in new business, the health of the environment is more important than any economic gains.

End with the Last Event If you're telling a story, you may end with the last thing that happens. Here, the ending includes an embarrassing moment for the narrator.

> **MODEL**
>
> When I pulled myself out of the pool, he growled, "You just set a new record for the 22-meter free. Too bad it was the wrong event." Suddenly, I realized I had swum four extra laps! It was one victory I never celebrated.

2.5 ELABORATION

Elaboration is the process of developing an idea by providing specific supporting details that are relevant and appropriate to the purpose and form of your writing.

Facts and Statistics A fact is a statement that can be verified, and a statistic is a fact expressed as a number. Make sure the facts and statistics you supply are from reliable, up-to-date sources.

> **MODEL**
>
> Women have aided U.S. military efforts for more than a century. Today, more than 200,000 women are on active military duty.

Sensory Details Details that show how something looks, sounds, tastes, smells, or feels can make readers feel they are actually experiencing what you are describing. Which senses does the writer appeal to in the following model?

> **MODEL**
>
> Anna Hawk got off her bike and sat beside the muddy road. The rain on her poncho made the only sound, and nothing on the prairie moved. Anna took a sip of warm, sweet cocoa from her thermos bottle.

Incidents From our earliest years, we are interested in hearing "stories." One way to illustrate a point powerfully is to relate an incident or tell a story, as shown in the example.

> **MODEL**
>
> Some of our most valuable sources of historical knowledge come from tragic events. The eruption of the volcano Vesuvius in A.D. 79 was a nightmare for the people of Pompeii. About 2,000 inhabitants may have died, and their homes were buried under tons of volcanic ash.

Examples An example can help make an abstract idea concrete or can serve to clarify a complex point for your reader.

> **MODEL**
>
> Realistic fiction is imaginative writing set in the real, modern world. For example, the short story "Tuesday of the Other June" is set in a realistic city, and its characters deal with ordinary human problems.

Quotations Choose quotations that clearly support your points, and be sure that you copy each quotation word for word. Always remember to credit the source.

> **MODEL**
>
> In Avi's short story "Scout's Honor," one of the characters tries to come up with an excuse for not crossing a scary-looking bridge. "I'm not so sure we should go," he says. "Maybe it doesn't have another side."

❸ Writing Descriptions

Descriptive writing allows you to paint word pictures about anything, from events of global importance to the most personal feelings. It is an essential part of almost every piece of writing.

> **CRITERIA: Standards for Writing**
>
> **Successful descriptive writing should**
> - have a clear focus and sense of purpose
> - use sensory details and precise words to create a vivid image, establish a mood, or express emotion
> - present details in a logical order

3.1 KEY TECHNIQUES

Consider Your Goals What do you want to accomplish with your description? Do you want to show why something is important to you? Do you want to make a person or scene more memorable? Do you want to explain an event?

Identify Your Audience Who will read your description? How familiar are they with your subject? What background information will they need? Which details will they find most interesting?

Think Figuratively What figures of speech might help make your description vivid and interesting? What similes, metaphors, or analogies come to mind? What imaginative comparisons can you make? What living thing does an inanimate object remind you of?

Gather Sensory Details Which sights, smells, tastes, sounds, and textures make your subject come alive? Which details stick in your mind when you observe or recall your subject? Which senses does it most strongly affect?

You might want to use a chart like the one shown here to collect sensory details about your subject.

Sights	Sounds	Textures	Smells	Tastes

Organize Your Details Details that are presented in a logical order help the reader form a mental picture of the subject. Descriptive details may be organized in spatial order, by order of impression, in order of importance, or in chronological order.

3.2 OPTIONS FOR ORGANIZATION

Option 1: Spatial Order Spatial order describes a space or scene and all of the objects or people in that space. Either of the following options will help readers "see" the place you are describing.

*For more information, see **Transitions**, page R32.*

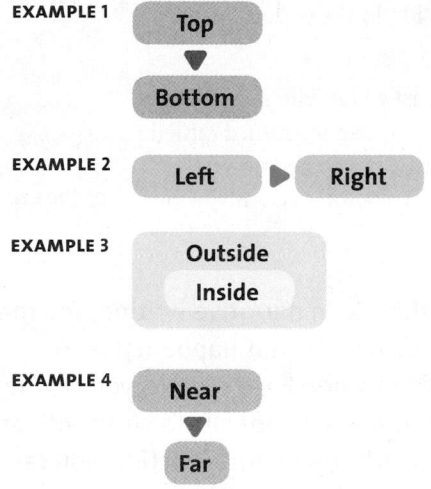

MODEL

Arthur and Chantal came to the bicycle race to cheer on their friends. As the first group of cyclists approached the finish line, Arthur and Chantal cheered wildly when they saw that their friend Lindsey was leading the pack. Another friend, Charles, was just behind her. Far off in the distance, they could just make out their friend Georgia's red bike.

Option 2: Order of Impression Order of impression is the order in which you notice details.

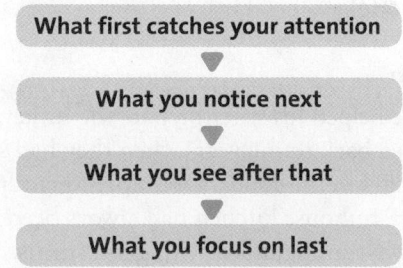

MODEL

Mike descended the stairs slowly, so we saw his shoes first—polished to a gleaming black so that they looked almost like patent leather. Then, the satin stripe on each trouser leg told us he was dressed for a formal event. Finally, we saw the white bow tie, just below the grin.

TIP Use transitions that help readers understand the order of the impressions you are describing. Some useful transitions are *after, next, during, first, before, finally,* and *then.*

*For more information, see **Transitions**, page R32.*

Option 3: Order of Importance You can use the order of importance as the organizing structure for a description. Organizing information from least important to most important is sometimes called **climactic order** because the most crucial information comes at the climax, or end.

MODEL

Most impressionist paintings were created outdoors. The paintings feature bright colors and loose brushwork. The painters used these techniques to portray the effects of sunlight on objects. The goal of the impressionists was to capture their immediate "impression" of a brief moment in time.

Option 4: Chronological Order You can use chronological order as the organizing structure for a description. See section 4.2 on page R36 for an example of how this is done.

④ Writing Narratives

Narrative writing tells a story. If you write a story from your imagination, it is a fictional narrative. A true story about actual events is a nonfictional narrative. Narrative writing can be found in short stories, novels, news articles, personal narratives, and biographies.

> ### CRITERIA: Standards for Writing
>
> **A successful narrative should**
>
> - hook the reader's attention with a strong introduction
> - include sensory details and concrete, specific language to develop the characters, setting, and plot
> - have a clear beginning, middle, and end
> - have a logical organization, with clues and transitions that help the reader understand the order of events
> - use a consistent tone and point of view
> - use language that is appropriate to the audience
> - include dialogue and suspense if appropriate

*For more information, see **Writing Workshop: Short Story**, page 414, and **Writing Workshop: Personal Narrative**, page 872.*

4.1 KEY TECHNIQUES

Identify the Main Events What are the most important events in your narrative? Is each event needed to tell the story? Consider organizing events in a way that builds suspense and keeps readers guessing about what will happen next.

Describe the Setting When do the events occur? Where do they take place? How can you use setting to create mood and to set the stage for the characters and their actions?

Depict Characters Vividly What do your characters look like? What do they think and say? How do they act? What details can show what they are like?

TIP One method of developing characters is to include dialogue. When writing dialogue, choose words that express the characters' personalities. Dialogue should show how characters feel about one another and about events in the narrative.

4.2 OPTIONS FOR ORGANIZATION

Option 1: Chronological Order One way to organize a piece of narrative writing is to arrange the events in chronological order, as shown.

EXAMPLE

Aunt Jessica gives Danielle her first horse to train.

He's a horse Danielle doesn't like. He's stubborn, and when Danielle tries to train him, nothing happens.

Danielle sees the horse running in the field. He looks proud and independent.

Aunt Jessica asks Danielle if she would like a different horse to train. Danielle says she wants to keep the horse she has. Aunt Jessica smiles warmly at her.

Introduction
Characters and setting
▼
Event 1
▼
Event 2
▼
End
Perhaps showing the significance of the events

Option 2: Flashback In narrative writing, you may want to include events that happened before the beginning of the story. For example, you can hook your reader's interest by opening a story with an exciting event. After your introduction, you can use a flashback to show how past events led up to the present situation or to provide background about a character or an event. Use clue words such as *last summer, as a young girl, the previous school year,* and *his earliest memories* to let your reader know that you are interrupting the main action to describe earlier events.

Notice how the flashback interrupts the action in the model.

MODEL

As he helped his sister prepare the turkey, his mind drifted back to the years when they had spent the holidays in the country with their grandparents. The farmhouse kitchen had always been so warm and welcoming, filled with good smells.

Option 3: Focus on Conflict When a fictional narrative focuses on a central conflict, the story's plot may be organized as in the following example.

EXAMPLE

Danielle lives on the Kansas prairie near her Aunt Jessica. Danielle excels at everything she does and is a little spoiled. She looks up to her aunt, who is quiet and thoughtful.

When Danielle asks for a horse to train, Jessica deliberately gives her a horse that will be hard to train.

- Danielle and Aunt Jessica have always been very close.

- Danielle is hurt that her aunt has given her a horse she dislikes.

- Danielle wants to train the horse quickly so that she can ride him in a competition.

By dealing with the challenge of training a difficult horse, Danielle becomes more mature. She and her aunt are brought closer together.

Describe main characters and setting.

Present conflict.

Relate events that create conflict and cause characters to change.

Present resolution or outcome of conflict.

5 Writing Informative Texts

Expository writing informs and explains. You can use it to explain how to cook spaghetti or to compare two pieces of literature. There are many types of expository writing, including description, explanation, problem and solution, responses to literature, and comparison and contrast. Think about your topic and select the type that presents the information most clearly.

5.1 COMPARISON AND CONTRAST

Compare-and-contrast writing examines the similarities and differences between two or more subjects. You might, for example, compare and contrast two short stories, the main characters in a novel, or two movies.

CRITERIA: Standards for Writing

Successful compare-and-contrast writing should

- explain the situation in the introduction
- clearly identify the subjects that are being compared
- state a thesis or purpose
- include specific, relevant details
- follow a clear plan of organization that is appropriate to the type of writing
- use language and details appropriate to the audience
- offer persuasive evidence to support arguments and conclusions
- use transitional words and phrases to clarify similarities and differences

For more information, see **Writing Workshop: Comparison-Contrast Essay,** *page 296.*

Options for Organization

Compare-and-contrast writing can be organized in different ways. The examples that follow demonstrate point-by-point organization and subject-by-subject organization. Both examples show ways of organizing information into categories.

Option 1: Point-by-Point Organization

EXAMPLE

I. Similarities in Appearance   **Point 1**

   Subject A. Domestic honeybees are about five-eighths of an inch long.

   Subject B. Africanized bees, contrary to rumor, are about the same size as domestic bees.

II. Differences in Temperament   **Point 2**

   Subject A. Domestic honeybees are bred to be gentle.

   Subject B. The Africanized bee is a "wild" bee that is quick-tempered around animals and people.

Option 2: Subject-by-Subject Organization

EXAMPLE

I. Domestic Honeybees   **Subject A**

   Point 1. Domestic honey-bees are about five-eighths of an inch long.

   Point 2. Domestic honeybees are bred to be gentle.

II. Africanized Bees   **Subject B**

   Point 1. Africanized bees are about five-eighths of an inch long.

   Point 2. The Africanized bee is a "wild" bee that is quick-tempered around animals and people.

5.2 CAUSE AND EFFECT

Cause-effect writing explains why something happened, why certain conditions exist, or what resulted from an action or a condition. You might use cause-effect writing to explain a character's actions, the progress of a disease, or the outcome of a war.

> **CRITERIA: Standards for Writing**
>
> **Successful cause-effect writing should**
>
> - hook the reader's attention with a strong introduction
> - include a thesis that clearly states the cause-and-effect relationship
> - have a sensible, appropriate pattern of organization
> - show clear connections between causes and effects
> - present causes and effects in a logical order and use transitions effectively
> - use facts, examples, and other details to illustrate each cause and effect
> - use language and details appropriate to the audience

*For more information, see **Writing Workshop: How-To Explanation**, page 780.*

Options for Organization

Your organization will depend on your topic and your purpose for writing.

Option 1: Effect-to-Cause Organization If you want to explain the causes of an event, such as the threat of Africanized bees to commercial beekeeping, you might first state the effect and then examine its causes.

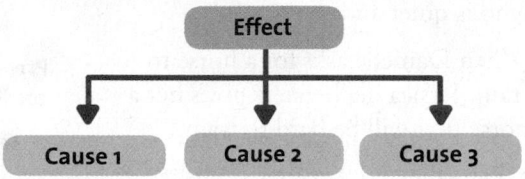

Option 2: Cause-to-Effect Organization If your focus is on explaining the effects of an event, such as the appearance of Africanized bees in the United States, you might first state the cause and then explain the effects.

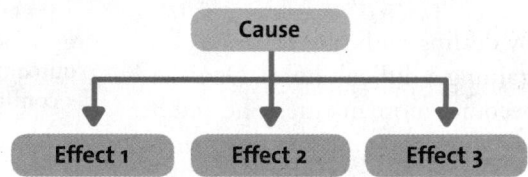

Option 3: Cause-Effect Chain Organization Sometimes you'll want to describe a chain of cause-and-effect relationships to explore a topic such as the myths about the Africanized honeybee.

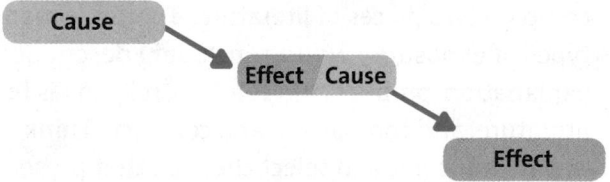

TIP Don't assume that a cause-effect relationship exists just because one event follows another. Look for evidence that the later event could not have happened if the first event had not caused it.

5.3 PROBLEM-SOLUTION

Problem-solution writing clearly states a problem, analyzes the problem, and proposes a solution to the problem. It can be used to identify and solve a conflict between characters, investigate global warming, or explain why a soccer team keeps losing games.

CRITERIA: Standards for Writing

Successful problem-solution writing should

- hook the reader's attention with a strong introduction
- identify the problem and help the reader understand the issues involved
- analyze the causes and effects of the problem
- include quotations, facts, and statistics
- explore possible solutions to the problem and recommend the best one(s)
- use language, details, and a tone appropriate to the audience

Options for Organization

How you organize a problem-solution piece will depend on your goal, your intended audience, and the specific problem you have chosen to address. The following organizational methods are effective for different kinds of problem-solution writing.

Option 1: Simple Problem-Solution

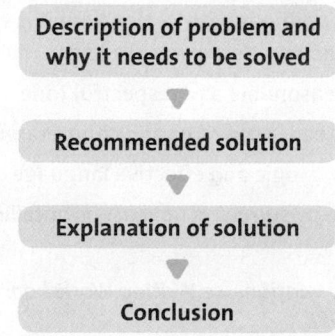

Description of problem and why it needs to be solved

▼

Recommended solution

▼

Explanation of solution

▼

Conclusion

Option 2: Deciding Between Solutions

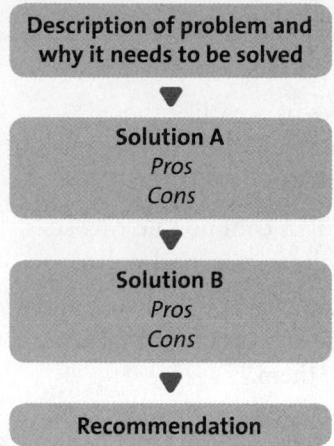

Description of problem and why it needs to be solved

▼

Solution A
Pros
Cons

▼

Solution B
Pros
Cons

▼

Recommendation

5.4 EXPLANATION

In writing an explanation, you analyze how something works, how it is defined, or what its parts are.

CRITERIA: Standards for Writing

A successful explanation should

- include a strong introduction
- state the thesis or purpose
- follow a specific organization to provide a logical flow of information
- show connections among facts and ideas through transitional words and phrases
- use language and details appropriate for the audience
- include persuasive supporting evidence

Options for Organization

Different types of analysis will require different methods of organization. Be sure that you organize details in an order that makes sense for the kind of analysis you are writing. Use one of the following options:

Option 1: Process Explanation What are the important steps or stages of a process? A process explanation is usually organized chronologically, with steps or stages in the order in which they occur. You might use one to explain how to program a cell phone or prepare for a test, or to explain the different stages of development in an insect's life.

MODEL

Keep your house safe from dangerous bees.

Introduce process.

Some types of bees, like the Africanized honeybee, can be a threat to your safety.

Give background.

Step 1: Fill in common nesting sites, such as holes in trees and walls.

Step 2: Look for active hives around your home and contact a beekeeper to remove them.

Explain steps.

Step 3: Watch for new hives in the spring and fall, when bees form new colonies.

Option 2: Extended Definition What are the most important characteristics of a subject? Use an extended definition to explain a quality (such as beauty), the characteristics of a limerick, or the characteristics of insects. You can organize the details in order of importance or impression.

MODEL

What is an Africanized honeybee?

An Africanized honeybee is a cross between a domestic honeybee and an aggressive African bee.

Introduce term and definition.

Feature 1: The aggressiveness of the African bee ancestors comes out in the hybrid bees.

Feature 2: The Africanized bee is not comfortable around animals or humans.

Explain features.

Feature 3: An individual who threatens the bees may receive hundreds of stings, and even die.

Option 3: Explanation of Parts What are the parts, groups, or types that make up your subject? The following explanation of parts analyzes the significance of the beekeeping industry.

MODEL

The beekeeping industry is a complex and productive industry.

Introduce subject.

Part 1: The primary product is honey. The United States produces 250 million pounds of honey per year.

Part 2: Other products are beeswax and royal jelly.

Explain parts.

Part 3: Honeybees pollinate more than 90 different types of crops, affecting every third bite of food that people eat.

6 Writing Arguments

Persuasive writing allows you to use the power of language to inform and influence others. It includes speeches, persuasive essays, newspaper editorials, advertisements, and critical reviews.

CRITERIA: Standards for Writing

Successful persuasive writing should

- have an attention-getting introduction
- state a clear position or claim in support of a proposition or proposal
- support opinions with evidence that is well-organized and clearly related to the main ideas
- have a reasonable and respectful tone
- answer reader concerns and counterarguments
- use sound logic and effective language
- conclude by summing up reasons or calling for action

*For more information, see **Writing Workshop: Persuasive Essay**, page 988.*

6.1 KEY TECHNIQUES

Clarify Your Claim What do you believe about the issue? How can you express your opinion most clearly?

Know Your Audience Who will read your writing? What do they already know and believe about the issue? What objections to your position might they have? What additional information might they need to understand your argument? What tone and approach would be most effective?

Support Your Opinion Why do you feel the way you do about the issue? What facts, statistics, examples, quotations, anecdotes, or expert opinions support your view? What reasons will convince your readers? What evidence can answer their objections?

Ways to Support Your Argument	
Statistics	facts that are stated in numbers
Examples	specific instances that explain points
Observations	events or situations you yourself have seen
Anecdotes	brief stories that illustrate points
Quotations	direct statements from authorities

*For more information, see **Identifying Faulty Reasoning**, page R24.*

Begin and End with a Bang How can you hook your readers and make a lasting impression? What memorable quotation, anecdote, or statistic will catch their attention at the beginning or stick in their minds at the end? What strong summary or call to action can you use as a conclusion?

MODEL

Beginning

Whether you are a bicyclist, a driver, or even a pedestrian, chances are you've been put in a dangerous situation because bikes must use the same lanes as cars.

End

Please help improve safety for everyone in our community by supporting the creation of bike lanes on all major streets.

6.2 OPTIONS FOR ORGANIZATION

In a two-sided persuasive essay, you want to show the weaknesses of other opinions as you explain the strengths of your own.

Option 1: Reasons for Your Opinion

Introduction states issue and your position on it.
▼
Reason 1 with evidence and support
▼
Reason 2 with evidence and support
▼
Reason 3 with evidence and support
▼
Objections to whole argument
▼
Response to objections
▼
Conclusion restates your position and suggests a course of action.

Option 2: Point-by-Point Basis

Introduction states issue and your position on it.
▼
Reason 1 with evidence and support
▼
Objections and responses for reason 1
▼
Reason 2 with evidence and support
▼
Objections and responses for reason 2
▼
Reason 3 with evidence and support
▼
Objections and responses for reason 3
▼
Conclusion restates your position and suggests a course of action.

7 Writing Functional Texts

You may need to do business writing to request information or complain about a product or service. Several types of formats, such as memos, letters, e-mails, and applications, have been developed to make communication easier.

CRITERIA: Standards for Writing

Successful business writing should

- be courteous
- use language that is appropriate for its audience
- state the purpose clearly in the opening sentences or paragraph
- have a formal tone and not contain slang or sentence fragments
- use precise words
- present only essential information
- present details in a logical order
- conclude with a summary of important points

7.1 KEY TECHNIQUES OF WORKPLACE WRITING

Think About Your Purpose Why are you writing? Do you want to order or complain about a product?

Identify Your Audience Who will read your writing? What background information will they need? What tone or language is appropriate?

Support Your Points What specific details and reasons might clarify your ideas?

Finish Strongly How can you best sum up your statements? What is your main point? What action do you want the recipients to take?

Revise and Proofread Your Writing Just as you are graded on the quality of an essay you write for a class, you will be judged on the quality of your writing in the workplace.

7.2 MATCH THE FORMAT TO THE OCCASION

Memos, e-mail messages, and letters have similar purposes but are used in different situations.

Format	Occasion
Memo	Use to send correspondence **inside** the workplace only.
E-mail message	Use to send correspondence **inside or outside** the company.
Letter	Use to send correspondence **outside** the company.

TIP Memos are often sent as e-mail messages in the workplace. Remember that both require formal language and standard spelling, capitalization, and punctuation.

Technical writing is used for detailed instructions or descriptions of items and processes. At work, at school, or in everyday life, you may have to use technical writing to leave instructions for another person.

CRITERIA: Standards for Writing

Instructions should

- present only essential information
- present steps in a logical order
- include sentences that are short and simple
- include definitions of unfamiliar terms if necessary
- use transitions and/or numbered steps
- use verbs that describe actions
- use the present tense
- include diagrams or drawings if necessary

7.3 KEY TECHNIQUES OF TECHNICAL WRITING

Think About Your Organization Present information in a sensible order. For example, list any necessary tools and materials early on. Then present the steps in order.

Keep Your Audience in Mind Explain what readers who are unfamiliar with the activity or process will need to know.

Evaluate Your Instructions Have a friend follow your instructions to make sure they are clear.

MODEL: BUSINESS LETTER

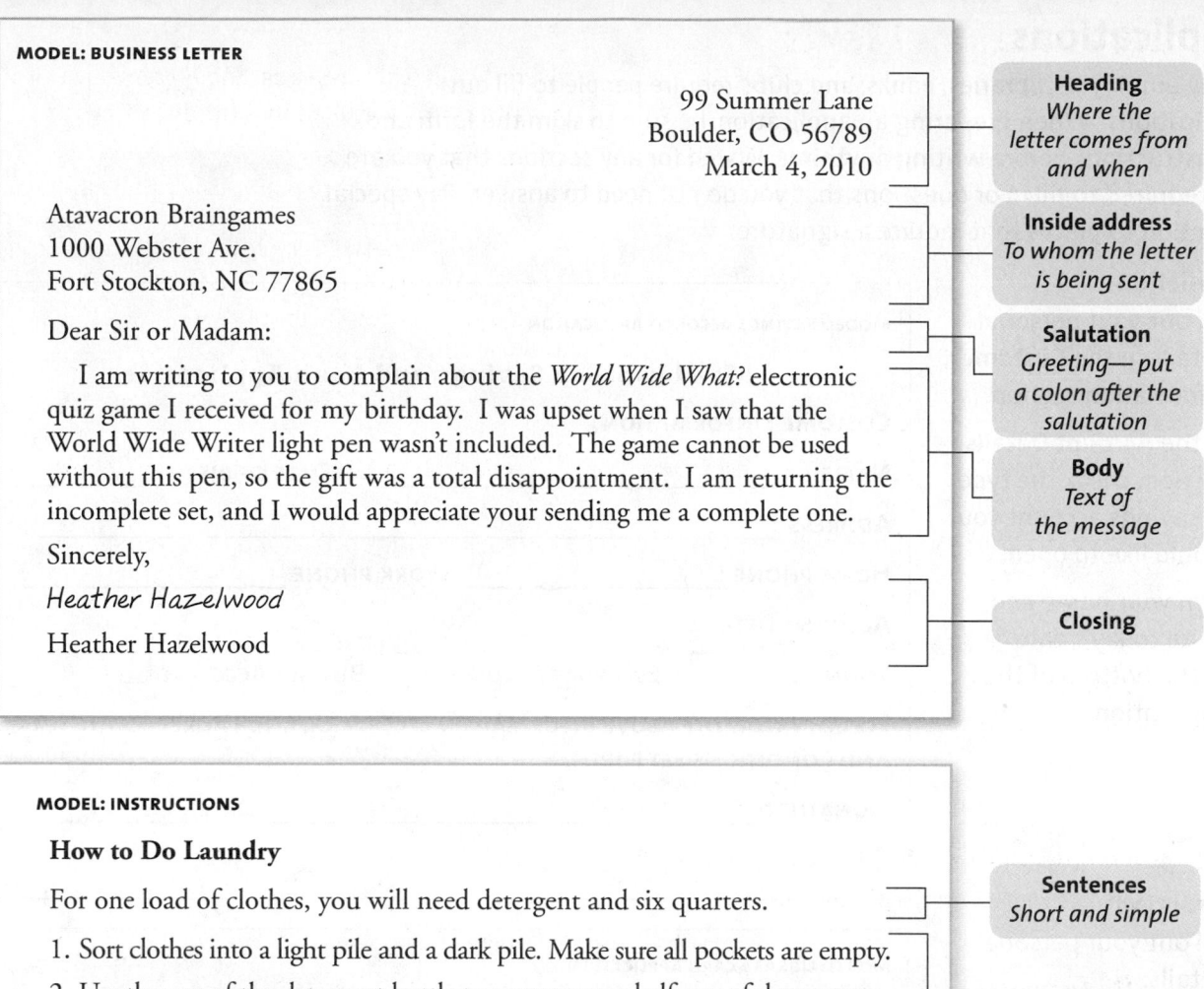

99 Summer Lane
Boulder, CO 56789
March 4, 2010

Heading
Where the letter comes from and when

Atavacron Braingames
1000 Webster Ave.
Fort Stockton, NC 77865

Inside address
To whom the letter is being sent

Dear Sir or Madam:

Salutation
Greeting— put a colon after the salutation

I am writing to you to complain about the *World Wide What?* electronic quiz game I received for my birthday. I was upset when I saw that the World Wide Writer light pen wasn't included. The game cannot be used without this pen, so the gift was a total disappointment. I am returning the incomplete set, and I would appreciate your sending me a complete one.

Body
Text of the message

Sincerely,

Heather Hazelwood

Heather Hazelwood

Closing

MODEL: INSTRUCTIONS

How to Do Laundry

For one load of clothes, you will need detergent and six quarters.

Sentences
Short and simple

1. Sort clothes into a light pile and a dark pile. Make sure all pockets are empty.

2. Use the cap of the detergent bottle to measure one-half cup of detergent.

3. Open the washer lid and add detergent.

Numbered list
Makes order clear

4. Add either light clothes or dark clothes to washer. Do not pack clothes tightly.

5. Close the lid and turn the dial to REGULAR COLD. Push the ON button.

6. Put six quarters in slots and push the tray forward so the quarters disappear.

Concise information
No unnecessary details

7. When clothes have completed the wash, rinse, and spin cycles, take them out of the washer and put them on hangers to air dry.

PRACTICE AND APPLY

1. Draft a response to the letter. Then revise your letter as necessary, using the rubric on page R42 in the left column. Check your grammar, spelling, punctuation, and capitalization.

2. Think about something you might want someone else to do because you won't be at home. The task might be preparing a meal, cleaning a pet's cage, or checking a computer for viruses. Write instructions, following the rubric on page R42 (right column).

8 Applications

Many employers, libraries, banks, and clubs require people to fill out applications. When preparing an application, be sure to skim the form and its instructions before writing anything. Watch for any sections that you are not required to fill in or questions that you do not need to answer. Pay special attention to places that require a signature.

Instructions

1. Fill out your personal details in the **Customer Information** section.

2. In the **Account Details** section, check the type of savings account you would like to open.

3. Sign your name and write today's date at the bottom of the application.

MODEL: SAVINGS ACCOUNT APPLICATION

Meadowbrook Savings and Loan Application

CUSTOMER INFORMATION

NAME _____ DATE OF BIRTH ___/___/___

ADDRESS _____

HOME PHONE _____ WORK PHONE _____

ACCOUNT DETAILS

YOUNG SAVER ☐   EVERYDAY ACCOUNT ☐   BUDGET ACCOUNT ☐

I CERTIFY THAT THE ABOVE INFORMATION IS CORRECT, AND I AGREE TO THE TERMS AND CONDITIONS SET FORTH.

SIGNATURE _____ DATE ___/___/___

Instructions

1. Fill out your personal details.

2. Sign and date the application.

3. Leave the bottom of the application blank.

MODEL: LIBRARY CARD APPLICATION

Millwood Public Library Card Application

(for office use only) **CARD NO.** _____

Please print clearly.

NAME _____
　　　　Last　　　　　　　First　　　　　　　Middle

LOCAL ADDRESS _____

CITY _____ STATE _____ ZIP CODE _____

HOME PHONE ( ) _____ WORK PHONE ( ) _____

SEX _____ _____ BIRTH DATE _____/_____/_____
　　　Male　Female　　　　　Month　Day　Year

I agree to be responsible for all materials borrowed from the Millwood Public Library in my name.

SIGNATURE _____ DATE _____

---

for office use only

STAFF INITIALS_____ REGISTRATION CLASS _____

MI　　CH　　NS　　OTHER　　FEE STAFF　　ISU　　KE　　NL　　TE

Instructions

1. Print your name, address, and phone number(s) in the **Applicant Information** section.

2. Fill out the **Emergency Contact Information.**

3. Put a check mark next to your payment type in the **Payment Method** section.

4. Sign and date the application.

MODEL: SPORTS CLUB APPLICATION

Riverdale Sports Club Application

APPLICANT INFORMATION

NAME _____

ADDRESS _____

HOME PHONE _____ WORK PHONE _____

EMERGENCY CONTACT INFORMATION

NAME _____ PHONE _____

RELATIONSHIP TO YOU _____

PAYMENT METHOD

CREDIT CARD ☐   CHECK ☐

SIGNATURE _____ DATE ___/___/___

Instructions

1. Fill out the information in the **Personal Details** section.

2. Under **Membership Type,** check whether you are a new or renewing member.

3. Under **Payment Method,** choose how you would like to pay for your membership.

4. Sign and date the application.

MODEL: LEAGUE MEMBERSHIP APPLICATION

SnoBowl Bowling League Application

PERSONAL DETAILS

NAME _____

ADDRESS _____

HOME PHONE _____ WORK PHONE _____

MEMBERSHIP TYPE

NEW ☐   RENEWING ☐

PAYMENT METHOD

CREDIT CARD ☐   CHECK ☐

SIGNATURE _____ DATE ___/___/___

Writing Online

THINK central

Go to **thinkcentral.com.**
KEYWORD: HML6N-R45

Writing that has a lot of mistakes can confuse or even annoy a reader. Punctuation errors in a letter might lead to a miscommunication or delay a reply. A sentence fragment might lower your grade on an essay. Paying attention to grammar, punctuation, and capitalization rules can make your writing clearer and easier to read.

COMMON CORE

Included in this handbook:
L 1 a–e, L 2a, L 3a

Quick Reference: Parts of Speech

PART OF SPEECH	FUNCTION	EXAMPLES
Noun	names a person, a place, a thing, an idea, a quality, or an action	
Common	serves as a general name, or a name common to an entire group	subway, fog, puzzle, tollbooth
Proper	names a specific, one-of-a-kind person, place, or thing	Mrs. Price, Pompeii, China, Meg
Singular	refers to a single person, place, thing, or idea	onion, waterfall, lamb, sofa
Plural	refers to more than one person, place, thing, or idea	dreams, commercials, men, tortillas
Concrete	names something that can be perceived by the senses	jacket, teacher, caterpillar, aroma
Abstract	names something that cannot be perceived by the senses	friendship, opportunities, fear, stubbornness
Compound	expresses a single idea through a combination of two or more words	jump rope, paycheck, Chinese-American, pine needles
Collective	refers to a group of people or things	colony, family, clan, flock
Possessive	shows who or what owns something	Mama's, Tito's, children's, waitresses'
Pronoun	takes the place of a noun or another pronoun	
Personal	refers to the person making a statement, the person(s) being addressed, or the person(s) or thing(s) the statement is about	I, me, my, mine, we, us, our, ours, you, your, yours, she, he, it, her, him, hers, his, its, they, them, their, theirs
Reflexive	follows a verb or preposition and refers to a preceding noun or pronoun	myself, yourself, herself, himself, itself, ourselves, yourselves, themselves
Intensive	emphasizes a noun or another pronoun	(same as reflexives)
Demonstrative	points to one or more specific persons or things	this, that, these, those
Interrogative	signals a question	who, whom, whose, which, what
Indefinite	refers to one or more persons or things not specifically mentioned	both, all, most, many, anyone, everybody, several, none, some
Relative	introduces an adjective clause by relating it to a word in the clause	who, whom, whose, which, that

PART OF SPEECH	FUNCTION	EXAMPLES
Verb	expresses an action, a condition, or a state of being	
Action	tells what the subject does or did, physically or mentally	run, reaches, listened, consider, decides, dreamed
Linking	connects the subject to something that identifies or describes it	am, is, are, was, were, sound, taste, appear, feel, become, remain, seem
Auxiliary	precedes the main verb in a verb phrase	be, have, do, can, could, will, would, may, might
Transitive	directs the action toward someone or something; always has an object	The storm **sank** the ship.
Intransitive	does not direct the action toward someone or something; does not have an object	The ship **sank.**
Adjective	modifies a noun or pronoun	**strong** women, **two** epics, **enough** time
Adverb	modifies a verb, an adjective, or another adverb	walked **out**, **really** funny, **far** away
Preposition	relates one word to another word	at, by, for, from, in, of, on, to, with
Conjunction	joins words or word groups	
Coordinating	joins words or word groups used the same way	and, but, or, for, so, yet, nor
Correlative	used as a pair to join words or word groups used the same way	both . . . and, either . . . or, neither . . . nor
Subordinating	introduces a clause that cannot stand by itself as a complete sentence	although, after, as, before, because, when, if, unless
Interjection	expresses emotion	wow, ouch, hurrah

Quick Reference: The Sentence and Its Parts

The diagrams that follow will give you a brief review of the essentials of a sentence and some of its parts.

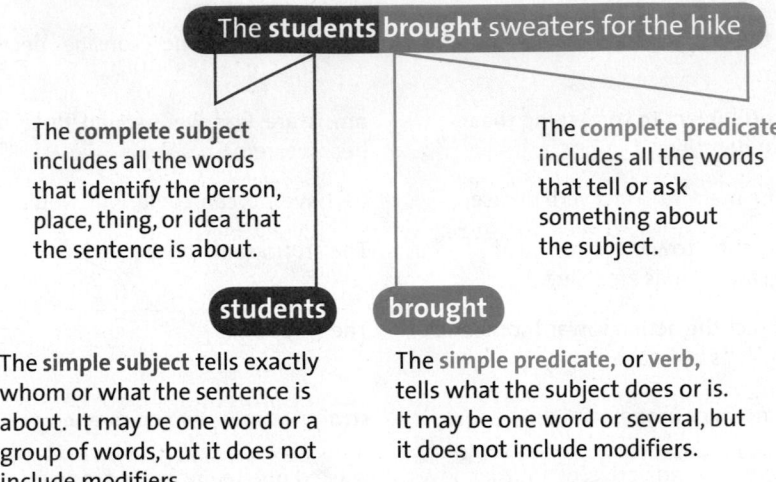

The **students brought** sweaters for the hike

The **complete subject** includes all the words that identify the person, place, thing, or idea that the sentence is about.

The **complete predicate** includes all the words that tell or ask something about the subject.

students

The **simple subject** tells exactly whom or what the sentence is about. It may be one word or a group of words, but it does not include modifiers.

brought

The **simple predicate**, or **verb**, tells what the subject does or is. It may be one word or several, but it does not include modifiers.

Every word in a sentence is part of a complete subject or a complete predicate.

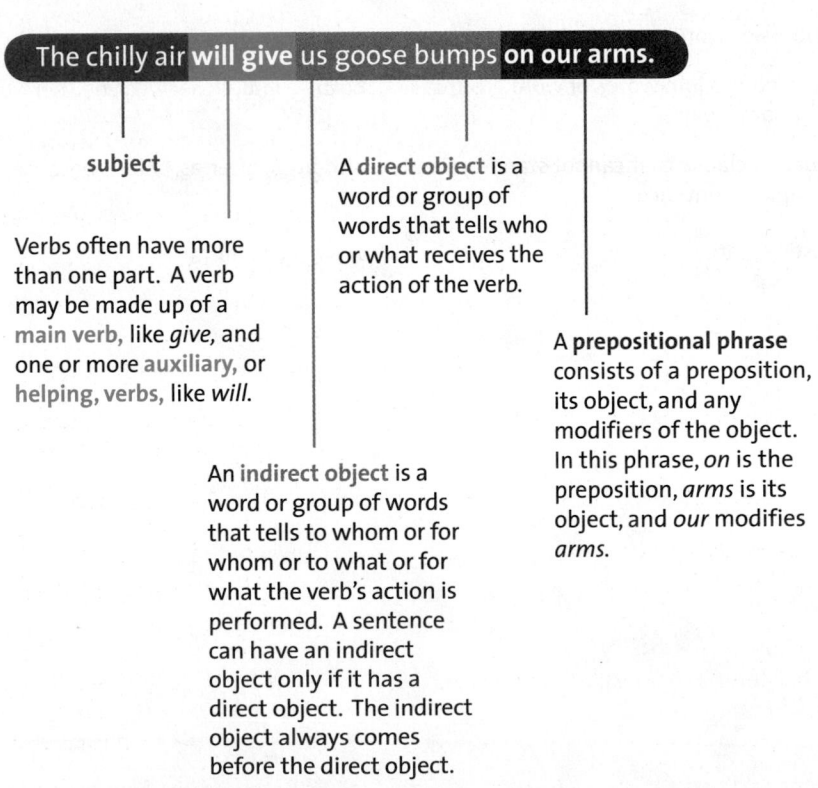

The chilly air **will give** us goose bumps **on our arms.**

subject

Verbs often have more than one part. A verb may be made up of a **main verb**, like *give*, and one or more **auxiliary**, or **helping**, **verbs**, like *will*.

A **direct object** is a word or group of words that tells who or what receives the action of the verb.

An **indirect object** is a word or group of words that tells to whom or for whom or to what or for what the verb's action is performed. A sentence can have an indirect object only if it has a direct object. The indirect object always comes before the direct object.

A **prepositional phrase** consists of a preposition, its object, and any modifiers of the object. In this phrase, *on* is the preposition, *arms* is its object, and *our* modifies *arms*.

Quick Reference: Punctuation

MARK	FUNCTION	EXAMPLES
End Marks period, question mark, exclamation point	ends a sentence	We can start now. When would you like to leave? What a fantastic hit!
period	follows an initial or abbreviation **Exception:** postal abbreviations of states	Mrs. Dorothy Parker, McDougal Littell Inc., C. P. Cavafy, P.M., A.D., lb., oz., Blvd., Dr. NE (Nebraska), NV (Nevada)
period	follows a number or letter in an outline or a list	I. Volcanoes A. Central-vent 1. Shield
Comma	separates parts of a compound sentence	I had never disliked poetry, but now I really love it.
	separates items in a series	She is brave, loyal, and kind.
	separates adjectives of equal rank that modify the same noun	The slow, easy route is best.
	sets off a term of address	Maria, how can I help you? You must do something, soldier.
	sets off a parenthetical expression	Hard workers, as you know, don't quit. I'm not a quitter, believe me.
	sets off an introductory word, phrase, or dependent clause	Yes, I forgot my key. At the beginning of the day, I feel fresh. While she was out, I was here. Having finished my chores, I went out.
	sets off a nonessential phrase or clause	Ed Pawn, the captain of the chess team, won. Ed Pawn, who is the captain, won. The two leading runners, sprinting toward the finish line, finished in a tie.
	sets off parts of dates and addresses	Mail it by May 14, 2010, to the Hauptman Company, 321 Market Street, Memphis, Tennessee.
	follows the salutation and closing of a letter	Dear Jim, Sincerely yours,
	separates words to avoid confusion	By noon, time had run out. What the minister does, does matter. While cooking, Jim burned his hand.
Semicolon	separates items in a series that contain commas	We spent the first week of summer vacation in Chicago, Illinois; the second week in St. Louis, Missouri; and the third week in Albany, New York.
	separates parts of a compound sentence that are not joined by a coordinating conjunction	The last shall be first; the first shall be last. I read the Bible; however, I have not memorized it.
	separates parts of a compound sentence when the parts contain commas	After I ran out of money, I called my parents; but only my sister was home, unfortunately.

MARK	FUNCTION	EXAMPLES
Colon	introduces a list	Those we wrote were the following: Dana, John, and Will.
	introduces a long quotation	Abraham Lincoln wrote: "Four score and seven years ago, our fathers brought forth on this continent a new nation...."
	follows the salutation of a business letter	To Whom It May Concern: Dear Leonard Atole:
	separates certain numbers	1:28 P.M., Genesis 2:5
Dash	indicates an abrupt break in thought	I was thinking of my mother—who is arriving tomorrow—just as you walked in.
Parentheses	enclose less important material	It was so unlike him (John is always on time) that I began to worry. The last World Series game (did you see it?) was fun.
Hyphen	joins parts of a compound adjective before a noun	That's a not-so-happy face.
	joins parts of a compound with *all-*, *ex-*, *self-*, or *-elect*	The ex-firefighter helped rescue him. Our president-elect is self-conscious.
	joins parts of a compound number (to ninety-nine)	My bicycle wheel has twenty-six spokes.
	joins parts of a fraction	My cup is one-third full.
	joins a prefix to a word beginning with a capital letter	Were your grandparents born post-World War II? The mid-April snowstorm surprised everyone.
	indicates that a word is divided at the end of a line	How could you have any reasonable expectations of getting a new computer?
Apostrophe	used with *s* to form the possessive of a noun or an indefinite pronoun	my friend's book, my friends' books, anyone's guess, somebody else's problem
	replaces one or more omitted letters in a contraction or numbers in a date	don't (omitted *o*), he'd (omitted *woul*), the class of '99 (omitted *19*)
	used with *s* to form the plural of a letter	I had two A's on my report card.
Quotation Marks	set off a speaker's exact words	Sara said, "I'm finally ready." "I'm ready," Sara said, "finally." Did Sara say, "I'm ready"? Sara said, "I'm ready!"
	set off the title of a story, an article, a short poem, an essay, a song, or a chapter	I like Bradbury's "All Summer in a Day" and Collins's "On Turning Ten." I learned to play Paul Simon's song "I Am a Rock."
Ellipses	replace material omitted from a quotation	"Early one morning, Mrs. Bunnin wobbled into the classroom lugging a large cardboard box.... Robert was at his desk scribbling a ballpoint tattoo ... on the tops of his knuckles."
Italics	indicate the title of a book, a play, a magazine, a long poem, an opera, a film, or a TV series, or the name of a ship	*In Search of Pompeii, The Phantom Tollbooth, Time,* the *Iliad, The Marriage of Figaro, Lemony Snicket's A Series of Unfortunate Events, American Idol, Titanic*

Quick Reference: Capitalization

CATEGORY	EXAMPLES
People and Titles	
Names and initials of people	Maya Angelou, E. E. Cummings
Titles used before a name	Mrs. Price, Scoutmaster Brenkman
Deities and members of religious groups	Jesus, Allah, Buddha, Zeus, Baptists, Roman Catholics
Names of ethnic and national groups	Hispanics, Jews, African Americans
Geographical Names	
Cities, states, countries, continents	Philadelphia, Kansas, Japan, Europe
Regions, bodies of water, mountains	the South, Lake Baikal, Mount Everest
Geographic features, parks	Great Basin, Yellowstone National Park
Streets and roads, planets	318 East Sutton Drive, Charles Court, Jupiter, Mars
Organizations, Events, Etc.	
Companies, organizations, teams	Ford Motor Company, Boy Scouts of America, St. Louis Cardinals
Buildings, bridges, monuments	Empire State Building, Eads Bridge, Washington Monument
Documents, awards	Declaration of Independence, Stanley Cup
Special named events	Mardi Gras, World Series
Government bodies, historical periods and events	U.S. Senate, House of Representatives, Middle Ages, Vietnam War
Days and months, holidays	Thursday, March, Thanksgiving, Labor Day
Specific cars, boats, trains, planes	Porsche, *Carpathia, Southwest Chief,* Concorde
Proper Adjectives	
Adjectives formed from proper nouns	French cooking, Spanish omelet, Edwardian age, Western movie
First Words and the Pronoun *I*	
First word in a sentence or quotation	This is it. He said, "Let's go."
First word of sentence in parentheses that is not within another sentence	The spelling rules are covered in another section. (Consult that section for more information.)
First words in the salutation and closing of a letter	Dear Madam, Very truly yours,
First word in each line of most poetry Personal pronoun *I*	Then am I A happy fly If I live Or if I die.
First word, last word, and all important words in a title	"Alone in the Nets," *Under the Royal Palms*

1 Nouns

A **noun** is a word used to name a person, a place, a thing, an idea, a quality, or an action. Nouns can be classified in several ways.

For more information on different types of nouns, see Quick Reference: Parts of Speech, page R46.

1.1 COMMON NOUNS

Common nouns are general names, common to entire groups.

1.2 PROPER NOUNS

Proper nouns name specific, one-of-a-kind people, places, and things.

Common	Proper
volcano, student, country, president	Mount Vesuvius, June, China, President Cleveland

For more information, see Quick Reference: Capitalization, page R51.

1.3 SINGULAR AND PLURAL NOUNS

A noun may take a singular or a plural form, depending on whether it names a single person, place, thing, or idea or more than one. Make sure you use appropriate spellings when forming plurals.

Singular	Plural
walrus, bully, lagoon, goose	walruses, bullies, lagoons, geese

For more information, see Forming Plural Nouns, page R73.

1.4 POSSESSIVE NOUNS

A **possessive noun** shows who or what owns something.

For more information, see Forming Possessives, page R74.

2 Pronouns

A **pronoun** is a word that is used in place of a noun or another pronoun. The word or word group to which the pronoun refers is called its **antecedent**.

2.1 PERSONAL PRONOUNS

Personal pronouns change their form to express person, number, gender, and case. The forms of these pronouns are shown in the following chart.

	Nominative	Objective	Possessive
Singular			
First person	I	me	my, mine
Second person	you	you	your, yours
Third person	she, he, it	her, him, it	her, hers, his, its
Plural			
First person	we	us	our, ours
Second person	you	you	your, yours
Third person	they	them	their, theirs

2.2 AGREEMENT WITH ANTECEDENT

Pronouns should agree with their antecedents in number, gender, and person.

If an antecedent is singular, use a singular pronoun.
> **EXAMPLE:** *That **poem** was fun to read. **It** rhymed.*

If an antecedent is plural, use a plural pronoun.
> **EXAMPLES:** ***Poets** choose **their** words carefully.*
> *I like **poems,** but Mischa doesn't care for **them.***

The gender of a pronoun must be the same as the gender of its antecedent.
> **EXAMPLE:** ***Eve Merriam's** creativity makes **her** poems easy to remember.*

The person of the pronoun must be the same as the person of its antecedent. As the chart in Section 2.1 shows, a pronoun can be in first-person, second-person, or third-person form.
> **EXAMPLE:** ***We** each have **our** favorite poets.*

Rewrite each sentence so that the underlined pronoun agrees with its antecedent.

1. The speaker in Maya Angelou's poem "Life Doesn't Frighten Me" talks about <u>their</u> fears.

2. When I read this poem, <u>we</u> felt braver already.

3. Scary things lose <u>its</u> power.

4. Even frogs and snakes don't seem as bad as <u>you</u> usually do.

5. I want to know how to be unafraid in <u>her</u> life.

2.3 PRONOUN FORMS

Personal pronouns change form to show how they function in sentences. The three forms are the subject form, the object form, and the possessive form. For examples of these pronouns, see the chart in Section 2.1.

A **subject pronoun** is used as a subject in a sentence.

> EXAMPLE: *"All Summer in a Day" was written by Ray Bradbury. He chose Venus as the setting.*

Also use the subject form when the pronoun follows a linking verb.

> EXAMPLE: *The girl in the closet was she.*

An **object pronoun** is used as a direct object, an indirect object, or the object of a preposition.

> SUBJECT   OBJECT
> *They locked her in it.*
>   OBJECT OF PREPOSITION

A **possessive pronoun** shows ownership. The pronouns *mine, yours, hers, his, its, ours,* and *theirs* can be used in place of nouns.

> EXAMPLE: *The poem about the sun was hers.*

The pronouns *my, your, her, his, its, our,* and *their* are used before nouns.

> EXAMPLE: *The other children got their revenge on Margot.*

WATCH OUT! Many spelling errors can be avoided if you watch out for *its* and *their.* Don't confuse the possessive pronoun *its* with the contraction *it's,* meaning "it is" or "it has." The homonyms *they're* (a contraction of *they are*) and *there* ("in that place") are often mistakenly used for *their.*

TIP To decide which pronoun to use in a comparison, such as "He tells better tales than (I *or* me)," fill in the missing word(s): *He tells better tales than I tell.*

Write the correct pronoun form to complete each sentence.

1. The children saw the sun in (their, they) dreams.

2. Margot really remembered that yellow flower and (its, her) warmth.

3. Margot was different, and the others feared (she, her).

4. The children thought, "(We, Us) will punish you."

5. The sun came out, but Margot didn't see (them, it).

2.4 REFLEXIVE AND INTENSIVE PRONOUNS

These pronouns are formed by adding *-self* or *-selves* to certain personal pronouns. Their forms are the same, and they differ only in how they are used.

A **reflexive pronoun** follows a verb or preposition and reflects back on an earlier noun or pronoun.

> EXAMPLES: *He likes himself too much.*
> *She is now herself again.*

Intensive pronouns intensify or emphasize the nouns or pronouns to which they refer.

> EXAMPLES: *They themselves will educate their children.*
> *You yourself did it.*

WATCH OUT! Avoid using *hisself* or *theirselves.* Standard English does not include these forms.

> NONSTANDARD: *The children congratulated theirselves.*
> STANDARD: *The children congratulated themselves.*

2.5 DEMONSTRATIVE PRONOUNS

Demonstrative pronouns point out things and persons near and far.

	Singular	Plural
Near	this	these
Far	that	those

2.6 INDEFINITE PRONOUNS

Indefinite pronouns do not refer to specific persons or things and usually have no antecedents. The chart shows some commonly used indefinite pronouns.

Singular	Plural	Singular or Plural	
another	both	all	none
anybody	few	any	some
no one	many	more	most
neither			

TIP Indefinite pronouns that end in *one, body,* or *thing* are always singular.

INCORRECT: *Did everybody play their part well?*

If the indefinite pronoun might refer to either a male or a female, *his or her* may be used to refer to it, or the sentence may be rewritten.

CORRECT: *Did everybody play his or her part well?*
Did all the students play their parts well?

2.7 INTERROGATIVE PRONOUNS

An **interrogative pronoun** tells a reader or listener that a question is coming. The interrogative pronouns are *who, whom, whose, which,* and *what.*

EXAMPLES: *Who is going to rehearse with you?*
From whom did you receive the script?

TIP *Who* is used as a subject; *whom,* as an object. To find out which pronoun you need to use in a question, change the question to a statement.

QUESTION: *(Who/Whom) did you meet there?*
STATEMENT: *You met (?) there.*

Since the verb has a subject (*you*), the needed word must be the object form, *whom.*

EXAMPLE: *Whom did you meet there?*

WATCH OUT! A special problem arises when you use an interrupter, such as *do you think,* within a question.

EXAMPLE: *(Who/Whom) do you think will win?*

If you eliminate the interrupter, it is clear that the word you need is *who.*

2.8 RELATIVE PRONOUNS

Relative pronouns relate, or connect, adjective clauses to the words they modify in sentences. The noun or pronoun that a relative clause modifies is the antecedent of the relative pronoun. Here are the relative pronouns and their uses.

	Subject	Object	Possessive
Person	who	whom	whose
Thing	which	which	whose
Thing/Person	that	that	whose

Often, short sentences with related ideas can be combined by using a relative pronoun to create a more effective sentence.

SHORT SENTENCE: *Lewis Carroll wrote "The Walrus and the Carpenter."*

RELATED SENTENCE: *"The Walrus and the Carpenter" is a poem in his book* Through the Looking Glass.

COMBINED SENTENCE: *Lewis Carroll wrote "The Walrus and the Carpenter," which is a poem in his book* Through the Looking Glass.

GRAMMAR PRACTICE

Write the correct form of each incorrect pronoun.

1. Whom eats the Oysters in Lewis Carroll's poem?
2. The Carpenter doesn't feel sympathy for who?
3. Everybody enjoys their walk.
4. Few of the Oysters believe what is happening to it.
5. The Walrus cries but eats the biggest Oysters hisself.

2.9 PRONOUN REFERENCE PROBLEMS

You should always be able to identify the word a pronoun refers to. Avoid problems by rewriting sentences.

An **indefinite reference** occurs when the pronoun *it, you,* or *they* does not clearly refer to a specific antecedent.

> UNCLEAR: *They told me how the story ended, and it was annoying.*

> CLEAR: *They told me how the story ended, and I was annoyed.*

A **general reference** occurs when the pronoun *it, this, that, which,* or *such* is used to refer to a general idea rather than a specific antecedent.

> UNCLEAR: *I'd rather not know what happens. That keeps me interested.*

> CLEAR: *I'd rather not know what happens. Not knowing keeps me interested.*

Ambiguous means "having more than one possible meaning." An **ambiguous reference** occurs when a pronoun could refer to two or more antecedents.

> UNCLEAR: *Jan told Danielle that she would read her story aloud.*

> CLEAR: *Jan told Danielle that she would read Danielle's story aloud.*

GRAMMAR PRACTICE

Rewrite the following sentences to correct indefinite, ambiguous, and general pronoun references.

1. In the story "Ghost of the Lagoon," it said even talking about Tupa could bring bad luck.

2. The shark came close to Afa. That made Mako throw the spear.

3. Mako told Afa that he would rescue him.

4. After Mako killed Tupa, they cheered.

3 Verbs

A **verb** is a word that expresses an action, a condition, or a state of being.

*For more information, see **Quick Reference: Parts of Speech**, page R47.*

3.1 ACTION VERBS

Action verbs express mental or physical activity.

> EXAMPLE: *Lucy ran several miles every day.*

3.2 LINKING VERBS

Linking verbs join subjects with words or phrases that rename or describe them.

> EXAMPLE: *After a few months, her shoes were worn out.*

3.3 PRINCIPAL PARTS

Action and linking verbs typically have four principal parts, which are used to form verb tenses. The principal parts are the **present,** the **present participle,** the **past,** and the **past participle.**

Action verbs and some linking verbs also fall into two categories: regular and irregular. A **regular verb** is a verb that forms its past and past participle by adding *-ed* or *-d* to the present form.

Present	Present Participle	Past	Past Participle
jump	(is) jumping	jumped	(has) jumped
solve	(is) solving	solved	(has) solved
grab	(is) grabbing	grabbed	(has) grabbed
carry	(is) carrying	carried	(has) carried

An **irregular verb** is a verb that forms its past and past participle in some other way than by adding *-ed* or *-d* to the present form.

Present	Present Participle	Past	Past Participle
begin	(is) beginning	began	(has) begun
break	(is) breaking	broke	(has) broken
go	(is) going	went	(has) gone

3.4 VERB TENSE

The **tense** of a verb indicates the time of the action or the state of being. An action or state of being can occur in the present, the past, or the future. There are six tenses, each expressing a different range of time.

The **present tense** expresses an action or state that is happening at the present time, occurs regularly, or is constant or generally true. Use the present part.

> NOW: *This apple is rotten.*
>
> REGULAR: *I eat an apple every day.*
>
> GENERAL: *Apples are round.*

The **past tense** expresses an action that began and ended in the past. Use the past part.

> EXAMPLE: *They settled the argument.*

The **future tense** expresses an action or state that will occur. Use *shall* or *will* with the present part.

> EXAMPLE: *You will understand someday.*

The **present perfect tense** expresses an action or state that (1) was completed at an indefinite time in the past or (2) began in the past and continues into the present. Use *have* or *has* with the past participle.

> EXAMPLE: *These buildings have existed for centuries.*

The **past perfect tense** expresses an action in the past that came before another action in the past. Use *had* with the past participle.

> EXAMPLE: *I had told you, but you forgot.*

The **future perfect tense** expresses an action in the future that will be completed before another action in the future. Use *shall have* or *will have* with the past participle.

> EXAMPLE: *She will have found the note by the time I get home.*

TIP A past-tense form of an irregular verb is not used with an auxiliary, or helping, verb, but a past-participle main irregular verb is always used with an auxiliary verb.

> INCORRECT: *He has did that too many times.* (*Did* is the past-tense form of an irregular verb and shouldn't be used with *has.*)
>
> INCORRECT: *He done that too many times.* (*Done* is the past participle of an irregular verb and shouldn't be used without an auxiliary verb.)
>
> CORRECT: *He has done that too many times.*

3.5 PROGRESSIVE FORMS

The progressive forms of the six tenses show ongoing actions. Use forms of *be* with the present participles of verbs.

> PRESENT PROGRESSIVE: *Angelo is taking the test.*
>
> PAST PROGRESSIVE: *Angelo was taking the test.*
>
> FUTURE PROGRESSIVE: *Angelo will be taking the test.*
>
> PRESENT PERFECT PROGRESSIVE: *Angelo has been taking the test.*
>
> PAST PERFECT PROGRESSIVE: *Angelo had been taking the test.*
>
> FUTURE PERFECT PROGRESSIVE: *Angelo will have been taking the test.*

WATCH OUT! Do not shift from tense to tense needlessly. Watch out for these special cases.

- In most compound sentences and in sentences with compound predicates, keep the tenses the same.

  > INCORRECT: *She smiled and shake his hand.*
  >
  > CORRECT: *She smiled and shook his hand.*

- If one past action happens before another, do shift tenses.

  > INCORRECT: *He remembered what he studied.*
  >
  > CORRECT: *He remembered what he had studied.*

GRAMMAR PRACTICE

Rewrite each sentence, using a form of the verb in parentheses. Identify each form that you use.

1. Helen Keller (become) blind and deaf before she (be) two.

2. A wonderful teacher (change) her life.

3. Anne Sullivan (be) almost blind before she (have) an operation.

4. Even now, Keller (be) an inspiration to everyone with a disability.

5. People (remember) both Helen and her teacher for years to come.

Rewrite each sentence to correct an error in tense.

1. Helen Keller writes a book about her life.

2. She described how she learns to understand language.

3. She felt like she knew it once and forgotten it.

4. Anne Sullivan was a determined teacher and does not give up.

5. Helen had began a life of learning.

3.6 ACTIVE AND PASSIVE VOICE

The voice of a verb tells whether its subject performs or receives the action expressed by the verb. When the subject performs the action, the verb is in the **active voice.** When the subject is the receiver of the action, the verb is in the **passive voice.**

Compare these two sentences:

ACTIVE: *May Swenson wrote "Analysis of Baseball."*

PASSIVE: *"Analysis of Baseball" was written by May Swenson.*

To form the passive voice, use a form of *be* with the past participle of the verb.

WATCH OUT! Use the passive voice sparingly. It can make writing awkward and less direct.

AWKWARD: *"Analysis of Baseball" is a poem that was written by May Swenson.*

BETTER: *May Swenson wrote the poem "Analysis of Baseball."*

There are occasions when you will choose to use the passive voice because

- you want to emphasize the receiver: *The king was shot.*

- the doer is unknown: *My books were stolen.*

- the doer is unimportant: *French is spoken here.*

4 Modifiers

Modifiers are words or groups of words that change or limit the meanings of other words. Adjectives and adverbs are common modifiers.

4.1 ADJECTIVES

Adjectives modify nouns and pronouns by telling which one, what kind, how many, or how much.

WHICH ONE: *this, that, these, those*
EXAMPLE: *This poem moves along quickly.*

WHAT KIND: *square, dirty, fast, regular*
EXAMPLE: *Fast runners make baseball exciting.*

HOW MANY: *some, few, both, thousands*
EXAMPLE: *Thousands of fans cheer in the stands.*

HOW MUCH: *more, less, enough, as much*
EXAMPLE: *I had more fun watching the game than I expected.*

4.2 PREDICATE ADJECTIVES

Most adjectives come before the nouns they modify, as in the examples above. A **predicate adjective,** however, follows a linking verb and describes the subject.

EXAMPLE: *Baseball players are strong.*

Be especially careful to use adjectives (not adverbs) after such linking verbs as *look, feel, grow, taste,* and *smell.*

EXAMPLE: *Exercising feels good.*

4.3 ADVERBS

Adverbs modify verbs, adjectives, and other adverbs by telling where, when, how, or to what extent.

WHERE: *The children played outside.*

WHEN: *The author spoke yesterday.*

HOW: *We walked slowly behind the leader.*

TO WHAT EXTENT: *He worked very hard.*

Adverbs may occur in many places in sentences, both before and after the words they modify.

EXAMPLES: *Suddenly the wind shifted.*

The wind suddenly shifted.

The wind shifted suddenly.

4.4 ADJECTIVE OR ADVERB?

Many adverbs are formed by adding *-ly* to adjectives.

EXAMPLES: *sweet, sweetly; gentle, gently*

However, *-ly* added to a noun will usually yield an adjective.

EXAMPLES: *friend, friendly; woman, womanly*

4.5 COMPARISON OF MODIFIERS

Modifiers can be used to compare two or more things. The form of a modifier shows the degree of comparison. Both adjectives and adverbs have **comparative** and **superlative** forms.

The **comparative form** is used to compare two things, groups, or actions.

EXAMPLES: *Today's weather is hotter than yesterday's.*

The boy got tired more quickly than his sister did.

The **superlative form** is used to compare more than two things, groups, or actions.

EXAMPLES: *This has been the hottest month ever recorded.*

Older people were most affected by the heat.

4.6 REGULAR COMPARISONS

Most one-syllable and some two-syllable adjectives and adverbs have comparatives and superlatives formed by adding *-er* and *-est*. All three-syllable and most two-syllable modifiers have comparatives and superlatives formed with *more* or *most*.

Modifier	Comparative	Superlative
messy	messier	messiest
quick	quicker	quickest
wild	wilder	wildest
tired	more tired	most tired
often	more often	most often

WATCH OUT! Note that spelling changes must sometimes be made to form the comparatives and superlatives of modifiers.

EXAMPLES: *friendly, friendlier* (Change *y* to *i* and add the ending.)

sad, sadder (Double the final consonant and add the ending.)

4.7 IRREGULAR COMPARISONS

Some commonly used modifiers have irregular comparative and superlative forms. They are listed in the following chart. You may wish to memorize them.

Modifier	Comparative	Superlative
good	better	best
bad	worse	worst
far	farther *or* further	farthest *or* furthest
little	less *or* lesser	least
many	more	most
well	better	best
much	more	most

4.8 PROBLEMS WITH MODIFIERS

Study the tips that follow to avoid common mistakes:

Farther and Further Use *farther* for distances; use *further* for everything else.

Double Comparisons Make a comparison by using *-er/-est* or by using *more/most*. Using *-er* with *more* or using *-est* with *most* is incorrect.

INCORRECT: *I like her more better than she likes me.*

CORRECT: *I like her better than she likes me.*

Illogical Comparisons An illogical or confusing comparison results when two unrelated things are compared or when something is compared with itself. The word *other* or the word *else* should be used when comparing an individual member to the rest of a group.

ILLOGICAL: *I like "Fog" more than any poem.* (implies that "Fog" isn't a poem)

LOGICAL: *I like "Fog" more than any other poem.* (identifies that "Fog" is a poem)

Bad vs. Badly *Bad*, always an adjective, is used before a noun or after a linking verb. *Badly*, always an adverb, never modifies a noun. Be sure to use the right form after a linking verb.

INCORRECT: *I felt badly that I missed the game.*

CORRECT: *I felt bad that I missed the game.*

Good vs. Well *Good* is always an adjective. It is used before a noun or after a linking verb. *Well* is often an adverb meaning "expertly" or "properly." *Well* can also be used as an adjective after a linking verb when it means "in good health."

INCORRECT: *I wrote my essay good.*

CORRECT: *I wrote my essay well.*

CORRECT: *I didn't feel well when I wrote it, though.*

Double Negatives If you add a negative word to a sentence that is already negative, the result will be an error known as a double negative. When using *not* or *-n't* with a verb, use *any-* words, such as *anybody* or *anything*, rather than *no-* words, such as *nobody* or *nothing*, later in the sentence.

INCORRECT: *The teacher didn't like nobody's paper.*

CORRECT: *The teacher didn't like anybody's paper.*

Using *hardly, barely,* or *scarcely* after a negative word is also incorrect.

INCORRECT: *My friends couldn't hardly catch up.*

CORRECT: *My friends could hardly catch up.*

Misplaced Modifiers Sometimes a modifier is placed so far away from the word it modifies that the intended meaning of the sentence is unclear.

Prepositional phrases and participial phrases are often misplaced. Place modifiers as close as possible to the words they modify.

MISPLACED: *We found the child in the park who was missing.*

CLEARER: *We found the child who was missing in the park.* (The child was missing, not the park.)

Dangling Modifiers Sometimes a modifier doesn't appear to modify any word in a sentence. Most dangling modifiers are participial phrases or infinitive phrases.

DANGLING: *Looking out the window, his brother was seen driving by.*

CLEARER: *Looking out the window, Josh saw his brother driving by.*

GRAMMAR PRACTICE

Choose the correct word or words from each pair in parentheses.

1. According to Gary Paulsen, bears were a (bad, badly) problem in the woods.

2. The (worse, worst) time of year was spring.

3. The bears didn't have (any, no) interest in the yard animals.

4. They stalked the dogs really (good, well), though.

5. Scarface was (more, most) daring than any other bear in the forest.

GRAMMAR PRACTICE

Rewrite each sentence that contains a misplaced or dangling modifier. Write "correct" if the sentence is written correctly.

1. Coyotes know how to survive in the wild.

2. Hunting their prey, we have seen them in the forest.

3. Looking out the window, a coyote was seen in the yard.

4. My brother and I found books about coyotes at the library.

5. We learned that wolves are their natural enemies reading about them.

5 The Sentence and Its Parts

A **sentence** is a group of words used to express a complete thought. A complete sentence has a subject and a predicate.

For more information, see **Quick Reference: The Sentence and Its Parts,** *page R48.*

5.1 KINDS OF SENTENCES

There are four basic types of sentences.

Type	Definition	Example
Declarative	states a fact, a wish, an intent, or a feeling	Avi remembers being young.
Interrogative	asks a question	Have you read "Scout's Honor"?
Imperative	gives a command or direction	Find a copy.
Exclamatory	expresses strong feeling or excitement	It's really funny!

5.2 COMPOUND SUBJECTS AND PREDICATES

A compound subject consists of two or more subjects that share the same verb. They are typically joined by the coordinating conjunction *and* or *or.*

> **EXAMPLE:** *A short story or novel will keep you interested.*

A compound predicate consists of two or more predicates that share the same subject. They too are usually joined by a coordinating conjunction: *and, but,* or *or.*

> **EXAMPLE:** *The class finished all the poetry but did not read the short stories.*

5.3 COMPLEMENTS

A **complement** is a word or group of words that completes the meaning of a sentence. Some sentences contain only a subject and a verb. Most sentences, however, require additional words placed after the verb to complete the meaning of the sentence. There are three kinds of complements: direct objects, indirect objects, and subject complements.

Direct objects are words or word groups that receive the action of action verbs. A direct object answers the question *what* or *whom.*

> **EXAMPLES:** *Daria caught the ball.* (Caught what?)
> *She tagged the runner.* (Tagged whom?)

Indirect objects tell to whom or what or for whom or what the actions of verbs are performed. Indirect objects come before direct objects. In the examples that follow, the indirect objects are highlighted.

> **EXAMPLES:** *The audience gave us a standing ovation.* (Gave to whom?)
> *We offered the newspaper an interview.* (Offered to what?)

Subject complements come after linking verbs and identify or describe the subjects. A subject complement that names or identifies a subject is called a **predicate nominative.** Predicate nominatives include **predicate nouns** and **predicate pronouns.**

> **EXAMPLES:** *The students were happy campers.*
> *The best actor in the play is he.*

A subject complement that describes a subject is called a **predicate adjective.**

> **EXAMPLE:** *The coach seemed thrilled.*

6 Phrases

A **phrase** is a group of related words that does not contain a subject and a predicate but functions in a sentence as a single part of speech.

6.1 PREPOSITIONAL PHRASES

A **prepositional phrase** is a phrase that consists of a preposition, its object, and any modifiers of the object. Prepositional phrases that modify nouns or pronouns are called **adjective phrases.** Prepositional phrases that modify verbs, adjectives, or adverbs are **adverb phrases.**

> **ADJECTIVE PHRASE:** *The central character of the story is a villain.*
> **ADVERB PHRASE:** *He reveals his nature in the first scene.*

6.2 APPOSITIVES AND APPOSITIVE PHRASES

An **appositive** is a noun or pronoun that identifies or renames another noun or pronoun. An **appositive phrase** includes an appositive and modifiers of it. An appositive usually follows the noun or pronoun it identifies.

An appositive can be either **essential** or **nonessential**. An **essential appositive** provides information that is needed to identify what is referred to by the preceding noun or pronoun.

> EXAMPLE: *Aesop's story is about the characters Ant and Grasshopper.*

A **nonessential appositive** adds extra information about a noun or pronoun whose meaning is already clear. Nonessential appositives and appositive phrases are set off with commas.

> EXAMPLE: *The story, a fable, has an important message.*

7 Verbals and Verbal Phrases

A **verbal** is a verb form that is used as a noun, an adjective, or an adverb. A **verbal phrase** consists of a verbal along with its modifiers and complements. There are three kinds of verbals: infinitives, participles, and gerunds.

7.1 INFINITIVES AND INFINITIVE PHRASES

An **infinitive** is a verb form that usually begins with *to* and functions as a noun, an adjective, or an adverb. An **infinitive phrase** consists of an infinitive plus its modifiers and complements.

> NOUN: *To be happy is not easy.* (subject)
> *I want to have fun.* (direct object)
> *My hope is to enjoy every day.* (predicate nominative)
> ADJECTIVE: *That's a goal to be proud of.* (adjective modifying *goal*)
> ADVERB: *I'll work to achieve it.* (adverb modifying *work*)

Because *to*, the sign of the infinitive, precedes infinitives, it is usually easy to recognize them. However, sometimes *to* may be omitted.

> EXAMPLE: *No one can help me [to] achieve my goal.*

7.2 PARTICIPLES AND PARTICIPIAL PHRASES

A **participle** is a verb form that functions as an adjective. Like adjectives, participles modify nouns and pronouns. Most participles are present-participle forms, ending in *-ing*, or past-participle forms ending in *-ed* or *-en*. In the examples below, the participles are highlighted.

> MODIFYING A NOUN: *The waxed floor was sticky.*
> MODIFYING A PRONOUN: *Sighing, she mopped up the mess.*

Participial phrases are participles with all their modifiers and complements.

> MODIFYING A NOUN: *The girls working on the project are very energetic.*
> MODIFYING A PRONOUN: *Having finished his work, he took a nap.*

7.3 DANGLING AND MISPLACED PARTICIPLES

A participle or participial phrase should be placed as close as possible to the word that it modifies. Otherwise the meaning of the sentence may not be clear.

> MISPLACED: *The boys were looking for squirrels searching the trees.*
> CLEARER: *The boys searching the trees were looking for squirrels.*

A participle or participial phrase that does not clearly modify anything in a sentence is called a **dangling participle.** A dangling participle causes confusion because it appears to modify a word that it cannot sensibly modify. Correct a dangling participle by providing a word for the participle to modify.

> DANGLING: *Waiting for the show to start, the phone rang.* (The phone wasn't waiting.)
> CLEARER: *Waiting for the show to start, I heard the phone ring.*

7.4 GERUNDS AND GERUND PHRASES

A **gerund** is a verb form ending in *-ing* that functions as a noun. Gerunds may perform any function nouns perform.

> SUBJECT: *Cooking is a good way to relax.*
> DIRECT OBJECT: *I enjoy cooking.*

INDIRECT OBJECT: *They should give cooking a chance.*

SUBJECT COMPLEMENT: *My favorite pastime is cooking.*

OBJECT OF PREPOSITION: *A love of cooking runs in the family.*

Gerund phrases are gerunds with all their modifiers and complements.

SUBJECT: *Depending on luck never got me far.*

OBJECT OF PREPOSITION: *I will finish before leaving the office.*

APPOSITIVE: *Her hobby, training horses, finally led to a career.*

GRAMMAR PRACTICE

Rewrite each sentence, adding the type of phrase shown in parentheses.

1. "The Jacket" is by Gary Soto. (appositive phrase)

2. He needed a new jacket. (infinitive phrase)

3. He didn't like it and was embarrassed. (prepositional phrase)

4. It brought him bad luck. (gerund phrase)

5. The ugly jacket was like a brother. (participial phrase)

8 Clauses

A **clause** is a group of words that contains a subject and a predicate. A sentence may contain one clause or more than one. The sentence in the following example contains two clauses. The subject and verb in each clause are highlighted.

EXAMPLE: *Some students like to play sports, but others prefer to play music.*

There are two kinds of clauses: independent clauses and subordinate clauses.

8.1 INDEPENDENT AND SUBORDINATE CLAUSES

An independent clause expresses a complete thought and can stand alone as a sentence.

INDEPENDENT CLAUSE: *I read "Night Journey."*

A sentence may contain more than one independent clause.

EXAMPLE: *I read it once, and I liked it.*

In the preceding example, the coordinating conjunction *and* joins two independent clauses.

For more information, see **Coordinating Conjunctions,** *page R47.*

A **subordinate (dependent) clause** cannot stand alone as a sentence because it does not express a complete thought. By itself, a subordinate clause is a sentence fragment. It needs an independent clause to complete its meaning. Most subordinate clauses are introduced by words such as *after, although, because, if, that, when,* and *while.*

SUBORDINATE CLAUSE : *Because they worked hard.*

A subordinate clause can be joined to an independent clause to make a sentence that expresses a complete thought. In the following example, the subordinate clause explains why the students did well on the test.

EXAMPLE: *The students did well on the test because they worked hard*

GRAMMAR PRACTICE

Identify the underlined group of words in each sentence as either an independent clause *(IC)* or a subordinate clause *(SC)*.

1. He stopped at the library before he came home.

2. You have to arrive early if you want to get a front-row seat.

3. She bought a ticket when she boarded the train.

4. I finished my homework while you were gone.

5. Because the test was long, the teacher gave the students extra time to finish it.

9 The Structure of Sentences

When classified by their structure, there are four kinds of sentences: simple, compound, complex, and compound-complex.

9.1 SIMPLE SENTENCES

A **simple sentence** is a sentence that has one independent clause and no subordinate clauses. Even a simple sentence can include many details.

EXAMPLES: *Chloe looked for the train.*

Seth drove to the station in an old red pickup truck.

A simple sentence may contain a compound subject or a compound verb. A compound subject is made up of two or more subjects that share the same verb. A compound verb is made up of two or more verbs that have the same subject.

EXAMPLES: *Seth and Chloe drove to the station.* (compound subject)

They waved and shouted as the train pulled in. (compound verb)

9.2 COMPOUND SENTENCES

A **compound sentence** consists of two or more independent clauses. The clauses in compound sentences are joined with commas and coordinating conjunctions (*and, but, or, nor, yet, for, so*) or with semicolons. Like simple sentences, compound sentences do not contain any subordinate clauses.

EXAMPLES: *We all get older, but not everyone gets wiser.*

Some young people don't want to grow up; others grow up too quickly.

WATCH OUT! Do not confuse compound sentences with simple sentences that have compound parts.

EXAMPLE: *Books and clothes were scattered all over her room.*

Here, the conjunction *and* is used to join the parts of a compound subject, not the clauses in a compound sentence.

GRAMMAR PRACTICE

Identify each sentence as simple *(S)* or compound *(CD)*.

1. Justin and his dad loved bikes.

2. They had their garage set up like a bike shop; they worked there all the time.

3. Justin bought a couple of old bikes and fixed them up.

4. He decided to donate them to a homeless shelter.

5. Many people offered him their old bikes for free.

6. Last year, Justin fixed 250 bikes and gave them all away.

9.3 COMPLEX SENTENCES

A **complex sentence** consists of one independent clause and one or more subordinate clauses. Most subordinate clauses start with words such as *when, until, who, where, because,* and *so that.*

EXAMPLES: *I often wonder what I'll be like in ten years.*

When I think about the future, I see a canvas that has nothing on it.

GRAMMAR PRACTICE

Write these sentences on a sheet of paper. Underline each independent clause once and each subordinate clause twice.

1. Although the Foster Grandparent Program is more than 40 years old, many people do not know about it.

2. This program was established so that children with special needs could get extra attention.

3. Anyone can volunteer who is at least 60 years old and meets other requirements.

4. After a volunteer is trained, he or she works 15 to 40 hours a week.

5. Foster grandparents often help with homework so that the children can improve in school.

6. Since this program was founded in 1965, there have been foster grandparent projects in all 50 states.

9.4 COMPOUND-COMPLEX SENTENCES

A **compound-complex** sentence contains two or more independent clauses and one or more subordinate clauses. Compound-complex sentences are both compound and complex. If you start with a compound sentence, all you need to do to form a compound-complex sentence is add a subordinate clause.

> COMPOUND: *All the students knew the answer, yet they were too shy to volunteer.*

> COMPOUND-COMPLEX: *All the students knew the answer that their teacher expected, yet they were too shy to volunteer.*

GRAMMAR PRACTICE

Identify each sentence as compound *(CD)*, complex *(C)*, or compound-complex *(CC)*.

1. In 1998, a hurricane swept through Central America, where it hit Honduras and Nicaragua especially hard.

2. Hurricane Mitch was one of the strongest storms ever in this region; it caused great destruction.

3. People on the coast tried to flee to higher ground, but flooding and mudslides made escape difficult.

4. More than 9,000 people were killed, and crops and roads were wiped out.

5. TV images of homeless and hungry people touched many Americans, who responded generously.

6. They donated money and supplies, which were flown to the region.

7. Volunteers helped clear roads so that supplies could get to villages that needed them.

8. Charity groups distributed food and safe drinking water, and they handed out sleeping bags and mosquito nets, which were needed in the tropical climate.

9. Medical volunteers treated people who desperately needed care.

10. Other volunteers rebuilt homes, and they helped restore the farm economy so that people could earn a living again.

10 Writing Complete Sentences

Remember, a sentence is a group of words that expresses a complete thought. In writing that you wish to share with a reader, try to avoid both sentence fragments and run-on sentences.

10.1 CORRECTING FRAGMENTS

A **sentence fragment** is a group of words that is only part of a sentence. It does not express a complete thought and may be confusing to a reader or listener. A sentence fragment may be lacking a subject, a predicate, or both.

> FRAGMENT: *Didn't care about sports.* (no subject)

> CORRECTED: *The lawyer didn't care about sports.*

> FRAGMENT: *Her middle-school son.* (no predicate)

> CORRECTED: *Her middle-school son played on the soccer team.*

> FRAGMENT: *Before every game.* (neither subject nor predicate)

> CORRECTED: *Before every game, he tried to teach his mom the rules.*

In your writing, fragments may be a result of haste or incorrect punctuation. Sometimes fixing a fragment will be a matter of attaching it to a preceding or following sentence.

> FRAGMENT: *She made an effort. But just couldn't make sense of the game.*

> CORRECTED: *She made an effort but just couldn't make sense of the game.*

10.2 CORRECTING RUN-ON SENTENCES

A **run-on sentence** is made up of two or more sentences written as though they were one. Some run-ons have no punctuation within them. Others may have only commas where conjunctions or stronger punctuation marks are necessary.

Use your judgment in correcting run-on sentences, as you have choices. You can change a run-on to two sentences if the thoughts are not closely connected. If the thoughts are closely related, you can keep the run-on as one sentence by adding a semicolon or a conjunction.

RUN-ON: *Most parents watched the game his mother read a book instead.*

MAKE TWO SENTENCES: *Most parents watched the game. His mother read a book instead.*

RUN-ON: *Most parents watched the game they played sports themselves.*

USE A SEMICOLON: *Most parents watched the game; they played sports themselves.*

ADD A CONJUNCTION: *Most parents watched the game since they played sports themselves.*

WATCH OUT! When you form compound sentences, make sure you use appropriate punctuation: a comma before a coordinating conjunction, a semicolon when there is no coordinating conjunction. A very common mistake is to use a comma without a conjunction or instead of a semicolon. This error is called a **comma splice.**

INCORRECT: *He finished the job, he left the village.*

CORRECT: *He finished the job, and he left the village.*

11 Subject-Verb Agreement

The subject and verb in a clause must agree in number. Agreement means that if the subject is singular, the verb is also singular, and if the subject is plural, the verb is also plural.

11.1 BASIC AGREEMENT

Fortunately, agreement between subjects and verbs in English is simple. Most verbs show the difference between singular and plural only in the third person of the present tense. In the present tense, the third-person singular form ends in -s.

Present-Tense Verb Forms	
Singular	**Plural**
I sleep	we sleep
you sleep	you sleep
she, he, it sleeps	they sleep

11.2 AGREEMENT WITH *BE*

The verb *be* presents special problems in agreement, because this verb does not follow the usual verb patterns.

Forms of *Be*			
Present Tense		**Past Tense**	
Singular	**Plural**	**Singular**	**Plural**
I am	we are	I was	we were
you are	you are	you were	you were
she, he, it is	they are	she, he, it was	they were

11.3 WORDS BETWEEN SUBJECT AND VERB

A verb agrees only with its subject. When words come between a subject and a verb, ignore them when considering proper agreement. Identify the subject and make sure the verb agrees with it.

EXAMPLES: *The poem I read describes a moose.*

The moose in the poem searches for a place where he belongs.

11.4 AGREEMENT WITH COMPOUND SUBJECTS

Use plural verbs with most compound subjects joined by the word *and*.

EXAMPLE: *My father and his friends play chess every day.*

To confirm that you need a plural verb, you could substitute the plural pronoun *they* for *my father and his friends.*

If a compound subject is thought of as a unit, use a singular verb. Test this by substituting the singular pronoun *it.*

EXAMPLE: *A bagel and cream cheese [it] is my usual breakfast.*

Use a singular verb with a compound subject that is preceded by *each, every,* or *many a.*

> EXAMPLE: *Each novel and short story seems grounded in personal experience.*

When the parts of a compound subject are joined by *or, nor,* or the correlative conjunctions *either . . . or* or *neither . . . nor,* make the verb agree with the noun or pronoun nearest the verb.

> EXAMPLES: *Cookies or ice cream is my favorite dessert.*
>
> *Either Cheryl or her parents are being invited.*
>
> *Neither ice storms nor snow is predicted today.*

11.5 PERSONAL PRONOUNS AS SUBJECTS

When using a personal pronoun as a subject, make sure to match it with the correct form of the verb *be.* (See the chart in Section 11.2.) Note especially that the pronoun *you* takes the forms *are* and *were,* regardless of whether it is singular or plural.

> **WATCH OUT!** *You is* and *you was* are nonstandard forms and should be avoided in writing and speaking. *We was* and *they was* are also forms to be avoided.
>
> INCORRECT: *You was a good student.*
> CORRECT: *You were a good student.*
> INCORRECT: *They was starting a new school.*
> CORRECT: *They were starting a new school.*

11.6 INDEFINITE PRONOUNS AS SUBJECTS

Some indefinite pronouns are always singular; some are always plural.

Singular Indefinite Pronouns			
another	either	neither	one
anybody	everybody	nobody	somebody
anyone	everyone	no one	someone
anything	everything	nothing	something
each	much		

> EXAMPLES: *Each of the writers was given an award.*
> *Somebody in the room upstairs is sleeping.*

Plural Indefinite Pronouns			
both	few	many	several

> EXAMPLES: *Many of the books in our library are not in circulation.*
>
> *Few have been returned recently.*

Still other indefinite pronouns may be either singular or plural.

Singular or Plural Indefinite Pronouns		
all	more	none
any	most	some

The number of the indefinite pronoun *any* or *none* often depends on the intended meaning.

> EXAMPLES: *Any of these stories has an important message.* (any one story)
>
> *Any of these stories have important messages.* (all of the many stories)

The indefinite pronouns *all, some, more, most,* and *none* are singular when they refer to quantities or parts of things. They are plural when they refer to numbers of individual things. Context will usually give a clue.

> EXAMPLES: *All of the flour is gone.* (referring to a quantity)
>
> *All of the flowers are gone.* (referring to individual items)

11.7 INVERTED SENTENCES

A sentence in which the subject follows the verb is called an **inverted sentence.** A subject can follow a verb or part of a verb phrase in a question; a sentence beginning with *here* or *there;* or a sentence in which an adjective, an adverb, or a phrase is placed first.

> EXAMPLES: *Here comes the scariest part.*
> *There goes the hero with a flashlight.*
> *Then, into the room rushes a big black cat!*

TIP To check subject-verb agreement in some inverted sentences, place the subject before the verb. For example, change *There are many people* to *Many people are there.*

11.8 SENTENCES WITH PREDICATE NOMINATIVES

In a sentence containing a predicate noun (nominative), the verb should agree with the subject, not the predicate noun.

> EXAMPLES: *Ogden Nash's limericks are a source of laughter.* (*Limericks* is the subject—not *source*—and it takes the plural verb *are.*)
>
> *One source of laughter is Ogden Nash's limericks.* (The subject is *source*—not *limericks*—and it takes the singular verb *is.*)

11.9 *DON'T* AND *DOESN'T* AS AUXILIARY VERBS

The auxiliary verb *doesn't* is used with singular subjects and with the personal pronouns *she, he,* and *it*. The auxiliary verb *don't* is used with plural subjects and with the personal pronouns *I, we, you,* and *they.*

> SINGULAR: *The humor doesn't escape us.*
> *Doesn't the limerick about Dougal MacDougal make you laugh?*
> PLURAL: *We don't usually forget such funny images.*
> *Don't people like to recite limericks?*

11.10 COLLECTIVE NOUNS AS SUBJECTS

Collective nouns are singular nouns that name groups of persons or things. *Team,* for example, is a collective name of a group of individuals. A collective noun takes a singular verb when the group acts as a single unit. It takes a plural verb when the members of the group act separately.

> EXAMPLES: *The class creates a bulletin board of limericks.* (The class as a whole creates the board.)
>
> *The faculty enjoy teaching poetry.* (The individual members enjoy teaching poetry.)

11.11 RELATIVE PRONOUNS AS SUBJECTS

When the relative pronoun *who, which,* or *that* is used as a subject in an adjective clause, the verb in the clause must agree in number with the antecedent of the pronoun.

> SINGULAR: *The **myth** from ancient Greece that interests me most is "Apollo's Tree."*

The antecedent of the relative pronoun *that* is the singular *myth;* therefore, *that* is singular and must take the singular verb *interests.*

> PLURAL: *Rafe Martin and Judith Ortiz Cofer are **writers** who tell folk tales.*

The antecedent of the relative pronoun *who* is the plural subject *writers.* Therefore *who* is plural, and it takes the plural verb *tell.*

GRAMMAR PRACTICE

Locate the subject of each verb in parentheses in the sentences below. Then choose the correct verb form.

1. Jim Haskins's "Matthew Henson at the Top of the World" (describes, describe) Henson's adventures in the Arctic.

2. The stories of the sea (is, are) inspiring to the young boy.

3. Nobody else (has, have) such courage and adventurousness.

4. Many of his experiences (brings, bring) danger and hardship, though.

5. The fishing boat's captain and crew (acts, act) cruel to Henson.

6. There (is, are) visions of hope when the explorer Robert Peary offers him a job.

7. With Peary, Henson (makes, make) five expeditions to the Arctic.

8. Henson's talents, such as his hunting ability, (endears, endear) him to the Eskimos.

9. None of his other achievements (equals, equal) his reaching the North Pole with Peary.

10. (Doesn't, Don't) the government feel ashamed for not recognizing Henson's contribution for so many years?

The key to becoming an independent reader is to develop a tool kit of vocabulary strategies. By learning and practicing the strategies, you'll know what to do when you encounter unfamiliar words while reading. You'll also know how to refine the words you use for different situations—personal, school, and work.

Being a good speller is important when communicating your ideas in writing. Learning basic spelling rules and checking your spelling in a dictionary will help you spell words that you may not use frequently.

COMMON CORE

Included in this handbook:
L 2b, L 4a–c, L 5a–c, L 6

1 Using Context Clues

The context of a word is made up of the punctuation marks, words, sentences, and paragraphs that surround the word. A word's context can give you important clues about its meaning.

1.1 GENERAL CONTEXT

Sometimes you need to determine the meaning of an unfamiliar word by reading all the information in a passage.

> Kevin set out the broom, a dustpan, and three trash bags before beginning the *monumental* task of cleaning his room.

You can figure out from the context that *monumental* means "huge."

1.2 SPECIFIC CONTEXT CLUES

Sometimes writers help you understand the meanings of words by providing specific clues such as those shown in the chart. When reading content area materials, use word, sentence, and paragraph clues to help you figure out meanings.

1.3 IDIOMS, SLANG, AND FIGURATIVE LANGUAGE

Use context clues to figure out the meanings of idioms, slang, and figurative language.

An **idiom** is an expression whose overall meaning differs from the meaning of the individual words.

The mosquitos drove us crazy on our hike.
(Drove us crazy *means "irritated."*)

Slang is informal language that features made-up words and ordinary words that are used to mean something different from their meanings in formal English.

That's a really cool backpack you're wearing.
(Cool *means "excellent."*)

Figurative language is language that communicates meaning beyond the literal meaning of the words.

Like a plunging horse, my car kicked up dirt, moved ahead quickly, and made a loud noise when I hit the gas. (Kicked up dirt, moved ahead, *and* made a loud noise *describe a plunging horse.*)

Specific Context Clues		
Type of Clue	**Key Words/ Phrases**	**Example**
Definition or restatement of the meaning of the word	or, which is, that is, in other words, also known as, also called	In 1909, a French inventor flew a *monoplane*, or a **single-winged plane.**
Example following an unfamiliar word	such as, like, as if, for example, especially, including	The stunt pilot performed *acrobatics*, such as **dives and wing-walking.**
Comparison with a more familiar word or concept	as, like, also, similar to, in the same way, likewise	The doctor prescribed a *bland* diet, similar to the **rice and potatoes** he was already eating.
Contrast with a familiar word or experience	unlike, but, however, although, on the other hand, on the contrary	The moon will *diminish* at the end of the month; however it **will grow** during the first part of the month.
Cause-and-effect relationship in which one term is familiar	because, since, when, consequently, as a result, therefore	Because their general was *valiant*, the rest of the soldiers **showed courage** in battle.

*For more information, see **Vocabulary Strategy: Context Clues**, pages 258, 758, 959, **Vocabulary Strategy: Idioms**, page 820, and **Vocabulary Strategy: Figurative Language**, pages 102 and 484.*

2 Analyzing Word Structure

Many words can be broken into smaller parts. These word parts include base words, roots, prefixes, and suffixes.

2.1 BASE WORDS

A **base word** is a word part that by itself is also a word. Other words or word parts can be added to base words to form new words.

*For more information, see **Vocabulary Strategy: Recognizing Base Words**, page 778.*

2.2 ROOTS

A **root** is a word part that contains the core meaning of the word. Many English words contain roots that come from older languages such as Greek and Latin. Knowing the meanings of a word's root can help you determine the word's meaning.

Root	Meaning	Example
auto (Greek)	self, same	**auto**mobile
hydr (Greek)	water	**hydr**ant
cent (Latin)	hundred	**cent**ury
circ (Latin)	ring	**circ**le
port (Latin)	carry	**port**able

*For more information, see **Vocabulary Strategy: Word Roots**, pages 124, 273, 338, 635.*

2.3 PREFIXES

A **prefix** is a word part attached to the beginning of a word. Most prefixes come from Greek, Latin, or Old English (OE).

Prefix	Meaning	Example
dis- (Latin)	not	**dis**honest
auto- (Greek)	self, same	**auto**biography
un- (OE)	the opposite of, not	**un**happy
re- (Latin)	carry, back	**re**pay

*For more information, see **Vocabulary Strategy: Prefixes**, page 124.*

2.4 SUFFIXES

A **suffix** is a word part that appears at the end of a root or base word to form a new word. Some suffixes do not change word meaning. These suffixes are
- added to nouns to change the number of persons or objects
- added to verbs to change the tense
- added to modifiers to change the degree of comparison

Suffix	Meaning	Example
-s, -es	to change the number of a noun	lock + s = locks
-d, -ed, -ing	to change verb tense	stew + ed = stewed
-er, -est	to indicate comparison in modifiers	mild + er = milder
		soft + est = softest

Other suffixes can be added to the root or base to change the word's meaning. These suffixes can also determine a word's part of speech.

Suffix	Meaning	Example
-ion (Latin)	process of	operat**ion**
-able (Latin)	capable of	read**able**
-ize (Greek)	to cause or become	legal**ize**

*For more information, see **Vocabulary Strategy: Suffixes**, page 64, and **Vocabulary Strategy: Noun-Forming Suffixes**, page 358.*

Strategies for Understanding New Words

- If you recognize elements—prefix, suffix, root, or base—of a word, you may be able to guess its meaning by analyzing one or two elements.

- Think about the way the word is used in the sentence. Use the context and the word parts to make a logical guess about the word's meaning.

- Look in a dictionary to see if you are correct.

Interactive Vocabulary — THINK central

Go to **thinkcentral.com**.
KEYWORD: HML6-R69

3 Understanding Word Origins

3.1 ETYMOLOGIES

Etymologies show the origin and historical development of a word. When you study a word's history and origin, you can find out when, where, and how the word came to be.

> **em•per•or** (ĕm′pər-ər) *n.* **1.** The male ruler of an empire. **2a.** The emperor butterfly. **b.** The emperor moth. [Middle English *emperour,* from Old French *empereor,* from Latin *imperātor,* from *imperāre,* to command : *in-,* in; see EN–¹ + *parāre,* to prepare.]

3.2 WORD FAMILIES

Words that have the same root make up a word family and have related meanings. The following chart shows a common Greek and a common Latin root. Notice how the meanings of the example words are related to the meanings of their roots.

Latin Root	*man:* "hand"
English	**manual** by hand
	manage handle
	manuscript document written by hand
Greek Root	*phon:* "sound"
English	**telephone** an instrument that transmits sound
	phonograph machine that reproduces sound
	phonetic representing sounds of speech

3.3 FOREIGN WORDS IN ENGLISH

The English language includes words from other languages, such as French, Dutch, Spanish, Italian, and Chinese. Many words have stayed the way they were in their original language.

French	Dutch	Spanish	Italian
ballet	boss	canyon	diva
vague	caboose	rodeo	cupola
mirage	dock	bronco	spaghetti

*For more information, see **Vocabulary Strategy: Spanish Words Used in English,** page 205, and **Foreign Words Used in English,** pages 858 and 965.*

PRACTICE AND APPLY

Look up the origin and meaning of each word listed in the preceding chart. Then use each word in a sentence.

4 Synonyms and Antonyms

4.1 SYNONYMS

A **synonym** is a word with a meaning similar to that of another word. You can find synonyms in a thesaurus or a dictionary. In a dictionary, synonyms are often given as part of the definition of a word. The following word pairs are synonyms:

satisfy/please   occasionally/sometimes

rob/steal   schedule/agenda

*For more information, see **Vocabulary Strategy: Synonyms,** pages 76 and 950.*

4.2 ANTONYMS

An **antonym** is a word with a meaning opposite that of another word. The following word pairs are antonyms:

accurate/incorrect   similar/different

fresh/stale   unusual/ordinary

5 Denotation and Connotation

5.1 DENOTATION

A word's dictionary meaning is called its **denotation.** For example, the denotation of the word *thin* is "having little flesh; spare; lean."

5.2 CONNOTATION

The images or feelings you connect to a word add a finer shade of meaning, called **connotation.** The connation of a word goes beyond its basic dictionary definition. Writers use connotations of words to communicate positive or negative feelings.

Positive	Negative
slender	scrawny
thrifty	cheap
young	immature

Make sure you understand the denotation and connotation of a word when you read it or use it in your writing.

*For more information, see **Vocabulary Strategy: Denotations and Connotations**, page 44.*

6 Analogies

An **analogy** is a comparison between two things that are similar in some way but are otherwise not alike. Analogies are sometimes used in writing when unfamiliar subjects or ideas are explained in terms of familiar ones. Analogies often appear on tests as well. In an analogy problem, the analogy is expressed using two groups of words. The relationship between the first pair of words is the same as the relationship between the second pair of words. Some analogy problems are expressed like this:

love : hate :: war: _____
a. soldier   **b.** peace   **c.** battle   **d.** argument

Follow these steps to determine the correct answer:

- Read the problem as "*Love* is to *hate* as ***war*** is to. . . ."

- Ask yourself how the words *love* and *hate* are related. (*Love* and *hate* are antonyms.)

- Ask yourself which answer choice is an antonym of *war*. (*Peace* is an antonym of *war*, therefore *peace* is the best answer.)

*For more information, see **Vocabulary Strategy: Analogies**, page pages 376, 745, 839, 914.*

7 Homonyms, Homographs, and Homophones

7.1 HOMONYMS

Homonyms are words that have the same spelling and sound but have different meanings.

The snake shed its skin in the shed behind the house.

Shed can mean "to lose by natural process," but an identically spelled word means "a small structure."

Sometimes only one of the meanings of a homonym may be familiar to you. Use context clues to help you figure out the meaning of an unfamiliar word.

7.2 HOMOGRAPHS

Homographs are words that are spelled the same but have different meanings and origins. Some are also pronounced differently, as in these examples:

Please close the door. (clōz)
That was a close call. (clōs)

If you see a word used in a way that is unfamiliar to you, check a dictionary to see if it is a homograph.

7.3 HOMOPHONES

Homophones are words that sound alike but have different meanings and spellings. The following homophones are frequently misused:

It's/its   they're/their/there
to/too/two   stationary/stationery

Many misused homophones are pronouns and contractions. Whenever you are unsure whether to write *your* or *you're* and *who's* or *whose*, ask yourself if you mean *you are* and *who is/has*. If you do, write the contraction. For other homophones, such as *fair* and *fare*, use the meaning of the word to help you decide which one to use.

8 Words with Multiple Meanings

Over time, some words have acquired additional meanings that are based on the original meaning.

I had to be replaced in the cast of the play because of the cast on my arm.

These two uses of *cast* have different meanings, but both of them have the same origin. You will find all the meanings of *cast* listed in one entry in the dictionary. Context can also help you figure out the meaning of the word.

*For more information, see **Vocabulary Strategy: Multiple-Meaning Words**, page 392.*

9 Specialized Vocabulary

Specialized vocabulary is a group of terms suited to a particular field of study or work. For example, science, mathematics, and history all have their own technical or specialized vocabularies. To figure out specialized terms, you can use context clues and reference sources, such as dictionaries on specific subjects, atlases, or manuals.

10 Using Reference Sources

10.1 DICTIONARIES

A **general dictionary** will tell you not only a word's definitions but also its pronunciation, syllabication, parts of speech, history, and origin.

❶ **tan·gi·ble** (tăn′jə-bəl) *adj.* **1a.** Discernible by the touch; palpable. **b.** Possible to touch. **c.** Possible to be treated as fact; real or concrete. **2.** Possible to understand or realize. **3.** *Law* That can be valued monetarily [Late Latin *tangibilis*, **❺** from Latin *tangere*, to touch.]

❶ Entry word
❷ Syllabication and pronunciation
❸ Part of speech
❹ Definitions
❺ Etymology

A **specialized dictionary** focuses on terms related to a particular field of study or work. Use a dictionary to check the spelling of any word you are unsure of in your reading.

For more information, see **Vocabulary Strategy: Reading a Dictionary Entry,** *page 136, and* **Use a Dictionary to Determine Parts of Speech,** *page 517.*

10.2 THESAURI

A **thesaurus** (plural, *thesauri*) is a dictionary of synonyms. A thesaurus can be especially helpful when you find yourself using the same modifiers over and over again.

10.3 SYNONYM FINDERS

A **synonym finder** is often included in word-processing software. It enables you to highlight a word and be shown a display of its synonyms.

10.4 GLOSSARIES

A **glossary** is a list of specialized terms and their definitions. It is often found in the back of a book and sometimes includes pronunciations. Many textbooks contain glossaries. In fact, this textbook has four glossaries: the **Glossary of Literary and Nonfiction Terms,** the **Glossary of Reading & Informational Terms,** the **Glossary of Academic Vocabulary in English and Spanish,** and the **Glossary of Vocabulary in English & Spanish.** Use these glossaries to help you understand how terms are used in this textbook.

For more information, see **Vocabulary Strategy: Reference Aids,** *page 723.*

11 Spelling Rules

11.1 WORDS ENDING IN A SILENT *E*

Before adding a suffix beginning with a vowel or *y* to a word ending in a silent *e*, drop the *e* (with some exceptions).

> **amaze + -ing = amazing**
> **love + -able = lovable**
> **create + -ed = created**
> **nerve + -ous = nervous**

Exceptions: *change + -able = changeable; courage + -ous = courageous*

When adding a suffix beginning with a consonant to a word ending in a silent *e*, keep the *e* (with some exceptions).

> **late + -ly = lately**
> **spite + -ful = spiteful**
> **noise + -less = noiseless**
> **state + -ment = statement**

Exceptions: *truly, argument, ninth, wholly, awful,* and others

When a suffix beginning with *a* or *o* is added to a word with a final silent *e*, the final *e* is usually retained if it is preceded by a soft *c* or a soft *g*.

> **bridge + -able = bridgeable**
> **peace + -able = peaceable**
> **outrage + -ous = outrageous**
> **advantage + -ous = advantageous**

When a suffix beginning with a vowel is added to words ending in *ee* or *oe*, the final, silent *e* is retained.

> **agree + -ing = agreeing**   **free + -ing = freeing**
> **hoe + -ing = hoeing**   **see + -ing = seeing**

11.2 WORDS ENDING IN Y

Before adding most suffixes to a word that ends in *y* preceded by a consonant, change the *y* to *i*.

> **easy + -est = easiest**
> **crazy + -est = craziest**
> **silly + -ness = silliness**
> **marry + -age = marriage**

Exceptions: *dryness, shyness,* and *slyness*

However, when you add *-ing,* the *y* does not change.

> **empty + -ed = emptied**   but
> **empty + -ing = emptying**

When adding a suffix to a word that ends in *y* preceded by a vowel, the *y* usually does not change.

> **play + -er = player**
> **employ + -ed = employed**
> **coy + -ness = coyness**
> **pay + -able = payable**

11.3 WORDS ENDING IN A CONSONANT

In one-syllable words that end in one consonant preceded by one short vowel, double the final consonant before adding a suffix beginning with a vowel, such as *-ed* or *-ing.* These are sometimes called 1+1+1 words.

> **dip + -ed = dipped**   **set + -ing = setting**
> **slim + -est = slimmest**   **fit + -er = fitter**

The rule does not apply to words of one syllable that end in a consonant preceded by two vowels.

> **feel + -ing = feeling**   **peel + -ed = peeled**
> **reap + -ed = reaped**   **loot + -ed = looted**

In words of more than one syllable, double the final consonant when (1) the word ends with one consonant preceded by one vowel and (2) when the word is accented on the last syllable.

> **be•gin´   per•mit´   re•fer´**

In the following examples, note that in the new words formed with suffixes, the accent remains on the same syllable:

> **be•gin´ + -ing = be•gin´ning = beginning**
> **per•mit´ + -ed = per•mit´ted = permitted**

Exceptions: In some words with more than one syllable, though the accent remains on the same syllable when a suffix is added, the final consonant is nevertheless not doubled, as in the following examples:

> **tra´vel + er = tra´vel•er = traveler**
> **mar´ket + er = mar´ket•er = marketer**

In the following examples, the accent does not remain on the same syllable; thus, the final consonant is not doubled:

> **re•fer´ + -ence = ref´er•ence = reference**
> **con•fer´ + -ence = con´fer•ence = conference**

11.4 PREFIXES AND SUFFIXES

When adding a prefix to a word, do not change the spelling of the base word. When a prefix creates a double letter, keep both letters.

> **dis- + approve = disapprove**
> **re- + build = rebuild**
> **ir- + regular = irregular**
> **mis- + spell = misspell**
> **anti- + trust = antitrust**
> **il- + logical = illogical**

When adding *-ly* to a word ending in *l,* keep both *l*'s. When adding *-ness* to a word ending in *n,* keep both *n*'s.

> **careful + -ly = carefully**
> **sudden + -ness = suddenness**
> **final + -ly = finally**
> **thin + -ness = thinness**

11.5 FORMING PLURAL NOUNS

To form the plural of most nouns, just add *-s.*

> **prizes   dreams   circles   stations**

For most singular nouns ending in *o,* add *-s.*

> **solos   halos   studios   photos   pianos**

For a few nouns ending in *o*, add *-es*.

heroes **tomatoes** **potatoes** **echoes**

When a singular noun ends in *s, sh, ch, x,* or *z,* add *-es*.

waitresses **brushes** **ditches**
axes **buzzes**

When a singular noun ends in *y* with a consonant before it, change the *y* to *i* and add *-es*.

army—armies **candy—candies**
baby—babies **diary—diaries**
ferry—ferries **conspiracy—conspiracies**

When a vowel (*a, e, i, o, u*) comes before the *y*, just add *-s*.

boy—boys **way—ways**
array—arrays **alloy—alloys**
weekday—weekdays **jockey—jockeys**

For most nouns ending in *f* or *fe*, change the *f* to *v* and add *-es* or *-s*.

life—lives **loaf—loaves**
calf—calves **knife—knives**
thief—thieves **shelf—shelves**

For some nouns ending in *f*, add *-s* to make the plural.

roofs **chiefs** **reefs** **beliefs**

Some nouns have the same form for both singular and plural.

deer **sheep** **moose** **salmon** **trout**

For some nouns, the plural is formed in a special way.

man—men **goose—geese**
ox—oxen **woman—women**
mouse—mice **child—children**

For a compound noun written as one word, form the plural by changing the last word in the compound to its plural form.

stepchild—stepchildren **firefly—fireflies**

If a compound noun is written as a hyphenated word or as two separate words, change the most important word to the plural form.

brother-in-law—brothers-in-law
life jacket—life jackets

11.6 FORMING POSSESSIVES

If a noun is singular, add *'s*.

mother—my mother's car **Ross—Ross's desk**

Exception: An apostrophe alone is used to indicate the possessive case with the names Jesus and Moses and with certain names in classical mythology (such as Zeus).

If a noun is plural and ends with *s*, add an apostrophe.

parents—my parents' car
the Santinis—the Santinis' house

If a noun is plural but does not end in *s*, add *'s*.

people—the people's choice
women—the women's coats

11.7 SPECIAL SPELLING PROBLEMS

Only one English word ends in *-sede: supersede.* Three words end in *-ceed: exceed, proceed,* and *succeed.* All other verbs ending in the sound "seed" are spelled with *-cede.*

concede **precede** **recede** **secede**

In words with **ie** or **ei,** when the sound is long *e* (as in *she*), the word is spelled *ie* except after *c* (with some exceptions).

i before *e*	**thief**	**relieve**	**field**
	piece	**grieve**	**pier**
except after *c*	**conceit**	**perceive**	**ceiling**
	receive	**receipt**	
Exceptions:	**either**	**neither**	**weird**
	leisure	**seize**	

11.8 USING A SPELL CHECKER

Most computer word processing programs have spell checkers to catch misspellings. Most computer spell checkers do not correct errors automatically. Instead, they stop at a word and highlight it. Sometimes the highlighted word may not be misspelled; it may be that the program's dictionary does not include the word. Keep in mind that spell checkers will identify only misspelled words, not misused words. For example, if you used *their* when you meant to use *there*, a spelling checker will not catch the error.

12 Commonly Confused Words

WORDS	DEFINITIONS	EXAMPLES
accept/except	The verb *accept* means "to receive" or "to believe." *Except* is usually a preposition meaning "excluding."	Did the teacher **accept** your report? Everyone smiled for the photographer **except** Jody.
advice/advise	*Advise* is a verb. *Advice* is a noun naming that which an *adviser* gives.	I **advise** you to take that job. Whom should I ask for **advice?**
affect/effect	As a verb, *affect* means "to influence." *Effect* as a verb means "to cause." If you want a noun, you will almost always want *effect*.	How deeply did the news **affect** him? The students tried to **effect** a change in school policy. What **effect** did the acidic soil produce in the plants?
all ready/already	*All ready* is an adjective meaning "fully ready." *Already* is an adverb meaning "before" or "by this time."	He was **all ready** to go at noon. I have **already** seen that movie.
desert/dessert	*Desert* (dĕz´ərt) means "a dry, sandy, barren region." *Desert* (dĭ-zûrt´) means "to abandon." *Dessert* (dĭ-zûrt´) is a sweet, such as cake.	The Sahara, in North Africa, is the world's largest **desert.** The night guard did not **desert** his post. Alison's favorite **dessert** is chocolate cake.
among/between	*Between* is used when you are speaking of only two things. *Among* is used for three or more.	**Between** ice cream and sherbet, I prefer the latter. Gary Soto is **among** my favorite authors.
bring/take	*Bring* is used to denote motion toward a speaker or place. *Take* is used to denote motion away from such a person or place.	**Bring** the books over here, and I will **take** them to the library.
fewer/less	*Fewer* refers to the number of separate, countable units. *Less* refers to bulk quantity.	We have **less** literature and **fewer** selections in this year's curriculum.
leave/let	*Leave* means "to allow something to remain behind." *Let* means "to permit."	The librarian will **leave** some books on display but will not **let** us borrow any.
lie/lay	To *lie* is "to rest or recline." It does not take an object. *Lay* always takes an object.	Rover loves to **lie** in the sun. We always **lay** some bones next to him.
loose/lose	*Loose* (lōōs) means "free, not restrained." *Lose* (lōōz) means "to misplace" or "to fail to find."	Who turned the horses **loose?** I hope we won't **lose** any of them.
passed/past	*Passed* is the past tense of *pass* and means "went by." *Past* is an adjective that means "of a former time." *Past* is also a noun that means "time gone by."	We **passed** through the Florida Keys during our vacation. My **past** experiences have taught me to set my alarm. Ebenezer Scrooge is a character who relives his **past.**
than/then	Use *than* in making comparisons. Use *then* on all other occasions.	Ramon is stronger **than** Mark. Cut the grass and **then** trim the hedges.
two/too/to	*Two* is the number. *Too* is an adverb meaning "also" or "very." Use *to* before a verb or as a preposition.	Meg had **to** go **to** town, **too.** We had **too** much reading **to** do. **Two** chapters is **too** many.
their/there/they're	*Their* means "belonging to them." *There* means "in that place." *They're* is the contraction for "they are."	**There** is a movie playing at 9 P.M. **They're** going to see it with me. Sakara and Jessica drove away in **their** car after the movie.

Good speakers and listeners do more than just talk and hear. They use specific techniques to present their ideas effectively, and they are attentive and critical listeners. Effective oral communication occurs when the audience understands a message the way the speaker intends it.

COMMON CORE

Included in this handbook:
SL 1a–d, SL 3, SL 4, SL 5, SL 6

1 Speech

In school, in business, and in community life, speaking directly to a live audience is an effective way to present information.

1.1 AUDIENCE, PURPOSE, AND OCCASION

When preparing and presenting a speech, think about your purpose in speaking as well as your audience's knowledge of and interest in your subject.

- **Know Your Audience** What kind of group are you presenting to? As you draft and revise your speech, match your purpose and message to the audience. Match your **vocal modulation** to them as well. In other words, change the loudness or softness of your voice depending on how audience members react to it.

- **Understand Your Purpose for Speaking** Are you trying to persuade the audience to do something? Perhaps you simply want to entertain them by sharing a story or an experience. Your purpose for speaking should affect your tone. Decide whether a serious or a humorous tone is more appropriate for your purpose.

- **Know the Occasion** Are you speaking at a special event? Is it formal? Will others be giving speeches besides you? Knowing what the occasion is will help you choose the proper language and the right length for your speech.

1.2 WRITING YOUR SPEECH

Once you understand your purpose and audience, use the following guidelines as you write:

- **Select Your Focus** Decide what your main message will be. Emphasize **salient** (important) points that will help your listeners follow your main or central ideas. As you draft and revise, make sure your speech is **unified.** In other words, every sentence of every paragraph should relate to the main message.

- **Clarify Your Ideas** Make sure that you show clear relationships between ideas. Transition words can help listeners follow your ideas.

*For more information on transitions, see the **Writing Handbook,** page R32.*

- **Use Appropriate Language** If you are telling a funny story to your classmates, you might use informal language, such as slang. However, if you are giving a speech at a school assembly, you will want to use formal, standard American English. In an informative presentation, be sure to explain any terms that might be unfamiliar to the audience.

- **Provide Detailed Evidence** Include relevant facts, statistics, and incidents; quote experts to support your ideas and opinions. Elaborate— provide specific details, perhaps with visual or media displays—to clarify what you are saying.

- **Arrange Details and Evidence Effectively** In a good presentation, your controlling idea, or thesis statement, should be supported by clearly stated evidence. The evidence can be presented as details, reasons, descriptions, or examples. Use the following chart to help you arrange your ideas.

Introduction	• Focus on one strong example or statistic. • Make sure your evidence is intense or even surprising, so that it grabs the audience's attention.
Main Body	• Try to provide at least one piece of evidence for every new idea you introduce. • Define unfamiliar terms clearly. • When possible, include well-labeled diagrams or illustrations.
Conclusion	• Leave your audience with one strong piece of evidence or a powerful detail.

- **Use Figurative Language** Help your audience follow the main ideas of your speech by using similes, metaphors, analogies, and sensory images to draw attention to important points.

- **Use Precise Language** Use precise language to express your ideas and give your sentences variety. Words that suggest strong emotions will capture the audience's attention. Asking questions will help you connect your experience or information with that of your audience.

- **Start Strong, Finish Strong** As you begin your speech, consider using a "hook"—an interesting question or statement that captures your audience's attention. At the end of the speech, restate your main ideas simply and clearly. Perhaps conclude with a powerful example or anecdote to reinforce your message.

- **Revise Your Speech** After you write your speech, revise, edit, and proofread it as you would a written report. Use a variety of sentence structures to achieve a natural rhythm. Check for correct subject-verb agreement and consistent verb tense. Correct run-on sentences and sentence fragments. Use parallel structure to emphasize ideas. Make sure you use complete sentences and correct punctuation and capitalization, even if no one else will see it. Your written speech should be clear and error free. If you notice an error in your notes during the speech, you may not remember what you actually wanted to say.

1.3 DELIVERING YOUR SPEECH

Confidence is the key to a successful presentation. Use these techniques to help you prepare and present your speech:

Prepare

- **Review Your Information** Reread your notes and review any background research. This will help you feel more confident during your speech.

- **Organize Your Notes** Some people prefer to write down only key points. Others prefer an entire script. Write each main point, or each paragraph, of your speech on a separate numbered index card. Be sure to include your most important evidence and examples.

- **Plan Your Visual Aids** If you are planning to use visual aids, such as slides, posters, charts, graphs, video clips, overhead transparencies, or media displays, now is the time to design them and decide how to work them into your speech.

Practice

- **Rehearse** Try out your speech several times, perhaps in front of a practice audience. Maintain good **posture** by standing with your shoulders back and your head up. Control your **rate** of speech—not too fast, not too slow. The **volume** of your speech should be loud enough for those in the back of the room to hear, but not loud enough to seem like shouting. As you speak, notice your **pitch.** Is your voice too high or too low?

- **Watch Your Attitude** Consider the **tone** (attitude) of your speech. Depending on your message, you might sound calm, urgent, or even a little sarcastic, but you should never sound bored.

- **Match Your Messages** Your **verbal messages** (words, rate, volume, pitch, and tone) should match your **nonverbal messages** (posture, gestures, movements, and facial expressions). For instance, if you are expressing someone else's opinion that you disagree with, you might lower the tone of your voice, frown, and shake your head from side to side.

- **Use Audience Feedback** If you had a practice audience, ask them specific questions about your delivery: Did I use enough eye contact? Was my voice at the right volume? Did I stand straight, or did I slouch? Use the audience's comments to evaluate the effectiveness of your delivery and to set goals for future rehearsals.

- **Evaluate Your Performance** When you have finished each rehearsal, evaluate your performance. Did you pause to let an important point sink in and use gestures for emphasis? Make a list of the aspects of your presentation that you wish to improve.

Present

- **Begin Your Speech** Try to look relaxed and smile.

- **Make Eye Contact** Try to make eye contact with as many audience members as possible. This will establish personal contact and help you determine if the audience understands your speech.

- **Remember to Pause** A slight pause after important points will provide emphasis and give your audience time to think about and connect with what you're saying.

- **Use Expressive Body Language** Use facial expressions to show your feelings toward your topic. Lean forward when you make an important point; move your hands and arms for emphasis. Use body language to show your own style and reflect your personality.

- **Watch the Audience for Responses** If they start fidgeting or yawning, speak a little louder or get to your conclusion a little sooner. Use what you learn to evaluate the effectiveness of your speech and to decide what areas need improvement.

Respond to Questions

Depending on the content of your speech, your audience may have questions. Follow these steps to make sure that you answer questions in an appropriate manner:

- Think about what your audience may ask, and prepare answers before your speech.

- Tell your audience at the beginning of your speech that you will take questions at the end. This helps avoid audience interruptions that may make your speech hard to follow.

- Call on audience members in the order in which they raise their hands.

- Repeat each question before you answer it to ensure that everyone has heard it. This step also gives you time to prepare your answer.

2 Different Types of Oral Presentations

2.1 INFORMATIVE SPEECH

When you deliver an informative speech, you give the audience new information, provide a better understanding of information, or enable the audience to use the information in a new way. Use the following questions to evaluate the presentation of a peer or a public figure, or your own presentation.

Evaluate an Informative Speech

- Did the speaker ask and answer questions that were specific enough to be completely and thoroughly answered during the presentation?

- Did the speaker use facts, details, examples and explanations to develop the topic?

- Did the speaker cite a variety of reliable sources, such as books, magazines, newspapers, speakers, and online information?

- Was the message balanced and unbiased?

- Did the speaker explain all unfamiliar terms?

2.2 PERSUASIVE SPEECH

When you deliver a persuasive speech, you offer a thesis or clear statement on a subject, you provide relevant evidence to support your position, and you attempt to convince the audience to accept your point of view.

*For more information, see **Speaking and Listening Workshop: Giving a Persuasive Speech**, page 998.*

Use the following guidelines to evaluate a persuasive presentation.

Evaluate a Persuasive Speech

- Did the speaker provide a clear statement of his or her position?
- Did the speaker anticipate and address audience concerns, biases, and counterarguments?
- Did the speaker use sound logic and reasoning in developing the argument?
- Did the speaker support the argument with evidence that was closely related to his or her main points?
- Did the speaker offer information in a logical sequence?
- Did the speaker engage listeners and encourage acceptance of the position or proposal?

2.3 PROBLEM-SOLUTION PRESENTATION

When delivering a presentation on problems and solutions, you need to be organized, logical, and persuasive.

- **Identify the Problem** Define the problem for your audience. Provide background information: How long has this problem existed? What are its causes?

- **Make Connections** Think about how similar or related problems have been solved. How might this information help solve the current problem?

- **Propose Solutions** Offer at least two or three possible solutions. Back them up with persuasive evidence and logical analysis of how they would work.

- **Encourage Discussion** Ask your audience if they have any questions or alternative suggestions. Have them discuss and evaluate what you said.

Use the following guidelines to evaluate a problem-solution presentation.

Evaluate a Problem-Solution Presentation

- Did the speaker define the purpose or problem clearly?
- Did the speaker theorize about (suggest explanations for) the causes and effects of each problem?
- Did the speaker make connections between the problem and at least one solution?
- Did the speaker give persuasive evidence to prove the correctness of how the problem was defined and how well the solution or solutions would work?
- Did the speaker invite the audience to respond, participate, and discuss ideas?

2.4 DESCRIPTIVE SPEECH

Most presentations will involve some description. In a descriptive speech, you describe a subject that you are personally involved with. Use the following questions to evaluate a speaker or your own presentation.

Evaluate a Descriptive Speech

- Did the speaker clearly express his or her point of view or perspective about the subject being described?
- Did the speaker use sensory details, figurative language, and factual details?
- Did the speaker use tone and pitch to emphasize important details?
- Did the speaker use facial expressions to emphasize his or her feelings toward the subject?

2.5 NARRATIVE SPEECH

A narrative speech tells a story or presents a subject using a story-type format. A good narrative keeps an audience informed and entertained. It also delivers a message in a creative way.

Use the following guidelines to evaluate a speaker or your own presentation.

Evaluate a Narrative Speech

- Did the speaker establish a context—in other words, explain when and where events took place?
- Was the plot clear? Did it flow well?
- Was there a consistent point of view, or did the speaker switch confusingly from *I* to *he* or *she* or *you*?
- Did the speaker use words that express the appropriate mood and tone?
- Did the speaker include sensory details and exact, specific language to develop the plot and characters?
- Did the speaker use narrative devices, such as dialogue, tension, and suspense, to keep the audience interested?

2.6 ORAL INTERPRETATION

When you read a poem, play, or story aloud, your voice can bring the literature to life. In a dramatic reading, several speakers participate in the reading of a play or other work.

Oral Reading

An oral reading can be a monologue, during which you assume the voice of a character, the narrator, or the speaker in a poem. Or it may be a dialogue, during which you take the roles of two or more characters.

Use these techniques when giving an oral reading:

- **Speak Clearly** As you speak, pronounce your words carefully and clearly.
- **Control Your Volume** Make sure that you are loud enough to be heard, but do not shout.
- **Pace Yourself** Read at a moderate rate, but vary your pace if it seems appropriate to the emotions of the character or to the action.
- **Vary Your Voice** Use a different voice for each character. Stress important words and phrases.

Use the following questions to evaluate an artistic performance by a peer, a media presentation, or your own performance.

Evaluate an Oral Interpretation

- Did the speaker speak clearly?
- Did the speaker maintain eye contact with the audience?
- Was the speaker's voice the right volume?
- Did the speaker vary the rate of speech appropriately to express emotion, mood, and action?
- Did the speaker use different voices for the different characters in the piece?
- Did the speaker stress important words or phrases?
- Did the speaker use voice, tone, and gestures to enhance meaning?
- How did the audience react to the performance?

PRACTICE AND APPLY

Listen to an oral reading by a classmate or view a dramatic performance in a theater or on television. Use the preceding guidelines to evaluate it.

2.7 ORAL RESPONSE TO LITERATURE

An oral response to literature is your own personal interpretation of a piece written by someone else. It is a way to show an audience what a piece means to you.

- **Choose Carefully** In choosing a piece, think about the assignment, your interests, and the audience.
- **Exhibit Understanding** Develop an interpretation that shows careful reading, understanding, and insight. Direct the audience's attention to specific words, sentences, or phrases that are rich with meaning. Discuss the writer's techniques in developing plot, characterization, setting, or theme and how they contribute to your interpretation.
- **Organize Clearly** Organize your presentation around several clear ideas or images. What elements of the literature are most important? How do they relate to the piece as a whole and help provide meaning? Support your interpretation with examples from the selection.

*For more information, see **Speaking and Listening Workshop: Giving an Oral Response to Literature,** page 566.*

Use the following questions to evaluate a speaker or your own presentation.

Evaluate an Oral Response to Literature

- Did the speaker choose an interesting piece that he or she enjoys and understands?
- Did the speaker present and explain an interpretation—an opinion about the main message of the piece?
- Was the speaker's interpretation based on careful reading, understanding, and in-depth knowledge of the piece?
- Did the speaker support the interpretation with repeated use of examples and evidence from the text?
- Did the speaker organize his or her interpretation around several clear ideas, beliefs, or images?

2.8 ORAL INSTRUCTIONS

When you give oral instructions, you tell someone how to complete a task. You follow oral instructions when you complete the task yourself. Use the following questions to evaluate a speaker or your own presentation.

For more information, see Speaking and Listening Workshop: Giving and Following Oral Instructions, page 790.

Evaluate Oral Instructions

- Did the speaker describe the task clearly?
- Did the speaker present each step so that it was clear, straightforward, and easily understood?
- Did the speaker list the steps in chronological order, including words like *first, next,* and *last?*
- Did the speaker monitor the listeners' understanding by asking and answering questions?

3 Other Types of Communication

3.1 GROUP DISCUSSION

Successful groups assign a role to each member. These roles distribute responsibility among the members and help keep discussions focused.

Role	Responsibilities
Chairperson	• Introduces topic
	• Explains goal or purpose
	• Participates in discussion and keeps it on track
	• Helps resolve conflicts
	• Helps group reach goal
Recorder	• Takes notes on discussion
	• Reports on suggestions and decisions
	• Organizes and writes up notes
	• Participates in discussion
Participants	• Contribute relevant facts or ideas to discussion
	• Respond constructively to one another's ideas
	• Reach agreement or vote on final decision

Guidelines for Discussion

- Be informed about the topic.
- Participate in the discussion; ask questions, contribute suggestions, and respond appropriately to questions.
- Don't talk while someone else is talking.
- Support statements and opinions with facts and examples.
- Listen attentively; be courteous and respectful of others' viewpoints.
- Work toward the goal by considering suggestions from other group members. Avoid getting sidetracked by unrelated topics.

For more information, see Speaking and Listening Workshop: Participating in a Discussion, page 180.

3.2 INTERVIEW

An **interview** is a formal type of conversation with a definite purpose and goal. Use the following guidelines to conduct a successful interview:

Prepare for the Interview

- Carefully select the person you want to interview. Identify who has the kind of knowledge and experience you are looking for.

- Set a time, a date, and a place. Ask permission to tape-record the interview.

- Learn all you can about the person you will interview and the subjects you will discuss.

- Prepare a list of questions. Create questions that encourage detailed responses instead of yes-or-no answers. Arrange your questions in order from most important to least important.

Conduct the Interview

- Ask your questions clearly and listen to the responses carefully. Give the person whom you are interviewing plenty of time to answer.

- Be flexible; follow up on interesting responses.

- Avoid arguments; be tactful and polite.

- Even if you tape the interview, take notes on important points.

- Thank the person for the interview, and ask if you can call with any follow-up questions.

Follow Up on the Interview

- Summarize your notes or make a written transcript of the tape recording as soon as possible.

- If any points are unclear or if information is missing, call and ask more questions.

- Select quotations to support your ideas.

- If possible, have the person you interviewed review your work to make sure you haven't misrepresented what he or she said.

- Send a thank-you note to the person in appreciation of his or her time and effort.

Evaluate an Interview

You can determine how effective your interview was by asking yourself these questions:

- Was the person being interviewed focused on the subject throughout the interview?

- Were your most important questions answered?

- Did you get the information you were looking for?

---

④ Active Listening

Active listening means receiving, interpreting, evaluating, and responding to a message. Whether you are listening to a class discussion, oral instructions, or a formal or an informal speech, use these strategies to get as much as you can from the message.

Listening with a Purpose

Situation	Reason for Listening	How to Listen
Your grandfather tells a story about his childhood.	For enjoyment	Maintain eye contact; react to the story.
You are watching a demonstration on television.	To follow step-by-step instructions	Listen for words such as *first, second, next,* and *finally;* take notes that you can refer to later.

Before Listening

- Learn what the topic is beforehand. You may need to read background information about the topic or learn new terms in order to understand the speaker's message.

- Think about what you know or want to know about the topic.

- Have a pen and paper to take notes.

While Listening

- Focus your attention on the speaker. Make eye contact, and use facial expressions and body language to demonstrate your interest in the topic. Try to ignore noises and other distractions.

- Listen for the speaker's purpose (usually stated at the beginning), which alerts you to main ideas. Note any ideas that are repeated for emphasis.

- Listen for words or phrases that signal important points, such as *to begin with, in addition, most important, finally,* and *in conclusion.*

- Listen for explanations of unfamiliar terms.

- Take notes on the most important points. You may want to organize your notes using an outline or a numbered list of steps.

- Note comparisons and contrasts, causes and effects, or problems and solutions.
- Note how the speaker uses word choice, voice pitch, posture, and gestures to convey meaning.

After Listening

- Review your notes right away to make sure you understand what was said.

- Ask questions to clarify anything that was unclear or confusing.

- Summarize and paraphrase the main points and supporting evidence.

- Ask other listeners if they had the same understanding of the message that you did.

- If you were listening to step-by-step directions or instructions, try following them to see if you understood correctly.

4.1 CRITICAL LISTENING

Critical listening involves analyzing a speaker's message in order to judge whether the message is accurate and reliable. Use the following strategies as you listen to public speakers:

- **Determine the Speaker's Purpose** Think about the background, viewpoint, and possible motives of the speaker. Separate facts from opinions. Listen carefully to details and evidence that a speaker uses to support the message.

- **Listen for the Main Idea** Figure out the speaker's main message before allowing yourself to be distracted by seemingly convincing details.

- **Recognize Persuasive Speech** Pay attention to a speaker's tone, mood, and emotion. Also, speakers may present information in a particular way to persuade you to accept an idea. Persuasive devices such as glittering generalities, either/or reasoning, and bandwagon or snob appeal may represent faulty reasoning and provide misleading information.

  *For more information, see **Recognizing Persuasive Techniques,** page R21.*

- **Recognize Rhetorical Devices** A speaker may draw attention to important ideas with **repetition** of words and phrases or by changing

the **cadence,** or rhythm and timing, of the speech. **Rhetorical questions,** or questions with assumed answers, involve the audience in the topic. A speaker may also make **allusions,** or indirect references, to something the audience will recognize. **Onomatopoeia,** a sound device in which words sound like the thing or action they represent, can express ideas creatively.

- **Observe Verbal and Nonverbal Messages** Note the speaker's movements, gestures, and posture. Compare your impressions of the speaker's appearance with his or her tone of voice to see if both support the message.

- **Give Appropriate Feedback** An effective speaker looks for verbal and nonverbal cues from his or her listeners to see how the message is being received. For example, if you agree with the speaker's message, you might nod your head.

4.2 VERBAL FEEDBACK

You may be asked to give a speaker feedback on a presentation's delivery and content.

Evaluate Delivery

- Did the speaker speak clearly and distinctly?
- Did the speaker pronounce words correctly?
- Did the speaker vary his or her rate of speaking?
- Did the speaker's voice sound natural and not strained?

Evaluate Content

Here's how to give constructive suggestions:

Be Specific Don't make statements like "Your examples need work." Offer concrete advice, such as "Consider dropping one of the last two examples, since they are very similar."

Discuss Only the Most Important Points Some points to focus on are:

- Is the topic appropriate for the audience?
- Are the supporting details and evidence well organized?
- Is the conclusion strong enough?

Give Balanced Feedback Tell the speaker what worked, as well as what didn't.

Movies, television, radio, newspapers, the Internet—media are all around us. You see hundreds of media images and messages every day. How can you be a smart media consumer? A person who is media literate *is familiar with the different types of media, their purposes, and how they are created. If you are media literate, you are able to analyze and evaluate media messages and the effects they have on you and your world. This section introduces the tools you will need to study media messages.*

COMMON CORE

Included in this handbook:
RI 4, SL 2, SL 3

1 Five Core Concepts in Media Literacy

from The Center for Media Literacy

The five core concepts of media literacy provide you with the basic ideas you can consider when examining media messages.

All media messages are "constructed." All media messages are made by someone. In fact, they are carefully thought out and researched and have attitudes and values built into them. Much of the information that you use to make sense of the world comes from the media. Therefore, it is important to know how a medium is put together so you can better understand the message it conveys.

Media messages are constructed using a creative language with its own rules. Each means of communication—whether it is film, television, newspapers, magazines, radio, or the Internet—has its own language and design. Therefore, the message must use the language and design of the medium that delivers the message. Thus, the medium actually shapes the message. For example, a horror film may use music to heighten suspense, or a newspaper may use a big headline to signal the importance of a story. Understanding the language of each medium can increase your enjoyment of it as well as help you recognize any subtle attempt to persuade you.

Different people experience the same media messages differently. Personal factors such as age, education, and experience will affect the way a person responds to a media message. How many times has your interpretation of a film or book differed from that of a friend? Everyone interprets media messages differently.

Media have embedded values and points of view. Media messages carry underlying values, which are purposely built into them by the creators of the message. For example, a commercial's main purpose may be to persuade you to buy something, but the commercial may also aim to convince you that the product is important to a particular way of life. Understanding not only the main message but also any other points of view will help you decide whether to accept or reject the message.

Most media messages are constructed to gain profit and/or power. The creators of media messages often provide a commodity, such as information or entertainment, in order to make money. The bigger the audience, the more the media outlet can charge for advertising. Consequently, media outlets want to build large audiences in order to bring in more revenue from advertising. For example, a television network will create programming to appeal to the largest audience possible, in the hope that the viewer ratings will attract more advertising dollars.

2 Media Basics

2.1 MESSAGE

When a film or TV show is created, it becomes a media product. Each media product is created to send a **message,** or an expression of a belief or opinion, that serves a specific purpose. In order to understand the message, you will need to deconstruct it.

Deconstruction of a media presentation is the process of analyzing it. To analyze a media presentation, ask why and how it was created, who created it, and whom it is trying to influence.

2.2 AUDIENCE

A **target audience** is the specific group of people at whom a product or presentation is aimed. The members of a target audience usually have certain characteristics in common, such as age, gender, ethnic background, values, or lifestyle. For example, a target audience may be kids ages 8 to 12 who like chewing gum.

Are you ready for bubbles **THAT JUST WON'T POP?** Amaze your friends with **SuperChew GUM!** NEW

Demographics are the characteristics of a population, including age, gender, profession, income, education, ethnicity, and geographical location. Media decision makers use demographics to shape their product's content to suit the needs and tastes of a target audience.

2.3 PURPOSE

The **purpose,** or intent, of a media presentation is the reason it was made. All media products—from news programs to video games—are created for a specific purpose. Identifying why a media product was invented is the first step in understanding how it can influence you. The following chart shows purposes of different media products.

Purposes of Media Products

Purpose	Example
To Inform	news reports and articles, public service announcements, some Web sites
To Persuade	advertisements, editorials, reviews, political cartoons
To Entertain	most TV shows, films, recorded music, video games, talk shows

Most media products have more than one purpose. For example, a documentary's main purpose is to inform people about a subject, but it also tries to entertain its audience. If you aren't aware of all of a media product's different purposes, you may become influenced without knowing it. This chart shows some examples of media products that have multiple purposes.

Multiple Purposes in Media

Media Product	Main Purpose	Other Purposes
News Broadcast	to inform	to persuade you that an issue or idea is important
Advertisement	to persuade	to entertain you; to inform you about a product
Sports Coverage	to entertain	to inform you about sports or athletes

2.4 TYPES AND GENRES OF MEDIA

The term *media* refers to television, newspapers, magazines, radio, movies, and the Internet. Each is a **medium,** or means for carrying information, entertainment, and advertisements to a large audience.

Media Tools THINK central

Go to thinkcentral.com.
KEYWORD: HML6-####

Each type of media has different characteristics, strengths, and weaknesses. The following chart shows how several types of media deliver their messages.

Type of Media	Characteristics
Newspaper Article	• Provides detailed information and dramatic photographs • Uses **headlines** and **subheads** to give main ideas • Can't be updated until next edition or next day
Television News Report	• Uses an **announcer,** or "anchor," to guide viewers through the news report • Uses **video footage** to bring news to life or clarify what happened • Uses **graphics** to give information at a glance • Can be updated quickly
Documentary	• Tells about historic people and places, major events, and important social, political, or environmental issues • Uses **footage,** or shots of photographs, interviews, news reports, and film clips, to help viewers understand the subject • Features **interviews** of experts or people directly involved with the subject • Uses a **voice-over narrator,** the voice of an unseen speaker, who tells viewers why the subject is important and how the information about the subject is organized
Web Site	• Gives in-depth information on specialized subjects • Allows users to interact socially and to share files • Uses **text, still images,** and **video** • Allows users to select the information they want to receive by clicking on links • Allows users to see when the site was last updated • Can be updated quickly

2.5 PRODUCERS AND CREATORS

People who control the media are known as **gatekeepers.** Gatekeepers decide what information to share with the public and the ways it will be presented. The following diagram gives some examples.

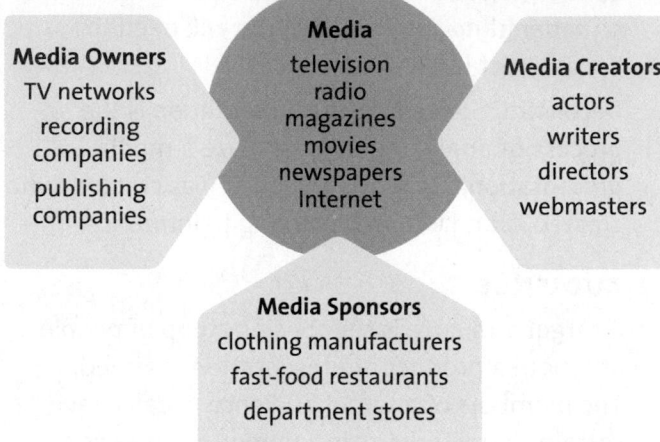

Media Owners — TV networks, recording companies, publishing companies

Media — television, radio, magazines, movies, newspapers, Internet

Media Creators — actors, writers, directors, webmasters

Media Sponsors — clothing manufacturers, fast-food restaurants, department stores

Media sponsors are companies that pay for their products to be advertised. It's important to be aware of sponsors and other gatekeepers, because they control much of what you see and hear. For example, if a fast-food chain sponsors a television show, you probably won't see characters on that show eating food from a competing restaurant.

2.6 INFLUENCE OF MEDIA

Everywhere you go, you're bombarded by media—advertisements, newspapers, magazines, radio, and television. Different kinds of media are all competing for your attention, telling you, "Buy this product. Listen to this music. Read this story. Look at this image. Think about this opinion." The creators of these media products are selling messages. But they may also be sending subtle messages about values that they want you to believe in.

For example, an ad for sneakers is meant to sell you shoes, but if you examine the ad more closely, you will see that it uses a set of values, such as athletic skill, to make the shoes more appealing. The ad suggests that if you buy the shoes, your athletic skills will improve. It also sends the message that athletic skill is a good thing to have. TV shows, movies, and news programs also convey values and beliefs.

Media can also shape your opinions about the world. For example, news about crime shapes our understanding of how much and what type of crime is common in the world around us. TV news items, magazine interviews, and commercials may shape what we think of a political candidate, a celebrity, an ethnic group, a country, or a region. As a result, our knowledge of a person or a place could be completely based on the information we receive from the media.

3 Film and TV

Films and television programs come in a variety of types. Films include comedies, dramas, documentaries, and animated features. Televison programs include dramas, sitcoms, talk shows, reality shows, and newscasts. Producers of films and producers of television programs rely on many of the same elements to make the action and settings seem real and also to affect the emotions of their audience members. Among these elements are scripts, visual and sound elements, special effects, and editing.

3.1 SCRIPT AND WRITTEN ELEMENTS

The writer and editor develop a story for television or film using a script and a storyboard. A **script** is the text, or words, of a film or television show. A **storyboard** is used to plan the shooting of a movie or TV show. A storyboard is made up of drawings and brief descriptions of what is happening in each shot of a scene. This helps a director visualize how a finished scene might look before the scene is filmed. Following are two scenes from a storyboard that a student created.

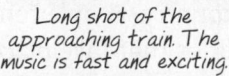

Long shot of the approaching train. The music is fast and exciting.

The train rumbles by loudly. Medium shot of Klaus and Violet.

For more information, see Media Study: Produce Your Own Media, page 113.

3.2 VISUAL ELEMENTS

Visual elements in film and television include camera shots and angles. A **camera shot** is a single, continuous view taken by a camera. A **camera angle** is the angle at which the camera is positioned during the recording of a shot or image. Each is carefully planned to create a certain effect. This chart shows what different shots are used for.

Camera Shot/Angle	Effect
Establishing shot introduces viewers to the location of a scene, usually by presenting a wide view of an area	establishes the setting of a film or television show
Close-up shot shows a close view of a person or object	helps to create emotion and make viewers feel as if they know the character
Medium shot shows a view wider than a close-up but narrower than an establishing or long shot	shows part of an object, or a character from the knees or waist up
Long shot gives a wide view of a scene, showing the full figure(s) of a person or group and the surroundings	allows the viewer to see the "big picture" and shows the relationship between characters and the environment
Reaction shot shows in some way what a character sees	allows the viewer to see how the character feels in order to create empathy in the viewer
Low-angle shot looks up at an object or person	makes a character, object, or scene appear more important or threatening
High-angle shot looks down on an object or person	makes a character, object, or scene seem weak or unimportant
Point-of-view (POV) shot shows a part of the story through a character's eyes	helps viewers identify with that character

3.3 SOUND ELEMENTS

Sound elements in film and television include music, voice-over, and sound effects.

Music may be used to create an atmosphere and mood in a scene. Music can have a powerful effect on the way viewers feel about a story. For example, fast-paced music can help give an action scene a mood of excitement and danger.

Voice-over is the voice of the unseen commentator or narrator of a film, TV program, or commercial.

Sound effects are the sounds added to films, TV programs, and commercials during the editing process. Sound effects, such as laugh tracks or the sounds of punches in a fight scene, can create humor, emphasize a point, or contribute to the mood.

3.4 SPECIAL EFFECTS

Special effects include computer-generated animation, altered video images, and fast- or slow-motion sequences in films, TV programs, and commercials.

Animation on film involves the frame-by-frame photography of a series of drawings or objects. When these frames are projected—at a rate of 24 per second—the illusion of movement is achieved.

A **split screen** is a special-effects shot in which two or more separate images are shown in the same frame. One example is when two people, actually a distance apart, are shown talking to each other.

3.5 EDITING

Editing is the process of selecting and arranging shots in a sequence. Moviemakers put shots together in ways that help you follow the action of a story. The editor decides which scenes or shots to use, as well as the length of each shot, the number of shots, and their sequence.

Cut is the transition from one shot to another. To create excitement, editors often use quick cuts, which are a series of short shots strung together.

Dissolve is a device in which one scene fades into another.

Fade-in is a device in which a white or black shot fades in to reveal the beginning of a new scene.

Fade-out is a device in which a shot fades to darkness to end a scene.

Jump cut is an abrupt and jarring change from one shot to another. A jump cut shows a break in time.

Pace is the length of time each shot stays on the screen and the rhythm that is created by the transitions between shots. Short, quick cuts create a fast pace in a story. Long cuts slow down a story.

4 News

The **news** is information on events, people, and places in your community, the region, the nation, and the world. It can be found in local newspapers, newscasts, online wire services, magazines, and documentaries. It would be impossible to publish all the news that happens in one day in any one source, though, so journalists have to make decisions about which stories will appear in each day's newspapers and on newscasts. Several factors help determine which events are "news."

4.1 CHOOSING THE NEWS

Newsworthiness is the importance of an event or action that makes it worthy of media reporting. Journalists and their editors often use the following guidelines in determining which stories are newsworthy:

Timeliness is the quality of being very current. Timely events usually take priority over previously reported events. For example, information about an election will be timely on the day the voting occurs. Election results may appear on the front page of a newspaper once the votes are counted.

Widespread impact is a characteristic of an event that could affect a number of people. The more widespread the impact of an event, the more likely it is to be newsworthy.

Proximity measures the nearness of an event to a particular city, region, or country. People tend to be more interested in stories that take place close to where they live and thus may affect them directly.

Human interest is a quality of stories that cause readers or listeners to feel emotions such as happiness, anger, or sadness. People are interested in reading or hearing stories about other people.

Uniqueness is the condition of being the only one of a kind. Unique or uncommon events or circumstances are likely to be interesting to an audience.

Compelling video and **photographs** grab people's attention and stay in their minds.

4.2 REPORTING THE NEWS

When developing a news story, a journalist must decide how to construct the story—what information to include, and how to organize it. The following elements are commonly used in news stories:

5 W's and H are the six questions reporters answer when writing news stories—*who, what, when, where, why*, and *how*. It is a journalist's job to answer these questions in any type of news report. These questions also provide a structure for writing and editing a story.

Inverted pyramid is a way of organizing information in the order of importance. In an inverted-pyramid organization, the most important information (the answers to the 5 W's and H) appears at the top of the pyramid. The less important details appear at the bottom. Not all stories are reported using the inverted-pyramid form. However, this form helps a reader to get the most important information without having to read the entire story. Following is an example of inverted-pyramid organization.

> This week, local officials passed a law making it illegal to ride a bicycle without a helmet.
>
> The mayor hopes this law will reduce bicycle-related injuries.
>
> Several other cities are planning to pass similar laws this summer.

Angle or slant is the point of view from which a story is written. Even an objective report must have an angle.

Consider these two headlines that describe the same tornado.

The headline on the right focuses on a fact. The headline on the left focuses on an opinion and has a negative slant.

Standards for News Reporting

The ideal of journalism is to present news in a way that is objective, accurate, and thorough. The best news stories contain the following elements:

- **Objectivity**—The story takes a balanced point of view on the issues. It is not biased, nor does it reflect a specific attitude or opinion.

- **Accuracy**—The story presents factual information that can be verified.

- **Thoroughness**—The story presents all sides of an issue. It includes background information, telling *who, what, when, where, why*, and *how*.

Balanced Versus Biased Reporting

Objectivity in news reporting can be measured by how balanced or biased the story is.

Balanced reporting presents all sides of an issue equally and fairly.

A balanced news story

- represents people and subjects in a neutral light

- treats all sides of an issue equally

- does not include inappropriate questions, such as "Will you seek counseling to help you recover from this terrible tragedy?"

- does not show stereotypes or prejudice toward people of a particular race, gender, age, religion, or other group
- does not leave out important background information that is needed to establish a context or perspective

Biased reporting is reporting in which one side is favored over another or in which the subject is unfairly represented. Biased reporting may show an overly negative view of a subject, or it may encourage racial, gender, or other stereotypes and prejudices. Sometimes biased reporting is apparent in the journalist's choice of sources.

Sources are the people interviewed for the news report, and also any written materials the journalist used for background information. From each source, the journalist gets a different point of view. To decide whether news reporting is balanced or biased, you will need to pay attention to the sources. Consider a magazine article about the safety of a new kind of car. If the journalist only interviews a spokesperson for the car company, then the article may be biased. If, on the other hand, the journalist also includes information from a neutral person, such as an engineer who studies automobile safety, the article might be more balanced. The following chart shows which sources are reliable.

Sources for News Stories	
Reliable Sources	**Weak Sources**
• experts in a field or subject area	• unnamed or anonymous sources
• people directly affected by the reported event (eyewitnesses)	• people who are not involved in the reported event (for example, people who heard about a story from a friend)
• published reports that are specifically mentioned or shown	• research, data, or reports that are not specifically named or are referred to only in vague terms (for example, "Research shows that …")

5 Advertising

Advertising is a sponsor's paid use of various media to promote products, services, or ideas. Some common forms of advertising are shown in the chart.

Type of Ad	Description
Billboard	a large outdoor advertising sign
Print Ad	an ad that appears in magazines and newspapers; typically uses eye-catching graphics and persuasive copy
Flyer	a print ad that is circulated by hand or mail
Infomercial	an extended ad on TV that includes detailed product information, demonstrations, and testimonials
Public Service Announcement	a message aired on radio or TV to promote ideas that are considered to be in the public interest
Political Ad	a message broadcast on radio or TV to promote political candidates
Trailer	a short film promoting an upcoming movie, TV show, or video game

Marketing is the process of transferring products and services from producer to consumer. It involves determining the packaging and pricing of a product, how it will be promoted and advertised, and where it will be sold. One way companies market their products is by becoming media sponsors.

Sponsors pay for their products to be advertised. These companies hire advertising agencies to create and produce specific campaigns for their products. They then buy television or radio airtime or magazine, newspaper, or billboard space to feature ads where the target audience is sure to see them. Because selling time and space to advertisers produces much of the income the media need to function, the media need advertisers just as much as advertisers need the media.

Product placement is the intentional and identifiable featuring of brand-name products in movies, television shows, video games, and other media. The intention is to have viewers feel positive about a product because they see a favorite character using it. Another purpose may be to promote product recognition.

5.1 PERSUASIVE TECHNIQUES

Persuasive techniques are the methods used to convince an audience to buy a product or adopt an idea. Advertisers use a combination of visuals, sound, special effects, and words to persuade their target audience. Recognizing the following techniques can help you evaluate persuasive media messages and identify misleading information:

Emotional appeals use strong feelings, such as fear and pity, rather than facts to persuade consumers. An example is "Our shelter has dozens of lonely puppies looking for homes. Won't you give one of them a chance?"

Bandwagon appeals use the argument that a person should believe or do something because "everyone else" does. These appeals take advantage of people's desire to be socially accepted by other people. An example of a bandwagon appeal is "Don't be left out! See why everyone's buying the new album by Gopher Broke."

Slogans are memorable phrases used in advertising campaigns. Slogans substitute catchy phrases for facts.

Logical appeals rely on logic and facts, appealing to a consumer's reason and his or her respect for authority. Two examples of logical appeals are expert opinions and product comparison.

Celebrity ads use one of the following two categories of spokesperson:

- **Celebrity authorities** are experts in a particular field. Advertisers hope that audiences will transfer the respect or admiration they have for the person to the product. For example, suppose a famous Hollywood hairstylist endorses, or recommends, a brand of shampoo. The shampoo manufacturer wants you to think that the product is good

enough for even the best professionals.

- **Celebrity spokespeople** are famous people who endorse a product. Advertisers hope that audiences will associate the product with the celebrity.

Product comparison is comparing between a product and its competition. Often mentioned by name, the competing product is portrayed as inferior. The intended effect is for people to question the quality of the competing product and to believe the featured product is better.

6 Elements of Design

The design of a media product is just as important as the words are in conveying the message. Like words, visual elements are used to persuade, inform, and entertain.

Graphics and images, such as charts, diagrams, maps, timelines, photographs, illustrations, and symbols, present information that can be quickly and easily understood. The following basic elements are used to give meaning to visuals:

Color can be used to highlight important elements such as headlines and subheads. It can also create mood, because many colors have strong emotional or psychological impacts on the reader or viewer. For example, warm colors are often associated with happiness and comfort. Cool colors are often associated with feelings of peace and contentment or sometimes with sadness.

Lines—strokes or marks—can be thick or thin, long or short, and smooth or jagged. They can focus attention and create a feeling of depth. They can frame an object. They can also direct a viewer's eye or create a sense of motion.

Texture is the apparent surface quality of an object. For example, an object's texture can be rough, wet, or shiny. Texture can be used to create contrast. It can also be used to make an object look "real." For example, a pattern on wrapping paper can create a feeling of depth even though the texture is only visual and cannot be felt.

Shape is the external outline of an object. Shapes can be used to symbolize living things or geometric objects. They can emphasize visual elements and add interest. Shapes can also symbolize ideas.

Notice how this movie poster uses design elements.

Lines The reader's eyes are led downward from the main image by the lamppost, to the smaller images around the edges of the poster.

Color Deep blues and bright golds suggest a dramatic story and hint at a conflict.

Shape The large image of the lion catches the reader's attention. The images surrounding the lion draw the eye to the film's title.

7 Evaluating Media Messages

By looking closely at media products, you can see how their messages influence your opinions and your buying habits. Here are six questions to ask about any media message:

Who made—and who sponsored—this message, and for what purpose? The source of the message is a clue to its purpose. If the source of the message is a private company, that company may be trying to sell you a product. If the source is a government agency, that agency may be trying to promote a program or particular point of view. To discover the purpose, think about why its creator paid for and produced the message.

Who is the target audience and how is the message specifically tailored to it? Think about the age group, ethnic group, gender, and/or profession the message is targeting. Decide how it relates to you.

What are the different techniques used to inform, persuade, entertain, and attract attention? Analyze the elements, such as humor, music, special effects, and graphics, that have been used to create the message. Think about how visual and sound effects, such as symbols, color, photographs, words, and music, support the purpose behind the message.

What messages are communicated (and/or implied) about certain people, places, events, behaviors, lifestyles, and so forth? The media try to influence who we are, what we believe in, how we view things, and what values we hold. Look or listen closely to determine whether certain types of behavior are being shown and if judgments or values are communicated through those behaviors. What are the biases in the message?

How current, accurate, and believable is the information in this message? Think about the reputation of the source. Note the broadcast or publication date of the message and whether the message might change quickly. If a report or account is not supported by facts, authoritative sources, or eyewitness accounts, you should question the message.

What is left out of this message that might be important to know? Think about what the message is asking you to believe. Also think about what questions come to mind as you watch, read, or listen to the message.

Strategies and Practice for State and Standardized Tests

The test questions in this section are modeled after many different kinds of tests that you may have to take while you are a student. The tips and strategies presented here will help you prepare for answering multiple-choice, short-constructed-response, and extended-constructed-response questions. This section also includes guidelines for writing an essay, as well as a sample essay. Read the tips in the margin, and then apply them to the practice questions. You can also apply the tips to the Assessment Practice *tests in this book.*

1 General Test-Taking Strategies

Getting Ready

- Arrive on time and be prepared. Be sure to bring either sharpened pencils with erasers or pens—whichever you are told to bring.

- If you have any questions, ask them before the test begins. Make sure you understand how to mark the answers, how much time you will have to take the test, and other test rules.

- Read the test directions carefully. Look at the passages and the types of questions to get an idea of what is expected.

Reading the Test

- Focus on one question at a time rather than thinking about the whole test.

- Look for main ideas as you read passages. They are often stated at the beginning or the end of a paragraph. Sometimes the main idea is implied, or suggested, rather than stated.

- Refer back to the passage as needed. For example, if a question asks about an author's attitude, you might have to reread a passage for clues.

Marking Your Answers

- If you are not sure of your answer, make a logical guess. You can often arrive at the correct answer by reasoning and rejecting wrong answers.

- As you fill in answers on your answer sheet, make sure you match each test item to its numbered space on the answer sheet.

- Don't look for patterns in the positions of correct choices.

- Only change an answer if you are sure your original choice is incorrect. If you do change an answer, erase your original choice neatly and thoroughly.

- Check your answers and reread your essay.

2 Critical Reading

In middle school, you will read many different types of writing, both fiction and nonfiction. You will read novels, persuasive essays, poems, historical documents, and scientific or technical information. Tests will measure your ability to read and analyze these kinds of writing.

Directions: Read the passage and then answer the questions that follow.

PASSAGE

Did you ever see an Egyptian mummy in a museum? Or statues dug from ancient cities? If so, you already have been introduced to archaeology.

Archaeology is a science. It is the study of very old objects such as buildings, bones, and tools.

The scientists who find and study old objects are called archaeologists. They look for objects that are many hundreds or thousands of years old. They study old objects to learn how people lived in ancient times.

Up until the 1700s, people had little interest in studying things from the past. When they found ancient objects (called artifacts), they kept the ones
10 made of gold. Less valuable ones were often thrown away!

In 1748 a farmer digging in a field in Italy struck an underground wall. A digging crew then unearthed an ancient city. It was Pompeii, which had been destroyed by a volcano nearly 1,700 years earlier. The excavation (digging) at Pompeii was one of the first done in an organized way. But archaeologists of the 1700s still mainly sought treasure. They tossed aside many other artifacts in search of it.

Sir Flinders Petrie (1853–1942) was one of the first archaeologists to study everything he found. Petrie worked in Egypt during the late 1800s. When Petrie dug, he searched the earth "inch by inch," as he described it.
20 Petrie found pottery, tools, and other items used by Egyptians in their daily life. Because he worked so carefully, Petrie is called the "Father of Modern Archaeology."

Today's archaeologists use the "inch by inch" method. They keep detailed records of everything they find. They know that the smallest artifact can help us understand how ancient people lived.

The world is a big place. How do archaeologists know where to look for ancient relics? They don't just guess. Like detectives, they search for clues.

Old books often provide good clues. The Bible, the works of Homer, and other old manuscripts describe ancient towns. Some of those towns are
30 still there—buried under layers of dirt. Archaeologists study the books to determine where the ancient sites may be located.

People often tell stories about past events. For example, people may tell of a sunken ship. Archaeologists listen to such stories for clues about the ship's location.

Tips: Reading Text

❶ Before you begin reading a passage, quickly skim over the questions that follow it to get an idea of the number and kinds of questions you will be answering.

❷ Look for key ideas as you read. The way in which the science of archaeology changed over time is a key idea in this passage. It is expressed in the opening lines.

❸ Watch for specialized or technical vocabulary words. This passage introduces *excavation* and *artifacts,* two terms used in archaeology.

❹ Pay attention to comparisons. In this passage, the author compares archaeologists to detectives because both follow clues to find what they are looking for.

Archaeologists often use photographs taken from airplanes. They show things that can't be seen from the ground. An aerial photo may show a piece of land to be more fertile than nearby land. This may be because ancient people worked the soil there. Cameras are also used to spot undersea wrecks.

40   Archaeologists have many other tools to help them decide where to work. These include magnets, metal detectors, soil studies, and electrical tests of the ground.

—from *Archaeology*
by Dennis B. Fradin

Directions: Answer these questions about the passage from *Archaeology*.

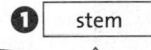

1. What is the author's purpose in this passage?

    A. to describe how ancient people lived

    B. to encourage readers to become archaeologists

    C. to explain the science and practice of archaeology

    D. to compare ancient and modern cities

2. From the details in lines 11–16, you can infer that archaeology in the 1700s was

    A. popular among Italian farmers

    B. concerned mainly with finding treasure

    C. a good way to become rich and famous

    D. a dangerous new branch of science

3. As explained in lines 28–31, archaeologists often use old books to

    A. distinguish fact from science

    B. find ancient sites to excavate

    C. learn how much artifacts are worth

    D. prove how archaeology has changed

4. Archaeologists use the "inch by inch" method of excavation to

    A. search a site very carefully

    B. calculate how deep to dig

    C. measure artifacts that are found

    D. sharpen their tiny digging tools

Tips: Multiple Choice

A multiple-choice question consists of a stem and a set of answer choices. The stem is in the form of a question or an incomplete sentence. One of the choices correctly answers the question or completes the sentence. Many tests offer four answer choices, but no matter how many choices are given, you can use the same strategies to guide you to the best answer.

❶ Read the stem carefully and try to answer the question before you look at the choices.

❷ Pay attention to key words in the stem. They may direct you to the correct answer. Note that question 1 is looking for the *author's purpose,* or the author's reason for writing the passage.

❸ Read all the answer choices before you decide which one is correct. For example, in question 2, you might be tempted to stop at choice A, because the passage mentions a farmer in Italy, but that is not the correct answer.

❹ Look for clues in the passage. Question 3 asks about the role of old books in archaeology. The passage says that archaeologists study old books "to determine where the ancient sites may be located." It says nothing about using books to establish historical facts, monetary values, or archaeological practices.

Answers: 1. C, **2.** B, **3.** B, **4.** A

3 Vocabulary

Most standardized tests include questions about the meanings of words. Some questions might be about words in a passage you just read, while others might be about words in a sentence or paragraph, followed by the answer choices.

1. Which word from the passage on pages R94–R95 has a negative connotation? ❶
   - A. objects (line 3)
   - B. artifacts (line 9)
   - C. underground (line 11)
   - D. tossed (line 15)

2. Which word from the passage comes from the Latin words that mean "written by hand"?
   - A. artifacts (line 9)
   - B. organized (line 14)
   - C. records (line 24)
   - D. manuscripts (line 29) ❷

3. Which line from the passage contains a simile? ❸
   - A. The scientists who find and study old objects are called archaeologists. (line 5)
   - B. Because he worked so carefully, Petrie is called the "Father of Modern Archaeology." (lines 21–22)
   - C. Like detectives, they search for clues. (line 27)
   - D. People often tell stories about past events. (line 32)

4. Read this dictionary entry for the word *spot*. Which definition best matches the meaning of the word *spot* as it is used in line 38 of the passage?

   > **DEFINITION**
   >
   > **spot** *noun.* **1.** A dirty area. **2.** A small place. **3.** A location.
   > *verb.* **1.** To stain. **2.** To locate. **3.** To schedule at a particular time.

   - A. *noun* meaning 1
   - B. *noun* meaning 2
   - C. *verb* meaning 1
   - D. *verb* meaning 2 ❹

Tips: Word Meaning

❶ Connotation is the suggestion or feeling a word or phrase carries beyond its literal meaning. *Objects* is a neutral word, while *artifacts* is more positive, suggesting something valuable. The word *tossed*, which is part of the phrase "tossed aside," has a negative connotation.

❷ If you don't know the exact meaning of a word, look for clues in nearby sentences. For the word *manuscripts* in line 29, read the sentence it appears in and the one before it. The information about books is a clue that manuscripts are written records.

❸ A simile is a figure of speech. The words *like* and *as* are clues that a comparison is a simile.

❹ Eliminate any answers that are not the same part of speech as the word as it is used in the passage. *Spot* is used as a verb in the passsage, so you can rule out answer choices A and B.

Answers: 1. D, **2.** D, **3.** C, **4.** D

④ Writing and Grammar

You will be asked to write essays and even research papers in middle school. When it comes to writing, good ideas aren't enough. You need to know how to express them. That requires knowledge of English grammar, sentence structure, and usage. To measure this knowledge, many standardized tests ask you to identify errors or to improve sentences and paragraphs.

Directions: Read this passage and then answer the questions.

> **PASSAGE**
>
> (1) Their is nothing better than a morning bike ride. (2) You should leave just as the sun rises. (3) It will be quiet with very little traffic. (4) The silence will allow you to enjoy the early morning sounds of nature. (5) When was the last time you heard the wind whispering through the trees? (6) The birds will be just waking up and trying out its songs soon. (7) Rising off the grass, you'll also see the mist. (8) As you pedal along, you'll feel free and happy.

1. What change, if any, should be made to sentence 1?
   - **A.** Change *Their* to *There*
   - **B.** Change *than* to *then*
   - **C.** Change *better* to *more better*
   - **D.** Make no change

2. The correct conjunction to join sentences 2 and 3 is
   - **A.** but
   - **B.** unless
   - **C.** because
   - **D.** nor

3. What change, if any, should be made to sentence 6?
   - **A.** Change *trying* to *tried*
   - **B.** Change *waking* to *has woken*
   - **C.** Change *its* to *their*
   - **D.** Make no change

4. What is the best way to rewrite sentence 7?
   - **A.** You'll also, rising off the grass, see the mist.
   - **B.** Rising off the grass, the mist you'll also see.
   - **C.** Also rising off the grass, you'll see the mist.
   - **D.** You'll also see the mist rising off the grass.

Tips: Grammar

❶ Read the entire passage to grasp its overall meaning. Pay particular attention to any underlined parts.

❷ Some items will test your knowledge of commonly confused words. In test item 1, choice A is a possible revision.

❸ In test items 1 and 3, choice D says, "Make no change." Choose this answer only if the sentence is correct as it is originally written.

❹ If you are asked to combine sentences, think about how the ideas relate to each other. When you understand the connection between the thoughts, you will know how to join them. The word *but* (choice A) can be used to show how two different ideas are related, but it is not the right word to express the cause-and-effect relationship between sentences 2 and 3.

❺ Some items will test your knowledge of language conventions. Make sure that pronouns agree with antecedents and that verbs agree with subjects.

❻ Before choosing a revision, read through all of the choices to decide which one is best. Your answer should produce a sentence that is grammatically correct.

Answers: 1. A, **2.** C, **3.** C, **4.** D

5 Responding to Writing Prompts

Not all tests are multiple choice. Sometimes you have to develop your ideas into a paragraph or a short essay. You might be asked to interpret, summarize, or react to a reading selection.

> **Directions:** Reread the passage from *Archaeology* on pages R94–R95 and follow the directions for the short and extended constructed responses.

SHORT CONSTRUCTED RESPONSE

Write a well-organized paragraph comparing and contrasting archaeology before the 1700s with archaeology today. Base your response on the information given in the passage.

> **SAMPLE SHORT CONSTRUCTED RESPONSE**
>
> Today, archaeology is practiced very differently than it was in the 1700s. In the 1700s, people usually did not search carefully for old objects or try to learn about ancient people. ❶ They were mainly interested in finding treasure and threw away anything that wasn't gold. Today, in contrast, archaeologists use the slow, careful "inch by inch" method developed by Sir Flinders Petrie. ❷ Modern archaeologists must pay close attention to everything they find, because anything can be a clue about ancient people and their lives.

EXTENDED CONSTRUCTED RESPONSE

What sources and tools do archaeologists use to help them make new discoveries? Express your ideas in two or three paragraphs.

> **SAMPLE EXTENDED CONSTRUCTED RESPONSE**
>
> One of the most important tools archaeologists need is curiosity about the way people lived long ago. In addition to this, they rely upon both high-tech and low-tech resources to help them in their search. ❸
>
> Old written records, such as the Bible or the works of Homer, can give clues about the locations of ancient cities or objects. Local legends and stories can also be a source of information and ideas for the scientists.
>
> ❹ Modern archaeologists also use technology in their work. Photographs taken underwater and from airplanes show features that can't be seen from the ground. Magnets and metal detectors can locate hidden metal objects. Electrical tests on the ground also can show the scientists where to begin digging for relics.

Tips: Responding to Writing Prompts

❶ Short-constructed-response prompts are often fact based rather than interpretive. Get right to the point in your answer, and stick to the facts.

❷ Make sure that you write about the assigned topic. Support your answer with details from the passage, such as a quotation, a paraphrase, or an example.

❸ Express your ideas clearly so that the reader will understand your viewpoint. You may also want to include any inferences you have made from your reading.

❹ When you are writing an extended constructed response, build your paragraphs around clear topic sentences that will pull your ideas together.

❺ Proofread your response for errors in capitalization, punctuation, spelling, or grammar.

6 Writing an Essay

Many tests will ask you to read a prompt and write an essay in response to it. You might be asked to write a narrative, persuasive, or expository essay. You might be asked to write a story, summarize an article, or respond to a piece of writing. It is important to read the prompt carefully and look for direction words that tell you what to write about. Because you will have a limited amount of time, this essay will represent a first draft. Even so, it should be complete. Essays are scored according to the following guidelines:

- **Focus** Establish a point of view in the opening paragraph. Stay with that focus throughout the essay.
- **Organization** Connect ideas and present information logically.
- **Support for ideas** Use details and examples to develop an argument or line of thinking.
- **Style/word choice** Use words accurately and vary sentences.
- **Grammar** Use standard English and proofread for errors.

WRITING PROMPT

Many stories, books, and movies make predictions about the future, describing a world with a changed environment or new technology. What do you think the world will be like when you are grown up? Describe your predictions in an essay of four or five paragraphs.

SAMPLE DESCRIPTIVE ESSAY

Today, I turned 60 years old. So many things have changed since I was in middle school! At the same time, some things haven't changed that much.

I stop in the doorway of my apartment and look at my street. It's a busy street in a big city, humming with activity. Dozens of glittering glass buildings tower over the mechanical sidewalks as they carry people along. My building is the tallest, at just over 400 stories. I live on the 385th floor. When I was a kid, just 50 stories seemed dizzying! **2**

1 Down the street is a garage where the city stores cars. Nobody has their own car anymore; they ride on the high-speed train or borrow a car from the city for a day. The garage looks like an enormous greenhouse—that's because **3** of the thousands of solar panels that cover its curved rooftop. The panels are used to charge the cars' batteries. All of our cars run on solar power, so they create much less pollution.

1 At the end of my street is the river. Unfortunately, no one can swim in it. **2** The water is sour smelling and greenish brown, and it foams at the edges. This pollution has gotten much worse over the last 50 years, although we are working hard to fix it.

All in all, though the world now still has some of the old problems I remember from my childhood, in many ways it has become a cleaner, safer place. **4**

Tips: Writing an Essay

Before you begin writing, take a minute or two to gather your thoughts. You don't need to prepare a complete outline, but write the main points you want to make. In the futuristic essay here, pollution and transportation are key issues.

1 When writing a descriptive essay, be sure to present your details in a logical order. In this essay, the information is arranged in spatial order, which describes all the details of a space or scene.

2 Sensory details make your subject come to life, no matter what the topic is. Use them in the body of your essay to create memorable images and experiences for your reader.

3 Figures of speech, such as similes, metaphors, and analogies, will help clarify your meaning to readers and strengthen your descriptions. In this essay, the author uses a simile to describe a futuristic building.

4 Make sure your essay has a conclusion, even if it's just a single sentence. A conclusion pulls your ideas together and lets the reader know you have finished.

5 Allow time to reread what you have written. If you have to make a correction, do so neatly and legibly.

Act An act is a major division within a play, similar to a chapter in a book. Each act may be further divided into smaller sections, called scenes.

Adventure Story An adventure story is a literary work in which action is the main element. An **adventure novel** usually focuses on a main character who is on a mission and faces many challenges and choices.

Alliteration Alliteration is the repetition of consonant sounds at the beginning of words. Note the repetition of the *w* sound in this line.

> To the gull's <u>w</u>ay and the <u>w</u>hale's <u>w</u>ay <u>w</u>here the <u>w</u>ind's
> like a <u>w</u>hetted knife;
> —John Masefield, "Sea-Fever"

See pages 580, 615.

Allusion An allusion is a reference to a famous person, place, event, or work of literature. In the personal essay "Role-Playing and Discovery," Jerry Pinkney makes an allusion to such men as movie cowboy Roy Rogers and pioneer Daniel Boone.

Analogy An analogy is a comparison between two things that are alike in some way. Often, writers use analogies to explain unfamiliar subjects or ideas in terms of familiar ones.
See also **Metaphor; Simile.**

Anecdote An anecdote is a short account of an event that is usually intended to entertain or make a point. In the short story "The All-American Slurp" by Lensey Namioka, the story's narrator uses a humorous anecdote about her family loudly slurping soup in a restaurant to show one of the many cultural differences her Chinese family faced after their immigration to the United States.
See page 851.

Antagonist The antagonist is a force working against the protagonist, or main character, in a story, play, or novel. The antagonist is usually another character but can be a force of nature, society itself, or an internal force within the main character. In Fan Kissen's dramatization of the Greek legend "Damon and Pythias," the king is the antagonist.
See also **Protagonist.**

Assonance Assonance is the repetition of vowel sounds within nonrhyming words. An example of assonance is the repetition of the $\overline{oo}$ sound in the following lines.

> I'm Nobody! Wh<u>o</u> are y<u>ou</u>?
> Are y<u>ou</u>—Nobody—T<u>oo</u>?
> —Emily Dickinson, "I'm Nobody! Who are You?"

Audience The audience of a piece of writing is the group of readers that the writer is addressing. A writer considers his or her audience when deciding on a subject, a purpose, a tone, and a style in which to write.

Author's Perspective An author's perspective is the combination of ideas, values, feelings, and beliefs that influences the way the writer looks at a topic. **Tone,** or attitude, often reveals an author's perspective. Helen Keller wrote "The Story of My Life" from the perspective of an adult looking back at an important moment that changed the course of her life.
See page 275.
See also **Author's Purpose; Tone.**

Author's Purpose A writer usually writes for one or more of these purposes: to express thoughts or feelings, to inform or explain, to persuade, or to entertain. For example, in "SuperCroc," author Peter Winkler's purpose was to inform readers about an important archaeological discovery.
See pages 138, 340, 822.
See also **Author's Perspective.**

Autobiography An autobiography is a writer's account of his or her own life. In almost every case, it is told from the first-person point of view. An autobiography focuses on the most important events and people in the writer's life over a period of time. Helen Keller's "The Story of My Life" is an autobiography.
See pages 265, 802, 833.
See also **Memoir; Personal Narrative.**

Ballad A ballad is a type of narrative poem that tells a story and was originally meant to be sung or recited. Because it tells a story, a ballad has a setting, a plot, and characters. **Folk ballads** were composed orally and handed down by word of mouth from generation to generation.

Biography A biography is the true account of a person's life, written by another person. As such, biographies are usually told from a third-person point of view. The writer of a biography—a **biographer**—usually researches his or her subject in order to present accurate information. The best biographers strive for honesty and balance in their accounts of their subjects' lives. Jim Haskins's "Matthew Henson at the Top of the World" is an example of a biography.

See pages 802, 809.

Cast of Characters In the script of a play, a cast of characters is a list of all the characters in the play, usually in order of appearance. It may include a brief description of each character.

Character Characters are the people, animals, or imaginary creatures who take part in the action of a work of literature. Like real people, characters display certain qualities, or **character traits,** that develop and change over time, and they usually have **motivations,** or reasons, for their behaviors.

> **Main character:** Main characters are the most important characters in literary works. Generally, the plot of a short story focuses on one main character, but a novel may have several main characters.
>
> **Minor characters:** The less important characters in a literary work are known as minor characters. The story is not centered on them, but they help carry out the action of the story and help the reader learn more about the main character.
>
> **Dynamic character:** A dynamic character is one who undergoes important changes as a plot unfolds. The changes occur because of the character's actions and experiences in the story. The changes are usually internal and may be good or bad. Main characters are usually, though not always, dynamic.
>
> **Static character:** A static character is one who remains the same throughout a story. The character may experience events and interact with other characters, but he or she is not changed because of them.

See pages 28, 194, 261, 361.
See also **Characterization; Character Traits.**

Character Development Characters that change during a story are said to undergo character development. Any character can change, but main characters usually develop the most. For example, in "President Cleveland, Where Are You?" Jerry changes from acting selfishly to acting on behalf of others.

See also **Character: Dynamic Character.**

Characterization The way a writer creates and develops characters is known as characterization. There are four basic methods of characterization:

- The writer may make direct comments about a character through the voice of the narrator.
- The writer may describe the character's physical appearance.
- The writer may present the character's own thoughts, speech, and actions.
- The writer may present the thoughts, speech, and actions of other characters.

See pages 194, 865.
See also **Character; Character Traits.**

Character Traits Character traits are the qualities shown by a character. Traits may be physical (tall) or expressions of personality (confidence). Writers reveal the traits of their characters through methods of characterization. Sometimes writers directly state a character's traits, but more often readers need to infer traits from a character's words, actions, thoughts, appearance, and relationships. Examples of words that describe traits include *brave, considerate,* and *rude.*

Climax The climax stage is the point of greatest interest in a story or play. The climax usually occurs toward the end of a story, after the reader has understood the **conflict** and become emotionally involved with the characters. At the climax, the conflict is resolved and the outcome of the plot usually becomes clear.

See pages 30, 35, 47.
See also **Plot.**

Comedy A comedy is a dramatic work that is light and often humorous in tone, usually ending happily with a peaceful resolution of the main conflict.

Conflict A conflict is a struggle between opposing forces. Almost every story has a main conflict—a conflict that is the story's focus. An **external conflict** involves a character who struggles against a force outside him- or herself, such as nature, a physical obstacle, or another character. An **internal conflict** is one that occurs within a character. For example, a character with an internal conflict might struggle with fear.
Examples: In Armstrong Sperry's "The Ghost of the Lagoon," young Mako becomes involved in an external conflict with a shark. In Sandra Cisneros's "Eleven," Rachel struggles with an internal conflict on her birthday. Rachel is torn between the idea of growing older and yet still feeling like a little girl.
See pages 28, 35, 47, 111, 151, 349.
See also **Plot.**

Connotation A word's connotations are the ideas and feelings associated with the word, as opposed to its dictionary definition. For example, the word *bread*, in addition to its basic meaning ("a baked food made from flour and other ingredients"), has connotations of life and general nourishment.
See also **Denotation.**

Couplet A couplet is a rhymed pair of lines. A couplet may be written in any rhythmic pattern.

> Before the coming of the night
> The moon shows papery white;
> —Christina Rossetti, "Is the Moon Tired?"

See also **Rhyme; Stanza.**

Critical Essay *See* **Essay.**

Cultural Values Cultural values are the behaviors that a society expects from its people.

Denotation A word's denotation is its dictionary definition.
See also **Connotation.**

Description Description is writing that helps a reader to picture events, objects, and characters. To create descriptions, writers often use **imagery**—words and phrases that appeal to the reader's senses.

Dialect A dialect is a form of a language that is spoken in a particular place or by a particular group of people. Dialects may feature unique pronunciations, vocabulary, and grammar. For example, the narrator in Walter Dean Myers's short story "Jeremiah's Song" uses dialect that reflects the community in which he lives. This dialect includes informal grammar.

> When he said that, Deacon Turner's wife started crying and goin' on and I give her a hard look, but she just went on.
> —Walter Dean Myers, "Jeremiah's Song"

See pages 195, 221.

Dialogue Dialogue is written conversation between two or more characters. Writers use dialogue to bring characters to life and to give readers insights into the characters' qualities, traits, and reactions to other characters. In fiction, dialogue is usually set off with quotation marks. In drama, stories are told primarily through dialogue.

Diary A diary is a daily record of a writer's thoughts, experiences, and feelings. As such, it is a type of autobiographical writing. A *journal* is another term for a diary.

Drama A drama, or play, is a form of literature meant to be performed by actors in front of an audience. In a drama, the characters' dialogue and actions tell the story. The written form of a drama is called a script. A script usually includes dialogue, a cast of characters, and stage directions that give instructions about performing the drama. The person who writes the drama is known as the playwright or dramatist.

Epic Poem An epic poem is a long narrative poem about the adventures of a hero whose actions reflect the ideals and values of a nation or a group of people.

Essay An essay is a short work of nonfiction that deals with a single subject. There are many types of essays. An **expository essay** presents or explains information and ideas. A **persuasive essay** attempts to convince the reader to adopt a certain viewpoint. A **critical essay** evaluates a situation or a work of art. A **personal essay** usually reflects the writer's experiences, feelings, and personality.

Exaggeration An extreme overstatement of an idea is called an exaggeration. It is often used for purposes of emphasis or humor. In "Uncle Septimus's Beard," author Herbert Shippey exaggerates the length and uses of Septimus's beard in order to create a humorous, larger-than-life description of Septimus.

Exposition Exposition is the first stage of a typical story plot. The exposition provides important background information and introduces the setting and the important characters. The conflict the characters face may also be introduced in the exposition, or it may be introduced later, in the rising action.
See pages 30, 35.
See also **Plot.**

Expository Essay *See* **Essay.**

External Conflict *See* **Conflict.**

Fable A fable is a brief tale told to illustrate a moral or teach a lesson. Often the moral of a fable appears in a distinct and memorable statement near the tale's beginning or end. "Ant and Grasshopper" by Aesop is an example of a fable.
See also **Moral.**

Falling Action The falling action is the stage of the plot in which the story begins to draw to a close. The falling action comes after the **climax** and before the **resolution,** also called denouement. Events in the falling action show the results of the important decision or action that happened at the climax. Tension eases as the falling action begins; however, the final outcome of the story is not yet fully worked out at this stage.

See pages 30, 35.

See also **Climax; Plot.**

Fantasy Fantasy is a type of fiction that is highly imaginative and portrays events, settings, or characters that are unrealistic. The setting might be a nonexistent world, the plot might involve magic or the supernatural, and the characters might have superhuman powers.

Fiction Fiction is prose writing that tells an imaginary story. The writer of a short story or novel might invent all the events and characters or might base parts of the story on real people and events. The basic elements of fiction are plot, character, setting, and theme. Different types of fiction include realistic fiction, historical fiction, science fiction, and fantasy.

See also **Novel; Novella; Short Story.**

Figurative Language In figurative language, words are used in an imaginative way to express ideas that are not literally true. "Megan has a bee in her bonnet" is an example of figurative language. The sentence does not mean that Megan is wearing a bonnet, nor that there is an actual bee in it. Instead, it means that Megan is angry or upset about something. Figurative language is used for comparison, emphasis, and emotional effect.

See pages 582, 629.

See also **Metaphor; Onomatopoeia; Personification; Simile.**

First-Person Point of View *See* **Point of View.**

Flashback In a literary work, a flashback is an interruption of the action to present events that took place at an earlier time. A flashback provides information that can help a reader better understand a character's current situation.

Example: In "Aaron's Gift," Myron Levoy uses a flashback to explain some of the experiences and behavior of Aaron's grandmother. It also helps readers understand the significance of Aaron's use of the word *Cossacks* to fight off his attackers.

Folklore The traditions, customs, and stories that are passed down within a culture are known as its folklore. Folklore includes various types of literature, such as legends, folk tales, myths, trickster tales, and fables.

See also **Fable; Folk Tale; Myth.**

Folk Tale A folk tale is a story that has been passed down from generation to generation by word of mouth. Folk tales may be set in the distant past and involve supernatural events. The characters in them may be animals, people, or superhuman beings. "The Crane Maiden" by Rafe Martin is an example of a folk tale.

Foreshadowing Foreshadowing occurs when a writer provides hints that suggest future events in a story. Foreshadowing creates suspense and makes readers eager to find out what will happen. For example, in Joan Aiken's short story "Lob's Girl," references to the steep hill near the Pengellys' house hint that it will play a part in the story's plot.

Form The structure or organization of a written work is often called its form. The form of a poem includes the arrangement of its words and lines on the page.

Free Verse Poetry without regular patterns of rhyme and rhythm is called free verse. Some poets use free verse to capture the sounds and rhythms of ordinary speech. The poem "On Turning Ten" by Billy Collins is written in free verse.

> This is the beginning of sadness, I say to myself,
> as I walk through the universe in my sneakers.
> It is time to say good-bye to my imaginary friends,
> time to turn the first big number.
> —Billy Collins, "On Turning Ten"

See page 637.

See also **Rhyme, Rhythm.**

Genre The term *genre* refers to a category in which a work of literature is classified. The major genres in literature are fiction, nonfiction, poetry, and drama.

Haiku Haiku is a form of Japanese poetry in which 17 syllables are arranged in three lines of 5, 7, and 5 syllables. The rules of haiku are strict. In addition to following the syllabic count, the poet must create a clear picture that will evoke a strong emotional response in the reader. Nature is a particularly important source of inspiration for Japanese haiku poets, and details from nature are often the subjects of their poems.

> Winter solitude—
> in a world of one color
> the sound of the wind.
> —Bashō

Hero A hero is a main character or protagonist in a story. They are typically courageous, strong, honorable, and intelligent. They are protectors of society who hold back the forces of evil and fight to make the world a better place. In modern literature, a hero may simply be the most important character in a story. Such a hero is often an ordinary person with ordinary problems.
See page 725.

Historical Fiction A short story or a novel can be called historical fiction when it is set in the past and includes real places and real events of historical importance. The short story "The Dog of Pompeii" by Louis Untermeyer is an example of historical fiction.
See pages 104, 325.

Humor Humor is a quality that provokes laughter or amusement. Writers create humor through exaggeration, amusing descriptions, irony, and witty and insightful dialogue. In the short story "The All-American Slurp," author Lensey Namioka uses humor to tell the story of a Chinese immigrant family learning to adjust to American culture.
See pages 492, 533.

Idiom An idiom is an expression that has a meaning different from the meaning of its individual words. For example, "to let the cat out of the bag" is an idiom meaning "to reveal a secret or surprise."

Imagery Imagery consists of words and phrases that appeal to a reader's five senses. Writers use sensory details to help the reader imagine how things look, feel, smell, sound, and taste.

> The winter
> still stings
> clean and cold and white
> as it did last year.
> —Charlotte Zolotow, "Change"

See pages 436, 525, 601.

Internal Conflict *See* **Conflict.**

Interview An interview is a conversation conducted by a writer or reporter, in which facts or statements are elicited from another person, recorded, and then broadcast or published. This book includes an interview with Ji-li Jiang.
See page 284.

Irony Irony is a contrast between what is expected and what actually exists or happens. Exaggeration and sarcasm are techniques writers use to express irony.

Journal *See* **Diary.**

Legend A legend is a story handed down from the past about a specific person, usually someone of heroic accomplishments. Legends usually have some basis in historical fact. "The Chenoo" by Joseph and James Bruchac is a Native-American legend.

Limerick A limerick is a short, humorous poem made up of five lines. It usually has the rhyme scheme *aabba*, created by two rhyming couplets followed by a fifth line that rhymes with the first couplet. A limerick typically has a sing-song rhythm.

> There was an Old Man with a beard, *a*
> Who said, "It is just as I feared!"— *a*
> Two Owls and a Hen, *b*
> Four Larks and a Wren, *b*
> Have all built their nests in my beard!" *a*
> —Edward Lear

Literary Nonfiction *See* **Narrative Nonfiction.**

Lyric Poetry Lyric poetry is poetry that presents the personal thoughts and feelings of a single speaker. Most poems, other than narrative poems, are lyric poems. Lyric poetry can be in a variety of forms and cover many subjects, from love and death to everyday experiences. Lilian Moore's "Message from a Caterpillar" is an example of a lyric poem.

Main Character *See* **Character.**

Memoir A memoir is a form of autobiographical writing in which a writer shares his or her personal experiences and observations of important events or people. Often informal in tone, memoirs usually give readers information about a particular person or period of time in the writer's life. In contrast, autobiographies focus on many important people and events in the writer's life over a long period of time. "The Red Guards" by Ji-li Jiang is a memoir.
See pages 115, 127, 509, 844.
See also **Autobiography; Personal Narrative.**

Metaphor A metaphor is a comparison of two things that are basically unlike but have some qualities in common.

Unlike a simile, a metaphor does not contain the word *like* or *as*. In "Mooses" by Ted Hughes, a moose's body is compared to a house frame, his ears to palms reaching out, and his front legs to a lectern.
See pages 499, 582, 629.
See also **Figurative Language; Simile.**

Meter In poetry, meter is the regular pattern of stressed (ˊ) and unstressed (ˇ) syllables. Although poems have rhythm, not all poems have regular meter. Each unit of meter is known as a **foot** and is made up of one stressed syllable and one or two unstressed syllables. Notice the meter marked in the following line.

> Ĭ mŭst gŏ dówn tŏ thĕ seas agaĭn, tŏ thĕ lónely̆ sea ănd thĕ sky̆,
>
> —John Masefield, "Sea-Fever"

See also **Rhythm.**

Minor Character *See* **Character.**

Mood Mood is the feeling or atmosphere that a writer creates for the reader. Descriptive words, imagery, and figurative language all influence the mood of a work. In "The Morning Walk," Mary Oliver creates a mood of thankfulness and contentment.
See page 525.

Moral A moral is a lesson that a story teaches. A moral is often stated at the end of a fable. For example, the moral of the fable "Ant and Grasshopper" is "In good times prepare for when the bad times come."
See also **Fable.**

Motivation Motivation is the reason why a character acts, feels, or thinks in a certain way. A character may have more than one motivation for his or her actions. Understanding these motivations helps readers get to know the character.

Myth A myth is a traditional story that attempts to answer basic questions about human nature, origins of the world, mysteries of nature, and social customs. For example, "The Story of Ceres and Proserpina" is a classical myth that explains the reason for the change of seasons.

Narrative Writing that tells a story is called a narrative. The events in a narrative may be real or imagined. Autobiographies and biographies are narratives that deal with real people or events. Fictional narratives include short stories, fables, myths, and novels. A narrative may also be in the form of a poem.
See also **Autobiography; Biography; Personal Narrative.**

Narrative Nonfiction Narrative nonfiction is writing that reads much like fiction, except that the characters, setting, and plot are real rather than imaginary. Narrative nonfiction includes autobiographies, biographies, and memoirs. "The First Emperor" by Daniel Cohen is an example of narrative nonfiction.

Narrative Poetry Poetry that tells a story is called narrative poetry. Like fiction, a narrative poem contains characters, a setting, and a plot. It might also contain such elements of poetry as rhyme, rhythm, imagery, and figurative language. Lewis Carroll's "The Walrus and the Carpenter" is a narrative poem.

Narrator The narrator is the voice that tells a story. Sometimes the narrator is a character in the story. At other times, the narrator is an outside voice created by the writer. The narrator is not the same as the writer.
See also **Point of View.**

Nonfiction Nonfiction is writing that tells about real people, places, and events. Unlike fiction, nonfiction is mainly written to convey factual information. Nonfiction includes a wide range of writing—newspaper articles, letters, essays, biographies, movie reviews, speeches, true-life adventure stories, advertising, and more.

Novel A novel is a long work of fiction. Like a short story, a novel is the product of a writer's imagination. Because a novel is considerably longer than a short story, a novelist can develop the characters and story line more thoroughly.
See also **Fiction.**

Novella A novella is a work of fiction that is longer than a short story but shorter than a novel. Due to its shorter length, a novella generally includes fewer characters and a less complex plot than a novel.
See also **Fiction; Novel; Short Story.**

Ode An ode is a type of lyric poem that deals with serious themes, such as justice, truth, or beauty.

Onomatopoeia Onomatopoeia is the use of words whose sounds echo their meanings, such as *buzz, whisper, gargle,* and *murmur.* In "The All-American Slurp," onomatopoeia is used to indicate the sound made as the Lin family pulls the strings out of celery stalks.

> I pulled the strings out of my stalk. *Z-z-zip, z-z-zip.*
>
> —Lensey Namioka, "The All-American Slurp"

Oral Literature Oral literature, or the oral tradition, consists of stories that have been passed down by word of mouth from generation to generation. Oral literature includes folk tales, legends, and myths. In more recent times, some examples of oral literature have been written down or recorded so that the stories can be preserved.

Parody A parody is a humorous imitation of another writer's work. Parodies can take the form of fiction, drama, or poetry. Jon Scieszka's "The True Story of the Three Little Pigs" is an example of a parody.

Personal Narrative A short essay told as a story in the first-person point of view. A personal narrative usually reflects the writer's experiences, feelings, and personality.
See pages 265, 802, 827.
See also **Autobiography; Memoir.**

Personification The giving of human qualities to an animal, object, or idea is known as personification. In "Ant and Grasshopper," the insects are personified. They have conversations with each other as if they were human.

> "Why haven't you saved anything up?" asked Ant. "*I* worked hard all through the summer, storing food for the winter. Very glad I am too, for as you say, it's bitterly cold."
> "I wasn't idle last summer, either," said Grasshopper.
> —Aesop, "Ant and Grasshopper"

See pages 582, 629.
See also **Figurative Language.**

Persuasive Essay *See* **Essay.**

Play *See* **Drama.**

Playwright *See* **Drama.**

Plot The series of events in a story is called the plot. The plot usually centers on a **conflict,** or struggle, faced by the main character. The action that the characters take to solve the problem builds toward a **climax** in the story. At this point, or shortly afterward, the problem is solved and the story ends. Most story plots have five stages: exposition, rising action, climax, falling action, and resolution.
See pages 30, 35, 151.
See also **Climax; Exposition; Falling Action; Rising Action.**

Poetry Poetry is a type of literature in which words are carefully chosen and arranged to create certain effects. Poets use a variety of sound devices, imagery, and figurative language to express emotions and ideas.
See also **Alliteration; Assonance; Ballad; Free Verse; Imagery; Meter; Narrative Poetry; Rhyme; Rhythm; Stanza.**

Point of View Point of view refers to how a writer chooses to narrate a story. When a story is told from the **first-person** point of view, the narrator is a character in the story and uses first-person pronouns, such as *I, me,* and *we.* In a story told from the **third-person** point of view, the narrator is not a character in the story. A writer's choice of narrator affects the information readers receive.
See pages 192, 199, 207.
See also **Narrator.**

Prop The word *prop,* originally an abbreviation of the word *property,* refers to any physical object that is used in a drama. In the play based on Norton Juster's *The Phantom Tollbooth,* the props include a clock and a toy car.

Prose The word *prose* refers to all forms of writing that are not in verse form. The term may be used to describe very different forms of writing, such as short stories and essays.

Protagonist A protagonist is the main character in a story, play, or novel. The protagonist is involved in the main conflict of the story. Usually, the protagonist undergoes changes as the plot runs its course. In "The Good Deed" by Marion Dane Bauer, Heather is the protagonist.

Pun A pun is a play on words based on similar senses of two or more words, or on various meanings of the same word. A pun is usually made for humorous effect.
Example: The fisherman was fired for playing hooky.

Radio Play A radio play is a drama that is written specifically to be broadcast over the radio. Because the audience is not meant to see a radio play, sound effects are often used to help listeners imagine the setting and the action. The stage directions in the play's script indicate the sound effects. Fan Kissen's drama *Damon and Pythias* was originally written as a radio play.

Realistic Fiction Realistic fiction is fiction that is set in the real, modern world. The characters behave like real people and use human abilities to cope with modern life's problems and conflicts. "Tuesday of the Other June" by Norma Fox Mazer is an example of realistic fiction.

Recurring Theme *See* **Theme.**

Refrain A refrain is one or more lines repeated in each stanza of a poem.
See pages 580, 601.

Repetition Repetition is a technique in which a sound, word, phrase, or line is repeated for emphasis or unity. Repetition often helps to reinforce meaning and create an appealing rhythm. Note how the use of repetition in the following lines emphasizes the rhythm of windshield wipers.

> fog smog   fog smog
> tissue paper   tissue paper
> clear the blear   clear the smear
> —Eve Merriam, "Windshield Wiper"

See also **Alliteration; Refrain; Sound Devices.**

Resolution *See* **Falling Action.**

Rhyme Rhyme Is the repetition of sounds at the end of words. Words rhyme when their accented vowels and the letters that follow have identical sounds. *Pig* and *dig* rhyme, as do *reaching* and *teaching*. The most common type of rhyme in poetry Is called **end rhyme,** in which rhyming words come at the ends of lines. Rhyme that occurs within a line of poetry is called **internal rhyme.** The following lines are examples of end rhyme.

> Shadows on the wall
> Noises down the hall
> Life doesn't frighten me at all
> —Maya Angelou, "Life Doesn't Frighten Me"

See pages 580, 593.

Rhyme Scheme A rhyme scheme is a pattern of end rhymes in a poem. A rhyme scheme is noted by assigning a letter of the alphabet, beginning with *a,* to each line. Lines that rhyme are given the same letter.

> Is the moon tired? she looks so pale   *a*
> Within her misty veil: *a*
> She scales the sky from east to west,   *b*
> And takes no rest.   *b*
> —Christina Rossetti, "Is the Moon Tired?"

See pages 580, 593.

Rhythm Rhythm is the musical quality created by the alternation of stressed and unstressed syllables in a line of poetry. Poets use rhythm to emphasize ideas and to create moods. Devices such as alliteration, rhyme, and assonance often contribute to creating rhythm.
See page 580.
See also **Meter.**

Rising Action The rising action is the stage of the plot that develops the **conflict,** or struggle. During this stage, events occur that make the conflict more complicated. The events in the rising action build toward a **climax,** or turning point.
See pages 30, 35.
See also **Plot.**

Scene In drama, the action is often divided into acts and scenes. Each scene presents an episode of the play's plot and typically occurs at a single place and time. The play based on Mark Twain's *The Prince and the Pauper* has eight scenes.
See also **Act.**

Scenery Scenery is a painted backdrop or other structures used to create the setting for a play.

Science Fiction Science fiction is fiction in which a writer explores unexpected possibilities of the past or the future, combining scientific information with his or her creative imagination. Most science fiction writers create believable worlds, although some create fantasy worlds that have familiar elements. Ray Bradbury, the author of "All Summer in a Day," is a famous writer of science fiction.
See also **Fantasy.**

Script The text of a play, film, or broadcast is called a script.

Sensory Details Sensory details are words and phrases that appeal to the reader's senses of sight, hearing, touch, smell, and taste. Note the sensory details in the following line. These details appeal to the sense of touch.

> But they were running and turning their faces up
> to the sky and feeling the sun on their cheeks like
> a warm iron; they were taking off their jackets and
> letting the sun burn their arms.
> —Ray Bradbury, "All Summer in a Day"

See also **Imagery.**

Setting The setting of a story, poem, or play is the time and place of the action. Sometimes the setting is clear and well-defined. At other times, it is left to the reader's imagination. Elements of setting include geographic location, historical period (past, present, or future), season, time of day, and culture.

See pages 28, 67, 111.

Short Story A short story is a work of fiction that centers on a single idea and can be read in one sitting. Generally, a short story has one main conflict that involves the characters and keeps the story moving.

See also **Fiction.**

Simile A simile is a figure of speech that makes a comparison between two unlike things using the word *like* or *as*.

> To find out, we studied the system map, which <u>looked like a noodle factory hit by a bomb.</u>
> —Avi, "Scout's Honor"

See pages 499, 582, 629.
See also **Figurative Language; Metaphor.**

Sound Devices Sound devices are ways of using words for the sound qualities they create. Sound devices can help convey meaning and mood in a writer's work. Some common sound devices include **alliteration, assonance, meter, onomatopoeia, repetition, rhyme,** and **rhythm.**

See pages 580, 615.
See also **Alliteration; Assonance; Meter; Onomatopoeia; Repetition; Rhyme; Rhythm.**

Speaker In poetry the speaker is the voice that "talks" to the reader, similar to the narrator in fiction. The speaker is not necessarily the poet. For example, in Sandra Cisneros's "Good Hotdogs," the experiences described may or may not have happened to the poet.

See pages 289, 579.

Speech A speech is a talk or public address. The purpose of a speech may be to entertain, to explain, to persuade, to inspire, or any combination of these purposes. Mawi Asgedom's speech "No Thought of Reward" was written to persuade people to give of themselves without expecting anything in return.

Stage Directions In the script of a play, the instructions to the actors, director, and stage crew are called the stage directions. Stage directions might suggest scenery, lighting, sound effects, and ways for actors to move and speak. Stage directions often appear in parentheses and in italic type.

> *(Suddenly he notices the package. He drags himself over to it, and disinterestedly reads the label.)*
> —Susan Nanus, *The Phantom Tollbooth*

See page 151.

Stanza A stanza is a group of two or more lines that form a unit in a poem. Each stanza may have the same number of lines, or the number of lines may vary.

See also **Couplet; Form; Poetry.**

Stereotype In literature, characters who are defined by a single trait are known as stereotypes. Such characters do not usually demonstrate the complexities of real people. Familiar stereotypes in popular literature include the absent-minded professor and the busybody.

Structure The structure of a work of literature is the way in which it is put together. In poetry, structure involves the arrangement of words and lines to produce a desired effect. One structural unit in poetry is the stanza. In prose, structure involves the arrangement of such elements as sentences, paragraphs, and events. **Sentence structure** refers to the length and types of sentences used in a work.

Style A style is a manner of writing. It involves how something is said rather than what is said. For example, "The First Skateboard in the History of the World" by Betsy Byars is written in a style that uses a humorous tone and realistic dialogue.

Subject The subject of a literary work is its focus or topic. In an autobiography, for example, the subject is the life of the person telling the story. Subject differs from **theme** in that theme is a deeper meaning, whereas the subject is the main situation or set of facts described by the text.

Surprise Ending A surprise ending is an unexpected plot twist at the end of a story. The surprise may be a sudden turn in the action or a piece of information that gives a different perspective to the entire story.

Suspense Suspense is a feeling of growing tension and excitement felt by a reader. Suspense makes a reader curious about the outcome of a story or an event within a story. A writer creates suspense by raising questions in the reader's mind. The use of **foreshadowing** is one way that writers create suspense.

See also **Foreshadowing.**

Symbol A symbol is a person, a place, an object, or an activity that stands for something beyond itself. For example, a flag is a colored piece of cloth that stands for a country. A white dove is a bird that represents peace.

Example: In "The Red Guards" by Ji-li Jiang, the photo album represents the Jiang family's history. To the Red Guards, it represents the past and "old ways," which are forbidden.

See pages 275, 713.

Tall Tale A tall tale is a humorously exaggerated story about impossible events, often involving the supernatural abilities of the main character. Stories about folk heroes such as Pecos Bill and Paul Bunyan are typical tall tales.

Teleplay A teleplay is a play written for television. In a teleplay, scenes can change quickly and dramatically. The camera can focus the viewer's attention on specific actions. The camera directions in teleplays are much like the stage directions in stage plays.

Theme A theme is a message about life or human nature that the writer shares with the reader. In many cases, readers must infer what the writer's message is. One way of figuring out a theme is to apply the lessons learned by the main characters to people in real life. For example, a theme of "Nadia the Willful" by Sue Alexander is that people we love live on in our memories even after they are gone.

   Recurring themes are themes found in a variety of works. For example, authors from different backgrounds might express similar themes having to do with the importance of family values. **Universal themes** are themes that are found throughout the literature of all time periods. For example, Cinderella stories contain a universal theme relating to goodness being rewarded.

See pages 318, 320, 325, 349, 361, 401, 407, 761.

See also **Moral.**

Third-Person Point of View *See* **Point of View.**

Title The title of a piece of writing is the name that is attached to it. A title often refers to an important aspect of the work. For example, "President Cleveland, Where Are You?" refers to the remaining trading card that the boys in the story are trying to find.

Tone The tone of a literary work expresses the writer's attitude toward his or her subject. Words such as *angry, sad,* and *humorous* can be used to describe different tones. For example, the tone of Betsy Byars's memoir "The First Skateboard in the History of the World" is humorous.

See pages 443, 643.

See also **Author's Perspective.**

Tragedy A tragedy is a dramatic work that presents the downfall of a character or characters. The events in a tragic plot are set in motion by a decision that is often an error in judgment on the part of the hero. Events are linked in a cause-and-effect relationship and lead to a disastrous conclusion, usually death.

Traits *See* **Character.**

Turning Point *See* **Climax.**

Universal Theme *See* **Theme.**

Voice The term *voice* refers to a writer's unique use of language that allows a reader to "hear" a human personality in the writer's work. Elements of style that contribute to a writer's voice can reveal much about the author's personality, beliefs, and attitudes.

Word Choice The success of any writing depends on the writer's choice of words. Words not only communicate ideas but also help describe events, characters, settings, and so on. Word choice can make a writer's work sound formal or informal, serious or humorous. A writer must choose words carefully depending on the goal of the piece of writing. For example, a writer working on a science article would probably use technical, formal words; a writer trying to establish the setting in a short story would probably use more descriptive words. Word choice is sometimes referred to as diction.

See also **Style.**

Almanac *See* **Reference Works.**

Analogy An analogy is a comparison between two things that are alike in some way. Often, writers use analogies in nonfiction to explain an unfamiliar subject or idea by showing how it is like a familiar one.

Appeal to Authority An appeal to authority is an attempt to persuade an audience by making reference to people who are experts on a subject.

Argument An argument is speaking or writing that expresses a position on a problem and supports it with reasons and evidence. An argument often takes into account other points of view, anticipating and answering objections that opponents might raise.
See also **Claim; Counterargument; Evidence.**

Assumption An assumption is an opinion or belief that is taken for granted. It can be about a specific situation, a person, or the world in general. Assumptions are often unstated.

Author's Message An author's message is the main idea or theme of a particular work.
See also **Main Idea; Theme,** *Glossary of Literary and Nonfiction Terms, page R109.*

Author's Perspective *See Glossary of Literary and Nonfiction Terms, page R100.*

Author's Position An author's position is his or her opinion on an issue or topic. *See also* **Claim.**

Author's Purpose *See Glossary of Literary and Nonfiction Terms, page R100.*

Autobiography *See Glossary of Literary and Nonfiction Terms, page R100.*

Bias In a piece of writing, the author's bias is the side of an issue that he or she favors. Words with extremely positive or negative connotations are often a signal of an author's bias.

Bibliography A bibliography is a list of related books and other materials used to write a text. Bibliographies can be good sources for further study on a subject.
See also **Works Consulted.**

Biography *See Glossary of Literary and Nonfiction Terms, page R100.*

Business Correspondence Business correspondence is written business communications such as business letters, e-mails, and memos. In general, business correspondence is brief, to the point, clear, courteous, and professional.

Cause and Effect Two events are related by cause and effect when one event brings about, or causes, the other. The event that happens first is the **cause;** the one that follows is the **effect.** Cause and effect is also a way of organizing an entire piece of writing. It helps writers show the relationships between events or ideas.
See also **False Cause,** *Reading Handbook, page R24.*

Chronological Order Chronological order is the arrangement of events by their order of occurrence. This type of organization is used in fictional narratives and in historical writing, biography, and autobiography.

Claim In an argument, a claim is the writer's position on an issue or problem. Although an argument focuses on supporting one claim, a writer may make more than one claim in a text.

Clarify Clarifying is a reading strategy that helps readers understand or make clear what they are reading. Readers usually clarify by rereading, reading aloud, or discussing.

Classification Classification is a pattern of organization in which objects, ideas, and/or information are presented in groups, or classes, based on common characteristics.

Cliché A cliché is an overused expression. "Better late than never" and "hard as nails" are common examples. Good writers generally avoid clichés unless they are using them in dialogue to indicate something about a character's personality.

Compare and Contrast To compare and contrast is to identify the similarities and differences of two or more subjects. Compare and contrast is also a pattern of organizing an entire piece of writing.
See also **Pattern of Organization.**

Conclusion A conclusion is a statement of belief based on evidence, experience, and reasoning. A valid conclusion is one that logically follows from the facts or statements upon which it is based.

Connect Connecting is a reader's process of relating the content of a text to his or her own knowledge and experience.

Consumer Documents Consumer documents are printed materials that accompany products and services. They usually provide information about the use, care, operation, or assembly of the product or service they accompany. Some common consumer documents are applications, contracts, warranties, manuals, instructions, labels, brochures, and schedules.

Context Clues When you encounter an unfamiliar word, you can often use context clues to understand it. Context clues are the words or phrases surrounding the word that provide hints about the word's meaning.

Counterargument A counterargument is an argument made to oppose another argument. A good argument anticipates opposing viewpoints and provides counterarguments to disprove them.

Credibility Credibility is the believability or trustworthiness of a source and the information it provides.

Critical Review A critical review is an evaluation or critique by a reviewer, or critic. Types of reviews include film reviews, book reviews, music reviews, and art show reviews.

Database A database is a collection of information that can be quickly and easily accessed and searched and from which information can be easily retrieved. It is frequently presented in an electronic format.

Debate A debate is an organized exchange of opinions on an issue. In school settings, debate is usually a formal contest in which two opposing teams defend and attack a proposition.
See also **Argument.**

Deductive Reasoning Deductive reasoning is a way of thinking that begins with a generalization, presents a specific situation, and then moves forward with facts and evidence toward a logical conclusion. The following passage has a deductive argument embedded in it: "All students in the math class must take the quiz on Friday. Since Lana is in the class, she had better show up." This deductive argument can be broken down as follows: generalization—All students in the math class must take the quiz on Friday; specific situation—Lana is a student in the math class; conclusion— Therefore, Lana must take the math quiz.
See also **Analyzing Logic and Reasoning,** *Reading Handbook, page R21.*

Diary *See Glossary of Literary and Nonfiction Terms, page R102.*

Dictionary *See* **Reference Works.**

Draw Conclusions To draw a conclusion is to make a judgment or arrive at a belief based on evidence, experience, and reasoning.

Editorial An editorial is an opinion piece that usually appears on the editorial page of a newspaper or as part of a news broadcast. The editorial section of the newspaper presents opinions rather than objective news reports.
See also **Op/Ed Piece.**

Either/Or Fallacy An either/or fallacy is a statement that suggests that there are only two choices available in a situation when in fact there are more than two.
See also **Identifying Faulty Reasoning,** *Reading Handbook, page R24.*

Emotional Appeal An emotional appeal is a message that creates strong feelings in order to make a point. An appeal to fear is a message that taps into people's fear of losing their safety or security. An appeal to pity is a message that taps into people's sympathy and compassion for others to build support for an idea, a cause, or a proposed action. An appeal to vanity is a message that attempts to persuade by tapping into people's desire to feel good about themselves.
See also **Recognizing Persuasive Techniques,** *Reading Handbook, page R21.*

Encyclopedia *See* **Reference Works.**

Essay *See Glossary of Literary and Nonfiction Terms, page R102.*

Ethical Appeal In an ethical appeal, a writer links a claim to a widely accepted value in order to gain moral support for the claim. The appeal also creates an image of the writer as a trustworthy, moral person.
See also **Recognizing Persuasive Techniques,** *Reading Handbook, page R21.*

Evaluate To evaluate is to examine something carefully and to judge its value or worth. A reader can evaluate the actions of a particular character, for example. A reader can also form opinions about the value of an entire work.

Evidence Evidence is a specific piece of information that supports a claim. Evidence can take the form of a fact, a quotation, an example, a statistic, or a personal experience, among other things.
See also **Strategies for Evaluating Evidence,** *Reading Handbook, page R25.*

Expository Essay *See* **Essay,** *Glossary of Literary and Nonfiction Terms, page R102.*

Fact Versus Opinion A **fact** is a statement that can be proved, or verified. An opinion, on the other hand, is a statement that cannot be proved because it expresses a person's beliefs, feelings, or thoughts.
See also **Generalization; Inference.**

Fallacious Reasoning Reasoning that includes errors in logic or fallacies.

Fallacy A fallacy is an error of reasoning. Typically, a fallacy is based on an incorrect inference or a misuse of evidence. *See also* **Either/Or Fallacy; Logical Appeal; Overgeneralization.**
See also **Identifying Faulty Reasoning,** *Reading Handbook, page R24.*

Faulty Reasoning *See* **Fallacy.**

Feature Article A feature article is an article in a newspaper or magazine about a topic of human interest or lifestyles.

Generalization A generalization is a broad statement about a class or category of people, ideas, or things based on a study of, or a belief about, only some of its members. *See also* **Overgeneralization; Stereotyping.**

Government Publications Government publications are documents produced by government organizations. Pamphlets, brochures, and reports are just some of the many forms these publications take. Government publications can be good resources for a wide variety of topics.

Graphic Aid A graphic aid is a visual tool that is printed, handwritten, or drawn. Charts, diagrams, graphs, photographs, and maps are examples of graphic aids.
See also **Graphic Aids,** *Reading Handbook, page R4.*

Graphic Organizer A graphic organizer is a "word picture"—a visual illustration of a verbal statement—that helps a reader understand a text. Charts, tables, webs, and diagrams can all be graphic organizers. Graphic organizers and graphic aids can look the same. However, graphic organizers and graphic aids do differ in how they are used. Graphic aids help deliver important information to students using a text. Graphic organizers are actually created by students themselves. They help students understand the text or organize information.

Historical Document Historical documents are writings that have played a significant role in human events. The Declaration of Independence, for example, is a historical document.

How-To Book A how-to book explains how to do something—usually an activity, a sport, or a household project.

Implied Main Idea *See* **Main Idea.**

Index The index of a book is an alphabetized list of important topics covered in the book and the page numbers on which they can be found. An index can be used to quickly find specific information about a topic.

Inductive Reasoning Inductive reasoning is the process of logical reasoning that starts with observations, examples, and facts and moves on to a general conclusion or principle.
See also **Analyzing Logic and Reasoning,** *Reading Handbook, pages R21–R22.*

Inference An inference is a logical guess that is made based on facts and one's own knowledge and experience.

Informational Text Informational text is writing that provides factual information. Examples include news reports, a science textbook, and lab reports. Informational text also includes literary nonfiction, such as personal essays, opinion pieces, speeches, biographies, and historical accounts.

Internet The Internet is a global, interconnected system of computer networks that allows for communication through e-mail, listservs, and the World Wide Web. The Internet connects computers and computer users throughout the world.

Journal A journal is a periodical publication issued by a legal, medical, or other professional organization. The term may also be used to refer to a diary or daily record.

Loaded Language Loaded language consists of words with strongly positive or negative connotations, intended to influence a reader's or listener's attitude.

Logical Appeal A logical appeal is a way of writing or speaking that relies on logic and facts. It appeals to people's reasoning or intellect rather than to their values or emotions. Flawed logical appeals—that is, errors in reasoning—are called logical fallacies.
See also **Fallacy.**

Logical Argument A logical argument is an argument in which the logical relationship between the support and claim is sound.

Main Idea The main idea, or central idea, is the most important idea about a topic that a writer or speaker conveys. It can be the central idea of an entire work or of just a paragraph. Often, the main idea of a paragraph is expressed in a topic sentence. However, a main idea may just be implied, or suggested, by details. A main idea is typically supported by details.
See also **Main Idea and Supporting Details,** *Reading Handbook, pages R8–R9.*

Make Inferences *See* **Inference.**

Monitor Monitoring is the strategy of checking your comprehension as you read and modifying the strategies you are using to suit your needs. Monitoring often includes the following strategies: questioning, clarifying, visualizing, predicting, connecting, and rereading.

Narrative Nonfiction *See Glossary of Literary and Nonfiction Terms, page R105.*

News Article A news article is writing that reports on a recent event. In newspapers, news articles are usually brief and to the point, presenting the most important facts first, followed by more detailed information.

Nonfiction *See Glossary of Literary and Nonfiction Terms, page R105.*

Op/Ed Piece An op/ed piece is an opinion piece that typically appears opposite ("op") the editorial page of a newspaper. Unlike editorials, op/ed pieces are written and submitted by readers.

Organization *See* **Pattern of Organization.**

Overgeneralization An overgeneralization is a statement that is too broad to be accurate. You can often recognize overgeneralizations by the appearance of words and phrases such as *all, everyone, every time, any, anything, no one,* or *none.* An example is "None of the city's workers really cares about keeping the environment clean." In all probability, there are many exceptions. The writer can't possibly know the feelings of every city worker.
See also **Identifying Faulty Reasoning,** *Reading Handbook, page R24.*

Overview An overview is a short summary of a story, a speech, or an essay.

Paraphrase Paraphrasing is the restating of information in one's own words. *See also* **Summarize.**

Pattern of Organization The term *pattern of organization* refers to the way ideas and information are arranged and organized. Patterns of organization include cause and effect, chronological, compare and contrast, classification, and problem-solution, among others.
See also **Cause and Effect; Chronological Order; Classification; Compare and Contrast; Problem-Solution Order; Sequential Order.**
See also **Reading Informational Texts: Patterns of Organization,** *Reading Handbook, page R8.*

Periodical A periodical is a magazine or other publication that is issued on a regular basis.

Personal Narrative *See Glossary of Literary and Nonfiction Terms, page R106.*

Persuasion Persuasion is the art of swaying others' feelings, beliefs, or actions. Persuasion normally appeals to both the mind and the emotions of readers.
See also **Appeal to Authority; Emotional Appeal; Ethical Appeal; Loaded Language; Logical Appeal.**
See also **Recognizing Persuasive Techniques,** *Reading Handbook, page R21.*

Predict Predicting is a reading strategy that involves using text clues to make a reasonable guess about what will happen next in a story.

Primary Source *See* **Sources.**

Prior Knowledge Prior knowledge is the knowledge a reader already possesses about a topic. This information might come from personal experiences, expert accounts, books, films, or other sources.

Problem-Solution Order Problem-solution order is a pattern of organization in which a problem is stated and analyzed and then one or more solutions are proposed and examined.

Propaganda Propaganda is any form of communication that is so distorted that it conveys false or misleading information to advance a specific belief or cause.

Public Document Public documents are documents that were written for the public to provide information that is of public interest or concern. They include government documents, speeches, signs, and rules and regulations.
See also **Government Publications.**

Reference Work Reference works are sources that contain facts and background information on a wide range of subjects. Most reference works are good sources of reliable information because they have been reviewed by experts. The following are some common reference works: encyclopedias, dictionaries, thesauri, almanacs, atlases, and directories.

Review *See* **Critical Review.**

Rhetorical Question Rhetorical questions are those that have such obvious answers that they do not require a reply. Writers often use them to suggest that their claim is so obvious that everyone should agree with it.

Scanning Scanning is the process used to search through a text for a particular fact or piece of information. When you scan, you sweep your eyes across a page, looking for key words that may lead you to the information you want.

Scope Scope refers to a work's focus. For example, an article about Austin, Texas, that focuses on the city's history, economy, and residents has a broad scope. An article that focuses only on the restaurants in Austin has a narrower scope.

Secondary Source *See* **Source.**

Sequential Order Sequential order is a pattern of organization that shows the order of steps or stages in a process.

Setting a Purpose The process of establishing specific reasons for reading a text is called setting a purpose. Readers can look at a text's title, headings, and illustrations to guess what it might be about. They can then use these guesses to figure out what they want to learn from reading the text.

Sidebar A sidebar is additional information set in a box alongside or within a news or feature article. Popular magazines often make use of sidebars.

Signal Words In a text, signal words are words and phrases that help show how events or ideas are related. Some common examples of signal words are *and, but, however, nevertheless, therefore,* and *in addition.*

Source A source is anything that supplies information. **Primary sources** are materials created by people who witnessed or took part in the event they supply information about. Letters, diaries, autobiographies, and eyewitness accounts are primary sources. **Secondary sources** are those made by people who were not directly involved in the event or even present when it occurred. Encyclopedias, textbooks, biographies, and most news articles are secondary sources.

Speech *See Glossary of Literary and Nonfiction Terms, page R108.*

Stereotyping Stereotyping is a dangerous type of overgeneralization. It can lead to unfair judgments of people based on their ethnic background, beliefs, practices, or physical appearance.

Summarize To summarize is to briefly retell the main ideas of a piece of writing in one's own words.
See also **Paraphrase.**

Support Support is any information that helps to prove a claim.

Supporting Detail *See* **Main Idea.**

Synthesize To synthesize information means to take individual pieces of information and combine them in order to gain a better understanding of a subject.

Text Feature Text features are elements of a text, such as boldface type, headings, and subheadings, that help organize and call attention to important information. Italic type, bulleted or numbered lists, sidebars, and graphic aids such as charts, tables, timelines, illustrations, and photographs are also considered text features.
See also **Understanding Text Features,** *Reading Handbook, page R3.*

Thesaurus *See* **Reference Works.**

Thesis Statement A thesis statement, or controlling idea, is the main proposition that a writer attempts to support in a piece of writing.

Topic Sentence The topic sentence of a paragraph states the paragraph's main idea. All other sentences in the paragraph provide supporting details.

Treatment The way a topic is handled in a work is referred to as its treatment. Treatment includes the form the writing takes as well as the writer's purpose and tone.

Unsupported Inference A guess that may seem logical but that is not supported by facts.

Visualize Visualizing is the process of forming a mental picture based on written or spoken information.

Web Site A Web site is a collection of "pages" on the World Wide Web that usually covers a specific subject. Linked pages are accessed by clicking hyperlinks or menus, which send the user from page to page within a Web site. Web sites are created by companies, organizations, educational institutions, government agencies, the military, and individuals.

Workplace Document Workplace documents are materials that are produced or used within a work setting, usually to aid in the functioning of the workplace. They include job applications, office memos, training manuals, job descriptions, and sales reports.

Works Cited The term *works cited* refers to a list of all the works a writer has referred to in his or her text. This list often includes not only books and articles but also Internet sources.

Works Consulted The term *works consulted* refers to a list of all the works a writer consulted in order to create his or her text. It is not limited just to those works cited in the text.
See also **Bibliography.**

The Glossary of Academic Vocabulary is an alphabetical list of the Academic Vocabulary words found in this textbook. Use this glossary just as you would a dictionary—to find out the meanings of words used in your literature class to talk about and write about literary and informational texts. You will also use these words to talk about and write about concepts and topics in your other academic classes.

For each word, the glossary includes the pronunciation, part of speech, and meaning. A Spanish version of each word and definition follows the English version. For more information about the words in the Academic Vocabulary Glossary, please consult a dictionary.

achieve (ə-chēv′) *v.* to bring about an intended result; accomplish
> **lograr** *v.* obtener el resultado esperado; alcanzar un objetivo

adequacy (ad′i-kwə-sē) *n.* quality of being enough to meet a need or requirement
> **adecuación** *s.* que cumple una necesidad o requisito

affect (a-fekt′) *v.* to produce a response or reaction
> **afectar** *v.* producir una respuesta o una reacción

analyze (an′ə-līz′) *v.* to separate, or break into parts and examine
> **analizar** *v.* separar o dividir en partes y examinar

appreciate (ə-prē′shē-āt) *v.* to think highly of; to recognize favorably the quality or value of
> **apreciar** *v.* tener una buena opinión de algo o alguien; reconocer de manera favorable la calidad o el valor de algo o alguien

aspect (as′pekt′) *n.* a quality, part, or element
> **aspecto** *s.* cualidad, parte o elemento

associations (ə-sō′sē-ā′shəns) *n.* connections or relations between thoughts, ideas, or images
> **asociaciones** *s.* conexiones o relaciones entre pensamientos, ideas o imágenes

attitude (at′ə-tōōd′) *n.* a state of mind or feeling
> **actitud** *s.* estado de ánimo o sentimiento

authority (ə-thôr′ə-tē) *n.* someone who is respected because of his or her knowledge about a subject
> **autoridad** *s.* alguien que es respetado por su conocimiento acerca de un tema

characteristics (kar′ək-tər-is′tiks) *n.* features or qualities that help identify, describe, or recognize something
> **características** *s.* rasgos o cualidades que ayudan a identificar, describir o reconocer algo

circumstance (sər′kəm-stans′) *n.* an event or condition that affects a person
> **circunstancia** *s.* evento o condición que afecta a una persona

communicate (kə-myōō′ni-kāt′) *v.* to express thoughts or feelings clearly so that other people can understand them
> **comunicar** *v.* expresar pensamientos o sentimientos de manera clara para que otras personas puedan comprenderlos

concept (kän′sept′) *n.* an idea of how something is or could be
> **concepto** *s.* idea de cómo es o podría ser algo

conclude (kən-klōōd′) *v.* to form an opinion about something based on evidence, experience, or reasoning
> **concluir** *v.* formar una opinión sobre algo a partir de pruebas, experiencias o razonamientos

context (kän′tekst′) *n.* words or phrases that become before and after a word in a passage that help explain its meaning
> **contexto** *s.* palabras o frases que están antes y después de una palabra en un pasaje y que ayudan a explicar su significado

contribute (kən-trib′yōōt) *v.* to give or add something, such as resources or ideas
> **contribuir** *v.* dar o añadir algo, como recursos o ideas

convey (kən-vā′) *v.* to make known, express
> **transmitir** *v.* dar a conocer, expresar

create (krē-āt′) *v.* to produce something; to use imagination to invent things
> **crear** *v.* producir algo; usar la imaginación para inventar cosas

device (di-vīs′) *n.* a way of achieving a particular purpose
> **recurso** *s.* manera de alcanzar un propósito particular

distinctive (di-stink′tiv) *adj.* unique; clearly different
> **distintivo** *adj.* único; claramente diferente

element (el′ə-mənt) *n.* a separate, identifiable part of something
   elemento *s.* parte individual e identificable de una cosa

evidence (ev′ə-dəns) *n.* specific information that supports a claim
   prueba *s.* información específica que respalda una afirmación

formulate (fôr′myoo-lāt′) *v.* to develop a plan, system, or method
   formular *v.* desarrollar un plan, sistema o método

illustrate (il′ə-strāt′) *v.* explain or make something clear
   ilustrar *v.* explicar o aclarar algo

impact (im-pakt′) *v.* to have a direct effect on
   impactar *v.* tener un efecto directo en algo

implicit (im-plis′it) *adj.* not stated directly, but understood in what is expressed
   implícito *adj.* no enunciado directamente, pero comprendido según lo expresado

influence (in-floo′əns) *n.* ability or power to affect thought, behavior, or development
   influencia *s.* capacidad o poder para afectar el pensamiento, la conducta o el desarrollo

insight (in′sīt′) *n.* a clear understanding of the true nature of something
   comprensión *s.* claro entendimiento de la verdadera naturaleza de algo

interact (in′tər-akt′) *v.* to talk to and deal with others
   interactuar *v.* hablar y tratar con otras personas

interpret (in-tər′prət) *v.* to explain the meaning of something
   interpretar *v.* explicar el significado de algo

obvious (äb′vē-əs) *adj.* easy to see or understand
   obvio *adj.* fácil de ver o comprender

perceive (pər-sēv′) *v.* to grasp mentally; understand
   percibir *v.* captar con la mente; comprender

provide (prə-vīd′) *v.* to supply; make something available
   proveer *v.* suministrar; hacer que algo esté disponible

purpose (pər′pəs) *n.* the goal or desired outcome of something
   propósito *s.* objetivo o resultado deseado de algo

qualities (kwôl′ə-tēz) *n.* traits; distinguishing characteristics
   cualidades *s.* rasgos; características distintivas

reaction (rē-ak′shən) *n.* response
   reacción *s.* respuesta

refine (ri-fīn′) *v.* to improve something to make it more effective
   refinar *v.* mejorar algo para que sea más eficaz

relevant (rel′ə-vənt) *adj.* having a logical connection with something else
   relevante *adj.* que tiene una conexión lógica con otra cosa

reliable (ri-lī′ə-bəl) *adj.* able to be trusted or accurate
   confiable *adj.* que inspira confianza o es preciso

sensory (sen′ser-ē) *adj.* of or relating to the senses
   sensorial *adj.* perteneciente o relativo a los sentidos

significant (sig-nif′ə-kənt) *adj.* important; meaningful
   significativo *adj.* importante; coherente

specific (spə-sif′ik) *adj.* detailed, exact
   específico *adj.* detallado, exacto

structural (struk′chər-al) *adj.* of or related to the manner of organization
   estructural *s.* perteneciente o relativo a la disposición de partes

systematically (sis′tə-mat′ik-lē) *adv.* carried on by step-by-step procedures; orderly
   sistemáticamente *adv.* paso a paso; en forma ordenada

tradition (trə-dish′ən) *n.* a set of beliefs or customs that have been handed down for generations
   tradición *s.* conjunto de creencias o costumbres que se transmiten de generación en generación

acclaim (ə-klām') *n.* enthusiastic praise
    aclamación *s.* elogio entusiasta

accusation (ăk'yōō-zā'shən) *n.* the act of charging someone with wrongdoing
    acusación *s.* acción de imputar un delito o maldad

acrid (ăk'rĭd) *adj.* harsh and sharp in taste or odor
    acre *adj.* de sabor u olor áspero y picante

administer (ăd-mĭn'ĭ-stər) *v.* to give or apply
    administrar *v.* dar o aplicar

affliction (ə-flĭk'shən) *n.* a cause of pain, suffering, or worry
    aflicción *s.* causa de dolor, sufrimiento o preocupación

aggressively (ə-grĕs'ĭv-lē) *adv.* in a manner showing readiness to attack
    agresivamente *adv.* de modo dispuesto a atacar

agility (ə-jĭl'ĭ-tē) *n.* quickness or ease of movement
    agilidad *s.* rapidez o facilidad de movimiento

agitated (ăj'ĭ-tāt'əd) *adj.* disturbed; upset **agitate** *v.*
    inquieto *adj.* perturbado; alterado **inquietar** *v.*

agonize (ăg'ə-nīz') *v.* to suffer extreme physical or mental pain
    padecer *v.* sufrir dolor físico o mental extremo

alley (ăl'ē) *n.* a narrow street behind or between buildings
    callejón *s.* calle angosta entre edificios o casas

allot (ə-lŏt') *v.* to parcel out; distribute
    repartir *v.* asignar; distribuir

ancestor (ăn'sĕs'tər) *n.* a person from whom another person or group is descended
    antepasado *s.* persona de la que descendemos

apparatus (ăp'ə-răt'əs) *n.* a device or set of equipment used for a specific purpose
    aparato *s.* instrumento o conjunto de instrumentos usados con un fin específico

appreciate (ə-prē'shē-āt') *v.* to admire or value
    apreciar *v.* admirar o valorar

archaeological (är'kē-ə-lŏj'ĭ-kəl) *adj.* relating to the study of past human life and culture
    arqueológico *adj.* relacionado con el estudio de la vida y la cultura humana en el pasado

ardent (är'dnt) *adj.* having strong enthusiasm or devotion
    ardiente *adj.* que tiene mucho entusiasmo o devoción

assassinate (ə-săs'ə-nāt') *v.* to murder by surprise attack for political reasons
    asesinar *v.* matar por razones políticas en un ataque sorpresa

assert (ə-sûrt') *v.* to put into words with force or confidence; maintain
    afirmar *v.* expresar en palabras con fuerza o confianza; sostener

assume (ə-sōōm') *v.* to take on
    asumir *v.* adoptar

atone (ə-tōn') *v.* to seek pardon; to make up for
    expiar *v.* pedir perdón; reparar una culpa

banish (băn'ĭsh) *v.* to send away; to exile
    desterrar *v.* expulsar; exilar

banquet (băng'kwĭt) *n.* a dinner honoring a particular guest or occasion
    banquete *s.* cena en honor de un invitado o de una ocasión

barbarian (bär-bâr'ē-ən) *n.* a person considered by those of another group to have a primitive culture
    bárbaro *s.* persona de cultura primitiva desde el punto de vista de otro grupo

barren (băr'ən) *adj.* unable to produce or without vegetation
    estéril *adj.* yermo o árido

blunder (blŭn'dər) *v.* to move clumsily
    andar a ciegas *v.* andar a tropezones

brawny (brô'nē) *adj.* strong and muscular
    musculoso *adj.* fuerte y muscular

cackle (kăk'əl) *v.* to make a sound of shrill laughter or chatter
    chillar *v.* emitir un sonido agudo de risa o parloteo

captivate (kăp'tə-vāt') *v.* to attract and hold interest
    cautivar *v.* atraer y conservar interés

captivity (kăp-tĭv'ĭ-tē) *n.* the condition of being confined or not free
    cautiverio *s.* encarcelamiento o privación de la libertad

certify (sûr'tə-fī') *v.* to confirm as true or genuine
    certificar *v.* confirmar la autenticidad

chariot (chăr'ē-ət) *n.* two-wheeled vehicle used in ancient times
    carroza *s.* carro antiguo de dos ruedas

clan (klăn) *n.* a family group; a group united by common interests or qualities
    clan *s.* grupo familiar; grupo unido por intereses o cualidades comunes

clarity (klăr'ĭ-tē) *n.* the quality of being clear
    claridad *s.* calidad de claro

clearing (klîr'ĭng) *n.* an open area of land, as in the middle of a forest
    claro *s.* terreno despejado, por ejemplo en medio de un bosque

coherent (kō-hîr'ənt) *adj.* clear; logical
    coherente *adj.* claro; lógico

collapse (kə-lăps') *v.* to fall down
    derrumbarse *v.* caerse

commence (kə-měns') *v.* to begin
    comenzar *v.* empezar

complexity (kəm-plěk'sĭ-tē) *n.* the quality of being complicated
    complejidad *s.* calidad de complicado

complicate (kŏm'plĭ-kāt') *v.* to make difficult or complex
    complicar *v.* hacer difícil o complejo

condition (kən-dĭsh'ən) *n.* a disease or state of health
    afección *s.* enfermedad

confiscate (kŏn'fĭ-skāt') *v.* to take and keep something that belongs to someone else
    confiscar *v.* quitarle a una persona sus bienes

congeal (kən-jēl') *v.* to make into a solid mass
    cuajar *v.* volverse sólido

consciousness (kŏn'shəs-nĭs) *n.* awareness of one's own thoughts
    conciencia *s.* reconocimiento de los pensamientos propios

console (kən-sōl') *v.* to ease someone's sorrow; to comfort
    consolar *v.* aliviar la pena; confortar

consumption (kən-sŭmp'shən) *n.* the act of taking in, eating, or drinking **consume** *v.*
    consumo *s.* acción de comer o beber **consumir** *v.*

contempt (kən-těmpt') *n.* the feeling produced by something disgraceful or worthless; scorn
    desprecio *s.* sentimiento que produce algo vergonzoso o sin valor; desdén

contribute (kən-trĭb'yōot) *v.* to offer a gift or a service
    contribuir *v.* ofrecer un regalo o servicio

cope (kōp) *v.* to struggle to overcome difficulties
    sobrellevar *v.* esforzarse por superar dificultades

corrupt (kə-rŭpt') *v.* to cause something to change from good to bad
    corromper *v.* hacer que algo se dañe

crag (krăg) *n.* a steep, rugged formation of rock
    risco *s.* peñasco escarpado

daze (dāz) *n.* a condition in which one cannot think clearly
    aturdimiento *s.* ofuscación que no permite pensar con claridad

dazzling (dăz'lĭng) *adj.* beautiful; amazing **dazzle** *v.*
    deslumbrante *adj.* hermoso; llamativo **deslumbrar** *v.*

decisively (dĭ-sī'sĭv'lē) *adv.* in a clear, definite way
    terminantemente *adv.* de modo claro y definitivo

dedicate (děd'ĭ-kāt') *v.* to set apart for a particular use
    dedicar *v.* destinar a cierto uso

dedication (děd'ĭ-kā'shən) *n.* commitment or devotion
    dedicación *s.* compromiso o devoción

dejectedly (dĭ-jěk'tĭd-lē) *adv.* unhappily; in a disheartened way
    abatidamente *adv.* afligidamente

desperately (děs'pər-ĭt-lē) *adv.* urgently
    desesperadamente *adv.* urgentemente

destination (děs'tə-nā'shən) *n.* the place to which a person is going
    destino *s.* lugar a donde va una persona

devise (dĭ-vīz') *v.* to plan or design
    ingeniar *v.* planear o idear

devoted (dĭ-vō'tĭd) *adj.* very loyal; faithful **devote** *v.*
    devoto *adj.* muy leal; fiel **dedicarse** *v.*

diagnosis (dī'əg-nō'sĭs) *n.* the identification of a disease through examination of a patient
    diagnóstico *s.* identificación de una enfermedad por medio de un examen

discard (dĭ-skärd′) *v.* to throw away
 descartar *v.* tirar

disintegrate (dĭs-ĭn′tĭ-grāt′) *v.* to break down into smaller parts
 desintegrar *v.* romper en partes pequeñas

dislodge (dĭs-lŏj′) *v.* to move from a settled position
 desastascar *v.* mover de una posición fija

distorted (dĭ-stôrt′əd) *adj.* twisted out of shape; misshapened
 distorsionado *adj.* torcido; deformado

divulge (dĭ-vŭlj′) *v.* to reveal, especially something private or secret
 divulgar *v.* revelar, especialmente algo privado o secreto

domesticate (də-měs′tĭ-kāt′) *v.* to tame a wild species of animal over generations
 domesticar *v.* amansar una especie a lo largo de generaciones

dreary (drîr′ē) *adj.* dismal, bleak, or boring
 deprimente *adj.* triste, pesado o aburrido

eject (ĭ-jĕkt′) *v.* to throw out from inside
 expulsar *v.* arrojar hacia fuera

eldest (ĕl′dĭst) *adj.* oldest
 mayor *adj.* más viejo

embrace (əm-brās′) *v.* to hold close
 abrazar *v.* rodear con los brazos

emerald (ĕm′ər-əld) *adj.* of a rich green color
 esmeralda *adj.* de color verde profundo

emerge (ĭ-mûrj′) *v.* to come into view
 emerger *v.* salir a la vista

engage (ĕn-gāj′) *v.* to involve; participate
 meterse *v.* participar

enhance (ĕn-hăns′) *v.* to increase in value or quality
 realzar *v.* aumentar el valor o la calidad

erupt (ĭ-rŭpt′) *v.* to release one's anger or enthusiasm in a sudden, noisy way
 estallar *v.* expresar furia o entusiasmo de modo repentino y explosivo

etiquette (ĕt′ĭ-kĕt′) *n.* the practice of social manners
 etiqueta *s.* práctica de buenos modales

excavation (ĕk′skə-vā′shən) *n.* the act or process of exposing by digging away a covering
 excavación *s.* acción o proceso de destapar lo que está cubierto de tierra

except (ĭk-sĕpt′) *prep.* but; however
 excepto *prep.* pero; sin embargo

expedition (ĕk′spĭ-dĭsh′ən) *n.* a journey taken by a group with a definite goal
 expedición *s.* viaje en que se embarca un grupo con una meta definida

expert (ĕk′spûrt′) *n.* one who is skilled in or knowledgeable about a particular thing
 experto *s.* persona que domina un campo de conocimiento

exquisite (ĕk′skwĭ-zĭt) *adj.* of extraordinary beauty or charm
 exquisito *adj.* de extraordinaria belleza o encanto

extinct (ĭk-stĭngkt′) *adj.* no longer existing
 extinto *adj.* que ya no existe

feasibility (fē′zə-bĭl-ə-tē′) *n.* the possibility of something being accomplished
 viabilidad *s.* posibilidad de realizarse

ferocious (fə-rō′shəs) *adj.* savage; fierce
 feroz *adj.* salvaje; fiero

fertile (fûr′tl) *adj.* able to produce farm crops or other vegetation
 fértil *adj.* bueno para cultivar

fossil (fŏs′əl) *n.* the remains of a living thing, preserved in soil or rock
 fósil *s.* restos de un organismo preservados en el suelo o en la roca

frenzied (frĕn′zēd) *adj.* wildly excited; frantic
 frenético *adj.* sumamente agitado

frugal (frōō′gəl) *adj.* avoiding waste; thrifty
 frugal *adj.* moderado; económico

gait (gāt) *n.* manner of walking or moving on foot
 paso *s.* modo de andar

generic (jə-nĕr′ĭk) *adj.* having no particularly distinctive or noteworthy quality
 genérico *adj.* que no tiene características distintivas o destacadas

glistening (glĭs′ən-ĭng) *adj.* sparkling
reluciente *adj.* brillante

graciousness (grā′shəs-nəs) *n.* the condition of being pleasant, courteous, and generous
gentileza *s.* simpatía, cortesía y generosidad

harsh (härsh) *adj.* rough; cruel
duro *adj.* severo; cruel

hibernation (hī′bər-nā′shən) *n.* the state of being inactive through the winter
hibernación *s.* estado de inactividad durante el invierno

hospitality (hŏs′pĭ-tăl′ĭ-tē) *n.* the friendly, generous treatment of guests
hospitalidad *s.* tratamiento amistoso y generoso de huéspedes

immense (ĭ-mĕns′) *adj.* extremely big; huge
inmenso *adj.* sumamente grande; enorme

immensely (ĭ-mĕns′lē) *adv.* extremely; very
inmensamente *adv.* sumamente; muy

immigrant (ĭm′ĭ-grənt) *n.* a person who leaves one country to live in another
inmigrante *s.* persona que llega a vivir a otro país

immortality (ĭm′ôr-tăl′ĭ-tē) *n.* endless life
inmortalidad *s.* vida eterna

impaired (ĭm-pârd′) *adj.* being in a less than perfect condition
deteriorado *adj.* que no está en perfectas condiciones

imposing (ĭm-pō′zĭng) *adj.* impressive; grand
imponente *adj.* impresionante; grandioso

impostor (ĭm-pŏs′tər) *n.* a person who uses a false name or identity
impostor *s.* persona que usa un nombre o una identidad falsos

impressionable (ĭm-prĕsh′ə-nə-bəl) *adj.* easily influenced
impresionable *adj.* fácil de influenciar

incident (ĭn′sĭ-dənt) *n.* a single event or occurrence
incidente *s.* suceso u ocurrencia

incredibly (ĭn-krĕd′ə-blē) *adv.* unbelievably
increíblemente *adv.* de modo imposible de creer

incredulous (ĭn-krĕj′ə-ləs) *adj.* unbelieving
incrédulo *adj.* que no cree

indignantly (ĭn-dĭg′nənt-lē) *adv.* angrily; in annoyance
con indignación *adv.* con furia

indistinct (ĭn′dĭ-stĭngkt′) *adj.* not clearly recognizable or understandable
indistinto *adj.* que no se distingue o diferencia

inefficient (ĭn′ĭ-fĭsh′ənt) *adj.* not able to produce without wasting time or energy
ineficaz *adj.* que desperdicia tiempo o energía

inevitable (ĭn-ĕv′ĭ-tə-bəl) *adj.* impossible to avoid or prevent
inevitable *adj.* que no se puede evitar o prevenir

inspect (ĭn-spĕkt′) *v.* to examine carefully
inspeccionar *v.* examinar con cuidado

inspiration (ĭn′spə-rā′shən) *n.* something that motivates or influences
inspiración *s.* algo que motiva o influencia

instinctive (ĭn-stĭngk′tĭv) *adj.* of or about the natural behaviors of a type of animal
instintivo *adj.* relativo a la conducta natural de un animal

intensity (ĭn-tĕn′sĭ-tē) *n.* extreme amount of energy or feeling
intensidad *s.* cantidad extrema de energía o sentimiento

intolerable (ĭn-tŏl′ər-ə-bəl) *adj.* unbearable; too much to be endured
intolerable *adj.* inaguantable; insoportable

invisible (ĭn-vĭz′ə-bəl) *adj.* not able to be seen
invisible *adj.* que no se ve

khaki (kăk′ē) *n.* cloth made of light yellowish brown cotton or wool
caqui *s.* tela de algodón o de lana de color pardo amarillento

lagoon (lə-gōōn′) *n.* a shallow body of water separated from a larger body of water by sandbars or other barriers
laguna *s.* masa de agua separada de una masa mayor por bancos de arena u otras barreras

lavishly (lăv′ĭsh-lē) *adv.* in a rich or plentiful way; abundantly
profusamente *adv.* derrochadoramente; abundantemente

lean (lēn) *adj.* having little to spare; thin
    flaco *adj.* delgado; escaso

lectern (lĕk′tərn) *n.* a stand that holds books, a computer, or papers for someone giving a speech or lecture
    atril *s.* soporte para sostener libros, una computadora o papeles al dar un discurso o conferencia

leisurely (lē′zhər-lē) *adj.* done slowly; unhurried
    despacio *adj.* pausadamente; sin prisa

leniency (lē′nē-ən-sē) *n.* tolerance; gentleness
    lenidad *s.* indulgencia; suavidad

manifestation (măn′ə-fĕ-stā′shən) *n.* evidence that something is present
    manifestación *s.* expresión pública

massacre (măs′ə-kər) *n.* the act of killing a number of helpless humans or animals
    masacre *s.* matanza de personas o animales indefensos

melancholy (mĕl′ən-kŏl′ē) *adj.* sad; gloomy
    melancólico *adj.* triste; abatido

mimic (mĭm′ĭk) *n.* one who imitates the speech and gestures of others
    imitador *s.* persona que imita las palabras y los gestos de otros

mortified (môr′tə-fīd′) *adj.* ashamed, humiliated **mortify** *v.*
    avergonzado *adj.* apenado, humillado **avergonzar** *v.*

mournful (môrn′fəl) *adj.* feeling or expressing sorrow or grief
    afligido *adj.* triste, dolorido

narrative (năr′ə-tĭv) *n.* a story
    narrativa *s.* relato

nocturnal (nŏk-tûr′nəl) *adj.* active at night
    nocturno *adj.* activo de noche

novelty (nŏv′əl-tē) *n.* something new and unusual
    novedad *s.* algo nuevo y poco común

obscure (ŏb-skyŏŏr′) *adj.* far from cities or other areas of human population
    alejado *adj.* lejos de ciudades u otros centros de población

obsess (əb-sĕs′) *v.* to occupy the mind of
    obsesionar *v.* ocupar la mente

obstacle (ŏb′stə-kəl) *n.* something that stands in the way or prevents progress
    obstáculo *s.* algo que presenta un inconveniente o dificultad

obstinacy (ŏb′stə-nə-sē) *n.* the act of being stubborn or disobedient
    obstinación *s.* terquedad; persistencia

ominous (ŏm′ə-nəs) *adj.* threatening; frightening
    ominoso *adj.* amenazante; siniestro

pauper (pô′pər) *n.* someone who is extremely poor
    indigente *s.* persona muy pobre

perception (pər-sĕp′shən) *n.* an impression or feeling
    percepción *s.* impresión o sentimiento

persuade (pər-swād′) *v.* to win someone over; convince
    persuadir *v.* convencer

pert (pûrt) *adj.* offensively bold; saucy
    descarado *adj.* insolente; fresco

petrify (pĕt′rə-fī′) *v.* to paralyze with astonishment or fear
    petrificar *v.* paralizar de sorpresa o miedo

ponder (pŏn′dər) *v.* to think seriously about; reflect on
    ponderar *v.* examinar; reflexionar

precise (prĭ-sīs′) *adj.* exact or correct
    preciso *adj.* exacto o correcto

predator (prĕd′ə-tər) *n.* an animal that feeds on other animals
    depredador *s.* animal que se alimenta de otros animales

preservation (prĕz′ər-vā′shən) *n.* the state of being mostly unchanged or kept from harm
    preservación *s.* protección contra algún daño

prestige (prĕ-stēzh′) *n.* recognition; fame
    prestigio *s.* reconocimiento; fama

proceed (prō-sēd′) *v.* to go forward or onward; continue
    proceder *v.* avanzar; continuar

proclaim (prō-klām′) *v.* to announce publicly; declare
    proclamar *v.* anunciar públicamente; declarar

profile (prō′fīl′) *n.* a side view of an object, especially of the human head
    perfil *s.* vista lateral de un objeto, especialmente de una cabeza humana

profound (prə-found') *adj.* very deep or great
　profundo *adj.* intenso, fuerte o muy grande

prop (prŏp) *n.* an object an actor uses in a play
　utilería *s.* accesorio que usa un actor en una obra

propeller (prə-pĕl'ər) *n.* a spinning blade used to move a boat or airplane forward　**propel** *v.*
　hélice *s.* palas rotativas que impulsa un bote o avión　**propulsar** *v.*

protest (prə-tĕst') *v.* to argue about or object to something
　protestar *v.* expresar disconformidad o queja

pursuit (pər-sōōt') *n.* the act of following or chasing
　persecución *s.* acción de seguir o perseguir

raggedy (răg'ĭ-dē) *adj.* tattered or worn out
　rasgado *adj.* andrajoso o gastado

recollection (rĕk'ə-lĕk'shən) *n.* something remembered
　recuerdo *s.* memoria

reconstruction (rē'kən-strŭk'shən) *n.* the act of building or assembling again
　reconstrucción *s.* acción de volver a armar o construir

reef (rēf) *n.* a ridge of rocks, sand, or coral that rises to the surface of a body of water
　arrecife *s.* saliente de rocas, arena o coral que se ve en la superficie del agua

relentless (rĭ-lĕnt'lĭs) *adj.* refusing to stop or give up
　implacable *adj.* que no para ni cede

reluctant (rĭ-lŭk'tənt) *adj.* unwilling
　reacio *adj.* mal dispuesto

repentance (rĭ-pĕn'təns) *n.* sorrow or regret
　arrepentimiento *s.* pena o remordimiento

repose (rĭ-pōz') *n.* freedom from work or worry; rest
　reposo *s.* descanso y tranquilidad

resilient (rĭ-zĭl'yənt) *adj.* flexible and springy
　elástico *adj.* flexible y adaptable

resounding (rĭ-zound'ĭng) *adj.* unmistakable; loud
　resonante *adj.* inconfundible; fuerte

resourcefulness (rĭ-sôrs'fəl-nĕs) *n.* the ability to act effectively, even in difficult situations
　ingenio *s.* capacidad de responder debidamente, inclusive en situaciones difíciles

restless (rĕst'lĭs) *adj.* unable to sleep or rest
　inquieto *adj.* que no puede dormir ni descansar

retort (rĭ-tôrt') *v.* to reply, especially in a quick or unkind way
　replicar *v.* contestar, especialmente a una ofensa

retrieve (rĭ-trēv') *v.* to get back again
　recuperar *v.* recobrar

revolting (rĭ-vōl'tĭng) *adj.* causing disgust　**revolt** *v.*
　repugnante *adj.* nauseabundo　**repugnar** *v.*

rigid (rĭj'ĭd) *adj.* stiff; not moving
　rígido *adj.* tieso; que no se mueve

sacred (sā'krĭd) *adj.* worthy of great respect; holy
　sagrado *adj.* que merece gran respeto; santo

sane (sān) *adj.* mentally healthy; reasonable
　cuerdo *adj.* sensato; razonable

savor (sā'vər) *v.* to take great pleasure in
　deleitarse *v.* gozar; apreciar

scavenge (skăv'ənj) *v.* to search for discarded scraps
　hurgar *v.* escarbar la basura

sensation (sĕn-sā'shən) *n.* a feeling
　sensación *s.* sentimiento

setback (sĕt'băk') *n.* an unexpected stop in progress; a change from better to worse
　revés *s.* contratiempo o fracaso; desmejora

shrivel (shrĭv'əl) *v.* to shrink or wrinkle
　secarse *v.* arrugarse o marchitarse

shrouded (shroud'əd) *adj.* concealed or hidden
　velado *adj.* envuelto u oculto

sibling (sĭb'lĭng) *n.* brother or sister
　hermano/a *s.* hijo o hija de los mismos padres

simulate (sĭm'yə-lāt') *v.* to imitate
　simular *v.* imitar

simultaneously (sī'məl-tā'nē-əs-lē) *adv.* at the same time
　simultáneamente *adv.* al mismo tiempo

sinewy (sĭn'yōō-ē) *adj.* lean
　fibroso *adj.* flaco

skirmish (skûr'mĭsh) *n.* a minor battle or conflict
　reyerta *s.* batalla o conflicto menor

slacken (slăk'ən) *v.* to slow down or lessen
aflojar *v.* disminuir o relajar

smirk (smûrk) *v.* to smile in an insulting way
regodearse *v.* sonreír con suficiencia

snare (snâr) *n.* a trap for catching small animals and birds
lazo *s.* trampa para animales pequeños y aves

species (spē'shēz) *n.* a variety or type of something
especie *s.* variedad o tipo

stalemate (stāl'māt') *n.* a situation in which no one playing a game is able to win
punto muerto *s.* situación en que ninguno de los jugadores puede ganar

stealthily (stĕl'thə-lē) *adv.* secretly; sneakily
clandestinamente *adv.* secretamente; furtivamente

stroke (strōk) *n.* a sudden, severe attack; a sudden loss of blood flow to the brain, often leading to physical or mental damage
apoplejía *s.* derrame cerebral que suele causar daño físico o mental

successor (sək-sĕs'ər) *n.* a person who follows another, taking on his or her rights or duties
sucesor *s.* persona que sucede a otra en el desempeño de un cargo

succumb (sə-kŭm') *v.* to give in; die
sucumbir *v.* ceder; morir

surmise (sər-mīz') *v.* to make a guess
suponer *v.* hacer una conjetura

surpass (sər-păs') *v.* to become greater than; to go beyond
sobrepasar *v.* superar; aventajar

tangible (tăn'jə-bəl) *adj.* possible to touch; real
tangible *adj.* que se puede tocar; real

taunt (tônt) *v.* to mock or insult
ridiculizar *v.* mofar o insultar

tense (tĕns) *adj.* nervous; feeling strain
tenso *adj.* nervioso; tirante

torment (tôr'mĕnt') *v.* to cause severe distress to the body or mind
atormentar *v.* causar profundo dolor físico o mental

trite (trīt) *adj.* boring because overused; not fresh or original
gastado *adj.* trillado y trivial

truce (trōōs) *n.* an agreement to end an argument or fight
tregua *s.* acuerdo que termina una discusión o una pelea

tumultuously (tōō-mŭl'chōō-əs'lē) *adv.* in a wild or disorderly way
tumultuosamente *adv.* de modo desordenado y ruidoso

tyrant (tī'rənt) *n.* a ruler who governs in a cruel manner
tirano *s.* gobernante que abusa del poder

uncomprehending (ŭn'kŏm-prĭ-hĕn'dĭng) *adj.* not understanding
atónito *adj.* que no entiende

unsuitable (ŭn-sōō'tə-bəl) *adj.* not appropriate or fitting
impropio *adj.* inservible o inadecuado

variation (vâr'ē-ā'shən) *n.* a slightly different form of something
variación *s.* forma ligeramente distinta

vicious (vĭsh'əs) *adj.* severe or fierce
feroz *adj.* malo; salvaje

vulnerable (vŭl'nər-ə-bəl) *adj.* open to attack or damage
vulnerable *adj.* fácil de atacar o dañar

zealous (zĕl'əs) *adj.* eager and enthusiastic
fervoroso *adj.* entusiasta

Using the Glossary

This glossary is an alphabetical list of vocabulary words found in the selections in this book. Use this glossary just as you would a dictionary—to determine the meanings, parts of speech, pronunciation, and syllabication of words. (Some technical, foreign, and more obscure words in this book are not listed here but are defined for you in the footnotes that accompany many of the selections.)

Many words in the English language have more than one meaning. This glossary gives the meanings that apply to the words as they are used in the selections in this book. Words closely related in form and meaning are listed together in one entry (for instance, *consumption* and *consume*), and the definition is given for the first form.

The following abbreviations are used to identify parts of speech of words:

adj. adjective   *adv.* adverb   *n.* noun   *v.* verb

Each word's pronunciation is given in parentheses. A guide to the pronunciation symbols appears in the Pronunciation Key below. The stress marks in the Pronunciation Key are used to indicate the force given to each syllable in a word. They can also help you determine where words are divided into syllables.

For more information about the words in this glossary or for information about words not listed here, consult a dictionary.

Pronunciation Key

Symbol	Examples	Symbol	Examples	Symbol	Examples
ă	**a**t, g**a**s	m	**m**an, see**m**	v	**v**an, sa**v**e
ā	**a**pe, d**ay**	n	**n**ight, mitt**en**	w	**w**eb, t**w**ice
ä	f**a**ther, b**a**rn	ng	si**ng**, ha**ng**er	y	**y**ard, law**y**er
âr	f**air**, d**are**	ŏ	**o**dd, n**o**t	z	**z**oo, rea**s**on
b	**b**ell, ta**b**le	ō	**o**pen, r**oa**d, gr**ow**	zh	trea**s**ure, gara**g**e
ch	**ch**in, lun**ch**	ô	**aw**ful, b**ough**t, h**o**rse	ə	**a**wake, ev**e**n, penc**i**l,
d	**d**ig, bor**ed**	oi	c**oi**n, b**oy**		pil**o**t, foc**u**s
ĕ	**e**gg, t**e**n	ŏŏ	l**oo**k, f**u**ll	ər	p**er**form, lett**er**
ē	**e**vil, s**ee**, m**ea**l	ōō	r**oo**t, gl**ue**, thr**ough**		
f	**f**all, lau**gh**, **ph**rase	ou	**ou**t, c**ow**	**Sounds in Foreign Words**	
g	**g**old, bi**g**	p	**p**ig, ca**p**	KH	*German* i**ch**, au**ch**;
h	**h**it, in**h**ale	r	**r**ose, sta**r**		*Scottish* lo**ch**
hw	**wh**ite, every**wh**ere	s	**s**it, fa**c**e	N	*French* e**n**tre, bo**n**, fi**n**
ĭ	**i**nch, f**i**t	sh	**sh**e, ma**sh**	œ	*French* f**eu**, c**œu**r;
ī	**i**dle, m**y**, tr**ie**d	t	**t**ap, hopp**ed**		*German* sch**ö**n
îr	d**ear**, h**ere**	th	**th**ing, wi**th**	ü	*French* **u**tile, r**ue**;
j	**j**ar, **g**em, ba**dge**	*th*	**th**en, o**th**er		*German* gr**ü**n
k	**k**eep, **c**at, lu**ck**	ŭ	**u**p, n**u**t		
l	**l**oad, ratt**le**	ûr	f**ur**, **ear**n, b**ir**d, w**or**m		

Stress Marks

ʹ   This mark indicates that the preceding syllable receives the primary stress. For example, in the word *language,* the first syllable is stressed: lăngʹgwĭj.

ˌ   This mark is used only in words in which more than one syllable is stressed. It indicates that the preceding syllable is stressed, but somewhat more weakly than the syllable receiving the primary stress. In the word *literature,* for example, the first syllable receives the primary stress, and the last syllable receives a weaker stress: lĭtʹər-ə-chŏŏrˌ.

-    This mark indicates that the preceding syllable is unstressed. In the word *literature* above, the second and third syllables are not stressed.

INDEX OF FINE ART

Index of Skills

A

Academic vocabulary, 16–19, 27, 44, 64, 76, 102, 124, 136, 191, 205, 218, 232, 258, 273, 286, 317, 338, 358, 376, 392, 435, 455, 484, 506, 517, 577, 599, 635, 675, 690, 704, 723, 745, 758, 778, 801, 820, 839, 858, 893, 906, 914, 930, 950, 959, 965, 1009, R115–116. *See also* Specialized vocabulary.

Active listening, 306, R82–R83

Active voice, R57

Adjective clauses, R62
    essential, R62
    nonessential, R62

Adjective phrases, R60

Adjectives, R48, R57–R59
    versus adverbs, R58
    commas with, 507
    comparative forms, 287, 303, 308, R58
    nouns formed from, 358
    predicate, 287, R57
    proper, 859, R51
    superlative forms, 287, 303, 308, R58
    vivid, 438

Adverb clauses, R62–R63

Adverb phrases, 299, R60

Adverbs, R48, R58–R59
    versus adjectives, R58
    comparative forms, 287, 303, R58
    superlative forms, 287, 303, R58

Advertising, 10, 966–983, 984–987, R90–R91
    billboard, R90
    celebrities in, R91
    demographics, 984–987, R85
    flyer, 859, R90
    infomercial, R90
    marketing, R90
    persuasive techniques in, 939, 966–983, 984–987
    political ad, R90
    print ad, R90
    product comparison, R91
    product placement, R90–R91
    public service announcement, 939, 966–971, R90
    sponsors, R90
    storyboard for, 987
    target audience, 984–987, R85
    television commercials, 984–987
    trailer, R90
    types of, R90

Affixes, 255, 286, 358, 506, 704, 778. *See also* Greek word parts; Latin word parts; Prefixes; Suffixes.

Agreement
    pronoun-antecedent, 125, R52–R53
    subject-verb, 607, 621, 666, R65

Alliteration, 580–581, 615–620, R100, R108. *See also* Sound devices.

Almanacs, 1016, 1018. *See also* References.

Ambiguous pronoun references, R55

Analogy, R71, R100, R110. *See also* Rhetorical devices.
    part-to-whole, 376, 745, 839, 914
    whole-to-part, 376, 745, 839, 914

Analysis, writing, 691, 821, R39–R40
    criteria for, R39
    options for organization, R39–R40

Analyzing Text Structure and Development of Ideas, FM44

Anecdotes, R100
    as nonfiction type, 851
    in student writing, 936, R30, R41

Antecedent-pronoun agreement, 125, R52–R53

Antonyms, R70

Apostrophes, 103, R50

Appeals, 938, R21. *See also* Arguments; Persuasive techniques.
    by association, 938
    to authority, 953, R110
    bandwagon, 938, R21, R91
    emotional, 938, 953, R21, R91, R111
    ethical, R21, R111
    to fear, pity, or vanity, 938, R21
    logical, R21, R91, R112
    to loyalty, R21
    snob appeal, R21
    testimonial, 938, R21

Applications, follow instructions to prepare, R16, R44–R45

Appositives and appositive phrases, R61

Argument: Supporting an Opinion, 170–179

Arguments, 936–941, 1000, R20, R110. *See also* Appeals; Persuasive techniques; Persuasive writing.
    analysis of, 940–941, 943–949, 956, R20
    claims, 936–937, 940–941, 943–949, R20, R110
    counterarguments, 943, 988, R20, R26, R111
    elements of, 936–937, 943–949, R20
    evidence, 913, 936, 943–949, R20, R22, R25–R26, R41, R111

facts in, 936–937, 940, 956
faulty, R24, R112
opposing. *See* counterarguments, *above*.
reasons, 949, R20
strategies for determining strong, R26
strategies for reading, R20
support, 936, 943–949, 1000, R20, R114
writing, 988, R40–R41

Art. *See* Visuals.

Articles (written). *See* Feature articles; Magazine articles; News articles.

Articulation. *See* Speaking strategies.

Assessment practice, 182–187, 308–313, 426–431, 568–573, 666–671, 792–797, 884–889, 1000–1005
    reading comprehension, 182–185, 308–311, 426–431, 568–571, 666–669, 792–795, 884–887, 1000–1003, R94–R95
    revising and editing, 187, 313, 431, 573, 671, 797, 889, 1005
    short constructed response, 185, 311, 429, 571, 669, 793, 795, 887, 1003, R97–R99
    vocabulary, 186, 312, 430, 572, 670, 796, 888, 1004, R96

Atlases, 1018. *See also* References.

Audience
    media, R85
    speech, R76
    target, 984–987, R85

Audio resources, 1016

Authority. *See* Arguments; Sources.

Author's background, 35, 47, 67, 87, 104, 115, 127, 143, 151, 199, 207, 221, 235, 265, 275, 289, 325, 349, 361, 383, 401, 407, 443, 459, 469, 499, 509, 525, 533, 585, 593, 601, 609, 615, 629, 637, 643, 683, 693, 713, 725, 737, 747, 761, 809, 833, 851, 865, 899, 909, 917, 943, 961

Author's intent. *See* Author's purpose.

Author's message, 961–964, R109, R110. *See also* Theme.

Author's perspective, 275–285, R100

Author's point of view. *See* Author's perspective.

Author's position, R110. *See also* Claims.

Author's purpose, 115–123, 125, 138–141, 340–347, 509–516, 521, 523, 568, 822–831, 871, R100
    comparing and contrasting, 138–141, 340–347, 521, 523, 822–831

Commonly confused words, R75

Comparative form of modifiers, 287, 308

Compare and contrast, reading and thinking, 43, 349–357, 505, 732–733, 809–819, R11–R13, R110

author's purpose, 138–141, 340–347, 521, 822–831

author's viewpoint 936, 940–941, 942–943

characters, 349–357, 454, 777

cultural and historical settings, 235, 239, 247, 257, 383–391

fables, 391

film and essay, 863

form, 641

information, 971, 977, 982

literary works, 63

memoir and autobiography, 279, 802–803, 844

mood, 530

organization, R11

personal narrative and autobiography, 265–272, 802–803, 827

persuasive techniques, 938–939, 940–941, 967–982

play and film, 166–169, 541, 550, 732–733

poetry, 413, 613, 634

style, 439

themes, universal, 769

tone, 653

versions of a story, 166–169

Comparing and Contrasting Texts, FM40

Comparison-and-contrast organization, 296, 299, 905, R11–R13, R37–R38. *See also* Analogy; Arguments.

point-by-point, 299, R11, R37

signal words for, 303, R11, R68

subject-by-subject, 299, R11, R37

Comparison-contrast essay, 296–305, R37–R38

Comparisons, illogical, R59

Complements

direct object, R48, R60

indirect object, R48, R60

subject, R60

Complex sentences. *See* Sentences, complex.

Compound sentences. *See* Sentences, compound.

Compound words, 232

Comprehension. *See* Reading skills and strategies; Assessment practice.

Computers. *See* Electronic media; Internet; Software; Web sites.

Computer software. *See* Software.

Conclusions, R110

deductive, R22

drawing, 135, 149, 247, 375, 530, 598, 689, 703, 905, R111

inductive, R21–R22

logical, R21–R22, R110

in own writing, R33, R39, R41

Conflict, 28, 30, 35, 47–61, 54, 63, 349–357, R37, R101. *See also* Falling action; Plot; Rising action.

analysis of, 34–43, 75, 137, 217

climax and, 30, 35

in drama, 151–165

in exposition, 30, 31, 35

external, 47, 54, 63, 75, R101

influence of setting on, 67–75, 101, 337

internal, 47, 54, 63, 75, R101

in narrative writing, R37

theme and, 349–357

Conjunctions

coordinating, 377

subordinating, 787

to correct run-on sentences, 65, R64

Connecting, 12, 47–63, 78–85, 123, 138, 166–169, 199–204, 235–257, 340–347, 378–381, 457, 469–483, 486–491, 518–523, 590, 622–627, 705, 706–711, 822–831, 870, R110. *See also* Cross-curricular connections.

Connect main ideas, 78–85, 347, 831, 917–929

Connotation, 44, R70, R102. *See also* Denotation.

Consumer documents, 8, R16, R110. *See also* Workplace and technical writing; Workplace documents.

Content-area vocabulary. *See* Academic vocabulary; Specialized vocabulary.

Context clues, 258, 308, 758, 1000, R68, R111. *See also* Vocabulary, in context.

for cause-and-effect, R68

for comparison, R68

for contrast, R68

for definition or restatement, 959, R68

examples as, R68

Conventions, grammar, R46–R67

Conversational voice, 199, 202, 204, 221–231, 365

Copyright page, 1019

Correspondence, business, R43–R45, R110

Counterarguments, 988, R20, R26, R111

Creative projects

art, 123, 135, 204, 405, 551, 703

drama, 43, 149, 467, 734, 757

music, 744

poem, 606

writing, 413, 634, 689

Credibility, 1021–1024, R111. *See also* Sources.

Credits, Web site, 1015

Crisis. *See* Climax.

Criteria

analysis writing, R39

business writing, R42

cause-effect writing, R38

compare-and-contrast essay, 303–304, R37

descriptive writing, R34

instruction writing, 787–788, R42

narrative writing, R36

online feature article, 562–563

opinion, 177–178

personal narratives, 879–880

persuasive writing, R40

problem-solution essay, R39

research paper, 1042–1043

short story, 421–422

workplace and technical writing, R42

Critical listening, R83

Critical reading. *See* Reading skills and strategies; Test-taking strategies.

Critical thinking. *See* Text analysis; Reading skills and strategies.

Cross-curricular connections

science, 75, 335, 337, 776, 815, 819

social studies, 91, 101, 131, 210, 217, 225, 231, 251, 272, 285, 329, 352, 357, 364, 375, 448, 454, 620, 716, 722, 871

Cultural and historical setting, 234–259, 383–391, 769

Cultural values, 140, 678, 792, R102

analysis of, 693–703, 725–734

Currency of sources. *See* Sources.

D

Dashes, 659, R50

Data, collecting own, 1018–1027

Databases, 1016, 1018, R111. *See also* References.

Deconstruction, of media presentation, R85

Deductive conclusion, R22

Deductive reasoning, R22, R111

Delivery. *See* Speaking strategies.

Demographics, 984, R85

Denotation, 44, R70, R102. *See also* Connotation.

Denouement. 30, 33, 42, 43. *See also* Resolution.

Dependent (subordinate) clauses, 456, 735, R62

Derivations of words. *See* Word parts; Word roots.

Descriptive language, R35, R102. *See also* Details.

Posture, in oral presentation, R77, R78, R83
Power presentations, 998, 1044–1045. *See also* Oral presentations.
Practicing keyboarding skills, 173
Predicate adjectives, R57
Predicate nominatives, R60, R67
Predicates, 45, R60
    complete, R48
    compound, R60, R64
    simple, R48
Predicting, 12, 207–217, 361–374, 693–703, R113
Prefixes, 93, 124, 182, 241, 286, 506, 704, 778, 815, 930, 1000, R69. *See also* Greek word parts; Latin word parts; Word parts.
    punctuation with, R50
    spelling with, R73
Prejudice. *See* Bias.
Preparing for Timed Writing, 179, 305, 423, 565, 789, 881, 997
Prepositional phrases, 879, 951, R60
Prepositions, R47, R48, R53, R60, R75
Presentations. *See* Oral presentations.
Present participle verb forms, R55, R61
Previewing, 12, 953–958, R4
Primary sources, 822, R28, R114. *See also* Sources, types of.
    versus secondary sources, 1018, R114
Prior knowledge, 12, R113
Problem. *See* Conflict.
Problem-solution essay
    criteria for, R39
    options for organization, R39
Problem-and-solution organizational pattern, 487, 490, 894–897, R13, R113
Procedures. *See* Business writing; Workplace and technical writing.
Process analysis, 518–523, R39
Prompts, responding to, 85, 169, 296, 347, 414, 491, 523, 556, 627, 656, 711, 780, 831, 843, 872, 931, 988, 1028, R98–R99. *See also* Conventions in writing; Writing for assessment.
Pronouns, R52–R55
    agreement with antecedent, 120, 125, R52–R53
    capitalization of, R51
    case of, 219, R52–R53
    common problems, 663
    demonstrative, R54
    first-person, R52
    forms, R53
    indefinite, R54, R66
    intensive, 177, R46, R53
    interrogative, R46, R54
    nominative, R52, R60

object, 214, 219, R52, R53
personal, R46, R52, R53, R54
possessive, 774, R52, R53, R54
predicate, R60
reference problems, R55
reflexive, R46, R53
relative, R46, R54, R67
second-person, R52
subject, 219, R52, R53
third-person, R52
verb agreement with, R66
Pronunciation, determining, 136, 218, R72, R115, R124
Proofreading, 21, 177, 303, 421, 563, 787, 879, 995, R29. *See also* Revising and editing.
    of test responses, R98, R99
Propaganda, 985, R25, R113
    persuasion and, 966–983
    techniques of, 978–983
Props, R106
Proposition-and support organizational pattern, 909–913
Public documents, R17, R113. *See also* Editorials; Government publications; Literary nonfiction, types of; Speech.
Public service announcements, 958, 967–971, R90
Publishing, 21, 177, 303, 421, 563, 663, 787, 879, 995, 1042, R29
Punctuation, 233, 884, R49–R50
    apostrophes, 103, R50
    colons, 821, R50
    commas, 65, 77, 339, 659, R49
    dashes, 659, R50
    in dialogue, 77, 331, 339, 417, 426
    ellipses, R50
    end marks, R49
    exclamation points, 233, R60
    hyphens, R50
    with italic type, 915, 1000
    parentheses, 659, R50
    periods, 65, 77, 230, 339, R49
    question marks, 230, R49
    quotation marks, 74, 77, 339, 915, 995, 1033, R50
    semicolons, R49
    of titles, 915, 1037
Puns, 551, R106
Purpose for reading, setting, 234–257, 383–391, 525–530, 643–653, 917–929, R114

Q

Qualities of a character. *See* Character traits.
Questioning, R2. *See also* Monitoring.
Question marks, R49

Questions, 306–307, R30, R33. *See also* Interviews; Research; Sentences.
    asking, 865–871
    research, 1012, 1030
    rhetorical, 961, R113
    as text feature, R3
Quick reference charts
    capitalization, R51
    parts of speech, R46
    punctuation, R49–R50
    sentence and its parts, R48
Quickwriting, 114, 220, 234, 288, 348, 406, 458, 524, 532, 600, 736, 832, 908, 916, 1010. *See also* Freewriting.
Quotation marks, R50
    commas with, 339, 995
    periods with, 339, 995
    to set off speaker's exact words, 339, 995, 1033, R50
    with titles, 915, R50
Quotations, 339, 995, 1033, R14, R28. *See also* Plagiarism; Works cited.
    capitalization in, R51
    direct, 995
    in elaboration, R34
    ellipses in, R50
    indirect, 995
    punctuation with, 74, 339, 1033, R50

R

Radio plays, 726, R106
Radio transcripts, 138–141
Reading comprehension, Assessment practice, 182–185, 308–311, 426–429, 568–571, 666–669, 792–795, 884–887, 1000–1003, R94–R95
Reading fluency, 104, 394, 492, 584, 591, 844
Reading for information. *See also* Informational texts; Reading skills and strategies.
    analyzing author's purpose, 138–141, 822–831
    citing evidence, R20, R111
    classification, 706–711
    comparing and contrasting, 166–169, 732–733, 831, R11–R13
    electronic texts, R19. *See also* online articles, *below*.
    feature articles, R112
    following instructions, 378–381
    handbook excerpt, 374
    illustrations, 84
    information, evaluating, 840–843, 1021–1024, R25–R26
    informational texts, 622, 894–897, R14–R19
    interviews, 284

INDEX OF TITLES & AUTHORS

Page numbers that appear in italics refer to biographical information.

ACKNOWLEDGMENTS

INTRODUCTORY UNIT

Houghton Mifflin Harcourt: Excerpt from *Number the Stars* by Lois Lowry. Copyright © 1989 by Lois Lowry. All rights reserved. Reprinted by permission of Houghton Mifflin Harcourt Publishing Company.

Simon & Schuster: "Quilt," from *A Suitcase of Seaweed and Other Poems* by Janet S. Wong. Copyright © 1996 by Janet S. Wong. Reprinted with the permission of Margaret K. McElderry Books, A Division of Simon & Schuster, Inc.

PLAYS/Sterling Partners: Excerpt from "The Little Princess" by Frances Hodgson Burnett, adapted by Adele Than, from *Plays from Famous Stories and Fairy Tales* and *PLAYS, The Drama Magazine for Young People*. Copyright © 1989 and © 1985. Reprinted with the permission of the publisher PLAYS/Sterling Partners, Inc., P.O. Box 60016, Newton, MA 02460.

Sterling Lord Literistic: Excerpt from *Steven Spielberg: Crazy for Movies* by Susan Goldman Rubin. Copyright © 2001 by Susan Goldman Rubin. Reprinted by permission of Sterling Lord Literistic, Inc.

Francisco Jiménez: Excerpt from "The Circuit" by Francisco Jiménez from *Arizona Quarterly,* Autumn 1973. Reprinted by the author.

UNIT 1

Viking Penguin: Excerpt from *Trouble River* by Betsy Byars. Copyright © 1969 by Betsy Byars. Used by permission of Viking Penguin, a division of Penguin Group (USA) Inc. All rights reserved.

HarperCollins Publishers: Excerpt from "Zlateh the Goat," from *Zlateh the Goat and Other Stories* by Isaac Bashevis Singer. Copyright © 1966 by Isaac Bashevis Singer, copyright renewed 1994 by Alma Singer. Reprinted by permission of HarperCollins Publishers.

Bancroft Library: Excerpt from "The Bracelet" by Yoshiko Uchida from *The Scribner Anthology for Young People,* edited by Anne Diven. Copyright © 1976 by Charles Scribner's Sons. Reprinted courtesy of the Bancroft Library, the University of California, Berkeley.

Brandt & Hochman Literary Agents: Excerpt from "You're Not a Winner Unless Your Picture's in the Paper" by Avi from *The Color of Absence: 12 Short Stories About Loss and Hope,* Atheneum Books. Copyright © 2001 by Avi. Reprinted by permission of Brandt and Hochman Literary Agents, Inc.

Simon & Schuster: "Boar Out There" by Cynthia Rylant from *Every Living Thing.* Copyright © 1985 by Cynthia Rylant. Reprinted with the permission of Atheneum Books for Young Readers, a Division of Simon & Schuster, Inc.

Random House: "The School Play" by Gary Soto from *Funny You Should Ask,* edited by David Gale. Copyright © 1992 by Gary Soto. Used by permission of Dell Publishing, a division of Random House, Inc.

Marion Dane Bauer: "The Good Deed" by Marion Dane Bauer from *Shelf Life: Stories by the Book* edited by Gary Paulsen. Copyright © 2003 by Marion Dane Bauer. Reprinted by permission of the author.

Henry Holt and Company: "The Pasture," from *The Poetry of Robert* Frost by Robert Frost, edited by Edward Connery Lathem. Copyright © 1939, 1967, 1969 by Henry Holt and Company. Reprinted by permission of Henry Holt and Company, LLC.

Don Congdon Associates: "All Summer in a Day" by Ray Bradbury, published in *Magazine of Fantasy and Science Fiction,* March 1954. Copyright © 1954, renewed 1982 by Ray Bradbury. Reprinted by permission of Don Congdon Associates, Inc.

Carus Publishing Company: "Weather That's Out of this World!" adapted from "Getting Caught Up in Earth's Atmosphere" by Alan Dyer from *Odyssey,* April 1993. Copyright © 1993 by Cobblestone Publishing, 30 Grove Street, Suite C, Peterborough, NH 03458. Used by permission of Carus Publishing Company.

NASA: "What Is an Orbital Space Colony?" by Al Globus. Copyright © NASA. Reprinted by courtesy of NASA.

Brandt & Hochman Literary Agents: "Lob's Girl," from *A Whisper in the Night: Tales of Terror and Suspense* by Joan Aiken. Copyright © 1984 by Joan Aiken Enterprises, Ltd., published by Delacorte Press. Used by permission of Brandt & Hochman Literary Agents, Inc.

Random House Children's Books: Excerpt from *Bud, Not Buddy* by Christopher Paul Curtis. Copyright © 1999 by Christopher Paul Curtis. Used by permission of Random House Children's Books, a division of Random House, Inc.

Simon & Schuster: Excerpt from *Woodsong* by Gary Paulsen. Copyright © 1990 by Gary Paulsen. Reprinted with the permission of Simon & Schuster Books for Young Readers, a Division of Simon & Schuster, Inc.

NI Syndication: "A Life in the Day of Gary Paulsen" by Caroline Scott from the *Sunday Times,* November 15, 1998. Copyright © 1998 NI Syndication. Reprinted by permission of NI Syndication Ltd.

HarperCollins Publishers: "The Horse Snake," from *The Land I Lost* by Huynh Quang Nhuong. Copyright © 1982 by Huynh Quang Nhuong. Reprinted by permission of HarperCollins Publishers.

PLAYS/Sterling Partners: "The Prince and the Pauper" by Mark Twain, adapted by Joellen Bland, from *Stage Plays from the Classics* and *PLAYS, The Drama Magazine for Young People.* Copyright © 1987, reprinted 1994 and 2005 and © 2000. Reprinted with the permission of the publisher PLAYS/Sterling Partners, Inc., P.O. Box 60016, Newton, MA 02460.

Scholastic: "Fish Story" by Mary Lou Brooks from *Scholastic Action,* May 6, 1983. Copyright © 1983 by Scholastic Inc. Reprinted by permission.

UNIT 2

HarperCollins Publishers: Excerpt from *Walk Two Moons* by Sharon Creech. Copyright © 1994 by Sharon Creech. Reprinted by permission of HarperCollins Publishers.

Houghton Mifflin Harcourt: Excerpt from "How Becky Garza Learned to Golf," from *Help Wanted* by Gary Soto. Copyright © 2005 by Gary Soto. Reprinted by permission of Houghton Mifflin Harcourt Publishing Company. All rights reserved.

Trident Media Group: Excerpt from "The Fable of the Three Princes," from *Magic: The Final Fantasy Collection* by Isaac Asimov. Copyright © 1996 by Nightfall, Inc./The Estate of Isaac Asimov. Reprinted with the permission of Trident Media Group, LLC on behalf of the Isaac Asimov Estate.

Dell Publishing: Excerpt from "Jeremiah's Song" by Walter Dean Myers from *Visions: Nineteen Short Stories for Outstanding Writers*, edited by Donald R. Gallo. Copyright © 1987 by Donald R. Gallo. Used by permission of Dell Publishing, a division of Random House, Inc.

Philomel Books: Excerpt from *Cousins* by Virginia Hamilton. Copyright © 1990 by Virginia Hamilton. Used by permission of Philomel Books, a division of Penguin Group (USA) Inc. All rights reserved.

Curtis Brown: Excerpt from "The King's Dragon," from *Spaceships & Spells* by Jane Yolen, published by Harper & Row. Copyright © 1987 by Jane Yolen. Reprinted by permission of Curtis Brown, Ltd.

Houghton Mifflin Harcourt: Excerpt from *Anastasia Krupnik* by Lois Lowry. Copyright © 1979 by Lois Lowry. Reprinted by permission of Houghton Mifflin Harcourt Publishing Company. All rights reserved.

Susan Bergholz Literary Services: "Eleven," from *Woman Hollering Creek* by Sandra Cisneros. Copyright © 1991 by Sandra Cisneros. Published by Vintage Books, a division of Random House, Inc., and originally in hardcover by Random House, Inc. Reprinted by permission of Susan Bergholz Literary Services, New York, NY and Lamy, NM. All rights reserved.

Barry N. Malzberg: "Ghost of the Lagoon" by Armstrong Sperry from *Children's Stories to Read or Tell*. Copyright © 1961 by Armstrong Sperry. Copyright © 1961 by the Estate of Armstrong Sperry. Reprinted by permission of Barry N. Malzberg.

Dell Publishing: "Jeremiah's Song" by Walter Dean Myers from *Visions: Nineteen Short Stories for Outstanding Writers*, edited by Donald R. Gallo. Copyright © 1987 by Walter Dean Myers. Used by permission of Dell Publishing, a division of Random House, Inc.

Random House: "President Cleveland, Where Are You?," from *Eight Plus One* by Robert Cormier. Copyright © 1965 by Robert Cormier. Used by permission of Random House Children's Books, a division of Random House, Inc.

HarperCollins Publishers: "Aaron's Gift," from *The Witch of Fourth Street and Other Stories* by Myron Levoy. Copyright © 1972 by Myron Levoy. Used by permission of HarperCollins Publishers.

Sheldon Fogelman Agency: "Role-Playing and Discovery" by Jerry Pinkney, published as part of the anthology *Guys Write for Guys Read* by Viking Books for Young Readers. Copyright © 2005 by Jerry Pinkney. All rights reserved. Used by permission of Sheldon Fogelman Agency, Inc.

HarperCollins Publishers: Excerpt from *Red Scarf Girl: A Memoir of the Cultural Revolution* by Ji-li Jiang. Copyright © 1997 by Ji-li Jiang. Foreward copyright © 1997 by HarperCollins Publishers. Reprinted by permission of HarperCollins Publishers.

Excerpt from "An Interview with Ji-li Jiang" by Ji-li Jiang. Copyright © 2002 by HarperCollins Publishers. Reprinted by permission of HarperCollins Publishers. All rights reserved.

Random House: "Life Doesn't Frighten Me," from *And Still I Rise* by Maya Angelou. Copyright © 1978 by Maya Angelou. Used by permission of Random House, Inc.

University of Pittsburgh Press: "On Turning Ten," from *The Art of Drowning* by Billy Collins. Copyright © 1995 by Billy Collins. Reprinted by permission of the University of Pittsburgh Press.

Curtis Brown: Excerpt from "Phoenix Farm" by Jane Yolen first appeared in *Bruce Coville's Book of Magic*, published by Scholastic, now appears in *Twelve Impossible Things Before Breakfast* by Jane Yolen, published by Harcourt Brace. Copyright © 1996 by Jane Yolen. Reprinted by permission of Curtis Brown, Ltd.

HarperCollins Publishers: Excerpt from *Ruby Holler* by Sharon Creech. Copyright © 2002 by Sharon Creech. Used by permission of HarperCollins Publishers.

UNIT 3

RP/Courage Books: "The Dog and His Reflection" by Aesop from *The Classic Treasury of Aesop's Fables,* illustrated by Don Daily. Copyright © 1999 by Running Press. Reprinted by permission of RP/Courage Books, a member of Perseus Books LLC.

Marian Reiner: "The Stray Cat" from *Catch a Little Rhyme* by Eve Merriam. Copyright © 1966 by Eve Merriam, renewed 1994. Used by permission of Marian Reiner.

Bancroft Library: Excerpt from "Gombei and the Wild Ducks," from *The Sea of Gold and Other Tales from Japan* adapted by Yoshiko Uchida. Copyright © 1965 by Yoshiko Uchida. Used by courtesy of the Bancroft Library, the University of California, Berkeley.

Professional Publishing Services Company: Excerpt from *The Donkey of God* by Louis Untermeyer. Copyright © 1932 by Harcourt, Brace and Company, Inc. Reprinted by arrangement with the Estate of Louis Untermeyer, Norma Anchin Untermeyer c/o Professional Publishing Services. The reprint is granted with the expressed permission by Laurence S. Untermeyer.

Hachette Children's Books: Excerpt from *In Search of Pompeii* by Giovanni Caselli, Copyright © 1999 by Giovanni Caselli. Reprinted by permission of Hachette Children's Books.

USA Today: Excerpt from "Italians trying to prevent a modern Pompeii" by Ellen Hale from USA Today.com, October 20, 2003. Copyright © 2003 by USA Today. Reprinted with permission.

Curtis Brown: *Nadia the Willful* by Sue Alexander, first published by Alfred A. Knopf. Copyright © 1983 by Sue Alexander. Reprinted by permission of Curtis Brown, Ltd.

Brandt & Hochman Literary Agents: "Scout's Honor," from *When I Was Your Age: Original Stories About Growing Up* by Avi. Copyright © 1996 by Avi. Reprinted by permission of Brandt & Hochman Literary Agents, Inc.

Boy Scouts of America: "Wilderness Survival Merit Badge Requirements" by the Boy Scouts of America. Copyright © 1979 the Boy Scouts of America. Reprinted by courtesy of the Boy Scouts of America.

Laura Cecil Literary Agency: "Ant and Grasshopper" by Aesop, retold by James Reeves from *Fables from Aesop*. Copyright © 1961 by James Reeves. Reprinted by permission of the James Reeves Estate.

Doubleday: "The Richer, the Poorer," from *The Richer, the Poorer: Stories, Sketches, and Reminiscences* by Dorothy West. Copyright © 1995 by Dorothy West. Used by permission of Doubleday, a division of Random House, Inc.

Scholastic: Excerpt from *Esperanza Rising* by Pam Muñoz Ryan. Copyright © 2000 by Pam Muñoz Ryan, published by Scholastic Inc. Reprinted by permission.

Random House and Harold Ober Associates: "Dreams," and "Words Like Freedom," from *The Collected Poems of Langston Hughes* by Langston Hughes, edited by Arnold Rampersad with David Roessel, Associate Editor. Copyright © 1994 by the Estate of Langston Hughes. Used by permission of Alfred A. Knopf, a division of Random House, Inc and Harold Ober Associates Incorporated.

Arte Público Press: "Same Song," from *Borders* by Pat Mora. Copyright ©1986 by Pat Mora. Reprinted by permission of Arte Público Press—University of Houston.

Houghton Mifflin Harcourt: "Without Commercials," from *Horses Make a Landscape Look More Beautiful: Poems* by Alice Walker. Copyright © 1984 by Alice Walker. Reprinted by permission of Harcourt Mifflin Harcourt Publishing Company. All rights reserved.

UNIT 4

Farrar, Straus and Giroux: Excerpt from "The Black Thing," from *A Wrinkle in Time* by Madeleine L'Engle. Copyright © 1962, renewed 1990 by Madeleine L'Engle Franklin. Reprinted by permission of Farrar, Straus and Giroux, LLC.

Random House: Excerpt from "Caesar the Giant," from *My Life in Dog Years* by Gary Paulsen. Copyright © 1998 by Gary Paulsen. Used by permission of Bantam Doubleday Dell Books for Young Readers, a division of Random House, Inc.

Random House: Excerpt from *Knots in My Yo-Yo String* by Jerry Spinelli. Copyright © 1998 by Jerry Spinelli. Used by permission of Alfred A. Knopf, a division of Random House, Inc.

HarperCollins Publishers: Excerpt from *Dragonwings* by Laurence Yep. Copyright © 1975 by Laurence Yep. Used by permission of HarperCollins Publishers.

Simon & Schuster: Excerpt from *From the Mixed-up Files of Mrs. Basil E. Frankweiler* by E. L. Konigsburg. Copyright © 1967 by E. L. Konigsburg. Reprinted with the permission of Atheneum Books for Young Readers, a Division of Simon & Schuster, Inc.

HarperCollins Publishers: Excerpt from *Julie of the Wolves* by Jean Craighead George. Copyright © 1972 by Jean Craighead George. Used by permission of HarperCollins Publishers.

Ashley Grayson Literary Agency: Excerpt from "Duffy's Jacket" by Bruce Coville from *Oddly Enough: Stories by Bruce Coville*. Copyright © 1989 by Bruce Coville, originally published in *Things That Go Bump in the Night* (HarperCollins). Reprinted by permission of Ashley Grayson Literary Agency.

Farrar, Straus and Giroux: Excerpt from *Tuck Everlasting* by Natalie Babbitt. Copyright © 1975, renewed 2003 by Natalie Babbitt. Reprinted by permission of Farrar, Straus and Giroux, LLC.

Jewell Parker Rhodes: Excerpt from "Block Party" by Jewell Parker Rhodes. Copyright © 1993 by Jewel Parker Rhodes. Reprinted by permission of the author.

Ruth Cohen: "All-American Slurp" by Lensey Namioka from *Visions: Nineteen Short Stories for Outstanding Writers,* edited by Donald R. Gallo. Copyright © 1987 by Lensey Namioka. Reprinted by permission of Lensey Namioka. All rights reserved.

Project Harmony: Excerpt from "American Lifestyles & Habits" by Project Harmony. Copyright © by Project Harmony. Reprinted by permission of Project Harmony (www.projectharmony.org).

Viking Penguin: *The True Story of the Three Little Pigs* by Jon Scieska, illustrated by Lane Smith. Text Copyright © 1989 by Jon Scieska, illustrations Copyright © 1989 by Lane Smith. Used by permission of Viking Penguin, a division of Penguin Group (USA) Inc. All rights reserved.

Elaine Markson Agency: "Tuesday of the Other June" by Norma Fox Mazer from *Short Takes,* selected by Elizabeth Segel. Copyright © 1986 by Norma Fox Mazer. Reprinted by permission of the Elaine Markson Agency. All rights reserved.

W. W. Norton & Company: "Primer," from *Mother Love* by Rita Dove. Copyright © 1995 by Rita Dove. Used by permission of the author and W. W. Norton & Company, Inc.

Scholastic: Adapted from "The Problem with Bullies" by Sean Price, from *Junior Scholastic,* February 9, 2004. Copyright © 2004 by Scholastic Inc. Used by permission.

Ray Lincoln Literary Agency: Excerpt from *Maniac Magee* by Jerry Spinelli. Copyright © 1990 by Jerry Spinelli. Reprinted by permission of the Ray Lincoln Literary Agency.

Da Capo Press: "The Jacket" by Gary Soto from *The Effects of Knut Hamsun on a Fresno Boy: Recollections and Short Essays*. Copyright © 1983, 2001 by Gary Soto. Reprinted by permission of Da Capo Press, a member of Persea Books, Inc.

Betsy Byars: "The First Skateboard in the History of the World," from *The Moon and I* by Betsy Byars. Copyright © 1991 by Betsy Byars. Reprinted by permission of the author.

Exploratorium: Excerpt from "Skateboard Science" by Pearl Tesler and Paul Doherty. Copyright © Exploratorium. Reprinted by permission of Exploratorium (www.exploratorium.edu).

Perseus Book Group: "The Morning Walk," from *Long Life: Essays and Other Writings* by Mary Oliver. Copyright © 2004 by Mary Oliver. Reprinted courtesy of Da Capo Press, a division of the Perseus Books Group.

Tall Mountain Estate: "There Is No Word for Goodbye," from *There Is No Word for Goodbye* by Mary Tall Mountain. Copyright © 1994 by Tall Mountain Estate. Reprinted by permission of the Tall Mountain Estate. All rights reserved.

Samuel French: *The Phantom Tollbooth* by Susan Nanus and Norton Juster. Copyright © 1977 by Susan Nanus and Norton Juster. Reprinted by permission of Samuel French, Inc. Caution: Professionals and amateurs are hereby warned that *The Phantom Tollbooth,* being fully protected under the copyright laws of the United States of America, the British Commonwealth countries, including Canada, and the other countries of the Copyright Union, is subject to a royalty. All rights, including professional, amateur, motion picture, recitation, public reading, radio, television, and cable broadcasting, and the rights of translation into foreign languages, are strictly reserved. Any inquiry regarding the availability of performance rights, or the purchase of individual copies of the authorized acting edition, must be directed to Samuel French, Inc., 45 West 25th Street, New York, NY 10010, with other locations in Hollywood and Toronto, Canada.

Farrar, Straus and Giroux: Excerpt from "Alan Mendelsohn, the Boy from Mars," from *Five Novels* by Daniel Pinkwater. Copyright © 1997 by Daniel Pinkwater. Reprinted by permission of Farrar, Straus and Giroux, LLC.

Diana Nightingale: "Sparky," from *Earl Nightingale's Greatest Discovery* by Earl Nightingale. Copyright © 1987 by Earl Nightingale. Reprinted by courtesy of Diana Nightingale, widow of Earl Nightingale.

UNIT 5

HarperCollins Publishers: "A Fine Head of Lettuce," from *A Pizza the Size of the Sun* by Jack Prelutsky. Copyright © 1996 by Jack Prelutsky. Reprinted by permission of HarperCollins Publishers.

Simon & Schuster: "Losing Face," from *Good Luck Gold and Other Poems* by Janet S. Wong. Copyright © 1994 by Janet S. Wong. Reprinted with the permission of Margaret K. McElderry Books, a Division of Simon & Schuster, Inc.

Scott Treimel NY: "People," from *All That Sunlight* by Charlotte Zolotow. Copyright © 1967 by Charlotte Zolotow, copyright renewed 1995. Used by permission of Scott Treimel NY.

Random House and Harold Ober Associates: Excerpt from "April Rain Song," from *The Collected Poems of Langston Hughes* by Langston Hughes, edited by Arnold Rampersad with David Roessel, Associate Editor. Copyright © 1994 by the Estate of Langston Hughes. Used by permission of Alfred A. Knopf, a division of Random House, Inc. and Harold Ober Associates Incorporated.

Brooks Permissions: "Pete at the Zoo," from *The Bean Eaters* by Gwendolyn Brooks. Copyright © 1950, 1959, 1960 by Gwendolyn Brooks. Reprinted by consent of Brooks Permissions.

Farrar, Straus and Giroux: "fireworks," from *more small poems* by Valerie Worth. Copyright © 1976 by Valerie Worth. Reprinted by permission of Farrar, Straus and Giroux, LLC.

W. W. Norton & Company: "Poem," from *The Really Short Poems of A. R. Ammons* by A. R. Ammons. Copyright © 1990 by A. R. Ammons. Used by permission of the author and W. W. Norton & Company, Inc.

Marian Reiner: Excerpt from "December Leave," from *Don't Ever Cross a Crocodile and Other Poems* by Kaye Starbird. Copyright © 1963, 1991 by Kaye Starbird. All rights reserved. Used by permission of Marian Reiner.

"New Sounds," from *Something new begins* by Lilian Moore. Copyright © 1967, 1969, 1972, 1975, 1980, 1982 by Lilian Moore. This poem originally appeared in *Little Raccoon and Poems from the Woods* by Lilian Moore. Used by permission of Marian Reiner.

"Like Bookends," from *If Only I Could Tell You* by Eve Merriam. Copyright © 1983 by Eve Merriam. Used by permission of Marian Reiner.

Farrar, Straus & Giroux and Faber and Faber: Excerpt from "Mooses," from *Under the North Star* by Ted Hughes. Copyright © 1981 by Ted Hughes. Used by permission of Farrar, Straus & Giroux, LLC and Faber and Faber Limited.

Rozanne Knudson: "Analysis of Baseball," from *More Poems to Solve* by May Swenson. Copyright © 1954 by May Swenson. Copyright renewed 1963, 1967, 1970, 1971 by May Swenson. Used with permission of the Literary Estate of May Swenson.

Arnold Adoff: "Alone in the Nets" by Arnold Adoff from *Sports Pages*. Copyright © 1986 by Arnold Adoff. Reprinted by permission of the author.

Scholastic: Adaption of "Teen Athletes: Many Kids Dream of Playing in the Big Leagues. But at What Cost?" by Victor Landauro. Published in *Junior Scholastic,* October 18, 2004. Copyright © 2004 by Scholastic Inc. All rights reserved. Used by permission.

Sally Andresen Stolte: "Fall" by Sally Andresen. Reprinted by permission of the author.

Scott Treimel NY: "Change," from *River Winding* by Charlotte Zolotow. Copyright © 1970 by Charlotte Zolotow. Used by permission of Scott Treimel NY.

Marian Reiner: "Message from a Caterpillar," from *Little Raccoon and Poems from the Woods* by Lilian Moore. Copyright © 1975 by Lilian Moore. All rights renewed and reserved. Used by permission of Marian Reiner.

Houghton Mifflin Harcourt: "Fog," from *Chicago Poems* by Carl Sandburg. Copyright © 1916 by Holt, Rinehart and Winston and renewed 1944 by Carl Sandburg. Reprinted by permission of Houghton Mifflin Harcourt Publishing Company. All rights reserved.

HarperCollins Publishers: "Winter solitude" and "A field of cotton" by Basho from *The Essential Haiku: Versions of Basho, Buson & Issa,* edited and with an introduction by Robert Haas. Copyright © 1994 by Robert Haas. Reprinted by permission of HarperCollins Publishers.

Marian Reiner: "Windshield Wiper," from *Chortles: New and Selected Wordplay Poems* by Eve Merriam. Copyright © 1962, 1964, 1973, 1976, 1989 by Eve Merriam. Used by permission of Marian Reiner.

Doubleday: "Night Journey," from *The Collected Poems of Theodore Roethke* by Theodore Roethke. Copyright © 1940 by Theodore Roethke. Used by permission of Doubleday, a division of Random House, Inc.

Walker & Co.: Excerpt from *A Long Hard Journey: The Story of the Pullman Porter* by Patricia and Frederick McKissack. Copyright © 1989 by Patricia and Frederick McKissack. Reprinted by permission of Walker & Co.

Harvard University Press: "I'm Nobody! Who are you?" from *The Poems of Emily Dickinson,* Thomas H. Johnson, editor, Cambridge, Mass. Copyright © 1951, 1955, 1979, 1983 by the President and Fellows of Harvard College. Reprinted with the permission of Harvard University Press and the Trustees of Amherst College.

Farrar, Straus & Giroux and Faber and Faber: "Mooses," from *Under the North Star* by Ted Hughes. Copyright © 1981 by Ted Hughes. Used by permission of Farrar, Straus & Giroux and Faber and Faber Limited.

Liveright Publishing Corporation: "who knows if the moon's," from *Complete Poems: 1904–1962* by E. E. Cummings, edited by George J. Firmage. Copyright © 1923, 1925, 1951, 1953, 1991 by the Trustees for the E. E. Cummings Trust. Copyright © 1976 by George James Firmage. Used by permission of Liveright Publishing Corporation.

Curtis Brown: "A bugler named Dougal MacDougal," from *Lots of Limericks* by Ogden Nash. Copyright 1934 by Ogden Nash. Reprinted by permission of Curtis Brown, Ltd.

Susan Bergholz Literary Services: "Good Hot Dogs," and "Ricos Hot Dogs," from *My Wicked Wicked Ways* by Sandra Cisneros, translated into Spanish by Liliana Valenzuela, published by Third Woman Press and in hardcover by Alfred A. Knopf. Copyright © 1987 by Sandra Cisneros. Reprinted by permission of Third Woman Press and Susan Bergholz Literary Services, New York, NY and Lamy, NM. All rights reserved.

Simon & Schuster: "Ode to an Artichoke" by Pablo Neruda from *The Yellow Canary Whose Eye Is So Black,* by Pablo Neruda, translated by Cheli Durán. Copyright © 1977 by Cheil Durán Ryan. Reprinted with the permission of Simon & Schuster Books for Young Readers, a Division of Simon & Schuster, Inc.

HarperCollins Publishers: "Rain Sizes," from *The Reason for the Pelican* by John Ciardi. Copyright © 1959 by John Ciardi. Reprinted by permission of HarperCollins Publishers.

Little, Brown and Company: "Rain in Ohio," from *American Primitive* by Mary Oliver. Copyright © 1978, 1979, 1980, 1981, 1982, 1983 by Mary Oliver. By permission of Little, Brown and Co., Inc.

UNIT 6

Virginia Pounds Brown: "How Day and Night Came," from *Southern Indian Myths and Legends,* edited by Virginia Pounds Brown and Laurella Owens. Copyright © 1985 by Virginia Pounds Brown and Laurella Owens. Reprinted by permission of Virginia Pounds Brown and Laurella Owens. All rights reserved.

Philomel Books: Excerpt from "Sal Fink," from *Cut from the Same Cloth* by Robert D. San Souci. Copyright © 1993 by Robert D. San Souci, text. Used by permission of Philomel Books, a Division of Penguin Group (USA) Inc. All rights reserved.

Gail B. Graham: Excerpt from *The Beggar In the Blanket & Other Vietnamese Tales* by Gail B. Graham. Copyright © 1970 by Gail B. Graham. Reprinted by permission of Gail B. Graham.

Houghton Mifflin Harcourt: Excerpt from "Baucis and Philemon" by Olivia Coolidge from *Greek Myths.* Copyright © 1949 by Olivia E. Coolidge. Adapted by permission of Houghton Mifflin Harcourt Publishing Company. All rights reserved.

HarperCollins Publishers: Excerpt from *Robin Hood Of Sherwood Forest* told by Ann McGovern. Copyright © 1968 by Ann McGovern. Reprinted by permission of HarperCollins Publishers.

Simon & Schuster: "Orion," from *The Macmillan Book of Greek Gods and Heroes* by Alice Low. Copyright © 1985 by Macmillan Publishing Company. Reprinted with the permission of Simon & Schuster Books for Young Readers, a Division of Simon & Schuster, Inc.

Scholastic: "The Story of Ceres and Proserpina" and "Apollo's Tree: The Story of Daphne and Apollo" retold by Mary Pope Osborne from *Favorite Greek Myths.* Copyright © 1989 by Mary Pope Osborne. Reprinted by permission of Scholastic Inc.

Houghton Mifflin Harcourt: "Arachne" by Olivia Coolidge from *Greek Myths.* Copyright © 1949 by Olivia E. Coolidge, copyright renewed 1977 by Olivia E. Coolidge. Adapted by permission of Houghton Mifflin Harcourt Publishing Company. All rights reserved.

BioKids Project: Excerpt from "Spider Webs" by BioKids Project (http://www.biokids.umich.edu) of the Animal Diversity Web (http://animaldiversity.org). Reprinted by permission of the BioKids Project.

Walker & Co.: "The Chenoo" by Joseph and James Bruchac from *When the Chenoo Howls: Native American Tales of Terror.* Copyright © 1998 by Jospeh and James Bruchac. Reprinted by permission of Walker & Co.

Houghton Mifflin Harcourt: "The Legend of Damon and Pythias" by Fan Kissen from *The Bag of Fire and Other Plays.* Copyright © 1964 by Houghton Mifflin Harcourt Publishing Company, renewed 1993 by John Kissen Heaslip. Reprinted by permission of Houghton Mifflin Company. All rights reserved.

Cricket Magazine: "Uncle Septimus's Beard" by Herbert Shippey from *Cricket,* August 2002, Vol. 29 No. 12. Copyright © 2002 by Herbert P. Shippey. Reprinted by permission of Cricket magazine.

Penguin Young Readers Group: "The Crane Maiden," from *Mysterious Tales of Japan* by Rafe Martin, text. Copyright © 1996 by Rafe Martin. Used by permission of Penguin Young Readers Group, a division of Penguin Group (USA) Inc. All rights reserved.

Judith Ortiz Cofer: "Aunty Misery" retold by Judith Ortiz Cofer from Third World: Pig Iron No. 15. Copyright © Judith Ortiz Cofer. Reprinted by permission of Judith Ortiz Cofer.

Philomel Books: *Yeh-Shen: A Cinderella Story from China* by Ai-Ling Louie, text. Copyright © 1982 by Ai-Ling Louie. Used by permission of Philomel Books, a division of Penguin Group (USA) Inc. All rights reserved.

Random House Children's Books: From *Sootface* by Robert D. San Souci. Copyright © 1994 by Robert D. San Souci. Used by permission of Random House Children's Books, a division of Random House, Inc.

Simon & Schuster: "Cassiopeia," and "Castor and Pollux," from *The Macmillan Book of Greek Gods and Heroes* retold by Alice Low. Copyright © 1995 by Macmillan Publishing Company. Reprinted with the permission of Simon & Schuster Books for Young Readers, a Division of Simon & Schuster, Inc.

UNIT 7

The Gale Group: Excerpt from *J.K. Rowling* by Bradley Steffens. Copyright © 2002 by Lucent Books. Reprinted by permission of The Gale Group.

HarperCollins Publishers: Excerpt from *No Pretty Pictures: A Child of War* by Anita Lobel. Copyright © 1998 by Anita Lobel. Reprinted by permission of HarperCollins Publishers.

Sports Illustrated: Excerpt from "Chairman of the Board" by Armen Keteyian, Sports Illustrated, November 24, 1986. Copyright © 1986 by Time Inc. Reprinted by permission of Sports Illustrated. All rights reserved.

Clarion Books: Excerpt from *The Voice That Challenged a Nation: Marian Anderson and the Struggle for Equal Rights* by Russell Freedman. Copyright © 2004 by Russell Freedman. Reprinted by permission of Clarion Books, an imprint of Houghton Mifflin Harcourt Publishing Company. All rights reserved.

Viking Penguin: Excerpt from "Easter Sunday," from *My Lord, What a Morning* by Marian Anderson. Copyright © 1956 by Marian Anderson. Copyright renewed 1984. Used by permission of Viking Penguin, a division of Penguin Group (USA) Inc.

The Estate of James Haskins: Excerpt from "Matthew Henson at the Top of the World," from *Against All Opposition: Black Explorers in America* by James Haskins. Copyright © 1992 by James Haskins. Reprinted by permission of the Estate of James Haskins.

Scholastic: Excerpt from *Over the Top of the World: Explorer Will Steger's Trek Across the Arctic* by Will Steger and Jon Bowermaster, published by Scholastic Press/Scholastic Inc. Copyright © 1997 by Expeditions Unlimited Inc. Used by permission.

William Morris Agency: "Up and Over the Top" by Bill Cosby, from *Relating Magazine*. Copyright © William H. Cosby, Jr. Reprinted by permission of William Morris Agency, LLC on behalf of the author.

How Stuff Works: Excerpt from "How Sign Language Works" by Jonathan Stickland from www.howstuffworks.com. Copyright © How Stuff Works. Reprinted by permission of How Stuff Works.

Simon & Schuster: Excerpt from *Under the Royal Palms* by Alma Flor Ada. Copyright © 1998 by Alma Flor Ada. Reprinted with the permission of Atheneum Books for Young Readers, a division of Simon & Schuster, Inc.

Tom Lalicki: Excerpt from *Spellbinder: The Life of Harry Houdini* by Tom Lalicki. Copyright © 2000 by Tom Lalicki. Reprinted by permission of the author.

Chronicle Books: "In a Neighborhood in Los Angeles," from *Body in Flames/Cuerpo en Llamas* by Francisco X. Alarcón. Copyright © 1990 by Francisco X. Alarcón. Used with permission of Chronicle Books LLC, San Francisco.

University of Georgia Press: "For Gwen, 1969," from *This Is My Century: New and Collected Poems* by Margaret Walker. Copyright © 1989 by Margaret Walker Alexander. Reprinted by permission of the University of Georgia Press, Athens, Georgia, 30602. All rights reserved.

Carus Publishing Company: Excerpt from "A Way with Words" by James C. Hall, adapted from *Footsteps* March/April 2005 Issue: Women Writers. Copyright © 2005 by Carus Publishing. Published by Cobblestone Publishing, 30 Grove Street, Suite C, Peterborough, NH 03458. Used by permission of the publisher.

Bantam Books: Excerpt from *John Glenn: A Memoir* by John Glenn with Nick Taylor. Copyright © 1999 by John Glenn. Used by permission of Bantam Books, a division of Random House, Inc.

UNIT 8

www.zillions.org: "Food Ad Tricks" from www. ConsumerReports.org., Copyright © 2000 by Consumers Union of U.S. Inc., Yonkers, NY 10703–1057, a nonprofit organization. Reprinted with permission from www.zillions.org for educational purposes only. No commercial use or reproduction permitted (www. ConsumerReports.org).

National Geographic Society: "Swimmers Beware: Jellyfish Are Everywhere" by Susan Jaques from *National Geographic Kids* magazine, August 1996. Copyright © 1996 National Geographic Society. Reprinted by permission of National Geographic Society.

Excerpt from "Hurricane Hunters" by Renee Skelton, National Geographic Explorer, September 2004. Copyright © 2004 National Geographic Society. Reprinted by permission of National Geographic Society.

Excerpt from "Super Croc" by Peter Winkler from *National Geographic for Kids,* March 2002. Copyright © 2002 National Geographic Society. Reprinted by permission of National Geographic Society.

Gareth Huw Davies: Excerpt from "Bird Brains" by Gareth Huw Davies from www.pbs.org. Copyright © Gareth Huw Davies. Reprinted by permission of the author.

Henry Morrison: Excerpt from *The Tomb Robbers* by Daniel Cohen. Copyright © 1980 by Daniel Cohen. Reprinted by permission of the author and his agents, Henry Morrison, Inc.

Carus Publishing Company: Excerpt from "Digging Up the Past: Discovery and Excavation of Shi-Huangdi's Tomb" by Helen Wieman Bledsoe adapted from *Calliope,* October 1997 issue: China's First Emperor: Shi-Huangdi. Copyright © 1997 by Cobblestone Publishing, 30 Grove Street, Suite C, Peterborough, NH 03458. All rights reserved. Used by permission of Carus Publishing Company.

National Association for Humane and Environmental Education: "Power in Numbers" by the National Association for Humane and Environmental Education (NAHEE) from www. humaneteen.org. Copyright © 2006 by NAHEE. Reprinted by permission of NAHEE.

Science News: Excerpts from "The Violent Side of Video Games" and "What Video Games Can Teach Us" by Emily Sohn from *Science News for Kids* (www.sciencenewsforkids.org). Copyright © 2004 by Science News for Kids. Reprinted by permission of Science News for Kids.

The Humane Society of the United States: "Should Wild Animals Be Kept as Pets?" from www.hsus.org. Copyright © 2005 the Humane Society of the United States. Reprinted by permission of the Humane Society of the United States (www.hsus.org).

Little, Brown and Company: "No Thought of Reward" from *The Code: The 5 Secrets of Teen Success* by Mawi Asgedom. Copyright © 2003 by Mawi Asgedom. By permission of Little, Brown and Co., Inc.

Free Spirit Publishing: Excerpt from *The Kids' Guide to Working Out Conflicts: How to Keep Cool, Stay Safe, and Get Along* by Naomi Drew, M.A. Copyright © 2004 by Naomi Drew, M.A. Reprinted by permission of Free Spirit Publishing, Inc.

STUDENT RESOURCE BANK

Janis Leibs Dworkis: Excerpt from "Young Peer Mediators Effectiveness is Hard to Dispute" by Janis Leibs Dworkis, *The Dallas Morning News,* February 4, 1997. Copyright © 1997 by Janis Leibs Dworkis. Reprinted by permission of the author.

Scholastic Library Publishing: Excerpt from *Archaeology* by Dennis B. Fradin. Copyright © 1983 Regensteiner Publishing Enterprises, Inc. Reprinted by permission of Children's Press, an imprint of Scholastic Library Publishing, Inc.

Harvard University Press: From "I'm Nobody! Who are you?" from *The Poems of Emily Dickinson,* Thomas H. Johnson, editor, Cambridge, Mass. Copyright © 1951, 1955, 1979, 1983 by the President and Fellows of Harvard College. Reprinted with the permission of Harvard University Press and the Trustees of Amherst College.

University of Pittsburgh Press: From "On Turning Ten," from *The Art of Drowning* by Billy Collins. Copyright © 1995 by Billy Collins. Reprinted by permission of the University of Pittsburgh Press.

HarperCollins Publishers: "Winter solitude" by Basho from *The Essential Haiku: Versions of Basho, Buson & Issa,* edited and with an introduction by Robert Haas. Copyright © 1994 by Robert Haas. Reprinted by permission of HarperCollins Publishers.

Scott Treimel NY: From "Change," from *River Winding* by Charlotte Zolotow. Copyright © 1970 by Charlotte Zolotow. Used by permission of Scott Treimel NY.

Laura Cecil Literary Agency: From "Ant and Grasshopper" by Aesop, retold by James Reeves from *Fables from Aesop.* Copyright © 1961 by James Reeves. Reprinted by permission of the James Reeves Estate.

Marian Reiner: From "Windshield Wiper," from *Chortles: New and Selected Wordplay Poems* by Eve Merriam. Copyright © 1962, 1964, 1973, 1976, 1989 by Eve Merriam. Used by permission of Marian Reiner.

Random House: From "Life Doesn't Frighten Me," from *And Still I Rise* by Maya Angelou. Copyright © 1978 by Maya Angelou. Used by permission of Random House, Inc.

CONSULTANTS

TABLE OF CONTENTS

STUDENT GUIDE TO ACADEMIC SUCCESS

INTRODUCTORY UNIT

UNIT 1

Kobal Collection; **67** © Bassouls Sophie/Corbis Sygma; **69** © Josh Westrich/zefa/Corbis; **70** © NASA/Roger Ressmeyer/Corbis; **73** © Jon Arnold/Getty Images; **75** *left* © NASA/Corbis; *right* © NASA/Roger Ressmeyer/Corbis; **79** NASA; **80** © NASA/Corbis; **81** © Phil Banko/Getty Images; **82** NASA; *background* © Phil Banko/Getty Images; **83** *top* © Roger Ressmeyer/Corbis; *center* NASA; *background* © Phil Banko/Getty Images; **84** NASA; **86** © Age Fotostock America, Inc.; **87** © Beth Gwinn; **89** *German Shepherd*, Keiler Sensenbrenner. © Keiler Sensenbrenner; **90** Illustration by Keiler Sensenbrenner; **91** © GeoNova LLC; **95, 99** Illustrations by Keiler Sensenbrenner; **104–105** AP/Wide World Photos; **104** *top* © Les Cunliffe/Age Fotostock America, Inc.; *center* © Time Life Pictures/Getty Images; **105** *right* The Newbery Awards are administered by the American Library Service to Children, a division of the American Library Association. Seal image used by permission of American Library Association; *left* Cover of *Bud, Not Buddy* by Christopher Paul Curtis. © 1999 by Christopher Paul Curtis. Cover art by Ernie Norcia. Reprinted by permission of Random House Children's Books, a division of Random House, Inc.; **106–107** The Granger Collection, New York; **108–109** © David Harriman/Getty Images; **110, 111, 112** *left*, *Lemony Snicket's A Series of Unfortunate Events* Courtesy of Paramount Pictures; **112** *bottom* © Sadik Demiroz/Getty Images; **114** © Mark Laricchia/Corbis; **115** © C. E. Mitchell/stockphoto.com; **117** *Ursus*, Susan Brearey. Oil and wax on wood with beech leaf and birch bark. 11 1/8″ × 11″ × 1 3/8″ © Susan Brearey/Courtesy Gerald Peters Gallery, Santa Fe, New Mexico; **118** *Golden Autumn* (1901), Stanislav Joukovski. Oil on canvas, 87.5 cm × 107.5 cm. Museum of Art, Serpukhov, Russia. © Bridgeman Art Library; **120** © Corbis; **126** © Paul King/Getty Images; **127** Huynh Quang Nhuong, Papers, 1956-2000, Western Historical Manuscript Collection, Columbia, Missouri; **129** *left* © Mark Kostich Photography; *bottom* © Alison Wright/Corbis; **131** © GeoNova LLC; **132** *left* © Martyn Chillmaid/Oxford Scientific Films Ltd.; *center* © Oxford Scientific Films Ltd.; *bottom* © Robert Francis/Getty Images; *background* © John and Lisa Merrill/Corbis; **133** © Michael Pole/Corbis; **134** *front* © Chris Rainier/Corbis; *bottom* © Joson/zefa/Corbis; *background* © Frans Lanting/Corbis; **139** © Jerry Redfern/www.onasia.com; **142** © Julian Beever; **143** © Bettmann/Corbis; **145, 146, 147, 148** Illustration by Sir John Tenniel from *Through the Looking-Glass* by Lewis Carroll; **150** *right* © Rubberball/Superstock; **151** Library of Congress; **153, 155, 156, 158, 163** © Crown Media Distribution, LLC. Sparrowhawk Distribution Limited; **165** The Granger Collection, New York; **167** © 2007 Albert L. Ortega/Getty Images; **170** © Craig Aurness/Corbis; **173** © Houghton Mifflin Harcourt; **181** © David Young-Wolff/PhotoEdit; **188** © Siede Preis/Getty Images.

UNIT 2

189 *left* Detail of *Room 13, Los Estudiantes* (2004), José Ramirez. Mixed media on canvas, 47″ × 19″. Courtesy the Tilford Art Group. © José Ramirez; *right* © Veer; **190–191** © Corbis Sygma; **198** © Age Fotostock/SuperStock; **199** © Gene Blevins/Corbis; **201** Detail of *Room 13, Los Estudiantes* (2004), José Ramirez. Mixed media on canvas, 47″ × 19″. Courtesy the Tilford Art Group. © José Ramirez; **206** © Getty Images; **207** Courtesy of Barry Malzberg/The Estate of Armstrong Sperry; **209** Detail of *New Moon Rising* (2000's), Peter Sickles. © Peter Sickles/SuperStock; **210** © GeoNova LLC; **211** Detail of *Fishermen, Finisterre* (1951), Keith Vaughan. Oil on canvas, 91.4 cm × 71.1 cm. Private collection. Photo © Bridgeman Art Library. © 2008 Artists Rights Society (ARS), New York/DACS, London; **212** © Andrew J. Martinez/Photo Researchers,

Inc.; **213** © Galen Rowell/Corbis; **215** © Images.com/Corbis; **220** © Corbis; **221** © Jerry Bauer; **223** *Howling Duet (Musical Interlude)* (1998), Benny Andrews. Oil and collage on paper, 29 8/10″ × 22 1/2″. Courtesy of ACA Galleries, New York. © Estate of Benny Andrews/Licensed by VAGA, New York; **225** © GeoNova LLC; **226** Detail of *Cookin Hog Cracklin* (1995), Jessie Coates. Acrylic on masonite. Private collection. © Jessie Coates/SuperStock; **229** *The Poverty of It All* (1965), Benny Andrews. Oil and collage on canvas, 26″ × 22″. Courtesy of ACA Galleries, New York. © Estate of Benny Andrews/Licensed by VAGA, New York; **231** © Getty Images; **235** *top* © Richard Howard Photography; *bottom* Courtesy of Myron Levoy; **237** Library of Congress, Prints and Photographs Division; **238** Courtesy Smoky Mountain Knife Works; **240** *top*, *Whelan's Drug Store, 44th Street and Eighth Avenue, Manhattan* (February 7, 1936), Berenice Abbott. Gelatin silver print, 8″ × 10″. Photography collection, Miriam and Ira D. Wallach Division of Art, Prints and Photographs. The New York Public Library. © Berenice Abbott/Commerce Graphics Ltd, New York. Photo © The New York Public Library/Art Resource, New York; *bottom* © Comstock Images/Age Fotostock America; **243** *left* Library of Congress, Prints and Photographs Division; *right* © Corbis; **244** Public Domain; **249** Detail of *The Rockefeller Center, New York* (1941), Israel Litwak. Oil on canvas. © Museum of the City of New York/ Bridgeman Art Library; **250** © Talent Factory/Age Fotostock America; **251** © GeoNova LLC; **252** *La Colombe*, Pablo Picasso. Embossed, cut out and painted copper, pencil strokes, 15 3/4″ × 10 3/4″. © 2008 Estate of Pablo Picasso/Artists Rights Society (ARS), New York; **254** *Head with a Bird II* (1971), Pablo Picasso. Oil on canvas, 55 cm × 46 cm. Private collection. Photo © Bridgeman Art Library © 2008 Estate of Pablo Picasso/Artists Rights Society (ARS), New York; **260** © Matthias Clamer/Getty Images; **261** *top* © Warner Bros./Courtesy Everett Collection; *bottom* © The WB/Warner Bros./Photofest; **262** *top left* © Warner Bros. /Courtesy Everett Collection; *background* © David Madison/Getty Images; **263** © Rubberball Productions/Getty Images; **264** © Kobi Israel/Alamy Images; **265** *top* © Myles Pinkney; *bottom* © Bettmann/Corbis; **267** *The Bull-dogger* (1923), Ritchey Lithography Corporation. Library of Congress, Prints and Photographs division [LC-USZC4-1946]; **268** *left* © Bettmann/Corbis; *center, right* The Granger Collection, New York; **269–270** Illustrations by Dan Page; **270** *inset* © GeoNova LLC; **272** © Bettmann/Corbis; **274** © Gary Moon/Age Fotostock America, Inc.; **275** © Michael A. Jones/Sacramento Bee/Zuma Press; **277** *September* (2003), Hung Liu. Oil on canvas, 66″ × 66″. © Hung Liu; **280** Detail of *Women Warriors I* (2004), Hung Liu. Oil on canvas, 24″ × 42″. © Hung Liu; **283** *Wildflower* (2003), Hung Liu. Five color lithograph with gold leaf and collage, Ed. 20, 25″ × 19″. © Hung Liu; **285** © Liu Liqun/Corbis; **288** © Photodisc Photography/Veer; **289** *top* © Deborah Feingold/Corbis; *bottom* © Christopher Felver/Corbis; **291** © David Alan Harvey/Magnum Photos; **293** © Comstock Images; **296** © Joseph Sohm/ChromoSohm Inc./Corbis; **307** © Corbis; **314** © Siede Preis/Getty Images.

UNIT 3

315 *left* © Images.com/Corbis; *right* © Chris North/Travel-Ink; **316–317** © DAJ/Getty Images; **318** © Louis Psihoyos/Corbis; **324** © Phillippe Eranian/Corbis; **325** © Getty Images; **327, 328, 333, 334** Illustrations © 1997 by Greg Ruhl. From *The Buried City of Pompeii* by Shelley Tanaka. A Hyperion/Madison Press Book. Published by permission of Madison Press Books, Toronto; **329** © GeoNova LLC; **335** AP/Wide World Photos; **341** © O. Louis Mazzatenta/National Geographic Image Collection; **342–343** Illustration by

Albert Lorenz; **342** *top* © Werner Forman/Art Resource, New York; *bottom left* © Scala/Art Resource, New York; *bottom right* © Erich Lessing/Art Resource, New York; **343** © Scala/Art Resource, New York; **344–345** Illustration by Garry Hincks; **345** *Pliny the Younger,* Annunzio da Lurago. Facade sculpture. South Abbondio, Como, Italy. © Alinari/Art Resource, New York; **348** © Corbis; **0349** Courtesy the Estate of Sue Alexander; **351** © Christine Osborne Pictures; **352** © Jean-Luc Manaud/Rapho/ImageState; **353** *top* © Gary Godby/ShutterStock; *bottom* © Keren Su/Corbis; **354** © Chris North/Travel-Ink; **360** © David Pu'u/Corbis; **361** Photo by Russ Wright/Courtesy of Avi; **363** *11th Floor Water Towers Looking East* (2005), Sonya Sklaroff. Oil on panel, 48″ × 48″. Private Collection. © 2005 Sonya Sklaroff 2005/www.goartonline.com; **364** © GeoNova LLC; **365** *Lafayette Street Morning* (2005), Lisbeth Firmin. Oil on panel, 16″ × 16″. Courtesy of Klaudia Marr Gallery, Santa Fe, New Mexico; **366** © Tom Schierlitz/Getty Images; **368–369** *The George Washington Bridge Seen from the Upper West Side,* Louis Aston Knight. Oil on board, 10.8″ × 17″. Photo courtesy of Spanierman Gallery, LLC, New York; **370** *Tent* (1984), Christopher Brown. Oil on canvas, 72″ × 96″. Private collection; **374** *Boy Scout Handbook, Tenth Edition* © 1990. Boy Scouts of America, Irving, Texas; **379, 380** *top background* © Co Rentmeester Inc./Getty Images; **380** *top foreground* Photos by Scott B. Rosen/Bill Smith Studio; *bottom* © Al Franklin/Corbis; **382** © Robert Rathe/Getty Images; **383** *top, Aesop.* Ancient marble bust. Museo di Villa Albani, Rome. Photo © Alinari/Art Resource, New York; *bottom* © Alison Shaw; **385** From *Aesop's Fables.* Illustration © 2000 by Jerry Pinkney. Published by Chronicle Books LLC, San Francisco. All rights reserved. Used with permission; **387** *left, Woman in Calico* (1944), William H. Johnson. Oil on paperboard, 26 ½″ × 20 ½″. Smithsonian American Art Museum, Washington, D.C. Gift of the Harmon Foundation. 1967.59.1014. © Smithsonian American Art Museum, Washington, D.C./Art Resource, New York; *right, Mom and Dad* (1944), William H. Johnson. Oil on paperboard, 31″ × 25 ⅜″. Gift of the Harmon Foundation. Smithsonian American Art Museum, Washington, D.C. © Smithsonian American Art Museum, Washington, D.C./Art Resource, New York; **388** *Street Life, Harlem* (1940), William H. Johnson. Smithsonian American Art Museum, Washington, D.C. © Smithsonian American Art Museum, Washington, D.C./Art Resource, New York; **394–395** © Garry Black/Masterfile; **394** *top* © Les Cunliffe/Age Fotostock America, Inc.; *center* © Steve Thanos Photography; **395** *right* The Belpré Awards are jointly administered by the Association for Library Service to Children, a division of the American Library Association. Seal image used by permission of American Library Association; **396–397** © Robert Stahl/Getty Images; **398–399** © Creatas/Superstock; **400** © Veer; **401** © Corbis; **403** © Images.com/Corbis; **404** *La Grande Famille* (1947), René Magritte. Oil on canvas, 100 cm × 81 cm. Private collection. Photo © Photothèque R. Magritte-ADAGP/Art Resource, New York. © 2007 C. Herscovici, Brussels/Artists Rights Society (ARS), New York; **406** *foreground* © Warner Brothers/The Kobal Collection; *background* © WizData, Inc./Alamy Images; **407** *top* Courtesy Pat Mora/Photo by Cheron Bayna; *bottom* © Getty Images; **409** *Lipsticks II,* Philip Le Bas. Enamel paints on panel, 20 cm × 20 cm. Portal Gallery www.portal-gallery.com. Photo © Bridgeman Art Library; **411** Detail of Quilt entitled *Bessie's Blues* from the series *The American Collection Number 5* (January 19, 1997), executed by Faith Ringgold. Center: cotton, warp-faced, weft-ribbed plain weave; painted with acrylic paint; quilted, 76 ⅞″ × 79 ¼″. Robert Allerton Endowment, 2002.381. Reproduction, The Art Institute of Chicago. © Faith Ringgold; **414** © Daryl Benson/Masterfile; **425** © Michael Pole/Corbis; **432** © Siede Preis/Getty Images.

UNIT 4

433 *left* From *The True Story of the 3 Little Pigs* by John Scieszka, illustrated by Lane Smith. Text © 1989 by John Scieszka. Illustrations © 1989 by Lane Smith. Used by permission of Viking Penguin, a division of Penguin Young Readers Group, a member of Penguin Group (USA) Inc., 345 Hudson Street, New York, NY 10014. All rights reserved; *right* © Christoph Wilhelm/Getty Images; **434–435** © Getty Images; **434** *left, Reader* (1999), William Wegman. Color polaroid, 24″ × 20″; *center, Lion King* (1999), William Wegman. Color polaroid, 24″ × 20″; *right, Glamour Puss* (1999), William Wegman. Color polaroid, 24″ × 20″; **436** *left* © Wilfried Krecichwost/Getty Images; *right* © Stockbyte/Getty Images; **438** *left* Cover of *From the Mixed-up Files of Mrs. Basil E. Frankweiler* by E. L. Konigsburg. © 1967, 1995 & 2002 by E. L. Konigsburg. Cover photo © 2002 by Barry David Marcus. Cover designed by Russell Gordon. Reprinted by permission of Simon Pulse, an imprint of Simon & Schuster Children's Publishing Division, New York; *right* Cover from *Julie of the Wolves* by Jean Craighead George. © 1972 by Jean Craighead George. Cover art © 1995 by Wendell Minor. Cover © 1995 by Harper Collins Publishers. The Newbery Awards are administered by the American Library Service to Children, a division of the American Library Association. Seal image used by permission of American Library Association. Used by permission of HarperCollins Publishers; **443** © Richard McNamee; **445** © Christoph Wilhelm/Getty Images; **447** © Romilly Lockyer/Getty Images; **448** © Beaconstox/Alamy Images; **451** © Owen Franken/Corbis; **452** © Food Collection/Age Fotostock America, Inc.; **458** © Ron Chapple/Alamy Images; **459** © Getty Images; **461–466** From *The True Story of the 3 Little Pigs* by John Scieszka, illustrated by Lane Smith. Text © 1989 by John Scieszka. Illustrations © 1989 by Lane Smith. Used by permission of Viking Penguin, a division of Penguin Young Readers Group, a member of Penguin Group (USA) Inc., 345 Hudson Street, New York 10014. All rights reserved; **467** Photograph by Sharon Hoogstraten/Public Domain; **468** *For Better or For Worse* © 1983 Lynn Johnston Productions. Distributed by Universal Press Syndicate. Reprinted with permission. All rights reserved; **469** © 2005 Judith S. Buck; **471** Detail of *Fire and Ice* (2004), Brian Calvin. Acrylic on canvas, 48″ × 60″. Courtesy of Anton Kern Gallery, New York. © Brian Calvin; **473** Left panel of *Le Plongeur (Paper Pool 18)* (1978), David Hockney. Coloured and pressed paper pulp. 72″ × 171″. Photo © Bradford Art Galleries and Museums, West Yorkshire, United Kingdom/Bridgeman Art Library. © David Hockney/The David Hockney U.S. No. 1 Trust; **477** Beth Reitmeyer/Houghton Mifflin Harcourt; **479** Detail of *Potrero* (2005), Michael Shankman. Oil on canvas, 18″ × 72″. © 2005 Michael Shankman. All rights reserved; **481** Detail of *Fire and Ice* (2004), Brian Calvin. Acrylic on canvas, 48″ × 60″. Courtesy of Anton Kern Gallery, New York. © Brian Calvin; **482** © Robert Daly/Getty Images; **487, 489, 490** Illustrations by James Yang; **492–493** © Andrew Gunners/Getty Images; **492** *top* © Les Cunliffe/Age Fotostock America, Inc.; *center* © Cully Craft Photography; **493** *right* The Newbery Awards are administered by the American Library Service to Children, a division of the American Library Association. Seal image used by permission of American Library Association; **494–495** © André Jenny/Alamy Images; **496–497** © Jack Hollingsworth/Getty Images; **496** © age fotostock/SuperStock; **497** © Comstock/Superstock; **498** © Alistair Berg/Getty Images; **499** © Gary Soto; **501** *jacket* © Hans Neleman/Getty Images; *teen guy* © Royalty-Free/Veer; **503** © Thomas Barwick/Getty Images; **508** © Ralph Hagen/CartoonStock; **509** © Ed Byars/Betsy Byars; **511, 512, 515** Illustrations by Juliette Borda; **519** ©

Al Fuchs/NewSport/Corbis; **522** © Terry Husebye/Getty Images; **524** AP/Wide World Photos; **525** *top* © Barbara Savage Cheresh; *bottom* © Lance Woodruff; **527** Detail of *Stag on Alert, In Wooded Clearing*, Rosa Bonheur. © SuperStock; **528–529** Detail of *Bluebells in Shakespeare's Wood* (2004), Timmy Mallett. Acrylic. © Timmy Mallett; **532** © Eureka/Alamy Images; **533** © Paul Franz; **535, 541** © MGM/Photofest; **545** © MGM/The Kobal Collection; **547** © MGM/Photofest; **550** © Courtesy Everett Collection; **552** © Dan Lim/Masterfile; **553** *La Bendicion en el Dia de la Boda* (1993), Carmen Lomas Garza. Alkyds on canvas, 24″ × 32″. © 1993 Carmen Lomas Garza. Collection of Smith College Museum, Northampton, Massachusetts. Photo by M. Lee Fatherree; **554** *top left, La Llorona* (1989), Carmen Lomas Garza. Gouache, 18″ × 26″. © 1989 Carmen Lomas Garza. Collection of Sonia Saldivar-Hull and Felix Hull, Austin, Texas. Photo by Wolfgang Dietze; *bottom left, Father and Son* (2003), Benny Andrews. From *Pictures for Miss Josie* by Sandra Belton. © 2004 by Sandra Belton. Reprinted by permission of Greenwillow Books, an imprint of HarperCollins Publishers, New York; *background/bottom* © Masterfile; **555** © David Young-Wolff/PhotoEdit; **556** © Richard Sisk/Jupiter Images; **567** © Jupiterimages Corporation; **574** © Siede Preis/Getty Images.

UNIT 5

575 *left Splash*, Nancy Glazier. Oil, 26″ × 34″; **575** *right Spoonbridge and Cherry* (1988), Claes Oldenburg and Coosje van Bruggen. Stainless steel and aluminum painted with polyurethane enamel, 29′ 6″ × 51′ 6″ × 13′ 6″. Minneapolis Sculpture Garden, Walker Art Center, Minneapolis. © Claes Oldenburg and Coosje van Bruggen. Photo by Attlio Maranzano; **576–577** © age fotostock/SuperStock; **578** © Turbo/zefa/Corbis; **582** © Mark Wiens/Masterfile; **584** © Getty Images; **585** *top* © The Literary Estate of Mary Swenson; *bottom* © 2006 by Arnold Adoff, used by permission of Arnold Adoff; **587** © Corbis; **588** © Lisa Pines/Getty Images; **592** © Corbis; **593** *top* The Granger Collection, New York; *bottom* © Stock Montage; **595** Unnamed clipper ship, Claude Marks. Private collection. Photo © Bridgeman Art Library; **596** *The Blacksmith* (1909), James Carroll Beckwith. Oil on canvas, 52 ¼″ × 32 ¼″. Smithsonian American Art Museum, Washington, D.C. Photo © Smithsonian American Art Museum, Washington, D.C./Art Resource, New York; **600** © Canopy Productions/Veer; **601** *top* © Les Stolte/Courtesy Sally Andresen Stolte; *bottom* © Andrew Kilgore; **603** © Bart Bemus/Getty Images; **605** *The Farewell* (1952), Bernard Perlin. Smithsonian American Art Museum, Washington, D.C. Photo © Smithsonian American Art Museum, Washington, D.C./Art Resource, New York; **608** © Michael Keller/Corbis; **609** *top* Photo © 1985 Joan Glazer; *center* © Bettmann/Corbis; *bottom* © Roger-Viollet/The Image Works, Inc.; **610** © Scott Tysick/Masterfile; **611** © Grant V. Faint/Getty Images; **612** © Ray Juno/Corbis; **614** © Tim McGuire/Corbis; **615** *top* © Miriam Berkley; *bottom* © Bettmann/Corbis; **617** © Grant Faint/Getty Images; **619** © Sylvia de Swaan/Jupiterimages; **623** © Getty Images; **625** Courtesy Archives of the Historic Pullman Foundation, Inc.; **626** Library of Congress, Prints and Photographs Division [LC-USW3-000054-D]; **628** *Garfield* © 1995 Paws, Inc. Reprinted with permission of Universal Press Syndicate. All rights reserved; **629** *top* The Granger Collection, New York; *center* © Bettmann/Corbis; *bottom* © UPPA/Topham/The Image Works, Inc.; **630** Detail of *The Son of Man* (1964), René Magritte. © 2008 C. Herscovici, Brussels/Artists Rights Society (ARS), New York. Photo © Christie's Images /Corbis; **631** Detail of *The Masterpiece on the Mysteries* (1955), René Magritte. Oil on canvas. © 2008 C. Herscovici, Brussels/Artists Rights Society (ARS), New York. Photo © Christie's Images/SuperStock; **633** *Splash*, Nancy Glazier. Oil, 26″ × 34″;

636 © Ron Chapple/Getty Images; **637** *top* © Bettmann/Corbis; *center* The Granger Collection, New York; *bottom* © Time Life Pictures/Getty Images; **639, 640** Illustrations by Kurt Devlaeminck/Houghton Mifflin Harcourt; **642** © Jupiterimages Corporation; **643** *top* © Gene Blevins/Corbis; *bottom* © Getty Images; **644, 645** © Jim Ballard/Getty Images; **646–647** © Ingram Publishing/Age Fotostock America, Inc.; **648, 649** © PunchStock; **650–651** © Paul Taylor/Getty Images; **652** © PunchStock; **656** © Daryl Benson/Masterfile; **665** © Corbis; **667** © Ed Kashi/Corbis; **672** © Siede Preis/Getty Images.

UNIT 6

673 *left* Illustration by Joel Priddy; *right* © Jean-Yves Bruel/Masterfile; **674–675** © Catherine Karnow/Corbis; **676** *left* Detail of *Prometheus Carrying Fire*, Jan Cossiers. Museo del Prado, Madrid, Spain/Art Resource, New York; *center* Illustration by Walter Crane in *King Arthur's Knights* by Henry Gilbert, 1911. Photo © Edwin Wallace/Mary Evans Picture Library; *right* Illustration by Joel Priddy; **678** Photograph by Sharon Hoogstraten; **680** © Phil Banko/Getty Images; **682** © Joy Tessman/Getty Images; **683** © Paul Coughlin; **685, 687, 688** From *The Pomegranate Seeds* retold by Laura Geringer. Illustrations © 1995 by Leonid Gore. Used by permission of Houghton Mifflin Company, Boston; **692** © Dreamworks/Courtesy of Photofest; **693** *top* © Paul Coughlin; *bottom* Courtesy of Julian Coolidge; **695** Detail of *Cupid*, manner of Jean-Baptiste Greuze. Oil on canvas. © Christie's Images/SuperStock; **697** *Apollo and Daphne* (1565-1570), Paolo Veronese. Oil on canvas, 109.4 cm. × 113.3 cm. © San Diego Museum of Art, San Diego, California/ Bridgeman Art Library; **699** From *Arachne Speaks* by Kate Hovey, illustrated by Blair Dawson. Illustration © 2000 Blair Dawson. Reprinted with the permission of Margaret K. McElderry Books, an imprint of Simon & Schuster Children's Publishing Division, New York; **700** © Alistair Dove/Alamy Images; **702** From *Arachne Speaks* by Kate Hovey, illustrated by Blair Dawson. Illustration © 2000 Blair Dawson. Reprinted with the permission of Margaret K. McElderry Books, an imprint of Simon & Schuster Children's Publishing Division, New York; **707** *top* © Anselm Spring/Getty Images; *bottom* © José Fuste Raga/Corbis; **708** *top* © Jerry Young/Dorling Kindersley; *bottom* © Adam Jones/Photo Researchers, Inc.; **709** *top* © Theo Allofs/Getty Images; *bottom* © Nancy Rotenberg/Animals Animals; **710** *top* © Hans Pfletschinger/Peter Arnold, Inc.; *bottom* © Kim Taylor/Nature Picture Library; **712** © Zia Soleil/Getty Images; **713** Photos by Carol Bruchac/© Joseph Bruchac; **715** © Kate Thompson/Getty Images; **716** © Bettmann/Corbis; **717** © Per Eriksson/Getty Images; **719** *ice cracks* © Staffan Andersson/Age Fotostock America, Inc.; *ice heart* © Kathy Collins/Getty Images; **720** © GeoNova LLC; **721** *top* Photograph by Sharon Hoogstraten; *bottom* Canoe model (1905), Tomah Joseph. Passamaquoddy. Peter Dana Point, Maine. L. 50 ½″ × 10 ½″. Eugene and Clair Thaw Collection, Fenimore Art Museum, Cooperstown, New York. © John Bigelow Taylor/Art Resource, New York; **725** Courtesy of John Heaslip; **727** *Poseidon and Apollo*. Detail from *Poseidon, Apollo and Artemis*. Relief from the east frieze of the Parthenon, Athens. Inv. 856. Acropolis Museum, Athens © Erich Lessing/Art Resource, New York; **731** *Reception in the Senate*, detail from the Arch of Trajan (100's). Marble. Benevento, Campania, Italy. © Bridgeman Art Library; **732** © DreamWorks Pictures/Courtesy Everett Collection; **736** © John Lund/Getty Images; **737** © Daniel Shippey; **739, 742** Illustrations by Joel Priddy; **743** © Adrian Davies/Nature Picture Library; **746** © Natalie Fobes/Getty Images; **747** *top* Courtesy Rafe Martin/© Moira Speer; *bottom* Photo of Judith Ortiz Cofer is reprinted with permission from the publisher Arte

UNIT 7

UNIT 8

UNIT 9 RESEARCH UNIT

1007 *left* © LWA-JDC/Corbis; *right* Photograph by Sharon Hoogstraten; **1008–1009** © Wizdata, Inc./Alamy Images; **1010** *foreground* © Tobin Rogers/Alamy Images; *background* © Harrison Smith/Alamy Images; **1014** © Jupiterimages Corporation; **1015** © Michael S. Quinton/National Geographic Image Collection; **1017** Image from www.library.phila.gov/The Free Library of Philadelphia; **1019** © Jim Gensheimer/Getty Images; **1020** From Gale. *InfoTrac* © Gale, a part of Cengage Learning, Inc. Reproduced by permission. www.cengage.com/permissions; **1022** © Malcolm Schuyl/Alamy Images; **1023** *left* © Larry Michael/Nature Picture Library; *right* © WireImageStock/Masterfile; **1027** © Stock4B/Getty Images; **1028** © Sam Barricklow/Jupiterimages Corporation; **1045** © Michael J. Doolittle/The Image Works, Inc.

STUDENT RESOURCE BANK

R3 © Jon Arnold/Alamy Images; **R6** © David Sutherland/Getty Images; **R7** © GeoNova LLC; **R14** Beatriz Terrazas/The Dallas Morning News; **R15** © Roger Wood/Corbis; **R19** Public Domain; **R85** © Digital Vision Ltd./Superstock; **R92** © Walt Disney Pictures/Walden Media/The Kobal Collection.

BACK COVER

© Kevin Schafer/Alamy Ltd.

Houghton Mifflin Harcourt has made every effort to locate the copyright holders of all copyrighted material in this book and to make full acknowledgment for its use. Omissions brought to our attention will be corrected in a subsequent edition.